Household Spending

Household Spending

Who Spends How Much on What

BY THE EDITORS OF NEW STRATEGIST PUBLICATIONS

New Strategist Publications, Inc.
P.O. Box 242, Ithaca, New York 14851
800/848-0842; 607/273-0913
www.newstrategist.com

ISBN 1-885070-87-X

Printed in the United States of America

Contents

Chapter 11. Spending on Transportation, 2003

List of Tables

Chapter 3. Spending on Entertainment, 2003

Chapter 4. Spending on Financial Products and Services, 2003

Chapter 5. Spending on Food and Alcoholic Beverages, 2003

Chapter 6. Spending on Gifts for Nonhousehold Members, 2003

Chapter 7. Spending on Health Care, 2003

Chapter 8. Spending on Household Operations, 2003

Chapter 9. Spending on Shelter and Utilities, 2003

Chapter 10. Spending on Personal Care, Reading, Education, Tobacco, 2003

Introduction

Welcome to the tenth edition of *Household Spending*: *Who Spends How Much on What*. This edition provides a comprehensive analysis of the spending of American households in the year 2003.

Since we published the first edition of *Household Spending* in 1991, the economy has cycled through good times and bad. The nation pulled out of a severe recession in the early 1990s, enjoyed a stunning economic recovery in the mid-to-late 1990s, then experienced another recession and terrorist attacks in 2001. Through these ups and downs, the average household has held a surprisingly steady course. While spending grew strongly at the national level during the decade, it rose more moderately at the household level. This caution served Americans well, insulating their day-to-day lives from the economy's gyrations.

During the past two decades, consumer spending at the national level has grown not only because of population and household growth, but also because the baby-boom generation entered the peak-spending age groups. While spending at the aggregate level soared, spending by the average household rose more slowly. In 2003, spending by the average household was only 5 percent greater than in 1990, after adjusting for inflation. The average household spent $40,817 in 2003, up from $38,733 in 1990.

Between 2000 and 2003, average household spending changed little—a gain of just 0.4 percent after adjusting for inflation. In many categories, spending fell during those years. Spending on food away from home (primarily restaurant and carry-out meals) declined 3 percent between 2000 and 2003, after adjusting for inflation. Spending on alcoholic beverages shrank 2 percent. Spending on "other lodging" (primarily hotels and motels) fell a substantial 13 percent. Entertainment spending climbed nearly 4 percent between 2000 and 2003, but spending on fees and admissions to entertainment events fell 10 percent. Spending on new cars and trucks rose a hefty 20 percent in response to low-interest and no-interest loans, but spending on used vehicles fell 15 percent. Average household spending on furniture declined 4 percent, and spending on clothes plummeted 17 percent.

In contrast, average household spending on many of life's necessities increased over the three-year period. The average household spent 10 percent more on property taxes in 2003 than in 2000, 3 percent more on water and other public services, 9 percent more on vehicle insurance, 19 percent more on out-of-pocket health insurance costs, and 16 percent more on education. Property tax is now Americans' fifth biggest expenditure, and health insurance ranks seventh. (See Appendix D for a ranking of expenditures in 2003.)

Analyzing spending trends at the individual household level, as *Household Spending* does, provides deeper insight into the nation's economic ups and downs than any examination of aggregate figures. Unfortunately, the complexity of household spending statistics discourages many from tackling the job of analyzing the data. It is much easier to analyze spending at the national level because it requires an examination of only two figures—today's and yesterday's. But analyzing trends in spending at the household level requires delving into the who, what, and why of spending—the mindset and motivations of individual consumers. The tenth edition of *Household Spending* is for those who want to know the who, what, and why.

Consumer spending is the result of a complex mix of wants and needs, hopes and fears. This mix determines the success of individual businesses and the health of our economy. Knowing how consumers spend their dollars is the key to understanding where our economy is headed, an insight of immense value as the nation copes with uncertainty.

How to use this book

Household Spending is based on unpublished data collected by the Bureau of Labor Statistics' Consumer Expenditure Survey, an ongoing, nationwide survey of household spending. The editors of New Strategist start with the average spending figures collected by the Bureau of Labor Statistics and analyze them in a variety of ways, calculating household spending indexes, aggregate (or total) spending, and market shares. We do this for hundreds of spending categories by age of householder, household income, household type, race and Hispanic origin of householder, region, and educational attainment of householder.

The Bureau of Labor Statistics' Consumer Expenditure Survey is a complete accounting of household expenditures, including everything from big-ticket items such as homes and cars, to small purchases like laundry detergent and film. The survey does not include expenditures by government, business, or institutions. The lag time between data collection and publication is about two years. The data in this book are from the 2003 Consumer Expenditure Survey, unless otherwise noted.

The Consumer Expenditure Survey uses consumer units as its sampling unit. The Bureau of Labor Statistics defines "consumer unit" as "a single person or group of persons in a sample household related by blood, marriage, adoption or other legal arrangement or who share responsibility for at least two out of three major types of expenses—food, housing, and other expenses." For convenience, consumer units are referred to as households in the text of this book. For more information about the Consumer Expenditure Survey and consumer units, see Appendix A.

Chapter 1 of *Household Spending* is devoted to summary household spending statistics. These are shown for the following consumer segments: age, income, household type, region, race and Hispanic origin, and education.

Chapters 2 through 11 present detailed spending statistics organized by major product and service category (food, housing, transportation, and so on) and include all typical household expenditures. Within each chapter, spending statistics are shown by age of householder, household income, household type, race and Hispanic origin of householder, region, and educational attainment of householder. For each of the demographic variables, tables show average spending, indexed spending, total (or aggregate) spending, and share of spending.

New to this edition of *Household Spending* are detailed spending tables for Asian households and for households with incomes as high as $150,000 or more. The new racial and ethnic categories were added in 2003, when the Bureau of Labor Statistics modified the questions on the Consumer

Expenditure Survey to comply with new standards for maintaining, collecting, and presenting federal data on race and ethnicity. The BLS expanded the high-income categories because the sample size of the previous top-income group ($70,000 or more) had become large enough to allow more detailed high-income breaks. *Household Spending* presents two sets of income tables, one showing the spending of households with incomes up to $100,000 or more, the other showing the spending of households with incomes above $100,000 to $150,000 or more.

How to use the tables in this book

The data in *Household Spending* reveal how American households allocate their spending dollars. The starting point for all calculations in *Household Spending* are the unpublished detailed average household spending data collected by the Consumer Expenditure Survey. These are shown in the average spending tables in chapters 2 through 11. The remaining tables in each chapter, produced by New Strategist's statisticians, are based on the average figures. The indexed spending tables reveal whether households in a given segment spend more or less than the average for all households (or for all households in that segment), and by how much. The total (or aggregate) spending tables show the overall size of a particular market. The market share tables reveal how much spending in a market is accounted for by a household segment. These four types of tables are described in detail below.

- **Average Spending Tables.** The average spending tables report the average annual spending of households on each item or category of items in 2003. The Consumer Expenditure Survey produces average spending data for all households in a segment. e.g, all households with a householder aged 25 to 34, not just for those who purchased an item. When reviewing the spending data, it is important to remember that by including both purchasers and nonpurchasers in the calculation, the average is diluted—especially for infrequently purchased items. For example, the average household spent $189 on day care centers in 2003. Since only a small percentage of households spend money on day care, this figure greatly underestimates the amount spent on day care centers by those who make use of them. To get a more realistic idea of how much buyers spend on an item, Appendix C shows the percentage of households purchasing individual products and services during an average quarter of 2003, and the amount spent by purchasers per quarter. According to Appendix C, only 5 percent of households spent on day care centers during an average quarter of 2003. The purchasers spent an average of $866 per quarter, for an estimated annual cost of $3,465—a much more realistic figure than the average of $189 for all households.

For frequently purchased items—such as bread—the average spending figures give a fairly accurate account of actual spending. But for most of the products and services examined in *Household Spending*, the average spending figures are less revealing than the indexes and market shares.

Average spending figures are useful in determining the market potential of a product or service in a local area. By multiplying the average amount married couples spend on children's clothing by the number of married couples in the Dallas metropolitan area, for example, marketers can estimate the size of the market for children's clothing in Dallas. The Dallas media could show those figures to potential advertisers as evidence of the local demand for children's clothing.

Note that because of sampling errors, average values can vary—especially for infrequently purchased items. To examine the standard errors associated with summary average spending figures (Chapter 1), go to http://www.bls.gov/cex/csxstnderror.htm. To examine the standard errors associated with detailed average spending data, contact the Bureau of Labor Statistics Consumer Expenditure Survey statisticians by phone at 202-691-6900 or by e-mail at cexinfo@bls.gov.

• **Indexed Spending Tables.** The indexed spending tables compare the spending of each household segment with that of the average household. To compute the indexes, New Strategist's statisticians divide the average amount a household segment spends on a particular item by how much the average household spends on the item, and multiply the resulting figure by 100.

An index of 100 thus is the average for all households. An index of 125 means the spending of a household segment is 25 percent above average (100 plus 25). An index of 75 indicates spending that is 25 percent below the average for all households (100 minus 25). Indexed spending figures identify the best customers for a product or service. Households with an index of 177 for outdoor furniture, for example, are a strong market for that product. Those with an index below 100 are either a weak or an underserved market.

Spending indexes can reveal hidden markets—household segments with a high propensity to buy a particular product or service but which are overshadowed by larger household segments that account for a bigger share of the total market. Householders aged 65 to 74, for example, spend 46 percent more than the average household on magazine subscriptions (with an index of 146). This is a higher index than that of any other age group, making householders aged 65 to 74 the best customers of this item. Householders aged 35 to 44 spend 24 percent less than average on magazine subscriptions (with an index of 76), meaning they are a weaker or underserved market for this product. But the market share of 35-to-44-year-olds is larger than that of 65-to-74-year-olds (16 versus 14 percent) because there are more households in the younger age group. Using the indexed spending tables, marketers can see that older householders are in fact their better customers and adjust their business strategy accordingly.

Note that because of sampling errors, small differences in index values usually are not significant. But the broader patterns revealed by indexes can guide marketers to the best customers.

• **Total Spending Tables.** To produce the total spending tables, New Strategist's statisticians multiplied average spending figures by the number of households in a segment. The result is the dollar size of the total household market and of each market segment. All totals are shown in thousands of dollars. To convert the numbers in the total spending tables to dollars, you must append "000" to the number. For example, households headed by people aged 45 to 54 spent approximately $11 billion (shown as $11,023,772) on alcoholic beverages in 2003.

When comparing the total spending figures in *Household Spending* with total spending estimates from the Bureau of Economic Analysis, other government agencies, or trade associations, keep in mind that the Consumer Expenditure Survey includes only household spending, not spending by businesses or institutions. Sales data also will differ from household spending totals, because sales figures for consumer products include the value of goods sold to industries, government, and foreign markets, which can be a significant proportion of sales.

• **Market Share Tables.** New Strategist's statisticians produced the market share tables by converting total spending data to percentages. To calculate the percentage of total household spending on an item that is controlled by each demographic segment—i.e., its market share—that segment's total spending on the item was divided by aggregate household spending on the item.

Market shares reveal the biggest customers—the demographic segments that account for the largest share of household spending on a particular product or service. Businesses can reach a large portion of their customers by targeting the demographic segments in control of the largest market shares. Of course, by single-mindedly targeting the biggest customers, businesses cannot nurture potential growth markets. An additional danger of focusing only on the biggest customers is that businesses may end up ignoring their best customers. This is especially problematic because market shares are unstable, thanks to baby booms and busts over the past half-century. Right now, for example, the biggest customers of lawn and garden supplies are householders aged 35 to 54, accounting for 49 percent of total household spending on this item because the age group is filled with the large baby-boom generation. But in fact the best customers of lawn and garden supplies are older householders. Those aged 55 to 74 spend 31 to 40 percent more than the average household on lawn and garden supplies. Although the older age group controls a smaller 33 percent of the market today, the share will expand as boomers age into their sixties and seventies. The best customers of lawn and garden supplies will become the biggest customers as well. Marketers who ignore their best customers in favor of the biggest customers may end up with no customers.

For more information

The tenth edition of *Household Spending* offers researchers a detailed analysis of the voluminous and unpublished spending data collected by the Bureau of Labor Statistics. It provides a convenient way to compare and contrast spending on goods and services by demographic characteristic such as age of householder or household type. For more about the Consumer Expenditure Survey, visit the Bureau of Labor Statistics web site (http://www.bls.gov/cex/), where summary average spending figures (as shown in chapter 1 of this book) are available online. The detailed average spending numbers (as shown in chapters 2 through 11) are available only by special request.

For household spending trends in single product categories, see New Strategist's Who's Buying reports. To find out more about these books, including tables of contents and sample pages, visit New Strategist's web site at www.newstrategist.com. All New Strategist books and reports are available as downloads or in print.

1

Spending Overview

Spending Trends: 1990 to 2003

Between 1990 and 2003, spending by the average household rose a modest 5 percent, after adjusting for inflation. Almost all the growth occurred before 2000, since average household spending inched up by only 0.4 percent between 2000 and 2003.

In 2003, the average household spent $40,817, according to the Bureau of Labor Statistics' Consumer Expenditure Survey. The 5 percent increase in spending since 1990 was much less than the 17 percent growth in household income during those years. While the media frequently claim that consumers spend beyond their means, in fact the steady rise in consumer spending at the national level is the consequence of demographic change rather than overindulgence. The spending driver is the aging of the baby-boom generation into its peak-earning and spending years.

The average household spent less in 2003 than in 1990 on many categories of products and services. Food spending fell 9 percent during those years, after adjusting for inflation. Both food-at-home (groceries) and food-away-from-home (restaurants) spending was down. Spending on alcoholic beverages fell 2 percent. Apparel spending was down 26 percent. The average household cut spending on gifts for people living in other households by a substantial 19 percent. The pattern of spending for the shorter time period, between 2000 and 2003, mirrors that of the 1990-to-2003 time period.

Spending rose on many nondiscretionary items between 1990 and 2003. Spending on property taxes ballooned an enormous 65 percent, for example, while spending on telephone services rose 18 percent. Spending on water and other public services increased 24 percent. Out-of-pocket spending on health insurance climbed 58 percent between 1990 and 2003, to $1,252. Spending on drugs rose 36 percent. Although spending on entertainment grew 6 percent, spending on fees and admissions to entertainment events fell 2 percent.

More belt tightening lies ahead for American households. During the next decade, the oldest members of the baby-boom generation will enter their sixties, moving out of the peak earning and spending years. The aging of boomers, combined with soaring costs for energy and health care, will crimp household budgets. Government and business will have to adapt.

Table 1.1 Spending Trends, 1990 to 2003

(average annual spending of consumer units by product and service category, 1990, 2000, and 2003; percent change 1990–2003 and 2000–03; in 2003 dollars)

	2003	2000	1990	percent change 2000–03	percent change 1990–2003
Number of consumer units (in 000s)	115,356	109,367	96,968	5.5%	19.0%
Average before-tax income	$51,128	$47,693	$43,521	7.2	17.5
Average annual spending	40,817	40,639	38,733	0.4	5.4
FOOD	**5,340**	**5,510**	**5,863**	**–3.1**	**–8.9**
Food at home	**3,129**	**3,227**	**3,391**	**–3.0**	**–7.7**
Cereals and bakery products	442	484	502	–8.7	–12.0
Cereals and cereal products	150	167	176	–10.0	–14.8
Bakery products	292	317	328	–8.0	–10.9
Meats, poultry, fish, and eggs	825	849	912	–2.9	–9.5
Beef	246	254	298	–3.2	–17.3
Pork	171	178	180	–4.1	–5.1
Other meats	102	108	135	–5.5	–24.5
Poultry	145	155	147	–6.4	–1.6
Fish and seafood	124	117	112	5.5	10.8
Eggs	37	36	41	1.9	–9.6
Dairy products	328	347	403	–5.5	–18.5
Fresh milk and cream	127	140	191	–9.2	–33.5
Other dairy products	201	206	212	–2.5	–5.0
Fruits and vegetables	535	557	557	–3.9	–3.9
Fresh fruits	171	174	173	–1.8	–1.3
Fresh vegetables	172	170	161	1.3	6.8
Processed fruits	108	123	127	–12.1	–14.9
Processed vegetables	84	90	96	–6.4	–12.1
Other food at home	999	990	1,018	0.9	–1.9
Sugar and other sweets	119	125	128	–4.8	–7.2
Fats and oils	86	89	93	–3.0	–7.3
Miscellaneous foods	490	467	459	5.0	6.9
Nonalcoholic beverages	268	267	291	0.4	–7.8
Food prepared by consumer unit on trips	36	43	48	–15.7	–24.6
Food away from home	**2,211**	**2,283**	**2,472**	**–3.1**	**–10.5**
ALCOHOLIC BEVERAGES	**391**	**397**	**400**	**–1.6**	**–2.2**
HOUSING	**13,432**	**13,159**	**11,877**	**2.1**	**13.1**
Shelter	**7,887**	**7,599**	**6,600**	**3.8**	**19.5**
Owned dwellings	5,263	4,916	4,030	7.1	30.6
Mortgage interest and charges	2,954	2,819	2,480	4.8	19.1
Property taxes	1,344	1,217	815	10.5	65.0
Maintenance, repairs, insurance, other expenses	965	881	737	9.5	30.9
Rented dwellings	2,179	2,173	2,092	0.3	4.2
Other lodging	445	511	476	–12.8	–6.6
Utilities, fuels, and public services	**2,811**	**2,659**	**2,579**	**5.7**	**9.0**
Natural gas	392	328	336	19.5	16.8
Electricity	1,028	973	1,034	5.6	–0.6
Fuel oil and other fuels	110	104	136	6.2	–19.4
Telephone services	956	937	808	2.1	18.3
Water and other public services	326	316	263	3.1	23.8
Household services	**707**	**731**	**609**	**–3.2**	**16.2**
Personal services	294	348	299	–15.6	–1.6
Other household services	414	382	310	8.3	33.6
Housekeeping supplies	**529**	**515**	**554**	**2.7**	**–4.5**
Laundry and cleaning supplies	132	140	154	–5.7	–14.4
Other household products	263	241	233	8.9	12.7
Postage and stationery	133	135	166	–1.2	–20.1
Household furnishings and equipment	**1,497**	**1,655**	**1,535**	**–9.5**	**–2.5**
Household textiles	113	113	135	–0.2	–16.4
Furniture	401	418	423	–4.0	–5.2
Floor coverings	52	47	126	10.6	–58.6

	2003	2000	1990	percent change 2000–03	percent change 1990–2003
Major appliances	$196	$202	$201	−2.9%	−2.3%
Small appliances, miscellaneous housewares	88	93	102	−5.3	−14.0
Miscellaneous household equipment	648	781	549	−17.0	18.1
APPAREL AND SERVICES	**1,640**	**1,983**	**2,208**	**−17.3**	**−25.7**
Men and boys	**372**	**470**	**536**	**−20.9**	**−30.6**
Men, aged 16 or older	282	367	442	−23.3	−36.2
Boys, aged 2 to 15	89	103	96	−13.2	−6.8
Women and girls	**634**	**774**	**918**	**−18.1**	**−31.0**
Women, aged 16 or older	529	648	800	−18.4	−33.9
Girls, aged 2 to 15	106	126	119	−15.9	−10.7
Children under age 2	**81**	**88**	**96**	**−7.5**	**−15.2**
Footwear	**294**	**366**	**307**	**−19.8**	**−4.3**
Other apparel products and services	**258**	**284**	**352**	**−9.2**	**−26.7**
TRANSPORTATION	**7,781**	**7,923**	**6,988**	**−1.8**	**11.4**
Vehicle purchases	**3,732**	**3,651**	**2,906**	**2.2**	**28.4**
Cars and trucks, new	2,052	1,714	1,582	19.7	29.7
Cars and trucks, used	1,611	1,891	1,294	−14.8	24.5
Gasoline and motor oil	**1,333**	**1,379**	**1,429**	**−3.3**	**−6.7**
Other vehicle expenses	**2,331**	**2,437**	**2,241**	**−4.3**	**4.0**
Vehicle finance charges	371	350	409	5.9	−9.4
Maintenance and repairs	619	667	804	−7.1	−23.0
Vehicle insurance	905	831	768	8.9	17.8
Vehicle rental, leases, licenses, other charges	436	589	259	−25.9	68.1
Public transportation	**385**	**456**	**412**	**−15.6**	**−6.6**
HEALTH CARE	**2,416**	**2,207**	**2,020**	**9.5**	**19.6**
Health insurance	1,252	1,050	793	19.2	57.9
Medical services	591	607	767	−2.6	−22.9
Drugs	467	444	344	5.1	35.8
Medical supplies	107	106	116	1.2	−7.8
ENTERTAINMENT	**2,060**	**1,990**	**1,941**	**3.5**	**6.1**
Fees and admissions	494	550	506	−10.2	−2.4
Television, radio, sound equipment	730	664	620	9.9	17.8
Pets, toys, and playground equipment	378	357	377	5.9	0.4
Other entertainment supplies, services	457	420	438	8.9	4.3
PERSONAL CARE PRODUCTS AND SERVICES	**527**	**602**	**497**	**−12.5**	**6.1**
READING	**127**	**156**	**209**	**−18.6**	**−39.2**
EDUCATION	**783**	**675**	**554**	**16.0**	**41.3**
TOBACCO PRODUCTS AND SMOKING SUPPLIES	**290**	**341**	**374**	**−14.9**	**−22.4**
MISCELLANEOUS	**606**	**829**	**1,149**	**−26.9**	**−47.3**
CASH CONTRIBUTIONS	**1,370**	**1,273**	**1,114**	**7.6**	**23.0**
PERSONAL INSURANCE AND PENSIONS	**4,055**	**3,594**	**3,537**	**12.8**	**14.6**
Life and other personal insurance	397	426	471	−6.9	−15.7
Pensions and Social Security	3,658	3,168	3,063	15.5	19.2
PERSONAL TAXES	**2,532**	**3,330**	**4,029**	**−24.0**	**−37.2**
Federal income taxes	1,843	2,573	3,165	−28.4	−41.8
State and local income taxes	502	600	762	−16.4	−34.1
Other taxes	187	156	102	19.9	82.7
GIFTS FOR NONHOUSEHOLD MEMBERS	**1,007**	**1,157**	**1,243**	**−13.0**	**−19.0**
Food	**78**	**75**	**130**	**4.3**	**−39.8**
Alcoholic beverages	**16**	**15**	**–**	**7.0**	**–**
Housing	**220**	**311**	**317**	**−29.2**	**−30.5**
Housekeeping supplies	42	42	48	0.8	−12.1
Household textiles	13	14	19	−6.4	−32.0

	2003	2000	1990	percent change	
				2000–03	1990–2003
Appliances and misc. housewares	$25	$30	$37	–16.4%	–32.2%
Major appliances	7	9	10	–18.1	–26.7
Small appliances and misc. housewares	18	22	27	–19.8	–34.1
Miscellaneous household equipment	57	75	68	–23.8	–16.5
Other housing	85	150	146	–43.2	–41.8
Apparel and services	**225**	**261**	**322**	**–13.7**	**–30.1**
Males, aged 2 or older	56	73	83	–22.9	–32.7
Females, aged 2 or older	80	91	130	–11.9	–38.3
Children under age 2	39	44	42	–10.9	–7.8
Other apparel products and services	50	54	66	–8.2	–23.7
Jewelry and watches	26	21	34	21.7	–23.8
All other apparel products and services	25	32	31	–22.0	–20.4
Transportation	**60**	**75**	**72**	**–19.8**	**–17.0**
Health care	**48**	**41**	**61**	**18.3**	**–21.8**
Entertainment	**69**	**100**	**90**	**–31.3**	**–23.4**
Toys, games, hobbies, and tricycles	26	32	34	–18.9	–23.8
Other entertainment	43	68	56	–37.1	–23.2
Personal care products and services	**16**	**20**	**–**	**–21.2**	**–**
Reading	**1**	**2**	**–**	**–53.2**	**–**
Education	**200**	**161**	**131**	**24.0**	**52.7**
All other gifts	**74**	**95**	**120**	**–22.2**	**–38.4**

Note: The Bureau of Labor Statistics uses consumer unit rather than household as the sampling unit in the Consumer Expenditure Survey. For the definition of consumer unit, see the glossary. Spending on gifts is also included in the preceding product and service categories. (–) means data are not available.
Source: Bureau of Labor Statistics, 1990, 2000, and 2003 Consumer Expenditure Surveys, Internet site http://www.bls.gov/cex/home.htm; calculations by New Strategist

Spending by Age, 2003

The average household spent $40,817 in 2003, but some spent more while others spent less. Because spending rises with income, affluent householders spend the most. Householders aged 45 to 54 are in their peak earning years, which explains why they spent 23 percent more than the average household in 2003, the highest level of spending among all age groups. Householders aged 35 to 44 were in second place, their spending being 16 percent above average.

Households headed by people under age 25 and aged 75 or older spend the least because their incomes are lowest. Householders under age 25 spend just 55 percent as much as the average household, while householders aged 75 or older spend 61 percent as much as the average.

Householders aged 45 to 54 spend the most overall, but other age groups spend more in some categories. Householders under age 25 are the biggest spenders on alcoholic beverages, for example. Householders aged 25 to 34 spend the most on used cars and trucks and infants' apparel. Householders aged 35 to 44 spend the most on children's clothes and entertainment. Spending on new cars and trucks, public transportation, and reading material is highest in the 55-to-64 age group. Households headed by people aged 65 or older spend the most on health care, including the individual categories of health insurance and drugs.

With the early retirement trend coming to an end, look for the two-earner couples of the baby-boom generation to boost spending by householders aged 55 to 64 in the years ahead.

Table 1.2 Average spending by age of householder, 2003

(average annual spending of consumer units by product and service category and age of consumer unit reference person, 2003)

	total consumer units	under 25	25 to 34	35 to 44	45 to 54	55 to 64	aged 65 or older total	65 to 74	75 or older
Number of consumer units (000)	115,356	8,584	19,737	24,413	23,131	16,580	22,912	11,495	11,417
Average number of persons per consumer unit	2.5	1.8	2.9	3.2	2.6	2.1	1.7	1.9	1.5
Average income before taxes	$51,128	$20,680	$50,389	$61,091	$68,028	$58,672	$30,437	$35,314	$25,492
Average annual spending	40,817	22,396	40,525	47,175	50,101	44,191	29,376	33,629	25,016
FOOD	**5,340**	**3,401**	**5,318**	**6,272**	**6,381**	**5,530**	**3,896**	**4,544**	**3,208**
Food at home	**3,129**	**1,766**	**2,976**	**3,600**	**3,693**	**3,315**	**2,575**	**2,888**	**2,241**
Cereals and bakery products	442	256	421	523	509	427	387	414	358
Cereals and cereal products	150	96	156	183	168	140	120	129	110
Bakery products	292	160	265	340	341	287	267	285	248
Meats, poultry, fish, and eggs	825	438	769	933	1,002	914	661	758	558
Beef	246	131	227	265	320	287	178	226	128
Pork	171	88	142	188	208	192	157	165	147
Other meats	102	53	90	123	123	108	83	92	74
Poultry	145	85	151	174	171	142	105	114	94
Fish and seafood	124	57	124	139	140	148	103	122	82
Eggs	37	23	35	44	40	36	36	39	32
Dairy products	328	193	317	388	378	326	277	308	243
Fresh milk and cream	127	76	127	157	138	118	108	118	97
Other dairy products	201	116	191	230	240	209	169	190	146
Fruits and vegetables	535	272	495	593	621	593	484	537	428
Fresh fruits	171	75	157	190	204	189	153	172	133
Fresh vegetables	172	87	157	187	199	192	160	182	136
Processed fruits	108	66	104	123	122	115	95	99	92
Processed vegetables	84	44	77	93	96	97	76	84	68
Other food at home	999	607	974	1,164	1,184	1,054	767	872	654
Sugar and other sweets	119	61	102	147	141	125	100	111	89
Fats and oils	86	44	76	95	101	93	80	89	70
Miscellaneous foods	490	331	509	562	570	498	366	416	313
Nonalcoholic beverages	268	159	256	317	329	291	191	217	164
Food prepared by consumer unit on trips	36	12	31	43	43	47	29	39	19
Food away from home	**2,211**	**1,636**	**2,342**	**2,672**	**2,688**	**2,215**	**1,321**	**1,656**	**968**
ALCOHOLIC BEVERAGES	**391**	**509**	**446**	**424**	**477**	**372**	**184**	**237**	**128**
HOUSING	**13,432**	**7,095**	**14,392**	**16,098**	**15,624**	**13,714**	**9,729**	**10,761**	**8,678**
Shelter	**7,887**	**4,574**	**8,915**	**9,678**	**9,237**	**7,571**	**5,201**	**5,764**	**4,635**
Owned dwellings	5,263	765	4,837	6,940	6,893	5,769	3,515	4,300	2,725
Mortgage interest and charges	2,954	449	3,373	4,541	4,088	2,739	851	1,349	350
Property taxes	1,344	230	910	1,479	1,625	1,770	1,399	1,472	1,325
Maintenance, repair, insurance, other expenses	965	87	554	921	1,180	1,260	1,266	1,480	1,050
Rented dwellings	2,179	3,593	3,835	2,315	1,656	1,179	1,331	1,045	1,619
Other lodging	445	216	243	423	688	623	355	419	291
Utilities, fuels, and public services	**2,811**	**1,329**	**2,580**	**3,142**	**3,335**	**3,089**	**2,484**	**2,723**	**2,244**
Natural gas	392	118	341	427	468	432	396	411	380
Electricity	1,028	470	915	1,145	1,199	1,153	946	1,046	845
Fuel oil and other fuels	110	23	62	109	129	146	138	140	135
Telephone	956	616	1,001	1,097	1,156	981	673	773	572
Water and other public services	326	102	261	365	383	376	332	352	312
Household services	**707**	**230**	**872**	**949**	**633**	**604**	**635**	**504**	**768**
Personal services	294	135	571	521	121	71	206	37	377
Other household services	414	95	301	428	512	533	429	467	391
Housekeeping supplies	**529**	**225**	**455**	**597**	**618**	**618**	**485**	**590**	**373**
Laundry and cleaning supplies	132	73	140	149	154	139	103	123	81
Other household products	263	101	204	311	312	308	247	313	176
Postage and stationery	133	51	111	137	151	171	136	154	116
Household furnishings and equipment	**1,497**	**737**	**1,571**	**1,731**	**1,801**	**1,831**	**923**	**1,180**	**657**
Household textiles	113	42	109	108	155	140	90	124	54
Furniture	401	203	499	518	450	447	184	225	142
Floor coverings	52	8	32	61	62	76	48	55	40

	total consumer units	under 25	25 to 34	35 to 44	45 to 54	55 to 64	aged 65 or older total	65 to 74	75 or older
Major appliances	$196	$67	$216	$209	$217	$231	$165	$219	$110
Small appliances, misc. housewares	88	48	69	92	111	127	63	79	47
Miscellaneous household equipment	648	369	647	743	807	810	373	477	265
APPAREL AND RELATED SERVICES	**1,640**	**1,117**	**1,849**	**2,091**	**1,953**	**1,562**	**908**	**1,190**	**611**
Men and boys	**372**	**259**	**391**	**530**	**467**	**314**	**170**	**216**	**122**
Men, aged 16 or older	282	233	274	349	372	273	150	186	112
Boys, aged 2 to 15	89	27	117	181	95	41	20	31	10
Women and girls	**634**	**352**	**625**	**764**	**809**	**654**	**419**	**552**	**277**
Women, aged 16 or older	529	326	485	547	708	602	386	496	268
Girls, aged 2 to 15	106	25	140	217	101	52	33	55	9
Children under age 2	**81**	**115**	**175**	**95**	**52**	**60**	**17**	**20**	**15**
Footwear	**294**	**206**	**331**	**413**	**334**	**237**	**167**	**214**	**116**
Other apparel products and services	**258**	**184**	**327**	**289**	**291**	**297**	**135**	**188**	**81**
TRANSPORTATION	**7,781**	**4,674**	**8,106**	**8,892**	**9,766**	**8,680**	**4,824**	**6,015**	**3,622**
Vehicle purchases	**3,732**	**2,241**	**3,932**	**4,255**	**4,632**	**4,289**	**2,247**	**2,770**	**1,721**
Cars and trucks, new	2,052	991	1,757	2,221	2,559	2,624	1,591	1,900	1,280
Cars and trucks, used	1,611	1,231	2,080	1,937	1,951	1,645	637	832	441
Other vehicles	68	19	96	98	113	20	19	38	1
Gasoline and motor oil	**1,333**	**947**	**1,388**	**1,582**	**1,644**	**1,411**	**792**	**1,019**	**563**
Other vehicle expenses	**2,331**	**1,299**	**2,446**	**2,643**	**3,013**	**2,484**	**1,487**	**1,857**	**1,112**
Vehicle finance charges	371	224	483	476	485	336	125	191	57
Maintenance and repairs	619	352	558	677	782	728	467	601	330
Vehicle insurance	905	504	910	997	1,197	932	640	724	555
Vehicle rentals, leases, licenses, other charges	436	218	495	493	549	488	255	340	170
Public transportation	**385**	**187**	**340**	**411**	**476**	**495**	**298**	**370**	**226**
HEALTH CARE	**2,416**	**546**	**1,468**	**2,105**	**2,479**	**3,059**	**3,741**	**3,626**	**3,856**
Health insurance	1,252	281	810	1,109	1,166	1,572	2,002	1,974	2,031
Medical services	591	129	394	598	718	742	688	681	695
Drugs	467	100	202	301	459	627	905	838	971
Medical supplies	107	37	62	97	137	118	146	133	159
ENTERTAINMENT	**2,060**	**950**	**1,958**	**2,519**	**2,407**	**2,414**	**1,469**	**2,016**	**909**
Fees and admissions	494	233	402	638	624	597	314	383	244
Television, radio, sound equipment	730	463	780	874	865	744	488	560	415
Pets, toys, and playground equipment	378	139	403	438	450	381	309	451	159
Other entertainment products and services	457	115	373	569	468	692	358	621	90
PERSONAL CARE PRODUCTS AND SERVICES	**527**	**326**	**498**	**602**	**616**	**549**	**440**	**491**	**387**
READING	**127**	**53**	**99**	**114**	**150**	**168**	**141**	**149**	**134**
EDUCATION	**783**	**1,490**	**684**	**694**	**1,377**	**743**	**129**	**176**	**81**
TOBACCO PRODUCTS AND SMOKING SUPPLIES	**290**	**230**	**285**	**312**	**385**	**337**	**162**	**219**	**105**
MISCELLANEOUS	**606**	**251**	**532**	**601**	**830**	**675**	**533**	**547**	**519**
CASH CONTRIBUTIONS	**1,370**	**371**	**754**	**1,256**	**1,651**	**1,568**	**1,969**	**1,811**	**2,127**
PERSONAL INSURANCE AND PENSIONS	**4,055**	**1,382**	**4,137**	**5,196**	**6,003**	**4,819**	**1,251**	**1,847**	**651**
Life and other personal insurance	397	40	200	382	600	570	388	504	270
Pensions and Social Security	3,658	1,342	3,937	4,814	5,403	4,249	864	1,342	382
PERSONAL TAXES	**2,532**	**421**	**1,979**	**2,817**	**3,949**	**2,827**	**1,878**	**1,455**	**2,307**
Federal income taxes	1,843	261	1,336	1,988	2,914	2,010	1,535	1,044	2,032
State and local income taxes	502	144	544	658	814	511	114	152	77
Other taxes	187	15	99	170	221	306	228	259	197
GIFTS FOR NONHOUSEHOLD MEMBERS	**1,007**	**321**	**639**	**741**	**1,588**	**1,572**	**873**	**952**	**788**
Food	**78**	**19**	**23**	**40**	**140**	**180**	**49**	**72**	**26**
Alcoholic beverages	**16**	**10**	**21**	**16**	**22**	**17**	**8**	**11**	**6**
Housing	**220**	**75**	**139**	**204**	**322**	**310**	**198**	**213**	**181**
Housekeeping supplies	42	17	31	54	49	52	31	41	21
Household textiles	13	2	5	10	21	23	10	15	6

	total consumer units	under 25	25 to 34	35 to 44	45 to 54	55 to 64	aged 65 or older total	65 to 74	75 or older
Appliances and misc. housewares	$25	$9	$14	$25	$31	$36	$24	$29	$18
Major appliances	7	1	3	9	8	7	9	8	9
Small appliances and misc. housewares	18	8	11	17	23	29	15	21	9
Miscellaneous household equipment	57	19	40	41	81	91	53	63	42
Other housing	85	28	48	73	140	107	79	65	94
Apparel and services	**225**	**116**	**220**	**220**	**250**	**314**	**188**	**265**	**108**
Males, aged 2 or older	56	30	38	55	71	80	48	57	39
Females, aged 2 or older	80	19	68	78	83	122	85	130	38
Children under age 2	39	28	51	45	41	52	14	18	11
Other apparel products and services	50	39	65	42	56	59	40	60	20
Jewelry and watches	26	27	49	14	24	27	19	28	9
All other apparel products and services	25	12	15	28	32	33	21	31	11
Transportation	**60**	**7**	**77**	**23**	**106**	**72**	**47**	**43**	**52**
Health care	**48**	**3**	**8**	**23**	**49**	**48**	**125**	**44**	**206**
Entertainment	**69**	**39**	**60**	**61**	**81**	**111**	**54**	**67**	**41**
Toys, games, hobbies, and tricycles	26	8	23	21	30	45	23	33	14
Other entertainment	43	31	37	40	51	66	31	34	27
Personal care products and services	**16**	**7**	**12**	**16**	**23**	**19**	**13**	**14**	**12**
Reading	**1**	–	**1**	–	**1**	**3**	**3**	**3**	**2**
Education	**200**	**23**	**31**	**97**	**510**	**373**	**83**	**111**	**54**
All other gifts	**74**	**22**	**47**	**41**	**84**	**126**	**106**	**110**	**101**

Note: Spending by category will not add to total spending because gift spending is also included in the preceding product and service categories and personal taxes are not included in the total. (–) means sample is too small to make a reliable estimate.
Source: Bureau of Labor Statistics, 2003 Consumer Expenditure Survey, Internet site http://www.bls.gov/cex/

Table 1.3 Indexed spending by age of householder, 2003

(indexed average annual spending of consumer units by product and service category and age of consumer unit reference person, 2003; index definition. an index of 100 is the average for all consumer units; an index of 132 means that spending by consumer units in that group is 32 percent above the average for all consumer units; an index of 68 indicates spending that is 32 percent below the average for all consumer units)

	total consumer units	under 25	25 to 34	35 to 44	45 to 54	55 to 64	aged 65 or older total	65 to 74	75 or older
Average spending of consumer unit, total	$40,817	$22,396	$40,525	$47,175	$50,101	$44,191	$29,376	$33,629	$25,016
Average spending of consumer unit, index	100	55	99	116	123	108	72	82	61
FOOD	100	64	100	117	119	104	73	85	60
Food at home	100	56	95	115	118	106	82	92	72
Cereals and bakery products	100	58	95	118	115	97	88	94	81
Cereals and cereal products	100	64	104	122	112	93	80	86	73
Bakery products	100	55	91	116	117	98	91	98	85
Meats, poultry, fish, and eggs	100	53	93	113	121	111	80	92	68
Beef	100	53	92	108	130	117	72	92	52
Pork	100	51	83	110	122	112	92	96	86
Other meats	100	52	88	121	121	106	81	90	73
Poultry	100	59	104	120	118	98	72	79	65
Fish and seafood	100	46	100	112	113	119	83	98	66
Eggs	100	62	95	119	108	97	97	105	86
Dairy products	100	59	97	118	115	99	84	94	74
Fresh milk and cream	100	60	100	124	109	93	85	93	76
Other dairy products	100	58	95	114	119	104	84	95	73
Fruits and vegetables	100	51	93	111	116	111	90	100	80
Fresh fruits	100	44	92	111	119	111	89	101	78
Fresh vegetables	100	51	91	109	116	112	93	106	79
Processed fruits	100	61	96	114	113	106	88	92	85
Processed vegetables	100	52	92	111	114	115	90	100	81
Other food at home	100	61	97	117	119	106	77	87	65
Sugar and other sweets	100	51	86	124	118	105	84	93	75
Fats and oils	100	51	88	110	117	108	93	103	81
Miscellaneous foods	100	68	104	115	116	102	75	85	64
Nonalcoholic beverages	100	59	96	118	123	109	71	81	61
Food prepared by consumer unit on trips	100	33	86	119	119	131	81	108	53
Food away from home	100	74	106	121	122	100	60	75	44
ALCOHOLIC BEVERAGES	100	130	114	108	122	95	47	61	33
HOUSING	100	53	107	120	116	102	72	80	65
Shelter	100	58	113	123	117	96	66	73	59
Owned dwellings	100	15	92	132	131	110	67	82	52
Mortgage interest and charges	100	15	114	154	138	93	29	46	12
Property taxes	100	17	68	110	121	132	104	110	99
Maintenance, repair, insurance, other expenses	100	9	57	95	122	131	131	153	109
Rented dwellings	100	165	176	106	75	54	61	48	74
Other lodging	100	49	55	95	155	140	80	94	65
Utilities, fuels, and public services	100	47	92	112	119	110	88	97	80
Natural gas	100	30	87	109	119	110	101	105	97
Electricity	100	46	89	111	117	112	92	102	82
Fuel oil and other fuels	100	21	56	99	117	133	125	127	123
Telephone	100	64	105	115	121	103	70	81	60
Water and other public services	100	31	80	112	117	115	102	108	96
Household services	100	33	123	134	90	85	90	71	109
Personal services	100	46	194	177	41	24	70	13	128
Other household services	100	23	73	103	124	129	104	113	94
Housekeeping supplies	100	43	86	113	117	117	92	112	71
Laundry and cleaning supplies	100	55	106	113	117	105	78	93	61
Other household products	100	38	78	118	119	117	94	119	67
Postage and stationery	100	38	83	103	114	129	102	116	87
Household furnishings and equipment	100	49	105	116	120	122	62	79	44
Household textiles	100	37	96	96	137	124	80	110	48
Furniture	100	51	124	129	112	111	46	56	35
Floor coverings	100	15	62	117	119	146	92	106	77

	total consumer units	under 25	25 to 34	35 to 44	45 to 54	55 to 64	aged 65 or older total	65 to 74	75 or older
Major appliances	100	34	110	107	111	118	84	112	56
Small appliances, misc. housewares	100	55	78	105	126	144	72	90	53
Miscellaneous household equipment	100	57	100	115	125	125	58	74	41
APPAREL AND RELATED SERVICES	**100**	**68**	**113**	**128**	**119**	**95**	**55**	**73**	**37**
Men and boys	**100**	**70**	**105**	**142**	**126**	**84**	**46**	**58**	**33**
Men, aged 16 or older	100	83	97	124	132	97	53	66	40
Boys, aged 2 to 15	100	30	131	203	107	46	22	35	11
Women and girls	**100**	**56**	**99**	**121**	**128**	**103**	**66**	**87**	**44**
Women, aged 16 or older	100	62	92	103	134	114	73	94	51
Girls, aged 2 to 15	100	24	132	205	95	49	31	52	8
Children under age 2	**100**	**142**	**216**	**117**	**64**	**74**	**21**	**25**	**19**
Footwear	**100**	**70**	**113**	**140**	**114**	**81**	**57**	**73**	**39**
Other apparel products and services	**100**	**71**	**127**	**112**	**113**	**115**	**52**	**73**	**31**
TRANSPORTATION	**100**	**60**	**104**	**114**	**126**	**112**	**62**	**77**	**47**
Vehicle purchases	**100**	**60**	**105**	**114**	**124**	**115**	**60**	**74**	**46**
Cars and trucks, new	100	48	86	108	125	128	78	93	62
Cars and trucks, used	100	76	129	120	121	102	40	52	27
Other vehicles	100	28	141	144	166	29	28	56	–
Gasoline and motor oil	**100**	**71**	**104**	**119**	**123**	**106**	**59**	**76**	**42**
Other vehicle expenses	**100**	**56**	**105**	**113**	**129**	**107**	**64**	**80**	**48**
Vehicle finance charges	100	60	130	128	131	91	34	51	15
Maintenance and repairs	100	57	90	109	126	118	75	97	53
Vehicle insurance	100	56	101	110	132	103	71	80	61
Vehicle rentals, leases, licenses, other charges	100	50	114	113	126	112	58	78	39
Public transportation	**100**	**49**	**88**	**107**	**124**	**129**	**77**	**96**	**59**
HEALTH CARE	**100**	**23**	**61**	**87**	**103**	**127**	**155**	**150**	**160**
Health insurance	100	22	65	89	93	126	160	158	162
Medical services	100	22	67	101	121	126	116	115	118
Drugs	100	21	43	64	98	134	194	179	208
Medical supplies	100	35	58	91	128	110	136	124	149
ENTERTAINMENT	**100**	**46**	**95**	**122**	**117**	**117**	**71**	**98**	**44**
Fees and admissions	100	47	81	129	126	121	64	78	49
Television, radio, sound equipment	100	63	107	120	118	102	67	77	57
Pets, toys, and playground equipment	100	37	107	116	119	101	82	119	42
Other entertainment products and services	100	25	82	125	102	151	78	136	20
PERSONAL CARE PRODUCTS AND SERVICES	**100**	**62**	**94**	**114**	**117**	**104**	**83**	**93**	**73**
READING	**100**	**42**	**78**	**90**	**118**	**132**	**111**	**117**	**106**
EDUCATION	**100**	**190**	**87**	**89**	**176**	**95**	**16**	**22**	**10**
TOBACCO PRODUCTS AND SMOKING SUPPLIES	**100**	**79**	**98**	**108**	**133**	**116**	**56**	**76**	**36**
MISCELLANEOUS	**100**	**41**	**88**	**99**	**137**	**111**	**88**	**90**	**86**
CASH CONTRIBUTIONS	**100**	**27**	**55**	**92**	**121**	**114**	**144**	**132**	**155**
PERSONAL INSURANCE AND PENSIONS	**100**	**34**	**102**	**128**	**148**	**119**	**31**	**46**	**16**
Life and other personal insurance	100	10	50	96	151	144	98	127	68
Pensions and Social Security	100	37	108	132	148	116	24	37	10
PERSONAL TAXES	**100**	**17**	**78**	**111**	**156**	**112**	**74**	**57**	**91**
Federal income taxes	100	14	72	108	158	109	83	57	110
State and local income taxes	100	29	108	131	162	102	23	30	15
Other taxes	100	8	53	91	118	164	122	139	105
GIFTS FOR NONHOUSEHOLD MEMBERS	**100**	**32**	**63**	**74**	**158**	**156**	**87**	**95**	**78**
Food	**100**	**24**	**29**	**51**	**179**	**231**	**63**	**92**	**33**
Alcoholic beverages	**100**	**63**	**131**	**100**	**138**	**106**	**50**	**69**	**38**
Housing	**100**	**34**	**63**	**93**	**146**	**141**	**90**	**97**	**82**
Housekeeping supplies	100	40	74	129	117	124	74	98	50
Household textiles	100	15	38	77	162	177	77	115	46

	total consumer units	under 25	25 to 34	35 to 44	45 to 54	55 to 64	aged 65 or older		
							total	65 to 74	75 or older
Appliances and misc. housewares	100	36	56	100	124	144	96	116	72
Major appliances	100	14	43	129	114	100	129	114	129
Small appliances and misc. housewares	100	44	61	94	128	161	83	117	50
Miscellaneous household equipment	100	33	70	72	142	160	93	111	74
Other housing	100	33	56	86	165	126	93	76	111
Apparel and services	**100**	52	98	98	**111**	**140**	84	**118**	**48**
Males, aged 2 or older	100	54	68	98	127	143	86	102	70
Females, aged 2 or older	100	24	85	98	104	153	106	163	48
Children under age 2	100	72	131	115	105	133	36	46	28
Other apparel products and services	100	78	130	84	112	118	80	120	40
Jewelry and watches	100	104	188	54	92	104	73	108	35
All other apparel products and services	100	48	60	112	128	132	84	124	44
Transportation	**100**	**12**	**128**	**38**	**177**	**120**	**78**	**72**	**87**
Health care	**100**	**6**	**17**	**48**	**102**	**100**	**260**	**92**	**429**
Entertainment	**100**	**57**	**87**	**88**	**117**	**161**	**78**	**97**	**59**
Toys, games, hobbies, and tricycles	100	31	88	81	115	173	88	127	54
Other entertainment	100	72	86	93	119	153	72	79	63
Personal care products and services	**100**	**44**	**75**	**100**	**144**	**119**	**81**	**88**	**75**
Reading	**100**	**–**	**100**	**–**	**100**	**300**	**300**	**300**	**200**
Education	**100**	**12**	**16**	**49**	**255**	**187**	**42**	**56**	**27**
All other gifts	**100**	**30**	**64**	**55**	**114**	**170**	**143**	**149**	**136**

Note: (–) means sample is too small to make a reliable estimate.
Source: Calculations by New Strategist based on the Bureau of Labor Statistics 2003 Consumer Expenditure Survey

Spending by Income, 2003

Among households reporting their incomes to Consumer Expenditure Survey interviewers, average spending was $42,742 in 2003. Not surprisingly, the most affluent households, those with incomes of $70,000 or more, spend the most—57 percent more than the average household. The highest income group spends the most on almost every product and service category, with a few exceptions such as rented dwellings and tobacco.

Households with incomes below $40,000 spend less than the average household on most categories. One of the few exceptions is rent. Many households with incomes below $40,000 spend more money than they make. The income they report to government interviewers is less than their reported expenditures. These households make up the difference through borrowing, the use of savings, and unreported income.

Income makes a bigger difference in the purchasing of some products than others. Everyone has to buy food, but only those who can afford to do so will buy a new car. The most affluent households spend close to the average on such items as eggs, drugs, and tobacco. They spend well over twice what the average household spends on other lodging (a category that includes hotel and motel expenses as well as housing for children in college), mortgage interest, and fees and admissions to entertainment events.

Table 1.4 Average spending by household income, 2003

(average annual spending of consumer units by product and service category and before-tax income of consumer unit, 2003, complete income reporters only)

	complete income reporters	under $10,000	$10,000–$19,999	$20,000–$29,999	$30,000–$39,999	$40,000–$49,999	$50,000–$69,999	$70,000 or more
Number of consumer units (000)	97,391	11,553	15,547	13,182	10,759	8,891	13,890	23,567
Average number of persons per consumer unit	2.5	1.6	2.0	2.3	2.5	2.6	2.8	3.0
Average income before taxes	$51,128	$5,287	$14,814	$24,655	$34,485	$44,294	$58,900	$117,960
Average annual spending	42,742	17,254	21,801	29,034	34,931	39,757	49,789	77,521
FOOD	5,593	3,016	3,564	4,338	4,993	5,486	6,511	8,794
Food at home	3,236	1,922	2,451	2,856	3,048	3,234	3,700	4,472
Cereals and bakery products	456	288	365	403	415	468	511	617
Cereals and cereal products	155	112	122	141	149	155	168	201
Bakery products	301	176	243	262	266	313	343	416
Meats, poultry, fish, and eggs	837	487	633	800	784	821	1,011	1,100
Beef	252	128	172	239	216	255	355	333
Pork	171	105	150	187	169	166	187	204
Other meats	104	61	84	95	96	103	129	132
Poultry	145	92	111	138	132	143	164	197
Fish and seafood	125	71	80	101	131	115	141	190
Eggs	38	29	35	41	40	40	36	44
Dairy products	343	195	262	302	321	367	384	475
Fresh milk and cream	132	84	110	124	126	142	140	168
Other dairy products	212	111	151	178	195	225	244	307
Fruits and vegetables	556	334	438	498	550	524	585	783
Fresh fruits	177	100	131	156	175	162	181	266
Fresh vegetables	179	107	137	165	187	159	179	259
Processed fruits	112	71	94	103	102	109	122	151
Processed vegetables	87	57	76	75	85	93	102	107
Other food at home	1,044	617	754	852	978	1,053	1,209	1,497
Sugar and other sweets	123	71	95	110	111	126	136	174
Fats and oils	87	55	72	80	85	90	93	113
Miscellaneous foods	513	295	371	395	483	524	591	755
Nonalcoholic beverages	281	182	201	248	269	285	344	374
Food prepared by consumer unit on trips	38	14	14	20	30	28	45	80
Food away from home	2,358	1,094	1,114	1,483	1,945	2,252	2,811	4,323
ALCOHOLIC BEVERAGES	442	195	205	247	309	407	556	858
HOUSING	13,653	6,443	7,987	9,828	11,259	12,728	15,106	23,693
Shelter	7,921	3,929	4,595	5,635	6,510	7,269	8,679	13,795
Owned dwellings	5,247	1,441	1,847	2,702	3,511	4,578	6,253	11,230
Mortgage interest and charges	2,947	574	584	1,286	1,875	2,635	3,821	6,689
Property taxes	1,310	528	689	742	924	1,056	1,409	2,636
Maintenance, repair, insurance, other expenses	989	339	575	673	712	887	1,024	1,904
Rented dwellings	2,220	2,336	2,615	2,780	2,794	2,389	1,986	1,400
Other lodging	455	152	133	154	204	303	439	1,165
Utilities, fuels, and public services	2,820	1,565	2,062	2,394	2,666	2,906	3,217	3,976
Natural gas	387	200	307	325	350	382	423	564
Electricity	1,021	618	789	901	1,001	1,068	1,153	1,354
Fuel oil and other fuels	112	55	87	91	108	106	119	167
Telephone	970	537	653	812	900	1,002	1,146	1,394
Water and other public services	330	155	226	265	307	349	376	497
Household services	730	181	366	414	449	560	749	1,597
Personal services	303	51	177	151	161	229	316	681
Other household services	427	130	189	264	288	331	433	916
Housekeeping supplies	582	258	378	426	494	542	628	1,010
Laundry and cleaning supplies	145	81	125	122	145	125	159	206
Other household products	287	118	161	192	226	288	283	549
Postage and stationery	149	58	91	113	122	129	186	255
Household furnishings and equipment	1,600	512	587	958	1,142	1,450	1,834	3,315
Household textiles	126	44	56	88	84	140	138	244
Furniture	419	122	123	229	271	334	493	922
Floor coverings	54	15	23	17	28	32	41	143

	complete income reporters	under $10,000	$10,000– $19,999	$20,000– $29,999	$30,000– $39,999	$40,000– $49,999	$50,000– $69,999	$70,000 or more
Major appliances	$205	$63	$90	$183	$175	$220	$221	$360
Small appliances, misc. housewares	95	39	52	68	79	68	107	178
Miscellaneous household equipment	701	229	242	372	503	656	832	1,468
APPAREL AND RELATED SERVICES	**1,744**	**878**	**987**	**1,112**	**1,503**	**1,515**	**1,967**	**3,139**
Men and boys	**385**	**203**	**167**	**204**	**363**	**342**	**455**	**720**
Men, aged 16 or older	294	159	111	145	274	264	349	566
Boys, aged 2 to 15	91	43	56	59	90	78	106	154
Women and girls	**699**	**314**	**413**	**445**	**598**	**602**	**771**	**1,285**
Women, aged 16 or older	588	276	354	366	515	506	651	1,071
Girls, aged 2 to 15	110	38	59	79	83	96	120	214
Children under age 2	**86**	**35**	**56**	**66**	**85**	**85**	**84**	**144**
Footwear	**311**	**227**	**239**	**245**	**268**	**263**	**396**	**434**
Other apparel products and services	**263**	**99**	**111**	**152**	**188**	**223**	**260**	**556**
TRANSPORTATION	**8,041**	**2,600**	**3,560**	**5,615**	**6,973**	**7,949**	**10,656**	**14,006**
Vehicle purchases	**3,871**	**1,075**	**1,488**	**2,607**	**3,264**	**3,686**	**5,407**	**6,964**
Cars and trucks, new	2,154	373	640	1,236	1,470	1,425	2,654	4,832
Cars and trucks, used	1,649	679	845	1,372	1,755	2,179	2,608	1,999
Other vehicles	68	61	7	–	38	82	145	133
Gasoline and motor oil	**1,353**	**576**	**773**	**1,053**	**1,309**	**1,494**	**1,712**	**2,041**
Other vehicle expenses	**2,416**	**784**	**1,141**	**1,686**	**2,145**	**2,486**	**3,104**	**4,161**
Vehicle finance charges	383	99	111	230	360	406	560	685
Maintenance and repairs	657	241	369	479	577	685	800	1,093
Vehicle insurance	929	294	514	729	901	983	1,158	1,484
Vehicle rentals, leases, licenses, other charges	447	150	147	247	306	412	585	899
Public transportation	**400**	**165**	**158**	**269**	**256**	**284**	**433**	**839**
HEALTH CARE	**2,495**	**1,158**	**1,920**	**2,286**	**2,460**	**2,629**	**2,811**	**3,429**
Health insurance	1,267	587	1,009	1,190	1,270	1,355	1,461	1,666
Medical services	612	204	342	451	591	660	717	1,008
Drugs	501	316	497	535	490	516	508	574
Medical supplies	115	51	72	111	110	99	125	182
ENTERTAINMENT	**2,155**	**681**	**826**	**1,517**	**1,742**	**1,925**	**2,363**	**4,270**
Fees and admissions	511	143	121	228	292	383	553	1,231
Television, radio, sound equipment	745	349	431	575	645	780	864	1,205
Pets, toys, and playground equipment	411	116	185	441	299	438	469	693
Other entertainment products and services	488	72	89	273	506	324	477	1,141
PERSONAL CARE PRODUCTS AND SERVICES	**559**	**261**	**348**	**384**	**452**	**533**	**637**	**966**
READING	**133**	**50**	**74**	**95**	**105**	**129**	**144**	**243**
EDUCATION	**792**	**724**	**347**	**251**	**320**	**400**	**600**	**1,902**
TOBACCO PRODUCTS AND SMOKING SUPPLIES	**307**	**216**	**280**	**324**	**323**	**415**	**345**	**290**
MISCELLANEOUS	**658**	**293**	**352**	**510**	**545**	**693**	**919**	**1,008**
CASH CONTRIBUTIONS	**1,458**	**398**	**559**	**904**	**1,138**	**1,070**	**1,383**	**3,217**
PERSONAL INSURANCE AND PENSIONS	**4,710**	**340**	**792**	**1,622**	**2,810**	**3,878**	**5,792**	**11,705**
Life and other personal insurance	414	111	196	217	281	347	429	894
Pensions and Social Security	4,296	229	596	1,405	2,529	3,532	5,363	10,811
PERSONAL TAXES	**2,532**	**–48**	**–71**	**1,458**	**1,115**	**1,452**	**2,472**	**7,204**
Federal income taxes	1,843	–82	–166	1,219	658	933	1,670	5,448
State and local income taxes	502	–4	20	132	280	367	578	1,380
Other taxes	187	37	74	107	177	152	224	376
GIFTS FOR NONHOUSEHOLD MEMBERS	**1,055**	**276**	**494**	**578**	**784**	**799**	**1,142**	**2,260**
Food	**84**	**19**	**34**	**46**	**64**	**27**	**94**	**198**
Alcoholic beverages	**19**	**7**	**16**	**6**	**12**	**13**	**24**	**38**
Housing	**238**	**64**	**113**	**154**	**212**	**220**	**227**	**485**
Housekeeping supplies	48	17	26	29	32	39	67	88
Household textiles	14	2	7	9	11	12	8	35

	complete income reporters	under $10,000	$10,000– $19,999	$20,000– $29,999	$30,000– $39,999	$40,000– $49,999	$50,000– $69,999	$70,000 or more
Appliances and misc. housewares	$28	$3	$10	$12	$32	$27	$28	$59
Major appliances	7	2	3	1	5	16	4	13
Small appliances and misc. housewares	21	2	7	11	27	11	23	45
Miscellaneous household equipment	62	10	32	41	52	53	76	121
Other housing	87	33	38	63	85	89	48	182
Apparel and services	**232**	**88**	**141**	**153**	**224**	**208**	**300**	**385**
Males, aged 2 or older	55	39	33	26	54	44	62	98
Females, aged 2 or older	89	22	57	51	79	69	124	158
Children under age 2	41	9	30	32	38	46	43	66
Other apparel products and services	47	18	21	44	53	49	71	64
Jewelry and watches	23	10	6	28	22	17	43	31
All other apparel products and services	24	22	15	16	30	33	29	33
Transportation	**56**	**8**	**29**	**35**	**21**	**54**	**89**	**106**
Health care	**52**	**25**	**71**	**19**	**69**	**28**	**45**	**76**
Entertainment	**74**	**22**	**27**	**70**	**56**	**58**	**84**	**143**
Toys, games, hobbies, and tricycles	26	8	12	22	25	26	32	44
Other entertainment	48	14	14	47	31	33	52	99
Personal care products and services	**19**	**9**	**12**	**9**	**10**	**35**	**25**	**27**
Reading	**1**	**1**	**1**	**1**	**1**	**3**	**2**	**2**
Education	**201**	**8**	**13**	**30**	**68**	**84**	**151**	**651**
All other gifts	**78**	**24**	**36**	**55**	**48**	**68**	**101**	**149**

Note: Spending by category will not add to total spending because gift spending is also included in the preceding product and service categories and personal taxes are not included in the total. (–) means sample is too small to make a reliable estimate.
Source: Bureau of Labor Statistics, 2003 Consumer Expenditure Survey, Internet site http://www.bls.gov/cex/; calculations by New Strategist

Table 1.5 Indexed spending by household income, 2003

(indexed average annual spending of consumer units by product and service category and before-tax income of consumer unit reference person, 2003; complete income reporters only; index definition: an index of 100 is the average for all consumer units; an index of 132 means that spending by consumer units in that group is 32 percent above the average for all consumer units; an index of 68 indicates spending that is 32 percent below the average for all consumer units)

	complete income reporters	under $10,000	$10,000–$19,999	$20,000–$29,999	$30,000–$39,999	$40,000–$49,999	$50,000–$69,999	$70,000 or more
Average spending of consumer unit, total	$42,742	17,254	21,801	$23,034	$34,931	$39,757	$49,789	$77,521
Average spending of consumer unit, index	100	40	51	68	82	93	116	181
FOOD	100	54	64	78	89	98	116	157
Food at home	100	59	76	88	94	100	114	138
Cereals and bakery products	100	63	80	88	91	103	112	135
Cereals and cereal products	100	72	78	91	96	100	108	130
Bakery products	100	58	81	87	88	104	114	138
Meats, poultry, fish, and eggs	100	58	76	96	94	98	121	131
Beef	100	51	68	95	86	101	141	132
Pork	100	62	88	109	99	97	109	119
Other meats	100	59	80	91	92	99	124	127
Poultry	100	63	76	95	91	99	113	136
Fish and seafood	100	57	64	81	105	92	113	152
Eggs	100	76	93	108	105	105	95	116
Dairy products	100	57	76	88	94	107	112	138
Fresh milk and cream	100	64	84	94	95	108	106	127
Other dairy products	100	52	71	84	92	106	115	145
Fruits and vegetables	100	60	79	90	99	94	105	141
Fresh fruits	100	56	74	88	99	92	102	150
Fresh vegetables	100	60	76	92	104	89	100	145
Processed fruits	100	63	84	92	91	97	109	135
Processed vegetables	100	65	88	86	98	107	117	123
Other food at home	100	59	72	82	94	101	116	143
Sugar and other sweets	100	58	77	89	90	102	111	141
Fats and oils	100	63	83	92	98	103	107	130
Miscellaneous foods	100	58	72	77	94	102	115	147
Nonalcoholic beverages	100	65	72	88	96	101	122	133
Food prepared by consumer unit on trips	100	37	36	53	79	74	118	211
Food away from home	100	46	47	63	82	96	119	183
ALCOHOLIC BEVERAGES	100	44	46	56	70	92	126	194
HOUSING	100	47	59	72	82	93	111	174
Shelter	100	50	58	71	82	92	110	174
Owned dwellings	100	27	35	51	67	87	119	214
Mortgage interest and charges	100	19	20	44	64	89	130	227
Property taxes	100	40	53	57	71	81	108	201
Maintenance, repair, insurance, other expenses	100	34	58	68	72	90	104	193
Rented dwellings	100	105	118	125	126	108	89	63
Other lodging	100	33	29	34	45	67	96	256
Utilities, fuels, and public services	100	55	73	85	95	103	114	141
Natural gas	100	52	79	84	90	99	109	146
Electricity	100	60	77	88	98	105	113	133
Fuel oil and other fuels	100	49	78	81	96	95	106	149
Telephone	100	55	67	84	93	103	118	144
Water and other public services	100	47	68	80	93	106	114	151
Household services	100	25	50	57	62	77	103	219
Personal services	100	17	58	50	53	76	104	225
Other household services	100	30	44	62	67	78	101	215
Housekeeping supplies	100	44	65	73	85	93	108	174
Laundry and cleaning supplies	100	56	86	84	100	86	110	142
Other household products	100	41	56	67	79	100	99	191
Postage and stationery	100	39	61	76	82	87	125	171
Household furnishings and equipment	100	32	37	60	71	91	115	207
Household textiles	100	35	44	70	67	111	110	194
Furniture	100	29	29	55	65	80	118	220
Floor coverings	100	27	43	31	52	59	76	265

	complete income reporters	under $10,000	$10,000– $19,999	$20,000– $29,999	$30,000– $39,999	$40,000– $49,999	$50,000– $69,999	$70,000 or more
Major appliances	100	31	44	89	85	107	108	176
Small appliances, misc. housewares	100	42	55	72	83	72	113	187
Miscellaneous household equipment	100	33	35	53	72	94	119	209
APPAREL AND RELATED SERVICES	**100**	**50**	**57**	**64**	**86**	**87**	**113**	**180**
Men and boys	**100**	**53**	**43**	**53**	**94**	**89**	**118**	**187**
Men, aged 16 or older	100	54	38	49	93	90	119	193
Boys, aged 2 to 15	100	47	62	65	99	86	116	169
Women and girls	**100**	**45**	**59**	**64**	**86**	**86**	**110**	**184**
Women, aged 16 or older	100	47	60	62	88	86	111	182
Girls, aged 2 to 15	100	35	53	72	75	87	109	195
Children under age 2	**100**	**41**	**66**	**77**	**99**	**99**	**98**	**167**
Footwear	**100**	**73**	**77**	**79**	**86**	**85**	**127**	**140**
Other apparel products and services	**100**	**38**	**42**	**58**	**71**	**85**	**99**	**211**
TRANSPORTATION	**100**	**32**	**44**	**70**	**87**	**99**	**133**	**174**
Vehicle purchases	**100**	**28**	**38**	**67**	**84**	**95**	**140**	**180**
Cars and trucks, new	100	17	30	57	68	66	123	224
Cars and trucks, used	100	41	51	83	106	132	158	121
Other vehicles	100	90	10	–	56	121	213	196
Gasoline and motor oil	**100**	**43**	**57**	**78**	**97**	**110**	**127**	**151**
Other vehicle expenses	**100**	**32**	**47**	**70**	**89**	**103**	**128**	**172**
Vehicle finance charges	100	26	29	60	94	106	146	179
Maintenance and repairs	100	37	56	73	88	104	122	166
Vehicle insurance	100	32	55	78	97	106	125	160
Vehicle rentals, leases, licenses, other charges	100	34	33	55	68	92	131	201
Public transportation	**100**	**41**	**40**	**67**	**64**	**71**	**108**	**210**
HEALTH CARE	**100**	**46**	**77**	**92**	**99**	**105**	**113**	**137**
Health insurance	100	46	80	94	100	107	115	131
Medical services	100	33	56	74	97	108	117	165
Drugs	100	63	99	107	98	103	101	115
Medical supplies	100	44	63	97	96	86	109	158
ENTERTAINMENT	**100**	**32**	**38**	**70**	**81**	**89**	**110**	**198**
Fees and admissions	100	28	24	45	57	75	108	241
Television, radio, sound equipment	100	47	58	77	87	105	116	162
Pets, toys, and playground equipment	100	28	45	107	73	107	114	169
Other entertainment products and services	100	15	18	56	104	66	98	234
PERSONAL CARE PRODUCTS AND SERVICES	**100**	**47**	**62**	**69**	**81**	**95**	**114**	**173**
READING	**100**	**37**	**56**	**71**	**79**	**97**	**108**	**183**
EDUCATION	**100**	**91**	**44**	**32**	**40**	**51**	**76**	**240**
TOBACCO PRODUCTS AND SMOKING SUPPLIES	**100**	**70**	**91**	**106**	**105**	**135**	**112**	**94**
MISCELLANEOUS	**100**	**45**	**53**	**78**	**83**	**105**	**140**	**153**
CASH CONTRIBUTIONS	**100**	**27**	**38**	**62**	**78**	**73**	**95**	**221**
PERSONAL INSURANCE AND PENSIONS	**100**	**7**	**17**	**34**	**60**	**82**	**123**	**249**
Life and other personal insurance	100	27	47	52	68	84	104	216
Pensions and Social Security	100	5	14	33	59	82	125	252
PERSONAL TAXES	**100**	**–2**	**–3**	**58**	**44**	**57**	**98**	**285**
Federal income taxes	100	–4	–9	66	36	51	91	296
State and local income taxes	100	–1	4	26	56	73	115	275
Other taxes	100	20	40	57	95	81	120	201
GIFTS FOR NONHOUSEHOLD MEMBERS	**100**	**26**	**47**	**55**	**74**	**76**	**108**	**214**
Food	**100**	**23**	**41**	**55**	**76**	**32**	**112**	**236**
Alcoholic beverages	**100**	**36**	**85**	**32**	**63**	**68**	**126**	**200**
Housing	**100**	**27**	**48**	**65**	**89**	**92**	**95**	**204**
Housekeeping supplies	100	35	54	60	67	81	140	183
Household textiles	100	13	53	64	79	86	57	250

	complete income reporters	under $10,000	$10,000– $19,999	$20,000– $29,999	$30,000– $39,999	$40,000– $49,999	$50,000– $69,999	$70,000 or more
Appliances and misc. housewares	100	10	36	43	114	96	100	211
Major appliances	100	29	43	14	71	229	57	186
Small appliances and misc. housewares	100	10	34	52	129	52	110	214
Miscellaneous household equipment	100	16	52	66	84	85	123	195
Other housing	100	38	43	72	98	102	55	209
Apparel and services	**100**	**38**	**61**	**66**	**97**	**90**	**129**	**166**
Males, aged 2 or older	100	71	60	47	98	80	113	178
Females, aged 2 or older	100	25	64	57	89	78	139	178
Children under age 2	100	22	73	78	93	112	105	161
Other apparel products and services	100	38	46	94	113	104	151	136
Jewelry and watches	100	43	26	122	96	74	187	135
All other apparel products and services	100	92	64	67	125	138	121	138
Transportation	**100**	**14**	**52**	**63**	**38**	**96**	**159**	**189**
Health care	**100**	**48**	**137**	**37**	**133**	**54**	**87**	**146**
Entertainment	**100**	**29**	**36**	**95**	**76**	**78**	**114**	**193**
Toys, games, hobbies, and tricycles	100	32	48	85	96	100	123	169
Other entertainment	100	29	30	98	65	69	108	206
Personal care products and services	**100**	**49**	**64**	**47**	**53**	**184**	**132**	**142**
Reading	**100**	**100**	**100**	**100**	**100**	**300**	**200**	**200**
Education	**100**	**4**	**6**	**15**	**34**	**42**	**75**	**324**
All other gifts	**100**	**31**	**46**	**71**	**62**	**87**	**129**	**191**

Note: (–) means sample is too small to make a reliable estimate.
Source: Calculations by New Strategist based on the Bureau of Labor Statistics 2003 Consumer Expenditure Survey

Spending by High-Income Consumer Units, 2002–03

Fully 24 percent of consumer units had an income of $70,000 or more in 2002–03, and 12 percent had an income of $100,000 or more. The Consumer Expenditure Survey now examines the spending patterns of households with incomes up to $150,000 or more. Not surprisingly, spending surges as income rises, in part because affluent households have more earners and more expenses than the average household. In 2002–03, the average household had 1.3 earners. Households with incomes of $100,000 or more had an average of 2.0 earners.

The most affluent households, those with incomes of $100,000 or more, spend more than twice as much as the average household ($93,515 versus $42,742 in 2002–03). On many products, the most affluent consumer units spend more than three times the average. These items include other lodging (motels, hotels, vacation homes, college dorms), fees and admissions to entertainment events, and education. The most affluent households spend more than four times the average on federal income taxes.

The most affluent households spend close to the average on a few items such as used cars and trucks. They spend less than average on rent and tobacco.

Table 1.6 Average spending by high-income consumer units, 2002–03

(average annual spending of consumer units by product and service category and before-tax income of consumer unit, 2002–03; complete income reporters only)

	total complete reporters	less than $70,000	$70,000–$79,999	$80,000–$99,999	$100,000 or more total	$100,000–$119,999	$120,000–$149,999	$150,000 or more
Number of consumer units (000)	97,391	73,824	5,121	6,909	11,537	4,384	3,151	4,002
Average number of persons per consumer unit	2.5	2.3	3.0	3.0	3.1	3.1	3.1	3.1
Average income before taxes	$51,128	$29,793	$74,560	$88,832	$154,665	$108,087	$131,885	$223,634
Average annual spending	42,742	31,737	57,128	65,957	93,515	75,601	86,451	118,674
FOOD	**5,593**	**4,619**	**7,548**	**7,840**	**9,926**	**8,714**	**9,689**	**11,435**
Food at home	**3,236**	**2,862**	**4,354**	**4,136**	**4,726**	**4,304**	**4,934**	**5,023**
Cereals and bakery products	456	408	617	591	632	606	619	670
Cereals and cereal products	155	141	210	196	200	182	204	218
Bakery products	301	267	406	396	432	424	416	452
Meats, poultry, fish, and eggs	837	757	1,094	967	1,183	1,042	1,264	1,274
Beef	252	228	349	313	337	298	352	368
Pork	171	161	198	190	216	179	254	227
Other meats	104	95	136	123	136	139	133	137
Poultry	145	130	209	171	207	178	244	208
Fish and seafood	125	106	161	130	240	207	226	286
Eggs	38	37	42	40	47	41	55	48
Dairy products	343	304	455	457	494	437	530	528
Fresh milk and cream	132	121	178	161	167	159	171	172
Other dairy products	212	183	277	296	327	278	359	356
Fruits and vegetables	556	488	780	704	830	741	916	861
Fresh fruits	177	151	265	236	284	240	323	300
Fresh vegetables	179	155	266	236	270	231	306	286
Processed fruits	112	100	151	133	161	153	169	164
Processed vegetables	87	81	99	99	115	117	118	111
Other food at home	1,044	906	1,407	1,417	1,586	1,478	1,605	1,690
Sugar and other sweets	123	108	159	160	190	192	173	202
Fats and oils	87	79	116	104	118	113	124	118
Miscellaneous foods	513	440	707	731	792	728	811	849
Nonalcoholic beverages	281	253	369	349	392	375	405	401
Food prepared by consumer unit on trips	38	25	57	73	94	71	92	120
Food away from home	**2,358**	**1,757**	**3,195**	**3,703**	**5,201**	**4,410**	**4,755**	**6,411**
ALCOHOLIC BEVERAGES	**442**	**316**	**618**	**589**	**1,127**	**785**	**865**	**1,703**
HOUSING	**13,653**	**10,464**	**17,081**	**19,841**	**28,941**	**23,204**	**26,719**	**36,971**
Shelter	**7,921**	**6,046**	**9,912**	**10,899**	**17,253**	**13,623**	**16,128**	**22,117**
Owned dwellings	5,247	3,336	7,643	8,858	14,242	11,269	13,211	18,310
Mortgage interest and charges	2,947	1,752	4,764	5,359	8,340	6,815	7,766	10,463
Property taxes	1,310	887	1,697	2,039	3,411	2,515	2,831	4,850
Maintenance, repair, insurance, other expenses	989	697	1,182	1,461	2,490	1,939	2,614	2,997
Rented dwellings	2,220	2,481	1,713	1,357	1,288	1,272	1,562	1,090
Other lodging	455	228	557	684	1,723	1,081	1,355	2,717
Utilities, fuels, and public services	**2,820**	**2,450**	**3,433**	**3,779**	**4,336**	**3,895**	**4,146**	**4,969**
Natural gas	387	331	468	472	661	570	608	802
Electricity	1,021	915	1,186	1,335	1,440	1,300	1,349	1,667
Fuel oil and other fuels	112	94	153	158	179	159	189	193
Telephone	970	834	1,190	1,350	1,512	1,388	1,494	1,662
Water and other public services	330	277	436	463	544	477	507	646
Household services	**730**	**453**	**912**	**1,168**	**2,158**	**1,438**	**1,848**	**3,191**
Personal services	303	183	429	569	859	677	825	1,085
Other household services	427	270	482	599	1,299	761	1,023	2,106
Housekeeping supplies	**582**	**453**	**769**	**897**	**1,186**	**1,072**	**1,083**	**1,390**
Laundry and cleaning supplies	145	127	226	213	192	170	165	239
Other household products	287	208	350	469	687	647	594	803
Postage and stationery	149	117	193	216	307	255	325	348
Household furnishings and equipment	**1,600**	**1,062**	**2,055**	**3,098**	**4,008**	**3,177**	**3,514**	**5,304**
Household textiles	126	90	183	211	290	269	280	321
Furniture	419	258	579	868	1,107	797	974	1,551
Floor coverings	54	26	58	98	207	140	193	292

	total complete reporters	less than $70,000	$70,000– $79,999	$80,000– $99,999	$100,000 or more			
					total	$100,000– $119,999	$120,000– $149,999	$150,000 or more
Major appliances	$205	$156	$232	$346	$424	$284	$353	$632
Small appliances, misc. housewares	95	69	134	170	203	152	149	302
Miscellaneous household equipment	701	463	868	1,404	1,777	1,536	1,565	2,205
APPAREL AND RELATED SERVICES	**1,744**	**1,314**	**2,549**	**2,546**	**3,756**	**2,695**	**3,541**	**5,083**
Men and boys	**385**	**283**	**583**	**664**	**814**	**566**	**750**	**1,135**
Men, aged 16 or older	294	211	450	537	634	433	609	874
Boys, aged 2 to 15	91	71	133	127	180	133	141	261
Women and girls	**699**	**521**	**1,164**	**967**	**1,529**	**1,131**	**1,347**	**2,104**
Women, aged 16 or older	588	442	939	790	1,298	946	1,166	1,783
Girls, aged 2 to 15	110	79	224	177	231	185	181	321
Children under age 2	**86**	**68**	**138**	**129**	**156**	**125**	**199**	**155**
Footwear	**311**	**274**	**411**	**398**	**467**	**424**	**541**	**455**
Other apparel products and services	**263**	**169**	**254**	**388**	**791**	**449**	**704**	**1,234**
TRANSPORTATION	**8,041**	**6,138**	**11,540**	**13,295**	**15,526**	**14,178**	**15,785**	**16,799**
Vehicle purchases	**3,871**	**2,884**	**5,698**	**6,834**	**7,604**	**7,295**	**7,932**	**7,683**
Cars and trucks, new	2,154	1,299	3,538	4,474	5,621	5,664	5,076	6,003
Cars and trucks, used	1,649	1,538	2,105	2,144	1,865	1,508	2,653	1,636
Other vehicles	68	47	55	216	117	123	203	44
Gasoline and motor oil	**1,353**	**1,134**	**1,861**	**2,038**	**2,123**	**2,063**	**2,195**	**2,133**
Other vehicle expenses	**2,416**	**1,860**	**3,531**	**3,842**	**4,632**	**4,191**	**4,612**	**5,130**
Vehicle finance charges	383	287	626	756	668	721	676	605
Maintenance and repairs	657	518	919	1,059	1,191	1,052	1,221	1,320
Vehicle insurance	929	752	1,284	1,421	1,611	1,583	1,600	1,651
Vehicle rentals, leases, licenses, other charges	447	303	702	606	1,161	834	1,115	1,555
Public transportation	**400**	**260**	**449**	**582**	**1,167**	**629**	**1,046**	**1,853**
HEALTH CARE	**2,495**	**2,199**	**2,700**	**3,335**	**3,809**	**3,465**	**3,478**	**4,447**
Health insurance	1,267	1,140	1,400	1,577	1,837	1,669	1,718	2,115
Medical services	612	485	716	1,032	1,122	972	890	1,470
Drugs	501	479	446	555	642	622	678	636
Medical supplies	115	94	138	171	208	203	192	226
ENTERTAINMENT	**2,155**	**1,484**	**3,243**	**3,607**	**5,124**	**3,810**	**4,382**	**7,147**
Fees and admissions	511	281	719	849	1,687	1,126	1,309	2,599
Television, radio, sound equipment	745	599	977	1,084	1,379	1,165	1,285	1,689
Pets, toys, and playground equipment	411	322	531	652	790	711	736	920
Other entertainment products and services	488	282	1,016	1,021	1,268	809	1,052	1,939
PERSONAL CARE PRODUCTS AND SERVICES	**559**	**433**	**722**	**871**	**1,131**	**874**	**1,139**	**1,405**
READING	**133**	**98**	**180**	**202**	**296**	**228**	**293**	**372**
EDUCATION	**792**	**439**	**855**	**1,082**	**2,858**	**2,093**	**2,165**	**4,243**
TOBACCO PRODUCTS AND SMOKING SUPPLIES	**307**	**313**	**325**	**358**	**234**	**243**	**259**	**204**
MISCELLANEOUS	**658**	**547**	**750**	**843**	**1,221**	**1,267**	**965**	**1,373**
CASH CONTRIBUTIONS	**1,458**	**896**	**1,627**	**2,173**	**4,547**	**2,238**	**2,698**	**8,534**
PERSONAL INSURANCE AND PENSIONS	**4,710**	**2,476**	**7,390**	**9,375**	**15,016**	**11,808**	**14,474**	**18,958**
Life and other personal insurance	414	261	490	659	1,214	729	944	1,958
Pensions and Social Security	4,296	2,215	6,901	8,715	13,802	11,079	13,530	17,001
PERSONAL TAXES	**2,532**	**1,040**	**3,172**	**4,656**	**10,519**	**6,216**	**10,245**	**15,448**
Federal income taxes	1,843	692	2,298	3,305	8,129	4,559	7,748	12,340
State and local income taxes	502	221	658	1,033	1,908	1,232	2,186	2,431
Other taxes	187	127	216	319	482	425	311	677
GIFTS FOR NONHOUSEHOLD MEMBERS	**1,055**	**676**	**1,225**	**1,369**	**3,255**	**2,461**	**2,295**	**4,877**
Food	**84**	**49**	**73**	**85**	**321**	**286**	**164**	**483**
Alcoholic beverages	**19**	**13**	**18**	**26**	**54**	**73**	**11**	**66**
Housing	**238**	**162**	**244**	**366**	**664**	**599**	**502**	**861**
Housekeeping supplies	48	35	60	66	114	83	144	125
Household textiles	14	8	13	24	52	56	34	61

	total complete reporters	less than $70,000	$70,000– $79,999	$80,000– $99,999	$100,000 or more			
					total	$100,000– $119,999	$120,000– $149,999	$150,000 or more
Appliances and misc. housewares	$28	$18	$30	$31	$89	$51	$40	$167
Major appliances	7	5	3	8	21	11	6	44
Small appliances and misc. housewares	21	13	26	23	67	40	34	123
Miscellaneous household equipment	62	44	72	122	142	131	108	182
Other housing	87	56	69	123	267	278	175	326
Apparel and services	**232**	**185**	**309**	**322**	**457**	**386**	**374**	**600**
Males, aged 2 or older	55	42	80	92	110	83	87	156
Females, aged 2 or older	89	68	144	108	194	173	129	267
Children under age 2	41	33	39	73	74	49	85	91
Other apparel products and services	47	42	47	50	80	81	73	85
Jewelry and watches	23	21	25	20	39	19	43	59
All other apparel products and services	24	21	21	30	41	62	30	26
Transportation	**56**	**40**	**137**	**73**	**112**	**80**	**58**	**189**
Health care	**52**	**44**	**20**	**39**	**124**	**68**	**40**	**251**
Entertainment	**74**	**52**	**110**	**101**	**184**	**141**	**133**	**270**
Toys, games, hobbies, and tricycles	26	21	36	37	52	42	48	65
Other entertainment	48	32	74	64	132	99	85	205
Personal care products and services	**19**	**16**	**18**	**24**	**32**	**22**	**15**	**56**
Reading	**1**	**1**	**3**	**1**	**2**	**2**	**2**	**3**
Education	**201**	**58**	**179**	**209**	**1,125**	**713**	**807**	**1,827**
All other gifts	**78**	**56**	**115**	**123**	**180**	**92**	**188**	**271**

Note: Spending by category will not add to total spending because gift spending is also included in the preceding product and service categories and personal taxes are not included in the total.
Source: Bureau of Labor Statistics, 2002 and 2003 Consumer Expenditure Surveys, Internet site http://www.bls.gov/cex/

Table 1.7 Indexed spending by high-income consumer units, 2002–03

(indexed average annual spending of consumer units by product and service category and before-tax income of consumer unit reference person, 2002–03; complete income reporters only; index definition: an index of 100 is the average for all consumer units; an index of 132 means that spending by consumer units in that group is 32 percent above the average for all consumer units; an index of 68 indicates spending that is 32 percent below the average for all consumer units)

	total complete reporters	less than $70,000	$70,000–$79,999	$80,000–$99,999	$100,000 or more total	$100,000–$119,999	$120,000–$149,999	$150,000 or more
Average spending of consumer unit, total	$42,742	$31,737	$57,128	$65,957	$93,515	$75,601	$86,451	$118,674
Average spending of consumer unit, index	100	74	134	154	219	177	202	278
FOOD	100	83	135	140	177	156	173	204
Food at home	100	88	135	128	146	133	152	155
Cereals and bakery products	100	89	135	130	139	133	136	147
Cereals and cereal products	100	91	135	126	129	117	132	141
Bakery products	100	89	135	132	144	141	138	150
Meats, poultry, fish, and eggs	100	90	131	116	141	124	151	152
Beef	100	90	138	124	134	118	140	146
Pork	100	94	116	111	126	105	149	133
Other meats	100	91	131	118	131	134	128	132
Poultry	100	90	144	118	143	123	168	143
Fish and seafood	100	85	129	104	192	166	181	229
Eggs	100	97	111	105	124	108	145	126
Dairy products	100	89	133	133	144	127	155	154
Fresh milk and cream	100	92	135	122	127	120	130	130
Other dairy products	100	86	131	140	154	131	169	168
Fruits and vegetables	100	88	140	127	149	133	165	155
Fresh fruits	100	85	150	133	160	136	182	169
Fresh vegetables	100	87	149	132	151	129	171	160
Processed fruits	100	89	135	119	144	137	151	146
Processed vegetables	100	93	114	114	132	134	136	128
Other food at home	100	87	135	136	152	142	154	162
Sugar and other sweets	100	88	129	130	154	156	141	164
Fats and oils	100	91	133	120	136	130	143	136
Miscellaneous foods	100	86	138	142	154	142	158	165
Nonalcoholic beverages	100	90	131	124	140	133	144	143
Food prepared by consumer unit on trips	100	66	150	192	247	187	242	316
Food away from home	100	75	135	157	221	187	202	272
ALCOHOLIC BEVERAGES	100	71	140	133	255	178	196	385
HOUSING	100	77	125	145	212	170	196	271
Shelter	100	76	125	138	218	172	204	279
Owned dwellings	100	64	146	169	271	215	252	349
Mortgage interest and charges	100	59	162	182	283	231	264	355
Property taxes	100	68	130	156	260	192	216	370
Maintenance, repair, insurance, other expenses	100	70	120	148	252	196	264	303
Rented dwellings	100	112	77	61	58	57	70	49
Other lodging	100	50	122	150	379	238	298	597
Utilities, fuels, and public services	100	87	122	134	154	138	147	176
Natural gas	100	86	121	122	171	147	157	207
Electricity	100	90	116	131	141	127	132	163
Fuel oil and other fuels	100	84	137	141	160	142	169	172
Telephone	100	86	123	139	156	143	154	171
Water and other public services	100	84	132	140	165	145	154	196
Household services	100	62	125	160	296	197	253	437
Personal services	100	60	142	188	283	223	272	358
Other household services	100	63	113	140	304	178	240	493
Housekeeping supplies	100	78	132	154	204	184	186	239
Laundry and cleaning supplies	100	88	156	147	132	117	114	165
Other household products	100	72	122	163	239	225	207	280
Postage and stationery	100	79	130	145	206	171	218	234
Household furnishings and equipment	100	66	128	194	251	199	220	332
Household textiles	100	71	145	167	230	213	222	255
Furniture	100	62	138	207	264	190	232	370
Floor coverings	100	48	107	181	383	259	357	541

	total complete reporters	less than $70,000	$70,000–$79,999	$80,000–$99,999	$100,000 or more total	$100,000–$119,999	$120,000–$149,999	$150,000 or more
Major appliances	100	76	113	169	207	139	172	308
Small appliances, misc. housewares	100	73	141	179	214	160	157	318
Miscellaneous household equipment	100	66	124	200	253	219	223	315
APPAREL AND RELATED SERVICES	**100**	**75**	**146**	**146**	**215**	**155**	**203**	**291**
Men and boys	**100**	**74**	**151**	**172**	**211**	**147**	**195**	**295**
Men, aged 16 or older	100	72	153	183	216	147	207	297
Boys, aged 2 to 15	100	78	146	140	198	146	155	287
Women and girls	**100**	**75**	**167**	**138**	**219**	**162**	**193**	**301**
Women, aged 16 or older	100	75	160	134	221	161	198	303
Girls, aged 2 to 15	100	72	204	161	210	168	165	292
Children under age 2	**100**	**79**	**160**	**150**	**181**	**145**	**231**	**180**
Footwear	**100**	**88**	**132**	**128**	**150**	**136**	**174**	**146**
Other apparel products and services	**100**	**64**	**97**	**148**	**301**	**171**	**268**	**469**
TRANSPORTATION	**100**	**76**	**144**	**165**	**193**	**176**	**196**	**209**
Vehicle purchases	**100**	**75**	**147**	**177**	**196**	**188**	**205**	**198**
Cars and trucks, new	100	60	164	208	261	263	236	279
Cars and trucks, used	100	93	128	130	113	91	161	99
Other vehicles	100	69	81	318	172	181	299	65
Gasoline and motor oil	**100**	**84**	**138**	**151**	**157**	**152**	**162**	**158**
Other vehicle expenses	**100**	**77**	**146**	**159**	**192**	**173**	**191**	**212**
Vehicle finance charges	100	75	163	197	174	188	177	158
Maintenance and repairs	100	79	140	161	181	160	186	201
Vehicle insurance	100	81	138	153	173	170	172	178
Vehicle rentals, leases, licenses, other charges	100	68	157	136	260	187	249	348
Public transportation	**100**	**65**	**112**	**146**	**292**	**157**	**262**	**463**
HEALTH CARE	**100**	**88**	**108**	**134**	**153**	**139**	**139**	**178**
Health insurance	100	90	110	124	145	132	136	167
Medical services	100	79	117	169	183	159	145	240
Drugs	100	96	89	111	128	124	135	127
Medical supplies	100	82	120	149	181	177	167	197
ENTERTAINMENT	**100**	**69**	**150**	**167**	**238**	**177**	**203**	**332**
Fees and admissions	100	55	141	166	330	220	256	509
Television, radio, sound equipment	100	80	131	146	185	156	172	227
Pets, toys, and playground equipment	100	78	129	159	192	173	179	224
Other entertainment products and services	100	58	208	209	260	166	216	397
PERSONAL CARE PRODUCTS AND SERVICES	**100**	**77**	**129**	**156**	**202**	**156**	**204**	**251**
READING	**100**	**74**	**135**	**152**	**223**	**171**	**220**	**280**
EDUCATION	**100**	**55**	**108**	**137**	**361**	**264**	**273**	**536**
TOBACCO PRODUCTS AND SMOKING SUPPLIES	**100**	**102**	**106**	**117**	**76**	**79**	**84**	**66**
MISCELLANEOUS	**100**	**83**	**114**	**128**	**186**	**193**	**147**	**209**
CASH CONTRIBUTIONS	**100**	**61**	**112**	**149**	**312**	**153**	**185**	**585**
PERSONAL INSURANCE AND PENSIONS	**100**	**53**	**157**	**199**	**319**	**251**	**307**	**403**
Life and other personal insurance	100	63	118	159	293	176	228	473
Pensions and Social Security	100	52	161	203	321	258	315	396
PERSONAL TAXES	**100**	**41**	**125**	**184**	**415**	**245**	**405**	**610**
Federal income taxes	100	38	125	179	441	247	420	670
State and local income taxes	100	44	131	206	380	245	435	484
Other taxes	100	68	116	171	258	227	166	362
GIFTS FOR NONHOUSEHOLD MEMBERS	**100**	**64**	**116**	**130**	**309**	**233**	**218**	**462**
Food	**100**	**58**	**87**	**101**	**382**	**340**	**195**	**575**
Alcoholic beverages	**100**	**68**	**95**	**137**	**284**	**384**	**58**	**347**
Housing	**100**	**68**	**103**	**154**	**279**	**252**	**211**	**362**
Housekeeping supplies	100	73	125	138	238	173	300	260
Household textiles	100	57	93	171	371	400	243	436

	total complete reporters	less than $70,000	$70,000– $79,999	$80,000– $99,999	$100,000 or more			
					total	$100,000– $119,999	$120,000– $149,999	$150,000 or more
Appliances and misc. housewares	100	64	107	111	318	182	143	596
Major appliances	100	71	43	114	300	157	86	629
Small appliances and misc. housewares	100	62	124	110	319	190	162	586
Miscellaneous household equipment	100	71	116	197	229	211	174	294
Other housing	100	64	79	141	307	320	201	375
Apparel and services	**100**	**80**	**133**	**139**	**197**	**166**	**161**	**259**
Males, aged 2 or older	100	76	145	157	200	151	158	284
Females, aged 2 or older	100	76	162	121	218	194	145	300
Children under age 2	100	80	95	178	180	120	207	222
Other apparel products and services	100	89	100	106	170	172	155	181
Jewelry and watches	100	91	109	87	170	83	187	257
All other apparel products and services	100	88	88	125	171	258	125	108
Transportation	**100**	**71**	**245**	**130**	**200**	**143**	**104**	**338**
Health care	**100**	**85**	**38**	**75**	**238**	**131**	**77**	**483**
Entertainment	**100**	**70**	**149**	**136**	**249**	**191**	**180**	**365**
Toys, games, hobbies, and tricycles	100	81	138	142	200	162	185	250
Other entertainment	100	67	154	133	275	206	177	427
Personal care products and services	**100**	**84**	**95**	**126**	**168**	**116**	**79**	**295**
Reading	**100**	**100**	**300**	**100**	**200**	**200**	**200**	**300**
Education	**100**	**29**	**89**	**104**	**560**	**355**	**401**	**909**
All other gifts	**100**	**72**	**147**	**158**	**231**	**118**	**241**	**347**

Source: Calculations by New Strategist based on the Bureau of Labor Statistics 2002 and 2003 Consumer Expenditure Surveys

Spending by Household Type, 2003

Married couples spent 30 percent more than the average household in 2003. Among married couples, those with children at home spend the most—$75,557 in 2003. Behind the higher spending levels of married couples are their higher incomes, stemming primarily from the greater number of earners in the household. Married couples with children at home have 2.0 earners per household. Those living with adult children average 2.6 earners. The more earners, the greater the spending—particularly on products and services needed by workers such as food away from home, men's and women's clothes, and transportation.

Married couples with children under age 18 at home have distinct spending patterns. Couples with school-aged children spend 45 percent more than the average household overall. They spend 62 percent more than the average household on milk and 60 percent more on cereal. They spend twice as much as the average household on fees and admissions to entertainment events and three times the average on children's clothes. The biggest spenders on household personal services (mostly day care) are married couples with preschoolers while couples without children at home (mostly empty-nesters) spend the most on alcoholic beverages, new cars and trucks, and public transportation (mostly airfare).

Single parents spend less than the average household on most items. Some of the exceptions are rent, children's clothes, and household personal services (mostly day care).

Table 1.8 Average spending by household type, 2003

(average annual spending of consumer units by product and service category and type of consumer unit, 2003)

	total married couples	married couples, no children	married couples with children total	oldest child under 6	oldest child 6 to 17	oldest child 18 or older	single parent, at least one child <18	single person
Number of consumer units (000)	58,448	25,132	28,584	5,496	15,047	8,041	6,999	33,929
Average number of persons per consumer unit	3.2	2.0	3.9	3.5	4.1	4.0	2.9	1.0
Average income before taxes	$69,472	$62,930	$75,557	$66,317	$77,508	$78,307	$29,154	$27,131
Average annual spending	53,030	47,896	57,702	51,503	59,183	59,180	30,535	23,657
FOOD	**6,864**	**5,927**	**7,553**	**6,224**	**7,844**	**7,937**	**4,804**	**2,831**
Food at home	4,047	3,402	4,476	3,952	4,551	4,710	2,979	1,525
Cereals and bakery products	571	458	652	547	691	650	445	217
Cereals and cereal products	193	147	225	198	240	215	160	71
Bakery products	378	311	427	349	451	435	285	146
Meats, poultry, fish, and eggs	1,077	912	1,169	890	1,213	1,283	787	359
Beef	333	288	360	235	381	408	212	94
Pork	221	193	235	158	249	263	163	73
Other meats	130	106	145	119	151	153	110	47
Poultry	186	145	211	175	218	225	142	66
Fish and seafood	162	140	169	158	165	186	125	59
Eggs	46	40	48	45	50	49	35	20
Dairy products	427	352	485	444	497	491	307	161
Fresh milk and cream	162	122	192	166	206	183	126	62
Other dairy products	265	230	293	277	291	308	181	99
Fruits and vegetables	688	606	735	672	723	808	455	280
Fresh fruits	221	197	235	207	233	260	144	88
Fresh vegetables	224	205	230	213	222	258	124	89
Processed fruits	136	111	154	150	153	159	106	60
Processed vegetables	106	93	116	102	114	131	81	44
Other food at home	1,285	1,074	1,435	1,399	1,428	1,479	985	507
Sugar and other sweets	152	131	168	146	176	168	124	60
Fats and oils	109	98	115	86	117	131	75	43
Miscellaneous foods	632	511	721	822	696	699	491	256
Nonalcoholic beverages	341	278	383	310	381	439	276	131
Food prepared by consumer unit on trips	51	56	49	36	57	42	19	17
Food away from home	**2,817**	**2,525**	**3,077**	**2,272**	**3,293**	**3,226**	**1,826**	**1,306**
ALCOHOLIC BEVERAGES	**447**	**478**	**440**	**445**	**429**	**459**	**220**	**280**
HOUSING	**16,648**	**14,352**	**18,679**	**19,303**	**19,235**	**17,215**	**11,772**	**8,768**
Shelter	**9,480**	**8,001**	**10,812**	**10,963**	**11,292**	**9,812**	**7,152**	**5,614**
Owned dwellings	7,433	5,973	8,773	8,440	9,213	8,175	3,234	2,692
Mortgage interest and charges	4,349	2,924	5,610	5,853	5,953	4,803	1,938	1,230
Property taxes	1,841	1,742	1,956	1,618	2,023	2,061	675	802
Maintenance, repair, insurance, other expenses	1,244	1,306	1,207	970	1,238	1,311	621	659
Rented dwellings	1,405	1,280	1,455	2,204	1,488	883	3,724	2,679
Other lodging	642	748	584	319	591	753	195	242
Utilities, fuels, and public services	**3,444**	**3,075**	**3,695**	**3,030**	**3,745**	**4,055**	**2,595**	**1,758**
Natural gas	473	413	517	429	517	578	335	254
Electricity	1,259	1,153	1,331	1,055	1,378	1,432	1,022	621
Fuel oil and other fuels	143	137	146	92	52	171	62	70
Telephone	1,145	991	1,252	1,094	1,338	1,388	932	623
Water and other public services	423	382	448	359	460	486	244	190
Household services	**970**	**596**	**1,316**	**2,365**	**1,286**	**656**	**725**	**343**
Personal services	416	68	725	1,850	652	92	478	93
Other household services	554	528	591	514	634	564	247	251
Housekeeping supplies	**699**	**659**	**734**	**645**	**728**	**813**	**349**	**284**
Laundry and cleaning supplies	171	149	185	152	133	214	122	68
Other household products	360	336	385	352	339	401	161	123
Postage and stationery	167	174	164	142	156	198	65	93
Household furnishings and equipment	**2,055**	**2,021**	**2,122**	**2,300**	**2,133**	**1,880**	**951**	**769**
Household textiles	157	168	149	125	142	178	67	52
Furniture	564	542	595	744	624	441	278	194
Floor coverings	71	73	72	50	79	75	38	26

	total married couples	married couples, no children	married couples with children				single parent, at least one child <18	single person
			total	oldest child under 6	oldest child 6 to 17	oldest child 18 or older		
Major appliances	$271	$251	$282	$345	$291	$221	$163	$91
Small appliances, misc. housewares	117	127	108	98	92	149	49	48
Miscellaneous household equipment	876	860	915	938	955	815	356	358
APPAREL AND RELATED SERVICES	**2,085**	**1,632**	**2,431**	**2,232**	**2,614**	**2,219**	**1,799**	**837**
Men and boys	**495**	**361**	**604**	**451**	**695**	**538**	**389**	**177**
Men, aged 16 or older	369	333	396	321	391	459	173	164
Boys, aged 2 to 15	125	28	209	130	304	79	216	13
Women and girls	**797**	**650**	**892**	**743**	**947**	**895**	**673**	**331**
Women, aged 16 or older	647	609	653	605	589	818	445	316
Girls, aged 2 to 15	149	41	239	138	357	77	228	15
Children under age 2	**115**	**44**	**168**	**469**	**117**	**51**	**111**	**17**
Footwear	**353**	**264**	**421**	**282**	**479**	**405**	**450**	**156**
Other apparel products and services	**325**	**314**	**346**	**286**	**376**	**331**	**177**	**156**
TRANSPORTATION	**10,627**	**9,580**	**11,546**	**9,832**	**11,526**	**12,755**	**4,592**	**3,839**
Vehicle purchases	**5,308**	**4,933**	**5,713**	**4,953**	**5,849**	**5,977**	**1,734**	**1,692**
Cars and trucks, new	3,020	3,249	2,997	2,499	3,188	2,979	450	1,027
Cars and trucks, used	2,194	1,604	2,607	2,353	2,553	2,883	1,268	620
Other vehicles	95	79	109	101	108	116	17	45
Gasoline and motor oil	**1,740**	**1,463**	**1,949**	**1,613**	**1,927**	**2,220**	**993**	**674**
Other vehicle expenses	**3,078**	**2,638**	**3,418**	**2,925**	**3,261**	**4,049**	**1,632**	**1,217**
Vehicle finance charges	520	399	613	603	597	650	227	144
Maintenance and repairs	793	734	833	652	809	1,003	476	362
Vehicle insurance	1,173	980	1,309	1,006	1,175	1,766	612	493
Vehicle rentals, leases, licenses, other charges	592	525	663	663	680	629	317	218
Public transportation	**501**	**547**	**466**	**342**	**489**	**509**	**234**	**256**
HEALTH CARE	**3,202**	**3,713**	**2,760**	**2,177**	**2,764**	**3,151**	**1,201**	**1,558**
Health insurance	1,663	1,906	1,455	1,253	1,429	1,642	644	779
Medical services	809	847	783	536	844	838	330	360
Drugs	584	792	391	296	361	514	164	356
Medical supplies	146	167	131	92	130	157	63	63
ENTERTAINMENT	**2,793**	**2,699**	**2,958**	**2,401**	**3,414**	**2,478**	**1,453**	**1,041**
Fees and admissions	706	586	849	437	1,072	712	336	253
Television, radio, sound equipment	887	750	997	938	1,061	919	635	475
Pets, toys, and playground equipment	516	517	528	531	578	429	296	177
Other entertainment products and services	684	846	584	495	703	419	187	137
PERSONAL CARE PRODUCTS AND SERVICES	**668**	**617**	**713**	**559**	**713**	**821**	**459**	**316**
READING	**163**	**186**	**149**	**121**	**151**	**167**	**64**	**93**
EDUCATION	**1,053**	**610**	**1,510**	**413**	**1,438**	**2,393**	**493**	**498**
TOBACCO PRODUCTS AND SMOKING SUPPLIES	**300**	**275**	**298**	**220**	**291**	**365**	**230**	**193**
MISCELLANEOUS	**712**	**638**	**778**	**626**	**696**	**1,035**	**510**	**423**
CASH CONTRIBUTIONS	**1,762**	**2,174**	**1,441**	**1,060**	**1,430**	**1,723**	**622**	**1,032**
PERSONAL INSURANCE AND PENSIONS	**5,707**	**5,015**	**6,445**	**5,891**	**6,638**	**6,462**	**2,315**	**1,948**
Life and other personal insurance	599	625	585	378	618	665	181	159
Pensions and Social Security	5,108	4,390	5,860	5,513	6,021	5,798	2,134	1,790
PERSONAL TAXES	**3,632**	**4,669**	**2,992**	**2,210**	**3,238**	**3,072**	**308**	**1,592**
Federal income taxes	2,670	3,667	2,033	1,429	2,245	2,052	–19	1,180
State and local income taxes	696	685	743	592	795	751	227	304
Other taxes	266	317	216	190	198	268	100	107
GIFTS FOR NONHOUSEHOLD MEMBERS	**1,316**	**1,630**	**1,122**	**690**	**1,185**	**1,303**	**505**	**733**
Food	**118**	**174**	**80**	**40**	**68**	**129**	**54**	**30**
Alcoholic beverages	**18**	**14**	**23**	**35**	**22**	**15**	**21**	**12**
Housing	**294**	**353**	**253**	**183**	**257**	**296**	**112**	**144**
Housekeeping supplies	50	47	56	38	55	72	19	33
Household textiles	19	24	15	8	9	31	1	5

	total married couples	married couples, no children	married couples with children				single parent, at least one child <18	single person
			total	oldest child under 6	oldest child 6 to 17	oldest child 18 or older		
Appliances and misc. housewares	$34	$47	$22	$25	$20	$23	$10	$12
Major appliances	8	9	7	9	7	4	3	3
Small appliances and misc. housewares	26	37	15	16	13	19	7	9
Miscellaneous household equipment	81	108	62	64	53	79	17	33
Other housing	109	127	98	48	120	92	64	62
Apparel and services	**261**	**316**	**216**	**250**	**196**	**230**	**156**	**182**
Males, aged 2 or older	71	90	55	35	58	63	33	38
Females, aged 2 or older	93	124	69	81	62	76	58	70
Children under age 2	53	43	59	105	49	45	34	17
Other apparel products and services	45	60	33	30	27	46	31	58
Jewelry and watches	20	25	15	9	10	28	8	38
All other apparel products and services	25	35	18	21	18	18	23	20
Transportation	**65**	**72**	**67**	**16**	**69**	**99**	**45**	**75**
Health care	**34**	**49**	**24**	**9**	**19**	**44**	**11**	**90**
Entertainment	**87**	**118**	**63**	**50**	**62**	**74**	**26**	**50**
Toys, games, hobbies, and tricycles	32	47	21	20	17	29	9	20
Other entertainment	55	72	42	30	45	46	17	29
Personal care products and services	**19**	**20**	**19**	**26**	**15**	**22**	**14**	**11**
Reading	**2**	**3**	**1**	–	**1**	**1**	–	**2**
Education	**329**	**390**	**314**	**13**	**433**	**299**	**41**	**72**
All other gifts	**89**	**122**	**63**	**67**	**44**	**94**	**25**	**65**

Note: Spending by category will not add to total spending because gift spending is also included in the preceding product and service categories and personal taxes are not included in the total. (–) means sample is too small to make a reliable estimate.
Source: Bureau of Labor Statistics, 2003 Consumer Expenditure Survey, Internet site http://www.bls.gov/cex/; calculations by New Strategist

Table 1.9 Indexed spending by household type, 2003

(indexed average annual spending of consumer units by product and service category and type of consumer unit, 2003; index definition: an index of 100 is the average for all consumer units; an index of 132 means that spending by consumer units in that group is 32 percent above the average for all consumer units; an index of 68 indicates spending that is 32 percent below the average for all consumer units)

| | total married couples | married couples, no children | married couples with children | | | | single parent, at least one child <18 | single person |
			total	oldest child under 6	oldest child 6 to 17	oldest child 18 or older		
Average spending of consumer unit, total	$53,030	$47,896	$57,702	$51,503	$59,183	$59,180	$30,535	$23,657
Average spending of consumer unit, index	130	117	141	126	145	145	75	58
FOOD	**129**	**111**	**141**	**117**	**147**	**149**	**90**	**53**
Food at home	**129**	**109**	**143**	**126**	**145**	**151**	**95**	**49**
Cereals and bakery products	129	104	148	124	156	147	101	49
Cereals and cereal products	129	98	150	132	160	143	107	47
Bakery products	129	107	146	120	154	149	98	50
Meats, poultry, fish, and eggs	131	111	142	108	147	156	95	44
Beef	135	117	146	96	155	166	86	38
Pork	129	113	137	92	146	154	95	43
Other meats	127	104	142	117	148	150	108	46
Poultry	128	100	146	121	150	155	98	46
Fish and seafood	131	113	136	127	133	150	101	48
Eggs	124	108	130	122	135	132	95	54
Dairy products	130	107	148	135	152	150	94	49
Fresh milk and cream	128	96	151	131	162	144	99	49
Other dairy products	132	114	146	138	145	153	90	49
Fruits and vegetables	129	113	137	126	135	151	85	52
Fresh fruits	129	115	137	121	136	152	84	51
Fresh vegetables	130	119	134	124	129	150	72	52
Processed fruits	126	103	143	139	142	147	98	56
Processed vegetables	126	111	138	121	136	156	96	52
Other food at home	129	108	144	140	143	148	99	51
Sugar and other sweets	128	110	141	123	148	141	104	50
Fats and oils	127	114	134	100	136	152	87	50
Miscellaneous foods	129	104	147	168	142	143	100	52
Nonalcoholic beverages	127	104	143	116	142	164	103	49
Food prepared by consumer unit on trips	142	156	136	100	158	117	53	47
Food away from home	**127**	**114**	**139**	**103**	**149**	**146**	**83**	**59**
ALCOHOLIC BEVERAGES	**114**	**122**	**113**	**114**	**110**	**117**	**56**	**72**
HOUSING	**124**	**107**	**139**	**144**	**143**	**128**	**88**	**65**
Shelter	**120**	**101**	**137**	**139**	**143**	**124**	**91**	**71**
Owned dwellings	141	113	167	160	175	155	61	51
Mortgage interest and charges	147	99	190	198	202	163	66	42
Property taxes	137	130	146	120	151	153	50	60
Maintenance, repair, insurance, other expenses	129	135	125	101	128	136	64	68
Rented dwellings	64	59	67	101	68	41	171	123
Other lodging	144	168	131	72	133	169	44	54
Utilities, fuels, and public services	**123**	**109**	**131**	**108**	**133**	**144**	**92**	**63**
Natural gas	121	105	132	109	132	147	85	65
Electricity	122	112	129	103	134	139	99	60
Fuel oil and other fuels	130	125	133	84	138	155	56	64
Telephone	120	104	131	114	129	145	97	65
Water and other public services	130	117	137	110	141	149	75	58
Household services	**137**	**84**	**186**	**335**	**182**	**93**	**103**	**49**
Personal services	141	23	247	629	222	31	163	32
Other household services	134	128	143	124	153	136	60	61
Housekeeping supplies	**132**	**125**	**139**	**122**	**138**	**154**	**66**	**54**
Laundry and cleaning supplies	130	113	140	115	139	162	92	52
Other household products	137	128	146	134	148	152	61	47
Postage and stationery	126	131	123	107	117	149	49	70
Household furnishings and equipment	**137**	**135**	**142**	**154**	**146**	**126**	**64**	**51**
Household textiles	139	149	132	111	126	158	59	46
Furniture	141	135	148	186	156	110	69	48
Floor coverings	137	140	138	96	152	144	73	50

	total married couples	married couples, no children	married couples with children				single parent, at least one child <18	single person
			total	oldest child under 6	oldest child 6 to 17	oldest child 18 or older		
Major appliances	138	128	144	176	148	113	83	46
Small appliances, misc. housewares	133	144	123	111	105	169	56	55
Miscellaneous household equipment	135	133	141	145	147	126	55	55
APPAREL AND RELATED SERVICES	**127**	**100**	**148**	**136**	**159**	**135**	**110**	**51**
Men and boys	**133**	**97**	**162**	**121**	**187**	**145**	**105**	**48**
Men, aged 16 or older	131	118	140	114	139	163	61	58
Boys, aged 2 to 15	140	31	235	146	342	89	243	15
Women and girls	**126**	**103**	**141**	**117**	**149**	**141**	**106**	**52**
Women, aged 16 or older	122	115	123	114	111	155	84	60
Girls, aged 2 to 15	141	39	225	130	337	73	215	14
Children under age 2	**142**	**54**	**207**	**579**	**144**	**63**	**137**	**21**
Footwear	**120**	**90**	**143**	**96**	**163**	**138**	**153**	**53**
Other apparel products and services	**126**	**122**	**134**	**111**	**146**	**128**	**69**	**60**
TRANSPORTATION	**137**	**123**	**148**	**126**	**148**	**164**	**59**	**49**
Vehicle purchases	**142**	**132**	**153**	**133**	**157**	**160**	**46**	**45**
Cars and trucks, new	147	158	146	122	155	145	22	50
Cars and trucks, used	136	100	162	146	158	179	79	38
Other vehicles	140	116	160	149	159	171	25	66
Gasoline and motor oil	**131**	**110**	**146**	**121**	**145**	**167**	**74**	**51**
Other vehicle expenses	**132**	**113**	**147**	**125**	**140**	**174**	**70**	**52**
Vehicle finance charges	140	108	165	163	161	175	61	39
Maintenance and repairs	128	119	135	105	131	162	77	58
Vehicle insurance	130	108	145	111	130	195	68	54
Vehicle rentals, leases, licenses, other charges	136	120	152	152	156	144	73	50
Public transportation	**130**	**142**	**121**	**89**	**127**	**132**	**61**	**66**
HEALTH CARE	**133**	**154**	**114**	**90**	**114**	**130**	**50**	**64**
Health insurance	133	152	116	100	114	131	51	62
Medical services	137	143	132	91	143	142	56	61
Drugs	125	170	84	63	77	110	35	76
Medical supplies	136	156	122	86	121	147	59	59
ENTERTAINMENT	**136**	**131**	**144**	**117**	**166**	**120**	**71**	**51**
Fees and admissions	143	119	172	88	217	144	68	51
Television, radio, sound equipment	122	103	137	128	145	126	87	65
Pets, toys, and playground equipment	137	137	140	140	153	113	78	47
Other entertainment products and services	150	185	128	108	154	92	41	30
PERSONAL CARE PRODUCTS AND SERVICES	**127**	**117**	**135**	**106**	**135**	**156**	**87**	**60**
READING	**128**	**146**	**117**	**95**	**119**	**131**	**50**	**73**
EDUCATION	**134**	**78**	**193**	**53**	**134**	**306**	**63**	**64**
TOBACCO PRODUCTS AND SMOKING SUPPLIES	**103**	**95**	**103**	**76**	**100**	**126**	**79**	**67**
MISCELLANEOUS	**117**	**105**	**128**	**103**	**115**	**171**	**84**	**70**
CASH CONTRIBUTIONS	**129**	**159**	**105**	**77**	**104**	**126**	**45**	**75**
PERSONAL INSURANCE AND PENSIONS	**141**	**124**	**159**	**145**	**164**	**159**	**57**	**48**
Life and other personal insurance	151	157	147	95	156	168	46	40
Pensions and Social Security	140	120	160	151	165	159	58	49
PERSONAL TAXES	**143**	**184**	**118**	**87**	**128**	**121**	**12**	**63**
Federal income taxes	145	199	110	78	122	111	–1	64
State and local income taxes	139	136	148	118	153	150	45	61
Other taxes	142	170	116	102	105	143	53	57
GIFTS FOR NONHOUSEHOLD MEMBERS	**131**	**162**	**111**	**69**	**118**	**129**	**50**	**73**
Food	**151**	**223**	**103**	**51**	**87**	**165**	**69**	**38**
Alcoholic beverages	**113**	**88**	**144**	**219**	**138**	**94**	**131**	**75**
Housing	**134**	**160**	**115**	**83**	**117**	**135**	**51**	**65**
Housekeeping supplies	119	112	133	90	131	171	45	79
Household textiles	146	185	115	62	69	238	8	38

	total married couples	married couples, no children	married couples with children				single parent, at least one child <18	single person
			total	oldest child under 6	oldest child 6 to 17	oldest child 18 or older		
Appliances and misc. housewares	136	188	88	100	80	92	40	48
Major appliances	114	129	100	129	100	57	43	43
Small appliances and misc. housewares	144	206	83	89	72	106	39	50
Miscellaneous household equipment	142	189	109	112	93	139	30	58
Other housing	128	149	115	56	141	108	75	73
Apparel and services	**116**	**140**	**96**	**111**	**87**	**102**	**69**	**81**
Males, aged 2 or older	127	161	98	63	104	113	59	68
Females, aged 2 or older	116	155	86	101	78	95	73	88
Children under age 2	136	110	151	269	126	115	87	44
Other apparel products and services	90	120	66	60	54	92	62	116
Jewelry and watches	77	96	58	35	38	108	31	146
All other apparel products and services	100	140	72	84	72	72	92	80
Transportation	**108**	**120**	**112**	**27**	**115**	**165**	**75**	**125**
Health care	**71**	**102**	**50**	**19**	**40**	**92**	**23**	**188**
Entertainment	**126**	**171**	**91**	**72**	**90**	**107**	**38**	**72**
Toys, games, hobbies, and tricycles	123	181	81	77	65	112	35	77
Other entertainment	128	167	98	70	105	107	40	67
Personal care products and services	**119**	**125**	**119**	**163**	**94**	**138**	**88**	**69**
Reading	**200**	**300**	**100**	**–**	**100**	**100**	**–**	**200**
Education	**165**	**195**	**157**	**7**	**217**	**150**	**21**	**36**
All other gifts	**120**	**165**	**85**	**91**	**59**	**127**	**34**	**88**

Note: Spending index for total consumer units is 100. (–) means sample is too small to make a reliable estimate.
Source: Calculations by New Strategist based on the Bureau of Labor Statistics 2003 Consumer Expenditure Survey

Spending by Race and Hispanic Origin, 2003

Asians spend more than the average household while Hispanics and blacks spend less. In 2003, for the first time, the Consumer Expenditure Survey collected information on the spending of Asian households. The $44,923 spent by Asians in 2003 was 10 percent above average and surpassed the spending of every other racial or ethnic group. Black households spent $28,708 in 2003, or 30 percent less than average. Hispanic spending, at $34,575, was 15 percent below average.

Asian spending reflects their above-average incomes, a consequence of their high educational attainment. Asian households spend more than twice the average on education.

Hispanic and black spending exceeds that of the average household in many categories. Because of their larger families, Hispanic households spend 15 percent more than the average household on food at home. They spend 25 percent more than the average household on laundry and cleaning supplies and 49 percent more on infants' apparel.

Blacks spend 20 percent more than the average household on pork and 22 percent more on poultry. They spend 7 percent more than average on telephone services, 11 to 28 percent more on clothes for children, and 50 percent more on shoes.

Table 1.10 Average spending by race and Hispanic origin of householder, 2003

(average annual spending of consumer units by product and service category and by race and Hispanic origin of consumer unit reference person, 2003)

	total consumer units	race			Hispanic origin	
		Asian	Black	white and other	Hispanic	non-Hispanic
Number of consumer units (000)	115,356	3,573	13,743	98,041	11,727	103,629
Average number of persons per consumer unit	2.5	2.8	2.6	2.5	3.3	2.4
Average income before taxes	$51,128	$60,393	$34,485	$53,039	$37,150	$52,797
Average annual spending	40,817	44,923	28,708	42,360	34,575	41,521
FOOD	5,340	6,285	4,007	5,488	5,717	5,291
Food at home	3,129	3,302	2,664	3,186	3,597	3,070
Cereals and bakery products	442	437	370	452	486	436
Cereals and cereal products	150	180	139	151	183	146
Bakery products	292	257	231	301	303	290
Meats, poultry, fish, and eggs	825	978	882	811	1,059	795
Beef	246	193	232	249	327	235
Pork	171	174	206	166	212	165
Other meats	102	81	90	104	113	101
Poultry	145	182	177	139	190	139
Fish and seafood	124	304	140	115	158	120
Eggs	37	43	36	37	59	35
Dairy products	328	247	227	345	374	322
Fresh milk and cream	127	112	94	132	160	122
Other dairy products	201	136	133	214	214	200
Fruits and vegetables	535	788	438	539	686	516
Fresh fruits	171	275	128	173	231	163
Fresh vegetables	172	322	133	172	240	163
Processed fruits	108	123	100	109	131	105
Processed vegetables	84	68	77	86	83	84
Other food at home	999	852	747	1,040	992	1,000
Sugar and other sweets	119	102	93	123	128	118
Fats and oils	86	63	80	87	97	84
Miscellaneous foods	490	400	360	511	452	494
Nonalcoholic beverages	268	248	202	278	289	266
Food prepared by consumer unit on trips	36	40	12	40	25	38
Food away from home	2,211	2,983	1,343	2,302	2,120	2,221
ALCOHOLIC BEVERAGES	391	308	169	425	315	401
HOUSING	13,432	16,326	10,622	13,719	12,300	13,562
Shelter	7,887	10,902	6,117	8,026	7,672	7,912
Owned dwellings	5,263	6,835	3,042	5,517	3,889	5,418
Mortgage interest and charges	2,954	4,348	1,848	3,058	2,471	3,009
Property taxes	1,344	1,713	748	1,414	779	1,408
Maintenance, repair, insurance, other expenses	965	774	446	1,045	638	1,002
Rented dwellings	2,179	3,661	2,946	2,018	3,560	2,023
Other lodging	445	406	129	491	224	470
Utilities, fuels, and public services	2,811	2,536	2,910	2,808	2,490	2,848
Natural gas	392	385	465	382	301	402
Electricity	1,028	780	1,094	1,028	860	1,047
Fuel oil and other fuels	110	27	46	121	57	116
Telephone	956	1,026	1,027	943	968	954
Water and other public services	326	318	278	333	305	329
Household services	707	783	453	740	454	736
Personal services	294	381	247	297	238	300
Other household services	414	403	206	443	216	436
Housekeeping supplies	529	471	357	555	476	536
Laundry and cleaning supplies	132	96	137	133	165	128
Other household products	263	228	168	278	199	271
Postage and stationery	133	146	53	144	111	136
Household furnishings and equipment	1,497	1,634	785	1,591	1,208	1,531
Household textiles	113	67	61	122	89	117
Furniture	401	334	234	427	403	401
Floor coverings	52	21	11	59	19	55

	total consumer units	race			Hispanic origin	
		Asian	black	white and other	Hispanic	non-Hispanic
Major appliances	$196	$283	$118	$203	$201	$195
Small appliances, misc. housewares	88	128	43	92	82	88
Miscellaneous household equipment	648	802	318	688	415	675
APPAREL AND RELATED SERVICES	**1,640**	**1,736**	**1,601**	**1,642**	**1,756**	**1,626**
Men and boys	**372**	**342**	**292**	**384**	**435**	**364**
Men, aged 16 or older	282	290	181	296	307	279
Boys, aged 2 to 15	89	52	112	88	128	85
Women and girls	**634**	**609**	**565**	**645**	**564**	**643**
Women, aged 16 or older	529	538	446	540	438	540
Girls, aged 2 to 15	106	71	118	105	126	103
Children under age 2	**81**	**125**	**104**	**77**	**121**	**77**
Footwear	**294**	**292**	**440**	**274**	**368**	**285**
Other apparel products and services	**258**	**368**	**201**	**263**	**268**	**257**
TRANSPORTATION	**7,781**	**7,454**	**5,074**	**8,172**	**6,780**	**7,894**
Vehicle purchases	3,732	2,992	2,097	3,988	3,063	3,807
Cars and trucks, new	2,052	2,156	929	2,206	1,441	2,122
Cars and trucks, used	1,611	836	1,164	1,702	1,562	1,617
Other vehicles	68	–	4	79	60	69
Gasoline and motor oil	**1,333**	**1,313**	**1,016**	**1,378**	**1,328**	**1,333**
Other vehicle expenses	**2,331**	**2,383**	**1,728**	**2,414**	**2,057**	**2,362**
Vehicle finance charges	371	282	308	383	331	375
Maintenance and repairs	619	546	413	651	520	630
Vehicle insurance	905	989	730	927	812	916
Vehicle rentals, leases, licenses, other charges	436	565	278	454	393	441
Public transportation	**385**	**766**	**233**	**393**	**331**	**391**
HEALTH CARE	**2,416**	**1,955**	**1,309**	**2,588**	**1,439**	**2,527**
Health insurance	1,252	1,071	774	1,325	747	1,309
Medical services	591	476	229	646	365	616
Drugs	467	340	263	500	263	490
Medical supplies	107	69	43	117	65	112
ENTERTAINMENT	**2,060**	**1,713**	**1,007**	**2,220**	**1,245**	**2,153**
Fees and admissions	494	516	163	540	250	522
Television, radio, sound equipment	730	621	616	750	621	742
Pets, toys, and playground equipment	378	197	123	421	194	400
Other entertainment products and services	457	378	105	509	179	489
PERSONAL CARE PRODUCTS AND SERVICES	**527**	**520**	**461**	**536**	**490**	**531**
READING	**127**	**111**	**52**	**138**	**48**	**136**
EDUCATION	**783**	**1,890**	**442**	**791**	**477**	**818**
TOBACCO PRODUCTS AND SMOKING SUPPLIES	**290**	**119**	**180**	**311**	**171**	**303**
MISCELLANEOUS	**606**	**432**	**447**	**635**	**419**	**627**
CASH CONTRIBUTIONS	**1,370**	**1,311**	**832**	**1,447**	**594**	**1,458**
PERSONAL INSURANCE AND PENSIONS	**4,055**	**4,762**	**2,504**	**4,247**	**2,824**	**4,195**
Life and other personal insurance	397	414	295	411	160	424
Pensions and Social Security	3,658	4,348	2,209	3,836	2,664	3,770
PERSONAL TAXES	**2,532**	**2,882**	**966**	**2,730**	**680**	**2,753**
Federal income taxes	1,843	1,993	592	2,006	413	2,014
State and local income taxes	502	650	317	521	197	538
Other taxes	187	240	57	203	70	201
GIFTS FOR NONHOUSEHOLD MEMBERS	**1,007**	**1,342**	**524**	**1,062**	**745**	**1,038**
Food	**78**	**116**	**32**	**83**	**74**	**78**
Alcoholic beverages	**16**	**12**	**4**	**18**	**13**	**17**
Housing	**220**	**139**	**96**	**241**	**138**	**230**
Housekeeping supplies	42	20	13	46	37	42
Household textiles	13	1	2	15	5	14

	total consumer units	race			Hispanic origin	
		Asian	black	white and other	Hispanic	non-Hispanic
Appliances and misc. housewares	$25	$20	$15	$26	$12	$26
Major appliances	7	5	8	7	1	7
Small appliances and misc. housewares	18	15	7	19	11	19
Miscellaneous household equipment	57	50	15	63	31	60
Other housing	85	47	50	91	52	89
Apparel and services	**225**	**179**	**222**	**227**	**187**	**230**
Males, aged 2 or older	56	57	30	59	52	56
Females, aged 2 or older	80	53	93	80	51	84
Children under age 2	39	46	44	38	49	38
Other apparel products and services	50	24	54	51	35	52
Jewelry and watches	26	20	21	27	13	27
All other apparel products and services	25	4	33	24	21	25
Transportation	**60**	**324**	**38**	**53**	**142**	**50**
Health care	**48**	**34**	**22**	**52**	**7**	**53**
Entertainment	**69**	**55**	**26**	**75**	**42**	**72**
Toys, games, hobbies, and tricycles	26	13	13	28	13	28
Other entertainment	43	43	14	47	28	45
Personal care products and services	**16**	**23**	**8**	**17**	**13**	**16**
Reading	**1**	**1**	–	**2**	–	**1**
Education	**200**	**388**	**45**	**215**	**98**	**211**
All other gifts	**74**	**71**	**30**	**81**	**33**	**79**

Note: Other includes Alaska Natives, American Indians, Native Hawaiians and other Pacific Islanders as well as approximately 1.3 percent reporting more than one race. Spending by category will not add to total spending because gift spending is also included in the preceding product and service categories and personal taxes are not included in the total. (–) means sample is too small to make a reliable estimate.
Source: Bureau of Labor Statistics, 2003 Consumer Expenditure Survey, Internet site http://www.bls.gov/cex/

Table 1.11 Indexed spending by race and Hispanic origin of householder, 2003

(indexed average annual spending of consumer units by product and service category and by race and Hispanic origin of consumer unit reference person, 2003; index definition: an index of 100 is the average for all consumer units; an index of 132 means that spending by consumer units in that group is 32 percent above the average for all consumer units; an index of 68 indicates spending that is 32 percent below the average for all consumer units)

	total consumer units	race			Hispanic origin	
		Asian	black	white and other	Hispanic	non-Hispanic
Average spending of consumer unit, total	$40,817	$44,923	$28,708	$42,360	$34,575	$41,521
Average spending of consumer unit, index	100	110	70	104	85	102
FOOD	100	118	75	103	107	99
Food at home	100	106	85	102	115	98
Cereals and bakery products	100	99	84	102	110	99
Cereals and cereal products	100	120	93	101	122	97
Bakery products	100	88	79	103	104	99
Meats, poultry, fish, and eggs	100	119	107	98	128	96
Beef	100	78	94	101	133	96
Pork	100	102	120	97	124	96
Other meats	100	79	88	102	111	99
Poultry	100	126	122	96	131	96
Fish and seafood	100	245	113	93	127	97
Eggs	100	116	97	100	159	95
Dairy products	100	75	69	105	114	98
Fresh milk and cream	100	88	74	104	126	96
Other dairy products	100	68	66	106	106	100
Fruits and vegetables	100	147	82	101	128	96
Fresh fruits	100	151	75	101	135	95
Fresh vegetables	100	137	77	100	140	95
Processed fruits	100	114	93	101	121	97
Processed vegetables	100	81	92	102	99	100
Other food at home	100	85	75	104	99	100
Sugar and other sweets	100	86	78	103	108	99
Fats and oils	100	73	93	101	113	98
Miscellaneous foods	100	82	73	104	92	101
Nonalcoholic beverages	100	93	75	104	108	99
Food prepared by consumer unit on trips	100	111	33	111	69	106
Food away from home	100	135	61	104	96	100
ALCOHOLIC BEVERAGES	100	79	43	109	81	103
HOUSING	100	122	79	102	92	101
Shelter	100	138	78	102	97	100
Owned dwellings	100	130	58	105	74	103
Mortgage interest and charges	100	147	63	104	84	102
Property taxes	100	127	56	105	58	105
Maintenance, repair, insurance, other expenses	100	80	46	108	66	104
Rented dwellings	100	168	135	93	163	93
Other lodging	100	91	29	110	50	106
Utilities, fuels, and public services	100	90	104	100	89	101
Natural gas	100	98	119	97	77	103
Electricity	100	76	106	100	84	102
Fuel oil and other fuels	100	25	42	110	52	105
Telephone	100	107	107	99	101	100
Water and other public services	100	98	85	102	94	101
Household services	100	111	64	105	64	104
Personal services	100	130	84	101	81	102
Other household services	100	97	50	107	52	105
Housekeeping supplies	100	89	67	105	90	101
Laundry and cleaning supplies	100	73	104	101	125	97
Other household products	100	87	64	106	76	103
Postage and stationery	100	110	40	108	83	102
Household furnishings and equipment	100	109	52	106	81	102
Household textiles	100	59	54	108	79	104
Furniture	100	83	58	106	100	100
Floor coverings	100	40	21	113	37	106

	total consumer units	race			Hispanic origin	
		Asian	Black	white and other	Hispanic	non-Hispanic
Major appliances	100	144	60	104	103	99
Small appliances, misc. housewares	100	145	49	105	93	100
Miscellaneous household equipment	100	124	49	106	64	104
APPAREL AND RELATED SERVICES	**100**	**106**	**98**	**100**	**107**	**99**
Men and boys	**100**	**92**	**78**	**103**	**117**	**98**
Men, aged 16 or older	100	103	64	105	109	99
Boys, aged 2 to 15	100	58	126	99	144	96
Women and girls	**100**	**96**	**89**	**102**	**89**	**101**
Women, aged 16 or older	100	102	84	102	83	102
Girls, aged 2 to 15	100	67	111	99	119	97
Children under age 2	**100**	**154**	**128**	**95**	**149**	**95**
Footwear	**100**	**99**	**150**	**93**	**125**	**97**
Other apparel products and services	**100**	**143**	**78**	**102**	**104**	**100**
TRANSPORTATION	**100**	**96**	**65**	**105**	**87**	**101**
Vehicle purchases	**100**	**80**	**56**	**107**	**82**	**102**
Cars and trucks, new	100	105	45	108	70	103
Cars and trucks, used	100	52	72	106	97	100
Other vehicles	100	–	6	116	88	101
Gasoline and motor oil	**100**	**98**	**76**	**103**	**100**	**100**
Other vehicle expenses	**100**	**102**	**74**	**104**	**88**	**101**
Vehicle finance charges	100	76	83	103	89	101
Maintenance and repairs	100	88	67	105	84	102
Vehicle insurance	100	109	81	102	90	101
Vehicle rentals, leases, licenses, other charges	100	130	64	104	90	101
Public transportation	**100**	**199**	**61**	**102**	**86**	**102**
HEALTH CARE	**100**	**81**	**54**	**107**	**60**	**105**
Health insurance	100	86	62	106	60	105
Medical services	100	81	39	109	62	104
Drugs	100	73	56	107	56	105
Medical supplies	100	64	40	109	61	105
ENTERTAINMENT	**100**	**83**	**49**	**108**	**60**	**105**
Fees and admissions	100	104	33	109	51	106
Television, radio, sound equipment	100	85	84	103	85	102
Pets, toys, and playground equipment	100	52	33	111	51	106
Other entertainment products and services	100	83	23	111	39	107
PERSONAL CARE PRODUCTS AND SERVICES	**100**	**99**	**87**	**102**	**93**	**101**
READING	**100**	**87**	**41**	**109**	**38**	**107**
EDUCATION	**100**	**241**	**56**	**101**	**61**	**104**
TOBACCO PRODUCTS AND SMOKING SUPPLIES	**100**	**41**	**62**	**107**	**59**	**104**
MISCELLANEOUS	**100**	**71**	**74**	**105**	**69**	**103**
CASH CONTRIBUTIONS	**100**	**96**	**61**	**106**	**43**	**106**
PERSONAL INSURANCE AND PENSIONS	**100**	**117**	**62**	**105**	**70**	**103**
Life and other personal insurance	100	104	74	104	40	107
Pensions and Social Security	100	119	60	105	73	103
PERSONAL TAXES	**100**	**114**	**38**	**108**	**27**	**109**
Federal income taxes	100	108	32	109	22	109
State and local income taxes	100	129	63	104	39	107
Other taxes	100	128	30	109	37	107
GIFTS FOR NONHOUSEHOLD MEMBERS	**100**	**133**	**52**	**105**	**74**	**103**
Food	**100**	**149**	**41**	**106**	**95**	**100**
Alcoholic beverages	**100**	**75**	**25**	**113**	**81**	**106**
Housing	**100**	**63**	**44**	**110**	**63**	**105**
Housekeeping supplies	100	48	31	110	88	100
Household textiles	100	8	15	115	38	108

	total	race			Hispanic origin	
	consumer units	Asian	black	white and other	Hispanic	non-Hispanic
Appliances and misc. housewares	100	80	60	104	48	104
Major appliances	100	71	114	100	14	100
Small appliances and misc. housewares	100	83	39	106	61	106
Miscellaneous household equipment	100	38	26	111	54	105
Other housing	100	55	59	107	61	105
Apparel and services	**100**	80	99	101	83	102
Males, aged 2 or older	100	102	54	105	93	100
Females, aged 2 or older	100	66	116	100	64	105
Children under age 2	100	118	113	97	126	97
Other apparel products and services	100	48	108	102	70	104
Jewelry and watches	100	77	81	104	50	104
All other apparel products and services	100	16	132	96	84	100
Transportation	**100**	540	63	88	237	83
Health care	**100**	71	46	108	15	110
Entertainment	**100**	80	38	109	61	104
Toys, games, hobbies, and tricycles	100	50	50	108	50	108
Other entertainment	100	100	33	109	65	105
Personal care products and services	**100**	144	50	106	81	100
Reading	**100**	100	–	200	–	100
Education	**100**	194	23	108	49	106
All other gifts	**100**	96	41	109	45	107

Note: Other includes Alaska Natives, American Indians, Native Hawaiians and other Pacific Islanders as well as approximately 1.3 percent reporting more than one race. (–) means sample is too small to make a reliable estimate.
Source: Calculations by New Strategist based on the Bureau of Labor Statistics 2003 Consumer Expenditure Survey

Spending by Region, 2003

Households in the West spent $45,381 in 2003, 11 percent more than the average household and more than households in any other region. Spending by households in the Northeast is only 3 percent above average, at $42,162 in 2003. Households in the Midwest spent $40,280, or just slightly below the average amount. In the South, average household spending was 8 percent below average at $37,625 in 2003.

Households in the Northeast and West spend more than the average household on most products and services. Those in the Midwest spend close to the average, while households in the South spend less than average on most items. Households in the Northeast spend the most on property taxes. Those in the West spend the most on mortgage interest and rent. Households in the Midwest spend the most on tobacco. Households in the South spend 12 percent less than average on alcoholic beverages.

The biggest consumers of natural gas are households in the Midwest, spending 51 percent more than the average household on this item. The South spends the most on electricity, while the Northeast spends the most on fuel oil. Western households spend 25 percent more than the average household on water and other public services.

Households in the West spend the most on entertainment. Public transportation spending is highest in the Northeast. Spending on laundry and cleaning supplies is 10 percent above average in the Midwest. Households in the South spend the most on prescription drugs.

Table 1.12 Average spending by region, 2003

(average annual spending of consumer units by product and service category and region of residence, 2003)

	total	Northeast	Midwest	South	West
Number of consumer units (000)	115,356	22,182	26,438	41,325	25,412
Average number of persons per consumer unit	2.5	2.4	2.5	2.5	2.6
Average income before taxes	$51,128	$56,513	$52,445	$46,729	$52,506
Average annual spending	**40,817**	**42,162**	**40,280**	**37,625**	**45,381**
FOOD	**5,340**	**5,730**	**5,088**	**4,960**	**5,876**
Food at home	**3,129**	**3,306**	**2,904**	**2,996**	**3,428**
Cereals and bakery products	442	485	411	413	482
Cereals and cereal products	150	158	135	142	173
Bakery products	292	327	276	271	310
Meats, poultry, fish, and eggs	825	889	734	835	849
Beef	246	239	225	262	247
Pork	171	168	161	181	167
Other meats	102	132	98	94	92
Poultry	145	165	123	141	157
Fish and seafood	124	146	97	121	141
Eggs	37	38	31	36	45
Dairy products	328	353	323	298	359
Fresh milk and cream	127	130	126	117	139
Other dairy products	201	222	197	181	220
Fruits and vegetables	535	586	472	489	633
Fresh fruits	171	185	152	149	213
Fresh vegetables	172	190	142	154	217
Processed fruits	108	123	96	98	125
Processed vegetables	84	88	81	88	78
Other food at home	999	994	962	961	1,104
Sugar and other sweets	119	126	118	107	135
Fats and oils	86	89	79	85	91
Miscellaneous foods	490	473	476	482	531
Nonalcoholic beverages	268	272	254	258	297
Food prepared by consumer unit on trips	36	34	35	30	50
Food away from home	**2,211**	**2,424**	**2,184**	**1,964**	**2,449**
ALCOHOLIC BEVERAGES	**391**	**427**	**403**	**345**	**421**
HOUSING	**13,432**	**14,811**	**12,634**	**12,006**	**15,371**
Shelter	**7,887**	**9,134**	**7,086**	**6,660**	**9,630**
Owned dwellings	5,263	5,932	4,908	4,528	6,244
Mortgage interest and charges	2,954	2,901	2,578	2,567	4,020
Property taxes	1,344	2,004	1,427	1,018	1,211
Maintenance, repair, insurance, other expenses	965	1,026	903	942	1,013
Rented dwellings	2,179	2,664	1,720	1,802	2,848
Other lodging	445	537	458	330	538
Utilities, fuels, and public services	**2,811**	**2,889**	**2,855**	**2,891**	**2,569**
Natural gas	392	512	593	243	320
Electricity	1,028	926	931	1,251	854
Fuel oil and other fuels	110	287	99	61	44
Telephone	956	932	917	1,002	941
Water and other public services	326	232	315	333	409
Household services	**707**	**813**	**614**	**666**	**778**
Personal services	294	373	274	265	291
Other household services	414	440	340	402	487
Housekeeping supplies	**529**	**523**	**575**	**496**	**537**
Laundry and cleaning supplies	132	125	145	132	126
Other household products	263	257	284	258	256
Postage and stationery	133	141	147	106	155
Household furnishings and equipment	**1,497**	**1,452**	**1,504**	**1,294**	**1,858**
Household textiles	113	126	105	91	147
Furniture	401	391	411	357	471
Floor coverings	52	66	44	38	71

	total	Northeast	Midwest	South	West
Major appliances	$196	$176	$195	$179	$240
Small appliances, misc. housewares	88	75	87	87	101
Miscellaneous household equipment	648	617	663	542	828
APPAREL AND RELATED SERVICES	**1,640**	**1,859**	**1,563**	**1,451**	**1,834**
Men and boys	**372**	**426**	**369**	**303**	**437**
Men, aged 16 or older	282	339	280	219	335
Boys, aged 2 to 15	89	87	88	84	101
Women and girls	**634**	**709**	**612**	**548**	**732**
Women, aged 16 or older	529	592	497	458	620
Girls, aged 2 to 15	106	118	115	89	112
Children under age 2	**81**	**76**	**92**	**74**	**87**
Footwear	**294**	**357**	**249**	**283**	**305**
Other apparel products and services	**258**	**291**	**242**	**242**	**273**
TRANSPORTATION	**7,781**	**7,043**	**7,817**	**7,621**	**8,645**
Vehicle purchases	**3,732**	**3,040**	**3,775**	**3,893**	**4,028**
Cars and trucks, new	2,052	1,688	2,039	2,208	2,131
Cars and trucks, used	1,611	1,294	1,654	1,627	1,820
Other vehicles	68	58	82	58	78
Gasoline and motor oil	**1,333**	**1,157**	**1,357**	**1,321**	**1,479**
Other vehicle expenses	**2,331**	**2,307**	**2,314**	**2,154**	**2,659**
Vehicle finance charges	371	268	391	408	379
Maintenance and repairs	619	565	580	555	811
Vehicle insurance	905	924	860	905	936
Vehicle rentals, leases, licenses, other charges	436	551	484	286	532
Public transportation	**385**	**539**	**371**	**253**	**479**
HEALTH CARE	**2,416**	**2,127**	**2,586**	**2,396**	**2,525**
Health insurance	1,252	1,237	1,332	1,223	1,227
Medical services	591	448	621	563	729
Drugs	467	358	513	520	426
Medical supplies	107	84	119	90	143
ENTERTAINMENT	**2,060**	**2,117**	**1,978**	**1,812**	**2,494**
Fees and admissions	494	614	489	365	606
Television, radio, sound equipment	730	776	738	696	736
Pets, toys, and playground equipment	378	447	378	307	434
Other entertainment products and services	457	279	373	444	718
PERSONAL CARE PRODUCTS AND SERVICES	**527**	**532**	**499**	**494**	**606**
READING	**127**	**153**	**141**	**93**	**146**
EDUCATION	**783**	**1,040**	**796**	**581**	**875**
TOBACCO PRODUCTS AND SMOKING SUPPLIES	**290**	**306**	**363**	**275**	**224**
MISCELLANEOUS	**606**	**548**	**647**	**556**	**695**
CASH CONTRIBUTIONS	**1,370**	**1,161**	**1,469**	**1,344**	**1,491**
PERSONAL INSURANCE AND PENSIONS	**4,055**	**4,308**	**4,295**	**3,690**	**4,179**
Life and other personal insurance	397	454	423	381	347
Pensions and Social Security	3,658	3,855	3,872	3,309	3,832
PERSONAL TAXES	**2,532**	**2,294**	**2,853**	**2,268**	**2,840**
Federal income taxes	1,843	1,536	1,904	1,786	2,133
State and local income taxes	502	543	672	348	546
Other taxes	187	215	277	133	161
GIFTS FOR NONHOUSEHOLD MEMBERS	**1,007**	**1,169**	**1,044**	**862**	**1,059**
Food	**78**	**122**	**66**	**58**	**82**
Alcoholic beverages	**16**	**18**	**16**	**14**	**17**
Housing	**220**	**216**	**214**	**200**	**263**
Housekeeping supplies	42	55	44	26	53
Household textiles	13	10	18	10	14

	total	Northeast	Midwest	South	West
Appliances and misc. housewares	$25	$15	$24	$26	$31
Major appliances	7	4	7	5	11
Small appliances and misc. housewares	18	11	13	21	20
Miscellaneous household equipment	57	56	59	45	74
Other housing	85	81	63	94	91
Apparel and services	**225**	**264**	**242**	**188**	**232**
Males, aged 2 or older	56	70	45	44	69
Females, aged 2 or older	80	88	96	66	80
Children under age 2	39	45	38	36	39
Other apparel products and services	50	62	60	42	44
Jewelry and watches	26	29	28	25	22
All other apparel products and services	25	33	32	17	22
Transportation	**60**	**32**	**57**	**46**	**108**
Health care	**48**	**30**	**86**	**43**	**32**
Entertainment	**69**	**70**	**74**	**60**	**77**
Toys, games, hobbies, and tricycles	26	26	29	25	25
Other entertainment	43	45	45	35	52
Personal care products and services	**16**	**19**	**15**	**13**	**19**
Reading	**1**	**2**	**1**	**1**	**2**
Education	**200**	**332**	**186**	**173**	**143**
All other gifts	**74**	**64**	**87**	**66**	**84**

Note: Spending by category will not add to total spending because gift spending is also included in the preceding product and service categories and personal taxes are not included in the total.
Source: Bureau of Labor Statistics, 2003 Consumer Expenditure Survey, Internet site http://www.bls.gov/cex/

Table 1.13 Indexed spending by region, 2003

(indexed average annual spending of consumer units by product and service category and region of residence, 2003; index definition: an index of 100 is the average for all consumer units; an index of 132 means that spending by consumer units in that group is 32 percent above the average for all consumer units; an index of 68 indicates spending that is 32 percent below the average for all consumer units)

	total	Northeast	Midwest	South	West
Average spending of consumer unit, total	$40,817	$42,162	$40,280	$37,625	$45,381
Average spending of consumer unit, index	100	103	99	92	111
FOOD	100	107	95	93	110
Food at home	100	106	93	96	110
Cereals and bakery products	100	110	93	93	109
Cereals and cereal products	100	105	90	95	115
Bakery products	100	112	95	93	106
Meats, poultry, fish, and eggs	100	108	89	101	103
Beef	100	97	91	107	100
Pork	100	98	94	106	98
Other meats	100	129	96	92	90
Poultry	100	114	85	97	108
Fish and seafood	100	118	78	98	114
Eggs	100	103	84	97	122
Dairy products	100	108	98	91	109
Fresh milk and cream	100	102	99	92	109
Other dairy products	100	110	98	90	109
Fruits and vegetables	100	110	88	91	118
Fresh fruits	100	108	89	87	125
Fresh vegetables	100	110	83	90	126
Processed fruits	100	114	89	91	116
Processed vegetables	100	105	96	105	93
Other food at home	100	99	96	96	111
Sugar and other sweets	100	106	99	90	113
Fats and oils	100	103	92	99	106
Miscellaneous foods	100	97	97	98	108
Nonalcoholic beverages	100	101	95	96	111
Food prepared by consumer unit on trips	100	94	97	83	139
Food away from home	100	110	99	89	111
ALCOHOLIC BEVERAGES	100	109	103	88	108
HOUSING	100	110	94	89	114
Shelter	100	116	90	84	122
Owned dwellings	100	113	93	86	119
Mortgage interest and charges	100	98	87	87	136
Property taxes	100	149	106	76	90
Maintenance, repair, insurance, other expenses	100	106	94	98	105
Rented dwellings	100	122	79	83	131
Other lodging	100	121	103	74	121
Utilities, fuels, and public services	100	103	102	103	91
Natural gas	100	131	151	62	82
Electricity	100	90	91	122	83
Fuel oil and other fuels	100	261	90	55	40
Telephone	100	97	96	105	98
Water and other public services	100	71	97	102	125
Household services	100	115	87	94	110
Personal services	100	127	93	90	99
Other household services	100	106	82	97	118
Housekeeping supplies	100	99	109	94	102
Laundry and cleaning supplies	100	95	110	100	95
Other household products	100	98	108	98	97
Postage and stationery	100	106	111	80	117
Household furnishings and equipment	100	97	100	86	124
Household textiles	100	112	93	81	130
Furniture	100	98	102	89	117
Floor coverings	100	127	85	73	137

	total	Northeast	Midwest	South	West
Major appliances	100	90	99	91	122
Small appliances, misc. housewares	100	85	99	99	115
Miscellaneous household equipment	100	95	102	84	128
APPAREL AND RELATED SERVICES	**100**	**113**	**95**	**88**	**112**
Men and boys	**100**	**115**	**99**	**81**	**117**
Men, aged 16 or older	100	120	99	78	119
Boys, aged 2 to 15	100	98	99	94	113
Women and girls	**100**	**112**	**97**	**86**	**115**
Women, aged 16 or older	100	112	94	87	117
Girls, aged 2 to 15	100	111	108	84	106
Children under age 2	**100**	**94**	**114**	**91**	**107**
Footwear	**100**	**121**	**85**	**96**	**104**
Other apparel products and services	**100**	**113**	**94**	**94**	**106**
TRANSPORTATION	**100**	**91**	**100**	**98**	**111**
Vehicle purchases	**100**	**81**	**101**	**104**	**108**
Cars and trucks, new	100	82	99	108	104
Cars and trucks, used	100	80	103	101	113
Other vehicles	100	85	121	85	115
Gasoline and motor oil	**100**	**87**	**102**	**99**	**111**
Other vehicle expenses	**100**	**99**	**99**	**92**	**114**
Vehicle finance charges	100	72	105	110	102
Maintenance and repairs	100	91	94	90	131
Vehicle insurance	100	102	95	100	103
Vehicle rentals, leases, licenses, other charges	100	126	111	66	122
Public transportation	**100**	**140**	**96**	**66**	**124**
HEALTH CARE	**100**	**88**	**107**	**99**	**105**
Health insurance	100	99	106	98	98
Medical services	100	76	105	95	123
Drugs	100	77	120	111	91
Medical supplies	100	79	111	84	134
ENTERTAINMENT	**100**	**103**	**96**	**88**	**121**
Fees and admissions	100	124	89	74	123
Television, radio, sound equipment	100	106	101	95	101
Pets, toys, and playground equipment	100	118	100	81	115
Other entertainment products and services	100	61	82	97	157
PERSONAL CARE PRODUCTS AND SERVICES	**100**	**101**	**95**	**94**	**115**
READING	**100**	**120**	**111**	**73**	**115**
EDUCATION	**100**	**133**	**102**	**74**	**112**
TOBACCO PRODUCTS AND SMOKING SUPPLIES	**100**	**106**	**125**	**95**	**77**
MISCELLANEOUS	**100**	**90**	**107**	**92**	**115**
CASH CONTRIBUTIONS	**100**	**85**	**107**	**98**	**109**
PERSONAL INSURANCE AND PENSIONS	**100**	**106**	**106**	**91**	**103**
Life and other personal insurance	100	114	107	96	87
Pensions and Social Security	100	105	106	90	105
PERSONAL TAXES	**100**	**91**	**113**	**90**	**112**
Federal income taxes	100	83	103	97	116
State and local income taxes	100	108	134	69	109
Other taxes	100	115	148	71	86
GIFTS FOR NONHOUSEHOLD MEMBERS	**100**	**116**	**104**	**86**	**105**
Food	**100**	**156**	**85**	**74**	**105**
Alcoholic beverages	**100**	**113**	**100**	**88**	**106**
Housing	**100**	**98**	**97**	**91**	**120**
Housekeeping supplies	100	131	105	62	126
Household textiles	100	77	138	77	108

	total	Northeast	Midwest	South	West
Appliances and misc. housewares	100	60	96	104	124
Major appliances	100	57	100	71	157
Small appliances and misc. housewares	100	61	100	117	111
Miscellaneous household equipment	100	98	104	79	130
Other housing	100	95	80	111	107
Apparel and services	**100**	**117**	**108**	**84**	**103**
Males, aged 2 or older	100	125	86	79	123
Females, aged 2 or older	100	110	120	83	100
Children under age 2	100	115	97	92	100
Other apparel products and services	100	124	120	84	88
Jewelry and watches	100	112	108	96	85
All other apparel products and services	100	132	128	68	88
Transportation	**100**	**53**	**95**	**77**	**180**
Health care	**100**	**63**	**179**	**90**	**67**
Entertainment	**100**	**101**	**107**	**87**	**112**
Toys, games, hobbies, and tricycles	100	100	112	96	96
Other entertainment	100	105	105	81	121
Personal care products and services	**100**	**119**	**94**	**81**	**119**
Reading	**100**	**200**	**100**	**100**	**200**
Education	**100**	**166**	**93**	**87**	**72**
All other gifts	**100**	**86**	**118**	**89**	**114**

Source: Calculations by New Strategist based on the Bureau of Labor Statistics 2003 Consumer Expenditure Survey

Spending by Education, 2003

Because college graduates have the highest incomes, their spending is well above average. The average household headed by a college graduate spent $58,480 in 2003, or 43 percent more than the average household. In contrast, households headed by people who did not graduate from high school spent only $23,901 in 2003, fully 41 percent less than the average household.

Households headed by the least educated—those without a high school diploma—spend more than average on only a few items. These include eggs, rent, and tobacco.

High school graduates spent $33,956 in 2003, or 17 percent less than the average household. Their spending is also below average in most categories with some exceptions such as tobacco.

Householders with some college experience or an associate's degree make up the largest share of households (31 percent). Their spending is close to the average on most items.

College graduates, who account for 27 percent of householders, far outspend the average household on most items—particularly those favored by the affluent. These include food away from home (42 percent above average) and alcoholic beverages (59 percent). They spend more than twice the average on other lodging (which includes vacation homes and hotel and motel expenses) and public transportation (which includes airfares). They are also big spenders on education and fees and admissions to entertainment events.

Table 1.14 Average spending by education of householder, 2003

(average annual spending of consumer units by product and service category and educational attainment of consumer unit reference person, 2003)

	total consumer units	not a high school graduate	high school graduate	some college or associate's degree	college degree or more
Number of consumer units (000)	115,356	17,721	31,552	35,495	30,589
Average number of persons per consumer unit	2.5	2.6	2.5	2.4	2.5
Average income before taxes	$51,128	$25,028	$40,113	$47,889	$81,842
Average annual spending	40,817	23,901	33,956	39,965	58,480
FOOD	**5,340**	**4,086**	**4,701**	**5,336**	**6,641**
Food at home	**3,129**	**2,913**	**2,986**	**3,028**	**3,491**
Cereals and bakery products	442	408	424	433	485
Cereals and cereal products	150	153	140	144	167
Bakery products	292	255	285	289	319
Meats, poultry, fish, and eggs	825	860	839	815	805
Beef	246	236	262	256	224
Pork	171	212	182	165	145
Other meats	102	98	104	102	103
Poultry	145	157	143	143	142
Fish and seafood	124	112	111	113	156
Eggs	37	45	38	35	36
Dairy products	328	290	307	315	382
Fresh milk and cream	127	132	123	123	132
Other dairy products	201	158	184	192	250
Fruits and vegetables	535	502	479	491	655
Fresh fruits	171	156	147	152	222
Fresh vegetables	172	167	148	158	214
Processed fruits	108	93	101	102	130
Processed vegetables	84	86	83	79	89
Other food at home	999	853	937	973	1,164
Sugar and other sweets	119	105	120	112	132
Fats and oils	86	91	84	82	88
Miscellaneous foods	490	387	451	478	590
Nonalcoholic beverages	268	255	258	266	289
Food prepared by consumer unit on trips	36	14	23	35	64
Food away from home	**2,211**	**1,173**	**1,715**	**2,309**	**3,150**
ALCOHOLIC BEVERAGES	**391**	**161**	**255**	**417**	**620**
HOUSING	**13,432**	**8,351**	**10,923**	**12,817**	**19,631**
Shelter	**7,887**	**4,865**	**6,178**	**7,403**	**11,963**
Owned dwellings	5,263	2,427	4,040	4,753	8,760
Mortgage interest and charges	2,954	1,144	2,210	2,770	4,984
Property taxes	1,344	766	1,057	1,152	2,196
Maintenance, repair, insurance, other expenses	965	517	773	830	1,580
Rented dwellings	2,179	2,346	1,917	2,280	2,238
Other lodging	445	92	222	371	966
Utilities, fuels, and public services	**2,811**	**2,311**	**2,740**	**2,731**	**3,268**
Natural gas	392	313	381	361	485
Electricity	1,028	903	1,046	989	1,127
Fuel oil and other fuels	110	101	116	102	117
Telephone	956	735	897	966	1,132
Water and other public services	326	260	301	313	407
Household services	**707**	**237**	**447**	**672**	**1,288**
Personal services	294	82	199	267	543
Other household services	414	155	248	404	745
Housekeeping supplies	**529**	**323**	**477**	**530**	**683**
Laundry and cleaning supplies	132	114	131	141	134
Other household products	263	153	238	257	350
Postage and stationery	133	55	108	132	199
Household furnishings and equipment	**1,497**	**615**	**1,080**	**1,481**	**2,429**
Household textiles	113	54	68	125	180
Furniture	401	191	278	370	685
Floor coverings	52	10	42	42	97

	total consumer units	not a high school graduate	high school graduate	some college or associate's degree	college degree or more
Major appliances	$196	$108	$168	$191	$277
Small appliances, misc. housewares	88	42	67	83	137
Miscellaneous household equipment	648	210	457	669	1,053
APPAREL AND RELATED SERVICES	**1,640**	**1,017**	**1,260**	**1,733**	**2,260**
Men and boys	**372**	**242**	**293**	**400**	**491**
Men, aged 16 or older	282	160	213	309	389
Boys, aged 2 to 15	89	82	80	91	101
Women and girls	**634**	**339**	**484**	**690**	**879**
Women, aged 16 or older	529	263	384	579	756
Girls, aged 2 to 15	106	77	100	111	123
Children under age 2	**81**	**68**	**73**	**77**	**102**
Footwear	**294**	**250**	**250**	**324**	**329**
Other apparel products and services	**258**	**117**	**150**	**243**	**459**
TRANSPORTATION	**7,781**	**4,412**	**7,236**	**7,919**	**10,068**
Vehicle purchases	**3,732**	**2,059**	**3,659**	**3,831**	**4,661**
Cars and trucks, new	2,052	719	1,969	2,083	2,876
Cars and trucks, used	1,611	1,310	1,653	1,659	1,689
Other vehicles	68	30	38	89	96
Gasoline and motor oil	**1,333**	**942**	**1,306**	**1,393**	**1,517**
Other vehicle expenses	**2,331**	**1,263**	**2,121**	**2,379**	**3,097**
Vehicle finance charges	371	192	384	424	398
Maintenance and repairs	619	348	544	608	863
Vehicle insurance	905	588	892	908	1,101
Vehicle rentals, leases, licenses, other charges	436	135	311	439	735
Public transportation	**385**	**148**	**200**	**316**	**793**
HEALTH CARE	**2,416**	**1,797**	**2,287**	**2,308**	**3,031**
Health insurance	1,252	976	1,246	1,176	1,506
Medical services	591	317	499	569	869
Drugs	467	445	447	456	510
Medical supplies	107	59	95	107	145
ENTERTAINMENT	**2,060**	**882**	**1,607**	**2,135**	**3,110**
Fees and admissions	494	91	285	447	1,000
Television, radio, sound equipment	730	441	661	759	934
Pets, toys, and playground equipment	378	166	372	363	516
Other entertainment products and services	457	183	289	566	661
PERSONAL CARE PRODUCTS AND SERVICES	**527**	**305**	**436**	**541**	**725**
READING	**127**	**42**	**83**	**120**	**230**
EDUCATION	**783**	**102**	**328**	**833**	**1,587**
TOBACCO PRODUCTS AND SMOKING SUPPLIES	**290**	**342**	**380**	**309**	**144**
MISCELLANEOUS	**606**	**312**	**515**	**629**	**840**
CASH CONTRIBUTIONS	**1,370**	**574**	**990**	**1,106**	**2,529**
PERSONAL INSURANCE AND PENSIONS	**4,055**	**1,519**	**2,895**	**3,760**	**7,064**
Life and other personal insurance	397	180	334	338	657
Pensions and Social Security	3,658	1,339	2,561	3,422	6,407
PERSONAL TAXES	**2,532**	**312**	**1,855**	**2,042**	**5,127**
Federal income taxes	1,843	113	1,386	1,425	3,835
State and local income taxes	502	124	310	452	983
Other taxes	187	75	158	165	309
GIFTS FOR NONHOUSEHOLD MEMBERS	**1,007**	**380**	**645**	**909**	**1,840**
Food	**78**	**17**	**54**	**67**	**147**
Alcoholic beverages	**16**	**7**	**7**	**22**	**25**
Housing	**220**	**93**	**146**	**198**	**391**
Housekeeping supplies	42	10	32	41	68
Household textiles	13	2	7	14	23

	total consumer units	not a high school graduate	high school graduate	some college or associate's degree	college degree or more
Appliances and misc. housewares	$25	$9	$13	$26	$42
Major appliances	7	4	3	10	8
Small appliances and misc. housewares	18	5	10	17	34
Miscellaneous household equipment	57	23	41	49	100
Other housing	85	49	54	68	158
Apparel and services	**225**	**122**	**174**	**226**	**331**
Males, aged 2 or older	56	33	36	61	82
Females, aged 2 or older	80	42	63	80	118
Children under age 2	39	25	37	34	52
Other apparel products and services	50	23	38	51	79
Jewelry and watches	26	5	19	17	54
All other apparel products and services	25	18	19	33	25
Transportation	**60**	**5**	**28**	**91**	**87**
Health care	**48**	**49**	**35**	**44**	**64**
Entertainment	**69**	**33**	**59**	**73**	**95**
Toys, games, hobbies, and tricycles	26	13	27	31	27
Other entertainment	43	20	33	43	68
Personal care products and services	**16**	**6**	**15**	**14**	**24**
Reading	**1**	**–**	**1**	**1**	**2**
Education	**200**	**11**	**70**	**110**	**546**
All other gifts	**74**	**37**	**56**	**63**	**127**

Note: Spending by category will not add to total spending because gift spending is also included in the preceding product and service categories and personal taxes are not included in the total. (–) means sample is too small to make a reliable estimate.
Source: Bureau of Labor Statistics, 2003 Consumer Expenditure Survey, Internet site http://www.bls.gov/cex/

Table 1.15 Indexed spending by education of householder, 2003

(indexed average annual spending of consumer units by product and service category and educational attainment of consumer unit reference person, 2003; index definition: an index of 100 is the average for all consumer units; an index of 132 means that spending by consumer units in that group is 32 percent above the average for all consumer units; an index of 68 indicates spending that is 32 percent below the average for all consumer units)

	total consumer units	not a high school graduate	high school graduate	some college or associate's degree	college degree or more
Average spending of consumer unit, total	$40,817	$23,901	$33,956	$39,965	$58,480
Average spending of consumer unit, index	100	59	83	98	143
FOOD	100	77	88	100	124
Food at home	100	93	95	97	112
Cereals and bakery products	100	92	96	98	110
Cereals and cereal products	100	102	93	96	111
Bakery products	100	87	98	99	109
Meats, poultry, fish, and eggs	100	104	102	99	98
Beef	100	95	107	104	91
Pork	100	124	106	97	85
Other meats	100	96	102	100	101
Poultry	100	108	99	99	98
Fish and seafood	100	90	90	91	126
Eggs	100	122	103	94	97
Dairy products	100	88	94	96	116
Fresh milk and cream	100	104	97	97	104
Other dairy products	100	75	92	96	124
Fruits and vegetables	100	94	90	92	122
Fresh fruits	100	91	86	89	130
Fresh vegetables	100	97	86	92	124
Processed fruits	100	86	94	95	120
Processed vegetables	100	102	99	94	106
Other food at home	100	85	94	97	117
Sugar and other sweets	100	88	101	94	111
Fats and oils	100	106	98	96	102
Miscellaneous foods	100	79	92	98	120
Nonalcoholic beverages	100	95	96	99	108
Food prepared by consumer unit on trips	100	39	64	98	178
Food away from home	100	53	78	104	142
ALCOHOLIC BEVERAGES	100	41	65	107	159
HOUSING	100	62	81	95	146
Shelter	100	62	78	94	152
Owned dwellings	100	46	77	90	166
Mortgage interest and charges	100	39	75	94	169
Property taxes	100	57	79	86	163
Maintenance, repair, insurance, other expenses	100	54	80	86	164
Rented dwellings	100	108	88	105	103
Other lodging	100	21	50	83	217
Utilities, fuels, and public services	100	82	97	97	116
Natural gas	100	80	97	92	124
Electricity	100	88	102	96	110
Fuel oil and other fuels	100	92	105	92	106
Telephone	100	77	94	101	118
Water and other public services	100	80	92	96	125
Household services	100	34	63	95	182
Personal services	100	28	68	91	185
Other household services	100	37	60	98	180
Housekeeping supplies	100	61	90	100	129
Laundry and cleaning supplies	100	86	99	107	102
Other household products	100	58	90	98	133
Postage and stationery	100	41	81	99	150
Household furnishings and equipment	100	41	72	99	162
Household textiles	100	48	60	111	159
Furniture	100	48	69	92	171
Floor coverings	100	19	81	82	187

	total consumer units	not a high school graduate	high school graduate	some college or associate's degree	college degree or more
Major appliances	100	55	86	97	141
Small appliances, misc. housewares	100	48	76	95	156
Miscellaneous household equipment	100	32	71	103	163
APPAREL AND RELATED SERVICES	**100**	**62**	**77**	**106**	**138**
Men and boys	**100**	**65**	**79**	**108**	**132**
Men, aged 16 or older	100	57	76	110	138
Boys, aged 2 to 15	100	92	90	102	113
Women and girls	**100**	**53**	**76**	**109**	**139**
Women, aged 16 or older	100	50	73	109	143
Girls, aged 2 to 15	100	73	94	104	116
Children under age 2	**100**	**84**	**90**	**94**	**126**
Footwear	**100**	**85**	**85**	**110**	**112**
Other apparel products and services	**100**	**45**	**62**	**94**	**178**
TRANSPORTATION	**100**	**57**	**94**	**102**	**129**
Vehicle purchases	**100**	**55**	**98**	**103**	**125**
Cars and trucks, new	100	35	96	101	140
Cars and trucks, used	100	81	103	103	105
Other vehicles	100	44	56	131	141
Gasoline and motor oil	**100**	**71**	**98**	**104**	**114**
Other vehicle expenses	**100**	**54**	**91**	**102**	**133**
Vehicle finance charges	100	52	104	114	107
Maintenance and repairs	100	56	88	98	139
Vehicle insurance	100	65	99	100	122
Vehicle rentals, leases, licenses, other charges	100	31	71	101	169
Public transportation	**100**	**38**	**52**	**82**	**206**
HEALTH CARE	**100**	**74**	**95**	**96**	**125**
Health insurance	100	78	100	94	120
Medical services	100	54	84	96	147
Drugs	100	95	96	98	109
Medical supplies	100	55	89	100	136
ENTERTAINMENT	**100**	**43**	**78**	**104**	**151**
Fees and admissions	100	18	58	90	202
Television, radio, sound equipment	100	60	91	104	128
Pets, toys, and playground equipment	100	44	98	96	137
Other entertainment products and services	100	40	63	124	145
PERSONAL CARE PRODUCTS AND SERVICES	**100**	**58**	**83**	**103**	**138**
READING	**100**	**33**	**65**	**95**	**181**
EDUCATION	**100**	**13**	**42**	**106**	**203**
TOBACCO PRODUCTS AND SMOKING SUPPLIES	**100**	**118**	**131**	**107**	**50**
MISCELLANEOUS	**100**	**51**	**85**	**104**	**139**
CASH CONTRIBUTIONS	**100**	**42**	**72**	**81**	**185**
PERSONAL INSURANCE AND PENSIONS	**100**	**37**	**71**	**93**	**174**
Life and other personal insurance	100	45	84	85	165
Pensions and Social Security	100	37	70	94	175
PERSONAL TAXES	**100**	**12**	**73**	**81**	**202**
Federal income taxes	100	6	75	77	208
State and local income taxes	100	25	62	90	196
Other taxes	100	40	84	88	165
GIFTS FOR NONHOUSEHOLD MEMBERS	**100**	**38**	**64**	**90**	**183**
Food	**100**	**22**	**69**	**86**	**188**
Alcoholic beverages	**100**	**44**	**44**	**136**	**156**
Housing	**100**	**42**	**66**	**90**	**178**
Housekeeping supplies	100	24	76	97	162
Household textiles	100	15	54	109	177

	total consumer units	not a high school graduate	high school graduate	some college or associate's degree	college degree or more
Appliances and misc. housewares	100	36	52	106	168
Major appliances	100	57	43	142	114
Small appliances and misc. housewares	100	28	56	92	189
Miscellaneous household equipment	100	40	72	86	175
Other housing	100	58	64	80	186
Apparel and services	**100**	**54**	**77**	**101**	**147**
Males, aged 2 or older	100	59	64	109	146
Females, aged 2 or older	100	53	79	100	148
Children under age 2	100	64	95	87	133
Other apparel products and services	100	46	76	102	158
Jewelry and watches	100	19	73	67	208
All other apparel products and services	100	72	76	134	100
Transportation	**100**	**8**	**47**	**152**	**145**
Health care	**100**	**102**	**73**	**92**	**133**
Entertainment	**100**	**48**	**86**	**107**	**138**
Toys, games, hobbies, and tricycles	100	50	104	119	104
Other entertainment	100	47	77	99	158
Personal care products and services	**100**	**38**	**94**	**85**	**150**
Reading	**100**	–	100	100	**200**
Education	**100**	**6**	**35**	**55**	**273**
All other gifts	**100**	**50**	**76**	**85**	**172**

Note: (–) means sample is too small to make a reliable estimate.
Source: Calculations by New Strategist based on the Bureau of Labor Statistics 2003 Consumer Expenditure Survey

Spending on Apparel, 2003

Americans spend much less on apparel than they once did. In 2003, the average household spent $1,640 on clothes, shoes, and related items. This figure is a substantial 17 percent less than the $1,983 spent by the average household on apparel in 2000, after adjusting for inflation. Overall, Americans devoted 4.0 percent of their spending to clothes, shoes, and related products and services in 2003, down from 4.9 percent in 2000.

Households headed by people aged 35 to 44 spend the most on apparel, more than $2,000 in 2003. Apparel spending patterns differ sharply by age. Householders aged 35 to 44 spend the most on boys' and girls' apparel. Those aged 25 to 34 spend the most on infants' apparel. Householders aged 45 to 54 spend the most on women's clothes—34 percent more than the average household.

Spending on apparel rises with income. Households with incomes of $100,000 or more spend more than twice the average on apparel. This income level accounts for just 12 percent of households but for 41 percent of the market for men's suits, 45 percent of the market for men's sports coats, 42 percent of the market for jewelry, and 46 percent of the market for professional dry cleaning. In contrast, only 18 percent of footwear spending is controlled by households with incomes of $100,000 or more.

Married couples with children under age 18 at home spend more on apparel than any other household type—more than $2,400 in 2003—in part because their households are larger than average. Married couples without children at home (most of them empty-nesters) spend 15 percent more than average on women's clothes and 18 percent more on men's clothes. Single-parent households spend more than twice the average on clothes for boys and girls.

Hispanic households are the biggest spenders on apparel, devoting $1,756 to this category in 2003, or 7 percent more than the average household. Asian households are not far behind, their spending on apparel being 6 percent above average. Blacks are the biggest spenders on footwear, devoting 50 percent more than the average household to shoes. Blacks and Hispanics together control more than 30 percent of the footwear market (although there is some overlap because Hispanics may be of any race and some are black).

Spending on apparel is greatest in the Northeast, where households devoted $1,859 to clothes in 2003—13 percent more than the average household. The West was not far behind, with spending 12 percent above average. In the Midwest, apparel spending is 5 percent below average, and in the South it is fully 12 percent below average. Spending on uniforms is higher than average in the South, however.

The most educated householders spend the most on clothes because they have the highest incomes. Householders with a college degree spent more than $2,200 on clothes in 2003—38 percent more than the average household. College graduates accounted for only one-third of the market for infants' clothes, but for more than half the markets for watches, jewelry, and professional dry cleaning.

Table 2.1 Apparel: Average spending by age, 2003

(average annual spending of consumer units (CU) on apparel, accessories, and related services, by age of consumer unit reference person, 2003)

	total consumer units	under 25	25 to 34	35 to 44	45 to 54	55 to 64	65 to 74	75+
Number of consumer units (000)	115,356	8,584	19,737	24,413	23,131	16,580	11,495	11,417
Average number of persons per CU	2.5	1.8	2.9	3.2	2.6	2.1	1.9	1.5
Average before-tax income of CU	$51,128.00	$20,680.00	$50,389.00	$61,091.00	$68,028.00	$58,672.00	$35,314.00	$25,492.00
Average spending of CU, total	40,817.33	22,395.53	40,525.22	47,175.06	50,100.86	44,190.65	33,629.17	25,016.38
Apparel, average spending	**1,639.99**	**1,116.75**	**1,848.81**	**2,091.00**	**1,953.44**	**1,561.85**	**1,190.00**	**610.79**
MEN'S APPAREL	**282.18**	**232.69**	**273.88**	**349.07**	**372.29**	**272.62**	**185.51**	**112.04**
Suits	23.68	19.99	25.42	23.68	32.20	27.75	13.57	10.41
Sport coats and tailored jackets	10.67	4.55	7.05	13.16	15.23	13.33	8.22	5.54
Coats and jackets	23.17	22.75	17.85	27.26	37.98	25.85	9.07	3.13
Underwear	14.51	10.60	15.07	21.05	19.34	8.87	10.58	4.26
Hosiery	11.61	10.78	8.23	12.09	18.07	11.95	6.81	8.01
Nightwear	2.02	1.34	1.61	2.11	2.37	2.59	2.38	1.14
Accessories	22.11	19.20	31.39	22.56	27.92	16.43	14.16	10.68
Sweaters and vests	11.59	10.87	9.34	12.40	15.91	13.70	10.15	3.93
Active sportswear	17.97	15.78	11.91	25.29	26.27	14.19	16.11	4.18
Shirts	61.38	38.73	65.15	81.39	75.81	62.67	36.80	21.48
Pants	60.98	58.74	55.98	70.55	77.64	56.32	47.69	35.57
Shorts and shorts sets	15.79	15.84	18.17	27.86	15.88	11.69	4.56	2.37
Uniforms	2.63	1.57	3.05	4.11	2.63	2.25	1.67	1.05
Costumes	4.09	1.93	3.67	5.55	5.05	5.05	3.74	0.29
BOYS' (AGED 2 TO 15) APPAREL	**89.48**	**26.75**	**117.23**	**180.90**	**95.21**	**41.28**	**30.64**	**9.71**
Coats and jackets	6.41	1.61	7.67	13.32	7.27	2.68	2.05	1.12
Sweaters	2.65	0.45	3.76	4.53	2.47	2.66	1.04	0.32
Shirts	19.17	6.04	25.80	37.37	21.35	6.60	10.06	0.99
Underwear	6.30	1.27	8.31	14.71	5.81	2.18	1.83	—
Nightwear	3.51	1.86	2.89	10.04	2.35	1.34	0.91	—
Hosiery	4.46	2.83	5.40	9.05	5.13	1.25	1.59	0.22
Accessories	4.54	1.83	5.10	8.79	5.75	2.22	1.80	0.08
Suits, sport coats, and vests	2.58	0.26	2.37	4.85	3.64	1.45	1.27	0.65
Pants	21.43	5.88	29.83	43.58	20.38	11.61	6.45	2.71
Shorts and shorts sets	7.78	2.83	12.66	13.98	8.01	4.70	0.95	0.71
Uniforms	3.37	0.55	5.58	5.54	4.11	1.31	0.41	1.49
Active sportswear	4.63	0.50	4.92	9.73	5.48	2.40	1.64	0.83
Costumes	2.65	0.85	2.93	5.41	3.44	0.88	0.65	0.62
WOMEN'S APPAREL	**528.63**	**326.43**	**485.38**	**547.12**	**708.49**	**602.41**	**496.35**	**268.27**
Coats and jackets	45.08	20.69	27.62	36.99	63.78	62.82	49.19	44.02
Dresses	47.94	24.47	32.00	52.31	74.32	57.72	26.82	37.64
Sport coats and tailored jackets	5.46	2.46	6.31	5.86	6.67	5.62	5.26	2.88
Sweaters and vests	45.69	23.17	47.47	33.84	68.70	63.22	43.60	13.51
Shirts, blouses, and tops	101.40	65.96	90.18	116.78	135.80	102.92	98.90	42.68
Skirts	12.88	12.61	12.36	14.09	14.21	14.33	15.14	3.94
Pants	88.11	60.72	97.71	86.04	115.76	93.36	91.44	26.18
Shorts and shorts sets	13.89	12.27	13.35	15.21	20.39	15.12	5.94	5.83
Active sportswear	26.04	27.71	33.95	23.35	27.11	19.64	31.31	17.67
Nightwear	26.50	14.49	17.76	35.06	28.93	33.52	30.09	13.95
Undergarments	31.51	20.88	35.81	37.15	37.04	31.13	23.31	17.16
Hosiery	17.07	8.04	11.42	17.59	24.20	22.19	18.43	9.19
Suits	22.18	11.77	16.99	25.75	27.18	26.69	21.17	15.70
Accessories	32.82	15.09	30.99	32.97	45.97	42.25	25.67	15.49
Uniforms	5.66	4.05	6.33	5.67	8.98	5.45	3.54	1.39
Costumes	6.40	2.06	5.12	8.47	9.45	6.44	6.53	1.04

	total consumer units	under 25	25 to 34	35 to 44	45 to 54	55 to 64	65 to 74	75+
GIRLS' (AGED 2 TO 15) APPAREL	**$105.80**	**$25.38**	**$139.61**	**$216.92**	**$100.81**	**$51.89**	**$55.29**	**$8.84**
Coats and jackets	6.79	1.06	8.65	13.71	7.56	3.13	3.07	0.54
Dresses and suits	10.55	4.18	13.87	25.94	5.84	5.47	4.11	0.15
Shirts, blouses, and sweaters	24.42	3.76	31.89	51.72	23.94	12.33	10.25	1.07
Skirts and pants	23.47	7.86	29.50	47.45	24.91	10.61	9.27	3.59
Shorts and shorts sets	7.68	3.16	11.78	14.71	6.97	4.39	2.22	0.68
Active sportswear	9.62	0.75	12.06	17.80	10.37	6.40	6.78	0.46
Underwear and nightwear	6.37	2.17	8.48	11.61	7.56	2.76	2.70	1.20
Hosiery	4.66	1.46	5.85	9.63	3.73	2.08	4.31	0.30
Accessories	5.73	0.30	7.38	11.01	3.83	3.17	8.39	0.49
Uniforms	2.61	0.30	3.45	5.75	1.82	0.72	3.05	0.07
Costumes	3.90	0.35	6.70	7.60	4.28	0.83	1.14	0.29
CHILDREN UNDER AGE 2	**81.48**	**115.30**	**175.30**	**94.92**	**51.57**	**60.29**	**19.74**	**14.86**
Coats, jackets, and snowsuits	2.09	2.27	4.90	1.73	1.47	1.94	1.23	0.21
Outerwear including dresses	20.51	25.20	38.31	17.09	19.74	19.66	11.01	5.85
Underwear	45.88	68.38	105.82	64.89	19.10	26.92	2.90	6.72
Nightwear and loungewear	4.07	3.70	7.86	3.47	4.49	3.55	2.21	0.89
Accessories	8.93	15.74	18.42	7.74	6.77	8.21	2.39	1.19
FOOTWEAR	**293.92**	**205.92**	**330.77**	**413.09**	**334.10**	**236.74**	**214.35**	**115.95**
Men's	83.38	87.22	100.59	106.83	87.87	59.22	64.38	42.64
Boys'	39.12	11.41	52.93	95.54	34.92	8.16	6.44	1.04
Women's	138.40	101.74	128.15	145.90	174.45	154.59	137.84	69.03
Girls'	33.02	5.55	49.09	64.82	36.86	14.77	5.69	3.25
OTHER APPAREL PRODUCTS AND SERVICES	**258.49**	**184.28**	**326.63**	**288.99**	**290.98**	**296.62**	**188.13**	**81.11**
Material for making clothes	5.33	1.71	5.28	3.93	6.18	9.92	5.50	2.70
Sewing patterns and notions	4.99	2.27	3.92	5.02	5.69	6.65	6.74	3.28
Watches	17.12	9.46	24.60	24.95	19.64	12.54	7.28	4.68
Jewelry	120.16	85.55	154.40	124.67	129.65	158.13	98.89	24.44
Shoe repair and other shoe services	1.15	0.45	0.49	0.95	1.88	1.62	1.30	0.92
Coin-operated apparel laundry and dry cleaning	36.41	61.52	62.54	42.58	27.61	21.61	18.02	16.94
Apparel alteration, repair, and tailoring services	5.62	2.66	5.02	4.28	8.33	7.08	6.36	3.43
Clothing rental	2.46	1.94	2.81	2.74	3.44	3.48	0.01	0.67
Watch and jewelry repair	3.59	0.69	2.57	3.20	3.98	4.96	6.68	2.47
Professional laundry, dry cleaning	61.18	17.92	63.99	76.27	34.10	70.06	37.10	21.47
Clothing storage	0.48	0.10	1.03	0.39	0.48	0.57	0.24	0.11

Note: Subcategories may not add to total because some are not shown. (–) means sample is too small to make a reliable estimate.
Source: Bureau of Labor Statistics, unpublished data from the 2003 Consumer Expenditure Survey

Table 2.2 Apparel: Indexed spending by age, 2003

(indexed average annual spending of consumer units (CU) on apparel, accessories, and related services, by age of consumer unit reference person, 2003; index definition: an index of 100 is the average for all consumer units; an index of 132 means that spending by consumer units in that group is 32 percent above the average for all consumer units; an index of 68 indicates spending that is 32 percent below the average for all consumer units)

	total consumer units	under 25	25 to 34	35 to 44	45 to 54	55 to 64	65 to 74	75+
Average spending of CU, total	$40,817	$22,396	$40,525	$47,175	$50,101	$44,191	$33,629	$25,016
Average spending of CU, index	100	55	99	116	123	108	82	61
Apparel, spending index	**100**	**68**	**113**	**128**	**119**	**95**	**73**	**37**
MEN'S APPAREL	**100**	**82**	**97**	**124**	**132**	**97**	**66**	**40**
Suits	100	84	107	100	136	117	57	44
Sport coats and tailored jackets	100	43	66	123	143	125	77	52
Coats and jackets	100	98	77	118	164	112	39	14
Underwear	100	73	104	145	133	61	73	29
Hosiery	100	93	71	104	156	103	59	69
Nightwear	100	66	80	104	117	128	118	56
Accessories	100	87	142	102	126	74	64	48
Sweaters and vests	100	94	81	107	137	118	88	34
Active sportswear	100	88	66	141	146	79	90	23
Shirts	100	63	106	133	124	102	60	35
Pants	100	96	92	116	127	92	78	58
Shorts and shorts sets	100	100	115	176	101	74	29	15
Uniforms	100	60	116	156	100	86	63	40
Costumes	100	47	90	136	123	123	91	7
BOYS' (AGED 2 TO 15) APPAREL	**100**	**30**	**131**	**202**	**106**	**46**	**34**	**11**
Coats and jackets	100	25	120	208	113	42	32	17
Sweaters	100	17	142	171	93	100	39	12
Shirts	100	32	135	195	111	34	52	5
Underwear	100	20	132	233	92	35	29	–
Nightwear	100	53	82	286	67	38	26	–
Hosiery	100	63	121	203	115	28	36	5
Accessories	100	40	112	194	127	49	40	2
Suits, sport coats, and vests	100	10	92	188	141	56	49	25
Pants	100	27	139	203	95	54	30	13
Shorts and shorts sets	100	36	163	180	103	60	12	9
Uniforms	100	16	166	164	122	39	12	44
Active sportswear	100	11	106	210	118	52	35	18
Costumes	100	32	111	204	130	33	25	23
WOMEN'S APPAREL	**100**	**62**	**92**	**103**	**134**	**114**	**94**	**51**
Coats and jackets	100	46	61	82	141	139	109	98
Dresses	100	51	67	109	155	120	56	79
Sport coats and tailored jackets	100	45	116	107	122	103	96	53
Sweaters and vests	100	51	104	74	150	138	95	30
Shirts, blouses, and tops	100	65	89	115	134	101	98	42
Skirts	100	98	96	109	110	111	118	31
Pants	100	69	111	98	131	106	104	30
Shorts and shorts sets	100	88	96	110	147	109	43	42
Active sportswear	100	106	130	90	104	75	120	68
Nightwear	100	55	67	132	109	126	114	53
Undergarments	100	66	114	118	118	99	74	54
Hosiery	100	47	67	103	142	130	108	54
Suits	100	53	77	116	123	120	95	71
Accessories	100	46	94	100	140	129	78	47
Uniforms	100	72	112	100	159	96	63	25
Costumes	100	32	80	132	148	101	102	16

	total consumer units	under 25	25 to 34	35 to 44	45 to 54	55 to 64	65 to 74	75+
GIRLS' (AGED 2 TO 15) APPAREL	100	24	132	205	95	49	52	8
Coats and jackets	100	16	127	202	111	46	45	8
Dresses and suits	100	40	131	246	55	52	39	1
Shirts, blouses, and sweaters	100	15	131	212	98	50	42	4
Skirts and pants	100	33	126	202	106	45	39	15
Shorts and shorts sets	100	41	153	192	91	57	29	9
Active sportswear	100	8	125	185	108	67	70	5
Underwear and nightwear	100	34	133	182	119	43	42	19
Hosiery	100	31	126	207	80	45	92	6
Accessories	100	5	129	192	67	55	146	9
Uniforms	100	11	132	220	70	28	117	3
Costumes	100	9	172	195	110	21	29	7
CHILDREN UNDER AGE 2	100	142	215	116	63	74	24	18
Coats, jackets, and snowsuits	100	109	234	83	70	93	59	10
Outerwear including dresses	100	123	137	83	96	96	54	29
Underwear	100	149	231	141	42	59	6	15
Nightwear and loungewear	100	91	193	35	110	87	54	22
Accessories	100	176	206	87	76	92	27	13
FOOTWEAR	100	70	113	141	114	81	73	39
Men's	100	105	121	128	105	71	77	51
Boys'	100	29	135	244	89	21	16	3
Women's	100	74	93	105	126	112	100	50
Girls'	100	17	149	196	112	45	17	10
OTHER APPAREL PRODUCTS AND SERVICES	100	71	125	112	113	115	73	31
Material for making clothes	100	32	99	74	116	186	103	51
Sewing patterns and notions	100	45	79	101	114	133	135	66
Watches	100	55	144	146	115	73	43	27
Jewelry	100	71	128	104	108	132	82	20
Shoe repair and other shoe services	100	39	43	83	163	141	113	80
Coin-operated apparel laundry and dry cleaning	100	169	172	117	76	59	49	47
Apparel alteration, repair, and tailoring services	100	47	89	76	148	126	113	61
Clothing rental	100	79	114	111	140	141	0	27
Watch and jewelry repair	100	19	72	89	111	138	186	69
Professional laundry, dry cleaning	100	29	105	125	137	115	61	35
Clothing storage	100	21	215	81	100	119	50	23

Note: (–) means sample is too small to make a reliable estimate.
Source: Calculations by New Strategist based on the 2003 Consumer Expenditure Survey

Table 2.3 Apparel: Total spending by age, 2003

(total annual spending on apparel, accessories, and related services, by consumer unit (CU) age group, 2003; numbers in thousands)

	total consumer units	under 25	25 to 34	35 to 44	45 to 54	55 to 64	65 to 74	75+
Number of consumer units	115,356	8,584	19,737	24,413	23,131	16,580	11,495	11,417
Total spending of all CUs	$4,708,523,919	$192,243,230	$799,846,267	$1,151,684,740	$1,158,882,993	$732,680,977	$386,567,309	$285,612,010
Apparel, total spending	189,182,686	9,586,182	36,489,963	51,047,583	45,185,021	25,895,473	13,679,050	6,973,389
MEN'S APPAREL	**32,551,156**	**1,997,411**	**5,405,570**	**8,522,846**	**8,611,440**	**4,520,040**	**2,132,437**	**1,279,161**
Suits	2,731,630	171,594	501,715	573,100	744,818	460,095	155,987	118,851
Sport coats and tailored jackets	1,230,849	39,057	139,146	321,275	352,285	221,011	94,489	63,250
Coats and jackets	2,672,799	195,286	352,305	665,498	878,515	428,593	104,260	35,735
Underwear	1,673,816	90,990	297,437	513,894	447,354	147,065	121,617	48,636
Hosiery	1,339,283	92,536	162,436	295,153	417,977	198,131	78,281	91,450
Nightwear	233,019	11,503	31,777	51,511	54,820	42,942	27,358	13,015
Accessories	2,550,521	164,813	619,544	550,757	645,818	272,409	162,769	121,934
Sweaters and vests	1,336,976	93,308	184,344	302,721	368,014	227,146	116,674	44,869
Active sportswear	2,072,947	135,456	235,068	627,405	607,651	235,270	185,184	47,723
Shirts	7,080,551	332,458	1,285,866	1,936,974	1,753,561	1,039,069	423,016	245,237
Pants	7,034,409	504,224	1,104,877	1,722,337	1,795,891	933,786	548,197	406,103
Shorts and shorts sets	1,821,471	135,971	358,621	680,146	367,320	193,820	52,417	27,058
Uniforms	**303,386**	**13,477**	**60,198**	**100,337**	**60,835**	**37,305**	**19,197**	**11,988**
Costumes	471,806	16,567	72,435	135,492	116,812	83,729	42,991	3,311
BOYS' (AGED 2 TO 15) APPAREL	**10,322,055**	**229,622**	**2,313,769**	**4,416,312**	**2,202,303**	**684,422**	**352,207**	**110,859**
Coats and jackets	739,432	13,820	151,383	325,181	168,162	44,434	23,565	12,787
Sweaters	305,693	3,863	74,211	110,591	57,134	44,103	11,955	3,653
Shirts	2,211,375	51,847	509,215	912,314	493,847	109,428	115,640	11,303
Underwear	726,743	10,902	164,014	359,115	134,391	36,144	21,036	–
Nightwear	404,900	15,966	57,040	245,107	54,358	22,217	10,460	–
Hosiery	514,488	24,293	106,580	220,938	118,662	20,725	18,277	2,512
Accessories	523,716	15,709	100,659	214,590	133,003	36,808	20,691	913
Suits, sport coats, and vests	297,618	2,232	46,777	118,403	84,197	24,041	14,599	7,421
Pants	2,472,079	50,474	588,755	1,063,919	471,410	192,494	74,143	30,940
Shorts and shorts sets	897,470	24,293	249,870	341,294	185,279	77,926	10,920	8,106
Uniforms	388,750	4,721	110,132	135,248	95,068	21,720	4,713	17,011
Active sportswear	534,098	4,292	97,106	237,538	126,758	39,792	18,852	9,476
Costumes	305,693	7,296	57,829	132,074	79,571	14,590	7,472	7,079
WOMEN'S APPAREL	**60,980,642**	**2,802,075**	**9,579,945**	**13,356,841**	**16,388,082**	**9,987,958**	**5,705,543**	**3,062,839**
Coats and jackets	5,200,248	177,603	545,136	903,037	1,475,295	1,041,556	565,439	502,576
Dresses	5,530,167	210,050	631,584	1,277,044	1,719,096	956,998	308,296	429,736
Sport coats and tailored jackets	629,844	21,117	124,540	143,060	154,284	93,180	60,464	32,881
Sweaters and vests	5,270,616	198,891	936,915	826,136	1,589,100	1,048,188	501,182	154,244
Shirts, blouses, and tops	11,697,098	566,201	1,779,883	2,850,950	3,141,190	1,706,414	1,136,856	487,278
Skirts	1,485,785	108,244	243,949	343,979	328,692	237,591	174,034	44,983
Pants	10,164,017	521,220	1,928,502	2,100,495	2,677,645	1,547,909	1,051,103	298,897
Shorts and shorts sets	1,602,295	105,326	263,489	371,322	471,641	250,690	68,280	66,561
Active sportswear	3,003,870	237,863	670,071	570,044	627,081	325,631	359,908	201,738
Nightwear	3,056,934	124,382	350,529	855,920	669,180	555,762	345,885	159,267
Undergarments	3,634,868	179,234	706,782	906,943	856,072	516,135	267,948	195,916
Hosiery	1,969,127	69,015	225,397	429,425	559,770	367,910	211,853	104,922
Suits	2,558,596	101,034	335,332	628,635	628,701	442,520	243,349	179,247
Accessories	3,785,984	129,533	611,650	804,897	1,063,332	700,505	295,077	176,849
Uniforms	652,915	34,765	124,935	138,422	207,716	90,361	40,692	15,870
Costumes	738,278	17,683	101,053	206,778	218,588	106,775	75,062	11,874

	total consumer units	under 25	25 to 34	35 to 44	45 to 54	55 to 64	65 to 74	75+
GIRLS' (AGED 2 TO 15) APPAREL	$12,204,665	$217,862	$2,755,483	$5,295,668	$2,331,836	$860,336	$635,559	$100,926
Coats and jackets	783,267	9,099	170,725	334,702	174,870	51,895	35,290	6,165
Dresses and suits	1,217,006	35,881	273,752	633,273	135,085	90,693	47,244	1,713
Shirts, blouses, and sweaters	2,816,994	32,276	629,413	1,262,640	553,756	204,431	117,824	12,216
Skirts and pants	2,707,405	67,470	582,242	1,158,397	576,193	175,914	106,559	40,987
Shorts and shorts sets	885,934	27,125	232,502	359,115	161,223	72,786	25,519	7,764
Active sportswear	1,109,725	6,438	238,028	434,551	239,868	106,112	77,936	5,252
Underwear and nightwear	734,818	18,627	167,370	283,435	174,870	45,761	31,037	13,700
Hosiery	537,559	12,533	115,461	235,097	86,279	34,486	49,543	3,425
Accessories	660,990	2,575	145,659	268,787	88,592	52,559	96,443	5,594
Uniforms	301,079	2,575	68,093	140,375	42,098	11,938	35,060	799
Costumes	449,888	3,004	132,238	185,539	99,001	13,761	13,104	3,311
CHILDREN UNDER AGE 2	9,399,207	989,735	3,459,896	2,317,282	1,192,866	999,608	226,911	169,657
Coats, jackets, and snowsuits	241,094	19,486	96,711	42,234	34,003	32,165	14,139	2,398
Outerwear including dresses	2,365,952	216,317	756,124	417,218	456,606	325,963	126,560	66,789
Underwear	5,292,533	586,974	2,038,569	1,584,160	441,802	446,334	33,336	76,722
Nightwear and loungewear	469,499	31,761	155,133	84,713	103,858	58,859	25,404	10,161
Accessories	1,030,129	135,112	363,556	188,957	156,597	136,122	27,473	13,586
FOOTWEAR	33,905,436	1,767,617	6,528,407	10,084,766	7,728,067	3,925,149	2,463,953	1,323,801
Men's	9,618,383	748,696	1,985,345	2,608,041	2,032,521	981,868	740,048	486,821
Boys'	4,512,727	97,943	1,044,679	2,332,418	807,735	135,293	74,028	11,874
Women's	15,965,270	873,336	2,529,297	3,561,857	4,035,203	2,563,102	1,584,471	788,116
Girls'	3,809,055	47,641	963,889	1,582,451	852,609	244,887	65,407	37,105
OTHER APPAREL PRODUCTS AND SERVICES	29,818,372	1,581,860	6,446,696	7,055,113	6,730,658	4,917,960	2,162,554	926,033
Material for making clothes	614,847	14,679	104,211	95,943	142,950	164,474	63,223	30,826
Sewing patterns and notions	575,626	19,486	77,369	122,553	131,615	110,257	77,476	37,448
Watches	1,974,895	81,205	485,530	609,104	454,293	207,913	83,684	53,432
Jewelry	13,861,177	734,361	3,047,393	3,043,569	2,998,934	2,621,795	1,136,741	279,031
Shoe repair and other shoe services	132,659	3,863	9,671	23,192	43,486	26,860	14,944	10,504
Coin-operated apparel laundry and dry cleaning	4,200,112	528,088	1,234,352	1,039,506	638,647	358,294	207,140	193,404
Apparel alteration, repair, and tailoring services	648,301	22,833	99,080	104,488	192,681	117,386	73,108	39,160
Clothing rental	283,776	16,653	55,461	66,892	79,571	57,698	115	7,649
Watch and jewelry repair	414,128	5,923	50,724	78,122	92,061	82,237	76,787	28,200
Professional laundry, dry cleaning	7,057,480	153,825	1,262,971	1,861,980	1,945,317	1,161,595	426,465	245,123
Clothing storage	55,371	858	20,329	9,521	11,103	9,451	2,759	1,256

Note: Numbers may not add to total because of rounding and missing subcategories. (–) means sample is too small to make a reliable estimate.
Source: Calculations by New Strategist based on the 2003 Consumer Expenditure Survey

Table 2.4 Apparel: Market shares by age, 2003

(percentage of total annual spending on apparel, accessories, and related services accounted for by consumer unit age groups, 2003)

	total consumer units	under 25	25 to 34	35 to 44	45 to 54	55 to 64	65 to 74	75+
Share of total consumer units	100.0%	7.4%	17.1%	21.2%	20.1%	14.4%	10.0%	9.9%
Share of total before-tax income	100.0	3.0	16.9	25.3	26.7	16.5	6.9	4.9
Share of total spending	100.0	4.1	17.0	24.5	24.6	15.6	8.2	6.1
Share of apparel spending	100.0	5.1	19.3	27.0	23.9	13.7	7.2	3.7
MEN'S APPAREL	**100.0**	**6.1**	**16.6**	**26.2**	**26.5**	**13.9**	**6.6**	**3.9**
Suits	100.0	6.3	18.4	21.2	27.3	16.8	5.7	4.4
Sport coats and tailored jackets	100.0	3.2	11.3	26.1	28.6	18.0	7.7	5.1
Coats and jackets	100.0	7.3	13.2	24.9	32.9	16.0	3.9	1.3
Underwear	100.0	5.4	17.8	30.7	26.7	8.8	7.3	2.9
Hosiery	100.0	6.9	12.1	22.0	31.2	14.8	5.8	6.8
Nightwear	100.0	4.9	13.6	22.1	23.5	18.4	11.7	5.6
Accessories	100.0	6.5	24.3	21.6	25.3	10.7	6.4	4.8
Sweaters and vests	100.0	7.0	13.8	22.6	27.5	17.0	8.7	3.4
Active sportswear	100.0	6.5	11.3	29.8	29.3	11.3	8.9	2.3
Shirts	100.0	4.7	18.2	28.1	24.8	14.7	6.0	3.5
Pants	100.0	7.2	15.7	24.5	25.5	13.3	7.8	5.8
Shorts and shorts sets	100.0	7.5	19.7	37.3	20.2	10.6	2.9	1.5
Uniforms	100.0	4.4	19.8	33.1	20.1	12.3	6.3	4.0
Costumes	100.0	3.5	15.4	28.7	24.8	17.7	9.1	0.7
BOYS' (AGED 2 TO 15) APPAREL	**100.0**	**2.2**	**22.4**	**42.8**	**21.3**	**6.6**	**3.4**	**1.1**
Coats and jackets	100.0	1.9	20.5	44.0	22.7	6.0	3.2	1.7
Sweaters	100.0	1.3	24.3	36.2	18.7	14.4	3.9	1.2
Shirts	100.0	2.3	23.0	41.3	22.3	4.9	5.2	0.5
Underwear	100.0	1.5	22.6	49.4	18.5	5.0	2.9	–
Nightwear	100.0	3.9	14.1	60.5	13.4	5.5	2.6	–
Hosiery	100.0	4.7	20.7	42.9	23.1	4.0	3.6	0.5
Accessories	100.0	3.0	19.2	41.0	25.4	7.0	4.0	0.2
Suits, sport coats, and vests	100.0	0.7	15.7	39.8	28.3	8.1	4.9	2.5
Pants	100.0	2.0	23.8	43.0	19.1	7.8	3.0	1.3
Shorts and shorts sets	100.0	2.7	27.8	38.0	20.6	8.7	1.2	0.9
Uniforms	100.0	1.2	28.3	34.8	24.5	5.6	1.2	4.4
Active sportswear	100.0	0.8	18.2	44.5	23.7	7.5	3.5	1.8
Costumes	100.0	2.4	18.9	43.2	26.0	4.8	2.4	2.3
WOMEN'S APPAREL	**100.0**	**4.6**	**15.7**	**21.9**	**26.9**	**16.4**	**9.4**	**5.0**
Coats and jackets	100.0	3.4	10.5	17.4	28.4	20.0	10.9	9.7
Dresses	100.0	3.8	11.4	23.1	31.1	17.3	5.6	7.8
Sport coats and tailored jackets	100.0	3.4	19.8	22.7	24.5	14.8	9.6	5.2
Sweaters and vests	100.0	3.8	17.8	15.7	30.2	19.9	9.5	2.9
Shirts, blouses, and tops	100.0	4.8	15.2	24.4	26.9	14.6	9.7	4.2
Skirts	100.0	7.3	16.4	23.2	22.1	16.0	11.7	3.0
Pants	100.0	5.1	19.0	20.7	26.3	15.2	10.3	2.9
Shorts and shorts sets	100.0	6.6	16.4	23.2	29.4	15.6	4.3	4.2
Active sportswear	100.0	7.9	22.3	19.0	20.9	10.8	12.0	6.7
Nightwear	100.0	4.1	11.5	28.0	21.9	18.2	11.3	5.2
Undergarments	100.0	4.9	19.4	25.0	23.6	14.2	7.4	5.4
Hosiery	100.0	3.5	11.4	21.8	28.4	18.7	10.8	5.3
Suits	100.0	3.9	13.1	24.6	24.6	17.3	9.5	7.0
Accessories	100.0	3.4	16.2	21.3	28.1	18.5	7.8	4.7
Uniforms	100.0	5.3	19.1	21.2	31.8	13.8	6.2	2.4
Costumes	100.0	2.4	13.7	28.0	29.6	14.5	10.2	1.6

	total consumer units	under 25	25 to 34	35 to 44	45 to 54	55 to 64	65 to 74	75+
GIRLS' (AGED 2 TO 15) APPAREL	**100.0%**	**1.8%**	**22.6%**	**43.4%**	**19.1%**	**7.0%**	**5.2%**	**0.8%**
Coats and jackets	100.0	1.2	21.8	42.7	22.3	6.6	4.5	0.8
Dresses and suits	100.0	2.9	22.5	52.0	11.1	7.5	3.9	0.1
Shirts, blouses, and sweaters	100.0	1.1	22.3	44.8	19.7	7.3	4.2	0.4
Skirts and pants	100.0	2.5	21.5	42.8	21.3	6.5	3.9	1.5
Shorts and shorts sets	100.0	3.1	26.2	40.5	18.2	8.2	2.9	0.9
Active sportswear	100.0	0.6	21.4	39.2	21.6	9.6	7.0	0.5
Underwear and nightwear	100.0	2.5	22.8	38.6	23.8	6.2	4.2	1.9
Hosiery	100.0	2.3	21.5	43.7	16.1	6.4	9.2	0.6
Accessories	100.0	0.4	22.0	40.7	13.4	8.0	14.6	0.8
Uniforms	100.0	0.9	22.6	46.6	14.0	4.0	11.6	0.3
Costumes	100.0	0.7	29.4	41.2	22.0	3.1	2.9	0.7
CHILDREN UNDER AGE 2	**100.0**	**10.5**	**36.8**	**24.7**	**12.7**	**10.6**	**2.4**	**1.8**
Coats, jackets, and snowsuits	100.0	8.1	40.1	17.5	14.1	13.3	5.9	1.0
Outerwear including dresses	100.0	9.1	32.0	17.6	19.3	13.8	5.3	2.8
Underwear	100.0	11.1	39.5	29.9	8.3	8.4	0.6	1.4
Nightwear and loungewear	100.0	6.8	33.0	18.0	22.1	12.5	5.4	2.2
Accessories	100.0	13.1	35.3	18.3	15.2	13.2	2.7	1.3
FOOTWEAR	**100.0**	**5.2**	**19.3**	**29.7**	**22.8**	**11.6**	**7.3**	**3.9**
Men's	100.0	7.8	20.6	27.1	21.1	10.2	7.7	5.1
Boys'	100.0	2.2	23.1	51.7	17.9	3.0	1.6	0.3
Women's	100.0	5.5	15.8	22.3	25.3	16.1	9.9	4.9
Girls'	100.0	1.3	25.4	41.5	22.4	6.4	1.7	1.0
OTHER APPAREL PRODUCTS AND SERVICES	**100.0**	**5.3**	**21.6**	**23.7**	**22.6**	**16.5**	**7.3**	**3.1**
Material for making clothes	100.0	2.4	16.9	15.6	23.2	26.8	10.3	5.0
Sewing patterns and notions	100.0	3.4	13.4	21.3	22.9	19.2	13.5	6.5
Watches	100.0	4.1	24.6	30.8	23.0	10.5	4.2	2.7
Jewelry	100.0	5.3	22.0	22.0	21.6	18.9	8.2	2.0
Shoe repair and other shoe services	100.0	2.9	7.3	17.5	32.8	20.2	11.3	7.9
Coin-operated apparel laundry and dry cleaning	100.0	12.6	29.4	24.7	15.2	8.5	4.9	4.6
Apparel alteration, repair, and tailoring services	100.0	3.5	15.3	16.1	29.7	18.1	11.3	6.0
Clothing rental	100.0	5.9	19.5	23.6	28.0	20.3	0.0	2.7
Watch and jewelry repair	100.0	1.4	12.2	18.9	22.2	19.9	18.5	6.8
Professional laundry, dry cleaning	100.0	2.2	17.9	26.4	27.6	16.5	6.0	3.5
Clothing storage	100.0	1.6	36.7	17.2	20.1	17.1	5.0	2.3

Note: Numbers may not add to total because of rounding. (–) means sample is too small to make a reliable estimate.
Source: Calculations by New Strategist based on the 2003 Consumer Expenditure Survey

Table 2.5 Apparel: Average spending by income, 2003

(average annual spending on apparel, accessories, and related services, by before-tax income of consumer units (CU), 2003; complete income reporters only)

	total complete reporters	under $20,000	$20,000–$39,999	$40,000–$49,999	$50,000–$69,999	$70,000–$79,999	$80,000–$99,999	$100,000 or more
Number of consumer units (000)	97,391	27,100	23,941	8,891	13,890	5,121	6,909	11,537
Average number of persons per CU	2.5	1.8	2.4	2.6	2.8	3.0	3.0	3.1
Average before-tax income of CU	$51,128.00	$10,752.55	$29,072.57	$44,294.00	$58,900.00	$74,560.00	$88,832.00	$154,665.00
Average spending of CU, total	42,741.66	19,862.52	31,684.32	39,755.91	49,788.99	57,128.14	65,957.39	93,514.86
Apparel, average spending	**1,744.04**	**940.45**	**1,287.87**	**1,515.01**	**1,966.68**	**2,549.39**	**2,546.27**	**3,756.44**
MEN'S APPAREL	**294.42**	**131.90**	**202.70**	**264.50**	**349.04**	**450.26**	**536.76**	**634.37**
Suits	24.54	6.93	13.90	12.28	26.06	36.60	33.67	84.76
Sport coats and tailored jackets	10.91	3.28	5.16	7.23	6.93	18.48	17.28	41.26
Coats and jackets	21.35	9.75	17.13	23.33	23.85	30.71	36.54	42.72
Underwear	14.96	9.41	11.23	2.72	25.17	20.26	23.16	19.51
Hosiery	12.42	5.45	12.66	7.86	12.72	17.69	22.85	23.98
Nightwear	2.17	0.75	1.55	1.38	2.39	2.47	2.82	6.60
Accessories	24.51	10.25	15.36	21.46	27.20	61.97	46.38	49.34
Sweaters and vests	11.63	6.12	6.61	8.56	11.47	14.98	15.75	33.61
Active sportswear	19.68	8.35	11.03	7.33	18.88	30.37	26.63	69.93
Shirts	64.99	28.56	36.22	44.82	93.73	98.28	151.51	134.48
Pants	63.71	32.76	56.00	105.23	64.70	84.67	113.11	79.38
Shorts and shorts sets	16.52	8.03	9.62	6.10	30.58	27.81	39.33	26.30
Uniforms	3.00	1.16	3.40	4.03	2.67	1.78	2.85	6.68
Costumes	4.02	1.09	2.83	2.18	2.69	4.20	4.87	15.81
BOYS' (AGED 2 TO 15) APPAREL	**91.05**	**50.78**	**72.68**	**77.66**	**106.15**	**132.98**	**127.08**	**179.69**
Coats and jackets	6.27	2.48	3.82	5.58	10.73	10.04	10.30	11.38
Sweaters	2.69	2.43	1.81	3.46	2.77	1.60	3.71	4.33
Shirts	21.05	14.58	19.42	13.93	21.62	37.64	20.27	39.40
Underwear	6.64	3.51	6.59	7.35	6.52	7.59	8.28	12.61
Nightwear	2.72	1.89	0.83	1.81	1.86	7.34	5.91	7.00
Hosiery	4.65	4.22	4.19	1.78	6.46	4.64	2.77	8.24
Accessories	3.98	2.31	3.10	0.96	6.39	8.12	6.81	6.33
Suits, sport coats, and vests	2.32	0.71	1.34	2.00	1.80	1.92	7.73	5.96
Pants	21.97	11.30	18.55	25.67	25.33	25.72	30.56	40.46
Shorts and shorts sets	7.89	4.27	5.80	7.37	9.67	13.32	13.93	12.99
Uniforms	3.28	1.40	2.90	1.63	2.39	4.14	4.41	9.77
Active sportswear	4.68	0.75	2.59	3.49	6.39	7.11	8.24	13.88
Costumes	2.89	0.93	1.75	2.62	4.21	3.80	4.17	7.32
WOMEN'S APPAREL	**588.43**	**320.83**	**432.74**	**506.02**	**651.21**	**939.28**	**790.43**	**1,298.02**
Coats and jackets	52.06	28.28	48.10	57.53	55.03	59.33	78.12	90.91
Dresses	51.99	25.24	28.65	61.05	70.86	129.66	38.71	110.39
Sport coats and tailored jackets	5.55	2.14	3.38	3.30	4.31	5.01	7.27	20.49
Sweaters and vests	51.83	29.69	31.48	34.87	44.23	74.86	81.22	148.03
Shirts, blouses, and tops	115.22	64.84	83.02	89.89	124.95	176.44	147.20	274.60
Skirts	15.24	8.23	14.25	21.70	15.74	20.05	9.27	30.10
Pants	95.23	47.74	80.30	60.24	106.13	194.08	105.10	210.68
Shorts and shorts sets	16.36	9.90	9.96	16.39	28.56	24.86	15.74	27.66
Active sportswear	28.74	19.04	30.20	24.45	26.85	26.71	38.96	50.67
Nightwear	29.43	22.60	18.89	24.77	40.85	41.39	52.31	40.21
Undergarments	34.85	18.95	31.64	37.70	37.87	54.66	42.98	60.15
Hosiery	18.28	11.68	10.51	19.36	18.43	22.24	30.12	41.57
Suits	23.82	8.86	14.18	16.42	24.49	28.63	35.80	74.60
Accessories	36.90	19.59	22.39	26.12	38.53	62.04	89.99	76.23
Uniforms	5.98	2.40	3.22	5.30	8.05	11.25	9.69	13.60
Costumes	6.94	1.64	2.56	6.94	6.33	8.09	7.94	28.12

	total complete reporters	under $20,000	$20,000– $39,999	$40,000– $49,999	$50,000– $69,999	$70,000– $79,999	$80,000– $99,999	$100,000 or more
GIRLS' (AGED 2 TO 15) APPAREL	**$110.46**	**$49.84**	**$81.20**	**$95.60**	**$119.88**	**$224.30**	**$176.71**	**$231.26**
Coats and jackets	7.29	2.74	6.06	8.42	8.81	11.44	10.05	14.33
Dresses and suits	11.41	–	–	–	–	–	–	–
Shirts, blouses, and sweaters	23.99	8.70	18.10	13.08	25.68	57.58	52.93	49.28
Skirts and pants	24.06	11.19	18.70	29.33	27.03	33.24	36.73	46.11
Shorts and shorts sets	8.01	3.56	6.07	8.92	10.44	9.64	15.49	13.70
Active sportswear	10.68	5.69	6.65	8.31	8.49	27.58	13.09	27.77
Underwear and nightwear	6.72	3.29	4.99	7.61	8.85	10.88	10.76	10.86
Hosiery	4.93	2.51	2.90	4.23	6.59	10.95	5.74	10.82
Accessories	6.21	3.25	2.79	5.03	10.98	9.57	11.59	11.90
Uniforms	2.95	1.40	2.13	2.02	2.04	8.92	5.50	5.94
Costumes	4.21	1.09	2.49	2.68	5.89	7.37	7.53	10.85
CHILDREN UNDER AGE 2	**85.75**	**47.19**	**74.82**	**84.99**	**83.96**	**137.85**	**129.21**	**155.54**
Coats, jackets, and snowsuits	2.20	1.20	1.92	1.96	2.68	2.53	3.71	3.69
Outerwear including dresses	21.62	10.36	19.49	23.72	22.81	27.01	32.01	40.83
Underwear	47.55	27.97	38.36	47.55	43.27	82.23	72.77	89.96
Nightwear and loungewear	4.12	1.42	4.66	3.16	4.21	3.93	8.36	7.54
Accessories	10.26	6.25	10.39	8.61	10.98	22.15	12.36	13.52
FOOTWEAR	**311.11**	**233.98**	**255.62**	**262.85**	**396.17**	**411.04**	**397.95**	**466.52**
Men's	90.56	59.78	74.35	88.66	119.96	142.09	156.68	103.64
Boys'	39.52	36.94	36.77	27.21	50.27	26.97	30.15	60.81
Women's	146.09	115.58	116.83	112.38	186.12	170.03	169.08	246.07
Girls'	34.95	21.68	27.68	34.59	39.82	71.95	42.05	56.01
OTHER APPAREL PRODUCTS AND SERVICES	**262.83**	**105.93**	**158.13**	**223.40**	**260.27**	**253.67**	**388.14**	**791.04**
Material for making clothes	5.82	1.74	6.46	4.58	5.85	4.56	13.65	11.51
Sewing patterns and notions	5.80	4.55	5.40	5.24	6.17	3.93	7.13	8.78
Watches	16.22	4.66	8.58	35.67	17.65	17.28	18.26	40.80
Jewelry	118.45	23.04	64.26	92.84	131.52	105.46	187.96	423.16
Shoe repair and other shoe services	1.29	0.42	0.80	0.81	1.20	1.99	1.44	4.40
Coin-operated apparel laundry and dry cleaning	38.77	54.30	51.13	37.48	25.64	19.75	15.12	16.02
Apparel alteration, repair, and tailoring services	6.21	1.93	3.53	2.52	6.34	8.58	10.53	20.85
Clothing rental	2.79	0.31	1.25	1.28	4.23	5.28	7.38	7.37
Watch and jewelry repair	3.90	2.06	2.20	3.96	3.37	6.65	5.05	10.44
Professional laundry, dry cleaning	63.06	12.56	24.38	37.87	57.57	80.19	118.79	247.02
Clothing storage	0.52	–	–	–	–	–	–	–

Note: Subcategories may not add to total because some are not shown. (–) means sample is too small to make a reliable estimate.
Source: Bureau of Labor Statistics, unpublished data from the 2003 Consumer Expenditure Survey; calculations by New Strategist

Table 2.6 Apparel: Indexed spending by income, 2003

(indexed average annual spending of consumer units (CU) on apparel, accessories, and related services, by before-tax income of consumer unit, 2003; complete income reporters only; index definition: an index of 100 is the average for all consumer units; an index of 132 means that spending by consumer units in that group is 32 percent above the average for all consumer units; an index of 68 indicates spending that is 32 percent below the average for all consumer units)

	total complete reporters	under $20,000	$20,000–$39,999	$40,000–$49,999	$50,000–$69,999	$70,000–$79,999	$80,000–$99,999	$100,000 or more
Average spending of CU, total	$42,742	$19,863	$31,684	$35,757	$49,789	$57,128	$65,957	$93,515
Average spending of CU, index	100	46	74	93	116	134	154	219
Apparel, spending index	100	54	74	87	113	146	146	215
MEN'S APPAREL	100	45	69	90	119	153	182	215
Suits	100	28	57	50	106	149	137	345
Sport coats and tailored jackets	100	30	47	66	64	169	158	378
Coats and jackets	100	46	80	109	112	144	171	200
Underwear	100	63	75	85	168	135	155	130
Hosiery	100	44	102	63	102	142	184	193
Nightwear	100	34	71	64	110	114	130	304
Accessories	100	42	63	88	111	253	189	201
Sweaters and vests	100	53	57	74	99	129	135	289
Active sportswear	100	42	56	37	96	154	135	355
Shirts	100	44	56	69	144	151	233	207
Pants	100	51	88	165	102	133	178	125
Shorts and shorts sets	100	49	58	37	185	168	238	159
Uniforms	100	39	113	134	89	59	95	223
Costumes	100	27	70	54	67	104	121	393
BOYS' (AGED 2 TO 15) APPAREL	100	56	80	85	117	146	140	197
Coats and jackets	100	39	61	89	171	160	164	181
Sweaters	100	90	67	129	103	59	138	161
Shirts	100	69	92	66	103	179	96	187
Underwear	100	53	99	111	98	114	125	190
Nightwear	100	69	31	67	68	270	217	257
Hosiery	100	91	90	38	139	100	60	177
Accessories	100	58	78	24	161	204	171	159
Suits, sport coats, and vests	100	31	58	86	78	83	333	257
Pants	100	51	84	117	115	117	139	184
Shorts and shorts sets	100	54	74	93	123	169	177	165
Uniforms	100	43	88	50	73	126	134	298
Active sportswear	100	16	55	75	137	152	176	297
Costumes	100	32	61	91	146	131	144	253
WOMEN'S APPAREL	100	55	74	86	111	160	134	221
Coats and jackets	100	54	92	111	106	114	150	175
Dresses	100	49	55	117	136	249	74	212
Sport coats and tailored jackets	100	39	61	59	78	90	131	369
Sweaters and vests	100	57	61	67	85	144	157	286
Shirts, blouses, and tops	100	56	72	78	108	153	128	238
Skirts	100	54	94	142	103	132	61	198
Pants	100	50	84	63	111	204	110	221
Shorts and shorts sets	100	61	61	100	175	152	96	169
Active sportswear	100	66	105	85	93	93	136	176
Nightwear	100	77	64	84	139	141	178	137
Undergarments	100	54	91	108	109	157	123	173
Hosiery	100	64	58	106	101	122	165	227
Suits	100	37	60	69	103	120	150	313
Accessories	100	53	61	71	104	168	244	207
Uniforms	100	40	54	89	135	188	162	227
Costumes	100	24	37	100	91	117	114	405

	total complete reporters	under $20,000	$20,000–$39,999	$40,000–$49,999	$50,000–$69,999	$70,000–$79,999	$80,000–$99,999	$100,000 or more
GIRLS' (AGED 2 TO 15) APPAREL	**100**	**45**	**74**	**87**	**109**	**203**	**160**	**209**
Coats and jackets	100	38	83	116	121	157	138	197
Dresses and suits	100	–	–	–	–	–	–	–
Shirts, blouses, and sweaters	100	36	75	55	107	240	221	205
Skirts and pants	100	47	78	122	112	138	153	192
Shorts and shorts sets	100	44	76	111	130	120	193	171
Active sportswear	100	53	62	78	79	258	123	260
Underwear and nightwear	100	49	74	113	132	162	160	162
Hosiery	100	51	59	86	134	222	116	219
Accessories	100	52	45	81	177	154	187	192
Uniforms	100	47	72	68	69	302	186	201
Costumes	100	26	59	64	140	175	179	258
CHILDREN UNDER AGE 2	**100**	**55**	**87**	**99**	**98**	**161**	**151**	**181**
Coats, jackets, and snowsuits	100	55	87	89	122	115	169	168
Outerwear including dresses	100	48	90	110	106	125	148	189
Underwear	100	59	81	100	91	173	153	189
Nightwear and loungewear	100	35	113	77	102	95	203	183
Accessories	100	61	101	84	107	216	120	132
FOOTWEAR	**100**	**75**	**82**	**84**	**127**	**132**	**128**	**150**
Men's	100	66	82	98	132	157	173	114
Boys'	100	93	93	69	127	68	76	154
Women's	100	79	80	77	127	116	116	168
Girls'	100	62	79	99	114	206	120	160
OTHER APPAREL PRODUCTS AND SERVICES	**100**	**40**	**64**	**85**	**99**	**97**	**148**	**301**
Material for making clothes	100	30	111	79	101	78	235	198
Sewing patterns and notions	100	78	93	108	106	68	123	151
Watches	100	29	53	220	109	107	113	252
Jewelry	100	19	54	78	111	89	159	357
Shoe repair and other shoe services	100	33	62	63	93	154	112	341
Coin-operated apparel laundry and dry cleaning	100	140	132	97	66	51	39	41
Apparel alteration, repair, and tailoring services	100	31	57	41	102	138	170	336
Clothing rental	100	11	45	46	152	189	265	264
Watch and jewelry repair	100	53	56	102	86	171	129	268
Professional laundry, dry cleaning	100	20	39	60	91	127	188	392
Clothing storage	100	–	–	–	–	–	–	–

Note: (–) means sample is too small to make a reliable estimate.
Source: Calculations by New Strategist based on the 2003 Consumer Expenditure Survey

Table 2.7 Apparel: Total spending by income, 2003

(total annual spending on apparel, accessories, and related services, by before-tax income group of consumer units (CU), 2003; complete income reporters only; numbers in thousands)

	total complete reporters	under $20,000	$20,000–$39,999	$40,000–$49,999	$50,000–$69,999	$70,000–$79,999	$80,000–$99,999	$100,000 or more
Number of consumer units	97,391	27,100	23,941	8,891	13,890	5,121	6,909	11,537
Total spending of all CUs	$4,162,653,009	$538,274,380	$758,554,310	$353,478,687	$691,569,071	$292,553,205	$455,699,608	$1,078,880,940
Apparel, total spending	169,853,800	25,486,177	30,832,989	13,469,954	27,317,185	13,055,426	17,592,179	43,338,048
MEN'S APPAREL	28,673,858	3,574,508	4,852,957	2,351,670	4,848,166	2,305,781	3,708,475	7,318,727
Suits	2,389,975	187,726	332,889	109,181	361,973	187,429	232,626	977,876
Sport coats and tailored jackets	1,062,536	88,899	123,571	64,282	96,258	94,636	119,388	476,017
Coats and jackets	2,079,298	264,238	410,126	207,427	331,277	157,266	252,455	492,861
Underwear	1,456,969	255,078	268,776	113,094	349,611	103,751	160,012	225,087
Hosiery	1,209,596	147,720	303,201	69,883	176,681	90,590	157,871	276,657
Nightwear	211,338	20,245	36,998	12,270	33,197	12,649	19,483	76,144
Accessories	2,387,053	277,783	367,712	190,801	377,808	317,348	320,439	569,236
Sweaters and vests	1,132,657	165,986	158,291	76,107	159,318	76,713	108,817	387,759
Active sportswear	1,916,655	226,260	264,057	65,171	262,243	155,525	183,987	806,782
Shirts	6,329,441	774,070	867,153	398,495	1,301,910	503,292	1,046,783	1,551,496
Pants	6,204,781	887,772	1,340,671	935,600	898,683	433,595	781,477	915,807
Shorts and shorts sets	1,608,899	217,741	230,292	54,235	424,756	142,415	271,731	303,423
Uniforms	292,173	31,500	81,388	35,831	37,086	9,115	19,691	77,067
Costumes	391,512	29,458	67,832	19,382	37,364	21,508	33,647	182,400
BOYS' (AGED 2 TO 15) APPAREL	8,867,451	1,376,213	1,739,944	690,475	1,474,424	680,991	877,996	2,073,084
Coats and jackets	610,642	67,102	91,406	49,612	149,040	51,415	71,163	131,291
Sweaters	261,982	65,748	43,423	30,763	38,475	8,194	25,632	49,955
Shirts	2,050,081	395,132	464,821	123,852	300,302	192,754	140,045	454,558
Underwear	646,676	95,186	157,769	65,349	90,563	38,868	57,207	145,482
Nightwear	264,904	51,120	19,929	16,093	25,835	37,588	40,832	80,759
Hosiery	452,868	114,356	100,245	15,826	89,729	23,761	19,138	95,065
Accessories	387,616	62,611	74,124	8,535	88,757	41,583	47,050	73,029
Suits, sport coats, and vests	225,947	19,335	32,039	17,782	25,002	9,832	53,407	68,761
Pants	2,139,680	306,279	444,054	228,232	351,834	131,712	211,139	466,787
Shorts and shorts sets	768,415	115,815	138,902	65,527	134,316	68,212	96,242	149,866
Uniforms	319,442	38,057	69,418	14,492	33,197	21,201	30,469	112,716
Active sportswear	455,790	20,286	61,933	31,030	88,757	36,410	56,930	160,134
Costumes	281,460	25,322	41,882	23,294	58,477	19,460	28,811	84,451
WOMEN'S APPAREL	57,307,786	8,694,455	10,360,125	4,499,024	9,045,307	4,810,053	5,461,081	14,975,257
Coats and jackets	5,070,175	766,509	1,151,563	511,499	764,367	303,829	539,731	1,048,829
Dresses	5,063,358	683,944	685,844	542,796	984,245	663,989	267,447	1,273,569
Sport coats and tailored jackets	540,520	57,907	80,979	29,340	59,866	25,656	50,228	236,393
Sweaters and vests	5,047,776	804,622	753,700	310,029	614,355	383,358	561,149	1,707,822
Shirts, blouses, and tops	11,221,391	1,757,221	1,987,483	799,212	1,735,556	903,549	1,017,005	3,168,060
Skirts	1,484,239	223,044	341,248	192,935	218,629	102,676	64,046	347,264
Pants	9,274,545	1,293,741	1,922,420	535,594	1,474,146	993,884	726,136	2,430,615
Shorts and shorts sets	1,593,317	268,377	238,444	145,723	396,698	127,308	108,748	319,113
Active sportswear	2,799,017	516,111	722,980	217,385	372,947	136,782	269,175	584,580
Nightwear	2,866,217	612,538	452,326	220,230	567,407	211,958	361,410	463,903
Undergarments	3,394,076	513,478	757,475	335,191	526,014	279,914	296,949	693,951
Hosiery	1,780,307	316,559	251,675	172,130	255,993	113,891	208,099	479,593
Suits	2,319,854	239,993	339,416	145,990	340,166	146,614	247,342	860,660
Accessories	3,593,728	530,968	535,992	232,233	535,182	317,707	621,741	879,466
Uniforms	582,398	64,919	77,195	47,122	111,815	57,611	66,948	156,903
Costumes	675,894	44,434	61,362	61,704	87,924	41,429	54,857	324,420

	total complete reporters	under $20,000	$20,000–$39,999	$40,000–$49,999	$50,000–$69,999	$70,000–$79,999	$80,000–$99,999	$100,000 or more
GIRLS' (AGED 2 TO 15) APPAREL	**$10,757,810**	**$1,350,708**	**$1,943,927**	**$849,980**	**$1,665,133**	**$1,148,640**	**$1,220,889**	**$2,668,047**
Coats and jackets	709,980	74,293	145,116	74,862	122,371	58,584	69,435	165,325
Dresses and suits	1,111,231	–	–	–	–	–	–	–
Shirts, blouses, and sweaters	2,336,410	235,810	433,248	116,294	356,695	294,867	365,693	568,543
Skirts and pants	2,343,227	303,199	447,776	260,773	375,447	170,222	253,768	531,971
Shorts and shorts sets	780,102	96,407	145,205	79,308	145,012	49,366	107,020	158,057
Active sportswear	1,040,136	154,237	159,175	73,884	117,926	141,237	90,439	320,382
Underwear and nightwear	654,468	89,088	119,548	57,661	122,927	55,716	74,341	125,292
Hosiery	480,138	68,019	69,438	37,609	91,535	56,075	39,658	124,830
Accessories	604,798	88,074	66,789	44,722	152,512	49,008	80,075	137,290
Uniforms	287,303	37,900	51,009	17,950	28,336	45,679	38,000	68,530
Costumes	410,016	29,539	59,567	23,828	81,812	37,742	52,025	125,176
CHILDREN UNDER AGE 2	**8,351,278**	**1,278,920**	**1,791,182**	**755,646**	**1,166,204**	**705,930**	**892,712**	**1,794,465**
Coats, jackets, and snowsuits	214,260	32,497	45,856	17,426	37,225	12,956	25,632	42,572
Outerwear including dresses	2,105,593	280,756	456,639	210,895	316,831	138,318	221,157	471,056
Underwear	4,630,942	757,920	918,375	422,767	601,020	421,100	502,768	1,037,869
Nightwear and loungewear	401,251	38,528	111,457	28,096	58,477	20,126	57,759	86,989
Accessories	999,232	169,248	248,855	76,552	152,512	113,430	85,395	155,980
FOOTWEAR	**30,299,314**	**6,340,734**	**6,119,810**	**2,336,999**	**5,502,801**	**2,104,936**	**2,749,437**	**5,382,241**
Men's	8,819,729	1,619,941	1,779,994	738,276	1,666,244	727,643	1,082,502	1,195,695
Boys'	3,848,892	1,001,012	880,278	241,924	698,250	138,113	208,306	701,565
Women's	14,227,851	3,132,237	2,796,987	999,171	2,585,207	870,724	1,168,174	2,838,910
Girls'	3,403,815	587,499	662,683	307,540	553,100	368,456	290,523	646,187
OTHER APPAREL PRODUCTS, SERVICES	**25,597,277**	**2,870,612**	**4,025,175**	**1,986,249**	**3,615,150**	**1,299,044**	**2,681,659**	**9,126,228**
Material for making clothes	566,816	47,236	154,726	40,721	81,257	23,352	94,308	132,791
Sewing patterns and notions	564,868	123,316	129,176	55,480	85,701	20,126	49,261	101,295
Watches	1,579,682	126,271	205,361	317,142	245,159	88,491	126,158	470,710
Jewelry	11,535,964	624,469	1,538,413	825,440	1,826,813	540,061	1,298,616	4,881,997
Shoe repair and other shoe services	125,634	11,422	19,247	7,202	16,668	10,191	9,949	50,763
Coin-operated apparel laundry and dry cleaning	3,775,849	1,471,579	1,224,173	333,235	356,140	101,140	104,464	184,823
Apparel alteration, repair, and tailoring services	604,798	52,354	84,617	22,405	88,063	43,938	72,752	240,546
Clothing rental	271,721	8,504	29,969	11,380	58,755	27,039	50,988	85,028
Watch and jewelry repair	379,825	55,944	52,715	35,208	46,809	34,055	34,890	120,446
Professional laundry, dry cleaning	6,141,476	340,418	583,644	336,702	799,647	410,653	820,720	2,849,870
Clothing storage	50,643	–	–	–	–	–	–	–

Note: Numbers may not add to total because of rounding and missing subcategories. (–) means sample is too small to make a reliable estimate.
Source: Calculations by New Strategist based on the 2003 Consumer Expenditure Survey

Table 2.8 Apparel: Market shares by income, 2003

(percentage of total annual spending on apparel, accessories, and related services accounted for by before-tax income group of consumer units, 2003; complete income reporters only)

	total complete reporters	under $20,000	$20,000– $39,999	$40,000– $49,999	$50,000– $69,999	$70,000– $79,999	$80,000– $99,999	$100,000 or more
Share of total consumer units	100.0%	27.8%	24.6%	9.1%	14.3%	5.3%	7.1%	11.8%
Share of total before-tax income	100.0	5.9	14.0	7.9	16.4	7.7	12.3	35.8
Share of total spending	100.0	12.9	18.2	8.5	16.6	7.0	10.9	25.9
Share of apparel spending	100.0	15.0	18.2	7.9	16.1	7.7	10.4	25.5
MEN'S APPAREL	**100.0**	**12.5**	**16.9**	**8.2**	**16.9**	**8.0**	**12.9**	**25.5**
Suits	100.0	7.9	13.9	4.6	15.1	7.8	9.7	40.9
Sport coats and tailored jackets	100.0	8.4	11.6	6.0	9.1	8.9	11.2	44.8
Coats and jackets	100.0	12.7	19.7	10.0	15.9	7.6	12.1	23.7
Underwear	100.0	17.5	18.4	7.8	24.0	7.1	11.0	15.4
Hosiery	100.0	12.2	25.1	5.8	14.6	7.5	13.1	22.9
Nightwear	100.0	9.6	17.5	5.8	15.7	6.0	9.2	36.0
Accessories	100.0	11.6	15.4	8.0	15.8	13.3	13.4	23.8
Sweaters and vests	100.0	14.7	14.0	6.7	14.1	6.8	9.6	34.2
Active sportswear	100.0	11.8	13.8	3.4	13.7	8.1	9.6	42.1
Shirts	100.0	12.2	13.7	6.3	20.6	8.0	16.5	24.5
Pants	100.0	14.3	21.6	15.1	14.5	7.0	12.6	14.8
Shorts and shorts sets	100.0	13.5	14.3	3.4	26.4	8.9	16.9	18.9
Uniforms	100.0	10.8	27.9	12.3	12.7	3.1	6.7	26.4
Costumes	100.0	7.5	17.3	5.0	9.5	5.5	8.6	46.6
BOYS' (AGED 2 TO 15) APPAREL	**100.0**	**15.5**	**19.6**	**7.8**	**16.6**	**7.7**	**9.9**	**23.4**
Coats and jackets	100.0	11.0	15.0	8.1	24.4	8.4	11.7	21.5
Sweaters	100.0	25.1	16.6	11.7	14.7	3.1	9.8	19.1
Shirts	100.0	19.3	22.7	6.0	14.6	9.4	6.8	22.2
Underwear	100.0	14.7	24.4	10.1	14.0	6.0	8.8	22.5
Nightwear	100.0	19.3	7.5	6.1	9.8	14.2	15.4	30.5
Hosiery	100.0	25.3	22.1	3.5	19.8	5.2	4.2	21.0
Accessories	100.0	16.2	19.1	2.2	22.9	10.7	12.1	18.8
Suits, sport coats, and vests	100.0	8.6	14.2	7.9	11.1	4.4	23.6	30.4
Pants	100.0	14.3	20.8	10.7	16.4	6.2	9.9	21.8
Shorts and shorts sets	100.0	15.1	18.1	8.5	17.5	8.9	12.5	19.5
Uniforms	100.0	11.9	21.7	4.5	10.4	6.6	9.5	35.3
Active sportswear	100.0	4.5	13.6	6.8	19.5	8.0	12.5	35.1
Costumes	100.0	9.0	14.9	8.3	20.8	6.9	10.2	30.0
WOMEN'S APPAREL	**100.0**	**15.2**	**18.1**	**7.9**	**15.8**	**8.4**	**9.5**	**26.1**
Coats and jackets	100.0	15.1	22.7	10.1	15.1	6.0	10.6	20.7
Dresses	100.0	13.5	13.5	10.7	19.4	13.1	5.3	25.2
Sport coats and tailored jackets	100.0	10.7	15.0	5.4	11.1	4.7	9.3	43.7
Sweaters and vests	100.0	15.9	14.9	6.1	12.2	7.6	11.1	33.8
Shirts, blouses, and tops	100.0	15.7	17.7	7.1	15.5	8.1	9.1	28.2
Skirts	100.0	15.0	23.0	13.0	14.7	6.9	4.3	23.4
Pants	100.0	13.9	20.7	5.8	15.9	10.7	7.8	26.2
Shorts and shorts sets	100.0	16.8	15.0	9.1	24.9	8.0	6.8	20.0
Active sportswear	100.0	18.4	25.8	7.8	13.3	4.9	9.6	20.9
Nightwear	100.0	21.4	15.8	7.7	19.8	7.4	12.6	16.2
Undergarments	100.0	15.1	22.3	9.9	15.5	8.2	8.7	20.4
Hosiery	100.0	17.8	14.1	9.7	14.4	6.4	11.7	26.9
Suits	100.0	10.3	14.6	6.3	14.7	6.3	10.7	37.1
Accessories	100.0	14.8	14.9	6.5	14.9	8.8	17.3	24.5
Uniforms	100.0	11.1	13.3	8.1	19.2	9.9	11.5	26.9
Costumes	100.0	6.6	9.1	9.1	13.0	6.1	8.1	48.0

	total complete reporters	under $20,000	$20,000– $39,999	$40,000– $49,999	$50,000– $69,999	$70,000– $79,999	$80,000– $99,999	$100,000 or more
GIRLS' (AGED 2 TO 15) APPAREL	100.0%	12.6%	18.1%	7.9%	15.5%	10.7%	11.3%	24.8%
Coats and jackets	100.0	10.5	20.4	10.5	17.2	8.3	9.8	23.3
Dresses and suits	100.0	–	–	–	–	–	–	–
Shirts, blouses, and sweaters	100.0	10.1	18.5	5.0	15.3	12.6	15.7	24.3
Skirts and pants	100.0	12.9	19.1	11.1	16.0	7.3	10.8	22.7
Shorts and shorts sets	100.0	12.4	18.6	10.2	18.6	6.3	13.7	20.3
Active sportswear	100.0	14.8	15.3	7.1	11.3	13.6	8.7	30.8
Underwear and nightwear	100.0	13.6	18.3	10.3	18.8	8.5	11.4	19.1
Hosiery	100.0	14.2	14.5	7.8	19.1	11.7	8.3	26.0
Accessories	100.0	14.6	11.0	7.4	25.2	8.1	13.2	22.7
Uniforms	100.0	13.2	17.8	6.3	9.9	15.9	13.2	23.9
Costumes	100.0	7.2	14.5	5.8	20.0	9.2	12.7	30.5
CHILDREN UNDER AGE 2	100.0	15.3	21.4	9.0	14.0	8.5	10.7	21.5
Coats, jackets, and snowsuits	100.0	15.2	21.4	8.1	17.4	6.0	12.0	19.9
Outerwear including dresses	100.0	13.3	22.2	10.0	15.0	6.6	10.5	22.4
Underwear	100.0	16.4	19.8	9.1	13.0	9.1	10.9	22.4
Nightwear and loungewear	100.0	9.6	27.8	7.0	14.6	5.0	14.4	21.7
Accessories	100.0	16.9	24.9	7.7	15.3	11.4	8.5	15.6
FOOTWEAR	100.0	20.9	20.2	7.7	18.2	6.9	9.1	17.8
Men's	100.0	18.4	20.2	8.9	18.9	8.3	12.3	13.6
Boys'	100.0	26.0	22.9	6.3	18.1	3.6	5.4	18.2
Women's	100.0	22.0	19.7	7.0	18.2	6.1	8.2	20.0
Girls'	100.0	17.3	19.5	9.0	16.2	10.8	8.5	19.0
OTHER APPAREL PRODUCTS AND SERVICES	100.0	11.2	15.7	7.8	14.1	5.1	10.5	35.7
Material for making clothes	100.0	8.3	27.3	7.2	14.3	4.1	16.6	23.4
Sewing patterns and notions	100.0	21.8	22.9	9.8	15.2	3.6	8.7	17.9
Watches	100.0	8.0	13.0	20.1	15.5	5.6	8.0	29.8
Jewelry	100.0	5.4	13.3	7.2	15.8	4.7	11.3	42.3
Shoe repair and other shoe services	100.0	9.1	15.3	5.7	13.3	8.1	7.9	40.4
Coin-operated apparel laundry and dry cleaning	100.0	39.0	32.4	8.8	9.4	2.7	2.8	4.9
Apparel alteration, repair, and tailoring services	100.0	8.7	14.0	3.7	14.6	7.3	12.0	39.8
Clothing rental	100.0	3.1	11.0	4.2	21.6	10.0	18.8	31.3
Watch and jewelry repair	100.0	14.7	13.9	9.3	12.3	9.0	9.2	31.7
Professional laundry, dry cleaning	100.0	5.5	9.5	5.5	13.0	6.7	13.4	46.4
Clothing storage	100.0	–	–	–	–	–	–	–

Note: Numbers may not add to total because of rounding. (–) means sample is too small to make a reliable estimate.
Source: Calculations by New Strategist based on the 2003 Consumer Expenditure Survey

Table 2.9 Apparel: Average spending by high-income consumer units, 2003

(average annual spending on apparel, accessories, and related services, by before-tax income of high-income consumer units (CU), 2003; complete income reporters only)

	total complete reporters	$100,000 or more	$100,000– $119,999	$120,000– $149,999	$150,000 or more
Number of consumer units (000)	97,391	11,537	4,384	3,151	4,002
Average number of persons per CU	2.5	3.1	3.1	3.1	3.1
Average before-tax income of CU	$51,128.00	$154,665.00	$108,087.00	$131,885.00	$223,634.00
Average spending of CU, total	42,741.66	93,514.86	75,601.50	86,451.46	118,674.11
Apparel, average spending	**1,744.04**	**3,756.44**	**2,695.05**	**3,540.81**	**5,082.92**
MEN'S APPAREL	**294.42**	**634.37**	**432.93**	**608.92**	**873.99**
Suits	24.54	84.76	39.52	81.65	136.79
Sport coats and tailored jackets	10.91	41.26	25.80	21.24	73.97
Coats and jackets	21.35	42.72	52.08	8.49	59.11
Underwear	14.96	19.51	9.26	20.13	30.19
Hosiery	12.42	23.98	12.82	29.41	31.90
Nightwear	2.17	6.60	4.88	5.85	9.07
Accessories	24.51	49.34	29.98	39.48	78.06
Sweaters and vests	11.63	33.61	25.47	34.99	41.45
Active sportswear	19.68	69.93	82.95	62.86	61.27
Shirts	64.99	134.48	68.27	160.08	186.57
Pants	63.71	79.38	54.68	98.00	91.76
Shorts and shorts sets	16.52	26.30	16.74	18.68	42.61
Uniforms	3.00	6.68	2.44	8.68	9.74
Costumes	4.02	15.81	8.03	19.40	21.52
BOYS' (AGED 2 TO 15) APPAREL	**91.05**	**179.69**	**133.23**	**140.90**	**260.62**
Coats and jackets	6.27	11.38	7.97	8.80	17.15
Sweaters	2.69	4.33	2.57	5.59	5.26
Shirts	21.05	39.40	34.47	25.75	55.36
Underwear	6.64	12.61	3.52	12.44	22.62
Nightwear	2.72	7.00	1.15	2.16	17.11
Hosiery	4.65	8.24	4.18	1.81	17.66
Accessories	3.98	6.33	3.84	4.64	10.36
Suits, sport coats, and vests	2.32	5.96	2.55	8.25	7.90
Pants	21.97	40.46	35.58	38.26	47.55
Shorts and shorts sets	7.89	12.99	12.41	11.68	14.65
Uniforms	3.28	9.77	7.75	3.57	16.87
Active sportswear	4.68	13.88	11.03	10.31	19.83
Costumes	2.89	7.32	6.20	7.64	8.31
WOMEN'S APPAREL	**588.43**	**1,298.02**	**946.36**	**1,165.61**	**1,783.29**
Coats and jackets	52.06	90.91	61.96	48.64	155.20
Dresses	51.99	110.39	51.89	95.67	185.42
Sport coats and tailored jackets	5.55	20.49	12.46	17.80	31.40
Sweaters and vests	51.83	148.03	98.60	109.41	231.76
Shirts, blouses, and tops	115.22	274.60	221.13	253.61	349.04
Skirts	15.24	30.10	39.11	15.50	31.64
Pants	95.23	210.68	155.66	209.83	271.16
Shorts and shorts sets	16.36	27.66	9.44	24.32	50.06
Active sportswear	28.74	50.67	39.48	54.69	59.70
Nightwear	29.43	40.21	36.98	39.38	44.36
Undergarments	34.85	60.15	44.47	66.62	72.16
Hosiery	18.28	41.57	24.05	42.57	59.85
Suits	23.82	74.60	53.96	88.15	86.55
Accessories	36.90	76.23	68.64	51.36	103.78
Uniforms	5.98	13.60	12.31	10.17	17.70
Costumes	6.94	28.12	16.22	37.86	33.50

	total complete reporters	$100,000 or more	$100,000– $119,999	$120,000– $149,999	$150,000 or more
GIRLS' (AGED 2 TO 15) APPAREL	**$110.46**	**$231.26**	**$184.84**	**$181.11**	**$320.78**
Coats and jackets	7.29	14.33	12.11	13.26	17.61
Dresses and suits	11.41	29.70	6.88	18.56	63.14
Shirts, blouses, and sweaters	23.99	49.28	56.21	30.70	56.18
Skirts and pants	24.06	46.11	44.12	39.00	53.89
Shorts and shorts sets	8.01	13.70	12.04	14.38	14.97
Active sportswear	10.68	27.77	14.66	19.89	48.14
Underwear and nightwear	6.72	10.86	8.23	12.08	12.77
Hosiery	4.93	10.82	7.65	4.98	18.81
Accessories	6.21	11.90	11.44	6.84	16.33
Uniforms	2.95	5.94	4.81	4.72	8.13
Costumes	4.21	10.85	6.68	16.71	10.80
CHILDREN UNDER AGE 2	**85.75**	**155.54**	**124.82**	**199.26**	**155.01**
Coats, jackets, and snowsuits	2.20	3.69	3.20	2.63	5.07
Outerwear including dresses	21.62	40.83	33.25	50.17	41.79
Underwear	47.55	89.96	78.55	114.66	83.19
Nightwear and loungewear	4.12	7.54	6.20	6.11	10.13
Accessories	10.26	13.52	3.63	25.69	14.83
FOOTWEAR	**311.11**	**466.52**	**423.56**	**540.89**	**455.49**
Men's	90.56	103.64	100.82	114.85	98.00
Boys'	39.52	60.81	62.11	58.62	61.09
Women's	146.09	246.07	227.96	295.58	227.31
Girls'	34.95	56.01	32.66	71.85	69.09
OTHER APPAREL PRODUCTS AND SERVICES	**262.83**	**791.04**	**449.31**	**704.11**	**1,233.75**
Material for making clothes	5.82	11.51	7.58	7.17	19.17
Sewing patterns and notions	5.80	8.78	11.48	2.02	11.09
Watches	16.22	40.80	30.48	41.54	51.54
Jewelry	118.45	423.16	198.53	395.24	691.24
Shoe repair and other shoe services	1.29	4.40	2.36	2.73	7.94
Coin-operated apparel laundry and dry cleaning	38.77	16.02	21.44	15.57	10.44
Apparel alteration, repair, and tailoring services	6.21	20.85	8.57	15.48	38.54
Clothing rental	2.79	7.37	7.97	6.03	7.77
Watch and jewelry repair	3.90	10.44	5.76	6.77	18.47
Professional laundry, dry cleaning	63.06	247.02	155.05	210.50	376.52
Clothing storage	0.52	0.68	0.07	1.05	1.05

Note: Subcategories may not add to total because some are not shown.
Source: Bureau of Labor Statistics, unpublished data from the 2003 Consumer Expenditure Survey; calculations by New Strategist

Table 2.10 Apparel: Indexed spending by high-income consumer units, 2003

(indexed average annual spending of high-income consumer units (CU) on apparel, accessories, and related services, by before-tax income of consumer unit, 2003; complete income reporters only; index definition: an index of 100 is the average for all consumer units; an index of 132 means that spending by consumer units in that group is 32 percent above the average for all consumer units; an index of 68 indicates spending that is 32 percent below the average for all consumer units)

	total complete reporters	$100,000 or more	$100,000–$119,999	$120,000–$149,999	$150,000 or more
Average spending of CU, total	$42,742	$93,515	$75,602	$86,451	$118,674
Average spending of CU, index	100	219	177	202	278
Apparel, spending index	**100**	**215**	**155**	**203**	**291**
MEN'S APPAREL	**100**	**215**	**147**	**207**	**297**
Suits	100	345	161	333	557
Sport coats and tailored jackets	100	378	236	195	678
Coats and jackets	100	200	244	40	277
Underwear	100	130	62	135	202
Hosiery	100	193	103	237	257
Nightwear	100	304	225	270	418
Accessories	100	201	122	161	318
Sweaters and vests	100	289	219	301	356
Active sportswear	100	355	421	319	311
Shirts	100	207	105	246	287
Pants	100	125	86	154	144
Shorts and shorts sets	100	159	101	113	258
Uniforms	100	223	81	289	325
Costumes	100	393	200	483	535
BOYS' (AGED 2 TO 15) APPAREL	**100**	**197**	**146**	**155**	**286**
Coats and jackets	100	181	127	140	274
Sweaters	100	161	96	208	196
Shirts	100	187	164	122	263
Underwear	100	190	53	187	341
Nightwear	100	257	42	79	629
Hosiery	100	177	90	39	380
Accessories	100	159	96	117	260
Suits, sport coats, and vests	100	257	110	356	341
Pants	100	184	162	174	216
Shorts and shorts sets	100	165	157	148	186
Uniforms	100	298	236	109	514
Active sportswear	100	297	236	220	424
Costumes	100	253	215	264	288
WOMEN'S APPAREL	**100**	**221**	**161**	**198**	**303**
Coats and jackets	100	175	119	93	298
Dresses	100	212	100	184	357
Sport coats and tailored jackets	100	369	225	321	566
Sweaters and vests	100	286	190	211	447
Shirts, blouses, and tops	100	238	192	220	303
Skirts	100	198	257	102	208
Pants	100	221	163	220	285
Shorts and shorts sets	100	169	58	149	306
Active sportswear	100	176	137	190	208
Nightwear	100	137	126	134	151
Undergarments	100	173	128	191	207
Hosiery	100	227	132	233	327
Suits	100	313	227	370	363
Accessories	100	207	186	139	281
Uniforms	100	227	206	170	296
Costumes	100	405	234	546	483

	total complete reporters	$100,000 or more	$100,000– $119,999	$120,000– $149,999	$150,000 or more
GIRLS' (AGED 2 TO 15) APPAREL	100	209	167	164	290
Coats and jackets	100	197	166	182	242
Dresses and suits	100	260	60	163	553
Shirts, blouses, and sweaters	100	205	234	128	234
Skirts and pants	100	192	183	162	224
Shorts and shorts sets	100	171	150	180	187
Active sportswear	100	260	137	186	451
Underwear and nightwear	100	162	122	180	190
Hosiery	100	219	155	101	382
Accessories	100	192	184	110	263
Uniforms	100	201	163	160	276
Costumes	100	258	159	397	257
CHILDREN UNDER AGE 2	100	181	146	232	181
Coats, jackets, and snowsuits	100	168	145	120	230
Outerwear including dresses	100	189	154	232	193
Underwear	100	189	165	241	175
Nightwear and loungewear	100	183	150	148	246
Accessories	100	132	35	250	145
FOOTWEAR	100	150	136	174	146
Men's	100	114	111	127	108
Boys'	100	154	157	148	155
Women's	100	168	156	202	156
Girls'	100	160	93	206	198
OTHER APPAREL PRODUCTS AND SERVICES	100	301	171	268	469
Material for making clothes	100	198	130	123	329
Sewing patterns and notions	100	151	198	35	191
Watches	100	252	188	256	318
Jewelry	100	357	163	334	584
Shoe repair and other shoe services	100	341	183	212	616
Coin-operated apparel laundry and dry cleaning	100	41	55	40	27
Apparel alteration, repair, and tailoring services	100	336	138	249	621
Clothing rental	100	264	286	216	278
Watch and jewelry repair	100	268	148	174	474
Professional laundry, dry cleaning	100	392	246	334	597
Clothing storage	100	131	13	202	202

Source: Calculations by New Strategist based on the 2003 Consumer Expenditure Survey

Table 2.11 Apparel: Total spending by high-income consumer units, 2003

(total annual spending on apparel, accessories, and related services, by before-tax income group of high-income consumer units (CU), 2003; complete income reporters only; numbers in thousands)

	total complete reporters	$100,000 or more	$100,000– $119,999	$120,000– $149,999	$150,000 or more
Number of consumer units	97,391	11,537	4,384	3,151	4,002
Total spending of all CUs	$4,162,653,009	$1,078,880,940	$331,436,976	$272,408,550	$474,933,788
Apparel, total spending	**169,853,800**	**43,338,048**	**11,815,099**	**11,157,092**	**20,341,846**
MEN'S APPAREL	**28,673,858**	**7,318,727**	**1,897,965**	**1,918,707**	**3,497,708**
Suits	2,389,975	977,876	173,256	257,279	547,434
Sport coats and tailored jackets	1,062,536	476,017	113,107	66,927	296,028
Coats and jackets	2,079,298	492,861	228,319	26,752	236,558
Underwear	1,456,969	225,087	40,596	63,430	120,820
Hosiery	1,209,596	276,657	56,203	92,671	127,664
Nightwear	211,338	76,144	21,394	18,433	36,298
Accessories	2,387,053	569,236	131,432	124,401	312,396
Sweaters and vests	1,132,657	387,759	111,660	110,253	165,883
Active sportswear	1,916,655	806,782	363,653	198,072	245,203
Shirts	6,329,441	1,551,496	299,296	504,412	746,653
Pants	6,204,781	915,807	239,717	308,798	367,224
Shorts and shorts sets	1,608,899	303,423	73,388	58,861	170,525
Uniforms	292,173	77,067	10,697	27,351	38,979
Costumes	391,512	182,400	35,204	61,129	86,123
BOYS' (AGED 2 TO 15) APPAREL	**8,867,451**	**2,073,084**	**584,080**	**443,976**	**1,043,001**
Coats and jackets	610,642	131,291	34,940	27,729	68,634
Sweaters	261,982	49,955	11,267	17,614	21,051
Shirts	2,050,081	454,558	151,116	81,138	221,551
Underwear	646,676	145,482	15,432	39,198	90,525
Nightwear	264,904	80,759	5,042	6,806	68,474
Hosiery	452,868	95,065	18,325	5,703	70,675
Accessories	387,616	73,029	16,835	14,621	41,461
Suits, sport coats, and vests	225,947	68,761	11,179	25,996	31,616
Pants	2,139,680	466,787	155,983	120,557	190,295
Shorts and shorts sets	768,415	149,866	54,405	36,804	58,629
Uniforms	319,442	112,716	33,976	11,249	67,514
Active sportswear	455,790	160,134	48,356	32,487	79,360
Costumes	281,460	84,451	27,181	24,074	33,257
WOMEN'S APPAREL	**57,307,786**	**14,975,257**	**4,148,842**	**3,672,837**	**7,136,727**
Coats and jackets	5,070,175	1,048,829	271,633	153,265	621,110
Dresses	5,063,358	1,273,569	227,486	301,456	742,051
Sport coats and tailored jackets	540,520	236,393	54,625	56,088	125,663
Sweaters and vests	5,047,776	1,707,822	432,262	344,751	927,504
Shirts, blouses, and tops	11,221,391	3,168,060	969,434	799,125	1,396,858
Skirts	1,484,239	347,264	171,458	48,841	126,623
Pants	9,274,545	2,430,615	682,413	661,174	1,085,182
Shorts and shorts sets	1,593,317	319,113	41,385	76,632	200,340
Active sportswear	2,799,017	584,580	173,080	172,328	238,919
Nightwear	2,866,217	463,903	162,120	124,086	177,529
Undergarments	3,394,076	693,951	194,956	209,920	288,784
Hosiery	1,780,307	479,593	105,435	134,138	239,520
Suits	2,319,854	860,660	236,561	277,761	346,373
Accessories	3,593,728	879,466	300,918	161,835	415,328
Uniforms	582,398	156,903	53,967	32,046	70,835
Costumes	675,894	324,420	71,108	119,297	134,067

	total complete reporters	$100,000 or more	$100,000–$119,999	$120,000–$149,999	$150,000 or more
GIRLS' (AGED 2 TO 15) APPAREL	**$10,757,810**	**$2,668,047**	**$810,339**	**$570,678**	**$1,283,762**
Coats and jackets	709,980	165,325	53,090	41,782	70,475
Dresses and suits	1,111,231	342,649	30,162	58,483	252.686
Shirts, blouses, and sweaters	2,336,410	568,543	246,425	96,736	224.832
Skirts and pants	2,343,227	531,971	193,422	122,889	215,668
Shorts and shorts sets	780,102	158,057	52,783	45,311	59,910
Active sportswear	1,040,136	320,382	64,269	62,673	192,656
Underwear and nightwear	654,468	125,292	35,080	38,064	51,106
Hosiery	480,138	124,830	33,538	15,692	75,278
Accessories	604,798	137,290	50,153	21,553	65,353
Uniforms	287,303	68,530	21,087	14,873	32,536
Costumes	410,016	125,176	29,285	52,653	43,222
CHILDREN UNDER AGE 2	**8,351,278**	**1,794,465**	**547,211**	**627,868**	**620,350**
Coats, jackets, and snowsuits	214,260	42,572	14,029	8,287	20,290
Outerwear including dresses	2,105,593	471,056	145,768	158,086	167,244
Underwear	4,630,942	1,037,869	344,363	361,294	332,926
Nightwear and loungewear	401,251	86,989	27,181	19,253	40,540
Accessories	999,232	155,980	15,914	80,949	59,350
FOOTWEAR	**30,299,314**	**5,382,241**	**1,856,887**	**1,704,344**	**1,822,871**
Men's	8,819,729	1,195,695	441,955	361,892	392,196
Boys'	3,848,892	701,565	272,290	184,712	244,482
Women's	14,227,851	2,838,910	999,377	931,373	909,695
Girls'	3,403,815	646,187	143,181	226,399	276,498
OTHER APPAREL PRODUCTS AND SERVICES	**25,597,277**	**9,126,228**	**1,969,775**	**2,218,651**	**4,937,468**
Material for making clothes	566,816	132,791	33,231	22,593	76,718
Sewing patterns and notions	564,868	101,295	50,323	6,365	44,382
Watches	1,579,682	470,710	133,624	130,893	206,263
Jewelry	11,535,964	4,881,997	870,356	1,245,401	2,766,342
Shoe repair and other shoe services	125,634	50,763	10,346	8,602	31,776
Coin-operated apparel laundry and dry cleaning	3,775,849	184,823	93,993	49,061	41,781
Apparel alteration, repair, and tailoring services	604,798	240,546	37,571	48,777	154,237
Clothing rental	271,721	85,028	34,940	19,001	31,096
Watch and jewelry repair	379,825	120,446	25,252	21,332	73,917
Professional laundry, dry cleaning	6,141,476	2,849,870	679,783	663,286	1,506,833
Clothing storage	50,643	7,845	307	3,309	4,202

Note: Numbers may not add to total because of rounding and missing subcategories.
Source: Calculations by New Strategist based on the 2003 Consumer Expenditure Survey

Table 2.12 Apparel: Market shares by high-income consumer units, 2003

(percentage of total annual spending on apparel, accessories, and related services accounted for by before-tax income group of high-income consumer units, 2003; complete income reporters only)

	total complete reporters	$100,000 or more	$100,000– $119,999	$120,000– $149,999	$150,000 or more
Share of total consumer units	100.0%	11.8%	4.5%	3.2%	4.1%
Share of total before-tax income	100.0	35.8	9.5	8.3	18.0
Share of total spending	100.0	25.9	8.0	6.5	11.4
Share of apparel spending	100.0	25.5	7.0	6.6	12.0
MEN'S APPAREL	**100.0**	**25.5**	**6.6**	**6.7**	**12.2**
Suits	100.0	40.9	7.2	10.8	22.9
Sport coats and tailored jackets	100.0	44.8	10.6	6.3	27.9
Coats and jackets	100.0	23.7	11.0	1.3	11.4
Underwear	100.0	15.4	2.8	4.4	8.3
Hosiery	100.0	22.9	4.6	7.7	10.6
Nightwear	100.0	36.0	10.1	8.7	17.2
Accessories	100.0	23.8	5.5	5.2	13.1
Sweaters and vests	100.0	34.2	9.9	9.7	14.6
Active sportswear	100.0	42.1	19.0	10.3	12.8
Shirts	100.0	24.5	4.7	8.0	11.8
Pants	100.0	14.8	3.9	5.0	5.9
Shorts and shorts sets	100.0	18.9	4.6	3.7	10.6
Uniforms	100.0	26.4	3.7	9.4	13.3
Costumes	100.0	46.6	9.0	15.6	22.0
BOYS' (AGED 2 TO 15) APPAREL	**100.0**	**23.4**	**6.6**	**5.0**	**11.8**
Coats and jackets	100.0	21.5	5.7	4.5	11.2
Sweaters	100.0	19.1	4.3	6.7	8.0
Shirts	100.0	22.2	7.4	4.0	10.8
Underwear	100.0	22.5	2.4	6.1	14.0
Nightwear	100.0	30.5	1.9	2.6	25.8
Hosiery	100.0	21.0	4.0	1.3	15.6
Accessories	100.0	18.8	4.3	3.8	10.7
Suits, sport coats, and vests	100.0	30.4	4.9	11.5	14.0
Pants	100.0	21.8	7.3	5.6	8.9
Shorts and shorts sets	100.0	19.5	7.1	4.8	7.6
Uniforms	100.0	35.3	10.6	3.5	21.1
Active sportswear	100.0	35.1	10.6	7.1	17.4
Costumes	100.0	30.0	9.7	8.6	11.8
WOMEN'S APPAREL	**100.0**	**26.1**	**7.2**	**6.4**	**12.5**
Coats and jackets	100.0	20.7	5.4	3.0	12.3
Dresses	100.0	25.2	4.5	6.0	14.7
Sport coats and tailored jackets	100.0	43.7	10.1	10.4	23.2
Sweaters and vests	100.0	33.8	8.6	6.8	18.4
Shirts, blouses, and tops	100.0	28.2	8.6	7.1	12.4
Skirts	100.0	23.4	11.6	3.3	8.5
Pants	100.0	26.2	7.4	7.1	11.7
Shorts and shorts sets	100.0	20.0	2.6	4.8	12.6
Active sportswear	100.0	20.9	6.2	6.2	8.5
Nightwear	100.0	16.2	5.7	4.3	6.2
Undergarments	100.0	20.4	5.7	6.2	8.5
Hosiery	100.0	26.9	5.9	7.5	13.5
Suits	100.0	37.1	10.2	12.0	14.9
Accessories	100.0	24.5	8.4	4.5	11.6
Uniforms	100.0	26.9	9.3	5.5	12.2
Costumes	100.0	48.0	10.5	17.7	19.8

	total complete reporters	$100,000 or more	$100,000– $119,999	$120,000– $149,999	$150,000 or more
GIRLS' (AGED 2 TO 15) APPAREL	**100.0%**	**24.8%**	**7.5%**	**5.3%**	**11.9%**
Coats and jackets	100.0	23.3	7.5	5.9	9.9
Dresses and suits	100.0	30.8	2.7	5.3	22.7
Shirts, blouses, and sweaters	100.0	24.3	10.5	4.1	9.6
Skirts and pants	100.0	22.7	3.3	5.2	9.2
Shorts and shorts sets	100.0	20.3	6.8	5.8	7.7
Active sportswear	100.0	30.8	6.2	6.0	18.5
Underwear and nightwear	100.0	19.1	5.5	5.8	7.8
Hosiery	100.0	26.0	7.0	3.3	15.7
Accessories	100.0	22.7	8.3	3.6	10.8
Uniforms	100.0	23.9	7.3	5.2	11.3
Costumes	100.0	30.5	7.1	12.8	10.5
CHILDREN UNDER AGE 2	**100.0**	**21.5**	**6.6**	**7.5**	**7.4**
Coats, jackets, and snowsuits	100.0	19.9	6.5	3.9	9.5
Outerwear including dresses	100.0	22.4	6.9	7.5	7.9
Underwear	100.0	22.4	7.4	7.8	7.2
Nightwear and loungewear	100.0	21.7	6.8	4.8	10.1
Accessories	100.0	15.6	1.6	8.1	5.9
FOOTWEAR	**100.0**	**17.8**	**6.1**	**5.6**	**6.0**
Men's	100.0	13.6	5.0	4.1	4.4
Boys'	100.0	18.2	7.1	4.8	6.4
Women's	100.0	20.0	7.0	6.5	6.4
Girls'	100.0	19.0	4.2	6.7	8.1
OTHER APPAREL PRODUCTS AND SERVICES	**100.0**	**35.7**	**7.7**	**8.7**	**19.3**
Material for making clothes	100.0	23.4	5.9	4.0	13.5
Sewing patterns and notions	100.0	17.9	8.9	1.1	7.9
Watches	100.0	29.8	8.5	8.3	13.1
Jewelry	100.0	42.3	7.5	10.8	24.0
Shoe repair and other shoe services	100.0	40.4	8.2	6.8	25.3
Coin-operated apparel laundry and dry cleaning	100.0	4.9	2.5	1.3	1.1
Apparel alteration, repair, and tailoring services	100.0	39.8	6.2	8.1	25.5
Clothing rental	100.0	31.3	12.9	7.0	11.4
Watch and jewelry repair	100.0	31.7	5.6	5.6	19.5
Professional laundry, dry cleaning	100.0	46.4	11.1	10.8	24.5
Clothing storage	100.0	15.5	0.6	6.5	8.3

Note: Numbers may not add to total because of rounding.
Source: Calculations by New Strategist based on the 2003 Consumer Expenditure Survey

Table 2.13 Apparel: Average spending by household type, 2003

(average annual spending of consumer units (CU) on apparel, accessories, and related services, by type of consumer unit, 2003)

	total married couples	married couples, no children	married couples with children				single parent, at least one child <18	single person
			total	oldest child under 6	oldest child 6 to 17	oldest child 18 or older		
Number of consumer units (000)	58,448	25,132	28,584	5,496	15,047	8,041	6,999	33,929
Average number of persons per CU	3.2	2.0	3.9	3.5	4.1	4.0	2.9	1.0
Average before-tax income of CU	$69,472.00	$62,930.00	$75,557.00	$66,317.00	$77,508.00	$78,307.00	$29,154.00	$27,131.00
Average spending of CU, total	53,030.03	47,895.65	57,702.32	51,503.24	59,183.18	59,180.36	30,534.75	23,657.35
Apparel, average spending	**2,084.78**	**1,632.28**	**2,430.58**	**2,231.56**	**2,613.72**	**2,218.68**	**1,799.32**	**837.31**
MEN'S APPAREL	**369.19**	**332.53**	**395.61**	**320.92**	**390.99**	**458.50**	**172.62**	**163.94**
Suits	30.27	29.07	31.12	23.18	30.04	38.58	4.35	17.73
Sport coats and tailored jackets	13.97	12.15	16.43	6.95	18.18	19.63	4.19	7.91
Coats and jackets	30.51	34.55	25.45	28.40	22.74	28.81	18.35	11.18
Underwear	17.82	15.68	18.87	12.60	19.25	22.72	6.53	9.68
Hosiery	15.07	11.16	18.09	11.15	15.06	29.39	8.23	4.89
Nightwear	2.82	2.94	2.84	2.68	2.30	3.97	0.96	1.02
Accessories	28.96	23.13	34.66	37.50	33.81	34.30	9.61	15.17
Sweaters and vests	15.77	13.86	17.47	15.07	15.82	22.21	5.49	6.87
Active sportswear	25.66	21.47	28.28	13.27	34.95	25.72	5.31	9.73
Shirts	83.11	74.39	87.94	92.85	75.97	108.71	48.79	28.42
Pants	76.52	74.62	77.31	43.23	81.10	94.64	35.53	39.50
Shorts and shorts sets	19.46	10.39	27.23	27.72	31.64	17.89	18.06	9.12
Uniforms	3.14	2.84	3.67	3.19	3.55	4.23	6.16	1.23
Costumes	6.09	6.30	6.24	3.12	6.60	7.69	1.08	1.50
BOYS' (AGED 2 TO 15) APPAREL	**125.44**	**28.16**	**208.61**	**129.97**	**303.80**	**79.13**	**216.14**	**13.07**
Coats and jackets	9.18	2.71	14.56	9.09	21.25	5.77	10.40	0.87
Sweaters	3.57	1.80	5.09	2.64	7.75	1.80	7.83	0.26
Shirts	28.38	6.61	46.52	29.58	66.76	17.71	44.41	2.10
Underwear	9.64	1.41	17.15	8.54	24.68	8.15	8.91	0.68
Nightwear	4.30	0.89	7.63	9.40	9.98	1.54	15.34	0.41
Hosiery	4.71	1.25	7.82	5.44	12.26	0.50	14.71	0.90
Accessories	5.80	0.80	10.15	7.72	14.87	2.29	17.05	0.61
Suits, sport coats, and vests	3.73	1.15	6.05	2.84	8.74	3.20	3.82	0.54
Pants	29.35	6.23	48.93	24.94	73.69	19.00	54.51	3.54
Shorts and shorts sets	10.88	2.16	18.45	16.76	24.73	7.86	20.02	1.31
Uniforms	4.83	0.73	7.92	3.70	12.41	2.38	6.95	0.77
Active sportswear	7.00	1.58	11.79	5.66	17.32	5.61	7.95	0.72
Costumes	4.07	0.83	6.56	3.64	9.36	3.32	4.25	0.35
WOMEN'S APPAREL	**647.44**	**609.35**	**653.00**	**604.67**	**589.36**	**817.84**	**445.27**	**315.68**
Coats and jackets	51.71	56.05	43.42	35.58	31.44	73.61	23.85	32.08
Dresses	64.19	57.79	56.71	53.96	48.74	74.98	27.46	26.80
Sport coats and tailored jackets	6.70	8.24	5.61	3.19	5.73	7.04	6.87	2.81
Sweaters and vests	57.59	59.42	54.39	54.45	51.98	59.25	28.11	25.13
Shirts, blouses, and tops	123.60	110.77	133.43	101.21	121.37	181.72	87.56	56.99
Skirts	13.86	14.02	13.03	11.12	13.87	12.72	11.82	8.83
Pants	109.00	89.47	120.04	141.24	97.87	149.65	74.87	47.77
Shorts and shorts sets	17.07	13.13	20.74	9.93	22.48	25.14	10.02	6.34
Active sportswear	29.37	29.04	29.57	48.03	27.24	20.76	11.80	22.40
Nightwear	29.98	28.54	28.24	28.84	22.88	38.74	55.92	14.13
Undergarments	39.41	36.84	41.13	34.03	38.35	52.01	26.72	19.94
Hosiery	22.16	22.01	22.57	14.42	22.02	29.69	15.56	9.38
Suits	26.58	27.67	27.74	20.52	28.65	30.97	17.61	16.08
Accessories	40.45	39.89	41.08	39.65	40.14	44.07	33.46	22.44
Uniforms	6.97	6.26	7.63	4.70	7.19	10.46	5.57	2.55
Costumes	8.80	10.21	7.65	3.79	9.40	7.02	8.08	2.01

	total married couples	married couples, no children	married couples with children				single parent, at least one child <18	single person
			total	oldest child under 6	oldest child 6 to 17	oldest child 18 or older		
GIRLS' (AGED 2 TO 15) APPAREL	**$149.45**	**$40.72**	**$238.61**	**$138.41**	**$357.35**	**$76.86**	**$227.63**	**$15.10**
Coats and jackets	9.61	2.15	15.64	6.26	24.11	6.18	15.54	0.87
Dresses and suits	13.46	5.07	20.34	13.84	31.94	1.47	22.07	1.68
Shirts, blouses, and sweaters	36.27	9.99	55.24	29.62	84.24	14.95	35.85	3.72
Skirts and pants	32.77	7.09	54.80	30.02	79.25	25.98	59.13	3.03
Shorts and shorts sets	11.10	2.66	18.64	11.77	27.46	6.85	18.57	0.77
Active sportswear	13.42	3.80	21.59	14.42	32.26	5.10	27.94	1.36
Underwear and nightwear	9.08	1.88	14.73	10.05	20.51	7.12	14.94	0.71
Hosiery	6.38	1.63	10.47	5.82	16.11	2.38	9.04	1.16
Accessories	7.37	4.28	10.23	5.96	16.27	1.04	12.36	1.52
Uniforms	3.87	0.78	6.42	4.00	9.49	2.32	6.01	0.11
Costumes	6.12	1.40	10.52	6.64	15.71	3.47	6.18	0.18
CHILDREN UNDER AGE 2	**115.22**	**43.50**	**167.67**	**469.24**	**116.72**	**50.93**	**110.54**	**16.85**
Coats, jackets, and snowsuits	2.79	1.45	3.59	10.65	2.19	1.38	2.50	0.82
Outerwear including dresses	28.18	19.28	34.05	99.75	18.65	17.96	19.83	6.18
Underwear	66.87	15.56	104.22	291.10	78.71	18.76	70.87	5.00
Nightwear and loungewear	5.42	3.16	7.40	18.50	5.18	3.98	3.74	1.79
Accessories	11.95	4.05	18.42	49.24	12.00	8.84	13.61	3.05
FOOTWEAR	**352.67**	**263.79**	**421.18**	**282.02**	**479.49**	**404.64**	**450.04**	**156.40**
Men's	100.00	93.40	105.10	61.65	111.93	123.12	77.40	49.59
Boys'	46.01	1.72	82.74	41.62	123.10	30.70	169.82	4.56
Women's	161.00	161.62	155.98	142.94	124.50	229.74	139.88	94.53
Girls'	45.66	7.06	77.37	35.82	119.96	21.09	62.94	7.72
OTHER APPAREL PRODUCTS AND SERVICES	**325.37**	**314.23**	**345.90**	**286.33**	**376.01**	**330.77**	**177.10**	**156.27**
Material for making clothes	8.21	10.38	5.99	8.52	2.84	10.55	4.45	2.01
Sewing patterns and notions	6.22	6.17	6.65	5.38	6.52	7.86	3.81	4.04
Watches	25.22	16.28	35.47	46.73	35.80	27.16	9.60	7.16
Jewelry	161.92	169.42	161.56	97.25	193.84	145.10	56.06	59.58
Shoe repair and other shoe services	1.64	2.02	1.44	0.79	1.36	2.04	0.64	0.81
Coin-operated apparel laundry and dry cleaning	23.63	15.74	27.46	40.30	25.83	21.75	68.79	37.98
Apparel alteration, repair, and tailoring services	7.31	8.44	7.00	4.37	7.51	7.84	1.80	3.91
Clothing rental	3.81	2.76	4.99	1.48	3.80	9.61	0.71	0.63
Watch and jewelry repair	4.95	5.63	4.82	3.86	5.50	4.18	1.27	2.36
Professional laundry, dry cleaning	82.19	77.23	90.28	77.34	92.86	94.31	29.71	36.86
Clothing storage	0.28	0.16	0.25	0.30	0.16	0.37	0.25	0.93

Note: Average spending figures for total consumer units can be found on Average Spending by Age and Average Spending by Region tables. Subcategories may not add to total because some are not shown.
Source: Bureau of Labor Statistics, unpublished data from the 2003 Consumer Expenditure Survey

Table 2.14 Apparel: Indexed spending by household type, 2003

(indexed average annual spending of consumer units (CU) on apparel, accessories, and related services, by type of consumer unit, 2003; index definition: an index of 100 is the average for all consumer units; an index of 132 means that spending by consumer units in that group is 32 percent above the average for all consumer units; an index of 68 indicates spending that is 32 percent below the average for all consumer units)

| | total married couples | married couples, no children | married couples with children | | | | single parent, at least one child <18 | single person |
			total	oldest child under 6	oldest child 6 to 17	oldest child 18 or older		
Average spending of CU, total	$53,030	$47,896	$57,702	$51,503	$59,183	$59,180	$30,535	$23,657
Average spending of CU, index	130	117	141	126	145	145	75	58
Apparel, spending index	**127**	**100**	**148**	**136**	**159**	**135**	**110**	**51**
MEN'S APPAREL	**131**	**118**	**140**	**114**	**139**	**162**	**61**	**58**
Suits	128	123	131	98	127	163	18	75
Sport coats and tailored jackets	131	114	154	65	170	184	39	74
Coats and jackets	132	149	110	123	98	124	79	48
Underwear	123	108	130	87	133	157	45	67
Hosiery	130	96	156	96	130	253	71	42
Nightwear	140	146	141	133	114	197	48	50
Accessories	131	105	157	170	153	155	43	69
Sweaters and vests	136	120	151	130	136	192	47	59
Active sportswear	143	119	157	74	194	143	30	54
Shirts	135	121	143	151	124	177	79	46
Pants	125	122	127	71	133	155	58	65
Shorts and shorts sets	123	66	172	176	200	113	114	58
Uniforms	119	108	140	121	135	161	234	47
Costumes	149	154	153	76	161	188	26	37
BOYS' (AGED 2 TO 15) APPAREL	**140**	**31**	**233**	**145**	**340**	**88**	**242**	**15**
Coats and jackets	143	42	227	142	332	90	162	14
Sweaters	135	68	192	100	292	68	295	10
Shirts	148	34	243	154	348	92	232	11
Underwear	153	22	272	136	392	129	141	11
Nightwear	123	25	217	268	284	44	437	12
Hosiery	106	28	175	122	275	11	330	20
Accessories	128	18	224	170	328	50	376	13
Suits, sport coats, and vests	145	45	234	110	339	124	148	21
Pants	137	29	228	116	344	89	254	17
Shorts and shorts sets	140	28	237	215	318	101	257	17
Uniforms	143	22	235	110	368	71	206	23
Active sportswear	151	34	255	122	374	121	172	16
Costumes	154	31	248	137	353	125	160	13
WOMEN'S APPAREL	**122**	**115**	**124**	**114**	**111**	**155**	**84**	**60**
Coats and jackets	115	124	96	79	70	163	53	71
Dresses	134	121	118	113	102	156	57	56
Sport coats and tailored jackets	123	151	103	58	105	129	126	51
Sweaters and vests	126	130	119	119	114	130	62	55
Shirts, blouses, and tops	122	109	132	100	120	179	86	56
Skirts	108	109	101	86	108	99	92	69
Pants	124	102	136	160	111	170	85	54
Shorts and shorts sets	123	95	149	71	162	181	72	46
Active sportswear	113	112	114	184	105	80	45	86
Nightwear	113	108	107	109	86	146	211	53
Undergarments	125	117	131	108	122	165	85	63
Hosiery	130	129	132	84	129	174	91	55
Suits	120	125	125	93	129	140	79	72
Accessories	123	122	125	121	122	134	102	68
Uniforms	123	111	135	83	127	185	98	45
Costumes	138	160	120	59	147	110	126	31

	total married couples	married couples, no children	married couples with children				single parent, at least one child <18	single person
			total	oldest child under 6	oldest child 6 to 17	oldest child 18 or older		
GIRLS' (AGED 2 TO 15) APPAREL	**141**	**38**	**226**	**131**	**338**	**73**	**215**	**14**
Coats and jackets	142	32	230	92	355	91	229	13
Dresses and suits	128	48	193	131	303	14	209	16
Shirts, blouses, and sweaters	149	41	226	121	345	61	147	15
Skirts and pants	140	30	233	128	338	111	252	13
Shorts and shorts sets	145	35	243	153	358	89	242	10
Active sportswear	140	40	224	150	335	53	290	14
Underwear and nightwear	143	30	231	158	322	112	235	11
Hosiery	137	35	225	125	346	51	194	25
Accessories	129	75	179	104	284	18	216	27
Uniforms	148	30	246	153	364	89	230	4
Costumes	157	36	270	170	403	89	158	5
CHILDREN UNDER AGE 2	**141**	**53**	**206**	**576**	**143**	**63**	**136**	**21**
Coats, jackets, and snowsuits	133	69	172	510	105	66	120	39
Outerwear including dresses	137	94	166	486	91	88	97	30
Underwear	146	34	227	634	172	41	154	11
Nightwear and loungewear	133	78	182	455	127	98	92	44
Accessories	134	45	206	551	134	99	152	34
FOOTWEAR	**120**	**90**	**143**	**96**	**163**	**138**	**153**	**53**
Men's	120	112	126	74	134	148	93	59
Boys'	118	4	212	106	315	78	434	12
Women's	116	117	113	103	90	166	101	68
Girls'	138	21	234	108	363	64	191	23
OTHER APPAREL PRODUCTS AND SERVICES	**126**	**122**	**134**	**111**	**145**	**128**	**69**	**60**
Material for making clothes	154	195	112	150	53	198	83	38
Sewing patterns and notions	125	124	133	108	131	158	76	81
Watches	147	95	207	273	209	159	56	42
Jewelry	135	141	134	81	161	121	47	50
Shoe repair and other shoe services	143	176	125	69	118	177	56	70
Coin-operated apparel laundry and dry cleaning	65	43	75	111	71	60	189	104
Apparel alteration, repair, and tailoring services	130	150	125	78	134	140	32	70
Clothing rental	155	112	203	60	154	391	29	26
Watch and jewelry repair	138	157	134	108	153	116	35	66
Professional laundry, dry cleaning	134	126	148	126	152	154	49	60
Clothing storage	58	33	52	63	33	77	52	194

Note: Spending index for total consumer units is 100.
Source: Calculations by New Strategist based on the 2003 Consumer Expenditure Survey

Table 2.15 Apparel: Total spending by household type, 2003

(total annual spending on apparel, accessories, and related services, by consumer unit (CU) type, 2003; numbers in thousands)

	total married couples	married couples, no children	married couples with children				single parent, at least one child <18	single person
			total	oldest child under 6	oldest child 6 to 17	oldest child 18 or older		
Number of consumer units	58,448	25,132	28,584	5,496	15,047	8,041	6,999	33,929
Total spending of all CUs	$3,099,499,193	$1,203,713,476	$1,649,363,115	$283,061,807	$890,529,309	$475,869,275	$213,712,715	$802,670,228
Apparel, total spending	**121,851,221**	**41,022,461**	**69,475,699**	**12,264,654**	**39,328,645**	**17,840,406**	**12,593,441**	**28,409,091**
MEN'S APPAREL	**21,578,417**	**8,357,144**	**11,308,116**	**1,763,776**	**5,883,227**	**3,686,799**	**1,208,167**	**5,562,320**
Suits	1,769,221	730,587	889,534	127,397	452,012	310,222	30,446	601,561
Sport coats and tailored jackets	816,519	305,354	469,635	38,197	273,554	157,845	29,326	268,378
Coats and jackets	1,783,248	868,311	727,463	156,086	342,169	231,661	128,432	379,326
Underwear	1,041,543	394,070	539,380	69,250	289,655	182,692	45,703	328,433
Hosiery	880,811	280,473	517,085	61,280	226,608	236,325	57,602	165,913
Nightwear	164,823	73,888	81,179	14,729	34,608	31,923	6,719	34,608
Accessories	1,692,654	581,303	990,721	206,100	508,739	275,806	67,260	514,703
Sweaters and vests	921,725	348,330	499,362	82,825	238,044	178,591	38,425	233,092
Active sportswear	1,499,776	539,584	808,356	72,932	525,893	206,815	37,165	330,129
Shirts	4,857,613	1,869,569	2,513,677	510,304	1,143,121	874,137	341,481	964,262
Pants	4,472,441	1,875,350	2,209,829	237,592	1,220,312	761,000	248,674	1,340,196
Shorts and shorts sets	1,137,398	261,121	778,342	152,349	476,087	143,853	126,402	309,432
Uniforms	183,527	71,375	104,903	17,532	53,417	34,013	43,114	41,733
Costumes	355,948	158,332	178,364	17,148	99,310	61,835	7,559	50,894
BOYS' (AGED 2 TO 15) APPAREL	**7,331,717**	**707,717**	**5,962,908**	**714,315**	**4,571,279**	**636,284**	**1,512,764**	**443,452**
Coats and jackets	536,553	68,108	416,183	49,959	319,749	46,397	72,790	29,518
Sweaters	208,659	45,238	145,493	14,509	116,614	14,474	54,802	8,822
Shirts	1,658,754	166,123	1,329,728	162,572	1,004,538	142,406	310,826	71,251
Underwear	563,439	35,436	490,216	46,936	371,360	65,534	62,361	23,072
Nightwear	251,326	22,367	218,096	51,662	150,169	12,383	107,365	13,911
Hosiery	275,290	31,415	223,527	29,898	184,476	4,021	102,955	30,536
Accessories	338,998	20,106	290,128	42,429	223,749	18,414	119,333	20,697
Suits, sport coats, and vests	218,011	28,902	172,933	15,609	131,511	25,731	26,736	18,322
Pants	1,715,449	156,572	1,398,615	137,070	1,108,813	152,779	381,515	120,109
Shorts and shorts sets	635,914	54,285	527,375	92,113	372,112	63,202	140,120	44,447
Uniforms	282,304	18,346	226,385	20,335	186,733	19,138	48,643	26,125
Active sportswear	409,136	39,709	337,005	31,107	260,614	45,110	55,642	24,429
Costumes	237,883	20,860	187,511	20,005	140,840	26,696	29,746	11,875
WOMEN'S APPAREL	**37,841,573**	**15,314,184**	**18,665,352**	**3,323,266**	**8,868,100**	**6,576,251**	**3,116,445**	**10,710,707**
Coats and jackets	3,022,346	1,408,649	1,241,117	195,548	473,078	591,898	166,926	1,088,442
Dresses	3,751,777	1,452,378	1,620,999	296,564	733,391	602,914	192,193	909,297
Sport coats and tailored jackets	391,602	207,088	160,356	17,532	86,219	56,609	48,083	95,340
Sweaters and vests	3,366,020	1,493,343	1,554,684	299,257	782,143	476,429	196,742	852,636
Shirts, blouses, and tops	7,224,173	2,783,872	3,813,963	556,250	1,826,254	1,461,211	612,832	1,933,614
Skirts	810,089	352,351	372,450	61,116	208,702	102,282	82,728	299,593
Pants	6,370,832	2,248,560	3,431,223	776,255	1,472,650	1,203,336	524,015	1,620,788
Shorts and shorts sets	997,707	329,983	592,832	54,575	338,257	202,151	70,130	215,110
Active sportswear	1,716,618	729,833	845,229	263,973	409,880	166,931	82,588	760,010
Nightwear	1,752,271	717,267	807,212	158,505	344,275	311,508	391,384	479,417
Undergarments	2,303,436	925,863	1,175,660	187,029	577,052	418,212	187,013	676,544
Hosiery	1,295,208	553,155	645,141	79,252	331,335	238,737	108,904	318,254
Suits	1,553,548	695,402	792,920	112,778	431,097	249,030	123,252	545,578
Accessories	2,364,222	1,002,515	1,174,231	217,916	603,987	354,367	234,187	761,367
Uniforms	407,383	157,326	218,096	25,831	108,188	84,109	38,984	86,519
Costumes	514,342	256,598	218,668	20,830	141,442	56,448	56,552	68,197

	total married couples	married couples, no children	married couples with children				single parent, at least one child <18	single person
			total	oldest child under 6	oldest child 6 to 17	oldest child 18 or older		
GIRLS' (AGED 2 TO 15) APPAREL	**$8,735,054**	**$1,023,375**	**$6,820,428**	**$760,701**	**$5,377,045**	**$618,031**	**$1,593,182**	**$512,328**
Coats and jackets	561,685	54,034	447,054	34,405	362,783	49,693	108,764	29,518
Dresses and suits	786,710	127,419	581,399	76,065	480,601	11,820	154,468	57,001
Shirts, blouses, and sweaters	2,119,909	251,069	1,578,980	162,792	1,267,559	120,213	250,914	126,216
Skirts and pants	1,915,341	178,186	1,566,403	164,990	1,192,475	208,905	413,851	102,805
Shorts and shorts sets	648,773	66,851	532,806	64,688	413,191	55,081	129,971	26,125
Active sportswear	784,372	95,502	617,129	79,252	485,416	41,009	195,552	46,143
Underwear and nightwear	530,708	47,248	421,042	55,235	308,614	57,252	104,565	24,090
Hosiery	372,898	40,965	299,274	31,987	242,407	19,138	63,271	39,358
Accessories	430,762	107,565	292,414	32,756	244,815	8,363	86,508	51,572
Uniforms	226,194	19,603	183,509	21,984	142,796	18,655	42,064	3,732
Costumes	357,702	35,185	300,704	36,493	236,388	27,902	43,254	6,107
CHILDREN UNDER AGE 2	**6,734,379**	**1,093,242**	**4,792,679**	**2,578,943**	**1,756,236**	**409,528**	**773,669**	**571,704**
Coats, jackets, and snowsuits	163,070	36,441	102,617	58,532	32,953	11,097	17,498	27,822
Outerwear including dresses	1,647,065	484,545	973,285	548,226	280,627	144,416	138,790	209,681
Underwear	3,908,418	391,054	2,979,024	1,599,386	1,184,349	150,849	496,019	169,645
Nightwear and loungewear	316,788	79,417	211,522	101,676	77,943	32,003	26,176	60,733
Accessories	698,454	101,785	526,517	270,623	180,554	71,082	95,256	103,483
FOOTWEAR	**20,612,856**	**6,629,570**	**12,039,009**	**1,549,982**	**7,214,836**	**3,253,710**	**3,149,830**	**5,306,496**
Men's	5,844,800	2,347,329	3,004,178	338,828	1,684,211	990,008	541,723	1,682,539
Boys'	2,689,192	43,227	2,365,040	228,744	1,852,236	246,859	1,188,570	154,716
Women's	9,410,128	4,061,834	4,458,532	785,598	1,873,352	1,847,339	979,020	3,207,308
Girls'	2,668,736	177,432	2,211,544	196,867	1,805,028	169,585	440,517	261,932
OTHER APPAREL PRODUCTS, SERVICES	**19,017,226**	**7,897,228**	**9,887,206**	**1,573,670**	**5,657,822**	**2,659,722**	**1,239,523**	**5,302,085**
Material for making clothes	479,858	260,870	171,218	46,826	42,713	84,833	31,146	68,197
Sewing patterns and notions	363,547	155,064	190,084	29,568	98,166	63,202	26,666	137,073
Watches	1,474,059	409,149	1,013,374	256,828	538,683	218,394	67,190	242,932
Jewelry	9,463,900	4,257,863	4,618,031	534,486	2,916,710	1,166,749	392,364	2,021,490
Shoe repair and other shoe services	95,855	50,767	41,161	4,342	20,464	16,404	4,479	27,482
Coin-operated apparel laundry and dry cleaning	1,381,126	395,578	784,917	221,489	388,664	174,892	481,461	1,288,623
Apparel alteration, repair, and tailoring services	427,255	212,114	200,088	24,018	113,003	63,041	12,598	132,662
Clothing rental	222,687	69,364	142,634	8,134	57,179	77,274	4,969	21,375
Watch and jewelry repair	289,318	141,493	137,775	21,215	82,759	33,611	8,889	80,072
Professional laundry, dry cleaning	4,803,841	1,940,944	2,580,564	425,061	1,397,264	758,347	207,940	1,250,623
Clothing storage	16,365	4,021	7,146	1,649	2,408	2,975	1,750	31,554

Note: Total spending figures for total consumer units can be found on Total Spending by Age and Total Spending by Region tables. Spending by type of consumer unit will not add to total because not all types of consumer units are shown. Numbers may not add to category total because of rounding and missing subcategories.
Source: Calculations by New Strategist based on the 2003 Consumer Expenditure Survey

Table 2.16 Apparel: Market shares by household type, 2003

(percentage of total annual spending on apparel, accessories, and related services accounted for by types of consumer units, 2003)

	total married couples	married couples, no children	married couples with children				single parent, at least one child <18	single person
			total	oldest child under 6	oldest child 6 to 17	oldest child 18 or older		
Share of total consumer units	50.7%	21.8%	24.8%	4.8%	13.0%	7.0%	6.1%	29.4%
Share of total before-tax income	68.8	26.8	36.6	6.2	19.8	10.7	3.5	15.6
Share of total spending	65.8	25.6	35.0	6.0	18.9	10.1	4.5	17.0
Share of apparel spending	64.4	21.7	36.7	6.5	20.8	9.4	6.7	15.0
MEN'S APPAREL	**66.3**	**25.7**	**34.7**	**5.4**	**18.1**	**11.3**	**3.7**	**17.1**
Suits	64.8	26.7	32.6	4.7	16.5	11.4	1.1	22.0
Sport coats and tailored jackets	66.3	24.8	38.2	3.1	22.2	12.8	2.4	21.8
Coats and jackets	66.7	32.5	27.2	5.8	12.8	8.7	4.8	14.2
Underwear	62.2	23.5	32.2	4.1	17.3	10.9	2.7	19.6
Hosiery	65.8	20.9	38.6	4.6	16.9	17.6	4.3	12.4
Nightwear	70.7	31.7	34.8	6.3	14.9	13.7	2.9	14.9
Accessories	66.4	22.8	38.8	8.1	19.9	10.8	2.6	20.2
Sweaters and vests	68.9	26.1	37.4	6.2	17.8	13.4	2.9	17.4
Active sportswear	72.3	26.0	39.0	3.5	25.4	10.0	1.8	15.9
Shirts	68.6	26.4	35.5	7.2	16.1	12.3	4.8	13.6
Pants	63.6	26.7	31.4	3.4	17.3	10.8	3.5	19.1
Shorts and shorts sets	62.4	14.3	42.7	8.4	26.1	7.9	6.9	17.0
Uniforms	60.5	23.5	34.6	5.8	17.6	11.2	14.2	13.8
Costumes	75.4	33.6	37.8	3.6	21.0	13.1	1.6	10.8
BOYS' (AGED 2 TO 15) APPAREL	**71.0**	**6.9**	**57.8**	**6.9**	**44.3**	**6.2**	**14.7**	**4.3**
Coats and jackets	72.6	9.2	56.3	6.8	43.2	6.3	9.8	4.0
Sweaters	68.3	14.8	47.6	4.7	38.1	4.7	17.9	2.9
Shirts	75.0	7.5	60.1	7.4	45.4	6.4	14.1	3.2
Underwear	77.5	4.9	67.5	6.5	51.1	9.0	8.6	3.2
Nightwear	62.1	5.5	53.9	12.8	37.1	3.1	26.5	3.4
Hosiery	53.5	6.1	43.4	5.8	35.9	0.8	20.0	5.9
Accessories	64.7	3.8	55.4	8.1	42.7	3.5	22.8	4.0
Suits, sport coats, and vests	73.3	9.7	58.1	5.2	44.2	8.6	9.0	6.2
Pants	69.4	6.3	56.6	5.5	44.9	6.2	15.4	4.9
Shorts and shorts sets	70.9	6.0	58.8	10.3	41.5	7.0	15.6	5.0
Uniforms	72.6	4.7	58.2	5.2	48.0	4.9	12.5	6.7
Active sportswear	76.6	7.4	63.1	5.8	48.8	8.4	10.4	4.6
Costumes	77.8	6.8	61.3	6.5	46.1	8.7	9.7	3.9
WOMEN'S APPAREL	**62.1**	**25.1**	**30.6**	**5.4**	**14.5**	**10.8**	**5.1**	**17.6**
Coats and jackets	58.1	27.1	23.9	3.8	9.1	11.4	3.2	20.9
Dresses	67.8	26.3	29.3	5.4	13.3	10.9	3.5	16.4
Sport coats and tailored jackets	62.2	32.9	25.5	2.8	13.7	9.0	7.6	15.1
Sweaters and vests	63.9	28.3	29.5	5.7	14.8	9.0	3.7	16.2
Shirts, blouses, and tops	61.8	23.8	32.6	4.8	15.6	12.5	5.2	16.5
Skirts	54.5	23.7	25.1	4.1	14.0	6.9	5.6	20.2
Pants	62.7	22.1	33.8	7.6	14.5	11.8	5.2	15.9
Shorts and shorts sets	62.3	20.6	37.0	3.4	21.1	12.6	4.4	13.4
Active sportswear	57.1	24.3	28.1	8.8	13.6	5.6	2.7	25.3
Nightwear	57.3	23.5	26.4	5.2	11.3	10.2	12.8	15.7
Undergarments	63.4	25.5	32.3	5.1	15.9	11.5	5.1	18.6
Hosiery	65.8	28.1	32.8	4.0	16.8	12.1	5.5	16.2
Suits	60.7	27.2	31.0	4.4	16.8	9.7	4.8	21.3
Accessories	62.4	26.5	31.0	5.8	16.0	9.4	6.2	20.1
Uniforms	62.4	24.1	33.4	4.0	16.6	12.9	6.0	13.3
Costumes	69.7	34.8	29.6	2.8	19.2	7.6	7.7	9.2

	total married couples	married couples, no children	married couples with children				single parent, at least one child <18	single person
			total	oldest child under 6	oldest child 6 to 17	oldest child 18 or older		
GIRLS' (AGED 2 TO 15) APPAREL	**71.6%**	**8.4%**	**55.9%**	**6.2%**	**44.1%**	**5.1%**	**13.1%**	**4.2%**
Coats and jackets	71.7	6.9	57.1	4.4	46.3	6.3	13.9	3.8
Dresses and suits	64.6	10.5	47.8	6.3	39.5	1.0	12.7	4.7
Shirts, blouses, and sweaters	75.3	8.9	56.1	5.8	45.0	4.3	8.9	4.5
Skirts and pants	70.7	6.6	57.9	6.1	44.0	7.7	15.3	3.8
Shorts and shorts sets	73.2	7.5	60.1	7.3	46.6	6.2	14.7	2.9
Active sportswear	70.7	8.6	55.6	7.1	43.7	3.7	17.6	4.2
Underwear and nightwear	72.2	6.4	57.3	7.5	42.0	7.8	14.2	3.3
Hosiery	69.4	7.6	55.7	6.0	45.1	3.6	11.8	7.3
Accessories	65.2	16.3	44.2	5.0	37.0	1.3	13.1	7.8
Uniforms	75.1	6.5	61.0	7.3	47.4	6.2	14.0	1.2
Costumes	79.5	7.8	66.8	8.1	52.5	6.2	9.6	1.4
CHILDREN UNDER AGE 2	**71.6**	**11.6**	**51.0**	**27.4**	**18.7**	**4.4**	**8.2**	**6.1**
Coats, jackets, and snowsuits	67.6	15.1	42.6	24.3	13.7	4.6	7.3	11.5
Outerwear including dresses	69.6	20.5	41.1	23.2	11.9	6.1	5.9	8.9
Underwear	73.8	7.4	56.3	30.2	22.4	2.9	9.4	3.2
Nightwear and loungewear	67.5	16.9	45.1	21.7	16.6	6.8	5.6	12.9
Accessories	67.8	9.9	51.1	26.3	17.5	6.9	9.2	10.0
FOOTWEAR	**60.8**	**19.6**	**35.5**	**4.6**	**21.3**	**9.6**	**9.3**	**15.7**
Men's	60.8	24.4	31.2	3.5	17.5	10.3	5.6	17.5
Boys'	59.6	1.0	52.4	5.1	41.0	5.5	26.3	3.4
Women's	58.9	25.4	27.9	4.9	11.7	11.6	6.1	20.1
Girls'	70.1	4.7	58.1	5.2	47.4	4.5	11.6	6.9
OTHER APPAREL PRODUCTS AND SERVICES	**63.8**	**26.5**	**33.2**	**5.3**	**19.0**	**8.9**	**4.2**	**17.8**
Material for making clothes	78.0	42.4	27.8	7.6	7.0	13.8	5.1	11.1
Sewing patterns and notions	63.2	26.9	33.0	5.1	17.0	11.0	4.6	23.8
Watches	74.6	20.7	51.3	13.0	27.3	11.1	3.4	12.3
Jewelry	68.3	30.7	33.3	3.9	21.0	8.4	2.8	14.6
Shoe repair and other shoe services	72.3	38.3	31.0	3.3	15.4	12.4	3.4	20.7
Coin-operated apparel laundry and dry cleaning	32.9	9.4	18.7	5.3	9.3	4.2	11.5	30.7
Apparel alteration, repair, and tailoring services	65.9	32.7	30.9	3.7	17.4	9.7	1.9	20.5
Clothing rental	78.5	24.4	50.3	2.9	20.1	27.2	1.8	7.5
Watch and jewelry repair	69.9	34.2	33.3	5.1	20.0	8.1	2.1	19.3
Professional laundry, dry cleaning	68.1	27.5	36.5	6.0	19.8	10.7	2.9	17.7
Clothing storage	29.6	7.3	12.9	3.0	4.3	5.4	3.2	57.0

Note: Market share for total consumer units is 100.0%. Market shares by type of consumer unit will not add to total because not all types of consumer units are shown.
Source: Calculations by New Strategist based on the 2003 Consumer Expenditure Survey

Table 2.17 Apparel: Average spending by race and Hispanic origin, 2003

(average annual spending of consumer units (CU) on apparel, accessories, and related services, by race and Hispanic origin of consumer unit reference person, 2003)

	total consumer units	race Asian	race black	race white and other	Hispanic origin Hispanic	Hispanic origin non-Hispanic
Number of consumer units (000)	115,356	3,573	13,743	98,041	11,727	103,629
Average number of persons per CU	2.5	2.8	2.6	2.5	3.3	2.4
Average before-tax income of CU	$51,128.00	$60,393.00	$34,485.00	$53,039.00	$37,150.00	$52,797.00
Average spending of CU, total	40,817.33	44,922.85	23,707.56	42,360.25	34,574.75	41,520.78
Apparel, average spending	**1,639.99**	**1,736.25**	**1,601.33**	**1,641.84**	**1,756.46**	**1,625.65**
MEN'S APPAREL	**282.18**	**290.05**	**180.53**	**295.96**	**306.50**	**279.05**
Suits	23.68	21.37	29.84	22.90	20.91	23.99
Sport coats and tailored jackets	10.67	8.72	6.58	11.31	7.56	11.02
Coats and jackets	23.17	7.80	26.81	23.27	18.51	23.76
Underwear	14.51	17.52	12.31	14.70	17.91	14.09
Hosiery	11.61	9.83	8.04	12.17	15.90	11.07
Nightwear	2.02	2.76	1.76	2.03	1.65	2.06
Accessories	22.11	46.08	7.98	23.13	14.89	23.01
Sweaters and vests	11.59	11.13	8.09	12.10	13.06	11.43
Active sportswear	17.97	7.68	12.63	19.11	10.00	18.97
Shirts	61.38	55.15	23.51	66.87	83.94	58.54
Pants	60.98	76.54	36.80	63.72	78.39	58.79
Shorts and shorts sets	15.79	17.59	3.35	17.44	18.84	15.41
Uniforms	2.63	2.29	1.15	2.85	3.34	2.55
Costumes	4.09	5.59	1.69	4.37	1.61	4.37
BOYS' (AGED 2 TO 15) APPAREL	**89.48**	**51.58**	**111.70**	**87.84**	**128.15**	**84.76**
Coats and jackets	6.41	2.79	7.17	6.43	7.59	6.27
Sweaters	2.65	2.57	3.29	2.56	2.80	2.63
Shirts	19.17	3.15	23.79	19.16	29.13	17.92
Underwear	6.30	4.32	8.30	6.10	11.10	5.70
Nightwear	3.51	–	2.12	3.84	9.76	2.72
Hosiery	4.46	3.84	8.58	3.91	8.00	4.01
Accessories	4.54	0.85	5.40	4.57	8.30	4.07
Suits, sport coats, and vests	2.58	4.65	4.53	2.23	2.71	2.57
Pants	21.43	17.47	27.11	20.78	29.56	20.51
Shorts and shorts sets	7.78	5.88	10.43	7.48	8.47	7.71
Uniforms	3.37	2.58	3.88	3.33	5.09	3.18
Active sportswear	4.63	1.31	4.64	4.74	3.60	4.74
Costumes	2.65	2.18	2.48	2.69	2.04	2.72
WOMEN'S APPAREL	**528.63**	**537.77**	**446.40**	**539.68**	**438.08**	**539.80**
Coats and jackets	45.08	19.60	44.85	46.11	30.67	46.89
Dresses	47.94	75.37	59.75	45.23	45.33	48.27
Sport coats and tailored jackets	5.46	11.38	3.76	5.48	4.59	5.56
Sweaters and vests	45.69	47.67	25.80	48.37	24.39	48.36
Shirts, blouses, and tops	101.40	95.25	70.71	105.89	96.34	102.03
Skirts	12.88	5.70	13.83	13.04	13.77	12.77
Pants	88.11	100.65	74.41	89.52	88.01	88.13
Shorts and shorts sets	13.89	3.75	8.94	14.97	16.08	13.62
Active sportswear	26.04	6.00	29.40	26.36	9.66	28.10
Nightwear	26.50	43.52	16.55	27.22	14.65	27.99
Undergarments	31.51	40.81	27.87	31.65	36.59	30.88
Hosiery	17.07	10.55	11.79	18.06	18.26	16.92
Suits	22.18	20.63	26.57	21.62	13.43	23.17
Accessories	32.82	42.64	20.12	34.19	20.73	34.33
Uniforms	5.66	4.67	8.00	5.37	3.68	5.88
Costumes	6.40	9.58	4.04	6.61	1.89	6.91

	total consumer units	race			Hispanic origin	
		Asian	black	white and other	Hispanic	non-Hispanic
GIRLS' (AGED 2 TO 15) APPAREL	$105.80	$71.29	$118.23	$105.36	$126.30	$103.36
Coats and jackets	6.79	7.45	8.94	6.46	7.24	6.73
Dresses and suits	10.55	8.05	20.65	9.25	16.93	9.75
Shirts, blouses, and sweaters	24.42	11.89	19.58	25.58	29.02	23.84
Skirts and pants	23.47	14.44	29.05	23.02	30.56	22.67
Shorts and shorts sets	7.68	1.83	10.43	7.51	7.86	7.66
Active sportswear	9.62	0.19	7.25	10.32	10.05	9.57
Underwear and nightwear	6.37	2.95	7.78	6.30	7.99	6.19
Hosiery	4.66	1.82	5.05	4.72	5.13	4.60
Accessories	5.73	18.03	2.87	5.64	3.97	5.95
Uniforms	2.61	1.86	3.95	2.45	3.80	2.48
Costumes	3.90	2.77	2.67	4.11	3.76	3.91
CHILDREN UNDER AGE 2	81.48	125.45	103.70	76.68	121.26	76.62
Coats, jackets, and snowsuits	2.09	3.49	3.18	1.89	2.99	1.99
Outerwear including dresses	20.51	21.96	20.91	20.40	30.72	19.35
Underwear	45.88	77.04	55.85	43.28	72.92	42.48
Nightwear and loungewear	4.07	3.68	4.83	3.98	4.28	4.05
Accessories	8.93	19.28	18.93	7.14	10.34	8.75
FOOTWEAR	293.92	291.67	439.59	273.81	368.42	284.56
Men's	83.38	87.27	106.23	80.05	121.02	78.65
Boys'	39.12	21.65	75.27	34.80	71.81	35.02
Women's	138.40	174.54	197.15	128.85	129.99	139.46
Girls'	33.02	8.21	60.95	30.11	45.60	31.44
OTHER APPAREL PRODUCTS AND SERVICES	258.49	368.43	201.18	262.50	267.77	257.50
Material for making clothes	5.33	7.11	1.42	5.80	2.84	5.65
Sewing patterns and notions	4.99	5.12	1.49	5.47	3.04	5.24
Watches	17.12	78.73	10.62	15.79	11.83	17.72
Jewelry	120.16	150.70	56.98	127.91	92.26	123.32
Shoe repair and other shoe services	1.15	0.68	0.83	1.21	0.36	1.24
Coin-operated apparel laundry and dry cleaning	36.41	57.41	59.28	32.43	112.22	27.83
Apparel alteration, repair, and tailoring services	5.62	6.03	3.65	5.89	4.30	5.77
Clothing rental	2.46	1.43	1.15	2.68	2.24	2.49
Watch and jewelry repair	3.59	2.02	1.72	3.91	1.84	3.79
Professional laundry, dry cleaning	61.18	59.18	63.76	60.89	36.21	64.00
Clothing storage	0.48	0.02	0.29	0.52	0.64	0.46

Note: Other races include Native Americans and Pacific Islanders. Subcategories may not add to total because some are not shown. (–) means sample is too small to make a reliable estimate.
Source: Bureau of Labor Statistics, unpublished data from the 2003 Consumer Expenditure Survey

Table 2.18 Apparel: Indexed spending by race and Hispanic origin, 2003

(indexed average annual spending of consumer units (CU) on apparel, accessories, and related services, by race and Hispanic origin of consumer unit reference person, 2003; index definition: an index of 100 is the average for all consumer units; an index of 132 means that spending by consumer units in that group is 32 percent above the average for all consumer units; an index of 68 indicates spending that is 32 percent below the average for all consumer units)

	total consumer units	race Asian	race black	race white and other	Hispanic origin Hispanic	Hispanic origin non-Hispanic
Average spending of CU, total	$40,817	$44,923	$28,708	$42,360	$34,575	$41,521
Average spending of CU, index	100	110	70	104	85	102
Apparel, spending index	**100**	**106**	**98**	**100**	**107**	**99**
MEN'S APPAREL	**100**	**103**	**64**	**105**	**109**	**99**
Suits	100	90	126	97	88	101
Sport coats and tailored jackets	100	82	62	106	71	103
Coats and jackets	100	34	116	100	80	103
Underwear	100	121	85	101	123	97
Hosiery	100	85	69	105	137	95
Nightwear	100	137	87	100	82	102
Accessories	100	208	36	105	67	104
Sweaters and vests	100	96	70	104	113	99
Active sportswear	100	43	70	106	56	106
Shirts	100	90	38	109	137	95
Pants	100	126	60	104	129	96
Shorts and shorts sets	100	111	21	110	119	98
Uniforms	100	87	44	108	127	97
Costumes	100	137	41	107	39	107
BOYS' (AGED 2 TO 15) APPAREL	**100**	**58**	**125**	**98**	**143**	**95**
Coats and jackets	100	44	112	100	118	98
Sweaters	100	97	124	97	106	99
Shirts	100	16	124	100	152	93
Underwear	100	69	132	97	176	90
Nightwear	100	–	60	109	278	77
Hosiery	100	86	192	88	179	90
Accessories	100	19	119	101	183	90
Suits, sport coats, and vests	100	180	176	86	105	100
Pants	100	82	127	97	138	96
Shorts and shorts sets	100	76	134	96	109	99
Uniforms	100	77	115	99	151	94
Active sportswear	100	28	100	102	78	102
Costumes	100	82	94	102	77	103
WOMEN'S APPAREL	**100**	**102**	**84**	**102**	**83**	**102**
Coats and jackets	100	43	99	102	68	104
Dresses	100	157	125	94	95	101
Sport coats and tailored jackets	100	208	69	100	84	102
Sweaters and vests	100	104	56	106	53	106
Shirts, blouses, and tops	100	94	70	104	95	101
Skirts	100	44	107	101	107	99
Pants	100	114	84	102	100	100
Shorts and shorts sets	100	27	64	108	116	98
Active sportswear	100	23	113	101	37	108
Nightwear	100	164	62	103	55	106
Undergarments	100	130	88	100	116	98
Hosiery	100	62	69	106	107	99
Suits	100	93	120	97	61	104
Accessories	100	130	61	104	63	105
Uniforms	100	83	141	95	65	104
Costumes	100	150	63	103	30	108

	total consumer units	race			Hispanic origin	
		Asian	black	white and other	Hispanic	non-Hispanic
GIRLS' (AGED 2 TO 15) APPAREL	100	67	112	100	119	98
Coats and jackets	100	110	132	95	107	99
Dresses and suits	100	76	196	88	160	92
Shirts, blouses, and sweaters	100	49	80	105	119	98
Skirts and pants	100	62	124	98	130	97
Shorts and shorts sets	100	24	136	98	102	100
Active sportswear	100	2	75	107	104	99
Underwear and nightwear	100	46	122	99	125	97
Hosiery	100	39	108	101	110	99
Accessories	100	315	50	98	69	104
Uniforms	100	71	151	94	146	95
Costumes	100	71	68	105	96	100
CHILDREN UNDER AGE 2	100	154	127	94	149	94
Coats, jackets, and snowsuits	100	167	152	90	143	95
Outerwear including dresses	100	107	102	99	150	94
Underwear	100	168	122	94	159	93
Nightwear and loungewear	100	50	119	98	105	100
Accessories	100	215	212	80	116	98
FOOTWEAR	100	99	150	93	125	97
Men's	100	105	127	96	145	94
Boys'	100	55	192	89	184	90
Women's	100	126	142	93	94	101
Girls'	100	25	185	91	138	95
OTHER APPAREL PRODUCTS AND SERVICES	100	143	78	102	104	100
Material for making clothes	100	133	27	109	53	106
Sewing patterns and notions	100	103	30	110	61	105
Watches	100	460	62	92	69	104
Jewelry	100	125	47	106	77	103
Shoe repair and other shoe services	100	59	72	105	31	108
Coin-operated apparel laundry and dry cleaning	100	153	163	89	308	76
Apparel alteration, repair, and tailoring services	100	107	65	105	77	103
Clothing rental	100	58	47	109	91	101
Watch and jewelry repair	100	56	48	109	51	106
Professional laundry, dry cleaning	100	97	104	100	59	105
Clothing storage	100	4	60	108	133	96

Note: Other races include Native Americans and Pacific Islanders. (–) means sample is too small to make a reliable estimate.
Source: Calculations by New Strategist based on the 2003 Consumer Expenditure Survey

Table 2.19 Apparel: Total spending by race and Hispanic origin, 2003

(total annual spending on apparel, accessories, and related services, by race and Hispanic origin groups, 2003; numbers in thousands)

	total consumer units	race			Hispanic origin	
		Asian	black	white and other	Hispanic	non-Hispanic
Number of consumer units	115,356	3,573	13,743	98,041	11,727	103629
Total spending of all consumer units	$4,708,523,919	$160,509,343	$394,527,997	$4,153,041,270	$405,458,093	4,302,756,911
Apparel, total spending	189,182,686	6,203,621	22,007,078	160,967,635	20,598,006	168,464,484
MEN'S APPAREL	**32,551,156**	**1,036,349**	**2,481,024**	**29,016,214**	**3,594,326**	**28,917,672**
Suits	2,731,630	76,355	410,091	2,245,139	245,212	2,486,060
Sport coats and tailored jackets	1,230,849	31,157	90,429	1,108,844	88,656	1,141,992
Coats and jackets	2,672,799	27,869	368,450	2,281,414	217,067	2,462,225
Underwear	1,673,816	62,599	69,176	1,441,203	210,031	1,460,133
Hosiery	1,339,283	35,123	10,494	1,193,159	186,459	1,147,173
Nightwear	233,019	9,861	24,188	199,023	19,350	213,476
Accessories	2,550,521	164,644	209,669	2,267,688	174,615	2,384,503
Sweaters and vests	1,336,976	39,767	111,181	1,186,296	153,155	1,184,479
Active sportswear	2,072,947	27,441	173,574	1,873,564	117,270	1,965,842
Shirts	7,080,551	197,051	323,098	6,556,002	984,364	6,066,442
Pants	7,034,409	273,477	505,742	6,247,173	919,280	6,092,349
Shorts and shorts sets	1,821,471	62,849	46,039	1,709,835	220,937	1,596,923
Uniforms	303,386	8,182	15,804	279,417	39,168	264,254
Costumes	471,806	19,973	23,226	428,439	18,880	452,859
BOYS' (AGED 2 TO 15) APPAREL	**10,322,055**	**184,295**	**1,535,093**	**8,611,921**	**1,502,815**	**8,783,594**
Coats and jackets	739,432	9,969	98,537	630,404	89,008	649,754
Sweaters	305,693	9,183	45,214	250,985	32,836	272,544
Shirts	2,211,375	11,255	326,946	1,878,466	341,608	1,857,032
Underwear	726,743	15,435	114,067	598,050	130,170	590,685
Nightwear	404,900	–	29,135	375,764	114,456	281,871
Hosiery	514,488	13,720	117,915	383,340	93,816	415,552
Accessories	523,716	3,037	74,212	448,047	97,334	421,770
Suits, sport coats, and vests	297,618	16,614	62,256	218,631	31,780	266,327
Pants	2,472,079	62,420	372,573	2,037,292	346,650	2,125,431
Shorts and shorts sets	897,470	21,009	143,339	733,347	99,328	798,980
Uniforms	388,750	9,218	53,323	326,477	59,690	329,540
Active sportswear	534,098	4,681	63,768	464,714	42,217	491,201
Costumes	305,693	7,789	34,083	263,730	23,923	281,871
WOMEN'S APPAREL	**60,980,642**	**1,921,452**	**5,134,875**	**52,910,767**	**5,137,364**	**55,938,934**
Coats and jackets	5,200,248	70,031	616,374	4,520,671	359,667	4,859,164
Dresses	5,530,167	269,297	821,144	4,434,394	531,585	5,002,172
Sport coats and tailored jackets	629,844	40,661	51,674	537,265	53,827	576,177
Sweaters and vests	5,270,616	170,325	354,569	4,742,243	286,022	5,011,498
Shirts, blouses, and tops	11,697,098	340,328	971,768	10,381,561	1,129,779	10,573,267
Skirts	1,485,785	20,366	190,066	1,278,455	161,481	1,323,342
Pants	10,164,017	359,622	1,022,617	8,776,630	1,032,093	9,132,824
Shorts and shorts sets	1,602,295	13,399	122,862	1,467,674	188,570	1,411,427
Active sportswear	3,003,870	21,438	404,044	2,584,361	113,283	2,911,975
Nightwear	3,056,934	155,497	227,447	2,668,676	171,801	2,900,576
Undergarments	3,634,868	145,814	383,017	3,102,998	429,091	3,200,064
Hosiery	1,969,127	37,695	162,030	1,770,620	214,135	1,753,403
Suits	2,558,596	73,711	365,152	2,119,646	157,494	2,401,084
Accessories	3,785,984	152,353	276,509	3,352,022	243,101	3,557,584
Uniforms	652,915	16,686	109,944	526,480	43,155	609,339
Costumes	738,278	34,229	55,522	648,051	22,164	716,076

	total consumer units	race			Hispanic origin	
		Asian	black	white and other	Hispanic	non-Hispanic
GIRLS' (AGED 2 TO 15) APPAREL	**$12,204,665**	**$254,719**	**$1,624,835**	**$10,329,600**	**$1,481,120**	**$10,711,093**
Coats and jackets	783,267	26,619	122,862	633,345	84,903	697,423
Dresses and suits	1,217,006	28,798	283,793	906,879	198,538	1,010,383
Shirts, blouses, and sweaters	2,816,994	42,483	269,088	2,507,889	340,318	2,470,515
Skirts and pants	2,707,405	51,594	399,234	2,256,904	358,377	2,349,269
Shorts and shorts sets	885,934	6,539	143,339	736,288	92,174	793,798
Active sportswear	1,109,725	679	99,637	1,011,783	117,856	991,730
Underwear and nightwear	734,818	10,540	106,921	617,658	93,699	641,464
Hosiery	537,559	6,503	69,402	462,754	60,160	476,693
Accessories	660,990	64,421	39,442	552,951	46,556	616,593
Uniforms	301,079	6,646	54,285	240,200	44,563	257,000
Costumes	449,888	9,897	36,694	402,949	44,094	405,189
CHILDREN UNDER AGE 2	**9,399,207**	**448,233**	**1,425,149**	**7,517,784**	**1,422,016**	**7,940,054**
Coats, jackets, and snowsuits	241,094	12,470	43,703	185,297	35,064	206,222
Outerwear including dresses	2,365,952	78,463	287,366	2,000,036	360,253	2,005,221
Underwear	5,292,533	275,264	767,547	4,243,214	855,133	4,402,160
Nightwear and loungewear	469,499	13,149	65,379	390,203	50,192	419,697
Accessories	1,030,129	68,887	260,155	700,013	121,257	906,754
FOOTWEAR	**33,905,436**	**1,042,137**	**6,041,285**	**26,844,606**	**4,320,461**	**29,488,668**
Men's	9,618,383	311,816	1,459,919	7,848,182	1,419,202	8,150,421
Boys'	4,512,727	77,355	1,034,436	3,411,827	842,116	3,629,088
Women's	15,965,270	623,631	2,709,432	12,632,583	1,524,393	14,452,100
Girls'	3,809,055	29,334	837,636	2,952,015	534,751	3,258,096
OTHER APPAREL PRODUCTS AND SERVICES	**29,818,372**	**1,316,400**	**2,764,817**	**25,735,763**	**3,140,139**	**26,684,468**
Material for making clothes	614,847	25,404	19,515	568,638	33,305	585,504
Sewing patterns and notions	575,626	18,294	20,477	536,284	35,650	543,016
Watches	1,974,895	281,302	145,951	1,548,067	138,730	1,836,306
Jewelry	13,861,177	538,451	783,076	12,540,424	1,081,933	12,779,528
Shoe repair and other shoe services	132,659	2,430	11,407	118,630	4,222	128,500
Coin-operated apparel laundry and dry cleaning	4,200,112	205,126	814,635	3,179,470	1,316,004	2,883,995
Apparel alteration, repair, and tailoring services	648,301	21,545	50,162	577,461	50,426	597,939
Clothing rental	283,776	5,109	15,804	262,750	26,268	258,036
Watch and jewelry repair	414,128	7,217	23,638	383,340	21,578	392,754
Professional laundry, dry cleaning	7,057,480	211,450	876,254	5,969,716	424,635	6,632,256
Clothing storage	55,371	71	3,985	50,981	7,505	47,669

Note: Other races include Native Americans and Pacific Islanders. Numbers may not add to total because of rounding and missing subcategories. (–) means sample is too small to make a reliable estimate.
Source: Calculations by New Strategist based on the 2003 Consumer Expenditure Survey

Table 2.20 Apparel: Market shares by race and Hispanic origin, 2003

(percentage of total annual spending on apparel, accessories, and related services accounted for by race and Hispanic origin groups, 2003)

	total consumer units	race			Hispanic origin	
		Asian	black	white and other	Hispanic	non-Hispanic
Share of total consumer units	100.0%	3.1%	11.9%	85.0%	10.2%	89.8%
Share of total before-tax income	100.0	3.7	8.0	88.2	7.4	92.8
Share of total spending	100.0	3.4	8.4	88.2	8.6	91.4
Share of apparel spending	100.0	3.3	11.6	85.1	10.9	89.0
MEN'S APPAREL	100.0	3.2	7.6	89.1	11.0	88.8
Suits	100.0	2.8	15.0	82.2	9.0	91.0
Sport coats and tailored jackets	100.0	2.5	7.3	90.1	7.2	92.8
Coats and jackets	100.0	1.0	13.8	85.4	8.1	92.1
Underwear	100.0	3.7	10.1	86.1	12.5	87.2
Hosiery	100.0	2.6	8.3	89.1	13.9	85.7
Nightwear	100.0	4.2	10.4	85.4	8.3	91.6
Accessories	100.0	6.5	4.3	88.9	6.8	93.5
Sweaters and vests	100.0	3.0	8.3	88.7	11.5	88.6
Active sportswear	100.0	1.3	8.4	90.4	5.7	94.8
Shirts	100.0	2.8	4.6	92.6	13.9	85.7
Pants	100.0	3.9	7.2	88.8	13.1	86.6
Shorts and shorts sets	100.0	3.5	2.5	93.9	12.1	87.7
Uniforms	100.0	2.7	5.2	92.1	12.9	87.1
Costumes	100.0	4.2	4.9	90.8	4.0	96.0
BOYS' (AGED 2 TO 15) APPAREL	100.0	1.8	14.9	83.4	14.6	85.1
Coats and jackets	100.0	1.3	13.3	85.3	12.0	87.9
Sweaters	100.0	3.0	14.8	82.1	10.7	89.2
Shirts	100.0	0.5	14.8	84.9	15.4	84.0
Underwear	100.0	2.1	15.7	82.3	17.9	81.3
Nightwear	100.0	–	7.2	92.8	28.3	69.6
Hosiery	100.0	2.7	22.9	74.5	18.2	80.8
Accessories	100.0	0.6	14.2	85.6	18.6	80.5
Suits, sport coats, and vests	100.0	5.6	20.9	73.5	10.7	89.5
Pants	100.0	2.5	15.1	82.4	14.0	86.0
Shorts and shorts sets	100.0	2.3	16.0	81.7	11.1	89.0
Uniforms	100.0	2.4	13.7	84.0	15.4	84.8
Active sportswear	100.0	0.9	11.9	87.0	7.9	92.0
Costumes	100.0	2.5	11.1	86.3	7.8	92.2
WOMEN'S APPAREL	100.0	3.2	10.1	86.8	8.4	91.7
Coats and jackets	100.0	1.3	11.9	86.9	6.9	93.4
Dresses	100.0	4.9	14.8	80.2	9.6	90.5
Sport coats and tailored jackets	100.0	6.5	8.2	85.3	8.5	91.5
Sweaters and vests	100.0	3.2	6.7	90.0	5.4	95.1
Shirts, blouses, and tops	100.0	2.9	8.3	88.8	9.7	90.4
Skirts	100.0	1.4	12.8	86.0	10.9	89.1
Pants	100.0	3.5	10.1	86.4	10.2	89.9
Shorts and shorts sets	100.0	0.8	7.7	91.6	11.8	88.1
Active sportswear	100.0	0.7	13.5	86.0	3.8	96.9
Nightwear	100.0	5.1	7.4	87.3	5.6	94.9
Undergarments	100.0	4.0	10.5	85.4	11.8	88.0
Hosiery	100.0	1.9	8.2	89.9	10.9	89.0
Suits	100.0	2.9	14.3	82.8	6.2	93.8
Accessories	100.0	4.0	7.3	88.5	6.4	94.0
Uniforms	100.0	2.6	16.8	80.6	6.6	93.3
Costumes	100.0	4.6	7.5	87.8	3.0	97.0

	total consumer units	race			Hispanic origin	
		Asian	black	white and other	Hispanic	
GIRLS' (AGED 2 TO 15) APPAREL	**100.0%**	**2.1%**	**13.3%**	**84.6%**	**12.1%**	**87.8%**
Coats and jackets	100.0	3.4	15.7	80.9	10.8	89.0
Dresses and suits	100.0	2.4	23.3	74.5	16.3	83.0
Shirts, blouses, and sweaters	100.0	1.5	9.6	89.0	12.1	87.7
Skirts and pants	100.0	1.9	14.7	83.4	13.2	86.8
Shorts and shorts sets	100.0	0.7	16.2	83.1	10.4	89.6
Active sportswear	100.0	0.1	9.0	91.2	10.6	89.4
Underwear and nightwear	100.0	1.4	14.6	84.1	12.8	87.3
Hosiery	100.0	1.2	12.9	86.1	11.2	88.7
Accessories	100.0	9.7	6.0	83.7	7.0	93.3
Uniforms	100.0	2.2	18.0	79.8	14.8	85.4
Costumes	100.0	2.2	8.2	89.6	9.8	90.1
CHILDREN UNDER AGE 2	**100.0**	**4.8**	**15.2**	**80.0**	**15.1**	**84.5**
Coats, jackets, and snowsuits	100.0	5.2	18.1	76.9	14.5	85.5
Outerwear including dresses	100.0	3.3	12.1	84.5	15.2	84.8
Underwear	100.0	5.2	14.5	80.2	16.2	83.2
Nightwear and loungewear	100.0	2.8	14.1	83.1	10.7	89.4
Accessories	100.0	6.7	25.3	68.0	11.8	88.0
FOOTWEAR	**100.0**	**3.1**	**17.8**	**79.2**	**12.7**	**87.0**
Men's	100.0	3.2	15.2	81.6	14.8	84.7
Boys'	100.0	1.7	22.9	75.6	18.7	80.4
Women's	100.0	3.9	17.0	79.1	9.5	90.5
Girls'	100.0	0.8	22.0	77.5	14.0	85.5
OTHER APPAREL PRODUCTS AND SERVICES	**100.0**	**4.4**	**9.3**	**86.3**	**10.5**	**89.5**
Material for making clothes	100.0	4.1	3.2	92.5	5.4	95.2
Sewing patterns and notions	100.0	3.2	3.6	93.2	6.2	94.3
Watches	100.0	14.2	7.4	78.4	7.0	93.0
Jewelry	100.0	3.9	5.6	90.5	7.8	92.2
Shoe repair and other shoe services	100.0	1.8	8.6	89.4	3.2	96.9
Coin-operated apparel laundry and dry cleaning	100.0	4.9	19.4	75.7	31.3	68.7
Apparel alteration, repair, and tailoring services	100.0	3.3	7.7	89.1	7.8	92.2
Clothing rental	100.0	1.8	5.6	92.6	9.3	90.9
Watch and jewelry repair	100.0	1.7	5.7	92.6	5.2	94.8
Professional laundry, dry cleaning	100.0	3.0	12.4	84.6	6.0	94.0
Clothing storage	100.0	0.1	7.2	92.1	13.6	86.1

Note: Other races include Native Americans and Pacific Islanders. Numbers may not add to total because of rounding. (–) means sample is too small to make a reliable estimate.
Source: Calculations by New Strategist based on the 2003 Consumer Expenditure Survey

Table 2.21 Apparel: Average spending by region, 2003

(average annual spending of consumer units (CU) on apparel, accessories, and related services, by region in which consumer unit lives, 2003)

	total consumer units	Northeast	Midwest	South	West
Number of consumer units (000)	115,356	22,182	26,438	41,325	25,412
Average number of persons per CU	2.5	2.4	2.5	2.5	2.6
Average before-tax income of CU	$48,596.00	$54,219.00	$49,591.00	$44,461.00	$49,667.00
Average spending of CU, total	40,817.33	42,162.29	40,280.39	37,624.55	45,380.67
Apparel, average spending	**1,639.99**	**1,859.49**	**1,562.84**	**1,450.63**	**1,833.53**
MEN'S APPAREL	**282.18**	**338.74**	**280.48**	**219.29**	**335.29**
Suits	23.68	38.19	21.89	19.16	20.20
Sport coats and tailored jackets	10.67	15.97	7.53	10.98	8.78
Coats and jackets	23.17	31.23	30.08	10.46	29.03
Underwear	14.51	16.04	14.74	11.09	18.40
Hosiery	11.61	13.47	10.73	9.43	14.40
Nightwear	2.02	2.45	2.11	1.48	2.42
Accessories	22.11	17.53	21.37	18.56	32.56
Sweaters and vests	11.59	19.39	10.95	8.70	10.14
Active sportswear	17.97	21.66	20.04	11.42	22.98
Shirts	61.38	67.77	60.12	49.13	76.69
Pants	60.98	74.22	58.12	50.65	68.95
Shorts and shorts sets	15.79	17.28	11.46	14.05	21.90
Uniforms	2.63	1.60	2.35	3.20	2.90
Costumes	4.09	1.94	8.97	0.98	5.93
BOYS' (AGED 2 TO 15) APPAREL	**89.48**	**87.16**	**88.41**	**84.04**	**101.32**
Coats and jackets	6.41	8.81	7.09	4.99	5.90
Sweaters	2.65	4.36	2.31	2.38	1.96
Shirts	19.17	16.45	19.14	15.97	26.70
Underwear	6.30	4.66	6.71	4.85	9.60
Nightwear	3.51	4.68	2.80	2.60	4.70
Hosiery	4.46	4.04	3.78	3.49	7.11
Accessories	4.54	5.83	4.31	3.84	4.80
Suits, sport coats, and vests	2.58	3.93	2.27	2.03	2.61
Pants	21.43	18.85	20.14	22.19	23.80
Shorts and shorts sets	7.78	5.67	8.40	9.35	6.45
Uniforms	3.37	2.34	3.12	4.57	2.57
Active sportswear	4.63	5.67	2.73	6.48	2.67
Costumes	2.65	1.87	5.62	1.29	2.46
WOMEN'S APPAREL	**528.63**	**591.58**	**497.15**	**458.43**	**619.69**
Coats and jackets	45.08	60.83	37.42	35.33	55.09
Dresses	47.94	49.68	48.47	49.96	42.62
Sport coats and tailored jackets	5.46	5.68	5.35	3.68	8.26
Sweaters and vests	45.69	61.38	49.24	29.58	53.88
Shirts, blouses, and tops	101.40	106.22	96.63	88.70	122.58
Skirts	12.88	16.39	13.54	10.84	12.38
Pants	88.11	86.00	76.41	73.78	125.42
Shorts and shorts sets	13.89	18.82	13.00	12.76	12.35
Active sportswear	26.04	31.32	24.56	25.50	23.89
Nightwear	26.50	32.79	23.82	25.16	26.02
Undergarments	31.51	27.83	26.44	31.04	40.93
Hosiery	17.07	21.13	17.49	13.23	19.19
Suits	22.18	29.14	18.04	22.65	19.65
Accessories	32.82	39.32	27.29	26.72	42.80
Uniforms	5.66	3.68	5.29	7.84	4.22
Costumes	6.40	1.39	14.15	1.66	10.42

	total consumer units	Northeast	Midwest	South	West
GIRLS' (AGED 2 TO 15) APPAREL	**$105.80**	**$117.78**	**$114.86**	**$89.31**	**$111.98**
Coats and jackets	6.79	9.95	6.57	5.58	6.20
Dresses and suits	10.55	11.72	11.95	6.68	14.22
Shirts, blouses, and sweaters	24.42	27.74	32.15	17.72	23.91
Skirts and pants	23.47	25.74	21.87	23.41	23.26
Shorts and shorts sets	7.68	5.33	7.24	10.22	6.06
Active sportswear	9.62	11.08	9.87	8.32	10.17
Underwear and nightwear	6.37	5.57	6.24	5.85	8.04
Hosiery	4.66	5.49	5.57	2.93	5.73
Accessories	5.73	8.55	4.59	3.58	7.91
Uniforms	2.61	3.16	2.36	2.88	1.95
Costumes	3.90	3.45	6.45	2.13	4.52
CHILDREN UNDER AGE 2	**81.48**	**75.85**	**91.74**	**74.35**	**86.93**
Coats, jackets, and snowsuits	2.09	3.18	2.49	1.33	1.96
Outerwear including dresses	20.51	19.82	22.39	19.29	21.12
Underwear	45.88	40.17	49.68	43.07	51.28
Nightwear and loungewear	4.07	5.81	3.80	3.55	3.70
Accessories	8.93	6.88	13.38	7.11	8.87
FOOTWEAR	**293.92**	**357.30**	**248.56**	**282.79**	**304.90**
Men's	83.38	104.26	62.16	79.69	93.76
Boys'	39.12	43.49	35.12	36.31	44.10
Women's	138.40	171.73	116.53	137.32	134.45
Girls'	33.02	37.82	34.75	29.48	32.60
OTHER APPAREL PRODUCTS AND SERVICES	**258.49**	**291.08**	**241.65**	**242.42**	**273.43**
Material for making clothes	5.33	6.55	7.50	2.86	5.89
Sewing patterns and notions	4.99	5.91	7.31	2.74	5.30
Watches	17.12	13.95	11.17	22.83	16.80
Jewelry	120.16	132.21	126.46	107.55	123.60
Shoe repair and other shoe services	1.15	1.45	1.02	0.98	1.30
Coin-operated apparel laundry and dry cleaning	36.41	47.02	33.02	28.08	44.20
Apparel alteration, repair, and tailoring services	5.62	6.81	5.04	4.39	7.19
Clothing rental	2.46	2.41	2.39	2.41	2.67
Watch and jewelry repair	3.59	4.21	2.74	2.71	5.37
Professional laundry, dry cleaning	61.18	70.40	44.71	67.41	60.12
Clothing storage	0.48	0.17	0.23	0.45	1.00

Note: Subcategories may not add to total because some are not shown.
Source: Bureau of Labor Statistics, unpublished data from the 2003 Consumer Expenditure Survey

Table 2.22 Apparel: Indexed spending by region, 2003

(indexed average annual spending of consumer units (CU) on apparel, accessories, and related services, by region in which consumer unit lives, 2003; index definition: an index of 100 is the average for all consumer units; an index of 132 means that spending by consumer units in that group is 32 percent above the average for all consumer units; an index of 68 indicates spending that is 32 percent below the average for all consumer units)

	total consumer units	Northeast	Midwest	South	West
Average spending of CU, total	$40,817	$42,162	$40,280	$37,625	$45,381
Average spending of CU, index	100	103	99	92	111
Apparel, spending index	**100**	**113**	**95**	**88**	**112**
MEN'S APPAREL	**100**	**120**	**99**	**78**	**119**
Suits	100	161	92	81	85
Sport coats and tailored jackets	100	150	71	103	82
Coats and jackets	100	135	130	45	125
Underwear	100	111	102	76	127
Hosiery	100	116	92	81	124
Nightwear	100	121	104	73	120
Accessories	100	79	97	84	147
Sweaters and vests	100	167	94	75	87
Active sportswear	100	121	112	64	128
Shirts	100	110	98	80	125
Pants	100	122	95	83	113
Shorts and shorts sets	100	109	73	89	139
Uniforms	100	61	89	122	110
Costumes	100	47	219	24	145
BOYS' (AGED 2 TO 15) APPAREL	**100**	**97**	**99**	**94**	**113**
Coats and jackets	100	137	111	78	92
Sweaters	100	165	87	90	74
Shirts	100	86	100	83	139
Underwear	100	74	107	77	152
Nightwear	100	133	80	74	134
Hosiery	100	91	85	78	159
Accessories	100	128	95	85	106
Suits, sport coats, and vests	100	152	88	79	101
Pants	100	88	94	104	111
Shorts and shorts sets	100	73	108	120	83
Uniforms	100	69	93	136	76
Active sportswear	100	122	59	140	58
Costumes	100	71	212	49	93
WOMEN'S APPAREL	**100**	**112**	**94**	**87**	**117**
Coats and jackets	100	135	83	78	122
Dresses	100	104	101	104	89
Sport coats and tailored jackets	100	104	98	67	151
Sweaters and vests	100	134	108	65	118
Shirts, blouses, and tops	100	105	95	87	121
Skirts	100	127	105	84	96
Pants	100	98	87	84	142
Shorts and shorts sets	100	135	94	92	89
Active sportswear	100	120	94	98	92
Nightwear	100	124	90	95	98
Undergarments	100	88	84	99	130
Hosiery	100	124	102	78	112
Suits	100	131	81	102	89
Accessories	100	120	83	81	130
Uniforms	100	65	93	139	75
Costumes	100	22	221	26	163

	total consumer units	Northeast	Midwest	South	West
GIRLS' (AGED 2 TO 15) APPAREL	**100**	**111**	**109**	**84**	**106**
Coats and jackets	100	147	97	82	91
Dresses and suits	100	111	113	63	135
Shirts, blouses, and sweaters	100	114	132	73	98
Skirts and pants	100	110	93	100	99
Shorts and shorts sets	100	69	94	133	79
Active sportswear	100	115	103	86	106
Underwear and nightwear	100	37	98	92	126
Hosiery	100	118	120	63	123
Accessories	100	149	80	62	138
Uniforms	100	121	90	110	75
Costumes	100	58	165	55	116
CHILDREN UNDER AGE 2	**100**	**93**	**113**	**91**	**107**
Coats, jackets, and snowsuits	100	152	119	64	94
Outerwear including dresses	100	97	109	94	103
Underwear	100	88	108	94	112
Nightwear and loungewear	100	143	93	87	91
Accessories	100	77	150	80	99
FOOTWEAR	**100**	**122**	**85**	**96**	**104**
Men's	100	125	75	96	112
Boys'	100	111	90	93	113
Women's	100	124	84	99	97
Girls'	100	115	105	89	99
OTHER APPAREL PRODUCTS AND SERVICES	**100**	**113**	**93**	**94**	**106**
Material for making clothes	100	123	141	54	111
Sewing patterns and notions	100	118	146	55	106
Watches	100	81	65	133	98
Jewelry	100	110	105	90	103
Shoe repair and other shoe services	100	126	89	85	113
Coin-operated apparel laundry and dry cleaning	100	129	91	77	121
Apparel alteration, repair, and tailoring services	100	121	90	78	128
Clothing rental	100	98	97	98	109
Watch and jewelry repair	100	117	76	75	150
Professional laundry, dry cleaning	100	115	73	110	98
Clothing storage	100	35	58	94	208

Source: Calculations by New Strategist based on the 2003 Consumer Expenditure Survey

Table 2.23 Apparel: Total spending by region, 2003

(total annual spending on apparel, accessories, and related services, by region in which consumer units live, 2003; numbers in thousands)

	total consumer units	Northeast	Midwest	South	West
Number of consumer units	115,356	22,182	26,438	41,325	25,412
Total spending of all consumer units	$4,708,523,919	$935,243,917	$1,064,932,951	$1,554,834,529	$1,153,213,586
Apparel, total spending	189,182,686	41,247,207	41,318,364	59,947,285	46,593,664
MEN'S APPAREL	32,551,156	7,513,931	7,415,330	9,062,159	8,520,389
Suits	2,731,630	847,131	578,728	791,787	513,322
Sport coats and tailored jackets	1,230,849	354,247	199,078	453,749	223,117
Coats and jackets	2,672,799	692,744	795,255	432,260	737,710
Underwear	1,673,816	355,799	389,696	458,294	467,581
Hosiery	1,339,283	298,792	283,680	389,695	365,933
Nightwear	233,019	54,346	55,784	61,161	61,497
Accessories	2,550,521	388,850	564,980	766,992	827,415
Sweaters and vests	1,336,976	430,109	289,496	359,528	257,678
Active sportswear	2,072,947	480,462	529,818	471,932	583,968
Shirts	7,080,551	1,503,274	1,589,453	2,030,297	1,948,846
Pants	7,034,409	1,646,348	1,536,577	2,093,111	1,752,157
Shorts and shorts sets	1,821,471	383,305	302,979	580,616	556,523
Uniforms	303,386	35,491	62,129	132,240	73,695
Costumes	471,806	43,033	237,149	40,499	150,693
BOYS' (AGED 2 TO 15) APPAREL	10,322,055	1,933,383	2,337,384	3,472,953	2,574,744
Coats and jackets	739,432	195,423	187,445	206,212	149,931
Sweaters	305,693	96,714	61,072	98,354	49,808
Shirts	2,211,375	364,894	506,023	659,960	678,500
Underwear	726,743	103,368	177,399	200,426	243,955
Nightwear	404,900	103,812	74,026	107,445	119,436
Hosiery	514,488	89,615	99,936	144,224	180,679
Accessories	523,716	129,321	113,948	158,688	121,978
Suits, sport coats, and vests	297,618	87,175	60,014	83,890	66,325
Pants	2,472,079	418,131	532,461	917,002	604,806
Shorts and shorts sets	897,470	125,772	222,079	386,389	163,907
Uniforms	388,750	51,906	82,487	188,855	65,309
Active sportswear	534,098	125,772	72,176	267,786	67,850
Costumes	305,693	41,480	148,582	53,309	62,514
WOMEN'S APPAREL	60,980,642	13,122,428	13,143,652	18,944,620	15,747,562
Coats and jackets	5,200,248	1,349,331	989,310	1,460,012	1,399,947
Dresses	5,530,167	1,102,002	1,281,450	2,064,597	1,083,059
Sport coats and tailored jackets	629,844	125,994	141,443	152,076	209,903
Sweaters and vests	5,270,616	1,361,531	1,301,807	1,222,394	1,369,199
Shirts, blouses, and tops	11,697,098	2,356,172	2,554,704	3,665,528	3,115,003
Skirts	1,485,785	363,563	357,971	447,963	314,601
Pants	10,164,017	1,907,652	2,020,128	3,048,959	3,187,173
Shorts and shorts sets	1,602,295	417,465	343,694	527,307	313,838
Active sportswear	3,003,870	694,740	649,317	1,053,788	607,093
Nightwear	3,056,934	727,348	629,753	1,039,737	661,220
Undergarments	3,634,868	617,325	699,021	1,282,728	1,040,113
Hosiery	1,969,127	468,706	462,401	546,730	487,656
Suits	2,558,596	646,383	476,942	936,011	499,346
Accessories	3,785,984	872,196	721,493	1,104,204	1,087,634
Uniforms	652,915	81,630	139,857	323,988	107,239
Costumes	738,278	30,833	374,098	68,600	264,793

	total consumer units	Northeast	Midwest	South	West
GIRLS' (AGED 2 TO 15) APPAREL	**$12,204,665**	**$2,612,596**	**$3,036,669**	**$3,690,736**	**$2,845,636**
Coats and jackets	783,267	220,711	173,698	230,594	157,554
Dresses and suits	1,217,006	259,973	315,934	276,051	361,359
Shirts, blouses, and sweaters	2,816,994	615,329	849,982	732,279	607,601
Skirts and pants	2,707,405	570,965	578,199	967,418	591,083
Shorts and shorts sets	885,934	118,230	191,411	422,342	153,997
Active sportswear	1,109,725	245,777	260,943	343,824	258,440
Underwear and nightwear	734,818	123,554	164,973	241,751	204,312
Hosiery	537,559	121,779	147,260	121,082	145,611
Accessories	660,990	189,656	121,350	147,944	201,009
Uniforms	301,079	70,095	62,394	119,016	49,553
Costumes	449,888	76,528	170,525	88,022	114,862
CHILDREN UNDER AGE 2	**9,399,207**	**1,682,505**	**2,425,422**	**3,072,514**	**2,209,065**
Coats, jackets, and snowsuits	241,094	70,539	65,831	54,962	49,808
Outerwear including dresses	2,365,952	439,647	591,947	797,159	536,701
Underwear	5,292,533	891,051	1,313,440	1,779,868	1,303,127
Nightwear and loungewear	469,499	128,877	100,464	146,704	94,024
Accessories	1,030,129	152,612	353,740	293,821	225,404
FOOTWEAR	**33,905,436**	**7,925,629**	**6,571,429**	**11,686,297**	**7,748,119**
Men's	9,618,383	2,312,695	1,643,386	3,293,189	2,382,629
Boys'	4,512,727	964,695	928,503	1,500,511	1,120,669
Women's	15,965,270	3,809,315	3,080,820	5,674,749	3,416,643
Girls'	3,809,055	838,923	918,721	1,218,261	828,431
OTHER APPAREL PRODUCTS AND SERVICES	**29,818,372**	**6,456,737**	**6,388,743**	**10,018,007**	**6,948,403**
Material for making clothes	614,847	145,292	198,285	118,190	149,677
Sewing patterns and notions	575,626	131,096	193,262	113,231	134,684
Watches	1,974,895	309,439	295,312	943,450	426,922
Jewelry	13,861,177	2,932,682	3,343,349	4,444,504	3,140,923
Shoe repair and other shoe services	132,659	32,164	26,967	40,499	33,036
Coin-operated apparel laundry and dry cleaning	4,200,112	1,042,998	872,983	1,160,406	1,123,210
Apparel alteration, repair, and tailoring services	648,301	151,059	133,248	181,417	182,712
Clothing rental	283,776	53,459	63,187	99,593	67,850
Watch and jewelry repair	414,128	93,386	72,440	111,991	136,462
Professional laundry, dry cleaning	7,057,480	1,551,613	1,182,043	2,785,718	1,527,769
Clothing storage	55,371	3,771	7,403	18,596	25,412

Note: Numbers may not add to total because of rounding and missing subcategories.
Source: Calculations by New Strategist based on the 2003 Consumer Expenditure Survey

Table 2.24 Apparel: Market shares by region, 2003

(percentage of total annual spending on apparel, accessories, and related services accounted for by consumer units by region, 2003)

	total consumer units	Northeast	Midwest	South	West
Share of total consumer units	100.0%	19.2%	22.9%	35.8%	22.0%
Share of total before-tax income	100.0	21.5	23.4	32.8	22.5
Share of total spending	100.0	19.9	22.6	33.0	24.5
Share of apparel spending	100.0	21.8	21.8	31.7	24.6
MEN'S APPAREL	**100.0**	**23.1**	**22.8**	**27.8**	**26.2**
Suits	100.0	31.0	21.2	29.0	18.8
Sport coats and tailored jackets	100.0	28.8	16.2	36.9	18.1
Coats and jackets	100.0	25.9	29.8	16.2	27.6
Underwear	100.0	21.3	23.3	27.4	27.9
Hosiery	100.0	22.3	21.2	29.1	27.3
Nightwear	100.0	23.3	23.9	26.2	26.4
Accessories	100.0	15.2	22.2	30.1	32.4
Sweaters and vests	100.0	32.2	21.7	26.9	19.3
Active sportswear	100.0	23.2	25.6	22.8	28.2
Shirts	100.0	21.2	22.4	28.7	27.5
Pants	100.0	23.4	21.8	29.8	24.9
Shorts and shorts sets	100.0	21.0	16.6	31.9	30.6
Uniforms	100.0	11.7	20.5	43.6	24.3
Costumes	100.0	9.1	50.3	8.6	31.9
BOYS' (AGED 2 TO 15) APPAREL	**100.0**	**18.7**	**22.6**	**33.6**	**24.9**
Coats and jackets	100.0	26.4	25.3	27.9	20.3
Sweaters	100.0	31.6	20.0	32.2	16.3
Shirts	100.0	16.5	22.9	29.8	30.7
Underwear	100.0	14.2	24.4	27.6	33.6
Nightwear	100.0	25.6	18.3	26.5	29.5
Hosiery	100.0	17.4	19.4	28.0	35.1
Accessories	100.0	24.7	21.8	30.3	23.3
Suits, sport coats, and vests	100.0	29.3	20.2	28.2	22.3
Pants	100.0	16.9	21.5	37.1	24.5
Shorts and shorts sets	100.0	14.0	24.7	43.1	18.3
Uniforms	100.0	13.4	21.2	48.6	16.8
Active sportswear	100.0	23.5	13.5	50.1	12.7
Costumes	100.0	13.6	48.6	17.4	20.4
WOMEN'S APPAREL	**100.0**	**21.5**	**21.6**	**31.1**	**25.8**
Coats and jackets	100.0	25.9	19.0	28.1	26.9
Dresses	100.0	19.9	23.2	37.3	19.6
Sport coats and tailored jackets	100.0	20.0	22.5	24.1	33.3
Sweaters and vests	100.0	25.8	24.7	23.2	26.0
Shirts, blouses, and tops	100.0	20.1	21.8	31.3	26.6
Skirts	100.0	24.5	24.1	30.1	21.2
Pants	100.0	18.8	19.9	30.0	31.4
Shorts and shorts sets	100.0	26.1	21.5	32.9	19.6
Active sportswear	100.0	23.1	21.6	35.1	20.2
Nightwear	100.0	23.8	20.6	34.0	21.6
Undergarments	100.0	17.0	19.2	35.3	28.6
Hosiery	100.0	23.8	23.5	27.8	24.8
Suits	100.0	25.3	18.6	36.6	19.5
Accessories	100.0	23.0	19.1	29.2	28.7
Uniforms	100.0	12.5	21.4	49.6	16.4
Costumes	100.0	4.2	50.7	9.3	35.9

	total consumer units	Northeast	Midwest	South	West
GIRLS' (AGED 2 TO 15) APPAREL	**100.0%**	**21.4%**	**24.9%**	**30.2%**	**23.3%**
Coats and jackets	100.0	28.2	22.2	29.4	20.1
Dresses and suits	100.0	21.4	26.0	22.7	29.7
Shirts, blouses, and sweaters	100.0	21.8	30.2	26.0	21.6
Skirts and pants	100.0	21.1	21.4	35.7	21.8
Shorts and shorts sets	100.0	13.3	21.6	47.7	17.4
Active sportswear	100.0	22.1	23.5	31.0	23.3
Underwear and nightwear	100.0	16.8	22.5	32.9	27.8
Hosiery	100.0	22.7	27.4	22.5	27.1
Accessories	100.0	28.7	18.4	22.4	30.4
Uniforms	100.0	23.3	20.7	39.5	16.5
Costumes	100.0	17.0	37.9	19.6	25.5
CHILDREN UNDER AGE 2	**100.0**	**17.9**	**25.8**	**32.7**	**23.5**
Coats, jackets, and snowsuits	100.0	29.3	27.3	22.8	20.7
Outerwear including dresses	100.0	18.6	25.0	33.7	22.7
Underwear	100.0	16.8	24.8	33.6	24.6
Nightwear and loungewear	100.0	27.4	21.4	31.2	20.0
Accessories	100.0	14.8	34.3	28.5	21.9
FOOTWEAR	**100.0**	**23.4**	**19.4**	**34.5**	**22.9**
Men's	100.0	24.0	17.1	34.2	24.8
Boys'	100.0	21.4	20.6	33.3	24.8
Women's	100.0	23.9	19.3	35.5	21.4
Girls'	100.0	22.0	24.1	32.0	21.7
OTHER APPAREL PRODUCTS AND SERVICES	**100.0**	**21.7**	**21.4**	**33.6**	**23.3**
Material for making clothes	100.0	23.6	32.2	19.2	24.3
Sewing patterns and notions	100.0	22.8	33.6	19.7	23.4
Watches	100.0	15.7	15.0	47.8	21.6
Jewelry	100.0	21.2	24.1	32.1	22.7
Shoe repair and other shoe services	100.0	24.2	20.3	30.5	24.9
Coin-operated apparel laundry and dry cleaning	100.0	24.8	20.8	27.6	26.7
Apparel alteration, repair, and tailoring services	100.0	23.3	20.6	28.0	28.2
Clothing rental	100.0	18.8	22.3	35.1	23.9
Watch and jewelry repair	100.0	22.6	17.5	27.0	33.0
Professional laundry, dry cleaning	100.0	22.1	16.7	39.5	21.6
Clothing storage	100.0	6.8	13.4	33.6	45.9

Note: Numbers may not add to total because of rounding.
Source: Calculations by New Strategist based on the 2003 Consumer Expenditure Survey

Table 2.25 Apparel: Average spending by education, 2003

(average annual spending of consumer units (CU) on apparel, accessories, and related services, by education of consumer unit reference person, 2003)

	total consumer units	less than high school graduate	high school graduate	some college	associate's degree	college graduate total	bachelor's degree	master's, professional, doctorate
Number of consumer units (000)	115,356	17,721	31,552	24,514	10,981	30,589	19,557	11,032
Average number of persons per CU	2.5	2.6	2.5	2.3	2.6	2.5	2.5	2.4
Average before-tax income of CU	$51,128.00	$25,028.00	$40,113.00	$45,113.00	$54,087.00	$81,842.00	$74,921.00	$93,948.00
Average spending of CU, total	40,817.33	23,901.14	33,955.56	37,912.41	44,547.12	58,480.00	54,725.85	65,202.73
Apparel, average spending	**1,639.99**	**1,017.30**	**1,259.80**	**1,713.34**	**1,778.66**	**2,260.15**	**2,197.04**	**2,377.05**
MEN'S APPAREL	**282.18**	**159.88**	**212.77**	**294.87**	**341.35**	**389.37**	**377.12**	**411.53**
Suits	23.68	6.97	14.94	24.29	17.03	44.26	37.10	56.95
Sport coats and tailored jackets	10.67	3.97	7.11	9.84	8.77	19.56	19.02	20.53
Coats and jackets	23.17	15.63	16.44	33.12	23.58	26.42	26.11	27.03
Underwear	14.51	9.98	10.66	16.03	17.91	18.53	16.00	23.38
Hosiery	11.61	8.16	10.00	14.50	16.32	11.39	9.79	14.44
Nightwear	2.02	1.23	1.53	2.26	1.32	3.03	2.46	4.05
Accessories	22.11	7.46	14.30	20.64	29.60	36.00	35.49	36.97
Sweaters and vests	11.59	4.66	8.38	11.95	7.81	19.99	19.22	21.37
Active sportswear	17.97	6.69	11.85	18.19	25.24	27.34	24.38	32.99
Shirts	61.38	32.88	50.27	58.78	79.91	82.80	85.32	77.97
Pants	60.98	50.53	49.52	65.07	78.70	69.38	69.69	68.81
Shorts and shorts sets	15.79	7.42	11.21	13.69	29.36	21.89	23.74	18.36
Uniforms	2.63	2.43	2.91	2.02	3.26	2.72	2.63	2.88
Costumes	4.09	1.86	3.66	4.50	2.54	6.04	6.17	5.82
BOYS' (AGED 2 TO 15) APPAREL	**89.48**	**82.45**	**80.31**	**89.23**	**95.33**	**101.44**	**101.28**	**101.37**
Coats and jackets	6.41	5.23	6.00	6.09	8.12	7.15	6.91	7.58
Sweaters	2.65	1.80	2.72	2.49	2.43	3.28	2.72	4.26
Shirts	19.17	20.59	19.96	17.50	16.88	19.60	20.76	17.37
Underwear	6.30	6.20	6.20	5.99	4.90	7.10	7.66	6.04
Nightwear	3.51	2.26	1.41	8.20	1.79	3.40	3.18	3.83
Hosiery	4.46	8.80	2.98	3.99	3.85	4.39	4.47	4.25
Accessories	4.54	4.05	2.88	7.07	2.73	5.22	6.16	3.43
Suits, sport coats, and vests	2.58	2.54	1.06	1.88	5.25	3.77	3.33	4.57
Pants	21.43	18.75	20.34	19.07	26.69	24.11	22.44	27.07
Shorts and shorts sets	7.78	5.71	7.87	7.53	10.13	8.26	8.00	8.73
Uniforms	3.37	2.12	2.29	3.08	3.95	5.23	5.04	5.58
Active sportswear	4.63	2.50	3.92	3.44	6.80	6.76	7.79	4.93
Costumes	2.65	1.89	2.69	2.90	1.80	3.16	2.83	3.74
WOMEN'S APPAREL	**528.63**	**262.50**	**384.14**	**582.25**	**573.37**	**755.88**	**703.84**	**854.11**
Coats and jackets	45.08	29.35	30.71	44.70	35.03	70.85	63.67	84.60
Dresses	47.94	26.60	35.78	71.49	68.44	47.41	48.77	44.83
Sport coats and tailored jackets	5.46	1.72	2.61	4.62	5.17	11.33	11.04	11.85
Sweaters and vests	45.69	15.35	28.05	51.66	46.03	74.12	69.13	83.65
Shirts, blouses, and tops	101.40	44.25	79.08	95.17	126.67	148.82	129.27	186.21
Skirts	12.88	2.16	9.18	13.97	15.03	20.46	18.73	23.76
Pants	88.11	52.60	70.01	97.03	75.65	121.36	120.63	122.75
Shorts and shorts sets	13.89	4.65	13.39	15.13	22.13	15.46	10.92	24.16
Active sportswear	26.04	14.91	18.39	29.87	22.69	37.58	36.48	39.66
Nightwear	26.50	16.95	24.72	31.46	18.18	31.96	32.79	30.37
Undergarments	31.51	21.02	21.95	39.22	27.81	41.99	42.57	40.87
Hosiery	17.07	10.77	12.86	16.85	21.83	23.14	20.14	28.88
Suits	22.18	7.87	10.51	22.13	26.26	41.08	34.56	52.64
Accessories	32.82	9.88	20.03	36.28	45.88	50.56	47.99	55.47
Uniforms	5.66	1.77	3.36	6.13	11.40	7.85	6.18	10.82
Costumes	6.40	2.64	3.50	6.52	5.17	11.91	10.96	13.59

	total consumer units	less than high school graduate	high school graduate	some college	associate's degree	college graduate total	bachelor's degree	master's, professional, doctorate
GIRLS' (AGED 2 TO 15) APPAREL	**$105.80**	**$76.72**	**$99.59**	**$99.66**	**$133.98**	**$122.80**	**$119.92**	**$128.18**
Coats and jackets	6.79	5.67	5.90	5.59	8.60	8.65	8.30	9.28
Dresses and suits	10.55	7.88	11.85	11.96	8.56	10.12	11.70	7.10
Shirts, blouses, and sweaters	24.42	14.24	23.99	21.77	42.20	26.24	25.81	27.05
Skirts and pants	23.47	19.67	23.81	21.91	25.55	25.84	25.72	26.05
Shorts and shorts sets	7.68	6.36	7.57	5.89	11.39	8.67	8.40	9.14
Active sportswear	9.62	7.10	6.03	11.78	10.45	12.71	11.59	14.87
Underwear and nightwear	6.37	5.02	5.51	7.18	7.93	6.83	6.49	7.43
Hosiery	4.66	3.75	3.63	4.54	5.96	5.84	5.49	6.53
Accessories	5.73	3.03	5.79	4.28	2.99	8.87	7.27	11.93
Uniforms	2.61	1.77	2.70	1.92	2.62	3.55	3.93	2.88
Costumes	3.90	2.21	2.82	2.83	7.72	5.47	5.22	5.92
CHILDREN UNDER AGE 2	**81.48**	**68.36**	**73.33**	**78.75**	**70.91**	**102.26**	**107.97**	**91.67**
Coats, jackets, and snowsuits	2.09	1.45	1.87	1.94	1.83	2.90	2.99	2.75
Outerwear including dresses	20.51	13.96	18.76	21.48	20.46	25.33	27.12	22.16
Underwear	45.88	45.19	40.00	43.18	36.00	57.24	61.03	50.00
Nightwear and loungewear	4.07	1.84	3.65	3.99	4.94	5.56	6.13	4.55
Accessories	8.93	5.92	9.05	8.15	7.68	11.22	10.71	12.21
FOOTWEAR	**293.92**	**250.21**	**249.65**	**341.40**	**284.74**	**329.06**	**336.23**	**315.34**
Men's	83.38	64.44	79.35	90.69	74.39	94.20	95.96	90.85
Boys'	39.12	47.14	31.49	55.00	33.22	33.38	32.27	35.49
Women's	138.40	117.00	107.18	149.11	153.49	168.45	174.22	157.41
Girls'	33.02	21.63	31.63	46.60	23.64	33.03	33.78	31.60
OTHER APPAREL PRODUCTS AND SERVICES	**258.49**	**117.18**	**160.00**	**227.18**	**278.97**	**459.33**	**450.68**	**474.84**
Material for making clothes	5.33	0.50	2.29	5.15	9.92	8.80	7.63	11.02
Sewing patterns and notions	4.99	1.99	4.22	6.60	4.48	6.23	6.28	6.16
Watches	17.12	6.65	9.27	13.05	12.35	36.27	37.39	34.29
Jewelry	120.16	23.85	71.40	101.95	154.50	228.53	233.30	220.06
Shoe repair and other shoe services	1.15	0.17	0.38	0.99	1.26	2.60	2.35	3.05
Coin-operated apparel laundry and dry cleaning	36.41	65.26	34.22	36.89	27.66	24.69	27.46	19.77
Apparel alteration, repair, and tailoring services	5.62	1.24	2.45	5.87	5.60	11.25	9.91	13.62
Clothing rental	2.46	1.49	2.22	2.35	3.51	2.98	3.54	1.99
Watch and jewelry repair	3.59	1.25	2.27	2.41	8.47	5.51	5.35	5.77
Professional laundry, dry cleaning	61.18	14.77	31.25	50.54	50.90	131.15	115.45	158.97
Clothing storage	0.48	–	0.04	0.39	0.32	1.33	2.01	0.13

Note: Subcategories may not add to total because some are not shown. (–) means sample is too small to make a reliable estimate.
Source: Bureau of Labor Statistics, unpublished data from the 2003 Consumer Expenditure Survey

Table 2.26 Apparel: Indexed spending by education, 2003

(indexed average annual spending of consumer units (CU) on apparel, accessories, and related services, by education of consumer unit reference person, 2003; index definition: an index of 100 is the average for all consumer units; an index of 132 means that spending by consumer units in that group is 32 percent above the average for all consumer units; an index of 68 indicates spending that is 32 percent below the average for all consumer units)

	total consumer units	less than high school graduate	high school graduate	some college	associate's degree	college graduate total	bachelor's degree	master's, professional, doctorate
Average spending of CU, total	$40,817	$23,901	$33,956	$37,912	$44,547	$58,480	$54,726	$65,203
Average spending of CU, index	100	59	83	93	109	143	134	160
Apparel, spending index	**100**	**62**	**77**	**104**	**108**	**138**	**134**	**145**
MEN'S APPAREL	**100**	**57**	**75**	**104**	**121**	**138**	**134**	**146**
Suits	100	29	63	103	72	187	157	240
Sport coats and tailored jackets	100	37	67	92	82	183	178	192
Coats and jackets	100	67	71	143	102	114	113	117
Underwear	100	69	73	110	123	128	110	161
Hosiery	100	70	86	125	141	98	84	124
Nightwear	100	61	76	112	65	150	122	200
Accessories	100	34	65	93	134	163	161	167
Sweaters and vests	100	40	72	103	67	172	166	184
Active sportswear	100	37	66	101	140	152	136	184
Shirts	100	54	82	96	130	135	139	127
Pants	100	83	81	107	129	114	114	113
Shorts and shorts sets	100	47	71	87	186	139	150	116
Uniforms	100	92	111	77	124	103	100	110
Costumes	100	45	89	110	62	148	151	142
BOYS' (AGED 2 TO 15) APPAREL	**100**	**92**	**90**	**100**	**107**	**113**	**113**	**113**
Coats and jackets	100	82	94	95	127	112	108	118
Sweaters	100	68	103	94	92	124	103	161
Shirts	100	107	104	91	88	102	108	91
Underwear	100	98	98	95	78	113	122	96
Nightwear	100	64	40	234	51	97	91	109
Hosiery	100	197	67	89	86	98	100	95
Accessories	100	89	63	156	60	115	136	76
Suits, sport coats, and vests	100	98	41	73	203	146	129	177
Pants	100	87	95	89	125	113	105	126
Shorts and shorts sets	100	73	101	97	130	106	103	112
Uniforms	100	63	68	91	117	155	150	166
Active sportswear	100	54	85	74	147	146	168	106
Costumes	100	71	102	109	68	119	107	141
WOMEN'S APPAREL	**100**	**50**	**73**	**110**	**108**	**143**	**133**	**162**
Coats and jackets	100	65	68	99	78	157	141	188
Dresses	100	55	75	149	143	99	102	94
Sport coats and tailored jackets	100	32	48	85	95	208	202	217
Sweaters and vests	100	34	61	113	101	162	151	183
Shirts, blouses, and tops	100	44	78	94	125	147	127	184
Skirts	100	17	71	108	117	159	145	184
Pants	100	60	79	110	86	138	137	139
Shorts and shorts sets	100	33	96	109	159	111	79	174
Active sportswear	100	57	71	115	87	144	140	152
Nightwear	100	64	93	119	69	121	124	115
Undergarments	100	67	70	124	88	133	135	130
Hosiery	100	63	75	99	128	136	118	169
Suits	100	35	47	100	118	185	156	237
Accessories	100	30	61	111	140	154	146	169
Uniforms	100	31	59	108	201	139	109	191
Costumes	100	41	55	102	81	186	171	212

	total consumer units	less than high school graduate	high school graduate	some college	associate's degree	college graduate		
						total	bachelor's degree	master's, professional, doctorate
GIRLS' (AGED 2 TO 15) APPAREL	**100**	**73**	**94**	**94**	**127**	**116**	**113**	**121**
Coats and jackets	100	84	87	82	127	127	122	137
Dresses and suits	100	75	112	113	81	96	111	67
Shirts, blouses, and sweaters	100	58	98	89	173	107	106	111
Skirts and pants	100	84	101	93	109	110	110	111
Shorts and shorts sets	100	83	99	77	148	113	109	119
Active sportswear	100	74	63	122	109	132	120	155
Underwear and nightwear	100	79	86	113	124	107	102	117
Hosiery	100	80	78	97	128	125	118	140
Accessories	100	53	101	75	52	155	127	208
Uniforms	100	68	103	74	100	136	151	110
Costumes	100	57	72	73	198	140	134	152
CHILDREN UNDER AGE 2	**100**	**84**	**90**	**97**	**87**	**126**	**133**	**113**
Coats, jackets, and snowsuits	100	69	89	93	88	139	143	132
Outerwear including dresses	100	68	91	105	100	124	132	108
Underwear	100	98	87	94	78	125	133	109
Nightwear and loungewear	100	45	90	98	121	137	151	112
Accessories	100	66	101	91	86	126	120	137
FOOTWEAR	**100**	**85**	**85**	**116**	**97**	**112**	**114**	**107**
Men's	100	77	95	109	89	113	115	109
Boys'	100	121	80	141	85	85	82	91
Women's	100	85	77	108	111	122	126	114
Girls'	100	66	96	141	72	100	102	96
OTHER APPAREL PRODUCTS AND SERVICES	**100**	**45**	**62**	**88**	**108**	**178**	**174**	**184**
Material for making clothes	100	9	43	115	186	165	143	207
Sewing patterns and notions	100	40	85	132	90	125	126	123
Watches	100	39	54	76	72	212	218	200
Jewelry	100	20	59	85	129	190	194	183
Shoe repair and other shoe services	100	15	33	86	110	226	204	265
Coin-operated apparel laundry and dry cleaning	100	179	94	101	76	68	75	54
Apparel alteration, repair, and tailoring services	100	22	44	104	100	200	176	242
Clothing rental	100	61	90	96	143	121	144	81
Watch and jewelry repair	100	35	63	67	236	153	149	161
Professional laundry, dry cleaning	100	24	51	83	83	214	189	260
Clothing storage	100	–	8	81	67	277	419	27

Note: (–) means sample is too small to make a reliable estimate.
Source: Calculations by New Strategist based on the 2003 Consumer Expenditure Survey

Table 2.27 Apparel: Total spending by education, 2003

(total annual spending on apparel, accessories, and related services, by consumer unit (CU) educational attainment group, 2003; numbers in thousands)

	total consumer units	less than high school graduate	high school graduate	some college	associate's degree	college graduate total	bachelor's degree	master's, professional, doctorate
Number of consumer units	115,356	17,721	31,552	24,514	10,981	30,589	19,557	11,032
Total spending of all CUs	$4,708,523,919	$423,552,102	$1,071,365,829	$929,384,819	$489,171,925	$1,788,844,720	$1,070,273,448	$719,316,517
Apparel, total spending	189,182,686	18,027,573	39,749,210	42,000,817	19,531,465	69,135,728	42,967,511	26,223,616
MEN'S APPAREL	**32,551,156**	**2,833,233**	**6,713,319**	**7,228,443**	**3,748,364**	**11,910,439**	**7,375,336**	**4,539,999**
Suits	2,731,630	123,515	471,387	595,445	187,006	1,353,869	725,565	628,272
Sport coats and tailored jackets	1,230,849	70,352	224,335	241,218	96,303	598,321	371,974	226,487
Coats and jackets	2,672,799	276,979	518,715	811,904	258,932	808,161	510,633	298,195
Underwear	1,673,816	176,856	336,344	392,959	196,670	566,814	312,912	257,928
Hosiery	1,339,283	144,603	315,520	355,453	179,210	348,409	191,463	159,302
Nightwear	233,019	21,797	48,275	55,402	14,495	92,685	48,110	44,680
Accessories	2,550,521	132,199	451,194	505,969	325,038	1,101,204	694,078	407,853
Sweaters and vests	1,336,976	82,580	264,406	292,942	85,762	611,474	375,886	235,754
Active sportswear	2,072,947	118,553	373,891	445,910	277,160	836,303	476,800	363,946
Shirts	7,080,551	582,666	1,586,119	1,440,933	877,492	2,532,769	1,668,603	860,165
Pants	7,034,409	895,442	1,562,455	1,595,126	864,205	2,122,265	1,362,927	759,112
Shorts and shorts sets	1,821,471	131,490	353,698	335,597	322,402	669,593	464,283	202,548
Uniforms	303,386	43,062	91,816	49,518	35,798	83,202	51,435	31,772
Costumes	471,806	32,961	115,480	110,313	27,892	184,758	120,667	64,206
BOYS' (AGED 2 TO 15) APPAREL	**10,322,055**	**1,461,096**	**2,533,941**	**2,187,384**	**1,046,819**	**3,102,948**	**1,980,733**	**1,118,314**
Coats and jackets	739,432	92,681	189,312	149,290	89,166	218,711	135,139	83,623
Sweaters	305,693	31,898	85,821	61,040	26,684	100,332	53,195	46,996
Shirts	2,211,375	364,875	629,778	428,995	185,359	599,544	406,003	191,626
Underwear	726,743	109,870	195,622	146,839	53,807	217,182	149,807	66,633
Nightwear	404,900	40,049	44,488	201,015	19,656	104,003	62,191	42,253
Hosiery	514,488	155,945	94,025	97,811	42,277	134,286	87,420	46,886
Accessories	523,716	71,770	90,870	173,314	29,978	159,675	120,471	37,840
Suits, sport coats, and vests	297,618	45,011	33,445	46,086	57,650	115,321	65,125	50,416
Pants	2,472,079	332,269	641,768	467,482	293,083	737,501	438,859	298,636
Shorts and shorts sets	897,470	101,187	248,314	184,590	111,238	252,665	156,456	96,309
Uniforms	388,750	37,569	72,254	75,503	43,375	159,980	98,567	61,559
Active sportswear	534,098	44,303	123,684	84,328	74,671	206,782	152,349	54,388
Costumes	305,693	33,493	84,875	71,091	19,766	96,661	55,346	41,260
WOMEN'S APPAREL	**60,980,642**	**4,651,763**	**12,120,385**	**14,273,277**	**6,296,176**	**23,121,613**	**13,764,999**	**9,422,542**
Coats and jackets	5,200,248	520,111	968,962	1,095,776	384,664	2,167,231	1,245,194	933,307
Dresses	5,530,167	471,379	1,128,931	1,752,506	751,540	1,450,224	953,795	494,565
Sport coats and tailored jackets	629,844	30,480	82,351	113,255	56,772	346,573	215,909	130,729
Sweaters and vests	5,270,616	272,017	885,034	1,266,393	505,455	2,267,257	1,351,975	922,827
Shirts, blouses, and tops	11,697,098	784,154	2,495,132	2,332,997	1,390,963	4,552,255	2,528,133	2,054,269
Skirts	1,485,785	38,277	289,647	342,461	165,044	625,851	366,303	262,120
Pants	10,164,017	932,125	2,208,956	2,378,593	830,713	3,712,281	2,359,161	1,354,178
Shorts and shorts sets	1,602,295	82,403	422,481	370,897	243,010	472,906	213,562	266,533
Active sportswear	3,003,870	264,220	580,241	732,233	249,159	1,149,535	713,439	437,529
Nightwear	3,056,934	300,371	779,965	771,210	199,635	977,624	641,274	335,042
Undergarments	3,634,868	372,495	692,566	961,439	305,382	1,284,432	832,541	450,878
Hosiery	1,969,127	190,855	405,759	413,061	239,715	707,829	393,878	318,604
Suits	2,558,596	139,464	331,612	542,495	288,361	1,256,596	675,890	580,724
Accessories	3,785,984	175,083	631,987	889,368	503,808	1,546,580	938,540	611,945
Uniforms	652,915	31,366	106,015	150,271	125,183	240,124	120,862	119,366
Costumes	738,278	46,783	110,432	159,831	56,772	364,315	214,345	149,925

	total consumer units	less than high school graduate	high school graduate	some college	associate's degree	college graduate total	bachelor's degree	master's, professional, doctorate
GIRLS' (AGED 2 TO 15) APPAREL	**$12,204,665**	**$1,359,555**	**$3,142,264**	**$2,443,065**	**$1,471,234**	**$3,756,329**	**$2,345,275**	**$1,414,082**
Coats and jackets	783,267	100,478	136,157	137,033	94,437	264,595	162,323	102,377
Dresses and suits	1,217,006	139,641	373,891	293,187	93,997	309,561	228,817	78,327
Shirts, blouses, and sweaters	2,816,994	252,347	756,932	533,670	463,398	802,655	504,766	298,416
Skirts and pants	2,707,405	348,572	751,253	537,102	280,565	790,420	503,006	287,384
Shorts and shorts sets	885,934	112,706	238,849	144,387	125,074	265,207	164,279	100,832
Active sportswear	1,109,725	125,819	190,259	288,775	114,751	388,786	226,666	164,046
Underwear and nightwear	734,818	88,959	173,852	176,011	87,079	208,923	126,925	81,968
Hosiery	537,559	66,454	114,534	111,294	65,447	178,640	107,368	72,039
Accessories	660,990	53,695	182,686	104,920	32,833	271,324	142,179	131,612
Uniforms	301,079	31,366	85,190	47,067	28,770	108,591	76,859	31,772
Costumes	449,888	39,163	88,977	69,375	84,773	167,322	102,088	65,309
CHILDREN UNDER AGE 2	**9,399,207**	**1,211,408**	**2,313,708**	**1,930,478**	**778,663**	**3,128,031**	**2,111,569**	**1,011,303**
Coats, jackets, and snowsuits	241,094	25,695	59,002	47,557	20,095	88,708	58,475	30,338
Outerwear including dresses	2,365,952	247,385	591,916	526,561	224,671	774,819	530,386	244,469
Underwear	5,292,533	800,812	1,262,080	1,058,515	395,316	1,750,914	1,193,564	551,600
Nightwear and loungewear	469,499	32,607	115,165	97,811	54,246	170,075	119,884	50,196
Accessories	1,030,129	104,908	285,546	199,789	84,334	343,209	209,455	134,701
FOOTWEAR	**33,905,436**	**4,433,971**	**7,876,957**	**8,369,080**	**3,126,730**	**10,065,616**	**6,575,650**	**3,478,831**
Men's	9,618,383	1,141,941	2,503,651	2,223,175	816,877	2,881,484	1,876,690	1,002,257
Boys'	4,512,727	835,368	993,572	1,348,270	364,789	1,021,061	631,104	391,526
Women's	15,965,270	2,073,357	3,381,743	3,655,283	1,685,474	5,152,717	3,407,221	1,736,547
Girls'	3,809,055	383,305	997,990	1,142,352	259,591	1,010,355	660,635	348,611
OTHER APPAREL PRODUCTS, SERVICES	**29,818,372**	**2,076,547**	**5,048,320**	**5,569,091**	**3,063,370**	**14,050,445**	**8,813,949**	**5,238,435**
Material for making clothes	614,847	8,861	72,254	150,761	108,932	269,183	149,220	121,573
Sewing patterns and notions	575,626	35,265	133,149	161,792	45,195	190,569	122,818	67,957
Watches	1,974,895	117,845	292,487	319,908	135,615	1,109,463	731,236	378,287
Jewelry	13,861,177	422,646	2,252,813	2,499,202	1,696,565	6,990,504	4,562,648	2,427,702
Shoe repair and other shoe services	132,659	3,013	11,990	24,269	13,836	79,531	45,959	33,648
Coin-operated apparel laundry and dry cleaning	4,200,112	1,156,472	1,079,709	904,321	303,734	755,242	537,035	218,103
Apparel alteration, repair, and tailoring services	648,301	21,974	77,302	143,897	61,494	344,126	193,810	150,256
Clothing rental	283,776	26,404	70,045	57,608	38,543	91,155	69,232	21,954
Watch and jewelry repair	414,128	22,151	71,623	59,079	93,009	168,545	104,630	63,655
Professional laundry, dry cleaning	7,057,480	261,739	986,000	1,238,938	558,933	4,011,747	2,257,856	1,753,757
Clothing storage	55,371	–	1,262	9,560	3,514	40,683	39,310	1,434

Note: Numbers may not add to total because of rounding and missing subcategories. (–) means sample is too small to make a reliable estimate.
Source: Calculations by New Strategist based on the 2003 Consumer Expenditure Survey

Table 2.28 Apparel: Market shares by education, 2003

(percentage of total annual spending on apparel, accessories, and related services accounted for by consumer unit educational attainment groups, 2003)

	total consumer units	less than high school graduate	high school graduate	some college	associate's degree	college graduate total	bachelor's degree	master's, professional, doctorate
Share of total consumer units	100.0%	15.4%	27.4%	21.3%	9.5%	26.5%	17.0%	9.6%
Share of total before-tax income	100.0	7.5	21.5	18.8	10.1	42.4	24.8	17.6
Share of total spending	100.0	9.0	22.8	19.7	10.4	38.0	22.7	15.3
Share of apparel spending	100.0	9.5	21.0	22.2	10.3	36.5	22.7	13.9
MEN'S APPAREL	100.0	8.7	20.6	22.2	11.5	36.6	22.7	13.9
Suits	100.0	4.5	17.3	21.8	6.8	49.6	26.6	23.0
Sport coats and tailored jackets	100.0	5.7	18.2	19.6	7.8	48.6	30.2	18.4
Coats and jackets	100.0	10.4	19.4	30.4	9.7	30.2	19.1	11.2
Underwear	100.0	10.6	20.1	23.5	11.7	33.9	18.7	15.4
Hosiery	100.0	10.8	23.6	26.5	13.4	26.0	14.3	11.9
Nightwear	100.0	9.4	20.7	23.8	6.2	39.8	20.6	19.2
Accessories	100.0	5.2	17.7	19.8	12.7	43.2	27.2	16.0
Sweaters and vests	100.0	6.2	19.8	21.9	6.4	45.7	28.1	17.6
Active sportswear	100.0	5.7	18.0	21.5	13.4	40.3	23.0	17.6
Shirts	100.0	8.2	22.4	20.4	12.4	35.8	23.6	12.1
Pants	100.0	12.7	22.2	22.7	12.3	30.2	19.4	10.8
Shorts and shorts sets	100.0	7.2	19.4	18.4	17.7	36.8	25.5	11.1
Uniforms	100.0	14.2	30.3	16.3	11.8	27.4	17.0	10.5
Costumes	100.0	7.0	24.5	23.4	5.9	39.2	25.6	13.6
BOYS' (AGED 2 TO 15) APPAREL	100.0	14.2	24.5	21.2	10.1	30.1	19.2	10.8
Coats and jackets	100.0	12.5	25.6	20.2	12.1	29.6	18.3	11.3
Sweaters	100.0	10.4	28.1	20.0	8.7	32.8	17.4	15.4
Shirts	100.0	16.5	28.5	19.4	8.4	27.1	18.4	8.7
Underwear	100.0	15.1	26.9	20.2	7.4	29.9	20.6	9.2
Nightwear	100.0	9.9	11.0	49.6	4.9	25.7	15.4	10.4
Hosiery	100.0	30.3	18.3	19.0	8.2	26.1	17.0	9.1
Accessories	100.0	13.7	17.4	33.1	5.7	30.5	23.0	7.2
Suits, sport coats, and vests	100.0	15.1	11.2	15.5	19.4	38.7	21.9	16.9
Pants	100.0	13.4	26.0	18.9	11.9	29.8	17.8	12.1
Shorts and shorts sets	100.0	11.3	27.7	20.6	12.4	28.2	17.4	10.7
Uniforms	100.0	9.7	18.6	19.4	11.2	41.2	25.4	15.8
Active sportswear	100.0	8.3	23.2	15.8	14.0	38.7	28.5	10.2
Costumes	100.0	11.0	27.8	23.3	6.5	31.6	18.1	13.5
WOMEN'S APPAREL	100.0	7.6	19.9	23.4	10.3	37.9	22.6	15.5
Coats and jackets	100.0	10.0	18.6	21.1	7.4	41.7	23.9	17.9
Dresses	100.0	8.5	20.4	31.7	13.6	26.2	17.2	8.9
Sport coats and tailored jackets	100.0	4.8	13.1	18.0	9.0	55.0	34.3	20.8
Sweaters and vests	100.0	5.2	16.8	24.0	9.6	43.0	25.7	17.5
Shirts, blouses, and tops	100.0	6.7	21.3	19.9	11.9	38.9	21.6	17.6
Skirts	100.0	2.6	19.5	23.0	11.1	42.1	24.7	17.6
Pants	100.0	9.2	21.7	23.4	8.2	36.5	23.2	13.3
Shorts and shorts sets	100.0	5.1	26.4	23.1	15.2	29.5	13.3	16.6
Active sportswear	100.0	8.8	19.3	24.4	8.3	38.3	23.8	14.6
Nightwear	100.0	9.8	25.5	25.2	6.5	32.0	21.0	11.0
Undergarments	100.0	10.2	19.1	26.5	8.4	35.3	22.9	12.4
Hosiery	100.0	9.7	20.6	21.0	12.2	35.9	20.0	16.2
Suits	100.0	5.5	13.0	21.2	11.3	49.1	26.4	22.7
Accessories	100.0	4.6	16.7	23.5	13.3	40.9	24.8	16.2
Uniforms	100.0	4.8	16.2	23.0	19.2	36.8	18.5	18.3
Costumes	100.0	6.3	15.0	21.6	7.7	49.3	29.0	20.3

	total consumer units	less than high school graduate	high school graduate	some college	associate's degree	college graduate total	bachelor's degree	master's, professional, doctorate
GIRLS' (AGED 2 TO 15) APPAREL	100.0%	11.1%	25.7%	20.0%	12.1%	30.8%	19.2%	11.6%
Coats and jackets	100.0	12.8	23.8	17.5	12.1	33.8	20.7	13.1
Dresses and suits	100.0	11.5	30.7	24.1	7.7	25.4	18.8	6.4
Shirts, blouses, and sweaters	100.0	9.0	26.9	18.9	16.5	28.5	17.9	10.6
Skirts and pants	100.0	12.9	27.7	19.8	10.4	29.2	18.6	10.6
Shorts and shorts sets	100.0	12.7	27.0	16.3	14.1	29.9	18.5	11.4
Active sportswear	100.0	11.3	17.1	26.0	10.3	35.0	20.4	14.8
Underwear and nightwear	100.0	12.1	23.7	24.0	11.9	28.4	17.3	11.2
Hosiery	100.0	12.4	21.3	20.7	12.2	33.2	20.0	13.4
Accessories	100.0	8.1	27.6	15.9	5.0	41.0	21.5	19.9
Uniforms	100.0	10.4	28.3	15.6	9.6	36.1	25.5	10.6
Costumes	100.0	8.7	19.8	15.4	18.8	37.2	22.7	14.5
CHILDREN UNDER AGE 2	100.0	12.9	24.6	20.5	8.3	33.3	22.5	10.8
Coats, jackets, and snowsuits	100.0	10.7	24.5	19.7	8.3	36.8	24.3	12.6
Outerwear including dresses	100.0	10.5	25.0	22.3	9.5	32.7	22.4	10.3
Underwear	100.0	15.1	23.8	20.0	7.5	33.1	22.6	10.4
Nightwear and loungewear	100.0	6.9	24.5	20.8	11.6	36.2	25.5	10.7
Accessories	100.0	10.2	27.7	19.4	8.2	33.3	20.3	13.1
FOOTWEAR	100.0	13.1	23.2	24.7	9.2	29.7	19.4	10.3
Men's	100.0	11.9	26.0	23.1	8.5	30.0	19.5	10.4
Boys'	100.0	18.5	22.0	29.9	8.1	22.6	14.0	8.7
Women's	100.0	13.0	21.2	22.9	10.6	32.3	21.3	10.9
Girls'	100.0	10.1	26.2	30.0	6.8	26.5	17.3	9.2
OTHER APPAREL PRODUCTS AND SERVICES	100.0	7.0	16.9	18.7	10.3	47.1	29.6	17.6
Material for making clothes	100.0	1.4	11.8	24.5	17.7	43.8	24.3	19.8
Sewing patterns and notions	100.0	6.1	23.1	28.1	8.5	33.1	21.3	11.8
Watches	100.0	6.0	14.8	16.2	6.9	56.2	37.0	19.2
Jewelry	100.0	3.0	16.3	18.0	12.2	50.4	32.9	17.5
Shoe repair and other shoe services	100.0	2.3	9.0	18.3	0.4	60.0	34.6	25.4
Coin-operated apparel laundry and dry cleaning	100.0	27.5	25.7	21.5	7.2	18.0	12.8	5.2
Apparel alteration, repair, and tailoring services	100.0	3.4	11.9	22.2	9.5	53.1	29.9	23.2
Clothing rental	100.0	9.3	24.7	20.3	13.6	32.1	24.4	7.7
Watch and jewelry repair	100.0	5.3	17.3	14.3	22.5	40.7	25.3	15.4
Professional laundry, dry cleaning	100.0	3.7	14.0	17.6	7.9	56.8	32.0	24.8
Clothing storage	100.0	–	2.3	17.3	5.3	73.5	71.0	2.6

Note: Numbers may not add to total because of rounding. (–) means sample is too small to make a reliable estimate.
Source: Calculations by New Strategist based on the 2003 Consumer Expenditure Survey

Spending on Entertainment, 2003

Entertainment spending has grown somewhat since 2000, despite the sluggish economic recovery. The average household spent $2,060 on entertainment in 2003, up from $1,991 in 2000, a 3 percent rise after adjusting for inflation. Overall, Americans devote 5.0 percent of their spending to entertainment, up slightly from 4.9 percent in 2000. The average American household now spends substantially more on entertainment than it does on clothes.

Households headed by people aged 35 to 44 spend the most on entertainment, a total of $2,519 in 2003—22 percent more than the average household. Interestingly, older householders spend more on entertainment than younger ones. Households headed by 55-to-64-year-olds spent $2,414 on entertainment in 2003 compared with the $1,958 spent by those aged 25 to 34. Householders aged 65 to 74 are the biggest spenders on pets.

Households with incomes of $100,000 or more spent $5,124 on entertainment in 2003, more than twice what the average household spends. High-income households spend far more than average on nearly every entertainment category. Households with incomes of $100,000 or more account for 12 percent of households, but they control a larger 28 percent of entertainment spending. They account for 50 percent of spending on fees for recreational lessons, 56 percent of spending on playground equipment, and 64 percent of spending on motorboats.

Married couples with children aged 6 to 17 at home spend much more on entertainment than other household types—66 percent more than the average household. They are especially big spenders on fees for recreational lessons, devoting nearly four times as much as the average household to this item. They spend nearly three times the average on video game hardware and software. Single parents spend 51 percent more than average on this item.

Asians, blacks, and Hispanics spend less than the average household on entertainment. In some categories, however, they spend more. Asians spend 68 percent more than average on fees for recreational lessons. Blacks spend more than average on tape recorders and players. Hispanics spend more than average on sound component systems. White and other consumer units spend 13 percent more than average on pets, while Asians, blacks, and Hispanics spend less than average on this item.

Households in the West spend much more on entertainment than households in other regions—$2,494 in 2003, or 21 percent more than average. Western households spend more than twice the average on motorized campers. Households in the South spend 12 percent less than average on entertainment, but they spend an average amount on cable television service.

College graduates spend 51 percent more than the average household on entertainment. They account for 64 percent of the market for social, recreation, and civic club memberships. They also control 60 percent of household spending on fees for recreational lessons. Householders without a college degree account for 69 percent of spending on pet food.

Table 3.1 Entertainment: Average spending by age, 2003

(average annual spending of consumer units (CU) on entertainment, by age of consumer unit reference person, 2003)

	total consumer units	under 25	25 to 34	35 to 44	45 to 54	55 to 64	65 to 74	75+
Number of consumer units (000)	115,356	8,584	19,737	24,413	23,131	16,580	11,495	11,417
Average number of persons per CU	2.5	1.8	2.9	3.2	2.6	2.1	1.9	1.5
Average before-tax income of CU	$51,128.00	$20,680.00	$50,389.00	$61,091.00	$68,028.00	$58,672.00	$35,314.00	$25,492.00
Average spending of CU, total	40,817.33	22,395.53	40,525.22	47,175.06	50,100.86	44,190.65	33,629.17	25,016.38
Entertainment, average spending	2,059.56	949.78	1,958.21	2,518.64	2,407.28	2,414.21	2,015.84	908.60
FEES AND ADMISSIONS	494.46	232.90	402.30	637.67	624.26	597.20	383.47	243.80
Recreation expenses on trips	22.87	7.00	17.37	26.83	26.66	34.04	22.72	12.03
Social, recreation, civic club membership	95.06	33.83	66.31	89.60	112.51	174.05	76.57	71.08
Fees for participant sports	65.73	27.63	54.50	71.94	70.87	76.59	78.37	61.60
Participant sports on trips	23.83	14.61	17.14	28.91	29.67	33.88	18.31	10.62
Movie, theater, opera, ballet	90.69	84.76	94.72	111.60	108.71	83.45	80.44	27.81
Movie, other admissions on trips	45.31	20.93	35.77	59.22	55.37	57.00	33.78	24.61
Admission to sports events	33.65	19.09	32.40	44.71	49.75	31.98	19.28	7.40
Admission to sports events on trips	15.10	6.98	11.92	19.74	18.45	19.00	11.25	8.20
Fees for recreational lessons	79.36	11.07	54.79	158.31	125.60	53.18	20.03	8.44
Other entertainment services on trips	22.87	7.00	17.37	26.83	26.66	34.04	22.72	12.03
TELEVISION, RADIO, SOUND EQUIPMENT	730.03	462.78	779.73	874.00	864.81	743.60	560.39	415.14
Television	597.36	341.56	613.52	673.24	707.87	645.10	510.38	393.82
Cable service and community antenna	423.79	202.60	397.00	449.26	498.11	483.61	424.22	344.12
Black-and-white TV sets	0.34	0.02	0.53	0.31	0.52	0.43	0.07	0.06
Color TV sets, consoles	56.50	31.92	66.67	71.52	75.01	60.84	29.01	9.18
Color TV sets, portable and table models	34.65	23.55	37.96	42.26	40.98	34.39	21.99	21.37
VCRs and video disc players	24.26	11.31	31.62	30.34	28.70	26.22	13.30	7.46
Video cassettes, tapes, and discs	35.92	43.91	53.53	44.99	40.45	26.40	14.13	6.71
Video game hardware and software	18.70	22.72	23.63	31.54	20.91	9.73	5.99	1.08
Repair of TV, radio, and sound equipment	2.60	2.81	1.81	2.06	3.11	3.30	1.67	3.84
Rental of television sets	0.58	2.72	0.77	0.97	0.08	0.19	–	–
Radio and sound equipment	132.68	121.22	166.21	200.76	156.94	98.50	50.01	21.32
Radios	5.46	3.05	2.23	7.99	11.42	1.92	1.99	3.74
Tape recorders and players	3.93	1.54	4.16	9.14	4.46	0.97	1.27	–
Sound components and component systems	17.05	17.07	17.40	28.76	20.00	12.11	7.44	2.28
Miscellaneous sound equipment	0.42	0.07	0.13	0.54	0.36	1.44	–	–
Sound equipment accessories	5.54	5.75	3.09	7.71	5.28	12.56	0.13	0.94
Satellite dishes	0.91	0.40	0.92	1.06	1.17	1.24	0.70	0.18
Compact disc, tape, record, video mail order clubs	4.38	2.77	5.37	5.51	4.99	3.80	4.43	1.03
Records, CDs, audio tapes, needles	33.31	38.26	40.60	41.57	43.81	25.44	15.73	7.23
Rental of VCR, radio, sound equipment	0.29	0.03	0.71	0.51	0.19	0.04	0.03	0.17
Musical instruments and accessories	23.32	7.28	38.21	44.84	22.04	9.25	9.18	0.92
Rental and repair of musical instruments	2.29	0.38	1.52	2.58	1.80	6.36	0.31	1.54
Rental of video cassettes, tapes, discs, films	35.76	44.62	51.85	50.55	41.41	23.38	8.81	3.29
PETS, TOYS, PLAYGROUND EQUIPMENT	378.21	139.27	403.10	438.18	450.20	381.43	451.32	159.44
Pets	274.25	87.88	238.98	287.16	358.01	293.43	388.50	132.13
Pet food	99.82	36.53	68.87	111.21	139.73	128.49	89.98	64.92
Pet purchase, supplies, and medicines	75.73	29.66	82.88	68.98	77.08	44.33	208.75	17.38
Pet services	24.52	4.10	19.21	27.42	39.52	25.12	20.91	15.25
Veterinarian services	74.18	17.59	68.02	79.56	101.69	95.49	68.85	34.58
Toys, games, hobbies, and tricycles	100.05	50.67	155.25	144.53	91.41	82.89	62.15	27.19
Playground equipment	3.91	0.71	8.87	6.49	0.78	5.11	0.67	0.12

	total consumer units	under 25	25 to 34	35 to 44	45 to 54	55 to 64	65 to 74	75+
OTHER ENTERTAINMENT SUPPLIES, EQUIPMENT, SERVICES	$456.86	$114.83	$373.08	$568.79	$468.01	$691.98	$620.66	$90.22
Unmotored recreational vehicles	60.28	0.07	16.70	117.92	50.26	115.17	53.37	5.13
Boat without motor and boat trailers	6.95	0.07	5.15	5.96	6.34	22.43	2.04	1.09
Trailer and other attachable campers	53.32	–	11.55	111.96	43.93	92.74	51.33	4.03
Motorized recreational vehicles	167.33	6.94	90.57	138.27	158.59	328.60	387.36	44.69
Motorized camper	83.89	–	–	15.41	64.69	238.74	329.67	5.01
Other vehicle	17.54	4.87	7.51	24.57	32.16	11.80	13.81	11.84
Motorboats	65.89	2.07	83.07	98.29	61.73	78.06	43.88	27.84
Rental of recreational vehicles	4.21	1.27	4.97	3.18	7.21	6.52	1.13	0.96
Docking and landing fees	3.57	0.28	1.31	2.70	2.22	5.32	14.96	0.56
Sports, recreation, exercise equipment	131.77	41.66	147.41	195.24	134.17	153.10	114.42	18.76
Athletic gear, game tables, exercise equipment	54.52	15.00	47.32	98.16	53.58	51.53	54.66	9.56
Bicycles	11.06	11.98	17.26	19.00	10.25	5.52	2.78	0.74
Camping equipment	9.31	0.69	10.90	14.79	12.54	10.34	2.52	–
Hunting and fishing equipment	30.49	5.60	47.02	19.20	23.71	63.25	37.37	4.35
Winter sports equipment	4.89	3.94	2.89	8.66	6.63	4.15	2.93	0.53
Water sports equipment	4.48	1.86	4.90	3.15	8.29	3.94	6.03	0.06
Other sports equipment	15.01	2.03	16.08	30.67	16.70	11.83	3.58	2.12
Rental and repair of miscellaneous sports equipment	2.01	0.55	1.04	1.61	2.47	2.54	4.56	1.39
Photographic equipment and supplies	79.18	58.94	91.50	94.99	106.11	80.77	45.29	16.10
Film	14.63	12.34	16.21	16.29	18.15	16.78	9.91	4.63
Other photographic supplies	1.26	6.10	0.44	0.79	2.29	0.18	0.45	–
Film processing	22.27	15.60	26.78	25.21	27.46	24.84	14.54	6.69
Repair and rental of photographic equipment	0.58	0.01	0.30	0.52	1.27	0.33	0.89	0.27
Photographic equipment	26.11	16.28	29.27	33.81	38.27	23.20	14.09	3.27
Photographer fees	14.34	8.61	18.61	18.37	18.67	15.45	5.40	1.24
Fireworks	2.33	2.07	4.81	2.03	3.08	0.11	0.78	1.99
Pinball, electronic video games	4.97	3.60	9.75	7.08	4.11	1.80	3.27	1.00

Note: Subcategories may not add to total because some are not shown. (–) means sample is too small to make a reliable estimate.
Source: Bureau of Labor Statistics, unpublished data from the 2003 Consumer Expenditure Survey

Table 3.2 Entertainment: Indexed spending by age, 2003

(indexed average annual spending of consumer units (CU) on entertainment by age of consumer unit reference person, 2003; index definition: an index of 100 is the average for all consumer units; an index of 132 means that spending by consumer units in that group is 32 percent above the average for all consumer units; an index of 68 indicates spending that is 32 percent below the average for all consumer units)

	total consumer units	under 25	25 to 34	35 to 44	45 to 54	55 to 64	65 to 74	75+
Average spending of CU, total	$40,817	$22,396	$40,525	$47,175	$50,101	$44,191	$33,629	$25,016
Average spending of CU, index	100	55	99	116	123	108	82	61
Entertainment, spending index	**100**	**46**	**95**	**122**	**117**	**117**	**98**	**44**
FEES AND ADMISSIONS	**100**	**47**	**81**	**129**	**126**	**121**	**78**	**49**
Recreation expenses on trips	100	31	76	117	117	149	99	53
Social, recreation, civic club membership	100	36	70	94	118	183	81	75
Fees for participant sports	100	42	83	109	108	117	119	94
Participant sports on trips	100	61	72	121	125	142	77	45
Movie, theater, opera, ballet	100	93	104	123	120	92	89	31
Movie, other admissions on trips	100	46	79	131	122	126	75	54
Admission to sports events	100	57	96	133	148	95	57	22
Admission to sports events on trips	100	46	79	131	122	126	75	54
Fees for recreational lessons	100	14	69	199	158	67	25	11
Other entertainment services on trips	100	31	76	117	117	149	99	53
TELEVISION, RADIO, SOUND EQUIPMENT	**100**	**63**	**107**	**120**	**118**	**102**	**77**	**57**
Television	**100**	**57**	**103**	**113**	**118**	**108**	**85**	**66**
Cable service and community antenna	100	48	94	106	118	114	100	81
Black-and-white TV sets	100	6	156	91	153	126	21	18
Color TV sets, consoles	100	56	118	127	133	108	51	16
Color TV sets, portable and table models	100	68	110	122	118	99	63	62
VCRs and video disc players	100	47	130	125	118	108	55	31
Video cassettes, tapes, and discs	100	122	149	125	113	73	39	19
Video game hardware and software	100	121	126	169	112	52	32	6
Repair of TV, radio, and sound equipment	100	108	70	79	120	127	64	148
Rental of television sets	100	469	133	167	14	33	–	–
Radio and sound equipment	**100**	**91**	**125**	**151**	**118**	**74**	**38**	**16**
Radios	100	56	41	146	209	35	36	68
Tape recorders and players	100	39	106	233	113	25	32	–
Sound components and component systems	100	100	102	169	117	71	44	13
Miscellaneous sound equipment	100	17	31	129	86	343	–	–
Sound equipment accessories	100	104	56	139	95	227	2	17
Satellite dishes	100	44	101	116	129	136	77	20
Compact disc, tape, record, video mail order clubs	100	63	123	126	114	87	101	24
Records, CDs, audio tapes, needles	100	115	122	125	132	76	47	22
Rental of VCR, radio, sound equipment	100	10	245	176	66	14	10	59
Musical instruments and accessories	100	31	164	192	95	40	39	4
Rental and repair of musical instruments	100	17	66	113	79	278	14	67
Rental of video cassettes, tapes, discs, films	100	125	145	141	116	65	25	9
PETS, TOYS, PLAYGROUND EQUIPMENT	**100**	**37**	**107**	**116**	**119**	**101**	**119**	**42**
Pets	**100**	**32**	**87**	**105**	**131**	**107**	**142**	**48**
Pet food	100	37	69	111	140	129	90	65
Pet purchase, supplies, and medicines	100	39	109	91	102	59	276	23
Pet services	100	17	78	112	161	102	85	62
Veterinarian services	100	24	92	107	137	129	93	47
Toys, games, hobbies, and tricycles	**100**	**51**	**155**	**144**	**91**	**83**	**62**	**27**
Playground equipment	**100**	**18**	**227**	**166**	**20**	**131**	**17**	**3**

	total consumer units	under 25	25 to 34	35 to 44	45 to 54	55 to 64	65 to 74	75+
OTHER ENTERTAINMENT SUPPLIES, EQUIPMENT, SERVICES	**100**	**25**	**82**	**124**	**102**	**151**	**136**	**20**
Unmotored recreational vehicles	**100**	**0**	**28**	**196**	**83**	**191**	**89**	**9**
Boat without motor and boat trailers	100	1	74	86	91	323	29	16
Trailer and other attachable campers	100	–	22	210	82	174	96	8
Motorized recreational vehicles	**100**	**4**	**54**	**83**	**95**	**196**	**231**	**27**
Motorized camper	100	–	–	18	77	285	393	6
Other vehicle	100	28	43	140	183	67	79	68
Motorboats	100	3	126	149	94	118	67	42
Rental of recreational vehicles	**100**	**30**	**118**	**76**	**171**	**155**	**27**	**23**
Docking and landing fees	**100**	**8**	**37**	**76**	**62**	**149**	**419**	**16**
Sports, recreation, exercise equipment	**100**	**32**	**112**	**148**	**102**	**116**	**87**	**14**
Athletic gear, game tables, exercise equipment	100	28	87	180	98	95	100	18
Bicycles	100	108	156	172	93	50	25	7
Camping equipment	100	7	117	159	135	111	27	–
Hunting and fishing equipment	100	18	154	63	78	207	123	14
Winter sports equipment	100	81	59	177	136	85	60	11
Water sports equipment	100	42	109	70	185	88	135	1
Other sports equipment	100	14	107	204	111	79	24	14
Rental and repair of miscellaneous sports equipment	100	27	52	80	123	126	227	69
Photographic equipment and supplies	**100**	**74**	**116**	**120**	**134**	**102**	**57**	**20**
Film	100	84	111	111	124	115	68	32
Other photographic supplies	100	484	35	63	182	14	36	–
Film processing	100	70	120	113	123	112	65	30
Repair and rental of photographic equipment	100	2	52	90	219	57	153	47
Photographic equipment	100	62	112	129	147	89	54	13
Photographer fees	100	60	130	128	130	108	38	9
Fireworks	**100**	**89**	**206**	**87**	**132**	**5**	**33**	**85**
Pinball, electronic video games	**100**	**72**	**196**	**142**	**83**	**36**	**66**	**20**

Note: (–) means sample is too small to make a reliable estimate.
Source: Calculations by New Strategist based on the 2003 Consumer Expenditure Survey

Table 3.3 Entertainment: Total spending by age, 2003

(total annual spending on entertainment, by consumer unit (CU) age groups, 2003; numbers in thousands)

	total consumer units	under 25	25 to 34	35 to 44	45 to 54	55 to 64	65 to 74	75+
Number of consumer units	115,356	8,584	19,737	24,413	23,131	16,580	11,495	11,417
Total spending of all CUs	$4,708,523,919	$192,243,230	$799,846,267	$1,151,684,740	$1,158,882,993	$732,680,977	$386,567,309	$285,612,010
Entertainment, total spending	237,582,603	8,152,912	38,649,191	61,487,558	55,682,794	40,027,602	23,172,081	10,373,486
FEES AND ADMISSIONS	57,038,928	1,999,214	7,940,195	15,567,438	14,439,758	9,901,576	4,407,988	2,783,465
Recreation expenses on trips	2,638,192	60,088	342,832	655,001	616,672	564,383	261,166	137,347
Social, recreation, civic club membership	10,965,741	290,397	1,308,760	2,187,405	2,602,469	2,885,749	880,172	811,520
Fees for participant sports	7,582,350	237,176	1,075,667	1,756,271	1,639,294	1,269,862	900,863	703,287
Participant sports on trips	2,748,933	125,412	338,292	705,780	686,297	561,730	210,473	121,249
Movie, theater, opera, ballet	10,461,636	727,580	1,869,489	2,724,491	2,514,571	1,383,601	924,658	317,507
Movie, other admissions on trips	5,226,780	179,663	705,992	1,445,738	1,280,763	945,060	388,301	280,972
Admission to sports events	3,881,729	163,869	639,479	1,091,505	1,150,767	530,228	221,624	84,486
Admission to sports events on trips	1,741,876	59,916	235,265	481,913	426,767	315,020	129,319	93,619
Fees for recreational lessons	9,154,652	95,025	1,081,390	3,864,822	2,905,254	881,724	230,245	96,359
Other entertainment services on trips	2,638,192	60,088	342,832	655,001	616,672	564,383	261,166	137,347
TELEVISION, RADIO, SOUND EQUIPMENT	84,213,341	3,972,504	15,389,531	21,336,962	20,003,920	12,328,888	6,441,683	4,739,653
Television	68,909,060	2,931,951	12,109,044	16,435,808	16,373,741	10,695,758	5,866,818	4,496,243
Cable service and community antenna	48,886,719	1,739,118	7,835,589	10,967,784	11,521,782	8,018,254	4,876,409	3,928,818
Black-and-white TV sets	39,221	172	10,461	7,568	12,028	7,129	805	685
Color TV sets, consoles	6,517,614	274,001	1,315,866	1,746,018	1,735,056	1,008,727	333,470	104,808
Color TV sets, portable and table models	3,997,085	202,153	749,217	1,031,693	947,908	570,186	252,775	243,981
VCRs and video disc players	2,798,537	97,085	624,084	740,690	663,860	434,728	152,884	85,171
Video cassettes, tapes, and discs	4,143,588	376,923	1,056,522	1,098,341	935,649	437,712	162,424	76,608
Video game hardware and software	2,157,157	195,028	466,385	769,986	483,669	161,323	68,855	12,330
Repair of TV, radio, and sound equipment	299,926	24,121	35,724	50,291	71,937	54,714	19,197	43,841
Rental of television sets	66,906	23,348	15,197	23,681	1,850	3,150	–	–
Radio and sound equipment	15,305,434	1,040,552	3,280,487	4,901,154	3,630,179	1,633,130	574,865	243,410
Radios	629,844	26,181	44,014	195,060	264,156	31,834	22,875	42,700
Tape recorders and players	453,349	13,219	82,106	223,135	103,164	16,083	14,599	–
Sound components and component systems	1,966,820	146,529	343,424	702,118	462,620	200,784	85,523	26,031
Miscellaneous sound equipment	48,450	601	2,566	13,183	8,327	23,875	–	–
Sound equipment accessories	639,072	49,358	60,987	188,224	122,132	208,245	1,494	10,732
Satellite dishes	104,974	3,434	18,158	25,878	27,063	20,559	8,047	2,055
Compact disc, tape, record, video mail order clubs	505,259	23,778	105,988	134,516	115,424	63,004	50,923	11,760
Records, CDs, audio tapes, needles	3,842,508	328,424	801,322	1,014,848	1,013,369	421,795	180,816	82,545
Rental of VCR, radio, sound equipment	33,453	258	14,013	12,451	4,395	663	345	1,941
Musical instruments and accessories	2,690,102	62,492	754,151	1,094,679	509,807	153,365	105,524	10,504
Rental and repair of musical instruments	264,165	3,262	30,000	62,986	41,636	105,449	3,563	17,582
Rental of video cassettes, tapes, discs, films	4,125,131	383,018	1,023,363	1,234,077	957,855	387,640	101,271	37,562
PETS, TOYS, PLAYGROUND EQUIPMENT	43,628,793	1,195,494	7,955,985	10,697,288	10,413,576	6,324,109	5,187,923	1,820,326
Pets	31,636,383	754,362	4,716,748	7,010,437	8,281,129	4,865,069	4,465,808	1,508,528
Pet food	11,514,836	313,574	1,359,287	2,714,970	3,232,095	2,130,364	1,034,320	741,192
Pet purchase, supplies, and medicines	8,735,910	254,601	1,635,803	1,684,009	1,782,937	734,991	2,399,581	198,427
Pet services	2,828,529	35,194	379,148	669,404	914,137	416,490	240,360	174,109
Veterinarian services	8,557,108	150,993	1,342,511	1,942,298	2,352,191	1,583,224	791,431	394,800
Toys, games, hobbies, and tricycles	11,541,368	434,951	3,064,169	3,528,411	2,114,405	1,374,316	714,414	310,428
Playground equipment	451,042	6,095	175,067	158,440	18,042	84,724	7,702	1,370

	total consumer units	under 25	25 to 34	35 to 44	45 to 54	55 to 64	65 to 74	75+
OTHER ENTERTAINMENT SUPPLIES, EQUIPMENT, SERVICES	$52,701,542	$985,701	$7,363,480	$13,885,870	$10,825,539	$11,473,028	$7,134,487	$1,030,042
Unmotored recreational vehicles	6,953,660	601	329,608	2,878,781	1,162,564	1,909,519	613,488	58,569
Boat without motor and boat trailers	801,724	601	101,646	145,501	146,651	371,889	23,450	12,445
Trailer and other attachable campers	6,150,782	–	227,962	2,733,279	1,016,145	1,537,629	590,038	46,011
Motorized recreational vehicles	19,302,519	59,573	1,787,580	3,375,586	3,668,345	5,448,188	4,452,703	510,226
Motorized camper	9,677,215	–	–	376,204	1,496,344	3,958,309	3,789,557	57,199
Other vehicle	2,023,344	41,804	148,225	599,827	743,893	195,644	158,746	135,177
Motorboats	7,600,807	17,769	1,639,553	2,399,554	1,427,877	1,294,235	504,401	317,849
Rental of recreational vehicles	485,649	10,902	98,093	77,633	166,775	108,102	12,989	10,960
Docking and landing fees	411,821	2,404	25,855	65,915	51,351	88,206	171,965	6,394
Sports, recreation, exercise equipment	15,200,460	357,609	2,909,431	4,766,394	3,103,486	2,538,398	1,315,258	214,183
Athletic gear, game tables, exercise equipment	6,289,209	128,760	933,955	2,396,380	1,239,359	854,367	628,317	109,147
Bicycles	1,275,837	102,836	340,661	463,847	237,093	91,522	31,956	8,449
Camping equipment	1,073,964	5,923	215,133	361,068	290,063	171,437	28,967	–
Hunting and fishing equipment	3,517,204	48,070	928,034	468,730	543,436	1,048,685	429,568	49,664
Winter sports equipment	564,091	33,821	57,040	211,417	153,359	68,807	33,680	6,051
Water sports equipment	516,795	15,966	96,711	76,901	191,756	65,325	69,315	685
Other sports equipment	1,731,494	17,426	317,371	748,747	386,288	196,141	41,152	24,204
Rental and repair of miscellaneous sports equipment	231,866	4,721	20,526	39,305	57,134	42,113	52,417	15,870
Photographic equipment and supplies	9,133,888	505,941	1,807,909	2,318,991	2,454,430	1,339,167	520,609	183,814
Film	1,687,658	105,927	319,937	397,688	419,828	278,212	113,915	52,861
Other photographic supplies	145,349	52,362	8,684	19,286	52,970	2,984	5,173	–
Film processing	2,568,978	133,910	528,557	615,452	635,177	411,847	167,137	76,380
Repair and rental of photographic equipment	66,906	86	5,921	12,695	29,376	5,471	10,231	3,083
Photographic equipment	3,011,945	139,748	577,702	825,404	885,223	384,656	161,965	37,334
Photographer fees	1,654,205	73,908	367,306	448,467	431,856	256,161	62,073	14,157
Fireworks	268,779	17,769	94,935	49,558	71,243	1,824	8,966	22,720
Pinball, electronic video games	573,319	30,902	192,436	172,844	95,068	29,844	37,589	11,417

Note: Numbers may not add to total because of rounding and missing subcategories. (–) means sample is too small to make a reliable estimate.
Source: Calculations by New Strategist based on the 2003 Consumer Expenditure Survey

Table 3.4 Entertainment: Market shares by age, 2003

(percentage of total annual spending on entertainment accounted for by consumer unit age groups, 2003)

	total consumer units	under 25	25 to 34	35 to 44	45 to 54	55 to 64	65 to 74	75+
Share of total consumer units	100.0%	7.4%	17.1%	21.2%	20.1%	14.4%	10.0%	9.9%
Share of total before-tax income	100.0	3.0	16.9	25.3	26.7	16.5	6.9	4.9
Share of total spending	100.0	4.1	17.0	24.5	24.6	15.6	8.2	6.1
Share of entertainment spending	100.0	3.4	16.3	25.9	23.4	16.8	9.8	4.4
FEES AND ADMISSIONS	100.0	3.5	13.9	27.3	25.3	17.4	7.7	4.9
Recreation expenses on trips	100.0	2.3	13.0	24.8	23.4	21.4	9.9	5.2
Social, recreation, civic club membership	100.0	2.6	11.9	19.9	23.7	26.3	8.0	7.4
Fees for participant sports	100.0	3.1	14.2	23.2	21.6	16.7	11.9	9.3
Participant sports on trips	100.0	4.6	12.3	25.7	25.0	20.4	7.7	4.4
Movie, theater, opera, ballet	100.0	7.0	17.9	26.0	24.0	13.2	8.8	3.0
Movie, other admissions on trips	100.0	3.4	13.5	27.7	24.5	18.1	7.4	5.4
Admission to sports events	100.0	4.2	16.5	28.1	29.6	13.7	5.7	2.2
Admission to sports events on trips	100.0	3.4	13.5	27.7	24.5	18.1	7.4	5.4
Fees for recreational lessons	100.0	1.0	11.8	42.2	31.7	9.6	2.5	1.1
Other entertainment services on trips	100.0	2.3	13.0	24.8	23.4	21.4	9.9	5.2
TELEVISION, RADIO, SOUND EQUIPMENT	100.0	4.7	18.3	25.3	23.8	14.6	7.6	5.6
Television	100.0	4.3	17.6	23.9	23.8	15.5	8.5	6.5
Cable service and community antenna	100.0	3.6	16.0	22.4	23.6	16.4	10.0	8.0
Black-and-white TV sets	100.0	0.4	26.7	19.3	30.7	18.2	2.1	1.7
Color TV sets, consoles	100.0	4.2	20.2	26.8	26.6	15.5	5.1	1.6
Color TV sets, portable and table models	100.0	5.1	18.7	25.8	23.7	14.3	6.3	6.1
VCRs and video disc players	100.0	3.5	22.3	26.5	23.7	15.5	5.5	3.0
Video cassettes, tapes, and discs	100.0	9.1	25.5	26.5	22.6	10.6	3.9	1.8
Video game hardware and software	100.0	9.0	21.6	35.7	22.4	7.5	3.2	0.6
Repair of TV, radio, and sound equipment	100.0	8.0	11.9	16.8	24.0	18.2	6.4	14.6
Rental of television sets	100.0	34.9	22.7	35.4	2.8	4.7	–	–
Radio and sound equipment	100.0	6.8	21.4	32.0	23.7	10.7	3.8	1.6
Radios	100.0	4.2	7.0	31.0	41.9	5.1	3.6	6.8
Tape recorders and players	100.0	2.9	18.1	49.2	22.8	3.5	3.2	–
Sound components and component systems	100.0	7.5	17.5	35.7	23.5	10.2	4.3	1.3
Miscellaneous sound equipment	100.0	1.2	5.3	27.2	17.2	49.3	–	–
Sound equipment accessories	100.0	7.7	9.5	29.5	19.1	32.6	0.2	1.7
Satellite dishes	100.0	3.3	17.3	24.7	25.8	19.6	7.7	2.0
Compact disc, tape, record, video mail order clubs	100.0	4.7	21.0	26.6	22.8	12.5	10.1	2.3
Records, CDs, audio tapes, needles	100.0	8.5	20.9	26.4	26.4	11.0	4.7	2.1
Rental of VCR, radio, sound equipment	100.0	0.8	41.9	37.2	13.1	2.0	1.0	5.8
Musical instruments and accessories	100.0	2.3	28.0	40.7	19.0	5.7	3.9	0.4
Rental and repair of musical instruments	100.0	1.2	11.4	23.8	15.8	39.9	1.3	6.7
Rental of video cassettes, tapes, discs, films	100.0	9.3	24.8	29.9	23.2	9.4	2.5	0.9
PETS, TOYS, PLAYGROUND EQUIPMENT	100.0	2.7	18.2	24.5	23.9	14.5	11.9	4.2
Pets	100.0	2.4	14.9	22.2	26.2	15.4	14.1	4.8
Pet food	100.0	2.7	11.8	23.6	28.1	18.5	9.0	6.4
Pet purchase, supplies, and medicines	100.0	2.9	18.7	19.3	20.4	8.4	27.5	2.3
Pet services	100.0	1.2	13.4	23.7	32.3	14.7	8.5	6.2
Veterinarian services	100.0	1.8	15.7	22.7	27.5	18.5	9.2	4.6
Toys, games, hobbies, and tricycles	100.0	3.8	26.5	30.6	18.3	11.9	6.2	2.7
Playground equipment	100.0	1.4	38.8	35.1	4.0	18.8	1.7	0.3

	total consumer units	under 25	25 to 34	35 to 44	45 to 54	55 to 64	65 to 74	75+
OTHER ENTERTAINMENT SUPPLIES, EQUIPMENT, SERVICES	**100.0%**	**1.9%**	**14.0%**	**26.3%**	**20.5%**	**21.8%**	**13.5%**	**2.0%**
Unmotored recreational vehicles	**100.0**	**0.0**	**4.7**	**41.4**	**16.7**	**27.5**	**8.8**	**0.8**
Boat without motor and boat trailers	100.0	0.1	12.7	18.1	18.3	46.4	2.9	1.6
Trailer and other attachable campers	100.0	–	3.7	44.4	16.5	25.0	9.6	0.7
Motorized recreational vehicles	**100.0**	**0.3**	**9.3**	**17.5**	**19.0**	**28.2**	**23.1**	**2.6**
Motorized camper	100.0	–	–	3.9	15.5	40.9	39.2	0.6
Other vehicle	100.0	2.1	7.3	29.6	36.8	9.7	7.8	6.7
Motorboats	100.0	0.2	21.6	31.6	18.8	17.0	6.6	4.2
Rental of recreational vehicles	**100.0**	**2.2**	**20.2**	**16.0**	**34.3**	**22.3**	**2.7**	**2.3**
Docking and landing fees	**100.0**	**0.6**	**6.3**	**16.0**	**12.5**	**21.4**	**41.8**	**1.6**
Sports, recreation, exercise equipment	**100.0**	**2.4**	**19.1**	**31.4**	**20.4**	**16.7**	**8.7**	**1.4**
Athletic gear, game tables, exercise equipment	100.0	2.0	14.9	38.1	19.7	13.6	10.0	1.7
Bicycles	100.0	8.1	26.7	36.4	18.6	7.2	2.5	0.7
Camping equipment	100.0	0.6	20.0	33.6	27.0	16.0	2.7	–
Hunting and fishing equipment	100.0	1.4	26.4	13.3	15.6	29.8	12.2	1.4
Winter sports equipment	100.0	6.0	10.1	37.5	27.2	12.2	6.0	1.1
Water sports equipment	100.0	3.1	18.7	14.9	37.1	12.6	13.4	0.1
Other sports equipment	100.0	1.0	18.3	43.2	22.3	11.3	2.4	1.4
Rental and repair of miscellaneous sports equipment	100.0	2.0	8.9	17.0	24.6	18.2	22.6	6.8
Photographic equipment and supplies	**100.0**	**5.5**	**19.8**	**25.4**	**26.9**	**14.7**	**5.7**	**2.0**
Film	100.0	6.3	19.0	23.6	24.9	16.5	6.7	3.1
Other photographic supplies	100.0	36.0	6.0	13.3	36.4	2.1	3.6	–
Film processing	100.0	5.2	20.6	24.0	24.7	16.0	6.5	3.0
Repair and rental of photographic equipment	100.0	0.1	8.8	19.0	43.9	8.2	15.3	4.6
Photographic equipment	100.0	4.6	19.2	27.4	29.4	12.8	5.4	1.2
Photographer fees	100.0	4.5	22.2	27.1	26.1	15.5	3.8	0.9
Fireworks	**100.0**	**6.6**	**35.3**	**18.4**	**26.5**	**0.7**	**3.3**	**8.5**
Pinball, electronic video games	**100.0**	**5.4**	**33.6**	**30.1**	**16.6**	**5.2**	**6.6**	**2.0**

Note: Numbers may not add to total because of rounding. (–) means sample is too small to make a reliable estimate.
Source: Calculations by New Strategist based on the 2003 Consumer Expenditure Survey

Table 3.5 Entertainment: Average spending by income, 2003

(average annual spending on entertainment, by before-tax income of consumer units (CU), 2003; complete income reporters only)

	total complete reporters	under $20,000	$20,000–$39,999	$40,000–$49,999	$50,000–$69,999	$70,000–$79,999	$80,000–$99,999	$100,000 or more
Number of consumer units (000)	97,391	27,100	23,941	8,891	13,890	5,121	6,909	11,537
Average number of persons per CU	2.5	1.8	2.4	2.6	2.8	3.0	3.0	3.1
Average before-tax income of CU	$51,128.00	$10,752.55	$29,072.57	$44,294.00	$58,900.00	$74,560.00	$88,832.00	$154,665.00
Average spending of CU, total	42,741.66	19,862.52	31,684.32	39,756.91	49,788.99	57,128.14	65,957.39	93,514.86
Entertainment, average spending	**2,155.48**	**763.77**	**1,618.22**	**1,925.19**	**2,362.72**	**3,242.80**	**3,606.89**	**5,124.28**
FEES AND ADMISSIONS	**511.12**	**130.25**	**256.72**	**383.11**	**553.20**	**718.88**	**849.34**	**1,686.90**
Recreation expenses on trips	23.69	6.17	13.65	23.20	32.04	31.03	37.84	64.25
Social, recreation, civic club membership	97.82	25.28	33.97	57.46	94.84	139.62	126.15	399.93
Fees for participant sports	65.57	18.68	42.18	55.47	77.23	85.28	127.38	172.24
Participant sports on trips	24.06	7.36	8.71	17.30	26.83	40.85	34.22	83.48
Movie, theater, opera, ballet	94.37	34.35	64.07	79.15	102.88	137.97	156.46	243.20
Movie, other admissions on trips	46.59	11.76	24.07	41.11	59.74	74.96	85.64	127.55
Admission to sports events	36.14	7.20	16.29	20.85	32.44	42.06	73.18	136.71
Admission to sports events on trips	15.53	3.92	8.02	13.70	19.91	24.98	28.54	42.51
Fees for recreational lessons	83.67	9.37	32.12	51.66	75.26	111.09	142.09	352.79
Other entertainment services on trips	23.69	6.17	13.65	23.20	32.04	31.03	37.84	64.25
TELEVISION, RADIO, SOUND EQUIPMENT	**745.25**	**396.17**	**606.21**	**780.01**	**863.65**	**976.74**	**1,083.95**	**1,379.48**
Television	**606.98**	**341.02**	**508.12**	**633.42**	**714.53**	**769.20**	**865.71**	**1,060.09**
Cable service and community antenna	428.83	270.43	385.51	468.21	510.50	523.62	561.49	640.62
Black-and-white TV sets	0.35	–	–	0.41	0.29	0.52	0.62	0.75
Color TV sets, consoles	53.47	13.70	27.08	55.24	51.70	92.85	102.41	155.57
Color TV sets, portable and table models	36.01	17.22	29.37	27.12	33.31	43.12	52.92	90.75
VCRs and video disc players	25.90	10.53	18.93	21.64	36.04	26.64	51.65	51.79
Video cassettes, tapes, and discs	38.78	18.05	28.38	35.19	51.72	51.14	63.28	76.12
Video game hardware and software	20.19	9.51	13.51	21.53	27.52	27.49	28.23	41.21
Repair of TV, radio, and sound equipment	2.80	0.81	3.34	3.79	3.41	3.83	4.75	3.21
Rental of television sets	0.65	0.58	1.73	0.28	0.04	–	0.37	0.06
Radio and sound equipment	**138.27**	**55.15**	**98.09**	**146.60**	**149.12**	**207.54**	**218.24**	**319.39**
Radios	4.85	1.81	2.81	8.26	1.18	10.94	3.49	16.38
Tape recorders and players	4.49	1.36	2.65	12.31	8.01	–	8.00	6.06
Sound components and component systems	16.33	5.56	13.45	13.57	19.28	24.75	21.55	39.36
Miscellaneous sound equipment	0.57	–	–	–	0.33	–	0.18	2.33
Sound equipment accessories	5.27	1.96	1.71	5.23	11.97	4.94	4.81	13.31
Satellite dishes	0.98	–	–	2.17	0.35	1.74	1.12	1.82
Compact disc, tape, record, video mail order clubs	4.83	1.54	4.60	7.03	7.17	6.88	5.54	7.22
Records, CDs, audio tapes, needles	34.95	17.75	26.06	31.62	39.81	47.59	53.73	73.69
Rental of VCR, radio, sound equipment	0.35	0.13	0.93	0.19	0.34	0.22	0.02	0.06
Musical instruments and accessories	25.80	5.82	13.21	16.66	13.57	48.49	59.91	90.14
Rental and repair of musical instruments	2.19	0.20	1.25	11.18	1.22	2.88	1.24	3.30
Rental of video cassettes, tapes, discs, films	37.66	18.1	30.59	38.39	45.90	59.11	58.66	65.72
PETS, TOYS, PLAYGROUND EQUIPMENT	**411.09**	**155.26**	**377.50**	**438.07**	**468.71**	**530.69**	**652.22**	**790.31**
Pets	**304.53**	**118.03**	**289.48**	**328.74**	**338.86**	**379.72**	**470.14**	**577.53**
Pet food	112.65	66.86	89.36	130.23	136.24	133.17	201.95	166.25
Pet purchase, supplies, and medicines	88.60	21.45	134.94	109.06	87.51	98.58	101.97	117.19
Pet services	25.87	7.25	14.72	26.43	21.93	24.25	37.89	90.61
Veterinarian services	77.41	22.46	50.47	63.03	93.18	123.71	128.33	203.49
Toys, games, hobbies, and tricycles	**102.46**	**36.96**	**87.05**	**107.85**	**126.49**	**148.90**	**171.05**	**193.56**
Playground equipment	**4.09**	**0.36**	**0.97**	**1.47**	**3.36**	**2.07**	**11.03**	**19.22**

	total complete reporters	under $20,000	$20,000–$39,999	$40,000–$49,999	$50,000–$69,999	$70,000–$79,999	$80,000–$99,999	$100,000 or more
OTHER ENTERTAINMENT SUPPLIES, EQUIPMENT, SERVICES	**$488.02**	**$82.09**	**$377.78**	**$324.01**	**$477.17**	**$1,016.50**	**$1,021.38**	**$1,267.59**
Unmotored recreational vehicles	**69.60**	**1.07**	**28.46**	**63.56**	**95.96**	**201.75**	**286.36**	**101.86**
Boat without motor and boat trailers	7.86	0.43	1.52	4.14	21.98	2.43	28.45	16.39
Trailer and other attachable campers	61.75	1.02	27.62	59.41	73.98	199.32	257.91	85.47
Motorized recreational vehicles	171.04	18.51	185.11	88.77	47.07	384.73	215.11	616.09
Motorized camper	**81.15**	–	**148.26**	**41.99**	**0.49**	**352.54**	**2.23**	**186.61**
Other vehicle	19.18	–	–	6.66	10.10	30.03	55.50	48.50
Motorboats	70.71	–	22.10	40.12	36.47	2.17	157.38	380.98
Rental of recreational vehicles	**4.55**	**1.21**	**2.95**	**1.17**	**4.70**	**10.29**	**6.02**	**14.74**
Docking and landing fees	**3.90**	**0.82**	**1.46**	**11.21**	**3.76**	**3.73**	**7.82**	**8.81**
Sports, recreation, exercise equipment	**144.02**	**41.89**	**97.76**	**89.03**	**220.31**	**269.78**	**314.44**	**283.09**
Athletic gear, game tables, exercise equipment	61.93	19.07	42.96	25.96	100.40	141.46	111.69	125.53
Bicycles	11.33	3.85	8.82	7.43	12.58	18.70	23.42	25.07
Camping equipment	10.40	3.50	6.87	4.54	6.81	27.91	31.91	24.11
Hunting and fishing equipment	31.34	9.93	24.02	27.78	58.18	39.26	105.61	20.54
Winter sports equipment	4.93	1.07	1.89	3.85	6.20	4.69	9.81	16.83
Water sports equipment	5.08	1.32	1.56	7.15	3.91	16.44	14.41	10.45
Other sports equipment	16.80	2.38	8.75	10.71	29.49	19.97	16.42	55.64
Rental and repair of miscellaneous sports equipment	2.2	0.77	2.90	1.61	2.73	1.34	1.19	4.92
Photographic equipment and supplies	**84.54**	**26.26**	**56.67**	**59.61**	**92.70**	**133.92**	**166.66**	**217.69**
Film	15.54	6.62	12.18	13.68	17.72	22.21	27.96	31.90
Other photographic supplies	0.98	–	–	0.74	0.32	–	0.91	4.75
Film processing	23.77	8.46	15.82	20.14	25.33	40.71	45.79	56.42
Repair and rental of photographic equipment	0.59	0.13	0.17	0.07	0.39	0.41	3.04	1.9
Photographic equipment	27.86	6.59	15.06	15.39	30.53	48.68	54.32	85.75
Photographer fees	15.80	3.88	13.13	9.60	18.42	21.91	34.62	36.97
Fireworks	**2.33**	–	–	**2.61**	**2.29**	**0.69**	**8.01**	**5.53**
Pinball, electronic video games	**5.15**	**2.41**	**3.33**	**3.01**	**9.71**	**2.67**	**7.71**	**12.52**

Note: Subcategories may not add to total because some are not shown. (–) means sample is too small to make a reliable estimate.
Source: Bureau of Labor Statistics, unpublished data from the 2003 Consumer Expenditure Survey; calculations by New Strategist

Table 3.6 Entertainment: Indexed spending by income, 2003

(indexed average annual spending of consumer units (CU) on entertainment by before-tax income of consumer unit, 2003; complete income reporters only; index definition: an index of 100 is the average for all consumer units; an index of 132 means that spending by consumer units in that group is 32 percent above the average for all consumer units; an index of 68 indicates spending that is 32 percent below the average for all consumer units)

	total complete reporters	under $20,000	$20,000–$39,999	$40,000–$49,999	$50,000–$69,999	$70,000–$79,999	$80,000–$99,999	$100,000 or more
Average spending of CU, total	$42,742	$19,863	$31,684	$39,757	$49,789	$57,128	$65,957	$93,515
Average spending of CU, index	100	46	74	93	116	134	154	219
Entertainment, spending index	**100**	**35**	**75**	**89**	**110**	**150**	**167**	**238**
FEES AND ADMISSIONS	**100**	**25**	**50**	**75**	**108**	**141**	**166**	**330**
Recreation expenses on trips	100	26	58	98	135	131	160	271
Social, recreation, civic club membership	100	26	35	59	97	143	129	409
Fees for participant sports	100	28	64	85	118	130	194	263
Participant sports on trips	100	31	36	72	112	170	142	347
Movie, theater, opera, ballet	100	36	68	84	109	146	166	258
Movie, other admissions on trips	100	25	52	88	128	161	184	274
Admission to sports events	100	20	45	58	90	116	202	378
Admission to sports events on trips	100	25	52	88	128	161	184	274
Fees for recreational lessons	100	11	38	62	90	133	170	422
Other entertainment services on trips	100	26	58	98	135	131	160	271
TELEVISION, RADIO, SOUND EQUIPMENT	**100**	**53**	**81**	**105**	**116**	**131**	**145**	**185**
Television	**100**	**56**	**84**	**104**	**118**	**127**	**143**	**175**
Cable service and community antenna	100	63	90	109	119	122	131	149
Black-and-white TV sets	100	–	–	117	83	149	177	214
Color TV sets, consoles	100	26	51	103	97	174	192	291
Color TV sets, portable and table models	100	48	82	75	93	120	147	252
VCRs and video disc players	100	41	73	84	139	103	199	200
Video cassettes, tapes, and discs	100	47	73	91	133	132	163	196
Video game hardware and software	100	47	67	107	136	136	140	204
Repair of TV, radio, and sound equipment	100	29	119	135	122	137	170	115
Rental of television sets	100	89	267	43	6	–	57	9
Radio and sound equipment	**100**	**40**	**71**	**106**	**108**	**150**	**158**	**231**
Radios	100	37	58	170	24	226	72	338
Tape recorders and players	100	30	59	274	178	–	178	135
Sound components and component systems	100	34	82	83	118	152	132	241
Miscellaneous sound equipment	100	–	–	–	58	–	32	409
Sound equipment accessories	100	37	32	99	227	94	91	253
Satellite dishes	100	–	–	221	36	178	114	186
Compact disc, tape, record, video mail order clubs	100	32	95	146	148	142	115	149
Records, CDs, audio tapes, needles	100	51	75	90	114	136	154	211
Rental of VCR, radio, sound equipment	100	36	266	54	97	63	6	17
Musical instruments and accessories	100	23	51	65	53	188	232	349
Rental and repair of musical instruments	100	9	57	511	56	132	57	151
Rental of video cassettes, tapes, discs, films	100	48	81	102	122	157	156	175
PETS, TOYS, PLAYGROUND EQUIPMENT	**100**	**38**	**92**	**107**	**114**	**129**	**159**	**192**
Pets	**100**	**39**	**95**	**108**	**111**	**125**	**154**	**190**
Pet food	100	59	79	116	121	118	179	148
Pet purchase, supplies, and medicines	100	24	152	123	99	111	115	132
Pet services	100	28	57	102	85	94	146	350
Veterinarian services	100	29	65	81	120	160	166	263
Toys, games, hobbies, and tricycles	**100**	**36**	**85**	**105**	**123**	**145**	**167**	**189**
Playground equipment	**100**	**9**	**24**	**36**	**82**	**51**	**270**	**470**

	total complete reporters	under $20,000	$20,000–$39,999	$40,000–$49,999	$50,000–$69,999	$70,000–$79,999	$80,000–$99,999	$100,000 or more
OTHER ENTERTAINMENT SUPPLIES, EQUIPMENT, SERVICES	**100**	**17**	**77**	**66**	**98**	**208**	**209**	**260**
Unmotored recreational vehicles	**100**	**2**	**41**	**91**	**138**	**290**	**411**	**146**
Boat without motor and boat trailers	100	5	19	53	280	31	362	209
Trailer and other attachable campers	100	2	45	96	120	323	418	138
Motorized recreational vehicles	**100**	**11**	**108**	**52**	**28**	**225**	**126**	**360**
Motorized camper	100	–	183	52	1	434	3	230
Other vehicle	100	–	–	35	53	157	289	253
Motorboats	100	–	31	57	52	3	223	539
Rental of recreational vehicles	**100**	**27**	**65**	**26**	**103**	**226**	**132**	**324**
Docking and landing fees	**100**	**21**	**37**	**287**	**96**	**96**	**201**	**226**
Sports, recreation, exercise equipment	**100**	**29**	**68**	**62**	**153**	**187**	**218**	**197**
Athletic gear, game tables, exercise equipment	100	31	69	42	162	228	180	203
Bicycles	100	34	78	66	111	165	207	221
Camping equipment	100	34	66	44	65	268	307	232
Hunting and fishing equipment	100	32	77	89	186	125	337	66
Winter sports equipment	100	22	38	78	126	95	199	341
Water sports equipment	100	26	31	141	77	324	284	206
Other sports equipment	100	14	52	64	176	119	98	331
Rental and repair of miscellaneous sports equipment	100	35	132	73	124	61	54	224
Photographic equipment and supplies	**100**	**31**	**67**	**71**	**110**	**158**	**197**	**257**
Film	100	43	78	88	114	143	180	205
Other photographic supplies	100	–	–	76	33	–	93	485
Film processing	100	36	67	85	107	171	193	237
Repair and rental of photographic equipment	100	22	28	12	66	69	515	322
Photographic equipment	100	24	54	55	110	175	195	308
Photographer fees	100	25	83	61	117	139	219	234
Fireworks	**100**	**–**	**–**	**112**	**98**	**30**	**344**	**237**
Pinball, electronic video games	**100**	**47**	**65**	**58**	**189**	**52**	**150**	**243**

Note: (–) means sample is too small to make a reliable estimate.
Source: Calculations by New Strategist based on the 2003 Consumer Expenditure Survey

Table 3.7 Entertainment: Total spending by income, 2003

(total annual spending on entertainment, by before-tax income group of consumer units (CU), 2003; complete income reporters only; numbers in thousands)

	total complete reporters	under $20,000	$20,000–$39,999	$40,000–$49,999	$50,000–$69,999	$70,000–$79,999	$80,000–$99,999	$100,000 or more
Number of consumer units	97,391	27,100	23,941	8,891	13,890	5,121	6,909	11,537
Total spending of all CUs	$4,162,653,009	$538,274,380	$758,554,310	$353,478,687	$691,569,071	$292,553,205	$455,699,608	$1,078,880,940
Entertainment, total spending	209,924,353	20,698,243	38,741,834	17,116,864	32,818,181	16,606,379	24,920,003	59,118,818
FEES AND ADMISSIONS	49,778,488	3,529,777	6,146,191	3,406,231	7,683,948	3,681,384	5,868,090	19,461,765
Recreation expenses on trips	2,307,193	167,325	326,734	206,271	445,036	158,905	261,437	741,252
Social, recreation, civic club membership	9,526,788	684,958	813,235	510,877	1,317,328	714,994	871,570	4,613,992
Fees for participant sports	6,385,928	506,127	1,009,728	493,184	1,072,725	436,719	880,068	1,987,133
Participant sports on trips	2,343,227	199,485	208,531	153,814	372,669	209,193	236,426	963,109
Movie, theater, opera, ballet	9,190,789	930,964	1,533,946	703,723	1,429,003	706,544	1,080,982	2,805,798
Movie, other admissions on trips	4,537,447	318,566	576,357	365,509	829,789	383,870	591,687	1,471,544
Admission to sports events	3,519,711	195,073	389,989	185,377	450,592	215,389	505,601	1,577,223
Admission to sports events on trips	1,512,482	106,201	192,031	121,807	276,550	127,923	197,183	490,438
Fees for recreational lessons	8,148,705	253,861	768,881	459,309	1,045,361	568,892	981,700	4,070,138
Other entertainment services on trips	2,307,193	167,325	326,734	206,271	445,036	158,905	261,437	741,252
TELEVISION, RADIO, SOUND EQUIPMENT	72,580,643	10,736,245	14,513,320	6,935,069	11,996,099	5,001,886	7,489,011	15,915,061
Television	59,114,389	9,241,627	12,164,985	5,631,737	9,924,822	3,939,073	5,981,190	12,230,258
Cable service and community antenna	41,764,183	7,328,552	9,229,502	4,162,855	7,090,845	2,681,458	3,879,334	7,390,833
Black-and-white TV sets	34,087	–	–	3,645	4,028	2,663	4,284	8,653
Color TV sets, consoles	5,207,497	371,353	648,268	491,139	718,113	475,485	707,551	1,794,811
Color TV sets, portable and table models	3,507,050	466,752	703,120	241,124	462,676	220,818	365,624	1,046,983
VCRs and video disc players	2,522,427	285,389	453,307	192,401	500,596	136,423	356,850	597,501
Video cassettes, tapes, and discs	3,776,823	489,068	679,518	312,874	718,391	261,888	437,202	878,196
Video game hardware and software	1,966,324	257,653	323,529	191,423	382,253	140,776	195,041	475,440
Repair of TV, radio, and sound equipment	272,695	22,072	79,979	33,697	47,365	19,613	32,818	37,034
Rental of television sets	63,304	15,750	41,485	2,489	556	–	2,556	692
Radio and sound equipment	13,466,254	1,494,618	2,348,335	1,303,421	2,071,277	1,062,812	1,507,820	3,684,802
Radios	472,346	48,967	67,384	73,440	16,390	56,024	24,112	188,976
Tape recorders and players	437,286	36,853	63,353	109,448	111,259	–	55,272	69,914
Sound components and component systems	1,590,395	150,617	322,021	120,651	267,799	126,745	148,889	454,096
Miscellaneous sound equipment	55,513	–	–	–	4,584	–	1,244	26,881
Sound equipment accessories	513,251	53,030	40,969	46,500	166,263	25,298	33,232	153,557
Satellite dishes	95,443	–	–	19,293	4,862	8,911	7,738	20,997
Compact disc, tape, record, video mail order clubs	470,399	41,701	110,069	62,504	99,591	35,232	38,276	83,297
Records, CDs, audio tapes, needles	3,403,815	481,013	623,858	281,133	552,961	243,708	371,221	850,162
Rental of VCR, radio, sound equipment	34,087	3,453	22,310	1,689	4,723	1,127	138	692
Musical instruments and accessories	2,512,688	157,838	316,326	148,124	188,487	248,317	413,918	1,039,945
Rental and repair of musical instruments	213,286	5,334	29,994	99,401	16,946	14,748	8,567	38,072
Rental of video cassettes, tapes, discs, films	3,667,745	490,607	732,401	341,325	637,551	302,702	405,282	758,212
PETS, TOYS, PLAYGROUND EQUIPMENT	40,036,466	4,207,491	9,037,673	3,894,880	6,510,382	2,717,663	4,506,188	9,117,806
Pets	29,658,481	3,198,574	6,930,416	2,922,827	4,706,765	1,944,546	3,248,197	6,662,964
Pet food	10,971,096	1,811,944	2,139,282	1,157,875	1,892,374	681,964	1,395,273	1,918,026
Pet purchase, supplies, and medicines	8,628,843	581,417	3,230,529	969,652	1,215,514	504,828	704,511	1,352,021
Pet services	2,519,505	196,566	352,377	234,989	304,608	124,184	261,782	1,045,368
Veterinarian services	7,539,037	608,728	1,208,227	560,400	1,294,270	633,519	886,632	2,347,664
Toys, games, hobbies, and tricycles	9,978,682	1,001,498	2,084,131	958,894	1,756,946	762,517	1,181,784	2,233,102
Playground equipment	398,329	9,869	23,258	13,070	46,670	10,600	76,206	221,741

	total complete reporters	under $20,000	$20,000– $39,999	$40,000– $49,999	$50,000– $69,999	$70,000– $79,999	$80,000– $99,999	$100,000 or more
OTHER ENTERTAINMENT SUPPLIES, EQUIPMENT, SERVICES	$47,528,756	$2,224,766	$9,044,519	$2,880,773	$6,627,891	$5,205,497	$7,056,714	$14,624,186
Unmotored recreational vehicles	6,778,414	28,901	681,312	565,112	1,332,884	1,033,162	1,978,461	1,175,159
Boat without motor and boat trailers	765,493	11,561	36,390	36,809	305,302	12,444	196,561	189,091
Trailer and other attachable campers	6,013,894	27,642	651,275	528,214	1,027,582	1,020,718	1,781,900	986,067
Motorized recreational vehicles	16,657,757	501,726	4,431,684	789,254	653,802	1,970,202	1,486,195	7,107,830
Motorized camper	7,903,280	–	3,549,509	373,333	6,806	1,805,357	15,407	2,152,920
Other vehicle	1,867,959	–	–	59,214	140,289	153,784	383,450	559,545
Motorboats	6,886,518	–	529,065	355,707	506,568	11,113	1,087,338	4,395,366
Rental of recreational vehicles	443,129	32,753	70,606	10,402	65,283	52,695	41,592	170,055
Docking and landing fees	379,825	22,321	34,904	99,668	52,226	19,101	54,028	101,641
Sports, recreation, exercise equipment	14,026,252	1,135,185	2,340,386	791,566	3,060,106	1,381,543	2,172,466	3,266,009
Athletic gear, game tables, exercise equipment	6,031,425	516,906	1,028,466	230,810	1,394,556	724,417	771,666	1,448,240
Bicycles	1,103,440	104,470	211,150	66,060	174,736	95,763	161,809	289,233
Camping equipment	1,012,866	94,896	164,411	40,365	94,591	142,927	220,466	278,157
Hunting and fishing equipment	3,052,234	269,148	574,982	246,992	808,120	201,050	729,659	236,970
Winter sports equipment	480,138	28,877	45,193	34,230	86,118	24,017	67,777	194,168
Water sports equipment	494,746	35,751	37,293	63,571	54,310	84,189	99,559	120,562
Other sports equipment	1,636,169	64,501	209,538	95,223	409,616	102,266	113,446	641,919
Rental and repair of miscellaneous sports equipment	214,260	20,762	69,330	14,315	37,920	6,862	8,222	56,762
Photographic equipment and supplies	8,233,435	711,666	1,355,789	529,993	1,287,603	685,804	1,151,454	2,511,490
Film	1,513,456	179,517	291,617	121,629	245,131	113,737	193,176	368,030
Other photographic supplies	95,443	–	–	6,579	4,445	–	6,287	54,801
Film processing	2,314,984	229,270	378,789	179,065	351,834	208,476	316,363	650,918
Repair and rental of photographic equipment	57,461	3,566	3,994	622	5,417	2,100	21,003	21,920
Photographic equipment	2,713,313	178,473	360,555	135,832	424,062	249,290	375,297	989,298
Photographer fees	1,538,778	105,098	314,458	85,354	255,854	112,201	239,190	426,523
Fireworks	226,921	–	–	23,206	31,808	3,533	55,341	63,800
Pinball, electronic video games	501,564	65,344	79,840	26,762	134,872	13,673	53,268	144,443

Note: Numbers may not add to total because of rounding and missing subcategories. (–) means sample is too small to make a reliable estimate.
Source: Calculations by New Strategist based on the 2003 Consumer Expenditure Survey

Table 3.8 Entertainment: Market shares by income, 2003

(percentage of total annual spending on entertainment accounted for by before-tax income group of consumer units, 2003; complete income reporters only)

	total complete reporters	under $20,000	$20,000–$39,999	$40,000–$49,999	$50,000–$69,999	$70,000–$79,999	$80,000–$99,999	$100,000 or more
Share of total consumer units	100.0%	27.8%	24.6%	9.1%	14.3%	5.3%	7.1%	11.8%
Share of total before-tax income	100.0	5.9	14.0	7.9	16.4	7.7	12.3	35.8
Share of total spending	100.0	12.9	18.2	8.5	16.6	7.0	10.9	25.9
Share of entertainment spending	100.0	9.9	18.5	8.2	15.6	7.9	11.9	28.2
FEES AND ADMISSIONS	100.0	7.1	12.3	6.8	15.4	7.4	11.8	39.1
Recreation expenses on trips	100.0	7.3	14.2	8.9	19.3	6.9	11.3	32.1
Social, recreation, civic club membership	100.0	7.2	8.5	5.4	13.8	7.5	9.1	48.4
Fees for participant sports	100.0	7.9	15.8	7.7	16.8	6.8	13.8	31.1
Participant sports on trips	100.0	8.5	8.9	6.6	15.9	8.9	10.1	41.1
Movie, theater, opera, ballet	100.0	10.1	16.7	7.7	15.5	7.7	11.8	30.5
Movie, other admissions on trips	100.0	7.0	12.7	8.1	18.3	8.5	13.0	32.4
Admission to sports events	100.0	5.5	11.1	5.3	12.8	6.1	14.4	44.8
Admission to sports events on trips	100.0	7.0	12.7	8.1	18.3	8.5	13.0	32.4
Fees for recreational lessons	100.0	3.1	9.4	5.6	12.8	7.0	12.0	49.9
Other entertainment services on trips	100.0	7.3	14.2	8.9	19.3	6.9	11.3	32.1
TELEVISION, RADIO, SOUND EQUIPMENT	100.0	14.8	20.0	9.6	16.5	6.9	10.3	21.9
Television	100.0	15.6	20.6	9.5	16.8	6.7	10.1	20.7
Cable service and community antenna	100.0	17.5	22.1	10.0	17.0	6.4	9.3	17.7
Black-and-white TV sets	100.0	–	–	10.7	11.8	7.8	12.6	25.4
Color TV sets, consoles	100.0	7.1	12.4	9.4	13.8	9.1	13.6	34.5
Color TV sets, portable and table models	100.0	13.3	20.0	6.9	13.2	6.3	10.4	29.9
VCRs and video disc players	100.0	11.3	18.0	7.6	19.8	5.4	14.1	23.7
Video cassettes, tapes, and discs	100.0	12.9	18.0	8.3	19.0	6.9	11.6	23.3
Video game hardware and software	100.0	13.1	16.5	9.7	19.4	7.2	9.9	24.2
Repair of TV, radio, and sound equipment	100.0	8.1	29.3	12.4	17.4	7.2	12.0	13.6
Rental of television sets	100.0	24.9	65.5	3.9	0.9	–	4.0	1.1
Radio and sound equipment	100.0	11.1	17.4	9.7	15.4	7.9	11.2	27.4
Radios	100.0	10.4	14.3	15.5	3.5	11.9	5.1	40.0
Tape recorders and players	100.0	8.4	14.5	25.0	25.4	–	12.6	16.0
Sound components and component systems	100.0	9.5	20.2	7.6	16.8	8.0	9.4	28.6
Miscellaneous sound equipment	100.0	–	–	–	8.3	–	2.2	48.4
Sound equipment accessories	100.0	10.3	8.0	9.1	32.4	4.9	6.5	29.9
Satellite dishes	100.0	–	–	20.2	5.1	9.3	8.1	22.0
Compact disc, tape, record, video mail order clubs	100.0	8.9	23.4	13.3	21.2	7.5	8.1	17.7
Records, CDs, audio tapes, needles	100.0	14.1	18.3	8.3	16.2	7.2	10.9	25.0
Rental of VCR, radio, sound equipment	100.0	10.1	65.4	5.0	13.9	3.3	0.4	2.0
Musical instruments and accessories	100.0	6.3	12.6	5.9	7.5	9.9	16.5	41.4
Rental and repair of musical instruments	100.0	2.5	14.1	46.6	7.9	6.9	4.0	17.9
Rental of video cassettes, tapes, discs, films	100.0	13.4	20.0	9.3	17.4	8.3	11.0	20.7
PETS, TOYS, PLAYGROUND EQUIPMENT	100.0	10.5	22.6	9.7	16.3	6.8	11.3	22.8
Pets	100.0	10.8	23.4	9.9	15.9	6.6	11.0	22.5
Pet food	100.0	16.5	19.5	10.6	17.2	6.2	12.7	17.5
Pet purchase, supplies, and medicines	100.0	6.7	37.4	11.2	14.1	5.9	8.2	15.7
Pet services	100.0	7.8	14.0	9.3	12.1	4.9	10.4	41.5
Veterinarian services	100.0	8.1	16.0	7.4	17.2	8.4	11.8	31.1
Toys, games, hobbies, and tricycles	100.0	10.0	20.9	9.6	17.6	7.6	11.8	22.4
Playground equipment	100.0	2.5	5.8	3.3	11.7	2.7	19.1	55.7

	total complete reporters	under $20,000	$20,000–$39,999	$40,000–$49,999	$50,000–$69,999	$70,000–$79,999	$80,000–$99,999	$100,000 or more
OTHER ENTERTAINMENT SUPPLIES, EQUIPMENT, SERVICES	**100.0%**	**4.7%**	**19.0%**	**6.1%**	**13.9%**	**11.0%**	**14.8%**	**30.8%**
Unmotored recreational vehicles	**100.0**	**0.4**	**10.1**	**8.3**	**19.7**	**15.2**	**29.2**	**17.3**
Boat without motor and boat trailers	100.0	1.5	4.8	4.8	39.9	1.6	25.7	24.7
Trailer and other attachable campers	100.0	0.5	11.0	8.8	17.1	17.0	29.6	16.4
Motorized recreational vehicles	**100.0**	**3.0**	**26.6**	**4.7**	**3.9**	**11.8**	**8.9**	**42.7**
Motorized camper	100.0	–	44.9	4.7	0.1	22.8	0.2	27.2
Other vehicle	100.0	–	–	3.2	7.5	8.2	20.5	30.0
Motorboats	100.0	–	7.7	5.2	7.4	0.2	15.8	63.8
Rental of recreational vehicles	**100.0**	**7.4**	**15.9**	**2.3**	**14.7**	**11.9**	**9.4**	**38.4**
Docking and landing fees	**100.0**	**5.9**	**9.2**	**26.2**	**13.8**	**5.0**	**14.2**	**26.8**
Sports, recreation, exercise equipment	**100.0**	**8.1**	**16.7**	**5.6**	**21.8**	**9.8**	**15.5**	**23.3**
Athletic gear, game tables, exercise equipment	100.0	8.6	17.1	3.8	23.1	12.0	12.8	24.0
Bicycles	100.0	9.5	19.1	6.0	15.8	8.7	14.7	26.2
Camping equipment	100.0	9.4	16.2	4.0	9.3	14.1	21.8	27.5
Hunting and fishing equipment	100.0	8.8	18.8	8.1	26.5	6.6	23.9	7.8
Winter sports equipment	100.0	6.0	9.4	7.1	17.9	5.0	14.1	40.4
Water sports equipment	100.0	7.2	7.5	12.8	11.0	17.0	20.1	24.4
Other sports equipment	100.0	3.9	12.8	5.8	25.0	6.3	6.9	39.2
Rental and repair of miscellaneous sports equipment	100.0	9.7	32.4	6.7	17.7	3.2	3.8	26.5
Photographic equipment and supplies	**100.0**	**8.6**	**16.5**	**6.4**	**15.6**	**8.3**	**14.0**	**30.5**
Film	100.0	11.9	19.3	8.0	16.3	7.5	12.8	24.3
Other photographic supplies	100.0	–	–	6.9	4.7	–	6.6	57.4
Film processing	100.0	9.9	16.4	7.7	15.2	9.0	13.7	28.1
Repair and rental of photographic equipment	100.0	6.2	7.0	1.1	9.4	3.7	36.6	38.1
Photographic equipment	100.0	6.6	13.3	5.0	15.6	9.2	13.8	36.5
Photographer fees	100.0	6.8	20.4	5.5	16.6	7.3	15.5	27.7
Fireworks	**100.0**	**–**	**–**	**10.2**	**14.0**	**1.6**	**24.4**	**28.1**
Pinball, electronic video games	**100.0**	**13.0**	**15.9**	**5.3**	**26.9**	**2.7**	**10.6**	**28.8**

Note: Numbers may not add to total because of rounding. (–) means sample is too small to make a reliable estimate.
Source: Calculations by New Strategist based on the 2003 Consumer Expenditure Survey

Table 3.9 Entertainment: Average spending by high-income consumer units, 2003

(average annual spending on entertainment, by before-tax income of high-income consumer units (CU), 2003; complete income reporters only)

	total complete reporters	$100,000 or more	$100,000– $119,999	$120,000– $149,999	$150,000 or more
Number of consumer units (000)	97,391	11,537	4,384	3,151	4,002
Average number of persons per CU	2.5	3.1	3.1	3.1	3.1
Average before-tax income of CU	$51,128.00	$154,665.00	$108,087.00	$131,885.00	$223,634.00
Average spending of CU, total	42,741.66	93,514.86	75,601.50	86,451.46	118,674.11
Entertainment, average spending	**2,155.48**	**5,124.28**	**3,810.37**	**4,381.82**	**7,146.80**
FEES AND ADMISSIONS	**511.12**	**1,686.90**	**1,126.11**	**1,308.59**	**2,599.22**
Recreation expenses on trips	23.69	64.25	49.07	53.89	89.04
Social, recreation, civic club membership	97.82	399.93	209.65	232.44	740.28
Fees for participant sports	65.57	172.24	149.24	160.33	206.82
Participant sports on trips	24.06	83.48	54.61	55.38	137.23
Movie, theater, opera, ballet	94.37	243.20	183.39	232.72	316.97
Movie, other admissions on trips	46.59	127.55	93.47	113.57	175.91
Admission to sports events	36.14	136.71	84.70	109.52	215.11
Admission to sports events on trips	15.53	42.51	31.15	37.84	58.63
Fees for recreational lessons	83.67	352.79	221.77	259.00	570.19
Other entertainment services on trips	23.69	64.25	49.07	53.89	89.04
TELEVISION, RADIO, SOUND EQUIPMENT	**745.25**	**1,379.48**	**1,164.68**	**1,285.29**	**1,688.88**
Television	**606.98**	**1,060.09**	**948.99**	**1,005.77**	**1,224.58**
Cable service and community antenna	428.83	640.62	617.40	608.90	691.05
Black-and-white TV sets	0.35	0.75	0.59	1.02	0.72
Color TV sets, consoles	53.47	155.57	101.16	118.98	244.01
Color TV sets, portable and table models	36.01	90.75	74.55	100.99	100.44
VCRs and video disc players	25.90	51.79	44.65	48.58	62.13
Video cassettes, tapes, and discs	38.78	76.12	67.87	86.55	76.96
Video game hardware and software	20.19	41.21	40.28	36.80	45.70
Repair of TV, radio, and sound equipment	2.80	3.21	2.49	3.73	3.58
Rental of television sets	0.65	0.06	–	0.22	–
Radio and sound equipment	**138.27**	**319.39**	**215.69**	**279.52**	**464.30**
Radios	4.85	16.38	24.98	–	19.76
Tape recorders and players	4.49	6.06	1.06	3.63	13.37
Sound components and component systems	16.33	39.36	23.66	38.28	57.41
Miscellaneous sound equipment	0.57	2.33	2.27	2.70	2.11
Sound equipment accessories	5.27	13.31	5.49	26.87	11.28
Satellite dishes	0.98	1.82	1.61	4.19	0.17
Compact disc, tape, record, video mail order clubs	4.83	7.22	8.68	7.10	5.72
Records, CDs, audio tapes, needles	34.95	73.69	67.60	78.29	76.73
Rental of VCR, radio, sound equipment	0.35	0.06	0.10	0.06	0.01
Musical instruments and accessories	25.80	90.14	17.67	50.79	200.52
Rental and repair of musical instruments	2.19	3.30	1.88	1.97	5.89
Rental of video cassettes, tapes, discs, films	37.66	65.72	60.68	65.63	71.32
PETS, TOYS, PLAYGROUND EQUIPMENT	**411.09**	**790.31**	**710.60**	**736.05**	**919.94**
Pets	**304.53**	**577.53**	**532.99**	**525.66**	**666.77**
Pet food	112.65	166.25	129.95	174.18	199.54
Pet purchase, supplies, and medicines	88.60	117.19	157.90	68.63	110.64
Pet services	25.87	90.61	51.37	92.52	132.10
Veterinarian services	77.41	203.49	193.77	190.33	224.49
Toys, games, hobbies, and tricycles	**102.46**	**193.56**	**169.21**	**181.53**	**229.71**
Playground equipment	**4.09**	**19.22**	**8.41**	**28.86**	**23.46**

	total complete reporters	$100,000 or more	$100,000– $119,999	$120,000– $149,999	$150,000 or more
OTHER ENTERTAINMENT SUPPLIES, EQUIPMENT, SERVICES	**$488.02**	**$1,267.59**	**$808.98**	**$1,051.89**	**$1,938.76**
Unmotored recreational vehicles	**69.60**	**101.86**	**22.29**	**159.41**	**143.70**
Boat without motor and boat trailers	7.86	16.39	2.08	–	44.96
Trailer and other attachable campers	61.75	85.47	20.21	159.41	98.74
Motorized recreational vehicles	**171.04**	**616.09**	**441.13**	**351.12**	**1,016.45**
Motorized camper	81.15	186.61	–	271.72	324.05
Other vehicle	19.18	48.50	0.44	79.41	76.83
Motorboats	70.71	380.98	440.69	–	615.56
Rental of recreational vehicles	**4.55**	**14.74**	**9.06**	**9.01**	**25.48**
Docking and landing fees	**3.90**	**8.81**	**6.46**	**16.05**	**5.67**
Sports, recreation, exercise equipment	**144.02**	**283.09**	**153.73**	**237.00**	**459.98**
Athletic gear, game tables, exercise equipment	61.93	125.53	42.50	106.76	230.36
Bicycles	11.33	25.07	23.69	20.32	30.32
Camping equipment	10.40	24.11	10.20	18.69	43.43
Hunting and fishing equipment	31.34	20.54	18.34	19.97	23.38
Winter sports equipment	4.93	16.83	13.58	10.85	25.09
Water sports equipment	5.08	10.45	13.49	5.71	10.85
Other sports equipment	16.80	55.64	26.23	50.86	91.63
Rental and repair of miscellaneous sports equipment	2.20	4.92	5.71	3.83	4.92
Photographic equipment and supplies	**84.54**	**217.69**	**162.55**	**259.04**	**245.60**
Film	15.54	31.90	28.88	34.52	33.14
Other photographic supplies	0.98	4.75	–	14.79	2.12
Film processing	23.77	56.42	46.31	61.66	63.37
Repair and rental of photographic equipment	0.59	1.90	0.17	0.34	5.04
Photographic equipment	27.86	85.75	53.52	118.39	95.35
Photographer fees	15.80	36.97	33.67	29.33	46.59
Fireworks	**2.33**	**5.53**	**–**	**–**	**15.82**
Pinball, electronic video games	**5.15**	**12.52**	**10.39**	**10.20**	**16.64**

Note: Subcategories may not add to total because some are not shown. (–) means sample is too small to make a reliable estimate.
Source: Bureau of Labor Statistics, unpublished data from the 2003 Consumer Expenditure Survey; calculations by New Strategist

Table 3.10 Entertainment: Indexed spending by high-income consumer units, 2003

(indexed average annual spending of high-income consumer units (CU) on entertainment by before-tax income of consumer unit, 2003; complete income reporters only; index definition: an index of 100 is the average for all consumer units; an index of 132 means that spending by consumer units in that group is 32 percent above the average for all consumer units; an index of 68 indicates spending that is 32 percent below the average for all consumer units)

	total complete reporters	$100,000 or more	$100,000–$119,999	$120,000–$149,999	$150,000 or more
Average spending of CU, total	$42,742	$93,515	$75,602	$86,451	$118,674
Average spending of CU, index	100	219	177	202	278
Entertainment, spending index	**100**	**238**	**177**	**203**	**332**
FEES AND ADMISSIONS	**100**	**330**	**220**	**256**	**509**
Recreation expenses on trips	100	271	207	227	376
Social, recreation, civic club membership	100	409	214	238	757
Fees for participant sports	100	263	228	245	315
Participant sports on trips	100	347	227	230	570
Movie, theater, opera, ballet	100	258	194	247	336
Movie, other admissions on trips	100	274	201	244	378
Admission to sports events	100	378	234	303	595
Admission to sports events on trips	100	274	201	244	378
Fees for recreational lessons	100	422	265	310	681
Other entertainment services on trips	100	271	207	227	376
TELEVISION, RADIO, SOUND EQUIPMENT	**100**	**185**	**156**	**172**	**227**
Television	**100**	**175**	**156**	**166**	**202**
Cable service and community antenna	100	149	144	142	161
Black-and-white TV sets	100	214	169	291	206
Color TV sets, consoles	100	291	189	223	456
Color TV sets, portable and table models	100	252	207	280	279
VCRs and video disc players	100	200	172	188	240
Video cassettes, tapes, and discs	100	196	175	223	198
Video game hardware and software	100	204	200	182	226
Repair of TV, radio, and sound equipment	100	115	89	133	128
Rental of television sets	100	9	–	34	–
Radio and sound equipment	**100**	**231**	**156**	**202**	**336**
Radios	100	338	515	–	407
Tape recorders and players	100	135	24	81	298
Sound components and component systems	100	241	145	234	352
Miscellaneous sound equipment	100	409	398	474	370
Sound equipment accessories	100	253	104	510	214
Satellite dishes	100	186	164	428	17
Compact disc, tape, record, video mail order clubs	100	149	180	147	118
Records, CDs, audio tapes, needles	100	211	193	224	220
Rental of VCR, radio, sound equipment	100	17	29	17	3
Musical instruments and accessories	100	349	68	197	777
Rental and repair of musical instruments	100	151	86	90	269
Rental of video cassettes, tapes, discs, films	100	175	161	174	189
PETS, TOYS, PLAYGROUND EQUIPMENT	**100**	**192**	**173**	**179**	**224**
Pets	**100**	**190**	**175**	**173**	**219**
Pet food	100	148	115	155	177
Pet purchase, supplies, and medicines	100	132	178	77	125
Pet services	100	350	199	358	511
Veterinarian services	100	263	250	246	290
Toys, games, hobbies, and tricycles	**100**	**189**	**165**	**177**	**224**
Playground equipment	**100**	**470**	**206**	**706**	**574**

	total complete reporters	$100,000 or more	$100,000–$119,999	$120,000–$149,999	$150,000 or more
OTHER ENTERTAINMENT SUPPLIES, EQUIPMENT, SERVICES	**100**	**260**	**166**	**216**	**397**
Unmotored recreational vehicles	**100**	**146**	**32**	**229**	**206**
Boat without motor and boat trailers	100	209	26	–	572
Trailer and other attachable campers	100	138	33	258	160
Motorized recreational vehicles	**100**	**360**	**258**	**205**	**594**
Motorized camper	100	230	–	335	399
Other vehicle	100	253	2	414	401
Motorboats	100	539	623	–	871
Rental of recreational vehicles	**100**	**324**	**199**	**198**	**560**
Docking and landing fees	**100**	**226**	**166**	**412**	**145**
Sports, recreation, exercise equipment	**100**	**197**	**107**	**165**	**319**
Athletic gear, game tables, exercise equipment	100	203	69	172	372
Bicycles	100	221	209	179	268
Camping equipment	100	232	98	180	418
Hunting and fishing equipment	100	66	59	64	75
Winter sports equipment	100	341	275	220	509
Water sports equipment	100	206	266	112	214
Other sports equipment	100	331	156	303	545
Rental and repair of miscellaneous sports equipment	100	224	260	174	224
Photographic equipment and supplies	**100**	**257**	**192**	**306**	**291**
Film	100	205	186	222	213
Other photographic supplies	100	485	–	1,509	216
Film processing	100	237	195	259	267
Repair and rental of photographic equipment	100	322	29	58	854
Photographic equipment	100	308	192	425	342
Photographer fees	100	234	213	186	295
Fireworks	**100**	**237**	**–**	**–**	**679**
Pinball, electronic video games	**100**	**243**	**202**	**198**	**323**

Note: (–) means sample is too small to make a reliable estimate.
Source: Calculations by New Strategist based on the 2003 Consumer Expenditure Survey

Table 3.11 Entertainment: Total spending by high-income consumer units, 2003

(total annual spending on entertainment, by before-tax income group of high-income consumer units (CU), 2003; complete income reporters only; numbers in thousands)

	total complete reporters	$100,000 or more	$100,000–$119,999	$120,000–$149,999	$150,000 or more
Number of consumer units	97,391	11,537	4,384	3,151	4,002
Total spending of all CUs	$4,162,653,009	$1,078,880,940	$331,436,976	$272,408,550	$474,933,788
Entertainment, total spending	209,924,353	59,118,818	16,704,662	13,807,115	28,601,494
FEES AND ADMISSIONS	49,778,488	19,461,765	4,936,866	4,123,367	10,402,078
Recreation expenses on trips	2,307,193	741,252	215,123	169,807	356,338
Social, recreation, civic club membership	9,526,788	4,613,992	919,106	732,418	2,962,601
Fees for participant sports	6,385,928	1,987,133	654,268	505,200	827,694
Participant sports on trips	2,343,227	963,109	239,410	174,502	549,194
Movie, theater, opera, ballet	9,190,789	2,805,798	803,982	733,301	1,268,514
Movie, other admissions on trips	4,537,447	1,471,544	409,772	357,859	703,992
Admission to sports events	3,519,711	1,577,223	371,325	345,098	860,870
Admission to sports events on trips	1,512,482	490,438	136,562	119,234	234,637
Fees for recreational lessons	8,148,705	4,070,138	972,240	816,109	2,281,900
Other entertainment services on trips	2,307,193	741,252	215,123	169,807	356,338
TELEVISION, RADIO, SOUND EQUIPMENT	72,580,643	15,915,061	5,105,957	4,049,949	6,758,898
Television	59,114,389	12,230,258	4,160,372	3,169,181	4,900,769
Cable service and community antenna	41,764,183	7,390,833	2,706,682	1,918,644	2,765,582
Black-and-white TV sets	34,087	8,653	2,587	3,214	2,881
Color TV sets, consoles	5,207,497	1,794,811	443,485	374,906	976,528
Color TV sets, portable and table models	3,507,050	1,046,983	326,827	318,219	401,961
VCRs and video disc players	2,522,427	597,501	195,746	153,076	248,644
Video cassettes, tapes, and discs	3,776,823	878,196	297,542	272,719	307,994
Video game hardware and software	1,966,324	475,440	176,588	115,957	182,891
Repair of TV, radio, and sound equipment	272,695	37,034	10,916	11,753	14,327
Rental of television sets	63,304	692	–	693	–
Radio and sound equipment	13,466,254	3,684,802	945,585	880,768	1,858,129
Radios	472,346	188,976	109,512	–	79,080
Tape recorders and players	437,286	69,914	4,647	11,438	53,507
Sound components and component systems	1,590,395	454,096	103,725	120,620	229,755
Miscellaneous sound equipment	55,513	26,881	9,952	8,508	8,444
Sound equipment accessories	513,251	153,557	24,068	84,667	45,143
Satellite dishes	95,443	20,997	7,058	13,203	680
Compact disc, tape, record, video mail order clubs	470,399	83,297	38,053	22,372	22,891
Records, CDs, audio tapes, needles	3,403,815	850,162	296,358	246,692	307,073
Rental of VCR, radio, sound equipment	34,087	692	438	189	40
Musical instruments and accessories	2,512,688	1,039,945	77,465	160,039	802,481
Rental and repair of musical instruments	213,286	38,072	8,242	6,207	23,572
Rental of video cassettes, tapes, discs, films	3,667,745	758,212	266,021	206,800	285,423
PETS, TOYS, PLAYGROUND EQUIPMENT	40,036,466	9,117,806	3,115,270	2,319,294	3,681,600
Pets	29,658,481	6,662,964	2,336,628	1,656,355	2,668,414
Pet food	10,971,096	1,918,026	569,701	548,841	798,559
Pet purchase, supplies, and medicines	8,628,843	1,352,021	692,234	216,253	442,781
Pet services	2,519,505	1,045,368	225,206	291,531	528,664
Veterinarian services	7,539,037	2,347,664	849,488	599,730	898,409
Toys, games, hobbies, and tricycles	9,978,682	2,233,102	741,817	572,001	919,299
Playground equipment	398,329	221,741	36,869	90,938	93,887

	total complete reporters	$100,000 or more	$100,000– $119,999	$120,000– $149,999	$150,000 or more
OTHER ENTERTAINMENT SUPPLIES, EQUIPMENT, SERVICES	**$47,528,756**	**$14,624,186**	**$3,546,568**	**$3,314,505**	**$7,758,918**
Unmotored recreational vehicles	**6,778,414**	**1,175,159**	**97,719**	**502,301**	**575,087**
Boat without motor and boat trailers	765,493	189,091	9,119	–	179,930
Trailer and other attachable campers	6,013,894	986,067	88,601	502,301	395,157
Motorized recreational vehicles	**16,657,757**	**7,107,830**	**1,933,914**	**1,106,379**	**4,067,833**
Motorized camper	7,903,280	2,152,920	–	856,190	1,296,848
Other vehicle	1,867,959	559,545	1,929	250,221	307,474
Motorboats	6,886,518	4,395,366	1,931,985	–	2,463,471
Rental of recreational vehicles	**443,129**	**170,055**	**39,719**	**28,391**	**101,971**
Docking and landing fees	**379,825**	**101,641**	**28,321**	**50,574**	**22,691**
Sports, recreation, exercise equipment	**14,026,252**	**3,266,009**	**673,952**	**746,787**	**1,840,840**
Athletic gear, game tables, exercise equipment	6,031,425	1,448,240	186,320	336,401	921,901
Bicycles	1,103,440	289,233	103,857	64,028	121,341
Camping equipment	1,012,866	278,157	44,717	58,892	173,807
Hunting and fishing equipment	3,052,234	236,970	80,403	62,925	93,567
Winter sports equipment	480,138	194,168	59,535	34,188	100,410
Water sports equipment	494,746	120,562	59,140	17,992	43,422
Other sports equipment	1,636,169	641,919	114,992	160,260	366,703
Rental and repair of miscellaneous sports equipment	214,260	56,762	25,033	12,063	19,690
Photographic equipment and supplies	**8,233,435**	**2,511,490**	**712,619**	**816,235**	**982,891**
Film	1,513,456	368,030	126,610	108,773	132,626
Other photographic supplies	95,443	54,801	–	46,603	8,484
Film processing	2,314,984	650,918	203,023	194,291	253,607
Repair and rental of photographic equipment	57,461	21,920	745	1,071	20,170
Photographic equipment	2,713,313	989,298	234,632	373,047	381,591
Photographer fees	1,538,778	426,523	147,609	92,419	186,453
Fireworks	**226,921**	**63,800**	**–**	**–**	**63,312**
Pinball, electronic video games	**501,564**	**144,443**	**45,550**	**32,140**	**66,593**

Note: Numbers may not add to total because of rounding and missing subcategories. (–) means sample is too small to make a reliable estimate.
Source: Calculations by New Strategist based on the 2003 Consumer Expenditure Survey

Table 3.12 Entertainment: Market shares by high-income consumer units, 2003

(percentage of total annual spending on entertainment accounted for by before-tax income group of high-income consumer units, 2003; complete income reporters only)

	total complete reporters	$100,000 or more	$100,000– $119,999	$120,000– $149,999	$150,000 or more
Share of total consumer units	100.0%	11.8%	4.5%	3.2%	4.1%
Share of total before-tax income	100.0	35.8	9.5	8.3	18.0
Share of total spending	100.0	25.9	8.0	6.5	11.4
Share of entertainment spending	100.0	28.2	8.0	6.6	13.6
FEES AND ADMISSIONS	100.0	39.1	9.9	8.3	20.9
Recreation expenses on trips	100.0	32.1	9.3	7.4	15.4
Social, recreation, civic club membership	100.0	48.4	9.6	7.7	31.1
Fees for participant sports	100.0	31.1	10.2	7.9	13.0
Participant sports on trips	100.0	41.1	10.2	7.4	23.4
Movie, theater, opera, ballet	100.0	30.5	8.7	8.0	13.8
Movie, other admissions on trips	100.0	32.4	9.0	7.9	15.5
Admission to sports events	100.0	44.8	10.5	9.8	24.5
Admission to sports events on trips	100.0	32.4	9.0	7.9	15.5
Fees for recreational lessons	100.0	49.9	11.9	10.0	28.0
Other entertainment services on trips	100.0	32.1	9.3	7.4	15.4
TELEVISION, RADIO, SOUND EQUIPMENT	100.0	21.9	7.0	5.6	9.3
Television	100.0	20.7	7.0	5.4	8.3
Cable service and community antenna	100.0	17.7	6.5	4.6	6.6
Black-and-white TV sets	100.0	25.4	7.6	9.4	8.5
Color TV sets, consoles	100.0	34.5	8.5	7.2	18.8
Color TV sets, portable and table models	100.0	29.9	9.3	9.1	11.5
VCRs and video disc players	100.0	23.7	7.8	6.1	9.9
Video cassettes, tapes, and discs	100.0	23.3	7.9	7.2	8.2
Video game hardware and software	100.0	24.2	9.0	5.9	9.3
Repair of TV, radio, and sound equipment	100.0	13.6	4.0	4.3	5.3
Rental of television sets	100.0	1.1	–	1.1	–
Radio and sound equipment	100.0	27.4	7.0	6.5	13.8
Radios	100.0	40.0	23.2	–	16.7
Tape recorders and players	100.0	16.0	1.1	2.6	12.2
Sound components and component systems	100.0	28.6	6.5	7.6	14.4
Miscellaneous sound equipment	100.0	48.4	17.9	15.3	15.2
Sound equipment accessories	100.0	29.9	4.7	16.5	8.8
Satellite dishes	100.0	22.0	7.4	13.8	0.7
Compact disc, tape, record, video mail order clubs	100.0	17.7	8.1	4.8	4.9
Records, CDs, audio tapes, needles	100.0	25.0	8.7	7.2	9.0
Rental of VCR, radio, sound equipment	100.0	2.0	1.3	0.6	0.1
Musical instruments and accessories	100.0	41.4	3.1	6.4	31.9
Rental and repair of musical instruments	100.0	17.9	3.9	2.9	11.1
Rental of video cassettes, tapes, discs, films	100.0	20.7	7.3	5.6	7.8
PETS, TOYS, PLAYGROUND EQUIPMENT	100.0	22.8	7.8	5.8	9.2
Pets	100.0	22.5	7.9	5.6	9.0
Pet food	100.0	17.5	5.2	5.0	7.3
Pet purchase, supplies, and medicines	100.0	15.7	8.0	2.5	5.1
Pet services	100.0	41.5	8.9	11.6	21.0
Veterinarian services	100.0	31.1	11.3	8.0	11.9
Toys, games, hobbies, and tricycles	100.0	22.4	7.4	5.7	9.2
Playground equipment	100.0	55.7	9.3	22.8	23.6

	total complete reporters	$100,000 or more	$100,000–$119,999	$120,000–$149,999	$150,000 or more
OTHER ENTERTAINMENT SUPPLIES, EQUIPMENT, SERVICES	**100.0%**	**30.8%**	**7.5%**	**7.0%**	**16.3%**
Unmotored recreational vehicles	**100.0**	**17.3**	**1.4**	**7.4**	**8.5**
Boat without motor and boat trailers	100.0	24.7	1.2	–	23.5
Trailer and other attachable campers	100.0	16.4	1.5	8.4	6.6
Motorized recreational vehicles	**100.0**	**42.7**	**11.6**	**6.6**	**24.4**
Motorized camper	100.0	27.2	–	10.8	16.4
Other vehicle	100.0	30.0	0.1	13.4	16.5
Motorboats	100.0	63.8	28.1	–	35.8
Rental of recreational vehicles	**100.0**	**38.4**	**9.0**	**6.4**	**23.0**
Docking and landing fees	**100.0**	**26.8**	**7.5**	**13.3**	**6.0**
Sports, recreation, exercise equipment	**100.0**	**23.3**	**4.8**	**5.3**	**13.1**
Athletic gear, game tables, exercise equipment	100.0	24.0	3.1	5.6	15.3
Bicycles	100.0	26.2	9.4	5.8	11.0
Camping equipment	100.0	27.5	4.4	5.8	17.2
Hunting and fishing equipment	100.0	7.8	2.6	2.1	3.1
Winter sports equipment	100.0	40.4	12.4	7.1	20.9
Water sports equipment	100.0	24.4	12.0	3.6	8.8
Other sports equipment	100.0	39.2	7.0	9.8	22.4
Rental and repair of miscellaneous sports equipment	100.0	26.5	11.7	5.6	9.2
Photographic equipment and supplies	**100.0**	**30.5**	**8.7**	**9.9**	**11.9**
Film	100.0	24.3	8.4	7.2	8.8
Other photographic supplies	100.0	57.4	–	48.8	8.9
Film processing	100.0	28.1	8.3	8.4	11.0
Repair and rental of photographic equipment	100.0	38.1	1.3	1.9	35.1
Photographic equipment	100.0	36.5	8.6	13.7	14.1
Photographer fees	100.0	27.7	9.6	6.0	12.1
Fireworks	**100.0**	**28.1**	**–**	**–**	**27.9**
Pinball, electronic video games	**100.0**	**28.8**	**9.1**	**6.4**	**13.3**

Note: Numbers may not add to total because of rounding. (–) means sample is too small to make a reliable estimate.
Source: Calculations by New Strategist based on the 2003 Consumer Expenditure Survey

Table 3.13 Entertainment: Average spending by household type, 2003

(average annual spending of consumer units (CU) on entertainment, by type of consumer unit, 2003)

	total married couples	married couples, no children	married couples with children				single parent, at least one child <18	single person
			total	oldest child under 6	oldest child 6 to 17	oldest child 18 or older		
Number of consumer units (000)	58,448	25,132	28,584	5,496	15,047	8,041	6,999	33,929
Average number of persons per CU	3.2	2.0	3.9	3.5	4.1	4.0	2.9	1.0
Average before-tax income of CU	$69,472.00	$62,930.00	$75,557.00	$66,317.00	$77,508.00	$78,307.00	$29,154.00	$27,131.00
Average spending of CU, total	53,030.03	47,895.65	57,702.32	51,503.24	59,183.18	59,180.36	30,534.75	23,657.35
Entertainment, average spending	**2,793.13**	**2,699.13**	**2,957.83**	**2,400.75**	**3,413.53**	**2,477.92**	**1,453.12**	**1,041.34**
FEES AND ADMISSIONS	**705.67**	**585.73**	**848.66**	**436.70**	**1,072.31**	**711.70**	**335.69**	**252.54**
Recreation expenses on trips	31.79	33.90	30.11	23.89	31.67	31.43	13.08	11.52
Social, recreation, civic club membership	142.41	134.98	162.27	69.33	225.54	107.39	44.40	43.54
Fees for participant sports	92.14	99.84	91.41	56.95	103.90	91.58	39.25	40.61
Participant sports on trips	34.29	36.17	34.52	27.22	37.75	33.48	10.10	12.72
Movie, theater, opera, ballet	112.36	91.05	133.04	65.42	151.23	145.22	73.50	63.21
Movie, other admissions on trips	63.62	58.18	68.27	31.82	82.64	66.29	28.18	24.05
Admission to sports events	45.87	36.17	59.69	31.23	67.88	63.80	21.71	20.11
Admission to sports events on trips	21.20	19.39	22.75	10.60	27.54	22.09	9.39	8.02
Fees for recreational lessons	130.20	42.15	216.49	96.33	312.49	118.98	82.98	17.25
Other entertainment services on trips	31.79	33.90	30.11	23.89	31.67	31.43	13.08	11.52
TELEVISION, RADIO, SOUND EQUIPMENT	**886.76**	**750.35**	**997.20**	**937.53**	**1,060.57**	**918.81**	**635.00**	**474.72**
Television	**718.39**	**645.37**	**773.17**	**731.21**	**800.61**	**750.51**	**519.94**	**398.65**
Cable service and community antenna	493.57	483.43	502.69	436.20	507.45	539.24	388.00	299.68
Black-and-white TV sets	0.56	0.43	0.71	1.19	0.91	0.02	–	0.09
Color TV sets, consoles	79.05	65.72	86.91	138.52	88.39	48.88	22.06	32.63
Color TV sets, portable and table models	42.50	37.77	43.28	34.99	46.34	43.20	22.65	21.46
VCRs and video disc players	32.00	18.44	42.24	40.25	43.86	40.58	22.07	11.66
Video cassettes, tapes, and discs	42.84	27.72	54.43	58.70	56.88	46.94	33.56	23.12
Video game hardware and software	24.21	8.26	39.42	19.77	52.27	28.80	28.26	7.91
Repair of TV, radio, and sound equipment	3.32	3.59	2.89	1.58	3.39	2.86	1.53	1.80
Rental of television sets	0.36	0.03	0.59	–	1.13	–	1.82	0.30
Radio and sound equipment	**168.37**	**104.97**	**224.03**	**206.32**	**259.96**	**168.30**	**115.06**	**76.07**
Radios	6.84	8.67	4.27	4.78	5.94	0.48	3.21	1.56
Tape recorders and players	5.66	0.78	7.15	10.81	8.41	1.88	6.09	0.44
Sound components and component systems	21.35	18.08	24.98	18.86	26.52	26.29	9.65	10.02
Miscellaneous sound equipment	0.47	0.40	0.56	0.10	0.78	0.44	–	0.61
Sound equipment accessories	8.34	7.42	9.59	13.87	7.51	10.69	1.57	1.20
Satellite dishes	1.27	1.13	1.50	1.01	1.31	2.19	0.15	0.39
Compact disc, tape, record, video mail order clubs	4.92	4.75	4.97	5.54	5.73	3.17	3.48	3.18
Records, CDs, audio tapes, needles	36.71	26.47	44.78	32.73	49.47	44.23	32.91	25.99
Rental of VCR, radio, sound equipment	0.29	0.02	0.56	1.24	0.39	0.40	0.01	0.17
Musical instruments and accessories	35.09	9.46	61.02	67.32	77.69	25.54	15.44	12.89
Rental and repair of musical instruments	3.22	4.03	3.00	0.28	5.23	0.69	1.99	1.43
Rental of video cassettes, tapes, discs, films	44.20	23.77	61.65	49.77	70.98	52.31	40.56	18.20
PETS, TOYS, PLAYGROUND EQUIPMENT	**516.28**	**516.56**	**527.67**	**531.46**	**578.12**	**428.91**	**295.59**	**177.10**
Pets	**371.18**	**437.22**	**324.80**	**236.58**	**349.20**	**337.66**	**169.41**	**139.78**
Pet food	120.80	119.46	119.14	74.34	126.48	137.11	73.71	57.30
Pet purchase, supplies, and medicines	115.43	158.68	83.23	74.20	103.20	49.14	42.38	27.14
Pet services	30.68	37.89	27.33	17.49	31.79	25.71	15.85	17.40
Veterinarian services	104.27	121.18	95.11	70.55	87.73	125.70	37.47	37.94
Toys, games, hobbies, and tricycles	**138.00**	**77.62**	**190.20**	**266.31**	**218.14**	**85.90**	**124.87**	**37.15**
Playground equipment	**7.10**	**1.72**	**12.67**	**28.57**	**10.78**	**5.34**	**1.31**	**0.17**

	total married couples	married couples, no children	married couples with children				single parent, at least one child <18	single person
			total	oldest child under 6	oldest child 6 to 17	oldest child 18 or older		
OTHER ENTERTAINMENT SUPPLIES, EQUIPMENT, SERVICES	**$684.43**	**$846.49**	**$584.29**	**$495.06**	**$702.53**	**$418.50**	**$186.84**	**$136.98**
Unmotored recreational vehicles	**90.58**	**75.86**	**89.94**	14.06	150.17	29.10	–	22.65
Boat without motor and boat trailers	11.30	19.27	6.03	14.06	3.39	5.46	–	2.68
Trailer and other attachable campers	79.28	56.59	83.92	–	146.77	23.64	–	19.97
Motorized recreational vehicles	**265.73**	**485.68**	**113.95**	**166.24**	**107.26**	**90.72**	**19.99**	**14.39**
Motorized camper	135.82	312.84	2.66	–	3.70	2.54	–	–
Other vehicle	25.98	34.01	20.84	17.15	24.49	16.52	19.85	8.65
Motorboats	103.93	138.83	90.45	149.09	79.08	71.65	0.14	5.74
Rental of recreational vehicles	**6.67**	**7.78**	**5.88**	**4.58**	**5.71**	**7.09**	**4.79**	**1.15**
Docking and landing fees	**6.24**	**10.06**	**3.86**	**4.41**	**3.52**	**4.13**	**0.67**	**0.96**
Sports, recreation, exercise equipment	**190.52**	**172.03**	**216.97**	**129.38**	**292.25**	**131.20**	**81.33**	**54.17**
Athletic gear, game tables, exercise equipment	74.66	59.00	87.93	29.13	116.84	72.22	27.45	21.12
Bicycles	14.02	7.49	20.74	23.57	27.21	6.70	12.20	6.64
Camping equipment	12.71	6.70	18.10	8.29	24.37	12.53	15.17	2.60
Hunting and fishing equipment	49.67	67.98	39.54	15.52	61.43	12.59	9.47	12.85
Winter sports equipment	7.27	5.68	9.42	5.10	14.33	3.18	5.04	2.02
Water sports equipment	5.70	7.38	4.19	1.75	6.36	1.81	0.68	1.36
Other sports equipment	23.88	14.58	34.66	45.36	38.51	20.14	8.53	6.55
Rental and repair of miscellaneous sports equipment	2.62	3.22	2.38	0.67	3.20	2.02	2.80	1.04
Photographic equipment and supplies	**112.70**	**89.26**	**136.24**	**159.33**	**122.25**	**146.57**	**63.80**	**36.21**
Film	19.53	14.73	23.95	27.04	23.60	22.51	12.54	7.59
Other photographic supplies	1.22	1.55	0.97	–	1.62	0.35	–	1.66
Film processing	32.10	25.00	39.53	55.55	36.02	35.17	15.85	10.14
Repair and rental of photographic equipment	1.09	1.49	0.90	0.43	0.86	1.30	–	0.10
Photographic equipment	36.56	29.75	43.42	44.60	36.74	55.11	22.17	14.41
Photographer fees	22.19	16.74	27.45	31.70	23.40	32.14	13.24	2.31
Fireworks	**2.51**	**0.36**	**4.63**	**0.23**	**6.73**	**3.60**	**4.96**	**0.14**
Pinball, electronic video games	**6.27**	**3.33**	**8.27**	**13.19**	**9.11**	**2.94**	**5.34**	**3.91**

Note: Average spending figures for total consumer units can be found on Average Spending by Age and Average Spending by Region tables. Subcategories may not add to total because some are not shown. (–) means sample is too small to make a reliable estimate.
Source: Bureau of Labor Statistics, unpublished data from the 2003 Consumer Expenditure Survey

Table 3.14 Entertainment: Indexed spending by household type, 2003

(indexed average annual spending of consumer units (CU) on entertainment by type of consumer unit, 2003; index definition: an index of 100 is the average for all consumer units; an index of 132 means that spending by consumer units in that group is 32 percent above the average for all consumer units; an index of 68 indicates spending that is 32 percent below the average for all consumer units)

	total married couples	married couples, no children	married couples with children				single parent, at least one child <18	single person
			total	oldest child under 6	oldest child 6 to 17	oldest child 18 or older		
Average spending of CU, total	$53,030	$47,896	$57,702	$51,503	$59,183	$59,180	$30,535	$23,657
Average spending of CU, index	130	117	141	126	145	145	75	58
Entertainment, spending index	**136**	**131**	**144**	**117**	**166**	**120**	**71**	**51**
FEES AND ADMISSIONS	**143**	**118**	**172**	**88**	**217**	**144**	**68**	**51**
Recreation expenses on trips	139	148	132	104	138	137	57	50
Social, recreation, civic club membership	150	142	171	73	237	113	47	46
Fees for participant sports	140	152	139	87	158	139	60	62
Participant sports on trips	144	152	145	114	158	140	42	53
Movie, theater, opera, ballet	124	100	147	72	167	160	81	70
Movie, other admissions on trips	140	128	151	70	182	146	62	53
Admission to sports events	136	107	177	93	202	190	65	60
Admission to sports events on trips	140	128	151	70	182	146	62	53
Fees for recreational lessons	164	53	273	121	394	150	105	22
Other entertainment services on trips	139	148	132	104	138	137	57	50
TELEVISION, RADIO, SOUND EQUIPMENT	**121**	**103**	**137**	**128**	**145**	**126**	**87**	**65**
Television	**120**	**108**	**129**	**122**	**134**	**126**	**87**	**67**
Cable service and community antenna	116	114	119	103	120	127	92	71
Black-and-white TV sets	165	126	209	350	268	6	–	26
Color TV sets, consoles	140	116	154	245	156	87	39	58
Color TV sets, portable and table models	123	109	125	101	134	125	65	62
VCRs and video disc players	132	76	174	166	181	167	91	48
Video cassettes, tapes, and discs	119	77	152	163	158	131	93	64
Video game hardware and software	129	44	211	106	280	154	151	42
Repair of TV, radio, and sound equipment	128	138	111	61	130	110	59	69
Rental of television sets	62	5	102	–	195	–	314	52
Radio and sound equipment	**127**	**79**	**169**	**156**	**196**	**127**	**87**	**57**
Radios	125	159	78	88	109	9	59	29
Tape recorders and players	144	20	182	275	214	48	155	11
Sound components and component systems	125	106	147	111	156	154	57	59
Miscellaneous sound equipment	112	95	133	24	186	105	–	145
Sound equipment accessories	151	134	173	250	136	193	28	22
Satellite dishes	140	124	165	111	144	241	16	43
Compact disc, tape, record, video mail order clubs	112	108	113	126	131	72	79	73
Records, CDs, audio tapes, needles	110	79	134	98	149	133	99	78
Rental of VCR, radio, sound equipment	100	7	193	428	134	138	3	59
Musical instruments and accessories	150	41	262	289	333	110	66	55
Rental and repair of musical instruments	141	176	131	12	228	30	87	62
Rental of video cassettes, tapes, discs, films	124	66	172	139	198	146	113	51
PETS, TOYS, PLAYGROUND EQUIPMENT	**137**	**137**	**140**	**141**	**153**	**113**	**78**	**47**
Pets	**135**	**159**	**118**	**86**	**127**	**123**	**62**	**51**
Pet food	121	120	119	74	127	137	74	57
Pet purchase, supplies, and medicines	152	210	110	98	136	65	56	36
Pet services	125	155	111	71	130	105	65	71
Veterinarian services	141	163	128	95	118	169	51	51
Toys, games, hobbies, and tricycles	**138**	**78**	**190**	**266**	**218**	**86**	**125**	**37**
Playground equipment	**182**	**44**	**324**	**731**	**276**	**137**	**34**	**4**

	total married couples	married couples, no children	married couples with children				single parent, at least one child <18	single person
			total	oldest child under 6	oldest child 6 to 17	oldest child 18 or older		
OTHER ENTERTAINMENT SUPPLIES, EQUIPMENT, SERVICES	**150**	**185**	**128**	**108**	**154**	**92**	**41**	**30**
Unmotored recreational vehicles	**150**	**126**	**149**	**23**	**249**	**48**	**–**	**38**
Boat without motor and boat trailers	163	277	87	202	49	79	–	39
Trailer and other attachable campers	149	106	157	–	275	44	–	37
Motorized recreational vehicles	**159**	**290**	**68**	**99**	**64**	**54**	**12**	**9**
Motorized camper	162	373	3	–	4	3	–	–
Other vehicle	148	194	119	98	140	94	113	49
Motorboats	158	211	137	226	120	109	0	9
Rental of recreational vehicles	**158**	**185**	**140**	**109**	**136**	**168**	**114**	**27**
Docking and landing fees	**175**	**282**	**108**	**124**	**99**	**116**	**19**	**27**
Sports, recreation, exercise equipment	**145**	**131**	**165**	**98**	**222**	**100**	**62**	**41**
Athletic gear, game tables, exercise equipment	137	108	161	53	214	132	50	39
Bicycles	127	68	188	213	246	61	110	60
Camping equipment	137	72	194	89	262	135	163	28
Hunting and fishing equipment	163	223	130	51	201	41	31	42
Winter sports equipment	149	116	193	104	293	65	103	41
Water sports equipment	127	165	94	39	142	40	15	30
Other sports equipment	159	97	231	302	257	134	57	44
Rental and repair of miscellaneous sports equipment	130	160	118	33	159	100	139	52
Photographic equipment and supplies	**142**	**113**	**172**	**201**	**154**	**185**	**81**	**46**
Film	133	101	164	185	161	154	86	52
Other photographic supplies	97	123	77	–	129	28	–	132
Film processing	144	112	178	249	162	158	71	46
Repair and rental of photographic equipment	188	257	155	74	148	224	–	17
Photographic equipment	140	114	166	171	141	211	85	55
Photographer fees	155	117	191	221	163	224	92	16
Fireworks	108	15	99	10	289	155	213	6
Pinball, electronic video games	126	67	66	265	183	59	107	79

Note: Spending index for total consumer units is 100. (–) means sample is too small to make a reliable estimate.
Source: Calculations by New Strategist based on the 2003 Consumer Expenditure Survey

Table 3.15 Entertainment: Total spending by household type, 2003

(total annual spending on entertainment, by consumer unit (CU) type, 2003; numbers in thousands)

	total married couples	married couples, no children	married couples with children				single parent, at least one child <18	single person
			total	oldest child under 6	oldest child 6 to 17	oldest child 18 or older		
Number of consumer units	58,448	25,132	28,584	5,496	15,047	8,041	6,999	33,929
Total spending of all CUs	$3,099,499,193	$1,203,713,476	$1,649,363,115	$283,061,807	$890,529,309	$475,869,275	$213,712,715	$802,670,228
Entertainment, total spending	**163,252,862**	**67,834,535**	**84,546,613**	**13,194,522**	**51,363,386**	**19,924,955**	**10,170,387**	**35,331,625**
FEES AND ADMISSIONS	**41,245,000**	**14,720,566**	**24,258,097**	**2,400,103**	**16,135,049**	**5,722,780**	**2,349,494**	**8,568,430**
Recreation expenses on trips	1,858,062	851,975	860,664	131,299	476,538	252,729	91,547	390,862
Social, recreation, civic club membership	8,323,580	3,392,317	4,638,326	381,038	3,393,700	863,523	310,756	1,477,269
Fees for participant sports	5,385,399	2,509,179	2,612,863	312,997	1,563,383	736,395	274,711	1,377,857
Participant sports on trips	2,004,182	909,024	986,720	149,601	568,024	269,213	70,690	431,577
Movie, theater, opera, ballet	6,567,217	2,288,269	3,802,815	359,548	2,275,558	1,167,714	514,427	2,144,652
Movie, other admissions on trips	3,718,462	1,462,180	1,951,430	174,883	1,243,484	533,038	197,232	815,992
Admission to sports events	2,681,010	909,024	1,706,179	171,640	1,021,390	513,016	151,948	682,312
Admission to sports events on trips	1,239,098	487,309	650,286	58,258	414,394	177,626	65,721	272,111
Fees for recreational lessons	7,609,930	1,059,314	6,188,150	529,430	4,702,037	956,718	580,777	585,275
Other entertainment services on trips	1,858,062	851,975	860,664	131,299	476,538	252,729	91,547	390,862
TELEVISION, RADIO, SOUND EQUIPMENT	**51,829,348**	**18,857,796**	**28,503,965**	**5,152,665**	**15,958,397**	**7,388,151**	**4,444,365**	**16,106,775**
Television	**41,988,459**	**16,219,439**	**22,100,291**	**4,018,730**	**12,046,779**	**6,034,851**	**3,639,060**	**13,525,796**
Cable service and community antenna	28,848,179	12,149,563	14,368,891	2,397,355	7,635,600	4,336,029	2,715,612	10,167,843
Black-and-white TV sets	32,731	10,807	20,295	6,540	13,693	161	–	3,054
Color TV sets, consoles	4,620,314	1,651,675	2,484,235	761,306	1,330,004	393,044	154,398	1,107,103
Color TV sets, portable and table models	2,484,040	949,236	1,237,116	192,305	697,278	347,371	158,527	728,116
VCRs and video disc players	1,870,336	463,434	1,207,388	221,214	659,961	326,304	154,468	395,612
Video cassettes, tapes, and discs	2,503,912	696,659	1,555,827	322,615	855,873	377,445	234,886	784,438
Video game hardware and software	1,415,026	207,590	1,126,781	108,656	786,507	231,581	197,792	268,378
Repair of TV, radio, and sound equipment	194,047	90,224	82,608	8,684	51,009	22,997	10,708	61,072
Rental of television sets	21,041	754	16,865	–	17,003	–	12,738	10,179
Radio and sound equipment	**9,840,890**	**2,638,106**	**6,403,674**	**1,133,935**	**3,911,618**	**1,353,300**	**805,305**	**2,580,979**
Radios	399,784	217,894	122,054	26,271	89,379	3,860	22,467	52,929
Tape recorders and players	330,816	19,603	204,376	59,412	126,545	15,117	42,624	14,929
Sound components and component systems	1,247,865	454,387	714,028	103,655	399,046	211,398	67,540	339,969
Miscellaneous sound equipment	27,471	10,053	16,007	550	11,737	3,538	–	20,697
Sound equipment accessories	487,456	186,479	274,121	76,230	113,003	85,958	10,988	40,715
Satellite dishes	74,229	28,399	42,876	5,551	19,712	17,610	1,050	13,232
Compact disc, tape, record, video mail order clubs	287,564	119,377	142,062	30,448	86,219	25,490	24,357	107,894
Records, CDs, audio tapes, needles	2,145,626	665,244	1,279,992	179,884	744,375	355,653	230,337	881,815
Rental of VCR, radio, sound equipment	16,950	503	16,007	6,815	5,868	3,216	70	5,768
Musical instruments and accessories	2,050,940	237,749	1,744,196	369,991	1,169,001	205,367	108,065	437,345
Rental and repair of musical instruments	188,203	101,282	85,752	1,539	78,696	5,548	13,928	48,518
Rental of video cassettes, tapes, discs, films	2,583,402	597,388	1,762,204	273,536	1,068,036	420,625	283,879	617,508
PETS, TOYS, PLAYGROUND EQUIPMENT	**30,175,533**	**12,982,186**	**15,082,919**	**2,920,904**	**8,698,972**	**3,448,865**	**2,068,834**	**6,008,826**
Pets	**21,694,729**	**10,988,213**	**9,284,083**	**1,300,244**	**5,254,412**	**2,715,124**	**1,185,701**	**4,742,596**
Pet food	7,060,518	3,002,269	3,405,498	408,573	1,903,145	1,102,502	515,896	1,944,132
Pet purchase, supplies, and medicines	6,746,653	3,987,946	2,379,046	407,803	1,552,850	395,135	296,618	920,833
Pet services	1,793,185	952,251	781,201	96,125	478,344	206,734	110,934	590,365
Veterinarian services	6,094,373	3,045,496	2,718,624	387,743	1,320,073	1,010,754	262,253	1,287,266
Toys, games, hobbies, and tricycles	**8,065,824**	**1,950,746**	**5,436,677**	**1,463,640**	**3,282,353**	**690,722**	**873,965**	**1,260,462**
Playground equipment	**414,981**	**43,227**	**362,159**	**157,021**	**162,207**	**42,939**	**9,169**	**5,768**

	total married couples	married couples, no children	married couples with children				single parent, at least one child <18	single person
			total	oldest child under 6	oldest child 6 to 17	oldest child 18 or older		
OTHER ENTERTAINMENT SUPPLIES, EQUIPMENT, SERVICES	**$40,003,565**	**$21,273,987**	**$16,701,345**	**$2,720,850**	**$10,570,969**	**$3,365,159**	**$1,307,693**	**$4,647,594**
Unmotored recreational vehicles	**5,294,220**	**1,906,514**	**2,570,845**	**77,274**	**2,259,608**	**233,993**	**–**	**768,492**
Boat without motor and boat trailers	660,462	484,294	172,362	77,274	51,009	43,904	–	90,930
Trailer and other attachable campers	4,633,757	1,422,220	2,398,769	–	2,208,448	190,089	–	677,562
Motorized recreational vehicles	**15,531,387**	**12,206,110**	**3,257,147**	**913,655**	**1,613,941**	**729,480**	**139,910**	**488,238**
Motorized camper	7,938,407	7,862,295	76,033	–	55,674	20,424	–	–
Other vehicle	1,518,479	854,739	595,691	94,256	368,501	132,837	138,930	293,486
Motorboats	6,074,501	3,489,076	2,585,423	819,399	1,189,917	576,138	980	194,752
Rental of recreational vehicles	**389,848**	**195,527**	**168,074**	**25,172**	**85,918**	**57,011**	**33,525**	**39,018**
Docking and landing fees	**364,716**	**252,828**	**110,334**	**24,237**	**52,965**	**33,209**	**4,689**	**32,572**
Sports, recreation, exercise equipment	**11,135,513**	**4,323,458**	**6,201,870**	**711,072**	**4,397,486**	**1,054,979**	**569,229**	**1,837,934**
Athletic gear, game tables, exercise equipment	4,363,728	1,482,788	2,513,391	160,098	1,753,091	580,721	192,123	716,580
Bicycles	819,441	188,239	592,832	129,541	409,429	53,875	85,388	225,289
Camping equipment	742,874	168,384	517,370	45,562	366,695	100,754	106,175	88,215
Hunting and fishing equipment	2,903,112	1,708,473	1,130,211	85,298	924,337	101,236	66,281	435,988
Winter sports equipment	424,917	142,750	269,261	28,030	215,624	25,570	35,275	68,537
Water sports equipment	333,154	185,474	119,767	9,618	95,699	14,554	4,759	46,143
Other sports equipment	1,395,738	366,425	990,721	249,299	579,460	161,946	59,701	222,235
Rental and repair of miscellaneous sports equipment	153,134	80,925	68,030	3,682	48,150	16,243	19,597	35,286
Photographic equipment and supplies	**6,587,090**	**2,243,282**	**3,894,284**	**875,678**	**1,839,496**	**1,178,569**	**446,536**	**1,228,569**
Film	1,141,489	370,194	684,587	148,612	355,109	181,003	87,767	257,521
Other photographic supplies	71,307	38,955	27,726	–	24,376	2,814	–	56,322
Film processing	1,876,181	628,300	1,129,926	305,303	541,993	282,802	110,934	344,040
Repair and rental of photographic equipment	63,708	37,447	25,726	2,363	12,940	10,453	–	3,393
Photographic equipment	2,136,859	747,677	1,241,117	245,122	552,827	443,140	155,168	488,917
Photographer fees	1,296,961	420,710	784,631	174,223	352,100	258,438	92,667	78,376
Fireworks	**146,704**	**9,048**	**132,344**	**1,264**	**101,266**	**28,948**	**34,715**	**4,750**
Pinball, electronic video games	**366,469**	**83,690**	**236,390**	**72,492**	**137,078**	**23,641**	**37,375**	**132,662**

Note: Total spending figures for total consumer units can be found on Total Spending by Age and Total Spending by Region tables. Spending by type of consumer unit will not add to total because not all types of consumer units are shown. Numbers may not add to category total because of rounding and missing subcategories. (–) means sample is too small to make a reliable estimate.
Source: Calculations by New Strategist based on the 2003 Consumer Expenditure Survey

Table 3.16 Entertainment: Market shares by household type, 2003

(percentage of total annual spending on entertainment accounted for by types of consumer units, 2003)

	total married couples	married couples, no children	married couples with children				single parent, at least one child <18	single person
			total	oldest child under 6	oldest child 6 to 17	oldest child 18 or older		
Share of total consumer units	50.7%	21.8%	24.8%	4.8%	13.0%	7.0%	6.1%	29.4%
Share of total before-tax income	68.8	26.8	36.6	6.2	19.8	10.7	3.5	15.6
Share of total spending	65.8	25.6	35.0	6.0	18.9	10.1	4.5	17.0
Share of entertainment spending	68.7	28.6	35.6	5.6	21.6	8.4	4.3	14.9
FEES AND ADMISSIONS	**72.3**	**25.8**	**42.5**	**4.2**	**28.3**	**10.0**	**4.1**	**15.0**
Recreation expenses on trips	70.4	32.3	32.6	5.0	18.1	9.6	3.5	14.8
Social, recreation, civic club membership	75.9	30.9	42.3	3.5	30.9	7.9	2.8	13.5
Fees for participant sports	71.0	33.1	34.5	4.1	20.6	9.7	3.6	18.2
Participant sports on trips	72.9	33.1	35.9	5.4	20.7	9.8	2.6	15.7
Movie, theater, opera, ballet	62.8	21.9	36.4	3.4	21.8	11.2	4.9	20.5
Movie, other admissions on trips	71.1	28.0	37.3	3.3	23.8	10.2	3.8	15.6
Admission to sports events	69.1	23.4	44.0	4.4	26.3	13.2	3.9	17.6
Admission to sports events on trips	71.1	28.0	37.3	3.3	23.8	10.2	3.8	15.6
Fees for recreational lessons	83.1	11.6	67.6	5.8	51.4	10.5	6.3	6.4
Other entertainment services on trips	70.4	32.3	32.6	5.0	18.1	9.6	3.5	14.8
TELEVISION, RADIO, SOUND EQUIPMENT	**61.5**	**22.4**	**33.8**	**6.1**	**18.9**	**8.8**	**5.3**	**19.1**
Television	**60.9**	**23.5**	**32.1**	**5.8**	**17.5**	**8.8**	**5.3**	**19.6**
Cable service and community antenna	59.0	24.9	29.4	4.9	15.6	8.9	5.6	20.8
Black-and-white TV sets	83.5	27.6	51.7	16.7	34.9	0.4	–	7.8
Color TV sets, consoles	70.9	25.3	38.1	11.7	20.4	6.0	2.4	17.0
Color TV sets, portable and table models	62.1	23.7	31.0	4.8	17.4	8.7	4.0	18.2
VCRs and video disc players	66.8	16.6	43.1	7.9	23.6	11.7	5.5	14.1
Video cassettes, tapes, and discs	60.4	16.8	37.5	7.8	20.7	9.1	5.7	18.9
Video game hardware and software	65.6	9.6	52.2	5.0	36.5	10.7	9.2	12.4
Repair of TV, radio, and sound equipment	64.7	30.1	27.5	2.9	17.0	7.7	3.6	20.4
Rental of television sets	31.4	1.1	25.2	–	25.4	–	19.0	15.2
Radio and sound equipment	**64.3**	**17.2**	**41.8**	**7.4**	**25.6**	**8.8**	**5.3**	**16.9**
Radios	63.5	34.6	19.4	4.2	14.2	0.6	3.6	8.4
Tape recorders and players	73.0	4.3	45.1	13.1	27.9	3.3	9.4	3.3
Sound components and component systems	63.4	23.1	36.3	5.3	20.3	10.7	3.4	17.3
Miscellaneous sound equipment	56.7	20.7	33.0	1.1	24.2	7.3	–	42.7
Sound equipment accessories	76.3	29.2	42.9	11.9	17.7	13.5	1.7	6.4
Satellite dishes	70.7	27.1	40.8	5.3	18.8	16.8	1.0	12.6
Compact disc, tape, record, video mail order clubs	56.9	23.6	28.1	6.0	17.1	5.0	4.8	21.4
Records, CDs, audio tapes, needles	55.8	17.3	33.3	4.7	19.4	9.3	6.0	22.9
Rental of VCR, radio, sound equipment	50.7	1.5	47.8	20.4	17.5	9.6	0.2	17.2
Musical instruments and accessories	76.2	8.8	64.8	13.8	43.5	7.6	4.0	16.3
Rental and repair of musical instruments	71.2	38.3	32.5	0.6	29.8	2.1	5.3	18.4
Rental of video cassettes, tapes, discs. films	62.6	14.5	42.7	6.6	25.9	10.2	6.9	15.0
PETS, TOYS, PLAYGROUND EQUIPMENT	**69.2**	**29.8**	**34.6**	**6.7**	**19.9**	**7.9**	**4.7**	**13.8**
Pets	**68.6**	**34.7**	**29.3**	**4.1**	**16.6**	**8.6**	**3.7**	**15.0**
Pet food	61.3	26.1	29.6	3.5	16.5	9.6	4.5	16.9
Pet purchase, supplies, and medicines	77.2	45.7	27.2	4.7	17.8	4.5	3.4	10.5
Pet services	63.4	33.7	27.6	3.4	16.9	7.3	3.9	20.9
Veterinarian services	71.2	35.6	31.8	4.5	15.4	11.8	3.1	15.0
Toys, games, hobbies, and tricycles	**69.9**	**16.9**	**47.1**	**12.7**	**28.4**	**6.0**	**7.6**	**10.9**
Playground equipment	**92.0**	**9.6**	**80.3**	**34.8**	**36.0**	**9.5**	**2.0**	**1.3**

	total married couples	married couples, no children	married couples with children				single parent, at least one child <18	single person
			total	oldest child under 6	oldest child 6 to 17	oldest child 18 or older		
OTHER ENTERTAINMENT SUPPLIES, EQUIPMENT, SERVICES	**75.9%**	**40.4%**	**31.7%**	**5.2%**	**20.1%**	**6.4%**	**2.5%**	**8.8%**
Unmotored recreational vehicles	**76.1**	**27.4**	**37.0**	**1.1**	**32.5**	**3.4**	**–**	**11.1**
Boat without motor and boat trailers	82.4	60.4	21.5	9.6	5.4	5.5	–	11.3
Trailer and other attachable campers	75.3	23.1	39.0	–	35.9	3.1	–	11.0
Motorized recreational vehicles	**80.5**	**63.2**	**16.9**	**4.7**	**8.4**	**3.8**	**0.7**	**2.5**
Motorized camper	82.0	81.2	0.8	–	0.6	0.2	–	–
Other vehicle	75.0	42.2	29.4	4.7	18.2	6.6	6.9	14.5
Motorboats	79.9	45.9	34.0	10.8	15.7	7.6	0.0	2.6
Rental of recreational vehicles	**80.3**	**40.3**	**34.6**	**5.2**	**17.7**	**11.7**	**6.9**	**8.0**
Docking and landing fees	**88.6**	**61.4**	**26.8**	**5.9**	**12.9**	**8.1**	**1.1**	**7.9**
Sports, recreation, exercise equipment	**73.3**	**28.4**	**40.8**	**4.7**	**28.9**	**6.9**	**3.7**	**12.1**
Athletic gear, game tables, exercise equipment	69.4	23.6	40.0	2.5	28.0	9.2	3.1	11.4
Bicycles	64.2	14.8	46.5	10.2	32.1	4.2	6.7	17.7
Camping equipment	69.2	15.7	48.2	4.2	34.1	9.4	9.9	8.2
Hunting and fishing equipment	82.5	48.6	32.1	2.4	26.3	2.9	1.9	12.4
Winter sports equipment	75.3	25.3	47.7	5.0	38.2	4.5	6.3	12.1
Water sports equipment	64.5	35.9	23.2	1.9	18.5	2.8	0.9	8.9
Other sports equipment	80.6	21.2	57.2	14.4	33.5	9.4	3.4	12.8
Rental and repair of miscellaneous sports equipment	66.0	34.9	29.3	1.6	20.8	7.0	8.5	15.2
Photographic equipment and supplies	**72.1**	**24.6**	**42.6**	**9.6**	**20.1**	**12.9**	**4.9**	**13.5**
Film	67.6	21.9	40.6	8.8	21.0	10.7	5.2	15.3
Other photographic supplies	49.1	26.8	19.1	–	16.8	1.9	–	38.7
Film processing	73.0	24.5	44.0	11.9	21.1	11.0	4.3	13.4
Repair and rental of photographic equipment	95.2	56.0	38.5	3.5	19.3	15.6	–	5.1
Photographic equipment	70.9	24.8	41.2	8.1	18.4	14.7	5.2	16.2
Photographer fees	78.4	25.4	47.4	10.5	21.3	15.6	5.6	4.7
Fireworks	**54.6**	**3.4**	**49.2**	**0.5**	**37.7**	**10.8**	**12.9**	**1.8**
Pinball, electronic video games	**63.9**	**14.6**	**41.2**	**12.6**	**23.9**	**4.1**	**6.5**	**23.1**

Note: Market share for total consumer units is 100.0%. Market shares by type of consumer unit will not add to total because not all types of consumer units are shown. (–) means sample is too small to make a reliable estimate.
Source: Calculations by New Strategist based on the 2003 Consumer Expenditure Survey

Table 3.17 Entertainment: Average spending by race and Hispanic origin, 2003

(average annual spending of consumer units (CU) on entertainment, by race and Hispanic origin of consumer unit reference person, 2003)

	total consumer units	race			Hispanic origin	
		Asian	black	white and other	Hispanic	non-Hispanic
Number of consumer units (000)	115,356	3,573	13,743	98,041	11,727	103,629
Average number of persons per CU	2.5	2.8	2.6	2.5	3.3	2.4
Average before-tax income of CU	$51,128.00	$60,393.00	$34,485.00	$53,039.00	$37,150.00	$52,797.00
Average spending of CU, total	40,817.33	44,922.85	28,707.56	42,360.25	34,574.75	41,520.78
Entertainment, average spending	**2,059.56**	**1,712.64**	**1,006.69**	**2,219.70**	**1,244.58**	**2,153.14**
FEES AND ADMISSIONS	**494.46**	**516.44**	**162.52**	**540.19**	**250.45**	**522.08**
Recreation expenses on trips	22.87	42.01	6.28	24.49	16.44	23.59
Social, recreation, civic club membership	95.06	51.04	30.04	105.78	31.58	102.25
Fees for participant sports	65.73	55.84	15.00	73.20	25.01	70.34
Participant sports on trips	23.83	19.95	3.58	26.81	7.85	25.64
Movie, theater, opera, ballet	90.69	92.04	44.28	97.15	68.31	93.22
Movie, other admissions on trips	45.31	49.72	15.62	49.31	28.19	47.24
Admission to sports events	33.65	13.80	9.54	37.76	12.14	36.09
Admission to sports events on trips	15.10	16.57	5.21	16.43	9.40	15.74
Fees for recreational lessons	79.36	133.46	26.70	84.77	35.09	84.37
Other entertainment services on trips	22.87	42.01	6.28	24.49	16.44	23.59
TELEVISION, RADIO, SOUND EQUIPMENT	**730.03**	**620.95**	**616.29**	**749.89**	**621.14**	**742.36**
Television	**597.36**	**468.18**	**531.13**	**611.35**	**494.41**	**609.01**
Cable service and community antenna	423.79	325.31	431.84	426.25	308.74	436.81
Black-and-white TV sets	0.34	0.10	0.14	0.37	0.68	0.30
Color TV sets, consoles	56.50	34.43	22.07	62.13	54.20	56.76
Color TV sets, portable and table models	34.65	17.97	26.13	36.46	49.64	32.96
VCRs and video disc players	24.26	35.16	13.83	25.32	25.26	24.15
Video cassettes, tapes, and discs	35.92	34.46	22.30	37.89	31.18	36.46
Video game hardware and software	18.70	15.35	11.81	19.79	21.24	18.42
Repair of TV, radio, and sound equipment	2.60	5.34	0.99	2.73	3.37	2.51
Rental of television sets	0.58	0.07	2.03	0.40	0.10	0.64
Radio and sound equipment	**132.68**	**152.77**	**85.16**	**138.54**	**126.72**	**133.36**
Radios	5.46	11.39	4.71	5.33	3.69	5.68
Tape recorders and players	3.93	12.10	6.64	3.24	1.49	4.24
Sound components and component systems	17.05	9.30	18.25	17.17	24.80	16.18
Miscellaneous sound equipment	0.42	–	0.10	0.48	0.14	0.45
Sound equipment accessories	5.54	12.22	0.77	5.94	9.19	5.08
Satellite dishes	0.91	0.42	0.44	1.00	0.64	0.94
Compact disc, tape, record, video mail order clubs	4.38	4.59	2.97	4.57	3.43	4.49
Records, CDs, audio tapes, needles	33.31	31.71	23.55	34.74	30.68	33.61
Rental of VCR, radio, sound equipment	0.29	0.12	0.41	0.29	0.01	0.33
Musical instruments and accessories	23.32	26.73	4.74	25.81	15.07	24.26
Rental and repair of musical instruments	2.29	0.51	0.89	2.55	0.62	2.48
Rental of video cassettes, tapes, discs, films	35.76	43.69	21.69	37.44	36.95	35.62
PETS, TOYS, PLAYGROUND EQUIPMENT	**378.21**	**197.31**	**123.04**	**420.56**	**194.36**	**400.00**
Pets	**274.25**	**118.68**	**53.41**	**310.86**	**125.66**	**292.06**
Pet food	99.82	24.35	31.54	112.24	68.00	103.81
Pet purchase, supplies, and medicines	75.73	78.43	9.71	84.77	27.71	81.76
Pet services	24.52	4.85	3.88	28.13	6.75	$26.53
Veterinarian services	74.18	11.04	8.28	85.72	23.20	79.95
Toys, games, hobbies, and tricycles	**100.05**	**78.19**	**69.18**	**105.17**	**67.07**	**103.78**
Playground equipment	**3.91**	**0.44**	**0.45**	**4.52**	**1.63**	**4.17**

	total consumer units	race			Hispanic origin	
		Asian	black	white and other	Hispanic	non-Hispanic
OTHER ENTERTAINMENT SUPPLIES, EQUIPMENT, SERVICES	**$456.86**	**$377.94**	**$104.83**	**$509.06**	**$178.63**	**$488.70**
Unmotored recreational vehicles	**60.28**	–	**36.02**	**65.87**	1.45	66.93
Boat without motor and boat trailers	6.95	–	–	8.18	1.39	7.58
Trailer and other attachable campers	53.32	–	36.02	57.69	0.06	59.35
Motorized recreational vehicles	**167.33**	**153.68**	–	**191.28**	**19.86**	**184.01**
Motorized camper	83.89	82.07	–	95.72	1.75	93.19
Other vehicle	17.54	–	–	20.64	16.56	17.65
Motorboats	65.89	71.61	–	74.92	1.55	73.17
Rental of recreational vehicles	**4.21**	**1.98**	**1.12**	**4.72**	**2.48**	**4.40**
Docking and landing fees	**3.57**	–	**0.28**	**4.16**	**0.29**	**3.94**
Sports, recreation, exercise equipment	131.77	84.31	34.90	147.10	95.58	136.18
Athletic gear, game tables, exercise equipment	54.52	12.07	17.42	61.32	59.58	53.88
Bicycles	11.06	13.04	5.02	11.84	10.18	11.16
Camping equipment	9.31	8.57	5.86	9.82	3.57	10.03
Hunting and fishing equipment	30.49	25.29	4.75	34.26	5.90	33.57
Winter sports equipment	4.89	0.92	0.04	5.71	2.04	5.21
Water sports equipment	4.48	16.99	0.71	4.55	0.97	4.88
Other sports equipment	15.01	7.15	0.84	17.28	12.93	15.25
Rental and repair of miscellaneous sports equipment	2.01	0.28	0.26	2.32	0.40	2.19
Photographic equipment and supplies	**79.18**	**113.67**	**26.69**	**85.29**	**51.06**	**82.38**
Film	14.63	11.99	7.05	15.79	11.99	14.93
Other photographic supplies	1.26	–	–	1.48	0.22	1.39
Film processing	22.27	23.62	8.25	24.18	12.72	23.35
Repair and rental of photographic equipment	0.58	1.50	0.08	0.62	–	0.65
Photographic equipment	26.11	51.91	5.46	28.06	13.14	27.58
Photographer fees	14.34	24.66	5.85	15.15	12.99	14.49
Fireworks	2.33	–	4.79	2.08	2.86	2.27
Pinball, electronic video games	4.97	6.76	1.04	5.44	4.47	5.03

Note: Other races include Native Americans and Pacific Islanders. Subcategories may not add to total because some are not shown. (–) means sample is too small to make a reliable estimate.
Source: Bureau of Labor Statistics, unpublished data from the 2003 Consumer Expenditure Survey

Table 3.18 Entertainment: Indexed spending by race and Hispanic origin, 2003

(indexed average annual spending of consumer units (CU) on entertainment by race and Hispanic origin of consumer unit reference person, 2003; index definition: an index of 100 is the average for all consumer units; an index of 132 means that spending by consumer units in that group is 32 percent above the average for all consumer units; an index of 68 indicates spending that is 32 percent below the average for all consumer units)

	total consumer units	race			Hispanic origin	
		Asian	black	white and other	Hispanic	non-Hispanic
Average spending of CU, total	$40,817	$44,923	$28,708	$42,360	$34,575	$41,521
Average spending of CU, index	100	110	70	104	85	102
Entertainment, spending index	**100**	**83**	**49**	**108**	**60**	**105**
FEES AND ADMISSIONS	**100**	**104**	**33**	**109**	**51**	**106**
Recreation expenses on trips	100	184	27	107	72	103
Social, recreation, civic club membership	100	54	32	111	33	108
Fees for participant sports	100	85	23	111	38	107
Participant sports on trips	100	84	15	113	33	108
Movie, theater, opera, ballet	100	101	49	107	75	103
Movie, other admissions on trips	100	110	34	109	62	104
Admission to sports events	100	41	28	112	36	107
Admission to sports events on trips	100	110	35	109	62	104
Fees for recreational lessons	100	168	34	107	44	106
Other entertainment services on trips	100	184	27	107	72	103
TELEVISION, RADIO, SOUND EQUIPMENT	**100**	**85**	**84**	**103**	**85**	**102**
Television	**100**	**78**	**89**	**102**	**83**	**102**
Cable service and community antenna	100	77	102	101	73	103
Black-and-white TV sets	100	29	41	109	200	88
Color TV sets, consoles	100	61	39	110	96	100
Color TV sets, portable and table models	100	52	75	105	143	95
VCRs and video disc players	100	145	57	104	104	100
Video cassettes, tapes, and discs	100	96	62	105	87	102
Video game hardware and software	100	82	63	106	114	99
Repair of TV, radio, and sound equipment	100	205	38	105	130	97
Rental of television sets	100	12	350	69	17	110
Radio and sound equipment	**100**	**115**	**64**	**104**	**96**	**101**
Radios	100	209	86	98	68	104
Tape recorders and players	100	308	169	82	38	108
Sound components and component systems	100	55	107	101	145	95
Miscellaneous sound equipment	100	–	24	114	33	107
Sound equipment accessories	100	221	14	107	166	92
Satellite dishes	100	46	48	110	70	103
Compact disc, tape, record, video mail order clubs	100	105	68	104	78	103
Records, CDs, audio tapes, needles	100	95	71	104	92	101
Rental of VCR, radio, sound equipment	100	41	141	100	3	114
Musical instruments and accessories	100	115	20	111	65	104
Rental and repair of musical instruments	100	22	39	111	27	108
Rental of video cassettes, tapes, discs, films	100	122	61	105	103	100
PETS, TOYS, PLAYGROUND EQUIPMENT	**100**	**52**	**33**	**111**	**51**	**106**
Pets	**100**	**43**	**19**	**113**	**46**	**106**
Pet food	100	24	32	112	68	104
Pet purchase, supplies, and medicines	100	104	13	112	37	108
Pet services	100	20	16	115	28	108
Veterinarian services	100	15	11	116	31	108
Toys, games, hobbies, and tricycles	**100**	**78**	**69**	**105**	**67**	**104**
Playground equipment	**100**	**11**	**12**	**116**	**42**	**107**

	total consumer units	race			Hispanic origin	
		Asian	black	white and other	Hispanic	non-Hispanic
OTHER ENTERTAINMENT SUPPLIES, EQUIPMENT, SERVICES	100	83	23	111	39	107
Unmotored recreational vehicles	100	–	60	109	2	111
Boat without motor and boat trailers	100	–	–	118	20	109
Trailer and other attachable campers	100	–	68	108	0	111
Motorized recreational vehicles	100	92	–	114	12	110
Motorized camper	100	98	–	114	2	111
Other vehicle	100	–	–	118	94	101
Motorboats	100	109	–	114	2	111
Rental of recreational vehicles	100	47	27	112	59	105
Docking and landing fees	100	–	8	117	8	110
Sports, recreation, exercise equipment	100	64	26	112	73	103
Athletic gear, game tables, exercise equipment	100	22	32	112	109	99
Bicycles	100	118	45	107	92	101
Camping equipment	100	92	63	105	38	108
Hunting and fishing equipment	100	83	16	112	19	110
Winter sports equipment	100	19	1	117	42	107
Water sports equipment	100	379	16	102	22	109
Other sports equipment	100	48	6	115	86	102
Rental and repair of miscellaneous sports equipment	100	14	13	115	20	109
Photographic equipment and supplies	100	144	34	108	64	104
Film	100	82	48	108	82	102
Other photographic supplies	100	–	–	117	17	110
Film processing	100	106	37	109	57	105
Repair and rental of photographic equipment	100	259	14	107	–	112
Photographic equipment	100	199	21	107	50	106
Photographer fees	100	172	41	106	91	101
Fireworks	100	–	206	89	123	97
Pinball, electronic video games	100	136	21	109	90	101

Note: Other races include Native Americans and Pacific Islanders. (–) means sample is too small to make a reliable estimate.
Source: Calculations by New Strategist based on the 2003 Consumer Expenditure Survey

Table 3.19 Entertainment: Total spending by race and Hispanic origin, 2003

(total annual spending on entertainment, by consumer unit race and Hispanic origin groups, 2003; numbers in thousands)

	total consumer units	race			Hispanic origin	
		Asian	black	white and other	Hispanic	non-Hispanic
Number of consumer units	115,356	3,573	13,743	98,041	11,727	103,629
Total spending of all consumer units	$4,708,523,919	$160,509,343	$394,527,997	$4,153,041,270	$405,458,093	$4,302,756,911
Entertainment, total spending	237,582,603	6,119,263	13,834,941	217,621,608	14,595,190	223,127,745
FEES AND ADMISSIONS	**57,038,928**	**1,845,240**	**2,233,512**	**52,960,768**	**2,937,027**	**54,102,628**
Recreation expenses on trips	2,638,192	150,102	86,306	2,401,024	192,792	2,444,608
Social, recreation, civic club membership	10,965,741	182,366	412,840	10,370,777	370,339	10,596,065
Fees for participant sports	7,582,350	199,516	206,145	7,176,601	293,292	7,289,264
Participant sports on trips	2,748,933	71,281	49,200	2,628,479	92,057	2,657,048
Movie, theater, opera, ballet	10,461,636	328,859	608,540	9,524,683	801,071	9,660,295
Movie, other admissions on trips	5,226,780	177,650	214,666	4,834,402	330,584	4,895,434
Admission to sports events	3,881,729	49,307	131,108	3,702,028	142,366	3,739,971
Admission to sports events on trips	1,741,876	59,205	71,601	1,610,814	110,234	1,631,120
Fees for recreational lessons	9,154,652	476,853	366,938	8,310,936	411,500	8,743,179
Other entertainment services on trips	2,638,192	150,102	86,306	2,401,024	192,792	2,444,608
TELEVISION, RADIO, SOUND EQUIPMENT	**84,213,341**	**2,218,654**	**8,469,673**	**73,519,965**	**7,284,109**	**76,930,024**
Television	**68,909,060**	**1,672,807**	**7,299,320**	**59,937,365**	**5,797,946**	**63,111,097**
Cable service and community antenna	48,886,719	1,162,333	5,934,777	41,789,976	3,620,594	45,266,183
Black-and-white TV sets	39,221	357	1,924	36,275	7,974	31,089
Color TV sets, consoles	6,517,614	123,018	303,308	6,091,287	635,603	5,881,982
Color TV sets, portable and table models	3,997,085	64,207	359,105	3,574,575	582,128	3,415,612
VCRs and video disc players	2,798,537	125,627	190,066	2,482,398	296,224	2,502,640
Video cassettes, tapes, and discs	4,143,588	123,126	306,469	3,714,773	365,648	3,778,313
Video game hardware and software	2,157,157	54,846	162,305	1,940,231	249,081	1,908,846
Repair of TV, radio, and sound equipment	299,926	19,080	13,606	267,652	39,520	260,109
Rental of television sets	66,906	250	27,898	39,216	1,173	66,323
Radio and sound equipment	**15,305,434**	**545,847**	**1,170,354**	**13,582,600**	**1,486,045**	**13,819,963**
Radios	629,844	40,696	64,730	522,559	43,273	588,613
Tape recorders and players	453,349	43,233	91,254	317,653	17,473	439,387
Sound components and component systems	1,966,820	33,229	250,810	1,683,364	290,830	1,676,717
Miscellaneous sound equipment	48,450	–	1,374	47,060	1,642	46,633
Sound equipment accessories	639,072	43,662	10,582	582,364	107,771	526,435
Satellite dishes	104,974	1,501	6,047	98,041	7,505	97,411
Compact disc, tape, record, video mail order clubs	505,259	16,400	40,817	448,047	40,224	465,294
Records, CDs, audio tapes, needles	3,842,508	113,300	323,648	3,405,944	359,784	3,482,971
Rental of VCR, radio, sound equipment	33,453	429	5,635	28,432	117	34,198
Musical instruments and accessories	2,690,102	95,506	65,142	2,530,438	176,726	2,514,040
Rental and repair of musical instruments	264,165	1,822	12,231	250,005	7,271	257,000
Rental of video cassettes, tapes, discs, films	4,125,131	156,104	298,086	3,670,655	433,313	3,691,265
PETS, TOYS, PLAYGROUND EQUIPMENT	**43,628,793**	**704,989**	**1,690,939**	**41,232,123**	**2,279,260**	**41,451,600**
Pets	**31,636,383**	**424,044**	**734,014**	**30,477,025**	**1,473,615**	**30,265,886**
Pet food	11,514,836	87,003	433,454	11,004,122	797,436	10,757,726
Pet purchase, supplies, and medicines	8,735,910	280,230	133,445	8,310,936	324,955	8,472,707
Pet services	2,828,529	17,329	53,323	2,757,893	79,157	2,749,277
Veterinarian services	8,557,108	39,446	113,792	8,404,075	272,066	8,285,139
Toys, games, hobbies, and tricycles	**11,541,368**	**279,373**	**950,741**	**10,310,972**	**786,530**	**10,754,618**
Playground equipment	**451,042**	**1,572**	**6,184**	**443,145**	**19,115**	**432,133**

	total consumer units	race			Hispanic origin	
		Asian	black	white and other	Hispanic	non-Hispanic
OTHER ENTERTAINMENT SUPPLIES, EQUIPMENT, SERVICES	**$52,701,542**	**$1,350,380**	**$1,440,679**	**$49,908,751**	**$2,094,794**	**$50,643,492**
Unmotored recreational vehicles	**6,953,660**	–	**495,023**	**6,457,961**	**17,004**	**6,935,889**
Boat without motor and boat trailers	801,724	–	–	801,724	16,301	785,508
Trailer and other attachable campers	6,150,782	–	495,023	5,655,759	704	6,150,381
Motorized recreational vehicles	**19,302,519**	**549,099**	–	**18,753,282**	**232,898**	**19,068,772**
Motorized camper	9,677,215	293,236	–	9,383,979	20,522	9,657,187
Other vehicle	2,023,344	–	–	2,023,344	194,199	1,829,052
Motorboats	7,600,307	255,863	–	7,344,944	18,177	7,582,534
Rental of recreational vehicles	**485,649**	**7,075**	**15,392**	**462,754**	**29,083**	**455,968**
Docking and landing fees	**411,821**	–	**3,848**	**407,851**	**3,401**	**408,298**
Sports, recreation, exercise equipment	**15,200,460**	**301,240**	**479,631**	**14,421,831**	**1,120,867**	**14,112,197**
Athletic gear, game tables, exercise equipment	6,289,209	43,126	239,403	6,011,874	698,695	5,583,531
Bicycles	1,275,837	46,592	68,990	1,160,805	119,381	1,156,500
Camping equipment	1,073,964	30,621	80,534	962,763	41,865	1,039,399
Hunting and fishing equipment	3,517,204	90,361	65,279	3,358,885	69,189	3,478,826
Winter sports equipment	564,091	3,287	550	559,814	23,923	539,907
Water sports equipment	516,795	60,705	9,758	446,087	11,375	505,710
Other sports equipment	1,731,494	25,547	11,544	1,694,148	151,630	1,580,342
Rental and repair of miscellaneous sports equipment	231,866	1,000	5,573	227,455	4,691	226,948
Photographic equipment and supplies	**9,133,888**	**406,143**	**366,801**	**8,361,917**	**598,781**	**8,536,957**
Film	1,687,658	42,840	96,888	1,548,067	140,607	1,547,181
Other photographic supplies	145,349	–	–	145,101	2,580	144,044
Film processing	2,568,978	84,394	113,380	2,370,631	149,167	2,419,737
Repair and rental of photographic equipment	66,906	5,360	1,099	60,785	–	66,906
Photographic equipment	3,011,945	185,474	75,037	2,751,030	154,093	2,858,088
Photographer fees	1,654,205	88,110	80,397	1,485,321	152,334	1,501,584
Fireworks	**268,779**	–	**65,829**	**202,951**	**33,539**	**235,238**
Pinball, electronic video games	**573,319**	**24,153**	**14,293**	**533,343**	**52,420**	**521,254**

Note: Other races include Native Americans and Pacific Islanders. Numbers may not add to total because of rounding and missing subcategories. (–) means sample is too small to make a reliable estimate.
Source: Calculations by New Strategist based on the 2003 Consumer Expenditure Survey

Table 3.20 Entertainment: Market shares by race and Hispanic origin, 2003

(percentage of total annual spending on entertainment accounted for by consumer unit race and Hispanic origin groups, 2003)

	total consumer units	race			Hispanic origin	
		Asian	black	white and other	Hispanic	non-Hispanic
Share of total consumer units	100.0%	3.1%	11.9%	85.0%	10.2%	89.8%
Share of total before-tax income	100.0	3.7	8.0	88.2	7.4	92.8
Share of total spending	100.0	3.4	8.4	88.2	8.6	91.4
Share of entertainment spending	100.0	2.6	5.8	91.6	6.1	93.9
FEES AND ADMISSIONS	100.0	3.2	3.9	92.9	5.1	94.9
Recreation expenses on trips	100.0	5.7	3.3	91.0	7.3	92.7
Social, recreation, civic club membership	100.0	1.7	3.8	94.6	3.4	96.6
Fees for participant sports	100.0	2.6	2.7	94.6	3.9	96.1
Participant sports on trips	100.0	2.6	1.8	95.6	3.3	96.7
Movie, theater, opera, ballet	100.0	3.1	5.8	91.0	7.7	92.3
Movie, other admissions on trips	100.0	3.4	4.1	92.5	6.3	93.7
Admission to sports events	100.0	1.3	3.4	95.4	3.7	96.3
Admission to sports events on trips	100.0	3.4	4.1	92.5	6.3	93.6
Fees for recreational lessons	100.0	5.2	4.0	90.8	4.5	95.5
Other entertainment services on trips	100.0	5.7	3.3	91.0	7.3	92.7
TELEVISION, RADIO, SOUND EQUIPMENT	100.0	2.6	10.1	87.3	8.6	91.4
Television	100.0	2.4	10.6	87.0	8.4	91.6
Cable service and community antenna	100.0	2.4	12.1	85.5	7.4	92.6
Black-and-white TV sets	100.0	0.9	4.9	92.5	20.3	79.3
Color TV sets, consoles	100.0	1.9	4.7	93.5	9.8	90.2
Color TV sets, portable and table models	100.0	1.6	9.0	89.4	14.6	85.5
VCRs and video disc players	100.0	4.5	6.8	88.7	10.6	89.4
Video cassettes, tapes, and discs	100.0	3.0	7.4	89.7	8.8	91.2
Video game hardware and software	100.0	2.5	7.5	89.9	11.5	88.5
Repair of TV, radio, and sound equipment	100.0	6.4	4.5	89.2	13.2	86.7
Rental of television sets	100.0	0.4	41.7	58.6	1.8	99.1
Radio and sound equipment	100.0	3.6	7.6	88.7	9.7	90.3
Radios	100.0	6.5	10.3	83.0	6.9	93.5
Tape recorders and players	100.0	9.5	20.1	70.1	3.9	96.9
Sound components and component systems	100.0	1.7	12.8	85.6	14.8	85.3
Miscellaneous sound equipment	100.0	–	2.8	97.1	3.4	96.3
Sound equipment accessories	100.0	6.8	1.7	91.1	16.9	82.4
Satellite dishes	100.0	1.4	5.8	93.4	7.1	92.8
Compact disc, tape, record, video mail order clubs	100.0	3.2	8.1	88.7	8.0	92.1
Records, CDs, audio tapes, needles	100.0	2.9	8.4	88.6	9.4	90.6
Rental of VCR, radio, sound equipment	100.0	1.2	16.5	84.0	0.4	100.0
Musical instruments and accessories	100.0	3.6	2.4	94.1	6.6	93.5
Rental and repair of musical instruments	100.0	0.7	4.6	94.6	2.8	97.3
Rental of video cassettes, tapes, discs, films	100.0	3.8	7.2	89.0	10.5	89.5
PETS, TOYS, PLAYGROUND EQUIPMENT	100.0	1.6	3.9	94.5	5.2	95.0
Pets	100.0	1.3	2.3	96.3	4.7	95.7
Pet food	100.0	0.8	3.8	95.6	6.9	93.4
Pet purchase, supplies, and medicines	100.0	3.2	1.5	95.1	3.7	97.0
Pet services	100.0	0.6	1.9	97.5	2.8	97.2
Veterinarian services	100.0	0.5	1.3	98.2	3.2	96.8
Toys, games, hobbies, and tricycles	100.0	2.4	8.2	89.3	6.8	93.2
Playground equipment	100.0	0.3	1.4	98.2	4.2	95.8

	total consumer units	race			Hispanic origin	
		Asian	black	white and other	Hispanic	non-Hispanic
OTHER ENTERTAINMENT SUPPLIES, EQUIPMENT, SERVICES	**100.0%**	**2.6%**	**2.7%**	**94.7%**	**4.0%**	**96.1%**
Unmotored recreational vehicles	**100.0**	–	**7.1**	**92.9**	**0.2**	**99.7**
Boat without motor and boat trailers	100.0	–	–	100.0	2.0	98.0
Trailer and other attachable campers	100.0	–	8.0	92.0	0.0	100.0
Motorized recreational vehicles	**100.0**	**2.8**	–	**97.2**	**1.2**	**98.8**
Motorized camper	100.0	3.0	–	97.0	0.2	99.8
Other vehicle	100.0	–	–	100.0	9.6	90.4
Motorboats	100.0	3.4	–	96.6	0.2	99.8
Rental of recreational vehicles	**100.0**	**1.5**	**3.2**	**95.3**	**6.0**	**93.9**
Docking and landing fees	**100.0**	–	**0.9**	**99.0**	**0.8**	**99.1**
Sports, recreation, exercise equipment	**100.0**	**2.0**	**3.2**	**94.9**	**7.4**	**92.8**
Athletic gear, game tables, exercise equipment	100.0	0.7	3.8	95.6	11.1	88.8
Bicycles	100.0	3.7	5.4	91.0	9.4	90.6
Camping equipment	100.0	2.9	7.5	89.6	3.9	96.8
Hunting and fishing equipment	100.0	2.6	1.9	95.5	2.0	98.9
Winter sports equipment	100.0	0.6	0.1	99.2	4.2	95.7
Water sports equipment	100.0	11.7	1.9	86.3	2.2	97.9
Other sports equipment	100.0	1.5	0.7	97.8	8.8	91.3
Rental and repair of miscellaneous sports equipment	100.0	0.4	1.5	98.1	2.0	97.9
Photographic equipment and supplies	**100.0**	**4.4**	**4.0**	**91.5**	**6.6**	**93.5**
Film	100.0	2.5	5.7	91.7	8.3	91.7
Other photographic supplies	100.0	–	–	99.8	1.8	99.1
Film processing	100.0	3.3	4.4	92.3	5.8	94.2
Repair and rental of photographic equipment	100.0	8.0	1.6	90.9	–	100.0
Photographic equipment	100.0	6.2	2.5	91.3	5.1	94.9
Photographer fees	100.0	5.3	4.9	89.8	9.2	90.8
Fireworks	**100.0**	–	**24.5**	**75.5**	**12.5**	**87.5**
Pinball, electronic video games	**100.0**	**4.2**	**2.5**	**93.0**	**9.1**	**90.9**

Note: Other races include Native Americans and Pacific Islanders. Numbers may not add to total because of rounding. (–) means sample is too small to make a reliable estimate.
Source: Calculations by New Strategist based on the 2003 Consumer Expenditure Survey

Table 3.21 Entertainment: Average spending by region, 2003

(average annual spending of consumer units (CU) on entertainment, by region in which consumer unit lives, 2003)

	total consumer units	Northeast	Midwest	South	West
Number of consumer units (000)	115,356	22,182	26,438	41,325	25,412
Average number of persons per CU	2.5	2.4	2.5	2.5	2.6
Average before-tax income of CU	$48,596.00	$54,219.00	$49,591.00	$44,461.00	$49,667.00
Average spending of CU, total	40,817.33	42,162.29	40,280.39	37,624.55	45,380.67
Entertainment, average spending	**2,059.56**	**2,116.88**	**1,977.83**	**1,812.38**	**2,494.25**
FEES AND ADMISSIONS	**494.46**	**614.13**	**488.88**	**365.07**	**606.22**
Recreation expenses on trips	22.87	23.57	25.38	17.01	29.15
Social, recreation, civic club membership	95.06	144.47	86.18	71.34	99.77
Fees for participant sports	65.73	62.37	68.52	53.21	86.12
Participant sports on trips	23.83	26.21	24.32	16.52	33.13
Movie, theater, opera, ballet	90.69	106.94	87.53	63.62	123.81
Movie, other admissions on trips	45.31	50.84	47.22	35.12	55.04
Admission to sports events	33.65	36.51	39.60	28.43	33.47
Admission to sports events on trips	15.10	16.94	15.74	11.71	18.34
Fees for recreational lessons	79.36	122.72	69.01	51.10	98.22
Other entertainment services on trips	22.87	23.57	25.38	17.01	29.15
TELEVISION, RADIO, SOUND EQUIPMENT	**730.03**	**776.32**	**737.62**	**696.34**	**736.14**
Television	**597.36**	**644.53**	**575.68**	**597.06**	**579.20**
Cable service and community antenna	423.79	478.46	409.03	435.29	372.73
Black-and-white TV sets	0.34	0.23	0.31	0.37	0.40
Color TV sets, consoles	56.50	56.12	47.61	57.96	63.72
Color TV sets, portable and table models	34.65	32.19	34.53	30.21	44.16
VCRs and video disc players	24.26	23.79	23.43	22.94	27.68
Video cassettes, tapes, and discs	35.92	30.43	39.77	30.41	45.68
Video game hardware and software	18.70	19.56	17.94	17.25	21.12
Repair of TV, radio, and sound equipment	2.60	2.80	2.11	2.24	3.51
Rental of television sets	0.58	0.96	0.94	0.39	0.19
Radio and sound equipment	**132.68**	**131.78**	**161.95**	**99.28**	**156.94**
Radios	5.46	2.11	9.31	4.89	5.17
Tape recorders and players	3.93	4.96	6.85	3.11	1.21
Sound components and component systems	17.05	21.63	17.59	11.07	22.22
Miscellaneous sound equipment	0.42	0.07	0.30	0.52	0.68
Sound equipment accessories	5.54	6.08	7.74	3.63	5.75
Satellite dishes	0.91	0.66	0.44	0.81	1.80
Compact disc, tape, record, video mail order clubs	4.38	4.50	5.74	3.14	4.86
Records, CDs, audio tapes, needles	33.31	32.40	36.30	25.77	43.28
Rental of VCR, radio, sound equipment	0.29	0.01	0.60	0.31	0.20
Musical instruments and accessories	23.32	30.90	35.25	13.48	20.32
Rental and repair of musical instruments	2.29	1.50	1.61	1.43	5.10
Rental of video cassettes, tapes, discs, films	35.76	26.97	40.21	31.12	46.34
PETS, TOYS, PLAYGROUND EQUIPMENT	**378.21**	**447.43**	**378.06**	**306.61**	**433.54**
Pets	**274.25**	**345.62**	**263.30**	**212.89**	**322.29**
Pet food	99.82	85.90	109.94	95.59	107.88
Pet purchase, supplies, and medicines	75.73	149.24	55.76	44.13	83.32
Pet services	24.52	22.52	20.56	17.98	41.02
Veterinarian services	74.18	87.96	77.04	55.19	90.07
Toys, games, hobbies, and tricycles	**100.05**	**93.54**	**107.21**	**92.86**	**109.96**
Playground equipment	**3.91**	**8.26**	**7.56**	**0.86**	**1.28**

	total consumer units	Northeast	Midwest	South	West
OTHER ENTERTAINMENT SUPPLIES, EQUIPMENT, SERVICES	**$456.86**	**$279.00**	**$373.27**	**$444.35**	**$718.35**
Unmotored recreational vehicles	**60.28**	**33.13**	**64.89**	**52.46**	**91.88**
Boat without motor and boat trailers	6.95	2.53	7.11	12.33	1.91
Trailer and other attachable campers	53.32	30.60	57.78	40.13	89.97
Motorized recreational vehicles	**167.33**	**41.91**	**51.71**	**213.80**	**321.52**
Motorized camper	83.89	8.43	0.84	91.66	223.53
Other vehicle	17.54	10.46	12.59	23.04	19.93
Motorboats	65.89	23.01	38.28	99.10	78.06
Rental of recreational vehicles	**4.21**	**5.46**	**3.87**	**2.05**	**6.97**
Docking and landing fees	**3.57**	**2.53**	**5.78**	**2.05**	**4.65**
Sports, recreation, exercise equipment	**131.77**	**110.20**	**143.43**	**104.53**	**181.81**
Athletic gear, game tables, exercise equipment	54.52	55.25	67.87	43.77	56.70
Bicycles	11.06	8.63	9.76	7.61	20.15
Camping equipment	9.31	2.97	14.13	6.11	14.81
Hunting and fishing equipment	30.49	4.89	30.72	30.05	53.33
Winter sports equipment	4.89	6.70	4.93	0.92	9.73
Water sports equipment	4.48	6.90	2.78	2.09	8.02
Other sports equipment	15.01	22.36	11.36	12.90	15.84
Rental and repair of miscellaneous sports equipment	2.01	2.49	1.88	1.09	3.23
Photographic equipment and supplies	**79.18**	**76.35**	**90.12**	**61.53**	**99.03**
Film	14.63	14.76	15.84	12.64	16.51
Other photographic supplies	1.26	1.73	0.52	1.82	0.73
Film processing	22.27	22.88	24.65	18.76	24.95
Repair and rental of photographic equipment	0.58	0.68	0.18	0.61	0.87
Photographic equipment	26.11	24.06	32.31	16.99	36.28
Photographer fees	14.34	12.24	16.63	10.70	19.69
Fireworks	**2.33**	**0.24**	**3.12**	**1.72**	**4.30**
Pinball, electronic video games	**4.97**	**5.18**	**6.44**	**4.20**	**4.43**

Note: Subcategories may not add to total because some are not shown.
Source: Bureau of Labor Statistics, unpublished data from the 2003 Consumer Expenditure Survey

Table 3.22 Entertainment: Indexed spending by region, 2003

(indexed average annual spending of consumer units (CU) on entertainment by region in which consumer unit lives, 2003; index definition: an index of 100 is the average for all consumer units; an index of 132 means that spending by consumer units in that group is 32 percent above the average for all consumer units; an index of 68 indicates spending that is 32 percent below the average for all consumer units)

	total consumer units	Northeast	Midwest	South	West
Average spending of CU, total	$40,817	$42,162	$40,280	$37,625	$45,381
Average spending of CU, index	100	103	99	92	111
Entertainment, spending index	100	103	96	88	121
FEES AND ADMISSIONS	100	124	99	74	123
Recreation expenses on trips	100	103	111	74	127
Social, recreation, civic club membership	100	152	91	75	105
Fees for participant sports	100	95	104	81	131
Participant sports on trips	100	110	102	69	139
Movie, theater, opera, ballet	100	118	97	70	137
Movie, other admissions on trips	100	112	104	78	121
Admission to sports events	100	108	118	84	99
Admission to sports events on trips	100	112	104	78	121
Fees for recreational lessons	100	155	87	64	124
Other entertainment services on trips	100	103	111	74	127
TELEVISION, RADIO, SOUND EQUIPMENT	100	106	101	95	101
Television	100	108	96	100	97
Cable service and community antenna	100	113	97	103	88
Black-and-white TV sets	100	68	91	109	118
Color TV sets, consoles	100	99	84	103	113
Color TV sets, portable and table models	100	93	100	87	127
VCRs and video disc players	100	98	97	95	114
Video cassettes, tapes, and discs	100	85	111	85	127
Video game hardware and software	100	105	96	92	113
Repair of TV, radio, and sound equipment	100	108	81	86	135
Rental of television sets	100	166	162	67	33
Radio and sound equipment	100	99	122	75	118
Radios	100	39	171	90	95
Tape recorders and players	100	126	174	79	31
Sound components and component systems	100	127	103	65	130
Miscellaneous sound equipment	100	17	71	124	162
Sound equipment accessories	100	110	140	66	104
Satellite dishes	100	73	48	89	198
Compact disc, tape, record, video mail order clubs	100	103	131	72	111
Records, CDs, audio tapes, needles	100	97	109	77	130
Rental of VCR, radio, sound equipment	100	3	207	107	69
Musical instruments and accessories	100	133	151	58	87
Rental and repair of musical instruments	100	66	70	62	223
Rental of video cassettes, tapes, discs, films	100	75	112	87	130
PETS, TOYS, PLAYGROUND EQUIPMENT	100	118	100	81	115
Pets	100	126	96	78	118
Pet food	100	86	110	96	108
Pet purchase, supplies, and medicines	100	197	74	58	110
Pet services	100	92	84	73	167
Veterinarian services	100	119	104	74	121
Toys, games, hobbies, and tricycles	100	93	107	93	110
Playground equipment	100	211	193	22	33

	total consumer units	Northeast	Midwest	South	West
OTHER ENTERTAINMENT SUPPLIES, EQUIPMENT, SERVICES	**100**	**61**	**82**	**97**	**157**
Unmotored recreational vehicles	**100**	**55**	**108**	**87**	**152**
Boat without motor and boat trailers	100	36	102	177	27
Trailer and other attachable campers	100	57	108	75	169
Motorized recreational vehicles	**100**	**25**	**31**	**128**	**192**
Motorized camper	100	10	1	109	266
Other vehicle	100	60	72	131	114
Motorboats	100	35	58	150	118
Rental of recreational vehicles	**100**	**130**	**92**	**49**	**166**
Docking and landing fees	**100**	**71**	**162**	**57**	**130**
Sports, recreation, exercise equipment	**100**	**84**	**109**	**79**	**138**
Athletic gear, game tables, exercise equipment	100	101	124	80	104
Bicycles	100	78	88	69	182
Camping equipment	100	32	152	66	159
Hunting and fishing equipment	100	16	101	99	175
Winter sports equipment	100	137	101	19	199
Water sports equipment	100	154	62	47	179
Other sports equipment	100	149	76	86	106
Rental and repair of miscellaneous sports equipment	100	124	94	54	161
Photographic equipment and supplies	**100**	**96**	**114**	**78**	**125**
Film	100	101	108	86	113
Other photographic supplies	100	137	41	144	58
Film processing	100	103	111	84	112
Repair and rental of photographic equipment	100	117	31	105	150
Photographic equipment	100	92	124	65	139
Photographer fees	100	85	116	75	137
Fireworks	**100**	**10**	**134**	**74**	**185**
Pinball, electronic video games	**100**	**104**	**130**	**85**	**89**

Source: Calculations by New Strategist based on the 2003 Consumer Expenditure Survey

Table 3.23 Entertainment: Total spending by region, 2003

(total annual spending on entertainment, by region in which consumer units live, 2003; numbers in thousands)

	total consumer units	Northeast	Midwest	South	West
Number of consumer units	115,356	22,182	26,438	41,325	25,412
Total spending of all consumer units	$4,708,523,919	$935,243,917	$1,064,932,951	$1,554,834,529	$1,153,213,586
Entertainment, total spending	237,582,603	46,956,632	52,289,870	74,896,604	63,383,881
FEES AND ADMISSIONS	57,038,928	13,622,632	12,925,009	15,086,518	15,405,263
Recreation expenses on trips	2,638,192	522,830	670,996	702,938	740,760
Social, recreation, civic club membership	10,965,741	3,204,634	2,278,427	2,948,126	2,535,355
Fees for participant sports	7,582,350	1,383,491	1,811,532	2,198,903	2,188,481
Participant sports on trips	2,748,933	581,390	642,972	682,689	841,900
Movie, theater, opera, ballet	10,461,636	2,372,143	2,314,118	2,629,097	3,146,260
Movie, other admissions on trips	5,226,780	1,127,733	1,248,402	1,451,334	1,398,676
Admission to sports events	3,881,729	809,865	1,046,945	1,174,870	850,540
Admission to sports events on trips	1,741,876	375,763	416,134	483,916	466,056
Fees for recreational lessons	9,154,652	2,722,175	1,824,486	2,111,708	2,495,967
Other entertainment services on trips	2,638,192	522,830	670,996	702,938	740,760
TELEVISION, RADIO, SOUND EQUIPMENT	84,213,341	17,220,330	19,501,198	28,776,251	18,706,790
Television	68,909,060	14,296,964	15,219,828	24,673,505	14,718,630
Cable service and community antenna	48,886,719	10,613,200	10,813,935	17,988,359	9,471,815
Black-and-white TV sets	39,221	5,102	8,196	15,290	10,165
Color TV sets, consoles	6,517,614	1,244,854	1,258,713	2,395,197	1,619,253
Color TV sets, portable and table models	3,997,085	714,039	912,904	1,248,428	1,122,194
VCRs and video disc players	2,798,537	527,710	619,442	947,996	703,404
Video cassettes, tapes, and discs	4,143,588	674,998	1,051,439	1,256,693	1,160,820
Video game hardware and software	2,157,157	433,880	474,298	712,856	536,701
Repair of TV, radio, and sound equipment	299,926	62,110	55,784	92,568	89,196
Rental of television sets	66,906	21,295	24,852	16,117	4,828
Radio and sound equipment	15,305,434	2,923,144	4,281,634	4,102,746	3,988,159
Radios	629,844	46,804	246,138	202,079	131,380
Tape recorders and players	453,349	110,023	181,100	128,521	30,749
Sound components and component systems	1,966,820	479,797	465,044	457,468	564,655
Miscellaneous sound equipment	48,450	1,553	7,931	21,489	17,280
Sound equipment accessories	639,072	134,867	204,630	150,010	146,119
Satellite dishes	104,974	14,640	11,633	33,473	45,742
Compact disc, tape, record, video mail order clubs	505,259	99,819	151,754	129,761	123,502
Records, CDs, audio tapes, needles	3,842,508	718,697	959,699	1,064,945	1,099,831
Rental of VCR, radio, sound equipment	33,453	222	15,863	12,811	5,082
Musical instruments and accessories	2,690,102	685,424	931,940	557,061	516,372
Rental and repair of musical instruments	264,165	33,273	42,565	59,095	129,601
Rental of video cassettes, tapes, discs, films	4,125,131	598,249	1,063,072	1,286,034	1,177,592
PETS, TOYS, PLAYGROUND EQUIPMENT	43,628,793	9,924,892	9,995,150	12,670,658	11,017,118
Pets	31,636,383	7,666,543	6,961,125	8,797,679	8,190,033
Pet food	11,514,836	1,905,434	2,906,594	3,950,257	2,741,447
Pet purchase, supplies, and medicines	8,735,910	3,310,442	1,474,183	1,823,672	2,117,328
Pet services	2,828,529	499,539	543,565	743,024	1,042,400
Veterinarian services	8,557,108	1,951,129	2,036,784	2,280,727	2,288,859
Toys, games, hobbies, and tricycles	11,541,368	2,074,904	2,834,418	3,837,440	2,794,304
Playground equipment	451,042	183,223	199,871	35,540	32,527

	total consumer units	Northeast	Midwest	South	West
OTHER ENTERTAINMENT SUPPLIES, EQUIPMENT, SERVICES	**$52,701,542**	**$6,188,778**	**$9,868,512**	**$18,362,764**	**$18,254,710**
Unmotored recreational vehicles	**6,953,660**	**734,890**	**1,715,562**	**2,167,910**	**2,334,855**
Boat without motor and boat trailers	801,724	56,120	187,974	509,537	48,537
Trailer and other attachable campers	6,150,782	678,769	1,527,588	1,658,372	2,286,318
Motorized recreational vehicles	**19,302,519**	**929,648**	**1,367,109**	**8,835,285**	**8,170,466**
Motorized camper	9,677,215	186,994	22,208	3,787,850	5,680,344
Other vehicle	2,023,344	232,024	332,854	952,128	506,461
Motorboats	7,600,807	510,408	1,012,047	4,095,308	1,983,661
Rental of recreational vehicles	**485,649**	**121,114**	**102,315**	**84,716**	**177,122**
Docking and landing fees	**411,821**	**56,120**	**152,812**	**84,716**	**118,166**
Sports, recreation, exercise equipment	**15,200,460**	**2,444,456**	**3,792,002**	**4,319,702**	**4,620,156**
Athletic gear, game tables, exercise equipment	6,289,209	1,225,556	1,794,347	1,808,795	1,440,860
Bicycles	1,275,837	191,431	258,035	314,483	512,052
Camping equipment	1,073,964	65,881	373,569	252,496	376,352
Hunting and fishing equipment	3,517,204	108,470	812,175	1,241,816	1,355,222
Winter sports equipment	564,091	148,619	130,339	38,019	247,259
Water sports equipment	516,795	153,056	73,498	86,369	203,804
Other sports equipment	1,731,494	495,990	300,336	533,093	402,526
Rental and repair of miscellaneous sports equipment	231,866	55,233	49,703	45,044	82,081
Photographic equipment and supplies	**9,133,888**	**1,693,596**	**2,382,593**	**2,542,727**	**2,516,550**
Film	1,687,658	327,406	418,778	522,348	419,552
Other photographic supplies	145,349	38,375	13,748	75,212	18,551
Film processing	2,568,978	507,524	651,697	775,257	634,029
Repair and rental of photographic equipment	66,906	15,084	4,759	25,208	22,108
Photographic equipment	3,011,945	533,699	854,212	702,112	921,947
Photographer fees	1,654,205	271,508	439,664	442,178	500,362
Fireworks	**268,779**	**5,324**	**82,487**	**71,079**	**109,272**
Pinball, electronic video games	**573,319**	**114,903**	**170,261**	**173,565**	**112,575**

Note: Numbers may not add to total because of rounding and missing subcategories.
Source: Calculations by New Strategist based on the 2003 Consumer Expenditure Survey

Table 3.24 Entertainment: Market shares by region, 2003

(percentage of total annual spending on entertainment accounted for by consumer units by region, 2003)

	total consumer units	Northeast	Midwest	South	West
Share of total consumer units	100.0%	19.2%	22.9%	35.8%	22.0%
Share of total before-tax income	100.0	21.5	23.4	32.8	22.5
Share of total spending	100.0	19.9	22.6	33.0	24.5
Share of entertainment spending	100.0	19.8	22.0	31.5	26.7
FEES AND ADMISSIONS	100.0	23.9	22.7	26.4	27.0
Recreation expenses on trips	100.0	19.8	25.4	26.6	28.1
Social, recreation, civic club membership	100.0	29.2	20.8	26.9	23.1
Fees for participant sports	100.0	18.2	23.9	29.0	28.9
Participant sports on trips	100.0	21.1	23.4	24.8	30.6
Movie, theater, opera, ballet	100.0	22.7	22.1	25.1	30.1
Movie, other admissions on trips	100.0	21.6	23.9	27.8	26.8
Admission to sports events	100.0	20.9	27.0	30.3	21.9
Admission to sports events on trips	100.0	21.6	23.9	27.8	26.8
Fees for recreational lessons	100.0	29.7	19.9	23.1	27.3
Other entertainment services on trips	100.0	19.8	25.4	26.6	28.1
TELEVISION, RADIO, SOUND EQUIPMENT	100.0	20.4	23.2	34.2	22.2
Television	100.0	20.7	22.1	35.8	21.4
Cable service and community antenna	100.0	21.7	22.1	36.8	19.4
Black-and-white TV sets	100.0	13.0	20.9	39.0	25.9
Color TV sets, consoles	100.0	19.1	19.3	36.7	24.8
Color TV sets, portable and table models	100.0	17.9	22.8	31.2	28.1
VCRs and video disc players	100.0	18.9	22.1	33.9	25.1
Video cassettes, tapes, and discs	100.0	16.3	25.4	30.3	28.0
Video game hardware and software	100.0	20.1	22.0	33.0	24.9
Repair of TV, radio, and sound equipment	100.0	20.7	18.6	30.9	29.7
Rental of television sets	100.0	31.8	37.1	24.1	7.2
Radio and sound equipment	100.0	19.1	28.0	26.8	26.1
Radios	100.0	7.4	39.1	32.1	20.9
Tape recorders and players	100.0	24.3	39.9	28.3	6.8
Sound components and component systems	100.0	24.4	23.6	23.3	28.7
Miscellaneous sound equipment	100.0	3.2	16.4	44.4	35.7
Sound equipment accessories	100.0	21.1	32.0	23.5	22.9
Satellite dishes	100.0	13.9	11.1	31.9	43.6
Compact disc, tape, record, video mail order clubs	100.0	19.8	30.0	25.7	24.4
Records, CDs, audio tapes, needles	100.0	18.7	25.0	27.7	28.6
Rental of VCR, radio, sound equipment	100.0	0.7	47.4	38.3	15.2
Musical instruments and accessories	100.0	25.5	34.6	20.7	19.2
Rental and repair of musical instruments	100.0	12.6	16.1	22.4	49.1
Rental of video cassettes, tapes, discs, films	100.0	14.5	25.8	31.2	28.5
PETS, TOYS, PLAYGROUND EQUIPMENT	100.0	22.7	22.9	29.0	25.3
Pets	100.0	24.2	22.0	27.8	25.9
Pet food	100.0	16.5	25.2	34.3	23.8
Pet purchase, supplies, and medicines	100.0	37.9	16.9	20.9	24.2
Pet services	100.0	17.7	19.2	26.3	36.9
Veterinarian services	100.0	22.8	23.8	26.7	26.7
Toys, games, hobbies, and tricycles	100.0	18.0	24.6	33.2	24.2
Playground equipment	100.0	40.6	44.3	7.9	7.2

	total consumer units	Northeast	Midwest	South	West
OTHER ENTERTAINMENT SUPPLIES, EQUIPMENT, SERVICES	100.0%	11.7%	18.7%	34.8%	34.6%
Unmotored recreational vehicles	100.0	10.6	24.7	31.2	33.6
Boat without motor and boat trailers	100.0	7.0	23.4	63.6	6.1
Trailer and other attachable campers	100.0	11.0	24.8	27.0	37.2
Motorized recreational vehicles	100.0	4.8	7.1	45.8	42.3
Motorized camper	100.0	1.9	0.2	39.1	58.7
Other vehicle	100.0	11.5	16.5	47.1	25.0
Motorboats	100.0	6.7	13.3	53.9	26.1
Rental of recreational vehicles	100.0	24.9	21.1	17.4	36.5
Docking and landing fees	100.0	13.6	37.1	20.6	28.7
Sports, recreation, exercise equipment	100.0	16.1	24.9	28.4	30.4
Athletic gear, game tables, exercise equipment	100.0	19.5	28.5	28.8	22.9
Bicycles	100.0	15.0	20.2	24.6	40.1
Camping equipment	100.0	6.1	34.8	23.5	35.0
Hunting and fishing equipment	100.0	3.1	23.1	35.3	38.5
Winter sports equipment	100.0	26.3	23.1	6.7	43.8
Water sports equipment	100.0	29.6	14.2	16.7	39.4
Other sports equipment	100.0	28.6	17.3	30.8	23.2
Rental and repair of miscellaneous sports equipment	100.0	23.8	21.4	19.4	35.4
Photographic equipment and supplies	100.0	18.5	26.1	27.8	27.6
Film	100.0	19.4	24.8	31.0	24.9
Other photographic supplies	100.0	26.4	9.5	51.7	12.8
Film processing	100.0	19.8	25.4	30.2	24.7
Repair and rental of photographic equipment	100.0	22.5	7.1	37.7	33.0
Photographic equipment	100.0	17.7	28.4	23.3	30.6
Photographer fees	100.0	16.4	26.6	26.7	30.2
Fireworks	100.0	2.0	30.7	26.4	40.7
Pinball, electronic video games	100.0	20.0	29.7	30.3	19.6

Note: Numbers may not add to total because of rounding.
Source: Calculations by New Strategist based on the 2003 Consumer Expenditure Survey

Table 3.25 Entertainment: Average spending by education, 2003

(average annual spending of consumer units (CU) on entertainment, by education of consumer unit reference person, 2003)

	total consumer units	less than high school graduate	high school graduate	some college	associate's degree	college graduate total	bachelor's degree	master's, professional, doctorate
Number of consumer units (000)	115,356	17,721	31,552	24,514	10,981	30,589	19,557	11,032
Average number of persons per CU	2.5	2.6	2.5	2.3	2.6	2.5	2.5	2.4
Average before-tax income of CU	$51,128.00	$25,028.00	$40,113.00	$45,113.00	$54,087.00	$81,842.00	$74,921.00	$93,948.00
Average spending of CU, total	40,817.33	23,901.14	33,955.56	37,912.41	44,547.12	58,480.00	54,725.85	65,202.73
Entertainment, average spending	**2,059.56**	**882.36**	**1,606.89**	**2,023.29**	**2,384.07**	**3,110.13**	**2,892.56**	**3,497.83**
FEES AND ADMISSIONS	**494.46**	**91.28**	**284.64**	**414.90**	**516.97**	**1,000.14**	**931.91**	**1,121.10**
Recreation expenses on trips	22.87	7.31	15.03	20.75	22.72	41.71	38.50	47.39
Social, recreation, civic club membership	95.06	11.98	45.85	64.13	68.56	228.26	228.61	227.64
Fees for participant sports	65.73	15.64	45.56	58.05	68.97	120.54	111.82	136.00
Participant sports on trips	23.83	2.87	10.84	22.77	18.95	51.99	45.87	62.84
Movie, theater, opera, ballet	90.69	21.76	56.07	89.42	100.57	163.81	148.31	191.29
Movie, other admissions on trips	45.31	8.92	31.02	39.87	56.84	81.35	71.92	98.06
Admission to sports events	33.65	4.14	20.70	33.50	35.55	63.55	66.78	57.82
Admission to sports events on trips	15.10	2.97	10.34	13.29	18.94	27.11	23.97	32.68
Fees for recreational lessons	79.36	8.39	34.22	52.37	103.16	180.12	157.63	219.98
Other entertainment services on trips	22.87	7.31	15.03	20.75	22.72	41.71	38.50	47.39
TELEVISION, RADIO, SOUND EQUIPMENT	**730.03**	**441.47**	**661.36**	**750.12**	**779.67**	**933.69**	**884.92**	**1,020.71**
Television	**597.36**	**390.49**	**573.68**	**589.75**	**652.01**	**728.09**	**706.39**	**766.56**
Cable service and community antenna	423.79	311.44	424.16	406.96	476.10	483.21	470.96	504.94
Black-and-white TV sets	0.34	0.38	0.33	0.26	0.31	0.39	0.32	0.50
Color TV sets, consoles	56.50	16.68	54.43	49.60	48.59	90.08	88.17	93.47
Color TV sets, portable and table models	34.65	21.90	30.40	37.22	29.78	46.13	42.87	51.91
VCRs and video disc players	24.26	14.30	18.73	24.94	25.43	34.76	32.53	38.73
Video cassettes, tapes, and discs	35.92	15.80	26.81	44.34	44.27	47.24	45.22	50.83
Video game hardware and software	18.70	7.15	15.86	23.14	22.36	23.46	23.09	24.12
Repair of TV, radio, and sound equipment	2.60	2.40	1.70	2.72	4.97	2.69	3.04	2.06
Rental of television sets	0.58	0.43	1.26	0.56	0.20	0.13	0.20	0.01
Radio and sound equipment	**132.68**	**50.98**	**87.68**	**160.37**	**127.66**	**205.60**	**178.53**	**254.15**
Radios	5.46	4.25	1.81	10.95	3.42	6.44	3.02	12.98
Tape recorders and players	3.93	–	1.56	9.62	4.63	3.94	4.29	3.27
Sound components and component systems	17.05	9.12	15.74	21.12	13.41	21.05	18.82	25.02
Miscellaneous sound equipment	0.42	1.37	0.12	0.21	–	0.54	0.12	1.33
Sound equipment accessories	5.54	1.09	3.24	3.14	2.49	12.74	12.14	13.88
Satellite dishes	0.91	0.67	0.96	0.99	0.52	1.08	1.37	0.58
Compact disc, tape, record, video mail order clubs	4.38	2.45	3.02	4.77	6.19	5.94	5.87	6.05
Records, CDs, audio tapes, needles	33.31	12.64	24.23	36.19	37.30	50.93	49.81	52.92
Rental of VCR, radio, sound equipment	0.29	0.72	0.23	0.17	0.36	0.18	0.25	0.08
Musical instruments and accessories	23.32	2.01	6.80	32.04	14.67	48.84	27.42	86.80
Rental and repair of musical instruments	2.29	0.03	1.05	1.06	1.06	6.32	8.10	3.16
Rental of video cassettes, tapes, discs, films	35.76	16.61	28.93	40.12	43.59	47.58	47.30	48.08
PETS, TOYS, PLAYGROUND EQUIPMENT	**378.21**	**166.43**	**372.21**	**332.11**	**431.00**	**515.75**	**467.15**	**604.03**
Pets	**274.25**	**116.78**	**276.44**	**230.80**	**295.25**	**381.16**	**332.13**	**470.23**
Pet food	99.82	66.29	92.03	98.73	129.46	115.76	111.00	124.87
Pet purchase, supplies, and medicines	75.73	24.15	112.94	46.35	60.37	88.69	78.22	108.70
Pet services	24.52	4.95	15.67	18.34	21.59	51.00	37.45	75.02
Veterinarian services	74.18	21.39	55.81	67.38	83.83	125.71	105.45	161.64
Toys, games, hobbies, and tricycles	**100.05**	**48.94**	**94.40**	**99.93**	**128.36**	**125.41**	**130.09**	**117.13**
Playground equipment	**3.91**	**0.71**	**1.37**	**1.38**	**7.38**	**9.17**	**4.93**	**16.68**

	total consumer units	less than high school graduate	high school graduate	some college	associate's degree	college graduate total	bachelor's degree	master's, professional, doctorate
OTHER ENTERTAINMENT SUPPLIES, EQUIPMENT, SERVICES	$456.86	$183.18	$288.67	$526.16	$656.43	$660.56	$608.57	$751.99
Unmotored recreational vehicles	60.28	9.15	69.19	58.26	113.35	63.26	44.86	95.89
Boat without motor and boat trailers	6.95	1.39	1.98	15.30	2.00	10.40	7.09	16.28
Trailer and other attachable campers	53.32	7.76	67.22	42.95	111.35	52.86	37.77	79.62
Motorized recreational vehicles	167.33	86.69	70.52	234.23	261.81	226.36	192.83	285.81
Motorized camper	83.89	3.53	18.90	163.25	212.84	87.60	29.72	190.22
Other vehicle	17.54	19.53	25.17	14.59	0.59	16.97	22.10	7.89
Motorboats	65.89	63.63	26.45	56.39	48.37	121.79	141.01	87.70
Rental of recreational vehicles	4.21	0.66	2.07	3.96	4.50	8.55	9.03	7.70
Docking and landing fees	3.57	0.03	1.11	9.80	1.80	3.81	4.24	3.05
Sports, recreation, exercise equipment	131.77	65.76	83.27	133.02	172.24	203.71	205.22	200.53
Athletic gear, game tables, exercise equipment	54.52	36.19	27.73	59.46	60.86	85.38	89.66	77.20
Bicycles	11.06	5.35	8.11	8.62	10.94	19.42	22.53	13.92
Camping equipment	9.31	2.55	9.05	6.76	11.08	14.18	13.34	15.78
Hunting and fishing equipment	30.49	15.31	15.12	42.25	63.61	34.90	35.11	34.52
Winter sports equipment	4.89	0.27	3.25	3.20	3.96	10.95	10.72	11.34
Water sports equipment	4.48	3.57	2.91	2.25	3.07	8.92	9.93	7.14
Other sports equipment	15.01	1.65	14.71	8.72	16.90	27.43	21.31	38.27
Rental and repair of miscellaneous sports equipment	2.01	0.87	2.40	1.76	1.83	2.53	2.63	2.36
Photographic equipment and supplies	79.18	19.95	51.48	74.79	87.37	142.74	138.90	149.59
Film	14.63	5.56	11.44	16.76	14.57	21.51	20.40	23.49
Other photographic supplies	1.26	1.20	0.49	0.11	5.02	1.73	1.48	2.22
Film processing	22.27	6.33	15.97	22.83	22.47	37.46	35.96	40.13
Repair and rental of photographic equipment	0.58	–	0.03	0.27	1.24	1.50	1.17	2.08
Photographic equipment	26.11	4.19	13.13	25.96	27.34	51.87	48.19	58.41
Photographer fees	14.34	2.67	10.42	8.86	16.72	28.66	31.71	23.27
Fireworks	2.33	0.24	3.89	2.09	7.12	0.45	0.23	0.87
Pinball, electronic video games	4.97	0.71	4.71	8.26	3.58	5.35	6.56	3.02

Note: Subcategories may not add to total because some are not shown. (–) means sample is too small to make a reliable estimate.
Source: Bureau of Labor Statistics, unpublished data from the 2003 Consumer Expenditure Survey

Table 3.26 Entertainment: Indexed spending by education, 2003

(indexed average annual spending of consumer units (CU) on entertainment by education of consumer unit reference person, 2003; index definition: an index of 100 is the average for all consumer units; an index of 132 means that spending by consumer units in that group is 32 percent above the average for all consumer units; an index of 68 indicates spending that is 32 percent below the average for all consumer units)

	total consumer units	less than high school graduate	high school graduate	some college	associate's degree	college graduate total	bachelor's degree	master's, professional, doctorate
Average spending of CU, total	$40,817	$23,901	$33,956	$37,912	$44,547	$58,480	$54,726	$65,203
Average spending of CU, index	100	59	83	93	109	143	134	160
Entertainment, spending index	**100**	**43**	**78**	**98**	**116**	**151**	**140**	**170**
FEES AND ADMISSIONS	**100**	**18**	**58**	**84**	**105**	**202**	**188**	**227**
Recreation expenses on trips	100	32	66	91	99	182	168	207
Social, recreation, civic club membership	100	13	48	67	72	240	240	239
Fees for participant sports	100	24	69	88	105	183	170	207
Participant sports on trips	100	12	45	96	80	218	192	264
Movie, theater, opera, ballet	100	24	62	99	111	181	164	211
Movie, other admissions on trips	100	20	68	88	125	180	159	216
Admission to sports events	100	12	62	100	106	189	198	172
Admission to sports events on trips	100	20	68	88	125	180	159	216
Fees for recreational lessons	100	11	43	66	130	227	199	277
Other entertainment services on trips	100	32	66	91	99	182	168	207
TELEVISION, RADIO, SOUND EQUIPMENT	**100**	**60**	**91**	**103**	**107**	**128**	**121**	**140**
Television	**100**	**65**	**96**	**99**	**109**	**122**	**118**	**128**
Cable service and community antenna	100	73	100	96	112	114	111	119
Black-and-white TV sets	100	112	97	76	91	115	94	147
Color TV sets, consoles	100	30	96	88	86	159	156	165
Color TV sets, portable and table models	100	63	88	107	86	133	124	150
VCRs and video disc players	100	59	77	103	105	143	134	160
Video cassettes, tapes, and discs	100	44	75	123	123	132	126	142
Video game hardware and software	100	38	85	124	120	125	123	129
Repair of TV, radio, and sound equipment	100	92	65	105	191	103	117	79
Rental of television sets	100	74	217	97	34	22	34	2
Radio and sound equipment	**100**	**38**	**66**	**121**	**96**	**155**	**135**	**192**
Radios	100	78	33	201	63	118	55	238
Tape recorders and players	100	–	40	245	118	100	109	83
Sound components and component systems	100	53	92	124	79	123	110	147
Miscellaneous sound equipment	100	326	29	50	–	129	29	317
Sound equipment accessories	100	20	58	57	45	230	219	251
Satellite dishes	100	74	105	109	57	119	151	64
Compact disc, tape, record, video mail order clubs	100	56	69	109	141	136	134	138
Records, CDs, audio tapes, needles	100	38	73	109	112	153	150	159
Rental of VCR, radio, sound equipment	100	248	79	59	124	62	86	28
Musical instruments and accessories	100	9	29	137	63	209	118	372
Rental and repair of musical instruments	100	1	46	46	46	276	354	138
Rental of video cassettes, tapes, discs, films	100	46	81	112	122	133	132	134
PETS, TOYS, PLAYGROUND EQUIPMENT	**100**	**44**	**98**	**88**	**114**	**136**	**124**	**160**
Pets	**100**	**43**	**101**	**84**	**108**	**139**	**121**	**171**
Pet food	100	66	92	99	130	116	111	125
Pet purchase, supplies, and medicines	100	32	149	61	80	117	103	144
Pet services	100	20	64	75	88	208	153	306
Veterinarian services	100	29	75	91	113	169	142	218
Toys, games, hobbies, and tricycles	**100**	**49**	**94**	**100**	**128**	**125**	**130**	**117**
Playground equipment	**100**	**18**	**35**	**35**	**189**	**235**	**126**	**427**

	total consumer units	less than high school graduate	high school graduate	some college	associate's degree	college graduate		
						total	bachelor's degree	master's, professional, doctorate
OTHER ENTERTAINMENT SUPPLIES, EQUIPMENT, SERVICES	**100**	**40**	**63**	**115**	**144**	**145**	**133**	**165**
Unmotored recreational vehicles	**100**	**15**	**115**	**97**	**188**	**105**	**74**	**159**
Boat without motor and boat trailers	100	20	28	220	29	150	102	234
Trailer and other attachable campers	100	15	126	81	209	99	71	149
Motorized recreational vehicles	**100**	**52**	**42**	**140**	**156**	**135**	**115**	**171**
Motorized camper	100	4	23	195	254	104	35	227
Other vehicle	100	111	144	83	3	97	126	45
Motorboats	100	97	40	86	73	185	214	133
Rental of recreational vehicles	**100**	**16**	**49**	**94**	**107**	**203**	**214**	**183**
Docking and landing fees	**100**	**1**	**31**	**275**	**50**	**107**	**119**	**85**
Sports, recreation, exercise equipment	**100**	**50**	**63**	**101**	**131**	**155**	**156**	**152**
Athletic gear, game tables, exercise equipment	100	66	51	109	112	157	164	142
Bicycles	100	48	73	78	99	176	204	126
Camping equipment	100	27	97	73	119	152	143	169
Hunting and fishing equipment	100	50	50	139	209	114	115	113
Winter sports equipment	100	6	66	65	81	224	219	232
Water sports equipment	100	80	65	50	69	199	222	159
Other sports equipment	100	11	98	58	113	183	142	255
Rental and repair of miscellaneous sports equipment	100	43	119	88	91	126	131	117
Photographic equipment and supplies	**100**	**25**	**65**	**94**	**110**	**180**	**175**	**189**
Film	100	38	78	115	100	147	139	161
Other photographic supplies	100	95	39	9	398	137	117	176
Film processing	100	28	72	103	101	168	161	180
Repair and rental of photographic equipment	100	–	5	47	214	259	202	359
Photographic equipment	100	16	50	99	105	199	185	224
Photographer fees	100	19	73	62	117	200	221	162
Fireworks	**100**	**10**	**167**	**90**	**306**	**19**	**10**	**37**
Pinball, electronic video games	**100**	**14**	**95**	**166**	**72**	**108**	**132**	**61**

Note: (–) means sample is too small to make a reliable estimate.
Source: Calculations by New Strategist based on the 2003 Consumer Expenditure Survey

Table 3.27 Entertainment: Total spending by education, 2003

(total annual spending on entertainment, by consumer unit (CU) educational attainment group, 2003; numbers in thousands)

	total consumer units	less than high school graduate	high school graduate	some college	associate's degree	college graduate total	college graduate bachelor's degree	college graduate master's, professional, doctorate
Number of consumer units	115,356	17,721	31,552	24,514	10,981	30,589	19,557	11,032
Total spending of all CUs	$4,708,523,919	$423,552,102	$1,071,365,829	$929,384,819	$489,171,925	$1,788,844,720	$1,070,273,448	$719,316,517
Entertainment, total spending	237,582,603	15,636,302	50,700,593	49,598,931	26,179,473	95,135,767	56,569,796	38,588,061
FEES AND ADMISSIONS	**57,038,928**	**1,617,573**	**8,980,961**	**10,170,859**	**5,676,848**	**30,593,282**	**18,225,364**	**12,367,975**
Recreation expenses on trips	2,638,192	129,541	474,227	508,666	249,488	1,275,867	752,945	522,806
Social, recreation, civic club membership	10,965,741	212,298	1,446,659	1,572,083	752,857	6,982,245	4,470,926	2,511,324
Fees for participant sports	7,582,350	277,156	1,437,509	1,423,038	757,360	3,687,198	2,186,864	1,500,352
Participant sports on trips	2,748,933	50,859	342,024	558,184	208,090	1,590,322	897,080	693,251
Movie, theater, opera, ballet	10,461,636	385,609	1,769,121	2,192,042	1,104,359	5,010,784	2,900,499	2,110,311
Movie, other admissions on trips	5,226,780	158,071	978,743	977,373	624,160	2,488,415	1,406,539	1,081,798
Admission to sports events	3,881,729	73,365	653,126	821,219	390,375	1,943,931	1,306,016	637,870
Admission to sports events on trips	1,741,876	52,631	326,248	325,791	207,980	829,268	468,781	360,526
Fees for recreational lessons	9,154,652	148,679	1,079,709	1,283,798	1,132,800	5,509,691	3,082,770	2,426,819
Other entertainment services on trips	2,638,192	129,541	474,227	508,666	249,488	1,275,867	752,945	522,806
TELEVISION, RADIO, SOUND EQUIPMENT	**84,213,341**	**7,823,290**	**20,867,231**	**18,388,442**	**8,561,556**	**28,560,643**	**17,306,380**	**11,260,473**
Television	**68,909,060**	**6,919,873**	**18,100,751**	**14,457,132**	**7,159,722**	**22,271,545**	**13,814,869**	**8,456,690**
Cable service and community antenna	48,886,719	5,519,028	13,383,096	9,976,217	5,228,054	14,780,911	9,210,565	5,570,498
Black-and-white TV sets	39,221	6,734	10,412	6,374	3,404	11,930	6,258	5,516
Color TV sets, consoles	6,517,614	295,586	1,717,375	1,215,894	533,567	2,755,457	1,724,341	1,031,161
Color TV sets, portable and table models	3,997,085	388,090	959,181	912,411	327,014	1,411,071	838,409	572,671
VCRs and video disc players	2,798,537	253,410	590,969	611,379	279,247	1,063,274	636,189	427,269
Video cassettes, tapes, and discs	4,143,588	279,992	845,909	1,086,951	486,129	1,445,024	884,368	560,757
Video game hardware and software	2,157,157	126,705	500,415	567,254	245,535	717,618	451,571	266,092
Repair of TV, radio, and sound equipment	299,926	42,530	53,638	66,678	54,576	82,284	59,453	22,726
Rental of television sets	66,906	7,620	39,756	13,728	2,196	3,977	3,911	110
Radio and sound equipment	**15,305,434**	**903,417**	**2,766,479**	**3,931,310**	**1,401,834**	**6,289,098**	**3,491,511**	**2,803,783**
Radios	629,844	75,314	57,109	268,428	37,555	196,993	59,062	143,195
Tape recorders and players	453,349	–	49,221	235,825	50,842	120,521	83,900	36,075
Sound components and component systems	1,966,820	161,616	496,628	517,736	147,255	643,898	368,063	276,021
Miscellaneous sound equipment	48,450	24,278	3,786	5,148	–	16,518	2,347	14,673
Sound equipment accessories	639,072	19,316	102,228	76,974	27,343	389,704	237,422	153,124
Satellite dishes	104,974	11,873	30,290	24,269	5,710	33,036	26,793	6,399
Compact disc, tape, record, video mail order clubs	505,259	43,416	95,287	116,932	67,972	181,699	114,800	66,744
Records, CDs, audio tapes, needles	3,842,508	223,993	764,505	387,162	409,591	1,557,898	974,134	583,813
Rental of VCR, radio, sound equipment	33,453	12,759	7,257	4,167	3,953	5,506	4,889	883
Musical instruments and accessories	2,690,102	35,619	214,554	785,429	161,091	1,493,967	536,253	957,578
Rental and repair of musical instruments	264,165	532	33,130	25,985	11,640	193,322	158,412	34,861
Rental of video cassettes, tapes, discs, films	4,125,131	294,346	912,799	983,502	478,662	1,455,425	925,046	530,419
PETS, TOYS, PLAYGROUND EQUIPMENT	**43,628,793**	**2,949,306**	**11,743,970**	**8,141,345**	**4,732,811**	**15,776,277**	**9,136,053**	**6,663,659**
Pets	**31,636,383**	**2,069,458**	**8,722,235**	**5,657,831**	**3,242,140**	**11,659,303**	**6,495,466**	**5,187,577**
Pet food	11,514,836	1,174,725	2,903,731	2,420,267	1,421,600	3,540,983	2,170,827	1,377,566
Pet purchase, supplies, and medicines	8,735,910	427,962	3,563,483	1,136,224	662,923	2,712,938	1,529,749	1,199,178
Pet services	2,828,529	87,719	494,420	449,587	237,080	1,560,039	732,410	827,621
Veterinarian services	8,557,108	379,052	1,760,917	1,651,753	920,537	3,845,343	2,062,286	1,783,212
Toys, games, hobbies, and tricycles	**11,541,368**	**867,266**	**2,978,509**	**2,449,684**	**1,409,521**	**3,836,166**	**2,544,170**	**1,292,178**
Playground equipment	**451,042**	**12,582**	**43,226**	**33,829**	**81,040**	**280,501**	**96,416**	**184,014**

	total consumer units	less than high school graduate	high school graduate	some college	associate's degree	college graduate total	bachelor's degree	master's, professional, doctorate
OTHER ENTERTAINMENT SUPPLIES, EQUIPMENT, SERVICES	**$52,701,542**	**$3,246,133**	**$9,108,116**	**$12,898,286**	**$7,208,258**	**$20,205,870**	**$11,901,803**	**$8,295,954**
Unmotored recreational vehicles	**6,953,660**	**162,147**	**2,183,083**	**1,428,186**	**1,244,696**	**1,935,060**	**877,327**	**1,057,858**
Boat without motor and boat trailers	801,724	24,632	62,473	575,064	21,962	318,126	138,659	179,601
Trailer and other attachable campers	6,150,782	137,515	2,120,925	1,052,876	1,222,734	1,616,935	738,668	878,368
Motorized recreational vehicles	**19,302,519**	**1,536,233**	**2,225,047**	**5,741,914**	**2,874,936**	**6,924,126**	**3,771,176**	**3,153,056**
Motorized camper	9,677,215	62,555	596,333	4,001,911	2,337,196	2,679,596	581,234	2,098,507
Other vehicle	2,023,344	346,091	794,164	357,659	6,479	519,095	432,210	87,042
Motorboats	7,600,807	1,127,587	834,550	1,382,344	531,151	3,725,434	2,757,733	967,506
Rental of recreational vehicles	**485,649**	**11,696**	**65,313**	**97,075**	**49,415**	**261,536**	**176,600**	**84,946**
Docking and landing fees	**411,821**	**532**	**35,023**	**240,237**	**19,766**	**116,544**	**82,922**	**33,648**
Sports, recreation, exercise equipment	**15,200,460**	**1,165,333**	**2,627,335**	**3,260,852**	**1,891,367**	**6,231,285**	**4,013,488**	**2,212,247**
Athletic gear, game tables, exercise equipment	6,289,209	641,323	874,937	1,457,602	668,304	2,611,689	1,753,481	851,670
Bicycles	1,275,837	94,807	255,887	211,311	120,132	594,038	440,619	153,565
Camping equipment	1,073,964	45,189	285,546	165,715	121,669	433,752	260,890	174,085
Hunting and fishing equipment	3,517,204	271,309	477,066	1,035,717	698,501	1,067,556	686,646	380,825
Winter sports equipment	564,091	4,785	102,544	78,445	43,485	334,950	209,651	125,103
Water sports equipment	516,795	63,264	91,816	55,157	33,712	272,854	194,201	78,768
Other sports equipment	1,731,494	29,240	464,130	213,762	185,579	839,056	416,760	422,195
Rental and repair of miscellaneous sports equipment	231,866	15,417	75,725	43,145	20,095	77,390	51,435	26,036
Photographic equipment and supplies	**9,133,888**	**353,534**	**1,624,297**	**1,833,402**	**959,410**	**4,366,274**	**2,716,467**	**1,650,277**
Film	1,687,658	98,529	360,955	410,855	159,993	657,969	398,963	259,142
Other photographic supplies	145,349	21,265	15,460	2,697	55,125	52,919	28,944	24,491
Film processing	2,568,978	112,174	503,885	559,655	246,743	1,145,864	703,270	442,714
Repair and rental of photographic equipment	66,906	–	947	6,619	13,616	45,884	22,882	22,947
Photographic equipment	3,011,945	74,251	414,278	636,383	300,221	1,586,651	942,452	644,379
Photographer fees	1,654,205	47,315	328,772	217,194	183,602	876,681	620,152	256,715
Fireworks	**268,779**	**4,253**	**122,737**	**51,234**	**78,185**	**13,765**	**4,498**	**9,598**
Pinball, electronic video games	**573,319**	**12,582**	**148,610**	**202,486**	**39,312**	**163,651**	**128,294**	**33,317**

Note: Numbers may not add to total because of rounding and missing subcategories. (–) means sample is too small to make a reliable estimate.
Source: Calculations by New Strategist based on the 2003 Consumer Expenditure Survey

Table 3.28 Entertainment: Market shares by education, 2003

(percentage of total annual spending on entertainment accounted for by consumer unit educational attainment groups, 2003)

	total consumer units	less than high school graduate	high school graduate	some college	associate's degree	college graduate total	bachelor's degree	master's, professional, doctorate
Share of total consumer units	100.0%	15.4%	27.4%	21.3%	9.5%	26.5%	17.0%	9.6%
Share of total before-tax income	100.0	7.5	21.5	18.8	10.1	42.4	24.8	17.6
Share of total spending	100.0	9.0	22.8	19.7	10.4	38.0	22.7	15.3
Share of entertainment spending	100.0	6.6	21.3	20.9	11.0	40.0	23.8	16.2
FEES AND ADMISSIONS	100.0	2.8	15.7	17.8	10.0	53.6	32.0	21.7
Recreation expenses on trips	100.0	4.9	18.0	19.3	9.5	48.4	28.5	19.8
Social, recreation, civic club membership	100.0	1.9	13.2	14.3	6.9	63.7	40.8	22.9
Fees for participant sports	100.0	3.7	19.0	18.8	10.0	48.6	28.8	19.8
Participant sports on trips	100.0	1.9	12.4	20.3	7.6	57.9	32.6	25.2
Movie, theater, opera, ballet	100.0	3.7	16.9	21.0	10.6	47.9	27.7	20.2
Movie, other admissions on trips	100.0	3.0	18.7	18.7	11.9	47.6	26.9	20.7
Admission to sports events	100.0	1.9	16.8	21.2	10.1	50.1	33.6	16.4
Admission to sports events on trips	100.0	3.0	18.7	18.7	11.9	47.6	26.9	20.7
Fees for recreational lessons	100.0	1.6	11.8	14.0	12.4	60.2	33.7	26.5
Other entertainment services on trips	100.0	4.9	18.0	19.3	9.5	48.4	28.5	19.8
TELEVISION, RADIO, SOUND EQUIPMENT	100.0	9.3	24.8	21.8	10.2	33.9	20.6	13.4
Television	100.0	10.0	26.3	21.0	10.4	32.3	20.0	12.3
Cable service and community antenna	100.0	11.3	27.4	20.4	10.7	30.2	18.8	11.4
Black-and-white TV sets	100.0	17.2	26.5	16.3	8.7	30.4	16.0	14.1
Color TV sets, consoles	100.0	4.5	26.3	18.7	8.2	42.3	26.5	15.8
Color TV sets, portable and table models	100.0	9.7	24.0	22.8	8.2	35.3	21.0	14.3
VCRs and video disc players	100.0	9.1	21.1	21.8	10.0	38.0	22.7	15.3
Video cassettes, tapes, and discs	100.0	6.8	20.4	26.2	11.7	34.9	21.3	13.5
Video game hardware and software	100.0	5.9	23.2	26.3	11.4	33.3	20.9	12.3
Repair of TV, radio, and sound equipment	100.0	14.2	17.9	22.2	18.2	27.4	19.8	7.6
Rental of television sets	100.0	11.4	59.4	20.5	3.3	5.9	5.8	0.2
Radio and sound equipment	100.0	5.9	18.1	25.7	9.2	41.1	22.8	18.3
Radios	100.0	12.0	9.1	42.6	6.0	31.3	9.4	22.7
Tape recorders and players	100.0	–	10.9	52.0	11.2	26.6	18.5	8.0
Sound components and component systems	100.0	8.2	25.3	26.3	7.5	32.7	18.7	14.0
Miscellaneous sound equipment	100.0	50.1	7.8	10.6	–	34.1	4.8	30.3
Sound equipment accessories	100.0	3.0	16.0	12.0	4.3	61.0	37.2	24.0
Satellite dishes	100.0	11.3	28.9	23.1	5.4	31.5	25.5	6.1
Compact disc, tape, record, video mail order clubs	100.0	8.6	18.9	23.1	13.5	36.0	22.7	13.2
Records, CDs, audio tapes, needles	100.0	5.8	19.9	23.1	10.7	40.5	25.4	15.2
Rental of VCR, radio, sound equipment	100.0	38.1	21.7	12.5	11.8	16.5	14.6	2.6
Musical instruments and accessories	100.0	1.3	8.0	29.2	6.0	55.5	19.9	35.6
Rental and repair of musical instruments	100.0	0.2	12.5	9.8	4.4	73.2	60.0	13.2
Rental of video cassettes, tapes, discs, films	100.0	7.1	22.1	23.8	11.6	35.3	22.4	12.9
PETS, TOYS, PLAYGROUND EQUIPMENT	100.0	6.8	26.9	18.7	10.8	36.2	20.9	15.3
Pets	100.0	6.5	27.6	17.9	10.2	36.9	20.5	16.4
Pet food	100.0	10.2	25.2	21.0	12.3	30.8	18.9	12.0
Pet purchase, supplies, and medicines	100.0	4.9	40.8	13.0	7.6	31.1	17.5	13.7
Pet services	100.0	3.1	17.5	15.9	8.4	55.2	25.9	29.3
Veterinarian services	100.0	4.4	20.6	19.3	10.8	44.9	24.1	20.8
Toys, games, hobbies, and tricycles	100.0	7.5	25.8	21.2	12.2	33.2	22.0	11.2
Playground equipment	100.0	2.8	9.6	7.5	18.0	62.2	21.4	40.8

	total consumer units	less than high school graduate	high school graduate	some college	associate's degree	college graduate total	bachelor's degree	master's, professional, doctorate
OTHER ENTERTAINMENT SUPPLIES, EQUIPMENT, SERVICES	**100.0%**	**6.2%**	**17.3%**	**24.5%**	**13.7%**	**38.3%**	**22.6%**	**15.7%**
Unmotored recreational vehicles	**100.0**	**2.3**	**31.4**	**20.5**	**17.9**	**27.8**	**12.6**	**15.2**
Boat without motor and boat trailers	100.0	3.1	7.8	46.8	2.7	39.7	17.3	22.4
Trailer and other attachable campers	100.0	2.2	34.5	17.1	19.9	26.3	12.0	14.3
Motorized recreational vehicles	**100.0**	**8.0**	**11.5**	**29.7**	**14.9**	**35.9**	**19.5**	**16.3**
Motorized camper	100.0	0.6	6.2	41.4	24.2	27.7	6.0	21.7
Other vehicle	100.0	17.1	39.3	17.7	0.3	25.7	21.4	4.3
Motorboats	100.0	14.8	11.0	18.2	7.0	49.0	36.3	12.7
Rental of recreational vehicles	**100.0**	**2.4**	**13.4**	**20.0**	**10.2**	**53.9**	**36.4**	**17.5**
Docking and landing fees	**100.0**	**0.1**	**8.5**	**58.3**	**4.8**	**28.3**	**20.1**	**8.2**
Sports, recreation, exercise equipment	**100.0**	**7.7**	**17.3**	**21.5**	**12.4**	**41.0**	**26.4**	**14.6**
Athletic gear, game tables, exercise equipment	100.0	10.2	13.9	23.2	10.6	41.5	27.9	13.5
Bicycles	100.0	7.4	20.1	16.6	9.4	46.6	34.5	12.0
Camping equipment	100.0	4.2	26.6	15.4	11.3	40.4	24.3	16.2
Hunting and fishing equipment	100.0	7.7	13.6	29.4	19.9	30.4	19.5	10.8
Winter sports equipment	100.0	0.8	18.2	13.9	7.7	59.4	37.2	22.2
Water sports equipment	100.0	12.2	17.8	10.7	6.5	52.8	37.6	15.2
Other sports equipment	100.0	1.7	26.8	12.3	10.7	48.5	24.1	24.4
Rental and repair of miscellaneous sports equipment	100.0	6.6	32.7	18.6	8.7	33.4	22.2	11.2
Photographic equipment and supplies	**100.0**	**3.9**	**17.8**	**20.1**	**10.5**	**47.8**	**29.7**	**18.1**
Film	100.0	5.8	21.4	24.3	9.5	39.0	23.6	15.4
Other photographic supplies	100.0	14.6	10.6	1.9	37.9	36.4	19.9	16.8
Film processing	100.0	4.4	19.6	21.8	9.6	44.6	27.4	17.2
Repair and rental of photographic equipment	100.0	–	1.4	9.9	20.4	68.6	34.2	34.3
Photographic equipment	100.0	2.5	13.8	21.1	10.0	52.7	31.3	21.4
Photographer fees	100.0	2.9	19.9	13.1	11.1	53.0	37.5	15.5
Fireworks	**100.0**	**1.6**	**45.7**	**19.1**	**29.1**	**5.1**	**1.7**	**3.6**
Pinball, electronic video games	**100.0**	**2.2**	**25.9**	**35.3**	**6.9**	**28.5**	**22.4**	**5.8**

Note: Numbers may not add to total because of rounding. (–) means sample is too small to make a reliable estimate.
Source: Calculations by New Strategist based on the 2003 Consumer Expenditure Survey

Spending on Financial Products and Services, 2003

Trends in spending on financial products and services have been mixed since 2000. Spending on financial services (such as bank fees, accounting fees, credit card fees, and legal fees) fell sharply between 2000 and 2003—down 27 percent after adjusting for inflation. One reason for the decline is the drop in interest rates during the time period. Spending on cash contributions (a category that includes child support as well as gifts to charities) rose 7.5 percent between 2000 and 2003. Spending on pensions and Social Security climbed 15 percent, while spending on life and other personal insurance fell 7 percent. Households spent less on federal and state taxes, but other taxes rose 20 percent.

Households headed by 45-to-54-year-olds spend more than other age groups on financial services. They are also the biggest spenders on personal insurance and pensions. Householders aged 65 or older spend the most on cash contributions—32 to 55 percent more than the average household. Support for college students peaks in the 45-to-54 age group, while child support spending is greatest among householders aged 35 to 44.

Households with incomes of $100,000 or more represent just 12 percent of consumer units but account for 34 percent of consumer spending on legal fees and 56 percent of spending on support for college students. These affluent households account for 58 percent of contributions to charities and for an even larger 75 percent of contributions to educational institutions.

Married couples with children at home spend more than other household types on most financial categories because their households are larger and more likely to include two or more wage earners. Married couples without children at home spend the most on cash gifts to nonhousehold members and on gifts to charities. Single parents spend more than twice the average on legal fees.

Blacks and Hispanics spend less than average on nearly every financial product and service, while whites and others spend more. Asian households spend 71 percent more than the average on support for college students.

Households in the West spend more than the average household on many financial products and services including accounting fees, finance charges, and credit card memberships. Households in the Northeast spend the most on life and other personal insurance. Households in the Midwest spend the most on lottery and gambling losses.

Households headed by college graduates account for 27 percent of households, but they control fully 70 percent of cash gifts to charities and 83 percent of cash contributions to educational institutions. Households headed by college graduates spend more than twice the average on credit card memberships and support for college students.

Table 4.1 Financial: Average spending by age, 2003

(average annual spending of consumer units (CU) on financial products and services, cash contributions, and miscellaneous items, by age of consumer unit reference person, 2003)

	total consumer units	under 25	25 to 34	35 to 44	45 to 54	55 to 64	65 to 74	75+
Number of consumer units (000)	115,356	8,584	19,737	24,413	23,131	16,580	11,495	11,417
Average number of persons per CU	2.5	1.8	2.9	3.2	2.6	2.1	1.9	1.5
Average before-tax income of CU	$51,128.00	$20,680.00	$50,389.00	$61,091.00	$68,028.00	$58,672.00	$35,314.00	$25,492.00
Average spending of CU, total	40,817.33	22,395.53	40,525.22	47,175.06	50,100.86	44,190.65	33,629.17	25,016.38
FINANCIAL PRODUCTS AND SERVICES	**605.93**	**251.39**	**531.81**	**600.55**	**830.45**	**674.52**	**547.39**	**519.27**
Miscellaneous fees	8.08	12.77	6.63	14.53	10.64	4.77	0.07	0.38
Lottery and gambling losses	35.37	10.02	35.39	19.76	28.03	43.02	39.12	91.77
Legal fees	108.09	38.49	77.05	93.21	207.40	134.84	34.41	80.07
Funeral expenses	57.51	1.24	24.62	22.92	39.25	93.47	108.69	163.89
Safe deposit box rental	3.48	0.22	1.26	1.96	4.47	4.70	5.54	7.14
Checking accounts, other bank service charges	20.01	18.65	25.25	26.43	23.29	17.63	10.90	4.27
Cemetery lots, vaults, and maintenance fees	13.27	0.18	4.30	5.52	15.83	21.38	34.00	17.36
Accounting fees	46.44	9.14	29.25	48.62	58.70	54.80	53.61	55.32
Miscellaneous personal services	26.87	13.16	25.94	38.75	38.87	15.91	18.77	12.34
Finance charges, except mortgage and vehicles	190.88	133.32	223.15	220.37	267.63	156.48	171.56	29.24
Occupational expenses	34.69	9.17	42.11	45.52	52.30	33.01	10.76	8.73
Expenses for other properties	53.45	3.15	30.00	55.20	74.54	82.50	51.99	44.64
Credit card memberships	2.34	0.98	2.37	3.01	2.94	2.77	1.38	1.04
Shopping club membership fees	4.92	0.91	4.24	4.74	6.22	6.66	6.13	3.09
CASH CONTRIBUTIONS	**1,369.89**	**371.39**	**753.76**	**1,255.92**	**1,651.02**	**1,568.21**	**1,811.40**	**2,127.33**
Support for college students	64.39	9.62	3.25	31.45	176.77	106.51	26.55	30.92
Alimony expenditures	42.18	3.80	3.52	39.43	90.02	60.05	47.19	15.84
Child support expenditures	166.12	78.26	220.75	354.51	182.88	59.33	18.87	4.33
Gifts to non–CU members of stocks, bonds, and mutual funds	24.68	0.05	5.41	2.61	5.42	29.43	33.82	146.67
Cash contributions to charities and other organizations	139.45	18.62	48.09	120.46	142.56	163.50	361.06	164.47
Cash contributions to church, religious organizations	564.41	194.54	312.29	502.85	766.69	719.55	741.53	596.52
Cash contributions to educational institutions	60.37	1.43	10.07	31.87	36.28	30.50	100.25	304.63
Cash contributions to political organizations	6.62	0.97	2.52	4.04	5.19	10.19	17.75	9.95
Other cash gifts	301.67	64.10	147.84	168.71	245.21	389.16	464.37	854.00
PERSONAL INSURANCE AND PENSIONS	**4,055.24**	**1,382.38**	**4,137.00**	**5,196.11**	**6,003.35**	**4,819.36**	**1,846.58**	**651.50**
Life and other personal insurance	**397.30**	**40.31**	**200.01**	**381.62**	**600.36**	**570.26**	**504.27**	**269.97**
Life, endowment, annuity, other personal insurance	380.22	38.14	190.86	371.42	583.88	542.46	481.96	232.90
Other nonhealth insurance	17.08	2.17	9.15	10.20	16.48	27.80	22.31	37.07
Pensions and Social Security	**3,657.94**	**1,342.06**	**3,936.99**	**4,814.48**	**5,402.98**	**4,249.09**	**1,342.31**	**381.53**
Deductions for government retirement	69.64	3.52	48.21	92.20	131.01	90.43	23.55	0.05
Deductions for railroad retirement	3.42	–	1.59	3.57	6.76	7.21	–	–
Deductions for private pensions	481.22	67.10	465.84	696.78	769.78	575.31	108.06	12.78
Nonpayroll deposit to retirement plans	388.15	32.53	264.90	370.15	630.68	717.35	237.01	89.88
Deductions for Social Security	2,715.50	1,238.91	3,156.45	3,651.78	3,864.76	2,858.79	973.68	278.82
PERSONAL TAXES	**2,531.74**	**420.52**	**1,979.13**	**2,816.57**	**3,948.87**	**2,827.41**	**1,455.17**	**2,306.73**
Federal income taxes	1,843.07	261.22	1,335.84	1,988.48	2,914.41	2,010.06	1,044.48	2,032.46
State and local income taxes	501.53	144.11	544.28	658.35	813.56	511.40	151.53	76.91
Other taxes	187.14	15.19	99.01	169.74	220.90	305.95	259.16	197.36

Note: Subcategories may not add to total because some are not shown. (–) means sample is too small to make a reliable estimate.
Source: Bureau of Labor Statistics, unpublished tables from the 2003 Consumer Expenditure Survey

Table 4.2 Financial: Indexed spending by age, 2003

(indexed average annual spending of consumer units (CU) on financial products and services, cash contributions, and miscellaneous items, by age of consumer unit reference person, 2003; index definition: an index of 100 is the average for all consumer units; an index of 132 means that spending by consumer units in that group is 32 percent above the average for all consumer units; an index of 68 indicates spending that is 32 percent below the average for all consumer units)

	total consumer units	under 25	25 to 34	35 to 44	45 to 54	55 to 64	65 to 74	75+
Average spending of CU, total	$40,817	$22,396	$40,525	$47,175	$50,101	$44,191	$33,629	$25,016
Average spending of CU, index	100	55	99	116	123	108	82	61
FINANCIAL PRODUCTS AND SERVICES	100	41	88	99	137	111	90	86
Miscellaneous fees	100	158	82	180	132	59	1	5
Lottery and gambling losses	100	28	100	56	79	122	111	259
Legal fees	100	36	71	86	192	125	32	74
Funeral expenses	100	2	43	40	68	163	189	285
Safe deposit box rental	100	6	36	56	128	135	159	205
Checking accounts, other bank service charges	100	93	126	132	116	88	54	21
Cemetery lots, vaults, and maintenance fees	100	1	32	42	119	161	256	131
Accounting fees	100	20	63	105	126	118	115	119
Miscellaneous personal services	100	49	97	144	145	59	70	46
Finance charges, except mortgage and vehicles	100	70	117	115	140	82	90	15
Occupational expenses	100	26	121	131	151	95	31	25
Expenses for other properties	100	6	56	103	139	154	97	84
Credit card memberships	100	42	101	129	126	118	59	44
Shopping club membership fees	100	18	86	96	126	135	125	63
CASH CONTRIBUTIONS	100	27	55	92	121	114	132	155
Support for college students	100	15	5	49	275	165	41	48
Alimony expenditures	100	9	8	93	213	142	112	38
Child support expenditures	100	47	133	213	110	36	11	3
Gifts to non–CU members of stocks, bonds, and mutual funds	100	0	22	11	22	119	137	594
Cash contributions to charities and other organizations	100	13	34	85	102	117	259	118
Cash contributions to church, religious organizations	100	34	55	89	136	127	131	106
Cash contributions to educational institutions	100	2	17	53	60	51	166	505
Cash contributions to political organizations	100	15	38	61	78	154	268	150
Other cash gifts	100	21	49	56	81	129	154	283
PERSONAL INSURANCE AND PENSIONS	100	34	102	128	148	119	46	16
Life and other personal insurance	100	10	50	96	151	144	127	68
Life, endowment, annuity, other personal insurance	100	10	50	98	154	143	127	61
Other nonhealth insurance	100	13	54	60	96	163	131	217
Pensions and Social Security	100	37	108	132	148	116	37	10
Deductions for government retirement	100	5	69	132	188	130	34	0
Deductions for railroad retirement	100	–	46	104	198	211	–	–
Deductions for private pensions	100	14	97	145	160	120	22	3
Nonpayroll deposit to retirement plans	100	8	68	95	162	185	61	23
Deductions for Social Security	100	46	116	134	142	105	36	10
PERSONAL TAXES	100	17	78	111	156	112	57	91
Federal income taxes	100	14	72	108	158	109	57	110
State and local income taxes	100	29	109	131	162	102	30	15
Other taxes	100	8	53	91	118	163	138	105

Note: (–) means sample is too small to make a reliable estimate.
Source: Calculations by New Strategist based on the 2003 Consumer Expenditure Survey

Table 4.3 Financial: Total spending by age, 2003

(total annual spending on financial products and services, cash contributions, and miscellaneous items, by consumer unit (CU) age groups, 2003; numbers in thousands)

	total consumer units	under 25	25 to 34	35 to 44	45 to 54	55 to 64	65 to 74	75+
Number of consumer units	115,356	8,584	19,737	24,413	23,131	16,580	11,495	11,417
Total spending of all CUs	$4,708,523,919	$192,243,230	$799,846,267	$1,151,684,740	$1,158,882,993	$732,680,977	$386,567,309	$285,612,010
FINANCIAL PRODUCTS AND SERVICES	69,897,661	2,157,932	10,496,334	14,661,227	19,209,139	11,183,542	6,292,248	5,928,506
Miscellaneous fees	932,076	109,618	130,856	354,721	246,114	79,087	805	4,338
Lottery and gambling losses	4,080,142	86,012	698,492	482,401	648,362	713,272	449,684	1,047,738
Legal fees	12,468,830	330,398	1,520,736	2,275,536	4,797,369	2,235,647	395,543	914,159
Funeral expenses	6,634,124	10,644	485,925	559,546	907,892	1,549,733	1,249,392	1,871,132
Safe deposit box rental	401,439	1,888	24,869	47,849	103,396	77,926	63,682	81,517
Checking accounts, other bank service charges	2,308,274	160,092	498,359	645,236	538,721	292,305	125,296	48,751
Cemetery lots, vaults, and maintenance fees	1,530,774	1,545	84,869	134,760	366,164	354,480	390,830	198,199
Accounting fees	5,357,133	78,458	577,307	1,186,960	1,357,790	908,584	616,247	631,588
Miscellaneous personal services	3,099,616	112,965	511,978	946,004	899,102	263,788	215,761	140,886
Finance charges, except mortgage and vehicles	22,019,153	1,144,419	4,404,312	5,379,893	6,190,550	2,594,438	1,972,082	333,833
Occupational expenses	4,001,700	78,715	831,125	1,111,280	1,209,751	547,306	123,686	99,670
Expenses for other properties	6,165,778	27,040	592,110	1,347,598	1,724,185	1,367,850	597,625	509,655
Credit card memberships	269,933	8,412	46,777	73,483	68,005	45,927	15,863	11,874
Shopping club membership fees	567,552	7,811	83,685	115,718	143,875	110,423	70,464	35,279
CASH CONTRIBUTIONS	158,025,031	3,188,012	14,876,961	30,660,775	38,189,744	26,000,922	20,822,043	24,287,727
Support for college students	7,427,773	82,578	64,145	767,789	4,088,867	1,765,936	305,192	353,014
Alimony expenditures	4,865,716	32,619	69,474	962,605	2,082,253	995,629	542,449	180,845
Child support expenditures	19,162,939	671,784	4,356,943	8,654,653	4,230,197	983,691	216,911	49,436
Gifts to non–CU members of stocks, bonds, and mutual funds	2,846,986	429	106,777	63,718	125,370	487,949	388,761	1,674,531
Cash contributions to charities and other organizations	16,086,394	159,834	949,152	2,940,790	3,297,555	2,710,830	4,150,385	1,877,754
Cash contributions to church, religious organizations	65,108,080	1,669,931	6,163,668	12,276,077	17,734,306	11,930,139	8,523,887	6,810,469
Cash contributions to educational institutions	6,964,042	12,275	198,752	778,042	839,193	505,690	1,152,374	3,477,961
Cash contributions to political organizations	763,657	8,326	49,737	98,629	120,050	168,950	204,036	113,599
Other cash gifts	34,799,445	550,234	2,917,918	4,118,717	5,671,953	6,452,273	5,337,933	9,750,118
PERSONAL INSURANCE AND PENSIONS	467,796,265	11,866,350	81,651,969	126,852,633	138,863,489	79,904,989	21,226,437	7,438,176
Life and other personal insurance	45,830,939	346,021	3,947,597	9,316,489	13,886,927	9,454,911	5,796,584	3,082,247
Life, endowment, annuity, other personal insurance	43,860,658	327,394	3,767,004	9,067,476	13,505,728	8,993,987	5,540,130	2,659,019
Other nonhealth insurance	1,970,280	18,627	180,594	249,013	381,199	460,924	256,453	423,228
Pensions and Social Security	421,965,327	11,520,243	77,704,372	117,535,900	124,976,330	70,449,912	15,429,853	4,355,928
Deductions for government retirement	8,033,392	30,216	951,521	2,250,879	3,030,392	1,499,329	270,707	571
Deductions for railroad retirement	394,518	–	31,382	87,154	156,366	119,542	–	–
Deductions for private pensions	55,511,614	575,986	9,194,284	17,010,490	17,805,781	9,538,640	1,242,150	145,909
Nonpayroll deposit to retirement plans	44,775,431	279,238	5,228,331	9,036,472	14,588,259	11,893,663	2,724,430	1,026,160
Deductions for Social Security	313,249,218	10,634,803	62,298,854	89,150,905	89,395,764	47,398,738	11,192,452	3,183,288
PERSONAL TAXES	292,051,399	3,609,744	39,062,089	68,760,923	91,341,312	46,878,458	16,727,179	26,335,936
Federal income taxes	212,609,183	2,242,312	26,365,474	48,544,762	67,413,218	33,326,795	12,006,298	23,204,596
State and local income taxes	57,854,495	1,237,040	10,742,454	16,072,299	18,818,456	8,479,012	1,741,837	878,081
Other taxes	21,587,722	130,391	1,954,160	4,143,863	5,109,638	5,072,651	2,979,044	2,253,259

Note: Numbers may not add to total because of rounding and missing subcategories. (–) means sample is too small to make a reliable estimate.
Source: Calculations by New Strategist based on the 2003 Consumer Expenditure Survey

Table 4.4 Financial: Market shares by age, 2003

(percentage of total annual spending on financial products and services, cash contributions, and miscellaneous items accounted for by consumer unit age groups, 2003)

	total consumer units	under 25	25 to 34	35 to 44	45 to 54	55 to 64	65 to 74	75+
Share of total consumer units	100.0%	7.4%	17.1%	21.2%	20.1%	14.4%	10.0%	9.9%
Share of total before-tax income	100.0	3.0	16.9	25.3	26.7	16.5	6.9	4.9
Share of total spending	100.0	4.1	17.0	24.5	24.6	15.6	8.2	6.1
FINANCIAL PRODUCTS AND SERVICES	100.0	3.1	15.0	21.0	27.5	16.0	9.0	8.5
Miscellaneous fees	100.0	11.8	14.0	38.1	26.4	8.5	0.1	0.5
Lottery and gambling losses	100.0	2.1	17.1	11.8	15.9	17.5	11.0	25.7
Legal fees	100.0	2.6	12.2	18.2	38.5	17.9	3.2	7.3
Funeral expenses	100.0	0.2	7.3	8.4	13.7	23.4	18.8	28.2
Safe deposit box rental	100.0	0.5	6.2	11.9	25.8	19.4	15.9	20.3
Checking accounts, other bank service charges	100.0	6.9	21.6	28.0	23.3	12.7	5.4	2.1
Cemetery lots, vaults, and maintenance fees	100.0	0.1	5.5	8.8	23.9	23.2	25.5	12.9
Accounting fees	100.0	1.5	10.8	22.2	25.3	17.0	11.5	11.8
Miscellaneous personal services	100.0	3.6	16.5	30.5	29.0	8.5	7.0	4.5
Finance charges, except mortgage and vehicles	100.0	5.2	20.0	24.4	28.1	11.8	9.0	1.5
Occupational expenses	100.0	2.0	20.8	27.8	30.2	13.7	3.1	2.5
Expenses for other properties	100.0	0.4	9.6	21.9	28.0	22.2	9.7	8.3
Credit card memberships	100.0	3.1	17.3	27.2	25.2	17.0	5.9	4.4
Shopping club membership fees	100.0	1.4	14.7	20.4	25.4	19.5	12.4	6.2
CASH CONTRIBUTIONS	100.0	2.0	9.4	19.4	24.2	16.5	13.2	15.4
Support for college students	100.0	1.1	0.9	10.3	55.0	23.8	4.1	4.8
Alimony expenditures	100.0	0.7	1.4	19.8	42.8	20.5	11.1	3.7
Child support expenditures	100.0	3.5	22.7	45.2	22.1	5.1	1.1	0.3
Gifts to non–CU members of stocks, bonds, and mutual funds	100.0	0.0	3.8	2.2	4.4	17.1	13.7	58.8
Cash contributions to charities and other organizations	100.0	1.0	5.9	18.3	20.5	16.9	25.8	11.7
Cash contributions to church, religious organizations	100.0	2.6	9.5	18.9	27.2	18.3	13.1	10.5
Cash contributions to educational institutions	100.0	0.2	2.9	11.2	12.1	7.3	16.5	49.9
Cash contributions to political organizations	100.0	1.1	6.5	12.9	15.7	22.1	26.7	14.9
Other cash gifts	100.0	1.6	8.4	11.8	16.3	18.5	15.3	28.0
PERSONAL INSURANCE AND PENSIONS	100.0	2.5	17.5	27.1	29.7	17.1	4.5	1.6
Life and other personal insurance	100.0	0.8	8.6	20.3	30.3	20.6	12.6	6.7
Life, endowment, annuity, other personal insurance	100.0	0.7	8.6	20.7	30.8	20.5	12.6	6.1
Other nonhealth insurance	100.0	0.9	9.2	12.6	19.3	23.4	13.0	21.5
Pensions and Social Security	100.0	2.7	18.4	27.9	29.6	16.7	3.7	1.0
Deductions for government retirement	100.0	0.4	11.8	28.0	37.7	18.7	3.4	0.0
Deductions for railroad retirement	100.0	–	8.0	22.1	39.6	30.3	–	–
Deductions for private pensions	100.0	1.0	16.6	30.6	32.1	17.2	2.2	0.3
Nonpayroll deposit to retirement plans	100.0	0.6	11.7	20.2	32.6	26.6	6.1	2.3
Deductions for Social Security	100.0	3.4	19.9	28.5	28.5	15.1	3.6	1.0
PERSONAL TAXES	100.0	1.2	13.4	23.5	31.3	16.1	5.7	9.0
Federal income taxes	100.0	1.1	12.4	22.8	31.7	15.7	5.6	10.9
State and local income taxes	100.0	2.1	18.6	27.8	32.5	14.7	3.0	1.5
Other taxes	100.0	0.6	9.1	19.2	23.7	23.5	13.8	10.4

Note: Numbers may not add to total because of rounding. (–) means sample is too small to make a reliable estimate.
Source: Calculations by New Strategist based on the 2003 Consumer Expenditure Survey

Table 4.5 Financial: Average spending by income, 2003

(average annual spending on financial products and services, cash contributions, and miscellaneous items, by before-tax income of consumer units (CU), 2003; complete income reporters only)

	total complete reporters	under $20,000	$20,000– $39,999	$40,000– $49,999	$50,000– $69,999	$70,000– $79,999	$80,000– $99,999	$100,000 or more
Number of consumer units (000)	97,391	27,100	23,941	8,891	13,890	5,121	6,909	11,537
Average number of persons per CU	2.5	1.8	2.4	2.6	2.8	3.0	3.0	3.1
Average before-tax income of CU	$51,128.00	$10,752.55	$29,072.57	$44,294.00	$58,900.00	$74,560.00	$88,832.00	$154,665.00
Average spending of CU, total	42,741.66	19,862.52	31,684.32	39,756.91	49,788.99	57,128.14	65,957.39	93,514.86
FINANCIAL PRODUCTS AND SERVICES	**658.42**	**326.87**	**525.86**	**692.53**	**919.29**	**749.63**	**843.43**	**1,221.27**
Miscellaneous fees	9.02	1.73	9.32	2.24	32.44	8.81	–	11.69
Lottery and gambling losses	43.67	21.67	48.80	56.80	66.57	56.99	27.38	48.70
Legal fees	109.38	42.79	77.53	111.86	153.29	67.42	85.81	309.88
Funeral expenses	61.68	60.85	70.01	43.90	64.11	39.99	56.59	69.77
Safe deposit box rental	3.67	1.45	3.25	2.63	5.22	5.89	4.20	7.35
Checking accounts, other bank service charges	21.68	11.76	18.99	24.97	27.11	30.84	30.27	32.29
Cemetery lots, vaults, and maintenance fees	13.39	10.43	14.63	13.72	9.93	12.86	26.74	13.96
Accounting fees	48.14	17.88	41.39	44.85	53.07	62.21	69.18	111.00
Miscellaneous personal services	31.35	15.49	12.88	38.01	60.33	21.92	61.81	54.88
Finance charges, except mortgage and vehicles	216.21	117.64	180.00	251.26	303.02	307.51	311.00	294.09
Occupational expenses	36.57	5.50	16.73	36.49	58.01	57.68	83.27	87.63
Expenses for other properties	55.35	18.59	27.18	57.46	76.03	64.82	70.75	160.19
Credit card memberships	2.48	0.82	1.53	2.45	3.15	5.09	3.93	5.52
Shopping club membership fees	5.27	1.54	3.62	5.90	6.86	7.56	10.31	11.00
CASH CONTRIBUTIONS	**1,457.65**	**489.80**	**1,008.95**	**1,070.04**	**1,382.75**	**1,626.52**	**2,173.34**	**4,547.45**
Support for college students	67.97	14.33	18.44	38.16	42.73	73.47	112.52	320.95
Alimony expenditures	44.00	3.64	21.57	20.78	55.85	37.24	69.04	179.53
Child support expenditures	178.77	52.06	144.43	177.45	287.37	262.82	259.21	332.44
Gifts to non–CU members of stocks, bonds, and mutual funds	28.81	5.28	61.58	5.62	27.34	4.70	10.21	62.86
Cash contributions to charities and other organizations	151.06	30.70	64.14	89.49	90.12	118.00	177.74	733.67
Cash contributions to church, religious organizations	598.13	214.35	392.00	536.07	623.70	727.83	1,078.70	1,598.99
Cash contributions to educational institutions	53.61	9.06	18.88	12.63	16.42	21.52	24.31	338.49
Cash contributions to political organizations	7.57	1.35	4.24	5.10	5.98	10.05	9.86	30.44
Other cash gifts	327.73	162.39	283.65	184.74	233.25	370.89	431.74	950.08
PERSONAL INSURANCE AND PENSIONS	**4,709.60**	**599.67**	**2,156.01**	**3,878.43**	**5,792.04**	**7,390.25**	**9,374.57**	**15,016.47**
Life and other personal insurance	**414.05**	**159.79**	**245.76**	**346.90**	**428.82**	**489.70**	**659.21**	**1,214.11**
Life, endowment, annuity, other personal insurance	395.24	150.16	229.14	324.74	410.42	476.35	630.58	1,174.68
Other nonhealth insurance	18.82	9.63	16.62	22.16	18.40	13.35	28.64	39.43
Pensions and Social Security	**4,295.55**	**439.88**	**1,910.25**	**3,531.53**	**5,363.22**	**6,900.55**	**8,715.36**	**13,802.36**
Deductions for government retirement	82.12	1.01	22.42	73.77	150.63	101.01	223.30	227.57
Deductions for railroad retirement	3.93	–	0.75	2.67	3.65	24.64	16.18	5.41
Deductions for private pensions	568.17	7.88	108.50	336.80	678.89	859.54	1,132.86	2,415.66
Nonpayroll deposit to retirement plans	449.89	55.11	128.76	240.07	481.49	576.07	976.89	1,795.58
Deductions for Social Security	3,191.43	375.87	1,650.23	2,878.22	4,048.56	5,339.29	6,366.13	9,358.14
PERSONAL TAXES	**2,531.74**	**–61.53**	**1,303.96**	**1,451.67**	**2,471.87**	**3,172.46**	**4,656.14**	**10,518.78**
Federal income taxes	1,843.07	–130.29	967.09	932.63	1,669.99	2,297.99	3,304.73	8,128.83
State and local income taxes	501.53	10.04	198.52	367.26	578.18	658.28	1,032.61	1,908.40
Other taxes	187.14	58.72	138.35	151.78	223.70	216.18	318.80	481.54

Note: Subcategories may not add to total because some are not shown. (–) means sample is too small to make a reliable estimate.
Source: Bureau of Labor Statistics, unpublished tables from the 2003 Consumer Expenditure Survey; calculations by New Strategist

Table 4.6 Financial: Indexed spending by income, 2003

(indexed average annual spending of consumer units (CU) on financial products and services, cash contributions, and miscellaneous items, by before-tax income of consumer unit, 2003; complete income reporters only; index definition: an index of 100 is the average for all consumer units; an index of 132 means that spending by consumer units in that group is 32 percent above the average for all consumer units; an index of 68 indicates spending that is 32 percent below the average for all consumer units)

	total complete reporters	under $20,000	$20,000– $39,999	$40,000– $49,999	$50,000– $69,999	$70,000– $79,999	$80,000– $99,999	$100,000 or more
Average spending of CU, total	$42,742	$19,863	$31,684	$39,757	$49,789	$57,128	$65,957	$93,515
Average spending of CU, index	100	46	74	93	116	134	154	219
FINANCIAL PRODUCTS AND SERVICES	**100**	**50**	**80**	**105**	**140**	**114**	**128**	**185**
Miscellaneous fees	100	19	103	25	360	98	–	130
Lottery and gambling losses	100	50	112	130	152	131	63	112
Legal fees	100	39	71	102	140	62	78	283
Funeral expenses	100	99	114	71	104	65	92	113
Safe deposit box rental	100	39	89	72	142	160	114	200
Checking accounts, other bank service charges	100	54	88	115	125	142	140	149
Cemetery lots, vaults, and maintenance fees	100	78	109	102	74	96	200	104
Accounting fees	100	37	86	93	110	129	144	231
Miscellaneous personal services	100	49	41	121	192	70	197	175
Finance charges, except mortgage and vehicles	100	54	83	116	140	142	144	136
Occupational expenses	100	15	46	100	159	158	228	240
Expenses for other properties	100	34	49	104	137	117	128	289
Credit card memberships	100	33	62	99	127	205	158	223
Shopping club membership fees	100	29	69	112	130	143	196	209
CASH CONTRIBUTIONS	**100**	**34**	**69**	**73**	**95**	**112**	**149**	**312**
Support for college students	100	21	27	56	63	108	166	472
Alimony expenditures	100	8	49	47	127	85	157	408
Child support expenditures	100	29	81	99	161	147	145	186
Gifts to non–CU members of stocks, bonds, and mutual funds	100	18	214	20	95	16	35	218
Cash contributions to charities and other organizations	100	20	42	59	60	78	118	486
Cash contributions to church, religious organizations	100	36	66	90	104	122	180	267
Cash contributions to educational institutions	100	17	35	24	31	40	45	631
Cash contributions to political organizations	100	18	56	67	79	133	130	402
Other cash gifts	100	50	87	56	71	113	132	290
PERSONAL INSURANCE AND PENSIONS	**100**	**13**	**46**	**82**	**123**	**157**	**199**	**319**
Life and other personal insurance	**100**	**39**	**59**	**84**	**104**	**118**	**159**	**293**
Life, endowment, annuity, other personal insurance	100	38	58	82	104	121	160	297
Other nonhealth insurance	100	51	88	118	98	71	152	210
Pensions and Social Security	**100**	**10**	**44**	**82**	**125**	**161**	**203**	**321**
Deductions for government retirement	100	1	27	90	183	123	272	277
Deductions for railroad retirement	100	–	19	68	93	627	412	138
Deductions for private pensions	100	1	19	59	119	151	199	425
Nonpayroll deposit to retirement plans	100	12	29	53	107	128	217	399
Deductions for Social Security	100	12	52	90	127	167	199	293
PERSONAL TAXES	**100**	**–2**	**52**	**57**	**98**	**125**	**184**	**415**
Federal income taxes	100	–7	52	51	91	125	179	441
State and local income taxes	100	2	40	73	115	131	206	381
Other taxes	100	31	74	81	120	116	170	257

Note: (–) means sample is too small to make a reliable estimate.
Source: Calculations by New Strategist based on the 2003 Consumer Expenditure Survey

Table 4.7 Financial: Total spending by income, 2003

(total annual spending on financial products and services, cash contributions, and miscellaneous items, by before-tax income group of consumer units (CU), 2003; complete income reporters only; numbers in thousands)

	total complete reporters	under $20,000	$20,000–$39,999	$40,000–$49,999	$50,000–$69,999	$70,000–$79,999	$80,000–$99,999	$100,000 or more
Number of consumer units	97,391	27,100	23,941	8,891	13,890	5,121	6,909	11,537
Total spending of all CUs	$4,162,653,009	$538,274,380	$758,554,310	$353,478,687	$691,569,071	$292,553,205	$455,699,608	$1,078,880,940
FINANCIAL PRODUCTS AND SERVICES	**64,124,182**	**8,858,181**	**12,589,523**	**6,157,284**	**12,768,938**	**3,838,855**	**5,827,258**	**14,089,792**
Miscellaneous fees	878,467	46,883	223,173	19,916	450,592	45,116	–	134,868
Lottery and gambling losses	4,253,065	587,227	1,168,249	505,009	924,657	291,846	189,168	561,852
Legal fees	10,652,628	1,159,570	1,856,187	994,547	2,129,198	345,258	592,861	3,575,086
Funeral expenses	6,007,077	1,649,023	1,676,120	390,315	890,488	204,789	390,980	804,936
Safe deposit box rental	357,425	39,273	77,814	23,383	72,506	30,163	29,018	84,797
Checking accounts, other bank service charges	2,111,437	318,714	454,729	222,008	376,558	157,932	209,135	372,530
Cemetery lots, vaults, and maintenance fees	1,304,065	282,555	350,276	121,985	137,928	65,856	184,747	161,057
Accounting fees	4,688,403	484,655	991,037	398,761	737,142	318,577	477,965	1,280,607
Miscellaneous personal services	3,053,208	419,707	308,320	337,947	837,984	112,252	427,045	633,151
Finance charges, except mortgage and vehicles	21,056,908	3,188,031	4,309,402	2,233,953	4,208,948	1,574,759	2,148,699	3,392,916
Occupational expenses	3,561,589	149,115	400,589	324,433	805,759	295,379	575,312	1,010,987
Expenses for other properties	5,390,592	503,785	650,618	510,877	1,056,057	331,943	488,812	1,848,112
Credit card memberships	241,530	22,120	36,525	21,783	43,754	26,066	27,152	63,684
Shopping club membership fees	513,251	41,739	86,593	52,457	95,285	38,715	71,232	126,907
CASH CONTRIBUTIONS	**141,961,991**	**13,273,715**	**24,155,258**	**9,513,726**	**19,206,398**	**8,329,409**	**15,015,606**	**52,463,931**
Support for college students	6,619,666	388,234	441,550	339,281	593,520	376,240	777,401	3,702,800
Alimony expenditures	4,285,204	98,516	516,445	184,755	775,757	190,706	476,997	2,071,238
Child support expenditures	17,410,589	1,410,845	3,457,826	1,577,708	3,991,569	1,345,901	1,790,882	3,835,360
Gifts to non–CU members of stocks, bonds, and mutual funds	2,805,835	142,993	1,474,360	49,967	379,753	24,069	70,541	725,216
Cash contributions to charities and other organizations	14,711,884	831,893	1,535,655	795,656	1,251,767	604,278	1,228,006	8,464,351
Cash contributions to church, religious organizations	58,252,479	5,808,775	9,384,808	4,766,198	8,663,193	3,727,217	7,452,738	18,447,548
Cash contributions to educational institutions	5,221,132	245,560	452,075	112,293	228,074	110,204	167,958	3,905,159
Cash contributions to political organizations	737,250	36,658	101,600	45,344	83,062	51,466	68,123	351,186
Other cash gifts	31,917,952	4,400,883	6,790,937	1,642,523	3,239,843	1,899,328	2,982,892	10,961,073
PERSONAL INSURANCE AND PENSIONS	**458,672,654**	**16,251,021**	**51,617,152**	**34,483,121**	**80,451,436**	**37,845,470**	**64,768,904**	**173,245,014**
Life and other personal insurance	**40,324,744**	**4,330,206**	**5,883,661**	**3,084,288**	**5,956,310**	**2,507,754**	**4,554,482**	**14,007,187**
Life, endowment, annuity, other personal insurance	38,492,819	4,069,422	5,485,841	2,887,263	5,700,734	2,439,388	4,356,677	13,552,283
Other nonhealth insurance	1,832,899	261,010	397,820	197,025	255,576	68,365	197,874	454,904
Pensions and Social Security	**418,347,910**	**11,920,660**	**45,733,252**	**31,398,833**	**74,495,126**	**35,337,717**	**60,214,422**	**159,237,827**
Deductions for government retirement	7,997,749	27,417	536,755	655,889	2,092,251	517,272	1,542,780	2,625,475
Deductions for railroad retirement	382,747	–	17,956	23,739	50,699	126,181	111,788	62,415
Deductions for private pensions	55,334,644	213,632	2,597,579	2,994,489	9,429,782	4,401,704	7,826,930	27,869,469
Nonpayroll deposit to retirement plans	43,815,237	1,493,464	3,082,758	2,134,462	6,687,896	2,950,054	6,749,333	20,715,606
Deductions for Social Security	310,816,559	10,186,076	39,508,090	25,590,254	56,234,498	27,342,504	43,983,592	107,964,861
PERSONAL TAXES	**246,568,690**	**–1,667,469**	**31,218,054**	**12,906,798**	**34,334,274**	**16,246,168**	**32,169,271**	**121,355,165**
Federal income taxes	179,498,430	–3,530,796	23,153,076	8,292,013	23,196,161	11,768,007	22,832,380	93,782,312
State and local income taxes	48,844,508	272,062	4,752,673	3,265,309	8,030,920	3,371,052	7,134,302	22,017,211
Other taxes	18,225,752	1,591,275	3,312,305	1,349,476	3,107,193	1,107,058	2,202,589	5,555,527

Note: Numbers may not add to total because of rounding and missing subcategories. (–) means sample is too small to make a reliable estimate.
Source: Calculations by New Strategist based on the 2003 Consumer Expenditure Survey

Table 4.8 Financial: Market shares by income, 2003

(percentage of total annual spending on financial products and services, cash contributions, and miscellaneous items accounted for by before-tax income group of consumer units, 2003; complete income reporters only)

	total complete reporters	under $20,000	$20,000–$39,999	$40,000–$49,999	$50,000–$69,999	$70,000–$79,999	$80,000–$99,999	$100,000 or more
Share of total consumer units	100.0%	27.8%	24.6%	9.1%	14.3%	5.3%	7.1%	11.8%
Share of total before-tax income	100.0	5.9	14.0	7.9	16.4	7.7	12.3	35.8
Share of total spending	100.0	12.9	18.2	8.5	16.6	7.0	10.9	25.9
FINANCIAL PRODUCTS AND SERVICES	**100.0**	**13.8**	**19.6**	**9.6**	**19.9**	**6.0**	**9.1**	**22.0**
Miscellaneous fees	100.0	5.3	25.4	2.3	51.3	5.1	–	15.4
Lottery and gambling losses	100.0	13.8	27.5	11.9	21.7	6.9	4.4	13.2
Legal fees	100.0	10.9	17.4	9.3	20.0	3.2	5.6	33.6
Funeral expenses	100.0	27.5	27.9	6.5	14.8	3.4	6.5	13.4
Safe deposit box rental	100.0	11.0	21.8	6.5	20.3	8.4	8.1	23.7
Checking accounts, other bank service charges	100.0	15.1	21.5	10.5	17.8	7.5	9.9	17.6
Cemetery lots, vaults, and maintenance fees	100.0	21.7	26.9	9.4	10.6	5.1	14.2	12.4
Accounting fees	100.0	10.3	21.1	8.5	15.7	6.8	10.2	27.3
Miscellaneous personal services	100.0	13.7	10.1	11.1	27.4	3.7	14.0	20.7
Finance charges, except mortgage and vehicles	100.0	15.1	20.5	10.6	20.0	7.5	10.2	16.1
Occupational expenses	100.0	4.2	1.2	9.1	22.6	8.3	16.2	28.4
Expenses for other properties	100.0	9.3	2.1	9.5	19.6	6.2	9.1	34.3
Credit card memberships	100.0	9.2	15.1	9.0	18.1	10.8	11.2	26.4
Shopping club membership fees	100.0	8.1	16.9	10.2	18.6	7.5	13.9	24.7
CASH CONTRIBUTIONS	**100.0**	**9.4**	**17.0**	**6.7**	**13.5**	**5.9**	**10.6**	**37.0**
Support for college students	100.0	5.9	5.7	5.1	9.0	5.7	11.7	55.9
Alimony expenditures	100.0	2.3	12.1	4.3	18.1	4.5	11.1	48.3
Child support expenditures	100.0	8.1	19.9	9.1	22.9	7.7	10.3	22.0
Gifts to non–CU members of stocks, bonds, and mutual funds	100.0	5.1	52.5	1.8	13.5	0.9	2.5	25.8
Cash contributions to charities and other organizations	100.0	5.7	10.4	5.4	8.5	4.1	8.3	57.5
Cash contributions to church, religious organizations	100.0	10.0	16.1	8.2	14.9	6.4	12.8	31.7
Cash contributions to educational institutions	100.0	4.7	8.7	2.2	4.4	2.1	3.2	74.8
Cash contributions to political organizations	100.0	5.0	13.3	6.2	11.3	7.0	9.2	47.6
Other cash gifts	100.0	13.8	21.3	5.1	10.2	6.0	9.3	34.3
PERSONAL INSURANCE AND PENSIONS	**100.0**	**3.5**	**11.3**	**7.5**	**17.5**	**8.3**	**14.1**	**37.8**
Life and other personal insurance	**100.0**	**10.7**	**14.6**	**7.6**	**14.8**	**6.2**	**11.3**	**34.7**
Life, endowment, annuity, other personal insurance	100.0	10.6	14.3	7.5	14.8	6.3	11.3	35.2
Other nonhealth insurance	100.0	14.2	21.7	10.7	13.9	3.7	10.8	24.8
Pensions and Social Security	**100.0**	**2.8**	**10.9**	**7.5**	**17.8**	**8.4**	**14.4**	**38.1**
Deductions for government retirement	100.0	0.3	6.7	8.2	26.2	6.5	19.3	32.8
Deductions for railroad retirement	100.0	–	4.7	6.2	13.2	33.0	29.2	16.3
Deductions for private pensions	100.0	0.4	4.7	5.4	17.0	8.0	14.1	50.4
Nonpayroll deposit to retirement plans	100.0	3.4	7.0	4.9	15.3	6.7	15.4	47.3
Deductions for Social Security	100.0	3.3	12.7	8.2	18.1	8.8	14.2	34.7
PERSONAL TAXES	**100.0**	**−0.7**	**12.7**	**5.2**	**13.9**	**6.6**	**13.0**	**49.2**
Federal income taxes	100.0	−2.0	12.9	4.6	12.9	6.6	12.7	52.2
State and local income taxes	100.0	0.6	9.7	6.7	16.4	6.9	14.6	45.1
Other taxes	100.0	8.7	18.2	7.4	17.0	6.1	12.1	30.5

Note: Numbers may not add to total because of rounding. (–) means sample is too small to make a reliable estimate.
Source: Calculations by New Strategist based on the 2003 Consumer Expenditure Survey

Table 4.9 Financial: Average spending by high-income consumer units, 2003

(average annual spending on financial products and services, cash contributions, and miscellaneous items, by before-tax income of high-income consumer units (CU), 2003; complete income reporters only)

	total complete reporters	$100,000 or more	$100,000– $119,999	$120,000– $149,999	$150,000 or more
Number of consumer units (000)	97,391	11,537	4,384	3,151	4,002
Average number of persons per CU	2.5	3.1	3.1	3.1	3.1
Average before-tax income of CU	$51,128.00	$154,665.00	$108,087.00	$131,885.00	$223,634.00
Average spending of CU, total	42,741.66	93,514.86	75,601.50	86,451.46	118,674.11
FINANCIAL PRODUCTS AND SERVICES	658.42	1,221.27	1,266.66	964.54	1,372.99
Miscellaneous fees	9.02	11.69	5.70	28.88	4.87
Lottery and gambling losses	43.67	48.70	39.33	27.42	75.40
Legal fees	109.38	309.88	427.05	142.72	313.15
Funeral expenses	61.68	69.77	58.68	98.83	59.04
Safe deposit box rental	3.67	7.35	6.58	6.85	8.57
Checking accounts, other bank service charges	21.68	32.29	33.35	32.99	30.56
Cemetery lots, vaults, and maintenance fees	13.39	13.96	8.10	28.04	9.29
Accounting fees	48.14	111.00	77.68	59.43	188.13
Miscellaneous personal services	31.35	54.88	21.98	29.26	110.53
Finance charges, except mortgage and vehicles	216.21	294.09	356.47	260.88	251.89
Occupational expenses	36.57	87.63	77.77	96.03	91.81
Expenses for other properties	55.35	160.19	132.69	140.27	206.01
Credit card memberships	2.48	5.52	3.37	3.92	9.15
Shopping club membership fees	5.27	11.00	11.58	9.03	11.93
CASH CONTRIBUTIONS	1,457.65	4,547.45	2,237.69	2,697.99	8,534.42
Support for college students	67.97	320.95	213.98	241.79	500.47
Alimony expenditures	44.00	179.53	65.11	36.15	417.81
Child support expenditures	178.77	332.44	266.26	300.66	429.97
Gifts to non–CU members of stocks, bonds, and mutual funds	28.81	62.86	7.92	4.27	169.18
Cash contributions to charities and other organizations	151.06	733.67	185.49	250.92	1,714.40
Cash contributions to church, religious organizations	598.13	1,598.99	1,116.87	1,246.87	2,404.49
Cash contributions to educational institutions	53.61	338.49	39.86	37.20	902.94
Cash contributions to political organizations	7.57	30.44	6.35	16.64	67.71
Other cash gifts	327.73	950.08	335.85	563.51	1,927.45
PERSONAL INSURANCE AND PENSIONS	4,709.60	15,016.47	11,808.17	14,474.24	18,958.45
Life and other personal insurance	414.05	1,214.11	729.48	944.17	1,957.63
Life, endowment, annuity, other personal insurance	395.24	1,174.68	700.46	923.81	1,891.80
Other nonhealth insurance	18.82	39.43	29.02	20.37	65.83
Pensions and Social Security	4,295.55	13,802.36	11,078.69	13,530.06	17,000.82
Deductions for government retirement	82.12	227.57	236.65	227.11	217.98
Deductions for railroad retirement	3.93	5.41	11.22	–	3.31
Deductions for private pensions	568.17	2,415.66	1,659.11	3,007.37	2,778.56
Nonpayroll deposit to retirement plans	449.89	1,795.58	1,392.50	1,266.62	2,653.74
Deductions for Social Security	3,191.43	9,358.14	7,779.21	9,028.97	11,347.22
PERSONAL TAXES	2,531.74	10,518.78	6,216.26	10,244.93	15,448.24
Federal income taxes	1,843.07	8,128.83	4,558.83	7,747.97	12,340.04
State and local income taxes	501.53	1,908.40	1,232.19	2,185.67	2,430.90
Other taxes	187.14	481.54	425.23	311.29	677.30

Note: Subcategories may not add to total because some are not shown. (–) means sample is too small to make a reliable estimate.
Source: Bureau of Labor Statistics, unpublished tables from the 2003 Consumer Expenditure Survey; calculations by New Strategist

Table 4.10 Financial: Indexed spending by high-income consumer units, 2003

(indexed average annual spending of consumer units (CU) on financial products and services, cash contributions, and miscellaneous items, by before-tax income of high-incomeconsumer unit, 2003; complete income reporters only; index definition: an index of 100 is the average for all consumer units; an index of 132 means that spending by consumer units in that group is 32 percent above the average for all consumer units; an index of 68 indicates spending that is 32 percent below the average for all consumer units)

	total complete reporters	$100,000 or more	$100,000–$119,999	$120,000–$149,999	$150,000 or more
Average spending of CU, total	$42,742	$93,515	$75,602	$86,451	$118,674
Average spending of CU, index	100	219	177	202	278
FINANCIAL PRODUCTS AND SERVICES	100	135	192	146	209
Miscellaneous fees	100	130	63	320	54
Lottery and gambling losses	100	1 2	90	63	173
Legal fees	100	253	390	130	286
Funeral expenses	100	113	95	160	96
Safe deposit box rental	100	200	179	187	234
Checking accounts, other bank service charges	100	149	154	152	141
Cemetery lots, vaults, and maintenance fees	100	104	60	209	69
Accounting fees	100	231	161	123	391
Miscellaneous personal services	100	175	70	93	353
Finance charges, except mortgage and vehicles	100	136	165	121	117
Occupational expenses	100	240	213	263	251
Expenses for other properties	100	289	240	253	372
Credit card memberships	100	223	136	158	369
Shopping club membership fees	100	205	220	171	226
CASH CONTRIBUTIONS	100	312	154	185	585
Support for college students	100	472	315	356	736
Alimony expenditures	100	408	148	82	950
Child support expenditures	100	186	149	168	241
Gifts to non–CU members of stocks, bonds, and mutual funds	100	218	27	15	587
Cash contributions to charities and other organizations	100	486	123	166	1,135
Cash contributions to church, religious organizations	100	257	137	208	402
Cash contributions to educational institutions	100	631	74	69	1,684
Cash contributions to political organizations	100	402	84	220	894
Other cash gifts	100	290	102	172	588
PERSONAL INSURANCE AND PENSIONS	100	319	251	307	403
Life and other personal insurance	100	293	176	228	473
Life, endowment, annuity, other personal insurance	100	297	177	234	479
Other nonhealth insurance	100	210	154	108	350
Pensions and Social Security	100	321	258	315	396
Deductions for government retirement	100	277	288	277	265
Deductions for railroad retirement	100	138	285	–	84
Deductions for private pensions	100	425	292	529	489
Nonpayroll deposit to retirement plans	100	399	310	282	590
Deductions for Social Security	100	293	244	283	356
PERSONAL TAXES	100	415	246	405	610
Federal income taxes	100	441	247	420	670
State and local income taxes	100	381	246	436	485
Other taxes	100	257	227	166	362

Note: (–) means sample is too small to make a reliable estimate.
Source: Calculations by New Strategist based on the 2003 Consumer Expenditure Survey

Table 4.11 Financial: Total spending by high-income consumer units, 2003

(total annual spending on financial products and services, cash contributions, and miscellaneous items, by before-tax income group of high-income consumer units (CU), 2003; complete income reporters only; numbers in thousands)

	total complete reporters	$100,000 or more	$100,000–$119,999	$120,000–$149,999	$150,000 or more
Number of consumer units	97,391	11,537	4,384	3,151	4,002
Total spending of all CUs	$4,162,653,009	$1,078,880,940	$331,436,976	$272,408,550	$474,933,788
FINANCIAL PRODUCTS AND SERVICES	**64,124,182**	**14,089,792**	**5,553,037**	**3,039,266**	**5,494,706**
Miscellaneous fees	878,467	134,868	24,989	91,001	19,490
Lottery and gambling losses	4,253,065	561,852	172,423	86,400	301,751
Legal fees	10,652,628	3,575,086	1,872,187	449,711	1,253,226
Funeral expenses	6,007,077	804,936	257,253	311,413	236,278
Safe deposit box rental	357,425	84,797	28,847	21,584	34,297
Checking accounts, other bank service charges	2,111,437	372,530	146,206	103,951	122,301
Cemetery lots, vaults, and maintenance fees	1,304,065	161,057	35,510	88,354	37,179
Accounting fees	4,688,403	1,280,607	340,549	187,264	752,896
Miscellaneous personal services	3,053,208	633,151	96,360	92,198	442,341
Finance charges, except mortgage and vehicles	21,056,908	3,392,916	1,562,764	822,033	1,008,064
Occupational expenses	3,561,589	1,010,987	340,944	302,591	367,424
Expenses for other properties	5,390,592	1,848,112	581,713	441,991	824,452
Credit card memberships	241,530	63,684	14,774	12,352	36,618
Shopping club membership fees	513,251	126,907	50,767	28,454	47,744
CASH CONTRIBUTIONS	**141,961,991**	**52,463,931**	**9,810,033**	**8,501,366**	**34,154,749**
Support for college students	6,619,666	3,702,800	938,088	761,880	2,002,881
Alimony expenditures	4,285,204	2,071,238	285,442	113,909	1,672,076
Child support expenditures	17,410,589	3,835,360	1,167,284	947,380	1,720,740
Gifts to non–CU members of stocks, bonds, and mutual funds	2,805,835	725,216	34,721	13,455	677,058
Cash contributions to charities and other organizations	14,711,884	8,464,351	813,188	790,649	6,861,029
Cash contributions to church, religious organizations	58,252,479	18,447,548	4,896,358	3,928,887	9,622,769
Cash contributions to educational institutions	5,221,132	3,905,159	174,746	117,217	3,613,566
Cash contributions to political organizations	737,250	351,186	27,838	52,433	270,975
Other cash gifts	31,917,952	10,961,073	1,472,366	1,775,620	7,713,655
PERSONAL INSURANCE AND PENSIONS	**458,672,654**	**173,245,014**	**51,767,017**	**45,608,330**	**75,871,717**
Life and other personal insurance	**40,324,744**	**14,007,187**	**3,198,040**	**2,975,080**	**7,834,435**
Life, endowment, annuity, other personal insurance	38,492,819	13,552,283	3,070,817	2,910,925	7,570,984
Other nonhealth insurance	1,832,899	454,904	127,224	64,186	263,452
Pensions and Social Security	**418,347,910**	**159,237,827**	**48,568,977**	**42,633,219**	**68,037,282**
Deductions for government retirement	7,997,749	2,625,475	1,037,474	715,624	872,356
Deductions for railroad retirement	382,747	62,415	49,188	–	13,247
Deductions for private pensions	55,334,644	27,869,469	7,273,538	9,476,223	11,119,797
Nonpayroll deposit to retirement plans	43,815,237	20,715,606	6,104,720	3,991,120	10,620,267
Deductions for Social Security	310,816,559	107,964,861	34,104,057	28,450,284	45,411,574
PERSONAL TAXES	**246,568,690**	**121,355,165**	**27,252,084**	**32,281,774**	**61,823,856**
Federal income taxes	179,498,430	93,782,312	19,985,911	24,413,853	49,384,840
State and local income taxes	48,844,508	22,017,211	5,401,921	6,887,046	9,728,462
Other taxes	18,225,752	5,555,527	1,864,208	980,875	2,710,555

Note: Numbers may not add to total because of rounding and missing subcategories. (–) means sample is too small to make a reliable estimate.
Source: Calculations by New Strategist based on the 2003 Consumer Expenditure Survey

Table 4.12 Financial: Market shares by high-income consumer units, 2003

(percentage of total annual spending on financial products and services, cash contributions, and miscellaneous items accounted for by before-tax income group of high-income consumer units, 2003; complete income reporters only)

	total complete reporters	$100,000 or more	$100,000–$119,999	$120,000–$149,999	$150,000 or more
Share of total consumer units	100.0%	11.8%	4.5%	3.2%	4.1%
Share of total before-tax income	100.0	35.8	9.5	8.3	18.0
Share of total spending	100.0	25.9	8.0	6.5	11.4
FINANCIAL PRODUCTS AND SERVICES	100.0	22.0	8.7	4.7	8.6
Miscellaneous fees	100.0	15.4	2.8	10.4	2.2
Lottery and gambling losses	100.0	13.2	4.1	2.0	7.1
Legal fees	100.0	33.6	17.6	4.2	11.8
Funeral expenses	100.0	13.4	4.3	5.2	3.9
Safe deposit box rental	100.0	23.7	8.1	6.0	9.6
Checking accounts, other bank service charges	100.0	17.6	6.9	4.9	5.8
Cemetery lots, vaults, and maintenance fees	100.0	12.4	2.7	6.8	2.9
Accounting fees	100.0	27.3	7.3	4.0	16.1
Miscellaneous personal services	100.0	20.7	3.2	3.0	14.5
Finance charges, except mortgage and vehicles	100.0	16.1	7.4	3.9	4.8
Occupational expenses	100.0	28.4	9.6	8.5	10.3
Expenses for other properties	100.0	34.3	10.8	8.2	15.3
Credit card memberships	100.0	26.4	6.1	5.1	15.2
Shopping club membership fees	100.0	24.7	9.9	5.5	9.3
CASH CONTRIBUTIONS	100.0	37.0	6.9	6.0	24.1
Support for college students	100.0	55.9	14.2	11.5	30.3
Alimony expenditures	100.0	48.3	6.7	2.7	39.0
Child support expenditures	100.0	22.0	6.7	5.4	9.9
Gifts to non–CU members of stocks, bonds, and mutual funds	100.0	25.8	1.2	0.5	24.1
Cash contributions to charities and other organizations	100.0	57.5	5.5	5.4	46.6
Cash contributions to church, religious organizations	100.0	31.7	8.4	6.7	16.5
Cash contributions to educational institutions	100.0	74.8	3.3	2.2	69.2
Cash contributions to political organizations	100.0	47.5	3.8	7.1	36.8
Other cash gifts	100.0	34.3	4.6	5.6	24.2
PERSONAL INSURANCE AND PENSIONS	100.0	37.8	11.3	9.9	16.5
Life and other personal insurance	100.0	34.7	7.9	7.4	19.4
Life, endowment, annuity, other personal insurance	100.0	35.2	8.0	7.6	19.7
Other nonhealth insurance	100.0	24.8	6.9	3.5	14.4
Pensions and Social Security	100.0	38.1	11.6	10.2	16.3
Deductions for government retirement	100.0	32.8	13.0	8.9	10.9
Deductions for railroad retirement	100.0	16.3	12.9	–	3.5
Deductions for private pensions	100.0	50.4	13.1	17.1	20.1
Nonpayroll deposit to retirement plans	100.0	47.3	13.9	9.1	24.2
Deductions for Social Security	100.0	34.7	11.0	9.2	14.6
PERSONAL TAXES	100.0	49.2	11.1	13.1	25.1
Federal income taxes	100.0	52.2	11.1	13.6	27.5
State and local income taxes	100.0	45.1	11.1	14.1	19.9
Other taxes	100.0	30.5	10.2	5.4	14.9

Note: Numbers may not add to total because of rounding. (–) means sample is too small to make a reliable estimate.
Source: Calculations by New Strategist based on the 2003 Consumer Expenditure Survey

Table 4.13 Financial: Average spending by household type, 2003

(average annual spending of consumer units (CU) on financial products and services, cash contributions, and miscellaneous items, by type of consumer unit, 2003)

	total married couples	married couples, no children	married couples with children total	oldest child under 6	oldest child 6 to 17	oldest child 18 or older	single parent, at least one child <18	single person
Number of consumer units (000)	58,448	25,132	28,584	5,496	15,047	8,041	6,999	33,929
Average number of persons per CU	3.2	2.0	3.9	3.5	4.1	4.0	2.9	1.0
Average spending of CU, total	$53,030.03	$47,895.65	$57,702.32	$51,503.24	$59,183.18	$59,180.36	$30,534.75	$23,657.35
FINANCIAL PRODUCTS AND SERVICES	**712.06**	**637.51**	**778.26**	**625.66**	**696.38**	**1,035.02**	**509.82**	**422.90**
Miscellaneous fees	14.22	4.67	24.00	37.45	24.77	12.53	–	1.21
Lottery and gambling losses	37.13	46.03	32.26	11.79	37.22	37.18	10.27	30.91
Legal fees	103.63	62.57	129.29	56.50	75.84	279.06	230.55	81.88
Funeral expenses	69.57	101.16	36.08	39.11	14.75	73.94	29.56	42.54
Safe deposit box rental	4.68	6.40	3.46	2.64	2.99	4.90	0.61	2.82
Checking accounts, other bank service charges	21.23	14.67	26.31	25.45	26.53	26.47	21.29	16.29
Cemetery lots, vaults, and maintenance fees	16.58	23.82	10.55	3.49	6.61	22.73	1.35	8.73
Accounting fees	56.44	60.65	55.52	59.94	54.99	53.47	34.20	33.41
Miscellaneous personal services	40.16	24.58	50.09	44.70	52.68	48.76	13.57	10.33
Finance charges, except mortgage and vehicles	216.15	159.08	274.25	236.79	264.91	317.33	130.10	148.56
Occupational expenses	47.42	38.99	57.02	47.59	63.54	51.25	22.36	18.88
Expenses for other properties	73.54	83.90	67.30	49.08	61.64	90.33	12.93	23.58
Credit card memberships	3.03	3.69	2.78	3.63	2.57	2.60	1.28	1.76
Shopping club membership fees	7.30	7.10	7.50	7.11	7.32	8.10	1.74	1.99
CASH CONTRIBUTIONS	**1,761.55**	**2,173.71**	**1,441.34**	**1,059.52**	**1,430.26**	**1,723.02**	**621.50**	**1,031.54**
Support for college students	99.10	103.98	98.42	0.97	86.03	188.20	37.56	29.53
Alimony expenditures	18.10	22.12	13.55	11.90	18.48	5.47	56.90	81.40
Child support expenditures	114.69	61.81	149.84	200.25	162.55	91.60	189.21	209.82
Gifts to non–CU members of stocks, bonds, and mutual funds	44.46	74.52	25.33	9.23	2.97	78.17	2.31	6.50
Cash contributions to charities and other organizations	182.76	248.22	143.42	78.81	164.34	148.41	50.71	119.29
Cash contributions to church, religious organizations	840.36	905.17	779.02	502.39	791.00	945.65	213.32	285.17
Cash contributions to educational institutions	76.21	122.71	45.71	13.10	68.71	24.97	5.77	23.78
Cash contributions to political organizations	8.25	12.69	5.28	0.66	6.85	5.48	1.35	5.72
Other cash gifts	377.60	622.49	180.77	242.20	129.32	235.07	64.37	270.33
PERSONAL INSURANCE AND PENSIONS	**5,707.00**	**5,015.07**	**6,445.13**	**5,891.44**	**6,638.23**	**6,462.20**	**2,314.89**	**1,948.26**
Life and other personal insurance	**599.20**	**624.92**	**584.79**	**378.19**	**617.63**	**664.51**	**181.25**	**158.53**
Life, endowment, annuity, other personal insurance	579.01	599.07	568.27	366.14	606.05	635.72	175.02	142.84
Other nonhealth insurance	20.19	25.85	16.52	12.06	11.59	28.79	6.24	15.69
Pensions and Social Security	**5,107.80**	**4,390.15**	**5,860.34**	**5,513.25**	**6,020.60**	**5,797.69**	**2,133.63**	**1,789.73**
Deductions for government retirement	97.71	86.18	113.41	45.61	119.00	149.27	46.22	42.95
Deductions for railroad retirement	4.06	4.38	3.65	2.14	4.56	2.99	–	4.38
Deductions for private pensions	699.53	666.23	782.76	713.54	865.27	675.66	199.62	249.01
Nonpayroll deposit to retirement plans	574.15	665.24	540.32	595.86	530.40	520.92	240.07	207.45
Deductions for Social Security	3,732.34	2,968.12	4,420.21	4,156.10	4,501.36	4,448.85	1,647.73	1,285.95
PERSONAL TAXES	**3,632.43**	**4,669.29**	**2,992.45**	**2,210.47**	**3,237.55**	**3,071.67**	**307.56**	**1,592.00**
Federal income taxes	2,670.32	3,666.81	2,033.15	1,428.62	2,244.51	2,052.40	−19.45	1,180.43
State and local income taxes	695.85	685.21	743.39	592.16	794.85	750.92	227.11	304.38
Other taxes	266.26	317.28	215.91	189.70	198.18	268.35	99.90	107.20

Note: Average spending figures for total consumer units can be found on Average Spending by Age and Average Spending by Region tables. Subcategories may not add to total because some are not shown. (–) means sample is too small to make a reliable estimate.
Source: Bureau of Labor Statistics, unpublished tables from the 2003 Consumer Expenditure Survey

Table 4.14 Financial: Indexed spending by household type, 2003

(indexed average annual spending of consumer units (CU) on financial products and services, cash contributions, and miscellaneous items, by type of consumer unit, 2003; index definition: an index of 100 is the average for all consumer units; an index of 132 means that spending by consumer units in that group is 32 percent above the average for all consumer units; an index of 68 indicates spending that is 32 percent below the average for all consumer units)

	total married couples	married couples, no children	married couples with children total	married couples with children oldest child under 6	married couples with children oldest child 6 to 17	married couples with children oldest child 18 or older	single parent, at least one child <18	single person
Average spending of CU, total	$53,030	$47,896	$57,702	$51,503	$59,183	$59,180	$30,535	$23,657
Average spending of CU, index	130	117	141	126	145	145	75	58
FINANCIAL PRODUCTS AND SERVICES	**118**	**105**	**128**	**103**	**115**	**171**	**84**	**70**
Miscellaneous fees	176	58	297	463	307	155	–	15
Lottery and gambling losses	105	130	91	33	105	105	29	87
Legal fees	96	58	120	52	70	258	213	76
Funeral expenses	121	176	63	68	26	129	51	74
Safe deposit box rental	134	184	99	75	86	141	18	81
Checking accounts, other bank service charges	106	73	131	127	133	132	106	81
Cemetery lots, vaults, and maintenance fees	125	180	80	26	50	171	10	66
Accounting fees	122	131	120	129	118	115	74	72
Miscellaneous personal services	149	91	186	166	196	181	51	38
Finance charges, except mortgage and vehicles	113	83	144	124	139	166	68	78
Occupational expenses	137	112	164	137	183	148	64	54
Expenses for other properties	138	157	126	92	115	169	24	44
Credit card memberships	129	158	119	155	110	111	55	75
Shopping club membership fees	148	144	152	145	149	165	35	40
CASH CONTRIBUTIONS	**129**	**159**	**105**	**77**	**104**	**126**	**45**	**75**
Support for college students	154	161	153	2	134	292	58	46
Alimony expenditures	43	52	32	28	44	13	135	193
Child support expenditures	69	37	90	121	98	55	114	126
Gifts to non–CU members of stocks, bonds, and mutual funds	180	302	103	37	12	317	9	26
Cash contributions to charities and other organizations	131	178	103	57	118	106	36	86
Cash contributions to church, religious organizations	149	160	138	89	140	168	38	51
Cash contributions to educational institutions	126	203	76	22	114	41	10	39
Cash contributions to political organizations	125	192	80	10	103	83	20	86
Other cash gifts	125	206	60	80	43	78	21	90
PERSONAL INSURANCE AND PENSIONS	**141**	**124**	**159**	**145**	**164**	**159**	**57**	**48**
Life and other personal insurance	**151**	**157**	**147**	**95**	**155**	**167**	**46**	**40**
Life, endowment, annuity, other personal insurance	152	158	149	96	159	167	46	38
Other nonhealth insurance	118	151	97	71	68	169	37	92
Pensions and Social Security	**140**	**120**	**160**	**151**	**165**	**158**	**58**	**49**
Deductions for government retirement	140	124	163	65	171	214	66	62
Deductions for railroad retirement	119	128	107	63	133	87	–	128
Deductions for private pensions	145	138	163	148	180	140	41	52
Nonpayroll deposit to retirement plans	148	171	139	154	137	134	62	53
Deductions for Social Security	137	109	163	153	166	164	61	47
PERSONAL TAXES	**143**	**184**	**118**	**87**	**128**	**121**	**12**	**63**
Federal income taxes	145	199	110	78	122	111	–1	64
State and local income taxes	139	137	148	118	158	150	45	61
Other taxes	142	170	115	101	106	143	53	57

Note: Spending index for total consumer units is 100. (–) means sample is too small to make a reliable estimate.
Source: Calculations by New Strategist based on the 2003 Consumer Expenditure Survey

Table 4.15 Financial: Total spending by household type, 2003

(total annual spending on financial products and services, cash contributions, and miscellaneous items, by consumer unit (CU) type, 2003; numbers in thousands)

	total married couples	married couples, no children	married couples with children total	oldest child under 6	oldest child 6 to 17	oldest child 18 or older	single parent, at least one child <18	single person
Number of consumer units	58,448	25,132	28,584	5,496	15,047	8,041	6,999	33,929
Total spending of all CUs	$3,099,499,193	$1,203,713,476	$1,649,363,115	$283,061,807	$890,529,309	$475,869,275	$213,712,715	$802,670,228
FINANCIAL PRODUCTS AND SERVICES	**41,618,483**	**16,021,901**	**22,245,784**	**3,438,627**	**10,478,430**	**8,322,596**	**3,568,230**	**14,348,574**
Miscellaneous fees	831,131	117,366	686,016	205,825	372,714	100,754	–	41,054
Lottery and gambling losses	2,170,174	1,156,826	922,120	64,798	560,049	298,964	71,880	1,048,745
Legal fees	6,056,966	1,572,509	3,695,625	310,524	1,141,164	2,243,921	1,613,619	2,778,107
Funeral expenses	4,066,227	2,542,353	1,031,311	214,949	221,943	594,552	206,890	1,443,340
Safe deposit box rental	273,537	160,845	98,901	14,509	44,991	39,401	4,269	95,680
Checking accounts, other bank service charges	1,240,851	368,686	752,045	139,873	399,197	212,845	149,009	552,703
Cemetery lots, vaults, and maintenance fees	969,068	598,644	301,561	19,181	99,461	182,772	9,449	296,200
Accounting fees	3,298,805	1,524,256	1,586,984	329,430	827,435	429,952	239,366	1,133,568
Miscellaneous personal services	2,347,272	617,745	1,431,773	245,671	792,676	392,079	94,976	350,487
Finance charges, except mortgage and vehicles	12,633,535	3,997,999	7,839,162	1,301,398	3,986,101	2,551,651	910,570	5,040,492
Occupational expenses	2,771,604	979,897	1,629,860	261,555	956,086	412,101	156,498	640,580
Expenses for other properties	4,298,266	2,108,575	1,923,703	269,744	927,497	726,344	90,497	800,046
Credit card memberships	177,097	92,737	79,464	19,950	38,671	20,907	8,959	59,715
Shopping club membership fees	426,670	178,437	214,380	39,077	110,144	65,132	12,178	67,519
CASH CONTRIBUTIONS	**102,959,074**	**54,629,680**	**41,199,263**	**5,823,122**	**21,521,122**	**13,854,804**	**4,349,879**	**34,999,121**
Support for college students	5,792,197	2,613,225	2,813,237	5,331	1,294,493	1,513,316	262,882	1,001,923
Alimony expenditures	1,057,909	555,920	387,313	65,402	278,069	43,984	398,243	2,761,821
Child support expenditures	6,703,401	1,553,409	4,283,027	1,100,574	2,445,890	736,556	1,324,281	7,118,983
Gifts to non–CU members of stocks, bonds, and mutual funds	2,598,598	1,872,837	724,033	50,728	44,690	628,565	16,168	220,539
Cash contributions to charities and other organizations	10,681,956	6,238,265	4,099,517	433,140	2,472,824	1,193,365	354,919	4,047,390
Cash contributions to church, religious organizations	49,117,361	22,748,732	22,267,508	2,761,135	11,902,177	7,603,972	1,493,027	9,675,533
Cash contributions to educational institutions	4,454,322	3,083,948	1,306,575	71,998	1,033,879	200,784	40,384	806,832
Cash contributions to political organizations	482,196	318,925	150,924	3,627	103,072	44,065	9,449	194,074
Other cash gifts	22,069,965	15,644,419	5,167,130	1,331,131	1,945,878	1,890,198	450,526	9,172,027
PERSONAL INSURANCE AND PENSIONS	**333,562,736**	**126,038,739**	**184,227,596**	**32,379,354**	**99,885,447**	**51,962,550**	**16,201,915**	**66,102,514**
Life and other personal insurance	**35,022,042**	**15,705,489**	**16,715,637**	**2,078,532**	**9,293,479**	**5,343,325**	**1,268,569**	**5,378,764**
Life, endowment, annuity, other personal insurance	33,841,976	15,055,827	16,243,430	2,012,305	9,119,234	5,111,825	1,224,965	4,846,418
Other nonhealth insurance	1,180,065	649,662	472,208	66,282	174,395	231,500	43,674	532,346
Pensions and Social Security	**298,540,694**	**110,333,250**	**167,511,959**	**30,300,822**	**90,591,968**	**46,619,225**	**14,933,276**	**60,723,749**
Deductions for government retirement	5,710,954	2,165,876	3,241,711	250,673	1,790,593	1,200,280	323,494	1,457,251
Deductions for railroad retirement	237,299	110,078	104,332	11,761	68,614	24,043	–	148,609
Deductions for private pensions	40,886,129	16,743,692	22,374,412	3,921,616	13,019,718	5,432,982	1,397,140	8,448,660
Nonpayroll deposit to retirement plans	33,557,919	16,718,812	15,444,507	3,274,847	7,980,929	4,188,718	1,680,250	7,038,571
Deductions for Social Security	218,147,808	74,594,792	126,347,283	22,841,926	67,731,964	35,773,203	11,532,462	43,630,998
PERSONAL TAXES	**212,308,269**	**117,348,596**	**85,536,191**	**12,148,743**	**48,715,415**	**24,699,298**	**2,152,612**	**54,014,968**
Federal income taxes	156,074,863	92,154,269	58,115,560	7,851,696	33,773,142	16,503,348	–136,131	40,050,809
State and local income taxes	40,671,041	17,220,698	21,249,060	3,254,511	11,960,108	6,038,148	1,589,543	10,327,309
Other taxes	15562364.48	7973880.96	6171571.44	1042591.2	2982014.46	2157802.35	699200.1	3637188.8

Note: Total spending figures for total consumer units can be found on Total Spending by Age and Total Spending by Region tables. Spending by type of consumer unit will not add to total because not all types of consumer units are shown. Numbers may not add to category total because of rounding and missing subcategories. (–) means sample is too small to make a reliable estimate.
Source: Calculations by New Strategist based on the 2003 Consumer Expenditure Survey

Table 4.16 Financial: Market shares by household type, 2003

(percentage of total annual spending on financial products and services, cash contributions, and miscellaneous items accounted for by types of consumer units, 2003)

	total married couples	married couples, no children	married couples with children				single parent, at least one child <18	single person
			total	oldest child under 6	oldest child 6 to 17	oldest child 18 or older		
Share of total consumer units	50.7%	21.8%	24.8%	4.8%	13.0%	7.0%	6.1%	29.4%
Share of total before-tax income	68.8	26.8	36.6	6.2	19.8	10.7	3.5	15.6
Share of total spending	65.8	25.6	35.0	6.0	18.9	10.1	4.5	17.0
FINANCIAL PRODUCTS AND SERVICES	**59.5**	**22.9**	**31.8**	**4.9**	**15.0**	**11.9**	**5.1**	**20.5**
Miscellaneous fees	89.2	12.6	73.6	22.1	40.0	10.8	–	4.4
Lottery and gambling losses	53.2	28.4	22.6	1.6	13.7	7.3	1.8	25.7
Legal fees	48.6	12.6	29.6	2.5	9.2	18.0	12.9	22.3
Funeral expenses	61.3	38.3	15.5	3.2	3.3	9.0	3.1	21.8
Safe deposit box rental	68.1	40.1	24.6	3.6	11.2	9.8	1.1	23.8
Checking accounts, other bank service charges	53.8	16.0	32.6	6.1	17.3	9.2	6.5	23.9
Cemetery lots, vaults, and maintenance fees	63.3	39.1	19.7	1.3	6.5	11.9	0.6	19.3
Accounting fees	61.6	28.5	29.6	6.1	15.4	8.0	4.5	21.2
Miscellaneous personal services	75.7	19.9	46.2	7.9	25.6	12.6	3.1	11.3
Finance charges, except mortgage and vehicles	57.4	18.2	35.6	5.9	18.1	11.6	4.1	22.9
Occupational expenses	69.3	24.5	40.7	6.5	23.9	10.3	3.9	16.0
Expenses for other properties	69.7	34.2	31.2	4.4	15.0	11.8	1.5	13.0
Credit card memberships	65.6	34.4	29.4	7.4	14.3	7.7	3.3	22.1
Shopping club membership fees	75.2	31.4	37.8	6.9	19.4	11.5	2.1	11.9
CASH CONTRIBUTIONS	**65.2**	**34.6**	**26.1**	**3.7**	**13.6**	**8.8**	**2.8**	**22.1**
Support for college students	78.0	35.2	37.9	0.1	17.4	20.4	3.5	13.5
Alimony expenditures	21.7	11.4	8.0	1.3	5.7	0.9	8.2	56.8
Child support expenditures	35.0	8.1	22.4	5.7	12.8	3.8	6.9	37.1
Gifts to non–CU members of stocks, bonds, and mutual funds	91.3	65.8	25.4	1.8	1.6	22.1	0.6	7.7
Cash contributions to charities and other organizations	66.4	38.8	25.5	2.7	15.4	7.4	2.2	25.2
Cash contributions to church, religious organizations	75.4	34.9	34.2	4.2	18.3	11.7	2.3	14.9
Cash contributions to educational institutions	64.0	44.3	18.8	1.0	14.8	2.9	0.6	11.6
Cash contributions to political organizations	63.1	41.8	19.8	0.5	13.5	5.8	1.2	25.4
Other cash gifts	63.4	45.0	14.8	3.8	5.6	5.4	1.3	26.4
PERSONAL INSURANCE AND PENSIONS	**71.3**	**26.9**	**39.4**	**6.9**	**21.4**	**11.1**	**3.5**	**14.1**
Life and other personal insurance	**76.4**	**34.3**	**36.5**	**4.5**	**20.3**	**11.7**	**2.8**	**11.7**
Life, endowment, annuity, other personal insurance	77.2	34.3	37.0	4.6	20.8	11.7	2.8	11.0
Other nonhealth insurance	59.9	33.0	24.0	3.4	8.9	11.7	2.2	27.0
Pensions and Social Security	**70.8**	**26.1**	**39.7**	**7.2**	**21.5**	**11.0**	**3.5**	**14.4**
Deductions for government retirement	71.1	27.0	40.4	3.1	22.3	14.9	4.0	18.1
Deductions for railroad retirement	60.1	27.9	26.4	3.0	17.4	6.1	–	37.7
Deductions for private pensions	73.7	30.2	40.3	7.1	23.5	9.8	2.5	15.2
Nonpayroll deposit to retirement plans	74.9	37.3	34.5	7.3	17.8	9.4	3.8	15.7
Deductions for Social Security	69.6	23.8	40.3	7.3	21.6	11.4	3.7	13.9
PERSONAL TAXES	**72.7**	**40.2**	**29.3**	**4.2**	**16.7**	**8.5**	**0.7**	**18.5**
Federal income taxes	73.4	43.3	27.3	3.7	15.9	7.8	–0.1	18.8
State and local income taxes	70.3	29.8	36.7	5.6	20.7	10.4	2.7	17.9
Other taxes	72.1	36.9	28.6	4.8	13.8	10.0	3.2	16.8

Note: Market share for total consumer units is 100.0%. Market shares by type of consumer unit will not add to total because not all types of consumer units are shown. (–) means sample is too small to make a reliable estimate.
Source: Calculations by New Strategist based on the 2003 Consumer Expenditure Survey

Table 4.17 Financial: Average spending by race and Hispanic origin, 2003

(average annual spending of consumer units (CU) on financial products and services, cash contributions, and miscellaneous items, by race and Hispanic origin of consumer unit reference person, 2003)

	total consumer units	race			Hispanic origin	
		Asian	black	white and other	Hispanic	non-Hispanic
Number of consumer units (000)	115,356	3,573	13,743	98,041	11,727	103,629
Average number of persons per CU	2.5	2.8	2.6	2.5	3.3	2.4
Average before-tax income of CU	$51,128.00	$60,393.00	$34,485.00	$53,039.00	$37,150.00	$52,797.00
Average spending of CU, total	40,817.33	44,922.85	28,707.56	42,360.25	34,574.75	41,520.78
FINANCIAL PRODUCTS AND SERVICES	605.93	432.29	446.78	634.69	418.61	627.39
Miscellaneous fees	8.08	–	1.28	9.34	1.09	8.96
Lottery and gambling losses	35.37	13.63	32.15	36.67	16.14	37.79
Legal fees	108.09	69.31	67.07	115.26	35.22	116.34
Funeral expenses	57.51	31.12	33.16	61.89	37.05	59.82
Safe deposit box rental	3.48	6.27	1.84	3.61	1.21	3.73
Checking accounts, other bank service charges	20.01	16.47	19.96	20.15	15.49	20.53
Cemetery lots, vaults, and maintenance fees	13.27	11.26	4.39	14.59	8.74	13.78
Accounting fees	46.44	46.03	17.13	50.56	28.53	48.46
Miscellaneous personal services	26.87	4.82	19.88	28.70	32.24	26.20
Finance charges, except mortgage and vehicles	190.88	133.76	197.35	192.05	191.16	190.85
Occupational expenses	34.69	34.49	14.59	37.51	20.96	36.24
Expenses for other properties	53.45	54.00	34.70	56.06	24.24	56.76
Credit card memberships	2.34	3.97	0.88	2.49	1.85	2.40
Shopping club membership fees	4.92	7.15	2.40	5.19	4.67	4.94
CASH CONTRIBUTIONS	1,369.89	1,310.98	832.29	1,447.39	593.51	1,457.75
Support for college students	64.39	110.15	37.68	66.46	10.95	70.43
Alimony expenditures	42.18	33.79	4.61	47.75	3.49	46.56
Child support expenditures	166.12	140.46	149.39	169.40	122.39	171.07
Gifts to non–CU members of stocks, bonds, and mutual funds	24.68	0.19	1.29	28.86	2.31	27.22
Cash contributions to charities and other organizations	139.45	128.20	28.42	155.42	27.16	152.16
Cash contributions to church, religious organizations	564.41	448.95	525.17	574.11	190.06	606.77
Cash contributions to educational institutions	60.37	13.68	3.38	70.06	2.92	66.87
Cash contributions to political organizations	6.62	2.19	0.55	7.63	0.61	7.30
Other cash gifts	301.67	433.37	81.80	327.69	233.61	309.37
PERSONAL INSURANCE AND PENSIONS	4,055.24	4,762.20	2,503.99	4,246.92	2,823.93	4,194.58
Life and other personal insurance	397.30	413.74	295.03	411.03	159.64	424.19
Life, endowment, annuity, other personal insurance	380.22	403.37	287.50	392.37	156.57	405.53
Other nonhealth insurance	17.08	10.37	7.53	18.66	3.08	18.66
Pensions and Social Security	3,657.94	4,348.46	2,208.96	3,835.89	2,664.28	3,770.39
Deductions for government retirement	69.64	43.07	67.26	70.94	25.15	74.68
Deductions for railroad retirement	3.42	–	–	4.02	–	3.81
Deductions for private pensions	481.22	601.98	230.32	511.99	206.16	512.35
Nonpayroll deposit to retirement plans	388.15	366.12	100.71	429.25	122.49	418.22
Deductions for Social Security	2,715.50	3,337.29	1,810.66	2,819.68	2,310.48	2,761.34
PERSONAL TAXES	2,531.74	2,882.20	965.74	2,730.13	680.13	2,752.78
Federal income taxes	1,843.07	1,992.52	591.70	2,006.24	412.57	2,013.83
State and local income taxes	501.53	649.51	317.22	521.09	197.21	537.86
Other taxes	187.14	240.17	56.82	202.80	70.36	201.08

Note: Other races include Native Americans and Pacific Islanders. Subcategories may not add to total because some are not shown. (–) means sample is too small to make a reliable estimate.
Source: Bureau of Labor Statistics, unpublished tables from the 2003 Consumer Expenditure Survey

Table 4.18 Financial: Indexed spending by race and Hispanic origin, 2003

(indexed average annual spending of consumer units (CU) on financial products and services, cash contributions, and miscellaneous items, by race and Hispanic origin of consumer unit reference person, 2003; index definition: an index of 100 is the average for all consumer units; an index of 132 means that spending by consumer units in that group is 32 percent above the average for all consumer units; an index of 68 indicates spending that is 32 percent below the average for all consumer units)

		race			Hispanic origin	
	total consumer units	Asian	black	white and other	Hispanic	non-Hispanic
Average spending of CU, total	$40,817	$44,923	$28,708	$42,360	$34,575	$41,521
Average spending of CU, index	100	110	70	104	85	102
FINANCIAL PRODUCTS AND SERVICES	**100**	**71**	**74**	**105**	**69**	**104**
Miscellaneous fees	100	–	16	116	13	111
Lottery and gambling losses	100	39	91	104	46	107
Legal fees	100	64	62	107	33	108
Funeral expenses	100	54	58	108	64	104
Safe deposit box rental	100	180	53	104	35	107
Checking accounts, other bank service charges	100	82	100	101	77	103
Cemetery lots, vaults, and maintenance fees	100	85	33	110	66	104
Accounting fees	100	99	37	109	61	104
Miscellaneous personal services	100	18	74	107	120	98
Finance charges, except mortgage and vehicles	100	70	103	101	100	100
Occupational expenses	100	99	42	108	60	104
Expenses for other properties	100	101	65	105	45	106
Credit card memberships	100	170	38	106	79	103
Shopping club membership fees	100	145	49	105	95	100
CASH CONTRIBUTIONS	**100**	**96**	**61**	**106**	**43**	**106**
Support for college students	100	171	59	103	17	109
Alimony expenditures	100	80	11	113	8	110
Child support expenditures	100	85	90	102	74	103
Gifts to non–CU members of stocks, bonds, and mutual funds	100	1	5	117	9	110
Cash contributions to charities and other organizations	100	92	20	111	19	109
Cash contributions to church, religious organizations	100	80	93	102	34	108
Cash contributions to educational institutions	100	23	6	116	5	111
Cash contributions to political organizations	100	33	8	115	9	110
Other cash gifts	100	144	27	109	77	103
PERSONAL INSURANCE AND PENSIONS	**100**	**117**	**62**	**105**	**70**	**103**
Life and other personal insurance	**100**	**104**	**74**	**103**	**40**	**107**
Life, endowment, annuity, other personal insurance	100	106	76	103	41	107
Other nonhealth insurance	100	61	44	109	18	109
Pensions and Social Security	**100**	**119**	**60**	**105**	**73**	**103**
Deductions for government retirement	100	62	97	102	36	107
Deductions for railroad retirement	100	–	–	118	–	111
Deductions for private pensions	100	125	48	106	43	106
Nonpayroll deposit to retirement plans	100	94	26	111	32	108
Deductions for Social Security	100	123	67	104	85	102
PERSONAL TAXES	**100**	**114**	**38**	**108**	**27**	**109**
Federal income taxes	100	108	32	109	22	109
State and local income taxes	100	130	63	104	39	107
Other taxes	100	128	30	108	38	107

Note: Other races include Native Americans and Pacific Islanders. (–) means sample is too small to make a reliable estimate.
Source: Calculations by New Strategist based on the 2003 Consumer Expenditure Survey

Table 4.19 Financial: Total spending by race and Hispanic origin, 2003

(total annual spending on financial products and services, cash contributions, and miscellaneous items, by consumer unit race and Hispanic origin groups, 2003; numbers in thousands)

	total consumer units	race Asian	race black	race white and other	Hispanic origin Hispanic	Hispanic origin non-Hispanic
Number of consumer units	115,356	3,573	13,743	98,041	11,727	103,629
Total spending of all consumer units	$4,708,523,919	$160,509,343	$394,527,997	$4,153,041,270	$405,458,093	$4,302,756,911
FINANCIAL PRODUCTS AND SERVICES	**69,897,661**	**1,544,572**	**6,140,098**	**62,225,642**	**4,909,039**	**65,015,798**
Miscellaneous fees	932,076	–	17,591	914,485	12,782	928,516
Lottery and gambling losses	4,080,142	48,700	441,837	3,595,163	189,274	3,916,140
Legal fees	12,468,830	247,645	921,743	11,300,206	413,025	12,056,198
Funeral expenses	6,634,124	111,192	455,718	6,067,757	434,485	6,199,087
Safe deposit box rental	401,439	22,403	25,287	353,928	14,190	386,536
Checking accounts, other bank service charges	2,308,274	58,847	274,310	1,975,526	181,651	2,127,503
Cemetery lots, vaults, and maintenance fees	1,530,774	40,232	60,332	1,430,418	102,494	1,428,008
Accounting fees	5,357,133	164,465	235,418	4,956,953	334,571	5,021,861
Miscellaneous personal services	3,099,616	17,222	273,211	2,813,777	378,078	2,715,080
Finance charges, except mortgage and vehicles	22,019,153	477,924	2,712,181	18,828,774	2,241,733	19,777,595
Occupational expenses	4,001,700	123,233	200,510	3,677,518	245,798	3,755,515
Expenses for other properties	6,165,778	192,942	476,882	5,496,178	284,262	5,881,982
Credit card memberships	269,933	14,185	12,094	244,122	21,695	248,710
Shopping club membership fees	567,552	25,547	32,983	508,833	54,765	511,927
CASH CONTRIBUTIONS	**158,025,031**	**4,684,132**	**11,438,161**	**141,903,563**	**6,960,092**	**151,065,175**
Support for college students	7,427,773	393,566	517,836	6,515,805	128,411	7,298,590
Alimony expenditures	4,865,716	120,732	63,355	4,681,458	40,927	4,824,966
Child support expenditures	19,162,939	501,864	2,053,067	16,608,145	1,435,268	17,727,813
Gifts to non–CU members of stocks, bonds, and mutual funds	2,846,986	679	17,728	2,829,463	27,089	2,820,781
Cash contributions to charities and other organizations	16,086,394	458,059	390,576	15,237,532	318,505	15,768,189
Cash contributions to church, religious organizations	65,108,080	1,604,098	7,217,411	56,286,319	2,228,834	62,878,968
Cash contributions to educational institutions	6,964,042	48,879	46,451	6,868,752	34,243	6,929,671
Cash contributions to political organizations	763,657	7,825	7,559	748,053	7,153	756,492
Other cash gifts	34,799,445	1,548,431	1,124,177	32,127,055	2,739,544	32,059,704
PERSONAL INSURANCE AND PENSIONS	**467,796,265**	**17,015,341**	**34,412,335**	**416,372,284**	**33,116,227**	**434,680,131**
Life and other personal insurance	**45,830,939**	**1,478,293**	**4,054,597**	**40,297,792**	**1,872,098**	**43,958,386**
Life, endowment, annuity, other personal insurance	43,860,658	1,441,241	3,951,113	38,468,347	1,836,096	42,024,668
Other nonhealth insurance	1,970,280	37,052	103,485	1,829,445	36,119	1,933,717
Pensions and Social Security	**421,965,327**	**15,537,048**	**30,357,737**	**376,074,491**	**31,244,012**	**390,721,745**
Deductions for government retirement	8,033,392	153,889	924,354	6,955,029	294,934	7,739,014
Deductions for railroad retirement	394,518	–	–	394,125	–	394,518
Deductions for private pensions	55,511,614	2,150,875	3,165,288	50,196,012	2,417,638	53,094,318
Nonpayroll deposit to retirement plans	44,775,431	1,308,147	1,384,058	42,084,099	1,436,440	43,339,720
Deductions for Social Security	313,249,218	11,924,137	24,883,900	276,444,247	27,094,999	286,154,903
PERSONAL TAXES	**292,051,399**	**10,298,101**	**13,272,165**	**267,664,675**	**7,975,885**	**285,267,839**
Federal income taxes	212,609,183	7,119,274	8,131,733	196,693,776	4,838,208	208,691,189
State and local income taxes	57,854,495	2,320,699	4,359,554	51,088,185	2,312,682	55,737,894
Other taxes	21,587,722	858,127	780,877	19,882,715	825,112	20,837,719

Note: Other races include Native Americans and Pacific Islanders. Numbers may not add to total because of rounding and missing subcategories. (–) means sample is too small to make a reliable estimate.
Source: Calculations by New Strategist based on the 2003 Consumer Expenditure Survey

Table 4.20 Financial: Market shares by race and Hispanic origin, 2003

(percentage of total annual spending on financial products and services, cash contributions, and miscellaneous items accounted for by consumer unit race and Hispanic origin groups, 2003)

	total consumer units	race			Hispanic origin	
		Asian	black	white and other	Hispanic	non-Hispanic
Share of total consumer units	100.0%	3.1%	11.9%	85.0%	10.2%	89.8%
Share of total before-tax income	100.0	3.7	8.0	88.2	7.4	92.8
Share of total spending	100.0	3.4	8.4	88.2	8.6	91.4
FINANCIAL PRODUCTS AND SERVICES	**100.0**	**2.2**	**8.8**	**89.0**	**7.0**	**93.0**
Miscellaneous fees	100.0	–	1.9	98.1	1.4	99.6
Lottery and gambling losses	100.0	1.2	10.8	88.1	4.6	96.0
Legal fees	100.0	2.0	7.4	90.6	3.3	96.7
Funeral expenses	100.0	1.7	6.9	91.5	6.5	93.4
Safe deposit box rental	100.0	5.6	6.3	88.2	3.5	96.3
Checking accounts, other bank service charges	100.0	2.5	11.9	85.6	7.9	92.2
Cemetery lots, vaults, and maintenance fees	100.0	2.6	3.9	93.4	6.7	93.3
Accounting fees	100.0	3.1	4.4	92.5	6.2	93.7
Miscellaneous personal services	100.0	0.6	8.8	90.8	12.2	87.6
Finance charges, except mortgage and vehicles	100.0	2.2	12.3	85.5	10.2	89.8
Occupational expenses	100.0	3.1	5.0	91.9	6.1	93.8
Expenses for other properties	100.0	3.1	7.7	89.1	4.6	95.4
Credit card memberships	100.0	5.3	4.5	90.4	8.0	92.1
Shopping club membership fees	100.0	4.5	5.8	89.7	9.6	90.2
CASH CONTRIBUTIONS	**100.0**	**3.0**	**7.2**	**89.8**	**4.4**	**95.6**
Support for college students	100.0	5.3	7.0	87.7	1.7	98.3
Alimony expenditures	100.0	2.5	1.3	96.2	0.8	99.2
Child support expenditures	100.0	2.6	10.7	86.7	7.5	92.5
Gifts to non–CU members of stocks, bonds, and mutual funds	100.0	0.0	0.5	99.4	1.0	99.1
Cash contributions to charities and other organizations	100.0	2.8	2.4	94.7	2.0	98.0
Cash contributions to church, religious organizations	100.0	2.5	11.1	86.5	3.4	96.6
Cash contributions to educational institutions	100.0	0.7	0.7	98.6	0.5	99.5
Cash contributions to political organizations	100.0	1.0	1.0	98.0	0.9	99.1
Other cash gifts	100.0	4.4	3.2	92.3	7.9	92.1
PERSONAL INSURANCE AND PENSIONS	**100.0**	**3.6**	**7.4**	**89.0**	**7.1**	**92.9**
Life and other personal insurance	**100.0**	**3.2**	**8.8**	**87.9**	**4.1**	**95.9**
Life, endowment, annuity, other personal insurance	100.0	3.3	9.0	87.7	4.2	95.8
Other nonhealth insurance	100.0	1.9	5.3	92.9	1.8	98.1
Pensions and Social Security	**100.0**	**3.7**	**7.2**	**89.1**	**7.4**	**92.6**
Deductions for government retirement	100.0	1.9	11.5	86.6	3.7	96.3
Deductions for railroad retirement	100.0	–	–	99.9	–	100.0
Deductions for private pensions	100.0	3.9	5.7	90.4	4.4	95.6
Nonpayroll deposit to retirement plans	100.0	2.9	3.1	94.0	3.2	96.8
Deductions for Social Security	100.0	3.8	7.9	88.3	8.6	91.4
PERSONAL TAXES	**100.0**	**3.5**	**4.5**	**91.6**	**2.7**	**97.7**
Federal income taxes	100.0	3.3	3.8	92.5	2.3	98.2
State and local income taxes	100.0	4.0	7.5	88.3	4.0	96.3
Other taxes	100.0	4.0	3.6	92.1	3.8	96.5

Note: Other races include Native Americans and Pacific Islanders. Numbers may not add to total because of rounding. (–) means sample is too small to make a reliable estimate.
Source: Calculations by New Strategist based on the 2003 Consumer Expenditure Survey

Table 4.21 Financial: Average spending by region, 2003

(average annual spending of consumer units (CU) on financial products and services, cash contributions, and miscellaneous items, by region in which consumer unit lives, 2003)

	total consumer units	Northeast	Midwest	South	West
Number of consumer units (000)	115,356	22,182	26,438	41,325	25,412
Average number of persons per CU	2.5	2.4	2.5	2.5	2.6
Average before-tax income of CU	$48,596.00	$54,219.00	$49,591.00	$44,461.00	$49,667.00
Average spending of CU, total	40,817.33	42,162.29	40,280.39	37,624.55	45,380.67
FINANCIAL PRODUCTS AND SERVICES	605.93	547.90	646.73	555.89	694.95
Miscellaneous fees	8.08	12.69	7.97	6.82	6.16
Lottery and gambling losses	35.37	38.46	42.96	26.53	38.66
Legal fees	108.09	118.64	113.63	100.02	106.26
Funeral expenses	57.51	33.25	79.30	58.60	54.25
Safe deposit box rental	3.48	4.01	4.13	2.94	3.21
Checking accounts, other bank service charges	20.01	18.39	18.24	19.60	23.94
Cemetery lots, vaults, and maintenance fees	13.27	14.94	15.69	13.43	9.03
Accounting fees	46.44	47.05	50.93	34.41	60.79
Miscellaneous personal services	26.87	13.64	28.35	26.53	37.40
Finance charges, except mortgage and vehicles	190.88	159.46	186.42	180.86	239.23
Occupational expenses	34.69	35.08	45.32	18.19	50.12
Expenses for other properties	53.45	45.39	47.90	61.36	53.42
Credit card memberships	2.34	2.93	1.46	1.67	3.85
Shopping club membership fees	4.92	3.96	3.85	3.83	8.63
CASH CONTRIBUTIONS	1,369.89	1,160.96	1,469.15	1,344.09	1,490.95
Support for college students	64.39	74.01	71.00	61.88	53.20
Alimony expenditures	42.18	76.57	23.41	38.16	38.22
Child support expenditures	166.12	145.23	187.67	156.95	176.86
Gifts to non–CU members of stocks, bonds, and mutual funds	24.68	9.65	23.01	30.63	29.88
Cash contributions to charities and other organizations	139.45	130.65	163.63	126.28	143.39
Cash contributions to church, religious organizations	564.41	385.38	643.76	587.84	600.01
Cash contributions to educational institutions	60.37	19.54	62.05	97.06	34.59
Cash contributions to political organizations	6.62	5.11	6.43	7.72	6.35
Other cash gifts	301.67	314.82	288.19	237.56	408.46
PERSONAL INSURANCE AND PENSIONS	4,055.24	4,308.46	4,294.99	3,689.84	4,178.98
Life and other personal insurance	397.30	453.51	423.24	381.24	347.34
Life, endowment, annuity, other personal insurance	380.22	435.70	401.19	367.32	330.93
Other nonhealth insurance	17.08	17.81	22.05	13.92	16.41
Pensions and Social Security	3,657.94	3,854.95	3,871.74	3,308.61	3,831.65
Deductions for government retirement	69.64	56.17	89.29	58.24	79.51
Deductions for railroad retirement	3.42	5.66	2.41	3.64	2.15
Deductions for private pensions	481.22	455.64	554.21	436.81	499.85
Nonpayroll deposit to retirement plans	388.15	474.59	459.97	267.12	434.81
Deductions for Social Security	2,715.50	2,862.88	2,765.86	2,542.80	2,815.33
PERSONAL TAXES	2,531.74	2,294.05	2,853.33	2,267.74	2,839.67
Federal income taxes	1,843.07	1,535.95	1,904.20	1,786.38	2,132.98
State and local income taxes	501.53	543.19	672.07	348.16	545.61
Other taxes	187.14	214.91	277.05	133.2	161.08

Note: Subcategories may not add to total because some are not shown.
Source: Bureau of Labor Statistics, unpublished tables from the 2003 Consumer Expenditure Survey

Table 4.22 Financial: Indexed spending by region, 2003

(indexed average annual spending of consumer units (CU) on financial products and services, cash contributions, and miscellaneous items, by region in which consumer unit lives, 2003; index definition: an index of 100 is the average for all consumer units; an index of 132 means that spending by consumer units in that group is 32 percent above the average for all consumer units; an index of 68 indicates spending that is 32 percent below the average for all consumer units)

	total consumer units	Northeast	Midwest	South	West
Average spending of CU, total	$40,817	$42,162	$40,280	$37,625	$45,381
Average spending of CU, index	100	103	99	92	111
FINANCIAL PRODUCTS AND SERVICES	**100**	**90**	**107**	**92**	**115**
Miscellaneous fees	100	157	99	84	76
Lottery and gambling losses	100	109	121	75	109
Legal fees	100	110	105	93	98
Funeral expenses	100	58	138	102	94
Safe deposit box rental	100	115	119	84	92
Checking accounts, other bank service charges	100	92	91	98	120
Cemetery lots, vaults, and maintenance fees	100	113	118	101	68
Accounting fees	100	101	110	74	131
Miscellaneous personal services	100	51	106	99	139
Finance charges, except mortgage and vehicles	100	84	98	95	125
Occupational expenses	100	101	131	52	144
Expenses for other properties	100	85	90	115	100
Credit card memberships	100	125	62	71	165
Shopping club membership fees	100	80	78	78	175
CASH CONTRIBUTIONS	**100**	**85**	**107**	**98**	**109**
Support for college students	100	115	110	96	83
Alimony expenditures	100	182	56	90	91
Child support expenditures	100	87	113	94	106
Gifts to non–CU members of stocks, bonds, and mutual funds	100	39	93	124	121
Cash contributions to charities and other organizations	100	94	117	91	103
Cash contributions to church, religious organizations	100	58	114	104	106
Cash contributions to educational institutions	100	32	103	161	57
Cash contributions to political organizations	100	77	97	117	96
Other cash gifts	100	104	96	79	135
PERSONAL INSURANCE AND PENSIONS	**100**	**106**	**106**	**91**	**103**
Life and other personal insurance	**100**	**114**	**107**	**96**	**87**
Life, endowment, annuity, other personal insurance	100	115	106	97	87
Other nonhealth insurance	100	104	129	81	96
Pensions and Social Security	**100**	**105**	**106**	**90**	**105**
Deductions for government retirement	100	81	128	84	114
Deductions for railroad retirement	100	165	70	106	63
Deductions for private pensions	100	95	115	91	104
Nonpayroll deposit to retirement plans	100	122	119	69	112
Deductions for Social Security	100	105	102	94	104
PERSONAL TAXES	**100**	**91**	**113**	**90**	**112**
Federal income taxes	100	83	103	97	116
State and local income taxes	100	108	134	69	109
Other taxes	100	115	148	71	86

Source: Calculations by New Strategist based on the 2003 Consumer Expenditure Survey

Table 4.23 Financial: Total spending by region, 2003

(total annual spending on financial products and services, cash contributions, and miscellaneous items, by region in which consumer units live, 2003; numbers in thousands)

	total consumer units	Northeast	Midwest	South	West
Number of consumer units	115,356	22,182	26,438	41,325	25,412
Total spending of all consumer units	$4,708,523,919	$935,243,917	$1,064,932,951	$1,554,834,529	$1,153,213,586
FINANCIAL PRODUCTS AND SERVICES	**69,897,661**	**12,153,518**	**17,098,248**	**22,972,154**	**17,660,069**
Miscellaneous fees	932,076	281,490	210,711	281,837	156,538
Lottery and gambling losses	4,080,142	853,120	1,135,776	1,096,352	982,428
Legal fees	12,468,830	2,631,672	3,004,150	4,133,327	2,700,279
Funeral expenses	6,634,124	737,552	2,096,533	2,421,645	1,378,601
Safe deposit box rental	401,439	88,950	109,189	121,496	81,573
Checking accounts, other bank service charges	2,308,274	407,927	482,229	809,970	608,363
Cemetery lots, vaults, and maintenance fees	1,530,774	331,399	414,812	554,995	229,470
Accounting fees	5,357,133	1,043,663	1,346,487	1,421,993	1,544,795
Miscellaneous personal services	3,099,616	302,562	749,517	1,096,352	950,409
Finance charges, except mortgage and vehicles	22,019,153	3,537,142	4,928,572	7,474,040	6,079,313
Occupational expenses	4,001,700	778,145	1,198,170	751,702	1,273,649
Expenses for other properties	6,165,778	1,006,841	1,266,380	2,535,702	1,357,509
Credit card memberships	269,933	64,993	38,599	69,013	97,836
Shopping club membership fees	567,552	87,841	101,786	158,275	219,306
CASH CONTRIBUTIONS	**158,025,031**	**25,752,415**	**38,841,388**	**55,544,519**	**37,888,021**
Support for college students	7,427,773	1,641,690	1,877,098	2,557,191	1,351,918
Alimony expenditures	4,865,716	1,698,476	618,914	1,576,962	971,247
Child support expenditures	19,162,939	3,221,492	4,961,619	6,485,959	4,494,366
Gifts to non–CU members of stocks, bonds, and mutual funds	2,846,986	214,056	608,338	1,265,785	759,311
Cash contributions to charities and other organizations	16,086,394	2,898,078	4,326,050	5,218,521	3,643,827
Cash contributions to church, religious organizations	65,108,080	8,548,499	17,019,727	24,292,488	15,247,454
Cash contributions to educational institutions	6,964,042	433,436	1,640,478	4,011,005	879,001
Cash contributions to political organizations	763,657	113,350	169,996	319,029	161,366
Other cash gifts	34,799,445	6,983,337	7,619,167	9,817,167	10,379,786
PERSONAL INSURANCE AND PENSIONS	**467,796,265**	**95,570,260**	**113,550,946**	**152,482,638**	**106,196,240**
Life and other personal insurance	**45,830,939**	**10,059,759**	**11,189,619**	**15,754,743**	**8,826,604**
Life, endowment, annuity, other personal insurance	43,860,658	9,664,697	10,606,661	15,179,499	8,409,593
Other nonhealth insurance	1,970,280	395,061	582,958	575,244	417,011
Pensions and Social Security	**421,965,327**	**85,510,501**	**102,361,062**	**136,728,308**	**97,369,890**
Deductions for government retirement	8,033,392	1,245,963	2,360,649	2,406,768	2,020,508
Deductions for railroad retirement	394,518	125,550	63,716	150,423	54,636
Deductions for private pensions	55,511,614	10,107,006	14,652,204	18,051,173	12,702,188
Nonpayroll deposit to retirement plans	44,775,431	10,527,355	12,160,687	11,038,734	11,049,392
Deductions for Social Security	313,249,218	63,504,404	73,123,807	105,081,210	71,543,166
PERSONAL TAXES	**292,051,399**	**50,886,617**	**75,436,339**	**93,714,356**	**72,161,694**
Federal income taxes	212,609,183	34,070,443	50,343,240	73,822,154	54,203,288
State and local income taxes	57,854,495	12,049,041	17,768,187	14,387,712	13,865,041
Other taxes	21,587,722	4,767,134	7,324,648	5,504,490	4,093,365

Note: Numbers may not add to total because of rounding and missing subcategories.
Source: Calculations by New Strategist based on the 2003 Consumer Expenditure Survey

Table 4.24 Financial: Market shares by region, 2003

(percentage of total annual spending on financial products and services, cash contributions, and miscellaneous items accounted for by consumer units (CU) by region, 2003)

	total consumer units	Northeast	Midwest	South	West
Share of total consumer units	100.0%	19.2%	22.9%	35.8%	22.0%
Share of total before-tax income	100.0	21.5	23.4	32.8	22.5
Share of total spending	100.0	19.9	22.6	33.0	24.5
FINANCIAL PRODUCTS AND SERVICES	100.0	17.4	24.5	32.9	25.3
Miscellaneous fees	100.0	30.2	22.6	30.2	16.8
Lottery and gambling losses	100.0	20.9	27.8	26.9	24.1
Legal fees	100.0	21.1	24.1	33.1	21.7
Funeral expenses	100.0	11.1	31.6	36.5	20.8
Safe deposit box rental	100.0	22.2	27.2	30.3	20.3
Checking accounts, other bank service charges	100.0	17.7	20.9	35.1	26.4
Cemetery lots, vaults, and maintenance fees	100.0	21.6	27.1	36.3	15.0
Accounting fees	100.0	19.5	25.1	26.5	28.8
Miscellaneous personal services	100.0	9.8	24.2	35.4	30.7
Finance charges, except mortgage and vehicles	100.0	16.1	22.4	33.9	27.6
Occupational expenses	100.0	19.4	29.9	18.8	31.8
Expenses for other properties	100.0	16.3	20.5	41.1	22.0
Credit card memberships	100.0	24.1	14.3	25.6	36.2
Shopping club membership fees	100.0	15.5	17.9	27.9	38.6
CASH CONTRIBUTIONS	100.0	16.3	24.6	35.1	24.0
Support for college students	100.0	22.1	25.3	34.4	18.2
Alimony expenditures	100.0	34.9	12.7	32.4	20.0
Child support expenditures	100.0	16.8	25.9	33.8	23.5
Gifts to non–CU members of stocks, bonds, and mutual funds	100.0	7.5	21.4	44.5	26.7
Cash contributions to charities and other organizations	100.0	18.0	26.9	32.4	22.7
Cash contributions to church, religious organizations	100.0	13.1	26.1	37.3	23.4
Cash contributions to educational institutions	100.0	6.2	23.6	57.6	12.6
Cash contributions to political organizations	100.0	14.8	22.3	41.8	21.1
Other cash gifts	100.0	20.1	21.9	28.2	29.8
PERSONAL INSURANCE AND PENSIONS	100.0	20.4	24.3	32.6	22.7
Life and other personal insurance	100.0	21.9	24.4	34.4	19.3
Life, endowment, annuity, other personal insurance	100.0	22.0	24.2	34.6	19.2
Other nonhealth insurance	100.0	20.1	29.6	29.2	21.2
Pensions and Social Security	100.0	20.3	24.3	32.4	23.1
Deductions for government retirement	100.0	15.5	29.4	30.0	25.2
Deductions for railroad retirement	100.0	31.8	16.2	38.1	13.8
Deductions for private pensions	100.0	18.2	26.4	32.5	22.9
Nonpayroll deposit to retirement plans	100.0	23.5	27.2	24.7	24.7
Deductions for Social Security	100.0	20.3	23.3	33.5	22.8
PERSONAL TAXES	100.0	17.4	25.8	32.1	24.7
Federal income taxes	100.0	16.0	23.7	34.7	25.5
State and local income taxes	100.0	20.8	30.7	24.9	24.0
Other taxes	100.0	22.1	33.9	25.5	19.0

Note: Numbers may not add to total because of rounding.
Source: Calculations by New Strategist based on the 2003 Consumer Expenditure Survey

Table 4.25 Financial: Average spending by education, 2003

(average annual spending of consumer units (CU) on financial products and services, cash contributions, and miscellaneous items, by education of consumer unit reference person, 2003)

	total consumer units	less than high school graduate	high school graduate	some college	associate's degree	college graduate total	college graduate bachelor's degree	college graduate master's, professional, doctorate
Number of consumer units (000)	115,356	17,721	31,552	24,514	10,981	30,589	19,557	11,032
Average number of persons per CU	2.5	2.6	2.5	2.3	2.6	2.5	2.5	2.4
Average before-tax income of CU	$51,128.00	$25,028.00	$40,113.00	$45,113.00	$54,087.00	$81,842.00	$74,921.00	$93,948.00
Average spending of CU, total	40,817.33	23,901.14	33,955.56	37,912.41	44,547.12	58,480.00	54,725.85	65,202.73
FINANCIAL PRODUCTS AND SERVICES	**605.93**	**311.85**	**514.60**	**633.41**	**618.71**	**840.02**	**790.93**	**927.66**
Miscellaneous fees	8.08	1.67	11.55	9.34	12.11	5.47	1.79	12.53
Lottery and gambling losses	35.37	21.26	43.31	31.90	21.13	41.01	45.24	32.94
Legal fees	108.09	36.76	67.28	125.65	70.58	190.91	194.22	185.05
Funeral expenses	57.51	70.10	68.50	36.87	35.17	63.44	70.86	50.28
Safe deposit box rental	3.48	1.31	2.81	2.43	3.39	6.29	5.46	7.77
Checking accounts, other bank service charges	20.01	9.85	17.61	23.05	24.08	24.49	25.45	22.78
Cemetery lots, vaults, and maintenance fees	13.27	14.33	16.34	7.40	7.74	16.18	14.79	18.65
Accounting fees	46.44	20.74	37.70	35.83	52.36	76.71	75.43	78.99
Miscellaneous personal services	26.87	11.70	23.56	39.29	8.70	34.27	29.29	43.80
Finance charges, except mortgage and vehicles	190.88	91.77	152.63	227.24	253.32	236.20	210.63	281.53
Occupational expenses	34.69	10.87	24.26	39.21	43.62	52.41	39.17	75.90
Expenses for other properties	53.45	18.51	42.74	48.28	79.29	79.62	66.43	103.02
Credit card memberships	2.34	0.62	1.01	2.48	1.47	4.92	4.34	5.95
Shopping club membership fees	4.92	2.35	3.95	4.44	5.54	7.55	7.17	8.24
CASH CONTRIBUTIONS	**1,369.89**	**573.55**	**989.70**	**1,043.41**	**1,248.48**	**2,528.61**	**2,306.88**	**2,921.70**
Support for college students	64.39	10.66	32.77	46.15	60.39	144.18	124.80	178.53
Alimony expenditures	42.18	24.44	62.88	18.39	32.79	53.55	50.00	59.84
Child support expenditures	166.12	75.00	209.40	155.87	179.18	177.80	181.82	170.66
Gifts to non–CU members of stocks, bonds, and mutual funds	24.68	5.13	32.04	2.87	3.78	53.41	62.63	37.07
Cash contributions to charities and other organizations	139.45	21.00	42.54	81.34	100.81	368.47	310.03	472.09
Cash contributions to church, religious organizations	564.41	242.52	372.26	482.47	538.76	1,023.95	915.16	1,216.81
Cash contributions to educational institutions	60.37	0.86	3.69	31.59	24.62	189.22	190.97	186.11
Cash contributions to political organizations	6.62	0.30	2.06	5.58	5.99	16.04	11.14	24.72
Other cash gifts	301.67	193.63	232.06	219.16	302.17	502.00	460.33	575.88
PERSONAL INSURANCE AND PENSIONS	**4,055.24**	**1,518.53**	**2,895.46**	**3,387.86**	**4,590.39**	**7,063.84**	**6,320.96**	**8,380.86**
Life and other personal insurance	**397.30**	**179.96**	**334.22**	**302.78**	**416.82**	**657.00**	**587.02**	**781.07**
Life, endowment, annuity, other personal insurance	380.22	171.63	318.98	287.33	402.43	630.68	564.76	747.56
Other nonhealth insurance	17.08	8.33	15.24	15.45	14.39	26.32	22.26	33.50
Pensions and Social Security	**3,657.94**	**1,338.56**	**2,561.24**	**3,085.08**	**4,173.57**	**6,406.84**	**5,733.94**	**7,599.79**
Deductions for government retirement	69.64	7.51	36.07	52.49	84.01	148.85	119.66	200.61
Deductions for railroad retirement	3.42	–	2.51	5.48	6.57	3.56	5.57	–
Deductions for private pensions	481.22	74.35	231.68	364.36	533.36	1,049.28	912.14	1,292.39
Nonpayroll deposit to retirement plans	388.15	58.47	162.70	254.46	387.99	918.91	665.79	1,367.64
Deductions for Social Security	2,715.50	1,198.24	2,128.28	2,408.30	3,161.63	4,286.24	4,030.78	4,739.15
PERSONAL TAXES	**2,531.74**	**311.78**	**1,855.13**	**1,808.82**	**2,561.12**	**5,126.62**	**4,546.38**	**6,141.53**
Federal income taxes	1,843.07	112.54	1,386.35	1,257.12	1,799.03	3,835.20	3,380.59	4,630.36
State and local income taxes	501.53	123.81	310.32	414.67	533.39	982.75	890.30	1,144.46
Other taxes	187.14	75.43	158.46	137.03	228.70	308.67	275.49	366.71

Note: Subcategories may not add to total because some are not shown. (–) means sample is too small to make a reliable estimate.
Source: Bureau of Labor Statistics, unpublished tables from the 2003 Consumer Expenditure Survey

Table 4.26 Financial: Indexed spending by education, 2003

(indexed average annual spending of consumer units (CU) on financial products and services, cash contributions, and miscellaneous items, by education of consumer unit reference person, 2003; index definition: an index of 100 is the average for all consumer units; an index of 132 means that spending by consumer units in that group is 32 percent above the average for all consumer units; an index of 68 indicates spending that is 32 percent below the average for all consumer units)

	total consumer units	less than high school graduate	high school graduate	some college	associate's degree	college graduate total	college graduate bachelor's degree	college graduate master's, professional, doctorate
Average spending of CU, total	$40,817	$23,901	$33,956	$37,912	$44,547	$58,480	$54,726	$65,203
Average spending of CU, index	100	59	83	93	109	143	134	160
FINANCIAL PRODUCTS AND SERVICES	**100**	**51**	**85**	**105**	**102**	**139**	**131**	**153**
Miscellaneous fees	100	21	143	116	150	68	22	155
Lottery and gambling losses	100	60	122	90	60	116	128	93
Legal fees	100	34	62	116	65	177	180	171
Funeral expenses	100	122	119	54	61	110	123	87
Safe deposit box rental	100	38	81	70	97	181	157	223
Checking accounts, other bank service charges	100	49	88	115	120	122	127	114
Cemetery lots, vaults, and maintenance fees	100	108	123	56	58	122	111	141
Accounting fees	100	45	81	77	113	165	162	170
Miscellaneous personal services	100	44	88	146	32	128	109	163
Finance charges, except mortgage and vehicles	100	48	80	119	133	124	110	147
Occupational expenses	100	31	70	113	126	151	113	219
Expenses for other properties	100	35	80	90	148	149	124	193
Credit card memberships	100	26	43	106	63	210	185	254
Shopping club membership fees	100	48	80	90	113	153	146	167
CASH CONTRIBUTIONS	**100**	**42**	**72**	**76**	**91**	**185**	**168**	**213**
Support for college students	100	17	51	72	94	224	194	277
Alimony expenditures	100	58	149	44	78	127	119	142
Child support expenditures	100	45	126	94	108	107	109	103
Gifts to non–CU members of stocks, bonds, and mutual funds	100	21	130	12	15	216	254	150
Cash contributions to charities and other organizations	100	15	31	58	72	264	222	339
Cash contributions to church, religious organizations	100	43	66	85	95	181	162	216
Cash contributions to educational institutions	100	1	6	52	41	313	316	308
Cash contributions to political organizations	100	5	31	84	90	242	168	373
Other cash gifts	100	64	77	73	100	166	153	191
PERSONAL INSURANCE AND PENSIONS	**100**	**37**	**71**	**84**	**113**	**174**	**156**	**207**
Life and other personal insurance	**100**	**45**	**84**	**76**	**105**	**165**	**148**	**197**
Life, endowment, annuity, other personal insurance	100	45	84	76	106	166	149	197
Other nonhealth insurance	100	49	89	90	84	154	130	196
Pensions and Social Security	**100**	**37**	**70**	**84**	**114**	**175**	**157**	**208**
Deductions for government retirement	100	11	52	75	121	214	172	288
Deductions for railroad retirement	100	–	73	160	192	104	163	–
Deductions for private pensions	100	15	48	76	111	218	190	269
Nonpayroll deposit to retirement plans	100	15	42	66	100	237	172	352
Deductions for Social Security	100	44	78	89	116	158	148	175
PERSONAL TAXES	**100**	**12**	**73**	**71**	**101**	**202**	**180**	**243**
Federal income taxes	100	6	75	68	98	208	183	251
State and local income taxes	100	25	62	83	106	196	178	228
Other taxes	100	40	85	73	122	165	147	196

Note: (–) means sample is too small to make a reliable estimate.
Source: Calculations by New Strategist based on the 2003 Consumer Expenditure Survey

Table 4.27 Financial: Total spending by education, 2003

(total annual spending on financial products and services, cash contributions, and miscellaneous items, by consumer unit (CU) educational attainment group, 2003; numbers in thousands)

	total consumer units	less than high school graduate	high school graduate	some college	associate's degree	college graduate total	college graduate bachelor's degree	college graduate master's, professional, doctorate
Number of consumer units	115,356	17,721	31,552	24,514	10,981	30,589	19,557	11,032
Total spending of all CUs	$4,708,523,919	$423,552,102	$1,071,365,829	$929,384,819	$489,171,925	$1,788,844,720	$1,070,273,448	$719,316,517
FINANCIAL PRODUCTS AND SERVICES	**69,897,661**	**5,526,294**	**16,236,659**	**15,527,413**	**6,794,055**	**25,695,372**	**15,468,218**	**10,233,945**
Miscellaneous fees	932,076	29,594	364,426	228,961	132,980	167,322	35,007	138,231
Lottery and gambling losses	4,080,142	376,748	1,366,517	781,997	232,029	1,254,455	884,759	363,394
Legal fees	12,468,830	651,424	2,122,819	3,080,184	775,039	5,839,746	3,798,361	2,041,472
Funeral expenses	6,634,124	1,242,242	2,161,312	903,831	386,202	1,940,566	1,385,809	554,689
Safe deposit box rental	401,439	23,215	88,661	59,569	37,226	192,405	106,781	85,719
Checking accounts, other bank service charges	2,308,274	174,552	555,631	555,048	264,422	749,125	497,726	251,309
Cemetery lots, vaults, and maintenance fees	1,530,774	253,942	515,560	181,404	84,993	494,930	289,248	205,747
Accounting fees	5,357,133	367,534	1,189,510	878,337	574,965	2,346,482	1,475,185	871,418
Miscellaneous personal services	3,099,616	207,336	743,365	963,155	95,535	1,048,285	572,825	483,202
Finance charges, except mortgage and vehicles	22,019,153	1,626,256	4,815,782	5,570,561	2,781,707	7,225,122	4,119,291	3,105,839
Occupational expenses	4,001,700	192,627	765,452	961,194	478,991	1,603,169	766,048	837,329
Expenses for other properties	6,165,778	328,016	1,348,532	1,183,536	870,683	2,435,496	1,299,172	1,136,517
Credit card memberships	269,933	10,987	31,868	60,795	16,142	150,498	84,877	65,640
Shopping club membership fees	567,552	41,644	124,630	108,842	60,835	230,947	140,224	90,904
CASH CONTRIBUTIONS	**158,025,031**	**10,163,880**	**31,227,014**	**25,578,153**	**13,709,559**	**77,347,651**	**45,115,652**	**32,232,194**
Support for college students	7,427,773	188,906	1,033,959	1,131,321	663,143	4,410,322	2,440,714	1,969,543
Alimony expenditures	4,865,716	433,101	1,983,990	450,812	360,067	1,638,041	977,850	660,155
Child support expenditures	19,162,939	1,329,075	6,606,989	3,320,997	1,967,576	5,438,724	3,555,854	1,882,721
Gifts to non–CU members of stocks, bonds, and mutual funds	2,846,986	90,909	1,010,926	70,355	41,508	1,633,758	1,224,855	408,956
Cash contributions to charities and other organizations	16,086,394	372,141	1,342,222	1,993,969	1,106,995	11,271,129	6,063,257	5,208,097
Cash contributions to church, religious organizations	65,108,080	4,297,697	11,745,548	11,827,270	5,916,124	31,321,607	17,897,784	13,423,848
Cash contributions to educational institutions	6,964,042	15,240	116,427	774,397	270,352	5,788,051	3,734,800	2,053,166
Cash contributions to political organizations	763,657	5,316	64,997	136,788	65,776	490,648	217,865	272,711
Other cash gifts	34,799,445	3,431,317	7,321,957	5,372,488	3,318,129	15,355,678	9,002,674	6,353,108
PERSONAL INSURANCE AND PENSIONS	**467,796,265**	**26,909,870**	**91,357,554**	**83,050,000**	**50,407,073**	**216,075,802**	**123,619,015**	**92,457,648**
Life and other personal insurance	**45,830,939**	**3,189,071**	**10,545,309**	**7,422,349**	**4,577,100**	**20,096,973**	**11,480,350**	**8,616,764**
Life, endowment, annuity, other personal insurance	43,860,658	3,041,455	10,064,457	7,043,608	4,419,084	19,291,871	11,045,011	8,247,082
Other nonhealth insurance	1,970,280	147,616	480,852	378,741	158,017	805,102	435,339	369,572
Pensions and Social Security	**421,965,327**	**23,720,622**	**80,812,244**	**75,627,651**	**45,829,972**	**195,978,829**	**112,138,665**	**83,840,883**
Deductions for government retirement	8,033,392	133,085	1,138,081	1,286,740	922,514	4,553,173	2,340,191	2,213,130
Deductions for railroad retirement	394,518	–	79,196	134,337	72,145	108,897	108,932	–
Deductions for private pensions	55,511,614	1,317,556	7,309,967	8,931,921	5,856,826	32,096,426	17,838,722	14,257,646
Nonpayroll deposit to retirement plans	44,775,431	1,036,147	5,133,510	6,237,832	4,260,518	28,108,538	13,020,855	15,087,804
Deductions for Social Security	313,249,218	21,234,011	67,151,491	59,037,066	34,717,859	131,111,795	78,829,964	52,282,303
PERSONAL TAXES	**292,051,399**	**5,525,053**	**58,533,062**	**44,341,413**	**28,123,659**	**156,818,179**	**88,913,554**	**67,753,359**
Federal income taxes	212,609,183	1,994,321	43,742,115	30,817,040	19,755,148	117,314,933	66,114,199	51,082,132
State and local income taxes	57,854,495	2,194,037	9,791,217	10,165,220	5,857,156	30,061,340	17,411,597	12,625,683
Other taxes	21,587,722	1,336,695	4,999,730	3,359,153	2,511,355	9,441,907	5,387,758	4,045,545

Note: Numbers may not add to total because of rounding and missing subcategories. (–) means sample is too small to make a reliable estimate.
Source: Calculations by New Strategist based on the 2003 Consumer Expenditure Survey

Table 4.28 Financial: Market shares by education, 2003

(percentage of total annual spending on financial products and services, cash contributions, and miscellaneous items accounted for by consumer unit educational attainment groups, 2003)

	total consumer units	less than high school graduate	high school graduate	some college	associate's degree	college graduate total	bachelor's degree	master's, professional, doctorate
Share of total consumer units	100.0%	15.4%	27.4%	21.3%	9.5%	26.5%	17.0%	9.6%
Share of total before-tax income	100.0	7.5	21.5	18.8	10.1	42.4	24.8	17.6
Share of total spending	100.0	9.0	22.8	19.7	10.4	38.0	22.7	15.3
FINANCIAL PRODUCTS AND SERVICES	100.0	7.9	23.2	22.2	9.7	36.8	22.1	14.6
Miscellaneous fees	100.0	3.2	39.1	24.6	14.3	18.0	3.8	14.8
Lottery and gambling losses	100.0	9.2	33.5	19.2	5.7	30.7	21.7	8.9
Legal fees	100.0	5.2	17.0	24.7	6.2	46.8	30.5	16.4
Funeral expenses	100.0	18.7	32.6	13.6	5.8	29.3	20.9	8.4
Safe deposit box rental	100.0	5.8	22.1	14.8	9.3	47.9	26.6	21.4
Checking accounts, other bank service charges	100.0	7.6	24.1	24.5	11.5	32.5	21.6	10.9
Cemetery lots, vaults, and maintenance fees	100.0	16.6	33.7	11.9	5.6	32.3	18.9	13.4
Accounting fees	100.0	6.9	22.2	16.4	10.7	43.8	27.5	16.3
Miscellaneous personal services	100.0	6.7	24.0	31.1	3.1	33.8	18.5	15.6
Finance charges, except mortgage and vehicles	100.0	7.4	21.9	25.3	12.6	32.8	18.7	14.1
Occupational expenses	100.0	4.8	19.1	24.0	12.0	40.1	19.1	20.9
Expenses for other properties	100.0	5.3	21.9	19.2	14.1	39.5	21.1	18.4
Credit card memberships	100.0	4.1	11.8	22.5	6.0	55.8	31.4	24.3
Shopping club membership fees	100.0	7.3	22.0	19.2	10.7	40.7	24.7	16.0
CASH CONTRIBUTIONS	100.0	6.4	19.8	16.2	8.7	48.9	28.5	20.4
Support for college students	100.0	2.5	13.9	15.2	8.9	59.4	32.9	26.5
Alimony expenditures	100.0	8.9	40.8	9.3	7.4	33.7	20.1	13.6
Child support expenditures	100.0	6.9	34.5	19.9	10.3	28.4	18.6	9.8
Gifts to non–CU members of stocks, bonds, and mutual funds	100.0	3.2	35.5	2.5	1.5	57.4	43.0	14.4
Cash contributions to charities and other organizations	100.0	2.3	8.3	12.4	6.9	70.1	37.7	32.4
Cash contributions to church, religious organizations	100.0	6.6	18.0	18.2	9.1	48.1	27.5	20.6
Cash contributions to educational institutions	100.0	0.2	1.7	11.1	3.9	83.1	53.6	29.5
Cash contributions to political organizations	100.0	0.7	8.5	17.9	8.6	64.2	28.5	35.7
Other cash gifts	100.0	9.9	21.0	15.4	9.5	44.1	25.9	18.3
PERSONAL INSURANCE AND PENSIONS	100.0	5.8	19.5	17.8	10.8	46.2	26.4	19.8
Life and other personal insurance	100.0	7.0	23.0	16.2	10.0	43.9	25.0	18.8
Life, endowment, annuity, other personal insurance	100.0	6.9	22.9	16.1	10.1	44.0	25.2	18.8
Other nonhealth insurance	100.0	7.5	24.4	19.2	8.0	40.9	22.1	18.8
Pensions and Social Security	100.0	5.6	19.2	17.9	10.9	46.4	26.6	19.9
Deductions for government retirement	100.0	1.7	14.2	16.0	11.5	56.7	29.1	27.5
Deductions for railroad retirement	100.0	–	20.1	34.1	18.3	27.6	27.6	–
Deductions for private pensions	100.0	2.4	13.2	16.1	10.6	57.8	32.1	25.7
Nonpayroll deposit to retirement plans	100.0	2.3	11.5	13.9	9.5	62.8	29.1	33.7
Deductions for Social Security	100.0	6.8	21.4	18.8	11.1	41.9	25.2	16.7
PERSONAL TAXES	100.0	1.9	20.0	15.2	9.6	53.7	30.4	23.2
Federal income taxes	100.0	0.9	20.6	14.5	9.3	55.2	31.1	24.0
State and local income taxes	100.0	3.8	16.9	17.6	10.1	52.0	30.1	21.8
Other taxes	100.0	6.2	23.2	15.6	11.6	43.7	25.0	18.7

Note: Numbers may not add to total because of rounding. (–) means sample is too small to make a reliable estimate.
Source: Calculations by New Strategist based on the 2003 Consumer Expenditure Survey

Spending on Food and Alcoholic Beverages, 2003

The average household spent 3 percent less on food away from home (primarily sit-down meals and take-outs from restaurants) in 2003 than in 2000, after adjusting for inflation. Spending on food at home (groceries) also fell 3 percent during those years. Overall, Americans devoted 13.1 percent of their expenditures to food in 2003, down from 13.6 percent in 2000. Spending on alcoholic beverages fell 1.5 percent between 2000 and 2003, after adjusting for inflation.

Householders aged 45 to 54 spend the most on food, both at home and away from home. In 2003, householders aged 45 to 54 spent an average of $6,381 on food, 20 percent more than the average household. When eating out, householders aged 25 to 44 spend the most on breakfast, lunch, and dinner at fast-food restaurants. Householders aged 45 to 54 are the biggest spenders on lunch and dinner at full-service restaurants, while householders aged 65 to 74 spend the most on breakfasts at full-service restaurants. Householders under age 25 spend the most on alcoholic beverages.

Households with incomes of $100,000 or more spend 46 percent more than the average household on food at home. They spend more than twice the average on restaurant meals and on alcoholic beverages. Only 12 percent of households have incomes of $100,000 or more, but they control one-third of consumer spending on dinners in full-service restaurants and 45 percent of spending on wine consumed at home.

Married couples with adult children at home spend more on food than any other household type—$7,937 in 2003. These households are not only larger than average, but also have the highest incomes. Married couples without children at home (most of them empty-nesters) and couples with adult children at home are the best customers of full-service restaurants. Married couples with school-aged children spend 44 percent more than the average household on fast-food lunches and 67 percent more on fast-food dinners. Spending on alcoholic beverages is highest among couples without children at home—22 percent above average.

Hispanic households spend more on food at home than any other racial or ethnic group—15 percent more than the average household in 2003. Behind the higher spending of Hispanics is their larger household size of 3.3 people versus 2.5 in the average household. Asians spend more on food away from home than any other racial or ethnic group—35 percent more than the average household. They spend 75 percent more than average on lunch at full-service restaurants. Whites and others spend the most on alcoholic beverages—9 percent more than average.

Spending on food at home is above average in the Northeast and West and below average in the Midwest and South. Households in the Northeast spend 10 percent more than average on food away from home, while households in the West spend 11 percent more. Spending on wine consumed at home is 18 percent above average in the Northeast and 20 percent above average in the West. Spending on beer consumed at home is highest in the Midwest, at 16 percent above average. Spending on alcoholic beverages is 12 percent below average in the South.

Because college graduates dominate the affluent, they account for a large share of the food-away-from-home market. College graduates control 44 percent of consumer spending on dinners at full-service restaurants, for example, a much greater percentage than their 27 percent share of all households. They account for 53 percent of household spending on wine consumed at home, but for only 27 percent of spending on beer consumed at home.

Table 5.1 Food and Alcohol: Average spending by age, 2003

(average annual spending of consumer units (CU) on food and alcoholic beverages, by age of consumer unit reference person, 2003)

	total consumer units	under 25	25 to 34	35 to 44	45 to 54	55 to 64	65 to 74	75+
Number of consumer units (000)	115,356	8,584	19,737	24,413	23,131	16,580	11,495	11,417
Average number of persons per CU	2.5	1.8	2.9	3.2	2.6	2.1	1.9	1.5
Average before-tax income of CU	$51,128.00	$20,680.00	$50,389.00	$61,091.00	$68,028.00	$58,672.00	$35,314.00	$25,492.00
Average spending of CU, total	40,817.33	22,395.53	40,525.22	47,175.06	50,100.86	44,190.65	33,629.17	25,016.38
Food, average spending	**5,339.50**	**3,401.29**	**5,317.89**	**6,272.20**	**6,381.31**	**5,530.09**	**4,544.42**	**3,208.44**
Alcoholic beverages, average spending	**391.21**	**509.04**	**446.21**	**423.90**	**476.58**	**371.90**	**236.70**	**128.20**
FOOD AT HOME	**3,128.78**	**1,765.69**	**2,975.71**	**3,600.17**	**3,693.40**	**3,314.80**	**2,888.42**	**2,240.59**
Cereals and bakery products	**441.72**	**255.72**	**421.22**	**523.11**	**508.90**	**426.87**	**413.88**	**357.88**
Cereals and cereal products	150.14	95.89	155.72	183.25	167.57	140.36	128.89	110.30
Flour	7.32	3.76	7.01	7.51	9.12	7.46	6.54	7.20
Prepared flour mixes	12.79	6.04	11.48	15.67	15.17	12.28	12.80	9.92
Ready-to-eat and cooked cereals	86.21	55.41	89.38	108.45	92.57	75.67	75.78	69.33
Rice	16.05	11.98	17.79	18.43	18.74	17.27	11.78	7.84
Pasta, cornmeal, and other cereal products	27.75	18.70	30.06	33.19	31.98	27.67	21.99	16.01
Bakery products	291.58	159.83	265.50	339.86	341.32	286.51	284.99	247.59
Bread	82.55	43.41	76.85	90.48	94.60	82.87	88.45	74.84
White bread	33.50	19.64	33.49	40.62	36.25	32.02	32.29	26.63
Bread, other than white	49.06	23.77	43.36	49.86	58.35	50.85	56.16	48.22
Crackers and cookies	69.58	39.26	60.02	77.31	85.91	67.70	70.28	61.62
Cookies	45.06	26.11	38.67	50.67	56.65	42.75	44.16	39.16
Crackers	24.52	13.15	21.34	26.64	29.25	24.95	26.12	22.46
Frozen and refrigerated bakery products	24.56	15.16	22.03	31.50	28.08	24.27	20.82	18.37
Other bakery products	114.89	62.01	106.60	140.57	132.74	111.67	105.44	92.75
Biscuits and rolls	37.24	17.34	32.06	44.62	46.12	37.18	36.85	28.00
Cakes and cupcakes	36.71	24.07	37.13	46.50	42.40	32.73	28.63	26.73
Bread and cracker products	3.57	2.09	2.99	3.53	4.22	4.68	3.48	3.03
Sweetrolls, coffee cakes, doughnuts	27.65	12.87	27.42	35.71	28.48	26.75	25.16	24.50
Pies, tarts, turnovers	9.72	5.64	6.99	10.21	11.52	10.34	11.32	10.49
Meats, poultry, fish, and eggs	**824.58**	**438.25**	**768.84**	**932.62**	**1,002.27**	**914.46**	**757.57**	**557.74**
Beef	245.55	131.23	226.75	265.02	320.38	287.27	225.63	127.83
Ground beef	89.27	54.14	85.76	108.54	106.80	91.28	80.47	50.14
Roast	39.63	14.52	37.05	38.11	51.47	44.10	47.71	27.53
Chuck roast	13.37	4.38	16.58	12.23	16.13	14.94	15.62	6.73
Round roast	9.78	4.86	7.69	8.87	12.09	13.51	11.67	7.10
Other roast	16.48	5.28	12.78	17.01	23.24	15.65	20.41	13.71
Steak	94.16	53.17	88.77	97.31	129.05	118.15	74.72	40.21
Round steak	15.65	9.38	13.80	14.59	20.41	24.23	12.37	6.93
Sirloin steak	31.35	16.75	29.81	32.80	44.62	43.18	19.43	9.29
Other steak	47.17	27.03	45.15	49.91	64.02	50.73	42.92	24.00
Other beef	22.49	9.40	15.19	21.07	33.06	33.74	22.73	9.95
Pork	170.61	88.44	141.69	187.56	207.67	191.95	165.39	147.46
Bacon	31.15	14.66	26.41	35.45	38.74	34.71	30.20	23.15
Pork chops	34.14	22.12	34.64	39.57	43.00	33.64	26.99	20.12
Ham	38.15	23.61	25.90	39.36	44.18	48.78	34.19	45.35
Ham, not canned	37.04	22.75	25.10	37.68	43.11	47.84	32.62	44.93
Canned ham	1.10	0.86	0.80	1.68	1.07	0.94	1.57	0.42
Sausage	25.82	14.10	24.12	28.52	31.89	25.17	27.56	18.60
Other pork	41.36	13.95	30.61	44.66	49.86	49.66	46.45	40.24
Other meats	102.01	53.19	90.43	122.71	122.61	108.49	91.76	74.15
Frankfurters	22.74	13.49	20.78	27.27	27.57	24.09	17.70	16.76
Lunch meats (cold cuts)	69.31	33.38	62.59	84.04	82.28	73.35	64.49	49.59
Bologna, liverwurst, salami	21.65	10.50	19.17	25.58	24.56	23.84	21.72	17.03
Other lunch meats	47.66	22.88	43.42	58.45	57.72	49.52	42.77	32.56
Lamb, organ meats, and others	9.96	6.32	7.05	11.41	12.75	11.05	9.57	7.80
Poultry	144.61	85.16	151.28	173.92	171.25	142.33	114.31	94.07
Fresh and frozen chicken	116.42	74.03	126.95	141.17	137.17	111.45	87.07	70.55

	total consumer units	under 25	25 to 34	35 to 44	45 to 54	55 to 64	65 to 74	75+
Fresh and frozen whole chicken	$32.82	$19.97	$33.28	$41.11	$40.45	$26.78	$28.45	$21.23
Fresh and frozen chicken parts	83.60	54.06	93.66	100.06	96.72	84.67	58.62	49.32
Other poultry	28.20	11.13	24.33	32.75	34.08	30.88	27.24	23.52
Fish and seafood	124.46	56.91	123.55	139.44	140.37	147.91	121.59	82.21
Canned fish and seafood	16.40	7.86	13.97	17.12	17.41	22.14	17.85	14.07
Fresh fish and shellfish	71.88	31.38	76.15	81.81	84.32	81.26	61.76	45.24
Frozen fish and shellfish	36.17	17.67	33.42	40.52	38.63	44.51	41.98	22.90
Eggs	37.34	23.33	35.14	43.96	40.00	36.50	38.89	32.02
Dairy products	**328.00**	**192.55**	**317.30**	**387.62**	**377.60**	**326.44**	**307.97**	**242.94**
Fresh milk and cream	126.53	76.28	126.62	157.46	137.83	117.56	118.09	96.87
Fresh milk, all types	112.58	70.05	114.64	141.12	122.52	101.70	101.57	86.79
Cream	13.95	6.23	11.98	16.34	15.31	15.86	16.52	10.09
Other dairy products	201.47	116.27	190.68	230.16	239.77	208.88	189.89	146.07
Butter	18.08	9.92	14.53	20.73	21.24	20.47	19.94	13.05
Cheese	97.04	56.68	93.89	110.08	116.77	103.77	83.41	68.89
Ice cream and related products	58.09	34.90	55.07	61.53	69.67	57.22	62.65	46.36
Miscellaneous dairy products	28.26	14.76	27.18	37.82	32.08	27.41	23.88	17.77
Fruits and vegetables	**535.42**	**272.03**	**494.80**	**592.63**	**620.80**	**593.31**	**536.69**	**427.71**
Fresh fruits	170.88	75.46	157.17	190.18	204.05	188.89	171.51	132.55
Apples	32.73	18.47	32.29	37.63	39.54	33.45	29.93	21.55
Bananas	28.41	15.48	27.73	29.33	32.01	30.16	29.49	26.75
Oranges	18.34	8.13	17.45	22.58	21.36	17.95	15.73	15.78
Citrus fruits, excl. oranges	14.14	5.84	12.41	14.88	17.42	17.36	14.24	10.55
Other fresh fruits	77.26	27.54	67.28	85.76	93.72	89.97	82.12	57.93
Fresh vegetables	171.96	87.05	157.40	186.84	199.08	192.24	182.31	135.74
Potatoes	30.11	18.51	26.32	32.78	33.74	33.74	31.87	25.63
Lettuce	22.10	11.58	19.41	24.55	25.79	24.45	23.26	17.55
Tomatoes	32.18	16.93	34.22	34.34	36.92	33.79	30.68	25.08
Other fresh vegetables	87.57	40.04	77.46	95.17	102.63	100.26	96.50	67.48
Processed fruits	108.39	65.70	103.60	122.71	121.51	115.38	99.11	91.64
Frozen fruits and fruit juices	11.54	6.07	10.46	12.05	15.46	11.97	9.54	9.89
Frozen orange juice	4.64	2.79	4.07	5.53	5.15	5.27	4.49	3.34
Frozen fruits	3.66	1.43	2.69	2.75	6.26	4.02	2.59	4.29
Frozen fruit juices, excl. orange	3.24	1.85	3.70	3.78	4.05	2.68	2.45	2.26
Canned fruits	15.96	7.84	12.81	16.47	18.13	18.87	16.98	17.18
Dried fruits	6.30	1.88	4.55	6.92	7.11	8.11	6.00	7.64
Fresh fruit juice	20.77	13.13	19.50	23.66	23.17	21.77	21.85	15.18
Canned and bottled fruit juice	53.82	36.77	56.27	63.61	57.64	54.66	44.73	41.76
Processed vegetables	84.19	43.82	76.63	92.91	96.16	96.80	83.77	67.77
Frozen vegetables	26.79	14.60	25.00	32.34	29.07	30.14	23.64	21.26
Canned and dried vegetables and juices	57.40	29.22	51.63	60.57	67.09	66.66	60.13	46.51
Canned beans	12.56	7.00	11.38	13.20	14.84	15.00	12.32	9.58
Canned corn	6.89	3.79	6.30	7.50	8.08	6.62	7.72	4.96
Canned miscellaneous vegetables	18.55	8.97	15.43	18.10	22.35	22.25	20.88	16.96
Dried peas	0.37	0.57	0.46	0.19	0.62	0.32	0.28	0.13
Dried beans	2.31	0.69	2.17	2.10	3.04	2.90	2.00	2.20
Dried miscellaneous vegetables	7.51	3.27	6.49	9.68	7.83	9.23	6.29	6.05
Dried processed vegetables	0.42	0.21	1.05	0.24	0.24	0.40	0.62	–
Fresh and canned vegetable juices	8.67	4.59	7.55	9.42	9.99	9.73	9.99	6.61
Sugar and other sweets	**119.08**	**61.25**	**101.68**	**147.44**	**140.69**	**124.80**	**110.93**	**89.01**
Candy and chewing gum	75.31	36.00	64.79	95.67	92.32	78.59	62.89	53.34
Sugar	16.89	10.18	15.76	19.90	18.09	18.02	18.26	11.99
Artificial sweeteners	5.67	2.91	3.90	5.63	6.80	6.75	7.97	4.82
Jams, preserves, other sweets	21.20	12.15	17.23	26.24	23.48	21.44	21.80	18.86
Fats and oils	**85.73**	**44.22**	**75.72**	**95.11**	**101.20**	**93.02**	**88.61**	**70.07**
Margarine	9.61	4.36	7.19	9.20	11.05	11.82	12.47	9.81
Fats and oils	26.29	15.06	24.46	30.24	30.33	30.47	23.03	18.73
Salad dressings	26.17	16.75	24.11	28.44	32.70	26.51	25.53	18.70
Nondairy cream and imitation milk	11.02	3.20	7.35	12.01	13.40	12.81	14.47	10.56
Peanut butter	12.64	4.85	12.67	15.22	13.71	11.40	13.10	12.26

	total consumer units	under 25	25 to 34	35 to 44	45 to 54	55 to 64	65 to 74	75+
Miscellaneous foods	$489.60	$331.28	$509.49	$562.15	$570.28	$497.94	$416.30	$312.74
Frozen prepared foods	104.79	80.66	107.03	121.63	119.95	93.04	87.87	85.75
Frozen meals	34.85	22.89	32.29	34.67	39.23	33.74	38.22	38.46
Other frozen prepared foods	69.94	57.77	74.74	86.96	80.72	59.30	49.65	47.29
Canned and packaged soups	35.19	20.76	31.49	36.94	38.65	37.51	39.44	34.59
Potato chips, nuts, and other snacks	105.68	60.05	96.13	131.13	129.12	113.75	92.33	55.67
Potato chips and other snacks	79.27	52.05	76.92	106.24	94.54	78.77	58.40	35.89
Nuts	26.41	8.00	19.21	24.89	34.58	34.98	33.93	19.77
Condiments and seasonings	90.22	50.84	88.87	106.44	108.84	96.00	77.59	53.59
Salt, spices, and other seasonings	20.77	11.58	19.89	24.59	24.36	22.64	19.20	12.61
Olives, pickles, relishes	11.41	5.64	9.70	12.75	13.34	14.93	9.89	8.50
Sauces and gravies	38.46	23.80	40.92	47.52	46.90	36.88	28.88	20.09
Baking needs and miscellaneous products	19.58	9.82	18.36	21.58	24.24	21.54	19.61	12.39
Other canned/packaged prepared foods	153.71	118.98	185.97	166.02	173.72	157.65	119.07	83.14
Prepared salads	20.51	10.18	18.27	19.28	26.79	25.15	22.41	13.30
Prepared desserts	11.10	6.37	8.30	12.48	14.02	10.87	10.70	11.49
Baby food	26.76	44.18	58.25	28.25	18.15	16.19	5.92	7.66
Miscellaneous prepared foods	95.13	58.25	100.87	105.83	114.15	105.44	80.04	50.70
Nonalcoholic beverages	268.37	158.68	256.14	316.92	328.66	290.80	217.18	163.68
Cola	88.27	54.26	86.10	101.83	109.43	101.05	71.79	42.73
Other carbonated drinks	45.64	34.26	45.13	58.68	55.63	46.48	30.91	19.72
Coffee	38.08	11.30	26.40	38.91	48.66	46.00	46.12	36.58
Roasted coffee	25.70	8.27	18.55	25.87	33.65	30.89	30.70	22.64
Instant and freeze-dried coffee	12.38	3.03	7.84	13.04	15.01	15.11	15.42	13.94
Noncarbonated fruit-flavored drinks, incl. nonfrozen lemonade	19.29	13.82	23.33	27.30	21.35	15.80	10.77	8.35
Tea	17.71	10.38	14.27	16.69	24.17	23.97	14.64	12.27
Other nonalcoholic beverages and ice	58.72	34.57	60.84	72.86	69.25	57.30	38.87	43.70
Food prepared by CU on trips	36.28	11.72	30.53	42.56	43.01	47.16	39.29	18.82
FOOD AWAY FROM HOME	2,210.73	1,635.60	2,342.17	2,672.03	2,687.91	2,215.29	1,655.99	967.85
Meals at restaurants, carry-outs, other	1,831.97	1,406.19	2,037.30	2,234.62	2,176.38	1,706.30	1,379.39	829.69
Lunch	658.16	505.21	763.29	859.39	780.16	550.75	444.14	265.57
• At fast food, take-out, delivery, concession stands, buffet, cafeteria (other than employer, school cafeteria)	369.02	347.37	480.77	469.27	431.68	277.14	226.75	109.86
• At full-service restaurants	210.10	117.93	203.65	229.30	254.33	226.03	198.55	147.94
• At vending machines, mobile vendors	5.56	2.13	7.50	6.31	6.80	5.46	3.46	2.82
• At employer and school cafeterias	73.48	37.77	71.36	154.51	87.35	42.12	15.38	4.95
Dinner	737.51	498.38	784.50	847.75	877.28	790.27	611.42	355.18
• At fast food, take-out, delivery, concession stands, buffet, cafeteria (other than employer, school cafeteria)	215.93	175.48	264.57	291.05	248.48	179.50	120.37	77.85
• At full-service restaurants	517.42	307.00	516.44	554.11	623.28	609.65	488.56	274.93
At vending machines, mobile vendors	1.32	3.69	–	1.37	1.76	–	1.56	2.40
• At employer and school cafeterias	2.83	12.21	3.48	1.23	3.76	1.12	0.93	–
Snacks and nonalcoholic beverages	248.42	264.43	290.46	307.91	302.26	200.50	157.13	76.73
• At fast food, take-out, delivery, concession stands, buffet, cafeteria (other than employer, school cafeteria)	180.26	189.26	214.00	222.59	218.71	145.65	116.33	52.41
• At full-service restaurants	26.66	22.04	27.61	26.57	32.71	24.26	25.38	20.74
• At vending machines, mobile vendors	31.33	41.21	40.22	41.71	38.77	21.64	11.66	2.84
• At employer and school cafeterias	10.16	11.92	8.63	17.04	12.07	8.95	3.75	0.75
Breakfast and brunch	187.89	138.18	199.06	219.57	216.69	164.78	166.71	132.21
• At fast food, take-out, delivery, concession stands, buffet, cafeteria (other than employer, school cafeteria)	92.82	88.14	113.99	116.48	109.90	65.54	59.63	43.88
• At full-service restaurants	89.42	45.21	79.89	93.74	101.22	91.95	105.44	87.45
• At vending machines, mobile vendors	1.37	1.09	1.56	1.83	1.07	2.23	0.51	0.52
• At employer and school cafeterias	4.27	3.74	3.63	7.52	4.51	5.07	1.12	0.34
Board (including at school)	33.25	69.12	5.68	13.17	78.00	37.72	15.68	17.45
Catered affairs	48.39	11.71	38.94	24.48	55.20	129.84	49.05	10.72
Food on trips	213.97	89.55	168.95	238.56	272.52	295.99	202.81	106.22
School lunches	56.87	6.49	47.78	133.36	83.04	19.02	4.36	1.77
Meals as pay	26.28	52.54	43.52	27.84	22.77	26.42	4.70	2.01

	total consumer units	under 25	25 to 34	35 to 44	45 to 54	55 to 64	65 to 74	75+
ALCOHOLIC BEVERAGES	**$391.21**	**$509.04**	**$446.21**	**$423.90**	**$476.58**	**$371.90**	**$236.70**	**$128.20**
At home	**240.08**	**327.01**	**238.93**	**268.26**	**304.62**	**229.26**	**151.86**	**77.30**
Beer and ale	111.17	217.68	135.77	126.08	121.32	85.32	53.39	22.39
Whiskey	14.29	11.51	10.20	11.31	20.69	12.96	22.96	9.54
Wine	89.93	69.72	65.21	101.77	134.66	109.01	59.91	32.21
Other alcoholic beverages	24.70	28.11	27.75	29.10	27.94	21.97	15.60	13.17
Away from home	**151.12**	**182.03**	**207.28**	**155.65**	**171.96**	**142.65**	**84.84**	**50.90**
Beer and ale	60.33	78.34	38.52	61.77	68.24	48.61	33.16	19.47
• At fast food, take-out, delivery, concession stands, buffet, and cafeteria	10.70	24.17	17.48	12.94	7.82	5.77	3.69	3.14
• At full-service restaurants	46.19	53.63	71.04	46.73	51.35	34.93	29.47	16.34
Wine	18.78	21.18	29.25	18.19	22.39	15.12	9.54	6.26
• At fast food, take-out, delivery, concession stands, buffet and cafeteria	1.66	3.89	3.11	1.92	0.72	0.92	0.91	0.51
• At full-service restaurants	16.72	17.26	26.14	16.05	20.52	13.36	8.63	5.75
Other alcoholic beverages	38.75	52.01	52.61	41.79	43.49	39.11	12.61	12.52
• At fast food, take-out, delivery, concession stands, buffet, and cafeteria	7.73	14.08	9.57	10.58	6.35	6.82	2.69	2.47
• At full-service restaurants	29.49	37.82	42.98	30.29	33.10	28.80	9.91	10.05
Alcoholic beverages purchased on trips	33.26	30.50	36.90	33.89	37.84	39.80	29.53	12.65

Note: Subcategories may not add to total because some are not shown. (–) means sample is too small to make a reliable estimate.
Source: Bureau of Labor Statistics, unpublished tables from the 2003 Consumer Expenditure Survey

Table 5.2 Food and Alcohol: Indexed spending by age, 2003

(indexed average annual spending of consumer units (CU) on food and alcoholic beverages, by age of consumer unit reference person, 2003; index definition: an index of 100 is the average for all consumer units; an index of 132 means that spending by consumer units in that group is 32 percent above the average for all consumer units; an index of 68 indicates spending that is 32 percent below the average for all consumer units)

	total consumer units	under 25	25 to 34	35 to 44	45 to 54	55 to 64	65 to 74	75+
Average spending of CU, total	$40,817	$22,396	$40,525	$47,175	$50,101	$44,191	$33,629	$25,016
Average spending of CU, index	100	55	99	116	123	108	82	61
Food, spending index	100	64	100	117	120	104	85	60
Alcoholic beverages, spending index	100	130	114	108	122	95	61	33
FOOD AT HOME	100	56	95	115	118	106	92	72
Cereals and bakery products	100	58	95	118	115	97	94	81
Cereals and cereal products	100	64	104	122	112	93	86	73
Flour	100	51	96	103	125	102	89	98
Prepared flour mixes	100	47	90	123	119	96	100	78
Ready-to-eat and cooked cereals	100	64	104	126	107	88	88	80
Rice	100	75	111	115	117	108	73	49
Pasta, cornmeal, and other cereal products	100	67	108	120	115	100	79	58
Bakery products	100	55	91	117	117	98	98	85
Bread	100	53	93	110	115	100	107	91
White bread	100	59	100	121	108	96	96	79
Bread, other than white	100	48	88	102	119	104	114	98
Crackers and cookies	100	56	86	111	123	97	101	89
Cookies	100	58	86	112	126	95	98	87
Crackers	100	54	87	109	119	102	107	92
Frozen and refrigerated bakery products	100	62	90	128	114	99	85	75
Other bakery products	100	54	93	122	116	97	92	81
Biscuits and rolls	100	47	86	120	124	100	99	75
Cakes and cupcakes	100	66	101	127	115	89	78	73
Bread and cracker products	100	59	84	99	118	131	97	85
Sweetrolls, coffee cakes, doughnuts	100	47	99	129	103	97	91	89
Pies, tarts, turnovers	100	58	72	105	119	106	116	108
Meats, poultry, fish, and eggs	100	53	93	113	122	111	92	68
Beef	100	53	92	108	130	117	92	52
Ground beef	100	61	96	122	120	102	90	56
Roast	100	37	93	96	130	111	120	69
Chuck roast	100	33	124	91	121	112	117	50
Round roast	100	50	79	91	124	138	119	73
Other roast	100	32	78	103	141	95	124	83
Steak	100	56	94	103	137	125	79	43
Round steak	100	60	88	93	130	155	79	44
Sirloin steak	100	53	95	105	142	138	62	30
Other steak	100	57	96	106	136	108	91	51
Other beef	100	42	68	94	147	150	101	44
Pork	100	52	83	110	122	113	97	86
Bacon	100	47	85	114	124	111	97	74
Pork chops	100	65	101	116	126	99	79	59
Ham	100	62	68	103	116	128	90	119
Ham, not canned	100	61	68	102	116	129	88	121
Canned ham	100	78	73	153	97	85	143	38
Sausage	100	55	93	110	124	97	107	72
Other pork	100	34	74	108	121	120	112	97
Other meats	100	52	89	120	120	106	90	73
Frankfurters	100	59	91	120	121	106	78	74
Lunch meats (cold cuts)	100	48	90	121	119	106	93	72
Bologna, liverwurst, salami	100	48	89	118	113	110	100	79
Other lunch meats	100	48	91	123	121	104	90	68
Lamb, organ meats, and others	100	63	71	115	128	111	96	78
Poultry	100	59	105	120	118	98	79	65
Fresh and frozen chicken	100	64	109	121	118	96	75	61
Fresh and frozen whole chicken	100	61	101	125	123	82	87	65

	total consumer units	under 25	25 to 34	35 to 44	45 to 54	55 to 64	65 to 74	75+
Fresh and frozen chicken parts	100	65	112	120	116	101	70	59
Other poultry	100	39	86	116	121	110	97	83
Fish and seafood	100	46	99	112	113	119	98	66
Canned fish and seafood	100	48	85	104	106	135	109	86
Fresh fish and shellfish	100	44	106	114	117	113	86	63
Frozen fish and shellfish	100	49	92	112	107	123	116	63
Eggs	100	62	94	118	107	98	104	86
Dairy products	**100**	**59**	**97**	**118**	**115**	**100**	**94**	**74**
Fresh milk and cream	100	60	100	124	109	93	93	77
Fresh milk, all types	100	62	102	125	109	90	90	77
Cream	100	45	86	117	110	114	118	72
Other dairy products	100	58	95	114	119	104	94	73
Butter	100	55	80	115	117	113	110	72
Cheese	100	58	97	113	120	107	86	71
Ice cream and related products	100	60	95	106	120	99	108	80
Miscellaneous dairy products	100	52	96	134	114	97	85	63
Fruits and vegetables	**100**	**51**	**92**	**111**	**116**	**111**	**100**	**80**
Fresh fruits	100	44	92	111	119	111	100	78
Apples	100	56	99	115	121	102	91	66
Bananas	100	54	98	103	113	106	104	94
Oranges	100	44	95	123	116	98	86	86
Citrus fruits, excl. oranges	100	41	88	105	123	123	101	75
Other fresh fruits	100	36	87	111	121	116	106	75
Fresh vegetables	100	51	92	109	116	112	106	79
Potatoes	100	61	87	109	112	112	106	85
Lettuce	100	52	88	111	117	111	105	79
Tomatoes	100	53	106	107	115	105	95	78
Other fresh vegetables	100	46	88	109	117	114	110	77
Processed fruits	100	61	96	113	112	106	91	85
Frozen fruits and fruit juices	100	53	91	104	134	104	83	86
Frozen orange juice	100	60	88	119	111	114	97	72
Frozen fruits	100	39	73	75	171	110	71	117
Frozen fruit juices, excl. orange	100	57	114	117	125	83	76	70
Canned fruits	100	49	80	103	114	118	106	108
Dried fruits	100	30	72	110	113	129	95	121
Fresh fruit juice	100	63	94	114	112	105	105	73
Canned and bottled fruit juice	100	68	105	118	107	102	83	78
Processed vegetables	100	52	91	110	114	115	100	80
Frozen vegetables	100	54	93	121	109	113	88	79
Canned and dried vegetables and juices	100	51	90	106	117	116	105	81
Canned beans	100	56	91	105	118	119	98	76
Canned corn	100	55	100	109	117	96	112	72
Canned miscellaneous vegetables	100	48	83	98	120	120	113	91
Dried peas	100	154	124	51	168	86	76	35
Dried beans	100	30	94	91	132	126	87	95
Dried miscellaneous vegetables	100	44	86	129	104	123	84	81
Dried processed vegetables	100	50	250	57	57	95	148	–
Fresh and canned vegetable juices	100	53	87	109	115	112	115	76
Sugar and other sweets	**100**	**51**	**85**	**124**	**118**	**105**	**93**	**75**
Candy and chewing gum	100	48	86	127	123	104	84	71
Sugar	100	60	93	118	107	107	108	71
Artificial sweeteners	100	51	69	99	120	119	141	85
Jams, preserves, other sweets	100	57	81	124	111	101	103	89
Fats and oils	**100**	**52**	**88**	**111**	**118**	**109**	**103**	**82**
Margarine	100	45	75	96	115	123	130	102
Fats and oils	100	57	93	115	115	116	88	71
Salad dressings	100	64	92	109	125	101	98	71
Nondairy cream and imitation milk	100	29	67	109	122	116	131	96
Peanut butter	100	38	100	120	108	90	104	97

	total consumer units	under 25	25 to 34	35 to 44	45 to 54	55 to 64	65 to 74	75+
Miscellaneous foods	**100**	**68**	**104**	**115**	**116**	**102**	**85**	**64**
Frozen prepared foods	100	77	102	116	114	89	84	82
Frozen meals	100	66	93	99	113	97	110	110
Other frozen prepared foods	100	83	107	124	115	85	71	68
Canned and packaged soups	100	59	89	105	110	107	112	98
Potato chips, nuts, and other snacks	100	57	91	124	122	108	87	53
Potato chips and other snacks	100	66	97	134	119	99	74	45
Nuts	100	30	73	94	131	132	128	75
Condiments and seasonings	100	56	99	118	121	106	86	59
Salt, spices, and other seasonings	100	56	96	118	117	109	92	61
Olives, pickles, relishes	100	49	85	112	117	131	87	74
Sauces and gravies	100	62	106	124	122	96	75	52
Baking needs and miscellaneous products	100	50	94	110	124	110	100	63
Other canned/packaged prepared foods	100	77	121	108	113	103	77	54
Prepared salads	100	50	89	94	131	123	109	65
Prepared desserts	100	57	75	112	126	98	96	104
Baby food	100	165	218	106	68	61	22	29
Miscellaneous prepared foods	100	61	106	111	120	111	84	53
Nonalcoholic beverages	**100**	**59**	**95**	**118**	**122**	**108**	**81**	**61**
Cola	100	61	98	115	124	114	81	48
Other carbonated drinks	100	75	99	129	122	102	68	43
Coffee	100	30	69	102	128	121	121	96
Roasted coffee	100	32	72	101	131	120	119	88
Instant and freeze-dried coffee	100	24	63	105	121	122	125	113
Noncarbonated fruit-flavored drinks, incl. nonfrozen lemonade	100	72	121	142	111	82	56	43
Tea	100	59	81	94	136	135	83	69
Other nonalcoholic beverages and ice	100	59	104	124	118	98	66	74
Food prepared by CU on trips	**100**	**32**	**84**	**117**	**119**	**130**	**108**	**52**
FOOD AWAY FROM HOME	**100**	**74**	**106**	**121**	**122**	**100**	**75**	**44**
Meals at restaurants, carry-outs, other	**100**	**77**	**111**	**122**	**119**	**93**	**75**	**45**
Lunch	100	77	116	131	119	84	67	40
• At fast food, take-out, delivery, concession stands, buffet, cafeteria (other than employer, school cafeteria)	100	94	130	127	117	75	61	30
• At full-service restaurants	100	56	97	109	121	108	95	70
• At vending machines, mobile vendors	100	38	135	113	122	98	62	51
• At employer and school cafeterias	100	51	97	210	119	57	21	7
Dinner	100	68	106	115	119	107	83	48
• At fast food, take-out, delivery, concession stands, buffet, cafeteria (other than employer, school cafeteria)	100	81	123	135	115	83	56	36
• At full-service restaurants	100	59	100	107	120	118	94	53
• At vending machines, mobile vendors	100	280	–	104	133	–	118	182
• At employer and school cafeterias	100	431	123	43	133	40	33	–
Snacks and nonalcoholic beverages	100	106	117	124	122	81	63	31
• At fast food, take-out, delivery, concession stands, buffet, cafeteria (other than employer, school cafeteria)	100	105	119	123	121	81	65	29
• At full-service restaurants	100	83	104	100	123	91	95	78
• At vending machines, mobile vendors	100	132	128	133	124	69	37	9
• At employer and school cafeterias	100	117	85	168	119	88	37	7
Breakfast and brunch	100	74	106	117	115	88	89	70
• At fast food, take-out, delivery, concession stands, buffet, cafeteria (other than employer, school cafeteria)	100	95	123	125	118	71	64	47
• At full-service restaurants	100	51	89	105	113	103	118	98
• At vending machines, mobile vendors	100	80	114	134	78	163	37	38
• At employer and school cafeterias	100	88	85	176	106	119	26	8
Board (including at school)	**100**	**208**	**17**	**40**	**235**	**113**	**47**	**52**
Catered affairs	**100**	**24**	**80**	**51**	**114**	**268**	**101**	**22**
Food on trips	**100**	**42**	**79**	**111**	**127**	**138**	**95**	**50**
School lunches	**100**	**11**	**84**	**234**	**146**	**33**	**8**	**3**
Meals as pay	**100**	**200**	**166**	**106**	**87**	**101**	**18**	**8**

	total consumer units	under 25	25 to 34	35 to 44	45 to 54	55 to 64	65 to 74	75+
ALCOHOLIC BEVERAGES	**100**	**130**	**114**	**108**	**122**	**95**	**61**	**33**
At home	**100**	**136**	**100**	**112**	**127**	**95**	**63**	**32**
Beer and ale	100	196	122	113	109	77	48	20
Whiskey	100	81	71	79	145	91	161	67
Wine	100	78	73	113	150	121	67	36
Other alcoholic beverages	100	114	112	113	113	89	63	53
Away from home	**100**	**120**	**137**	**103**	**114**	**94**	**56**	**34**
Beer and ale	100	130	147	102	113	81	55	32
• At fast food, take-out, delivery, concession stands, buffet, and cafeteria	100	226	163	121	73	54	34	29
• At full-service restaurants	100	116	154	101	111	76	64	35
Wine	100	113	156	97	119	81	51	33
• At fast food, take-out, delivery, concession stands, buffet and cafeteria	100	234	187	116	43	55	55	31
• At full-service restaurants	100	103	156	96	123	80	52	34
Other alcoholic beverages	100	134	136	108	112	101	33	32
• At fast food, take-out, delivery, concession stands, buffet, and cafeteria	100	182	124	137	82	88	35	32
• At full-service restaurants	100	128	146	103	112	98	34	34
Alcoholic beverages purchased on trips	100	92	111	102	114	120	89	38

Note: (–) means sample is too small to make a reliable estimate.
Source: Calculations by New Strategist based on the 2003 Consumer Expenditure Survey

Table 5.3 Food and Alcohol: Total spending by age, 2003

(total annual spending on food and alcoholic beverages, by consumer unit (CU) age groups, 2003; numbers in thousands)

	total consumer units	under 25	25 to 34	35 to 44	45 to 54	55 to 64	65 to 74	75+
Number of consumer units	115,356	8,584	19,737	24,413	23,131	16,580	11,495	11,417
Total spending of all CUs	$4,708,523,919	$192,243,230	$799,846,267	$1,151,584,740	$1,158,882,993	$732,680,977	$386,567,309	$285,612,010
Food, total spending	615,943,362	29,196,673	104,959,195	153,123,219	147,606,082	91,688,892	52,238,108	36,630,759.48
Alcoholic beverages, total spending	45,128,421	4,369,599	8,806,847	10,348,671	11,023,772	6,166,102	2,720,867	1,463,659.40
FOOD AT HOME	360,923,546	15,156,683	58,731,588	87,890,950	85,432,035	54,959,384	33,202,388	25,580,816
Cereals and bakery products	50,955,052	2,195,100	8,313,619	12,770,684	11,771,366	7,077,505	4,757,551	4,085,916
Cereals and cereal products	17,319,550	823,120	3,073,446	4,473,682	3,876,062	2,327,169	1,481,591	1,259,295
Flour	844,406	32,276	138,356	183,342	210,955	123,687	75,177	82,202
Prepared flour mixes	1,475,403	51,847	226,581	382,552	350,897	203,602	147,136	113,257
Ready-to-eat and cooked cereals	9,944,841	475,639	1,764,093	2,547,590	2,141,237	1,254,609	871,091	791,541
Rice	1,851,464	102,836	351,121	449,932	433,475	286,337	135,411	89,509
Pasta, cornmeal, and other cereal products	3,201,129	160,521	593,294	810,267	739,729	458,769	252,775	182,786
Bakery products	33,635,502	1,371,981	5,240,174	8,297,002	7,895,073	4,750,336	3,275,960	2,826,735
Bread	9,522,638	372,631	1,516,788	2,208,888	2,188,193	1,373,985	1,016,733	854,448
White bread	3,864,426	168,590	660,992	991,656	838,499	530,892	371,174	304,035
Bread, other than white	5,659,365	204,042	855,796	1,217,232	1,349,694	843,093	645,559	550,528
Crackers and cookies	8,026,470	337,008	1,184,615	1,887,369	1,987,184	1,122,466	807,869	703,516
Cookies	5,197,941	224,128	763,230	1,237,007	1,310,371	708,795	507,619	447,090
Crackers	2,828,529	112,880	421,188	650,362	676,582	413,671	300,249	256,426
Frozen and refrigerated bakery products	2,833,143	130,133	434,806	769,010	649,518	402,397	239,326	209,730
Other bakery products	13,253,251	532,294	2,103,964	3,431,735	3,070,409	1,851,489	1,212,033	1,058,927
Biscuits and rolls	4,295,857	148,847	632,768	1,089,308	1,066,802	616,444	423,591	319,676
Cakes and cupcakes	4,234,719	206,617	732,835	1,135,205	980,754	542,663	329,102	305,176
Bread and cracker products	411,821	17,941	59,014	86,178	97,613	77,594	40,003	34,594
Sweetrolls, coffee cakes, doughnuts	3,189,593	110,476	541,189	871,788	658,771	443,515	289,214	279,717
Pies, tarts, turnovers	1,121,260	48,414	137,962	249,257	266,469	171,437	130,123	119,764
Meats, poultry, fish, and eggs	95,120,250	3,761,938	15,174,595	22,768,052	23,183,507	15,161,747	8,708,267	6,367,718
Beef	28,325,666	1,126,478	4,475,365	6,469,933	7,410,710	4,762,937	2,593,617	1,459,435
Ground beef	10,297,830	464,738	1,692,645	2,649,787	2,470,391	1,513,422	925,003	572,448
Roast	4,571,558	124,640	731,256	930,379	1,190,553	731,178	548,426	314,310
Chuck roast	1,542,310	37,598	327,239	298,571	373,103	247,705	179,552	76,836
Round roast	1,128,182	41,718	151,778	216,543	279,654	223,996	134,147	81,061
Other roast	1,901,067	45,324	252,239	415,265	537,564	259,477	234,613	156,527
Steak	10,861,921	456,411	1,752,053	2,375,629	2,985,056	1,958,927	858,906	459,078
Round steak	1,805,321	80,518	272,371	356,186	472,104	401,733	142,193	79,120
Sirloin steak	3,616,411	143,782	588,360	800,746	1,032,105	715,924	223,348	106,064
Other steak	5,441,343	232,026	891,126	1,218,453	1,480,847	841,103	493,365	274,008
Other beef	2,594,356	80,690	299,805	514,382	764,711	559,409	261,281	113,599
Pork	19,680,887	759,169	2,796,536	4,578,902	4,803,615	3,182,531	1,901,158	1,683,551
Bacon	3,593,339	125,841	521,254	865,441	896,095	575,492	347,149	264,304
Pork chops	3,938,254	189,878	683,690	966,022	994,633	557,751	310,250	229,710
Ham	4,400,831	202,668	511,188	960,896	1,021,928	808,772	393,014	517,761
Ham, not canned	4,272,786	195,286	495,399	919,882	997,177	793,187	374,967	512,966
Canned ham	126,892	7,382	15,790	41,014	24,750	15,585	18,047	4,795
Sausage	2,978,492	121,034	476,056	696,259	737,648	417,319	316,802	212,356
Other pork	4,771,124	119,747	604,150	1,090,285	1,153,312	823,363	533,943	459,420
Other meats	11,767,466	456,583	1,784,817	2,995,719	2,836,092	1,798,764	1,054,781	846,571
Frankfurters	2,623,195	115,798	410,135	665,743	637,722	399,412	203,462	191,349
Lunch meats (cold cuts)	7,995,324	286,534	1,235,339	2,051,669	1,903,219	1,216,143	741,313	566,169
Bologna, liverwurst, salami	2,497,457	90,132	378,358	624,485	568,097	395,267	249,671	194,432
Other lunch meats	5,497,867	196,402	856,981	1,426,940	1,335,121	821,042	491,641	371,738
Lamb, organ meats, and others	1,148,946	54,251	139,146	278,552	294,920	183,209	110,007	89,053
Poultry	16,681,631	731,013	2,985,813	4,245,909	3,961,184	2,359,831	1,313,993	1,073,997
Fresh and frozen chicken	13,429,746	635,474	2,505,612	3,446,383	3,172,879	1,847,841	1,000,870	805,469

	total consumer units	under 25	25 to 34	35 to 44	45 to 54	55 to 64	65 to 74	75+
Fresh and frozen whole chicken	$3,785,984	$171,422	$656,847	$1,003,618	$935,649	$444,012	$327,033	$242,383
Fresh and frozen chicken parts	9,643,762	464,051	1,848,567	2,442,765	2,237,230	1,403,829	673,837	563,086
Other poultry	3,253,039	95,540	480,201	799,526	788,304	511,990	313,124	268,528
Fish and seafood	14,357,208	488,515	2,438,506	3,404,149	3,246,898	2,452,348	1,397,677	938,592
Canned fish and seafood	1,891,838	67,470	275,726	417,951	402,711	367,081	205,186	160,637
Fresh fish and shellfish	8,291,789	269,366	1,502,973	1,997,228	1,950,406	1,347,291	709,931	516,505
Frozen fish and shellfish	4,172,427	151,679	659,611	989,215	893,551	737,976	482,560	261,449
Eggs	4,307,393	200,265	693,558	1,073,195	925,240	605,170	447,041	365,572
Dairy products	**37,836,768**	**1,652,849**	**6,262,550**	**9,462,967**	**8,734,266**	**5,412,375**	**3,540,115**	**2,773,646**
Fresh milk and cream	14,595,995	654,788	2,499,099	3,844,071	3,188,146	1,949,145	1,357,445	1,105,965
Fresh milk, all types	12,986,778	601,309	2,262,650	3,445,163	2,834,010	1,686,186	1,167,547	990,881
Cream	1,609,216	53,478	236,449	398,908	354,136	262,959	189,897	115,198
Other dairy products	23,240,773	998,062	3,763,451	5,618,896	5,546,120	3,463,230	2,182,786	1,667,681
Butter	2,085,636	85,153	286,779	506,081	491,302	339,393	229,210	148,992
Cheese	11,194,146	486,541	1,853,107	2,687,383	2,701,007	1,720,507	958,798	786,517
Ice cream and related products	6,701,030	299,582	1,085,917	1,502,132	1,611,537	948,708	720,162	529,292
Miscellaneous dairy products	3,259,961	126,700	535,452	923,300	742,042	454,458	274,501	202,880
Fruits and vegetables	**61,763,910**	**2,335,106**	**9,765,868**	**14,467,876**	**14,359,725**	**9,837,080**	**6,169,252**	**4,883,165**
Fresh fruits	19,712,033	647,749	3,102,064	4,642,864	4,719,881	3,131,796	1,971,507	1,513,323
Apples	3,775,602	158,546	637,308	918,661	914,600	554,601	344,045	246,036
Bananas	3,277,264	132,880	547,307	716,033	740,423	500,053	338,988	305,405
Oranges	2,115,629	69,788	344,411	551,246	494,078	297,611	180,816	180,160
Citrus fruits, excl. oranges	1,631,134	50,131	244,936	363,265	402,942	287,829	163,689	120,449
Other fresh fruits	8,912,405	236,403	1,327,905	2,093,659	2,167,837	1,491,703	943,969	661,387
Fresh vegetables	19,836,618	747,237	3,106,604	4,561,325	4,604,919	3,187,339	2,095,653	1,549,744
Potatoes	3,473,369	158,890	519,478	800,258	780,440	559,409	366,346	292,618
Lettuce	2,549,368	99,403	383,095	599,339	596,548	405,381	267,374	200,368
Tomatoes	3,712,156	145,327	675,400	838,342	853,997	560,238	352,667	286,338
Other fresh vegetables	10,101,725	343,703	1,528,828	2,323,385	2,373,935	1,662,311	1,109,268	770,419
Processed fruits	12,503,437	563,969	2,044,753	2,995,719	2,810,648	1,913,000	1,139,269	1,046,254
Frozen fruits and fruit juices	1,331,208	52,105	206,449	294,177	357,605	198,463	109,662	112,914
Frozen orange juice	535,252	23,949	80,330	135,004	119,125	87,377	51,613	38,133
Frozen fruits	422,203	12,275	53,093	67,136	144,800	66,652	29,772	48,979
Frozen fruit juices, excl. orange	373,753	15,880	73,027	92,281	93,681	44,434	28,163	25,802
Canned fruits	1,841,082	67,299	252,831	402,082	419,365	312,865	195,185	196,144
Dried fruits	726,743	16,138	89,803	168,938	164,461	134,464	68,970	87,226
Fresh fruit juice	2,395,944	112,708	384,872	577,612	535,945	360,947	251,166	173,310
Canned and bottled fruit juice	6,208,460	315,634	1,110,501	1,552,911	1,333,271	906,263	514,171	476,774
Processed vegetables	9,711,822	376,151	1,512,446	2,268,212	2,224,277	1,604,944	962,936	773,730
Frozen vegetables	3,090,387	125,326	493,425	789,516	672,418	499,721	271,742	242,725
Canned and dried vegetables and juices	6,621,434	250,824	1,019,021	1,478,695	1,551,859	1,105,223	691,194	531,005
Canned beans	1,448,871	50,088	224,607	322,252	343,264	248,700	141,618	109,375
Canned corn	794,803	32,533	136,185	183,098	186,898	109,760	88,741	56,628
Canned miscellaneous vegetables	2,139,854	76,998	304,542	441,875	516,978	368,905	240,016	193,632
Dried peas	42,682	4,893	9,379	4,538	14,341	5,306	3,219	1,484
Dried beans	266,472	5,923	42,329	51,267	70,318	48,082	22,990	25,117
Dried miscellaneous vegetables	866,324	28,070	128,093	236,318	181,116	153,033	72,304	69,073
Dried processed vegetables	48,450	1,803	20,724	5,859	5,551	6,632	7,127	–
Fresh and canned vegetable juices	1,000,137	39,401	149,014	229,970	231,079	161,323	114,835	75,466
Sugar and other sweets	**13,736,592**	**525,770**	**2,006,858**	**3,599,453**	**3,254,300**	**2,069,184**	**1,275,140**	**1,016,227**
Candy and chewing gum	8,687,460	309,024	1,278,760	2,335,592	2,135,454	1,303,022	722,921	608,983
Sugar	1,948,363	87,385	311,055	485,819	418,440	298,772	209,899	136,890
Artificial sweeteners	654,069	24,979	76,974	137,445	157,291	111,915	91,615	55,030
Jams, preserves, other sweets	2,445,547	104,296	340,069	640,597	543,116	355,475	250,591	215,325
Fats and oils	**9,889,470**	**379,584**	**1,494,486**	**2,321,920**	**2,340,857**	**1,542,272**	**1,018,572**	**799,989**
Margarine	1,108,571	37,426	141,509	224,600	255,829	195,976	143,343	112,001
Fats and oils	3,032,709	129,275	481,583	738,249	701,563	505,193	264,730	213,840
Salad dressings	3,018,867	143,782	475,859	694,306	756,384	439,536	293,467	213,498
Nondairy cream and imitation milk	1,271,223	27,469	145,067	293,200	309,955	212,390	166,333	120,564
Peanut butter	1,458,100	41,632	250,068	371,566	317,126	189,012	150,585	139,972

	total consumer units	under 25	25 to 34	35 to 44	45 to 54	55 to 64	65 to 74	75+
Miscellaneous foods	**$56,478,298**	**$2,843,708**	**$10,055,804**	**$13,723,768**	**$13,191,147**	**$8,255,845**	**$4,785,369**	**$3,570,553**
Frozen prepared foods	12,088,155	692,385	2,112,451	2,969,353	2,774,563	1,542,603	1,010,066	979,008
Frozen meals	4,020,157	196,488	637,308	846,399	907,429	559,409	439,339	439,098
Other frozen prepared foods	8,067,999	495,898	1,475,143	2,122,954	1,867,134	983,194	570,727	539,910
Canned and packaged soups	4,059,378	178,204	621,518	901,816	894,013	621,916	453,363	394,914
Potato chips, nuts, and other snacks	12,190,822	515,469	1,897,318	3,201,277	2,986,675	1,885,975	1,061,333	635,584
Potato chips and other snacks	9,144,270	446,797	1,518,170	2,593,637	2,186,805	1,306,007	671,308	409,756
Nuts	3,046,552	68,672	379,148	607,640	799,870	579,968	390,025	225,714
Condiments and seasonings	10,407,418	436,411	1,754,027	2,598,520	2,517,578	1,591,680	891,897	611,837
Salt, spices, and other seasonings	2,395,944	99,403	392,569	600,316	563,471	375,371	220,704	143,968
Olives, pickles, relishes	1,316,212	48,414	191,449	311,266	308,568	247,539	113,686	97,045
Sauces and gravies	4,436,592	204,299	807,638	1,160,105	1,084,844	611,470	331,976	229,368
Baking needs and miscellaneous products	2,258,670	84,295	362,371	526,833	560,695	357,133	225,417	141,457
Other canned/packaged prepared foods	17,731,371	1,021,324	3,670,490	4,053,046	4,018,317	2,613,837	1,368,710	949,209
Prepared salads	2,365,952	87,385	360,595	470,683	619,679	416,987	257,603	151,846
Prepared desserts	1,280,452	54,680	163,817	304,674	324,297	180,225	122,997	131,181
Baby food	3,086,927	379,241	1,149,680	589,667	419,828	268,430	68,050	87,454
Miscellaneous prepared foods	10,973,816	500,018	1,990,871	2,583,628	2,640,404	1,748,195	920,060	578,842
Nonalcoholic beverages	**30,958,090**	**1,362,109**	**5,055,435**	**7,736,968**	**7,602,234**	**4,821,464**	**2,496,484**	**1,868,735**
Cola	10,182,474	465,768	1,699,356	2,485,976	2,531,225	1,675,409	825,226	487,848
Other carbonated drinks	5,264,848	294,088	890,731	1,432,555	1,286,778	770,638	355,310	225,143
Coffee	4,392,756	96,999	521,057	949,910	1,125,554	762,680	530,149	417,634
Roasted coffee	2,964,649	70,990	366,121	631,564	778,358	512,156	352,897	258,481
Instant and freeze-dried coffee	1,428,107	26,010	154,738	318,346	347,196	250,524	177,253	159,153
Noncarbonated fruit-flavored drinks, incl. nonfrozen lemonade	2,225,217	118,631	460,464	666,475	493,847	261,964	123,801	95,332
Tea	2,042,955	89,102	281,647	407,453	559,076	397,423	168,287	140,087
Other nonalcoholic beverages and ice	6,773,704	296,749	1,200,799	1,778,731	1,601,822	950,034	446,811	498,923
Food prepared by CU on trips	**4,185,116**	**100,604**	**602,571**	**1,039,017**	**994,864**	**781,913**	**451,639**	**214,868**
FOOD AWAY FROM HOME	255,020,970	14,039,990	46,227,409	65,232,268	62,174,046	36,729,508	19,035,605	11,049,943
Meals at restaurants, carry-outs, other	211,328,731	12,070,735	40,210,190	54,553,778	50,341,846	28,290,454	15,856,088	9,472,571
Lunch	75,922,705	4,336,723	15,065,055	20,980,288	18,045,881	9,131,435	5,105,389	3,032,013
• At fast food, take-out, delivery, concession stands, buffet, cafeteria (other than employer, school cafeteria)	42,568,671	2,981,824	9,488,957	11,456,289	9,985,190	4,594,981	2,606,491	1,254,272
• At full-service restaurants	24,236,296	1,012,311	4,019,440	5,597,901	5,882,907	3,747,577	2,282,332	1,689,031
• At vending machines, mobile vendors	641,379	18,284	148,028	154,046	157,291	90,527	39,773	32,196
• At employer and school cafeterias	8,476,359	324,218	1,408,432	3,772,053	2,020,493	698,350	176,793	56,514
Dinner	85,076,204	4,278,094	15,483,677	20,696,121	20,292,364	13,102,677	7,028,273	4,055,090
• At fast food, take-out, delivery, concession stands, buffet, cafeteria (other than employer, school cafeteria)	24,908,821	1,506,320	5,221,818	7,105,404	5,747,591	2,976,110	1,383,653	888,813
• At full-service restaurants	59,687,502	2,635,288	10,192,976	13,527,487	14,417,090	10,107,997	5,615,997	3,138,876
• At vending machines, mobile vendors	152,270	31,675	–	33,446	40,711	–	17,932	27,401
• At employer and school cafeterias	326,457	104,811	68,685	30,028	86,973	18,570	10,690	–
Snacks and nonalcoholic beverages	28,656,738	2,269,867	5,732,809	7,517,007	6,991,576	3,324,290	1,806,209	876,026
• At fast food, take-out, delivery, concession stands, buffet, cafeteria (other than employer, school cafeteria)	20,794,073	1,624,608	4,223,718	5,434,090	5,058,981	2,414,877	1,337,213	598,365
• At full-service restaurants	3,075,391	189,191	544,939	648,653	756,615	402,231	291,743	236,789
• At vending machines, mobile vendors	3,614,103	353,747	793,822	1,018,266	896,789	358,791	134,032	32,424
• At employer and school cafeterias	1,172,017	102,321	170,330	415,998	279,191	148,391	43,106	8,563
Breakfast and brunch	21,674,239	1,186,137	3,928,847	5,360,362	5,012,256	2,732,052	1,916,331	1,509,442
• At fast food, take-out, delivery, concession stands, buffet, cafeteria (other than employer, school cafeteria)	10,707,344	756,594	2,249,821	2,843,626	2,542,097	1,086,653	685,447	500,978
• At full-service restaurants	10,315,134	388,083	1,576,789	2,288,475	2,341,320	1,524,531	1,212,033	998,417
• At vending machines, mobile vendors	158,038	9,357	30,790	44,676	24,750	36,973	5,862	5,937
• At employer and school cafeterias	492,570	32,104	71,645	183,586	104,321	84,061	12,874	3,882
Board (including at school)	**3,835,587**	**593,326**	**112,106**	**321,519**	**1,804,218**	**625,398**	**180,242**	**199,227**
Catered affairs	**5,582,077**	**100,519**	**768,559**	**597,630**	**1,276,831**	**2,152,747**	**563,830**	**122,390**
Food on trips	**24,682,723**	**768,697**	**3,334,566**	**5,823,965**	**6,303,660**	**4,907,514**	**2,331,301**	**1,212,714**
School lunches	**6,560,296**	**55,710**	**943,034**	**3,255,718**	**1,920,798**	**315,352**	**50,118**	**20,208**
Meals as pay	**3,031,556**	**451,003**	**858,954**	**679,658**	**526,693**	**438,044**	**54,027**	**22,948**

	total consumer units	under 25	25 to 34	35 to 44	45 to 54	55 to 64	65 to 74	75+
ALCOHOLIC BEVERAGES	$45,128,421	$4,369,599	$8,806,847	$10,348,671	$11,023,772	$6,166,102	$2,720,867	$1,463,659
At home	27,694,668	2,807,054	4,715,761	6,549,031	7,046,165	3,801,131	1,745,631	882,534
Beer and ale	12,824,127	1,868,565	2,679,692	3,077,991	2,806,253	1,414,606	613,718	255,627
Whiskey	1,648,437	98,802	201,317	276,111	478,580	214,877	263,925	108,918
Wine	10,373,965	598,476	1,287,050	2,484,511	3,114,820	1,807,386	688,665	367,742
Other alcoholic beverages	2,849,293	241,296	547,702	710,418	646,280	364,263	179,322	150,362
Away from home	17,432,599	1,562,546	4,091,085	3,799,883	3,977,607	2,365,137	975,236	581,125
Beer and ale	6,959,427	672,471	1,747,119	1,507,991	1,578,459	805,954	381,174	222,289
• At fast food, take-out, delivery, concession stands, buffet, and cafeteria	1,234,309	207,475	345,003	315,904	180,884	95,667	42,417	35,849
• At full-service restaurants	5,328,294	460,360	1,402,116	1,140,819	1,187,777	579,139	338,758	186,554
Wine	2,166,386	181,809	577,307	444,072	517,903	250,690	109,662	71,470
• At fast food, take-out, delivery, concession stands, buffet and cafeteria	191,491	33,392	61,382	46,873	16,654	15,254	10,460	5,823
• At full-service restaurants	1,928,752	148,160	515,925	391,829	474,648	221,509	99,202	65,648
Other alcoholic beverages	4,470,045	446,454	1,033,364	1,020,219	1,005,967	648,444	144,952	142,941
• At fast food, take-out, delivery, concession stands, buffet, and cafeteria	891,702	120,863	188,883	258,290	146,882	113,076	30,922	28,200
• At full-service restaurants	3,401,848	324,647	848,296	739,470	765,636	477,504	113,915	114,741
Alcoholic beverages purchased on trips	3,836,741	261,812	728,295	827,357	875,277	659,884	339,447	144,425

Note: Numbers may not add to total because of rounding and missing subcategories. (–) means sample is too small to make a reliable estimate.
Source: Calculations by New Strategist based on the 2003 Consumer Expenditure Survey

Table 5.4 Food and Alcohol: Market shares by age, 2003

(percentage of total annual spending on food and alcoholic beverages accounted for by consumer unit age groups, 2003)

	total consumer units	under 25	25 to 34	35 to 44	45 to 54	55 to 64	65 to 74	75+
Share of total consumer units	100.0%	7.4%	17.1%	21.2%	20.1%	14.4%	10.0%	9.9%
Share of total before-tax income	100.0	3.0	16.9	25.3	26.7	16.5	6.9	4.9
Share of total spending	100.0	4.1	17.0	24.5	24.6	15.6	8.2	6.1
Share of food spending	100.0	4.7	17.0	24.9	24.0	14.9	8.5	5.9
Share of alcoholic beverages spending	100.0	9.7	19.5	22.9	24.4	13.7	6.0	3.2
FOOD AT HOME	100.0	4.2	16.3	24.4	23.7	15.2	9.2	7.1
Cereals and bakery products	100.0	4.3	16.3	25.1	23.1	13.9	9.3	8.0
Cereals and cereal products	100.0	4.8	17.7	25.8	22.4	13.4	8.6	7.3
Flour	100.0	3.8	16.4	21.7	25.0	14.6	8.9	9.7
Prepared flour mixes	100.0	3.5	15.4	25.9	23.8	13.8	10.0	7.7
Ready-to-eat and cooked cereals	100.0	4.8	17.7	26.6	21.5	12.6	8.8	8.0
Rice	100.0	5.6	19.0	24.3	23.4	15.5	7.3	4.8
Pasta, cornmeal, and other cereal products	100.0	5.0	18.5	25.3	23.1	14.3	7.9	5.7
Bakery products	100.0	4.1	15.6	24.7	23.5	14.1	9.7	8.4
Bread	100.0	3.9	15.9	23.2	23.0	14.4	10.7	9.0
White bread	100.0	4.4	17.1	25.7	21.7	13.7	9.6	7.9
Bread, other than white	100.0	3.6	15.1	21.5	23.8	14.9	11.4	9.7
Crackers and cookies	100.0	4.2	14.8	23.5	24.8	14.0	10.1	8.8
Cookies	100.0	4.3	14.7	23.8	25.2	13.6	9.8	8.6
Crackers	100.0	4.0	14.9	23.0	23.9	14.6	10.6	9.1
Frozen and refrigerated bakery products	100.0	4.6	15.3	27.1	22.9	14.2	8.4	7.4
Other bakery products	100.0	4.0	15.9	25.9	23.2	14.0	9.1	8.0
Biscuits and rolls	100.0	3.5	14.7	25.4	24.8	14.3	9.9	7.4
Cakes and cupcakes	100.0	4.9	17.3	26.8	23.2	12.8	7.8	7.2
Bread and cracker products	100.0	4.4	14.3	20.9	23.7	18.8	9.7	8.4
Sweetrolls, coffee cakes, doughnuts	100.0	3.5	17.0	27.3	20.7	13.9	9.1	8.8
Pies, tarts, turnovers	100.0	4.3	12.3	22.2	23.8	15.3	11.6	10.7
Meats, poultry, fish, and eggs	100.0	4.0	16.0	23.9	24.4	15.9	9.2	6.7
Beef	100.0	4.0	15.8	22.8	26.2	16.8	9.2	5.2
Ground beef	100.0	4.5	16.4	25.7	24.0	14.7	9.0	5.6
Roast	100.0	2.7	16.0	20.4	26.0	16.0	12.0	6.9
Chuck roast	100.0	2.4	21.2	19.4	24.2	16.1	11.6	5.0
Round roast	100.0	3.7	13.5	19.2	24.8	19.9	11.9	7.2
Other roast	100.0	2.4	13.3	21.8	28.3	13.6	12.3	8.2
Steak	100.0	4.2	16.1	21.9	27.5	18.0	7.9	4.2
Round steak	100.0	4.5	15.1	19.7	26.2	22.3	7.9	4.4
Sirloin steak	100.0	4.0	16.3	22.1	28.5	19.8	6.2	2.9
Other steak	100.0	4.3	16.4	22.4	27.2	15.5	9.1	5.0
Other beef	100.0	3.1	11.6	19.8	29.5	21.6	10.1	4.4
Pork	100.0	3.9	14.2	23.3	24.4	16.2	9.7	8.6
Bacon	100.0	3.5	14.5	24.1	24.9	16.0	9.7	7.4
Pork chops	100.0	4.8	17.4	24.5	25.3	14.2	7.9	5.8
Ham	100.0	4.6	11.6	21.8	23.2	18.4	8.9	11.8
Ham, not canned	100.0	4.6	11.6	21.5	23.3	18.6	8.8	12.0
Canned ham	100.0	5.8	12.4	32.3	19.5	12.3	14.2	3.8
Sausage	100.0	4.1	16.0	23.4	24.8	14.0	10.6	7.1
Other pork	100.0	2.5	12.7	22.9	24.2	17.3	11.2	9.6
Other meats	100.0	3.9	15.2	25.5	24.1	15.3	9.0	7.2
Frankfurters	100.0	4.4	15.6	25.4	24.3	15.2	7.8	7.3
Lunch meats (cold cuts)	100.0	3.6	15.5	25.7	23.8	15.2	9.3	7.1
Bologna, liverwurst, salami	100.0	3.6	15.1	25.0	22.7	15.8	10.0	7.8
Other lunch meats	100.0	3.6	15.6	26.0	24.3	14.9	8.9	6.8
Lamb, organ meats, and others	100.0	4.7	12.1	24.2	25.7	15.9	9.6	7.8
Poultry	100.0	4.4	17.9	25.5	23.7	14.1	7.9	6.4
Fresh and frozen chicken	100.0	4.7	18.7	25.7	23.6	13.8	7.5	6.0

	total consumer units	under 25	25 to 34	35 to 44	45 to 54	55 to 64	65 to 74	75+
Fresh and frozen whole chicken	100.0%	4.5%	17.3%	26.5%	24.7%	11.7%	8.6%	6.4%
Fresh and frozen chicken parts	100.0	4.8	19.2	25.3	23.2	14.6	7.0	5.8
Other poultry	100.0	2.9	14.8	24.6	24.2	15.7	9.6	8.3
Fish and seafood	100.0	3.4	17.0	23.7	22.6	17.1	9.7	6.5
Canned fish and seafood	100.0	3.6	14.6	22.1	21.3	19.4	10.8	8.5
Fresh fish and shellfish	100.0	3.2	18.1	24.1	23.5	16.2	8.6	6.2
Frozen fish and shellfish	100.0	3.6	15.8	23.7	21.4	17.7	11.6	6.3
Eggs	100.0	4.6	16.1	24.9	21.5	14.0	10.4	8.5
Dairy products	**100.0**	**4.4**	**16.6**	**25.0**	**23.1**	**14.3**	**9.4**	**7.3**
Fresh milk and cream	100.0	4.5	17.1	26.3	21.8	13.4	9.3	7.6
Fresh milk, all types	100.0	4.6	17.4	26.5	21.8	13.0	9.0	7.6
Cream	100.0	3.3	14.7	24.8	22.0	16.3	11.8	7.2
Other dairy products	100.0	4.3	16.2	24.2	23.9	14.9	9.4	7.2
Butter	100.0	4.1	13.8	24.3	23.6	16.3	11.0	7.1
Cheese	100.0	4.3	16.6	24.0	24.1	15.4	8.6	7.0
Ice cream and related products	100.0	4.5	16.2	22.4	24.0	14.2	10.7	7.9
Miscellaneous dairy products	100.0	3.9	16.5	28.3	22.8	13.9	8.4	6.2
Fruits and vegetables	**100.0**	**3.8**	**15.8**	**23.4**	**23.2**	**15.9**	**10.0**	**7.9**
Fresh fruits	100.0	3.3	15.7	23.6	23.9	15.9	10.0	7.7
Apples	100.0	4.2	16.9	24.3	24.2	14.7	9.1	6.5
Bananas	100.0	4.1	16.7	21.8	22.6	15.3	10.3	9.3
Oranges	100.0	3.3	16.3	26.1	23.4	14.1	8.5	8.5
Citrus fruits, excl. oranges	100.0	3.1	15.0	22.3	24.7	17.6	10.0	7.4
Other fresh fruits	100.0	2.7	14.9	23.5	24.3	16.7	10.6	7.4
Fresh vegetables	100.0	3.8	15.7	23.0	23.2	16.1	10.6	7.8
Potatoes	100.0	4.6	15.0	23.0	22.5	16.1	10.5	8.4
Lettuce	100.0	3.9	15.0	23.5	23.4	15.9	10.5	7.9
Tomatoes	100.0	3.9	18.2	22.6	23.0	15.1	9.5	7.7
Other fresh vegetables	100.0	3.4	15.1	23.0	23.5	16.5	11.0	7.6
Processed fruits	100.0	4.5	16.4	24.0	22.5	15.3	9.1	8.4
Frozen fruits and fruit juices	100.0	3.9	15.5	22.1	26.9	14.9	8.2	8.5
Frozen orange juice	100.0	4.5	15.0	25.2	22.3	16.3	9.6	7.1
Frozen fruits	100.0	2.9	12.6	15.9	34.3	15.8	7.1	11.6
Frozen fruit juices, excl. orange	100.0	4.2	19.5	24.7	25.1	11.9	7.5	6.9
Canned fruits	100.0	3.7	13.7	21.8	22.8	17.0	10.6	10.7
Dried fruits	100.0	2.2	12.4	23.2	22.6	18.5	9.5	12.0
Fresh fruit juice	100.0	4.7	16.1	24.1	22.4	15.1	10.5	7.2
Canned and bottled fruit juice	100.0	5.1	17.9	25.0	21.5	14.6	8.3	7.7
Processed vegetables	100.0	3.9	15.6	23.4	22.9	16.5	9.9	8.0
Frozen vegetables	100.0	4.1	16.0	25.5	21.8	16.2	8.8	7.9
Canned and dried vegetables and juices	100.0	3.8	15.4	22.3	23.4	16.7	10.4	8.0
Canned beans	100.0	4.1	15.5	22.2	23.7	17.2	9.8	7.5
Canned corn	100.0	4.1	17.1	23.0	23.5	13.8	11.2	7.1
Canned miscellaneous vegetables	100.0	3.6	14.2	20.6	24.2	17.2	11.2	9.0
Dried peas	100.0	11.5	21.3	10.9	33.6	12.4	7.5	3.5
Dried beans	100.0	2.2	16.1	19.2	26.4	18.0	8.6	9.4
Dried miscellaneous vegetables	100.0	3.2	14.8	27.3	20.9	17.7	8.3	8.0
Dried processed vegetables	100.0	3.7	42.8	12.1	11.5	13.7	14.7	–
Fresh and canned vegetable juices	100.0	3.9	14.9	23.0	23.1	16.1	11.5	7.5
Sugar and other sweets	**100.0**	**3.8**	**14.6**	**26.2**	**23.7**	**15.1**	**9.3**	**7.4**
Candy and chewing gum	100.0	3.6	14.7	26.9	24.6	15.0	8.3	7.0
Sugar	100.0	4.5	15.0	24.9	21.5	15.3	10.8	7.0
Artificial sweeteners	100.0	3.8	11.8	21.0	24.0	17.1	14.0	8.4
Jams, preserves, other sweets	100.0	4.3	13.9	26.2	22.2	14.5	10.2	8.8
Fats and oils	**100.0**	**3.8**	**15.1**	**23.5**	**23.7**	**15.6**	**10.3**	**8.1**
Margarine	100.0	3.4	12.8	20.3	23.1	17.7	12.9	10.1
Fats and oils	100.0	4.3	15.9	24.3	23.1	16.7	8.7	7.1
Salad dressings	100.0	4.8	15.8	23.0	25.1	14.6	9.7	7.1
Nondairy cream and imitation milk	100.0	2.2	11.4	23.1	24.4	16.7	13.1	9.5
Peanut butter	100.0	2.9	17.2	25.5	21.7	13.0	10.3	9.6

	total consumer units	under 25	25 to 34	35 to 44	45 to 54	55 to 64	65 to 74	75+
Miscellaneous foods	100.0%	5.0%	17.8%	24.3%	23.4%	14.6%	8.5%	6.3%
Frozen prepared foods	100.0	5.7	17.5	24.6	23.0	12.8	8.4	8.1
Frozen meals	100.0	4.9	15.9	21.1	22.6	13.9	10.9	10.9
Other frozen prepared foods	100.0	6.1	18.3	26.3	23.1	12.2	7.1	6.7
Canned and packaged soups	100.0	4.4	15.3	22.2	22.0	15.3	11.2	9.7
Potato chips, nuts, and other snacks	100.0	4.2	15.6	26.3	24.5	15.5	8.7	5.2
Potato chips and other snacks	100.0	4.9	16.6	28.4	23.9	14.3	7.3	4.5
Nuts	100.0	2.3	12.4	19.9	26.3	19.0	12.8	7.4
Condiments and seasonings	100.0	4.2	16.9	25.0	24.2	15.3	8.6	5.9
Salt, spices, and other seasonings	100.0	4.1	16.4	25.1	23.5	15.7	9.2	6.0
Olives, pickles, relishes	100.0	3.7	14.5	23.6	23.4	18.8	8.6	7.4
Sauces and gravies	100.0	4.6	18.2	26.1	24.5	13.8	7.5	5.2
Baking needs and miscellaneous products	100.0	3.7	16.0	23.3	24.8	15.8	10.0	6.3
Other canned/packaged prepared foods	100.0	5.8	20.7	22.9	22.7	14.7	7.7	5.4
Prepared salads	100.0	3.7	15.2	19.9	26.2	17.6	10.9	6.4
Prepared desserts	100.0	4.3	12.8	23.8	25.3	14.1	9.6	10.2
Baby food	100.0	12.3	37.2	22.3	13.6	8.7	2.2	2.8
Miscellaneous prepared foods	100.0	4.6	18.1	23.5	24.1	15.9	8.4	5.3
Nonalcoholic beverages	100.0	4.4	16.3	25.0	24.6	15.6	8.1	6.0
Cola	100.0	4.6	16.7	24.4	24.9	16.5	8.1	4.8
Other carbonated drinks	100.0	5.6	16.9	27.2	24.4	14.6	6.7	4.3
Coffee	100.0	2.2	11.9	21.6	25.6	17.4	12.1	9.5
Roasted coffee	100.0	2.4	12.3	21.3	26.3	17.3	11.9	8.7
Instant and freeze-dried coffee	100.0	1.8	10.8	22.3	24.3	17.5	12.4	11.1
Noncarbonated fruit-flavored drinks, incl. nonfrozen lemonade	100.0	5.3	20.7	30.0	22.2	11.8	5.6	4.3
Tea	100.0	4.4	13.8	19.9	27.4	19.5	8.2	6.9
Other nonalcoholic beverages and ice	100.0	4.4	17.7	26.3	23.6	14.0	6.6	7.4
Food prepared by CU on trips	100.0	2.4	14.4	24.8	23.8	18.7	10.8	5.1
FOOD AWAY FROM HOME	100.0	5.5	18.1	25.6	24.4	14.4	7.5	4.3
Meals at restaurants, carry-outs, other	100.0	5.7	19.0	25.8	23.8	13.4	7.5	4.5
Lunch	100.0	5.7	19.8	27.6	23.8	12.0	6.7	4.0
• At fast food, take-out, delivery, concession stands, buffet, cafeteria (other than employer, school cafeteria)	100.0	7.0	22.3	26.9	23.5	10.8	6.1	2.9
• At full-service restaurants	100.0	4.2	16.6	23.1	24.3	15.5	9.4	7.0
• At vending machines, mobile vendors	100.0	2.9	23.1	24.0	24.5	14.1	6.2	5.0
• At employer and school cafeterias	100.0	3.8	16.6	44.5	23.8	8.2	2.1	0.7
Dinner	100.0	5.0	18.2	24.3	23.9	15.4	8.3	4.8
• At fast food, take-out, delivery, concession stands, buffet, cafeteria (other than employer, school cafeteria)	100.0	6.0	21.0	28.5	23.1	11.9	5.6	3.6
• At full-service restaurants	100.0	4.4	17.1	22.7	24.2	16.9	9.4	5.3
• At vending machines, mobile vendors	100.0	20.8	–	22.0	26.7	–	11.8	18.0
• At employer and school cafeterias	100.0	32.1	21.0	9.2	26.6	5.7	3.3	–
Snacks and nonalcoholic beverages	100.0	7.9	20.0	26.2	24.4	11.6	6.3	3.1
• At fast food, take-out, delivery, concession stands, buffet, cafeteria (other than employer, school cafeteria)	100.0	7.8	20.3	26.1	24.3	11.6	6.4	2.9
• At full-service restaurants	100.0	6.2	17.7	21.1	24.6	13.1	9.5	7.7
• At vending machines, mobile vendors	100.0	9.8	22.0	28.2	24.8	9.9	3.7	0.9
• At employer and school cafeterias	100.0	8.7	14.5	35.5	23.8	12.7	3.7	0.7
Breakfast and brunch	100.0	5.5	18.1	24.7	23.1	12.6	8.8	7.0
• At fast food, take-out, delivery, concession stands, buffet, cafeteria (other than employer, school cafeteria)	100.0	7.1	21.0	26.6	23.7	10.1	6.4	4.7
• At full-service restaurants	100.0	3.8	15.3	22.2	22.7	14.8	11.8	9.7
• At vending machines, mobile vendors	100.0	5.9	19.5	28.3	15.7	23.4	3.7	3.8
• At employer and school cafeterias	100.0	6.5	14.5	37.3	21.2	17.1	2.6	0.8
Board (including at school)	100.0	15.5	2.9	8.4	47.0	16.3	4.7	5.2
Catered affairs	100.0	1.8	13.8	10.7	22.9	38.6	10.1	2.2
Food on trips	100.0	3.1	13.5	23.6	25.5	19.9	9.4	4.9
School lunches	100.0	0.8	14.4	49.6	29.3	4.8	0.8	0.3
Meals as pay	100.0	14.9	28.3	22.4	17.4	14.4	1.8	0.8

	total consumer units	under 25	25 to 34	35 to 44	45 to 54	55 to 64	65 to 74	75+
ALCOHOLIC BEVERAGES	100.0%	9.7%	19.5%	22.9%	24.4%	13.7%	6.0%	3.2%
At home	100.0	10.1	17.0	23.6	25.4	13.7	6.3	3.2
Beer and ale	100.0	14.6	20.9	24.0	21.9	11.0	4.8	2.0
Whiskey	100.0	6.0	12.2	16.7	29.0	13.0	16.0	6.6
Wine	100.0	5.8	12.4	23.9	30.0	17.4	6.6	3.5
Other alcoholic beverages	100.0	8.5	19.2	24.9	22.7	12.8	6.3	5.3
Away from home	100.0	9.0	23.5	21.8	22.8	13.6	5.6	3.3
Beer and ale	100.0	9.7	25.1	21.7	22.7	11.6	5.5	3.2
• At fast food, take-out, delivery, concession stands, buffet, and cafeteria	100.0	16.8	28.0	25.5	14.7	7.8	3.4	2.9
• At full-service restaurants	100.0	8.6	26.3	21.4	22.3	10.9	6.4	3.5
Wine	100.0	8.4	26.6	20.5	23.9	11.6	5.1	3.3
• At fast food, take-out, delivery, concession stands, buffet and cafeteria	100.0	17.4	32.1	24.5	8.7	8.0	5.5	3.0
• At full-service restaurants	100.0	7.7	26.7	20.3	24.6	11.5	5.1	3.4
Other alcoholic beverages	100.0	10.0	23.2	22.8	22.5	14.5	3.2	3.2
• At fast food, take-out, delivery, concession stands, buffet, and cafeteria	100.0	13.6	21.2	29.0	16.5	12.7	3.5	3.2
• At full-service restaurants	100.0	9.5	24.9	21.7	22.5	14.0	3.3	3.4
Alcoholic beverages purchased on trips	100.0	6.8	19.0	21.6	22.8	17.2	8.8	3.8

Note: Numbers may not add to total because of rounding. (–) means sample is too small to make a reliable estimate.
Source: Calculations by New Strategist based on the 2003 Consumer Expenditure Survey

Table 5.5 Food and Alcohol: Average spending by income, 2003

(average annual spending on food and alcoholic beverages, by before-tax income of consumer units (CU), 2003; complete income reporters only)

	total complete reporters	under $20,000	$20,000– $39,999	$40,000– $49,999	$50,000– $69,999	$70,000– $79,999	$80,000– $99,999	$100,000 or more
Number of consumer units (000)	97,391	27,100	23,941	8,891	13,890	5,121	6,909	11,537
Average number of persons per CU	2.5	1.8	2.4	2.6	2.8	3.0	3.0	3.1
Average before-tax income of CU	$51,128.00	$10,752.55	$29,072.57	$44,294.00	$58,900.00	$74,560.00	$88,832.00	$154,665.00
Average spending of CU, total	42,741.66	19,862.52	31,684.32	39,756.91	49,788.99	57,128.14	65,957.39	93,514.86
Food, average spending	**5,593.46**	**3,330.65**	**4,632.44**	**5,485.64**	**6,510.70**	**7,548.35**	**7,839.61**	**9,926.45**
Alcoholic beverages, average spending	**442.41**	**200.86**	**274.68**	**407.20**	**555.81**	**617.95**	**588.82**	**1,126.82**
FOOD AT HOME	**3,235.68**	**2,225.26**	**2,942.08**	**3.233.65**	**3,700.01**	**4,353.67**	**4,136.12**	**4,725.79**
Cereals and bakery products	**456.14**	**331.97**	**408.63**	**468.29**	**510.72**	**616.79**	**591.37**	**632.04**
Cereals and cereal products	154.67	117.69	144.81	154.83	168.18	210.37	195.63	200.48
Flour	7.49	7.26	6.51	10.35	6.36	9.91	7.09	8.12
Prepared flour mixes	13.29	9.67	12.01	14.77	17.31	12.86	12.37	19.54
Ready-to-eat and cooked cereals	89.87	66.01	83.90	88.35	99.73	124.07	118.89	118.16
Rice	15.97	12.56	16.01	14.67	16.42	21.71	21.97	18.74
Pasta, cornmeal, and other cereal products	28.04	22.19	26.37	26.69	28.36	41.82	35.31	35.91
Bakery products	301.48	214.28	263.83	313.46	342.55	406.42	395.74	431.56
Bread	84.96	66.15	80.94	85.56	90.58	103.07	106.89	110.36
White bread	34.08	28.05	34.45	35.90	37.32	43.07	33.95	37.92
Bread, other than white	50.88	38.10	46.49	49.66	53.26	60.00	72.94	72.44
Crackers and cookies	72.65	52.68	61.73	78.52	81.11	95.82	98.20	103.89
Cookies	46.69	35.24	39.33	47.57	52.70	63.27	64.41	64.39
Crackers	25.96	17.44	22.40	30.94	28.41	32.55	33.79	39.51
Frozen and refrigerated bakery products	25.29	18.17	21.14	24.75	26.77	38.05	37.49	37.54
Other bakery products	118.58	77.28	100.02	124.63	144.09	169.48	153.16	179.77
Biscuits and rolls	38.86	23.77	30.60	37.39	48.62	53.34	50.37	69.90
Cakes and cupcakes	37.34	25.82	32.86	39.80	43.02	55.02	46.95	52.35
Bread and cracker products	3.77	2.06	3.47	4.02	4.75	6.51	5.15	5.11
Sweetrolls, coffee cakes, doughnuts	28.79	18.82	25.49	31.20	36.89	41.65	39.03	36.17
Pies, tarts, turnovers	9.81	6.80	7.60	12.22	10.81	12.96	11.66	16.23
Meats, poultry, fish, and eggs	**836.78**	**570.66**	**792.77**	**821.19**	**1,011.38**	**1,093.87**	**967.11**	**1,183.17**
Beef	252.49	152.97	228.74	255.25	355.32	348.76	313.33	336.96
Ground beef	91.95	66.56	85.30	95.84	128.46	117.69	98.60	103.35
Roast	40.87	27.61	42.49	50.60	42.97	37.13	49.40	54.95
Chuck roast	14.24	9.70	14.76	21.52	13.24	11.14	17.54	18.39
Round roast	9.82	5.28	12.09	6.79	17.22	10.33	7.76	10.20
Other roast	16.81	12.63	15.64	22.30	12.50	15.67	24.10	26.37
Steak	95.57	46.70	82.72	89.77	147.36	152.68	126.66	139.54
Round steak	16.10	9.18	13.98	14.10	30.24	23.76	16.53	18.12
Sirloin steak	32.60	12.54	24.83	28.39	65.63	54.70	37.81	48.19
Other steak	46.87	24.98	43.91	47.28	51.49	74.23	72.32	73.23
Other beef	24.09	12.10	18.22	19.04	36.53	41.26	38.67	39.11
Pork	171.42	131.40	178.54	165.58	186.51	197.91	189.89	216.10
Bacon	31.49	23.23	30.69	30.57	35.62	35.55	40.02	42.12
Pork chops	33.92	26.43	33.41	31.44	46.86	44.25	28.39	37.79
Ham	37.70	29.24	39.31	38.96	37.52	26.27	49.20	52.28
Ham, not canned	36.49	28.04	38.66	37.22	36.40	26.27	46.88	50.31
Canned ham	1.22	1.43	0.64	1.75	1.12	–	2.32	1.98
Sausage	25.73	23.47	26.25	22.92	24.68	34.06	28.82	28.29
Other pork	42.57	29.04	48.89	41.69	41.83	57.78	43.45	55.62
Other meats	103.84	74.46	95.29	102.85	129.43	135.78	123.26	136.44
Frankfurters	23.14	17.38	23.01	23.72	29.48	25.60	23.21	27.63
Lunch meats (cold cuts)	70.85	51.06	64.13	72.54	89.09	93.95	91.20	86.73
Bologna, liverwurst, salami	21.47	18.98	20.05	23.32	24.06	25.72	23.81	22.13
Other lunch meats	49.38	32.08	44.08	49.22	65.03	68.23	67.38	64.60
Lamb, organ meats, and others	9.84	6.03	8.14	6.59	10.86	16.23	8.85	22.08
Poultry	145.42	102.85	135.12	143.09	163.73	208.83	170.57	206.76
Fresh and frozen chicken	117.08	84.50	110.61	114.62	132.30	169.68	137.04	157.55

	total complete reporters	under $20,000	$20,000– $39,999	$40,000– $49,999	$50,000– $69,999	$70,000– $79,999	$80,000– $99,999	$100,000 or more
Fresh and frozen whole chicken	$32.93	$23.61	$36.25	$28.32	$35.37	$46.10	$30.79	$44.56
Fresh and frozen chicken parts	84.15	60.90	74.36	86.30	96.93	123.58	106.24	112.99
Other poultry	28.34	18.35	24.51	28.47	31.42	39.15	33.53	49.21
Fish and seafood	125.25	76.63	114.40	114.68	140.65	160.92	130.29	239.69
Canned fish and seafood	15.83	12.00	14.56	14.67	19.51	21.33	16.30	22.23
Fresh fish and shellfish	71.24	41.20	65.40	61.80	70.01	95.95	77.62	153.14
Frozen fish and shellfish	38.12	23.44	34.44	38.21	51.13	43.64	36.37	64.32
Eggs	38.37	32.34	40.69	39.74	35.74	41.68	39.77	47.22
Dairy products	**343.30**	**233.14**	**310.82**	**366.56**	**383.81**	**455.33**	**456.79**	**493.95**
Fresh milk and cream	131.66	99.27	124.99	141.97	139.80	178.50	160.84	166.66
Fresh milk, all types	117.54	91.50	111.50	127.44	124.74	162.07	142.52	140.67
Cream	14.12	7.77	13.50	14.53	15.05	16.43	18.32	25.99
Other dairy products	211.63	133.88	185.83	224.59	244.02	276.83	295.95	327.29
Butter	17.78	12.58	16.75	19.55	17.18	21.01	23.73	26.80
Cheese	103.74	63.11	94.20	107.95	121.58	130.40	146.21	160.86
Ice cream and related products	60.69	41.02	53.05	68.70	73.40	87.60	79.51	79.28
Miscellaneous dairy products	29.42	17.16	21.84	28.38	31.85	37.82	46.49	60.35
Fruits and vegetables	**555.96**	**393.67**	**521.10**	**524.32**	**584.88**	**780.41**	**704.31**	**830.41**
Fresh fruits	177.31	117.80	164.45	162.49	181.49	264.58	236.07	283.71
Apples	33.54	21.05	32.56	32.14	36.22	44.77	46.60	51.40
Bananas	28.89	22.26	29.82	29.19	27.71	40.10	32.72	36.74
Oranges	18.45	11.70	18.13	16.77	21.32	31.51	22.56	25.10
Citrus fruits, excl. oranges	14.77	10.87	12.75	14.79	14.97	24.38	17.36	22.43
Other fresh fruits	81.66	51.91	71.20	69.61	81.27	123.82	116.83	148.05
Fresh vegetables	179.41	123.72	175.08	159.25	179.28	265.97	235.70	270.38
Potatoes	30.86	23.13	33.07	31.61	30.38	43.42	37.58	34.94
Lettuce	22.56	14.43	22.56	20.57	26.11	29.61	25.96	34.70
Tomatoes	32.70	22.26	31.25	30.98	36.55	48.01	37.29	48.28
Other fresh vegetables	93.29	63.91	88.20	76.09	86.24	144.94	134.88	152.46
Processed fruits	112.03	84.33	102.45	109.12	121.66	151.07	133.27	161.17
Frozen fruits and fruit juices	12.22	10.72	9.05	11.21	14.91	17.73	16.51	15.27
Frozen orange juice	4.90	5.30	3.20	5.01	5.61	6.75	6.22	5.02
Frozen fruits	3.93	2.76	3.21	3.13	5.92	5.04	5.00	5.48
Frozen fruit juices, excl. orange	3.39	2.66	2.64	3.07	3.38	5.94	5.30	4.77
Canned fruits	16.94	14.19	14.93	14.53	18.42	22.67	18.04	25.20
Dried fruits	6.66	4.57	5.48	6.22	7.55	8.89	6.91	12.53
Fresh fruit juice	20.58	13.35	21.65	22.56	19.78	27.26	24.04	29.92
Canned and bottled fruit juice	55.62	41.50	51.35	54.60	61.00	74.53	67.77	78.25
Processed vegetables	87.21	67.82	79.11	93.45	102.45	98.79	99.27	115.15
Frozen vegetables	28.02	17.91	24.41	29.02	34.85	36.58	40.63	39.91
Canned and dried vegetables and juices	59.20	49.91	54.70	64.43	67.60	62.22	58.64	75.24
Canned beans	12.74	10.19	11.87	13.48	14.20	17.29	13.93	15.48
Canned corn	7.05	6.61	6.79	8.52	6.75	7.16	7.43	7.40
Canned miscellaneous vegetables	19.51	15.14	17.09	19.44	25.50	19.95	20.09	27.35
Dried peas	0.38	0.72	0.39	0.29	0.18	0.35	0.37	0.16
Dried beans	2.35	2.10	2.65	1.62	3.23	1.68	1.77	2.52
Dried miscellaneous vegetables	7.64	6.12	7.12	9.35	8.75	8.51	5.63	10.42
Dried processed vegetables	0.44	0.47	0.69	0.15	0.39	0.61	–	0.36
Fresh and canned vegetable juices	8.95	8.59	8.03	11.31	8.44	6.58	9.37	11.31
Sugar and other sweets	**123.46**	**85.07**	**110.31**	**126.16**	**135.79**	**158.82**	**159.64**	**190.27**
Candy and chewing gum	78.58	48.04	66.95	79.50	89.63	105.35	111.66	132.23
Sugar	17.12	15.38	17.73	18.82	17.12	21.69	18.01	15.61
Artificial sweeteners	5.99	5.05	4.71	7.03	6.46	10.54	4.95	8.08
Jams, preserves, other sweets	21.77	16.61	20.91	20.81	22.58	21.24	25.02	34.36
Fats and oils	**87.00**	**64.92**	**82.03**	**90.20**	**92.90**	**115.99**	**103.95**	**117.65**
Margarine	9.80	7.36	9.69	13.87	10.92	10.92	10.42	10.12
Fats and oils	26.62	22.71	24.79	23.64	24.23	35.64	29.63	39.53
Salad dressings	26.53	18.90	23.85	25.12	29.78	40.66	35.71	36.24
Nondairy cream and imitation milk	11.56	6.54	11.64	14.21	13.50	16.11	12.66	16.05
Peanut butter	12.49	9.41	12.05	13.36	14.47	12.67	15.53	15.72

	total complete reporters	under $20,000	$20,000–$39,999	$40,000–$49,999	$50,000–$69,999	$70,000–$79,999	$80,000–$99,999	$100,000 or more
Miscellaneous foods	**$513.36**	**$339.08**	**$434.43**	**$523.85**	**$591.16**	**$706.65**	**$730.59**	**$792.36**
Frozen prepared foods	109.63	76.47	96.00	114.11	127.16	162.51	139.66	153.96
Frozen meals	36.41	25.04	36.20	38.55	35.86	53.79	38.97	54.54
Other frozen prepared foods	73.22	51.43	59.80	75.57	91.30	108.72	100.69	99.42
Canned and packaged soups	37.25	27.52	33.08	39.81	43.72	49.03	47.38	48.63
Potato chips, nuts, and other snacks	111.97	70.98	93.54	115.33	128.90	155.63	167.17	177.01
Potato chips and other snacks	85.18	55.16	72.07	91.26	100.33	124.42	129.75	119.44
Nuts	26.79	15.82	21.46	24.07	28.57	31.21	37.42	57.57
Condiments and seasonings	94.00	59.42	80.19	89.37	109.15	128.53	135.99	153.66
Salt, spices, and other seasonings	21.71	14.01	19.63	19.90	25.66	31.49	28.76	33.15
Olives, pickles, relishes	11.32	6.92	10.57	11.31	12.55	13.82	15.14	18.78
Sauces and gravies	40.42	24.88	34.18	36.23	46.40	61.26	61.38	66.55
Baking needs and miscellaneous products	20.56	13.61	15.81	21.93	24.54	21.96	30.71	35.19
Other canned/packaged prepared foods	160.50	104.68	131.63	165.22	182.23	210.95	240.40	259.09
Prepared salads	21.08	12.27	15.96	18.83	23.03	28.51	32.88	43.23
Prepared desserts	11.62	7.29	9.49	11.47	14.67	13.55	17.67	18.60
Baby food	26.99	22.40	25.26	28.45	28.73	24.77	36.46	34.08
Miscellaneous prepared foods	100.54	62.73	80.92	105.09	115.33	143.48	152.84	163.18
Nonalcoholic beverages	**281.48**	**192.79**	**257.67**	**284.67**	**344.26**	**369.18**	**349.04**	**391.94**
Cola	93.37	66.43	91.62	96.00	125.06	113.59	120.77	96.37
Other carbonated drinks	48.87	33.32	46.13	50.37	60.62	62.18	52.84	69.04
Coffee	40.22	26.12	36.64	46.05	39.02	51.26	45.79	70.49
Roasted coffee	26.84	16.35	23.57	31.84	26.99	38.03	29.72	48.35
Instant and freeze-dried coffee	13.38	9.77	13.07	14.22	12.03	13.23	16.07	22.15
Noncarbonated fruit-flavored drinks, incl. nonfrozen lemonade	19.71	13.42	18.39	21.67	23.51	29.33	23.81	24.65
Tea	17.94	15.61	12.05	14.38	23.26	20.50	23.86	29.22
Other nonalcoholic beverages and ice	60.59	37.10	50.97	55.72	72.80	91.80	81.97	101.90
Food prepared by CU on trips	**38.20**	**13.95**	**24.32**	**28.40**	**45.10**	**56.63**	**73.32**	**94.00**
FOOD AWAY FROM HOME	**2,357.77**	**1,105.40**	**1,690.36**	**2,251.98**	**2,810.69**	**3,194.68**	**3,703.49**	**5,200.66**
Meals at restaurants, carry-outs, other	**1,956.55**	**973.26**	**1,445.26**	**1,959.55**	**2,346.98**	**2,686.70**	**3,077.75**	**4,016.64**
Lunch	706.60	348.87	550.11	727.62	869.03	1,027.69	1,072.71	1,347.36
• At fast food, take-out, delivery, concession stands, buffet, cafeteria (other than employer, school cafeteria)	395.14	226.17	331.71	425.06	450.43	621.94	556.25	658.36
• At full-service restaurants	225.04	97.49	157.94	207.46	286.03	275.29	337.76	535.52
• At vending machines, mobile vendors	6.88	2.46	7.77	2.74	15.96	4.67	9.11	7.75
• At employer and school cafeterias	79.54	22.75	52.68	92.36	116.61	125.79	169.58	145.74
Dinner	774.13	345.90	507.04	712.90	879.42	1,043.59	1,291.26	1,909.31
• At fast food, take-out, delivery, concession stands, buffet, cafeteria (other than employer, school cafeteria)	233.57	129.41	187.07	237.34	285.96	332.96	367.28	400.11
• At full-service restaurants	535.73	213.04	315.01	467.78	585.44	708.04	920.45	1,506.10
• At vending machines, mobile vendors	1.45	1.78	1.22	1.99	3.77	–	–	0.60
• At employer and school cafeterias	3.39	2.21	3.74	5.79	4.25	2.60	3.53	2.50
Snacks and nonalcoholic beverages	274.05	165.49	215.68	306.88	340.65	359.52	428.20	428.21
• At fast food, take-out, delivery, concession stands, buffet, cafeteria (other than employer, school cafeteria)	198.42	115.74	153.48	230.17	240.61	266.53	308.81	324.46
• At full-service restaurants	28.59	20.21	24.27	28.62	41.58	27.59	37.55	37.62
• At vending machines, mobile vendors	35.06	21.68	28.92	39.17	47.96	51.52	61.18	38.61
• At employer and school cafeterias	11.98	7.86	9.01	8.93	10.49	13.89	20.65	27.52
Breakfast and brunch	201.77	113.00	172.43	212.15	257.89	255.89	285.59	331.75
• At fast food, take-out, delivery, concession stands, buffet, cafeteria (other than employer, school cafeteria)	99.14	62.14	91.14	116.55	117.86	135.79	124.05	138.16
• At full-service restaurants	95.93	47.48	76.24	85.35	132.26	109.45	151.52	183.26
• At vending machines, mobile vendors	1.67	1.50	1.69	0.49	2.17	4.60	0.78	1.80
• At employer and school cafeterias	5.02	1.88	3.35	9.77	5.60	6.05	9.24	8.53
Board (including at school)	**37.17**	**23.70**	**9.17**	**11.99**	**20.56**	**19.21**	**43.43**	**170.52**
Catered affairs	**53.40**	**5.16**	**39.14**	**15.39**	**68.63**	**39.04**	**78.79**	**198.40**
Food on trips	**221.47**	**65.07**	**120.28**	**174.52**	**256.83**	**324.62**	**380.13**	**651.64**
School lunches	**60.91**	**10.66**	**38.14**	**68.73**	**87.47**	**102.99**	**114.48**	**137.44**
Meals as pay	**28.28**	**27.54**	**38.39**	**21.81**	**30.22**	**22.13**	**8.92**	**26.03**

	total complete reporters	under $20,000	$20,000–$39,999	$40,000–$49,999	$50,000–$69,999	$70,000–$79,999	$80,000–$99,999	$100,000 or more
ALCOHOLIC BEVERAGES	**$442.41**	**$200.86**	**$274.68**	**$407.20**	**$555.81**	**$617.95**	**$588.82**	**$1,126.82**
At home	**275.87**	**133.15**	**183.79**	**271.05**	**349.32**	**351.33**	**348.14**	**668.32**
Beer and ale	124.90	82.92	99.13	144.51	175.45	174.20	139.58	176.51
Whiskey	14.74	9.71	10.28	15.33	21.29	14.49	27.91	20.49
Wine	106.75	27.60	52.75	93.61	108.12	122.66	136.58	405.40
Other alcoholic beverages	29.48	12.92	21.62	17.60	44.46	39.98	44.08	65.93
Away from home	**166.54**	**67.71**	**90.90**	**136.15**	**206.49**	**266.61**	**240.68**	**458.50**
Beer and ale	66.94	28.80	39.99	55.78	89.49	102.58	99.08	167.23
• At fast food, take-out, delivery, concession stands, buffet, and cafeteria	12.08	7.69	11.14	10.18	15.59	14.08	17.61	18.24
• At full-service restaurants	52.43	20.65	28.52	45.59	72.82	80.71	81.47	134.13
Wine	20.64	7.63	8.41	19.92	23.51	35.56	31.46	63.18
• At fast food, take-out, delivery, concession stands, buffet and cafeteria	1.68	1.32	0.74	2.44	2.16	3.01	2.61	2.21
• At full-service restaurants	18.66	6.27	7.64	17.48	21.25	31.73	28.85	58.92
Other alcoholic beverages	43.49	18.11	22.73	38.32	56.61	64.53	51.38	125.55
• At fast food, take-out, delivery, concession stands, buffet, and cafeteria	9.03	5.98	7.99	10.39	10.92	8.82	9.70	15.02
• At full-service restaurants	33.37	11.97	14.66	27.93	45.06	51.96	41.68	104.02
Alcoholic beverages purchased on trips	35.47	13.17	19.72	22.14	36.88	63.94	58.76	102.54

Note: Subcategories may not add to total because some are not shown. (–) means sample is too small to make a reliable estimate.
Source: Bureau of Labor Statistics, unpublished tables from the 2003 Consumer Expenditure Survey; calculations by New Strategist

Table 5.6 Food and Alcohol: Indexed spending by income, 2003

(Indexed average annual spending of consumer units (CU) on food and beverages, by before-tax income of consumer unit, 2003; complete income reporters only; index definition: an index of 100 is the average for all consumer units; an index of 132 means that spending by consumer units in that group is 32 percent above the average for all consumer units; an index of 68 indicates spending that is 32 percent below the average for all consumer units)

	total complete reporters	under $20,000	$20,000–$39,999	$40,000–$49,999	$50,000–$69,999	$70,000–$79,999	$80,000–$99,999	$100,000 or more
Average spending of CU, total	$42,742	$19,863	$31,684	$39,757	$49,789	$57,128	$65,957	$93,515
Average spending of CU, index	100	46	74	93	116	134	154	219
Food, spending index	100	60	83	98	116	135	140	177
Alcoholic beverages, spending index	100	45	62	92	126	140	133	255
FOOD AT HOME	100	69	91	100	114	135	128	146
Cereals and bakery products	100	73	90	103	112	135	130	139
Cereals and cereal products	100	76	94	100	109	136	126	130
Flour	100	97	87	138	85	132	95	108
Prepared flour mixes	100	73	90	111	130	97	93	147
Ready-to-eat and cooked cereals	100	73	93	98	111	138	132	131
Rice	100	79	100	92	103	136	138	117
Pasta, cornmeal, and other cereal products	100	79	94	95	101	149	126	128
Bakery products	100	71	88	104	114	135	131	143
Bread	100	78	95	101	107	121	126	130
White bread	100	82	101	105	110	126	100	111
Bread, other than white	100	75	91	98	105	118	143	142
Crackers and cookies	100	73	85	108	112	132	135	143
Cookies	100	75	84	102	113	136	138	138
Crackers	100	67	86	119	109	125	130	152
Frozen and refrigerated bakery products	100	72	84	98	106	150	148	148
Other bakery products	100	65	84	105	122	143	129	152
Biscuits and rolls	100	61	79	96	125	137	130	180
Cakes and cupcakes	100	69	88	107	115	147	126	140
Bread and cracker products	100	55	92	107	126	173	137	136
Sweetrolls, coffee cakes, doughnuts	100	65	89	108	128	145	136	126
Pies, tarts, turnovers	100	69	77	125	110	132	119	165
Meats, poultry, fish, and eggs	100	68	95	98	121	131	116	141
Beef	100	61	91	101	141	138	124	133
Ground beef	100	72	93	104	140	128	107	112
Roast	100	68	104	124	105	91	121	134
Chuck roast	100	68	104	151	93	78	123	129
Round roast	100	54	123	69	175	105	79	104
Other roast	100	75	93	133	74	93	143	157
Steak	100	49	87	94	154	160	133	146
Round steak	100	57	87	88	188	148	103	113
Sirloin steak	100	38	76	87	201	168	116	148
Other steak	100	53	94	101	110	158	154	156
Other beef	100	50	76	79	152	171	161	162
Pork	100	77	104	97	109	115	111	126
Bacon	100	74	97	97	113	113	127	134
Pork chops	100	78	98	93	138	130	84	111
Ham	100	78	104	103	100	70	131	139
Ham, not canned	100	77	106	102	100	72	128	138
Canned ham	100	117	52	143	92	–	190	162
Sausage	100	91	102	89	96	132	112	110
Other pork	100	68	115	98	98	136	102	131
Other meats	100	72	92	99	125	131	119	131
Frankfurters	100	75	99	103	127	111	100	119
Lunch meats (cold cuts)	100	72	91	102	126	133	129	122
Bologna, liverwurst, salami	100	88	93	109	112	120	111	103
Other lunch meats	100	65	89	100	132	138	136	131
Lamb, organ meats, and others	100	61	83	67	110	165	90	224
Poultry	100	71	93	98	113	144	117	142
Fresh and frozen chicken	100	72	94	98	113	145	117	135

	total complete reporters	under $20,000	$20,000– $39,999	$40,000– $49,999	$50,000– $69,999	$70,000– $79,999	$80,000– $99,999	$100,000 or more
Fresh and frozen whole chicken	100	72	110	86	107	140	94	135
Fresh and frozen chicken parts	100	72	88	103	115	147	126	134
Other poultry	100	65	86	100	111	138	118	174
Fish and seafood	100	61	91	92	112	128	104	191
Canned fish and seafood	100	76	92	92	123	134	103	140
Fresh fish and shellfish	100	58	92	87	98	135	109	215
Frozen fish and shellfish	100	61	90	100	134	114	95	169
Eggs	100	84	106	104	93	109	104	123
Dairy products	**100**	**68**	**91**	**107**	**112**	**133**	**133**	**144**
Fresh milk and cream	100	75	95	108	106	136	122	127
Fresh milk, all types	100	78	95	108	106	138	121	120
Cream	100	55	96	103	107	116	130	184
Other dairy products	100	63	88	106	115	131	140	155
Butter	100	71	94	110	97	118	133	151
Cheese	100	61	91	104	117	126	141	155
Ice cream and related products	100	68	87	113	121	144	131	131
Miscellaneous dairy products	100	58	74	96	108	129	158	205
Fruits and vegetables	**100**	**71**	**94**	**94**	**105**	**140**	**127**	**149**
Fresh fruits	100	66	93	92	102	149	133	160
Apples	100	63	97	96	108	133	139	153
Bananas	100	77	103	101	96	139	113	127
Oranges	100	63	98	91	116	171	122	136
Citrus fruits, excl. oranges	100	74	86	100	101	165	118	152
Other fresh fruits	100	64	87	85	100	152	143	181
Fresh vegetables	100	69	98	89	100	148	131	151
Potatoes	100	75	107	102	98	141	122	113
Lettuce	100	64	100	91	116	131	115	154
Tomatoes	100	68	96	95	112	147	114	148
Other fresh vegetables	100	69	95	82	92	155	145	163
Processed fruits	100	75	91	97	109	135	119	144
Frozen fruits and fruit juices	100	88	74	92	122	145	135	125
Frozen orange juice	100	108	65	102	114	138	127	102
Frozen fruits	100	70	82	80	151	128	127	139
Frozen fruit juices, excl. orange	100	78	78	91	100	175	156	141
Canned fruits	100	84	88	86	109	134	106	149
Dried fruits	100	69	82	93	113	133	104	188
Fresh fruit juice	100	65	105	110	96	132	117	145
Canned and bottled fruit juice	100	75	92	98	110	134	122	141
Processed vegetables	100	78	91	107	117	113	114	132
Frozen vegetables	100	64	87	104	124	131	145	142
Canned and dried vegetables and juices	100	84	92	109	114	105	99	127
Canned beans	100	80	93	106	111	136	109	122
Canned corn	100	94	96	121	96	102	105	105
Canned miscellaneous vegetables	100	78	88	100	131	102	103	140
Dried peas	100	190	102	76	47	92	97	42
Dried beans	100	89	113	69	137	71	75	107
Dried miscellaneous vegetables	100	80	93	122	115	111	74	136
Dried processed vegetables	100	106	156	34	89	139	–	82
Fresh and canned vegetable juices	100	96	90	126	94	74	105	126
Sugar and other sweets	**100**	**69**	**89**	**102**	**110**	**129**	**129**	**154**
Candy and chewing gum	100	61	85	101	114	134	142	168
Sugar	100	90	104	110	100	127	105	91
Artificial sweeteners	100	84	79	117	108	176	83	135
Jams, preserves, other sweets	100	76	96	96	104	98	115	158
Fats and oils	**100**	**75**	**94**	**104**	**107**	**133**	**119**	**135**
Margarine	100	75	99	142	111	111	106	103
Fats and oils	100	85	93	89	91	134	111	148
Salad dressings	100	71	90	95	112	153	135	137
Nondairy cream and imitation milk	100	57	101	123	117	139	110	139
Peanut butter	100	75	97	107	116	101	124	126

	total complete reporters	under $20,000	$20,000– $39,999	$40,000– $49,999	$50,000– $69,999	$70,000– $79,999	$80,000– $99,999	$100,000 or more
Miscellaneous foods	**100**	**66**	**85**	**102**	**115**	**138**	**142**	**154**
Frozen prepared foods	100	70	88	104	116	148	127	140
Frozen meals	100	69	99	106	98	148	107	150
Other frozen prepared foods	100	70	82	103	125	148	138	136
Canned and packaged soups	100	74	89	107	117	132	127	131
Potato chips, nuts, and other snacks	100	63	84	103	115	139	149	158
Potato chips and other snacks	100	65	85	107	118	146	152	140
Nuts	100	59	80	90	107	116	140	215
Condiments and seasonings	100	63	85	95	116	137	145	163
Salt, spices, and other seasonings	100	65	90	92	118	145	132	153
Olives, pickles, relishes	100	61	93	100	111	122	134	166
Sauces and gravies	100	62	85	90	115	152	152	165
Baking needs and miscellaneous products	100	66	77	107	119	107	149	171
Other canned/packaged prepared foods	100	65	82	103	114	131	150	161
Prepared salads	100	58	76	89	109	135	156	205
Prepared desserts	100	63	82	99	126	117	152	160
Baby food	100	83	94	105	106	92	135	126
Miscellaneous prepared foods	100	62	80	105	115	143	152	162
Nonalcoholic beverages	**100**	**68**	**92**	**101**	**122**	**131**	**124**	**139**
Cola	100	71	98	103	134	122	129	103
Other carbonated drinks	100	68	94	103	124	127	108	141
Coffee	100	65	91	114	97	127	114	175
Roasted coffee	100	61	88	119	101	142	111	180
Instant and freeze-dried coffee	100	73	98	106	90	99	120	166
Noncarbonated fruit-flavored drinks, incl. nonfrozen lemonade	100	68	93	110	119	149	121	125
Tea	100	87	67	80	130	114	133	163
Other nonalcoholic beverages and ice	100	61	84	92	120	152	135	168
Food prepared by CU on trips	**100**	**37**	**64**	**74**	**118**	**148**	**192**	**246**
FOOD AWAY FROM HOME	**100**	**47**	**72**	**96**	**119**	**135**	**157**	**221**
Meals at restaurants, carry-outs, other	**100**	**50**	**74**	**100**	**120**	**137**	**157**	**205**
Lunch	100	49	78	103	123	145	152	191
• At fast food, take-out, delivery, concession stands, buffet, cafeteria (other than employer, school cafeteria)	100	57	84	108	114	157	141	167
• At full-service restaurants	100	43	70	92	127	122	150	238
• At vending machines, mobile vendors	100	36	113	40	232	68	132	113
• At employer and school cafeterias	100	29	66	116	147	158	213	183
Dinner	100	45	65	92	114	135	167	247
• At fast food, take-out, delivery, concession stands, buffet, cafeteria (other than employer, school cafeteria)	100	55	80	102	122	143	157	171
• At full-service restaurants	100	40	59	87	109	132	172	281
• At vending machines, mobile vendors	100	123	84	137	260	–	–	41
• At employer and school cafeterias	100	65	110	171	125	77	104	74
Snacks and nonalcoholic beverages	100	60	79	112	124	131	156	156
• At fast food, take-out, delivery, concession stands, buffet, cafeteria (other than employer, school cafeteria)	100	58	77	116	121	134	156	164
• At full-service restaurants	100	71	85	100	145	97	131	132
• At vending machines, mobile vendors	100	62	82	112	137	147	175	110
• At employer and school cafeterias	100	66	75	75	88	116	172	230
Breakfast and brunch	100	56	85	105	128	127	142	164
• At fast food, take-out, delivery, concession stands, buffet, cafeteria (other than employer, school cafeteria)	100	63	92	118	119	137	125	139
• At full-service restaurants	100	49	79	89	138	114	158	191
• At vending machines, mobile vendors	100	90	101	29	130	275	47	108
• At employer and school cafeterias	100	37	67	195	112	121	184	170
Board (including at school)	**100**	**64**	**25**	**32**	**55**	**52**	**117**	**459**
Catered affairs	**100**	**10**	**73**	**29**	**129**	**73**	**148**	**372**
Food on trips	**100**	**29**	**54**	**79**	**116**	**147**	**172**	**294**
School lunches	**100**	**18**	**63**	**113**	**144**	**169**	**188**	**226**
Meals as pay	**100**	**97**	**136**	**77**	**107**	**78**	**32**	**92**

	total complete reporters	under $20,000	$20,000–$39,999	$40,000–$49,999	$50,000–$69,999	$70,000–$79,999	$80,000–$99,999	$100,000 or more
ALCOHOLIC BEVERAGES	**100**	**45**	**62**	**92**	**126**	**140**	**133**	**255**
At home	**100**	**48**	**67**	**98**	**127**	**127**	**126**	**242**
Beer and ale	100	66	79	116	140	139	112	141
Whiskey	100	66	70	104	144	98	189	139
Wine	100	26	49	88	101	115	128	380
Other alcoholic beverages	100	44	73	60	151	136	150	224
Away from home	**100**	**41**	**55**	**82**	**124**	**160**	**145**	**275**
Beer and ale	100	43	60	83	134	153	148	250
• At fast food, take-out, delivery, concession stands, buffet, and cafeteria	100	64	92	84	129	117	146	151
• At full-service restaurants	100	39	54	87	139	154	155	256
Wine	100	37	41	97	114	172	152	306
• At fast food, take-out, delivery, concession stands, buffet and cafeteria	100	79	44	145	129	179	155	132
• At full-service restaurants	100	34	41	94	114	170	155	316
Other alcoholic beverages	100	42	52	88	130	148	118	289
• At fast food, take-out, delivery, concession stands, buffet, and cafeteria	100	66	88	115	121	98	107	166
• At full-service restaurants	100	36	44	84	135	156	125	312
Alcoholic beverages purchased on trips	100	37	56	62	104	180	166	289

Note: (–) means sample is too small to make a reliable estimate.
Source: Calculations by New Strategist based on the 2003 Consumer Expenditure Survey

Table 5.7 Food and Alcohol: Total spending by income, 2003

(total annual spending on food and alcoholic beverages, by before-tax income group of consumer units (CU), 2003; complete income reporters only; numbers in thousands)

	total complete reporters	under $20,000	$20,000–$39,999	$40,000–$49,999	$50,000–$69,999	$70,000–$79,999	$80,000–$99,999	$100,000 or more
Number of consumer units	97,391	27,100	23,941	8,891	13,890	5,121	6,909	11,537
Total spending of all CUs	$4,162,653,009	$538,274,380	$758,554,310	$353,478,687	$691,569,071	$292,553,205	$455,699,608	$1,078,880,940
Food, total spending	544,752,663	90,260,728	110,905,207	48,772,825	90,433,623	38,655,100	54,163,865	114,521,454
Alcoholic beverages, total spending	43,086,752	5,443,213	6,576,171	3,620,415	7,720,201	3,164,522	4,068,157	13,000,122
FOOD AT HOME	315,126,111	60,304,488	70,436,290	28,750,382	51,393,139	22,295,144	28,576,453	54,521,439
Cereals and bakery products	44,423,931	8,996,414	9,783,107	4,163,566	7,093,901	3,158,582	4,085,775	7,291,845
Cereals and cereal products	15,063,466	3,189,435	3,466,861	1,376,594	2,336,020	1,077,305	1,351,608	2,312,938
Flour	729,459	196,864	155,870	92,022	88,340	50,749	48,985	93,680
Prepared flour mixes	1,294,326	262,077	287,630	131,320	240,436	65,856	85,464	225,433
Ready-to-eat and cooked cereals	8,752,529	1,788,763	2,008,694	785,520	1,385,250	635,362	821,411	1,363,212
Rice	1,555,334	340,428	383,329	130,431	228,074	111,177	151,791	216,203
Pasta, cornmeal, and other cereal products	2,730,844	601,375	631,338	237,301	393,920	214,160	243,957	414,294
Bakery products	29,361,439	5,806,897	6,316,246	2,786,973	4,758,020	2,081,277	2,734,168	4,978,908
Bread	8,274,339	1,792,598	1,937,748	760,714	1,258,156	527,821	738,503	1,273,223
White bread	3,319,085	760,111	824,754	319,187	518,375	220,561	234,561	437,483
Bread, other than white	4,955,254	1,032,487	1,112,994	441,527	739,781	307,260	503,942	835,740
Crackers and cookies	7,075,456	1,427,728	1,477,802	698,121	1,126,618	490,694	678,464	1,198,579
Cookies	4,547,186	955,008	941,627	422,945	732,003	324,006	445,009	742,867
Crackers	2,528,270	472,720	536,175	275,088	394,615	166,689	233,455	455,827
Frozen and refrigerated bakery products	2,463,018	492,458	506,115	220,052	371,835	194,854	259,018	433,099
Other bakery products	11,548,625	2,094,194	2,394,581	1,108,085	2,001,410	867,907	1,058,182	2,074,006
Biscuits and rolls	3,784,614	644,052	732,599	332,434	675,332	273,154	348,006	806,436
Cakes and cupcakes	3,636,580	699,646	786,736	353,862	597,548	281,757	324,378	603,962
Bread and cracker products	367,164	55,936	83,043	35,742	65,978	33,338	35,581	58,954
Sweetrolls, coffee cakes, doughnuts	2,803,887	510,036	610,320	277,399	512,402	213,290	269,658	417,293
Pies, tarts, turnovers	955,406	184,370	181,883	108,648	150,151	66,368	80,559	187,246
Meats, poultry, fish, and eggs	81,494,841	15,464,968	18,979,725	7,301,200	14,048,068	5,601,708	6,681,763	13,650,232
Beef	24,590,254	4,145,569	5,476,248	2,269,428	4,935,395	1,786,000	2,164,797	3,887,508
Ground beef	8,955,102	1,803,763	2,042,156	852,113	1,784,309	602,690	681,227	1,192,349
Roast	3,980,370	748,213	1,017,272	449,885	596,853	190,143	341,305	633,958
Chuck roast	1,386,848	262,903	353,471	191,334	183,904	57,048	121,184	212,165
Round roast	956,380	143,117	289,408	60,370	239,186	52,900	53,614	117,677
Other roast	1,637,143	342,311	374,393	198,269	173,625	80,246	166,507	304,231
Steak	9,307,658	1,265,622	1,980,461	798,145	2,046,830	781,874	875,094	1,609,873
Round steak	1,567,995	248,713	334,684	125,363	420,034	121,675	114,206	209,050
Sirloin steak	3,174,947	339,896	594,494	252,415	911,601	280,119	261,229	555,968
Other steak	4,564,716	677,057	1,051,284	420,366	715,196	380,132	499,659	844,855
Other beef	2,346,149	327,826	436,120	169,285	507,402	211,292	267,171	451,212
Pork	16,694,765	3,561,072	4,274,503	1,472,172	2,590,624	1,013,497	1,311,950	2,493,146
Bacon	3,066,843	629,559	734,647	271,798	494,762	182,052	276,498	485,938
Pork chops	3,303,503	716,164	799,828	279,533	650,885	226,604	196,147	435,983
Ham	3,671,641	792,499	941,047	346,393	521,153	134,529	339,923	603,154
Ham, not canned	3,553,798	759,886	925,636	330,923	505,596	134,529	323,894	580,426
Canned ham	118,817	38,843	15,303	15,559	15,557	–	16,029	22,843
Sausage	2,505,870	635,931	628,433	203,782	342,805	174,421	199,117	326,382
Other pork	4,145,935	786,952	1,170,524	370,666	581,019	295,891	300,196	641,688
Other meats	10,113,081	2,017,931	2,281,242	914,439	1,797,783	695,329	851,603	1,574,108
Frankfurters	2,253,628	471,057	550,941	210,895	409,477	131,098	160,358	318,767
Lunch meats (cold cuts)	6,900,152	1,383,620	1,535,447	644,953	1,237,460	481,118	630,101	1,000,604
Bologna, liverwurst, salami	2,090,985	514,427	480,056	207,338	334,193	131,712	164,503	255,314
Other lunch meats	4,809,168	869,275	1,055,390	437,615	903,267	349,406	465,528	745,290
Lamb, organ meats, and others	958,327	163,297	194,854	58,592	150,845	83,114	61,145	254,737
Poultry	14,162,599	2,787,292	3,234,828	1,272,213	2,274,210	1,069,418	1,178,468	2,385,390
Fresh and frozen chicken	11,402,538	2,289,967	2,648,126	1,019,086	1,837,647	868,931	946,809	1,817,654

	total complete reporters	under $20,000	$20,000–$39,999	$40,000–$49,999	$50,000–$69,999	$70,000–$79,999	$80,000–$99,999	$100,000 or more
Fresh and frozen whole chicken	$3,207,086	$639,771	$867,805	$251,793	$491,289	$236,078	$212,728	$514,089
Fresh and frozen chicken parts	8,195,453	1,650,267	1,780,189	767,293	1,346,358	632,853	734,012	1,303,566
Other poultry	2,760,061	497,325	586,702	253,127	436,424	200,487	231,659	567,736
Fish and seafood	12,198,223	2,076,667	2,738,742	1,019,620	1,953,629	824,071	900,174	2,765,304
Canned fish and seafood	1,546,569	325,177	348,488	130,431	270,994	109,231	112,617	256,468
Fresh fish and shellfish	6,938,135	1,116,393	1,565,672	549,464	972,439	491,360	536,277	1,766,776
Frozen fish and shellfish	3,712,545	635,097	824,582	339,725	710,196	223,480	251,280	742,060
Eggs	3,736,893	876,437	974,163	353,328	496,429	213,443	274,771	544,777
Dairy products	**33,434,330**	**6,318,080**	**7,441,379**	**3,259,085**	**5,331,121**	**2,331,745**	**3,155,962**	**5,698,701**
Fresh milk and cream	12,822,499	2,690,099	2,992,448	1,262,255	1,941,822	914,099	1,111,244	1,922,756
Fresh milk, all types	11,447,338	2,479,549	2,669,363	1,133,069	1,732,639	829,960	984,671	1,622,910
Cream	1,375,161	210,550	323,084	129,186	209,045	84,138	126,573	299,847
Other dairy products	20,610,857	3,628,137	4,449,063	1,996,830	3,389,438	1,417,646	2,044,719	3,775,945
Butter	1,731,612	341,029	401,018	173,319	238,630	107,592	163,951	309,192
Cheese	10,103,342	1,710,281	2,255,193	959,783	1,688,746	667,778	1,010,165	1,855,842
Ice cream and related products	5,910,660	1,111,746	1,270,106	610,312	1,019,526	448,600	549,335	914,653
Miscellaneous dairy products	2,865,243	465,027	522,770	252,327	442,397	193,676	321,199	696,258
Fruits and vegetables	**54,145,500**	**10,668,539**	**12,475,541**	**4,661,729**	**8,123,983**	**3,996,480**	**4,866,078**	**9,580,440**
Fresh fruits	17,268,398	3,192,264	3,937,207	1,444,699	2,520,896	1,354,914	1,631,008	3,273,162
Apples	3,266,494	570,570	779,427	285,757	503,096	229,267	321,959	593,002
Bananas	2,813,626	603,268	713,938	259,528	384,892	205,352	226,062	423,869
Oranges	1,796,864	317,077	434,127	149,102	296,135	161,363	155,867	289,579
Citrus fruits, excl. oranges	1,438,465	294,499	305,259	131,498	207,933	124,850	119,940	258,775
Other fresh fruits	7,952,949	1,406,780	1,704,588	618,903	1,128,840	634,082	807,178	1,708,053
Fresh vegetables	17,472,919	3,352,929	4,191,603	1,415,892	2,490,199	1,362,032	1,628,451	3,119,374
Potatoes	3,005,486	626,745	791,618	281,045	421,978	222,354	259,640	403,103
Lettuce	2,197,141	390,977	540,160	182,888	362,668	151,633	179,358	400,334
Tomatoes	3,184,686	603,143	748,095	275,443	507,680	245,859	257,637	557,006
Other fresh vegetables	9,085,606	1,732,029	2,111,623	676,516	1,197,874	742,238	931,886	1,758,931
Processed fruits	10,910,714	2,285,390	2,452,869	970,186	1,689,857	773,629	920,762	1,859,418
Frozen fruits and fruit juices	1,190,118	290,554	216,733	99,668	207,100	90,795	114,068	176,170
Frozen orange juice	477,216	143,727	76,511	44,544	77,923	34,567	42,974	57,916
Frozen fruits	382,747	74,752	76,796	27,829	82,229	25,810	34,545	63,223
Frozen fruit juices, excl. orange	330,155	72,001	63,293	27,295	46,948	30,419	36,618	55,031
Canned fruits	1,649,804	384,440	357,430	129,186	255,854	116,093	124,638	290,732
Dried fruits	648,624	123,905	131,106	55,302	104,870	45,526	47,741	144,559
Fresh fruit juice	2,004,307	361,724	518,314	200,581	274,744	139,598	166,092	345,187
Canned and bottled fruit juice	5,416,887	1,124,649	1,229,287	485,449	847,290	381,668	468,223	902,770
Processed vegetables	8,493,469	1,838,000	1,893,863	830,864	1,423,031	505,904	685,856	1,328,486
Frozen vegetables	2,728,896	485,459	584,384	258,017	484,067	187,326	280,713	460,442
Canned and dried vegetables and juices	5,765,547	1,352,467	1,309,611	572,847	938,964	318,629	405,144	868,044
Canned beans	1,240,761	276,274	284,132	119,851	197,238	88,542	96,242	178,593
Canned corn	686,607	179,094	162,461	75,751	93,758	36,666	51,334	85,374
Canned miscellaneous vegetables	1,900,098	410,353	409,251	172,841	354,195	102,164	138,802	315,537
Dried peas	37,009	19,532	9,305	2,578	2,500	1,792	2,556	1,846
Dried beans	228,869	56,877	53,481	14,403	44,865	8,603	12,229	29,073
Dried miscellaneous vegetables	744,067	165,837	170,450	83,131	121,538	43,580	38,898	120,216
Dried processed vegetables	42,852	12,653	16,429	1,334	5,417	3,124	–	4,153
Fresh and canned vegetable juices	871,649	232,672	192,245	100,557	117,232	33,696	64,737	130,483
Sugar and other sweets	**12,023,893**	**2,305,427**	**2,640,885**	**1,121,689**	**1,886,123**	**813,317**	**1,102,953**	**2,195,145**
Candy and chewing gum	7,652,985	1,301,842	1,602,942	706,835	1,244,961	539,497	771,459	1,525,538
Sugar	1,667,334	416,703	424,392	167,329	237,797	111,074	124,431	180,093
Artificial sweeteners	583,372	136,946	112,750	62,504	89,729	53,975	34,200	93,219
Jams, preserves, other sweets	2,120,202	450,039	500,669	185,022	313,636	108,770	172,863	396,411
Fats and oils	**8,473,017**	**1,759,328**	**1,963,846**	**801,968**	**1,290,381**	**593,985**	**718,191**	**1,357,328**
Margarine	954,432	199,429	231,882	123,318	151,679	55,921	71,992	116,754
Fats and oils	2,592,548	615,516	593,570	210,183	336,555	182,512	204,714	456,058
Salad dressings	2,583,783	512,069	571,069	223,342	413,644	208,220	246,720	418,101
Nondairy cream and imitation milk	1,125,840	177,215	278,724	126,341	187,515	82,499	87,468	185,169
Peanut butter	1,216,414	255,071	288,601	118,784	200,988	64,883	107,297	181,362

	total complete reporters	under $20,000	$20,000– $39,999	$40,000– $49,999	$50,000– $69,999	$70,000– $79,999	$80,000– $99,999	$100,000 or more
Miscellaneous foods	**$49,996,644**	**$9,188,985**	**$10,400,710**	**$4,657,550**	**$8,211,212**	**$3,618,755**	**$5,047,646**	**$9,141,457**
Frozen prepared foods	10,676,975	2,072,334	2,298,320	1,014,552	1,766,252	832,214	964,911	1,776,237
Frozen meals	3,546,006	678,581	866,610	342,748	498,095	275,459	269,244	629,228
Other frozen prepared foods	7,130,969	1,393,834	1,431,710	671,893	1,268,157	556,755	695,667	1,147,009
Canned and packaged soups	3,627,815	745,827	791,937	353,951	607,271	251,083	327,348	561,044
Potato chips, nuts, and other snacks	10,904,870	1,923,564	2,239,456	1,025,399	1,790,421	796,981	1,154,978	2,042,164
Potato chips and other snacks	8,295,765	1,494,788	1,725,469	811,393	1,393,584	637,155	896,443	1,377,979
Nuts	2,609,105	428,776	513,879	214,006	396,837	159,826	258,535	664,185
Condiments and seasonings	9,154,754	1,610,308	1,919,852	794,589	1,516,094	658,202	939,555	1,772,775
Salt, spices, and other seasonings	2,114,359	379,679	470,067	175,931	356,417	161,260	198,703	382,452
Olives, pickles, relishes	1,102,466	187,532	253,063	100,557	174,320	70,772	104,602	216,665
Sauces and gravies	3,936,544	674,171	818,345	322,121	644,496	313,712	424,074	767,787
Baking needs and miscellaneous products	2,002,359	368,935	378,485	194,980	340,861	112,457	212,175	405,987
Other canned/packaged prepared foods	15,631,256	2,836,825	3,151,253	1,468,971	2,531,175	1,080,275	1,660,924	2,989,121
Prepared salads	2,053,002	332,456	382,045	167,418	319,887	146,000	227,168	498,745
Prepared desserts	1,131,683	197,564	227,157	101,980	203,766	69,390	122,082	214,588
Baby food	2,628,583	606,934	604,793	252,949	399,060	126,847	251,902	393,181
Miscellaneous prepared foods	9,791,691	1,699,880	1,937,258	934,355	1,601,934	734,761	1,055,972	1,882,608
Nonalcoholic beverages	**27,413,619**	**5,224,640**	**6,168,786**	**2,531,001**	**4,781,771**	**1,890,571**	**2,411,517**	**4,521,812**
Cola	9,093,398	1,800,306	2,193,453	853,536	1,737,083	581,694	834,400	1,111,821
Other carbonated drinks	4,759,498	903,086	1,104,332	447,840	842,012	318,424	365,072	796,514
Coffee	3,917,066	707,952	877,247	409,431	541,988	262,502	316,363	813,243
Roasted coffee	2,613,974	443,144	564,364	283,089	374,891	194,752	205,335	557,814
Instant and freeze-dried coffee	1,303,092	264,771	312,884	126,430	167,097	67,751	111,028	255,545
Noncarbonated fruit-flavored drinks, incl. nonfrozen lemonade	1,919,577	363,589	440,336	192,668	326,554	150,199	164,503	284,387
Tea	1,747,195	423,013	288,437	127,853	323,081	104,981	164,849	337,111
Other nonalcoholic beverages and ice	5,900,921	1,005,336	1,220,333	495,407	1,011,192	470,108	566,331	1,175,620
Food prepared by CU on trips	**3,720,336**	**377,952**	**582,310**	**252,504**	**626,439**	**290,002**	**506,568**	**1,084,478**
FOOD AWAY FROM HOME	**229,625,578**	**29,956,240**	**40,468,917**	**20,022,354**	**39,040,484**	**16,359,956**	**25,587,412**	**60,000,014**
Meals at restaurants, carry-outs, other	**190,550,361**	**26,375,366**	**34,600,876**	**17,422,359**	**32,599,552**	**13,758,591**	**21,264,175**	**46,339,976**
Lunch	68,816,481	9,454,348	13,170,175	6,459,269	12,070,827	5,262,800	7,411,353	15,544,492
• At fast food, take-out, delivery, concession stands, buffet, cafeteria (other than employer, school cafeteria)	38,483,080	6,129,081	7,941,375	3,779,208	6,256,473	3,184,955	3,843,131	7,595,499
• At full-service restaurants	21,916,871	2,642,066	3,781,268	1,844,527	3,972,957	1,409,760	2,333,584	6,178,294
• At vending machines, mobile vendors	670,050	66,772	186,138	24,361	221,684	23,915	62,941	89,412
• At employer and school cafeterias	7,746,480	616,429	1,261,261	821,173	1,619,713	644,171	1,171,628	1,681,402
Dinner	75,393,295	9,373,782	12,139,002	6,338,394	12,215,144	5,344,224	8,921,315	22,027,709
• At fast food, take-out, delivery, concession stands, buffet, cafeteria (other than employer, school cafeteria)	22,747,616	3,506,918	4,478,669	2,110,190	3,971,984	1,705,088	2,537,538	4,616,069
• At full-service restaurants	52,175,280	5,773,386	7,541,737	4,159,032	8,131,762	3,625,873	6,359,389	17,375,876
• At vending machines, mobile vendors	141,217	48,221	29,153	17,693	52,365	–	–	6,922
• At employer and school cafeterias	330,155	59,896	89,551	51,479	59,033	13,315	24,389	28,843
Snacks and nonalcoholic beverages	26,690,004	4,484,885	5,163,605	2,728,470	4,731,629	1,841,102	2,958,434	4,940,259
• At fast food, take-out, delivery, concession stands, buffet, cafeteria (other than employer, school cafeteria)	19,324,322	3,136,421	3,674,488	2,046,441	3,342,073	1,364,900	2,133,568	3,743,295
• At full-service restaurants	2,784,409	547,799	581,098	254,460	577,546	141,288	259,433	434,022
• At vending machines, mobile vendors	3,414,528	587,527	692,358	348,260	666,164	263,834	422,693	445,444
• At employer and school cafeterias	1,166,744	213,026	215,660	79,397	145,706	71,131	142,671	317,498
Breakfast and brunch	19,650,582	3,062,423	4,128,095	1,886,226	3,582,092	1,310,413	1,973,141	3,827,400
• At fast food, take-out, delivery, concession stands, buffet, cafeteria (other than employer, school cafeteria)	9,655,344	1,683,943	2,182,040	1,036,246	1,637,075	695,381	857,061	1,593,952
• At full-service restaurants	9,342,719	1,286,766	1,825,201	758,847	1,837,091	560,493	1,046,852	2,114,271
• At vending machines, mobile vendors	162,643	40,781	40,572	4,357	30,141	23,557	5,389	20,767
• At employer and school cafeterias	488,903	50,934	80,282	86,865	77,784	30,982	63,839	98,411
Board (including at school)	**3,620,023**	**642,284**	**219,464**	**106,603**	**285,578**	**98,374**	**300,058**	**1,967,289**
Catered affairs	**5,200,679**	**139,958**	**936,950**	**136,832**	**953,271**	**199,924**	**544,360**	**2,288,941**
Food on trips	**21,569,185**	**1,763,361**	**2,879,742**	**1,551,657**	**3,567,369**	**1,662,379**	**2,626,318**	**7,517,971**
School lunches	**5,932,086**	**288,945**	**913,035**	**611,078**	**1,214,958**	**527,412**	**790,942**	**1,585,645**
Meals as pay	**2,754,217**	**746,400**	**918,981**	**193,913**	**419,756**	**113,328**	**61,628**	**300,308**

	total complete reporters	under $20,000	$20,000–$39,999	$40,000–$49,999	$50,000–$69,999	$70,000–$79,999	$80,000–$99,999	$100,000 or more
ALCOHOLIC BEVERAGES	**$43,086,752**	**$5,443,213**	**$6,576,171**	**$3,620,415**	**$7,720,201**	**$3,164,522**	**$4,068,157**	**$13,000,122**
At home	**26,867,255**	**3,608,354**	**4,400,107**	**2,409,906**	**4,852,055**	**1,799,161**	**2,405,299**	**7,710,408**
Beer and ale	12,164,136	2,247,239	2,373,352	1,284,838	2,437,001	892,078	964,358	2,036,396
Whiskey	1,435,543	263,086	246,208	136,299	295,718	74,203	192,830	236,393
Wine	10,396,489	747,890	1,262,789	832,287	1,501,787	628,142	943,631	4,677,100
Other alcoholic beverages	2,871,087	350,139	517,626	156,482	617,549	204,738	304,549	760,634
Away from home	**16,219,497**	**1,834,859**	**2,176,172**	**1,210,510**	**2,868,146**	**1,365,310**	**1,662,858**	**5,289,715**
Beer and ale	6,519,354	780,480	957,303	495,940	1,243,016	525,312	684,544	1,929,333
• At fast food, take-out, delivery, concession stands, buffet, and cafeteria	1,176,483	208,330	266,756	90,510	216,545	72,104	121,667	210,435
• At full-service restaurants	5,106,210	559,529	682,769	405,341	1,011,470	413,316	562,876	1,547,458
Wine	2,010,150	206,719	201,263	177,109	326,554	182,103	217,357	728,908
• At fast food, take-out, delivery, concession stands, buffet and cafeteria	163,617	35,774	17,773	21,694	30,002	15,414	18,032	25,497
• At full-service restaurants	1,817,316	169,933	182,807	155,415	295,163	162,489	199,325	679,760
Other alcoholic beverages	4,235,535	490,743	545,455	340,703	786,313	330,458	354,984	1,448,470
• At fast food, take-out, delivery, concession stands, buffet, and cafeteria	879,441	162,052	191,287	92,377	151,679	45,167	67,017	173,286
• At full-service restaurants	3,249,938	324,439	350,873	248,326	625,883	266,087	287,967	1,200,079
Alcoholic beverages purchased on trips	3,454,459	356,989	472,044	196,847	512,263	327,437	405,973	1,183,004

Note: Numbers may not add to total because of rounding and missing subcategories. (–) means sample is too small to make a reliable estimate.
Source: Calculations by New Strategist based on the 2003 Consumer Expenditure Survey

Table 5.8 Food and Alcohol: Market shares by income, 2003

(percentage of total annual spending on food and alcoholic beverages accounted for by before-tax income group of consumer units, 2003; complete income reporters only)

	total complete reporters	under $20,000	$20,000– $39,999	$40,000– $49,999	$50,000– $69,999	$70,000– $79,999	$80,000– $99,999	$100,000 or more
Share of total consumer units	100.0%	27.8%	24.6%	9.1%	14.3%	5.3%	7.1%	11.8%
Share of total before-tax income	100.0	5.9	14.0	7.9	16.4	7.7	12.3	35.8
Share of total spending	100.0	12.9	18.2	8.5	16.6	7.0	10.9	25.9
Share of food spending	100.0	16.6	20.4	9.0	16.6	7.1	9.9	21.0
Share of alcoholic beverages spending	100.0	12.6	15.3	8.4	17.9	7.3	9.4	30.2
FOOD AT HOME	100.0	19.1	22.4	9.1	16.3	7.1	9.1	17.3
Cereals and bakery products	100.0	20.3	22.0	9.4	16.0	7.1	9.2	16.4
Cereals and cereal products	100.0	21.2	23.0	9.1	15.5	7.2	9.0	15.4
Flour	100.0	27.0	21.4	12.6	12.1	7.0	6.7	12.8
Prepared flour mixes	100.0	20.2	22.2	10.1	18.6	5.1	6.6	17.4
Ready-to-eat and cooked cereals	100.0	20.4	22.9	9.0	15.8	7.3	9.4	15.6
Rice	100.0	21.9	24.6	8.4	14.7	7.1	9.8	13.9
Pasta, cornmeal, and other cereal products	100.0	22.0	23.1	8.7	14.4	7.8	8.9	15.2
Bakery products	100.0	19.8	21.5	9.5	16.2	7.1	9.3	17.0
Bread	100.0	21.7	23.4	9.2	15.2	6.4	8.9	15.4
White bread	100.0	22.9	24.8	9.6	15.6	6.6	7.1	13.2
Bread, other than white	100.0	20.8	22.5	8.9	14.9	6.2	10.2	16.9
Crackers and cookies	100.0	20.2	20.9	9.9	15.9	6.9	9.6	16.9
Cookies	100.0	21.0	20.7	9.3	16.1	7.1	9.8	16.3
Crackers	100.0	18.7	21.2	10.9	15.6	6.6	9.2	18.0
Frozen and refrigerated bakery products	100.0	20.0	20.5	8.9	15.1	7.9	10.5	17.6
Other bakery products	100.0	18.1	20.7	9.6	17.3	7.5	9.2	18.0
Biscuits and rolls	100.0	17.0	19.4	8.8	17.8	7.2	9.2	21.3
Cakes and cupcakes	100.0	19.2	21.6	9.7	16.4	7.7	8.9	16.6
Bread and cracker products	100.0	15.2	22.6	9.7	18.0	9.1	9.7	16.1
Sweetrolls, coffee cakes, doughnuts	100.0	18.2	21.8	9.9	18.3	7.6	9.6	14.9
Pies, tarts, turnovers	100.0	19.3	19.0	11.4	15.7	6.9	8.4	19.6
Meats, poultry, fish, and eggs	100.0	19.0	23.3	9.0	17.2	6.9	8.2	16.7
Beef	100.0	16.9	22.3	9.2	20.1	7.3	8.8	15.8
Ground beef	100.0	20.1	22.8	9.5	19.9	6.7	7.6	13.3
Roast	100.0	18.8	25.6	11.3	15.0	4.8	8.6	15.9
Chuck roast	100.0	19.0	25.5	13.8	13.3	4.1	8.7	15.3
Round roast	100.0	15.0	30.3	6.3	25.0	5.5	5.6	12.3
Other roast	100.0	20.9	22.9	12.1	10.6	4.9	10.2	18.6
Steak	100.0	13.6	21.3	8.6	22.0	8.4	9.4	17.3
Round steak	100.0	15.9	21.3	8.0	26.8	7.8	7.3	13.3
Sirloin steak	100.0	10.7	18.7	8.0	28.7	8.8	8.2	17.5
Other steak	100.0	14.8	23.0	9.2	15.7	8.3	10.9	18.5
Other beef	100.0	14.0	18.6	7.2	21.6	9.0	11.4	19.2
Pork	100.0	21.3	25.6	8.8	15.5	6.1	7.9	14.9
Bacon	100.0	20.5	24.0	8.9	16.1	5.9	9.0	15.8
Pork chops	100.0	21.7	24.2	8.5	19.7	6.9	5.9	13.2
Ham	100.0	21.6	25.6	9.4	14.2	3.7	9.3	16.4
Ham, not canned	100.0	21.4	26.0	9.3	14.2	3.8	9.1	16.3
Canned ham	100.0	32.7	12.9	13.1	13.1	–	13.5	19.2
Sausage	100.0	25.4	25.1	8.1	13.7	7.0	7.9	13.0
Other pork	100.0	19.0	28.2	8.9	14.0	7.1	7.2	15.5
Other meats	100.0	20.0	22.6	9.0	17.8	6.9	8.4	15.6
Frankfurters	100.0	20.9	24.4	9.4	18.2	5.8	7.1	14.1
Lunch meats (cold cuts)	100.0	20.1	22.3	9.3	17.9	7.0	9.1	14.5
Bologna, liverwurst, salami	100.0	24.6	23.0	9.9	16.0	6.3	7.9	12.2
Other lunch meats	100.0	18.1	21.9	9.1	18.8	7.3	9.7	15.5
Lamb, organ meats, and others	100.0	17.0	20.3	6.1	15.7	8.7	6.4	26.6
Poultry	100.0	19.7	22.8	9.0	16.1	7.6	8.3	16.8
Fresh and frozen chicken	100.0	20.1	23.2	8.9	16.1	7.6	8.3	15.9

	total complete reporters	under $20,000	$20,000—$39,999	$40,000—$49,999	$50,000—$69,999	$70,000—$79,999	$80,000—$99,999	$100,000 or more
Fresh and frozen whole chicken	100.0%	19.9%	27.1%	7.9%	15.3%	7.4%	6.6%	16.0%
Fresh and frozen chicken parts	100.0	20.1	21.7	9.4	16.4	7.7	9.0	15.9
Other poultry	100.0	18.0	21.3	9.2	15.8	7.3	8.4	20.6
Fish and seafood	100.0	17.0	22.5	8.4	16.0	6.8	7.4	22.7
Canned fish and seafood	100.0	21.0	22.5	8.4	17.5	7.1	7.3	16.6
Fresh fish and shellfish	100.0	16.1	22.6	7.9	14.0	7.1	7.7	25.5
Frozen fish and shellfish	100.0	17.1	22.2	9.2	19.1	6.0	6.8	20.0
Eggs	100.0	23.5	26.1	9.5	13.3	5.7	7.4	14.6
Dairy products	**100.0**	**18.9**	**22.3**	**9.7**	**15.9**	**7.0**	**9.4**	**17.0**
Fresh milk and cream	100.0	21.0	23.3	9.8	15.1	7.1	8.7	15.0
Fresh milk, all types	100.0	21.7	23.3	9.9	15.1	7.3	8.6	14.2
Cream	100.0	15.3	23.5	9.4	15.2	6.1	9.2	21.8
Other dairy products	100.0	17.6	21.6	9.7	16.4	6.9	9.9	18.3
Butter	100.0	19.7	23.2	10.0	13.8	6.2	9.5	17.9
Cheese	100.0	16.9	22.3	9.5	16.7	6.6	10.0	18.4
Ice cream and related products	100.0	18.8	21.5	10.3	17.2	7.6	9.3	15.5
Miscellaneous dairy products	100.0	16.2	18.2	8.8	15.4	6.8	11.2	24.3
Fruits and vegetables	**100.0**	**19.7**	**23.0**	**8.6**	**15.0**	**7.4**	**9.0**	**17.7**
Fresh fruits	100.0	18.5	22.8	8.4	14.6	7.8	9.4	19.0
Apples	100.0	17.5	23.9	8.7	15.4	7.0	9.9	18.2
Bananas	100.0	21.4	25.4	9.2	13.7	7.3	8.0	15.1
Oranges	100.0	17.6	24.2	8.3	16.5	9.0	8.7	16.1
Citrus fruits, excl. oranges	100.0	20.5	21.2	9.1	14.5	8.7	8.3	18.0
Other fresh fruits	100.0	17.7	21.4	7.8	14.2	8.0	10.1	21.5
Fresh vegetables	100.0	19.2	24.0	8.1	14.3	7.8	9.3	17.9
Potatoes	100.0	20.9	26.3	9.4	14.0	7.4	8.6	13.4
Lettuce	100.0	17.8	24.6	8.3	16.5	6.9	8.2	18.2
Tomatoes	100.0	18.9	23.5	8.6	15.9	7.7	8.1	17.5
Other fresh vegetables	100.0	19.1	23.2	7.4	13.2	8.2	10.3	19.4
Processed fruits	100.0	20.9	22.5	8.9	15.5	7.1	8.4	17.0
Frozen fruits and fruit juices	100.0	24.4	18.2	8.4	17.4	7.6	9.6	14.8
Frozen orange juice	100.0	30.1	16.0	9.3	16.3	7.2	9.0	12.1
Frozen fruits	100.0	19.5	20.1	7.3	21.5	6.7	9.0	16.5
Frozen fruit juices, excl. orange	100.0	21.8	19.2	8.3	14.2	9.2	11.1	16.7
Canned fruits	100.0	23.3	21.7	7.8	15.5	7.0	7.6	17.6
Dried fruits	100.0	19.1	20.2	8.5	16.2	7.0	7.4	22.3
Fresh fruit juice	100.0	18.0	25.9	10.0	13.7	7.0	8.3	17.2
Canned and bottled fruit juice	100.0	20.8	22.7	9.0	15.6	7.0	8.6	16.7
Processed vegetables	100.0	21.6	22.3	9.8	16.8	6.0	8.1	15.6
Frozen vegetables	100.0	17.8	21.4	9.5	17.7	6.9	10.3	16.9
Canned and dried vegetables and juices	100.0	23.5	22.7	9.9	16.3	5.5	7.0	15.1
Canned beans	100.0	22.3	22.9	9.7	15.9	7.1	7.8	14.4
Canned corn	100.0	26.1	23.7	11.0	13.7	5.3	7.5	12.4
Canned miscellaneous vegetables	100.0	21.6	21.5	9.1	18.6	5.4	7.3	16.6
Dried peas	100.0	52.8	25.1	7.0	6.8	4.8	6.9	5.0
Dried beans	100.0	24.9	27.7	6.3	19.6	3.8	5.3	12.7
Dried miscellaneous vegetables	100.0	22.3	22.9	11.2	16.3	5.9	5.2	16.2
Dried processed vegetables	100.0	29.5	38.3	3.1	12.6	7.3	–	9.7
Fresh and canned vegetable juices	100.0	26.7	22.1	11.5	13.4	3.9	7.4	15.0
Sugar and other sweets	**100.0**	**19.2**	**22.0**	**9.3**	**15.7**	**6.8**	**9.2**	**18.3**
Candy and chewing gum	100.0	17.0	20.9	9.2	16.3	7.0	10.1	19.9
Sugar	100.0	25.0	25.5	10.0	14.3	6.7	7.5	10.8
Artificial sweeteners	100.0	23.5	19.3	10.7	15.4	9.3	5.9	16.0
Jams, preserves, other sweets	100.0	21.2	23.6	8.7	14.8	5.1	8.2	18.7
Fats and oils	**100.0**	**20.8**	**23.2**	**9.5**	**15.2**	**7.0**	**8.5**	**16.0**
Margarine	100.0	20.9	24.3	12.9	15.9	5.9	7.5	12.2
Fats and oils	100.0	23.7	22.9	8.1	13.0	7.0	7.9	17.6
Salad dressings	100.0	19.8	22.1	8.6	16.0	8.1	9.5	16.2
Nondairy cream and imitation milk	100.0	15.7	24.8	11.2	16.7	7.3	7.8	16.4
Peanut butter	100.0	21.0	23.7	9.8	16.5	5.3	8.8	14.9

	total complete reporters	under $20,000	$20,000–$39,999	$40,000–$49,999	$50,000–$69,999	$70,000–$79,999	$80,000–$99,999	$100,000 or more
Miscellaneous foods	100.0%	18.4%	20.8%	9.3%	16.4%	7.2%	10.1%	18.3%
Frozen prepared foods	100.0	19.4	21.5	9.5	16.5	7.8	9.0	16.6
Frozen meals	100.0	19.1	24.4	9.7	14.0	7.8	7.6	17.7
Other frozen prepared foods	100.0	19.5	20.1	9.4	17.8	7.8	9.8	16.1
Canned and packaged soups	100.0	20.6	21.8	9.8	16.7	6.9	9.0	15.5
Potato chips, nuts, and other snacks	100.0	17.6	20.5	9.4	16.4	7.3	10.6	18.7
Potato chips and other snacks	100.0	18.0	20.8	9.8	16.8	7.7	10.8	16.6
Nuts	100.0	16.4	19.7	8.2	15.2	6.1	9.9	25.5
Condiments and seasonings	100.0	17.6	21.0	8.7	16.6	7.2	10.3	19.4
Salt, spices, and other seasonings	100.0	18.0	22.2	8.4	16.9	7.6	9.4	18.1
Olives, pickles, relishes	100.0	17.0	23.0	9.1	15.8	6.4	9.5	19.7
Sauces and gravies	100.0	17.1	20.8	8.2	16.4	8.0	10.8	19.5
Baking needs and miscellaneous products	100.0	18.4	18.9	9.7	17.0	5.6	10.6	20.3
Other canned/packaged prepared foods	100.0	18.1	20.2	9.4	16.2	6.9	10.6	19.1
Prepared salads	100.0	16.2	18.6	8.2	15.6	7.1	11.1	24.3
Prepared desserts	100.0	17.5	20.1	9.0	18.0	6.1	10.8	19.0
Baby food	100.0	23.1	23.0	9.6	15.2	4.8	9.6	15.0
Miscellaneous prepared foods	100.0	17.4	19.8	9.5	16.4	7.5	10.8	19.2
Nonalcoholic beverages	100.0	19.1	22.5	9.2	17.4	6.9	8.8	16.5
Cola	100.0	19.8	24.1	9.4	19.1	6.4	9.2	12.2
Other carbonated drinks	100.0	19.0	23.2	9.4	17.7	6.7	7.7	16.7
Coffee	100.0	18.1	22.4	10.5	13.8	6.7	8.1	20.8
Roasted coffee	100.0	17.0	21.6	10.8	14.3	7.5	7.9	21.3
Instant and freeze-dried coffee	100.0	20.3	24.0	9.7	12.8	5.2	8.5	19.6
Noncarbonated fruit-flavored drinks, incl. nonfrozen lemonade	100.0	18.9	22.9	10.0	17.0	7.8	8.6	14.8
Tea	100.0	24.2	16.5	7.3	18.5	6.0	9.4	19.3
Other nonalcoholic beverages and ice	100.0	17.0	20.7	8.4	17.1	8.0	9.6	19.9
Food prepared by CU on trips	100.0	10.2	15.7	6.8	16.8	7.8	13.6	29.1
FOOD AWAY FROM HOME	100.0	13.0	17.6	8.7	17.0	7.1	11.1	26.1
Meals at restaurants, carry-outs, other	100.0	13.8	18.2	9.1	17.1	7.2	11.2	24.3
Lunch	100.0	13.7	19.1	9.4	17.5	7.6	10.8	22.6
• At fast food, take-out, delivery, concession stands, buffet, cafeteria (other than employer, school cafeteria)	100.0	15.9	20.6	9.8	16.3	8.3	10.0	19.7
• At full-service restaurants	100.0	12.1	17.3	8.4	18.1	6.4	10.6	28.2
• At vending machines, mobile vendors	100.0	10.0	27.8	3.6	33.1	3.6	9.4	13.3
• At employer and school cafeterias	100.0	8.0	16.3	10.6	20.9	8.3	15.1	21.7
Dinner	100.0	12.4	16.1	8.4	16.2	7.1	11.8	29.2
• At fast food, take-out, delivery, concession stands, buffet, cafeteria (other than employer, school cafeteria)	100.0	15.4	19.7	9.3	17.5	7.5	11.2	20.3
• At full-service restaurants	100.0	11.1	14.5	8.0	15.6	6.9	12.2	33.3
• At vending machines, mobile vendors	100.0	34.1	20.6	12.5	37.1	–	–	4.9
• At employer and school cafeterias	100.0	18.1	27.1	15.6	17.9	4.0	7.4	8.7
Snacks and nonalcoholic beverages	100.0	16.8	19.3	10.2	17.7	6.9	11.1	18.5
• At fast food, take-out, delivery, concession stands, buffet, cafeteria (other than employer, school cafeteria)	100.0	16.2	19.0	10.6	17.3	7.1	11.0	19.4
• At full-service restaurants	100.0	19.7	20.9	9.1	20.7	5.1	9.3	15.6
• At vending machines, mobile vendors	100.0	17.2	20.3	10.2	19.5	7.7	12.4	13.0
• At employer and school cafeterias	100.0	18.3	18.5	6.8	12.5	6.1	12.2	27.2
Breakfast and brunch	100.0	15.6	21.0	9.6	18.2	6.7	10.0	19.5
• At fast food, take-out, delivery, concession stands, buffet, cafeteria (other than employer, school cafeteria)	100.0	17.4	22.6	10.7	17.0	7.2	8.9	16.5
• At full-service restaurants	100.0	13.8	19.5	8.1	19.7	6.0	11.2	22.6
• At vending machines, mobile vendors	100.0	25.1	24.9	2.7	18.5	14.5	3.3	12.8
• At employer and school cafeterias	100.0	10.4	16.4	17.8	15.9	6.3	13.1	20.1
Board (including at school)	100.0	17.7	6.1	2.9	7.9	2.7	8.3	54.3
Catered affairs	100.0	2.7	18.0	2.6	18.3	3.8	10.5	44.0
Food on trips	100.0	8.2	13.4	7.2	16.5	7.7	12.2	34.9
School lunches	100.0	4.9	15.4	10.3	20.5	8.9	13.3	26.7
Meals as pay	100.0	27.1	33.4	7.0	15.2	4.1	2.2	10.9

	total complete reporters	under $20,000	$20,000–$39,999	$40,000–$49,999	$50,000–$69,999	$70,000–$79,999	$80,000–$99,999	$100,000 or more
ALCOHOLIC BEVERAGES	100.0%	12.6%	15.3%	8.4%	17.9%	7.3%	9.4%	30.2%
At home	100.0	13.4	16.4	9.0	18.1	6.7	9.0	28.7
Beer and ale	100.0	18.5	19.5	10.6	20.0	7.3	7.9	16.7
Whiskey	100.0	18.3	17.2	9.5	20.6	5.2	13.4	16.5
Wine	100.0	7.2	12.1	8.0	14.4	6.0	9.1	45.0
Other alcoholic beverages	100.0	12.2	18.0	5.5	21.5	7.1	10.6	26.5
Away from home	**100.0**	**11.3**	**13.4**	**7.5**	**17.7**	**8.4**	**10.3**	**32.6**
Beer and ale	100.0	12.0	14.7	7.6	19.1	8.1	10.5	29.6
• At fast food, take-out, delivery, concession stands, buffet, and cafeteria	100.0	17.7	22.7	7.7	18.4	6.1	10.3	17.9
• At full-service restaurants	100.0	11.0	13.4	7.9	19.8	8.1	11.0	30.3
Wine	100.0	10.3	10.0	8.8	16.2	9.1	10.8	36.3
• At fast food, take-out, delivery, concession stands, buffet and cafeteria	100.0	21.9	10.9	13.3	18.3	9.4	11.0	15.6
• At full-service restaurants	100.0	9.4	10.1	8.6	16.2	8.9	11.0	37.4
Other alcoholic beverages	100.0	11.6	12.9	8.0	18.6	7.8	8.4	34.2
• At fast food, take-out, delivery, concession stands, buffet, and cafeteria	100.0	18.4	21.3	10.5	17.2	5.1	7.6	19.7
• At full-service restaurants	100.0	10.0	10.3	7.6	19.3	8.2	8.9	36.9
Alcoholic beverages purchased on trips	100.0	10.3	13.7	5.7	14.8	9.5	11.8	34.2

Note: Numbers may not add to total because of rounding. (–) means sample is too small to make a reliable estimate
Source: Calculations by New Strategist based on the 2003 Consumer Expenditure Survey

Table 5.9 Food and Alcohol: Average spending by high-income consumer units, 2003

(average annual spending on food and alcoholic beverages, by before-tax income of high-income consumer units (CU), 2003; complete income reporters only)

	total complete reporters	$100,000 or more	$100,000– $119,999	$120,000– $149,999	$150,000 or more
Number of consumer units (000)	97,391	11,537	4,384	3,151	4,002
Average number of persons per CU	2.5	3.1	3.1	3.1	3.1
Average before-tax income of CU	$51,128.00	$154,665.00	$108,087.00	$131,885.00	$223,634.00
Average spending of CU, total	42,741.66	93,514.86	75,601.50	86,451.46	118,674.11
Food, average spending	5,593.46	9,926.45	8,713.88	9,688.59	11,434.56
Alcoholic beverages, average spending	442.41	1,126.82	784.77	864.64	1,702.64
FOOD AT HOME	**3,235.68**	**4,725.79**	**4,303.64**	**4,933.93**	**5,023.34**
Cereals and bakery products	**456.14**	**632.04**	**606.13**	**619.14**	**670.21**
Cereals and cereal products	154.67	200.48	182.20	203.50	218.00
Flour	7.49	8.12	5.42	11.79	8.21
Prepared flour mixes	13.29	19.54	16.34	21.16	21.77
Ready-to-eat and cooked cereals	89.87	118.16	113.36	118.53	123.10
Rice	15.97	18.74	17.54	14.40	23.42
Pasta, cornmeal, and other cereal products	28.04	35.91	29.55	37.63	41.50
Bakery products	301.48	431.56	423.93	415.63	452.21
Bread	84.96	110.36	107.80	97.79	122.89
White bread	34.08	37.92	39.50	32.19	40.64
Bread, other than white	50.88	72.44	68.30	65.59	82.25
Crackers and cookies	72.65	103.89	107.06	112.89	93.47
Cookies	46.69	64.39	62.89	70.60	61.19
Crackers	25.96	39.51	44.17	42.28	32.28
Frozen and refrigerated bakery products	25.29	37.54	32.42	28.20	50.34
Other bakery products	118.58	179.77	176.64	176.75	185.51
Biscuits and rolls	38.86	69.90	67.65	70.91	71.55
Cakes and cupcakes	37.34	52.35	49.61	42.75	62.79
Bread and cracker products	3.77	5.11	6.21	3.92	4.85
Sweetrolls, coffee cakes, doughnuts	28.79	36.17	32.55	48.82	30.29
Pies, tarts, turnovers	9.81	16.23	20.62	10.36	16.03
Meats, poultry, fish, and eggs	**836.78**	**1,183.17**	**1,041.66**	**1,264.15**	**1,274.15**
Beef	252.49	336.96	297.82	351.99	367.84
Ground beef	91.95	103.35	104.00	113.06	95.11
Roast	40.87	54.95	37.99	70.92	61.00
Chuck roast	14.24	18.39	7.72	27.78	22.69
Round roast	9.82	10.20	6.63	17.84	8.14
Other roast	16.81	26.37	23.64	25.30	30.17
Steak	95.57	139.54	119.91	136.83	163.00
Round steak	16.10	18.12	16.85	15.43	21.60
Sirloin steak	32.60	48.19	42.27	50.08	53.16
Other steak	46.87	73.23	60.78	71.33	88.24
Other beef	24.09	39.11	35.93	31.18	48.73
Pork	171.42	216.10	179.02	253.67	227.25
Bacon	31.49	42.12	33.53	48.95	46.14
Pork chops	33.92	37.79	26.88	52.96	37.87
Ham	37.70	52.28	39.66	64.48	56.53
Ham, not canned	36.49	50.31	38.22	59.68	56.17
Canned ham	1.22	1.98	1.44	4.81	0.36
Sausage	25.73	28.29	27.70	27.21	29.77
Other pork	42.57	55.62	51.25	60.06	56.94
Other meats	103.84	136.44	138.65	132.94	136.76
Frankfurters	23.14	27.63	23.79	33.64	27.13
Lunch meats (cold cuts)	70.85	86.73	91.67	85.36	82.43
Bologna, liverwurst, salami	21.47	22.13	22.52	27.93	17.21
Other lunch meats	49.38	64.60	69.15	57.43	65.22
Lamb, organ meats, and others	9.84	22.08	23.19	13.94	27.20
Poultry	145.42	206.76	178.26	244.48	208.46
Fresh and frozen chicken	117.08	157.55	139.58	190.39	151.59

	total complete reporters	$100,000 or more	$100,000–$119,999	$120,000–$149,999	$150,000 or more
Fresh and frozen whole chicken	$32.93	$44.56	$37.48	$51.62	$46.77
Fresh and frozen chicken parts	84.15	112.99	102.09	138.78	104.82
Other poultry	28.34	49.21	38.68	54.09	56.87
Fish and seafood	125.25	239.69	207.20	226.02	285.61
Canned fish and seafood	15.88	22.23	21.02	23.27	22.75
Fresh fish and shellfish	71.24	153.14	134.47	133.58	188.61
Frozen fish and shellfish	38.12	64.32	51.71	69.17	74.25
Eggs	38.37	47.22	40.70	55.04	48.23
Dairy products	**343.30**	**493.95**	**436.62**	**530.02**	**528.26**
Fresh milk and cream	131.66	166.66	158.92	170.59	172.01
Fresh milk, all types	117.54	140.67	134.37	141.80	146.63
Cream	14.12	25.99	24.55	28.78	25.38
Other dairy products	211.63	327.29	277.70	359.44	356.25
Butter	17.78	26.80	23.60	31.38	26.73
Cheese	103.74	150.86	139.49	178.70	170.25
Ice cream and related products	60.69	79.28	64.14	85.16	91.18
Miscellaneous dairy products	29.42	50.35	50.47	64.19	68.09
Fruits and vegetables	**555.96**	**830.41**	**741.25**	**915.99**	**860.89**
Fresh fruits	177.31	233.71	240.31	323.23	300.21
Apples	33.54	51.40	45.17	57.37	53.54
Bananas	28.89	36.74	34.25	34.90	40.87
Oranges	18.45	25.10	17.59	29.51	29.82
Citrus fruits, excl. oranges	14.77	22.43	20.15	25.34	22.64
Other fresh fruits	81.66	148.05	123.15	176.11	153.33
Fresh vegetables	179.41	270.38	231.10	305.83	285.55
Potatoes	30.36	34.94	33.25	37.26	34.99
Lettuce	22.56	34.70	27.51	37.65	40.22
Tomatoes	32.70	48.28	47.13	53.48	45.49
Other fresh vegetables	93.29	152.46	123.22	177.44	164.85
Processed fruits	112.03	161.17	152.70	169.04	164.26
Frozen fruits and fruit juices	12.22	15.27	18.16	14.09	13.04
Frozen orange juice	4.90	5.02	5.04	6.99	3.48
Frozen fruits	3.93	5.48	6.76	4.52	4.83
Frozen fruit juices, excl. orange	3.39	4.77	6.36	2.58	4.73
Canned fruits	16.94	25.20	27.51	29.16	19.62
Dried fruits	6.66	12.53	10.06	16.40	12.22
Fresh fruit juice	20.58	29.92	23.34	26.62	39.63
Canned and bottled fruit juice	55.62	73.25	73.63	82.77	79.75
Processed vegetables	87.21	115.15	117.13	117.89	110.88
Frozen vegetables	28.02	39.91	42.72	40.67	36.27
Canned and dried vegetables and juices	59.20	75.24	74.42	77.22	74.61
Canned beans	12.74	15.48	17.09	16.68	12.80
Canned corn	7.05	7.40	7.56	8.59	6.30
Canned miscellaneous vegetables	19.51	27.35	24.84	32.45	26.12
Dried peas	0.33	0.16	0.06	0.18	0.23
Dried beans	2.35	2.52	3.09	1.22	2.90
Dried miscellaneous vegetables	7.64	10.42	10.70	7.96	12.03
Dried processed vegetables	0.44	0.36	0.32	–	0.68
Fresh and canned vegetable juices	8.95	11.31	10.40	10.14	13.21
Sugar and other sweets	**123.46**	**190.27**	**191.87**	**172.70**	**202.18**
Candy and chewing gum	78.58	132.23	145.44	114.68	131.49
Sugar	17.12	15.61	14.08	11.95	20.12
Artificial sweeteners	5.99	8.08	8.27	9.77	6.55
Jams, preserves, other sweets	21.77	34.36	24.08	36.31	44.01
Fats and oils	**87.00**	**117.65**	**112.69**	**124.18**	**117.98**
Margarine	9.80	10.12	9.98	10.78	9.75
Fats and oils	26.62	39.53	33.11	41.27	45.15
Salad dressings	26.53	36.24	36.65	36.18	35.83
Nondairy cream and imitation milk	11.56	16.05	16.52	18.98	13.27
Peanut butter	12.49	15.72	16.42	16.96	13.99

	total complete reporters	$100,000 or more	$100,000–$119,999	$120,000–$149,999	$150,000 or more
Miscellaneous foods	**$513.36**	**$792.36**	**$727.52**	**$810.60**	**$848.69**
Frozen prepared foods	109.63	153.96	162.97	151.09	146.40
Frozen meals	36.41	54.54	66.35	42.89	50.75
Other frozen prepared foods	73.22	99.42	96.62	108.21	95.65
Canned and packaged soups	37.25	48.63	40.54	53.34	53.77
Potato chips, nuts, and other snacks	111.97	177.01	151.49	200.43	186.56
Potato chips and other snacks	85.18	119.44	116.35	127.91	116.23
Nuts	26.79	57.57	35.14	72.53	70.33
Condiments and seasonings	94.00	153.66	144.88	164.45	154.84
Salt, spices, and other seasonings	21.71	33.15	25.72	42.08	34.28
Olives, pickles, relishes	11.32	18.78	22.38	13.81	18.73
Sauces and gravies	40.42	66.55	66.41	69.12	64.70
Baking needs and miscellaneous products	20.56	35.19	30.37	39.43	37.13
Other canned/packaged prepared foods	160.50	259.09	227.64	241.28	307.11
Prepared salads	21.08	43.23	36.04	41.99	52.00
Prepared desserts	11.62	18.60	21.68	18.26	15.53
Baby food	26.99	34.08	37.91	31.71	31.76
Miscellaneous prepared foods	100.54	163.18	132.02	149.33	207.81
Nonalcoholic beverages	**281.48**	**391.94**	**374.63**	**404.82**	**400.74**
Cola	93.37	96.37	96.09	100.72	93.31
Other carbonated drinks	48.87	69.04	68.13	77.52	63.45
Coffee	40.22	70.49	64.48	63.39	82.55
Roasted coffee	26.84	48.35	42.94	45.89	56.13
Instant and freeze-dried coffee	13.38	22.15	21.54	17.50	26.42
Noncarbonated fruit-flavored drinks, incl. nonfrozen lemonade	19.71	24.65	26.23	32.02	17.21
Tea	17.94	29.22	32.21	31.17	24.47
Other nonalcoholic beverages and ice	60.59	101.90	86.82	100.00	119.76
Food prepared by CU on trips	**38.20**	**94.00**	**71.27**	**92.34**	**120.23**
FOOD AWAY FROM HOME	**2,357.77**	**5,200.66**	**4,410.24**	**4,754.67**	**6,411.22**
Meals at restaurants, carry-outs, other	**1,956.55**	**4,016.64**	**3,501.12**	**3,813.56**	**4,734.74**
Lunch	706.60	1,347.36	1,120.56	1,377.01	1,570.91
• At fast food, take-out, delivery, concession stands, buffet, cafeteria (other than employer, school cafeteria)	395.14	658.36	635.27	625.19	709.21
• At full-service restaurants	225.04	535.52	352.08	526.06	742.28
• At vending machines, mobile vendors	6.88	7.75	12.63	5.24	4.39
• At employer and school cafeterias	79.54	145.74	120.58	220.51	115.03
Dinner	774.13	1,909.31	1,695.72	1,644.60	2,347.03
• At fast food, take-out, delivery, concession stands, buffet, cafeteria (other than employer, school cafeteria)	233.57	400.11	378.18	368.21	448.72
• At full-service restaurants	535.73	1,506.10	1,317.32	1,267.65	1,896.47
• At vending machines, mobile vendors	1.45	0.60	–	2.22	–
• At employer and school cafeterias	3.39	2.50	0.23	6.52	1.84
Snacks and nonalcoholic beverages	274.05	428.21	355.19	428.81	507.14
• At fast food, take-out, delivery, concession stands, buffet, cafeteria (other than employer, school cafeteria)	198.42	324.46	275.83	318.50	381.95
• At full-service restaurants	28.59	37.62	23.51	32.30	57.10
• At vending machines, mobile vendors	35.06	38.61	37.79	35.74	41.73
• At employer and school cafeterias	11.98	27.52	18.06	42.26	26.36
Breakfast and brunch	201.77	331.75	329.65	363.15	309.66
• At fast food, take-out, delivery, concession stands, buffet, cafeteria (other than employer, school cafeteria)	99.14	138.16	146.59	151.36	118.75
• At full-service restaurants	95.93	183.26	171.74	201.39	181.71
• At vending machines, mobile vendors	1.67	1.80	2.30	0.01	2.65
• At employer and school cafeterias	5.02	8.53	9.02	10.39	6.55
Board (including at school)	**37.17**	**170.52**	**132.49**	**92.50**	**273.62**
Catered affairs	**53.40**	**198.40**	**198.70**	**92.49**	**281.48**
Food on trips	**221.47**	**651.64**	**439.79**	**594.82**	**928.49**
School lunches	**60.91**	**137.44**	**131.32**	**136.14**	**145.16**
Meals as pay	**28.28**	**26.03**	**6.84**	**25.16**	**47.74**

	total complete reporters	$100,000 or more	$100,000– $119,999	$120,000– $149,999	$150,000 or more
ALCOHOLIC BEVERAGES	**$442.41**	**$1,126.82**	**$784.77**	**$864.64**	**$1,702.64**
At home	**275.87**	**668.32**	**446.31**	**501.11**	**1,039.49**
Beer and ale	124.90	176.51	168.43	157.35	200.16
Whiskey	14.74	20.49	4.57	36.56	25.30
Wine	106.75	405.40	206.85	265.44	729.90
Other alcoholic beverages	29.48	65.93	66.45	41.76	84.13
Away from home	**166.54**	**458.50**	**338.47**	**363.54**	**663.15**
Beer and ale	66.94	167.23	140.65	135.41	220.85
• At fast food, take-out, delivery, concession stands, buffet, and cafeteria	12.08	18.24	20.43	14.95	18.41
• At full-service restaurants	52.43	134.13	120.22	120.46	159.88
Wine	20.64	63.18	45.30	52.06	91.24
• At fast food, take-out, delivery, concession stands, buffet and cafeteria	1.68	2.21	3.58	1.09	1.58
• At full-service restaurants	18.66	58.92	40.43	50.97	85.18
Other alcoholic beverages	43.49	125.55	94.55	78.07	196.11
• At fast food, take-out, delivery, concession stands, buffet, and cafeteria	9.03	15.02	14.19	11.71	18.50
• At full-service restaurants	33.37	104.02	80.36	66.36	158.97
Alcoholic beverages purchased on trips	35.47	102.54	57.97	98.00	154.95

Note: Subcategories may not add to total because some are not shown. (–) means sample is too small to make a reliable estimate.
Source: Bureau of Labor Statistics, unpublished tables from the 2003 Consumer Expenditure Survey; calculations by New Strategist

Table 5.10 Food and Alcohol: Indexed spending by high-income consumer units, 2003

(indexed average annual spending of consumer units (CU) on food and beverages, by before-tax income of high-income consumer unit, 2003; complete income reporters only; index definition: an index of 100 is the average for all consumer units; an index of 132 means that spending by consumer units in that group is 32 percent above the average for all consumer units; an index of 68 indicates spending that is 32 percent below the average for all consumer units)

	total complete reporters	$100,000 or more	$100,000–$119,999	$120,000–$149,999	$150,000 or more
Average spending of CU, total	$42,742	$93,515	$75,602	$86,451	$118,674
Average spending of CU, index	100	219	177	202	278
Food, spending index	100	177	156	173	204
Alcoholic beverages, spending index	100	255	177	195	385
FOOD AT HOME	100	146	133	152	155
Cereals and bakery products	100	139	133	136	147
Cereals and cereal products	100	130	118	132	141
Flour	100	108	72	157	110
Prepared flour mixes	100	147	123	159	164
Ready-to-eat and cooked cereals	100	131	126	132	137
Rice	100	117	110	90	147
Pasta, cornmeal, and other cereal products	100	128	105	134	148
Bakery products	100	143	141	138	150
Bread	100	130	127	115	145
White bread	100	111	116	94	119
Bread, other than white	100	142	134	129	162
Crackers and cookies	100	143	147	155	129
Cookies	100	138	135	151	131
Crackers	100	152	170	163	124
Frozen and refrigerated bakery products	100	148	128	112	199
Other bakery products	100	152	149	149	156
Biscuits and rolls	100	180	174	182	184
Cakes and cupcakes	100	140	133	114	168
Bread and cracker products	100	136	165	104	129
Sweetrolls, coffee cakes, doughnuts	100	126	113	170	105
Pies, tarts, turnovers	100	165	210	106	163
Meats, poultry, fish, and eggs	100	141	124	151	152
Beef	100	133	118	139	146
Ground beef	100	112	113	123	103
Roast	100	134	93	174	149
Chuck roast	100	129	54	195	159
Round roast	100	104	68	182	83
Other roast	100	157	141	151	179
Steak	100	146	125	143	171
Round steak	100	113	105	96	134
Sirloin steak	100	148	130	154	163
Other steak	100	156	130	152	188
Other beef	100	162	149	129	202
Pork	100	126	104	148	133
Bacon	100	134	106	155	147
Pork chops	100	111	79	156	112
Ham	100	139	105	171	150
Ham, not canned	100	138	105	164	154
Canned ham	100	162	118	394	30
Sausage	100	110	108	106	116
Other pork	100	131	120	141	134
Other meats	100	131	134	128	132
Frankfurters	100	119	103	145	117
Lunch meats (cold cuts)	100	122	129	120	116
Bologna, liverwurst, salami	100	103	105	130	80
Other lunch meats	100	131	140	116	132
Lamb, organ meats, and others	100	224	236	142	276
Poultry	100	142	123	168	143
Fresh and frozen chicken	100	135	119	163	129

	total complete reporters	$100,000 or more	$100,000–$119,999	$120,000–$149,999	$150,000 or more
Fresh and frozen whole chicken	100	135	114	157	142
Fresh and frozen chicken parts	100	134	121	165	125
Other poultry	100	174	136	191	201
Fish and seafood	100	191	165	180	228
Canned fish and seafood	100	140	132	147	143
Fresh fish and shellfish	100	215	189	188	265
Frozen fish and shellfish	100	169	136	181	195
Eggs	100	123	106	143	126
Dairy products	**100**	**144**	**127**	**154**	**154**
Fresh milk and cream	100	127	121	130	131
Fresh milk, all types	100	120	114	121	125
Cream	100	184	174	204	180
Other dairy products	100	155	131	170	168
Butter	100	151	133	176	150
Cheese	100	155	134	172	164
Ice cream and related products	100	131	106	140	150
Miscellaneous dairy products	100	205	172	218	231
Fruits and vegetables	**100**	**149**	**133**	**165**	**155**
Fresh fruits	100	160	136	182	169
Apples	100	153	135	171	160
Bananas	100	127	119	121	141
Oranges	100	136	95	160	162
Citrus fruits, excl. oranges	100	152	136	172	153
Other fresh fruits	100	181	151	216	188
Fresh vegetables	100	151	129	170	159
Potatoes	100	113	108	121	113
Lettuce	100	154	122	167	178
Tomatoes	100	148	144	164	139
Other fresh vegetables	100	163	132	190	177
Processed fruits	100	144	136	151	147
Frozen fruits and fruit juices	100	125	149	115	107
Frozen orange juice	100	102	103	143	71
Frozen fruits	100	139	172	115	123
Frozen fruit juices, excl. orange	100	141	188	76	140
Canned fruits	100	149	162	172	116
Dried fruits	100	188	151	246	183
Fresh fruit juice	100	145	113	129	193
Canned and bottled fruit juice	100	141	132	149	143
Processed vegetables	100	132	134	135	127
Frozen vegetables	100	142	152	145	129
Canned and dried vegetables and juices	100	127	126	130	126
Canned beans	100	122	134	131	100
Canned corn	100	105	107	122	89
Canned miscellaneous vegetables	100	140	127	166	134
Dried peas	100	42	16	47	61
Dried beans	100	107	131	52	123
Dried miscellaneous vegetables	100	136	140	104	157
Dried processed vegetables	100	82	73	–	155
Fresh and canned vegetable juices	100	126	116	113	148
Sugar and other sweets	**100**	**154**	**155**	**140**	**164**
Candy and chewing gum	100	168	185	146	167
Sugar	100	91	82	70	118
Artificial sweeteners	100	135	138	163	109
Jams, preserves, other sweets	100	158	111	167	202
Fats and oils	**100**	**135**	**130**	**143**	**136**
Margarine	100	103	102	110	99
Fats and oils	100	148	124	155	170
Salad dressings	100	137	138	136	135
Nondairy cream and imitation milk	100	139	143	164	115
Peanut butter	100	126	131	136	112

	total complete reporters	$100,000 or more	$100,000– $119,999	$120,000– $149,999	$150,000 or more
Miscellaneous foods	100	154	142	158	165
Frozen prepared foods	100	140	149	138	134
Frozen meals	100	150	182	118	139
Other frozen prepared foods	100	136	132	148	131
Canned and packaged soups	100	131	109	143	144
Potato chips, nuts, and other snacks	100	158	135	179	167
Potato chips and other snacks	100	140	137	150	136
Nuts	100	215	131	271	263
Condiments and seasonings	100	163	154	175	165
Salt, spices, and other seasonings	100	153	118	194	158
Olives, pickles, relishes	100	166	198	122	165
Sauces and gravies	100	165	164	171	160
Baking needs and miscellaneous products	100	171	148	192	181
Other canned/packaged prepared foods	100	161	142	150	191
Prepared salads	100	205	171	199	247
Prepared desserts	100	160	187	157	134
Baby food	100	126	140	117	118
Miscellaneous prepared foods	100	162	131	149	207
Nonalcoholic beverages	100	139	133	144	142
Cola	100	103	103	108	100
Other carbonated drinks	100	141	139	159	130
Coffee	100	175	160	158	205
Roasted coffee	100	180	160	171	209
Instant and freeze-dried coffee	100	166	161	131	197
Noncarbonated fruit-flavored drinks, incl. nonfrozen lemonade	100	125	133	162	87
Tea	100	163	180	174	136
Other nonalcoholic beverages and ice	100	168	143	165	198
Food prepared by CU on trips	100	246	187	242	315
FOOD AWAY FROM HOME	100	221	187	202	272
Meals at restaurants, carry-outs, other	100	205	179	195	242
Lunch	100	191	159	195	222
• At fast food, take-out, delivery, concession stands, buffet, cafeteria (other than employer, school cafeteria)	100	167	161	158	179
• At full-service restaurants	100	238	156	234	330
• At vending machines, mobile vendors	100	113	184	76	64
• At employer and school cafeterias	100	183	152	277	145
Dinner	100	247	219	212	303
• At fast food, take-out, delivery, concession stands, buffet, cafeteria (other than employer, school cafeteria)	100	171	162	158	192
• At full-service restaurants	100	281	246	237	354
• At vending machines, mobile vendors	100	41	–	153	–
• At employer and school cafeterias	100	74	7	192	54
Snacks and nonalcoholic beverages	100	156	130	156	185
• At fast food, take-out, delivery, concession stands, buffet, cafeteria (other than employer, school cafeteria)	100	164	139	161	192
• At full-service restaurants	100	132	82	113	200
• At vending machines, mobile vendors	100	110	108	102	119
• At employer and school cafeterias	100	230	151	353	220
Breakfast and brunch	100	164	163	180	153
• At fast food, take-out, delivery, concession stands, buffet, cafeteria (other than employer, school cafeteria)	100	139	148	153	120
• At full-service restaurants	100	191	179	210	189
• At vending machines, mobile vendors	100	108	138	1	159
• At employer and school cafeterias	100	170	180	207	130
Board (including at school)	100	459	356	249	736
Catered affairs	100	372	372	173	527
Food on trips	100	294	199	269	419
School lunches	100	226	216	224	238
Meals as pay	100	92	24	89	169

	total complete reporters	$100,000 or more	$100,000– $119,999	$120,000– $149,999	$150,000 or more
ALCOHOLIC BEVERAGES	100	255	177	195	385
At home	100	242	162	182	377
Beer and ale	100	141	135	126	160
Whiskey	100	139	31	248	172
Wine	100	380	194	249	684
Other alcoholic beverages	100	224	225	142	285
Away from home	100	275	203	218	398
Beer and ale	100	250	210	202	330
• At fast food, take-out, delivery, concession stands, buffet, and cafeteria	100	151	169	124	152
• At full-service restaurants	100	256	229	230	305
Wine	100	306	219	252	442
• At fast food, take-out, delivery, concession stands, buffet and cafeteria	100	132	213	65	94
• At full-service restaurants	100	316	217	273	456
Other alcoholic beverages	100	239	217	180	451
• At fast food, take-out, delivery, concession stands, buffet, and cafeteria	100	156	157	130	205
• At full-service restaurants	100	312	241	199	476
Alcoholic beverages purchased on trips	100	239	163	276	437

Note: (–) means sample is too small to make a reliable estimate.
Source: Calculations by New Strategist based on the 2003 Consumer Expenditure Survey

Table 5.11 Food and Alcohol: Total spending by high-income consumer units, 2003

(total annual spending on food and alcoholic beverages, by before-tax income group of high-income consumer units (CU), 2003; complete income reporters only; numbers in thousands)

	total complete reporters	$100,000 or more	$100,000– $119,999	$120,000– $149,999	$150,000 or more
Number of consumer units	97,391	11,537	4,384	3,151	4,002
Total spending of all CUs	$4,162,653,009	$1,078,880,940	$331,436,976	$272,408,550	$474,933,788
Food, total spending	544,752,663	114,521,454	38,201,650	30,528,747	45,761,109
Alcoholic beverages, total spending	43,086,752	13,000,122	3,440,432	2,724,481	6,813,965
FOOD AT HOME	**315,126,111**	**54,521,439**	**18,867,158**	**15,546,813**	**20,103,407**
Cereals and bakery products	**44,423,931**	**7,291,845**	**2,657,274**	**1,950,910**	**2,682,180**
Cereals and cereal products	15,063,466	2,312,938	798,765	641,229	872,436
Flour	729,459	93,680	23,761	37,150	32,856
Prepared flour mixes	1,294,326	225,433	71,635	66,675	87,124
Ready-to-eat and cooked cereals	8,752,529	1,363,212	496,970	373,488	492,646
Rice	1,555,334	216,203	76,895	45,374	93,727
Pasta, cornmeal, and other cereal products	2,730,844	414,294	129,547	118,572	166,083
Bakery products	29,361,439	4,978,908	1,858,509	1,309,650	1,809,744
Bread	8,274,339	1,273,223	472,595	308,136	491,806
White bread	3,319,085	437,483	173,168	101,431	162,641
Bread, other than white	4,955,254	835,740	299,427	206,674	329,165
Crackers and cookies	7,075,456	1,198,579	469,351	355,716	374,067
Cookies	4,547,186	742,867	275,710	222,461	244,882
Crackers	2,528,270	455,827	193,641	133,224	129,185
Frozen and refrigerated bakery products	2,463,018	433,099	142,129	88,858	201,461
Other bakery products	11,548,625	2,074,006	774,390	556,939	742,411
Biscuits and rolls	3,784,614	806,436	296,578	223,437	286,343
Cakes and cupcakes	3,636,580	603,962	217,490	134,705	251,286
Bread and cracker products	367,164	58,954	27,225	12,352	19,410
Sweetrolls, coffee cakes, doughnuts	2,803,887	417,293	142,699	153,832	121,221
Pies, tarts, turnovers	955,406	187,246	90,398	32,644	64,152
Meats, poultry, fish, and eggs	**81,494,841**	**13,650,232**	**4,566,637**	**3,983,337**	**5,099,148**
Beef	24,590,254	3,887,508	1,305,643	1,109,120	1,472,096
Ground beef	8,955,102	1,192,349	455,936	356,252	380,630
Roast	3,980,370	633,958	166,548	223,469	244,122
Chuck roast	1,386,848	212,165	33,844	87,535	90,805
Round roast	956,380	117,677	29,066	56,214	32,576
Other roast	1,637,143	304,231	103,638	79,720	120,740
Steak	9,307,658	1,609,873	525,685	431,151	652,326
Round steak	1,567,995	209,050	73,870	48,620	86,443
Sirloin steak	3,174,947	555,968	185,312	157,802	212,746
Other steak	4,564,716	844,855	266,460	224,761	353,136
Other beef	2,346,149	451,212	157,517	98,248	195,017
Pork	16,694,765	2,493,146	784,824	799,314	909,455
Bacon	3,066,843	485,938	146,996	154,241	184,652
Pork chops	3,303,503	435,983	117,842	166,877	151,556
Ham	3,671,641	603,154	173,869	203,176	226,233
Ham, not canned	3,553,798	580,426	167,556	188,052	224,792
Canned ham	118,817	22,843	6,313	15,156	1,441
Sausage	2,505,870	326,382	121,437	85,739	119,140
Other pork	4,145,935	641,688	224,680	189,249	227,874
Other meats	10,113,081	1,574,108	607,842	418,894	547,314
Frankfurters	2,253,628	318,767	104,295	106,000	108,574
Lunch meats (cold cuts)	6,900,152	1,000,604	401,881	268,969	329,885
Bologna, liverwurst, salami	2,090,985	255,314	98,728	88,007	68,874
Other lunch meats	4,809,168	745,290	303,154	180,962	261,010
Lamb, organ meats, and others	958,327	254,737	101,665	43,925	108,854
Poultry	14,162,599	2,385,390	781,492	770,356	834,257
Fresh and frozen chicken	11,402,538	1,817,654	611,919	599,919	606,663

	total complete reporters	$100,000 or more	$100,000– $119,999	$120,000– $149,999	$150,000 or more
Fresh and frozen whole chicken	$3,207,086	$514,089	$164,312	$162,655	$187,174
Fresh and frozen chicken parts	8,195,453	1,203,566	427,363	437,296	419,490
Other poultry	2,760,061	567,736	169,573	170,438	227,594
Fish and seafood	12,198,223	2,765,304	908,365	712,189	1,143,011
Canned fish and seafood	1,546,569	256,468	92,152	73,324	91,046
Fresh fish and shellfish	6,938,135	1,766,776	589,516	420,911	754,817
Frozen fish and shellfish	3,712,545	742,060	226,697	217,955	297,149
Eggs	3,736,893	544,777	178,429	173,431	193,016
Dairy products	**33,434,330**	**5,698,701**	**1,914,142**	**1,670,093**	**2,114,097**
Fresh milk and cream	12,822,499	1,922,756	695,705	537,529	688,384
Fresh milk, all types	11,447,338	1,622,910	589,078	446,812	586,813
Cream	1,375,161	299,847	107,627	90,686	101,571
Other dairy products	20,610,857	3,775,945	1,217,437	1,132,595	1,425,713
Butter	1,731,612	309,192	108,462	98,878	106,973
Cheese	10,103,342	1,855,842	611,524	563,084	681,341
Ice cream and related products	5,910,660	914,653	281,190	268,339	364,902
Miscellaneous dairy products	2,865,243	696,258	221,260	202,263	272,496
Fruits and vegetables	**54,145,500**	**9,580,440**	**3,249,640**	**2,886,284**	**3,445,282**
Fresh fruits	17,268,398	3,273,162	1,053,519	1,018,498	1,201,440
Apples	3,266,494	593,002	198,025	180,773	214,267
Bananas	2,813,626	423,869	150,152	109,970	163,562
Oranges	1,796,864	239,579	77,115	92,986	119,340
Citrus fruits, excl. oranges	1,438,465	258,775	85,358	79,846	90,605
Other fresh fruits	7,952,949	1,708,053	539,890	554,923	613,627
Fresh vegetables	17,472,919	3,119,374	1,012,142	963,670	1,142,771
Potatoes	3,005,486	403,103	145,758	117,406	140,030
Lettuce	2,197,141	400,334	120,634	118,635	160,960
Tomatoes	3,184,686	557,006	206,618	168,515	182,051
Other fresh vegetables	9,085,606	1,758,931	540,196	559,113	659,730
Processed fruits	10,910,714	1,859,418	669,437	532,645	657,369
Frozen fruits and fruit juices	1,190,118	176,170	79,613	44,398	52,186
Frozen orange juice	477,216	57,916	22,095	22,025	13,927
Frozen fruits	382,747	63,223	29,636	14,243	19,330
Frozen fruit juices, excl. orange	330,155	55,031	27,882	8,130	18,929
Canned fruits	1,649,804	290,732	120,604	91,883	78,519
Dried fruits	648,624	144,559	44,103	51,676	48,904
Fresh fruit juice	2,004,307	345,187	102,323	83,880	158,599
Canned and bottled fruit juice	5,416,887	902,770	322,794	260,808	319,160
Processed vegetables	8,493,469	1,328,486	513,498	371,471	443,742
Frozen vegetables	2,728,896	460,442	187,284	128,151	145,153
Canned and dried vegetables and juices	5,765,547	868,044	326,257	243,320	298,589
Canned beans	1,240,761	173,593	74,923	52,559	51,226
Canned corn	686,607	85,374	33,143	27,067	25,213
Canned miscellaneous vegetables	1,900,098	315,537	108,899	102,250	104,532
Dried peas	37,009	1,846	263	567	920
Dried beans	228,869	29,073	13,547	3,844	11,606
Dried miscellaneous vegetables	744,067	120,216	46,909	25,082	48,144
Dried processed vegetables	42,852	4,153	1,403	–	2,721
Fresh and canned vegetable juices	871,649	130,483	45,594	31,951	52,866
Sugar and other sweets	**12,023,893**	**2,195,145**	**841,158**	**544,178**	**809,124**
Candy and chewing gum	7,652,985	1,525,538	637,609	361,357	526,223
Sugar	1,667,334	180,093	61,727	37,654	80,520
Artificial sweeteners	583,372	93,219	36,256	30,785	26,213
Jams, preserves, other sweets	2,120,202	396,411	105,567	114,413	176,128
Fats and oils	**8,473,017**	**1,357,328**	**494,035**	**391,291**	**472,156**
Margarine	954,432	116,754	43,752	33,968	39,020
Fats and oils	2,592,548	456,058	145,154	130,042	180,690
Salad dressings	2,583,783	418,101	160,674	114,003	143,392
Nondairy cream and imitation milk	1,125,840	185,159	72,624	59,806	53,107
Peanut butter	1,216,414	181,362	71,985	53,441	55,988

	total complete reporters	$100,000 or more	$100,000– $119,999	$120,000– $149,999	$150,000 or more
Miscellaneous foods	**$49,996,644**	**$9,141,457**	**$3,189,448**	**$2,554,201**	**$3,396,457**
Frozen prepared foods	10,676,975	1,776,237	714,460	476,085	585,893
Frozen meals	3,546,006	629,228	290,878	135,146	203,102
Other frozen prepared foods	7,130,969	1,147,009	423,582	340,970	382,791
Canned and packaged soups	3,627,815	561,044	177,727	168,074	215,188
Potato chips, nuts, and other snacks	10,904,870	2,042,164	664,132	631,555	746,613
Potato chips and other snacks	8,295,765	1,377,979	510,078	403,044	465,152
Nuts	2,609,105	664,185	154,054	228,542	281,461
Condiments and seasonings	9,154,754	1,772,775	635,154	518,182	619,670
Salt, spices, and other seasonings	2,114,359	382,452	112,756	132,594	137,189
Olives, pickles, relishes	1,102,466	216,665	98,114	43,515	74,957
Sauces and gravies	3,936,544	767,787	291,141	217,797	258,929
Baking needs and miscellaneous products	2,002,359	405,987	133,142	124,244	148,594
Other canned/packaged prepared foods	15,631,256	2,989,121	997,974	760,273	1,229,054
Prepared salads	2,053,002	498,745	157,999	132,310	208,104
Prepared desserts	1,131,683	214,588	95,045	57,537	62,151
Baby food	2,628,583	393,181	166,197	99,918	127,104
Miscellaneous prepared foods	9,791,691	1,882,608	578,776	470,539	831,656
Nonalcoholic beverages	**27,413,619**	**4,521,812**	**1,642,378**	**1,275,588**	**1,603,761**
Cola	9,093,398	1,111,821	421,259	317,369	373,427
Other carbonated drinks	4,759,498	796,514	298,682	244,266	253,927
Coffee	3,917,066	813,243	282,680	199,742	330,365
Roasted coffee	2,613,974	557,814	188,249	144,599	224,632
Instant and freeze-dried coffee	1,303,092	255,545	94,431	55,143	105,733
Noncarbonated fruit-flavored drinks, incl. nonfrozen lemonade	1,919,577	284,387	114,992	100,895	68,874
Tea	1,747,195	337,111	141,209	98,217	97,929
Other nonalcoholic beverages and ice	5,900,921	1,175,620	380,619	315,100	479,280
Food prepared by CU on trips	**3,720,336**	**1,084,478**	**312,448**	**290,963**	**481,160**
FOOD AWAY FROM HOME	**229,625,578**	**60,000,014**	**19,334,492**	**14,981,965**	**25,657,702**
Meals at restaurants, carry-outs, other	**190,550,361**	**46,339,976**	**15,348,910**	**12,016,528**	**18,948,429**
Lunch	68,816,481	15,544,492	4,912,535	4,338,959	6,286,782
• At fast food, take-out, delivery, concession stands, buffet, cafeteria (other than employer, school cafeteria)	38,483,080	7,595,499	2,785,024	1,969,974	2,838,258
• At full-service restaurants	21,916,871	6,178,294	1,543,519	1,657,615	2,970,605
• At vending machines, mobile vendors	670,050	89,412	55,370	16,511	17,569
• At employer and school cafeterias	7,746,480	1,681,402	528,623	694,827	460,350
Dinner	75,393,295	22,027,709	7,434,036	5,182,135	9,392,814
• At fast food, take-out, delivery, concession stands, buffet, cafeteria (other than employer, school cafeteria)	22,747,616	4,616,069	1,657,941	1,160,230	1,795,777
• At full-service restaurants	52,175,280	17,375,876	5,775,131	3,994,365	7,589,673
• At vending machines, mobile vendors	141,217	6,922	–	6,995	–
• At employer and school cafeterias	330,155	28,843	1,008	20,545	7,364
Snacks and nonalcoholic beverages	26,690,004	4,940,259	1,557,153	1,351,180	2,029,574
• At fast food, take-out, delivery, concession stands, buffet, cafeteria (other than employer, school cafeteria)	19,324,322	3,743,295	1,209,239	1,003,594	1,528,564
• At full-service restaurants	2,784,409	434,022	103,068	101,777	228,514
• At vending machines, mobile vendors	3,414,528	445,444	165,671	112,617	167,003
• At employer and school cafeterias	1,166,744	317,498	79,175	133,161	105,493
Breakfast and brunch	19,650,582	3,827,400	1,445,186	1,144,286	1,239,259
• At fast food, take-out, delivery, concession stands, buffet, cafeteria (other than employer, school cafeteria)	9,655,344	1,593,952	642,651	476,935	475,238
• At full-service restaurants	9,342,719	2,114,271	752,908	634,580	727,203
• At vending machines, mobile vendors	162,643	20,767	10,083	32	10,605
• At employer and school cafeterias	488,903	98,411	39,544	32,739	26,213
Board (including at school)	**3,620,023**	**1,967,289**	**580,836**	**291,468**	**1,095,027**
Catered affairs	**5,200,679**	**2,288,941**	**871,101**	**291,436**	**1,126,483**
Food on trips	**21,569,185**	**7,517,971**	**1,928,039**	**1,874,278**	**3,715,817**
School lunches	**5,932,086**	**1,585,645**	**575,707**	**428,977**	**580,930**
Meals as pay	**2,754,217**	**300,308**	**29,987**	**79,279**	**191,055**

	total complete reporters	$100,000 or more	$100,000– $119,999	$120,000– $149,999	$150,000 or more
ALCOHOLIC BEVERAGES	$43,086,752	$13,000,122	$3,440,432	$2,724,481	$6,813,965
At home	26,867,255	7,710,408	1,956,623	1,578,998	4,160,039
Beer and ale	12,164,136	2,036,396	738,397	495,810	801,040
Whiskey	1,435,543	236,393	20,035	115,201	101,251
Wine	10,395,489	4,677,100	906,830	836,401	2,921,060
Other alcoholic beverages	2,871,087	760,634	291,317	131,586	336,688
Away from home	16,219,497	5,289,715	1,483,852	1,145,515	2,653,926
Beer and ale	6,519,354	929,333	616,610	426,677	883,842
• At fast food, take-out, delivery, concession stands, buffet, and cafeteria	1,176,483	210,435	89,565	47,107	73,677
• At full-service restaurants	5,106,210	547,458	527,044	379,569	639,840
Wine	2,010,150	728,908	198,595	164,041	365,142
• At fast food, take-out, delivery, concession stands, buffet and cafeteria	163,617	25,497	15,695	3,435	6,323
• At full-service restaurants	1,817,316	679,760	177,245	160,606	340,890
Other alcoholic beverages	4,235,535	1,448,470	414,507	245,999	784,832
• At fast food, take-out, delivery, concession stands, buffet, and cafeteria	879,441	173,286	62,209	36,898	74,037
• At full-service restaurants	3,249,938	1,200,079	352,298	209,100	636,198
Alcoholic beverages purchased on trips	3,454,459	1,183,034	254,140	308,798	620,110

Note: Numbers may not add to total because of rounding and missing subcategories. (–) means sample is too small to make a reliable estimate.
Source: Calculations by New Strategist based on the 2003 Consumer Expenditure Survey

Table 5.12 Food and Alcohol: Market shares by high-income consumer units, 2003

(percentage of total annual spending on food and alcoholic beverages accounted for by before-tax income group of high-income consumer units, 2003; complete income reporters only)

	total complete reporters	$100,000 or more	$100,000– $119,999	$120,000– $149,999	$150,000 or more
Share of total consumer units	100.0%	11.8%	4.5%	3.2%	4.1%
Share of total before-tax income	100.0	35.8	9.5	8.3	18.0
Share of total spending	100.0	25.9	8.0	6.5	11.4
Share of food spending	100.0	21.0	7.0	5.6	8.4
Share of alcoholic beverages spending	100.0	30.2	8.0	6.3	15.8
FOOD AT HOME	100.0	17.3	6.0	4.9	6.4
Cereals and bakery products	100.0	16.4	6.0	4.4	6.0
Cereals and cereal products	100.0	15.4	5.3	4.3	5.8
Flour	100.0	12.8	3.3	5.1	4.5
Prepared flour mixes	100.0	17.4	5.5	5.2	6.7
Ready-to-eat and cooked cereals	100.0	15.6	5.7	4.3	5.6
Rice	100.0	13.9	4.9	2.9	6.0
Pasta, cornmeal, and other cereal products	100.0	15.2	4.7	4.3	6.1
Bakery products	100.0	17.0	6.3	4.5	6.2
Bread	100.0	15.4	5.7	3.7	5.9
White bread	100.0	13.2	5.2	3.1	4.9
Bread, other than white	100.0	16.9	6.0	4.2	6.6
Crackers and cookies	100.0	16.9	6.6	5.0	5.3
Cookies	100.0	16.3	6.1	4.9	5.4
Crackers	100.0	18.0	7.7	5.3	5.1
Frozen and refrigerated bakery products	100.0	17.6	5.8	3.6	8.2
Other bakery products	100.0	18.0	6.7	4.8	6.4
Biscuits and rolls	100.0	21.3	7.8	5.9	7.6
Cakes and cupcakes	100.0	16.6	6.0	3.7	6.9
Bread and cracker products	100.0	16.1	7.4	3.4	5.3
Sweetrolls, coffee cakes, doughnuts	100.0	14.9	5.1	5.5	4.3
Pies, tarts, turnovers	100.0	19.6	9.5	3.4	6.7
Meats, poultry, fish, and eggs	100.0	16.7	5.6	4.9	6.3
Beef	100.0	15.8	5.3	4.5	6.0
Ground beef	100.0	13.3	5.1	4.0	4.3
Roast	100.0	15.9	4.2	5.6	6.1
Chuck roast	100.0	15.3	2.4	6.3	6.5
Round roast	100.0	12.3	3.0	5.9	3.4
Other roast	100.0	18.6	6.3	4.9	7.4
Steak	100.0	17.3	5.6	4.6	7.0
Round steak	100.0	13.3	4.7	3.1	5.5
Sirloin steak	100.0	17.5	5.8	5.0	6.7
Other steak	100.0	18.5	5.8	4.9	7.7
Other beef	100.0	19.2	6.7	4.2	8.3
Pork	100.0	14.9	4.7	4.8	5.4
Bacon	100.0	15.8	4.8	5.0	6.0
Pork chops	100.0	13.2	3.6	5.1	4.6
Ham	100.0	16.4	4.7	5.5	6.2
Ham, not canned	100.0	16.3	4.7	5.3	6.3
Canned ham	100.0	19.2	5.3	12.8	1.2
Sausage	100.0	13.0	4.8	3.4	4.8
Other pork	100.0	15.5	5.4	4.6	5.5
Other meats	100.0	15.6	6.0	4.1	5.4
Frankfurters	100.0	14.1	4.6	4.7	4.8
Lunch meats (cold cuts)	100.0	14.5	5.8	3.9	4.8
Bologna, liverwurst, salami	100.0	12.2	4.7	4.2	3.3
Other lunch meats	100.0	15.5	6.3	3.8	5.4
Lamb, organ meats, and others	100.0	26.6	10.6	4.6	11.4
Poultry	100.0	16.8	5.5	5.4	5.9
Fresh and frozen chicken	100.0	15.9	5.4	5.3	5.3

	total complete reporters	$100,000 or more	$100,000–$119,999	$120,000–$149,999	$150,000 or more
Fresh and frozen whole chicken	100.0%	16.0%	5.1%	5.1%	5.8%
Fresh and frozen chicken parts	100.0	15.9	5.5	5.3	5.1
Other poultry	100.0	20.6	6.1	6.2	8.2
Fish and seafood	100.0	22.7	7.4	5.8	9.4
Canned fish and seafood	100.0	16.6	6.0	4.7	5.9
Fresh fish and shellfish	100.0	25.5	8.5	6.1	10.9
Frozen fish and shellfish	100.0	20.0	6.1	5.9	8.0
Eggs	100.0	14.6	4.8	4.6	5.2
Dairy products	**100.0**	**17.0**	**5.7**	**5.0**	**6.3**
Fresh milk and cream	100.0	15.0	5.4	4.2	5.4
Fresh milk, all types	100.0	14.2	5.1	3.9	5.1
Cream	100.0	21.8	7.8	6.6	7.4
Other dairy products	100.0	13.3	5.9	5.5	6.9
Butter	100.0	17.9	6.0	5.7	6.2
Cheese	100.0	13.4	6.1	5.6	6.7
Ice cream and related products	100.0	15.5	4.8	4.5	6.2
Miscellaneous dairy products	100.0	24.3	7.7	7.1	9.5
Fruits and vegetables	**100.0**	**17.7**	**6.0**	**5.3**	**6.4**
Fresh fruits	100.0	19.0	6.1	5.9	7.0
Apples	100.0	18.2	6.1	5.5	6.6
Bananas	100.0	15.1	5.3	3.9	5.8
Oranges	100.0	16.1	4.3	5.2	6.6
Citrus fruits, excl. oranges	100.0	18.0	6.1	5.6	6.3
Other fresh fruits	100.0	21.5	6.8	7.0	7.7
Fresh vegetables	100.0	17.9	5.8	5.5	6.5
Potatoes	100.0	13.4	4.9	3.9	4.7
Lettuce	100.0	18.2	5.5	5.4	7.3
Tomatoes	100.0	17.5	6.5	5.3	5.7
Other fresh vegetables	100.0	19.4	5.9	6.2	7.3
Processed fruits	100.0	17.0	6.1	4.9	6.0
Frozen fruits and fruit juices	100.0	14.8	6.7	3.7	4.4
Frozen orange juice	100.0	12.1	4.6	4.6	2.9
Frozen fruits	100.0	16.5	7.7	3.7	5.1
Frozen fruit juices, excl. orange	100.0	16.7	8.4	2.5	5.7
Canned fruits	100.0	17.6	7.3	5.6	4.8
Dried fruits	100.0	22.3	6.8	8.0	7.5
Fresh fruit juice	100.0	17.2	5.1	4.2	7.9
Canned and bottled fruit juice	100.0	16.7	6.0	4.8	5.9
Processed vegetables	100.0	15.5	6.0	4.4	5.2
Frozen vegetables	100.0	16.9	6.9	4.7	5.3
Canned and dried vegetables and juices	100.0	15.1	5.7	4.2	5.2
Canned beans	100.0	14.4	6.0	4.2	4.1
Canned corn	100.0	12.4	4.8	3.9	3.7
Canned miscellaneous vegetables	100.0	16.6	5.7	5.4	5.5
Dried peas	100.0	5.0	0.7	1.5	2.5
Dried beans	100.0	12.7	5.9	1.7	5.1
Dried miscellaneous vegetables	100.0	16.2	6.3	3.4	6.5
Dried processed vegetables	100.0	9.7	3.3	–	6.4
Fresh and canned vegetable juices	100.0	15.0	5.2	3.7	6.1
Sugar and other sweets	**100.0**	**18.3**	**7.0**	**4.5**	**6.7**
Candy and chewing gum	100.0	19.9	8.3	4.7	6.9
Sugar	100.0	10.8	3.7	2.3	4.8
Artificial sweeteners	100.0	16.0	5.2	5.3	4.5
Jams, preserves, other sweets	100.0	18.7	5.0	5.4	8.3
Fats and oils	**100.0**	**16.0**	**5.8**	**4.6**	**5.6**
Margarine	100.0	12.2	4.6	3.6	4.1
Fats and oils	100.0	17.6	5.6	5.0	7.0
Salad dressings	100.0	16.2	6.2	4.4	5.5
Nondairy cream and imitation milk	100.0	16.4	6.4	5.3	4.7
Peanut butter	100.0	14.9	5.9	4.4	4.6

	total complete reporters	$100,000 or more	$100,000–$119,999	$120,000–$149,999	$150,000 or more
Miscellaneous foods	100.0%	18.3%	6.4%	5.1%	6.8%
Frozen prepared foods	100.0	16.6	6.7	4.5	5.5
Frozen meals	100.0	17.7	8.2	3.8	5.7
Other frozen prepared foods	100.0	16.1	5.9	4.8	5.4
Canned and packaged soups	100.0	15.5	4.9	4.6	5.9
Potato chips, nuts, and other snacks	100.0	18.7	6.1	5.8	6.8
Potato chips and other snacks	100.0	16.6	6.1	4.9	5.6
Nuts	100.0	25.5	5.9	8.8	10.8
Condiments and seasonings	100.0	19.4	6.9	5.7	6.8
Salt, spices, and other seasonings	100.0	18.1	5.3	6.3	6.5
Olives, pickles, relishes	100.0	19.7	8.9	3.9	6.8
Sauces and gravies	100.0	19.5	7.4	5.5	6.6
Baking needs and miscellaneous products	100.0	20.3	6.6	6.2	7.4
Other canned/packaged prepared foods	100.0	19.1	6.4	4.9	7.9
Prepared salads	100.0	24.3	7.7	6.4	10.1
Prepared desserts	100.0	19.0	8.4	5.1	5.5
Baby food	100.0	15.0	6.3	3.8	4.8
Miscellaneous prepared foods	100.0	19.2	5.9	4.8	8.5
Nonalcoholic beverages	100.0	16.5	6.0	4.7	5.9
Cola	100.0	12.2	4.6	3.5	4.1
Other carbonated drinks	100.0	16.7	6.3	5.1	5.3
Coffee	100.0	20.8	7.2	5.1	8.4
Roasted coffee	100.0	21.3	7.2	5.5	8.6
Instant and freeze-dried coffee	100.0	19.6	7.2	4.2	8.1
Noncarbonated fruit-flavored drinks, incl. nonfrozen lemonade	100.0	14.8	6.0	5.3	3.6
Tea	100.0	19.3	8.1	5.6	5.6
Other nonalcoholic beverages and ice	100.0	19.9	6.5	5.3	8.1
Food prepared by CU on trips	100.0	29.1	8.4	7.8	12.9
FOOD AWAY FROM HOME	100.0	26.1	8.4	6.5	11.2
Meals at restaurants, carry-outs, other	100.0	24.3	8.1	6.3	9.9
Lunch	100.0	22.6	7.1	6.3	9.1
• At fast food, take-out, delivery, concession stands, buffet, cafeteria (other than employer, school cafeteria)	100.0	19.7	7.2	5.1	7.4
• At full-service restaurants	100.0	28.2	7.0	7.6	13.6
• At vending machines, mobile vendors	100.0	13.3	8.3	2.5	2.6
• At employer and school cafeterias	100.0	21.7	6.8	9.0	5.9
Dinner	100.0	29.2	9.9	6.9	12.5
• At fast food, take-out, delivery, concession stands, buffet, cafeteria (other than employer, school cafeteria)	100.0	20.3	7.3	5.1	7.9
• At full-service restaurants	100.0	33.3	11.1	7.7	14.5
• At vending machines, mobile vendors	100.0	4.9	–	5.0	–
• At employer and school cafeterias	100.0	8.7	0.3	6.2	2.2
Snacks and nonalcoholic beverages	100.0	18.5	5.8	5.1	7.6
• At fast food, take-out, delivery, concession stands, buffet, cafeteria (other than employer, school cafeteria)	100.0	19.4	6.3	5.2	7.9
• At full-service restaurants	100.0	15.6	3.7	3.7	8.2
• At vending machines, mobile vendors	100.0	13.0	4.9	3.3	4.9
• At employer and school cafeterias	100.0	27.2	6.8	11.4	9.0
Breakfast and brunch	100.0	19.5	7.4	5.8	6.3
• At fast food, take-out, delivery, concession stands, buffet, cafeteria (other than employer, school cafeteria)	100.0	16.5	6.7	4.9	4.9
• At full-service restaurants	100.0	22.6	8.1	6.8	7.8
• At vending machines, mobile vendors	100.0	12.8	6.2	0.0	6.5
• At employer and school cafeterias	100.0	20.1	8.1	6.7	5.4
Board (including at school)	100.0	54.3	16.0	8.1	30.2
Catered affairs	100.0	44.0	16.7	5.6	21.7
Food on trips	100.0	34.9	8.9	8.7	17.2
School lunches	100.0	26.7	9.7	7.2	9.8
Meals as pay	100.0	10.9	1.1	2.9	6.9

	total complete reporters	$100,000 or more	$100,000– $119,999	$120,000– $149,999	$150,000 or more
ALCOHOLIC BEVERAGES	100.0%	30.2%	8.0%	6.3%	15.8%
At home	100.0	28.7	7.3	5.9	15.5
Beer and ale	100.0	16.7	6.1	4.1	6.6
Whiskey	100.0	16.5	1.4	8.0	7.1
Wine	100.0	45.0	8.7	8.0	28.1
Other alcoholic beverages	100.0	26.5	10.1	4.6	11.7
Away from home	100.0	32.6	9.1	7.1	16.4
Beer and ale	100.0	29.6	9.5	6.5	13.6
• At fast food, take-out, delivery, concession stands, buffet, and cafeteria	100.0	17.9	7.6	4.0	6.3
• At full-service restaurants	100.0	30.3	10.3	7.4	12.5
Wine	100.0	36.3	9.9	8.2	18.2
• At fast food, take-out, delivery, concession stands, buffet and cafeteria	100.0	15.6	9.6	2.1	3.9
• At full-service restaurants	100.0	37.4	9.8	8.8	18.8
Other alcoholic beverages	100.0	34.2	9.8	5.8	18.5
• At fast food, take-out, delivery, concession stands, buffet, and cafeteria	100.0	19.7	7.1	4.2	8.4
• At full-service restaurants	100.0	35.9	10.8	6.4	19.6
Alcoholic beverages purchased on trips	100.0	34.2	7.4	8.9	18.0

Note: Numbers may not add to total because of rounding. (–) means sample is too small to make a reliable estimate.
Source: Calculations by New Strategist based on the 2003 Consumer Expenditure Survey

Table 5.13 Food and Alcohol: Average spending by household type, 2003

(average annual spending of consumer units (CU) on food and alcoholic beverages, by type of consumer unit, 2003)

	total married couples	married couples, no children	married couples with children				single parent, at least one child <18	single person
			total	oldest child under 6	oldest child 6 to 17	oldest child 18 or older		
Number of consumer units (000)	58,448	25,132	28,584	5,496	15,047	8,041	6,999	33,929
Average number of persons per CU	3.2	2.0	3.9	3.5	4.1	4.0	2.9	1.0
Average before-tax income of CU	$69,472.00	$62,930.00	$75,557.00	$66,317.00	$77,508.00	$78,307.00	$29,154.00	$27,131.00
Average spending of CU, total	53,030.03	47,895.65	57,702.32	51,503.24	59,183.18	59,180.36	30,534.75	23,657.35
Food, average spending	6,863.66	5,927.28	7,553.31	6,223.84	7,844.17	7,936.70	4,804.12	2,830.95
Alcoholic beverages, average spending	447.08	478.43	440.26	445.12	429.25	459.39	220.34	279.88
FOOD AT HOME	4,046.99	3,402.17	4,476.43	3,952.04	4,551.14	4,710.50	2,978.55	1,524.82
Cereals and bakery products	571.22	458.08	652.01	547.22	690.80	649.99	444.55	217.48
Cereals and cereal products	193.33	146.78	225.01	198.11	239.77	214.69	159.95	71.17
Flour	9.11	7.32	9.80	10.60	8.68	11.49	6.14	4.00
Prepared flour mixes	17.18	13.56	19.30	18.38	20.21	18.12	13.13	6.11
Ready-to-eat and cooked cereals	110.54	82.08	133.00	106.41	147.27	123.46	91.14	43.67
Rice	20.65	15.73	22.41	24.55	21.10	23.51	15.12	6.42
Pasta, cornmeal, and other cereal products	35.85	28.09	40.50	38.17	42.52	38.11	34.42	10.98
Bakery products	377.89	311.30	427.00	349.11	451.03	435.30	284.61	146.31
Bread	104.23	89.33	113.66	95.74	114.45	125.20	71.73	45.30
White bread	41.12	31.89	46.74	39.48	48.63	48.23	36.93	16.98
Bread, other than white	63.11	57.44	66.92	56.26	65.83	76.97	34.80	28.32
Crackers and cookies	90.84	78.35	100.87	88.67	103.37	104.75	63.71	37.15
Cookies	58.27	50.41	64.23	57.74	66.33	64.74	42.23	24.56
Crackers	32.56	27.94	36.64	30.93	37.03	40.02	21.48	12.58
Frozen and refrigerated bakery products	32.21	23.25	39.69	38.91	42.71	34.13	27.62	11.56
Other bakery products	150.61	120.37	172.78	125.79	190.50	171.21	121.54	52.31
Biscuits and rolls	49.52	40.47	57.19	43.21	58.91	63.97	34.97	17.59
Cakes and cupcakes	48.48	36.52	56.76	42.29	65.80	48.96	45.62	13.94
Bread and cracker products	4.91	4.19	5.25	3.63	5.14	6.66	2.95	1.50
Sweetrolls, coffee cakes, doughnuts	35.93	27.52	42.00	29.53	48.14	38.67	29.72	13.70
Pies, tarts, turnovers	11.77	11.67	11.58	7.13	12.51	12.96	8.29	5.58
Meats, poultry, fish, and eggs	1,076.51	912.02	1,168.61	890.17	1,212.74	1,283.41	787.15	358.94
Beef	332.61	288.35	359.70	235.21	380.94	407.97	212.07	94.18
Ground beef	116.37	91.13	133.13	88.35	140.35	151.34	104.84	34.21
Roast	54.98	45.52	61.34	34.75	61.28	81.00	30.55	14.30
Chuck roast	18.32	15.63	20.44	12.20	20.85	25.65	13.01	4.11
Round roast	13.08	8.72	15.92	6.46	18.08	18.48	8.82	4.19
Other roast	23.57	21.16	24.98	16.09	22.36	36.87	8.72	6.00
Steak	127.52	116.96	133.20	92.63	143.54	141.96	66.99	39.21
Round steak	21.84	22.49	20.54	13.05	20.99	25.12	13.79	5.62
Sirloin steak	44.27	40.67	45.37	24.34	48.69	54.06	18.94	11.79
Other steak	61.41	53.80	67.30	55.24	73.86	62.78	34.26	21.80
Other beef	33.75	34.74	32.04	19.48	35.77	33.67	9.68	6.46
Pork	221.14	192.80	234.94	158.20	248.76	263.22	163.34	73.41
Bacon	39.99	32.36	44.91	32.96	46.34	50.78	30.63	14.88
Pork chops	43.67	34.16	48.54	32.49	50.28	56.81	31.71	12.92
Ham	48.25	45.07	49.49	35.26	52.53	53.76	34.60	18.91
Ham, not canned	46.89	44.51	47.41	34.39	49.49	52.75	33.67	18.26
Canned ham	1.36	0.56	2.08	0.87	3.04	1.01	0.93	0.65
Sausage	32.29	26.12	36.03	24.22	39.99	36.63	28.72	12.43
Other pork	56.95	55.08	55.97	33.26	59.62	65.24	37.68	14.26
Other meats	130.02	105.55	145.26	118.82	151.24	152.51	109.78	47.09
Frankfurters	28.90	20.04	34.88	25.45	33.88	43.88	27.45	10.06
Lunch meats (cold cuts)	88.80	73.89	97.97	85.56	101.32	100.27	72.94	32.42
Bologna, liverwurst, salami	26.38	22.47	28.64	22.26	29.74	31.10	28.27	10.54
Other lunch meats	62.42	51.42	69.33	63.30	71.58	69.17	44.67	21.88
Lamb, organ meats, and others	12.33	11.62	12.40	7.81	16.05	8.36	9.39	4.60
Poultry	185.52	145.48	211.40	175.33	217.73	225.04	141.79	65.67
Fresh and frozen chicken	149.05	111.97	173.15	147.09	179.23	179.94	117.20	52.38

	total married couples	married couples, no children	married couples with children				single parent, at least one child <18	single person
			total	oldest child under 6	oldest child 6 to 17	oldest child 18 or older		
Fresh and frozen whole chicken	$42.69	$31.34	$49.01	$37.86	$52.15	$50.80	$28.61	$13.94
Fresh and frozen chicken parts	106.36	80.63	124.15	109.23	127.08	129.15	88.59	38.44
Other poultry	36.48	33.51	38.25	28.24	38.50	45.10	24.59	13.29
Fish and seafood	161.63	140.32	168.95	158.07	164.56	185.90	124.84	58.78
Canned fish and seafood	20.42	17.84	21.52	17.87	22.09	23.06	11.65	10.20
Fresh fish and shellfish	92.61	79.00	98.01	100.44	87.76	117.12	73.51	31.75
Frozen fish and shellfish	48.60	43.49	49.41	39.76	54.71	45.72	39.68	16.84
Eggs	45.58	39.53	48.35	44.55	49.51	48.78	35.34	19.81
Dairy products	**426.85**	**352.03**	**485.01**	**443.58**	**497.13**	**490.76**	**306.82**	**161.03**
Fresh milk and cream	161.63	121.84	192.05	166.34	205.71	183.11	126.20	62.15
Fresh milk, all types	143.11	104.59	172.30	150.57	184.50	163.40	116.30	55.05
Cream	18.52	17.25	19.75	15.77	21.21	19.71	9.90	7.10
Other dairy products	265.22	230.19	292.96	277.24	291.42	307.66	180.62	98.88
Butter	23.36	19.31	26.37	25.44	23.21	33.50	16.56	7.79
Cheese	127.84	114.65	139.97	131.27	140.28	145.74	86.15	47.58
Ice cream and related products	76.27	68.00	82.25	69.74	83.79	88.32	52.75	29.03
Miscellaneous dairy products	37.74	28.23	44.37	50.79	44.14	40.10	25.17	14.48
Fruits and vegetables	**687.54**	**606.40**	**735.31**	**671.61**	**722.86**	**807.55**	**455.36**	**280.33**
Fresh fruits	220.96	197.32	235.18	206.72	233.17	260.20	143.91	87.63
Apples	42.04	35.71	46.85	39.11	47.60	51.04	28.85	16.17
Bananas	35.18	32.14	36.66	33.99	34.31	43.40	24.74	16.50
Oranges	23.79	19.68	26.50	18.91	28.12	28.79	15.23	8.95
Citrus fruits, excl. oranges	18.34	16.57	19.31	16.02	18.90	22.58	11.05	7.44
Other fresh fruits	101.62	93.23	105.85	98.70	104.23	114.39	64.04	38.56
Fresh vegetables	223.91	205.04	229.74	212.64	222.04	258.02	124.34	88.50
Potatoes	38.46	35.35	39.65	41.57	36.30	45.05	28.50	14.62
Lettuce	28.46	26.52	29.99	24.57	29.34	35.29	18.78	11.80
Tomatoes	41.34	36.35	42.62	32.63	44.57	45.99	24.42	16.83
Other fresh vegetables	115.65	106.81	117.49	113.88	111.83	131.68	52.64	45.26
Processed fruits	136.18	111.21	154.11	149.81	153.39	158.72	105.84	59.72
Frozen fruits and fruit juices	14.64	12.46	15.72	14.45	15.28	17.54	9.06	5.65
Frozen orange juice	5.75	4.44	6.39	3.95	7.17	6.60	3.83	2.56
Frozen fruits	4.71	5.50	3.98	3.88	3.78	4.44	2.21	1.68
Frozen fruit juices, excl. orange	4.18	2.52	5.35	6.62	4.32	6.51	3.01	1.41
Canned fruits	20.35	17.75	22.11	22.09	21.71	22.93	13.14	9.56
Dried fruits	8.63	7.71	9.61	7.65	8.95	12.39	4.32	2.93
Fresh fruit juice	24.89	22.38	27.23	22.96	29.34	26.06	24.71	11.87
Canned and bottled fruit juice	67.67	50.91	79.45	82.66	78.12	79.80	54.62	29.71
Processed vegetables	106.49	92.82	116.29	102.44	114.26	130.60	81.27	44.47
Frozen vegetables	34.42	28.95	39.04	34.52	39.32	41.80	29.84	12.91
Canned and dried vegetables and juices	72.08	63.88	77.25	67.92	74.94	88.80	51.42	31.56
Canned beans	15.27	12.92	16.80	14.23	16.63	19.04	11.40	7.10
Canned corn	8.40	7.15	9.41	7.16	9.20	11.49	6.58	3.90
Canned miscellaneous vegetables	23.29	22.10	24.48	21.36	23.66	28.43	14.18	10.52
Dried peas	0.57	0.43	0.72	1.43	0.40	0.83	0.12	0.14
Dried beans	2.94	2.80	2.81	2.38	2.58	3.60	2.78	0.65
Dried miscellaneous vegetables	9.87	7.58	10.42	8.43	9.89	12.95	5.62	3.84
Dried processed vegetables	0.56	0.44	0.72	2.42	0.30	0.30	0.98	0.18
Fresh and canned vegetable juices	10.98	10.36	11.63	9.87	12.19	11.80	9.75	5.25
Sugar and other sweets	**151.78**	**130.61**	**168.11**	**145.82**	**176.30**	**167.82**	**123.93**	**60.00**
Candy and chewing gum	95.59	80.57	108.68	88.57	118.31	103.84	78.48	38.60
Sugar	20.96	18.51	21.54	20.69	21.38	22.51	21.20	7.20
Artificial sweeteners	7.33	8.42	6.56	6.47	5.48	8.84	4.24	3.80
Jams, preserves, other sweets	27.90	23.11	31.32	30.09	31.13	32.63	20.00	10.40
Fats and oils	**109.13**	**98.43**	**114.74**	**85.51**	**117.35**	**130.89**	**75.06**	**43.36**
Margarine	12.60	12.41	12.73	8.74	12.09	16.99	5.65	4.91
Fats and oils	33.21	29.24	34.87	27.21	37.68	34.79	23.89	11.89
Salad dressings	32.92	29.53	34.78	25.69	34.36	42.34	27.13	13.60
Nondairy cream and imitation milk	14.61	14.10	14.56	9.68	14.28	18.73	6.42	5.80
Peanut butter	15.79	13.15	17.79	14.20	18.95	18.06	11.98	7.17

	total married couples	married couples, no children	married couples with children			single parent, at least one child <18	single person
			total	oldest child under 6	oldest child 6 to 17	oldest child 18 or older	
Miscellaneous foods	**$631.84**	**$510.56**	**$720.99**	**$821.74**	**$695.54**	**$698.75**	**$491.31**	**$255.51**
Frozen prepared foods	127.69	103.59	146.04	138.39	151.98	139.56	116.53	65.88
Frozen meals	39.65	41.75	38.76	48.58	38.43	32.19	32.15	30.72
Other frozen prepared foods	88.04	61.84	107.29	89.82	113.55	107.37	84.38	35.16
Canned and packaged soups	43.47	37.70	47.81	47.82	45.69	52.14	31.10	21.04
Potato chips, nuts, and other snacks	139.10	114.26	159.78	128.07	163.25	176.01	106.47	54.14
Potato chips and other snacks	103.55	73.48	127.65	105.09	135.04	129.18	91.51	38.91
Nuts	35.55	40.78	32.13	22.99	28.21	46.83	14.96	15.22
Condiments and seasonings	117.19	100.67	128.66	120.48	127.06	137.95	83.93	44.49
Salt, spices, and other seasonings	26.64	24.25	27.91	28.34	26.56	30.33	18.58	9.73
Olives, pickles, relishes	14.50	13.01	15.50	15.35	15.68	15.24	10.63	6.75
Sauces and gravies	50.80	40.48	58.38	53.26	59.82	59.22	37.86	16.88
Baking needs and miscellaneous products	25.27	22.92	26.88	23.54	25.01	33.15	16.86	11.13
Other canned/packaged prepared foods	204.39	154.34	238.69	386.98	207.56	193.09	153.27	69.96
Prepared salads	25.56	25.45	25.46	23.96	23.51	30.53	17.82	12.25
Prepared desserts	14.30	12.91	15.07	13.79	15.99	14.15	9.44	5.38
Baby food	38.48	10.64	59.43	207.40	26.93	16.85	49.90	4.21
Miscellaneous prepared foods	125.83	105.12	138.59	141.82	140.86	131.57	76.10	48.12
Nonalcoholic beverages	**340.78**	**277.87**	**382.86**	**310.17**	**381.43**	**439.25**	**275.53**	**130.75**
Cola	112.29	89.42	125.15	99.67	125.45	143.27	92.33	39.93
Other carbonated drinks	59.05	43.35	69.95	52.65	69.30	83.99	53.38	20.66
Coffee	49.97	52.11	48.13	40.35	44.98	60.28	23.62	20.62
Roasted coffee	34.17	36.55	32.19	26.80	29.80	41.01	17.93	13.35
Instant and freeze-dried coffee	15.81	15.56	15.95	13.55	15.18	19.27	5.69	7.27
Noncarbonated fruit-flavored drinks, incl. nonfrozen lemonade	24.51	12.87	32.86	30.54	38.43	23.21	31.21	6.96
Tea	22.69	18.66	26.10	16.96	22.97	39.19	13.62	9.35
Other nonalcoholic beverages and ice	71.27	59.42	80.43	70.01	79.85	89.30	60.65	32.94
Food prepared by CU on trips	**51.33**	**56.17**	**48.79**	**36.22**	**56.98**	**42.06**	**18.84**	**17.42**
FOOD AWAY FROM HOME	**2,816.67**	**2,525.11**	**3,076.89**	**2,271.81**	**3,293.03**	**3,226.21**	**1,825.57**	**1,306.13**
Meals at restaurants, carry-outs, other	**2,279.14**	**2,023.47**	**2,494.82**	**1,987.69**	**2,630.95**	**2,590.24**	**1,553.33**	**1,127.43**
Lunch	811.81	645.86	942.13	730.52	1,018.52	942.02	618.38	393.63
• At fast food, take-out, delivery, concession stands, buffet, cafeteria (other than employer, school cafeteria)	439.18	316.58	525.48	505.02	532.82	525.57	379.05	218.23
• At full-service restaurants	260.00	294.79	242.57	179.93	240.30	293.27	126.52	149.40
• At vending machines, mobile vendors	7.01	3.94	7.32	4.19	8.77	6.66	2.83	4.09
• At employer and school cafeterias	105.63	30.55	166.76	41.39	236.63	116.51	109.97	21.91
Dinner	952.14	943.96	968.53	768.40	998.32	1,054.98	484.44	441.87
• At fast food, take-out, delivery, concession stands, buffet, cafeteria (other than employer, school cafeteria)	274.46	186.25	341.19	303.57	359.73	331.03	238.96	106.01
• At full-service restaurants	675.00	754.65	625.08	463.80	636.10	721.22	243.71	330.14
• At vending machines, mobile vendors	1.00	1.45	0.75	—	1.39	—	0.71	0.89
• At employer and school cafeterias	1.68	1.60	1.52	1.03	1.09	2.73	1.06	4.84
Snacks and nonalcoholic beverages	290.44	221.28	348.51	298.58	361.71	358.34	269.37	163.58
• At fast food, take-out, delivery, concession stands, buffet, cafeteria (other than employer, school cafeteria)	211.98	158.65	255.55	230.46	259.18	266.61	196.56	117.64
• At full-service restaurants	29.49	32.94	27.61	21.96	25.91	35.23	26.55	21.28
• At vending machines, mobile vendors	36.92	21.94	49.67	40.41	55.65	44.28	29.57	19.45
• At employer and school cafeterias	12.05	7.76	15.69	5.75	20.97	12.22	16.68	5.21
Breakfast and brunch	224.75	212.37	235.64	190.19	252.41	234.89	181.15	128.34
• At fast food, take-out, delivery, concession stands, buffet, cafeteria (other than employer, school cafeteria)	103.85	79.03	121.97	96.91	132.51	118.91	120.13	63.68
• At full-service restaurants	115.09	130.89	104.81	88.07	108.31	109.98	49.90	60.05
• At vending machines, mobile vendors	1.61	0.68	2.57	1.97	3.56	1.00	2.45	0.75
• At employer and school cafeterias	4.21	1.77	6.30	3.24	8.03	5.01	8.68	3.86
Board (including at school)	**45.75**	**36.56**	**54.12**	**3.62**	**35.88**	**122.75**	**12.38**	**24.64**
Catered affairs	**74.92**	**109.10**	**43.24**	**17.26**	**25.84**	**93.55**	**31.02**	**7.45**
Food on trips	**306.86**	**341.58**	**292.16**	**211.11**	**322.70**	**290.40**	**85.24**	**110.34**
School lunches	**89.48**	**0.12**	**170.19**	**9.95**	**259.85**	**111.94**	**121.62**	**0.08**
Meals as pay	**20.52**	**14.27**	**22.36**	**42.18**	**17.81**	**17.33**	**21.98**	**36.17**

	total married couples	married couples, no children	married couples with children				single parent, at least one child <18	single person
			total	oldest child under 6	oldest child 6 to 17	oldest child 18 or older		
ALCOHOLIC BEVERAGES	**$447.08**	**$478.43**	**$440.26**	**$445.12**	**$429.25**	**$459.39**	**$220.34**	**$279.88**
At home	**282.12**	**283.59**	**294.14**	**330.73**	**286.19**	**283.45**	**141.26**	**147.26**
Beer and ale	119.34	109.37	129.24	143.25	126.62	124.28	62.13	73.91
Whiskey	19.66	28.06	13.86	6.42	10.69	25.81	3.05	7.18
Wine	115.42	117.84	123.43	146.18	122.19	109.24	58.59	47.60
Other alcoholic beverages	27.71	28.32	27.60	34.89	26.68	24.12	17.49	18.57
Away from home	**164.96**	**194.85**	**146.12**	**114.39**	**143.07**	**175.94**	**79.07**	**132.63**
Beer and ale	65.02	76.70	57.95	48.41	50.32	80.52	33.09	54.49
• At fast food, take-out, delivery, concession stands, buffet, and cafeteria	10.05	10.06	9.02	14.66	7.98	6.99	11.05	11.19
• At full-service restaurants	48.46	62.04	39.99	33.75	40.61	43.32	22.04	43.16
Wine	19.50	21.93	18.09	15.72	19.24	17.50	8.91	15.69
• At fast food, take-out, delivery, concession stands, buffet and cafeteria	1.18	0.86	1.39	1.09	1.44	1.49	1.93	1.95
• At full-service restaurants	17.55	20.41	15.76	14.53	17.62	12.80	6.98	13.74
Other alcoholic beverages	39.47	43.49	36.89	21.36	37.32	47.08	24.60	36.16
• At fast food, take-out, delivery, concession stands, buffet, and cafeteria	6.98	6.12	7.14	8.04	7.26	6.24	8.49	7.94
• At full-service restaurants	29.63	35.36	25.83	13.82	29.33	27.53	16.11	28.19
Alcoholic beverages purchased on trips	40.96	52.72	33.19	28.40	36.19	30.84	12.48	26.28

Note: Average spending figures for total consumer units can be found on Average Spending by Age and Average Spending by Region tables. Subcategories may not add to total because some are not shown. (–) means sample is too small to make a reliable estimate.
Source: Bureau of Labor Statistics, unpublished tables from the 2003 Consumer Expenditure Survey

Table 5.14 Food and Alcohol: Indexed spending by household type, 2003

(indexed average annual spending of consumer units (CU) on food and alcoholic beverages, by type of consumer unit, 2003; index definition: an index of 100 is the average for all consumer units; an index of 132 means that spending by consumer units in that group is 32 percent above the average for all consumer units; an index of 68 indicates spending that is 32 percent below the average for all consumer units)

	total married couples	married couples, no children	married couples with children				single parent, at least one child <18	single person
			total	oldest child under 6	oldest child 6 to 17	oldest child 18 or older		
Average spending of CU, total	$53,030	$47,896	$57,702	$51,503	$59,183	$59,180	$30,535	$23,657
Average spending of CU, index	130	117	141	126	145	145	75	58
Food, spending index	129	111	141	117	147	149	90	53
Alcoholic beverages, spending index	114	122	113	114	110	117	56	72
FOOD AT HOME	129	109	143	126	145	151	95	49
Cereals and bakery products	129	104	148	124	156	147	101	49
Cereals and cereal products	129	98	150	132	160	143	107	47
Flour	124	100	134	145	119	157	84	55
Prepared flour mixes	134	106	151	144	158	142	103	48
Ready-to-eat and cooked cereals	128	95	154	123	171	143	106	51
Rice	129	98	140	153	131	146	94	40
Pasta, cornmeal, and other cereal products	129	101	146	138	153	137	124	40
Bakery products	130	107	146	120	155	149	98	50
Bread	126	108	138	116	139	152	87	55
White bread	123	95	140	118	145	144	110	51
Bread, other than white	129	117	136	115	134	157	71	58
Crackers and cookies	131	113	145	127	149	151	92	53
Cookies	129	112	143	128	147	144	94	55
Crackers	133	114	149	126	151	163	88	51
Frozen and refrigerated bakery products	131	95	162	158	174	139	112	47
Other bakery products	131	105	150	109	166	149	106	46
Biscuits and rolls	133	109	154	116	158	172	94	47
Cakes and cupcakes	132	99	155	115	179	133	124	38
Bread and cracker products	138	117	147	102	144	187	83	42
Sweetrolls, coffee cakes, doughnuts	130	100	152	107	174	140	107	50
Pies, tarts, turnovers	121	120	119	73	129	133	85	57
Meats, poultry, fish, and eggs	131	111	142	108	147	156	95	44
Beef	135	117	146	96	155	166	86	38
Ground beef	130	102	149	99	157	170	117	38
Roast	139	115	155	88	155	204	77	36
Chuck roast	137	117	153	91	156	192	97	31
Round roast	134	89	163	66	185	189	90	43
Other roast	143	128	152	98	136	224	53	36
Steak	135	124	141	98	152	151	71	42
Round steak	140	144	131	83	134	161	88	36
Sirloin steak	141	130	145	78	155	172	60	38
Other steak	130	114	143	117	157	133	73	46
Other beef	150	154	142	87	159	150	43	29
Pork	130	113	138	93	146	154	96	43
Bacon	128	104	144	106	149	163	98	48
Pork chops	128	100	142	95	147	166	93	38
Ham	126	118	130	92	138	141	91	50
Ham, not canned	127	120	128	93	134	142	91	49
Canned ham	124	51	189	79	276	92	85	59
Sausage	125	101	140	94	155	142	111	48
Other pork	138	133	135	80	144	158	91	34
Other meats	127	103	142	116	148	150	108	46
Frankfurters	127	88	153	112	149	193	121	44
Lunch meats (cold cuts)	128	107	141	123	146	145	105	47
Bologna, liverwurst, salami	122	104	132	103	137	144	131	49
Other lunch meats	131	108	145	133	150	145	94	46
Lamb, organ meats, and others	124	117	124	78	161	84	94	46
Poultry	128	101	146	121	151	156	98	45
Fresh and frozen chicken	128	96	149	126	154	155	101	45

	total married couples	married couples, no children	married couples with children				single parent, at least one child <18	single person
			total	oldest child under 6	oldest child 6 to 17	oldest child 18 or older		
Fresh and frozen whole chicken	130	95	149	115	159	155	87	42
Fresh and frozen chicken parts	127	96	149	131	152	154	106	46
Other poultry	129	119	136	100	137	160	87	47
Fish and seafood	130	113	136	127	132	149	100	47
Canned fish and seafood	125	109	131	109	135	141	71	62
Fresh fish and shellfish	129	110	136	140	122	163	102	44
Frozen fish and shellfish	134	120	137	110	151	126	110	47
Eggs	122	106	129	119	133	131	95	53
Dairy products	**130**	**107**	**148**	**135**	**152**	**150**	**94**	**49**
Fresh milk and cream	128	96	152	131	163	145	100	49
Fresh milk, all types	127	93	153	134	164	145	103	49
Cream	133	124	142	113	152	141	71	51
Other dairy products	132	114	145	138	145	153	90	49
Butter	129	107	146	141	128	185	92	43
Cheese	132	118	144	135	145	150	89	49
Ice cream and related products	131	117	142	120	144	152	91	50
Miscellaneous dairy products	134	100	157	180	156	142	89	51
Fruits and vegetables	**128**	**113**	**137**	**125**	**135**	**151**	**85**	**52**
Fresh fruits	129	115	133	121	136	152	84	51
Apples	128	109	143	119	145	156	88	49
Bananas	124	113	129	120	121	153	87	58
Oranges	130	107	144	103	153	157	83	49
Citrus fruits, excl. oranges	130	117	137	113	134	160	78	53
Other fresh fruits	132	121	137	128	135	148	83	50
Fresh vegetables	130	119	134	124	129	150	72	51
Potatoes	128	117	132	138	121	150	95	49
Lettuce	129	120	136	111	133	160	85	53
Tomatoes	128	113	132	101	139	143	76	52
Other fresh vegetables	132	122	134	130	128	150	60	52
Processed fruits	126	103	142	138	142	146	98	55
Frozen fruits and fruit juices	127	108	136	125	132	152	79	49
Frozen orange juice	124	96	138	85	155	142	83	55
Frozen fruits	129	150	109	106	103	121	60	46
Frozen fruit juices, excl. orange	129	78	165	204	133	201	93	44
Canned fruits	128	111	139	138	136	144	82	60
Dried fruits	137	122	153	121	142	197	69	47
Fresh fruit juice	120	108	131	111	141	125	119	57
Canned and bottled fruit juice	126	95	148	154	145	148	101	55
Processed vegetables	126	110	138	122	136	155	97	53
Frozen vegetables	128	108	146	129	147	156	111	48
Canned and dried vegetables and juices	126	111	135	118	131	155	90	55
Canned beans	122	103	134	113	132	152	91	57
Canned corn	122	104	137	104	134	167	96	57
Canned miscellaneous vegetables	126	119	132	115	128	153	76	57
Dried peas	154	116	195	386	108	224	32	38
Dried beans	127	121	122	103	112	156	120	28
Dried miscellaneous vegetables	131	101	139	112	132	172	75	51
Dried processed vegetables	133	105	171	576	71	71	233	43
Fresh and canned vegetable juices	127	119	134	114	141	136	112	61
Sugar and other sweets	**127**	**110**	**141**	**122**	**148**	**141**	**104**	**50**
Candy and chewing gum	127	107	144	118	157	138	104	51
Sugar	124	110	128	122	127	133	126	43
Artificial sweeteners	129	149	116	114	97	156	75	67
Jams, preserves, other sweets	132	109	148	142	147	154	94	49
Fats and oils	**127**	**115**	**134**	**100**	**137**	**153**	**88**	**51**
Margarine	131	129	132	91	126	177	59	51
Fats and oils	126	111	133	103	143	132	91	45
Salad dressings	126	113	133	98	131	162	104	52
Nondairy cream and imitation milk	133	128	132	88	130	170	58	53
Peanut butter	125	104	141	112	150	143	95	57

	total married couples	married couples, no children	married couples with children				single parent, at least one child <18	single person
			total	oldest child under 6	oldest child 6 to 17	oldest child 18 or older		
Miscellaneous foods	**129**	**104**	**147**	**168**	**142**	**143**	**100**	**52**
Frozen prepared foods	122	99	139	132	145	133	111	63
Frozen meals	114	120	111	139	110	92	92	88
Other frozen prepared foods	126	88	153	128	162	154	121	50
Canned and packaged soups	124	107	136	136	130	148	88	60
Potato chips, nuts, and other snacks	132	108	151	121	154	167	101	51
Potato chips and other snacks	131	93	161	133	170	163	115	49
Nuts	135	154	122	87	107	177	57	58
Condiments and seasonings	130	112	143	134	141	153	93	49
Salt, spices, and other seasonings	128	117	134	136	128	146	89	47
Olives, pickles, relishes	127	114	136	135	137	134	93	59
Sauces and gravies	132	105	152	138	156	154	98	44
Baking needs and miscellaneous products	129	117	137	120	128	169	86	57
Other canned/packaged prepared foods	133	100	155	252	135	126	100	46
Prepared salads	125	124	124	117	115	149	87	60
Prepared desserts	129	116	136	124	144	127	85	48
Baby food	144	40	222	775	101	63	186	16
Miscellaneous prepared foods	132	111	146	149	148	138	80	51
Nonalcoholic beverages	**127**	**104**	**143**	**116**	**142**	**164**	**103**	**49**
Cola	127	101	142	113	142	162	105	45
Other carbonated drinks	129	95	153	115	152	184	117	45
Coffee	131	137	126	106	118	158	62	54
Roasted coffee	133	142	125	104	116	160	70	52
Instant and freeze-dried coffee	128	126	129	109	123	156	46	59
Noncarbonated fruit-flavored drinks, incl. nonfrozen lemonade	127	67	170	158	199	120	162	36
Tea	128	105	147	96	130	221	77	53
Other nonalcoholic beverages and ice	121	101	137	119	136	152	103	56
Food prepared by CU on trips	**141**	**155**	**134**	**100**	**157**	**116**	**52**	**48**
FOOD AWAY FROM HOME	**127**	**114**	**139**	**103**	**149**	**146**	**83**	**59**
Meals at restaurants, carry-outs, other	**124**	**110**	**136**	**109**	**144**	**141**	**85**	**62**
Lunch	123	98	143	111	155	143	94	60
• At fast food, take-out, delivery, concession stands, buffet, cafeteria (other than employer, school cafeteria)	119	86	142	137	144	142	103	59
• At full-service restaurants	124	140	115	86	114	140	60	71
• At vending machines, mobile vendors	126	71	132	75	158	120	51	74
• At employer and school cafeterias	144	42	227	56	322	159	150	30
Dinner	129	128	131	104	135	143	66	60
• At fast food, take-out, delivery, concession stands, buffet, cafeteria (other than employer, school cafeteria)	127	86	158	141	167	153	111	49
• At full-service restaurants	130	146	121	90	123	139	47	64
• At vending machines, mobile vendors	76	110	57	–	105	–	54	67
• At employer and school cafeterias	59	57	54	36	39	96	37	171
Snacks and nonalcoholic beverages	117	89	140	120	146	144	108	66
• At fast food, take-out, delivery, concession stands, buffet, cafeteria (other than employer, school cafeteria)	118	88	142	128	144	148	109	65
• At full-service restaurants	111	124	104	82	97	132	100	80
• At vending machines, mobile vendors	118	70	159	129	178	141	94	62
• At employer and school cafeterias	119	76	154	57	206	120	164	51
Breakfast and brunch	120	113	125	101	134	125	96	68
• At fast food, take-out, delivery, concession stands, buffet, cafeteria (other than employer, school cafeteria)	112	85	131	104	143	128	129	69
• At full-service restaurants	129	146	117	98	121	123	56	67
• At vending machines, mobile vendors	118	50	188	144	260	73	179	55
• At employer and school cafeterias	99	41	148	76	188	117	203	90
Board (including at school)	**138**	**110**	**163**	**11**	**108**	**369**	**37**	**74**
Catered affairs	**155**	**225**	**89**	**36**	**53**	**193**	**64**	**15**
Food on trips	**143**	**160**	**137**	**99**	**151**	**136**	**40**	**52**
School lunches	**157**	**0**	**299**	**17**	**457**	**197**	**214**	**0**
Meals as pay	**78**	**54**	**85**	**161**	**68**	**66**	**84**	**138**

	total married couples	married couples, no children	married couples with children				single parent, at least one child <18	single person
			total	oldest child under 6	oldest child 6 to 17	oldest child 18 or older		
ALCOHOLIC BEVERAGES	**114**	**122**	**113**	**114**	**110**	**117**	**56**	**72**
At home	**118**	**118**	**123**	**138**	**119**	**118**	**59**	**61**
Beer and ale	107	98	116	129	114	112	56	66
Whiskey	138	196	97	45	75	181	21	50
Wine	128	131	137	163	136	121	65	53
Other alcoholic beverages	112	115	112	141	108	98	71	75
Away from home	**109**	**129**	**97**	**76**	**95**	**116**	**52**	**88**
Beer and ale	108	127	96	80	83	133	55	90
• At fast food, take-out, delivery, concession stands, buffet, and cafeteria	94	94	84	137	75	65	103	105
• At full-service restaurants	105	134	87	73	88	94	48	93
Wine	104	117	96	84	102	93	47	84
• At fast food, take-out, delivery, concession stands, buffet and cafeteria	71	52	84	66	87	90	116	117
• At full-service restaurants	105	122	94	88	105	77	42	82
Other alcoholic beverages	102	112	95	56	96	121	63	93
• At fast food, take-out, delivery, concession stands, and cafeteria	90	79	92	104	94	81	110	103
• At full-service restaurants	100	120	88	47	99	93	55	96
Alcoholic beverages purchased on trips	123	159	100	85	109	93	38	79

Note: Spending index for total consumer units is 100. (–) means sample is too small to make a reliable estimate.
Source: Calculations by New Strategist based on the 2003 Consumer Expenditure Survey

Table 5.15 Food and Alcohol: Total spending by household type, 2003

(total annual spending on food and alcoholic beverages, by consumer unit (CU) type, 2003; numbers in thousands)

	total married couples	married couples, no children	married couples with children				single parent, at least one child <18	single person
			total	oldest child under 6	oldest child 6 to 17	oldest child 18 or older		
Number of consumer units	58,448	25,132	28,584	5,496	15,047	8,041	6,999	33,929
Total spending of all CUs	$3,099,499,193	$1,203,713,476	$1,649,363,115	$283,061,807	$890,529,309	$475,869,275	$213,712,715	$802,670,228
Food, total spending	401,167,200	148,964,401	215,903,813	34,206,225	118,031,226	63,819,005	33,624,036	96,051,303
Alcoholic beverages, total spending	26,130,932	12,023,903	12,584,392	2,446,380	6,458,925	3,693,955	1,542,160	9,496,049
FOOD AT HOME	236,538,472	85,503,336	127,954,275	21,720,412	68,481,004	37,877,131	20,846,871	51,735,618
Cereals and bakery products	33,386,667	11,512,467	18,637,054	3,007,521	10,394,468	5,226,570	3,111,405	7,378,879
Cereals and cereal products	11,299,752	3,688,875	6,431,686	1,088,813	3,607,819	1,726,322	1,119,490	2,414,727
Flour	532,461	183,966	280,123	58,258	130,608	92,391	42,974	135,716
Prepared flour mixes	1,004,137	340,790	551,671	101,016	304,100	145,703	91,897	207,306
Ready-to-eat and cooked cereals	6,460,842	2,062,835	3,801,672	584,829	2,215,972	992,742	637,889	1,481,679
Rice	1,206,951	395,326	640,567	134,927	317,492	189,044	105,825	217,824
Pasta, cornmeal, and other cereal products	2,095,361	705,958	1,157,652	209,782	639,798	306,443	240,906	372,540
Bakery products	22,086,915	7,823,592	12,205,368	1,918,709	6,786,648	3,500,247	1,991,985	4,964,152
Bread	6,092,035	2,245,042	3,248,857	526,187	1,722,129	1,006,733	502,038	1,536,984
White bread	2,403,382	801,459	1,336,016	216,982	731,736	387,817	258,473	576,114
Bread, other than white	3,688,653	1,443,582	1,912,841	309,205	990,544	618,916	243,565	960,869
Crackers and cookies	5,309,416	1,969,092	2,883,268	487,330	1,555,408	842,295	445,906	1,260,462
Cookies	3,405,765	1,266,904	1,835,950	317,339	998,068	520,574	295,568	833,296
Crackers	1,903,067	702,188	1,047,318	169,991	557,190	321,801	150,339	426,827
Frozen and refrigerated bakery products	1,882,610	584,319	1,134,499	213,849	642,657	274,439	193,312	392,219
Other bakery products	8,802,853	3,025,139	4,938,744	691,342	2,866,454	1,376,700	850,658	1,774,826
Biscuits and rolls	2,894,345	1,017,092	1,634,719	237,482	886,419	514,383	244,755	596,811
Cakes and cupcakes	2,833,559	917,821	1,622,428	232,426	990,093	393,687	319,294	472,970
Bread and cracker products	286,980	105,303	150,066	19,950	77,342	53,553	20,647	50,894
Sweetrolls, coffee cakes, doughnuts	2,100,037	691,633	1,200,528	162,297	724,363	310,945	208,010	464,827
Pies, tarts, turnovers	687,933	293,290	331,003	39,186	188,238	104,211	58,022	189,324
Meats, poultry, fish, and eggs	62,919,856	22,920,887	33,403,548	4,892,374	18,248,099	10,319,900	5,509,263	12,178,475
Beef	19,440,389	7,246,812	10,281,665	1,292,714	5,732,004	3,280,487	1,484,278	3,195,433
Ground beef	6,801,594	2,290,279	3,805,388	485,572	2,111,846	1,216,925	733,775	1,160,711
Roast	3,213,471	1,144,009	1,753,343	190,986	922,080	651,321	213,819	485,185
Chuck roast	1,070,767	392,813	584,257	67,051	313,730	206,252	91,057	139,448
Round roast	764,500	219,151	455,057	35,504	272,050	148,598	61,731	142,163
Other roast	1,377,619	531,793	714,028	88,431	336,451	296,472	61,031	203,574
Steak	7,453,289	2,939,439	3,807,389	509,094	2,159,846	1,141,500	468,863	1,330,356
Round steak	1,276,504	565,219	587,115	71,723	315,837	201,990	96,516	190,681
Sirloin steak	2,587,493	1,022,118	1,296,856	133,773	732,638	434,696	132,561	400,023
Other steak	3,589,292	1,352,102	1,923,703	303,599	1,111,371	504,814	239,786	739,652
Other beef	1,972,620	873,086	915,831	107,062	538,231	270,740	67,750	219,181
Pork	12,925,191	4,845,450	6,715,525	369,467	3,743,092	2,116,552	1,143,217	2,490,728
Bacon	2,337,336	813,272	1,283,707	181,148	697,278	408,322	214,379	504,864
Pork chops	2,552,424	858,509	1,387,467	178,565	756,563	456,809	221,938	438,363
Ham	2,820,116	1,132,699	1,414,622	193,789	790,419	432,284	242,165	641,597
Ham, not canned	2,740,627	1,118,625	1,355,167	189,007	744,676	424,163	235,656	619,544
Canned ham	79,489	14,074	59,455	4,782	45,743	8,121	6,509	22,054
Sausage	1,887,286	656,448	1,029,882	133,113	601,730	294,542	201,011	421,737
Other pork	3,328,614	1,384,271	1,599,846	182,797	897,102	524,595	263,722	483,828
Other meats	7,599,409	2,652,683	4,152,112	653,035	2,275,708	1,226,333	768,350	1,597,717
Frankfurters	1,689,147	503,645	997,010	139,873	509,792	352,839	192,123	341,326
Lunch meats (cold cuts)	5,190,182	1,857,003	2,800,374	470,238	1,524,562	806,271	510,507	1,099,978
Bologna, liverwurst, salami	1,541,858	564,716	818,646	122,341	447,498	250,075	197,862	357,612
Other lunch meats	3,648,324	1,292,287	1,981,729	347,897	1,077,064	556,196	312,645	742,367
Lamb, organ meats, and others	720,664	292,034	354,442	42,924	241,504	67,223	65,721	156,073
Poultry	10,843,273	3,656,203	6,042,658	963,614	3,276,183	1,809,547	992,388	2,228,117
Fresh and frozen chicken	8,711,674	2,814,030	4,949,320	808,407	2,696,874	1,446,898	820,283	1,777,201

	total married couples	married couples, no children	married couples with children				single parent, at least one child <18	single person
			total	oldest child under 6	oldest child 6 to 17	oldest child 18 or older		
Fresh and frozen whole chicken	$2,495,145	$787,637	$1,400,902	$208,079	$784,701	$408,483	$200,241	$472,970
Fresh and frozen chicken parts	6,216,529	2,026,393	3,548,704	600,328	1,912,173	1,038,495	620,041	1,304,231
Other poultry	2,132,183	842,173	1,093,338	155,207	579,310	362,649	172,105	450,916
Fish and seafood	9,446,950	3,526,522	4,829,267	868,753	2,476,134	1,494,822	873,755	1,994,347
Canned fish and seafood	1,193,508	448,355	615,128	98,214	332,388	185,425	81,538	346,076
Fresh fish and shellfish	5,412,869	1,985,428	2,801,518	552,018	1,320,525	941,762	514,496	1,077,246
Frozen fish and shellfish	2,840,573	1,092,991	1,412,335	218,521	823,221	367,635	277,720	571,364
Eggs	2,664,060	993,468	1,382,036	244,847	744,977	392,240	247,345	672,133
Dairy products	**24,948,529**	**8,847,218**	**13,863,526**	**2,437,916**	**7,480,315**	**3,946,201**	**2,147,433**	**5,463,587**
Fresh milk and cream	9,446,950	3,062,083	5,489,557	914,205	3,095,318	1,472,388	883,274	2,108,687
Fresh milk, all types	8,364,493	2,628,556	4,925,023	827,533	2,776,172	1,313,899	813,984	1,867,791
Cream	1,082,457	433,527	564,534	86,572	319,147	158,488	69,290	240,896
Other dairy products	15,501,579	5,785,135	8,373,969	1,523,711	4,384,997	2,473,894	1,264,159	3,354,900
Butter	1,365,345	485,299	753,760	139,818	349,241	269,374	115,903	264,307
Cheese	7,471,992	2,881,384	4,000,902	721,460	2,110,793	1,171,895	602,964	1,614,342
Ice cream and related products	4,457,829	1,708,976	2,351,034	383,291	1,260,788	710,181	369,197	984,959
Miscellaneous dairy products	2,205,828	709,476	1,268,272	279,142	664,175	322,444	176,165	491,292
Fruits and vegetables	**40,185,338**	**15,240,045**	**21,018,101**	**3,691,169**	**10,876,874**	**6,493,510**	**3,187,065**	**9,511,317**
Fresh fruits	12,914,670	4,959,046	6,722,385	1,136,133	3,508,509	2,092,268	1,007,226	2,973,198
Apples	2,457,154	897,464	1,339,160	214,949	716,237	410,413	201,921	548,632
Bananas	2,056,201	807,742	1,047,889	186,809	516,263	348,979	173,155	559,829
Oranges	1,390,478	494,598	757,476	103,929	423,122	231,500	106,595	303,665
Citrus fruits, excl. oranges	1,071,936	416,437	551,957	88,046	284,388	181,566	77,339	252,432
Other fresh fruits	5,939,486	2,343,056	3,025,616	542,455	1,568,349	919,810	448,216	1,308,302
Fresh vegetables	13,087,092	5,153,065	6,566,888	1,168,669	3,341,036	2,074,739	870,256	3,002,717
Potatoes	2,247,910	888,416	1,133,355	228,469	546,206	362,247	199,472	496,042
Lettuce	1,663,430	666,501	857,234	135,037	441,479	283,767	131,441	400,362
Tomatoes	2,416,240	913,548	1,218,250	179,334	670,645	369,806	170,916	571,025
Other fresh vegetables	6,759,511	2,684,349	3,358,334	625,834	1,682,706	1,058,839	368,427	1,535,627
Processed fruits	7,959,449	2,794,930	4,405,080	823,356	2,308,059	1,276,268	740,774	2,026,240
Frozen fruits and fruit juices	855,679	313,145	449,340	79,417	229,918	141,039	63,411	191,699
Frozen orange juice	336,076	111,586	182,652	21,709	107,887	53,071	26,806	86,858
Frozen fruits	275,290	138,226	113,764	21,324	56,878	35,702	15,468	57,001
Frozen fruit juices, excl. orange	244,313	63,333	152,924	36,384	65,003	52,347	21,067	47,840
Canned fruits	1,189,417	446,093	631,992	121,407	326,670	184,380	91,967	324,361
Dried fruits	504,406	193,768	274,692	42,044	134,671	99,628	30,236	99,412
Fresh fruit juice	1,454,771	562,454	778,342	126,188	441,479	209,548	172,945	402,737
Canned and bottled fruit juice	3,955,176	1,279,470	2,270,999	454,299	1,175,472	641,672	382,285	1,008,031
Processed vegetables	6,224,128	2,332,752	3,324,033	563,010	1,719,270	1,050,155	568,809	1,508,823
Frozen vegetables	2,011,780	727,571	1,115,919	189,722	591,648	336,114	208,850	438,023
Canned and dried vegetables and juices	4,212,932	1,605,432	2,208,114	373,288	1,127,622	714,041	359,889	1,070,799
Canned beans	892,501	324,705	480,211	78,208	250,232	153,101	79,789	240,896
Canned corn	490,963	179,694	268,975	39,351	138,432	92,391	46,053	132,323
Canned miscellaneous vegetables	1,361,254	555,417	699,736	117,395	356,012	228,606	99,246	356,933
Dried peas	33,315	10,807	20,580	7,859	6,019	6,674	840	4,750
Dried beans	171,837	70,370	80,321	13,080	38,821	28,948	19,457	22,054
Dried miscellaneous vegetables	576,882	190,501	297,845	46,331	148,815	104,131	39,334	130,287
Dried processed vegetables	32,731	11,058	20,580	13,300	4,514	2,412	6,859	6,107
Fresh and canned vegetable juices	641,759	260,368	332,432	54,246	183,423	94,884	68,240	178,127
Sugar and other sweets	**8,871,237**	**3,282,491**	**4,805,256**	**801,427**	**2,652,786**	**1,349,441**	**867,386**	**2,035,740**
Candy and chewing gum	5,587,044	2,024,885	3,106,509	486,781	1,780,211	834,977	549,282	1,309,659
Sugar	1,225,070	465,193	615,699	113,712	321,705	181,003	148,379	244,289
Artificial sweeteners	428,424	211,611	187,511	35,559	82,458	71,082	29,676	128,930
Jams, preserves, other sweets	1,630,699	580,801	895,251	165,375	468,413	262,378	139,980	352,862
Fats and oils	**6,378,430**	**2,473,743**	**3,279,728**	**469,963**	**1,765,765**	**1,052,486**	**525,345**	**1,471,161**
Margarine	736,445	311,888	363,874	48,035	181,918	136,617	39,544	166,591
Fats and oils	1,941,058	734,860	996,724	149,546	566,971	279,746	167,206	403,416
Salad dressings	1,924,108	742,148	994,152	141,192	517,015	340,456	189,883	461,434
Nondairy cream and imitation milk	853,925	354,361	416,183	53,201	214,871	150,608	44,934	196,788
Peanut butter	922,894	330,486	508,509	78,043	285,141	145,220	83,848	243,271

| | total married couples | married couples, no children | married couples with children | | | single parent, at least one | single |
			total	oldest child under 6	oldest child 6 to 17	oldest child 18 or older	child <18	person
Miscellaneous foods	**$36,929,784**	**$12,831,394**	**$20,608,778**	**$4,516,283**	**$10,465,790**	**$5,618,649**	**$3,438,679**	**$8,669,199**
Frozen prepared foods	7,463,225	2,603,424	4,174,407	760,591	2,286,843	1,122,202	815,593	2,235,243
Frozen meals	2,317,463	1,049,261	1,107,916	266,996	578,256	258,840	225,018	1,042,299
Other frozen prepared foods	5,145,762	1,554,163	3,066,777	493,651	1,708,587	863,362	590,576	1,192,944
Canned and packaged soups	2,540,735	947,476	1,366,601	262,819	687,497	419,258	217,669	713,866
Potato chips, nuts, and other snacks	8,130,117	2,871,582	4,567,152	703,873	2,456,423	1,415,296	745,184	1,836,916
Potato chips and other snacks	6,052,290	1,846,699	3,648,748	577,575	2,031,947	1,038,736	640,478	1,320,177
Nuts	2,077,826	1,024,883	918,404	126,353	424,476	376,560	104,705	516,399
Condiments and seasonings	6,849,521	2,530,038	3,677,617	662,158	1,911,872	1,109,256	587,426	1,509,501
Salt, spices, and other seasonings	1,557,055	609,451	797,779	155,757	399,648	243,884	130,041	330,129
Olives, pickles, relishes	847,496	326,967	443,052	84,364	235,937	122,545	74,399	229,021
Sauces and gravies	2,969,158	1,017,343	1,668,734	292,717	900,112	476,188	264,982	572,722
Baking needs and miscellaneous products	1,476,981	576,025	768,338	129,376	376,325	266,559	118,003	377,630
Other canned/packaged prepared foods	11,946,187	3,878,873	6,822,715	2,125,842	3,123,155	1,552,637	1,072,737	2,373,673
Prepared salads	1,493,931	639,609	727,749	131,684	353,755	245,492	124,722	415,630
Prepared desserts	835,806	324,454	430,761	75,790	240,602	113,780	66,071	182,538
Baby food	2,249,079	267,404	1,698,747	1,139,870	405,216	135,491	349,250	142,841
Miscellaneous prepared foods	7,354,512	2,641,876	3,961,457	779,443	2,119,520	1,057,954	532,624	1,632,663
Nonalcoholic beverages	**19,917,909**	**6,983,429**	**10,943,670**	**1,704,694**	**5,739,377**	**3,532,009**	**1,928,434**	**4,436,217**
Cola	6,563,126	2,247,303	3,577,288	547,786	1,887,646	1,152,034	646,218	1,354,785
Other carbonated drinks	3,451,354	1,089,472	1,999,451	289,364	1,042,757	675,364	373,607	700,973
Coffee	2,920,647	1,309,629	1,375,748	221,764	676,814	484,711	165,316	699,616
Roasted coffee	1,997,168	918,575	920,119	147,293	448,401	329,761	125,492	452,952
Instant and freeze-dried coffee	924,063	391,054	455,915	74,471	228,413	154,950	39,824	246,664
Noncarbonated fruit-flavored drinks, incl. nonfrozen lemonade	1,432,560	323,449	939,270	167,848	578,256	186,632	218,439	236,146
Tea	1,326,185	468,963	746,042	93,212	345,630	315,127	95,326	317,236
Other nonalcoholic beverages and ice	4,165,589	1,493,343	2,299,011	334,775	1,201,503	718,061	424,489	1,117,621
Food prepared by CU on trips	**3,000,136**	**1,411,664**	**1,394,613**	**199,065**	**857,378**	**338,204**	**131,861**	**591,043**
FOOD AWAY FROM HOME	164,628,728	63,461,065	87,949,824	12,485,868	49,550,222	25,941,955	12,777,164	44,315,685
Meals at restaurants, carry-outs, other	133,211,175	50,853,848	71,311,935	10,924,344	39,587,905	20,828,120	10,871,757	38,252,572
Lunch	47,448,671	16,231,754	26,929,844	4,014,938	15,325,670	7,574,783	4,328,042	13,355,472
• At fast food, take-out, delivery, concession stands, buffet, cafeteria (other than employer, school cafeteria)	25,669,193	7,956,289	15,020,320	2,775,590	8,017,343	4,226,108	2,652,971	7,404,326
• At full-service restaurants	15,196,480	7,408,662	6,933,621	988,895	3,615,794	2,358,184	885,513	5,068,993
• At vending machines, mobile vendors	409,720	99,020	209,235	23,028	131,962	53,553	19,807	138,770
• At employer and school cafeterias	6,173,862	767,783	4,766,668	227,479	3,560,572	936,857	769,680	743,384
Dinner	55,650,679	23,723,603	27,684,462	4,223,126	15,021,721	8,483,094	3,390,596	14,992,207
• At fast food, take-out, delivery, concession stands, buffet, cafeteria (other than employer, school cafeteria)	16,041,638	4,680,835	9,752,575	1,668,421	5,412,857	2,661,812	1,672,481	3,596,813
• At full-service restaurants	39,452,400	18,965,864	17,867,287	2,549,045	9,571,397	5,799,330	1,705,726	11,201,320
• At vending machines, mobile vendors	58,448	36,441	21,438	#VALUE!	20,915	#VALUE!	4,969	30,197
• At employer and school cafeterias	98,193	40,211	43,448	5,661	16,401	21,952	7,419	164,216
Snacks and nonalcoholic beverages	16,975,637	5,561,209	9,961,810	1,540,996	5,442,650	2,881,412	1,885,321	5,550,106
• At fast food, take-out, delivery, concession stands, buffet, cafeteria (other than employer, school cafeteria)	12,389,807	3,987,192	7,304,641	1,266,608	3,899,881	2,143,811	1,375,723	3,991,408
• At full-service restaurants	1,723,632	827,848	789,204	120,692	389,868	283,284	185,823	722,009
• At vending machines, mobile vendors	2,157,900	551,396	1,419,767	222,093	837,366	356,055	206,960	659,919
• At employer and school cafeterias	704,298	195,024	448,483	31,602	315,536	98,261	116,743	176,770
Breakfast and brunch	13,136,188	5,337,283	6,735,534	1,045,284	3,798,013	1,888,750	1,267,869	4,354,448
• At fast food, take-out, delivery, concession stands, buffet, cafeteria (other than employer, school cafeteria)	6,069,825	1,986,182	3,486,390	532,617	1,993,878	956,155	840,790	2,160,599
• At full-service restaurants	6,726,780	3,289,527	2,995,889	484,033	1,629,741	884,349	349,250	2,037,436
• At vending machines, mobile vendors	94,101	17,090	73,461	10,827	53,567	8,041	17,148	25,447
• At employer and school cafeterias	246,066	44,484	180,079	17,807	120,827	40,285	60,751	130,966
Board (including at school)	**2,673,996**	**918,826**	**1,546,966**	**19,896**	**539,886**	**987,033**	**86,648**	**836,011**
Catered affairs	**4,378,924**	**2,741,901**	**1,235,972**	**94,861**	**388,814**	**752,236**	**217,109**	**252,771**
Food on trips	**17,935,353**	**8,584,589**	**8,351,101**	**1,160,261**	**4,855,667**	**2,335,106**	**596,595**	**3,743,726**
School lunches	**5,229,927**	**3,016**	**4,864,711**	**54,685**	**3,909,963**	**900,110**	**851,218**	**2,714**
Meals as pay	**1,199,353**	**358,634**	**639,138**	**231,821**	**267,987**	**139,351**	**153,838**	**1,227,212**

	total married couples	married couples, no children	married couples with children				single parent, at least one child <18	single person
			total	oldest child under 6	oldest child 6 to 17	oldest child 18 or older		
ALCOHOLIC BEVERAGES	$26,130,932	$12,023,903	$12,584,392	$2,446,380	$6,458,925	$3,693,955	$1,542,160	$9,496,049
At home	**16,489,350**	**7,127,184**	**8,407,698**	**1,817,692**	**4,306,301**	**2,279,221**	**988,679**	**4,996,385**
Beer and ale	6,975,184	2,748,687	3,694,196	787,302	1,905,251	999,335	434,848	2,507,692
Whiskey	1,149,088	705,204	396,174	35,284	160,852	207,538	21,347	243,610
Wine	6,746,068	2,961,555	3,528,123	803,405	1,838,593	878,399	410,071	1,615,020
Other alcoholic beverages	1,619,594	711,738	788,918	191,755	401,454	193,949	122,413	630,062
Away from home	**9,641,582**	**4,896,970**	**4,176,694**	**628,687**	**2,152,774**	**1,414,734**	**553,411**	**4,500,003**
Beer and ale	3,800,289	1,927,624	1,656,443	266,061	757,165	647,461	231,597	1,848,791
• At fast food, take-out, delivery, concession stands, buffet, and cafeteria	587,402	252,828	257,828	80,571	120,075	56,207	77,339	379,666
• At full-service restaurants	2,832,390	1,559,189	1,143,074	185,490	611,059	348,336	154,258	1,464,376
Wine	1,139,736	551,145	517,085	86,397	289,504	140,718	62,361	532,346
• At fast food, take-out, delivery, concession stands, buffet and cafeteria	68,969	21,614	39,752	5,991	21,668	11,981	13,508	66,162
• At full-service restaurants	1,025,762	512,944	450,484	80,406	265,128	102,925	48,853	466,184
Other alcoholic beverages	2,306,943	1,092,991	1,054,464	120,143	561,554	378,570	172,175	1,226,873
• At fast food, take-out, delivery, concession stands, buffet, and cafeteria	407,967	153,808	204,090	44,188	109,241	50,176	59,422	269,396
• At full-service restaurants	1,731,814	888,668	738,325	75,955	441,329	221,369	112,754	956,459
Alcoholic beverages purchased on trips	2,394,030	1,324,959	948,703	156,086	544,551	247,984	87,348	891,654

Note: Total spending figures for total consumer units can be found on Total Spending by Age and Total Spending by Region tables. Spending by type of consumer unit will not add to total because not all types of consumer units are shown. Numbers may not add to category total because of rounding and missing subcategories. (–) means sample is too small to make a reliable estimate.
Source: Calculations by New Strategist based on the 2003 Consumer Expenditure Survey

Table 5.16 Food and Alcohol: Market shares by household type, 2003

(percentage of total annual spending on food and alcoholic beverages accounted for by types of consumer units, 2003)

	total married couples	married couples, no children	married couples with children				single parent, at least one child <18	single person
			total	oldest child under 6	oldest child 6 to 17	oldest child 18 or older		
Share of total consumer units	50.7%	21.8%	24.8%	4.8%	13.0%	7.0%	6.1%	29.4%
Share of total before-tax income	68.8	26.8	36.6	6.2	19.8	10.7	3.5	15.6
Share of total spending	65.8	25.6	35.0	6.0	18.9	10.1	4.5	17.0
Share of food spending	65.1	24.2	35.1	5.6	19.2	10.4	5.5	15.6
Share of alcoholic beverages spending	57.9	26.6	27.9	5.4	14.3	8.2	3.4	21.0
FOOD AT HOME	65.5	23.7	35.5	6.0	19.0	10.5	5.8	14.3
Cereals and bakery products	65.5	22.6	36.6	5.9	20.4	10.3	6.1	14.5
Cereals and cereal products	65.2	21.3	37.1	6.3	20.8	10.0	6.5	13.9
Flour	63.1	21.8	33.2	6.9	15.5	10.9	5.1	16.1
Prepared flour mixes	68.1	23.1	37.4	6.8	20.6	9.9	6.2	14.1
Ready-to-eat and cooked cereals	65.0	20.7	38.2	5.9	22.3	10.0	6.4	14.9
Rice	65.2	21.4	34.6	7.3	17.1	10.2	5.7	11.8
Pasta, cornmeal, and other cereal products	65.5	22.1	36.2	6.6	20.0	9.6	7.5	11.6
Bakery products	65.7	23.3	36.3	5.7	20.2	10.4	5.9	14.8
Bread	64.0	23.6	34.1	5.5	18.1	10.6	5.3	16.1
White bread	62.2	20.7	34.6	5.6	18.9	10.0	6.7	14.9
Bread, other than white	65.2	25.5	33.8	5.5	17.5	10.9	4.3	17.0
Crackers and cookies	66.1	24.5	35.9	6.1	19.4	10.5	5.6	15.7
Cookies	65.5	24.4	35.3	6.1	19.2	10.0	5.7	16.0
Crackers	67.3	24.8	37.0	6.0	19.7	11.4	5.3	15.1
Frozen and refrigerated bakery products	66.4	20.6	40.0	7.5	22.7	9.7	6.8	13.8
Other bakery products	66.4	22.8	37.3	5.2	21.6	10.4	6.4	13.4
Biscuits and rolls	67.4	23.7	38.1	5.5	20.6	12.0	5.7	13.9
Cakes and cupcakes	66.9	21.7	38.3	5.5	23.4	9.3	7.5	11.2
Bread and cracker products	69.7	25.6	36.4	4.8	18.8	13.0	5.0	12.4
Sweetrolls, coffee cakes, doughnuts	65.8	21.7	37.6	5.1	22.7	9.7	6.5	14.6
Pies, tarts, turnovers	61.4	26.2	29.5	3.5	16.8	9.3	5.2	16.9
Meats, poultry, fish, and eggs	66.1	24.1	35.1	5.1	19.2	10.8	5.8	12.8
Beef	68.6	25.6	36.3	4.6	20.2	11.6	5.2	11.3
Ground beef	66.0	22.2	37.0	4.7	20.5	11.8	7.1	11.3
Roast	70.3	25.0	38.4	4.2	20.2	14.2	4.7	10.6
Chuck roast	69.4	25.5	37.9	4.3	20.3	13.4	5.9	9.0
Round roast	67.8	19.4	40.3	3.1	24.1	13.2	5.5	12.6
Other roast	72.5	28.0	37.6	4.7	17.7	15.6	3.2	10.7
Steak	68.6	27.1	35.1	4.7	19.9	10.5	4.3	12.2
Round steak	70.7	31.3	32.5	4.0	17.5	11.2	5.3	10.6
Sirloin steak	71.5	28.3	35.9	3.7	20.3	12.0	3.7	11.1
Other steak	66.0	24.8	35.4	5.6	20.4	9.3	4.4	13.6
Other beef	76.0	33.7	35.3	4.1	20.7	10.4	2.6	8.4
Pork	65.7	24.6	34.1	4.4	19.0	10.8	5.8	12.7
Bacon	65.0	22.6	35.7	5.0	19.4	11.4	6.0	14.0
Pork chops	64.8	21.8	35.2	4.5	19.2	11.6	5.6	11.1
Ham	64.1	25.7	32.1	4.4	18.0	9.8	5.5	14.6
Ham, not canned	64.1	26.2	31.7	4.4	17.4	9.9	5.5	14.5
Canned ham	62.6	11.1	46.9	3.8	36.0	6.4	5.1	17.4
Sausage	63.4	22.0	34.6	4.5	20.2	9.9	6.7	14.2
Other pork	69.8	29.0	33.5	3.8	18.8	11.0	5.5	10.1
Other meats	64.6	22.5	35.3	5.5	19.3	10.4	6.5	13.6
Frankfurters	64.4	19.2	38.0	5.3	19.4	13.5	7.3	13.0
Lunch meats (cold cuts)	64.9	23.2	35.0	5.9	19.1	10.1	6.4	13.8
Bologna, liverwurst, salami	61.7	22.6	32.8	4.9	17.9	10.0	7.9	14.3
Other lunch meats	66.4	23.5	36.0	6.3	19.6	10.1	5.7	13.5
Lamb, organ meats, and others	62.7	25.4	30.8	3.7	21.0	5.9	5.7	13.6
Poultry	65.0	21.9	36.2	5.8	19.6	10.8	5.9	13.4
Fresh and frozen chicken	64.9	21.0	36.9	6.0	20.1	10.8	6.1	13.2

	total married couples	married couples, no children	married couples with children			single parent, at least one child <18	single person
			total	oldest child under 6	oldest child 6 to 17	oldest child 18 or older	
Fresh and frozen whole chicken	65.9%	20.8%	37.0%	5.5%	20.7%	10.8%	5.3%	12.5%
Fresh and frozen chicken parts	64.5	21.0	36.8	6.2	19.8	10.8	6.4	13.5
Other poultry	65.5	25.9	33.6	4.8	17.8	11.1	5.3	13.9
Fish and seafood	65.8	24.6	33.6	6.1	17.2	10.4	6.1	13.9
Canned fish and seafood	63.1	23.7	32.5	5.2	17.6	9.8	4.3	18.3
Fresh fish and shellfish	65.3	23.9	33.8	6.7	15.9	11.4	6.2	13.0
Frozen fish and shellfish	68.1	26.2	33.8	5.2	19.7	8.8	6.7	13.7
Eggs	61.8	23.1	32.1	5.7	17.3	9.1	5.7	15.6
Dairy products	**65.9**	**23.4**	**36.6**	**6.4**	**19.8**	**10.4**	**5.7**	**14.4**
Fresh milk and cream	64.7	21.0	37.6	6.3	21.2	10.1	6.1	14.4
Fresh milk, all types	64.4	20.2	37.9	6.4	21.4	10.1	6.3	14.4
Cream	67.3	26.9	35.1	5.4	19.8	9.8	4.3	15.0
Other dairy products	66.7	24.9	36.0	5.6	18.9	10.6	5.4	14.4
Butter	65.5	23.3	36.1	5.7	16.7	12.9	5.6	12.7
Cheese	66.7	25.7	35.7	5.4	18.9	10.5	5.4	14.4
Ice cream and related products	66.5	25.5	35.1	5.7	18.8	10.6	5.5	14.7
Miscellaneous dairy products	67.7	21.8	38.9	3.6	20.4	9.9	5.4	15.1
Fruits and vegetables	**65.1**	**24.7**	**34.0**	**6.0**	**17.6**	**10.5**	**5.2**	**15.4**
Fresh fruits	65.5	25.2	34.1	5.8	17.8	10.6	5.1	15.1
Apples	65.1	23.8	35.5	5.7	19.0	10.9	5.3	14.5
Bananas	62.7	24.6	32.0	5.7	15.8	10.6	5.3	17.1
Oranges	65.7	23.4	35.8	4.9	20.0	10.9	5.0	14.4
Citrus fruits, excl. oranges	65.7	25.5	33.8	5.4	17.4	11.1	4.7	15.5
Other fresh fruits	66.6	26.3	33.9	6.1	17.6	10.3	5.0	14.7
Fresh vegetables	66.0	26.0	33.1	5.9	16.8	10.5	4.4	15.1
Potatoes	64.7	25.6	32.5	6.6	15.7	10.4	5.7	14.3
Lettuce	65.2	26.1	33.5	5.3	17.3	11.1	5.2	15.7
Tomatoes	65.1	24.6	32.3	4.8	18.1	10.0	4.6	15.4
Other fresh vegetables	66.9	26.6	33.2	6.2	16.7	10.5	3.6	15.2
Processed fruits	63.7	22.4	35.2	6.6	18.5	10.2	5.9	16.2
Frozen fruits and fruit juices	64.3	23.5	33.8	6.0	17.3	10.6	4.8	14.4
Frozen orange juice	62.8	20.8	34.1	4.1	20.2	9.9	5.0	16.2
Frozen fruits	65.2	32.7	26.9	5.1	13.5	8.5	3.7	13.5
Frozen fruit juices, excl. orange	65.4	16.9	40.9	9.7	17.4	14.0	5.6	12.8
Canned fruits	64.6	24.2	34.3	6.6	17.7	10.0	5.0	17.6
Dried fruits	69.4	26.7	37.8	5.8	18.5	13.7	4.2	13.7
Fresh fruit juice	60.7	23.5	32.5	5.3	18.4	8.7	7.2	16.8
Canned and bottled fruit juice	63.7	20.6	36.6	7.3	18.9	10.3	6.2	16.2
Processed vegetables	64.1	24.0	34.2	5.8	17.7	10.8	5.9	15.5
Frozen vegetables	65.1	23.5	35.1	6.1	19.1	10.9	6.8	14.2
Canned and dried vegetables and juices	63.6	24.2	33.3	5.6	17.0	10.8	5.4	16.2
Canned beans	61.6	22.4	33.1	5.4	17.3	10.6	5.5	16.6
Canned corn	61.8	22.6	33.8	5.0	17.4	11.6	5.8	16.6
Canned miscellaneous vegetables	63.6	26.0	32.7	5.5	16.6	10.7	4.6	16.7
Dried peas	78.1	25.3	48.2	18.4	14.1	15.6	2.0	11.1
Dried beans	64.5	26.4	30.1	4.9	14.6	10.9	7.3	8.3
Dried miscellaneous vegetables	66.6	22.0	34.4	5.3	17.2	12.0	4.5	15.0
Dried processed vegetables	67.6	22.8	42.5	27.5	9.3	5.0	14.2	12.6
Fresh and canned vegetable juices	64.2	26.0	33.2	5.4	18.3	9.5	6.8	17.8
Sugar and other sweets	**64.6**	**23.9**	**35.0**	**5.8**	**19.3**	**9.8**	**6.3**	**14.8**
Candy and chewing gum	64.3	23.3	35.8	5.6	20.5	9.6	6.3	15.1
Sugar	62.9	23.9	31.6	5.8	16.5	9.3	7.6	12.5
Artificial sweeteners	65.5	32.4	28.7	5.4	12.6	10.9	4.5	19.7
Jams, preserves, other sweets	66.7	23.7	36.6	6.3	19.2	10.7	5.7	14.4
Fats and oils	**64.5**	**25.0**	**33.2**	**4.8**	**17.9**	**10.6**	**5.3**	**14.9**
Margarine	66.4	28.1	32.8	4.3	16.4	12.3	3.6	15.0
Fats and oils	64.0	24.2	32.9	4.9	18.7	9.2	5.5	13.3
Salad dressings	63.7	24.6	32.9	4.7	17.1	11.3	6.3	15.3
Nondairy cream and imitation milk	67.2	27.9	32.7	4.2	16.9	11.8	3.5	15.5
Peanut butter	63.3	22.7	34.9	5.4	19.6	10.0	5.8	16.7

	total married couples	married couples, no children	married couples with children				single parent, at least one child <18	single person
			total	oldest child under 6	oldest child 6 to 17	oldest child 18 or older		
Miscellaneous foods	**65.4%**	**22.7%**	**36.5%**	**8.0%**	**18.5%**	**9.9%**	**6.1%**	**15.3%**
Frozen prepared foods	61.7	21.5	34.5	6.3	18.9	9.3	6.7	18.5
Frozen meals	57.6	26.1	27.6	6.6	14.4	6.4	5.6	25.9
Other frozen prepared foods	63.8	19.3	38.0	6.1	21.2	10.7	7.3	14.8
Canned and packaged soups	62.6	23.3	33.7	6.5	16.9	10.3	5.4	17.6
Potato chips, nuts, and other snacks	66.7	23.6	37.5	5.8	20.1	11.6	6.1	15.1
Potato chips and other snacks	66.2	20.2	39.9	6.3	22.2	11.4	7.0	14.4
Nuts	68.2	33.6	30.1	4.1	13.9	12.4	3.4	17.0
Condiments and seasonings	65.8	24.3	35.3	6.4	18.4	10.7	5.6	14.5
Salt, spices, and other seasonings	65.0	25.4	33.3	6.5	16.7	10.2	5.4	13.8
Olives, pickles, relishes	64.4	24.8	33.7	6.4	17.9	9.3	5.7	17.4
Sauces and gravies	66.9	22.9	37.6	6.6	20.3	10.7	6.0	12.9
Baking needs and miscellaneous products	65.4	25.5	34.0	5.7	16.7	11.8	5.2	16.7
Other canned/packaged prepared foods	67.4	21.9	38.5	12.0	17.6	8.8	6.0	13.4
Prepared salads	63.1	27.0	30.8	5.6	15.0	10.4	5.3	17.6
Prepared desserts	65.3	25.3	33.6	5.9	18.8	8.9	5.2	14.3
Baby food	72.9	8.7	55.0	36.9	13.1	4.4	11.3	4.6
Miscellaneous prepared foods	67.0	24.1	36.1	7.1	19.3	9.6	4.9	14.9
Nonalcoholic beverages	**64.3**	**22.6**	**35.3**	**5.5**	**18.5**	**11.4**	**6.2**	**14.3**
Cola	64.5	22.1	35.1	5.4	18.5	11.3	6.3	13.3
Other carbonated drinks	65.6	20.7	38.0	5.5	19.8	12.8	7.1	13.3
Coffee	66.5	29.8	31.3	5.0	15.4	11.0	3.8	15.9
Roasted coffee	67.4	31.0	31.0	5.0	15.1	11.1	4.2	15.3
Instant and freeze-dried coffee	64.7	27.4	31.9	5.2	16.0	10.9	2.8	17.3
Noncarbonated fruit-flavored drinks, incl. nonfrozen lemonade	64.4	14.5	42.2	7.5	26.0	8.4	9.8	10.6
Tea	64.9	23.0	36.5	4.6	16.9	15.4	4.7	15.5
Other nonalcoholic beverages and ice	61.5	22.0	33.9	5.7	17.7	10.6	6.3	16.5
Food prepared by CU on trips	**71.7**	**33.7**	**33.3**	**4.8**	**20.5**	**8.1**	**3.2**	**14.1**
FOOD AWAY FROM HOME	**64.6**	**24.9**	**34.5**	**4.9**	**19.4**	**10.2**	**5.0**	**17.4**
Meals at restaurants, carry-outs, other	**63.0**	**24.1**	**33.7**	**5.2**	**18.7**	**9.9**	**5.1**	**18.1**
Lunch	62.5	21.4	35.5	5.3	20.2	10.0	5.7	17.6•
• At fast food, take-out, delivery, concession stands, buffet, cafeteria (other than employer, school cafeteria)	60.3	18.7	35.3	6.5	18.8	9.9	6.2	17.4
• At full-service restaurants	62.7	30.6	28.6	4.1	14.9	9.7	3.7	20.9
• At vending machines, mobile vendors	63.9	15.4	32.6	3.6	20.6	8.3	3.1	21.6
• At employer and school cafeterias	72.8	9.1	56.2	2.7	42.0	11.1	9.1	8.8
Dinner	65.4	27.9	32.5	5.0	17.7	10.0	4.0	17.6
• At fast food, take-out, delivery, concession stands, buffet, cafeteria (other than employer, school cafeteria)	64.4	18.8	39.2	6.7	21.7	10.7	6.7	14.4
• At full-service restaurants	66.1	31.8	29.9	4.3	16.0	9.7	2.9	18.8
• At vending machines, mobile vendors	38.4	23.9	14.1	–	13.7	–	3.3	19.8
• At employer and school cafeterias	30.1	12.3	13.3	1.7	5.0	6.7	2.3	50.3
Snacks and nonalcoholic beverages	59.2	19.4	34.8	5.7	19.0	10.1	6.6	19.4
• At fast food, take-out, delivery, concession stands, buffet, cafeteria (other than employer, school cafeteria)	59.6	19.2	35.1	6.1	18.8	10.3	6.6	19.2
• At full-service restaurants	56.0	26.9	25.7	3.9	12.7	9.2	6.0	23.5
• At vending machines, mobile vendors	59.7	15.3	39.3	6.1	23.2	9.9	5.7	18.3
• At employer and school cafeterias	60.1	16.6	38.3	2.7	26.9	8.4	10.0	15.1
Breakfast and brunch	60.6	24.6	31.1	4.8	17.5	8.7	5.8	20.1
• At fast food, take-out, delivery, concession stands, buffet, cafeteria (other than employer, school cafeteria)	56.7	18.5	32.6	5.0	18.6	8.9	7.9	20.2
• At full-service restaurants	65.2	31.9	29.0	4.7	15.8	8.6	3.4	19.8
• At vending machines, mobile vendors	59.5	10.8	46.5	6.9	33.9	5.1	10.9	16.1
• At employer and school cafeterias	50.0	9.0	36.6	3.6	24.5	8.2	12.3	26.6
Board (including at school)	**69.7**	**24.0**	**40.3**	**0.5**	**14.1**	**25.7**	**2.3**	**21.8**
Catered affairs	**78.4**	**49.1**	**22.1**	**1.7**	**7.0**	**13.5**	**3.9**	**4.5**
Food on trips	**72.7**	**34.8**	**33.8**	**4.7**	**19.7**	**9.5**	**2.4**	**15.2**
School lunches	**79.7**	**0.0**	**74.2**	**0.8**	**59.6**	**13.7**	**13.0**	**0.0**
Meals as pay	**39.6**	**11.8**	**21.1**	**7.6**	**8.8**	**4.6**	**5.1**	**40.5**

	total married couples	married couples, no children	married couples with children				single parent, at least one child <18	single person
			total	oldest child under 6	oldest child 6 to 17	oldest child 18 or older		
ALCOHOLIC BEVERAGES	**57.9%**	**26.6%**	**27.9%**	**5.4%**	**14.3%**	**8.2%**	**3.4%**	**21.0%**
At home	**59.5**	**25.7**	**30.4**	**6.6**	**15.5**	**8.2**	**3.6**	**18.0**
Beer and ale	54.4	21.4	28.8	6.1	14.9	7.8	3.4	19.6
Whiskey	69.7	42.8	24.0	2.1	9.8	12.6	1.3	14.8
Wine	65.0	28.5	34.0	7.7	17.7	8.5	4.0	15.6
Other alcoholic beverages	56.8	25.0	27.7	6.7	14.1	6.8	4.3	22.1
Away from home	**55.3**	**28.1**	**24.0**	**3.6**	**12.3**	**8.1**	**3.2**	**25.8**
Beer and ale	54.6	27.7	23.8	3.8	10.9	9.3	3.3	26.6
• At fast food, take-out, delivery, concession stands, buffet, and cafeteria	47.6	20.5	20.9	6.5	9.7	4.6	6.3	30.8•
• At full-service restaurants	53.2	29.3	21.5	3.5	11.5	6.5	2.9	27.5
Wine	52.6	25.4	23.9	4.0	13.4	6.5	2.9	24.6
• At fast food, take-out, delivery, concession stands, buffet and cafeteria	36.0	11.3	20.7	3.1	11.3	6.3	7.1	34.6
• At full-service restaurants	53.2	26.6	23.4	4.2	13.7	5.3	2.5	24.2
Other alcoholic beverages	51.6	24.5	23.6	2.7	12.6	8.5	3.9	27.4
• At fast food, take-out, delivery, concession stands, buffet, and cafeteria	45.8	17.2	22.9	5.0	12.3	5.6	6.7	30.2
• At full-service restaurants	50.9	26.1	21.7	2.2	13.0	6.5	3.3	28.1
Alcoholic beverages purchased on trips	62.4	34.5	24.7	4.1	14.2	6.5	2.3	23.2

Note: Market share for total consumer units is 100.0%. Market shares by type of consumer unit will not add to total because not all types of consumer units are shown. (–) means sample is too small to make a reliable estimate.
Source: Calculations by New Strategist based on the 2003 Consumer Expenditure Survey

Table 5.17 Food and Alcohol: Average spending by race and Hispanic origin, 2003

(average annual spending of consumer units (CU) on food and alcoholic beverages, by race and Hispanic origin of consumer unit reference person, 2003)

	total consumer units	race			Hispanic origin	
		Asian	black	white and other	Hispanic	non-Hispanic
Number of consumer units (000)	115,356	3,573	13,743	98,041	11,727	103,629
Average number of persons per CU	2.5	2.8	2.6	2.5	3.3	2.4
Average before-tax income of CU	$51,128.00	$60,393.00	$34,485.00	$53,039.00	$37,150.00	$52,797.00
Average spending of CU, total	40,817.33	44,922.85	28,707.56	42,360.25	34,574.75	41,520.78
Food, average spending	**5,339.50**	**6,284.83**	**4,006.72**	**5,488.34**	**5,717.03**	**5,290.54**
Alcoholic beverages, average spending	**391.21**	**308.30**	**159.43**	**425.24**	**315.26**	**400.53**
FOOD AT HOME	**3,128.78**	**3,301.77**	**2,663.86**	**3,186.49**	**3,597.34**	**3,069.79**
Cereals and bakery products	**441.72**	**436.62**	**370.22**	**451.83**	**486.40**	**436.11**
Cereals and cereal products	150.14	179.56	139.14	150.51	182.93	146.02
Flour	7.32	8.91	8.28	7.13	14.70	6.40
Prepared flour mixes	12.79	8.50	10.96	13.21	10.88	13.03
Ready-to-eat and cooked cereals	86.21	61.28	76.02	88.60	93.45	85.30
Rice	16.05	63.90	17.68	13.96	29.05	14.42
Pasta, cornmeal, and other cereal products	27.75	36.96	26.20	27.61	34.85	26.86
Bakery products	291.58	257.06	231.07	301.32	303.47	290.09
Bread	82.55	79.09	68.76	84.60	96.33	80.82
White bread	33.50	31.11	33.21	33.63	44.10	32.16
Bread, other than white	49.06	47.98	35.54	50.97	52.23	48.66
Crackers and cookies	69.58	62.70	54.44	71.95	63.00	70.41
Cookies	45.06	45.24	35.60	46.36	43.01	45.31
Crackers	24.52	17.47	18.84	25.59	19.99	25.09
Frozen and refrigerated bakery products	24.56	15.22	22.08	25.27	22.00	24.89
Other bakery products	114.89	100.04	85.80	119.50	122.15	113.97
Biscuits and rolls	37.24	35.62	22.98	39.28	30.92	38.03
Cakes and cupcakes	36.71	33.27	35.29	37.04	43.83	35.81
Bread and cracker products	3.57	3.17	2.63	3.72	3.03	3.64
Sweetrolls, coffee cakes, doughnuts	27.65	16.76	19.11	29.26	31.30	27.19
Pies, tarts, turnovers	9.72	11.22	5.78	10.21	13.07	9.30
Meats, poultry, fish, and eggs	**824.58**	**977.63**	**881.60**	**810.68**	**1,059.39**	**795.09**
Beef	245.55	193.17	232.17	249.45	326.95	235.33
Ground beef	89.27	54.36	94.86	89.86	105.23	87.26
Roast	39.63	28.60	39.49	40.08	53.57	37.88
Chuck roast	13.37	10.62	12.35	13.62	20.23	12.51
Round roast	9.78	6.84	11.71	9.62	12.40	9.45
Other roast	16.48	11.15	15.43	16.83	20.95	15.92
Steak	94.16	92.03	80.22	96.18	134.55	89.09
Round steak	15.65	14.03	11.14	16.33	26.16	14.32
Sirloin steak	31.35	36.75	26.51	31.81	45.75	29.54
Other steak	47.17	41.25	42.57	48.04	62.63	45.22
Other beef	22.49	18.16	17.60	23.34	33.60	21.09
Pork	170.61	174.47	206.13	165.54	212.26	165.38
Bacon	31.15	17.96	40.93	30.31	32.24	31.01
Pork chops	34.14	43.50	46.13	32.11	49.50	32.21
Ham	38.15	27.69	38.94	38.45	49.32	36.74
Ham, not canned	37.04	26.02	38.08	37.33	47.97	35.67
Canned ham	1.10	1.67	0.86	1.12	1.34	1.08
Sausage	25.82	21.42	36.16	24.56	28.02	25.55
Other pork	41.36	63.91	43.97	40.11	53.19	39.87
Other meats	102.01	80.66	90.46	104.45	112.73	100.66
Frankfurters	22.74	15.53	23.92	22.86	27.66	22.12
Lunch meats (cold cuts)	69.31	36.31	55.50	72.52	75.00	68.60
Bologna, liverwurst, salami	21.65	12.03	21.57	22.04	31.01	20.48
Other lunch meats	47.66	24.28	33.93	50.48	43.99	48.13
Lamb, organ meats, and others	9.96	28.82	11.04	9.07	10.07	9.94
Poultry	144.61	181.94	177.09	138.65	189.85	138.93
Fresh and frozen chicken	116.42	155.45	137.55	111.96	163.95	110.45

	total consumer units	race			Hispanic origin	
		Asian	black	white and other	Hispanic	non-Hispanic
Fresh and frozen whole chicken	$32.82	$67.46	$39.01	$30.61	$53.23	$30.26
Fresh and frozen chicken parts	83.60	87.59	98.54	81.35	110.71	80.19
Other poultry	28.20	26.49	39.54	26.69	25.90	28.48
Fish and seafood	124.46	304.12	139.96	115.27	158.14	120.23
Canned fish and seafood	16.40	21.00	12.49	16.76	19.11	16.06
Fresh fish and shellfish	71.88	197.78	96.38	63.56	98.14	68.58
Frozen fish and shellfish	36.17	85.34	31.09	34.95	40.89	35.58
Eggs	37.34	43.27	35.79	37.32	59.45	34.56
Dairy products	**328.00**	**247.34**	**226.84**	**345.19**	**373.79**	**322.26**
Fresh milk and cream	126.53	111.70	94.07	131.61	160.12	122.31
Fresh milk, all types	112.58	103.63	87.18	116.45	144.76	108.54
Cream	13.95	8.06	6.89	15.16	15.35	13.77
Other dairy products	201.47	135.64	132.77	213.58	213.67	199.94
Butter	18.08	13.63	15.07	18.67	18.52	18.02
Cheese	97.04	40.05	57.75	104.73	100.03	96.67
Ice cream and related products	58.09	50.80	43.79	60.35	65.51	57.16
Miscellaneous dairy products	28.26	31.17	16.16	29.83	29.62	28.09
Fruits and vegetables	**535.42**	**788.02**	**437.83**	**539.05**	**686.08**	**516.50**
Fresh fruits	170.88	274.83	128.19	172.72	231.22	163.30
Apples	32.73	53.37	25.48	32.93	37.26	32.16
Bananas	28.41	42.10	23.33	28.58	42.62	26.63
Oranges	18.34	36.27	15.71	18.00	29.38	16.95
Citrus fruits, excl. oranges	14.14	21.33	9.77	14.47	24.75	12.81
Other fresh fruits	77.26	121.75	53.90	78.75	97.21	74.75
Fresh vegetables	171.96	321.97	132.52	171.55	240.41	163.37
Potatoes	30.11	38.83	30.32	29.74	37.50	29.19
Lettuce	22.10	29.59	15.15	22.77	27.93	21.37
Tomatoes	32.18	46.64	21.28	33.12	57.60	28.99
Other fresh vegetables	87.57	206.92	65.78	85.92	117.38	83.83
Processed fruits	108.39	123.32	100.39	108.91	131.49	105.49
Frozen fruits and fruit juices	11.54	12.65	9.32	11.80	11.86	11.50
Frozen orange juice	4.64	3.01	3.86	4.81	6.44	4.41
Frozen fruits	3.66	3.46	2.69	3.80	1.99	3.87
Frozen fruit juices, excl. orange	3.24	6.18	2.78	3.19	3.43	3.22
Canned fruits	15.96	11.46	12.00	16.68	14.63	16.13
Dried fruits	6.30	6.01	3.32	6.72	5.93	6.34
Fresh fruit juice	20.77	24.78	19.66	20.77	26.44	20.06
Canned and bottled fruit juice	53.82	68.41	56.09	52.93	72.63	51.46
Processed vegetables	84.19	67.91	76.73	85.86	82.96	84.34
Frozen vegetables	26.79	18.96	23.34	27.58	20.24	27.61
Canned and dried vegetables and juices	57.40	48.94	53.39	58.28	62.72	56.73
Canned beans	12.56	4.77	13.21	12.78	12.16	12.61
Canned corn	6.89	5.83	8.81	6.66	6.51	6.93
Canned miscellaneous vegetables	18.55	13.39	14.46	19.32	15.31	18.95
Dried peas	0.37	0.44	0.19	0.40	0.75	0.33
Dried beans	2.31	1.62	2.39	2.32	6.15	1.82
Dried miscellaneous vegetables	7.51	16.81	7.45	7.15	8.85	7.34
Dried processed vegetables	0.42	0.85	0.34	0.41	0.34	0.43
Fresh and canned vegetable juices	8.67	5.23	6.33	9.13	12.34	8.21
Sugar and other sweets	**119.08**	**101.94**	**93.45**	**123.30**	**128.33**	**117.92**
Candy and chewing gum	75.31	66.34	49.30	79.27	76.25	75.20
Sugar	16.89	16.96	22.09	16.16	22.38	16.20
Artificial sweeteners	5.67	1.42	4.74	5.97	6.31	5.59
Jams, preserves, other sweets	21.20	17.22	17.33	21.90	23.39	20.93
Fats and oils	**85.73**	**62.54**	**79.53**	**87.50**	**97.45**	**84.26**
Margarine	9.61	3.78	9.34	9.88	7.52	9.87
Fats and oils	26.29	32.01	29.74	25.58	44.32	24.02
Salad dressings	26.17	15.04	22.98	27.05	24.85	26.34
Nondairy cream and imitation milk	11.02	5.33	7.08	11.79	10.59	11.08
Peanut butter	12.64	6.38	10.39	13.19	10.16	12.95

	total consumer units	race			Hispanic origin	
		Asian	black	white and other	Hispanic	non-Hispanic
Miscellaneous foods	**$489.60**	**$399.75**	**$359.72**	**$511.13**	**$451.80**	**$494.35**
Frozen prepared foods	104.79	65.86	76.09	110.30	69.16	109.27
Frozen meals	34.85	27.61	25.72	36.40	19.24	36.82
Other frozen prepared foods	69.94	38.25	50.38	73.89	49.92	72.45
Canned and packaged soups	35.19	34.39	22.91	36.93	30.22	35.82
Potato chips, nuts, and other snacks	105.68	98.92	65.36	111.54	92.81	107.30
Potato chips and other snacks	79.27	66.61	51.23	83.66	71.05	80.31
Nuts	26.41	32.31	14.13	27.88	21.76	27.00
Condiments and seasonings	90.22	89.73	70.99	92.91	83.98	91.01
Salt, spices, and other seasonings	20.77	28.24	19.47	20.66	25.77	20.15
Olives, pickles, relishes	11.41	7.78	8.59	11.94	9.32	11.67
Sauces and gravies	38.46	36.90	31.63	39.47	33.99	39.02
Baking needs and miscellaneous products	19.58	16.81	11.29	20.84	14.90	20.17
Other canned/packaged prepared foods	153.71	110.85	124.36	159.46	175.64	150.95
Prepared salads	20.51	9.71	12.94	21.98	12.23	21.54
Prepared desserts	11.10	4.64	7.14	11.90	11.61	11.03
Baby food	26.76	13.61	24.00	27.66	43.71	24.63
Miscellaneous prepared foods	95.13	82.18	80.28	97.70	108.08	93.51
Nonalcoholic beverages	**268.37**	**248.32**	**202.27**	**278.32**	**289.48**	**265.72**
Cola	88.27	50.75	65.15	92.94	108.63	85.71
Other carbonated drinks	45.64	30.78	35.37	47.65	46.86	45.49
Coffee	38.08	29.42	20.54	40.85	38.50	38.03
Roasted coffee	25.70	18.43	13.84	27.63	23.82	25.94
Instant and freeze-dried coffee	12.38	10.99	6.70	13.22	14.68	12.09
Noncarbonated fruit-flavored drinks, incl. nonfrozen lemonade	19.29	14.07	23.76	18.88	25.41	18.52
Tea	17.71	33.20	13.75	17.65	14.15	18.15
Other nonalcoholic beverages and ice	58.72	90.10	43.66	59.58	55.75	59.09
Food prepared by CU on trips	**36.28**	**39.62**	**12.41**	**39.51**	**24.63**	**37.60**
FOOD AWAY FROM HOME	**2,210.73**	**2,983.06**	**1,342.86**	**2,301.85**	**2,119.69**	**2,220.74**
Meals at restaurants, carry-outs, other	**1,831.97**	**2,346.25**	**1,197.91**	**1,899.72**	**1,855.13**	**1,829.06**
Lunch	658.16	952.83	479.64	671.36	706.16	652.13
• At fast food, take-out, delivery, concession stands, buffet, cafeteria (other than employer, school cafeteria)	369.02	495.99	311.69	372.00	437.83	360.38
• At full-service restaurants	210.10	367.97	83.70	221.44	181.28	213.72
• At vending machines, mobile vendors	5.56	4.98	2.93	5.95	16.07	4.24
• At employer and school cafeterias	73.48	83.89	81.32	71.98	70.99	73.79
Dinner	737.51	962.34	381.54	778.04	670.90	745.87
• At fast food, take-out, delivery, concession stands, buffet, cafeteria (other than employer, school cafeteria)	215.93	240.69	173.67	220.82	253.15	211.26
• At full-service restaurants	517.42	719.15	200.86	553.40	414.67	530.33
• At vending machines, mobile vendors	1.32	–	–	1.55	1.57	1.28
• At employer and school cafeterias	2.83	2.49	7.01	2.27	1.51	3.00
Snacks and nonalcoholic beverages	248.42	243.36	198.68	255.51	267.56	246.01
• At fast food, take-out, delivery, concession stands, buffet, cafeteria (other than employer, school cafeteria)	180.26	177.64	131.52	187.12	181.27	180.14
• At full-service restaurants	26.66	27.51	21.58	27.33	28.45	26.44
• At vending machines, mobile vendors	31.33	20.22	34.51	31.32	46.56	29.41
• At employer and school cafeterias	10.16	17.99	11.08	9.73	11.28	10.02
Breakfast and brunch	187.89	187.72	138.04	194.80	210.51	185.05
• At fast food, take-out, delivery, concession stands, buffet, cafeteria (other than employer, school cafeteria)	92.82	94.79	89.63	93.19	116.07	89.91
• At full-service restaurants	89.42	90.01	40.60	96.17	85.12	89.96
• At vending machines, mobile vendors	1.37	0.61	1.5	1.38	2.54	1.22
• At employer and school cafeterias	4.27	2.32	6.31	4.07	6.78	3.96
Board (including at school)	**33.25**	**79.58**	**20.68**	**33.33**	**12.1**	**35.65**
Catered affairs	**48.39**	**92.55**	**4.54**	**52.93**	**57.46**	**47.36**
Food on trips	**213.97**	**268.03**	**63.67**	**233.06**	**110.38**	**225.69**
School lunches	**56.87**	**65.36**	**39.77**	**58.96**	**47.96**	**57.88**
Meals as pay	**26.28**	**131.29**	**16.3**	**23.85**	**36.67**	**25.1**

		race			Hispanic origin	
	total consumer units	Asian	black	white and other	Hispanic	non-Hispanic
ALCOHOLIC BEVERAGES	**$391.21**	**$308.3**	**$169.43**	**$425.24**	**$315.26**	**$400.53**
At home	**240.08**	**180.06**	**122.45**	**258.74**	**207.15**	**244.22**
Beer and ale	111.17	64.94	69.49	118.75	115.97	110.56
Whiskey	14.29	6.97	4.53	15.93	20.22	13.54
Wine	89.93	89.79	32.09	97.95	55.96	94.2
Other alcoholic beverages	24.7	18.36	16.34	26.11	14.99	25.92
Away from home	**151.12**	**128.24**	**46.98**	**166.5**	**108.11**	**156.31**
Beer and ale	60.33	41.49	20.39	66.61	48.33	61.84
• At fast food, take-out, delivery, concession stands, buffet, and cafeteria	10.7	2.78	3.79	11.97	18.02	9.78
• At full-service restaurants	46.19	38.71	14.07	50.93	27.84	48.49
Wine	18.78	14.37	6.38	20.67	13.65	19.43
• At fast food, take-out, delivery, concession stands, buffet and cafeteria	1.66	1.78	1.03	1.74	2.61	1.54
• At full-service restaurants	16.72	12.59	5.08	18.49	10.77	17.47
Other alcoholic beverages	38.75	36.77	12.89	42.41	30.23	39.82
• At fast food, take-out, delivery, concession stands, buffet, and cafeteria	7.73	5.8	4.43	8.26	9.74	7.48
• At full-service restaurants	29.49	30.97	7.35	32.51	19.41	30.76
Alcoholic beverages purchased on trips	33.26	35.6	7.32	36.81	15.91	35.22

Note: Other races include Native Americans and Pacific Islanders. Subcategories may not add to total because some are not shown. (–) means sample is too small to make a reliable estimate.
Source: Bureau of Labor Statistics, unpublished tables from the 2003 Consumer Expenditure Survey

Table 5.18 Food and Alcohol: Indexed spending by race and Hispanic origin, 2003

(indexed average annual spending of consumer units (CU) on food and alcoholic beverages, by race and Hispanic origin of consumer unit reference person, 2003; index definition: an index of 100 is the average for all consumer units; an index of 132 means that spending by consumer units in that group is 32 percent above the average for all consumer units; an index of 68 indicates spending that is 32 percent below the average for all consumer units)

	total consumer units	race			Hispanic origin	
		Asian	black	white and other	Hispanic	non-Hispanic
Average spending of CU, total	$40,817	$44,923	$28,708	$42,360	$34,575	$41,521
Average spending of CU, index	100	110	70	104	85	102
Food, spending index	100	118	75	103	107	99
Alcoholic beverages, spending index	100	79	43	109	81	102
FOOD AT HOME	100	106	85	102	115	98
Cereals and bakery products	100	99	84	102	110	99
Cereals and cereal products	100	120	93	100	122	97
Flour	100	122	113	97	201	87
Prepared flour mixes	100	66	86	103	85	102
Ready-to-eat and cooked cereals	100	71	88	103	108	99
Rice	100	398	110	87	181	90
Pasta, cornmeal, and other cereal products	100	133	94	99	126	97
Bakery products	100	88	79	103	104	99
Bread	100	96	83	102	117	98
White bread	100	93	99	100	132	96
Bread, other than white	100	98	72	104	106	99
Crackers and cookies	100	90	78	103	91	101
Cookies	100	100	79	103	95	101
Crackers	100	71	77	104	82	102
Frozen and refrigerated bakery products	100	62	90	103	90	101
Other bakery products	100	87	75	104	106	99
Biscuits and rolls	100	96	62	105	83	102
Cakes and cupcakes	100	91	96	101	119	98
Bread and cracker products	100	89	74	104	85	102
Sweetrolls, coffee cakes, doughnuts	100	61	69	106	113	98
Pies, tarts, turnovers	100	115	59	105	134	96
Meats, poultry, fish, and eggs	100	119	107	98	128	96
Beef	100	79	95	102	133	96
Ground beef	100	61	106	101	118	98
Roast	100	72	100	101	135	96
Chuck roast	100	79	92	102	151	94
Round roast	100	70	120	98	127	97
Other roast	100	68	94	102	127	97
Steak	100	98	85	102	143	95
Round steak	100	90	71	104	167	92
Sirloin steak	100	117	85	101	146	94
Other steak	100	87	90	102	133	96
Other beef	100	81	78	104	149	94
Pork	100	102	121	97	124	97
Bacon	100	58	131	97	103	100
Pork chops	100	127	135	94	145	94
Ham	100	73	102	101	129	96
Ham, not canned	100	70	103	101	130	96
Canned ham	100	152	78	102	122	98
Sausage	100	83	140	95	109	99
Other pork	100	155	106	97	129	96
Other meats	100	79	89	102	111	99
Frankfurters	100	68	105	101	122	97
Lunch meats (cold cuts)	100	52	80	105	108	99
Bologna, liverwurst, salami	100	56	100	102	143	95
Other lunch meats	100	51	71	106	92	101
Lamb, organ meats, and others	100	289	111	91	101	100
Poultry	100	126	122	96	131	96
Fresh and frozen chicken	100	134	118	96	141	95

		race			Hispanic origin	
	total consumer units	Asian	black	white and other	Hispanic	non-Hispanic
Fresh and frozen whole chicken	100	206	119	93	162	92
Fresh and frozen chicken parts	100	105	118	97	132	96
Other poultry	100	94	140	95	92	101
Fish and seafood	100	244	112	93	127	97
Canned fish and seafood	100	128	76	102	117	98
Fresh fish and shellfish	100	275	134	88	137	95
Frozen fish and shellfish	100	236	86	97	113	98
Eggs	100	116	96	100	159	93
Dairy products	**100**	**75**	**69**	**105**	**114**	**98**
Fresh milk and cream	100	88	74	104	127	97
Fresh milk, all types	100	92	77	103	129	96
Cream	100	58	49	109	110	99
Other dairy products	100	67	66	106	106	99
Butter	100	75	83	103	102	100
Cheese	100	41	60	108	103	100
Ice cream and related products	100	87	75	104	113	98
Miscellaneous dairy products	100	110	57	106	105	99
Fruits and vegetables	**100**	**147**	**82**	**101**	**128**	**96**
Fresh fruits	100	161	75	101	135	96
Apples	100	163	78	101	114	98
Bananas	100	143	82	101	150	94
Oranges	100	198	86	98	160	92
Citrus fruits, excl. oranges	100	151	69	102	175	91
Other fresh fruits	100	158	70	102	126	97
Fresh vegetables	100	187	77	100	140	95
Potatoes	100	129	101	99	125	97
Lettuce	100	134	69	103	126	97
Tomatoes	100	145	66	103	179	90
Other fresh vegetables	100	236	75	98	134	96
Processed fruits	100	114	93	100	121	97
Frozen fruits and fruit juices	100	110	81	102	103	100
Frozen orange juice	100	65	83	104	139	95
Frozen fruits	100	95	73	104	54	106
Frozen fruit juices, excl. orange	100	191	86	98	106	99
Canned fruits	100	72	75	105	92	101
Dried fruits	100	95	53	107	94	101
Fresh fruit juice	100	119	95	100	127	97
Canned and bottled fruit juice	100	127	104	98	135	96
Processed vegetables	100	81	91	102	99	100
Frozen vegetables	100	71	87	103	76	103
Canned and dried vegetables and juices	100	85	93	102	109	99
Canned beans	100	38	105	102	97	100
Canned corn	100	85	128	97	94	101
Canned miscellaneous vegetables	100	72	78	104	83	102
Dried peas	100	119	51	108	203	89
Dried beans	100	70	103	100	266	79
Dried miscellaneous vegetables	100	224	99	95	118	98
Dried processed vegetables	100	202	81	98	81	102
Fresh and canned vegetable juices	100	60	73	105	142	95
Sugar and other sweets	**100**	**86**	**78**	**104**	**108**	**99**
Candy and chewing gum	100	88	65	105	101	100
Sugar	100	100	131	96	133	96
Artificial sweeteners	100	25	84	105	111	99
Jams, preserves, other sweets	100	81	82	103	110	99
Fats and oils	**100**	**73**	**93**	**102**	**114**	**98**
Margarine	100	39	97	103	78	103
Fats and oils	100	122	113	97	169	91
Salad dressings	100	57	88	103	95	101
Nondairy cream and imitation milk	100	48	64	107	96	101
Peanut butter	100	50	82	104	80	102

	total consumer units	race			Hispanic origin	
		Asian	black	white and other	Hispanic	non-Hispanic
Miscellaneous foods	**100**	**82**	**73**	**104**	**92**	**101**
Frozen prepared foods	100	63	73	105	66	104
Frozen meals	100	79	74	104	55	106
Other frozen prepared foods	100	55	72	106	71	104
Canned and packaged soups	100	98	65	105	86	102
Potato chips, nuts, and other snacks	100	94	62	106	88	102
Potato chips and other snacks	100	84	65	106	90	101
Nuts	100	122	54	106	82	102
Condiments and seasonings	100	99	79	103	93	101
Salt, spices, and other seasonings	100	136	94	99	124	97
Olives, pickles, relishes	100	68	75	105	82	102
Sauces and gravies	100	96	82	103	88	101
Baking needs and miscellaneous products	100	86	58	106	76	103
Other canned/packaged prepared foods	100	72	81	104	114	98
Prepared salads	100	47	63	107	60	105
Prepared desserts	100	42	64	107	105	99
Baby food	100	51	90	103	163	92
Miscellaneous prepared foods	100	86	84	103	114	98
Nonalcoholic beverages	**100**	**93**	**75**	**104**	**108**	**99**
Cola	100	57	74	105	123	97
Other carbonated drinks	100	67	77	104	103	100
Coffee	100	77	54	107	101	100
Roasted coffee	100	72	54	108	93	101
Instant and freeze-dried coffee	100	89	54	107	119	98
Noncarbonated fruit-flavored drinks, incl. nonfrozen lemonade	100	73	123	98	132	96
Tea	100	187	78	100	80	102
Other nonalcoholic beverages and ice	100	153	74	101	95	101
Food prepared by CU on trips	**100**	**109**	**34**	**109**	**68**	**104**
FOOD AWAY FROM HOME	**100**	**135**	**61**	**104**	**96**	**100**
Meals at restaurants, carry-outs, other	**100**	**128**	**65**	**104**	**101**	**100**
Lunch	100	145	73	102	107	99
• At fast food, take-out, delivery, concession stands, buffet, cafeteria (other than employer, school cafeteria)	100	134	84	101	119	98
• At full-service restaurants	100	175	40	105	86	102
• At vending machines, mobile vendors	100	90	53	107	289	76
• At employer and school cafeterias	100	114	111	98	97	100
Dinner	100	130	52	105	91	101
• At fast food, take-out, delivery, concession stands, buffet, cafeteria (other than employer, school cafeteria)	100	111	80	102	117	98
• At full-service restaurants	100	139	39	107	80	102
• At vending machines, mobile vendors	100	–	–	117	119	97
• At employer and school cafeterias	100	88	248	80	53	106
Snacks and nonalcoholic beverages	100	98	80	103	108	99
• At fast food, take-out, delivery, concession stands, buffet, cafeteria (other than employer, school cafeteria)	100	99	73	104	101	100
• At full-service restaurants	100	103	81	103	107	99
• At vending machines, mobile vendors	100	65	110	100	149	94
• At employer and school cafeterias	100	177	109	96	111	99
Breakfast and brunch	100	100	73	104	112	98
• At fast food, take-out, delivery, concession stands, buffet, cafeteria (other than employer, school cafeteria)	100	102	97	100	125	97
• At full-service restaurants	100	101	45	108	95	101
• At vending machines, mobile vendors	100	45	109	101	185	89
• At employer and school cafeterias	100	54	148	95	159	93
Board (including at school)	**100**	**239**	**62**	**100**	**36**	**107**
Catered affairs	**100**	**191**	**9**	**109**	**119**	**98**
Food on ttrips	**100**	**125**	**30**	**109**	**52**	**105**
School lunches	**100**	**115**	**70**	**104**	**84**	**102**
Meals as pay	**100**	**500**	**62**	**91**	**140**	**96**

	total consumer units	race			Hispanic origin	
		Asian	black	white and other	Hispanic	non-Hispanic
ALCOHOLIC BEVERAGES	**100**	**79**	**43**	**109**	**81**	**102**
At home	**100**	**75**	**51**	**108**	**86**	**102**
Beer and ale	100	58	63	107	104	99
Whiskey	100	49	32	111	141	95
Wine	100	103	36	109	62	105
Other alcoholic beverages	100	74	65	106	61	105
Away from home	**100**	**85**	**31**	**110**	**72**	**103**
Beer and ale	100	69	34	110	80	103
• At fast food, take-out, delivery, concession stands, buffet, and cafeteria	100	26	35	112	168	91
• At full-service restaurants	100	84	30	110	60	105
Wine	100	77	34	110	73	103
• At fast food, take-out, delivery, concession stands, buffet and cafeteria	100	107	62	105	157	93
• At full-service restaurants	100	75	30	111	64	104
Other alcoholic beverages	100	95	33	109	78	103
• At fast food, take-out, delivery, concession stands, buffet, and cafeteria	100	75	57	107	126	97
• At full-service restaurants	100	105	25	110	66	104
Alcoholic beverages purchased on trips	100	107	22	111	48	106

Note: Other races include Native Americans and Pacific Islanders. (–) means sample is too small to make a reliable estimate.
Source: Calculations by New Strategist based on the 2003 Consumer Expenditure Survey

Table 5.19 Food and Alcohol: Total spending by race and Hispanic origin, 2003

(total annual spending on food and alcoholic beverages, by consumer unit race and Hispanic origin groups, 2003; numbers in thousands)

| | | | race | | Hispanic origin | |
	total consumer units	Asian	black	white and other	Hispanic	non-Hispanic
Number of consumer units	115,356	3,573	13,743	98,041	11,727	103,629
Total spending of all consumer units	$4,708,523,919	$160,509,343	$394,527,997	$4,153,041,270	$405,458,093	$4,302,756,911
Food, total spending	615,943,362	22,455,698	55,064,353	538,082,342	67,043,611	548,253,370
Alcoholic beverages, total spending	45,128,421	1,101,556	2,328,476	41,690,955	3,697,054	41,506,523
FOOD AT HOME	**360,923,546**	**11,797,224**	**36,609,428**	**312,406,666**	**42,186,006**	**318,119,268**
Cereals and bakery products	**50,955,052**	**1,560,043**	**5,087,933**	**44,297,865**	**5,704,013**	**45,193,643**
Cereals and cereal products	17,319,550	641,568	1,912,201	14,756,151	2,145,220	15,131,907
Flour	844,406	31,835	113,792	699,032	172,387	663,226
Prepared flour mixes	1,475,403	30,371	150,623	1,295,122	127,590	1,350,286
Ready-to-eat and cooked cereals	9,944,841	218,953	1,044,743	8,686,433	1,095,888	8,839,554
Rice	1,851,464	228,315	242,976	1,368,652	340,669	1,494,330
Pasta, cornmeal, and other cereal products	3,201,129	132,058	360,067	2,706,912	408,686	2,783,475
Bakery products	33,635,502	918,475	3,175,595	29,541,714	3,558,793	30,061,737
Bread	9,522,638	282,589	944,969	8,294,269	1,129,662	8,375,296
White bread	3,864,426	111,156	456,405	3,297,119	517,161	3,332,709
Bread, other than white	5,659,365	171,433	488,426	4,997,150	612,501	5,042,587
Crackers and cookies	8,026,470	224,027	748,169	7,054,050	738,801	7,296,518
Cookies	5,197,941	161,643	489,251	4,545,181	504,378	4,695,430
Crackers	2,828,529	62,420	258,918	2,508,869	234,423	2,600,052
Frozen and refrigerated bakery products	2,833,143	54,381	303,445	2,477,496	257,994	2,579,326
Other bakery products	13,253,251	357,443	1,179,149	11,715,900	1,432,453	11,810,597
Biscuits and rolls	4,295,857	127,270	315,814	3,851,050	362,599	3,941,011
Cakes and cupcakes	4,234,719	118,874	484,990	3,631,439	513,994	3,710,954
Bread and cracker products	411,821	11,326	36,144	364,713	35,533	377,210
Sweetrolls, coffee cakes, doughnuts	3,189,593	59,883	262,629	2,868,680	367,055	2,817,673
Pies, tarts, turnovers	1,121,260	40,089	79,435	1,000,999	153,272	963,750
Meats, poultry, fish, and eggs	**95,120,250**	**3,493,072**	**12,115,829**	**79,479,878**	**12,423,467**	**82,394,382**
Beef	28,325,666	690,196	3,190,712	24,456,327	3,834,143	24,387,013
Ground beef	10,297,830	194,228	1,303,661	8,809,964	1,234,032	9,042,667
Roast	4,571,558	102,188	542,711	3,929,483	628,215	3,925,467
Chuck roast	1,542,310	37,945	169,726	1,335,318	237,237	1,296,399
Round roast	1,128,182	24,439	160,931	943,154	145,415	979,294
Other roast	1,901,067	39,839	212,054	1,650,030	245,681	1,649,774
Steak	10,861,921	328,823	1,102,463	9,429,583	1,577,868	9,232,308
Round steak	1,805,321	50,129	153,097	1,601,010	306,778	1,483,967
Sirloin steak	3,616,411	131,308	364,327	3,118,684	536,510	3,061,201
Other steak	5,441,343	147,386	585,040	4,709,890	734,462	4,686,103
Other beef	2,594,356	64,886	241,877	2,288,277	394,027	2,185,536
Pork	19,680,887	623,381	2,832,845	16,229,707	2,489,173	17,138,164
Bacon	3,593,339	64,171	562,501	2,971,623	378,078	3,213,535
Pork chops	3,938,254	155,426	633,965	3,148,097	580,487	3,337,890
Ham	4,400,831	98,936	535,152	3,769,676	578,376	3,807,329
Ham, not canned	4,272,786	92,969	523,333	3,659,871	562,544	3,696,446
Canned ham	126,892	5,967	11,819	109,806	15,714	111,919
Sausage	2,978,492	76,534	496,947	2,407,887	328,591	2,647,721
Other pork	4,771,124	228,350	604,280	3,932,425	623,759	4,131,688
Other meats	11,767,466	288,198	1,243,192	10,240,382	1,321,985	10,431,295
Frankfurters	2,623,195	55,489	328,733	2,241,217	324,369	2,292,273
Lunch meats (cold cuts)	7,995,324	129,736	762,737	7,109,933	879,525	7,108,949
Bologna, liverwurst, salami	2,497,457	42,983	296,437	2,160,824	363,654	2,122,322
Other lunch meats	5,497,867	86,752	466,300	4,949,110	515,871	4,987,664
Lamb, organ meats, and others	1,148,946	102,974	151,723	889,232	118,091	1,030,072
Poultry	16,681,631	650,072	2,433,748	13,593,385	2,226,371	14,397,177
Fresh and frozen chicken	13,429,746	555,423	1,890,350	10,976,670	1,922,642	11,445,823

		race			Hispanic origin	
	total consumer units	Asian	black	white and other	Hispanic	non-Hispanic
Fresh and frozen whole chicken	$3,785,984	$241,035	$536,114	3,001,035	$624,228	$3,135,814
Fresh and frozen chicken parts	9,643,762	314,388	1,354,235	7,975,635	1,298,296	8,310,010
Other poultry	3,253,039	94,649	543,398	2,616,714	303,729	2,951,354
Fish and seafood	14,357,208	1,086,621	1,923,470	11,301,186	1,854,508	12,459,315
Canned fish and seafood	1,891,838	75,033	171,650	1,643,167	224,103	1,664,282
Fresh fish and shellfish	8,291,789	706,668	1,324,550	6,231,486	1,150,888	7,106,877
Frozen fish and shellfish	4,172,427	304,920	427,270	3,426,533	479,517	3,687,120
Eggs	4,307,393	154,604	491,862	3,658,890	697,170	3,581,418
Dairy products	**37,836,768**	**883,746**	**3,117,462**	**33,842,773**	**4,383,435**	**33,395,482**
Fresh milk and cream	14,595,995	399,104	1,292,804	12,903,176	1,877,727	12,674,863
Fresh milk, all types	12,986,778	370,270	1,198,115	11,416,874	1,697,601	11,247,892
Cream	1,609,216	28,798	94,689	1,486,302	180,009	1,426,971
Other dairy products	23,240,773	484,642	1,824,658	20,939,597	2,505,708	20,719,582
Butter	2,085,636	48,700	207,107	1,830,425	217,184	1,867,395
Cheese	11,194,146	143,099	793,658	10,267,834	1,173,052	10,017,815
Ice cream and related products	6,701,030	181,508	601,806	5,916,774	768,236	5,923,434
Miscellaneous dairy products	3,259,961	111,370	222,087	2,924,563	347,354	2,910,939
Fruits and vegetables	**61,763,910**	**2,815,595**	**6,017,098**	**52,849,001**	**8,045,660**	**53,524,379**
Fresh fruits	19,712,033	981,968	1,761,715	16,933,642	2,711,517	16,922,616
Apples	3,775,602	190,691	350,172	3,228,490	436,948	3,332,709
Bananas	3,277,264	150,423	320,624	2,802,012	499,805	2,759,640
Oranges	2,115,629	129,593	215,903	1,764,738	344,539	1,756,512
Citrus fruits, excl. oranges	1,631,134	76,212	134,269	1,418,653	290,243	1,327,487
Other fresh fruits	8,912,405	435,013	740,748	7,720,729	1,139,982	7,746,268
Fresh vegetables	19,836,618	1,150,399	1,821,222	16,818,934	2,819,288	16,929,870
Potatoes	3,473,369	138,740	416,688	2,915,739	439,763	3,024,931
Lettuce	2,549,368	105,725	208,206	2,232,394	327,535	2,214,552
Tomatoes	3,712,156	166,645	292,451	3,247,118	675,475	3,004,205
Other fresh vegetables	10,101,725	739,325	904,015	8,423,683	1,376,515	8,687,219
Processed fruits	12,503,437	440,622	1,379,660	10,677,645	1,541,983	10,931,823
Frozen fruits and fruit juices	1,331,208	45,198	128,085	1,156,884	139,082	1,191,734
Frozen orange juice	535,252	10,755	53,048	471,577	75,522	457,004
Frozen fruits	422,203	12,363	36,969	372,556	23,337	401,044
Frozen fruit juices, excl. orange	373,753	22,081	38,206	312,751	40,224	333,685
Canned fruits	1,841,082	40,947	164,916	1,635,324	171,566	1,671,536
Dried fruits	726,743	21,474	45,627	658,836	69,541	657,008
Fresh fruit juice	2,395,944	88,539	270,187	2,036,312	310,062	2,078,798
Canned and bottled fruit juice	6,208,460	244,429	770,845	5,189,310	851,732	5,332,748
Processed vegetables	9,711,822	242,642	1,054,500	8,417,800	972,872	8,740,070
Frozen vegetables	3,090,387	67,744	320,762	2,703,971	237,354	2,861,197
Canned and dried vegetables and juices	6,621,434	174,863	733,739	5,713,829	735,517	5,878,873
Canned beans	1,448,871	17,043	181,545	1,252,964	142,600	1,306,762
Canned corn	794,803	20,831	121,076	652,953	76,343	718,149
Canned miscellaneous vegetables	2,139,854	47,842	198,724	1,894,152	179,540	1,963,770
Dried peas	42,682	1,572	2,511	39,216	8,795	34,198
Dried beans	266,472	5,788	32,846	227,455	72,121	188,605
Dried miscellaneous vegetables	866,324	60,062	102,385	700,993	103,784	760,637
Dried processed vegetables	48,450	3,037	4,673	40,197	3,987	44,560
Fresh and canned vegetable juices	1,000,137	18,687	86,993	895,114	144,711	850,794
Sugar and other sweets	**13,736,592**	**364,232**	**1,284,283**	**12,088,455**	**1,504,926**	**12,219,932**
Candy and chewing gum	8,687,460	237,033	677,530	7,771,710	894,184	7,792,901
Sugar	1,948,363	60,598	303,583	1,584,343	262,450	1,678,790
Artificial sweeteners	654,069	5,074	65,142	585,305	73,997	579,286
Jams, preserves, other sweets	2,445,547	61,527	238,166	2,147,098	274,295	2,168,955
Fats and oils	**9,889,470**	**223,455**	**1,092,981**	**8,578,588**	**1,142,796**	**8,731,780**
Margarine	1,108,571	13,506	128,360	968,645	88,187	1,022,818
Fats and oils	3,032,709	114,372	408,717	2,507,889	519,741	2,489,169
Salad dressings	3,018,867	53,738	315,814	2,652,009	291,416	2,729,588
Nondairy cream and imitation milk	1,271,223	19,044	97,300	1,155,903	124,189	1,148,209
Peanut butter	1,458,100	22,796	142,790	1,293,161	119,146	1,341,996

	total consumer units	race			Hispanic origin	
		Asian	black	white and other	Hispanic	non-Hispanic
Miscellaneous foods	**$56,478,298**	**$1,428,307**	**$4,943,632**	**$50,111,696**	**$5,298,259**	**$51,228,996**
Frozen prepared foods	12,088,155	235,318	1,045,705	10,813,922	811,039	11,323,541
Frozen meals	4,020,157	98,651	353,470	3,568,692	225,627	3,815,620
Other frozen prepared foods	8,067,999	136,667	692,372	7,244,249	585,412	7,507,921
Canned and packaged soups	4,059,378	122,875	314,852	3,620,654	354,390	3,711,991
Potato chips, nuts, and other snacks	12,190,822	353,441	898,242	10,935,493	1,088,383	11,119,392
Potato chips and other snacks	9,144,270	237,998	704,054	8,202,110	833,203	8,322,445
Nuts	3,046,552	115,444	194,189	2,733,383	255,180	2,797,983
Condiments and seasonings	10,407,418	320,605	975,616	9,108,989	984,833	9,431,275
Salt, spices, and other seasonings	2,395,944	100,902	267,576	2,025,527	302,205	2,088,124
Olives, pickles, relishes	1,316,212	27,798	118,052	1,170,610	109,296	1,209,350
Sauces and gravies	4,436,592	131,844	434,691	3,869,678	398,601	4,043,604
Baking needs and miscellaneous products	2,258,670	60,062	155,158	2,043,174	174,732	2,090,197
Other canned/packaged prepared foods	17,731,371	396,067	1,709,079	15,633,618	2,059,730	15,642,798
Prepared salads	2,365,952	34,694	177,834	2,154,941	143,421	2,232,169
Prepared desserts	1,280,452	16,579	98,125	1,166,688	136,150	1,143,028
Baby food	3,086,927	48,629	329,832	2,711,814	512,587	2,552,382
Miscellaneous prepared foods	10,973,816	293,629	1,103,288	9,578,606	1,267,454	9,690,348
Nonalcoholic beverages	**30,958,090**	**887,247**	**2,779,797**	**27,286,771**	**3,394,732**	**27,536,298**
Cola	10,182,474	181,330	895,356	9,111,931	1,273,904	8,882,042
Other carbonated drinks	5,264,848	109,977	486,090	4,671,654	549,527	4,714,083
Coffee	4,392,756	105,118	282,281	4,004,975	451,490	3,941,011
Roasted coffee	2,964,649	65,850	190,203	2,708,873	279,337	2,688,136
Instant and freeze-dried coffee	1,428,107	39,267	92,078	1,296,102	172,152	1,252,875
Noncarbonated fruit-flavored drinks, incl. nonfrozen lemonade	2,225,217	50,272	326,534	1,851,014	297,983	1,919,209
Tea	2,042,955	118,624	188,966	1,730,424	165,937	1,880,866
Other nonalcoholic beverages and ice	6,773,704	321,927	600,019	5,841,283	653,780	6,123,438
Food prepared by CU on trips	**4,185,116**	**141,562**	**170,551**	**3,873,600**	**288,836**	**3,896,450**
FOOD AWAY FROM HOME	**255,020,970**	**10,658,473**	**18,454,925**	**225,675,676**	**24,857,605**	**230,133,065**
Meals at restaurants, carry-outs, other	**211,328,731**	**8,383,151**	**16,462,877**	**186,250,449**	**21,755,110**	**189,543,659**
Lunch	75,922,705	3,404,462	6,591,693	65,820,806	8,281,138	67,579,580
• At fast food, take-out, delivery, concession stands, buffet, cafeteria (other than employer, school cafeteria)	42,568,671	1,772,172	4,283,556	36,471,252	5,134,432	37,345,819
• At full-service restaurants	24,236,296	1,314,757	1,150,289	21,710,199	2,125,871	22,147,590
• At vending machines, mobile vendors	641,379	17,794	40,267	583,344	188,453	439,387
• At employer and school cafeterias	8,476,359	299,739	1,117,581	7,056,991	832,500	7,646,784
Dinner	85,076,204	3,438,441	5,243,504	76,279,820	7,867,644	77,293,762
• At fast food, take-out, delivery, concession stands, buffet, cafeteria (other than employer, school cafeteria)	24,908,821	859,985	2,386,747	21,649,414	2,968,690	21,892,663
• At full-service restaurants	59,687,502	2,569,523	2,760,419	54,255,889	4,862,835	54,957,568
• At vending machines, mobile vendors	152,270	–	–	151,964	18,411	132,645
• At employer and school cafeterias	326,457	8,897	96,338	222,553	17,708	310,887
Snacks and nonalcoholic beverages	28,656,738	869,525	2,730,459	25,050,456	3,137,676	25,493,770
• At fast food, take-out, delivery, concession stands, buffet, cafeteria (other than employer, school cafeteria)	20,794,073	634,708	1,807,479	18,345,432	2,125,753	18,667,728
• At full-service restaurants	3,075,391	98,293	296,574	2,679,461	333,633	2,739,951
• At vending machines, mobile vendors	3,614,103	72,246	474,271	3,070,644	546,009	3,047,729
• At employer and school cafeterias	1,172,017	64,278	152,272	953,939	132,281	1,038,363
Breakfast and brunch	21,674,239	670,724	1,897,084	19,098,387	2,468,651	19,176,546
• At fast food, take-out, delivery, concession stands, buffet, cafeteria (other than employer, school cafeteria)	10,707,344	338,685	1,231,785	9,136,441	1,361,153	9,317,283
• At full-service restaurants	10,315,134	321,606	557,966	9,428,603	998,202	9,322,465
• At vending machines, mobile vendors	158,038	2,180	20,615	135,297	29,787	126,427
• At employer and school cafeterias	492,570	8,289	86,718	399,027	79,509	410,371
Board (including at school)	**3,835,587**	**284,339**	**284,205**	**3,267,707**	**141,897**	**3,694,374**
Catered affairs	**5,582,077**	**330,681**	**62,393**	**5,189,310**	**673,833**	**4,907,869**
Food on trips	**24,682,723**	**957,671**	**875,017**	**22,849,435**	**1,294,426**	**23,388,029**
School lunches	**6,560,296**	**233,531**	**546,559**	**5,780,497**	**562,427**	**5,998,047**
Meals as pay	**3,031,556**	**469,099**	**224,011**	**2,338,278**	**430,029**	**2,601,088**

		race			Hispanic origin	
	total consumer units	Asian	black	white and other	Hispanic	non-Hispanic
ALCOHOLIC BEVERAGES	**$45,128,421**	**$1,101,555**	**$2,328,476**	**$41,690,955**	**$3,697,054**	**$41,506,523**
At home	**27,694,668**	**643,354**	**1,682,830**	**25,367,128**	**2,429,248**	**25,308,274**
Beer and ale	12,824,127	232,031	955,001	11,642,369	1,359,980	11,457,222
Whiskey	1,648,437	24,904	62,256	1,561,793	237,120	1,403,137
Wine	10,373,965	320,829	441,013	9,603,116	656,243	9,761,852
Other alcoholic beverages	2,849,293	65,600	224,561	2,559,851	175,788	2,686,064
Away from home	**17,432,599**	**458,202**	**645,646**	**16,323,827**	**1,267,806**	**16,198,249**
Beer and ale	6,959,427	148,244	280,220	6,530,511	566,766	6,408,417
• At fast food, take-out, delivery, concession stands, buffet, and cafeteria	1,234,309	9,933	52,086	1,173,551	211,321	1,013,492
• At full-service restaurants	5,328,294	138,311	193,364	4,993,228	326,480	5,024,970
Wine	2,166,386	51,344	87,680	2,026,507	160,074	2,013,511
• At fast food, take-out, delivery, concession stands, buffet and cafeteria	191,491	6,360	14,155	170,591	30,607	159,589
• At full-service restaurants	1,928,752	44,984	69,814	1,312,778	126,300	1,810,399
Other alcoholic beverages	4,470,045	131,379	177,147	4,157,919	354,507	4,126,507
• At fast food, take-out, delivery, concession stands, buffet, and cafeteria	891,702	20,725	60,881	809,819	114,221	775,145
• At full-service restaurants	3,401,848	110,656	101,011	3,187,313	227,621	3,187,628
Alcoholic beverages purchased on trips	3,836,741	127,199	100,599	3,608,889	186,577	3,649,813

Note: Other races include Native Americans and Pacific Islanders. Numbers may not add to total because of rounding and missing subcategories. (–) means sample is too small to make a reliable estimate.
Source: Calculations by New Strategist based on the 2003 Consumer Expenditure Survey

Table 5.20 Food and Alcohol: Market shares by race and Hispanic origin, 2003

(percentage of total annual spending on food and alcoholic beverages accounted for by consumer unit race and Hispanic origin groups, 2003)

	total consumer units	race			Hispanic origin	
		Asian	black	white and other	Hispanic	non-Hispanic
Share of total consumer units	100.0%	3.1%	11.9%	85.0%	10.2%	89.8%
Share of total before-tax income	100.0	3.7	8.0	88.2	7.4	92.8
Share of total spending	100.0	3.4	8.4	88.2	8.6	91.4
Share of food spending	100.0	3.6	8.9	87.4	10.9	89.0
Share of alcoholic beverages spending	100.0	2.4	5.2	92.4	8.2	92.0
FOOD AT HOME	100.0	3.3	10.1	86.6	11.7	88.1
Cereals and bakery products	100.0	3.1	10.0	86.9	11.2	88.7
Cereals and cereal products	100.0	3.7	11.0	85.2	12.4	87.4
Flour	100.0	3.8	13.5	82.8	20.4	78.5
Prepared flour mixes	100.0	2.1	10.2	87.8	8.6	91.5
Ready-to-eat and cooked cereals	100.0	2.2	10.5	87.3	11.0	88.9
Rice	100.0	12.3	13.1	73.9	18.4	80.7
Pasta, cornmeal, and other cereal products	100.0	4.1	11.2	84.6	12.8	87.0
Bakery products	100.0	2.7	9.4	87.8	10.6	89.4
Bread	100.0	3.0	9.9	87.1	11.9	88.0
White bread	100.0	2.9	11.8	85.3	13.4	86.2
Bread, other than white	100.0	3.0	8.6	88.3	10.8	89.1
Crackers and cookies	100.0	2.8	9.3	87.9	9.2	90.9
Cookies	100.0	3.1	9.4	87.4	9.7	90.3
Crackers	100.0	2.2	9.2	88.7	8.3	91.9
Frozen and refrigerated bakery products	100.0	1.9	10.7	87.4	9.1	91.0
Other bakery products	100.0	2.7	8.9	88.4	10.8	89.1
Biscuits and rolls	100.0	3.0	7.4	89.6	8.4	91.7
Cakes and cupcakes	100.0	2.8	11.5	85.8	12.1	87.6
Bread and cracker products	100.0	2.8	8.8	88.6	8.6	91.6
Sweetrolls, coffee cakes, doughnuts	100.0	1.9	8.2	89.9	11.5	88.3
Pies, tarts, turnovers	100.0	3.6	7.1	89.3	13.7	86.0
Meats, poultry, fish, and eggs	100.0	3.7	12.7	83.6	13.1	86.6
Beef	100.0	2.4	11.3	86.3	13.5	86.1
Ground beef	100.0	1.9	12.7	85.6	12.0	87.8
Roast	100.0	2.2	11.9	86.0	13.7	85.9
Chuck roast	100.0	2.5	11.0	86.6	15.4	84.1
Round roast	100.0	2.2	14.3	83.6	12.9	86.8
Other roast	100.0	2.1	11.2	86.8	12.9	86.8
Steak	100.0	3.0	10.1	86.8	14.5	85.0
Round steak	100.0	2.8	8.5	88.7	17.0	82.2
Sirloin steak	100.0	3.6	10.1	86.2	14.8	84.6
Other steak	100.0	2.7	10.8	86.6	13.5	86.1
Other beef	100.0	2.5	9.3	88.2	15.2	84.2
Pork	100.0	3.2	14.4	82.5	12.6	87.1
Bacon	100.0	1.8	15.7	82.7	10.5	89.4
Pork chops	100.0	3.9	16.1	79.9	14.7	84.8
Ham	100.0	2.2	12.2	85.7	13.1	86.5
Ham, not canned	100.0	2.2	12.2	85.7	13.2	86.5
Canned ham	100.0	4.7	9.3	86.5	12.4	88.2
Sausage	100.0	2.6	16.7	80.8	11.0	88.9
Other pork	100.0	4.8	12.7	82.4	13.1	86.6
Other meats	100.0	2.4	10.6	87.0	11.2	88.6
Frankfurters	100.0	2.1	12.5	85.4	12.4	87.4
Lunch meats (cold cuts)	100.0	1.6	9.5	88.9	11.0	88.9
Bologna, liverwurst, salami	100.0	1.7	11.9	86.5	14.6	85.0
Other lunch meats	100.0	1.6	8.5	90.0	9.4	90.7
Lamb, organ meats, and others	100.0	9.0	13.2	77.4	10.3	89.7
Poultry	100.0	3.9	14.6	81.5	13.3	86.3
Fresh and frozen chicken	100.0	4.1	14.1	81.7	14.3	85.2

		race			Hispanic origin	
	total consumer units	Asian	black	white and other	Hispanic	non-Hispanic
Fresh and frozen whole chicken	100.0%	6.4%	14.2%	79.3%	16.5%	82.8%
Fresh and frozen chicken parts	100.0	3.3	14.0	82.7	13.5	86.2
Other poultry	100.0	2.9	16.7	80.4	9.3	90.7
Fish and seafood	100.0	7.6	13.4	78.7	12.9	86.8
Canned fish and seafood	100.0	4.0	9.1	86.9	11.8	88.0
Fresh fish and shellfish	100.0	8.5	16.0	75.2	13.9	85.7
Frozen fish and shellfish	100.0	7.3	10.2	82.1	11.5	88.4
Eggs	100.0	3.6	11.4	84.9	16.2	83.1
Dairy products	**100.0**	**2.3**	**8.2**	**89.4**	**11.6**	**88.3**
Fresh milk and cream	100.0	2.7	8.9	88.4	12.9	86.8
Fresh milk, all types	100.0	2.9	9.2	87.9	13.1	86.6
Cream	100.0	1.8	5.9	92.4	11.2	88.7
Other dairy products	100.0	2.1	7.9	90.1	10.8	89.2
Butter	100.0	2.3	9.9	87.8	10.4	89.5
Cheese	100.0	1.3	7.1	91.7	10.5	89.5
Ice cream and related products	100.0	2.7	9.0	88.3	11.5	88.4
Miscellaneous dairy products	100.0	3.4	6.8	89.7	10.7	89.3
Fruits and vegetables	**100.0**	**4.6**	**9.7**	**85.6**	**13.0**	**86.7**
Fresh fruits	100.0	5.0	8.9	85.9	13.8	85.8
Apples	100.0	5.1	9.3	85.5	11.6	88.3
Bananas	100.0	4.5	9.8	85.5	15.3	84.2
Oranges	100.0	6.1	10.2	83.4	16.3	83.0
Citrus fruits, excl. oranges	100.0	4.7	8.2	87.0	17.8	81.4
Other fresh fruits	100.0	4.9	8.3	86.6	12.8	86.9
Fresh vegetables	100.0	5.8	9.2	84.8	14.2	85.3
Potatoes	100.0	4.0	12.0	83.9	12.7	87.1
Lettuce	100.0	4.1	8.2	87.6	12.8	86.9
Tomatoes	100.0	4.5	7.9	87.5	18.2	80.9
Other fresh vegetables	100.0	7.3	8.9	83.4	13.6	86.0
Processed fruits	100.0	3.5	11.0	85.4	12.3	87.4
Frozen fruits and fruit juices	100.0	3.4	9.6	86.9	10.4	89.5
Frozen orange juice	100.0	2.0	9.9	88.1	14.1	85.4
Frozen fruits	100.0	2.9	8.8	88.2	5.5	95.0
Frozen fruit juices, excl. orange	100.0	5.5	10.2	83.7	10.8	89.3
Canned fruits	100.0	2.2	9.0	88.8	9.3	90.8
Dried fruits	100.0	3.0	6.3	90.7	9.6	90.4
Fresh fruit juice	100.0	3.7	11.3	85.0	12.9	86.8
Canned and bottled fruit juice	100.0	3.9	12.4	83.6	13.7	85.9
Processed vegetables	100.0	2.5	10.9	86.7	10.0	90.0
Frozen vegetables	100.0	2.2	10.4	87.5	7.7	92.6
Canned and dried vegetables and juices	100.0	2.6	11.1	86.3	11.1	88.8
Canned beans	100.0	1.2	12.5	86.5	9.8	90.2
Canned corn	100.0	2.6	15.2	82.2	9.6	90.4
Canned miscellaneous vegetables	100.0	2.2	9.3	88.5	8.4	91.8
Dried peas	100.0	3.7	6.1	91.9	20.6	80.1
Dried beans	100.0	2.2	12.3	85.4	27.2	71.1
Dried miscellaneous vegetables	100.0	6.9	11.8	80.9	12.0	87.8
Dried processed vegetables	100.0	6.3	9.6	83.0	8.2	92.0
Fresh and canned vegetable juices	100.0	1.9	8.7	89.5	14.5	85.1
Sugar and other sweets	**100.0**	**2.7**	**9.3**	**88.0**	**11.0**	**89.0**
Candy and chewing gum	100.0	2.7	7.8	89.5	10.3	89.7
Sugar	100.0	3.1	15.6	81.3	13.5	86.2
Artificial sweeteners	100.0	0.8	10.0	89.5	11.3	88.6
Jams, preserves, other sweets	100.0	2.5	9.7	87.8	11.2	88.7
Fats and oils	**100.0**	**2.3**	**11.1**	**86.7**	**11.6**	**88.3**
Margarine	100.0	1.2	11.6	87.4	8.0	92.3
Fats and oils	100.0	3.8	13.5	82.7	17.1	82.1
Salad dressings	100.0	1.8	10.5	87.8	9.7	90.4
Nondairy cream and imitation milk	100.0	1.5	7.7	90.9	9.8	90.3
Peanut butter	100.0	1.6	9.8	88.7	8.2	92.0

	total consumer units	race			Hispanic origin	
		Asian	black	white and other	Hispanic	non-Hispanic
Miscellaneous foods	**100.0%**	**2.5%**	**8.8%**	**88.7%**	**9.4%**	**90.7%**
Frozen prepared foods	100.0	1.9	8.7	89.5	6.7	93.7
Frozen meals	100.0	2.5	8.8	88.8	5.6	94.9
Other frozen prepared foods	100.0	1.7	8.6	89.8	7.3	93.1
Canned and packaged soups	100.0	3.0	7.8	89.2	8.7	91.4
Potato chips, nuts, and other snacks	100.0	2.9	7.4	89.7	8.9	91.2
Potato chips and other snacks	100.0	2.6	7.7	89.7	9.1	91.0
Nuts	100.0	3.8	6.4	89.7	8.4	91.8
Condiments and seasonings	100.0	3.1	9.4	87.5	9.5	90.6
Salt, spices, and other seasonings	100.0	4.2	11.2	84.5	12.6	87.2
Olives, pickles, relishes	100.0	2.1	9.0	88.9	8.3	91.9
Sauces and gravies	100.0	3.0	9.8	87.2	9.0	91.1
Baking needs and miscellaneous products	100.0	2.7	6.9	90.5	7.7	92.5
Other canned/packaged prepared foods	100.0	2.2	9.6	88.2	11.6	88.2
Prepared salads	100.0	1.5	7.5	91.1	6.1	94.3
Prepared desserts	100.0	1.3	7.7	91.1	10.6	89.3
Baby food	100.0	1.6	10.7	87.8	16.6	82.7
Miscellaneous prepared foods	100.0	2.7	10.1	87.3	11.5	88.3
Nonalcoholic beverages	**100.0**	**2.9**	**9.0**	**88.1**	**11.0**	**88.9**
Cola	100.0	1.8	8.8	89.5	12.5	87.2
Other carbonated drinks	100.0	2.1	9.2	88.7	10.4	89.5
Coffee	100.0	2.4	6.4	91.2	10.3	89.7
Roasted coffee	100.0	2.2	6.4	91.4	9.4	90.7
Instant and freeze-dried coffee	100.0	2.7	6.4	90.8	12.1	87.7
Noncarbonated fruit-flavored drinks, incl. nonfrozen lemonade	100.0	2.3	14.7	83.2	13.4	86.2
Tea	100.0	5.8	9.2	84.7	8.1	92.1
Other nonalcoholic beverages and ice	100.0	4.8	8.9	86.2	9.7	90.4
Food prepared by CU on trips	**100.0**	**3.4**	**4.1**	**92.6**	**6.9**	**93.1**
FOOD AWAY FROM HOME	**100.0**	**4.2**	**7.2**	**88.5**	**9.7**	**90.2**
Meals at restaurants, carry-outs, other	**100.0**	**4.0**	**7.8**	**88.1**	**10.3**	**89.7**
Lunch	100.0	4.5	8.7	86.7	10.9	89.0
• At fast food, take-out, delivery, concession stands, buffet, cafeteria (other than employer, school cafeteria)	100.0	4.2	10.1	85.7	12.1	87.7
• At full-service restaurants	100.0	5.4	4.7	89.6	8.8	91.4
• At vending machines, mobile vendors	100.0	2.8	6.3	91.0	29.4	68.5
• At employer and school cafeterias	100.0	3.5	13.2	83.3	9.8	90.2
Dinner	100.0	4.0	6.2	89.7	9.2	90.9
• At fast food, take-out, delivery, concession stands, buffet, cafeteria (other than employer, school cafeteria)	100.0	3.5	9.6	86.9	11.9	87.9
• At full-service restaurants	100.0	4.3	4.6	90.9	8.1	92.1
• At vending machines, mobile vendors	100.0	–	–	99.8	12.1	87.1
• At employer and school cafeterias	100.0	2.7	29.5	68.2	5.4	95.2
Snacks and nonalcoholic beverages	100.0	3.0	9.5	87.4	10.9	89.0
• At fast food, take-out, delivery, concession stands, buffet, cafeteria (other than employer, school cafeteria)	100.0	3.1	8.7	88.2	10.2	89.8
• At full-service restaurants	100.0	3.2	9.6	87.1	10.8	89.1
• At vending machines, mobile vendors	100.0	2.0	13.1	85.0	15.1	84.3
• At employer and school cafeterias	100.0	5.5	13.0	81.4	11.3	88.6
Breakfast and brunch	100.0	3.1	8.8	88.1	11.4	88.5
• At fast food, take-out, delivery, concession stands, buffet, cafeteria (other than employer, school cafeteria)	100.0	3.2	11.5	85.3	12.7	87.0
• At full-service restaurants	100.0	3.1	5.4	91.4	9.7	90.4
• At vending machines, mobile vendors	100.0	1.4	13.0	85.6	18.8	80.0
• At employer and school cafeterias	100.0	1.7	17.6	81.0	16.1	83.3
Board (including at school)	**100.0**	**7.4**	**7.4**	**85.2**	**3.7**	**96.3**
Catered affairs	**100.0**	**5.9**	**1.1**	**93.0**	**12.1**	**87.9**
Food on trips	**100.0**	**3.9**	**3.5**	**92.6**	**5.2**	**94.8**
School lunches	**100.0**	**3.6**	**8.3**	**88.1**	**8.6**	**91.4**
Meals as pay	**100.0**	**15.5**	**7.4**	**77.1**	**14.2**	**85.8**

	total consumer units	race			Hispanic origin	
		Asian	black	white and other	Hispanic	non-Hispanic
ALCOHOLIC BEVERAGES	100.0%	2.4%	5.2%	92.4%	8.2%	92.0%
At home	100.0	2.3	6.1	91.6	8.8	91.4
Beer and ale	100.0	1.8	7.4	90.8	10.6	89.3
Whiskey	100.0	1.5	3.8	94.7	14.4	85.1
Wine	100.0	3.1	4.3	92.6	6.3	94.1
Other alcoholic beverages	100.0	2.3	7.9	89.8	6.2	94.3
Away from home	100.0	2.6	3.7	93.6	7.3	92.9
Beer and ale	100.0	2.1	4.0	93.8	8.1	92.1
• At fast food, take-out, delivery, concession stands, buffet, and cafeteria	100.0	0.8	4.2	95.1	17.1	82.1
• At full-service restaurants	100.0	2.6	3.6	93.7	6.1	94.3
Wine	100.0	2.4	4.0	93.5	7.4	92.9
• At fast food, take-out, delivery, concession stands, buffet and cafeteria	100.0	3.3	7.4	89.1	16.0	83.3
• At full-service restaurants	100.0	2.3	3.6	94.0	6.5	93.9
Other alcoholic beverages	100.0	2.9	4.0	93.0	7.9	92.3
• At fast food, take-out, delivery, concession stands, buffet, and cafeteria	100.0	2.3	6.8	90.8	12.8	86.9
• At full-service restaurants	100.0	3.3	3.0	93.7	6.7	93.7
Alcoholic beverages purchased on trips	100.0	3.3	2.6	94.1	4.9	95.1

Note: Other races include Native Americans and Pacific Islanders. Numbers may not add to total because of rounding. (–) means sample is too small to make a reliable estimate.
Source: Calculations by New Strategist based on the 2003 Consumer Expenditure Survey

Table 5.21 Food and Alcohol: Average spending by region, 2003

(average annual spending of consumer units (CU) on food and alcoholic beverages, by region in which consumer unit lives, 2003)

	total consumer units	Northeast	Midwest	South	West
Number of consumer units (000)	115,356	22,182	26,438	41,325	25,412
Average number of persons per CU	2.5	2.4	2.5	2.5	2.6
Average before-tax income of CU	$48,596.00	$54,219.00	$49,591.00	$44,461.00	$49,667.00
Average spending of CU, total	40,817.33	42,162.29	40,280.39	37,624.55	45,380.67
Food, average spending	5,339.50	5,730.36	5,088.38	4,959.74	5,876.43
Alcoholic beverages, average spending	391.21	427.23	403.10	345.25	420.72
FOOD AT HOME	**3,128.78**	**3,305.93**	**2,903.91**	**2,995.83**	**3,427.59**
Cereals and bakery products	**441.72**	**484.66**	**411.48**	**412.98**	**482.50**
Cereals and cereal products	150.14	158.14	135.44	141.50	172.68
Flour	7.32	6.55	5.39	7.61	9.63
Prepared flour mixes	12.79	13.36	12.34	12.31	13.54
Ready-to-eat and cooked cereals	86.21	88.37	83.58	79.57	97.76
Rice	16.05	19.11	10.42	16.16	19.27
Pasta, cornmeal, and other cereal products	27.75	30.75	23.72	25.86	32.48
Bakery products	291.58	326.52	276.03	271.47	309.81
Bread	82.55	89.76	82.16	73.39	91.30
White bread	33.50	36.79	33.38	31.67	33.65
Bread, other than white	49.06	52.97	48.78	41.72	57.65
Crackers and cookies	69.58	74.06	65.29	67.82	73.07
Cookies	45.06	47.80	42.52	43.94	47.15
Crackers	24.52	26.26	22.77	23.87	25.92
Frozen and refrigerated bakery products	24.56	25.30	23.08	26.66	22.16
Other bakery products	114.89	137.40	105.50	103.61	123.28
Biscuits and rolls	37.24	47.31	36.50	31.56	38.30
Cakes and cupcakes	36.71	43.91	30.49	36.01	38.20
Bread and cracker products	3.57	4.81	3.06	3.20	3.63
Sweetrolls, coffee cakes, doughnuts	27.65	30.41	27.32	25.25	29.40
Pies, tarts, turnovers	9.72	10.96	8.11	7.59	13.76
Meats, poultry, fish, and eggs	**824.58**	**888.61**	**734.42**	**834.84**	**848.90**
Beef	245.55	239.44	224.99	261.66	247.21
Ground beef	89.27	89.06	87.17	94.66	83.08
Roast	39.63	32.13	41.29	40.58	42.88
Chuck roast	13.37	11.46	13.96	13.59	14.07
Round roast	9.78	8.55	10.86	9.59	9.98
Other roast	16.48	12.11	16.47	17.40	18.83
Steak	94.16	94.02	82.44	98.91	99.28
Round steak	15.65	13.56	12.65	18.25	16.52
Sirloin steak	31.35	34.89	27.16	31.04	33.26
Other steak	47.17	45.57	42.63	49.63	49.50
Other beef	22.49	24.23	14.09	27.50	21.97
Pork	170.61	167.59	161.00	181.09	166.85
Bacon	31.15	28.78	30.16	35.27	27.71
Pork chops	34.14	35.26	33.12	36.41	30.61
Ham	38.15	45.21	37.00	36.40	35.99
Ham, not canned	37.04	44.27	36.34	35.29	34.27
Canned ham	1.10	0.94	0.66	1.11	1.72
Sausage	25.82	25.24	23.84	28.72	23.83
Other pork	41.36	33.10	36.87	44.29	48.71
Other meats	102.01	131.85	98.18	94.50	92.02
Frankfurters	22.74	28.81	20.94	22.48	19.76
Lunch meats (cold cuts)	69.31	88.19	70.79	62.67	61.83
Bologna, liverwurst, salami	21.65	26.92	21.19	19.81	20.47
Other lunch meats	47.66	61.27	49.60	42.86	41.36
Lamb, organ meats, and others	9.96	14.85	6.44	9.35	10.43
Poultry	144.61	165.09	122.76	140.58	156.60
Fresh and frozen chicken	116.42	132.16	96.52	113.96	127.92

	total consumer units	Northeast	Midwest	South	West
Fresh and frozen whole chicken	$32.82	$38.00	$24.40	$31.33	$39.71
Fresh and frozen chicken parts	83.60	94.16	72.12	82.63	88.21
Other poultry	28.20	32.92	26.24	26.61	28.68
Fish and seafood	124.46	146.35	96.88	120.64	140.99
Canned fish and seafood	16.40	18.29	15.35	14.97	18.17
Fresh fish and shellfish	71.88	95.25	44.21	70.10	83.99
Frozen fish and shellfish	36.17	32.81	37.32	35.57	38.83
Eggs	37.34	38.30	30.61	36.37	45.25
Dairy products	**328.00**	**352.54**	**323.36**	**298.44**	**358.75**
Fresh milk and cream	126.53	130.21	125.86	117.47	138.52
Fresh milk, all types	112.58	114.28	113.81	105.24	121.51
Cream	13.95	15.93	12.05	12.23	17.01
Other dairy products	201.47	222.33	197.50	180.97	220.24
Butter	18.08	22.97	16.67	15.58	19.30
Cheese	97.04	103.99	99.83	85.04	107.16
Ice cream and related products	58.09	63.10	55.74	56.20	59.24
Miscellaneous dairy products	28.26	32.27	25.27	24.15	34.54
Fruits and vegetables	**535.42**	**585.91**	**472.18**	**488.96**	**633.32**
Fresh fruits	170.88	185.24	152.45	149.29	212.57
Apples	32.73	34.64	33.02	27.75	38.70
Bananas	28.41	29.08	24.55	25.67	36.35
Oranges	18.34	23.07	15.60	14.65	23.02
Citrus fruits, excl. oranges	14.14	14.70	10.64	13.12	19.05
Other fresh fruits	77.26	83.75	68.63	68.10	95.46
Fresh vegetables	171.96	190.02	142.17	153.94	216.91
Potatoes	30.11	33.66	27.07	31.27	28.43
Lettuce	22.10	26.88	20.14	18.66	25.50
Tomatoes	32.18	34.53	23.67	28.92	44.46
Other fresh vegetables	87.57	94.95	71.29	75.09	118.53
Processed fruits	108.39	122.83	96.08	98.06	125.46
Frozen fruits and fruit juices	11.54	9.55	12.85	9.32	15.42
Frozen orange juice	4.64	3.59	4.82	4.11	6.21
Frozen fruits	3.66	3.44	4.91	2.40	4.52
Frozen fruit juices, excl. orange	3.24	2.52	3.12	2.81	4.70
Canned fruits	15.96	15.81	16.80	14.54	17.45
Dried fruits	6.30	6.89	5.53	5.53	7.83
Fresh fruit juice	20.77	28.01	13.30	17.24	22.74
Canned and bottled fruit juice	53.82	62.58	42.60	51.43	62.01
Processed vegetables	84.19	87.82	81.48	87.66	78.37
Frozen vegetables	26.79	31.75	25.27	27.02	23.72
Canned and dried vegetables and juices	57.40	56.07	56.21	60.65	54.65
Canned beans	12.56	11.79	13.07	14.41	9.73
Canned corn	6.89	6.31	7.17	7.82	5.60
Canned miscellaneous vegetables	18.55	17.25	18.84	20.17	16.78
Dried peas	0.37	0.17	0.30	0.56	0.35
Dried beans	2.31	1.78	1.66	2.51	3.14
Dried miscellaneous vegetables	7.51	8.92	6.41	7.06	8.15
Dried processed vegetables	0.42	0.76	0.35	0.34	0.32
Fresh and canned vegetable juices	8.67	9.09	8.34	7.70	10.21
Sugar and other sweets	**119.08**	**125.58**	**117.69**	**106.71**	**134.64**
Candy and chewing gum	75.31	81.30	76.96	62.56	88.69
Sugar	16.89	15.02	14.57	19.25	17.23
Artificial sweeteners	5.67	6.08	5.56	6.31	4.42
Jams, preserves, other sweets	21.20	23.19	20.60	18.59	24.29
Fats and oils	**85.73**	**89.20**	**79.42**	**84.54**	**91.36**
Margarine	9.61	9.98	11.00	9.37	8.18
Fats and oils	26.29	28.56	21.50	27.85	26.82
Salad dressings	26.17	26.80	24.36	25.30	28.95
Nondairy cream and imitation milk	11.02	10.54	9.67	10.45	13.81
Peanut butter	12.64	13.31	12.79	11.56	13.60

	total consumer units	Northeast	Midwest	South	West
Miscellaneous foods	**$489.60**	**$473.20**	**$475.72**	**$481.93**	**$531.10**
Frozen prepared foods	104.79	95.81	113.04	106.22	101.51
Frozen meals	34.85	34.97	35.49	35.10	33.68
Other frozen prepared foods	69.94	60.85	77.55	71.12	67.84
Canned and packaged soups	35.19	35.86	35.65	32.51	38.42
Potato chips, nuts, and other snacks	105.68	103.06	113.07	100.84	107.78
Potato chips and other snacks	79.27	77.45	87.22	75.61	78.20
Nuts	26.41	25.62	25.84	25.24	29.59
Condiments and seasonings	90.22	87.26	85.71	87.39	102.18
Salt, spices, and other seasonings	20.77	19.38	17.80	21.40	24.20
Olives, pickles, relishes	11.41	10.45	12.16	10.26	13.27
Sauces and gravies	38.46	37.76	36.50	37.78	42.26
Baking needs and miscellaneous products	19.58	19.68	19.25	17.95	22.46
Other canned/packaged prepared foods	153.71	151.20	128.25	154.97	181.21
Prepared salads	20.51	20.48	18.75	19.38	24.21
Prepared desserts	11.10	12.32	9.70	10.41	12.62
Baby food	26.76	28.88	19.78	32.48	23.26
Miscellaneous prepared foods	95.13	89.21	79.92	92.61	120.66
Nonalcoholic beverages	**268.37**	**271.95**	**254.28**	**257.93**	**297.03**
Cola	88.27	79.41	98.60	86.29	88.09
Other carbonated drinks	45.64	45.56	47.64	44.18	45.89
Coffee	38.08	39.64	36.12	33.61	45.96
Roasted coffee	25.70	26.42	24.91	22.59	30.90
Instant and freeze-dried coffee	12.38	13.22	11.20	11.02	15.06
Noncarbonated fruit-flavored drinks, incl. nonfrozen lemonade	19.29	22.03	14.82	19.10	22.00
Tea	17.71	22.91	12.43	18.99	16.77
Other nonalcoholic beverages and ice	58.72	60.43	44.06	55.64	77.86
Food prepared by CU on trips	**36.28**	**34.28**	**35.37**	**29.52**	**49.98**
FOOD AWAY FROM HOME	**2,210.73**	**2,424.43**	**2,184.47**	**1,963.91**	**2,448.84**
Meals at restaurants, carry-outs, other	**1,831.97**	**1,963.62**	**1,806.23**	**1,671.43**	**2,000.85**
Lunch	658.16	654.59	620.45	642.51	726.73
• At fast food, take-out, delivery, concession stands, buffet, cafeteria (other than employer, school cafeteria)	369.02	363.82	341.25	357.69	421.48
• At full-service restaurants	210.10	210.93	187.45	200.84	248.45
• At vending machines, mobile vendors	5.56	5.03	5.92	5.86	5.17
• At employer and school cafeterias	73.48	74.81	85.83	78.12	51.64
Dinner	737.51	879.32	727.94	634.16	788.78
• At fast food, take-out, delivery, concession stands, buffet, cafeteria (other than employer, school cafeteria)	215.93	208.67	224.82	192.53	250.13
• At full-service restaurants	517.42	668.14	496.53	436.15	537.82
• At vending machines, mobile vendors	1.32	0.76	0.93	2.46	0.39
• At employer and school cafeterias	2.83	1.75	5.66	3.01	0.45
Snacks and nonalcoholic beverages	248.42	253.24	260.08	220.50	276.28
• At fast food, take-out, delivery, concession stands, buffet, cafeteria (other than employer, school cafeteria)	180.26	193.32	182.04	153.17	210.22
• At full-service restaurants	26.66	21.05	29.26	25.11	31.27
• At vending machines, mobile vendors	31.33	25.45	36.77	33.19	27.64
• At employer and school cafeterias	10.16	13.43	12.01	9.03	7.15
Breakfast and brunch	187.89	176.47	197.77	174.26	209.05
• At fast food, take-out, delivery, concession stands, buffet, cafeteria (other than employer, school cafeteria)	92.82	83.47	100.80	94.85	89.22
• At full-service restaurants	89.42	88.78	91.77	72.42	114.61
• At vending machines, mobile vendors	1.37	0.83	1.25	1.43	1.87
• At employer and school cafeterias	4.27	3.39	3.95	5.55	3.35
Board (including at school)	**33.25**	**39.86**	**27.04**	**32.22**	**35.62**
Catered affairs	**48.39**	**90.84**	**35.03**	**25.52**	**62.42**
Food on trips	**213.97**	**241.59**	**225.37**	**169.45**	**250.38**
School lunches	**56.87**	**59.15**	**69.87**	**50.65**	**51.49**
Meals as pay	**26.28**	**29.37**	**20.93**	**14.63**	**48.08**

	total consumer units	Northeast	Midwest	South	West
ALCOHOLIC BEVERAGES	**$391.21**	**$427.23**	**$403.10**	**$345.25**	**$420.72**
At home	**240.08**	**234.95**	**249.23**	**222.18**	**263.36**
Beer and ale	111.17	96.42	129.41	106.63	111.72
Whiskey	14.29	10.78	20.71	12.33	13.58
Wine	89.93	106.23	73.70	80.65	107.90
Other alcoholic beverages	24.70	21.52	25.40	22.56	30.15
Away from home	**151.12**	**192.28**	**153.88**	**123.06**	**157.37**
Beer and ale	60.33	79.54	64.90	48.20	57.99
• At fast food, take-out, delivery, concession stands, buffet, and cafeteria	10.70	11.25	15.47	5.04	14.14
• At full-service restaurants	46.19	65.10	46.55	37.54	43.05
Wine	18.78	23.60	17.50	17.50	17.98
• At fast food, take-out, delivery, concession stands, buffet and cafeteria	1.66	1.70	1.47	1.61	1.92
• At full-service restaurants	15.72	21.57	15.73	15.18	15.99
Other alcoholic beverages	33.75	43.14	36.33	34.78	39.49
• At fast food, take-out, delivery, concession stands, buffet, and cafeteria	7.73	8.43	7.89	6.61	8.75
• At full-service restaurants	29.49	38.33	27.19	25.65	30.37
Alcoholic beverages purchased on trips	33.26	41.00	35.14	22.58	41.90

Note: Subcategories may not add to total because some are not shown.
Source: Bureau of Labor Statistics, unpublished tables from the 2003 Consumer Expenditure Survey

Table 5.22 Food and Alcohol: Indexed spending by region, 2003

(indexed average annual spending of consumer units (CU) on food and alcoholic beverages, by region in which consumer unit lives, 2003; index definition: an index of 100 is the average for all consumer units; an index of 132 means that spending by consumer units in that group is 32 percent above the average for all consumer units; an index of 68 indicates spending that is 32 percent below the average for all consumer units)

	total consumer units	Northeast	Midwest	South	West
Average spending of CU, total	$40,817	$42,162	$40,280	$37,625	$45,381
Average spending of CU, index	100	103	99	92	111
Food, spending index	**100**	**107**	**95**	**93**	**110**
Alcoholic beverages, spending index	**100**	**109**	**103**	**88**	**108**
FOOD AT HOME	**100**	**106**	**93**	**96**	**110**
Cereals and bakery products	**100**	**110**	**93**	**93**	**109**
Cereals and cereal products	100	105	90	94	115
Flour	100	89	74	104	132
Prepared flour mixes	100	104	96	96	106
Ready-to-eat and cooked cereals	100	103	97	92	113
Rice	100	119	65	101	120
Pasta, cornmeal, and other cereal products	100	111	85	93	117
Bakery products	100	112	95	93	106
Bread	100	109	100	89	111
White bread	100	110	100	95	100
Bread, other than white	100	108	99	85	118
Crackers and cookies	100	106	94	97	105
Cookies	100	106	94	98	105
Crackers	100	107	93	97	106
Frozen and refrigerated bakery products	100	103	94	109	90
Other bakery products	100	120	92	90	107
Biscuits and rolls	100	127	98	85	103
Cakes and cupcakes	100	120	83	98	104
Bread and cracker products	100	135	86	90	102
Sweetrolls, coffee cakes, doughnuts	100	110	99	91	106
Pies, tarts, turnovers	100	113	83	78	142
Meats, poultry, fish, and eggs	**100**	**108**	**89**	**101**	**103**
Beef	100	98	92	107	101
Ground beef	100	100	98	106	93
Roast	100	81	104	102	108
Chuck roast	100	86	104	102	105
Round roast	100	87	111	98	102
Other roast	100	73	100	106	114
Steak	100	100	88	105	105
Round steak	100	87	81	117	106
Sirloin steak	100	111	87	99	106
Other steak	100	97	90	105	105
Other beef	100	108	63	122	98
Pork	100	98	94	106	98
Bacon	100	92	97	113	89
Pork chops	100	103	97	107	90
Ham	100	119	97	95	94
Ham, not canned	100	120	98	95	93
Canned ham	100	85	60	101	156
Sausage	100	98	92	111	92
Other pork	100	80	89	107	118
Other meats	100	129	96	93	90
Frankfurters	100	127	92	99	87
Lunch meats (cold cuts)	100	127	102	90	89
Bologna, liverwurst, salami	100	124	98	92	95
Other lunch meats	100	129	104	90	87
Lamb, organ meats, and others	100	149	65	94	105
Poultry	100	114	85	97	108
Fresh and frozen chicken	100	114	83	98	110

	total consumer units	Northeast	Midwest	South	West
Fresh and frozen whole chicken	100	116	74	95	121
Fresh and frozen chicken parts	100	113	86	99	106
Other poultry	100	117	93	94	102
Fish and seafood	100	118	78	97	113
Canned fish and seafood	100	112	94	91	111
Fresh fish and shellfish	100	133	62	98	117
Frozen fish and shellfish	100	91	103	98	107
Eggs	100	103	82	97	121
Dairy products	**100**	**107**	**99**	**91**	**109**
Fresh milk and cream	100	103	99	93	109
Fresh milk, all types	100	102	101	93	108
Cream	100	114	86	88	122
Other dairy products	100	110	98	90	109
Butter	100	127	92	86	107
Cheese	100	107	103	88	110
Ice cream and related products	100	109	96	97	102
Miscellaneous dairy products	100	114	89	85	122
Fruits and vegetables	**100**	**109**	**88**	**91**	**118**
Fresh fruits	100	108	89	87	124
Apples	100	106	101	85	118
Bananas	100	102	86	90	128
Oranges	100	126	85	80	126
Citrus fruits, excl. oranges	100	104	75	93	135
Other fresh fruits	100	108	89	88	124
Fresh vegetables	100	111	83	90	126
Potatoes	100	112	90	104	94
Lettuce	100	122	91	84	115
Tomatoes	100	107	74	90	138
Other fresh vegetables	100	108	81	86	135
Processed fruits	100	113	89	90	116
Frozen fruits and fruit juices	100	83	111	81	134
Frozen orange juice	100	77	104	89	134
Frozen fruits	100	94	134	66	123
Frozen fruit juices, excl. orange	100	78	96	87	145
Canned fruits	100	99	105	91	109
Dried fruits	100	109	88	88	124
Fresh fruit juice	100	135	88	83	109
Canned and bottled fruit juice	100	116	79	96	115
Processed vegetables	100	104	97	104	93
Frozen vegetables	100	119	94	101	89
Canned and dried vegetables and juices	100	98	98	106	95
Canned beans	100	94	104	115	77
Canned corn	100	92	104	113	81
Canned miscellaneous vegetables	100	93	102	109	90
Dried peas	100	46	81	151	95
Dried beans	100	77	72	109	136
Dried miscellaneous vegetables	100	119	85	94	109
Dried processed vegetables	100	181	83	81	76
Fresh and canned vegetable juices	100	105	96	89	118
Sugar and other sweets	**100**	**105**	**99**	**90**	**113**
Candy and chewing gum	100	108	102	83	118
Sugar	100	89	86	114	102
Artificial sweeteners	100	107	98	111	78
Jams, preserves, other sweets	100	109	97	88	115
Fats and oils	**100**	**104**	**93**	**99**	**107**
Margarine	100	104	114	98	85
Fats and oils	100	109	82	106	102
Salad dressings	100	102	93	97	111
Nondairy cream and imitation milk	100	95	88	95	125
Peanut butter	100	105	101	91	108

	total consumer units	Northeast	Midwest	South	West
Miscellaneous foods	100	97	97	98	108
Frozen prepared foods	100	91	108	101	97
Frozen meals	100	100	102	101	97
Other frozen prepared foods	100	87	111	102	97
Canned and packaged soups	100	102	101	92	109
Potato chips, nuts, and other snacks	100	98	107	95	102
Potato chips and other snacks	100	98	110	95	99
Nuts	100	97	98	96	112
Condiments and seasonings	100	97	95	97	113
Salt, spices, and other seasonings	100	93	86	103	117
Olives, pickles, relishes	100	92	107	90	116
Sauces and gravies	100	98	95	98	110
Baking needs and miscellaneous products	100	101	98	92	115
Other canned/packaged prepared foods	100	98	83	101	118
Prepared salads	100	100	91	94	118
Prepared desserts	100	111	87	94	114
Baby food	100	108	74	121	87
Miscellaneous prepared foods	100	94	84	97	127
Nonalcoholic beverages	100	101	95	96	111
Cola	100	90	112	98	100
Other carbonated drinks	100	100	104	97	101
Coffee	100	104	95	88	121
Roasted coffee	100	103	97	88	120
Instant and freeze-dried coffee	100	107	90	89	122
Noncarbonated fruit-flavored drinks, incl. nonfrozen lemonade	100	114	77	99	114
Tea	100	129	70	107	95
Other nonalcoholic beverages and ice	100	103	75	95	133
Food prepared by CU on trips	100	94	97	81	138
FOOD AWAY FROM HOME	100	110	99	89	111
Meals at restaurants, carry-outs, other	100	107	99	91	109
Lunch	100	99	94	98	110
• At fast food, take-out, delivery, concession stands, buffet, and cafeteria (other than employer and school cafeteria)	100	99	92	97	114
• At full-service restaurants	100	100	89	96	118
• At vending machines, mobile vendors	100	90	106	105	93
• At employer and school cafeterias	100	102	117	106	70
Dinner	100	119	99	86	107
• At fast food, take-out, delivery, concession stands, buffet, and cafeteria (other than employer and school cafeteria)	100	97	104	89	116
• At full-service restaurants	100	129	96	84	104
• At vending machines, mobile vendors	100	58	70	186	30
• At employer and school cafeterias	100	62	200	106	16
Snacks and nonalcoholic beverages	100	102	105	89	111
• At fast food, take-out, delivery, concession stands, buffet, and cafeteria (other than employer and school cafeteria)	100	107	101	85	117
• At full-service restaurants	100	79	110	94	117
• At vending machines, mobile vendors	100	81	117	106	88
• At employer and school cafeterias	100	132	118	89	70
Breakfast and brunch	100	94	105	93	111
• At fast food, take-out, delivery, concession stands, buffet, and cafeteria (other than employer and school cafeteria)	100	90	109	102	96
• At full-service restaurants	100	99	103	81	128
• At vending machines, mobile vendors	100	61	91	104	136
• At employer and school cafeterias	100	79	93	130	78
Board (including at school)	100	120	81	97	107
Catered affairs	100	188	72	53	129
Food on trips	100	113	105	79	117
School lunches	100	104	123	89	91
Meals as pay	100	112	80	56	183

	total consumer units	Northeast	Midwest	South	West
ALCOHOLIC BEVERAGES	**100**	**109**	**103**	**88**	**108**
At home	**100**	**98**	**104**	**93**	**110**
Beer and ale	100	87	116	96	100
Whiskey	100	75	145	86	95
Wine	100	118	82	90	120
Other alcoholic beverages	100	87	103	91	122
Away from home	**100**	**127**	**102**	**81**	**104**
Beer and ale	100	132	108	80	96
• At fast food, take-out, delivery, concession stands, buffet, and cafeteria	100	105	145	47	132
• At full-service restaurants	100	141	101	81	93
Wine	100	126	93	93	96
• At fast food, take-out, delivery, concession stands, buffet and cafeteria	100	102	89	97	116
• At full-service restaurants	100	129	94	91	96
Other alcoholic beverages	100	124	94	90	102
• At fast food, take-out, delivery, concession stands, buffet, and cafeteria	100	109	102	86	113
• At full-service restaurants	100	130	92	87	103
Alcoholic beverages purchased on trips	100	123	106	68	126

Source: Calculations by New Strategist based on the 2003 Consumer Expenditure Survey

Table 5.23 Food and Alcohol: Total spending by region, 2003

(total annual spending on food and alcoholic beverages, by region in which consumer units live, 2003; numbers in thousands)

	total consumer units	Northeast	Midwest	South	West
Number of consumer units	115,356	22,182	26,438	41,325	25,412
Total spending of all consumer units	$4,708,523,919	$935,243,917	$1,064,932,951	$1,554,834,529	$1,153,213,586
Food, total spending	615,943,362	127,110,846	134,526,590	204,961,256	149,331,839
Alcoholic beverages, total spending	45,128,421	9,476,816	10,657,158	14,267,456	10691336.64
FOOD AT HOME	**360,923,546**	**73,332,139**	**76,773,573**	**123,802,675**	**87,101,917**
Cereals and bakery products	**50,955,052**	**10,750,728**	**10,878,708**	**17,066,399**	**12,261,290**
Cereals and cereal products	17,319,550	3,507,861	3,580,763	5,847,488	4,388,144
Flour	844,406	145,292	142,501	314,483	244,718
Prepared flour mixes	1,475,403	296,352	326,245	508,711	344,078
Ready-to-eat and cooked cereals	9,944,841	1,960,223	2,209,688	3,288,230	2,484,277
Rice	1,851,464	423,898	275,484	667,812	489,689
Pasta, cornmeal, and other cereal products	3,201,129	682,097	627,109	1,068,665	825,382
Bakery products	33,635,502	7,242,867	7,297,681	11,218,498	7,872,892
Bread	9,522,638	1,991,056	2,172,146	3,032,842	2,320,116
White bread	3,864,426	816,076	882,500	1,308,763	855,114
Bread, other than white	5,659,365	1,174,981	1,289,646	1,724,079	1,465,002
Crackers and cookies	8,026,470	1,642,799	1,726,137	2,802,662	1,856,855
Cookies	5,197,941	1,060,300	1,124,144	1,815,821	1,198,176
Crackers	2,828,529	582,499	601,993	986,428	658,679
Frozen and refrigerated bakery products	2,833,143	561,205	610,189	1,101,725	563,130
Other bakery products	13,253,251	3,047,807	2,789,209	4,281,683	3,132,791
Biscuits and rolls	4,295,857	1,049,430	964,987	1,304,217	973,280
Cakes and cupcakes	4,234,719	974,012	806,095	1,488,113	970,738
Bread and cracker products	411,821	106,695	80,900	132,240	92,246
Sweetrolls, coffee cakes, doughnuts	3,189,593	674,555	722,286	1,043,456	747,113
Pies, tarts, turnovers	1,121,260	243,115	214,412	313,657	349,669
Meats, poultry, fish, and eggs	**95,120,250**	**19,711,147**	**19,416,596**	**34,499,763**	**21,572,247**
Beef	28,325,666	5,311,258	5,948,286	10,813,100	6,282,101
Ground beef	10,297,830	1,975,529	2,304,600	3,911,825	2,111,229
Roast	4,571,558	712,708	1,091,625	1,676,969	1,089,667
Chuck roast	1,542,310	254,206	369,074	561,607	357,547
Round roast	1,128,182	189,656	287,117	396,307	253,612
Other roast	1,901,067	268,624	435,434	719,055	478,508
Steak	10,861,921	2,085,552	2,179,549	4,087,456	2,522,903
Round steak	1,805,321	300,788	334,441	754,181	419,806
Sirloin steak	3,616,411	773,930	718,056	1,282,728	845,203
Other steak	5,441,343	1,010,834	1,127,052	2,050,960	1,257,894
Other beef	2,594,356	537,470	372,511	1,136,438	558,302
Pork	19,680,887	3,717,481	4,256,518	7,483,544	4,239,992
Bacon	3,593,339	638,398	797,370	1,457,533	704,167
Pork chops	3,938,254	782,137	875,627	1,504,643	777,861
Ham	4,400,831	1,002,848	978,206	1,504,230	914,578
Ham, not canned	4,272,786	981,997	960,757	1,458,359	870,869
Canned ham	126,892	20,851	17,449	45,871	43,709
Sausage	2,978,492	559,874	630,282	1,186,854	605,568
Other pork	4,771,124	734,224	974,769	1,830,284	1,237,819
Other meats	11,767,466	2,924,697	2,595,683	3,905,213	2,338,412
Frankfurters	2,623,195	639,063	553,612	928,986	502,141
Lunch meats (cold cuts)	7,995,324	1,956,231	1,871,546	2,589,838	1,571,224
Bologna, liverwurst, salami	2,497,457	597,139	560,221	818,648	520,184
Other lunch meats	5,497,867	1,359,091	1,311,325	1,771,190	1,051,040
Lamb, organ meats, and others	1,148,946	329,403	170,261	386,389	265,047
Poultry	16,681,631	3,662,026	3,245,529	5,809,469	3,979,519
Fresh and frozen chicken	13,429,746	2,931,573	2,551,796	4,709,397	3,250,703

	total consumer units	Northeast	Midwest	South	West
Fresh and frozen whole chicken	$3,785,984	$842,916	$645,087	$1,294,712	$1,009,111
Fresh and frozen chicken parts	9,643,762	2,088,657	1,906,709	3,414,685	2,241,593
Other poultry	3,253,039	730,231	693,733	1,099,658	728,816
Fish and seafood	14,357,208	3,246,336	2,561,313	4,985,448	3,582,838
Canned fish and seafood	1,891,838	405,709	405,823	618,635	461,736
Fresh fish and shellfish	8,291,789	2,112,836	1,168,824	2,896,883	2,134,354
Frozen fish and shellfish	4,172,427	727,791	986,666	1,469,930	986,748
Eggs	4,307,393	849,571	809,267	1,502,990	1,149,893
Dairy products	**37,836,768**	**7,820,042**	**8,548,992**	**12,333,033**	**9,116,555**
Fresh milk and cream	14,595,995	2,888,318	3,327,487	4,854,448	3,520,070
Fresh milk, all types	12,986,778	2,534,959	3,008,909	4,349,043	3,087,812
Cream	1,609,216	353,359	318,578	505,405	432,258
Other dairy products	23,240,773	4,931,724	5,221,505	7,478,585	5,596,739
Butter	2,035,636	509,521	440,721	643,844	490,452
Cheese	11,194,146	2,306,706	2,639,306	3,514,278	2,723,150
Ice cream and related products	6,701,030	1,399,684	1,473,654	2,322,465	1,505,407
Miscellaneous dairy products	3,259,961	715,813	668,088	997,999	877,730
Fruits and vegetables	**61,763,910**	**12,996,656**	**12,483,495**	**20,206,272**	**16,093,928**
Fresh fruits	19,712,033	4,108,994	4,030,473	6,169,409	5,401,829
Apples	3,775,602	768,384	872,983	1,146,769	983,444
Bananas	3,277,264	645,053	649,053	1,060,813	923,726
Oranges	2,115,629	511,739	412,433	605,411	584,984
Citrus fruits, excl. oranges	1,631,134	326,075	281,300	542,184	484,099
Other fresh fruits	8,912,405	1,857,743	1,814,440	2,814,233	2,425,830
Fresh vegetables	19,836,618	4,215,024	3,758,690	6,361,571	5,512,117
Potatoes	3,473,369	746,546	715,677	1,292,233	722,463
Lettuce	2,549,368	596,252	552,461	771,125	648,006
Tomatoes	3,712,156	765,944	625,787	1,195,119	1,129,818
Other fresh vegetables	10,101,725	2,106,181	1,884,765	3,103,094	3,012,084
Processed fruits	12,503,437	2,724,615	2,540,163	4,052,330	3,188,190
Frozen fruits and fruit juices	1,331,208	211,838	339,728	385,149	391,853
Frozen orange juice	535,252	79,633	127,431	169,846	157,809
Frozen fruits	422,203	76,306	129,811	99,180	114,862
Frozen fruit juices, excl. orange	373,753	55,899	82,487	116,123	119,436
Canned fruits	1,841,082	350,697	444,158	600,866	443,439
Dried fruits	726,743	152,834	146,202	228,527	198,976
Fresh fruit juice	2,395,944	621,318	483,815	712,443	577,869
Canned and bottled fruit juice	6,208,460	1,388,150	1,126,259	2,125,345	1,575,798
Processed vegetables	9,711,822	1,948,023	2,154,168	3,622,550	1,991,538
Frozen vegetables	3,090,387	704,279	668,088	1,116,602	602,773
Canned and dried vegetables and juices	6,621,434	1,243,745	1,486,080	2,506,361	1,388,766
Canned beans	1,448,871	261,526	345,545	595,493	247,259
Canned corn	794,803	139,968	189,560	323,162	142,307
Canned miscellaneous vegetables	2,139,854	382,640	498,092	833,525	426,413
Dried peas	42,682	3,771	7,931	23,142	8,894
Dried beans	266,472	39,484	43,887	103,726	79,794
Dried miscellaneous vegetables	866,324	197,863	169,468	291,755	207,108
Dried processed vegetables	48,450	16,858	9,253	14,051	8,132
Fresh and canned vegetable juices	1,000,137	201,634	220,493	318,203	259,457
Sugar and other sweets	**13,736,592**	**2,785,616**	**3,111,488**	**4,409,791**	**3,421,472**
Candy and chewing gum	8,687,460	1,803,397	2,034,668	2,585,292	2,253,790
Sugar	1,948,363	333,174	385,202	795,506	437,849
Artificial sweeteners	654,069	134,867	146,995	260,761	112,321
Jams, preserves, other sweets	2,445,547	514,401	544,623	768,232	617,257
Fats and oils	**9,889,470**	**1,978,634**	**2,099,706**	**3,493,616**	**2,321,640**
Margarine	1,108,571	221,375	290,818	387,215	207,870
Fats and oils	3,032,709	633,513	571,061	1,150,901	681,550
Salad dressings	3,018,867	594,478	644,030	1,045,523	735,677
Nondairy cream and imitation milk	1,271,223	233,798	255,655	431,846	350,940
Peanut butter	1,458,100	295,242	338,142	477,717	345,603

	total consumer units	Northeast	Midwest	South	West
Miscellaneous foods	**$56,478,298**	**$10,496,522**	**$12,577,085**	**$19,915,757**	**$13,496,313**
Frozen prepared foods	12,088,155	2,125,257	2,988,552	4,389,542	2,579,572
Frozen meals	4,020,157	775,705	938,285	1,450,508	855,876
Other frozen prepared foods	8,067,999	1,349,775	2,050,267	2,939,034	1,723,950
Canned and packaged soups	4,059,378	795,447	942,515	1,343,476	976,329
Potato chips, nuts, and other snacks	12,190,822	2,286,077	2,989,345	4,167,213	2,738,905
Potato chips and other snacks	9,144,270	1,717,996	2,305,922	3,124,583	1,987,218
Nuts	3,046,552	568,303	683,158	1,043,043	751,941
Condiments and seasonings	10,407,418	1,935,601	2,266,001	3,611,392	2,596,598
Salt, spices, and other seasonings	2,395,944	429,887	470,596	884,355	614,970
Olives, pickles, relishes	1,316,212	231,802	321,486	423,995	337,217
Sauces and gravies	4,436,592	837,592	964,987	1,561,259	1,073,911
Baking needs and miscellaneous products	2,258,670	436,542	508,932	741,784	570,754
Other canned/packaged prepared foods	17,731,371	3,353,918	3,390,674	6,404,135	4,604,909
Prepared salads	2,365,952	454,287	495,713	800,879	615,225
Prepared desserts	1,280,452	273,282	256,449	430,193	320,699
Baby food	3,086,927	640,616	522,944	1,342,236	591,083
Miscellaneous prepared foods	10,973,816	1,978,856	2,112,925	3,827,108	3,066,212
Nonalcoholic beverages	**30,958,090**	**6,032,395**	**6,722,655**	**10,658,957**	**7,548,126**
Cola	10,182,474	1,761,473	2,606,787	3,565,934	2,238,543
Other carbonated drinks	5,264,848	1,010,612	1,259,506	1,825,739	1,166,157
Coffee	4,392,756	879,294	954,941	1,388,933	1,167,936
Roasted coffee	2,964,649	586,048	658,571	933,532	785,231
Instant and freeze-dried coffee	1,428,107	293,246	296,106	455,402	382,705
Noncarbonated fruit-flavored drinks, incl. nonfrozen lemonade	2,225,217	488,669	391,811	789,308	559,064
Tea	2,042,955	508,190	328,624	784,762	426,159
Other nonalcoholic beverages and ice	6,773,704	1,340,458	1,164,858	2,299,323	1,978,578
Food prepared by CU on trips	**4,185,116**	**760,399**	**935,112**	**1,219,914**	**1,270,092**
FOOD AWAY FROM HOME	**255,020,970**	**53,778,706**	**57,753,018**	**81,158,581**	**62,229,922**
Meals at restaurants, carry-outs, other	**211,328,731**	**43,557,019**	**47,753,109**	**69,071,845**	**50,845,600**
Lunch	75,922,705	14,520,115	16,403,457	26,551,726	18,467,663
• At fast food, take-out, delivery, concession stands, buffet, and cafeteria (other than employer and school cafeteria)	42,568,671	8,070,255	9,021,968	14,781,539	10,710,650
• At full-service restaurants	24,236,296	4,678,849	4,955,803	8,299,713	6,313,611
• At vending machines, mobile vendors	641,379	111,575	156,513	242,165	131,380
• At employer and school cafeterias	8,476,359	1,659,435	2,269,174	3,228,309	1,312,276
Dinner	85,076,204	19,505,076	19,245,278	26,206,662	20,044,477
• At fast food, take-out, delivery, concession stands, buffet, and cafeteria (other than employer and school cafeteria)	24,908,821	4,628,718	5,943,791	7,956,302	6,356,304
• At full-service restaurants	59,687,502	14,820,681	13,127,260	18,023,899	13,667,082
• At vending machines, mobile vendors	152,270	16,858	24,587	101,660	9,911
• At employer and school cafeterias	326,457	38,819	149,639	124,388	11,435
Snacks and nonalcoholic beverages	28,656,738	5,617,370	6,875,995	9,112,163	7,020,827
• At fast food, take-out, delivery, concession stands, buffet, and cafeteria (other than employer and school cafeteria)	20,794,073	4,288,224	4,812,774	6,329,750	5,342,111
• At full-service restaurants	3,075,391	466,931	773,576	1,037,671	794,633
• At vending machines, mobile vendors	3,614,103	564,532	972,125	1,371,577	702,388
• At employer and school cafeterias	1,172,017	297,904	317,520	373,165	181,696
Breakfast and brunch	21,674,239	3,914,458	5,228,643	7,201,295	5,312,379
• At fast food, take-out, delivery, concession stands, buffet, and cafeteria (other than employer and school cafeteria)	10,707,344	1,851,532	2,664,950	3,919,676	2,267,259
• At full-service restaurants	10,315,134	1,969,318	2,426,215	2,992,757	2,912,469
• At vending machines, mobile vendors	158,038	18,411	33,048	59,095	47,520
• At employer and school cafeterias	492,570	75,197	104,430	229,354	85,130
Board (including at school)	**3,835,587**	**884,175**	**714,884**	**1,331,492**	**905,175**
Catered affairs	**5,582,077**	**2,015,013**	**926,123**	**1,054,614**	**1,586,217**
Food on trips	**24,682,723**	**5,358,949**	**5,958,332**	**7,002,521**	**6,362,657**
School lunches	**6,560,296**	**1,312,065**	**1,847,223**	**2,093,111**	**1,308,464**
Meals as pay	**3,031,556**	**651,485**	**553,347**	**604,585**	**1,221,809**

	total consumer units	Northeast	Midwest	South	West
ALCOHOLIC BEVERAGES	$45,128,421	$9,476,816	$10,657,158	$14,267,456	$10,691,337
At home	27,694,668	5,211,661	6,589,143	9,181,589	6,692,504
Beer and ale	12,824,127	2,138,788	3,421,342	4,406,485	2,839,029
Whiskey	1,648,437	239,122	547,531	509,537	345,095
Wine	10,373,965	2,356,394	1,948,481	3,332,861	2,741,955
Other alcoholic beverages	2,849,293	477,357	671,525	932,292	766,172
Away from home	17,432,599	4,265,155	4,068,279	5,085,455	3,999,086
Beer and ale	6,959,427	1,764,356	1,715,826	1,991,865	1,473,642
• At fast food, take-out, delivery, concession stands, buffet, and cafeteria	1,234,309	249,548	408,996	208,278	359,326
• At full-service restaurants	5,328,294	1,444,048	1,230,689	1,551,341	1,093,987
Wine	2,166,386	523,495	462,665	723,188	456,908
• At fast food, take-out, delivery, concession stands, buffet and cafeteria	191,491	37,709	38,864	66,533	48,791
• At full-service restaurants	1,928,752	478,466	415,870	627,314	406,338
Other alcoholic beverages	4,470,045	1,067,841	960,493	1,437,284	1,003,520
• At fast food, take-out, delivery, concession stands, buffet, and cafeteria	391,702	185,994	208,596	273,158	222,355
• At full-service restaurants	3,401,848	850,236	718,849	1,059,986	771,762
Alcoholic beverages purchased on trips	3,835,741	909,462	929,031	933,119	1,064,763

Note: Numbers may not add to total because of rounding and missing subcategories.
Source: Calculations by New Strategist based on the 2003 Consumer Expenditure Survey

Table 5.24 Food and Alcohol: Market shares by region, 2003

(percentage of total annual spending on food and alcoholic beverages accounted for by consumer units by region, 2003)

	total consumer units	Northeast	Midwest	South	West
Share of total consumer units	100.0%	19.2%	22.9%	35.8%	22.0%
Share of total before-tax income	100.0	21.5	23.4	32.8	22.5
Share of total spending	100.0	19.9	22.6	33.0	24.5
Share of food spending	100.0	20.6	21.8	33.3	24.2
Share of alcoholic beverages spending	100.0	21.0	23.6	31.6	23.7
FOOD AT HOME	100.0	20.3	21.3	34.3	24.1
Cereals and bakery products	100.0	21.1	21.3	33.5	24.1
Cereals and cereal products	100.0	20.3	20.7	33.8	25.3
Flour	100.0	17.2	16.9	37.2	29.0
Prepared flour mixes	100.0	20.1	22.1	34.5	23.3
Ready-to-eat and cooked cereals	100.0	19.7	22.2	33.1	25.0
Rice	100.0	22.9	14.9	36.1	26.4
Pasta, cornmeal, and other cereal products	100.0	21.3	19.6	33.4	25.8
Bakery products	100.0	21.5	21.7	33.4	23.4
Bread	100.0	20.9	22.8	31.8	24.4
White bread	100.0	21.1	22.8	33.9	22.1
Bread, other than white	100.0	20.8	22.8	30.5	25.9
Crackers and cookies	100.0	20.5	21.5	34.9	23.1
Cookies	100.0	20.4	21.6	34.9	23.1
Crackers	100.0	20.6	21.3	34.9	23.3
Frozen and refrigerated bakery products	100.0	19.8	21.5	38.9	19.9
Other bakery products	100.0	23.0	21.0	32.3	23.6
Biscuits and rolls	100.0	24.4	22.5	30.4	22.7
Cakes and cupcakes	100.0	23.0	19.0	35.1	22.9
Bread and cracker products	100.0	25.9	19.6	32.1	22.4
Sweetrolls, coffee cakes, doughnuts	100.0	21.1	22.6	32.7	23.4
Pies, tarts, turnovers	100.0	21.7	19.1	28.0	31.2
Meats, poultry, fish, and eggs	100.0	20.7	20.4	36.3	22.7
Beef	100.0	18.8	21.0	38.2	22.2
Ground beef	100.0	19.2	22.4	38.0	20.5
Roast	100.0	15.6	23.9	36.7	23.8
Chuck roast	100.0	16.5	23.9	36.4	23.2
Round roast	100.0	16.8	25.4	35.1	22.5
Other roast	100.0	14.1	22.9	37.8	25.2
Steak	100.0	19.2	20.1	37.6	23.2
Round steak	100.0	16.7	18.5	41.8	23.3
Sirloin steak	100.0	21.4	19.9	35.5	23.4
Other steak	100.0	18.6	20.7	37.7	23.1
Other beef	100.0	20.7	14.4	43.8	21.5
Pork	100.0	18.9	21.6	38.0	21.5
Bacon	100.0	17.8	22.2	40.6	19.6
Pork chops	100.0	19.9	22.2	38.2	19.8
Ham	100.0	22.8	22.2	34.2	20.8
Ham, not canned	100.0	23.0	22.5	34.1	20.4
Canned ham	100.0	16.4	13.8	36.1	34.4
Sausage	100.0	18.8	21.2	39.8	20.3
Other pork	100.0	15.4	20.4	38.4	25.9
Other meats	100.0	24.9	22.1	33.2	19.9
Frankfurters	100.0	24.4	21.1	35.4	19.1
Lunch meats (cold cuts)	100.0	24.5	23.4	32.4	19.7
Bologna, liverwurst, salami	100.0	23.9	22.4	32.8	20.8
Other lunch meats	100.0	24.7	23.9	32.2	19.1
Lamb, organ meats, and others	100.0	28.7	14.8	33.6	23.1
Poultry	100.0	22.0	19.5	34.8	23.9
Fresh and frozen chicken	100.0	21.8	19.0	35.1	24.2

	total consumer units	Northeast	Midwest	South	West
Fresh and frozen whole chicken	100.0%	22.3%	17.0%	34.2%	26.7%
Fresh and frozen chicken parts	100.0	21.7	19.8	35.4	23.2
Other poultry	100.0	22.4	21.3	33.8	22.4
Fish and seafood	100.0	22.6	17.8	34.7	25.0
Canned fish and seafood	100.0	21.4	21.5	32.7	24.4
Fresh fish and shellfish	100.0	25.5	14.1	34.9	25.7
Frozen fish and shellfish	100.0	17.4	23.6	35.2	23.6
Eggs	100.0	19.7	18.8	34.9	26.7
Dairy products	**100.0**	**20.7**	**22.6**	**32.6**	**24.1**
Fresh milk and cream	100.0	19.8	22.8	33.3	24.1
Fresh milk, all types	100.0	19.5	23.2	33.5	23.8
Cream	100.0	22.0	19.8	31.4	26.9
Other dairy products	100.0	21.2	22.5	32.2	24.1
Butter	100.0	24.4	21.1	30.9	23.5
Cheese	100.0	20.6	23.6	31.4	24.3
Ice cream and related products	100.0	20.9	22.0	34.7	22.5
Miscellaneous dairy products	100.0	22.0	20.5	30.6	26.9
Fruits and vegetables	**100.0**	**21.0**	**20.2**	**32.7**	**26.1**
Fresh fruits	100.0	20.8	20.4	31.3	27.4
Apples	100.0	20.4	23.1	30.4	26.0
Bananas	100.0	19.7	19.8	32.4	28.2
Oranges	100.0	24.2	19.5	28.6	27.7
Citrus fruits, excl. oranges	100.0	20.0	17.2	33.2	29.7
Other fresh fruits	100.0	20.8	20.4	31.6	27.2
Fresh vegetables	100.0	21.2	18.9	32.1	27.8
Potatoes	100.0	21.5	20.6	37.2	20.8
Lettuce	100.0	23.4	20.9	30.2	25.4
Tomatoes	100.0	20.6	16.9	32.2	30.4
Other fresh vegetables	100.0	20.8	18.7	30.7	29.8
Processed fruits	100.0	21.8	20.3	32.4	25.5
Frozen fruits and fruit juices	100.0	15.9	25.5	28.9	29.4
Frozen orange juice	100.0	14.9	23.8	31.7	29.5
Frozen fruits	100.0	18.1	30.7	23.5	27.2
Frozen fruit juices, excl. orange	100.0	15.0	22.1	31.1	32.0
Canned fruits	100.0	19.0	24.1	32.6	24.1
Dried fruits	100.0	21.0	20.1	31.4	27.4
Fresh fruit juice	100.0	25.9	20.2	29.7	24.1
Canned and bottled fruit juice	100.0	22.4	18.1	34.2	25.4
Processed vegetables	100.0	20.1	22.2	37.3	20.5
Frozen vegetables	100.0	22.8	21.6	36.1	19.5
Canned and dried vegetables and juices	100.0	18.8	22.4	37.9	21.0
Canned beans	100.0	18.1	23.8	41.1	17.1
Canned corn	100.0	17.6	23.8	40.7	17.9
Canned miscellaneous vegetables	100.0	17.9	23.3	39.0	19.9
Dried peas	100.0	8.8	18.6	54.2	20.8
Dried beans	100.0	14.8	15.5	38.9	29.9
Dried miscellaneous vegetables	100.0	22.8	19.6	33.7	23.9
Dried processed vegetables	100.0	34.8	19.1	29.0	16.8
Fresh and canned vegetable juices	100.0	20.2	22.0	31.8	25.9
Sugar and other sweets	**100.0**	**20.3**	**22.7**	**32.1**	**24.9**
Candy and chewing gum	100.0	20.8	23.4	29.8	25.9
Sugar	100.0	17.1	19.8	40.8	22.5
Artificial sweeteners	100.0	20.6	22.5	39.9	17.2
Jams, preserves, other sweets	100.0	21.0	22.3	31.4	25.2
Fats and oils	**100.0**	**20.0**	**21.2**	**35.3**	**23.5**
Margarine	100.0	20.0	26.2	34.9	18.8
Fats and oils	100.0	20.9	18.8	37.9	22.5
Salad dressings	100.0	19.7	21.3	34.6	24.4
Nondairy cream and imitation milk	100.0	18.4	20.1	34.0	27.6
Peanut butter	100.0	20.2	23.2	32.8	23.7

	total consumer units	Northeast	Midwest	South	West
Miscellaneous foods	**100.0%**	**18.6%**	**22.3%**	**35.3%**	**23.9%**
Frozen prepared foods	100.0	17.6	24.7	36.3	21.3
Frozen meals	100.0	19.3	23.3	36.1	21.3
Other frozen prepared foods	100.0	16.7	25.4	36.4	21.4
Canned and packaged soups	100.0	19.6	23.2	33.1	24.1
Potato chips, nuts, and other snacks	100.0	18.8	24.5	34.2	22.5
Potato chips and other snacks	100.0	18.8	25.2	34.2	21.7
Nuts	100.0	18.7	22.4	34.2	24.7
Condiments and seasonings	100.0	18.6	21.8	34.7	24.9
Salt, spices, and other seasonings	100.0	17.9	19.6	36.9	25.7
Olives, pickles, relishes	100.0	17.6	24.4	32.2	25.6
Sauces and gravies	100.0	18.9	21.8	35.2	24.2
Baking needs and miscellaneous products	100.0	19.3	22.5	32.8	25.3
Other canned/packaged prepared foods	100.0	18.9	19.1	36.1	26.0
Prepared salads	100.0	19.2	21.0	33.9	26.0
Prepared desserts	100.0	21.3	20.0	33.6	25.0
Baby food	100.0	20.8	16.9	43.5	19.1
Miscellaneous prepared foods	100.0	18.0	19.3	34.9	27.9
Nonalcoholic beverages	**100.0**	**19.5**	**21.7**	**34.4**	**24.4**
Cola	100.0	17.3	25.6	35.0	22.0
Other carbonated drinks	100.0	19.2	23.9	34.7	22.1
Coffee	100.0	20.0	21.7	31.6	26.6
Roasted coffee	100.0	19.8	22.2	31.5	26.5
Instant and freeze-dried coffee	100.0	20.5	20.7	31.9	26.8
Noncarbonated fruit-flavored drinks, incl. nonfrozen lemonade	100.0	22.0	17.6	35.5	25.1
Tea	100.0	24.9	16.1	38.4	20.9
Other nonalcoholic beverages and ice	100.0	19.8	17.2	33.9	29.2
Food prepared by CU on trips	**100.0**	**18.2**	**22.3**	**29.1**	**30.3**
FOOD AWAY FROM HOME	**100.0**	**21.1**	**22.6**	**31.8**	**24.4**
Meals at restaurants, carry-outs, other	**100.0**	**20.6**	**22.6**	**32.7**	**24.1**
Lunch	100.0	19.1	21.6	35.0	24.3
• At fast food, take-out, delivery, concession stands, buffet, cafeteria (other than employer, school cafeteria)	100.0	19.0	21.2	34.7	25.2
• At full-service restaurants	100.0	19.3	20.4	34.2	26.1
• At vending machines, mobile vendors	100.0	17.4	24.4	37.8	20.5
• At employer and school cafeterias	100.0	19.6	26.8	38.1	15.5
Dinner	100.0	22.9	22.6	30.8	23.6
• At fast food, take-out, delivery, concession stands, buffet, cafeteria (other than employer, school cafeteria)	100.0	18.6	23.9	31.9	25.5
• At full-service restaurants	100.0	24.8	22.0	30.2	22.9
• At vending machines, mobile vendors	100.0	11.1	16.1	66.8	6.5
• At employer and school cafeterias	100.0	11.9	45.8	38.1	3.5
Snacks and nonalcoholic beverages	100.0	19.6	24.0	31.8	24.5
• At fast food, take-out, delivery, concession stands, buffet, cafeteria (other than employer, school cafeteria)	100.0	20.6	23.1	30.4	25.7
• At full-service restaurants	100.0	15.2	25.2	33.7	25.8
• At vending machines, mobile vendors	100.0	15.6	26.9	38.0	19.4
• At employer and school cafeterias	100.0	25.4	27.1	31.8	15.5
Breakfast and brunch	100.0	18.1	24.1	33.2	24.5
• At fast food, take-out, delivery, concession stands, buffet, cafeteria (other than employer, school cafeteria)	100.0	17.3	24.9	36.6	21.2
• At full-service restaurants	100.0	19.1	23.5	29.0	28.2
• At vending machines, mobile vendors	100.0	11.6	20.9	37.4	30.1
• At employer and school cafeterias	100.0	15.3	21.2	46.6	17.3
Board (including at school)	**100.0**	**23.1**	**18.6**	**34.7**	**23.6**
Catered affairs	**100.0**	**36.1**	**16.6**	**18.9**	**28.4**
Food on trips	**100.0**	**21.7**	**24.1**	**28.4**	**25.8**
School lunches	**100.0**	**20.0**	**28.2**	**31.9**	**19.9**
Meals as pay	**100.0**	**21.5**	**18.3**	**19.9**	**40.3**

	total consumer units	Northeast	Midwest	South	West
ALCOHOLIC BEVERAGES	**100.0%**	**21.0%**	**23.6%**	**31.6%**	**23.7%**
At home	**100.0**	**18.8**	**23.8**	**33.2**	**24.2**
Beer and ale	100.0	16.7	26.7	34.4	22.1
Whiskey	100.0	14.5	33.2	30.9	20.9
Wine	100.0	22.7	18.8	32.1	26.4
Other alcoholic beverages	100.0	16.8	23.6	32.7	26.9
Away from home	**100.0**	**24.5**	**23.3**	**29.2**	**22.9**
Beer and ale	100.0	25.4	24.7	28.6	21.2
• At fast food, take-out, delivery, concession stands, buffet, and cafeteria	100.0	20.2	33.1	16.9	29.1
• At full-service restaurants	100.0	27.1	23.1	29.1	20.5
Wine	100.0	24.2	21.4	33.4	21.1
• At fast food, take-out, delivery, concession stands, buffet and cafeteria	100.0	19.7	20.3	34.7	25.5
• At full-service restaurants	100.0	24.8	21.6	32.5	21.1
Other alcoholic beverages	100.0	23.9	21.5	32.2	22.4
• At fast food, take-out, delivery, concession stands, buffet, and cafeteria	100.0	21.0	23.4	30.6	24.9
• At full-service restaurants	100.0	25.0	21.1	31.2	22.7
Alcoholic beverages purchased on trips	100.0	23.7	24.2	24.3	27.8

Note: Numbers may not add to total because of rounding.
Source: Calculations by New Strategist based on the 2003 Consumer Expenditure Survey

Table 5.25 Food and Alcohol: Average spending by education, 2003

(average annual spending of consumer units (CU) on food and alcoholic beverages, by education of consumer unit reference person, 2003)

	total consumer units	less than high school graduate	high school graduate	some college	associate's degree	college graduate total	bachelor's degree	master's, professional, doctorate
Number of consumer units (000)	115,356	17,721	31,552	24,514	10,981	30,589	19,557	11,032
Average number of persons per CU	2.5	2.6	2.5	2.3	2.6	2.5	2.5	2.4
Average before-tax income of CU	$51,128.00	$25,028.00	$40,113.00	$45,113.00	$54,087.00	$81,842.00	$74,921.00	$93,948.00
Average spending of CU, total	40,817.33	23,901.14	33,955.56	37,912.41	44,547.12	58,480.00	54,725.85	65,202.73
Food, average spending	5,339.50	4,086.37	4,700.70	5,136.20	5,783.42	6,641.10	6,381.45	7,126.56
Alcoholic beverages, average spending	391.21	160.69	254.51	401.47	453.45	619.98	564.87	724.75
FOOD AT HOME	3128.78	2913.47	2986.08	2906.76	3297.80	3490.87	3413.98	3636.72
Cereals and bakery products	441.72	407.94	424.33	422.74	456.07	485.31	481.54	492.54
Cereals and cereal products	150.14	153.16	139.54	138.56	154.59	166.54	166.96	165.74
Flour	7.32	10.26	7.01	7.33	3.95	7.26	7.10	7.56
Prepared flour mixes	12.79	11.66	11.91	12.85	14.54	13.66	13.47	14.03
Ready-to-eat and cooked cereals	86.21	81.29	80.28	80.52	94.91	96.13	99.44	89.81
Rice	16.05	21.96	13.98	12.14	16.56	18.00	16.71	20.46
Pasta, cornmeal, and other cereal products	27.75	27.99	26.37	25.72	24.64	31.49	30.25	33.87
Bakery products	291.58	254.79	284.79	284.18	301.48	318.77	314.57	326.80
Bread	82.55	81.53	82.27	73.92	88.36	87.80	85.79	91.63
White bread	33.50	40.48	35.23	30.56	33.84	30.34	30.61	29.82
Bread, other than white	49.06	41.05	47.04	43.36	54.52	57.46	55.18	61.81
Crackers and cookies	69.58	58.45	66.58	65.44	70.99	80.63	78.35	85.00
Cookies	45.06	38.73	44.21	41.95	46.81	50.71	49.45	53.12
Crackers	24.52	19.72	22.37	23.49	24.18	29.92	28.90	31.88
Frozen and refrigerated bakery products	24.56	20.51	23.31	26.38	27.56	25.58	26.54	23.74
Other bakery products	114.89	94.30	112.62	118.44	114.57	124.76	123.89	126.43
Biscuits and rolls	37.24	24.35	35.35	33.63	42.57	46.43	43.91	51.24
Cakes and cupcakes	36.71	32.46	37.18	41.45	33.57	35.82	36.66	34.21
Bread and cracker products	3.57	2.36	3.40	3.18	5.43	4.04	4.16	3.83
Sweetrolls, coffee cakes, doughnuts	27.65	25.00	27.24	30.62	23.14	28.58	29.66	26.53
Pies, tarts, turnovers	9.72	10.12	9.44	9.56	9.85	9.89	9.51	10.62
Meats, poultry, fish, and eggs	824.58	860.27	839.14	757.68	941.49	804.63	793.96	825.04
Beef	245.55	235.72	262.28	211.94	353.00	224.36	231.69	210.34
Ground beef	89.27	94.83	97.95	84.20	119.66	71.94	77.00	62.27
Roast	39.63	39.96	45.81	34.62	40.68	36.43	39.71	30.15
Chuck roast	13.37	13.06	15.79	12.73	12.32	11.85	12.59	10.42
Round roast	9.78	10.13	13.44	6.31	7.05	9.20	10.58	6.55
Other roast	16.48	16.76	16.58	15.58	21.32	15.39	16.54	13.18
Steak	94.16	84.34	95.85	74.33	151.38	93.93	98.02	86.12
Round steak	15.65	17.94	13.72	11.86	34.65	13.38	13.10	13.92
Sirloin steak	31.35	25.13	31.67	23.61	63.85	29.63	32.50	24.16
Other steak	47.17	41.27	50.46	38.86	52.88	50.92	52.42	48.04
Other beef	22.49	16.60	22.67	18.79	41.27	22.05	16.96	31.79
Pork	170.61	212.43	181.82	163.81	167.86	144.53	144.03	145.51
Bacon	31.15	37.06	32.75	30.33	35.12	26.00	27.09	23.91
Pork chops	34.14	46.29	37.72	31.93	35.32	25.77	25.83	25.64
Ham	38.15	53.37	41.61	32.71	30.15	33.58	31.98	36.64
Ham, not canned	37.04	51.97	40.43	31.77	29.44	32.46	30.51	36.19
Canned ham	1.10	1.41	1.18	0.93	0.72	1.12	1.47	0.45
Sausage	25.82	33.91	27.30	27.35	21.90	20.48	20.50	20.44
Other pork	41.36	41.79	42.44	41.49	45.37	38.71	38.62	38.87
Other meats	102.01	97.72	103.55	98.19	110.73	102.60	103.27	101.31
Frankfurters	22.74	26.73	25.09	20.73	24.52	19.28	20.51	16.92
Lunch meats (cold cuts)	69.31	64.35	71.46	66.76	77.95	68.72	68.24	69.63
Bologna, liverwurst, salami	21.65	24.93	25.12	21.02	20.70	17.25	17.18	17.37
Other lunch meats	47.66	39.42	46.34	45.74	57.24	51.47	51.06	52.26
Lamb, organ meats, and others	9.96	6.64	7.00	10.69	8.26	14.60	14.52	14.75
Poultry	144.61	156.66	143.11	139.47	152.22	141.67	137.23	150.16
Fresh and frozen chicken	116.42	130.40	114.18	114.44	122.72	111.39	109.31	115.38

	total consumer units	less than high school graduate	high school graduate	some college	associate's degree	college graduate total	bachelor's degree	master's, professional, doctorate
Fresh and frozen whole chicken	$32.82	$44.77	$32.79	$29.10	$35.82	$28.81	$27.83	$30.69
Fresh and frozen chicken parts	83.60	85.62	81.39	85.34	86.90	82.58	81.48	84.69
Other poultry	28.20	26.26	28.93	25.03	29.51	30.27	27.92	34.78
Fish and seafood	124.46	112.45	110.76	111.40	118.36	155.69	141.45	182.94
Canned fish and seafood	16.40	14.50	16.56	16.47	16.89	16.86	15.81	18.87
Fresh fish and shellfish	71.88	62.81	59.72	62.05	73.03	95.55	83.22	119.13
Frozen fish and shellfish	36.17	35.14	34.39	32.87	28.44	43.28	42.41	44.94
Eggs	37.34	45.29	37.62	32.83	39.33	35.79	36.30	34.79
Dairy products	**328.00**	**290.40**	**306.83**	**301.90**	**344.04**	**382.00**	**374.31**	**396.70**
Fresh milk and cream	126.53	132.29	123.00	115.62	137.59	131.85	133.17	129.30
Fresh milk, all types	112.58	122.14	111.15	102.11	122.97	113.78	116.28	108.99
Cream	13.95	10.15	11.85	13.51	14.62	18.07	16.89	20.31
Other dairy products	201.47	158.11	183.83	186.28	206.45	250.15	241.14	267.39
Butter	18.08	16.63	17.81	16.47	20.24	19.55	19.36	19.93
Cheese	97.04	72.90	90.79	87.85	102.06	120.33	112.67	134.98
Ice cream and related products	58.09	47.50	54.55	57.55	56.42	67.77	69.55	64.37
Miscellaneous dairy products	28.26	21.09	20.67	24.41	27.72	42.50	39.56	48.12
Fruits and vegetables	**535.42**	**502.20**	**479.03**	**479.11**	**519.50**	**655.14**	**620.97**	**720.50**
Fresh fruits	170.88	155.89	147.48	148.31	161.08	221.55	202.36	258.25
Apples	32.73	30.77	29.05	28.86	31.28	40.71	37.28	47.26
Bananas	28.41	30.91	26.84	23.94	29.50	31.71	30.44	34.14
Oranges	18.34	18.85	17.13	15.24	13.88	22.96	22.10	24.61
Citrus fruits, excl. oranges	14.14	14.03	11.62	12.66	11.08	18.80	16.87	22.50
Other fresh fruits	77.26	61.33	62.84	67.61	75.33	107.38	95.68	129.75
Fresh vegetables	171.96	166.82	147.54	156.88	160.26	214.05	201.99	237.11
Potatoes	30.11	33.18	30.39	27.90	29.94	30.00	28.91	32.10
Lettuce	22.10	20.16	18.69	20.96	21.94	27.41	26.00	30.12
Tomatoes	32.18	36.64	27.27	28.62	31.54	37.81	34.77	43.61
Other fresh vegetables	87.57	76.84	71.19	79.40	76.84	118.83	112.32	131.29
Processed fruits	108.39	93.05	100.51	99.73	107.68	130.43	127.39	136.26
Frozen fruits and fruit juices	11.54	11.10	9.73	10.11	11.91	14.54	15.13	13.40
Frozen orange juice	4.64	5.71	4.01	3.95	5.64	4.95	5.03	4.80
Frozen fruits	3.66	2.40	2.79	3.02	3.06	5.82	6.51	4.50
Frozen fruit juices, excl. orange	3.24	3.00	2.93	3.13	3.21	3.76	3.58	4.11
Canned fruits	15.96	11.91	17.24	13.76	15.55	18.33	17.71	19.51
Dried fruits	6.30	4.61	5.92	5.94	5.34	8.05	7.51	9.09
Fresh fruit juice	20.77	19.13	17.76	19.14	16.87	27.06	25.44	30.15
Canned and bottled fruit juice	53.82	46.30	49.87	50.77	53.01	62.45	61.59	64.10
Processed vegetables	84.19	86.45	83.50	74.19	90.48	89.10	89.22	88.87
Frozen vegetables	26.79	22.20	26.64	23.54	33.06	29.60	29.37	30.03
Canned and dried vegetables and juices	57.40	64.24	56.86	50.64	57.42	59.50	59.85	58.84
Canned beans	12.56	13.54	13.66	10.99	13.26	11.88	11.31	12.96
Canned corn	6.89	8.88	8.06	6.56	6.60	5.04	5.14	4.85
Canned miscellaneous vegetables	18.55	16.97	18.78	16.45	18.51	20.61	21.16	19.57
Dried peas	0.37	0.24	0.41	0.30	0.36	0.46	0.52	0.34
Dried beans	2.31	5.18	2.06	1.43	1.56	2.02	1.57	2.89
Dried miscellaneous vegetables	7.51	8.82	6.61	6.88	5.73	8.79	9.52	7.38
Dried processed vegetables	0.42	0.77	0.24	0.16	1.51	0.27	0.31	0.20
Fresh and canned vegetable juices	8.67	9.73	6.96	7.64	9.87	10.28	10.22	10.40
Sugar and other sweets	**119.08**	**105.37**	**120.15**	**106.00**	**124.76**	**132.37**	**133.56**	**130.09**
Candy and chewing gum	75.31	56.95	74.92	66.80	78.90	89.72	89.38	90.37
Sugar	16.89	23.50	18.02	14.41	16.99	14.26	14.70	13.40
Artificial sweeteners	5.67	4.53	6.72	5.29	4.91	5.67	6.18	4.69
Jams, preserves, other sweets	21.20	20.39	20.49	19.50	23.96	22.72	23.30	21.62
Fats and oils	**85.73**	**91.23**	**84.19**	**79.40**	**89.88**	**87.93**	**85.90**	**91.81**
Margarine	9.61	10.03	10.72	9.72	8.77	8.44	8.98	7.41
Fats and oils	26.29	37.60	25.33	21.30	24.03	26.08	24.31	29.46
Salad dressings	26.17	22.54	24.55	25.76	29.61	28.74	27.78	30.56
Nondairy cream and imitation milk	11.02	9.31	10.97	10.45	14.74	11.17	11.46	10.63
Peanut butter	12.64	11.74	12.52	12.18	12.72	13.50	13.38	13.74

	total consumer units	less than high school graduate	high school graduate	some college	associate's degree	college graduate total	college graduate bachelor's degree	college graduate master's, professional, doctorate
Miscellaneous foods	$489.60	$387.18	$451.46	$468.34	$501.36	$590.37	$588.78	$593.40
Frozen prepared foods	104.79	81.69	103.54	103.46	106.70	117.71	124.57	104.57
Frozen meals	34.85	28.70	33.75	30.50	37.94	41.19	44.97	33.94
Other frozen prepared foods	69.94	52.99	69.79	72.96	68.76	76.52	79.60	70.63
Canned and packaged soups	35.19	27.76	36.54	33.59	33.88	38.99	37.27	42.29
Potato chips, nuts, and other snacks	105.68	74.78	95.88	99.72	126.37	128.73	126.22	133.51
Potato chips and other snacks	79.27	55.49	75.05	78.20	96.54	90.63	94.04	84.10
Nuts	26.41	19.29	20.82	21.52	29.83	38.10	32.19	49.41
Condiments and seasonings	90.22	70.14	83.27	83.50	90.88	111.80	112.54	110.39
Salt, spices, and other seasonings	20.77	18.95	18.92	19.81	19.84	24.55	23.32	26.92
Olives, pickles, relishes	11.41	9.13	11.44	9.49	9.60	14.42	14.66	13.98
Sauces and gravies	38.46	28.16	36.60	37.39	42.44	44.92	45.61	43.62
Baking needs and miscellaneous products	19.58	13.90	16.30	16.81	19.01	27.90	28.96	25.88
Other canned/packaged prepared foods	153.71	132.81	132.24	148.07	143.52	193.14	188.18	202.63
Prepared salads	20.51	9.95	17.06	19.80	21.08	29.52	27.87	32.67
Prepared desserts	11.10	10.05	10.16	10.60	10.72	13.05	13.14	12.88
Baby food	26.76	33.07	22.83	30.56	24.93	25.53	25.08	26.39
Miscellaneous prepared foods	95.13	79.74	81.84	86.98	86.67	124.78	121.82	130.45
Nonalcoholic beverages	268.37	254.51	257.84	256.74	284.63	289.32	279.77	307.58
Cola	88.27	96.52	94.52	82.81	89.83	81.29	80.11	83.56
Other carbonated drinks	45.64	42.09	48.11	45.54	50.07	43.54	42.73	45.08
Coffee	38.08	31.53	32.03	35.91	41.28	48.07	45.22	53.53
Roasted coffee	25.70	20.10	21.33	23.86	29.54	33.07	31.14	36.77
Instant and freeze-dried coffee	12.38	11.43	10.70	12.05	11.73	14.99	14.08	16.75
Noncarbonated fruit-flavored drinks, incl. nonfrozen lemonade	19.29	18.73	20.39	19.38	18.71	18.55	19.44	16.85
Tea	17.71	14.35	16.74	17.88	19.44	19.68	18.05	22.80
Other nonalcoholic beverages and ice	58.72	50.72	44.80	55.18	64.82	77.56	73.96	84.45
Food prepared by CU on trips	36.28	14.37	23.10	34.86	36.07	63.79	55.18	79.05
FOOD AWAY FROM HOME	2210.73	1172.90	1714.62	2229.44	2485.62	3150.23	2967.47	3489.85
Meals at restaurants, carry-outs, other	1831.97	1036.65	1455.84	1877.83	2075.36	2496.77	2385.04	2710.48
Lunch	658.16	400.89	538.89	698.72	743.74	849.99	826.91	894.11
• At fast food, take-out, delivery, concession stands, buffet, cafeteria (other than employer, school cafeteria)	369.02	252.32	311.64	415.03	417.93	436.30	442.12	425.19
• At full-service restaurants	210.10	112.42	156.31	189.15	212.42	327.30	295.64	387.84
• At vending machines, mobile vendors	5.56	5.22	6.68	6.11	9.92	2.82	2.83	2.81
• At employer and school cafeterias	73.48	30.93	64.26	88.43	103.48	83.56	86.32	78.28
Dinner	737.51	349.03	547.17	715.21	825.18	1111.03	1019.58	1285.92
• At fast food, take-out, delivery, concession stands, buffet, cafeteria (other than employer, school cafeteria)	215.93	144.64	188.18	228.65	258.64	256.73	266.44	238.14
• At full-service restaurants	517.42	200.46	356.56	475.93	565.15	852.12	750.73	1046.03
• At vending machines, mobile vendors	1.32	1.28	1.23	3.22	–	0.45	0.50	0.36
• At employer and school cafeterias	2.83	2.64	1.20	7.40	1.39	1.73	1.91	1.39
Snacks and nonalcoholic beverages	248.42	149.50	209.16	266.91	296.21	308.71	307.47	311.08
• At fast food, take-out, delivery, concession stands, buffet, cafeteria (other than employer, school cafeteria)	180.26	100.74	146.23	195.96	214.58	231.94	232.78	230.34
• At full-service restaurants	26.66	18.16	23.63	26.09	26.30	34.45	31.57	39.96
• At vending machines, mobile vendors	31.33	24.51	30.72	34.73	42.02	29.50	30.56	27.47
• At employer and school cafeterias	10.16	6.09	8.59	10.13	13.31	12.82	12.57	13.30
Breakfast and brunch	187.89	137.23	160.62	196.98	210.23	227.05	231.06	219.36
• At fast food, take-out, delivery, concession stands, buffet, cafeteria (other than employer, school cafeteria)	92.82	70.42	86.38	101.08	107.38	99.87	108.15	84.01
• At full-service restaurants	89.42	62.63	68.65	88.55	95.51	122.53	118.67	129.89
• At vending machines, mobile vendors	1.37	1.28	2.02	1.72	0.52	0.75	0.90	0.48
• At employer and school cafeterias	4.27	2.90	3.56	5.63	6.81	3.90	3.34	4.97
Board (including at school)	33.25	6.84	13.38	40.79	20.14	67.73	48.18	102.38
Catered affairs	48.39	11.71	34.98	39.42	64.85	84.75	85.72	83.01
Food on trips	213.97	52.52	131.84	192.56	213.55	409.51	356.59	503.32
School lunches	56.87	23.79	55.53	52.79	81.18	71.96	72.11	71.71
Meals as pay	26.28	41.38	23.05	26.05	30.54	19.51	19.84	18.94

	total consumer units	less than high school graduate	high school graduate	some college	associate's degree	college graduate total	bachelor's degree	master's, professional, doctorate
ALCOHOLIC BEVERAGES	**$391.21**	**$160.69**	**$254.51**	**$401.47**	**$453.45**	**$619.98**	**$564.87**	**$724.75**
At home	**240.08**	**113.96**	**174.21**	**251.00**	**282.18**	**348.17**	**317.51**	**406.81**
Beer and ale	111.17	80.48	111.65	124.83	125.78	111.21	121.28	91.95
Whiskey	14.29	7.15	13.92	12.57	22.42	16.79	14.88	20.45
Wine	89.93	17.68	33.53	84.93	109.82	180.46	142.23	253.58
Other alcoholic beverages	24.70	8.64	15.12	28.57	24.16	39.71	39.12	40.83
Away from home	**151.12**	**46.73**	**80.29**	**150.47**	**171.28**	**271.81**	**247.36**	**317.94**
Beer and ale	60.33	21.95	30.36	63.29	72.60	103.83	95.00	120.73
• At fast food, take-out, delivery, concession stands, buffet, and cafeteria	10.70	9.43	4.83	12.77	13.69	14.91	18.03	8.95
• At full-service restaurants	46.19	10.25	25.53	48.54	50.06	81.97	76.77	91.93
Wine	18.78	4.33	10.60	18.62	20.70	33.74	28.89	43.00
• At fast food, take-out, delivery, concession stands, buffet and cafeteria	1.66	0.97	0.97	1.94	2.96	2.10	2.55	1.24
• At full-service restaurants	16.72	3.11	9.53	16.48	16.80	30.77	26.11	39.67
Other alcoholic beverages	38.75	15.42	20.06	36.93	47.19	67.97	61.77	79.86
• At fast food, take-out, delivery, concession stands, buffet, and cafeteria	7.73	7.37	4.86	8.74	12.21	8.74	9.84	6.65
• At full-service restaurants	29.49	7.04	15.20	27.27	31.08	56.21	51.87	64.51
Alcoholic beverages purchased on trips	33.26	5.04	19.27	31.58	30.78	66.27	61.71	74.34

Note: Subcategories may not add to total because some are not shown. (–) means sample is too small to make a reliable estimate.
Source: Bureau of Labor Statistics, unpublished tables from the 2003 Consumer Expenditure Survey

Table 5.26 Food and Alcohol: Indexed spending by education, 2003

(indexed average annual spending of consumer units (CU) on food and alcoholic beverages, by education of consumer unit reference person, 2003; index definition: an index of 100 is the average for all consumer units; an index of 132 means that spending by consumer units in that group is 32 percent above the average for all consumer units; an index of 68 indicates spending that is 32 percent below the average for all consumer units)

	total consumer units	less than high school graduate	high school graduate	some college	associate's degree	college graduate total	bachelor's degree	master's, professional, doctorate
Average spending of CU, total	$40,817	$23,901	$33,956	$37,912	$44,547	$58,480	$54,726	$65,203
Average spending of CU, index	100	59	83	93	109	143	134	160
Food, spending index	100	77	88	96	108	124	120	133
Alcoholic beverages, spending index	100	41	65	103	116	158	144	185
FOOD AT HOME	100	93	95	93	105	112	109	116
Cereals and bakery products	100	92	96	96	103	110	109	112
Cereals and cereal products	100	102	93	92	103	111	111	110
Flour	100	140	96	100	54	99	97	103
Prepared flour mixes	100	91	93	100	114	107	105	110
Ready-to-eat and cooked cereals	100	94	93	93	110	112	115	104
Rice	100	137	87	76	103	112	104	127
Pasta, cornmeal, and other cereal products	100	101	95	93	89	113	109	122
Bakery products	100	87	98	97	103	109	108	112
Bread	100	99	100	90	107	106	104	111
White bread	100	121	105	91	101	91	91	89
Bread, other than white	100	84	96	88	111	117	112	126
Crackers and cookies	100	84	96	94	102	116	113	122
Cookies	100	86	98	93	104	113	110	118
Crackers	100	80	91	96	99	122	118	130
Frozen and refrigerated bakery products	100	84	95	107	112	104	108	97
Other bakery products	100	82	98	103	100	109	108	110
Biscuits and rolls	100	65	95	90	114	125	118	138
Cakes and cupcakes	100	88	101	113	91	98	100	93
Bread and cracker products	100	66	95	89	152	113	117	107
Sweetrolls, coffee cakes, doughnuts	100	90	99	111	84	103	107	96
Pies, tarts, turnovers	100	104	97	98	101	102	98	109
Meats, poultry, fish, and eggs	100	104	102	92	114	98	96	100
Beef	100	96	107	86	144	91	94	86
Ground beef	100	106	110	94	134	81	86	70
Roast	100	101	116	87	103	92	100	76
Chuck roast	100	98	118	95	92	89	94	78
Round roast	100	104	137	65	72	94	108	67
Other roast	100	102	101	95	129	93	100	80
Steak	100	90	102	79	161	100	104	91
Round steak	100	115	88	76	221	85	84	89
Sirloin steak	100	80	101	75	204	95	104	77
Other steak	100	87	107	82	112	108	111	102
Other beef	100	74	101	84	184	98	75	141
Pork	100	125	107	96	98	85	84	85
Bacon	100	119	105	97	113	83	87	77
Pork chops	100	136	110	94	103	75	76	75
Ham	100	140	109	86	79	88	84	96
Ham, not canned	100	140	109	86	79	88	82	98
Canned ham	100	128	107	85	65	102	134	41
Sausage	100	131	106	106	85	79	79	79
Other pork	100	101	103	100	110	94	93	94
Other meats	100	96	102	96	109	101	101	99
Frankfurters	100	118	110	91	108	85	90	74
Lunch meats (cold cuts)	100	93	103	96	112	99	98	100
Bologna, liverwurst, salami	100	115	116	97	96	80	79	80
Other lunch meats	100	83	97	96	120	108	107	110
Lamb, organ meats, and others	100	67	70	107	83	147	146	148
Poultry	100	108	99	96	105	98	95	104
Fresh and frozen chicken	100	112	98	98	105	96	94	99

	total consumer units	less than high school graduate	high school graduate	some college	associate's degree	college graduate total	bachelor's degree	master's, professional, doctorate
Fresh and frozen whole chicken	100	136	100	89	109	88	85	94
Fresh and frozen chicken parts	100	102	97	102	104	99	97	101
Other poultry	100	93	103	89	105	107	99	123
Fish and seafood	100	90	89	90	95	125	114	147
Canned fish and seafood	100	88	102	100	103	103	96	115
Fresh fish and shellfish	100	87	83	86	102	133	116	166
Frozen fish and shellfish	100	97	95	91	79	120	117	124
Eggs	100	121	101	88	105	96	97	93
Dairy products	**100**	**89**	**94**	**92**	**105**	**116**	**114**	**121**
Fresh milk and cream	100	105	97	91	109	104	105	102
Fresh milk, all types	100	108	99	91	109	101	103	97
Cream	100	73	85	97	105	130	121	146
Other dairy products	100	78	91	92	102	124	120	133
Butter	100	92	99	91	112	108	107	110
Cheese	100	75	94	91	105	124	116	139
Ice cream and related products	100	82	94	99	97	117	120	111
Miscellaneous dairy products	100	75	73	85	98	150	140	170
Fruits and vegetables	**100**	**94**	**89**	**89**	**97**	**122**	**116**	**135**
Fresh fruits	100	91	86	87	94	130	118	151
Apples	100	94	89	88	96	124	114	144
Bananas	100	109	94	84	104	112	107	120
Oranges	100	103	93	83	76	125	121	134
Citrus fruits, excl. oranges	100	99	82	90	78	133	119	159
Other fresh fruits	100	79	81	88	98	139	124	168
Fresh vegetables	100	97	86	91	93	124	117	138
Potatoes	100	110	101	93	99	100	96	107
Lettuce	100	91	85	95	99	124	118	136
Tomatoes	100	114	85	89	98	117	108	136
Other fresh vegetables	100	88	81	91	88	136	128	150
Processed fruits	100	86	93	92	99	120	118	126
Frozen fruits and fruit juices	100	96	84	88	103	126	131	116
Frozen orange juice	100	123	86	85	122	107	108	103
Frozen fruits	100	66	76	83	84	159	178	123
Frozen fruit juices, excl. orange	100	93	90	97	99	116	110	127
Canned fruits	100	75	103	86	97	115	111	122
Dried fruits	100	73	94	94	85	128	119	144
Fresh fruit juice	100	92	86	92	81	130	122	145
Canned and bottled fruit juice	100	86	93	94	108	116	114	119
Processed vegetables	100	103	99	88	107	106	106	106
Frozen vegetables	100	83	99	88	123	110	110	112
Canned and dried vegetables and juices	100	112	99	88	100	104	104	103
Canned beans	100	108	109	88	106	95	90	103
Canned corn	100	129	117	95	96	73	75	70
Canned miscellaneous vegetables	100	91	101	89	100	111	114	105
Dried peas	100	65	111	81	97	124	141	92
Dried beans	100	224	89	62	68	87	68	125
Dried miscellaneous vegetables	100	117	88	92	76	117	127	98
Dried processed vegetables	100	183	57	38	360	64	74	48
Fresh and canned vegetable juices	100	112	80	88	114	119	118	120
Sugar and other sweets	**100**	**88**	**101**	**89**	**105**	**111**	**112**	**109**
Candy and chewing gum	100	76	99	89	105	119	119	120
Sugar	100	139	107	85	101	84	87	79
Artificial sweeteners	100	80	119	93	87	100	109	83
Jams, preserves, other sweets	100	96	97	92	113	107	110	102
Fats and oils	**100**	**106**	**98**	**93**	**105**	**103**	**100**	**107**
Margarine	100	104	112	101	91	88	93	77
Fats and oils	100	143	96	81	91	99	92	112
Salad dressings	100	86	94	98	113	110	106	117
Nondairy cream and imitation milk	100	84	100	95	134	101	104	96
Peanut butter	100	93	99	96	101	107	106	109

	total consumer units	less than high school graduate	high school graduate	some college	associate's degree	college graduate total	bachelor's degree	master's, professional, doctorate
Miscellaneous foods	100	79	92	96	102	121	120	121
Frozen prepared foods	100	78	99	99	102	112	119	100
Frozen meals	100	82	97	88	109	118	129	97
Other frozen prepared foods	100	76	100	104	98	109	114	101
Canned and packaged soups	100	79	104	95	96	111	106	120
Potato chips, nuts, and other snacks	100	71	91	94	120	122	119	126
Potato chips and other snacks	100	70	95	99	122	114	119	106
Nuts	100	73	79	81	113	144	122	187
Condiments and seasonings	100	78	92	93	101	124	125	122
Salt, spices, and other seasonings	100	91	91	95	96	118	112	130
Olives, pickles, relishes	100	80	100	83	84	126	128	123
Sauces and gravies	100	73	95	97	110	117	119	113
Baking needs and miscellaneous products	100	71	83	86	97	142	148	132
Other canned/packaged prepared foods	100	86	86	96	93	126	122	132
Prepared salads	100	49	83	97	103	144	136	159
Prepared desserts	100	91	92	95	97	118	118	116
Baby food	100	124	85	114	93	95	94	99
Miscellaneous prepared foods	100	84	86	91	91	131	128	137
Nonalcoholic beverages	100	95	96	96	106	108	104	115
Cola	100	109	107	94	102	92	91	95
Other carbonated drinks	100	92	105	100	110	95	94	99
Coffee	100	83	84	94	108	126	119	141
Roasted coffee	100	78	83	93	115	129	121	143
Instant and freeze-dried coffee	100	92	86	97	95	121	114	135
Noncarbonated fruit-flavored drinks, incl. nonfrozen lemonade	100	97	106	100	97	96	101	87
Tea	100	81	95	101	110	111	102	129
Other nonalcoholic beverages and ice	100	86	76	94	110	132	126	144
Food prepared by CU on trips	100	40	64	96	99	176	152	218
FOOD AWAY FROM HOME	100	53	78	101	112	142	134	158
Meals at restaurants, carry-outs, other	100	57	79	103	113	136	130	148
Lunch	100	61	82	106	113	129	126	136
• At fast food, take-out, delivery, concession stands, buffet, cafeteria (other than employer, school cafeteria)	100	68	84	112	113	118	120	115
• At full-service restaurants	100	54	74	90	101	156	141	185
• At vending machines, mobile vendors	100	94	120	110	178	51	51	51
• At employer and school cafeterias	100	42	87	120	141	114	117	107
Dinner	100	47	74	97	112	151	138	174
• At fast food, take-out, delivery, concession stands, buffet, cafeteria (other than employer, school cafeteria)	100	67	87	106	120	119	123	110
• At full-service restaurants	100	39	69	92	109	165	145	202
• At vending machines, mobile vendors	100	97	93	244	–	34	38	27
• At employer and school cafeterias	100	93	42	261	49	61	67	49
Snacks and nonalcoholic beverages	100	60	84	107	119	124	124	125
• At fast food, take-out, delivery, concession stands, buffet, cafeteria (other than employer, school cafeteria)	100	56	81	109	119	129	129	128
• At full-service restaurants	100	68	89	98	99	129	118	150
• At vending machines, mobile vendors	100	78	98	111	134	94	98	88
• At employer and school cafeterias	100	60	85	100	131	126	124	131
Breakfast and brunch	100	73	85	105	112	121	123	117
• At fast food, take-out, delivery, concession stands, buffet, cafeteria (other than employer, school cafeteria)	100	76	93	109	116	108	117	91
• At full-service restaurants	100	70	77	99	107	137	133	145
• At vending machines, mobile vendors	100	93	147	126	38	55	66	35
• At employer and school cafeterias	100	68	83	132	159	91	78	116
Board (including at school)	100	21	40	123	61	204	145	308
Catered affairs	100	24	72	81	134	175	177	172
Food on trips	100	25	62	90	100	191	167	235
School lunches	100	42	98	93	143	127	127	126
Meals as pay	100	157	88	99	116	74	75	72

	total consumer units	less than high school graduate	high school graduate	some college	associate's degree	college graduate total	bachelor's degree	master's, professional, doctorate
ALCOHOLIC BEVERAGES	**100**	**41**	**65**	**103**	**116**	**158**	**144**	**185**
At home	**100**	**47**	**73**	**105**	**118**	**145**	**132**	**169**
Beer and ale	100	72	100	112	113	100	109	83
Whiskey	100	50	97	89	157	117	104	143
Wine	100	20	37	94	122	201	158	282
Other alcoholic beverages	100	35	61	116	98	161	158	165
Away from home	**100**	**31**	**53**	**100**	**113**	**180**	**164**	**210**
Beer and ale	100	36	50	105	120	172	157	200
• At fast food, take-out, delivery, concession stands, buffet, and cafeteria	100	88	45	119	128	139	169	84
• At full-service restaurants	100	22	55	105	108	177	166	199
Wine	100	23	56	99	110	180	154	229
• At fast food, take-out, delivery, concession stands, buffet and cafeteria	100	58	58	117	178	127	154	75
• At full-service restaurants	100	19	58	99	100	184	156	237
Other alcoholic beverages	100	40	52	95	122	175	159	206
• At fast food, take-out, delivery, concession stands, buffet, and cafeteria	100	95	63	113	158	113	127	86
• At full-service restaurants	100	24	52	92	105	191	176	219
Alcoholic beverages purchased on trips	100	15	58	95	93	199	186	224

Note: (–) means sample is too small to make a reliable estimate.
Source: Calculations by New Strategist based on the 2003 Consumer Expenditure Survey

Table 5.27 Food and Alcohol: Total spending by education, 2003

(total annual spending on food and alcoholic beverages, by consumer unit (CU) educational attainment group, 2003; numbers in thousands)

	total consumer units	less than high school graduate	high school graduate	some college	associate's degree	college graduate total	bachelor's degree	master's, professional, doctorate
Number of consumer units	115,356	17,721	31,552	24,514	10,981	30,589	19,557	11,032
Total spending of all CUs	$4,708,523,919	$423,552,102	$1,071,365,829	$929,384,819	$489,171,925	$1,788,844,720	$1,070,273,448	$719,316,517
Food, total spending	615,943,362	72,414,563	148,316,486	125,908,807	63,507,735	203,144,608	124,802,018	78,620,210
Alcoholic beverages, total spending	45,128,421	2,847,587	8,030,300	9,841,636	4,979,334	18,964,568	11,047,163	7,995,442
FOOD AT HOME	360,923,546	51,629,602	94,216,796	71,256,315	36,213,142	106,782,222	66,767,207	40,120,295
Cereals and bakery products	50,955,052	7,229,105	13,388,460	10,363,048	5,008,105	14,845,148	9,417,478	5,433,701
Cereals and cereal products	17,319,550	2,714,148	4,402,766	3,396,660	1,697,553	5,094,292	3,265,237	1,828,444
Flour	844,406	181,817	221,180	179,688	43,375	222,076	138,855	83,402
Prepared flour mixes	1,475,403	206,627	375,784	315,005	159,664	417,846	263,433	154,779
Ready-to-eat and cooked cereals	9,944,841	1,440,540	2,532,995	1,973,867	1,042,207	2,940,521	1,944,748	990,784
Rice	1,851,464	389,153	441,097	297,600	181,845	550,602	326,797	225,715
Pasta, cornmeal, and other cereal products	3,201,129	496,011	832,026	630,500	270,572	963,248	591,599	373,654
Bakery products	33,635,502	4,515,134	8,985,694	6,966,389	3,310,552	9,750,856	6,152,045	3,605,258
Bread	9,522,638	1,444,793	2,595,783	1,812,075	970,281	2,685,714	1,677,795	1,010,862
White bread	3,864,426	717,346	1,111,577	749,148	371,597	928,070	598,640	328,974
Bread, other than white	5,659,365	727,447	1,484,206	1,062,927	598,684	1,757,644	1,079,155	681,888
Crackers and cookies	8,026,470	1,035,792	2,100,732	1,604,196	779,541	2,466,391	1,532,291	937,720
Cookies	5,197,941	686,334	1,394,914	1,028,362	514,021	1,551,168	967,094	586,020
Crackers	2,828,529	349,458	705,818	575,834	265,521	915,223	565,197	351,700
Frozen and refrigerated bakery products	2,833,143	363,458	735,477	646,679	302,636	782,467	519,043	261,900
Other bakery products	13,253,251	1,671,090	3,553,386	2,903,438	1,258,093	3,816,284	2,422,917	1,394,776
Biscuits and rolls	4,295,857	431,506	1,115,363	824,406	467,461	1,420,247	858,748	565,280
Cakes and cupcakes	4,234,719	575,224	1,173,103	1,016,105	368,632	1,095,698	716,960	377,405
Bread and cracker products	411,821	41,822	107,277	77,955	59,627	123,580	81,357	42,253
Sweetrolls, coffee cakes, doughnuts	3,189,593	443,025	859,476	750,619	254,100	874,234	580,061	292,679
Pies, tarts, turnovers	1,121,260	179,337	297,851	234,354	108,163	302,525	185,987	117,160
Meats, poultry, fish, and eggs	95,120,250	15,244,845	26,476,545	18,573,768	10,338,502	24,612,827	15,527,476	9,101,841
Beef	28,325,666	4,177,194	8,275,459	5,195,497	3,876,293	6,862,948	4,531,161	2,320,471
Ground beef	10,297,830	1,680,482	3,090,518	2,064,079	1,313,986	2,200,573	1,505,889	686,963
Roast	4,571,558	708,131	1,445,397	848,675	446,707	1,114,357	776,608	332,615
Chuck roast	1,542,310	231,436	498,206	312,063	135,286	362,480	246,223	114,953
Round roast	1,128,182	179,514	424,059	154,683	77,416	281,419	206,913	72,260
Other roast	1,901,067	297,004	523,132	381,928	234,115	470,765	323,473	145,402
Steak	10,861,921	1,494,589	3,024,259	1,822,126	1,662,304	2,873,225	1,916,977	950,076
Round steak	1,805,321	317,915	432,893	290,736	380,492	409,281	256,197	153,565
Sirloin steak	3,616,411	445,329	999,252	578,776	701,137	906,352	635,603	266,533
Other steak	5,441,343	731,346	1,592,114	952,614	580,675	1,557,592	1,025,178	529,977
Other beef	2,594,356	294,169	715,284	460,618	453,186	674,487	331,687	350,707
Pork	19,680,887	3,764,472	5,736,785	4,015,638	1,843,271	4,421,028	2,816,795	1,605,266
Bacon	3,593,339	656,740	1,033,328	743,510	385,653	795,314	529,799	263,775
Pork chops	3,938,254	820,305	1,190,141	782,732	387,849	788,279	505,157	282,860
Ham	4,400,831	945,770	1,312,879	801,853	331,077	1,027,179	625,433	404,212
Ham, not canned	4,272,786	920,960	1,275,647	778,810	323,281	992,919	596,684	399,248
Canned ham	126,892	24,987	37,231	22,798	7,906	34,260	28,749	4,964
Sausage	2,978,492	600,919	861,370	670,458	240,484	626,463	400,919	225,494
Other pork	4,771,124	740,561	1,339,067	1,017,086	498,208	1,184,100	755,291	428,814
Other meats	11,767,466	1,731,696	3,267,210	2,407,030	1,215,926	3,138,431	2,019,651	1,117,652
Frankfurters	2,623,195	473,682	791,640	508,175	269,254	589,756	401,114	186,661
Lunch meats (cold cuts)	7,995,324	1,140,346	2,254,706	1,636,555	855,969	2,102,076	1,334,570	768,158
Bologna, liverwurst, salami	2,497,457	441,785	792,586	515,284	227,307	527,660	335,989	191,626
Other lunch meats	5,497,867	698,562	1,462,120	1,121,270	628,552	1,574,416	998,580	576,532
Lamb, organ meats, and others	1,148,946	117,667	220,864	262,055	90,703	446,599	283,968	162,722
Poultry	16,681,631	2,776,172	4,515,407	3,418,968	1,671,528	4,333,544	2,683,807	1,656,565
Fresh and frozen chicken	13,429,746	2,310,818	3,602,607	2,805,382	1,347,588	3,407,309	2,137,776	1,272,872

	total consumer units	less than high school graduate	high school graduate	some college	associate's degree	college graduate total	bachelor's degree	master's, professional, doctorate
Fresh and frozen whole chicken	$3,785,984	$793,369	$1,034,590	$713,357	$393,339	$881,269	$544,271	$338,572
Fresh and frozen chicken parts	9,643,762	1,517,272	2,568,017	2,092,025	954,249	2,526,040	1,593,504	934,300
Other poultry	3,253,039	465,353	912,799	613,585	324,049	925,929	546,031	383,693
Fish and seafood	14,357,208	1,992,726	3,494,700	2,730,860	1,299,711	4,762,401	2,766,338	2,018,194
Canned fish and seafood	1,891,838	256,955	525,656	403,746	185,469	515,731	309,196	208,174
Fresh fish and shellfish	8,291,789	1,113,056	1,884,285	1,521,094	801,942	2,922,779	1,627,534	1,314,242
Frozen fish and shellfish	4,172,427	622,716	1,085,073	805,775	312,300	1,323,892	829,412	495,778
Eggs	4,307,393	802,584	1,136,986	806,020	431,883	1,094,780	709,919	383,803
Dairy products	**37,836,768**	**5,146,178**	**9,631,100**	**7,400,777**	**3,777,903**	**11,684,998**	**7,320,381**	**4,376,394**
Fresh milk and cream	14,595,995	2,344,311	3,880,896	2,834,309	1,510,876	4,033,160	2,604,406	1,426,438
Fresh milk, all types	12,986,778	2,164,443	3,507,005	2,503,125	1,350,334	3,480,416	2,274,088	1,202,378
Cream	1,609,216	179,868	373,891	331,184	160,542	552,743	330,318	224,060
Other dairy products	23,240,773	2,801,867	5,800,204	4,566,468	2,267,027	7,651,838	4,715,975	2,949,846
Butter	2,085,636	294,700	561,941	403,746	222,255	598,015	378,624	219,868
Cheese	11,194,146	1,291,861	2,864,606	2,153,555	1,120,721	3,680,774	2,203,487	1,489,099
Ice cream and related products	6,701,030	841,748	1,721,162	1,410,781	619,548	2,073,017	1,360,189	710,130
Miscellaneous dairy products	3,259,961	373,736	652,180	598,387	304,393	1,300,033	773,675	530,860
Fruits and vegetables	**61,763,910**	**8,899,486**	**15,114,355**	**11,744,903**	**5,704,630**	**20,040,077**	**12,144,310**	**7,948,556**
Fresh fruits	19,712,033	2,762,527	4,653,289	3,635,671	1,768,819	6,776,993	3,957,555	2,849,014
Apples	3,775,602	545,275	916,586	707,474	343,486	1,245,278	729,085	521,372
Bananas	3,277,264	547,756	846,856	586,865	323,940	969,977	595,315	376,632
Oranges	2,115,629	334,041	540,486	373,593	152,416	702,323	432,210	271,498
Citrus fruits, excl. oranges	1,631,134	248,626	365,634	310,347	121,669	575,073	329,927	248,220
Other fresh fruits	8,912,405	1,086,829	1,982,728	1,657,392	827,199	3,284,647	1,871,214	1,431,402
Fresh vegetables	19,836,618	2,956,217	4,655,182	3,845,756	1,759,815	6,547,575	3,950,318	2,615,798
Potatoes	3,473,369	587,983	958,865	683,941	323,771	917,670	565,393	354,127
Lettuce	2,549,368	357,255	589,707	513,813	240,923	838,444	508,482	332,284
Tomatoes	3,712,156	649,297	860,423	701,591	346,341	1,156,570	679,997	481,106
Other fresh vegetables	10,101,725	1,361,682	2,246,187	1,946,412	848,780	3,634,891	2,196,642	1,448,391
Processed fruits	12,503,437	1,548,939	3,171,292	2,444,781	1,182,434	3,989,723	2,491,366	1,503,220
Frozen fruits and fruit juices	1,331,208	196,703	307,001	247,837	130,784	444,764	295,897	147,829
Frozen orange juice	535,252	101,187	126,524	96,830	61,933	151,416	98,372	52,954
Frozen fruits	422,203	42,530	88,030	74,032	35,602	178,028	127,316	49,644
Frozen fruit juices, excl. orange	373,753	53,163	92,447	76,729	35,249	115,015	70,014	45,342
Canned fruits	1,841,082	211,057	543,956	337,313	170,755	560,696	346,354	215,234
Dried fruits	726,743	81,694	186,788	145,613	58,639	246,241	146,873	100,281
Fresh fruit juice	2,395,944	339,003	560,364	469,198	185,249	827,738	497,530	332,615
Canned and bottled fruit juice	6,208,460	820,482	1,573,498	1,244,576	637,008	1,910,283	1,204,516	707,151
Processed vegetables	9,711,822	1,531,980	2,634,592	1,818,694	993,561	2,725,480	1,744,876	980,414
Frozen vegetables	3,090,387	393,406	840,545	577,060	363,032	905,434	574,389	331,291
Canned and dried vegetables and juices	6,621,434	1,138,397	1,794,047	1,241,389	630,529	1,820,046	1,170,486	649,123
Canned beans	1,448,871	239,942	431,000	269,409	145,608	363,397	221,190	142,975
Canned corn	794,803	157,362	254,309	160,812	72,475	154,169	100,523	53,505
Canned miscellaneous vegetables	2,139,854	300,725	592,547	403,255	233,258	630,439	413,826	215,896
Dried peas	42,682	4,253	12,936	7,354	3,953	14,071	10,170	3,751
Dried beans	266,472	91,795	64,997	35,055	17,130	61,790	30,704	31,882
Dried miscellaneous vegetables	866,324	156,299	208,559	168,656	62,921	268,877	186,183	81,416
Dried processed vegetables	48,450	13,645	7,572	3,922	6,581	8,259	6,063	2,206
Fresh and canned vegetable juices	1,000,137	172,425	219,602	187,287	108,382	314,455	199,873	114,733
Sugar and other sweets	**13,736,592**	**1,867,262**	**3,790,573**	**2,598,484**	**1,369,990**	**4,049,066**	**2,612,033**	**1,435,153**
Candy and chewing gum	8,687,460	1,009,211	2,363,876	1,637,535	866,401	2,744,445	1,748,005	996,962
Sugar	1,948,363	416,444	568,567	353,247	186,567	436,199	287,488	147,829
Artificial sweeteners	654,069	80,276	212,029	129,679	53,917	173,440	120,862	51,740
Jams, preserves, other sweets	2,445,547	361,331	646,500	478,023	263,105	694,982	455,678	238,512
Fats and oils	**9,889,470**	**1,616,687**	**2,656,363**	**1,946,412**	**956,972**	**2,689,691**	**1,679,946**	**1,012,848**
Margarine	1,108,571	177,742	338,237	238,276	96,303	258,171	175,622	81,747
Fats and oils	3,032,709	666,310	799,212	522,148	263,873	797,761	475,431	325,003
Salad dressings	3,018,867	399,431	777,757	631,481	325,147	879,128	543,293	337,138
Nondairy cream and imitation milk	1,271,223	164,983	346,125	256,171	161,860	341,679	224,123	117,270
Peanut butter	1,458,100	208,045	395,031	298,581	139,678	412,952	261,673	151,580

	total consumer units	less than high school graduate	high school graduate	some college	associate's degree	college graduate total	bachelor's degree	master's, professional, doctorate
Miscellaneous foods	$56,478,298	$6,861,217	$14,244,466	$11,480,887	$5,505,434	$18,058,828	$11,514,770	$6,546,389
Frozen prepared foods	12,088,155	1,447,628	3,266,894	2,536,218	1,171,673	3,600,631	2,436,215	1,153,616
Frozen meals	4,020,157	508,593	1,064,880	747,677	416,619	1,259,961	879,478	374,426
Other frozen prepared foods	8,067,999	939,036	2,202,014	1,788,541	755,054	2,340,670	1,556,737	779,190
Canned and packaged soups	4,059,378	491,935	1,152,910	823,425	372,036	1,192,665	728,889	466,543
Potato chips, nuts, and other snacks	12,190,822	1,325,176	3,025,206	2,444,536	1,387,669	3,937,722	2,468,485	1,472,882
Potato chips and other snacks	9,144,270	983,338	2,367,978	1,916,995	1,060,106	2,772,281	1,839,140	927,791
Nuts	3,046,552	341,838	656,913	527,541	327,563	1,165,441	629,540	545,091
Condiments and seasonings	10,407,418	1,242,951	2,627,335	2,046,919	997,953	3,419,850	2,200,945	1,217,822
Salt, spices, and other seasonings	2,395,944	335,813	596,964	485,622	217,863	750,960	456,069	296,981
Olives, pickles, relishes	1,316,212	161,793	360,955	232,638	105,418	441,093	286,706	154,227
Sauces and gravies	4,436,592	499,023	1,154,803	916,578	466,034	1,374,058	891,995	481,216
Baking needs and miscellaneous products	2,258,670	246,322	514,298	412,080	208,749	853,433	566,371	285,508
Other canned/packaged prepared foods	17,731,371	2,353,526	4,172,436	3,629,788	1,575,993	5,907,959	3,680,236	2,235,414
Prepared salads	2,365,952	176,324	538,277	485,377	231,479	902,987	545,054	360,415
Prepared desserts	1,280,452	178,096	320,568	259,848	117,716	399,186	256,979	142,092
Baby food	3,086,927	586,033	720,332	749,148	273,756	780,937	490,490	291,134
Miscellaneous prepared foods	10,973,816	1,413,073	2,582,216	2,132,228	951,723	3,816,895	2,382,434	1,439,124
Nonalcoholic beverages	30,958,090	4,510,172	8,135,368	6,293,724	3,125,522	8,850,009	5,471,462	3,393,223
Cola	10,182,474	1,710,431	2,982,295	2,030,004	986,423	2,486,580	1,566,711	921,834
Other carbonated drinks	5,264,848	745,877	1,517,967	1,116,368	549,819	1,331,845	835,671	497,323
Coffee	4,392,756	558,743	1,010,611	880,298	453,296	1,470,413	884,368	590,543
Roasted coffee	2,964,649	356,192	673,004	584,904	324,379	1,011,578	609,005	405,647
Instant and freeze-dried coffee	1,428,107	202,551	337,606	295,394	128,807	458,529	275,363	184,786
Noncarbonated fruit-flavored drinks, incl. nonfrozen lemonade	2,225,217	331,914	643,345	475,081	205,455	567,426	380,188	185,889
Tea	2,042,955	254,296	528,180	438,310	213,471	601,992	353,004	251,530
Other nonalcoholic beverages and ice	6,773,704	898,809	1,413,530	1,352,683	711,788	2,372,483	1,446,436	931,652
Food prepared by CU on trips	4,185,116	254,651	728,851	854,558	396,085	1,951,272	1,079,155	872,080
FOOD AWAY FROM HOME	255,020,970	20,784,961	54,099,690	54,652,492	27,294,593	96,362,385	58,034,811	38,500,025
Meals at restaurants, carry-outs, other	211,328,731	18,370,475	45,934,664	46,033,125	22,789,528	76,373,698	46,644,227	29,902,015
Lunch	75,922,705	7,104,172	17,003,057	17,128,422	8,167,009	26,000,344	16,171,879	9,863,822
• At fast food, take-out, delivery, concession stands, buffet, cafeteria (other than employer, school cafeteria)	42,568,671	4,471,363	9,832,865	10,174,045	4,589,289	13,345,981	8,646,541	4,690,696
• At full-service restaurants	24,236,296	1,992,195	4,931,893	4,636,823	2,332,584	10,011,780	5,781,831	4,278,651
• At vending machines, mobile vendors	641,379	92,504	210,767	149,781	108,932	86,261	55,346	31,000
• At employer and school cafeterias	8,476,359	548,111	2,027,532	2,167,773	1,136,314	2,556,017	1,688,160	863,585
Dinner	85,076,204	6,185,161	17,264,308	17,532,658	9,061,302	33,985,297	19,939,926	14,186,269
• At fast food, take-out, delivery, concession stands, buffet, cafeteria (other than employer, school cafeteria)	24,908,821	2,563,165	5,937,455	5,605,126	2,840,126	7,853,114	5,210,767	2,627,160
• At full-service restaurants	59,687,502	3,552,352	11,250,181	11,666,948	6,205,912	26,065,499	14,682,027	11,539,803
• At vending machines, mobile vendors	152,270	22,683	38,809	78,935	–	13,765	9,779	3,972
• At employer and school cafeterias	326,457	46,783	37,862	181,404	15,264	52,919	37,354	15,334
Snacks and nonalcoholic beverages	28,656,738	2,649,290	6,599,416	6,543,032	3,252,682	9,443,130	6,013,191	3,431,835
• At fast food, take-out, delivery, concession stands, buffet, cafeteria (other than employer, school cafeteria)	20,794,073	1,785,214	4,613,849	4,803,763	2,356,303	7,094,813	4,552,478	2,541,111
• At full-service restaurants	3,075,391	321,813	745,574	639,570	288,800	1,053,791	617,414	440,839
• At vending machines, mobile vendors	3,614,103	434,342	969,277	851,371	461,422	902,376	597,662	303,049
• At employer and school cafeterias	1,172,017	107,921	271,032	248,327	146,157	392,151	245,831	146,726
Breakfast and brunch	21,674,239	2,431,853	5,067,882	4,828,768	2,308,536	6,945,232	4,518,840	2,419,980
• At fast food, take-out, delivery, concession stands, buffet, cafeteria (other than employer, school cafeteria)	10,707,344	1,247,913	2,725,462	2,477,875	1,179,140	3,054,923	2,115,090	926,798
• At full-service restaurants	10,315,134	1,109,866	2,166,045	2,170,715	1,048,795	3,748,070	2,320,829	1,432,946
• At vending machines, mobile vendors	158,038	22,683	63,735	42,164	5,710	22,942	17,601	5,295
• At employer and school cafeterias	492,570	51,391	112,325	138,014	74,781	119,297	65,320	54,829
Board (including at school)	3,835,587	121,212	422,166	999,926	221,157	2,071,793	942,256	1,129,456
Catered affairs	5,582,077	207,513	1,103,689	966,342	712,118	2,592,418	1,676,426	915,766
Food on trips	24,682,723	930,707	4,159,816	4,720,416	2,344,993	12,526,501	6,973,831	5,552,626
School lunches	6,560,296	421,583	1,752,083	1,294,094	891,438	2,201,184	1,410,255	791,105
Meals as pay	3,031,556	733,295	727,274	638,590	335,360	596,791	388,011	208,946

	total consumer units	less than high school graduate	high school graduate	some college	associate's degree	college graduate total	bachelor's degree	master's, professional, doctorate
ALCOHOLIC BEVERAGES	$45,128,421	$2,847,587	$8,030,300	$9,841,636	$4,979,334	$18,964,568	$11,047,163	$7,995,442
At home	27,694,668	2,019,485	5,496,674	6,153,014	3,098,619	10,650,172	6,209,543	4,487,928
Beer and ale	12,824,127	1,426,186	3,522,781	3,060,083	1,381,190	3,401,803	2,371,873	1,014,392
Whiskey	1,648,437	126,705	439,204	310,592	246,194	513,589	291,008	225,604
Wine	10,373,965	313,307	1,057,939	2,081,974	1,205,933	5,520,091	2,781,592	2,797,495
Other alcoholic beverages	2,849,293	153,109	477,066	700,365	265,301	1,214,689	765,070	450,437
Away from home	17,432,599	828,102	2,533,310	3,688,622	1,880,826	8,314,396	4,837,620	3,507,514
Beer and ale	6,959,427	388,976	957,919	1,551,491	797,221	3,176,056	1,857,915	1,331,893
• At fast food, take-out, delivery, concession stands, buffet, and cafeteria	1,234,309	167,109	152,596	313,044	150,330	456,082	352,613	98,736
• At full-service restaurants	5,328,294	181,640	805,523	1,189,910	549,709	2,507,380	1,501,391	1,014,172
Wine	2,166,386	76,732	334,451	456,451	227,307	1,032,073	565,002	474,376
• At fast food, take-out, delivery, concession stands, buffet and cafeteria	191,491	17,189	30,605	47,557	32,504	64,237	49,870	13,680
• At full-service restaurants	1,928,752	55,112	303,846	403,991	184,481	941,224	510,633	437,639
Other alcoholic beverages	4,470,045	273,258	632,933	906,528	518,193	2,079,134	1,208,036	881,016
• At fast food, take-out, delivery, concession stands, buffet, and cafeteria	891,702	130,604	153,343	214,252	134,078	267,348	192,441	73,363
• At full-service restaurants	3,401,848	124,756	479,590	668,497	341,289	1,719,408	1,014,422	711,674
Alcoholic beverages purchased on trips	3,836,741	89,314	608,007	774,152	337,995	2,027,133	1,206,862	820,119

Note: Numbers may not add to total because of rounding and missing subcategories. (–) means sample is too small to make a reliable estimate.
Source: Calculations by New Strategist based on the 2003 Consumer Expenditure Survey

Table 5.28 Food and Alcohol: Market shares by education, 2003

(percentage of total annual spending on food and alcoholic beverages accounted for by consumer unit educational attainment groups, 2003)

	total consumer units	less than high school graduate	high school graduate	some college	associate's degree	college graduate total	bachelor's degree	master's, professional, doctorate
Share of total consumer units	100.0%	15.4%	27.4%	21.3%	9.5%	26.5%	17.0%	9.6%
Share of total before-tax income	100.0	7.5	21.5	18.8	10.1	42.4	24.8	17.6
Share of total spending	100.0	9.0	22.8	19.7	10.4	38.0	22.7	15.3
Share of food spending	100.0	11.8	24.1	20.4	10.3	33.0	20.3	12.8
Share of alcoholic beverages spending	100.0	6.3	17.8	21.8	11.0	42.0	24.5	17.7
FOOD AT HOME	100.0	14.3	26.1	19.7	10.0	29.6	18.5	11.1
Cereals and bakery products	100.0	14.2	26.3	20.3	9.8	29.1	18.5	10.7
Cereals and cereal products	100.0	15.7	25.4	19.6	9.8	29.4	18.9	10.6
Flour	100.0	21.5	26.2	21.3	5.1	26.3	16.4	9.9
Prepared flour mixes	100.0	14.0	25.5	21.4	10.8	28.3	17.9	10.5
Ready-to-eat and cooked cereals	100.0	14.5	25.5	19.8	10.5	29.6	19.6	10.0
Rice	100.0	21.0	23.8	16.1	9.8	29.7	17.7	12.2
Pasta, cornmeal, and other cereal products	100.0	15.5	26.0	19.7	8.5	30.1	18.5	11.7
Bakery products	100.0	13.4	26.7	20.7	9.8	29.0	18.3	10.7
Bread	100.0	15.2	27.3	19.0	10.2	28.2	17.6	10.6
White bread	100.0	18.6	28.8	19.4	9.6	24.0	15.5	8.5
Bread, other than white	100.0	12.9	26.2	18.8	10.6	31.1	19.1	12.0
Crackers and cookies	100.0	12.9	26.2	20.0	9.7	30.7	19.1	11.7
Cookies	100.0	13.2	26.8	19.8	9.9	29.8	18.6	11.3
Crackers	100.0	12.4	25.0	20.4	9.4	32.4	20.0	12.4
Frozen and refrigerated bakery products	100.0	12.8	26.0	22.8	10.7	27.6	18.3	9.2
Other bakery products	100.0	12.6	26.8	21.9	9.5	28.8	18.3	10.5
Biscuits and rolls	100.0	10.0	26.0	19.2	10.9	33.1	20.0	13.2
Cakes and cupcakes	100.0	13.6	27.7	24.0	8.7	25.9	16.9	8.9
Bread and cracker products	100.0	10.2	26.0	18.9	14.5	30.0	19.8	10.3
Sweetrolls, coffee cakes, doughnuts	100.0	13.9	26.9	23.5	8.0	27.4	18.2	9.2
Pies, tarts, turnovers	100.0	16.0	26.6	20.9	9.6	27.0	16.6	10.4
Meats, poultry, fish, and eggs	100.0	16.0	27.8	19.5	10.9	25.9	16.3	9.6
Beef	100.0	14.7	29.2	18.3	13.7	24.2	16.0	8.2
Ground beef	100.0	16.3	30.0	20.0	12.8	21.4	14.6	6.7
Roast	100.0	15.5	31.6	18.6	9.8	24.4	17.0	7.3
Chuck roast	100.0	15.0	32.3	20.2	8.8	23.5	16.0	7.5
Round roast	100.0	15.9	37.6	13.7	6.9	24.9	18.3	6.4
Other roast	100.0	15.6	27.5	20.1	12.3	24.8	17.0	7.6
Steak	100.0	13.8	27.8	16.8	15.3	26.5	17.6	8.7
Round steak	100.0	17.6	24.0	16.1	21.1	22.7	14.2	8.5
Sirloin steak	100.0	12.3	27.6	16.0	19.4	25.1	17.6	7.4
Other steak	100.0	13.4	29.3	17.5	10.7	28.6	18.8	9.7
Other beef	100.0	11.3	27.6	17.8	17.5	26.0	12.8	13.5
Pork	100.0	19.1	29.1	20.4	9.4	22.5	14.3	8.2
Bacon	100.0	18.3	28.8	20.7	10.7	22.1	14.7	7.3
Pork chops	100.0	20.8	30.2	19.9	9.8	20.0	12.8	7.2
Ham	100.0	21.5	29.8	18.2	7.5	23.3	14.2	9.2
Ham, not canned	100.0	21.6	29.9	18.2	7.6	23.2	14.0	9.3
Canned ham	100.0	19.7	29.3	18.0	6.2	27.0	22.7	3.9
Sausage	100.0	20.2	28.9	22.5	8.1	21.0	13.5	7.6
Other pork	100.0	15.5	28.1	21.3	10.4	24.8	15.8	9.0
Other meats	100.0	14.7	27.8	20.5	10.3	26.7	17.2	9.5
Frankfurters	100.0	18.1	30.2	19.4	10.3	22.5	15.3	7.1
Lunch meats (cold cuts)	100.0	14.3	28.2	20.5	10.7	26.3	16.7	9.6
Bologna, liverwurst, salami	100.0	17.7	31.7	20.6	9.1	21.1	13.5	7.7
Other lunch meats	100.0	12.7	26.6	20.4	11.4	28.6	18.2	10.5
Lamb, organ meats, and others	100.0	10.2	19.2	22.8	7.9	38.9	24.7	14.2
Poultry	100.0	16.6	27.1	20.5	10.0	26.0	16.1	9.9
Fresh and frozen chicken	100.0	17.2	26.8	20.9	10.0	25.4	15.9	9.5

	total consumer units	less than high school graduate	high school graduate	some college	associate's degree	college graduate total	bachelor's degree	master's, professional, doctorate
Fresh and frozen whole chicken	100.0%	21.0%	27.3%	18.8%	10.4%	23.3%	14.4%	8.9%
Fresh and frozen chicken parts	100.0	15.7	26.6	21.7	9.9	26.2	16.5	9.7
Other poultry	100.0	14.3	28.1	18.9	10.0	28.5	16.8	11.8
Fish and seafood	100.0	13.9	24.3	19.0	9.1	33.2	19.3	14.1
Canned fish and seafood	100.0	13.6	27.8	21.3	9.8	27.3	16.3	11.0
Fresh fish and shellfish	100.0	13.4	22.7	18.3	9.7	35.2	19.6	15.8
Frozen fish and shellfish	100.0	14.9	26.0	19.3	7.5	31.7	19.9	11.9
Eggs	100.0	18.6	27.6	18.7	10.0	25.4	16.5	8.9
Dairy products	**100.0**	**13.6**	**25.6**	**19.6**	**10.0**	**30.9**	**19.3**	**11.6**
Fresh milk and cream	100.0	16.1	26.6	19.4	10.4	27.6	17.8	9.8
Fresh milk, all types	100.0	16.7	27.0	19.3	10.4	26.8	17.5	9.3
Cream	100.0	11.2	23.2	20.6	10.0	34.3	20.5	13.9
Other dairy products	100.0	12.1	25.0	19.6	9.8	32.9	20.3	12.7
Butter	100.0	14.1	26.9	19.4	10.7	28.7	18.2	10.5
Cheese	100.0	11.5	25.6	19.2	10.0	32.9	19.7	13.3
Ice cream and related products	100.0	12.6	25.7	21.1	9.2	30.9	20.3	10.6
Miscellaneous dairy products	100.0	11.5	20.0	18.4	9.3	39.9	23.7	16.3
Fruits and vegetables	**100.0**	**14.4**	**24.5**	**19.0**	**9.2**	**32.4**	**19.7**	**12.9**
Fresh fruits	100.0	14.0	23.6	18.4	9.0	34.4	20.1	14.5
Apples	100.0	14.4	24.3	18.7	9.1	33.0	19.3	13.8
Bananas	100.0	16.7	25.8	17.9	9.9	29.6	18.2	11.5
Oranges	100.0	15.8	25.5	17.7	7.2	33.2	20.4	12.8
Citrus fruits, excl. oranges	100.0	15.2	22.5	19.0	7.5	35.3	20.2	15.2
Other fresh fruits	100.0	12.2	22.2	18.6	9.3	36.9	21.0	16.1
Fresh vegetables	100.0	14.9	23.5	19.4	8.9	33.0	19.9	13.2
Potatoes	100.0	16.9	27.6	19.7	9.5	26.4	16.3	10.2
Lettuce	100.0	14.0	23.1	20.2	9.5	32.9	19.9	13.0
Tomatoes	100.0	17.5	23.2	18.9	9.3	31.2	18.3	13.0
Other fresh vegetables	100.0	13.5	22.2	19.3	8.4	36.0	21.7	14.3
Processed fruits	100.0	13.2	25.4	19.6	9.5	31.9	19.9	12.0
Frozen fruits and fruit juices	100.0	14.8	23.1	18.6	9.8	33.4	22.2	11.1
Frozen orange juice	100.0	18.9	23.6	18.1	11.6	28.3	18.4	9.9
Frozen fruits	100.0	10.1	20.9	17.5	8.0	42.2	30.2	11.8
Frozen fruit juices, excl. orange	100.0	14.2	24.7	20.5	9.4	30.8	18.7	12.1
Canned fruits	100.0	11.5	29.5	18.3	9.3	30.5	18.8	11.7
Dried fruits	100.0	11.2	25.7	20.0	8.1	33.9	20.2	13.8
Fresh fruit juice	100.0	14.1	23.4	19.6	7.7	34.5	20.8	13.9
Canned and bottled fruit juice	100.0	13.2	25.3	20.0	10.3	30.8	19.4	11.4
Processed vegetables	100.0	15.8	27.1	18.7	10.2	28.1	18.0	10.1
Frozen vegetables	100.0	12.7	27.2	18.7	11.7	29.3	18.6	10.7
Canned and dried vegetables and juices	100.0	17.2	27.1	18.7	9.5	27.5	17.7	9.8
Canned beans	100.0	16.6	29.7	18.6	10.0	25.1	15.3	9.9
Canned corn	100.0	19.8	32.0	20.2	9.1	19.4	12.6	6.7
Canned miscellaneous vegetables	100.0	14.1	27.7	18.8	9.5	29.5	19.3	10.1
Dried peas	100.0	10.0	30.3	17.2	9.3	33.0	23.8	8.8
Dried beans	100.0	34.4	24.4	13.2	6.4	23.2	11.5	12.0
Dried miscellaneous vegetables	100.0	18.0	24.1	19.5	7.3	31.0	21.5	9.4
Dried processed vegetables	100.0	28.2	15.6	8.1	34.2	17.0	12.5	4.6
Fresh and canned vegetable juices	100.0	17.2	22.0	18.7	10.8	31.4	20.0	11.5
Sugar and other sweets	**100.0**	**13.6**	**27.6**	**18.9**	**10.0**	**29.5**	**19.0**	**10.4**
Candy and chewing gum	100.0	11.6	27.2	18.8	10.0	31.6	20.1	11.5
Sugar	100.0	21.4	29.2	18.1	9.6	22.4	14.8	7.6
Artificial sweeteners	100.0	12.3	32.4	19.8	8.2	26.5	18.5	7.9
Jams, preserves, other sweets	100.0	14.8	26.4	19.5	10.8	28.4	18.6	9.8
Fats and oils	**100.0**	**16.3**	**26.9**	**19.7**	**10.0**	**27.2**	**17.0**	**10.2**
Margarine	100.0	16.0	30.5	21.5	8.7	23.3	15.8	7.4
Fats and oils	100.0	22.0	26.4	17.2	8.7	26.3	15.7	10.7
Salad dressings	100.0	13.2	25.8	20.9	10.8	29.1	18.0	11.2
Nondairy cream and imitation milk	100.0	13.0	27.2	20.2	12.7	26.9	17.6	9.2
Peanut butter	100.0	14.3	27.1	20.5	9.6	28.3	17.9	10.4

	total consumer units	less than high school graduate	high school graduate	some college	associate's degree	college graduate total	college graduate bachelor's degree	college graduate master's, professional, doctorate
Miscellaneous foods	100.0%	12.1%	25.2%	20.3%	9.7%	32.0%	20.4%	11.6%
Frozen prepared foods	100.0	12.0	27.0	21.0	9.7	29.8	20.2	9.5
Frozen meals	100.0	12.7	26.5	18.6	10.4	31.3	21.9	9.3
Other frozen prepared foods	100.0	11.6	27.3	22.2	9.4	29.0	19.3	9.7
Canned and packaged soups	100.0	12.1	28.4	20.3	9.2	29.4	18.0	11.5
Potato chips, nuts, and other snacks	100.0	10.9	24.8	20.1	11.4	32.3	20.2	12.1
Potato chips and other snacks	100.0	10.8	25.9	21.0	11.6	30.3	20.1	10.1
Nuts	100.0	11.2	21.6	17.3	10.8	38.3	20.7	17.9
Condiments and seasonings	100.0	11.9	25.2	19.7	9.6	32.9	21.1	11.7
Salt, spices, and other seasonings	100.0	14.0	24.9	20.3	9.1	31.3	19.0	12.4
Olives, pickles, relishes	100.0	12.3	27.4	17.7	8.0	33.5	21.8	11.7
Sauces and gravies	100.0	11.2	26.0	20.7	10.5	31.0	20.1	10.8
Baking needs and miscellaneous products	100.0	10.9	22.8	18.2	9.2	37.8	25.1	12.6
Other canned/packaged prepared foods	100.0	13.3	23.5	20.5	8.9	33.3	20.8	12.6
Prepared salads	100.0	7.5	22.8	20.5	9.8	38.2	23.0	15.2
Prepared desserts	100.0	13.9	25.0	20.3	9.2	31.2	20.1	11.1
Baby food	100.0	19.0	23.3	24.3	8.9	25.3	15.9	9.4
Miscellaneous prepared foods	100.0	12.9	23.5	19.4	8.7	34.8	21.7	13.1
Nonalcoholic beverages	100.0	14.6	26.3	20.3	10.1	28.6	17.7	11.0
Cola	100.0	16.8	29.3	19.9	9.7	24.4	15.4	9.1
Other carbonated drinks	100.0	14.2	28.8	21.2	10.4	25.3	15.9	9.4
Coffee	100.0	12.7	23.0	20.0	10.3	33.5	20.1	13.4
Roasted coffee	100.0	12.0	22.7	19.7	10.9	34.1	20.5	13.7
Instant and freeze-dried coffee	100.0	14.2	23.6	20.7	9.0	32.1	19.3	12.9
Noncarbonated fruit-flavored drinks, incl. nonfrozen lemonade	100.0	14.9	28.9	21.3	9.2	25.5	17.1	8.4
Tea	100.0	12.4	25.9	21.5	10.4	29.5	17.3	12.3
Other nonalcoholic beverages and ice	100.0	13.3	20.9	20.0	10.5	35.0	21.4	13.8
Food prepared by CU on trips	100.0	6.1	17.4	20.4	9.5	46.6	25.8	20.8
FOOD AWAY FROM HOME	100.0	8.2	21.2	21.4	10.7	37.8	22.8	15.1
Meals at restaurants, carry-outs, other	100.0	8.7	21.7	21.8	10.8	36.1	22.1	14.1
Lunch	100.0	9.4	22.4	22.6	10.8	34.2	21.3	13.0
• At fast food, take-out, delivery, concession stands, buffet, cafeteria (other than employer, school cafeteria)	100.0	10.5	23.1	23.9	10.8	31.4	20.3	11.0
• At full-service restaurants	100.0	8.2	20.3	19.1	9.6	41.3	23.9	17.7
• At vending machines, mobile vendors	100.0	14.4	32.9	23.4	17.0	13.4	8.6	4.8
• At employer and school cafeterias	100.0	6.5	23.9	25.6	13.4	30.2	19.9	10.2
Dinner	100.0	7.3	20.3	20.6	10.7	39.9	23.4	16.7
• At fast food, take-out, delivery, concession stands, buffet, cafeteria (other than employer, school cafeteria)	100.0	10.3	23.8	22.5	11.4	31.5	20.9	10.5
• At full-service restaurants	100.0	6.0	18.8	19.5	10.4	43.7	24.6	19.3
• At vending machines, mobile vendors	100.0	14.9	25.5	51.8	–	9.0	6.4	2.6
• At employer and school cafeterias	100.0	14.3	11.6	55.6	4.7	16.2	11.4	4.7
Snacks and nonalcoholic beverages	100.0	9.2	23.0	22.8	11.4	33.0	21.0	12.0
• At fast food, take-out, delivery, concession stands, buffet, cafeteria (other than employer, school cafeteria)	100.0	8.6	22.2	23.1	11.3	34.1	21.9	12.2
• At full-service restaurants	100.0	10.5	24.2	20.8	9.4	34.3	20.1	14.3
• At vending machines, mobile vendors	100.0	12.0	26.8	23.6	12.8	25.0	16.5	8.4
• At employer and school cafeterias	100.0	9.2	23.1	21.2	12.5	33.5	21.0	12.5
Breakfast and brunch	100.0	11.2	23.4	22.3	10.7	32.0	20.8	11.2
• At fast food, take-out, delivery, concession stands, buffet, cafeteria (other than employer, school cafeteria)	100.0	11.7	25.5	23.1	11.0	28.5	19.8	8.7
• At full-service restaurants	100.0	10.8	21.0	21.0	10.2	36.3	22.5	13.9
• At vending machines, mobile vendors	100.0	14.4	40.3	26.7	3.6	14.5	11.1	3.4
• At employer and school cafeterias	100.0	10.4	22.8	28.0	15.2	24.2	13.3	11.1
Board (including at school)	100.0	3.2	11.0	26.1	5.8	54.0	24.6	29.4
Catered affairs	100.0	3.7	19.8	17.3	12.8	46.4	30.0	16.4
Food on trips	100.0	3.8	16.9	19.1	9.5	50.8	28.3	22.5
School lunches	100.0	6.4	26.7	19.7	13.6	33.6	21.5	12.1
Meals as pay	100.0	24.2	24.0	21.1	11.1	19.7	12.8	6.9

	total consumer units	less than high school graduate	high school graduate	some college	associate's degree	college graduate total	bachelor's degree	master's, professional, doctorate
ALCOHOLIC BEVERAGES	**100.0%**	**6.3%**	**17.8%**	**21.8%**	**11.0%**	**42.0%**	**24.5%**	**17.7%**
At home	**100.0**	**7.3**	**19.8**	**22.2**	**11.2**	**38.5**	**22.4**	**16.2**
Beer and ale	100.0	11.1	27.5	23.9	10.8	26.5	18.5	7.9
Whiskey	100.0	7.7	26.6	13.8	14.9	31.2	17.7	13.7
Wine	100.0	3.0	10.2	20.1	11.6	53.2	26.8	27.0
Other alcoholic beverages	100.0	5.4	16.7	24.6	9.3	42.6	26.9	15.8
Away from home	**100.0**	**4.8**	**14.5**	**21.2**	**10.8**	**47.7**	**27.8**	**20.1**
Beer and ale	100.0	5.6	13.8	22.3	11.5	45.6	26.7	19.1
• At fast food, take-out, delivery, concession stands, buffet, and cafeteria	100.0	13.5	12.3	25.4	12.2	37.0	28.6	8.0
• At full-service restaurants	100.0	3.4	15.1	22.3	10.3	47.1	28.2	19.0
Wine	100.0	3.5	15.4	21.1	10.5	47.6	26.1	21.9
• At fast food, take-out, delivery, concession stands, buffet and cafeteria	100.0	9.0	16.0	24.8	17.0	33.5	26.0	7.1
• At full-service restaurants	100.0	2.9	15.8	20.9	9.6	48.8	26.5	22.7
Other alcoholic beverages	100.0	6.1	14.2	20.3	11.6	46.5	27.0	19.7
• At fast food, take-out, delivery, concession stands, buffet, and cafeteria	100.0	14.6	17.2	24.0	15.0	30.0	21.6	8.2
• At full-service restaurants	100.0	3.7	14.1	19.7	10.0	50.5	29.8	20.9
Alcoholic beverages purchased on trips	100.0	2.3	15.8	20.2	8.8	52.8	31.5	21.4

Note: Numbers may not add to total because of rounding. (–) means sample is too small to make a reliable estimate.
Source: Calculations by New Strategist based on the 2003 Consumer Expenditure Survey

Spending on Gifts for Nonhousehold Members, 2003

Spending on gifts for nonhousehold members stood at $1,007 in 2003, fully 13 percent less than in 2000 after adjusting for inflation. Households cut their spending on many gift categories. Spending on gifts of apparel fell 14 percent, while spending on gifts of small appliances was down 19 percent. Bucking the trend, spending on gifts of jewelry for nonhousehold members climbed 35 percent, and gifts of college tuition was up 28 percent.

Households headed by 45-to-54-year-olds spend the most on gifts for nonhousehold members, a total of $1,588 in 2003—58 percent more than the average household. This age group, the most affluent, accounts for 32 percent of all spending on gifts for people in other households—much greater than its 20 percent share of households. Householders aged 55 to 64 spend 56 percent more than the average household on gifts for nonhousehold members, accounting for another 22 percent of the market. Every other age group spends less than average on gifts for nonhousehold members.

Households with incomes of more than $100,000 spent $3,255 on gifts for nonhousehold members in 2003, more than three times as much as the average household. While overall spending on gifts is less in lower-income households, gift spending by category varies by household income. Lower-income households spend more than average on practical gifts such as paying someone's utility bills.

Among household types, married couples without children at home (most of them empty-nesters) spend the most on gifts for nonhousehold members—62 percent more than the average household. Spending on gifts for nonhousehold members is well below average for married couples with preschoolers, for single parents, and for people living alone.

Asian households spend far more than any other racial or ethnic group on gifts for nonhousehold members. In 2003, the average Asian household devoted $1,342 to this item, 33 percent more than average. Black households spent 48 percent less than average on gifts for nonhousehold members in 2003, while Hispanic households spent 26 percent less.

Households in the Northeast spend the most on gifts for nonhousehold members, 16 percent more than the average household. In the South, spending on gifts is 14 percent below average.

Because college graduates dominate the nation's affluent households, they spend the most on gifts for nonhousehold members. In 2003, households headed by college graduates spent $1,840 on gifts for nonhousehold members, 83 percent more than the average household. College graduates spend more than twice the average on gifts of educational expenses. They account for 57 percent of the market for gifts of jewelry for nonhousehold members.

Table 6.1 Gifts for Nonhousehold Members: Average spending by age, 2003

(average annual spending of consumer units (CU) on selected gifts of products and services for nonhousehold members by age of consumer unit reference person, 2003)

	total consumer units	under 25	25 to 34	35 to 44	45 to 54	55 to 64	65 to 74	75+
Number of consumer units (000)	115,356	8,584	19,737	24,413	23,131	16,580	11,495	11,417
Average number of persons per CU	2.5	1.8	2.9	3.2	2.6	2.1	1.9	1.5
Average before-tax income of CU	$51,128.00	$20,680.00	$50,389.00	$61,091.00	$68,028.00	$58,672.00	$35,314.00	$25,492.00
Average spending of CU, total	40,817.33	22,395.53	40,525.22	47,175.06	50,100.86	44,190.65	33,629.17	25,016.38
Gifts, average spending	**1,007.01**	**320.79**	**639.28**	**740.96**	**1,587.52**	**1,571.92**	**952.27**	**788.23**
FOOD	**77.59**	**18.74**	**23.34**	**40.46**	**139.71**	**179.69**	**72.00**	**26.22**
Fresh fruit other than apples, bananas, and citrus	2.36	0.25	0.51	2.11	3.89	6.38	0.72	0.50
Candy and chewing gum	9.41	4.11	4.45	11.84	15.83	11.03	6.07	4.73
Board (including at school)	16.71	2.29	0.93	3.63	51.26	29.86	6.79	3.69
Catered affairs	25.42	0.11	2.73	3.69	31.32	103.17	28.90	1.73
ALCOHOLIC BEVERAGES	**16.11**	**9.67**	**21.01**	**16.10**	**21.64**	**16.63**	**10.52**	**5.52**
Beer and ale	3.93	6.05	5.68	3.09	3.68	4.63	3.39	0.92
Wine	9.58	3.51	12.58	10.47	14.54	9.42	4.37	2.09
HOUSING	**220.43**	**75.07**	**139.22**	**203.55**	**321.82**	**309.52**	**213.17**	**180.85**
Housekeeping supplies	**41.56**	**17.09**	**31.33**	**54.38**	**49.19**	**51.91**	**40.52**	**21.22**
Laundry and cleaning supplies	2.25	0.65	1.47	2.10	3.52	3.19	2.38	1.07
Other household products	12.41	1.89	4.84	23.62	13.07	15.77	11.71	4.44
Miscellaneous household products	5.57	1.56	3.57	9.96	5.65	8.10	3.36	1.21
Lawn and garden supplies	5.42	–	0.82	12.30	5.34	5.39	6.90	1.63
Postage and stationery	26.89	14.55	25.02	28.65	32.60	32.95	26.42	15.72
Stationery, stationery supplies, giftwrap	19.13	9.90	20.48	19.49	22.88	18.91	22.96	11.49
Postage	7.17	3.95	4.52	8.31	9.44	13.42	1.26	4.23
Household textiles	**12.72**	**1.71**	**5.46**	**9.78**	**20.87**	**23.48**	**14.80**	**5.71**
Bathroom linens	3.30	0.22	1.89	2.26	4.19	9.79	1.50	1.08
Bedroom linens	5.95	–	1.72	3.70	12.59	9.63	8.10	1.47
Appliances and miscellaneous housewares	**24.51**	**8.84**	**13.71**	**25.45**	**30.94**	**36.35**	**29.21**	**18.49**
Major appliances	6.65	0.93	2.64	8.71	7.94	7.13	7.78	9.25
Small appliances and miscellaneous housewares	17.87	7.91	11.07	16.74	23.00	29.22	21.43	9.24
China and other dinnerware	2.04	–	0.31	0.90	1.75	4.64	5.80	2.20
Glassware	2.15	4.69	1.35	2.21	0.73	5.16	1.06	1.17
Nonelectric cookware	3.62	–	2.16	5.67	2.89	5.90	3.98	2.55
Tableware, nonelectric kitchenware	5.09	0.72	3.28	4.09	12.47	3.56	4.20	1.39
Small electric kitchen appliances	2.28	1.06	2.79	1.13	2.28	4.48	2.82	1.04
Miscellaneous household equipment	**56.73**	**19.26**	**40.25**	**40.99**	**81.12**	**91.16**	**63.40**	**41.92**
Infants' equipment	4.69	0.86	6.27	3.62	1.74	8.53	12.22	
Household decorative items	18.91	6.78	17.71	11.34	21.09	36.77	21.34	14.12
Indoor plants, fresh flowers	10.86	6.96	6.16	8.57	13.53	17.37	12.39	10.45
Computers and computer hardware, nonbusiness use	8.04	1.37	1.67	4.67	23.19	8.74	6.22	1.38
Miscellaneous household equipment and parts	4.33	1.10	3.15	4.41	6.25	2.55	3.85	8.02
Other housing	**84.91**	**28.17**	**48.47**	**72.96**	**139.70**	**106.61**	**65.24**	**93.50**
Repair or maintenance services	4.18	1.83	2.18	4.07	4.26	2.74	0.08	15.73
Materials for additions, finishing basements, remodeling rooms	2.23	–	2.22	7.84	–	0.62	1.05	–
Housing while attending school	28.03	1.78	0.76	13.51	89.18	36.94	14.80	2.41
Lodging on trips	2.49	0.30	0.66	1.32	2.36	4.16	8.99	1.05
Utility: natural gas (renter)	2.82	1.86	3.05	2.38	1.70	3.32	2.58	5.88
Electricity (renter)	9.55	8.88	11.99	7.92	6.67	10.05	9.45	14.49
Day care centers, nurseries, and preschools	9.49	2.58	11.77	13.81	9.21	10.76	0.75	9.02
Bedroom furniture other than mattresses and springs	2.57	–	0.20	0.51	4.01	2.61	2.45	10.17
APPAREL AND SERVICES	**225.14**	**116.09**	**220.44**	**220.00**	**250.46**	**313.56**	**264.97**	**107.62**
Men and boys, aged 2 or older	**55.56**	**30.15**	**37.58**	**55.20**	**70.83**	**80.02**	**57.23**	**38.54**
Men's suits	2.93	1.52	1.63	2.05	5.13	4.52	2.88	1.43
Men's coats and jackets	3.95	2.06	6.43	3.69	6.15	4.57	–	–
Men's accessories	2.76	2.64	1.27	1.36	3.49	5.28	2.57	3.59
Men's sweaters and vests	2.29	1.22	1.49	2.01	3.14	4.32	1.80	0.94
Men's active sportswear	4.09	2.68	1.33	7.39	6.20	1.36	4.97	1.50
Men's shirts	8.37	4.45	5.37	7.48	10.43	11.32	11.32	7.06
Men's pants	6.03	6.57	2.25	3.12	8.26	9.88	4.05	10.58
Boys' shirts	3.68	1.22	2.53	3.24	3.74	4.59	9.81	0.76
Boys' pants	4.23	1.11	2.70	4.65	4.44	8.01	4.35	2.31
Women and girls, aged 2 or older	**80.28**	**18.83**	**67.62**	**78.45**	**82.69**	**122.15**	**129.74**	**38.23**
Women's coats and jackets	7.09	3.86	3.32	3.68	1.95	21.50	9.53	11.47
Women's dresses	4.76	–	6.77	5.69	3.98	5.23	8.48	–
Women's vests and sweaters	7.06	1.40	4.67	8.04	8.97	11.89	7.19	2.53
Women's shirts, tops, blouses	8.50	3.59	8.19	9.88	8.47	9.22	11.33	6.03

	total consumer units	under 25	25 to 34	35 to 44	45 to 54	55 to 64	65 to 74	75+
Women's pants	$6.42	$1.35	$7.69	$5.99	$7.31	$9.62	$7.87	$0.98
Women's active sportswear	3.27	2.49	5.44	1.21	1.85	4.34	4.58	4.62
Women's sleepwear	5.62	1.40	4.15	7.47	4.67	5.27	12.10	3.36
Women's undergarments	3.14	0.32	3.95	4.29	2.28	4.00	4.98	–
Women's accessories	4.55	0.12	1.69	4.92	4.94	11.51	4.85	1.15
Girls' dresses and suits	2.12	–	3.35	2.58	2.18	1.76	2.90	0.15
Girls' shirts, blouses, sweaters	5.42	1.13	2.71	6.12	7.38	7.20	9.58	1.07
Girls' skirts and pants	4.58	1.77	2.60	4.59	5.95	6.40	7.43	1.75
Girls' active sportswear	2.07	0.75	1.54	0.94	1.23	4.69	5.89	0.46
Girls' accessories	2.24	–	4.17	0.68	1.74	1.63	7.86	–
Children under age 2	**38.81**	**27.99**	**50.73**	**44.53**	**41.00**	**52.22**	**18.19**	**10.63**
Infant dresses, outerwear	11.89	8.31	11.71	8.33	15.99	18.96	10.27	5.57
Infant underwear	19.44	15.59	32.15	30.24	13.81	21.32	2.19	3.04
Infant nightwear, loungewear	2.49	1.59	2.75	1.59	3.84	3.50	2.11	0.86
Infant accessories	3.96	1.67	3.09	3.65	6.26	6.58	2.39	0.94
Other apparel products and services	**50.49**	**39.12**	**64.51**	**41.82**	**55.93**	**59.17**	**59.81**	**20.23**
Jewelry and watches	25.85	27.16	49.09	14.15	24.23	26.57	28.33	9.47
Jewelry	24.28	25.97	47.60	13.01	22.03	25.20	26.09	8.25
All other apparel products and services	24.63	11.96	15.42	27.67	31.70	32.60	31.48	10.76
Men's footwear	5.05	7.67	1.90	4.13	7.26	3.17	8.36	5.15
Boys' footwear	4.10	–	3.92	8.68	3.03	2.48	5.30	1.04
Women's footwear	7.98	3.01	4.16	5.93	14.55	10.81	10.54	2.48
Girls' footwear	5.88	0.97	4.65	7.54	4.92	12.95	5.13	0.89
TRANSPORTATION	**59.73**	**7.37**	**77.28**	**23.25**	**105.87**	**72.16**	**42.73**	**52.17**
New cars	11.55	–	21.57	–	24.04	9.40	16.90	–
New trucks	13.10	–	37.61	–	–	25.69	–	30.04
Used cars	13.37	–	2.26	12.66	40.17	6.48	0.05	13.33
Used trucks	3.78	–	0.78	0.63	13.24	5.73	0.37	–
Airline fares	7.28	3.36	5.86	4.12	9.93	10.29	12.35	4.63
Ship fares	3.74	1.32	1.43	3.29	5.48	7.69	3.36	1.69
HEALTH CARE	**47.89**	**2.84**	**7.85**	**22.78**	**49.07**	**48.35**	**43.67**	**205.84**
Physician's services	3.33	0.14	0.39	4.32	5.14	2.56	1.74	7.72
Dental services	3.66	0.55	0.47	1.38	9.80	1.81	2.03	7.20
Hospital services other than room	2.20	–	0.58	0.98	1.14	8.48	0.81	3.71
Care in convalescent or nursing home	20.37	–	–	0.48	8.33	4.54	10.89	170.30
Nonprescription drugs	3.09	0.50	0.58	0.98	2.61	2.60	16.55	1.95
Prescription drugs	2.89	0.58	0.40	1.38	5.62	1.54	3.93	7.58
ENTERTAINMENT	**68.97**	**38.80**	**59.74**	**61.07**	**80.87**	**111.14**	**66.74**	**41.13**
Toys, games, hobbies, and tricycles	26.07	7.80	22.61	21.16	29.79	45.42	32.65	14.07
Other entertainment	42.89	31.00	37.13	39.91	51.08	65.71	34.08	27.06
Fees for recreational lessons	6.02	0.05	0.92	4.05	10.40	14.83	5.17	2.73
Community antenna or cable TV	3.53	6.68	4.42	2.02	2.88	2.63	2.30	6.73
VCRs and video disc players	2.52	1.32	2.61	2.71	3.28	4.07	0.97	0.61
Pet purchase, supplies, and medicine	2.33	1.07	5.96	1.53	1.44	3.57	0.45	0.53
Athletic gear, game tables, exercise equipment	6.00	11.01	6.61	8.72	4.40	8.24	1.18	–
Photographic equipment	2.10	2.26	1.59	1.76	4.20	1.97	1.38	0.28
PERSONAL CARE PRODUCTS AND SERVICES	**15.77**	**7.26**	**11.82**	**15.53**	**23.03**	**19.40**	**13.72**	**11.61**
Cosmetics, perfume, bath preparation	9.98	4.18	6.74	11.66	14.80	10.95	5.83	9.54
EDUCATION	**199.83**	**23.06**	**31.50**	**96.80**	**509.66**	**373.03**	**111.12**	**54.28**
College tuition	155.43	16.03	19.50	65.98	446.03	252.85	78.48	33.79
Elementary and high school tuition	10.44	–	4.47	5.91	11.48	23.87	16.02	11.05
Other school expenses including rentals	15.75	0.30	0.71	6.80	18.69	69.33	0.64	4.00
College books and supplies	9.97	6.49	2.93	5.13	23.87	16.89	4.75	2.15
Miscellaneous school supplies	6.20	0.07	1.73	10.70	7.93	7.13	7.75	2.71
ALL OTHER GIFTS	**74.21**	**21.60**	**46.56**	**40.93**	**84.25**	**125.91**	**110.30**	**100.78**
Gifts of trip expenses	40.70	12.83	28.70	22.58	46.66	84.25	54.35	32.08
Legal fees	4.50	0.78	0.82	2.83	4.90	12.77	2.13	6.80
Funeral expenses	21.80	0.87	14.90	6.60	23.89	20.00	46.17	55.82
Cemetery lots, vaults, and maintenance fees	2.24	–	0.72	0.69	2.31	3.66	6.14	3.72
Miscellaneous personal services	2.49	0.35	0.87	6.44	4.02	0.50	0.65	–

Note: (–) means sample is too small to make a reliable estimate. Expenditures for items in a given category may not add to category total because categories with annual spending of less than $2.00 for the average household are omitted. Spending on gifts is also included in the product and service categories in other chapters.
Source: Bureau of Labor Statistics, unpublished tables from the 2003 Consumer Expenditure Survey

Table 6.2 Gifts for Nonhousehold Members: Indexed spending by age, 2003

(indexed average annual spending of consumer units (CU) on selected gifts of products and services for nonhousehold members by age of consumer unit reference person, 2003; index definition: an index of 100 is the average for all consumer units; an index of 132 means that spending by consumer units in that group is 32 percent above the average for all consumer units; an index of 68 indicates spending that is 32 percent below the average for all consumer units)

	total consumer units	under 25	25 to 34	35 to 44	45 to 54	55 to 64	65 to 74	75+
Average spending of CU, total	$40,817	$22,396	$40,525	$47,175	$50,101	$44,191	$33,629	$25,016
Average spending of CU, index	100	55	99	116	123	108	82	61
Gifts, spending index	100	32	63	74	158	156	95	78
FOOD	100	24	30	52	180	232	93	34
Fresh fruit other than apples, bananas, and citrus	100	11	22	89	165	270	31	21
Candy and chewing gum	100	44	47	126	168	117	65	50
Board (including at school)	100	14	6	22	307	179	41	22
Catered affairs	100	0	11	15	123	406	114	7
ALCOHOLIC BEVERAGES	100	60	130	100	134	103	65	34
Beer and ale	100	154	145	79	94	118	86	23
Wine	100	37	131	109	152	98	46	22
HOUSING	100	34	63	92	146	140	97	82
Housekeeping supplies	100	41	75	131	118	125	97	51
Laundry and cleaning supplies	100	29	65	93	156	142	106	48
Other household products	100	15	39	190	105	127	94	36
Miscellaneous household products	100	28	64	179	101	145	60	22
Lawn and garden supplies	100	–	15	227	99	99	127	30
Postage and stationery	100	54	93	107	121	123	98	58
Stationery, stationery supplies, giftwrap	100	52	107	102	120	99	120	60
Postage	100	55	63	116	132	187	18	59
Household textiles	100	13	43	77	164	185	116	45
Bathroom linens	100	7	57	68	127	297	45	33
Bedroom linens	100	–	29	62	212	162	136	25
Appliances and miscellaneous housewares	100	36	56	104	126	148	119	75
Major appliances	100	14	40	131	119	107	117	139
Small appliances and miscellaneous housewares	100	44	62	94	129	164	120	52
China and other dinnerware	100	–	15	44	86	227	284	108
Glassware	100	218	63	103	34	240	49	54
Nonelectric cookware	100	–	60	157	80	163	110	70
Tableware, nonelectric kitchenware	100	14	64	80	245	70	83	27
Small electric kitchen appliances	100	46	122	50	100	196	124	46
Miscellaneous household equipment	100	34	71	72	143	161	112	74
Infants' equipment	100	18	134	77	37	182	261	–
Household decorative items	100	36	94	60	112	194	113	75
Indoor plants, fresh flowers	100	64	57	79	125	160	114	96
Computers and computer hardware, nonbusiness use	100	17	21	58	288	109	77	17
Miscellaneous household equipment and parts	100	25	73	102	144	59	89	185
Other housing	100	33	57	86	165	126	77	110
Repair or maintenance services	100	44	52	97	102	66	2	376
Materials for additions, finishing basements, remodeling rooms	100	–	100	352	–	28	47	–
Housing while attending school	100	6	3	48	318	132	53	9
Lodging on trips	100	12	27	53	95	167	361	42
Utility: natural gas (renter)	100	66	108	84	60	118	91	209
Electricity (renter)	100	93	126	83	70	105	99	152
Day care centers, nurseries, and preschools	100	27	124	146	97	113	8	95
Bedroom furniture other than mattresses and springs	100	–	8	20	156	102	95	396
APPAREL AND SERVICES	100	52	98	98	111	139	118	48
Men and boys, aged 2 or older	100	54	68	99	127	144	103	69
Men's suits	100	52	56	70	175	154	98	49
Men's coats and jackets	100	52	163	93	156	116	–	–
Men's accessories	100	96	46	49	126	191	93	130
Men's sweaters and vests	100	53	65	88	137	189	79	41
Men's active sportswear	100	66	33	181	152	33	122	37
Men's shirts	100	53	64	89	125	135	135	84
Men's pants	100	109	37	52	137	164	67	175
Boys' shirts	100	33	69	88	102	125	267	21
Boys' pants	100	26	64	110	105	189	103	55
Women and girls, aged 2 or older	100	23	84	98	103	152	162	48
Women's coats and jackets	100	54	47	52	28	303	134	162
Women's dresses	100	–	142	120	84	110	178	–
Women's vests and sweaters	100	20	66	114	127	168	102	36

	total consumer units	under 25	25 to 34	35 to 44	45 to 54	55 to 64	65 to 74	75+
Women's shirts, tops, blouses	100	42	96	116	100	108	133	71
Women's pants	100	21	120	93	114	150	123	15
Women's active sportswear	100	76	166	37	57	133	140	141
Women's sleepwear	100	25	74	133	83	94	215	60
Women's undergarments	100	10	126	137	73	127	159	–
Women's accessories	100	3	37	108	109	253	107	25
Girls' dresses and suits	100	–	158	122	103	83	137	7
Girls' shirts, blouses, sweaters	100	21	50	113	136	133	177	20
Girls' skirts and pants	100	39	57	100	130	140	162	38
Girls' active sportswear	100	36	74	45	59	227	285	22
Girls' accessories	100	–	186	30	78	73	351	–
Children under age 2	**100**	**72**	**131**	**115**	**106**	**135**	**47**	**27**
Infant dresses, outerwear	100	70	98	70	134	159	86	47
Infant underwear	100	80	165	156	71	110	11	16
Infant nightwear, loungewear	100	64	110	64	154	141	85	35
Infant accessories	100	42	78	92	158	166	60	24
Other apparel products and services	**100**	**77**	**128**	**83**	**111**	**117**	**118**	**40**
Jewelry and watches	100	105	190	55	94	103	110	37
Jewelry	100	107	196	54	91	104	107	34
All other apparel products and services	100	49	63	112	129	132	128	44
Men's footwear	100	152	38	82	144	63	166	102
Boys' footwear	100	–	96	212	74	60	129	25
Women's footwear	100	38	52	74	182	135	132	31
Girls' footwear	100	16	79	128	84	220	87	15
TRANSPORTATION	**100**	**12**	**129**	**39**	**177**	**121**	**72**	**87**
New cars	100	–	187	–	208	81	146	–
New trucks	100	–	287	–	–	196	–	229
Used cars	100	–	17	95	300	48	0	100
Used trucks	100	–	21	17	350	152	10	–
Airline fares	100	46	80	57	136	141	170	64
Ship fares	100	35	38	88	147	206	90	45
HEALTH CARE	**100**	**6**	**16**	**48**	**102**	**101**	**91**	**430**
Physician's services	100	4	12	130	154	77	52	232
Dental services	100	15	13	51	268	49	55	197
Hospital services other than room	100	–	26	45	52	385	37	169
Care in convalescent or nursing home	100	–	–	2	41	22	53	836
Nonprescription drugs	100	16	19	32	84	84	536	63
Prescription drugs	100	20	14	48	194	53	136	262
ENTERTAINMENT	**100**	**56**	**87**	**89**	**117**	**161**	**97**	**60**
Toys, games, hobbies, and tricycles	100	30	87	81	114	174	125	54
Other entertainment	100	72	87	93	119	153	79	63
Fees for recreational lessons	100	1	15	67	173	246	86	45
Community antenna or cable TV	100	189	125	57	82	75	65	191
VCRs and video disc players	100	52	104	108	130	162	38	24
Pet purchase, supplies, and medicine	100	46	256	66	62	153	19	23
Athletic gear, game tables, exercise equipment	100	184	110	145	73	137	20	–
Photographic equipment	100	108	76	84	200	94	66	13
PERSONAL CARE PRODUCTS AND SERVICES	**100**	**46**	**75**	**98**	**146**	**123**	**87**	**74**
Cosmetics, perfume, bath preparation	100	42	68	117	148	110	58	96
EDUCATION	**100**	**12**	**16**	**48**	**255**	**187**	**56**	**27**
College tuition	100	10	13	42	287	163	50	22
Elementary and high school tuition	100	–	43	57	110	229	153	106
Other school expenses including rentals	100	2	5	43	119	440	4	25
College books and supplies	100	65	29	51	239	169	48	22
Miscellaneous school supplies	100	1	28	173	128	115	125	44
ALL OTHER GIFTS	**100**	**29**	**63**	**55**	**114**	**170**	**149**	**136**
Gifts of trip expenses	100	32	71	55	115	207	134	79
Legal fees	100	17	18	63	109	284	47	151
Funeral expenses	100	4	68	30	110	92	212	256
Cemetery lots, vaults, and maintenance fees	100	–	32	31	103	163	274	166
Miscellaneous personal services	100	14	35	259	161	20	26	–

Note: (–) means sample is too small to make a reliable estimate. Categories with annual spending of less than $2.00 for the average household are omitted. Spending on gifts is also included in the product and service categories in other chapters.
Source: Calculations by New Strategist based on the 2003 Consumer Expenditure Survey

Table 6.3 Gifts for Nonhousehold Members: Total spending by age, 2003

(total annual spending on selected gifts of products and services for nonhousehold members by consumer unit (CU) age groups, 2003; numbers in thousands)

	total consumer units	under 25	25 to 34	35 to 44	45 to 54	55 to 64	65 to 74	75+
Number of consumer units	115,356	8,584	19,737	24.413	23,131	16,580	11,495	11,417
Total spending of all CUs	$4,708,523,919	$192,243,230	$799,846,267	$1,151,684,740	$1,158,882,993	$732,680,977	$386,567,309	$285,612,010
Gifts, total spending	**116,164,646**	**2,753,661**	**12,617,469**	**18,089,056**	**36,720,925**	**26,062,434**	**10,946,344**	**8,999,222**
FOOD	**8,950,472**	**160,864**	**460,662**	**987,750**	**3,231,632**	**2,979,260**	**827,640**	**299,354**
Fresh fruit other than apples, bananas, and citrus	272,240	2,146	10,066	51,511	89,980	105,780	8,276	5,709
Candy and chewing gum	1,085,500	35,280	87,830	289,050	366,164	182,877	69,775	54,002
Board (including at school)	1,927,599	19,657	18,355	88,619	1,185,695	495,079	78,051	42,129
Catered affairs	2,932,350	944	53,882	90,084	724,463	1,710,559	332,206	19,751
ALCOHOLIC BEVERAGES	**1,858,385**	**83,007**	**414,674**	**393,049**	**500,555**	**275,725**	**120,927**	**63,022**
Beer and ale	453,349	51,933	112,106	75,436	85,122	76,765	38,968	10,504
Wine	1,105,110	30,130	248,291	255,604	336,325	156,184	50,233	23,862
HOUSING	**25,427,923**	**644,401**	**2,747,785**	**4,969,266**	**7,444,018**	**5,131,842**	**2,450,389**	**2,064,764**
Housekeeping supplies	**4,794,195**	**146,701**	**618,360**	**1,327,579**	**1,137,814**	**860,668**	**465,777**	**242,269**
Laundry and cleaning supplies	259,551	5,580	29,013	51,267	81,421	52,890	27,358	12,216
Other household products	1,431,568	16,224	95,527	576,635	302,322	261,467	134,606	50,691
Miscellaneous household products	642,533	13,391	70,461	243,153	130,690	134,298	38,623	13,815
Lawn and garden supplies	625,230	–	16,184	300,280	123,520	89,366	79,316	18,610
Postage and stationery	3,101,923	124,897	493,820	699,432	754,071	546,311	303,698	179,475
Stationery, stationery supplies, giftwrap	2,206,760	84,982	404,214	475,809	529,237	313,528	263,925	131,181
Postage	827,103	33,907	89,211	202,872	218,357	222,504	14,484	48,294
Household textiles	**1,467,328**	**14,679**	**107,764**	**238,759**	**482,744**	**389,298**	**170,126**	**65,191**
Bathroom linens	380,675	1,888	37,303	55,173	96,919	162,318	17,243	12,330
Bedroom linens	686,368	–	33,948	90,328	291,219	159,665	93,110	16,783
Appliances and miscellaneous housewares	**2,827,376**	**75,883**	**270,594**	**621,311**	**715,673**	**602,683**	**335,769**	**211,100**
Major appliances	767,117	7,983	52,106	212,637	183,660	118,215	89,431	105,607
Small appliances and miscellaneous housewares	2,061,412	67,899	218,489	408,674	532,013	484,468	246,338	105,493
China and other dinnerware	235,326	–	6,118	21,972	40,479	76,931	66,671	25,117
Glassware	248,015	40,259	26,645	53,953	16,886	85,553	12,185	13,358
Nonelectric cookware	417,589	–	42,632	138,422	66,849	97,822	45,750	29,113
Tableware, nonelectric kitchenware	587,162	6,180	64,737	99,849	288,444	59,025	48,279	15,870
Small electric kitchen appliances	263,012	9,099	55,066	27,587	52,739	74,278	32,416	11,874
Miscellaneous household equipment	**6,544,146**	**165,328**	**794,414**	**1,000,689**	**1,876,387**	**1,511,433**	**728,783**	**478,601**
Infants' equipment	541,020	7,382	123,751	38,375	40,248	141,427	140,469	–
Household decorative items	2,181,382	58,200	349,542	276,843	487,833	609,647	245,303	161,208
Indoor plants, fresh flowers	1,252,766	59,745	121,580	209,219	312,962	287,995	142,423	119,308
Computers and computer hardware, nonbusiness use	927,462	11,760	32,961	114,009	536,408	144,909	71,499	15,755
Miscellaneous household equipment and parts	499,491	9,442	62,172	107,661	144,569	42,279	44,256	91,564
Other housing	**9,794,878**	**241,811**	**956,652**	**1,781,172**	**3,231,401**	**1,767,594**	**749,934**	**1,067,490**
Repair or maintenance services	482,188	15,709	43,027	99,361	98,538	45,429	920	179,589
Materials for additions, finishing basements, remodeling rooms	257,244	–	43,816	191,398	–	10,280	12,070	–
Housing while attending school	3,233,429	15,280	15,000	329,820	2,062,823	612,465	170,126	27,515
Lodging on trips	287,236	2,575	13,026	32,225	54,589	68,973	103,340	11,988
Utility: natural gas (renter)	325,304	15,966	60,198	58,103	39,323	55,046	29,657	67,132
Electricity (renter)	1,101,650	76,226	236,647	193,351	154,284	166,629	108,628	165,432
Day care centers, nurseries, and preschools	1,094,728	22,147	232,304	337,144	213,037	178,401	8,621	102,981
Bedroom furniture other than mattresses and springs	296,465	–	3,947	12,451	92,755	43,274	28,163	116,111
APPAREL AND SERVICES	**25,971,250**	**996,517**	**4,350,824**	**5,370,860**	**5,793,390**	**5,198,825**	**3,045,830**	**1,228,698**
Men and boys, aged 2 or older	**6,409,179**	**258,808**	**741,716**	**1,347,598**	**1,638,369**	**1,326,732**	**657,859**	**440,011**
Men's suits	337,993	13,048	32,171	50,047	118,662	74,942	33,106	16,326
Men's coats and jackets	455,656	17,683	126,909	90,084	142,256	75,771	–	–
Men's accessories	318,383	22,662	25,066	33,202	80,727	87,542	29,542	40,987
Men's sweaters and vests	264,165	10,472	29,408	49,070	72,631	71,626	20,691	10,732
Men's active sportswear	471,806	23,005	26,250	180,412	143,412	22,549	57,130	17,126
Men's shirts	965,530	38,199	105,988	182,609	241,256	187,686	130,123	80,604
Men's pants	695,597	56,397	44,408	76,169	191,062	163,810	46,555	120,792
Boys' shirts	424,510	10,472	49,935	79,098	86,510	76,102	112,766	8,677
Boys' pants	487,956	9,528	53,290	113,520	102,702	132,806	50,003	26,373
Women and girls, aged 2 or older	**9,260,780**	**161,637**	**1,334,616**	**1,915,200**	**1,912,702**	**2,025,247**	**1,491,361**	**436,472**
Women's coats and jackets	817,874	33,134	65,527	89,840	45,105	356,470	109,547	130,953
Women's dresses	549,095	–	133,619	138,910	92,061	86,713	97,478	–
Women's vests and sweaters	814,413	12,018	92,172	196,281	207,485	197,136	82,649	28,885

	total consumer units	under 25	25 to 34	35 to 44	45 to 54	55 to 64	65 to 74	75+
Women's shirts, tops, blouses	$980,526	$30,817	$151,646	$241,200	$195,920	$152,868	$130,238	$68,845
Women's pants	740,586	11,588	151,778	146,234	169,088	159,500	90,466	11,189
Women's active sportswear	377,214	21,374	137,369	29,540	42,792	71,957	52,647	52,747
Women's sleepwear	648,301	12,018	51,909	182,365	108,022	87,377	139,090	38,361
Women's undergarments	362,218	2,747	77,961	104,732	52,739	66,320	57,245	–
Women's accessories	524,870	1,030	33,356	120,112	114,267	190,836	55,751	13,130
Girls' dresses and suits	244,555	–	66,119	62,986	50,426	29,181	33,336	1,713
Girls' shirts, blouses, sweaters	625,230	9,700	53,487	149,408	170,707	119,376	110,122	12,216
Girls' skirts and pants	528,330	15,194	51,316	112,056	137,629	106,112	85,408	19,980
Girls' active sportswear	238,787	6,438	30,395	22,948	28,451	77,760	67,706	5,252
Girls' accessories	258,397		82,303	16,601	40,248	27,025	90,351	–
Children under age 2	**4,476,966**	**240,266**	**1,001,258**	**1,087,111**	**948,371**	**865,808**	**209,094**	**121,363**
Infant dresses, outerwear	1,371,583	71,333	221,120	203,360	369,865	314,357	118,054	63,593
Infant underwear	2,242,521	133,825	634,545	738,249	319,439	353,486	25,174	34,708
Infant nightwear, loungewear	287,236	13,649	54,277	38,817	88,823	58,030	24,254	9,819
Infant accessories	456,810	14,335	60,987	89,107	144,800	109,096	27,473	10,732
Other apparel products and services	**5,824,324**	**335,806**	**1,273,234**	**1,020,952**	**1,293,717**	**981,039**	**687,516**	**230,966**
Jewelry and watches	2,981,953	233,141	968,889	345,444	560,464	440,531	325,653	108,119
Jewelry	2,800,844	222,926	939,481	317,613	509,576	417,816	299,905	94,190
All other apparel products and services	2,841,218	102,665	304,345	675,508	733,253	540,508	361,863	122,847
Men's footwear	582,548	65,839	37,500	100,826	167,931	52,559	96,098	58,798
Boys' footwear	472,960	–	77,369	211,905	70,087	41,118	60,924	11,874
Women's footwear	920,541	25,838	82,106	144,769	336,556	179,230	121,157	28,314
Girls' footwear	678,293	8,326	91,777	184,074	113,805	214,711	58,969	10,161
TRANSPORTATION	**6,890,214**	**63,264**	**1,525,275**	**567,602**	**2,448,879**	**1,196,413**	**491,181**	**595,625**
New cars	1,332,362		425,727	–	556,069	155,852	194,266	–
New trucks	1,511,164	–	742,309	–	–	425,940	–	342,967
Used cars	1,542,310	–	44,606	309,069	929,172	107,438	575	152,189
Used trucks	436,046	–	15,395	15,380	306,254	95,003	4,253	–
Airline fares	839,792	28,842	115,659	100,582	229,691	170,608	141,963	52,861
Ship fares	431,431	11,331	28,224	80,319	126,758	127,500	38,623	19,295
HEALTH CARE	**5,524,399**	**24,379**	**154,935**	**556,128**	**1,135,038**	**801,643**	**501,987**	**2,350,075**
Physician's services	384,135	1,202	7,697	105,464	118,893	42,445	20,001	88,139
Dental services	422,203	4,721	9,276	45,896	226,684	30,010	23,335	82,202
Hospital services other than room	253,783	–	11,447	23,925	26,369	140,598	9,311	42,357
Care in convalescent or nursing home	2,349,802	–	–	11,718	192,681	75,273	125,181	1,944,315
Nonprescription drugs	356,450	4,292	11,447	23,925	60,372	43,108	190,242	22,263
Prescription drugs	333,379	4,979	7,895	33,690	129,996	25,533	45,175	86,541
ENTERTAINMENT	**7,956,103**	**333,059**	**1,179,088**	**1,490,902**	**1,870,604**	**1,842,701**	**767,176**	**469,581**
Toys, games, hobbies, and tricycles	3,007,331	66,955	446,254	516,579	589,072	753,064	375,312	160,637
Other entertainment	4,947,619	266,104	732,835	974,323	1,181,531	1,089,472	391,750	308,944
Fees for recreational lessons	694,443	429	18,158	98,873	240,562	245,881	59,429	31,168
Community antenna or cable TV	407,207	57,341	87,238	49,314	66,617	43,605	26,439	76,836
VCRs and video disc players	290,697	11,331	51,514	66,159	75,870	67,481	11,150	6,964
Pet purchase, supplies, and medicine	268,779	9,185	117,533	37,352	33,309	59,191	5,173	6,051
Athletic gear, game tables, exercise equipment	692,136	94,510	130,462	212,881	101,776	136,619	13,564	–
Photographic equipment	242,248	19,400	31,382	42,967	97,150	32,663	15,863	3,197
PERSONAL CARE PRODUCTS, SERVICES	**1,819,164**	**62,320**	**233,291**	**379,134**	**532,707**	**321,652**	**157,711**	**132,551**
Cosmetics, perfume, bath preparation	1,151,253	35,881	133,027	284,656	342,339	181,551	67,016	108,918
EDUCATION	**23,051,589**	**197,947**	**621,716**	**2,363,178**	**11,788,945**	**6,184,837**	**1,277,324**	**619,715**
College tuition	17,929,783	137,602	384,872	1,610,770	10,317,120	4,192,253	902,128	385,780
Elementary and high school tuition	1,204,317	–	88,224	144,281	265,544	395,765	184,150	126,158
Other school expenses including rentals	1,816,857	2,575	14,013	156,008	432,318	1,149,491	7,357	45,668
College books and supplies	1,150,099	55,710	57,829	125,239	552,137	280,036	54,601	24,547
Miscellaneous school supplies	715,207	601	34,145	261,219	133,429	118,215	89,086	30,940
ALL OTHER GIFTS	**8,560,569**	**185,414**	**918,955**	**999,224**	**1,948,787**	**2,087,588**	**1,267,899**	**1,150,605**
Gifts of trip expenses	4,694,989	110,133	566,452	551,246	1,079,292	1,396,865	624,753	366,257
Legal fees	519,102	6,696	16,184	69,089	113,342	211,727	24,484	77,636
Funeral expenses	2,514,761	7,468	294,081	161,126	552,600	331,600	530,724	637,297
Cemetery lots, vaults, and maintenance fees	258,397	–	14,211	16,845	53,433	60,683	70,579	42,471
Miscellaneous personal services	287,236	3,004	17,171	157,220	92,987	8,290	7,472	–

Note: Numbers may not add to total because of rounding. (–) means sample is too small to make a reliable estimate. Expenditures for items in a given category may not add to category total because categories with annual spending of less than $2.00 for the average household are omitted. Spending on gifts is also included in the product and service categories in other chapters.
Source: Calculations by New Strategist based on the 2003 Consumer Expenditure Survey

Table 6.4 Gifts for Nonhousehold Members: Market shares by age, 2003

(percentage of total annual spending on selected gifts of products and services for nonhousehold members accounted for by consumer unit age groups, 2003)

	total consumer units	under 25	25 to 34	35 to 44	45 to 54	55 to 64	65 to 74	75+
Share of total consumer units	100.0%	7.4%	17.1%	21.2%	20.1%	14.4%	10.0%	9.9%
Share of total before-tax income	100.0	3.0	16.9	25.3	26.7	16.5	6.9	4.9
Share of total spending	100.0	4.1	17.0	24.5	24.6	15.6	8.2	6.1
Share of gifts spending	100.0	2.4	10.9	15.6	31.6	22.4	9.4	7.7
FOOD	100.0	1.8	5.1	11.0	36.1	33.3	9.2	3.3
Fresh fruit other than apples, bananas, and citrus	100.0	0.8	3.7	18.9	33.1	38.9	3.0	2.1
Candy and chewing gum	100.0	3.3	8.1	26.6	33.7	16.8	6.4	5.0
Board (including at school)	100.0	1.0	1.0	4.6	61.5	25.7	4.0	2.2
Catered affairs	100.0	0.0	1.8	3.1	24.7	58.3	11.3	0.7
ALCOHOLIC BEVERAGES	100.0	4.5	22.3	21.2	26.9	14.8	6.5	3.4
Beer and ale	100.0	11.5	24.7	16.6	18.8	16.9	8.6	2.3
Wine	100.0	2.7	22.5	23.1	30.4	14.1	4.5	2.2
HOUSING	100.0	2.5	10.8	19.5	29.3	20.2	9.6	8.1
Housekeeping supplies	100.0	3.1	12.9	27.7	23.7	18.0	9.7	5.1
Laundry and cleaning supplies	100.0	2.1	11.2	19.8	31.4	20.4	10.5	4.7
Other household products	100.0	1.1	6.7	40.3	21.1	18.3	9.4	3.5
Miscellaneous household products	100.0	2.1	11.0	37.8	20.3	20.9	6.0	2.2
Lawn and garden supplies	100.0	–	2.6	48.0	19.8	14.3	12.7	3.0
Postage and stationery	100.0	4.0	15.9	22.5	24.3	17.6	9.8	5.8
Stationery, stationery supplies, giftwrap	100.0	3.9	18.3	21.6	24.0	14.2	12.0	5.9
Postage	100.0	4.1	10.8	24.5	26.4	26.9	1.8	5.8
Household textiles	100.0	1.0	7.3	16.3	32.9	26.5	11.6	4.4
Bathroom linens	100.0	0.5	9.8	14.5	25.5	42.6	4.5	3.2
Bedroom linens	100.0	–	4.9	13.2	42.4	23.3	13.6	2.4
Appliances and miscellaneous housewares	100.0	2.7	9.6	22.0	25.3	21.3	11.9	7.5
Major appliances	100.0	1.0	6.8	27.7	23.9	15.4	11.7	13.8
Small appliances and miscellaneous housewares	100.0	3.3	10.6	19.8	25.8	23.5	11.9	5.1
China and other dinnerware	100.0	–	2.6	9.3	17.2	32.7	28.3	10.7
Glassware	100.0	16.2	10.7	21.8	6.8	34.5	4.9	5.4
Nonelectric cookware	100.0	–	10.2	33.1	16.0	23.4	11.0	7.0
Tableware, nonelectric kitchenware	100.0	1.1	11.0	17.0	49.1	10.1	8.2	2.7
Small electric kitchen appliances	100.0	3.5	20.9	10.5	20.1	28.2	12.3	4.5
Miscellaneous household equipment	100.0	2.5	12.1	15.3	28.7	23.1	11.1	7.3
Infants' equipment	100.0	1.4	22.9	16.3	7.4	26.1	26.0	–
Household decorative items	100.0	2.7	16.0	12.7	22.4	27.9	11.2	7.4
Indoor plants, fresh flowers	100.0	4.8	9.7	16.7	25.0	23.0	11.4	9.5
Computers and computer hardware, nonbusiness use	100.0	1.3	3.6	12.3	57.8	15.6	7.7	1.7
Miscellaneous household equipment and parts	100.0	1.9	12.4	21.6	28.9	8.5	8.9	18.3
Other housing	100.0	2.5	9.8	18.2	33.0	18.0	7.7	10.9
Repair or maintenance services	100.0	3.3	8.9	20.6	20.4	9.4	0.2	37.2
Materials for additions, finishing basements, remodeling rooms	100.0	–	17.0	74.4	–	4.0	4.7	–
Housing while attending school	100.0	0.5	0.5	10.2	63.8	18.9	5.3	0.9
Lodging on trips	100.0	0.9	4.5	11.2	19.0	24.0	36.0	4.2
Utility: natural gas (renter)	100.0	4.9	18.5	17.9	12.1	16.9	9.1	20.6
Electricity (renter)	100.0	6.9	21.5	17.6	14.0	15.1	9.9	15.0
Day care centers, nurseries, and preschools	100.0	2.0	21.2	30.8	19.5	16.3	0.8	9.4
Bedroom furniture other than mattresses and springs	100.0	–	1.3	4.2	31.3	14.6	9.5	39.2
APPAREL AND SERVICES	100.0	3.8	16.8	20.7	22.3	20.0	11.7	4.7
Men and boys, aged 2 or older	100.0	4.0	11.6	21.0	25.6	20.7	10.3	6.9
Men's suits	100.0	3.9	9.5	14.8	35.1	22.2	9.8	4.8
Men's coats and jackets	100.0	3.9	27.9	19.8	31.2	16.6	–	–
Men's accessories	100.0	7.1	7.9	10.4	25.4	27.5	9.3	12.9
Men's sweaters and vests	100.0	4.0	11.1	18.6	27.5	27.1	7.8	4.1
Men's active sportswear	100.0	4.9	5.6	38.2	30.4	4.8	12.1	3.6
Men's shirts	100.0	4.0	11.0	18.9	25.0	19.4	13.5	8.3
Men's pants	100.0	8.1	6.4	11.0	27.5	23.5	6.7	17.4
Boys' shirts	100.0	2.5	11.8	18.6	20.4	17.9	26.6	2.0
Boys' pants	100.0	2.0	10.9	23.3	21.0	27.2	10.2	5.4
Women and girls, aged 2 or older	100.0	1.7	14.4	20.7	20.7	21.9	16.1	4.7
Women's coats and jackets	100.0	4.1	8.0	11.0	5.5	43.6	13.4	16.0
Women's dresses	100.0	–	24.3	25.3	16.8	15.8	17.8	–
Women's vests and sweaters	100.0	1.5	11.3	24.1	25.5	24.2	10.1	3.5

	total consumer units	under 25	25 to 34	35 to 44	45 to 54	55 to 64	65 to 74	75+
Women's shirts, tops, blouses	100.0%	3.1%	16.5%	24.6%	20.0%	15.6%	13.3%	7.0%
Women's pants	100.0	1.6	20.5	19.7	22.8	21.5	12.2	1.5
Women's active sportswear	100.0	5.7	28.5	7.8	11.3	19.1	14.0	14.0
Women's sleepwear	100.0	1.9	12.6	28.1	16.7	13.5	21.5	5.9
Women's undergarments	100.0	0.8	21.5	28.9	14.6	18.3	15.8	–
Women's accessories	100.0	0.2	6.4	22.9	21.8	36.4	10.6	2.5
Girls' dresses and suits	100.0	–	27.0	25.8	20.6	11.9	13.6	0.7
Girls' shirts, blouses, sweaters	100.0	1.6	8.6	23.9	27.3	19.1	17.6	2.0
Girls' skirts and pants	100.0	2.9	9.7	21.2	26.0	20.1	16.2	3.8
Girls' active sportswear	100.0	2.7	12.7	9.6	11.9	32.6	28.4	2.2
Girls' accessories	100.0	–	31.9	6.4	15.6	10.5	35.0	–
Children under age 2	**100.0**	**5.4**	**22.4**	**24.3**	**21.2**	**19.3**	**4.7**	**2.7**
Infant dresses, outerwear	100.0	5.2	16.9	14.8	27.0	22.9	8.6	4.6
Infant underwear	100.0	6.0	28.3	32.9	14.2	15.8	1.1	1.5
Infant nightwear, loungewear	100.0	4.8	18.9	13.5	30.9	20.2	8.4	3.4
Infant accessories	100.0	3.1	13.4	19.5	31.7	23.9	6.0	2.3
Other apparel products and services	**100.0**	**5.8**	**21.9**	**17.5**	**22.2**	**16.8**	**11.8**	**4.0**
Jewelry and watches	100.0	7.8	32.5	11.6	18.8	14.8	10.9	3.6
Jewelry	100.0	8.0	33.5	11.3	18.2	14.9	10.7	3.4
All other apparel products and services	100.0	3.6	10.7	23.8	25.8	19.0	12.7	4.3
Men's footwear	100.0	11.3	6.4	17.3	28.8	9.0	16.5	10.1
Boys' footwear	100.0	–	16.4	44.8	14.8	8.7	12.9	2.5
Women's footwear	100.0	2.8	8.9	15.7	36.6	19.5	13.2	3.1
Girls' footwear	100.0	1.2	13.5	27.1	16.8	31.7	8.7	1.5
TRANSPORTATION	**100.0**	**0.9**	**22.1**	**8.2**	**35.5**	**17.4**	**7.1**	**8.6**
New cars	100.0	–	32.0	–	41.7	11.7	14.6	–
New trucks	100.0	–	49.1	–	–	28.2	–	22.7
Used cars	100.0	–	2.9	20.0	60.2	7.0	0.0	9.9
Used trucks	100.0	–	3.5	3.5	70.2	21.8	1.0	–
Airline fares	100.0	3.4	13.8	12.0	27.4	20.3	16.9	6.3
Ship fares	100.0	2.6	6.5	18.6	29.4	29.6	9.0	4.5
HEALTH CARE	**100.0**	**0.4**	**2.8**	**10.1**	**20.5**	**14.5**	**9.1**	**42.5**
Physician's services	100.0	0.3	2.0	27.5	31.0	11.0	5.2	22.9
Dental services	100.0	1.1	2.2	10.9	53.7	7.1	5.5	19.5
Hospital services other than room	100.0	–	4.5	9.4	10.4	55.4	3.7	16.7
Care in convalescent or nursing home	100.0	–	–	0.5	8.2	3.2	5.3	82.7
Nonprescription drugs	100.0	1.2	3.2	6.7	16.9	12.1	53.4	6.2
Prescription drugs	100.0	1.5	2.4	10.1	39.0	7.7	13.6	26.0
ENTERTAINMENT	**100.0**	**4.2**	**14.8**	**18.7**	**23.5**	**23.2**	**9.6**	**5.9**
Toys, games, hobbies, and tricycles	100.0	2.2	14.8	17.2	22.9	25.0	12.5	5.3
Other entertainment	100.0	5.4	14.8	19.7	23.9	22.0	7.9	6.2
Fees for recreational lessons	100.0	0.1	2.6	14.2	34.6	35.4	8.6	4.5
Community antenna or cable TV	100.0	14.1	21.4	12.1	16.4	10.7	6.5	18.9
VCRs and video disc players	100.0	3.9	17.7	22.8	26.1	23.2	3.8	2.4
Pet purchase, supplies, and medicine	100.0	3.4	43.8	13.9	12.4	22.0	1.9	2.3
Athletic gear, game tables, exercise equipment	100.0	13.7	18.3	30.8	14.7	19.7	2.0	–
Photographic equipment	100.0	8.0	13.0	17.7	40.1	13.5	6.5	1.3
PERSONAL CARE PRODUCTS AND SERVICES	**100.0**	**3.4**	**12.8**	**20.8**	**29.3**	**17.7**	**8.7**	**7.3**
Cosmetics, perfume, bath preparation	100.0	3.1	11.6	24.7	29.7	15.8	5.8	9.5
EDUCATION	**100.0**	**0.9**	**2.7**	**10.3**	**51.1**	**26.8**	**5.5**	**2.7**
College tuition	100.0	0.8	2.2	9.0	57.5	23.4	5.0	2.2
Elementary and high school tuition	100.0	–	7.3	12.0	22.0	32.9	15.3	10.5
Other school expenses including rentals	100.0	0.1	0.8	9.1	23.8	63.3	0.4	2.5
College books and supplies	100.0	4.8	5.6	10.9	48.0	24.3	4.7	2.1
Miscellaneous school supplies	100.0	0.1	4.8	36.5	25.6	16.5	12.5	4.3
ALL OTHER GIFTS	**100.0**	**2.2**	**10.7**	**11.7**	**22.8**	**24.4**	**14.8**	**13.4**
Gifts of trip expenses	100.0	2.3	12.1	11.7	23.0	29.8	13.3	7.8
Legal fees	100.0	1.3	3.1	13.3	21.8	40.8	4.7	15.0
Funeral expenses	100.0	0.3	11.7	6.4	22.0	13.2	21.1	25.3
Cemetery lots, vaults, and maintenance fees	100.0	–	5.5	6.5	20.7	23.5	27.3	16.4
Miscellaneous personal services	100.0	1.0	6.0	54.7	32.4	2.9	2.6	–

Note: Numbers may not add to total because of rounding. (–) means sample is too small to make a reliable estimate. Expenditures for items in a given category may not add to category total because categories with annual spending of less than $2.00 for the average household are omitted. Spending on gifts is also included in the product and service categories in other chapters.
Source: Calculations by New Strategist based on the 2003 Consumer Expenditure Survey

Table 6.5 Gifts for Nonhousehold Members: Average spending by income, 2003

(average annual spending on selected gifts of products and services for nonhousehold members by before-tax income of consumer units (CU), 2003; complete income reporters only)

	total complete reporters	under $20,000	$20,000–$39,999	$40,000–$49,999	$50,000–$69,999	$70,000–$79,999	$80,000–$99,999	$100,000 or more
Number of consumer units (000)	97,391	27,100	23,941	8,891	13,890	5,121	6,909	11,537
Average number of persons per CU	2.5	1.8	2.4	2.6	2.8	3.0	3.0	3.1
Average before-tax income of CU	$51,128.00	$10,752.55	$29,072.57	$44,294.00	$58,900.00	$74,560.00	$88,832.00	$154,665.00
Average spending of CU, total	42,741.66	19,862.52	31,684.32	39,756.91	49,788.99	57,128.14	65,957.39	93,514.86
Gifts, average spending	**1,055.13**	**400.94**	**670.63**	**799.33**	**1,141.98**	**1,225.24**	**1,369.38**	**3,254.95**
FOOD	**84.32**	**27.60**	**54.36**	**27.32**	**94.07**	**73.21**	**84.79**	**321.45**
Fresh fruit other than apples, bananas, and citrus	2.54	2.80	1.15	0.59	1.25	14.78	4.10	1.86
Candy and chewing gum	9.37	5.33	6.20	4.68	8.56	10.34	8.63	31.28
Board (including at school)	18.55	1.65	1.14	3.27	10.44	5.15	13.39	127.06
Catered affairs	28.57	0.70	34.37	1.69	41.42	8.02	20.10	101.46
ALCOHOLIC BEVERAGES	**19.07**	**12.38**	**8.47**	**13.46**	**24.01**	**17.99**	**26.11**	**53.60**
Beer and ale	4.41	3.54	3.46	3.37	4.95	8.19	6.18	6.28
Wine	11.83	7.80	3.93	8.82	14.08	8.10	17.85	36.72
HOUSING	**238.46**	**92.62**	**179.85**	**219.73**	**227.03**	**243.91**	**366.36**	**663.51**
Housekeeping supplies	**47.59**	**22.15**	**30.52**	**39.06**	**67.35**	**59.54**	**66.23**	**114.13**
Laundry and cleaning supplies	2.44	1.98	2.36	1.21	4.05	1.93	1.61	3.58
Other household products	14.66	5.83	10.94	8.20	9.98	20.09	13.18	54.62
Miscellaneous household products	6.35	1.98	5.38	4.96	6.93	11.40	9.68	15.45
Lawn and garden supplies	6.61	2.76	3.78	2.31	1.64	5.77	0.80	36.17
Postage and stationery	30.50	14.33	17.22	29.64	53.33	37.51	51.43	55.94
Stationery, stationery supplies, giftwrap	22.31	11.15	13.23	20.75	43.80	28.96	28.21	37.75
Postage	7.48	2.91	3.27	7.86	7.45	8.56	23.22	17.74
Household textiles	**14.41**	**4.95**	**9.77**	**12.27**	**7.99**	**13.25**	**24.49**	**51.97**
Bathroom linens	3.30	1.01	1.37	1.87	2.99	4.66	15.46	7.01
Bedroom linens	7.08	–	6.90	6.45	1.53	5.15	3.44	31.94
Appliances and miscellaneous housewares	**27.61**	**7.01**	**21.00**	**27.24**	**27.96**	**29.86**	**30.55**	**88.58**
Major appliances	6.72	1.97	2.92	16.39	4.48	3.47	7.79	21.10
Small appliances and miscellaneous housewares	20.89	5.04	18.09	10.85	23.48	26.39	22.76	67.48
China and other dinnerware	2.58	–	–	0.22	4.32	1.85	2.49	3.93
Glassware	2.76	–	2.17	5.47	2.91	5.78	3.00	6.36
Nonelectric cookware	3.99	2.38	4.33	0.23	3.86	4.68	0.60	12.37
Tableware, nonelectric kitchenware	6.11	0.55	3.43	1.91	7.75	1.35	7.20	28.96
Small electric kitchen appliances	2.50	0.67	1.98	2.34	2.57	2.87	2.18	7.94
Miscellaneous household equipment	**62.16**	**22.69**	**45.84**	**52.66**	**76.02**	**72.21**	**121.63**	**142.27**
Infants' equipment	4.75	–	6.19	0.25	0.19	8.47	16.84	1.42
Household decorative items	21.06	8.67	13.84	18.53	26.48	14.80	51.50	47.34
Indoor plants, fresh flowers	11.70	4.48	11.58	7.51	12.47	16.30	17.79	25.54
Computers and computer hardware, nonbusiness use	8.71	0.78	1.12	11.23	6.87	17.89	6.70	40.77
Miscellaneous household equipment and parts	5.37	0.88	7.08	8.30	7.68	1.76	3.13	10.10
Other housing	**86.70**	**35.82**	**72.72**	**88.50**	**47.72**	**69.05**	**123.45**	**266.56**
Repair or maintenance services	4.50	0.94	8.95	13.06	3.69	–	2.37	1.28
Materials for additions, finishing basements, remodeling rooms	2.60	0.01	2.39	3.74	0.58	–	–	13.44
Housing while attending school	26.45	1.65	2.88	14.02	8.05	32.73	40.50	156.23
Lodging on trips	2.86	1.09	0.69	6.89	4.08	1.03	3.41	7.87
Utility: natural gas (renter)	2.98	4.06	3.01	3.57	1.50	4.56	1.36	1.95
Electricity (renter)	9.57	16.90	10.30	6.92	6.62	6.57	2.37	2.04
Day care centers, nurseries, and preschools	10.48	2.09	12.36	17.11	6.25	10.31	28.46	17.05
Bedroom furniture other than mattresses and springs	2.91	0.24	2.16	1.06	3.59	0.80	15.63	4.91
APPAREL AND SERVICES	**232.08**	**118.57**	**185.09**	**208.27**	**300.38**	**308.73**	**322.27**	**457.34**
Men and boys, aged 2 or older	**55.46**	**35.74**	**38.81**	**43.88**	**61.99**	**79.77**	**91.70**	**109.51**
Men's suits	3.09	0.46	1.53	0.71	3.45	8.72	2.18	12.60
Men's coats and jackets	2.60	–	1.65	–	4.60	–	1.92	9.90
Men's accessories	2.98	–	2.79	1.30	2.31	2.24	2.20	8.62
Men's sweaters and vests	2.27	0.69	1.70	1.26	2.11	4.41	3.75	6.26
Men's active sportswear	4.70	–	1.69	1.60	8.40	–	7.13	17.56
Men's shirts	8.52	7.81	4.60	5.96	8.87	9.71	24.10	10.88
Men's pants	6.03	4.53	4.84	12.95	3.25	11.16	12.15	3.66
Boys' shirts	4.33	4.61	3.66	2.10	2.59	15.71	0.15	6.66
Boys' pants	3.97	2.27	3.21	5.25	5.71	3.43	5.24	5.87
Women and girls, aged 2 or older	**88.62**	**42.08**	**63.60**	**68.66**	**124.20**	**143.81**	**107.58**	**194.05**
Women's coats and jackets	9.40	2.52	8.92	17.66	10.88	10.31	4.20	24.21
Women's dresses	5.17	–	0.92	0.68	4.33	24.29	0.52	20.63
Women's vests and sweaters	8.37	5.31	5.02	4.59	13.13	16.56	8.30	17.19

	total complete reporters	under $20,000	$20,000–$39,999	$40,000–$49,999	$50,000–$69,999	$70,000–$79,999	$80,000–$99,999	$100,000 or more
Women's shirts, tops, blouses	$10.34	$4.61	$7.62	$6.90	$16.23	$20.94	$17.28	$17.36
Women's pants	6.94	–	4.10	1.78	18.11	5.76	6.13	15.98
Women's active sportswear	3.17	3.35	2.72	2.77	0.93	–	5.70	6.71
Women's sleepwear	6.89	–	4.17	4.19	10.66	4.03	12.71	10.42
Women's undergarments	3.08	1.32	3.14	6.84	1.18	3.80	1.08	7.99
Women's accessories	5.02	–	4.51	3.22	6.74	3.16	10.64	10.70
Girls' dresses and suits	2.30	–	2.62	2.60	0.12	6.60	3.72	5.35
Girls' shirts, blouses, sweaters	4.60	–	3.88	2.98	5.20	14.74	11.41	4.69
Girls' skirts and pants	4.34	2.55	3.74	3.16	5.84	4.69	6.22	7.60
Girls' active sportswear	2.28	–	2.59	1.68	1.17	7.91	0.97	5.91
Girls' accessories	2.38	–	1.69	0.90	7.81	2.09	3.42	1.57
Children under age 2	**40.68**	**20.78**	**34.89**	**46.27**	**42.91**	**38.61**	**73.28**	**73.64**
Infant dresses, outerwear	12.69	5.14	11.26	13.82	13.26	15.42	18.59	27.11
Infant underwear	19.85	11.47	14.66	23.86	20.21	17.54	39.11	36.50
Infant nightwear, loungewear	2.62	0.80	2.90	1.99	2.19	1.97	6.05	5.56
Infant accessories	4.41	3.51	5.21	5.82	5.81	2.25	7.48	2.15
Other apparel products and services	**47.32**	**19.97**	**47.78**	**49.46**	**71.28**	**46.55**	**49.72**	**80.14**
Jewelry and watches	23.28	7.55	25.07	15.92	42.65	25.50	19.84	39.13
Jewelry	21.55	6.62	23.75	15.41	40.14	23.02	17.32	36.29
All other apparel products and services	24.04	12.42	22.71	32.54	28.63	21.05	29.88	41.01
Men's footwear	4.69	–	2.83	10.60	7.06	1.81	7.95	3.66
Boys' footwear	4.13	–	5.05	5.44	4.63	0.82	–	6.10
Women's footwear	8.53	–	6.20	3.91	7.85	4.65	16.39	26.43
Girls' footwear	5.00	–	6.30	11.16	6.48	13.07	3.81	1.78
TRANSPORTATION	**55.89**	**20.20**	**28.44**	**54.14**	**88.77**	**136.92**	**72.77**	**112.14**
New cars	13.68	–	–	–	13.99	83.16	33.04	41.91
New trucks	3.52	–	–	–	–	–	–	–
Used cars	15.84	0.08	15.11	20.09	48.72	27.13	6.06	12.52
Used trucks	3.32	–	–	13.80	–	–	4.25	9.23
Airline fares	7.91	2.08	4.61	8.37	11.71	10.13	11.38	21.27
Ship fares	4.28	0.32	1.44	2.45	4.63	9.48	10.11	14.79
HEALTH CARE	**51.96**	**51.40**	**41.63**	**28.32**	**44.80**	**20.02**	**38.75**	**123.72**
Physician's services	2.46	1.17	1.48	0.66	4.88	1.26	1.50	7.14
Dental services	3.94	0.93	4.39	1.91	3.82	3.01	3.40	13.16
Hospital services other than room	2.06	–	–	1.36	4.76	0.01	1.02	1.92
Care in convalescent or nursing home	23.32	–	19.84	8.12	3.58	0.74	17.62	62.32
Nonprescription drugs	3.89	7.95	1.87	0.80	3.74	0.59	1.76	3.79
Prescription drugs	3.09	3.26	3.25	1.88	1.72	5.35	1.07	5.13
ENTERTAINMENT	**74.22**	**24.61**	**63.29**	**58.31**	**83.89**	**109.57**	**101.24**	**183.68**
Toys, games, hobbies, and tricycles	26.19	10.44	23.35	25.77	31.99	35.86	36.81	51.76
Other entertainment	48.03	14.17	39.94	32.53	51.90	73.70	64.43	131.92
Fees for recreational lessons	6.42	0.41	2.92	2.22	3.77	4.58	4.90	36.33
Community antenna or cable TV	3.59	6.08	3.95	2.14	2.32	1.98	1.39	1.69
VCRs and video disc players	2.68	0.81	1.44	2.10	4.98	3.21	4.42	6.06
Pet purchase, supplies, and medicine	3.00	–	1.13	0.42	10.38	0.64	2.31	7.99
Athletic gear, game tables, exercise equipment	8.04	1.94	11.40	3.46	3.92	22.30	9.89	19.74
Photographic equipment	2.26	0.72	0.89	0.49	2.27	1.29	5.67	8.93
PERSONAL CARE PRODUCTS AND SERVICES	**18.65**	**11.14**	**9.61**	**35.03**	**24.91**	**17.90**	**24.06**	**32.18**
Cosmetics, perfume, bath preparation	12.03	7.13	4.80	23.63	16.07	9.89	21.10	19.95
EDUCATION	**200.89**	**10.73**	**46.82**	**83.91**	**150.58**	**178.99**	**208.76**	**1,124.83**
College tuition	152.71	4.22	31.36	72.48	117.72	125.67	165.64	861.54
Elementary and high school tuition	11.51	2.49	4.05	1.63	13.02	8.21	17.63	54.97
Other school expenses including rentals	16.85	0.99	2.58	2.58	3.44	9.96	6.80	119.86
College books and supplies	10.23	2.53	4.09	2.95	7.29	14.57	12.74	46.83
Miscellaneous school supplies	7.40	1.36	3.04	3.32	6.55	7.82	5.19	37.79
ALL OTHER GIFTS	**78.11**	**31.05**	**52.08**	**68.27**	**101.46**	**114.57**	**122.85**	**180.39**
Gifts of trip expenses	42.35	11.42	22.86	35.90	63.06	56.02	62.55	117.32
Legal fees	5.17	–	4.84	7.66	4.98	10.25	2.76	4.81
Funeral expenses	22.84	13.16	22.65	21.43	23.38	38.33	44.99	26.28
Cemetery lots, vaults, and maintenance fees	2.16	1.21	0.71	1.79	1.79	0.61	8.07	5.31
Miscellaneous personal services	3.29	–	0.32	0.02	1.74	1.14	1.71	24.06

Note: (–) means sample is too small to make a reliable estimate. Expenditures for items in a given category may not add to category total because categories with annual spending of less than $2.00 for the average household are omitted. Spending on gifts is also included in the product and service categories in other chapters.
Source: Bureau of Labor Statistics, unpublished tables from the 2003 Consumer Expenditure Survey; calculations by New Strategist

Table 6.6 Gifts for Nonhousehold Members: Indexed spending by income, 2003

(indexed average annual spending of consumer units (CU) on selected gifts of products and services for nonhousehold members by before-tax income of consumer unit, 2003; complete income reporters only; index definition: an index of 100 is the average for all consumer units; an index of 132 means that spending by consumer units in that group is 32 percent above the average for all consumer units; an index of 68 indicates spending that is 32 percent below the average for all consumer units)

	total complete reporters	under $20,000	$20,000–$39,999	$40,000–$49,999	$50,000–$69,999	$70,000–$79,999	$80,000–$99,999	$100,000 or more
Average spending of CU, total	$42,742	$19,863	$31,684	$39,757	$49,789	$57,128	$65,957	$93,515
Average spending of CU, index	100	46	74	93	116	134	154	219
Gifts, spending index	**100**	**38**	**64**	**76**	**108**	**116**	**130**	**308**
FOOD	**100**	**33**	**64**	**32**	**112**	**87**	**101**	**381**
Fresh fruit other than apples, bananas, and citrus	100	110	45	23	49	582	161	73
Candy and chewing gum	100	57	66	50	91	110	92	334
Board (including at school)	100	9	6	18	56	28	72	685
Catered affairs	100	2	120	6	145	28	70	355
ALCOHOLIC BEVERAGES	**100**	**65**	**44**	**71**	**126**	**94**	**137**	**281**
Beer and ale	100	80	78	76	112	186	140	142
Wine	100	66	33	75	119	68	151	310
HOUSING	**100**	**39**	**75**	**92**	**95**	**102**	**154**	**278**
Housekeeping supplies	**100**	**47**	**64**	**82**	**142**	**125**	**139**	**240**
Laundry and cleaning supplies	100	81	97	50	166	79	66	147
Other household products	100	40	75	56	68	137	90	373
Miscellaneous household products	100	31	85	78	109	180	152	243
Lawn and garden supplies	100	42	57	35	25	87	12	547
Postage and stationery	100	47	56	97	175	123	169	183
Stationery, stationery supplies, giftwrap	100	50	59	93	196	130	126	169
Postage	100	39	44	105	100	114	310	237
Household textiles	**100**	**34**	**68**	**85**	**55**	**92**	**170**	**361**
Bathroom linens	100	31	41	57	91	141	468	212
Bedroom linens	100	–	98	91	22	73	49	451
Appliances and miscellaneous housewares	**100**	**25**	**76**	**99**	**101**	**108**	**111**	**321**
Major appliances	100	29	43	244	67	52	116	314
Small appliances and miscellaneous housewares	100	24	87	52	112	126	109	323
China and other dinnerware	100	–	–	9	167	72	97	152
Glassware	100	–	78	198	105	209	109	230
Nonelectric cookware	100	60	109	6	97	117	15	310
Tableware, nonelectric kitchenware	100	9	56	31	127	22	118	474
Small electric kitchen appliances	100	27	79	94	103	115	87	318
Miscellaneous household equipment	**100**	**37**	**74**	**85**	**122**	**116**	**196**	**229**
Infants' equipment	100	–	130	5	4	178	355	30
Household decorative items	100	41	66	88	126	70	245	225
Indoor plants, fresh flowers	100	38	99	64	107	139	152	218
Computers and computer hardware, nonbusiness use	100	9	13	129	79	205	77	468
Miscellaneous household equipment and parts	100	16	132	155	143	33	58	188
Other housing	**100**	**41**	**84**	**102**	**55**	**80**	**142**	**307**
Repair or maintenance services	100	21	199	290	82	–	53	28
Materials for additions, finishing basements, remodeling rooms	100	0	92	144	22	–	–	517
Housing while attending school	100	6	11	53	30	124	153	591
Lodging on trips	100	38	24	241	143	36	119	275
Utility: natural gas (renter)	100	-136	101	120	50	153	46	65
Electricity (renter)	100	177	108	72	69	69	25	21
Day care centers, nurseries, and preschools	100	20	118	163	60	98	272	163
Bedroom furniture other than mattresses and springs	100	8	74	36	123	27	537	169
APPAREL AND SERVICES	**100**	**51**	**80**	**90**	**129**	**133**	**139**	**197**
Men and boys, aged 2 or older	**100**	**64**	**70**	**79**	**112**	**144**	**165**	**197**
Men's suits	100	15	49	23	112	282	71	408
Men's coats and jackets	100	–	64	–	177	–	74	381
Men's accessories	100	–	94	44	78	75	74	289
Men's sweaters and vests	100	30	75	56	93	194	165	276
Men's active sportswear	100	–	36	34	179	–	152	374
Men's shirts	100	92	54	70	104	114	283	128
Men's pants	100	75	80	215	54	185	201	61
Boys' shirts	100	106	85	48	60	363	3	154
Boys' pants	100	57	81	132	144	86	132	148
Women and girls, aged 2 or older	**100**	**47**	**72**	**77**	**140**	**162**	**121**	**219**
Women's coats and jackets	100	27	95	188	116	110	45	258
Women's dresses	100	–	18	13	84	470	10	399
Women's vests and sweaters	100	63	60	55	157	198	99	205

	total complete reporters	under $20,000	$20,000–$39,999	$40,000–$49,999	$50,000–$69,999	$70,000–$79,999	$80,000–$99,999	$100,000 or more
Women's shirts, tops, blouses	100	45	74	67	157	203	167	168
Women's pants	100	–	59	26	261	83	88	230
Women's active sportswear	100	106	86	87	29	–	180	212
Women's sleepwear	100	–	50	61	155	58	184	151
Women's undergarments	100	43	102	222	38	123	35	259
Women's accessories	100	–	90	64	134	63	212	213
Girls' dresses and suits	100	–	114	113	5	287	162	233
Girls' shirts, blouses, sweaters	100	–	84	65	113	320	248	102
Girls' skirts and pants	100	59	86	73	135	108	143	175
Girls' active sportswear	100	–	–	74	51	347	43	259
Girls' accessories	100	–	71	38	328	88	144	66
Children under age 2	**100**	**51**	**86**	**114**	**105**	**95**	**180**	**181**
Infant dresses, outerwear	100	40	89	109	104	122	146	214
Infant underwear	100	58	74	120	102	88	197	184
Infant nightwear, loungewear	100	31	111	76	84	75	231	212
Infant accessories	100	80	118	132	132	51	170	49
Other apparel products and services	**100**	**42**	**101**	**105**	**151**	**98**	**105**	**169**
Jewelry and watches	100	32	118	73	183	110	85	168
Jewelry	100	31	110	72	186	107	80	168
All other apparel products and services	100	52	94	135	119	88	124	171
Men's footwear	100	–	60	226	151	39	170	78
Boys' footwear	100	–	122	132	112	20	–	148
Women's footwear	100	–	73	46	92	55	192	310
Girls' footwear	100	–	125	223	130	261	76	36
TRANSPORTATION	**100**	**36**	**51**	**97**	**159**	**245**	**130**	**201**
New cars	100	–	–	–	102	608	242	306
New trucks	100	–	–	–	–	–	–	–
Used cars	100	1	95	127	308	171	38	79
Used trucks	100	–	–	416	–	–	128	278
Airline fares	100	26	58	106	148	128	144	269
Ship fares	100	7	34	57	108	221	236	346
HEALTH CARE	**100**	**99**	**80**	**55**	**86**	**39**	**75**	**238**
Physician's services	100	48	60	27	198	51	61	290
Dental services	100	24	111	48	97	76	86	334
Hospital services other than room	100	–	–	66	231	0	50	93
Care in convalescent or nursing home	100	–	85	35	15	3	76	267
Nonprescription drugs	100	204	43	21	96	15	45	97
Prescription drugs	100	106	105	61	56	173	35	166
ENTERTAINMENT	**100**	**33**	**85**	**79**	**113**	**148**	**136**	**247**
Toys, games, hobbies, and tricycles	100	40	89	98	122	137	141	198
Other entertainment	100	30	83	68	108	153	134	275
Fees for recreational lessons	100	6	45	35	59	71	76	566
Community antenna or cable TV	100	169	110	60	65	55	39	47
VCRs and video disc players	100	30	54	78	186	120	165	226
Pet purchase, supplies, and medicine	100	–	38	14	346	21	77	266
Athletic gear, game tables, exercise equipment	100	24	142	43	49	277	123	246
Photographic equipment	100	32	39	22	100	57	251	395
PERSONAL CARE PRODUCTS AND SERVICES	**100**	**60**	**52**	**188**	**134**	**96**	**129**	**173**
Cosmetics, perfume, bath preparation	100	59	40	196	134	82	175	166
EDUCATION	**100**	**5**	**23**	**42**	**75**	**89**	**104**	**560**
College tuition	100	3	21	47	77	82	108	564
Elementary and high school tuition	100	22	35	14	113	71	153	478
Other school expenses including rentals	100	6	15	16	20	59	40	711
College books and supplies	100	25	40	29	71	142	125	458
Miscellaneous school supplies	100	18	41	45	89	106	70	511
ALL OTHER GIFTS	**100**	**40**	**67**	**87**	**130**	**147**	**157**	**231**
Gifts of trip expenses	100	27	54	85	149	132	148	277
Legal fees	100	–	94	148	96	198	53	93
Funeral expenses	100	58	99	94	102	168	197	115
Cemetery lots, vaults, and maintenance fees	100	56	33	83	83	28	374	246
Miscellaneous personal services	100	–	10	1	53	35	52	731

Note: (–) means sample is too small to make a reliable estimate. Categories with annual spending of less than $2.00 for the average household are omitted. Spending on gifts is also included in the product and service categories in other chapters.
Source: Calculations by New Strategist based on the 2003 Consumer Expenditure Survey

Table 6.7 Gifts for Nonhousehold Members: Total spending by income, 2003

(total annual spending on selected gifts of products and services for nonhousehold members by before-tax income group of consumer units (CU), 2003; complete income reporters only; numbers in thousands)

	total complete reporters	under $20,000	$20,000–$39,999	$40,000–$49,999	$50,000–$69,999	$70,000–$79,999	$80,000–$99,999	$100,000 or more
Number of consumer units	97,391	27,100	23,941	8,891	13,890	5,121	6,909	11,537
Total spending of all CUs	$4,162,653,009	$538,274,380	$758,554,310	$353,478,687	$691,569,071	$292,553,205	$455,699,608	$1,078,880,940
Gifts, total spending	**102,760,166**	**10,865,418**	**16,055,468**	**7,106,843**	**15,862,102**	**6,274,454**	**9,461,046**	**37,552,358**
FOOD	**8,212,009**	**748,043**	**1,301,359**	**242,902**	**1,306,632**	**374,908**	**585,814**	**3,708,569**
Fresh fruit other than apples, bananas, and citrus	247,373	75,909	27,593	5,246	17,363	75,688	28,327	21,459
Candy and chewing gum	912,554	144,329	148,455	41,610	118,898	52,951	59,625	360,877
Board (including at school)	1,806,603	44,662	27,339	29,074	145,012	26,373	92,512	1,465,891
Catered affairs	2,782,461	19,012	822,759	15,026	575,324	41,070	138,871	1,170,544
ALCOHOLIC BEVERAGES	**1,857,246**	**335,456**	**202,750**	**119,673**	**333,499**	**92,127**	**180,394**	**618,383**
Beer and ale	429,494	95,995	82,805	29,963	68,756	41,941	42,698	72,452
Wine	1,152,136	211,354	94,124	78,419	195,571	41,480	123,326	423,639
HOUSING	**23,223,858**	**2,509,914**	**4,305,720**	**1,953,619**	**3,153,447**	**1,249,063**	**2,531,181**	**7,654,915**
Housekeeping supplies	**4,634,838**	**600,157**	**730,669**	**347,282**	**935,492**	**304,904**	**457,583**	**1,316,718**
Laundry and cleaning supplies	237,634	53,678	56,619	10,758	56,255	9,884	11,123	41,302
Other household products	1,427,752	158,019	261,796	72,906	138,622	102,881	91,061	630,151
Miscellaneous household products	618,433	53,742	128,886	44,099	96,258	58,379	66,879	178,247
Lawn and garden supplies	643,755	74,840	90,533	20,538	22,780	29,548	5,527	417,293
Postage and stationery	2,970,426	388,470	412,361	263,529	740,754	192,089	355,330	645,380
Stationery, stationery supplies, giftwrap	2,172,793	302,280	316,674	184,488	608,382	148,304	194,903	435,522
Postage	728,485	78,923	78,287	69,883	103,481	43,836	160,427	204,666
Household textiles	**1,403,404**	**134,037**	**233,831**	**109,093**	**110,981**	**67,853**	**169,201**	**599,578**
Bathroom linens	321,390	27,371	32,732	16,626	41,531	23,864	106,813	80,874
Bedroom linens	689,528	–	165,310	57,347	21,252	26,373	23,767	368,492
Appliances and miscellaneous housewares	**2,688,966**	**190,082**	**502,870**	**242,191**	**388,364**	**152,913**	**211,070**	**1,021,947**
Major appliances	654,468	53,499	69,809	145,723	62,227	17,770	53,821	243,431
Small appliances and miscellaneous housewares	2,034,498	136,504	433,193	96,467	326,137	135,143	157,249	778,517
China and other dinnerware	251,269	–	–	1,956	60,005	9,474	17,203	45,340
Glassware	268,799	–	51,865	48,634	40,420	29,599	20,727	73,375
Nonelectric cookware	388,590	64,574	103,729	2,045	53,615	23,966	4,145	142,713
Tableware, nonelectric kitchenware	595,059	14,831	82,194	16,982	107,648	6,913	49,745	334,112
Small electric kitchen appliances	243,478	18,251	47,491	20,805	35,697	14,697	15,062	91,604
Miscellaneous household equipment	**6,053,825**	**614,887**	**1,097,391**	**468,200**	**1,055,918**	**369,787**	**840,342**	**1,641,369**
Infants' equipment	462,607	–	148,314	2,223	2,639	43,375	116,348	16,383
Household decorative items	2,051,054	235,022	331,379	164,750	367,807	75,791	355,814	546,162
Indoor plants, fresh flowers	1,139,475	121,415	277,187	66,771	173,208	83,472	122,911	294,655
Computers and computer hardware, nonbusiness use	848,276	21,169	26,785	99,846	95,424	91,615	46,290	470,363
Miscellaneous household equipment and parts	522,990	23,937	169,552	73,795	106,675	9,013	21,625	116,524
Other housing	**8,443,800**	**970,823**	**1,740,959**	**786,854**	**662,831**	**353,605**	**852,916**	**3,075,303**
Repair or maintenance services	438,260	25,539	214,390	116,116	51,254	–	16,374	14,767
Materials for additions, finishing basements, remodeling rooms	253,217	271	57,325	33,252	8,056	–	–	155,057
Housing while attending school	2,575,992	44,803	68,988	124,652	111,815	167,610	279,815	1,802,426
Lodging on trips	278,538	29,458	16,548	61,259	56,671	5,275	23,560	90,796
Utility: natural gas (renter)	290,225	110,036	72,115	31,741	20,835	23,352	9,396	22,497
Electricity (renter)	932,032	457,982	246,557	61,526	91,952	33,645	16,374	23,535
Day care centers, nurseries, and preschools	1,020,658	56,680	295,813	152,125	86,813	52,798	196,630	196,706
Bedroom furniture other than mattresses and springs	283,408	6,369	51,803	9,424	49,865	4,097	107,988	56,647
APPAREL AND SERVICES	**22,602,503**	**3,213,276**	**4,431,132**	**1,851,729**	**4,172,278**	**1,581,006**	**2,226,563**	**5,276,332**
Men and boys, aged 2 or older	**5,401,305**	**968,525**	**929,130**	**390,137**	**861,041**	**408,502**	**633,555**	**1,263,417**
Men's suits	300,938	12,503	36,562	6,313	47,921	44,655	15,062	145,366
Men's coats and jackets	253,217	–	39,594	–	63,894	–	13,265	114,216
Men's accessories	290,225	–	66,759	11,558	32,086	11,471	15,200	99,449
Men's sweaters and vests	221,078	18,645	40,774	11,203	29,308	22,584	25,909	72,222
Men's active sportswear	457,738	–	40,454	14,226	116,676	–	49,261	202,590
Men's shirts	829,771	211,645	110,089	52,990	123,204	49,725	166,507	125,523
Men's pants	587,268	122,718	115,898	115,227	45,143	57,150	83,944	42,225
Boys' shirts	421,703	124,825	87,688	18,671	35,975	80,451	1,036	76,836
Boys' pants	386,642	61,644	76,858	46,678	79,312	17,565	36,203	67,722
Women and girls, aged 2 or older	**8,630,790**	**1,140,483**	**1,522,738**	**610,456**	**1,725,138**	**736,451**	**743,270**	**2,238,755**
Women's coats and jackets	915,475	68,223	213,473	157,015	151,123	52,798	29,018	279,311
Women's dresses	503,511	–	21,971	6,046	60,144	124,389	3,593	238,008
Women's vests and sweaters	815,163	143,801	120,265	40,810	182,376	84,804	57,345	198,321

	total complete reporters	under $20,000	$20,000–$39,999	$40,000–$49,999	$50,000–$69,999	$70,000–$79,999	$80,000–$99,999	$100,000 or more
Women's shirts, tops, blouses	$1,007,023	$125,055	$182,337	$61,348	$225,435	$107,234	$119,388	$200,282
Women's pants	675,894	–	98,208	15,826	251,548	29,497	42,352	184,361
Women's active sportswear	308,729	90,897	65,275	24,628	12,918	–	39,381	77,413
Women's sleepwear	671,024	–	99,797	37,253	148,067	20,638	87,813	120,216
Women's undergarments	299,964	35,896	75,064	60,814	16,390	19,460	7,462	92,181
Women's accessories	488,903	–	108,004	28,529	93,619	16,182	73,512	123,446
Girls' dresses and suits	223,999	–	62,303	23,117	1,667	33,799	25,701	61,723
Girls' shirts, blouses, sweaters	447,999	–	92,343	26,495	72,228	75,484	78,832	54,109
Girls' skirts and pants	422,677	69,189	85,553	28,096	81,118	24,017	42,974	87,681
Girls' active sportswear	222,051	–	–	14,937	16,251	40,507	6,702	68,184
Girls' accessories	231,791	–	40,375	8,002	108,481	10,703	23,629	18,113
Children under age 2	**3,961,866**	**563,136**	**835,392**	**411,387**	**596,020**	**197,722**	**506,292**	**849,585**
Infant dresses, outerwear	1,235,892	139,249	269,621	122,874	184,181	78,966	128,438	312,768
Infant underwear	1,933,211	310,716	350,558	212,139	280,717	89,822	270,211	421,101
Infant nightwear, loungewear	255,164	21,774	69,491	17,693	30,419	10,088	41,799	64,146
Infant accessories	429,494	95,103	124,789	51,746	80,701	11,522	51,679	24,805
Other apparel products and services	**4,608,542**	**541,162**	**1,144,003**	**439,749**	**990,079**	**238,383**	**343,515**	**924,575**
Jewelry and watches	2,267,262	204,605	600,171	150,436	592,409	130,586	137,075	451,443
Jewelry	2,098,776	179,527	568,633	137,010	557,545	117,885	119,664	418,678
All other apparel products and services	2,341,280	336,556	543,699	289,313	397,671	107,797	206,441	473,132
Men's footwear	456,764	–	67,820	54,245	98,063	9,269	54,927	42,225
Boys' footwear	402,225	–	120,504	48,367	64,311	4,199	–	70,376
Women's footwear	830,745	–	148,500	34,764	109,037	23,813	113,239	304,923
Girls' footwear	486,955	–	150,761	99,224	90,007	66,931	26,323	20,536
TRANSPORTATION	**5,443,183**	**547,426**	**680,858**	**481,359**	**1,233,015**	**701,167**	**502,768**	**1,293,759**
New cars	1,332,309	–	–	–	194,321	425,862	228,273	483,516
New trucks	342,816	–	–	–	–	–	–	–
Used cars	1,542,673	2,168	361,714	178,620	576,721	138,933	41,869	144,443
Used trucks	323,338	–	–	122,696	–	–	29,363	106,487
Airline fares	770,363	56,333	110,457	74,418	162,652	51,876	78,624	245,392
Ship fares	416,833	8,633	34,530	21,733	64,311	48,547	69,850	170,632
HEALTH CARE	**5,060,436**	**1,392,832**	**996,665**	**251,793**	**622,272**	**102,522**	**267,724**	**1,427,358**
Physician's services	239,582	31,819	35,442	5,868	67,783	6,452	10,364	82,374
Dental services	383,721	25,335	105,127	16,982	53,060	15,414	23,491	151,827
Hospital services other than room	200,625	–	–	12,092	66,116	51	7,047	22,151
Care in convalescent or nursing home	2,271,158	–	474,947	72,195	49,726	3,790	121,737	718,986
Nonprescription drugs	378,851	215,380	44,872	7,113	51,949	3,021	12,160	43,725
Prescription drugs	300,938	88,375	77,778	16,715	23,891	27,397	7,393	59,185
ENTERTAINMENT	**7,228,360**	**666,964**	**1,515,342**	**518,434**	**1,165,232**	**561,108**	**699,467**	**2,119,116**
Toys, games, hobbies, and tricycles	2,550,670	282,980	559,130	229,121	444,341	183,639	254,320	597,155
Other entertainment	4,677,690	384,059	956,212	289,224	720,891	377,418	445,147	1,521,961
Fees for recreational lessons	625,250	11,238	69,513	19,738	52,365	23,454	33,854	419,139
Community antenna or cable TV	349,634	164,759	94,641	19,027	32,225	10,140	9,604	19,498
VCRs and video disc players	261,008	21,902	34,431	18,671	69,172	16,438	30,538	69,914
Pet purchase, supplies, and medicine	292,173	–	26,936	3,734	144,178	3,277	15,960	92,181
Athletic gear, game tables, exercise equipment	783,024	52,485	273,003	30,763	54,449	114,198	68,330	227,740
Photographic equipment	220,104	19,585	21,225	4,357	31,530	6,606	39,174	103,025
PERSONAL CARE PRODUCTS AND SERVICES	**1,816,342**	**301,906**	**230,112**	**311,452**	**346,000**	**91,666**	**166,231**	**371,261**
Cosmetics, perfume, bath preparation	1,171,614	193,339	114,952	210,094	223,212	50,647	145,780	230,163
EDUCATION	**19,564,878**	**290,744**	**1,120,901**	**746,044**	**2,091,556**	**916,608**	**1,442,323**	**12,977,164**
College tuition	14,872,580	114,427	750,695	644,420	1,635,131	643,556	1,144,407	9,939,587
Elementary and high school tuition	1,120,970	67,407	96,843	14,492	180,848	42,043	121,806	634,189
Other school expenses including rentals	1,641,038	26,722	61,655	23,828	47,782	51,005	46,981	1,382,825
College books and supplies	996,310	68,441	97,814	26,228	101,258	74,613	88,021	540,278
Miscellaneous school supplies	720,693	36,806	72,770	29,518	90,980	40,046	35,858	435,983
ALL OTHER GIFTS	**7,607,211**	**841,417**	**1,246,777**	**606,989**	**1,409,279**	**586,713**	**848,771**	**2,081,159**
Gifts of trip expenses	4,124,509	309,386	547,378	319,187	875,903	286,878	432,158	1,353,521
Legal fees	503,511	–	115,758	68,105	69,172	52,490	19,069	55,493
Funeral expenses	2,224,410	356,757	542,161	190,534	324,748	196,288	310,836	303,192
Cemetery lots, vaults, and maintenance fees	210,365	32,920	17,027	15,915	24,863	3,124	55,756	61,261
Miscellaneous personal services	320,416	–	7,717	178	24,169	5,838	11,814	277,580

Note: Numbers may not add to total because of rounding. (–) means sample is too small to make a reliable estimate. Expenditures for items in a given category may not add to category total because categories with annual spending of less than $2.00 for the average household are omitted. Spending on gifts is also included in the product and service categories in other chapters.

Source: Calculations by New Strategist based on the 2003 Consumer Expenditure Survey

Table 6.8 Gifts for Nonhousehold Members: Market shares by income, 2003

(percentage of total annual spending on selected gifts of products and services for nonhousehold members accounted for by before-tax income group of consumer units, 2003; complete income reporters only)

	total complete reporters	under $20,000	$20,000–$39,999	$40,000–$49,999	$50,000–$69,999	$70,000–$79,999	$80,000–$99,999	$100,000 or more
Share of total consumer units	100.0%	27.8%	24.6%	9.1%	14.3%	5.3%	7.1%	11.8%
Share of total before-tax income	100.0	5.9	14.0	7.9	16.4	7.7	12.3	35.8
Share of total spending	100.0	12.9	18.2	8.5	16.6	7.0	10.9	25.9
Share of gifts spending	100.0	10.6	15.6	6.9	15.4	6.1	9.2	36.5
FOOD	100.0	9.1	15.8	3.0	15.9	4.6	7.1	45.2
Fresh fruit other than apples, bananas, and citrus	100.0	30.7	11.2	2.1	7.0	30.6	11.5	8.7
Candy and chewing gum	100.0	15.8	16.3	4.6	13.0	5.8	6.5	39.5
Board (including at school)	100.0	2.5	1.5	1.6	8.0	1.5	5.1	81.1
Catered affairs	100.0	0.7	29.6	0.5	20.7	1.5	5.0	42.1
ALCOHOLIC BEVERAGES	100.0	18.1	10.9	6.4	18.0	5.0	9.7	33.3
Beer and ale	100.0	22.4	19.3	7.0	16.0	9.8	9.9	16.9
Wine	100.0	18.3	8.2	6.8	17.0	3.6	10.7	36.8
HOUSING	100.0	10.8	18.5	8.4	13.6	5.4	10.9	33.0
Housekeeping supplies	100.0	12.9	15.8	7.5	20.2	6.6	9.9	28.4
Laundry and cleaning supplies	100.0	22.6	23.8	4.5	23.7	4.2	4.7	17.4
Other household products	100.0	11.1	18.3	5.1	9.7	7.2	6.4	44.1
Miscellaneous household products	100.0	8.7	20.8	7.1	15.6	9.4	10.8	28.8
Lawn and garden supplies	100.0	11.6	14.1	3.2	3.5	4.6	0.9	64.8
Postage and stationery	100.0	13.1	13.9	8.9	24.9	6.5	12.0	21.7
Stationery, stationery supplies, giftwrap	100.0	13.9	14.6	8.5	28.0	6.8	9.0	20.0
Postage	100.0	10.8	10.7	9.6	14.2	6.0	22.0	28.1
Household textiles	100.0	9.6	16.7	7.8	7.9	4.8	12.1	42.7
Bathroom linens	100.0	8.5	10.2	5.2	12.9	7.4	33.2	25.2
Bedroom linens	100.0	–	24.0	8.3	3.1	3.8	3.4	53.4
Appliances and miscellaneous housewares	100.0	7.1	18.7	9.0	14.4	5.7	7.8	38.0
Major appliances	100.0	8.2	10.7	22.3	9.5	2.7	8.2	37.2
Small appliances and miscellaneous housewares	100.0	6.7	21.3	4.7	16.0	6.6	7.7	38.3
China and other dinnerware	100.0	–	–	0.8	23.9	3.8	6.8	18.0
Glassware	100.0	–	19.3	18.1	15.0	11.0	7.7	27.3
Nonelectric cookware	100.0	16.6	26.7	0.5	13.8	6.2	1.1	36.7
Tableware, nonelectric kitchenware	100.0	2.5	13.8	2.9	18.1	1.2	8.4	56.1
Small electric kitchen appliances	100.0	7.5	19.5	8.5	14.7	6.0	6.2	37.6
Miscellaneous household equipment	100.0	10.2	18.1	7.7	17.4	6.1	13.9	27.1
Infants' equipment	100.0	–	32.1	0.5	0.6	9.4	25.2	3.5
Household decorative items	100.0	11.5	16.2	8.0	17.9	3.7	17.3	26.6
Indoor plants, fresh flowers	100.0	10.7	24.3	5.9	15.2	7.3	10.8	25.9
Computers and computer hardware, nonbusiness use	100.0	2.5	3.2	11.8	11.2	10.8	5.5	55.4
Miscellaneous household equipment and parts	100.0	4.6	32.4	14.1	20.4	1.7	4.1	22.3
Other housing	100.0	11.5	20.6	9.3	7.8	4.2	10.1	36.4
Repair or maintenance services	100.0	5.8	48.9	26.5	11.7	–	3.7	3.4
Materials for additions, finishing basements, remodeling rooms	100.0	0.1	22.6	13.1	3.2	–	–	61.2
Housing while attending school	100.0	1.7	2.7	4.8	4.3	6.5	10.9	70.0
Lodging on trips	100.0	10.6	5.9	22.0	20.3	1.9	8.5	32.6
Utility: natural gas (renter)	100.0	37.9	24.8	10.9	7.2	8.0	3.2	7.8
Electricity (renter)	100.0	49.1	26.5	6.6	9.9	3.6	1.8	2.5
Day care centers, nurseries, and preschools	100.0	5.6	29.0	14.9	8.5	5.2	19.3	19.3
Bedroom furniture other than mattresses and springs	100.0	2.2	18.3	3.3	17.6	1.4	38.1	20.0
APPAREL AND SERVICES	100.0	14.2	19.6	8.2	18.5	7.0	9.9	23.3
Men and boys, aged 2 or older	100.0	17.9	17.2	7.2	15.9	7.6	11.7	23.4
Men's suits	100.0	4.2	12.1	2.1	15.9	14.8	5.0	48.3
Men's coats and jackets	100.0	–	15.6	–	25.2	–	5.2	45.1
Men's accessories	100.0	–	23.0	4.0	11.1	4.0	5.2	34.3
Men's sweaters and vests	100.0	8.4	18.4	5.1	13.3	10.2	11.7	32.7
Men's active sportswear	100.0	–	8.8	3.1	25.5	–	10.8	44.3
Men's shirts	100.0	25.5	13.3	6.4	14.8	6.0	20.1	15.1
Men's pants	100.0	20.9	19.7	19.6	7.7	9.7	14.3	7.2
Boys' shirts	100.0	29.6	20.8	4.4	8.5	19.1	0.2	18.2
Boys' pants	100.0	15.9	19.9	12.1	20.5	4.5	9.4	17.5
Women and girls, aged 2 or older	100.0	13.2	17.6	7.1	20.0	8.5	8.6	25.9
Women's coats and jackets	100.0	7.5	23.3	17.2	16.5	5.8	3.2	30.5
Women's dresses	100.0	–	4.4	1.2	11.9	24.7	0.7	47.3
Women's vests and sweaters	100.0	17.6	14.8	5.0	22.4	10.4	7.0	24.3

	total complete reporters	under $20,000	$20,000– $39,999	$40,000– $49,999	$50,000– $69,999	$70,000– $79,999	$80,000– $99,999	$100,000 or more
Women's shirts, tops, blouses	100.0%	12.4%	18.1%	6.1%	22.4%	10.6%	11.9%	19.9%
Women's pants	100.0	–	14.5	2.3	37.2	4.4	6.3	27.3
Women's active sportswear	100.0	29.4	21.1	8.0	4.2	–	12.8	25.1
Women's sleepwear	100.0	–	14.9	5.6	22.1	3.1	13.1	17.9
Women's undergarments	100.0	12.0	25.0	20.3	5.5	6.5	2.5	30.7
Women's accessories	100.0	–	22.1	5.9	19.1	3.3	15.0	25.2
Girls' dresses and suits	100.0	–	28.0	10.3	0.7	15.1	11.5	27.6
Girls' shirts, blouses, sweaters	100.0	–	20.7	5.9	16.1	16.8	17.6	12.1
Girls' skirts and pants	100.0	16.4	21.2	6.6	19.2	5.7	10.2	20.7
Girls' active sportswear	100.0	–	–	6.7	7.3	18.2	3.0	30.7
Girls' accessories	100.0	–	17.4	3.5	46.8	4.6	10.2	7.8
Children under age 2	**100.0**	**14.2**	**21.1**	**10.4**	**15.0**	**5.0**	**12.8**	**21.4**
Infant dresses, outerwear	100.0	11.3	21.8	9.9	14.9	6.4	10.4	25.3
Infant underwear	100.0	16.1	13.1	11.0	14.5	4.6	14.0	21.8
Infant nightwear, loungewear	100.0	8.5	27.2	6.9	11.9	4.0	16.4	25.1
Infant accessories	100.0	22.1	29.1	12.0	18.8	2.7	12.0	5.8
Other apparel products and services	**100.0**	**11.7**	**24.8**	**9.5**	**21.5**	**5.2**	**7.5**	**20.1**
Jewelry and watches	100.0	9.0	26.5	6.6	26.1	5.8	6.0	19.9
Jewelry	100.0	8.6	27.1	6.5	26.6	5.6	5.7	19.9
All other apparel products and services	100.0	14.4	25.2	12.4	17.0	4.6	8.8	20.2
Men's footwear	100.0	–	14.8	20.5	21.5	2.0	12.0	9.2
Boys' footwear	100.0	–	30.0	12.0	16.0	1.0	–	17.5
Women's footwear	100.0	–	17.9	4.2	13.1	2.9	13.6	36.7
Girls' footwear	100.0	–	31.0	20.4	18.5	13.7	5.4	4.2
TRANSPORTATION	**100.0**	**10.1**	**12.5**	**8.8**	**22.7**	**12.9**	**9.2**	**23.8**
New cars	100.0	–	–	–	14.6	32.0	17.1	36.3
New trucks	100.0	–	–	–	–	–	–	–
Used cars	100.0	0.1	23.4	11.6	43.9	9.0	2.7	9.4
Used trucks	100.0	–	–	37.9	–	–	9.1	32.9
Airline fares	100.0	7.3	14.3	9.7	21.1	6.7	10.2	31.9
Ship fares	100.0	2.1	8.3	5.2	15.4	11.6	16.8	40.9
HEALTH CARE	**100.0**	**27.5**	**19.7**	**5.0**	**12.3**	**2.0**	**5.3**	**28.2**
Physician's services	100.0	13.3	14.8	2.4	28.3	2.7	4.3	34.4
Dental services	100.0	6.6	27.4	4.4	13.8	4.0	6.1	39.6
Hospital services other than room	100.0	–	–	6.0	33.0	0.0	3.5	11.0
Care in convalescent or nursing home	100.0	–	20.9	3.2	2.2	0.2	5.4	31.7
Nonprescription drugs	100.0	56.9	11.3	1.9	13.7	0.8	3.2	11.5
Prescription drugs	100.0	29.4	25.8	5.6	7.9	9.1	2.5	19.7
ENTERTAINMENT	**100.0**	**9.2**	**21.0**	**7.2**	**16.1**	**7.8**	**9.7**	**29.3**
Toys, games, hobbies, and tricycles	100.0	11.1	21.9	9.0	17.4	7.2	10.0	23.4
Other entertainment	100.0	8.2	20.4	6.2	15.4	8.1	9.5	32.5
Fees for recreational lessons	100.0	1.8	11.2	3.2	8.4	3.8	5.4	67.0
Community antenna or cable TV	100.0	47.1	27.1	5.4	9.2	2.9	2.7	5.6
VCRs and video disc players	100.0	8.4	13.2	7.2	26.5	6.3	11.7	26.8
Pet purchase, supplies, and medicine	100.0	–	9.2	1.3	49.3	1.1	5.5	31.6
Athletic gear, game tables, exercise equipment	100.0	6.7	34.9	3.9	7.0	14.6	8.7	29.1
Photographic equipment	100.0	8.9	9.6	2.0	14.3	3.0	17.8	46.8
PERSONAL CARE PRODUCTS AND SERVICES	**100.0**	**16.6**	**12.7**	**17.1**	**19.0**	**5.0**	**9.2**	**20.4**
Cosmetics, perfume, bath preparation	100.0	16.5	9.8	17.9	19.1	4.3	12.4	19.6
EDUCATION	**100.0**	**1.5**	**5.7**	**3.8**	**10.7**	**4.7**	**7.4**	**66.3**
College tuition	100.0	0.8	5.0	4.3	11.0	4.3	7.7	66.8
Elementary and high school tuition	100.0	6.0	8.6	1.3	16.1	3.8	10.9	56.6
Other school expenses including rentals	100.0	1.6	3.8	1.5	2.9	3.1	2.9	84.3
College books and supplies	100.0	6.9	9.8	2.6	10.2	7.5	8.8	54.2
Miscellaneous school supplies	100.0	5.1	10.1	4.1	12.6	5.6	5.0	60.5
ALL OTHER GIFTS	**100.0**	**11.1**	**15.4**	**8.0**	**18.5**	**7.7**	**11.2**	**27.4**
Gifts of trip expenses	100.0	7.5	13.3	7.7	21.2	7.0	10.5	32.8
Legal fees	100.0	–	23.0	13.5	13.7	10.4	3.8	11.0
Funeral expenses	100.0	16.0	24.4	8.6	14.6	8.8	14.0	13.6
Cemetery lots, vaults, and maintenance fees	100.0	15.6	8.1	7.6	11.8	1.5	26.5	29.1
Miscellaneous personal services	100.0	–	2.4	0.1	7.5	1.8	3.7	86.6

Note: Numbers may not add to total because of rounding. (–) means sample is too small to make a reliable estimate. Expenditures for items in a given category may not add to category total because categories with annual spending of less than $2.00 for the average household are omitted. Spending on gifts is also included in the product and service categories in other chapters.

Source: Calculations by New Strategist based on the 2003 Consumer Expenditure Survey

Table 6.9 Gifts for Nonhousehold Members: Average spending by high-income consumer units, 2003

(average annual spending on selected gifts of products and services for nonhousehold members by before-tax income of high-income consumer units (CU), 2003; complete income reporters only)

	total complete reporters	$100,000 or more	$100,000– $119,999	$120,000– $149,999	$150,000 or more
Number of consumer units (000)	97,391	11,537	4,384	3,151	4,002
Average number of persons per CU	2.5	3.1	3.1	3.1	3.1
Average before-tax income of CU	$51,128.00	$154,665.00	$108,087.00	$131,885.00	$223,634.00
Average spending of CU, total	42,741.66	93,514.86	75,601.50	86,451.46	118,674.11
Gifts, average spending	**1,055.13**	**3,254.95**	**2,461.19**	**2,294.83**	**4,876.65**
FOOD	**84.32**	**321.45**	**286.08**	**164.48**	**483.36**
Fresh fruit other than apples, bananas, and citrus	2.54	1.86	1.90	1.01	2.49
Candy and chewing gum	9.37	31.28	41.57	14.85	32.85
Board (including at school)	18.55	127.06	89.49	64.27	217.66
Catered affairs	28.57	101.46	125.33	32.67	129.47
ALCOHOLIC BEVERAGES	**19.07**	**53.60**	**73.09**	**10.69**	**65.74**
Beer and ale	4.41	6.28	8.08	0.05	9.15
Wine	11.83	36.72	52.04	5.87	44.01
HOUSING	**238.46**	**663.51**	**598.55**	**501.86**	**861.02**
Housekeeping supplies	**47.59**	**114.13**	**82.62**	**144.31**	**124.97**
Laundry and cleaning supplies	2.44	3.58	0.91	3.18	6.80
Other household products	14.66	54.62	32.05	104.63	40.32
Miscellaneous household products	6.35	15.45	13.45	8.93	22.69
Lawn and garden supplies	6.61	36.17	17.14	92.82	12.87
Postage and stationery	30.50	55.94	49.66	36.51	77.85
Stationery, stationery supplies, giftwrap	22.31	37.75	43.86	29.71	37.36
Postage	7.48	17.74	5.80	6.79	39.23
Household textiles	**14.41**	**51.97**	**56.23**	**34.18**	**61.14**
Bathroom linens	3.30	7.01	6.84	5.80	8.13
Bedroom linens	7.08	31.94	34.34	22.81	36.43
Appliances and miscellaneous housewares	**27.61**	**88.58**	**50.72**	**40.24**	**167.41**
Major appliances	6.72	21.10	10.72	5.77	44.34
Small appliances and miscellaneous housewares	20.89	67.48	40.00	34.48	123.07
China and other dinnerware	2.58	3.93	–	3.62	8.45
Glassware	2.76	6.36	0.49	–	17.68
Nonelectric cookware	3.99	12.37	22.00	10.11	3.66
Tableware, nonelectric kitchenware	6.11	28.96	8.08	10.80	65.77
Small electric kitchen appliances	2.50	7.94	4.92	3.74	14.56
Miscellaneous household equipment	**62.16**	**142.27**	**130.68**	**108.33**	**181.57**
Infants' equipment	4.75	1.42	2.20	–	1.68
Household decorative items	21.06	47.34	45.67	39.52	55.23
Indoor plants, fresh flowers	11.70	25.54	28.05	24.18	23.86
Computers and computer hardware, nonbusiness use	8.71	40.77	28.88	24.70	66.44
Miscellaneous household equipment and parts	5.37	10.10	8.41	12.33	10.22
Other housing	**86.70**	**266.56**	**278.31**	**174.80**	**325.94**
Repair or maintenance services	4.50	1.28	–	–	3.69
Materials for additions, finishing basements, remodeling rooms	2.60	13.44	35.36	–	–
Housing while attending school	26.45	156.23	120.30	114.72	228.29
Lodging on trips	2.86	7.87	5.53	12.43	6.84
Utility: natural gas (renter)	2.98	1.95	2.44	–	2.97
Electricity (renter)	9.57	2.04	1.13	0.61	4.15
Day care centers, nurseries, and preschools	10.48	17.05	28.39	13.24	7.64
Bedroom furniture other than mattresses and springs	2.91	4.91	3.49	0.52	9.92
APPAREL AND SERVICES	**232.08**	**457.34**	**386.30**	**373.74**	**599.84**
Men and boys, aged 2 or older	**55.46**	**109.51**	**82.85**	**86.67**	**156.33**
Men's suits	3.09	12.60	4.68	15.91	18.68
Men's coats and jackets	2.60	9.90	–	–	28.35
Men's accessories	2.98	8.62	–	8.93	17.76
Men's sweaters and vests	2.27	6.26	6.49	1.79	9.52
Men's active sportswear	4.70	17.56	39.97	–	6.83
Men's shirts	8.52	10.88	8.61	10.77	13.45
Men's pants	6.03	3.66	–	6.44	5.47
Boys' shirts	4.33	6.66	7.91	7.75	4.44
Boys' pants	3.97	5.87	2.45	7.42	8.41
Women and girls, aged 2 or older	**88.62**	**194.05**	**172.87**	**129.28**	**267.41**
Women's coats and jackets	9.40	24.21	17.00	–	50.83
Women's dresses	5.17	20.63	17.54	27.35	18.76
Women's vests and sweaters	8.37	17.19	20.44	3.78	24.07

	total complete reporters	$100,000 or more	$100,000–$119,999	$120,000–$149,999	$150,000 or more
Women's shirts, tops, blouses	$10.34	$17.36	$13.85	$16.68	$21.71
Women's pants	6.94	15.98	13.22	10.32	23.37
Women's active sportswear	3.17	6.71	16.92	–	0.82
Women's sleepwear	6.89	10.42	9.41	6.35	14.67
Women's undergarments	3.08	7.99	13.37	–	8.34
Women's accessories	5.02	0.70	6.98	8.90	16.16
Girls' dresses and suits	2.30	5.35	–	3.06	12.95
Girls' shirts, blouses, sweaters	4.60	4.69	1.70	12.04	2.25
Girls' skirts and pants	4.34	7.60	5.95	7.48	9.51
Girls' active sportswear	2.28	5.91	6.75	5.55	5.28
Girls' accessories	2.38	1.57	–	0.41	4.19
Children under age 2	**40.68**	**73.64**	**49.45**	**84.82**	**91.32**
Infant dresses, outerwear	12.69	27.11	20.96	30.74	30.99
Infant underwear	19.85	36.50	22.75	43.01	46.41
Infant nightwear, loungewear	2.62	5.56	4.43	4.28	7.81
Infant accessories	4.41	2.15	–	5.05	2.23
Other apparel products and services	**47.32**	**80.14**	**81.12**	**72.97**	**84.78**
Jewelry and watches	23.28	39.13	18.65	42.83	58.67
Jewelry	21.55	36.29	14.95	40.19	56.60
All other apparel products and services	24.04	41.01	62.48	30.14	26.11
Men's footwear	4.69	3.66	6.97	–	2.90
Boys' footwear	4.13	5.10	1.92	7.81	9.31
Women's footwear	8.53	26.43	47.30	20.41	8.42
Girls' footwear	5.00	1.78	3.62	0.98	0.41
TRANSPORTATION	**55.89**	**112.14**	**80.49**	**58.38**	**189.14**
New cars	13.68	41.91	33.47	–	84.16
New trucks	3.52	–	–	–	–
Used cars	15.84	12.52	11.13	14.16	12.76
Used trucks	3.32	9.23	–	–	26.60
Airline fares	7.91	21.27	16.74	24.53	23.65
Ship fares	4.28	14.79	11.08	10.93	21.90
HEALTH CARE	**51.96**	**123.72**	**67.72**	**40.11**	**250.98**
Physician's services	2.46	7.14	13.71	2.26	3.78
Dental services	3.94	13.16	22.82	6.82	7.56
Hospital services other than room	2.06	1.92	1.36	–	4.04
Care in convalescent or nursing home	23.32	62.32	1.75	–	177.77
Nonprescription drugs	3.89	3.79	4.48	1.12	5.13
Prescription drugs	3.09	5.13	6.84	2.09	5.65
ENTERTAINMENT	**74.22**	**183.68**	**140.76**	**133.21**	**270.06**
Toys, games, hobbies, and tricycles	26.19	51.76	42.25	48.31	64.88
Other entertainment	48.03	131.92	98.51	84.90	205.18
Fees for recreational lessons	6.42	36.33	26.45	8.62	68.99
Community antenna or cable TV	3.59	1.69	0.91	0.74	3.28
VCRs and video disc players	2.68	6.06	5.24	6.27	6.79
Pet purchase, supplies, and medicine	3.00	7.99	4.17	0.84	17.69
Athletic gear, game tables, exercise equipment	8.04	19.74	–	16.70	43.56
Photographic equipment	2.26	8.93	3.09	7.94	16.11
PERSONAL CARE PRODUCTS AND SERVICES	**18.65**	**32.18**	**22.07**	**15.44**	**56.15**
Cosmetics, perfume, bath preparation	12.03	19.95	16.46	10.27	31.27
EDUCATION	**200.89**	**1,124.83**	**712.80**	**806.73**	**1,826.71**
College tuition	152.71	861.54	510.91	657.24	1,406.58
Elementary and high school tuition	11.51	54.97	70.95	0.66	80.23
Other school expenses including rentals	16.85	119.86	45.06	79.81	233.33
College books and supplies	10.23	46.83	42.99	34.12	61.05
Miscellaneous school supplies	7.40	37.79	40.42	33.71	38.09
ALL OTHER GIFTS	**78.11**	**180.39**	**91.77**	**188.21**	**270.87**
Gifts of trip expenses	42.35	117.32	61.64	123.28	173.64
Legal fees	5.17	4.31	0.12	–	13.72
Funeral expenses	22.84	26.28	23.97	50.29	9.89
Cemetery lots, vaults, and maintenance fees	2.16	5.31	3.84	12.16	1.53
Miscellaneous personal services	3.29	24.06	0.67	0.06	68.14

Note: (–) means sample is too small to make a reliable estimate. Expenditures for items in a given category may not add to category total because categories with annual spending of less than $2.00 for the average household are omitted. Spending on gifts is also included in the product and service categories in other chapters.
Source: Bureau of Labor Statistics, unpublished tables from the 2003 Consumer Expenditure Survey; calculations by New Strategist

Table 6.10 Gifts for Nonhousehold Members: Indexed spending by high-income consumer units, 2003

(indexed average annual spending of consumer units (CU) on selected gifts of products and services for nonhousehold members by before-tax income of high-income consumer unit, 2003; complete income reporters only; index definition: an index of 100 is the average for all consumer units; an index of 132 means that spending by consumer units in that group is 32 percent above the average for all consumer units; an index of 68 indicates spending that is 32 percent below the average for all consumer units)

	total complete reporters	$100,000 or more	$100,000–$119,999	$120,000–$149,999	$150,000 or more
Average spending of CU, total	$42,742	$93,515	$75,602	$86,451	$118,674
Average spending of CU, index	100	219	177	202	278
Gifts, spending index	100	308	233	217	462
FOOD	100	381	339	195	573
Fresh fruit other than apples, bananas, and citrus	100	73	75	40	98
Candy and chewing gum	100	334	444	158	351
Board (including at school)	100	685	482	346	1,173
Catered affairs	100	355	439	114	453
ALCOHOLIC BEVERAGES	100	281	383	56	345
Beer and ale	100	142	183	1	207
Wine	100	310	440	50	372
HOUSING	100	278	251	210	361
Housekeeping supplies	100	240	174	303	263
Laundry and cleaning supplies	100	147	37	130	279
Other household products	100	373	219	714	275
Miscellaneous household products	100	243	212	141	357
Lawn and garden supplies	100	547	259	1,404	195
Postage and stationery	100	183	163	120	255
Stationery, stationery supplies, giftwrap	100	169	197	133	167
Postage	100	237	78	91	524
Household textiles	100	361	390	237	424
Bathroom linens	100	212	207	176	246
Bedroom linens	100	451	485	322	515
Appliances and miscellaneous housewares	100	321	184	146	606
Major appliances	100	314	160	86	660
Small appliances and miscellaneous housewares	100	323	191	165	589
China and other dinnerware	100	152	–	140	328
Glassware	100	230	18	–	641
Nonelectric cookware	100	310	551	253	92
Tableware, nonelectric kitchenware	100	474	132	177	1,076
Small electric kitchen appliances	100	318	197	150	582
Miscellaneous household equipment	100	229	210	174	292
Infants' equipment	100	30	46	–	35
Household decorative items	100	225	217	188	262
Indoor plants, fresh flowers	100	218	240	207	204
Computers and computer hardware, nonbusiness use	100	468	332	284	763
Miscellaneous household equipment and parts	100	188	157	230	190
Other housing	100	307	321	202	376
Repair or maintenance services	100	28	–	–	82
Materials for additions, finishing basements, remodeling rooms	100	517	1,360	–	–
Housing while attending school	100	591	455	434	863
Lodging on trips	100	275	193	435	239
Utility: natural gas (renter)	100	65	82	–	100
Electricity (renter)	100	21	12	6	43
Day care centers, nurseries, and preschools	100	163	271	126	73
Bedroom furniture other than mattresses and springs	100	169	120	18	341
APPAREL AND SERVICES	100	197	166	161	258
Men and boys, aged 2 or older	100	197	149	156	282
Men's suits	100	408	151	515	605
Men's coats and jackets	100	381	–	–	1,090
Men's accessories	100	289	–	300	596
Men's sweaters and vests	100	276	286	79	419
Men's active sportswear	100	374	850	–	145
Men's shirts	100	128	101	126	158
Men's pants	100	61	–	107	91
Boys' shirts	100	154	183	179	103
Boys' pants	100	148	62	187	212
Women and girls, aged 2 or older	100	219	195	146	302
Women's coats and jackets	100	258	181	–	541
Women's dresses	100	399	339	529	363
Women's vests and sweaters	100	205	244	45	288

	total complete reporters	$100,000 or more	$100,000–$119,999	$120,000–$149,999	$150,000 or more
Women's shirts, tops, blouses	100	168	134	161	210
Women's pants	100	230	190	149	337
Women's active sportswear	100	212	534	–	26
Women's sleepwear	100	151	137	92	213
Women's undergarments	100	259	434	–	271
Women's accessories	100	213	139	177	322
Girls' dresses and suits	100	233	–	133	563
Girls' shirts, blouses, sweaters	100	102	37	262	49
Girls' skirts and pants	100	175	137	172	219
Girls' active sportswear	100	259	296	243	232
Girls' accessories	100	66	–	17	176
Children under age 2	**100**	**181**	**122**	**209**	**224**
Infant dresses, outerwear	100	214	165	242	244
Infant underwear	100	184	115	217	234
Infant nightwear, loungewear	100	212	169	163	298
Infant accessories	100	49	–	115	51
Other apparel products and services	**100**	**169**	**171**	**154**	**179**
Jewelry and watches	100	168	80	184	252
Jewelry	100	168	69	186	263
All other apparel products and services	100	171	260	125	109
Men's footwear	100	78	149	–	62
Boys' footwear	100	148	46	189	225
Women's footwear	100	310	555	239	99
Girls' footwear	100	36	72	20	8
TRANSPORTATION	**100**	**201**	**144**	**104**	**338**
New cars	100	306	245	–	615
New trucks	100	–	–	–	–
Used cars	100	79	70	89	81
Used trucks	100	278	–	–	801
Airline fares	100	269	212	310	299
Ship fares	100	346	259	255	512
HEALTH CARE	**100**	**238**	**130**	**77**	**483**
Physician's services	100	290	557	92	154
Dental services	100	334	579	173	192
Hospital services other than room	100	93	66	–	196
Care in convalescent or nursing home	100	267	8	–	762
Nonprescription drugs	100	97	115	29	132
Prescription drugs	100	166	221	68	183
ENTERTAINMENT	**100**	**247**	**190**	**179**	**364**
Toys, games, hobbies, and tricycles	100	198	161	184	248
Other entertainment	100	275	205	177	427
Fees for recreational lessons	100	566	412	134	1,075
Community antenna or cable TV	100	47	25	21	91
VCRs and video disc players	100	226	196	234	253
Pet purchase, supplies, and medicine	100	266	139	28	590
Athletic gear, game tables, exercise equipment	100	246	–	208	542
Photographic equipment	100	395	137	351	713
PERSONAL CARE PRODUCTS AND SERVICES	**100**	**173**	**118**	**83**	**301**
Cosmetics, perfume, bath preparation	100	166	137	85	260
EDUCATION	**100**	**560**	**355**	**402**	**909**
College tuition	100	564	335	430	921
Elementary and high school tuition	100	478	616	6	697
Other school expenses including rentals	100	711	267	474	1,385
College books and supplies	100	458	420	334	597
Miscellaneous school supplies	100	511	546	456	515
ALL OTHER GIFTS	**100**	**231**	**117**	**241**	**347**
Gifts of trip expenses	100	277	146	291	410
Legal fees	100	93	2	–	265
Funeral expenses	100	115	105	220	43
Cemetery lots, vaults, and maintenance fees	100	246	178	563	71
Miscellaneous personal services	100	731	20	2	2,071

Note: (–) means sample is too small to make a reliable estimate. Categories with annual spending of less than $2.00 for the average household are omitted. Spending on gifts is also included in the product and service categories in other chapters.
Source: Calculations by New Strategist based on the 2003 Consumer Expenditure Survey

Table 6.11 Gifts for Nonhousehold Members: Total spending by high-income consumer units, 2003

(total annual spending on selected gifts of products and services for nonhousehold members by before-tax income group of high-income consumer units (CU), 2003; complete income reporters only; numbers in thousands)

	total complete reporters	$100,000 or more	$100,000–$119,999	$120,000–$149,999	$150,000 or more
Number of consumer units	97,391	11,537	4,384	3,151	4,002
Total spending of all CUs	$4,162,653,009	$1,078,880,940	$331,436,976	$272,408,550	$474,933,788
Gifts, total spending	**102,760,166**	**37,552,358**	**10,789,857**	**7,231,009**	**19,516,353**
FOOD	**8,212,009**	**3,708,569**	**1,254,175**	**518,276**	**1,934,407**
Fresh fruit other than apples, bananas, and citrus	247,373	21,459	8,330	3,183	9,965
Candy and chewing gum	912,554	360,877	182,243	46,792	131,466
Board (including at school)	1,806,603	1,465,891	392,324	202,515	871,075
Catered affairs	2,782,461	1,170,544	549,447	102,943	518,139
ALCOHOLIC BEVERAGES	**1,857,246**	**618,383**	**320,427**	**33,684**	**263,091**
Beer and ale	429,494	72,452	35,423	158	36,618
Wine	1,152,136	423,639	228,143	18,496	176,128
HOUSING	**23,223,858**	**7,654,915**	**2,624,043**	**1,581,361**	**3,445,802**
Housekeeping supplies	**4,634,838**	**1,316,718**	**362,206**	**454,721**	**500,130**
Laundry and cleaning supplies	237,634	41,302	3,989	10,020	27,214
Other household products	1,427,752	630,151	140,507	329,689	161,361
Miscellaneous household products	618,433	178,247	58,965	28,138	90,805
Lawn and garden supplies	643,755	417,293	75,142	292,476	51,506
Postage and stationery	2,970,426	645,380	217,709	115,043	311,556
Stationery, stationery supplies, giftwrap	2,172,793	435,522	192,282	93,616	149,515
Postage	728,485	204,666	25,427	21,395	156,998
Household textiles	**1,403,404**	**599,578**	**246,512**	**107,701**	**244,682**
Bathroom linens	321,390	80,874	29,987	18,276	32,536
Bedroom linens	689,528	368,492	150,547	71,874	145,793
Appliances and miscellaneous housewares	**2,688,966**	**1,021,947**	**222,356**	**126,796**	**669,975**
Major appliances	654,468	243,431	46,996	18,181	177,449
Small appliances and miscellaneous housewares	2,034,498	778,517	175,360	108,646	492,526
China and other dinnerware	251,269	45,340	–	11,407	33,817
Glassware	268,799	73,375	2,148	–	70,755
Nonelectric cookware	388,590	142,713	96,448	31,857	14,647
Tableware, nonelectric kitchenware	595,059	334,112	35,423	34,031	263,212
Small electric kitchen appliances	243,478	91,604	21,569	11,785	58,269
Miscellaneous household equipment	**6,053,825**	**1,641,369**	**572,901**	**341,348**	**726,643**
Infants' equipment	462,607	16,383	9,645	–	6,723
Household decorative items	2,051,054	546,162	200,217	124,528	221,030
Indoor plants, fresh flowers	1,139,475	294,655	122,971	76,191	95,488
Computers and computer hardware, nonbusiness use	848,276	470,363	126,610	77,830	265,893
Miscellaneous household equipment and parts	522,990	116,524	36,869	38,852	40,900
Other housing	**8,443,800**	**3,075,303**	**1,220,111**	**550,795**	**1,304,412**
Repair or maintenance services	438,260	14,767	–	–	14,767
Materials for additions, finishing basements, remodeling rooms	253,217	155,057	155,018	–	–
Housing while attending school	2,575,992	1,802,426	527,395	361,483	913,617
Lodging on trips	278,538	90,796	24,244	39,167	27,374
Utility: natural gas (renter)	290,225	22,497	10,697	–	11,886
Electricity (renter)	932,032	23,535	4,954	1,922	16,608
Day care centers, nurseries, and preschools	1,020,658	196,706	124,462	41,719	30,575
Bedroom furniture other than mattresses and springs	283,408	56,647	15,300	1,639	39,700
APPAREL AND SERVICES	**22,602,503**	**5,276,332**	**1,693,539**	**1,177,655**	**2,400,560**
Men and boys, aged 2 or older	**5,401,305**	**1,263,417**	**363,214**	**273,097**	**625,633**
Men's suits	300,938	145,366	20,517	50,132	74,757
Men's coats and jackets	253,217	114,216	–	–	113,457
Men's accessories	290,225	99,449	–	28,138	71,076
Men's sweaters and vests	221,078	72,222	28,452	5,640	38,099
Men's active sportswear	457,738	202,590	175,228	–	27,334
Men's shirts	829,771	125,523	37,746	33,936	53,827
Men's pants	587,268	42,225	–	20,292	21,891
Boys' shirts	421,703	76,836	34,677	24,420	17,769
Boys' pants	386,642	67,722	10,741	23,380	33,657
Women and girls, aged 2 or older	**8,630,790**	**2,238,755**	**757,862**	**407,361**	**1,070,175**
Women's coats and jackets	915,475	279,311	74,528	–	203,422
Women's dresses	503,511	238,008	76,895	86,180	75,078
Women's vests and sweaters	815,163	198,321	89,609	11,911	96,328

	total complete reporters	$130,000 or more	$100,000– $119,999	$120,000– $149,999	$150,000 or more
Women's shirts, tops, blouses	$1,007,023	$200,282	$60,718	$52,559	$86,883
Women's pants	675,894	184,361	57,956	32,518	93,527
Women's active sportswear	308,729	77,413	74,177	–	3,282
Women's sleepwear	671,024	120,216	41,253	20,009	58,709
Women's undergarments	299,964	92,181	58,614	–	33,377
Women's accessories	488,903	123,446	30,600	28,044	64,672
Girls' dresses and suits	223,999	51,723	–	9,642	51,826
Girls' shirts, blouses, sweaters	447,999	54,109	7,453	37,938	9,005
Girls' skirts and pants	422,677	87,681	26,085	23,569	38,059
Girls' active sportswear	222,051	68,184	29,592	17,488	21,131
Girls' accessories	231,791	18,113	–	1,292	16,768
Children under age 2	**3,961,866**	**849,585**	**216,789**	**267,268**	**365,463**
Infant dresses, outerwear	1,235,892	312,768	91,889	96,862	124,022
Infant underwear	1,933,211	421,101	99,736	135,525	185,733
Infant nightwear, loungewear	255,164	64,146	19,421	13,486	31,256
Infant accessories	429,494	24,805		15,913	8,924
Other apparel products and services	**4,608,542**	**924,575**	**355,630**	**229,928**	**339,290**
Jewelry and watches	2,267,262	451,443	81,762	134,957	234,797
Jewelry	2,098,776	418,678	65,541	126,639	226,513
All other apparel products and services	2,341,280	473,132	273,912	94,971	104,492
Men's footwear	456,764	42,225	30,556	–	11,606
Boys' footwear	402,225	79,376	8,417	24,609	37,259
Women's footwear	830,745	304,923	207,363	64,312	33,697
Girls' footwear	486,955	20,536	15,870	3,088	1,641
TRANSPORTATION	**5,443,183**	**1,293,759**	**352,868**	**183,955**	**756,938**
New cars	1,332,309	483,516	146,732	–	336,808
New trucks	342,816	–	–	–	–
Used cars	1,542,673	144,443	48,794	44,618	51,066
Used trucks	323,338	105,437	–	–	106,453
Airline fares	770,363	245,392	73,388	77,294	94,647
Ship fares	416,833	170,532	48,575	34,440	87,644
HEALTH CARE	**5,060,436**	**1,427,358**	**296,884**	**126,387**	**1,004,422**
Physician's services	239,582	82,374	60,105	7,121	15,128
Dental services	383,721	151,827	100,043	21,490	30,255
Hospital services other than room	200,625	22,51	5,962	–	16,168
Care in convalescent or nursing home	2,271,158	718,986	7,672	–	711,436
Nonprescription drugs	378,851	43,725	19,640	3,529	20,530
Prescription drugs	300,938	59,185	29,937	6,586	22,611
ENTERTAINMENT	**7,228,360**	**2,119,116**	**617,092**	**419,745**	**1,080,780**
Toys, games, hobbies, and tricycles	2,550,670	597,155	185,224	152,225	259,650
Other entertainment	4,677,690	1,521,561	431,868	267,520	821,130
Fees for recreational lessons	625,250	419,139	115,957	27,162	276,098
Community antenna or cable TV	349,634	19,498	3,989	2,332	13,127
VCRs and video disc players	261,008	69,514	22,972	19,757	27,174
Pet purchase, supplies, and medicine	292,173	92,181	18,281	2,647	70,795
Athletic gear, game tables, exercise equipment	783,024	227,740	–	52,622	174,327
Photographic equipment	220,104	103,025	13,547	25,019	64,472
PERSONAL CARE PRODUCTS AND SERVICES	**1,816,342**	**371,251**	**96,755**	**48,651**	**224,712**
Cosmetics, perfume, bath preparation	1,171,614	230,153	72,161	32,361	125,143
EDUCATION	**19,564,878**	**12,977,154**	**3,124,915**	**2,542,006**	**7,310,493**
College tuition	14,872,580	9,539,537	2,239,829	2,070,963	5,629,133
Elementary and high school tuition	1,120,970	634,139	311,045	2,080	321,080
Other school expenses including rentals	1,641,038	1,382,825	197,543	251,481	933,787
College books and supplies	996,310	540,278	188,468	107,512	244,322
Miscellaneous school supplies	720,693	435,923	177,201	106,220	152,436
ALL OTHER GIFTS	**7,607,211**	**2,081,259**	**402,320**	**593,050**	**1,084,022**
Gifts of trip expenses	4,124,509	1,353,521	270,230	388,455	694,907
Legal fees	503,511	55,493	525	–	54,907
Funeral expenses	2,224,410	333,192	105,084	158,464	39,580
Cemetery lots, vaults, and maintenance fees	210,365	51,361	16,835	38,316	6,123
Miscellaneous personal services	320,416	277,580	2,937	189	272,696

Note: Numbers may not add to total because of rounding. (–) means sample is too small to make a reliable estimate. Expenditures for items in a given category may not add to category total because categories with annual spending of less than $2.00 for the average household are omitted. Spending on gifts is also included in the product and service categories in other chapters.
Source: Calculations by New Strategist based on the 2003 Consumer Expenditure Survey

Table 6.12 Gifts for Nonhousehold Members: Market shares by high-income consumer units, 2003

(percentage of total annual spending on selected gifts of products and services for nonhousehold members accounted for by before-tax income group of high-income consumer units, 2003; complete income reporters only)

	total complete reporters	$100,000 or more	$100,000– $119,999	$120,000– $149,999	$150,000 or more
Share of total consumer units	100.0%	11.8%	4.5%	3.2%	4.1%
Share of total before-tax income	100.0	35.8	9.5	8.3	18.0
Share of total spending	100.0	25.9	8.0	6.5	11.4
Share of gifts spending	100.0	36.5	10.5	7.0	19.0
FOOD	100.0	45.2	15.3	6.3	23.6
Fresh fruit other than apples, bananas, and citrus	100.0	8.7	3.4	1.3	4.0
Candy and chewing gum	100.0	39.5	20.0	5.1	14.4
Board (including at school)	100.0	81.1	21.7	11.2	48.2
Catered affairs	100.0	42.1	19.7	3.7	18.6
ALCOHOLIC BEVERAGES	100.0	33.3	17.3	1.8	14.2
Beer and ale	100.0	16.9	8.2	0.0	8.5
Wine	100.0	36.8	19.8	1.6	15.3
HOUSING	100.0	33.0	11.3	6.8	14.8
Housekeeping supplies	100.0	28.4	7.8	9.8	10.8
Laundry and cleaning supplies	100.0	17.4	1.7	4.2	11.5
Other household products	100.0	44.1	9.8	23.1	11.3
Miscellaneous household products	100.0	28.8	9.5	4.5	14.7
Lawn and garden supplies	100.0	64.8	11.7	45.4	8.0
Postage and stationery	100.0	21.7	7.3	3.9	10.5
Stationery, stationery supplies, giftwrap	100.0	20.0	8.8	4.3	6.9
Postage	100.0	28.1	3.5	2.9	21.6
Household textiles	100.0	42.7	17.6	7.7	17.4
Bathroom linens	100.0	25.2	9.3	5.7	10.1
Bedroom linens	100.0	53.4	21.8	10.4	21.1
Appliances and miscellaneous housewares	100.0	38.0	8.3	4.7	24.9
Major appliances	100.0	37.2	7.2	2.8	27.1
Small appliances and miscellaneous housewares	100.0	38.3	8.6	5.3	24.2
China and other dinnerware	100.0	18.0	–	4.5	13.5
Glassware	100.0	27.3	0.8	–	26.3
Nonelectric cookware	100.0	36.7	24.8	8.2	3.8
Tableware, nonelectric kitchenware	100.0	56.1	6.0	5.7	44.2
Small electric kitchen appliances	100.0	37.6	8.9	4.8	23.9
Miscellaneous household equipment	100.0	27.1	9.5	5.6	12.0
Infants' equipment	100.0	3.5	2.1	–	1.5
Household decorative items	100.0	26.6	9.8	6.1	10.8
Indoor plants, fresh flowers	100.0	25.9	10.8	6.7	8.4
Computers and computer hardware, nonbusiness use	100.0	55.4	14.9	9.2	31.3
Miscellaneous household equipment and parts	100.0	22.3	7.0	7.4	7.8
Other housing	100.0	36.4	14.4	6.5	15.4
Repair or maintenance services	100.0	3.4	–	–	3.4
Materials for additions, finishing basements, remodeling rooms	100.0	61.2	61.2	–	–
Housing while attending school	100.0	70.0	20.5	14.0	35.5
Lodging on trips	100.0	32.6	8.7	14.1	9.8
Utility: natural gas (renter)	100.0	7.8	3.7	–	4.1
Electricity (renter)	100.0	2.5	0.5	0.2	1.8
Day care centers, nurseries, and preschools	100.0	19.3	12.2	4.1	3.0
Bedroom furniture other than mattresses and springs	100.0	20.0	5.4	0.6	14.0
APPAREL AND SERVICES	100.0	23.3	7.5	5.2	10.6
Men and boys, aged 2 or older	100.0	23.4	6.7	5.1	11.6
Men's suits	100.0	48.3	6.8	16.7	24.8
Men's coats and jackets	100.0	45.1	–	–	44.8
Men's accessories	100.0	34.3	–	9.7	24.5
Men's sweaters and vests	100.0	32.7	12.9	2.6	17.2
Men's active sportswear	100.0	44.3	38.3	–	6.0
Men's shirts	100.0	15.1	4.5	4.1	6.5
Men's pants	100.0	7.2	–	3.5	3.7
Boys' shirts	100.0	18.2	8.2	5.8	4.2
Boys' pants	100.0	17.5	2.8	6.0	8.7
Women and girls, aged 2 or older	100.0	25.9	8.8	4.7	12.4
Women's coats and jackets	100.0	30.5	8.1	–	22.2
Women's dresses	100.0	47.3	15.3	17.1	14.9
Women's vests and sweaters	100.0	24.3	11.0	1.5	11.8

	total complete reporters	$100,000 or more	$100,000– $119,999	$120,000– $149,999	$150,000 or more
Women's shirts, tops, blouses	100.0%	19.9%	6.0%	5.2%	8.6%
Women's pants	100.0	27.3	8.6	4.8	13.8
Women's active sportswear	100.0	25.1	24.0	–	1.1
Women's sleepwear	100.0	17.9	6.1	3.0	8.7
Women's undergarments	100.0	30.7	19.5	–	11.1
Women's accessories	100.0	25.2	6.3	5.7	13.2
Girls' dresses and suits	100.0	27.6	–	4.3	23.1
Girls' shirts, blouses, sweaters	100.0	12.1	1.7	8.5	2.0
Girls' skirts and pants	100.0	20.7	6.2	5.6	9.0
Girls' active sportswear	100.0	30.7	13.3	7.9	9.5
Girls' accessories	100.0	7.8	–	0.6	7.2
Children under age 2	**100.0**	**21.4**	**5.5**	**6.7**	**9.2**
Infant dresses, outerwear	100.0	25.3	7.4	7.8	10.0
Infant underwear	100.0	21.8	5.2	7.0	9.6
Infant nightwear, loungewear	100.0	25.1	7.6	5.3	12.2
Infant accessories	100.0	5.8	–	3.7	2.1
Other apparel products and services	**100.0**	**20.1**	**7.7**	**5.0**	**7.4**
Jewelry and watches	100.0	19.9	3.6	6.0	10.4
Jewelry	100.0	19.9	3.1	6.0	10.8
All other apparel products and services	100.0	20.2	11.7	4.1	4.5
Men's footwear	100.0	9.2	6.7	–	2.5
Boys' footwear	100.0	17.5	2.1	6.1	9.3
Women's footwear	100.0	36.7	25.0	7.7	4.1
Girls' footwear	100.0	4.2	3.3	0.6	0.3
TRANSPORTATION	**100.0**	**23.8**	**6.5**	**3.4**	**13.9**
New cars	100.0	36.3	11.0	–	25.3
New trucks	100.0	–	–	–	–
Used cars	100.0	9.4	3.2	2.9	3.3
Used trucks	100.0	32.9	–	–	32.9
Airline fares	100.0	31.9	9.5	10.0	12.3
Ship fares	100.0	40.9	11.7	8.3	21.0
HEALTH CARE	**100.0**	**28.2**	**5.9**	**2.5**	**19.8**
Physician's services	100.0	34.4	25.1	3.0	6.3
Dental services	100.0	39.6	26.1	5.6	7.9
Hospital services other than room	100.0	11.0	3.0	–	8.1
Care in convalescent or nursing home	100.0	31.7	0.3	–	31.3
Nonprescription drugs	100.0	11.5	5.2	0.9	5.4
Prescription drugs	100.0	19.7	10.0	2.2	7.5
ENTERTAINMENT	**100.0**	**29.3**	**8.5**	**5.8**	**15.0**
Toys, games, hobbies, and tricycles	100.0	23.4	7.3	6.0	10.2
Other entertainment	100.0	32.5	9.2	5.7	17.6
Fees for recreational lessons	100.0	67.0	18.5	4.3	44.2
Community antenna or cable TV	100.0	5.6	1.1	0.7	3.8
VCRs and video disc players	100.0	26.8	8.8	7.6	10.4
Pet purchase, supplies, and medicine	100.0	31.6	6.3	0.9	24.2
Athletic gear, game tables, exercise equipment	100.0	29.1	–	6.7	22.3
Photographic equipment	100.0	46.8	6.2	11.4	29.3
PERSONAL CARE PRODUCTS AND SERVICES	**100.0**	**20.4**	**5.3**	**2.7**	**12.4**
Cosmetics, perfume, bath preparation	100.0	19.5	6.2	2.8	10.7
EDUCATION	**100.0**	**66.3**	**16.0**	**13.0**	**37.4**
College tuition	100.0	66.8	15.1	13.9	37.8
Elementary and high school tuition	100.0	56.6	27.7	0.2	28.6
Other school expenses including rentals	100.0	84.3	12.0	15.3	56.9
College books and supplies	100.0	54.2	18.9	10.8	24.5
Miscellaneous school supplies	100.0	60.5	24.6	14.7	21.2
ALL OTHER GIFTS	**100.0**	**27.4**	**5.3**	**7.8**	**14.2**
Gifts of trip expenses	100.0	32.8	6.5	9.4	16.8
Legal fees	100.0	11.0	0.1	–	10.9
Funeral expenses	100.0	13.6	4.7	7.1	1.8
Cemetery lots, vaults, and maintenance fees	100.0	29.1	8.0	18.2	2.9
Miscellaneous personal services	100.0	86.6	0.9	0.1	85.1

Note: Numbers may not add to total because of rounding. (–) means sample is too small to make a reliable estimate. Expenditures for items in a given category may not add to category total because categories with annual spending of less than $2.00 for the average household are omitted. Spending on gifts is also included in the product and service categories in other chapters.
Source: Calculations by New Strategist based on the 2003 Consumer Expenditure Survey

Table 6.13 Gifts for Nonhousehold Members: Average spending by household type, 2003

(average annual spending of consumer units (CU) on selected gifts of products and services for nonhousehold members by type of consumer unit, 2003)

	total married couples	married couples, no children	married couples with children				single parent, at least one child <18	single person
			total	oldest child under 6	oldest child 6 to 17	oldest child 18 or older		
Number of consumer units (000)	58,448	25,132	28,584	5,496	15,047	8,041	6,999	33,929
Average number of persons per CU	3.2	2.0	3.9	3.5	4.1	4.0	2.9	1.0
Average before-tax income of CU	$69,472.00	$62,930.00	$75,557.00	$66,317.00	$77,508.00	$78,307.00	$29,154.00	$27,131.00
Average spending of CU, total	53,030.03	47,895.65	57,702.32	51,503.24	59,183.18	59,180.36	30,534.75	23,657.35
Gifts, average spending	**1,316.11**	**1,630.47**	**1,122.22**	**689.57**	**1,185.10**	**1,303.16**	**504.65**	**733.30**
FOOD	**118.44**	**173.77**	**79.76**	**40.22**	**67.99**	**129.17**	**53.82**	**29.91**
Fresh fruit other than apples, bananas, and citrus	3.20	4.05	2.66	0.66	2.76	3.91	1.91	0.98
Candy and chewing gum	10.82	9.68	12.63	18.46	9.39	14.97	14.45	5.94
Board (including at school)	29.05	33.84	23.76	–	27.93	32.19	4.49	5.31
Catered affairs	47.10	86.94	19.63	4.17	6.29	55.14	9.31	2.20
ALCOHOLIC BEVERAGES	**17.95**	**14.08**	**22.59**	**35.28**	**21.66**	**15.14**	**20.67**	**11.70**
Beer and ale	4.13	4.44	3.81	7.50	3.30	2.12	2.66	2.81
Wine	11.02	6.06	16.54	27.56	16.28	8.98	15.16	6.43
HOUSING	**293.55**	**353.46**	**253.05**	**182.65**	**257.05**	**296.17**	**112.03**	**143.88**
Housekeeping supplies	**50.39**	**47.49**	**55.87**	**37.74**	**54.51**	**71.98**	**19.36**	**32.71**
Laundry and cleaning supplies	2.89	2.65	3.36	1.44	2.75	6.00	0.93	1.62
Other household products	14.24	12.63	16.24	10.91	19.71	13.09	7.14	12.07
Miscellaneous household products	7.94	5.83	10.12	8.61	12.60	6.16	3.02	2.72
Lawn and garden supplies	4.49	4.44	4.62	1.42	6.08	3.98	3.60	8.62
Postage and stationery	33.27	32.21	36.27	25.39	32.05	52.89	11.28	19.03
Stationery, stationery supplies, giftwrap	22.03	20.08	24.60	20.56	24.51	27.73	7.69	15.47
Postage	10.44	11.00	11.06	4.33	7.13	24.02	3.59	3.38
Household textiles	**18.86**	**23.94**	**14.60**	**8.00**	**9.03**	**30.66**	**1.36**	**4.61**
Bathroom linens	5.59	9.87	2.57	4.48	1.55	3.23	–	0.81
Bedroom linens	8.73	8.46	8.28	1.69	4.73	20.37	0.86	2.07
Appliances and miscellaneous housewares	**33.53**	**46.69**	**21.99**	**24.92**	**20.38**	**22.92**	**9.83**	**11.68**
Major appliances	7.93	9.21	6.67	8.53	7.38	3.75	2.89	3.03
Small appliances and miscellaneous housewares	25.60	37.48	15.31	16.40	13.00	19.17	6.94	8.66
China and other dinnerware	3.33	6.03	1.34	0.67	0.56	3.43	–	0.92
Glassware	2.38	4.30	1.05	2.28	0.43	1.40	2.73	2.20
Nonelectric cookware	4.91	5.86	3.69	4.90	3.86	2.45	0.24	1.69
Tableware, nonelectric kitchenware	8.04	12.37	4.37	5.64	3.19	5.82	2.23	1.24
Small electric kitchen appliances	3.04	3.16	2.59	1.23	3.05	2.64	0.44	1.29
Miscellaneous household equipment	**81.34**	**107.94**	**62.38**	**63.66**	**53.22**	**78.92**	**17.14**	**33.19**
Infants' equipment	8.27	13.25	4.86	2.29	6.86	2.67	0.14	0.99
Household decorative items	27.75	32.60	25.21	33.93	18.09	33.32	6.52	10.21
Indoor plants, fresh flowers	12.78	17.95	8.84	4.84	9.04	11.18	6.28	9.65
Computers and computer hardware, nonbusiness use	11.83	15.61	10.45	1.80	8.16	20.66	1.87	5.54
Miscellaneous household equipment and parts	6.63	10.19	4.28	9.51	2.89	3.26	1.41	0.23
Other housing	**109.44**	**127.40**	**98.21**	**48.32**	**119.92**	**91.70**	**64.33**	**61.68**
Repair or maintenance services	4.10	7.68	1.60	0.46	2.74	0.23	0.09	6.09
Materials for additions, finishing basements, remodeling rooms	3.15	0.32	6.16	0.01	11.69	–	–	2.09
Housing while attending school	48.21	55.19	47.21	0.08	60.88	53.86	9.71	7.01
Lodging on trips	2.77	4.32	1.68	0.95	1.61	2.31	0.36	3.09
Utility: natural gas (renter)	2.64	2.42	1.49	0.80	1.64	1.68	2.97	2.82
Electricity (renter)	6.71	5.27	6.75	4.10	8.27	5.73	18.29	12.39
Day care centers, nurseries, and preschools	9.73	7.43	11.93	17.48	10.96	9.96	10.83	8.78
Bedroom furniture other than mattresses and springs	4.34	6.11	2.26	–	0.80	6.55	0.59	1.13
APPAREL AND SERVICES	**261.47**	**316.20**	**216.22**	**250.43**	**196.18**	**229.77**	**155.52**	**182.48**
Men and boys, aged 2 or older	**70.55**	**89.51**	**54.89**	**34.84**	**58.08**	**62.99**	**32.77**	**38.01**
Men's suits	4.24	5.15	3.57	1.06	4.39	3.76	0.74	1.21
Men's coats and jackets	6.66	11.62	2.75	–	2.43	5.41	0.20	0.73
Men's accessories	3.06	4.30	2.14	0.59	0.86	5.90	2.33	2.47
Men's sweaters and vests	3.28	3.53	2.82	2.74	2.03	4.36	1.02	1.36
Men's active sportswear	4.92	4.08	5.78	1.94	7.36	5.38	1.80	3.72
Men's shirts	11.41	15.97	6.91	6.30	5.88	9.47	8.22	3.87
Men's pants	6.38	9.59	3.43	0.64	4.76	2.78	2.72	7.09
Boys' shirts	5.16	6.31	4.08	3.50	5.26	2.08	1.87	2.10
Boys' pants	5.20	6.23	4.55	2.44	5.69	3.85	1.88	3.54
Women and girls, aged 2 or older	**92.85**	**123.98**	**69.41**	**81.41**	**61.82**	**75.65**	**57.85**	**69.84**
Women's coats and jackets	5.53	10.84	1.72	2.79	1.32	1.74	–	10.01
Women's dresses	6.52	10.20	4.11	15.57	0.89	2.24	1.42	4.18
Women's vests and sweaters	8.58	11.21	7.24	7.42	7.59	6.39	5.62	4.94

	total married couples	married couples, no children	married couples with children			single parent, at least one child <18	single person
			total	oldest child under 6	oldest child 6 to 17	oldest child 18 or older		
Women's shirts, tops, blouses	$9.27	$10.58	$8.26	$11.43	$6.73	$9.04	$8.95	$8.66
Women's pants	6.35	8.59	4.79	7.89	3.32	5.52	9.44	6.86
Women's active sportswear	2.67	4.02	1.85	2.58	1.83	1.37	0.20	4.39
Women's sleepwear	6.41	6.99	4.72	5.13	2.32	9.31	15.19	3.10
Women's undergarments	2.80	3.01	2.96	5.03	1.97	3.46	1.03	4.72
Women's accessories	6.31	7.34	5.46	4.23	4.59	8.12	1.49	3.46
Girls' dresses and suits	2.79	5.07	1.21	–	2.24	–	–	1.68
Girls' shirts, blouses, sweaters	7.11	9.78	5.04	1.05	7.53	2.90	6.52	3.72
Girls' skirts and pants	5.69	7.09	4.69	3.54	4.06	6.65	2.26	3.03
Girls' active sportswear	2.60	3.61	1.92	4.21	2.04	–	–	1.36
Girls' accessories	2.65	4.28	1.33	1.17	1.52	1.04	1.17	1.52
Children under age 2	52.75	42.95	59.01	104.57	48.97	45.49	34.31	16.85
Infant dresses, outerwear	15.55	19.00	12.71	13.18	10.15	17.17	7.02	6.18
Infant underwear	27.99	15.36	36.84	83.64	30.88	14.55	23.74	5.00
Infant nightwear, loungewear	3.08	3.11	3.04	2.29	2.89	3.84	2.11	1.79
Infant accessories	4.94	4.05	5.56	4.90	4.18	8.84	1.07	3.05
Other apparel products and services	45.31	59.75	32.91	29.62	27.30	45.63	30.60	57.77
Jewelry and watches	20.03	24.83	14.57	8.71	9.60	27.85	7.87	37.92
Jewelry	18.25	23.05	12.70	7.66	7.84	25.23	6.55	36.59
All other apparel products and services	25.28	34.93	18.35	20.91	17.70	17.78	22.73	19.85
Men's footwear	5.53	6.90	4.38	5.10	3.41	5.83	5.70	2.83
Boys' footwear	2.07	1.72	2.13	0.72	2.24	2.93	13.44	4.32
Women's footwear	9.66	15.46	5.66	13.61	3.30	4.64	3.14	4.25
Girls' footwear	5.37	7.06	4.20	0.62	6.64	1.87	–	7.72
TRANSPORTATION	65.30	71.50	67.06	16.39	68.84	98.92	44.82	75.33
New cars	11.60	–	23.71	–	32.13	24.17	–	19.28
New trucks	12.70	29.54	–	–	–	–	–	22.67
Used cars	14.43	17.40	12.71	–	18.65	10.26	32.42	13.92
Used trucks	5.17	1.65	9.11	2.12	–	30.94	2.20	3.50
Airline fares	8.82	11.24	7.30	6.53	6.64	9.07	2.54	7.22
Ship fares	4.65	5.01	4.67	4.04	4.28	5.82	2.60	3.21
HEALTH CARE	34.24	48.80	23.79	8.60	18.83	43.56	11.31	90.28
Physician's services	3.42	4.95	2.46	1.43	1.60	4.78	1.54	4.35
Dental services	4.18	4.14	4.31	–	2.61	10.43	3.41	3.68
Hospital services other than room	2.06	3.72	0.84	–	0.95	1.20	1.53	1.06
Care in convalescent or nursing home	4.01	7.95	0.90	–	1.71	–	–	61.27
Nonprescription drugs	3.57	6.53	0.85	0.30	0.31	2.38	1.78	1.29
Prescription drugs	2.04	1.78	2.18	0.89	1.78	3.81	1.66	5.37
ENTERTAINMENT	86.92	118.39	63.31	49.92	62.41	74.48	25.94	49.53
Toys, games, hobbies, and tricycles	31.84	46.51	20.86	19.59	17.10	28.76	8.62	20.34
Other entertainment	55.08	71.88	42.45	30.33	45.32	45.73	17.32	29.19
Fees for recreational lessons	9.82	14.19	7.24	2.50	11.00	3.46	1.61	2.97
Community antenna or cable TV	2.44	2.44	2.40	3.07	2.85	1.12	4.41	4.95
VCRs and video disc players	3.03	2.13	3.23	3.07	2.71	4.31	1.46	2.18
Pet purchase, supplies, and medicine	3.98	7.72	1.31	1.58	1.10	1.53	0.34	0.85
Athletic gear, game tables, exercise equipment	7.27	7.39	7.20	1.99	5.17	15.15	1.47	3.70
Photographic equipment	2.97	4.20	1.98	2.99	1.06	3.01	0.93	1.38
PERSONAL CARE PRODUCTS AND SERVICES	18.87	19.79	18.78	25.63	14.52	22.42	14.36	10.95
Cosmetics, perfume, bath preparation	11.44	10.80	12.03	13.07	10.10	11.51	5.91	7.94
EDUCATION	329.15	389.58	314.30	13.20	432.73	298.68	41.17	72.33
College tuition	261.95	294.70	262.73	6.06	366.32	244.29	32.15	47.42
Elementary and high school tuition	12.63	21.66	6.77	–	10.65	4.13	0.84	9.53
Other school expenses including rentals	28.30	49.97	13.54	0.19	17.09	16.04	0.63	4.28
College books and supplies	14.63	13.15	16.86	0.36	23.25	16.17	2.01	6.80
Miscellaneous school supplies	8.75	7.24	11.02	3.02	12.31	14.26	3.12	3.23
ALL OTHER GIFTS	88.61	122.29	62.74	66.92	44.25	94.08	24.95	65.35
Gifts of trip expenses	47.03	72.96	26.79	15.80	24.06	39.40	5.83	43.36
Legal fees	3.48	4.96	1.66	0.07	2.95	0.32	17.00	1.89
Funeral expenses	27.31	31.39	25.30	38.37	7.99	48.77	1.23	17.16
Cemetery lots, vaults, and maintenance fees	2.64	3.69	1.23	–	2.00	0.61	–	1.23
Miscellaneous personal services	4.56	6.13	3.68	2.27	5.90	0.22	0.23	0.43

Note: Average spending figures for total consumer units can be found on Average Spending by Age and Average Spending by Region tables. (–) means sample is too small to make a reliable estimate. Expenditures for items in a given category may not add to category total because categories with annual spending of less than $2.00 for the average household are omitted. Spending on gifts is also included in the product and service categories in other chapters.
Source: Bureau of Labor Statistics, unpublished tables from the 2003 Consumer Expenditure Survey

Table 6.14 Gifts for Nonhousehold Members: Indexed spending by household type, 2003

(indexed average annual spending of consumer units (CU) on selected gifts of products and services for nonhousehold members by type of consumer unit, 2003; index definition: an index of 100 is the average for all consumer units; an index of 132 means that spending by consumer units in that group is 32 percent above the average for all consumer units; an index of 68 indicates spending that is 32 percent below the average for all consumer units)

	total married couples	married couples, no children	married couples with children total	oldest child under 6	oldest child 6 to 17	oldest child 18 or older	single parent, at least one child <18	single person
Average spending of CU, total	$53,030	$47,896	$57,702	$51,503	$59,183	$59,180	$30,535	$23,657
Average spending of CU, index	130	117	141	126	145	145	75	58
Gifts, spending index	**131**	**162**	**111**	**68**	**118**	**129**	**50**	**73**
FOOD	**153**	**224**	**103**	**52**	**88**	**166**	**69**	**39**
Fresh fruit other than apples, bananas, and citrus	136	172	113	28	117	166	81	42
Candy and chewing gum	115	103	134	196	100	159	154	63
Board (including at school)	174	203	142	–	167	193	27	32
Catered affairs	185	342	77	16	25	217	37	9
ALCOHOLIC BEVERAGES	**111**	**87**	**140**	**219**	**134**	**94**	**128**	**73**
Beer and ale	105	113	97	191	84	54	68	72
Wine	115	63	173	288	170	94	158	67
HOUSING	**133**	**160**	**115**	**83**	**117**	**134**	**51**	**65**
Housekeeping supplies	**121**	**114**	**134**	**91**	**131**	**173**	**47**	**79**
Laundry and cleaning supplies	128	118	149	64	122	267	41	72
Other household products	115	102	131	88	159	105	58	97
Miscellaneous household products	143	105	182	155	226	111	54	49
Lawn and garden supplies	83	82	85	26	112	73	66	159
Postage and stationery	124	120	135	94	119	197	42	71
Stationery, stationery supplies, giftwrap	115	105	129	107	128	145	40	81
Postage	146	153	154	60	99	335	50	47
Household textiles	**148**	**188**	**115**	**63**	**71**	**241**	**11**	**36**
Bathroom linens	169	299	78	136	47	98	–	25
Bedroom linens	147	142	139	28	79	342	14	35
Appliances and miscellaneous housewares	**137**	**190**	**90**	**102**	**83**	**94**	**40**	**48**
Major appliances	119	138	100	128	111	56	43	46
Small appliances and miscellaneous housewares	143	210	86	92	73	107	39	48
China and other dinnerware	163	296	66	33	27	168	–	45
Glassware	111	200	49	106	20	65	127	102
Nonelectric cookware	136	162	102	135	107	68	7	47
Tableware, nonelectric kitchenware	158	243	86	111	63	114	44	24
Small electric kitchen appliances	133	139	114	54	134	116	19	57
Miscellaneous household equipment	**143**	**190**	**110**	**112**	**94**	**139**	**30**	**59**
Infants' equipment	176	283	104	49	146	57	3	21
Household decorative items	147	172	133	179	96	176	34	54
Indoor plants, fresh flowers	118	165	81	45	83	103	58	89
Computers and computer hardware, nonbusiness use	147	194	130	22	101	257	23	69
Miscellaneous household equipment and parts	153	235	99	220	67	75	33	5
Other housing	**129**	**150**	**116**	**57**	**141**	**108**	**76**	**73**
Repair or maintenance services	98	184	38	11	66	6	2	146
Materials for additions, finishing basements, remodeling rooms	141	14	276	0	524	–	–	94
Housing while attending school	172	197	168	0	217	192	35	25
Lodging on trips	111	173	67	38	65	93	14	124
Utility: natural gas (renter)	94	86	53	28	58	60	105	100
Electricity (renter)	70	55	71	43	87	60	192	130
Day care centers, nurseries, and preschools	103	78	126	184	115	105	114	93
Bedroom furniture other than mattresses and springs	169	238	88	–	31	255	23	44
APPAREL AND SERVICES	**116**	**140**	**96**	**111**	**87**	**102**	**69**	**81**
Men and boys, aged 2 or older	**127**	**161**	**99**	**63**	**105**	**113**	**59**	**68**
Men's suits	145	176	122	36	150	128	25	41
Men's coats and jackets	169	294	70	–	62	137	5	18
Men's accessories	111	156	78	21	31	214	84	89
Men's sweaters and vests	143	154	123	120	89	190	45	59
Men's active sportswear	120	100	141	47	180	132	44	91
Men's shirts	136	191	83	75	70	113	98	46
Men's pants	106	159	57	11	79	46	45	118
Boys' shirts	140	171	111	95	143	57	51	57
Boys' pants	123	147	108	58	135	91	44	84
Women and girls, aged 2 or older	**116**	**154**	**86**	**101**	**77**	**94**	**72**	**87**
Women's coats and jackets	78	153	24	39	19	25	–	141
Women's dresses	137	214v	86	327	19	47	30	88
Women's vests and sweaters	122	159	103	105	108	91	80	70

	total married couples	married couples, no children	married couples with children				single parent, at least one child <18	single person
			total	oldest child under 6	oldest child 6 to 17	oldest child 18 or older		
Women's shirts, tops, blouses	109	124	97	134	79	106	105	102
Women's pants	99	134	75	123	52	86	147	107
Women's active sportswear	82	123	57	79	56	42	6	134
Women's sleepwear	114	124	84	91	41	166	270	55
Women's undergarments	89	96	94	150	63	110	33	150
Women's accessories	139	161	120	93	101	178	33	76
Girls' dresses and suits	132	239	57	–	106	–	–	79
Girls' shirts, blouses, sweaters	131	180	93	19	139	54	120	69
Girls' skirts and pants	124	155	102	77	89	145	49	66
Girls' active sportswear	126	174	93	203	99	–	–	66
Girls' accessories	118	191	59	52	68	46	52	68
Children under age 2	**136**	**111**	**152**	**269**	**126**	**117**	**88**	**43**
Infant dresses, outerwear	131	160	107	111	85	144	59	52
Infant underwear	144	79	190	430	159	75	122	26
Infant nightwear, loungewear	124	125	122	92	116	154	85	72
Infant accessories	125	102	140	124	106	223	27	77
Other apparel products and services	**90**	**118**	**65**	**59**	**54**	**90**	**61**	**114**
Jewelry and watches	77	96	56	34	37	108	30	147
Jewelry	75	95	52	32	32	104	27	151
All other apparel products and services	103	142	75	85	72	72	92	81
Men's footwear	110	137	87	101	68	115	113	56
Boys' footwear	50	42	52	18	55	71	328	105
Women's footwear	121	194	71	171	41	58	39	53
Girls' footwear	91	120	71	11	113	32	–	131
TRANSPORTATION	**109**	**120**	**112**	**27**	**115**	**166**	**75**	**126**
New cars	100	–	205	–	278	209	–	167
New trucks	97	225	–	–	–	–	–	173
Used cars	108	130	95	–	139	77	242	104
Used trucks	137	44	241	56	–	819	58	93
Airline fares	121	154	100	90	91	125	35	99
Ship fares	124	134	125	108	114	156	70	86
HEALTH CARE	**71**	**102**	**50**	**18**	**39**	**91**	**24**	**189**
Physician's services	103	149	74	43	48	144	46	131
Dental services	114	113	118	–	71	285	93	101
Hospital services other than room	94	169	38	–	43	55	70	48
Care in convalescent or nursing home	20	39	4	–	8	–	–	301
Nonprescription drugs	116	211	28	10	10	77	58	42
Prescription drugs	71	62	75	31	62	132	57	186
ENTERTAINMENT	**126**	**172**	**92**	**72**	**90**	**108**	**38**	**72**
Toys, games, hobbies, and tricycles	122	178	80	75	66	110	33	78
Other entertainment	128	168	99	71	106	107	40	68
Fees for recreational lessons	163	236	120	42	183	57	27	49
Community antenna or cable TV	69	69	68	87	81	32	125	140
VCRs and video disc players	120	85	128	122	108	171	58	87
Pet purchase, supplies, and medicine	171	331	55	68	47	66	15	36
Athletic gear, game tables, exercise equipment	121	123	120	33	86	253	25	62
Photographic equipment	141	200	94	142	50	143	44	66
PERSONAL CARE PRODUCTS AND SERVICES	**120**	**125**	**119**	**163**	**92**	**142**	**91**	**69**
Cosmetics, perfume, bath preparation	115	108	121	181	101	115	59	80
EDUCATION	**165**	**195**	**157**	**7**	**217**	**149**	**21**	**36**
College tuition	169	190	169	4	236	157	21	31
Elementary and high school tuition	121	207	65	–	102	40	8	91
Other school expenses including rentals	180	317	86	1	109	102	4	27
College books and supplies	147	132	169	4	233	162	20	68
Miscellaneous school supplies	141	117	178	49	199	230	50	52
ALL OTHER GIFTS	**119**	**165**	**85**	**90**	**60**	**127**	**34**	**88**
Gifts of trip expenses	116	179	66	39	59	97	14	107
Legal fees	77	110	37	2	66	7	378	42
Funeral expenses	125	144	116	176	37	224	6	79
Cemetery lots, vaults, and maintenance fees	118	165	55	–	89	27	–	55
Miscellaneous personal services	183	246	148	91	237	9	9	17

Note: Spending index for total consumer units is 100. (–) means sample is too small to make a reliable estimate. Categories with annual spending of less than $2.00 for the average household are omitted. Spending on gifts is also included in the product and service categories in other chapters.
Source: Calculations by New Strategist based on the 2003 Consumer Expenditure Survey

Table 6.15 Gifts for Nonhousehold Members: Total spending by household type, 2003

(total annual spending on selected gifts of products and services for nonhousehold members by consumer unit (CU) type, 2003; numbers in thousands)

	total married couples	married couples, no children	married couples with children				single parent, at least one child <18	single person
			total	oldest child under 6	oldest child 6 to 17	oldest child 18 or older		
Number of consumer units	58,448	25,132	28,584	5,496	15,047	8,061	6,999	33,929
Total spending of all CUs	$3,099,499,193	$1,203,713,476	$1,649,363,115	$283,061,807	$890,529,309	$475,869,275	$213,712,715	$802,670,228
Gifts, total spending	**76,923,997**	**40,976,972**	**32,077,536**	**3,789,877**	**17,832,200**	**10,478,710**	**3,532,045**	**24,880,136**
FOOD	**6,922,581**	**4,367,188**	**2,279,860**	**221,049**	**1,023,046**	**1,038,656**	**376,686**	**1,014,816**
Fresh fruit other than apples, bananas, and citrus	187,034	101,785	76,033	3,627	41,530	31,440	13,368	33,250
Candy and chewing gum	632,407	243,278	361,016	101,456	141,291	120,374	101,136	201,538
Board (including at school)	1,697,914	850,467	679,156	–	420,263	258,840	31,426	180,163
Catered affairs	2,752,901	2,184,976	561,104	22,918	94,646	443,381	65,161	74,644
ALCOHOLIC BEVERAGES	**1,049,142**	**353,859**	**645,713**	**193,899**	**325,918**	**121,741**	**144,669**	**396,969**
Beer and ale	241,390	111,586	108,905	41,220	49,655	17,047	18,617	95,340
Wine	644,097	152,300	472,779	151,470	244,965	72,208	106,105	218,163
HOUSING	**17,157,410**	**8,883,157**	**7,233,181**	**1,003,844**	**3,867,831**	**2,381,503**	**784,098**	**4,881,705**
Housekeeping supplies	**2,945,195**	**1,193,519**	**1,596,988**	**207,419**	**820,212**	**578,791**	**135,501**	**1,109,818**
Laundry and cleaning supplies	168,915	66,600	96,042	7,914	41,379	48,246	6,509	54,965
Other household products	832,300	317,417	464,204	59,961	296,576	105,257	49,973	409,523
Miscellaneous household products	464,077	146,520	289,270	47,321	189,592	49,533	21,137	92,287
Lawn and garden supplies	262,432	111,586	132,058	7,804	91,486	32,003	25,196	292,468
Postage and stationery	1,944,565	809,502	1,036,742	139,543	482,256	425,288	78,949	645,669
Stationery, stationery supplies, giftwrap	1,287,609	504,651	703,166	112,998	368,802	222,977	53,822	524,882
Postage	610,197	276,452	316,139	23,798	107,285	193,145	25,126	114,680
Household textiles	**1,102,329**	**601,660**	**417,326**	**43,968**	**135,874**	**246,537**	**9,519**	**156,413**
Bathroom linens	326,724	248,053	73,461	24,622	23,323	25,972	–	27,482
Bedroom linens	510,251	212,617	236,676	9,288	71,172	163,795	6,019	70,233
Appliances and miscellaneous housewares	**1,959,761**	**1,173,413**	**628,562**	**136,960**	**306,658**	**184,300**	**68,800**	**396,291**
Major appliances	463,493	231,466	190,655	46,881	111,047	30,154	20,227	102,805
Small appliances and miscellaneous housewares	1,496,269	941,947	437,621	90,134	195,611	154,146	48,573	293,825
China and other dinnerware	194,632	151,546	38,303	3,682	8,426	27,581	–	31,215
Glassware	139,106	108,068	30,013	12,531	6,470	11,257	19,107	74,644
Nonelectric cookware	286,980	147,274	105,475	26,930	58,081	19,700	1,680	57,340
Tableware, nonelectric kitchenware	469,922	310,883	124,912	30,997	48,000	46,799	15,608	42,072
Small electric kitchen appliances	177,682	79,417	74,033	6,760	45,893	21,228	3,080	43,768
Miscellaneous household equipment	**4,754,160**	**2,712,748**	**1,783,070**	**349,875**	**800,801**	**634,596**	**119,963**	**1,126,104**
Infants' equipment	483,365	332,999	138,918	12,586	103,222	21,469	980	33,590
Household decorative items	1,621,932	819,303	720,603	186,479	272,200	267,926	45,633	346,415
Indoor plants, fresh flowers	746,965	451,119	252,683	26,601	136,025	89,898	43,954	327,415
Computers and computer hardware, nonbusiness use	691,440	392,311	298,703	9,893	122,784	166,127	13,088	187,967
Miscellaneous household equipment and parts	387,510	256,095	122,340	52,267	43,486	26,214	9,869	7,804
Other housing	**6,396,549**	**3,201,817**	**2,807,235**	**265,567**	**1,804,436**	**737,360**	**450,246**	**2,092,741**
Repair or maintenance services	239,637	193,014	45,734	2,528	41,229	1,849	630	206,628
Materials for additions, finishing basements, remodeling rooms	184,111	8,042	176,077	55	175,899	–	–	70,912
Housing while attending school	2,817,778	1,387,035	1,349,451	440	916,061	433,088	67,960	237,842
Lodging on trips	161,901	108,570	48,021	5,221	24,226	18,575	2,520	104,841
Utility: natural gas (renter)	154,303	60,819	42,590	4,397	24,677	13,509	20,787	95,680
Electricity (renter)	392,186	132,446	192,942	22,534	124,439	46,075	128,012	420,380
Day care centers, nurseries, and preschools	568,699	186,731	341,007	96,070	164,915	80,088	75,799	297,897
Bedroom furniture other than mattresses and springs	253,664	153,557	64,600	–	12,038	52,669	4,129	38,340
APPAREL AND SERVICES	**15,282,399**	**7,946,738**	**6,180,432**	**1,376,363**	**2,951,920**	**1,847,581**	**1,088,484**	**6,191,364**
Men and boys, aged 2 or older	**4,123,506**	**2,249,565**	**1,568,976**	**191,481**	**873,930**	**506,503**	**229,357**	**1,289,641**
Men's suits	247,820	129,430	102,045	5,826	66,056	30,234	5,179	41,054
Men's coats and jackets	389,264	292,034	78,606	–	36,564	43,502	1,400	24,768
Men's accessories	178,851	108,068	61,170	3,243	12,940	47,442	16,308	83,805
Men's sweaters and vests	191,709	88,716	80,607	15,059	30,545	35,059	7,139	46,143
Men's active sportswear	287,564	102,539	165,216	10,662	110,746	43,261	12,598	126,216
Men's shirts	666,892	401,358	197,515	34,625	88,476	76,148	57,532	131,305
Men's pants	372,898	241,016	98,043	3,517	71,624	22,354	19,037	240,557
Boys' shirts	301,592	158,583	116,623	19,236	79,147	16,725	13,088	71,251
Boys' pants	303,930	156,572	130,057	13,410	85,617	30,958	13,158	120,109
Women and girls, aged 2 or older	**5,426,897**	**3,115,865**	**1,984,015**	**447,429**	**930,206**	**608,302**	**404,892**	**2,369,601**
Women's coats and jackets	323,217	272,431	49,164	15,334	19,862	13,991	–	339,629
Women's dresses	381,081	256,346	117,480	85,573	13,392	18,012	9,939	141,823
Women's vests and sweaters	501,484	281,730	206,948	40,780	114,207	51,382	39,334	167,609

	total married couples	married couples, no children	married couples with children				single parent, at least one child <18	single person
			total	oldest child under 6	oldest child 6 to 17	oldest child 18 or older		
Women's shirts, tops, blouses	$541,813	$265,897	$236,104	$62,819	$101,266	$72,691	$62,641	$293,825
Women's pants	371,145	215,884	136,917	43,363	49,956	44,386	66,071	232,753
Women's active sportswear	156,056	101,031	52,830	14,180	27,536	11,016	1,400	148,948
Women's sleepwear	374,652	175,673	134,916	28,194	34,909	74,862	106,315	105,180
Women's undergarments	163,654	75,647	84,509	27,545	29,643	27,822	7,209	160,145
Women's accessories	368,807	184,469	156,069	23,248	69,066	65,293	10,429	117,394
Girls' dresses and suits	163,070	127,419	34,587	–	33,705	–	–	57,001
Girls' shirts, blouses, sweaters	415,565	245,791	144,063	5,771	113,304	23,319	45,633	126,216
Girls' skirts and pants	332,569	178,186	134,059	19,456	61,091	53,473	15,818	102,805
Girls' active sportswear	151,965	90,727	54,881	23,138	30,696	–	–	46,143
Girls' accessories	154,887	107,565	38,017	6,430	22,871	8,363	8,189	51,572
Children under age 2	**3,083,132**	**1,079,419**	**1,686,742**	**574,717**	**736,852**	**365,785**	**240,136**	**571,704**
Infant dresses, outerwear	908,866	477,508	363,203	72,437	152,727	138,064	49,133	209,681
Infant underwear	1,635,960	386,028	1,053,035	459,685	464,651	116,997	166,156	169,645
Infant nightwear, loungewear	180,020	78,161	86,855	12,586	43,486	30,877	14,768	60,733
Infant accessories	288,733	101,785	158,927	26,930	62,896	71,082	7,489	103,483
Other apparel products and services	**2,648,279**	**1,501,637**	**940,699**	**162,792**	**410,783**	**366,911**	**214,169**	**1,960,078**
Jewelry and watches	1,170,713	624,028	416,469	47,870	144,451	223,942	55,082	1,286,588
Jewelry	1,066,676	579,293	363,017	42,099	117,968	202,874	45,843	1,241,462
All other apparel products and services	1,477,565	877,861	524,516	114,921	266,332	142,969	159,087	673,491
Men's footwear	323,217	173,411	125,198	28,030	51,310	46,879	39,894	96,019
Boys' footwear	120,987	43,227	60,884	3,957	33,705	23,560	94,067	146,573
Women's footwear	564,608	388,541	161,735	74,801	49,655	37,310	21,977	144,198
Girls' footwear	313,866	177,432	120,053	3,408	99,912	15,037	–	261,932
TRANSPORTATION	**3,816,654**	**1,796,938**	**1,916,343**	**90,079**	**1,035,835**	**795,416**	**313,695**	**2,555,872**
New cars	677,997	–	677,727	–	483,460	194,351	–	654,151
New trucks	742,290	742,399	–	–	–	–	–	769,170
Used cars	843,405	437,297	363,303	–	280,627	82,501	226,908	472,292
Used trucks	302,176	41,468	260,400	11,652	–	248,789	15,398	118,752
Airline fares	515,511	282,484	208,663	35,889	99,912	72,932	17,777	244,967
Ship fares	271,783	125,911	133,487	22,204	64,401	46,799	18,197	108,912
HEALTH CARE	**2,001,260**	**1,226,442**	**680,012**	**47,266**	**283,335**	**350,266**	**79,159**	**3,063,110**
Physician's services	199,892	124,403	70,317	7,859	24,075	38,436	10,778	147,591
Dental services	244,313	104,046	123,197	–	39,273	83,868	23,867	124,859
Hospital services other than room	120,403	93,491	24,011	–	14,295	9,649	10,708	35,965
Care in convalescent or nursing home	234,376	199,799	25,726	–	25,730	–	–	2,078,830
Nonprescription drugs	208,659	164,112	24,296	1,649	4,665	19,138	12,458	43,768
Prescription drugs	119,234	44,735	52,313	4,891	26,784	30,636	11,618	182,199
ENTERTAINMENT	**5,080,300**	**2,975,377**	**1,809,653**	**274,360**	**939,083**	**598,894**	**181,554**	**1,680,503**
Toys, games, hobbies, and tricycles	1,860,984	1,168,889	596,252	107,667	257,304	231,259	60,331	690,116
Other entertainment	3,219,316	1,806,488	1,213,391	166,694	631,930	367,715	121,223	990,388
Fees for recreational lessons	573,959	356,623	206,543	13,740	165,517	27,822	11,268	100,769
Community antenna or cable TV	142,613	61,322	68,602	16,873	42,884	9,006	30,866	167,949
VCRs and video disc players	177,097	53,531	92,326	16,873	40,777	34,657	10,219	73,965
Pet purchase, supplies, and medicine	232,623	194,019	37,445	8,684	16,552	12,303	2,380	28,840
Athletic gear, game tables, exercise equipment	424,917	185,725	205,805	10,937	77,793	121,821	10,289	125,537
Photographic equipment	173,591	105,554	56,596	16,433	15,950	24,203	6,509	46,822
PERSONAL CARE PRODUCTS AND SERVICES	**1,102,914**	**497,362**	**536,808**	**140,862**	**218,482**	**180,279**	**100,506**	**371,523**
Cosmetics, perfume, bath preparation	668,645	271,426	343,856	99,313	151,975	92,552	41,364	269,396
EDUCATION	**19,238,159**	**9,790,925**	**8,983,951**	**72,547**	**6,511,288**	**2,401,686**	**288,149**	**2,454,085**
College tuition	15,310,454	7,406,400	7,509,874	33,306	5,512,017	1,964,336	225,018	1,608,913
Elementary and high school tuition	738,198	544,359	193,514	–	160,251	33,209	5,879	323,343
Other school expenses including rentals	1,654,078	1,255,846	387,027	1,044	257,153	128,978	4,409	145,216
College books and supplies	855,094	330,486	481,926	1,979	349,843	130,023	14,068	230,717
Miscellaneous school supplies	511,420	181,956	314,996	16,598	185,229	114,665	21,837	109,591
ALL OTHER GIFTS	**5,179,077**	**3,073,392**	**1,793,360**	**367,792**	**665,830**	**756,497**	**174,625**	**2,217,260**
Gifts of trip expenses	2,748,809	1,833,631	765,765	86,837	362,031	316,815	40,804	1,471,161
Legal fees	203,399	124,655	47,449	385	44,389	2,573	118,983	64,126
Funeral expenses	1,596,215	788,893	723,175	210,882	120,226	392,160	8,609	582,222
Cemetery lots, vaults, and maintenance fees	154,303	92,737	35,158	–	30,094	4,905	–	41,733
Miscellaneous personal services	266,523	154,059	105,189	12,476	88,777	1,769	1,610	14,589

Note: Total spending figures for total consumer units can be found on Total Spending by Age and Total Spending by Region tables. Spending by type of consumer unit will not add to total because not all types of consumer units are shown. (–) means sample is too small to make a reliable estimate. Expenditures for items in a given category may not add to category total because categories with annual spending of less than $2.00 for the average household are omitted. Spending on gifts is also included in the product and service categories in other chapters.
Source: Calculations by New Strategist based on the 2003 Consumer Expenditure Survey

Table 6.16 Gifts for Nonhousehold Members: Market shares by household type, 2003

(percentage of total annual spending on selected gifts of products and services for nonhousehold members accounted for by types of consumer units, 2003)

	total married couples	married couples, no children	married couples with children				single parent, at least one child <18	single person
			total	oldest child under 6	oldest child 6 to 17	oldest child 18 or older		
Share of total consumer units	50.7%	21.8%	24.8%	4.8%	13.0%	7.0%	6.1%	29.4%
Share of total before-tax income	68.8	26.8	36.6	6.2	19.8	10.7	3.5	15.6
Share of total spending	65.8	25.6	35.0	6.0	18.9	10.1	4.5	17.0
Share of gifts spending	66.2	35.3	27.6	3.3	15.4	9.0	3.0	21.4
FOOD	**77.3**	**48.8**	**25.5**	**2.5**	**11.4**	**11.6**	**4.2**	**11.3**
Fresh fruit other than apples, bananas, and citrus	68.7	37.4	27.9	1.3	15.3	11.5	4.9	12.2
Candy and chewing gum	58.3	22.4	33.3	9.3	13.0	11.1	9.3	18.6
Board (including at school)	88.1	44.1	35.2	–	21.8	13.4	1.6	9.3
Catered affairs	93.9	74.5	19.1	0.8	3.2	15.1	2.2	2.5
ALCOHOLIC BEVERAGES	**56.5**	**19.0**	**34.7**	**10.4**	**17.5**	**6.6**	**7.8**	**21.4**
Beer and ale	53.2	24.6	24.0	9.1	11.0	3.8	4.1	21.0
Wine	58.3	13.8	42.8	13.7	22.2	6.5	9.6	19.7
HOUSING	**67.5**	**34.9**	**28.4**	**3.9**	**15.2**	**9.4**	**3.1**	**19.2**
Housekeeping supplies	**61.4**	**24.9**	**33.3**	**4.3**	**17.1**	**12.1**	**2.8**	**23.1**
Laundry and cleaning supplies	65.1	25.7	37.0	3.0	15.9	18.6	2.5	21.2
Other household products	58.1	22.2	32.4	4.2	20.7	7.4	3.5	28.6
Miscellaneous household products	72.2	22.8	45.0	7.4	29.5	7.7	3.3	14.4
Lawn and garden supplies	42.0	17.8	21.1	1.2	14.6	5.1	4.0	46.8
Postage and stationery	62.7	26.1	33.4	4.5	15.5	13.7	2.5	20.8
Stationery, stationery supplies, giftwrap	58.3	22.9	31.9	5.1	16.7	10.1	2.4	23.8
Postage	73.8	33.4	38.2	2.9	13.0	23.4	3.0	13.9
Household textiles	**75.1**	**41.0**	**28.4**	**3.0**	**9.3**	**16.8**	**0.6**	**10.7**
Bathroom linens	85.8	65.2	19.3	6.5	6.1	6.8	–	7.2
Bedroom linens	74.3	31.0	34.5	1.4	10.4	23.9	0.9	10.2
Appliances and miscellaneous housewares	**69.3**	**41.5**	**22.2**	**4.8**	**10.8**	**6.5**	**2.4**	**14.0**
Major appliances	60.4	30.2	24.9	6.1	14.5	3.9	2.6	13.4
Small appliances and miscellaneous housewares	72.6	45.7	21.2	4.4	9.5	7.5	2.4	14.3
China and other dinnerware	82.7	64.4	16.3	1.6	3.6	11.7	–	13.3
Glassware	56.1	43.6	12.1	5.1	2.6	4.5	7.7	30.1
Nonelectric cookware	68.7	35.3	25.3	6.4	13.9	4.7	0.4	13.7
Tableware, nonelectric kitchenware	80.0	52.9	21.3	5.3	8.2	8.0	2.7	7.2
Small electric kitchen appliances	67.6	30.2	28.1	2.6	17.4	8.1	1.2	16.6
Miscellaneous household equipment	**72.6**	**41.5**	**27.2**	**5.3**	**12.2**	**9.7**	**1.8**	**17.2**
Infants' equipment	89.3	61.6	25.7	2.3	19.1	4.0	0.2	6.2
Household decorative items	74.4	37.6	33.0	8.5	12.5	12.3	2.1	15.9
Indoor plants, fresh flowers	59.6	36.0	20.2	2.1	10.9	7.2	3.5	26.1
Computers and computer hardware, nonbusiness use	74.6	42.3	32.2	1.1	13.2	17.9	1.4	20.3
Miscellaneous household equipment and parts	77.6	51.3	24.5	10.5	8.7	5.2	2.0	1.6
Other housing	**65.3**	**32.7**	**28.7**	**2.7**	**18.4**	**7.5**	**4.6**	**21.4**
Repair or maintenance services	49.7	40.0	9.5	0.5	8.6	0.4	0.1	42.9
Materials for additions, finishing basements, remodeling rooms	71.6	3.1	68.4	0.0	68.4	–	–	27.6
Housing while attending school	87.1	42.9	41.7	0.0	28.3	13.4	2.1	7.4
Lodging on trips	56.4	37.8	16.7	1.8	8.4	6.5	0.9	36.5
Utility: natural gas (renter)	47.4	18.7	13.1	1.4	7.6	4.2	6.4	29.4
Electricity (renter)	35.6	12.0	17.5	2.0	11.3	4.2	11.6	38.2
Day care centers, nurseries, and preschools	51.9	17.1	31.1	8.8	15.1	7.3	6.9	27.2
Bedroom furniture other than mattresses and springs	85.6	51.8	21.8	–	4.1	17.8	1.4	12.9
APPAREL AND SERVICES	**58.8**	**30.6**	**23.8**	**5.3**	**11.4**	**7.1**	**4.2**	**23.8**
Men and boys, aged 2 or older	**64.3**	**35.1**	**24.5**	**3.0**	**13.6**	**7.9**	**3.6**	**20.1**
Men's suits	73.3	38.3	30.2	1.7	19.5	8.9	1.5	12.1
Men's coats and jackets	85.4	64.1	17.3	–	8.0	9.5	0.3	5.4
Men's accessories	56.2	33.9	19.2	1.0	4.1	14.9	5.1	26.3
Men's sweaters and vests	72.6	33.6	30.5	5.7	11.6	13.3	2.7	17.5
Men's active sportswear	60.9	21.7	35.0	2.3	23.5	9.2	2.7	26.8
Men's shirts	69.1	41.6	20.5	3.6	9.2	7.9	6.0	13.6
Men's pants	53.6	34.6	14.1	0.5	10.3	3.2	2.7	34.6
Boys' shirts	71.0	37.4	27.5	4.5	18.6	3.9	3.1	16.8
Boys' pants	62.3	32.1	26.7	2.7	17.5	6.3	2.7	24.6
Women and girls, aged 2 or older	**58.6**	**33.6**	**21.4**	**4.8**	**10.0**	**6.6**	**4.4**	**25.6**
Women's coats and jackets	39.5	33.3	6.0	1.9	2.4	1.7	–	41.5
Women's dresses	69.4	46.7	21.4	15.6	2.4	3.3	1.8	25.8
Women's vests and sweaters	61.6	34.6	25.4	5.0	14.0	6.3	4.8	20.6

	total married couples	married couples, no children	married couples with children				single parent, at least one child <18	single person
			total	oldest child under 6	oldest child 6 to 17	oldest child 18 or older		
Women's shirts, tops, blouses	55.3%	27.1%	24.1%	6.4%	10.3%	7.4%	6.4%	30.0%
Women's pants	50.1	29.2	18.5	5.9	6.7	6.0	8.9	31.4
Women's active sportswear	41.4	26.8	14.0	3.8	7.3	2.9	0.4	39.5
Women's sleepwear	57.8	27.1	20.8	4.3	5.4	11.5	16.4	16.2
Women's undergarments	45.2	20.9	23.4	7.6	8.2	7.7	2.0	44.2
Women's accessories	70.3	35.1	29.7	4.4	13.2	12.4	2.0	22.4
Girls' dresses and suits	66.7	52.1	14.1	–	13.8	–	–	23.3
Girls' shirts, blouses, sweaters	66.5	39.3	23.0	0.9	18.1	3.7	7.3	20.2
Girls' skirts and pants	62.9	33.7	25.4	3.7	11.6	10.1	3.0	19.5
Girls' active sportswear	63.6	38.0	23.0	9.7	12.9	–	–	19.3
Girls' accessories	59.9	41.6	14.7	2.5	8.9	3.2	3.2	20.0
Children under age 2	**68.9**	**24.1**	**37.7**	**12.8**	**16.5**	**8.2**	**5.4**	**12.8**
Infant dresses, outerwear	66.3	34.8	26.5	5.3	11.1	10.1	3.6	15.3
Infant underwear	73.0	17.2	47.0	20.5	20.7	5.2	7.4	7.6
Infant nightwear, loungewear	62.7	27.2	30.3	4.4	15.1	10.7	5.1	21.1
Infant accessories	63.2	22.3	34.8	5.9	13.8	15.6	1.6	22.7
Other apparel products and services	**45.5**	**25.8**	**15.2**	**2.8**	**7.1**	**6.3**	**3.7**	**33.7**
Jewelry and watches	39.3	20.9	14.0	1.6	4.8	7.5	1.8	43.1
Jewelry	38.1	20.7	13.0	1.5	4.2	7.2	1.6	44.3
All other apparel products and services	52.0	30.9	18.5	4.0	9.4	5.0	5.6	23.7
Men's footwear	55.5	29.8	21.5	4.8	8.8	8.0	6.8	16.5
Boys' footwear	25.6	9.1	12.9	0.8	7.1	5.0	19.9	31.0
Women's footwear	61.3	42.2	17.6	8.1	5.4	4.1	2.4	15.7
Girls' footwear	46.3	26.2	17.7	0.5	14.7	2.2	–	38.6
TRANSPORTATION	**55.4**	**26.1**	**27.8**	**1.3**	**15.0**	**11.5**	**4.6**	**37.1**
New cars	50.9	–	50.9	–	36.3	14.6	–	49.1
New trucks	49.1	49.1	–	–	–	–	–	50.9
Used cars	54.7	28.4	23.6	–	18.2	5.3	14.7	30.6
Used trucks	69.3	9.5	55.7	2.7	–	57.1	3.5	27.2
Airline fares	61.4	33.6	24.8	4.3	11.9	8.7	2.1	29.2
Ship fares	63.0	29.2	30.9	5.1	14.9	10.8	4.2	25.2
HEALTH CARE	**36.2**	**22.2**	**12.3**	**0.9**	**5.1**	**6.3**	**1.4**	**55.4**
Physician's services	52.0	32.4	18.3	2.0	6.3	10.0	2.8	38.4
Dental services	57.9	24.6	29.2	–	9.3	19.9	5.7	29.6
Hospital services other than room	47.4	36.8	9.5	–	5.6	3.8	4.2	14.2
Care in convalescent or nursing home	10.0	8.5	1.1	–	1.1	–	–	88.5
Nonprescription drugs	58.5	46.0	6.8	0.5	1.3	5.4	3.5	12.3
Prescription drugs	35.8	13.4	18.7	1.5	8.0	9.2	3.5	54.7
ENTERTAINMENT	**63.9**	**37.4**	**22.7**	**3.4**	**11.8**	**7.5**	**2.3**	**21.1**
Toys, games, hobbies, and tricycles	61.9	38.9	19.8	3.6	8.6	7.7	2.0	22.9
Other entertainment	65.1	36.5	24.5	3.4	13.8	7.4	2.5	20.0
Fees for recreational lessons	82.7	51.4	29.8	2.0	23.8	4.0	1.6	14.5
Community antenna or cable TV	35.0	15.1	16.8	4.1	10.5	2.2	7.6	41.2
VCRs and video disc players	60.9	18.4	31.8	5.8	14.0	11.9	3.5	25.4
Pet purchase, supplies, and medicine	86.5	72.2	13.9	3.2	6.2	4.6	0.9	10.7
Athletic gear, game tables, exercise equipment	61.4	26.8	29.7	1.6	11.2	17.6	1.5	18.1
Photographic equipment	71.7	43.6	23.4	6.8	6.6	10.0	2.7	19.3
PERSONAL CARE PRODUCTS AND SERVICES	**60.6**	**27.3**	**29.5**	**7.7**	**12.0**	**9.9**	**5.5**	**20.4**
Cosmetics, perfume, bath preparation	58.1	23.6	29.9	8.6	13.2	8.0	3.6	23.4
EDUCATION	**83.5**	**42.5**	**39.0**	**0.3**	**28.2**	**10.4**	**1.3**	**10.6**
College tuition	85.4	41.3	41.9	0.2	30.7	11.0	1.3	9.0
Elementary and high school tuition	61.3	45.2	16.1	–	13.3	2.8	0.5	26.8
Other school expenses including rentals	91.0	69.1	21.3	0.1	14.2	7.1	0.2	8.0
College books and supplies	74.3	28.7	41.9	0.2	30.4	11.3	1.2	20.1
Miscellaneous school supplies	71.5	25.4	44.0	2.3	25.9	16.0	3.1	15.3
ALL OTHER GIFTS	**60.5**	**35.9**	**20.5**	**4.3**	**7.8**	**8.8**	**2.0**	**25.9**
Gifts of trip expenses	58.5	39.1	16.3	1.8	7.7	6.7	0.9	31.3
Legal fees	39.2	24.0	9.1	0.1	8.6	0.5	22.9	12.4
Funeral expenses	63.5	31.4	28.8	8.4	4.8	15.6	0.3	23.2
Cemetery lots, vaults, and maintenance fees	59.7	35.9	13.6	–	11.6	1.9	–	16.2
Miscellaneous personal services	92.8	53.6	36.6	4.3	30.9	0.6	0.6	5.1

Note: Market share for total consumer units is 100.0%. Market shares by type of consumer unit will not add to total because not all types of consumer units are shown. (–) means sample is too small to make a reliable estimate.
Source: Calculations by New Strategist based on the 2003 Consumer Expenditure Survey

Table 6.17 Gifts for Nonhousehold Members: Average spending by race and Hispanic origin, 2003

(average annual spending of consumer units (CU) on selected gifts of products and services for nonhousehold members by race and Hispanic origin of consumer unit reference person, 2003)

		race			Hispanic origin	
	total consumer units	Asian	black	white and other	Hispanic	non-Hispanic
Number of consumer units (000)	115,356	3,573	13,743	98,041	11,727	103,629
Average number of persons per CU	2.5	2.8	2.6	2.5	3.3	2.4
Average before-tax income of CU	$51,128.00	$60,393.00	$34,485.00	$53,039.00	$37,150.00	$52,797.00
Average spending of CU, total	40,817.33	44,922.85	28,707.56	42,360.25	34,574.75	41,520.78
Gifts, average spending	1,007.01	1,342.33	523.63	1,062.43	745.37	1,037.61
FOOD	**77.59**	**115.92**	**31.65**	**82.59**	**73.71**	**78.09**
Fresh fruit other than apples, bananas, and citrus	2.36	3.68	2.71	2.26	2.20	2.38
Candy and chewing gum	9.41	13.94	9.50	9.22	8.06	9.58
Board (including at school)	16.71	66.66	5.67	16.43	5.06	18.03
Catered affairs	25.42	4.32	1.79	29.50	39.22	23.85
ALCOHOLIC BEVERAGES	**16.11**	**12.00**	**4.21**	**17.92**	**12.63**	**16.54**
Beer and ale	3.93	1.97	1.37	4.36	4.45	3.87
Wine	9.58	8.53	2.75	10.57	7.86	9.80
HOUSING	**220.43**	**138.70**	**95.95**	**240.85**	**137.92**	**230.18**
Housekeeping supplies	**41.56**	**19.63**	**12.73**	**46.41**	**37.35**	**42.09**
Laundry and cleaning supplies	2.25	2.16	2.06	2.28	1.94	2.29
Other household products	12.41	1.63	3.17	14.12	6.76	13.12
Miscellaneous household products	5.57	0.80	1.84	6.27	4.96	5.64
Lawn and garden supplies	5.42	0.63	0.86	6.23	–	6.08
Postage and stationery	26.89	15.84	7.50	30.01	28.65	26.67
Stationery, stationery supplies, giftwrap	19.13	9.87	6.99	21.17	20.46	18.96
Postage	7.17	5.97	0.52	8.14	8.19	7.04
Household textiles	**12.72**	**1.03**	**2.30**	**14.62**	**4.66**	**13.72**
Bathroom linens	3.30	0.85	0.57	3.77	1.63	3.51
Bedroom linens	5.95	0.15	1.41	6.81	1.09	6.56
Appliances and miscellaneous housewares	**24.51**	**20.14**	**15.31**	**25.96**	**12.28**	**25.98**
Major appliances	6.65	4.64	8.23	6.51	1.37	7.27
Small appliances and miscellaneous housewares	17.87	15.50	7.08	19.45	10.91	18.71
China and other dinnerware	2.04	–	1.39	2.21	1.15	2.28
Glassware	2.15	–	1.10	2.38	1.15	2.28
Nonelectric cookware	3.62	2.93	0.62	4.06	4.18	3.55
Tableware, nonelectric kitchenware	5.09	9.96	2.37	5.27	4.11	5.21
Small electric kitchen appliances	2.28	0.40	0.84	2.55	0.28	2.51
Miscellaneous household equipment	**56.73**	**50.49**	**15.18**	**62.75**	**31.38**	**59.79**
Infants' equipment	4.69	2.15	1.11	5.29	7.24	4.37
Household decorative items	18.91	6.06	3.93	21.49	7.39	20.36
Indoor plants, fresh flowers	10.86	6.83	4.21	11.94	8.32	11.15
Computers and computer hardware, nonbusiness use	8.04	10.50	3.69	8.56	3.42	8.56
Miscellaneous household equipment and parts	4.33	0.56	0.16	5.06	1.82	4.65
Other housing	**84.91**	**47.40**	**50.42**	**91.11**	**52.24**	**88.61**
Repair or maintenance services	4.18	6.53	0.47	4.62	0.16	4.64
Materials for additions, finishing basements, remodeling rooms	2.23	–	–	2.63	2.67	2.18
Housing while attending school	28.03	13.60	9.12	31.20	5.78	30.54
Lodging on trips	2.49	2.84	0.63	2.73	0.93	2.66
Utility: natural gas (renter)	2.82	5.49	4.02	2.56	1.89	2.93
Electricity (renter)	9.55	5.61	13.75	9.10	5.26	10.03
Day care centers, nurseries, and preschools	9.49	7.71	9.59	9.54	7.83	9.67
Bedroom furniture other than mattresses and springs	2.57	–	0.21	3.00	4.44	2.36
APPAREL AND SERVICES	**225.14**	**179.45**	**221.50**	**227.39**	**186.68**	**229.74**
Men and boys, aged 2 or older	**55.56**	**57.20**	**30.19**	**59.00**	**51.61**	**56.03**
Men's suits	2.93	–	1.75	3.20	2.12	3.02
Men's coats and jackets	3.95	0.68	9.47	3.31	2.49	4.13
Men's accessories	2.76	13.39	–	2.73	1.46	2.92
Men's sweaters and vests	2.29	4.14	1.00	2.41	2.61	2.26
Men's active sportswear	4.09	3.69	–	4.67	0.91	4.49
Men's shirts	8.37	10.24	1.90	9.19	9.85	8.18
Men's pants	6.03	3.73	3.31	6.50	2.18	6.51
Boys' shirts	3.68	0.60	0.79	4.20	6.69	3.30
Boys' pants	4.23	3.08	2.95	4.45	3.84	4.27
Women and girls, aged 2 or older	**80.28**	**52.72**	**93.16**	**79.56**	**51.30**	**83.86**
Women's coats and jackets	7.09	1.00	2.79	7.93	3.74	7.51
Women's dresses	4.76	3.46	11.82	3.84	2.88	5.00
Women's vests and sweaters	7.06	0.68	7.37	7.27	2.65	7.62

	total consumer units	race			Hispanic origin	
		Asian	black	white and other	Hispanic	non-Hispanic
Women's shirts, tops, blouses	$8.50	$7.24	$10.32	$8.30	$7.92	$8.57
Women's pants	6.42	1.66	11.11	5.95	4.77	6.63
Women's active sportswear	3.27	0.99	8.40	2.65	0.40	3.63
Women's sleepwear	5.62	7.48	4.91	5.64	1.72	6.11
Women's undergarments	3.14	1.05	4.44	3.04	2.70	3.19
Women's accessories	4.55	–	2.92	4.95	2.77	4.77
Girls' dresses and suits	2.12	2.86	4.64	1.74	0.53	2.32
Girls' shirts, blouses, sweaters	5.42	–	2.44	6.05	4.45	5.54
Girls' skirts and pants	4.58	0.70	3.94	4.81	3.87	4.66
Girls' active sportswear	2.07	–	0.95	2.30	2.44	2.02
Girls' accessories	2.24	17.93	1.79	1.69	1.78	2.30
Children under age 2	**38.81**	**45.67**	**44.29**	**37.77**	**49.03**	**37.55**
Infant dresses, outerwear	11.89	5.70	10.56	12.27	14.19	11.63
Infant underwear	19.44	32.00	21.75	18.63	27.66	18.41
Infant nightwear, loungewear	2.49	0.88	2.72	2.52	2.04	2.55
Infant accessories	3.96	5.32	7.77	3.38	4.39	3.91
Other apparel products and services	**50.49**	**23.86**	**53.86**	**51.06**	**34.74**	**52.30**
Jewelry and watches	25.85	19.78	21.26	26.72	13.34	27.27
Jewelry	24.28	18.43	20.55	25.02	11.92	25.68
All other apparel products and services	24.63	4.08	32.60	24.34	21.40	25.03
Men's footwear	5.05	–	2.05	5.66	5.76	4.96
Boys' footwear	4.10	–	7.85	3.74	3.52	4.17
Women's footwear	7.98	2.70	12.50	7.56	6.15	8.21
Girls' footwear	5.88	–	9.67	5.58	5.60	5.91
TRANSPORTATION	**59.73**	**323.95**	**38.42**	**53.09**	**141.79**	**50.44**
New cars	11.55	173.55	16.61	4.93	36.31	8.74
New trucks	13.10	119.23	–	11.07	63.30	7.42
Used cars	13.37	–	–	15.73	25.90	11.96
Used trucks	3.78	–	11.10	2.89	–	4.21
Airline fares	7.28	15.69	4.45	7.38	6.22	7.40
Ship fares	3.74	6.93	2.81	3.76	1.44	4.01
HEALTH CARE	**47.89**	**34.06**	**22.38**	**51.92**	**7.15**	**52.55**
Physician's services	3.33	1.08	0.44	3.81	0.71	3.62
Dental services	3.66	0.10	1.94	4.03	0.97	3.97
Hospital services other than room	2.20	–	3.10	2.16	0.91	2.35
Care in convalescent or nursing home	20.37	–	–	23.96	–	22.67
Nonprescription drugs	3.09	17.04	0.98	2.84	0.71	3.39
Prescription drugs	2.89	0.76	1.62	3.15	0.88	3.12
ENTERTAINMENT	**68.97**	**55.45**	**26.42**	**75.37**	**41.57**	**72.16**
Toys, games, hobbies, and tricycles	26.07	12.72	12.88	28.41	13.21	27.53
Other entertainment	42.89	42.73	13.54	46.96	28.36	44.63
Fees for recreational lessons	6.02	1.97	0.86	6.89	3.47	6.31
Community antenna or cable TV	3.53	3.64	3.70	3.50	2.90	3.60
VCRs and video disc players	2.52	1.98	0.70	2.79	1.02	2.69
Pet purchase, supplies, and medicine	2.33	11.54	0.18	2.26	–	2.62
Athletic gear, game tables, exercise equipment	6.00	–	0.07	7.06	4.09	6.24
Photographic equipment	2.10	0.62	0.21	2.42	2.41	2.07
PERSONAL CARE PRODUCTS AND SERVICES	**15.77**	**23.20**	**8.36**	**16.50**	**13.23**	**16.09**
Cosmetics, perfume, bath preparation	9.98	13.04	3.71	10.73	9.37	10.06
EDUCATION	**199.83**	**387.51**	**44.89**	**214.71**	**97.70**	**211.41**
College tuition	155.43	299.54	29.13	167.89	31.68	169.44
Elementary and high school tuition	10.44	–	2.28	11.96	0.26	11.59
Other school expenses including rentals	15.75	63.35	1.55	16.01	54.85	11.33
College books and supplies	9.97	18.01	6.78	10.12	6.59	10.35
Miscellaneous school supplies	6.20	2.74	2.56	6.84	3.97	6.48
ALL OTHER GIFTS	**74.21**	**71.25**	**29.68**	**80.56**	**32.77**	**78.92**
Gifts of trip expenses	40.70	53.99	12.27	44.20	14.66	43.65
Legal fees	4.50	–	3.66	4.78	0.69	4.93
Funeral expenses	21.80	15.85	11.31	23.49	13.27	22.77
Cemetery lots, vaults, and maintenance fees	2.24	0.82	1.92	2.34	1.87	2.28
Miscellaneous personal services	2.49	–	–	2.93	1.58	2.60

Note: Other races include Native Americans and Pacific Islanders. (–) means sample is too small to make a reliable estimate. Expenditures for items in a given category may not add to category total because categories with annual spending of less than $2.00 for the average household are omitted. Spending on gifts is also included in the product and service categories in other chapters.
Source: Bureau of Labor Statistics, unpublished tables from the 2003 Consumer Expenditure Survey

Table 6.18 Gifts for Nonhousehold Members: Indexed spending by race and Hispanic origin, 2003

(indexed average annual spending of consumer units (CU) on selected gifts of products and services for nonhousehold members by race and Hispanic origin of consumer unit reference person, 2003; index definition: an index of 100 is the average for all consumer units; an index of 132 means that spending by consumer units in that group is 32 percent above the average for all consumer units; an index of 68 indicates spending that is 32 percent below the average for all consumer units)

	total consumer units	race			Hispanic origin	
		Asian	black	white and other	Hispanic	non-Hispanic
Average spending of CU, total	$40,817	$44,923	$28,708	$42,360	$34,575	$41,521
Average spending of CU, index	100	110	70	104	85	102
Gifts, spending index	**100**	**133**	**52**	**106**	**74**	**103**
FOOD	**100**	**149**	**41**	**106**	**95**	**101**
Fresh fruit other than apples, bananas, and citrus	100	156	115	96	93	101
Candy and chewing gum	100	148	101	98	86	102
Board (including at school)	100	399	34	98	30	108
Catered affairs	100	17	7	116	154	94
ALCOHOLIC BEVERAGES	**100**	**74**	**26**	**111**	**78**	**103**
Beer and ale	100	50	35	111	113	98
Wine	100	89	29	110	82	102
HOUSING	**100**	**63**	**44**	**109**	**63**	**104**
Housekeeping supplies	**100**	**47**	**31**	**112**	**90**	**101**
Laundry and cleaning supplies	100	96	92	101	86	102
Other household products	100	13	26	114	54	106
Miscellaneous household products	100	14	33	113	89	101
Lawn and garden supplies	100	12	16	115	–	112
Postage and stationery	100	59	28	112	107	99
Stationery, stationery supplies, giftwrap	100	52	37	111	107	99
Postage	100	83	7	114	114	98
Household textiles	**100**	**8**	**18**	**115**	**37**	**108**
Bathroom linens	100	26	17	114	49	106
Bedroom linens	100	3	24	114	18	110
Appliances and miscellaneous housewares	**100**	**82**	**62**	**106**	**50**	**106**
Major appliances	100	70	124	98	21	109
Small appliances and miscellaneous housewares	100	87	40	109	61	105
China and other dinnerware	100	–	68	108	–	112
Glassware	100	–	51	111	53	106
Nonelectric cookware	100	81	17	112	115	98
Tableware, nonelectric kitchenware	100	196	47	104	81	102
Small electric kitchen appliances	100	18	37	112	12	110
Miscellaneous household equipment	**100**	**89**	**27**	**111**	**55**	**105**
Infants' equipment	100	46	24	113	154	93
Household decorative items	100	32	21	114	39	108
Indoor plants, fresh flowers	100	63	39	110	77	103
Computers and computer hardware, nonbusiness use	100	131	46	106	43	106
Miscellaneous household equipment and parts	100	13	4	117	42	107
Other housing	**100**	**56**	**59**	**107**	**62**	**104**
Repair or maintenance services	100	156	11	111	4	111
Materials for additions, finishing basements, remodeling rooms	100	–	–	118	120	98
Housing while attending school	100	49	33	111	21	109
Lodging on trips	100	114	25	110	37	107
Utility: natural gas (renter)	100	195	143	91	67	104
Electricity (renter)	100	59	144	95	55	105
Day care centers, nurseries, and preschools	100	81	101	101	83	102
Bedroom furniture other than mattresses and springs	100	–	8	117	173	92
APPAREL AND SERVICES	**100**	**80**	**98**	**101**	**83**	**102**
Men and boys, aged 2 or older	**100**	**103**	**54**	**106**	**93**	**101**
Men's suits	100	–	60	109	72	103
Men's coats and jackets	100	17	240	84	63	105
Men's accessories	100	485	–	99	53	106
Men's sweaters and vests	100	181	44	105	114	99
Men's active sportswear	100	90	–	114	22	110
Men's shirts	100	122	23	110	118	98
Men's pants	100	62	55	108	36	108
Boys' shirts	100	16	21	114	182	90
Boys' pants	100	73	70	105	91	101
Women and girls, aged 2 or older	**100**	**66**	**116**	**99**	**64**	**104**
Women's coats and jackets	100	14	39	112	53	106
Women's dresses	100	73	248	81	61	105
Women's vests and sweaters	100	10	104	103	38	108

	total consumer units	race			Hispanic origin	
		Asian	black	white and other	Hispanic	non-Hispanic
Women's shirts, tops, blouses	100	85	121	98	93	101
Women's pants	100	26	173	93	74	103
Women's active sportswear	100	30	257	81	12	111
Women's sleepwear	100	133	87	100	31	109
Women's undergarments	100	33	141	97	86	102
Women's accessories	100	–	64	109	61	105
Girls' dresses and suits	100	135	219	82	25	109
Girls' shirts, blouses, sweaters	100	–	45	112	82	102
Girls' skirts and pants	100	15	86	105	84	102
Girls' active sportswear	100	–	46	111	118	98
Girls' accessories	100	800	80	75	79	103
Children under age 2	**100**	**118**	**114**	**97**	**126**	**97**
Infant dresses, outerwear	100	56	89	103	119	98
Infant underwear	100	165	112	96	142	95
Infant nightwear, loungewear	100	35	109	101	82	102
Infant accessories	100	134	196	85	111	99
Other apparel products and services	**100**	**47**	**107**	**101**	**69**	**104**
Jewelry and watches	100	77	82	103	52	105
Jewelry	100	76	85	103	49	106
All other apparel products and services	100	17	132	99	87	102
Men's footwear	100	–	41	112	114	98
Boys' footwear	100	–	191	91	86	102
Women's footwear	100	34	157	95	77	103
Girls' footwear	100	–	164	95	95	101
TRANSPORTATION	**100**	**542**	**64**	**89**	**237**	**84**
New cars	100	1503	144	43	314	76
New trucks	100	910	–	85	483	57
Used cars	100	–	–	118	194	89
Used trucks	100	–	294	76	–	111
Airline fares	100	216	61	101	85	102
Ship fares	100	185	75	101	39	107
HEALTH CARE	**100**	**71**	**47**	**108**	**15**	**110**
Physician's services	100	32	13	114	21	109
Dental services	100	3	53	110	27	108
Hospital services other than room	100	–	141	98	41	107
Care in convalescent or nursing home	100	–	–	118	–	111
Nonprescription drugs	100	551	32	92	23	110
Prescription drugs	100	26	56	109	30	108
ENTERTAINMENT	**100**	**80**	**38**	**109**	**60**	**105**
Toys, games, hobbies, and tricycles	100	49	49	109	51	106
Other entertainment	100	100	32	109	66	104
Fees for recreational lessons	100	33	4	114	58	105
Community antenna or cable TV	100	103	105	99	82	102
VCRs and video disc players	100	79	28	111	40	107
Pet purchase, supplies, and medicine	100	495	8	97	–	112
Athletic gear, game tables, exercise equipment	100	–	1	118	68	104
Photographic equipment	100	30	10	115	115	99
PERSONAL CARE PRODUCTS AND SERVICES	**100**	**147**	**53**	**105**	**84**	**102**
Cosmetics, perfume, bath preparation	100	131	37	108	94	101
EDUCATION	**100**	**194**	**22**	**107**	**49**	**106**
College tuition	100	193	19	108	20	109
Elementary and high school tuition	100	–	22	115	2	111
Other school expenses including rentals	100	402	10	102	348	72
College books and supplies	100	181	68	102	66	104
Miscellaneous school supplies	100	44	41	110	64	105
ALL OTHER GIFTS	**100**	**96**	**40**	**109**	**44**	**106**
Gifts of trip expenses	100	133	30	109	36	107
Legal fees	100	–	81	106	15	110
Funeral expenses	100	73	52	108	61	104
Cemetery lots, vaults, and maintenance fees	100	37	85	104	83	102
Miscellaneous personal services	100	–	–	118	63	104

Note: Other races include Native Americans and Pacific Islanders. (–) means sample is too small to make a reliable estimate. Categories with annual spending of less than $2.00 for the average household are omitted. Spending on gifts is also included in the product and service categories in other chapters.
Source: Calculations by New Strategist based on the 2003 Consumer Expenditure Survey

Table 6.19 Gifts for Nonhousehold Members: Total spending by race and Hispanic origin, 2003

(total annual spending on selected gifts of products and services for nonhousehold members by consumer unit race and Hispanic origin groups, 2003; numbers in thousands)

	total consumer units	race Asian	race black	race white and other	Hispanic origin Hispanic	Hispanic origin non-Hispanic
Number of consumer units	115,356	3,573	13,743	98,041	11,727	103,629
Total spending of all consumer units	$4,708,523,919	$160,509,343	$394,527,997	$4,153,041,270	$405,458,093	$4,302,756,911
Gifts, total spending	116,164,646	4,796,145	7,196,247	104,161,700	8,740,954	107,526,487
FOOD	**8,950,472**	**414,182**	**434,966**	**8,097,206**	**864,397**	**8,092,389**
Fresh fruit other than apples, bananas, and citrus	272,240	13,149	37,244	221,573	25,799	246,637
Candy and chewing gum	1,085,500	49,808	130,559	903,938	94,520	992,766
Board (including at school)	1,927,599	238,176	77,923	1,610,814	59,339	1,868,431
Catered affairs	2,932,350	15,435	24,600	2,892,210	459,933	2,471,552
ALCOHOLIC BEVERAGES	**1,858,385**	**42,876**	**57,858**	**1,756,895**	**148,112**	**1,714,024**
Beer and ale	453,349	7,039	18,828	427,459	52,185	401,044
Wine	1,105,110	30,478	37,793	1,036,293	92,174	1,015,564
HOUSING	**25,427,923**	**495,575**	**1,318,641**	**23,613,175**	**1,617,388**	**23,853,323**
Housekeeping supplies	**4,794,195**	**70,138**	**174,948**	**4,550,083**	**438,003**	**4,361,745**
Laundry and cleaning supplies	259,551	7,718	28,311	223,533	22,750	237,310
Other household products	1,431,568	5,824	45,565	1,384,339	79,275	1,359,612
Miscellaneous household products	642,533	2,858	25,287	614,717	58,166	584,468
Lawn and garden supplies	625,230	2,251	11,819	610,795	–	630,064
Postage and stationery	3,101,923	56,596	103,073	2,942,210	335,979	2,763,785
Stationery, stationery supplies, giftwrap	2,206,760	35,266	96,064	2,075,528	239,934	1,964,806
Postage	827,103	21,331	7,146	798,054	96,044	729,548
Household textiles	**1,467,328**	**3,680**	**31,609**	**1,433,359**	**54,648**	**1,421,790**
Bathroom linens	380,675	3,037	7,834	369,615	19,115	363,738
Bedroom linens	686,368	536	19,378	667,659	12,782	679,806
Appliances and miscellaneous housewares	**2,827,376**	**71,960**	**210,405**	**2,545,144**	**144,008**	**2,692,281**
Major appliances	767,117	16,579	113,105	638,247	16,066	753,383
Small appliances and miscellaneous housewares	2,061,412	55,382	97,300	1,906,897	127,942	1,938,899
China and other dinnerware	235,326	–	19,103	216,223	–	236,274
Glassware	248,015	–	15,117	232,898	13,486	236,274
Nonelectric cookware	417,589	10,469	8,521	398,046	49,019	367,883
Tableware, nonelectric kitchenware	587,162	35,587	32,571	516,676	48,198	539,907
Small electric kitchen appliances	263,012	1,429	11,544	250,005	3,284	260,109
Miscellaneous household equipment	**6,544,146**	**180,401**	**208,619**	**6,152,073**	**367,993**	**6,195,978**
Infants' equipment	541,020	7,682	15,255	518,637	84,903	452,859
Household decorative items	2,181,382	21,652	54,010	2,106,901	86,663	2,109,886
Indoor plants, fresh flowers	1,252,766	24,404	57,858	1,170,610	97,569	1,155,463
Computers and computer hardware, nonbusiness use	927,462	37,517	50,712	839,231	40,106	887,064
Miscellaneous household equipment and parts	499,491	2,001	2,199	496,087	21,343	481,875
Other housing	**9,794,878**	**169,360**	**692,922**	**8,932,516**	**612,618**	**9,182,566**
Repair or maintenance services	482,188	23,332	6,459	452,949	1,876	480,839
Materials for additions, finishing basements, remodeling rooms	257,244	–	–	257,244	31,311	225,911
Housing while attending school	3,233,429	48,593	125,336	3,058,879	67,782	3,164,830
Lodging on trips	287,236	10,147	8,658	267,652	10,906	275,653
Utility: natural gas (renter)	325,304	19,616	55,247	250,985	22,164	303,633
Electricity (renter)	1,101,650	20,045	188,966	892,173	61,684	1,039,399
Day care centers, nurseries, and preschools	1,094,728	27,548	131,795	935,311	91,822	1,002,092
Bedroom furniture other than mattresses and springs	296,465	–	2,886	293,579	52,068	244,564
APPAREL AND SERVICES	**25,971,250**	**641,175**	**3,044,075**	**22,293,543**	**2,189,196**	**23,807,726**
Men and boys, aged 2 or older	**6,409,179**	**204,376**	**414,901**	**5,784,419**	**605,230**	**5,806,333**
Men's suits	337,993	–	24,050	313,731	24,861	312,960
Men's coats and jackets	455,656	2,430	130,146	324,516	29,200	427,988
Men's accessories	318,383	47,842	–	267,652	17,121	302,597
Men's sweaters and vests	264,165	14,792	13,743	236,279	30,607	234,202
Men's active sportswear	471,806	13,184	–	457,851	10,672	465,294
Men's shirts	965,530	36,588	26,112	900,997	115,511	847,685
Men's pants	695,597	13,327	45,489	637,267	25,565	674,625
Boys' shirts	424,510	2,144	10,857	411,772	78,454	341,976
Boys' pants	487,956	11,005	40,542	436,282	45,032	442,496
Women and girls, aged 2 or older	**9,260,780**	**188,369**	**1,280,298**	**7,800,142**	**601,595**	**8,690,328**
Women's coats and jackets	817,874	3,573	38,343	777,465	43,859	778,254
Women's dresses	549,095	12,363	162,442	376,477	33,774	518,145
Women's vests and sweaters	814,413	2,430	101,286	712,758	31,077	789,653

	total consumer units	race			Hispanic origin	
		Asian	black	white and other	Hispanic	non-Hispanic
Women's shirts, tops, blouses	$980,526	$25,869	$141,823	$813,740	$92,878	$888,101
Women's pants	740,586	5,931	152,685	583,344	55,938	687,060
Women's active sportswear	377,214	3,537	115,441	259,809	4,691	376,173
Women's sleepwear	648,301	26,726	67,478	552,951	20,170	633,173
Women's undergarments	362,218	3,752	61,019	298,045	31,663	330,577
Women's accessories	524,870	–	40,130	484,740	32,484	494,310
Girls' dresses and suits	244,555	10,219	63,768	170,591	6,215	240,419
Girls' shirts, blouses, sweaters	625,230	–	33,533	591,697	52,185	574,105
Girls' skirts and pants	528,330	2,501	54,147	471,577	45,383	482,911
Girls' active sportswear	233,787	–	13,056	225,494	28,614	209,331
Girls' accessories	258,397	64,064	24,600	165,689	20,874	238,347
Children under age 2	**4,476,966**	**163,179**	**603,677**	**3,703,009**	**574,975**	**3,891,269**
Infant dresses, outerwear	1,371,583	23,939	145,126	1,202,963	166,406	1,205,205
Infant underwear	2,242,521	114,336	293,910	1,826,504	324,369	1,907,810
Infant nightwear, loungewear	287,236	3,144	37,381	247,063	23,923	264,254
Infant accessories	456,810	19,008	105,783	331,379	51,482	405,189
Other apparel products and services	**5,824,324**	**85,252**	**740,198**	**5,005,973**	**407,396**	**5,419,797**
Jewelry and watches	2,981,953	70,674	292,176	2,619,656	156,438	2,825,963
Jewelry	2,800,844	65,850	282,419	2,452,986	139,786	2,661,193
All other apparel products and services	2,841,218	14,578	448,022	2,386,318	250,958	2,593,834
Men's footwear	582,548	–	28,173	554,375	67,548	514,000
Boys' footwear	472,960	–	107,883	365,077	41,279	432,133
Women's footwear	920,541	9,647	171,788	741,190	72,121	850,794
Girls' footwear	678,293	–	132,895	545,398	65,671	612,447
TRANSPORTATION	**6,890,214**	**1,157,473**	**528,006**	**5,204,997**	**1,662,771**	**5,227,047**
New cars	1,332,362	620,094	228,271	483,342	425,807	905,717
New trucks	1,511,164	426,009	–	1,085,314	742,319	768,927
Used cars	1,542,310	–	–	1,541,760	303,729	1,239,403
Used trucks	436,046	–	152,547	283,338	–	436,046
Airline fares	839,792	55,060	61,156	723,543	72,942	766,855
Ship fares	431,431	24,761	38,618	368,634	16,887	415,552
HEALTH CARE	**5,524,399**	**121,696**	**307,568**	**5,090,289**	**83,848**	**5,445,704**
Physician's services	384,135	3,859	6,047	373,536	8,326	375,137
Dental services	422,203	357	26,661	395,105	11,375	411,407
Hospital services other than room	253,783	–	42,603	211,180	10,672	243,528
Care in convalescent or nursing home	2,349,802	–	–	2,349,062	–	2,349,269
Nonprescription drugs	356,450	60,884	13,468	278,436	8,326	351,302
Prescription drugs	333,379	2,715	22,264	308,829	10,320	323,322
ENTERTAINMENT	**7,956,103**	**198,123**	**363,090**	**7,389,350**	**487,491**	**7,477,869**
Toys, games, hobbies, and tricycles	3,007,331	45,449	177,010	2,785,345	154,914	2,852,906
Other entertainment	4,947,619	152,574	186,080	4,604,005	332,578	4,624,962
Fees for recreational lessons	694,443	7,039	11,819	675,502	40,693	653,899
Community antenna or cable TV	407,207	13,006	50,849	343,144	34,008	373,064
VCRs and video disc players	290,697	7,375	9,620	273,534	11,962	278,762
Pet purchase, supplies, and medicine	268,779	41,232	2,474	221,573	–	268,779
Athletic gear, game tables, exercise equipment	692,136	–	962	691,174	47,963	646,645
Photographic equipment	242,248	2,215	2,886	237,259	28,262	214,512
PERSONAL CARE PRODUCTS AND SERVICES	**1,819,164**	**82,894**	**114,891**	**1,617,677**	**155,148**	**1,667,391**
Cosmetics, perfume, bath preparation	1,151,253	46,592	50,987	1,051,980	109,882	1,042,508
EDUCATION	**23,051,589**	**1,384,573**	**616,923**	**21,050,383**	**1,145,728**	**21,908,207**
College tuition	17,929,783	1,070,256	400,334	16,460,103	371,511	17,558,898
Elementary and high school tuition	1,204,317	–	31,334	1,172,570	3,049	1,201,060
Other school expenses including rentals	1,816,857	226,350	21,302	1,569,636	643,226	1,174,117
College books and supplies	1,150,099	64,350	93,178	992,175	77,281	1,072,560
Miscellaneous school supplies	715,207	9,790	35,182	670,600	46,556	671,516
ALL OTHER GIFTS	**8,560,569**	**254,576**	**407,892**	**7,898,183**	**384,294**	**8,178,401**
Gifts of trip expenses	4,694,989	192,906	168,627	4,333,412	171,918	4,523,406
Legal fees	519,102	–	50,299	468,636	8,092	510,891
Funeral expenses	2,514,761	56,632	155,433	2,302,983	155,617	2,359,632
Cemetery lots, vaults, and maintenance fees	258,397	2,530	26,387	229,416	21,929	236,274
Miscellaneous personal services	287,236	–	–	287,094	18,529	269,435

Note. Other races include Native Americans and Pacific Islanders. Numbers may not add to total because of rounding. (–) means sample is too small to make a reliable estimate. Expenditures for items in a given category may not add to category total because categories with annual spending of less than $2.00 for the average household are omitted. Spending on gifts is also included in the product and service categories in other chapters.
Source: Calculations by New Strategist based on the 2003 Consumer Expenditure Survey

Table 6.20 Gifts for Nonhousehold Members: Market shares by race and Hispanic origin, 2003

(percentage of total annual spending on selected gifts of products and services for nonhousehold members accounted for by consumer unit race and Hispanic origin groups, 2003)

	total consumer units	race Asian	race black	race white and other	Hispanic origin Hispanic	Hispanic origin non-Hispanic
Share of total consumer units	100.0%	3.1%	11.9%	85.0%	10.2%	89.8%
Share of total before-tax income	100.0	3.7	8.0	88.2	7.4	92.8
Share of total spending	100.0	3.4	8.4	88.2	8.6	91.4
Share of gifts spending	**100.0**	**4.1**	**6.2**	**89.7**	**7.5**	**92.6**
FOOD	**100.0**	**4.6**	**4.9**	**90.5**	**9.7**	**90.4**
Fresh fruit other than apples, bananas, and citrus	100.0	4.8	13.7	81.4	9.5	90.6
Candy and chewing gum	100.0	4.6	12.0	83.3	8.7	91.5
Board (including at school)	100.0	12.4	4.0	83.6	3.1	96.9
Catered affairs	100.0	0.5	0.8	98.6	15.7	84.3
ALCOHOLIC BEVERAGES	**100.0**	**2.3**	**3.1**	**94.5**	**8.0**	**92.2**
Beer and ale	100.0	1.6	4.2	94.3	11.5	88.5
Wine	100.0	2.8	3.4	93.8	8.3	91.9
HOUSING	**100.0**	**1.9**	**5.2**	**92.9**	**6.4**	**93.8**
Housekeeping supplies	**100.0**	**1.5**	**3.6**	**94.9**	**9.1**	**91.0**
Laundry and cleaning supplies	100.0	3.0	10.9	86.1	8.8	91.4
Other household products	100.0	0.4	3.0	96.7	5.5	95.0
Miscellaneous household products	100.0	0.4	3.9	95.7	9.1	91.0
Lawn and garden supplies	100.0	0.4	1.9	97.7	–	100.0
Postage and stationery	100.0	1.8	3.3	94.9	10.8	89.1
Stationery, stationery supplies, giftwrap	100.0	1.6	4.4	94.1	10.9	89.0
Postage	100.0	2.6	0.9	96.5	11.6	88.2
Household textiles	**100.0**	**0.3**	**2.2**	**97.7**	**3.7**	**96.9**
Bathroom linens	100.0	0.8	2.1	97.1	5.0	95.6
Bedroom linens	100.0	0.1	2.8	97.3	1.9	99.0
Appliances and miscellaneous housewares	**100.0**	**2.5**	**7.4**	**90.0**	**5.1**	**95.2**
Major appliances	100.0	2.2	14.7	83.2	2.1	98.2
Small appliances and miscellaneous housewares	100.0	2.7	4.7	92.5	6.2	94.1
China and other dinnerware	100.0	–	8.1	91.9	–	100.0
Glassware	100.0	–	6.1	93.9	5.4	95.3
Nonelectric cookware	100.0	2.5	2.0	95.3	11.7	88.1
Tableware, nonelectric kitchenware	100.0	6.1	5.5	88.0	8.2	92.0
Small electric kitchen appliances	100.0	0.5	4.4	95.1	1.2	98.9
Miscellaneous household equipment	**100.0**	**2.8**	**3.2**	**94.0**	**5.6**	**94.7**
Infants' equipment	100.0	1.4	2.8	95.9	15.7	83.7
Household decorative items	100.0	1.0	2.5	96.6	4.0	96.7
Indoor plants, fresh flowers	100.0	1.9	4.6	93.4	7.8	92.2
Computers and computer hardware, nonbusiness use	100.0	4.0	5.5	90.5	4.3	95.6
Miscellaneous household equipment and parts	100.0	0.4	0.4	99.3	4.3	96.5
Other housing	**100.0**	**1.7**	**7.1**	**91.2**	**6.3**	**93.7**
Repair or maintenance services	100.0	4.8	1.3	93.9	0.4	99.7
Materials for additions, finishing basements, remodeling rooms	100.0	–	–	100.0	12.2	87.8
Housing while attending school	100.0	1.5	3.9	94.6	2.1	97.9
Lodging on trips	100.0	3.5	3.0	93.2	3.8	96.0
Utility: natural gas (renter)	100.0	6.0	17.0	77.2	6.8	93.3
Electricity (renter)	100.0	1.8	17.2	81.0	5.6	94.3
Day care centers, nurseries, and preschools	100.0	2.5	12.0	85.4	8.4	91.5
Bedroom furniture other than mattresses and springs	100.0	–	1.0	99.0	17.6	82.5
APPAREL AND SERVICES	**100.0**	**2.5**	**11.7**	**85.8**	**8.4**	**91.7**
Men and boys, aged 2 or older	**100.0**	**3.2**	**6.5**	**90.3**	**9.4**	**90.6**
Men's suits	100.0	–	7.1	92.8	7.4	92.6
Men's coats and jackets	100.0	0.5	28.6	71.2	6.4	93.9
Men's accessories	100.0	15.0	–	84.1	5.4	95.0
Men's sweaters and vests	100.0	5.6	5.2	89.4	11.6	88.7
Men's active sportswear	100.0	2.8	–	97.0	2.3	98.6
Men's shirts	100.0	3.8	2.7	93.3	12.0	87.8
Men's pants	100.0	1.9	6.5	91.6	3.7	97.0
Boys' shirts	100.0	0.5	2.6	97.0	18.5	80.6
Boys' pants	100.0	2.3	8.3	89.4	9.2	90.7
Women and girls, aged 2 or older	**100.0**	**2.0**	**13.8**	**84.2**	**6.5**	**93.8**
Women's coats and jackets	100.0	0.4	4.7	95.1	5.4	95.2
Women's dresses	100.0	2.3	29.6	68.6	6.2	94.4
Women's vests and sweaters	100.0	0.3	12.4	87.5	3.8	97.0

	total consumer units	race			Hispanic origin	
		Asian	black	white and other	Hispanic	non-Hispanic
Women's shirts, tops, blouses	100.0%	2.6%	14.5%	83.0%	9.5%	90.6%
Women's pants	100.0	0.8	20.5	78.8	7.6	92.8
Women's active sportswear	100.0	0.9	30.6	68.9	1.2	99.7
Women's sleepwear	100.0	4.1	10.4	85.3	3.1	97.7
Women's undergarments	100.0	1.0	16.8	82.3	8.7	91.3
Women's accessories	100.0	–	7.6	92.4	6.2	94.2
Girls' dresses and suits	100.0	4.2	26.1	69.8	2.5	98.3
Girls' shirts, blouses, sweaters	100.0	–	5.4	94.6	8.3	91.8
Girls' skirts and pants	100.0	0.5	10.2	89.3	8.6	91.4
Girls' active sportswear	100.0	–	5.5	94.4	12.0	87.7
Girls' accessories	100.0	24.8	9.5	64.1	8.1	92.2
Children under age 2	**100.0**	**3.6**	**13.6**	**82.7**	**12.8**	**86.9**
Infant dresses, outerwear	100.0	1.7	10.6	87.7	12.1	87.9
Infant underwear	100.0	5.1	13.3	81.4	14.5	85.1
Infant nightwear, loungewear	100.0	1.1	13.0	86.0	8.3	92.0
Infant accessories	100.0	4.2	23.4	72.5	11.3	88.7
Other apparel products and services	**100.0**	**1.5**	**12.7**	**85.9**	**7.0**	**93.1**
Jewelry and watches	100.0	2.4	9.8	87.9	5.2	94.8
Jewelry	100.0	2.4	10.1	87.6	5.0	95.0
All other apparel products and services	100.0	0.5	15.8	84.0	8.8	91.3
Men's footwear	100.0	–	4.8	95.2	11.6	88.2
Boys' footwear	100.0	–	22.8	77.2	8.7	91.4
Women's footwear	100.0	1.0	18.7	80.5	7.8	92.4
Girls' footwear	100.0	–	19.6	80.4	9.7	90.3
TRANSPORTATION	**100.0**	**16.8**	**7.7**	**75.5**	**24.1**	**75.9**
New cars	100.0	46.5	17.1	36.3	32.0	68.0
New trucks	100.0	28.2	–	71.8	49.1	50.9
Used cars	100.0	–	–	100.0	19.7	80.4
Used trucks	100.0	–	35.0	65.0	–	100.0
Airline fares	100.0	6.7	7.3	86.2	8.7	91.3
Ship fares	100.0	5.7	9.0	85.4	3.9	96.3
HEALTH CARE	**100.0**	**2.2**	**5.6**	**92.1**	**1.5**	**98.6**
Physician's services	100.0	1.0	1.6	97.2	2.2	97.7
Dental services	100.0	0.1	6.3	93.6	2.7	97.4
Hospital services other than room	100.0	–	16.8	83.2	4.2	96.0
Care in convalescent or nursing home	100.0	–	–	100.0	–	100.0
Nonprescription drugs	100.0	17.1	3.8	78.1	2.3	98.6
Prescription drugs	100.0	0.8	6.7	92.6	3.1	97.0
ENTERTAINMENT	**100.0**	**2.5**	**4.6**	**92.9**	**6.1**	**94.0**
Toys, games, hobbies, and tricycles	100.0	1.5	5.9	92.6	5.2	94.9
Other entertainment	100.0	3.1	3.8	93.1	6.7	93.5
Fees for recreational lessons	100.0	1.0	1.7	97.3	5.9	94.2
Community antenna or cable TV	100.0	3.2	12.5	84.3	8.4	91.6
VCRs and video disc players	100.0	2.4	3.3	94.1	4.1	95.9
Pet purchase, supplies, and medicine	100.0	15.3	0.9	82.4	–	100.0
Athletic gear, game tables, exercise equipment	100.0	–	0.1	99.9	6.9	93.4
Photographic equipment	100.0	0.9	1.2	97.9	11.7	88.6
PERSONAL CARE PRODUCTS AND SERVICES	**100.0**	**4.6**	**6.3**	**88.9**	**8.5**	**91.7**
Cosmetics, perfume, bath preparation	100.0	4.0	4.4	91.4	9.5	90.6
EDUCATION	**100.0**	**6.0**	**2.7**	**91.3**	**5.0**	**95.0**
College tuition	100.0	6.0	2.2	91.8	2.1	97.9
Elementary and high school tuition	100.0	–	2.6	97.4	0.3	99.7
Other school expenses including rentals	100.0	12.5	1.2	86.4	35.4	64.6
College books and supplies	100.0	5.6	8.1	86.3	6.7	93.3
Miscellaneous school supplies	100.0	1.4	4.9	93.8	6.5	93.9
ALL OTHER GIFTS	**100.0**	**3.0**	**4.8**	**92.3**	**4.5**	**95.5**
Gifts of trip expenses	100.0	4.1	3.6	92.3	3.7	96.3
Legal fees	100.0	–	9.7	90.3	1.6	98.4
Funeral expenses	100.0	2.3	6.2	91.6	6.2	93.8
Cemetery lots, vaults, and maintenance fees	100.0	1.1	10.2	88.8	8.5	91.4
Miscellaneous personal services	100.0	–	–	100.0	6.5	93.8

Note: Other races include Native Americans and Pacific Islanders. Numbers may not add to total because of rounding. (–) means sample is too small to make a reliable estimate. Expenditures for items in a given category may not add to category total because categories with annual spending of less than $2.00 for the average household are omitted. Spending on gifts is also included in the product and service categories in other chapters.
Source: Calculations by New Strategist based on the 2003 Consumer Expenditure Survey

Table 6.21 Gifts for Nonhousehold Members: Average spending by region, 2003

(average annual spending of consumer units (CU) on selected gifts of products and services for nonhousehold members by region in which consumer unit lives, 2003)

	total consumer units	Northeast	Midwest	South	West
Number of consumer units (000)	115,356	22,182	26,438	41,325	25,412
Average number of persons per CU	2.5	2.4	2.5	2.5	2.6
Average before-tax income of CU	$48,596.00	$54,219.00	$49,591.00	$44,461.00	$49,667.00
Average spending of CU, total	40,817.33	42,162.29	40,280.39	37,624.55	45,380.67
Gifts, average spending	**1,007.01**	**1,168.80**	**1,043.62**	**862.37**	**1,059.23**
FOOD	**77.59**	**122.08**	**66.12**	**58.21**	**81.90**
Fresh fruit other than apples, bananas, and citrus	2.36	4.30	1.40	2.44	1.56
Candy and chewing gum	9.41	12.48	10.53	5.09	12.43
Board (including at school)	16.71	22.26	11.05	17.77	16.01
Catered affairs	25.42	54.82	17.52	11.51	30.59
ALCOHOLIC BEVERAGES	**16.11**	**17.62**	**16.19**	**14.46**	**17.32**
Beer and ale	3.93	4.10	5.03	2.96	4.16
Wine	9.58	12.18	8.42	8.08	10.95
HOUSING	**220.43**	**216.45**	**214.20**	**199.83**	**262.82**
Housekeeping supplies	**41.56**	**54.59**	**44.00**	**25.71**	**52.86**
Laundry and cleaning supplies	2.25	3.27	2.79	1.58	1.86
Other household products	12.41	25.37	11.53	6.62	11.28
Miscellaneous household products	5.57	7.81	5.23	3.12	7.88
Lawn and garden supplies	5.42	15.04	4.90	2.59	2.07
Postage and stationery	26.89	25.94	29.68	17.51	39.72
Stationery, stationery supplies, giftwrap	19.13	18.03	23.18	11.36	28.13
Postage	7.17	7.65	6.26	5.47	10.43
Household textiles	**12.72**	**10.13**	**18.28**	**9.66**	**13.94**
Bathroom linens	3.30	3.56	5.09	2.52	2.39
Bedroom linens	5.95	4.56	7.54	5.63	5.98
Appliances and miscellaneous housewares	**24.51**	**14.92**	**24.32**	**25.95**	**30.83**
Major appliances	6.65	4.42	6.62	4.98	11.25
Small appliances and miscellaneous housewares	17.87	10.50	17.70	20.97	19.58
China and other dinnerware	2.04	0.44	3.68	0.86	3.57
Glassware	2.15	1.12	1.34	3.63	1.57
Nonelectric cookware	3.62	2.10	3.38	4.18	4.31
Tableware, nonelectric kitchenware	5.09	3.02	3.82	7.31	4.70
Small electric kitchen appliances	2.28	1.73	3.24	2.08	2.07
Miscellaneous household equipment	**56.73**	**55.80**	**59.10**	**44.56**	**74.44**
Infants' equipment	4.69	3.07	0.52	3.70	12.17
Household decorative items	18.91	21.54	25.61	11.78	20.82
Indoor plants, fresh flowers	10.86	11.97	11.74	9.83	10.67
Computers and computer hardware, nonbusiness use	8.04	10.70	5.25	8.79	7.37
Miscellaneous household equipment and parts	4.33	1.08	3.62	2.56	10.77
Other housing	**84.91**	**81.03**	**68.50**	**93.94**	**90.75**
Repair or maintenance services	4.18	4.97	3.95	4.54	3.16
Materials for additions, finishing basements, remodeling rooms	2.23	–	0.10	1.56	7.49
Housing while attending school	28.03	35.21	25.41	24.35	30.45
Lodging on trips	2.49	3.34	3.45	1.68	2.05
Utility: natural gas (renter)	2.82	5.17	3.22	2.00	1.68
Electricity (renter)	9.55	5.72	7.62	15.57	5.09
Day care centers, nurseries, and preschools	9.49	8.44	5.35	14.95	5.83
Bedroom furniture other than mattresses and springs	2.57	2.06	2.91	1.63	4.19
APPAREL AND SERVICES	**225.14**	**264.02**	**241.63**	**188.44**	**232.20**
Men and boys, aged 2 or older	**55.56**	**69.55**	**47.95**	**44.39**	**69.26**
Men's suits	2.93	4.99	1.89	3.01	2.10
Men's coats and jackets	3.95	7.85	5.88	2.09	1.42
Men's accessories	2.76	2.95	2.06	2.32	4.06
Men's sweaters and vests	2.29	3.23	2.63	1.80	1.93
Men's active sportswear	4.09	4.87	2.79	2.25	7.73
Men's shirts	8.37	10.06	5.18	6.69	12.97
Men's pants	6.03	9.16	4.77	4.03	7.84
Boys' shirts	3.68	4.09	3.54	2.39	5.52
Boys' pants	4.23	3.18	4.21	4.44	4.82
Women and girls, aged 2 or older	**80.28**	**88.16**	**96.22**	**65.61**	**79.74**
Women's coats and jackets	7.09	4.16	6.53	6.60	11.05
Women's dresses	4.76	3.04	8.27	3.51	4.51
Women's vests and sweaters	7.06	9.81	10.26	3.95	6.20

	total consumer units	Northeast	Midwest	South	West
Women's shirts, tops, blouses	$8.50	$8.54	$10.90	$7.33	$7.76
Women's pants	6.42	5.97	7.39	6.98	4.87
Women's active sportswear	3.27	3.83	6.22	2.04	1.58
Women's sleepwear	5.62	6.07	6.58	5.76	3.97
Women's undergarments	3.14	1.49	5.35	3.36	1.84
Women's accessories	4.55	7.30	4.53	2.02	6.21
Girls' dresses and suits	2.12	2.91	0.49	2.40	2.71
Girls' shirts, blouses, sweaters	5.42	9.88	6.64	2.68	4.60
Girls' skirts and pants	4.58	4.62	4.85	4.67	4.11
Girls' active sportswear	2.07	2.60	1.65	2.06	2.05
Girls' accessories	2.24	3.81	1.08	0.76	4.47
Children under age 2	**38.81**	**44.56**	**37.65**	**36.43**	**38.90**
Infant dresses, outerwear	11.89	12.55	12.83	11.07	11.66
Infant underwear	19.44	23.10	16.21	18.34	21.48
Infant nightwear, loungewear	2.49	3.73	2.31	2.42	1.73
Infant accessories	3.96	3.29	5.14	4.02	3.18
Other apparel products and services	**50.49**	**61.75**	**59.80**	**42.01**	**44.30**
Jewelry and watches	25.85	29.03	28.18	24.96	22.11
Jewelry	24.28	27.59	26.68	23.55	20.11
All other apparel products and services	24.63	32.71	31.62	17.04	22.19
Men's footwear	5.05	3.88	7.49	3.48	5.94
Boys' footwear	4.10	8.02	3.57	3.01	2.97
Women's footwear	7.98	11.44	10.69	5.66	5.76
Girls' footwear	5.88	8.30	8.48	3.99	3.99
TRANSPORTATION	**59.73**	**32.14**	**57.19**	**46.35**	**108.17**
New cars	11.55	8.76	–	9.08	30.01
New trucks	13.10	–	–	8.30	45.98
Used cars	13.37	–	28.58	12.93	9.95
Used trucks	3.78	2.40	12.70	0.77	0.61
Airline fares	7.28	8.41	6.53	6.73	7.99
Ship fares	3.74	5.61	2.34	3.32	4.26
HEALTH CARE	**47.89**	**30.05**	**85.67**	**42.80**	**32.22**
Physician's services	3.33	4.00	2.90	2.78	4.07
Dental services	3.66	2.78	4.04	2.05	6.66
Hospital services other than room	2.20	–	2.71	2.93	2.41
Care in convalescent or nursing home	20.37	9.67	51.45	17.64	1.81
Nonprescription drugs	3.09	2.76	4.81	0.94	4.98
Prescription drugs	2.89	1.13	5.33	3.50	0.92
ENTERTAINMENT	**68.97**	**70.09**	**73.73**	**60.12**	**77.08**
Toys, games, hobbies, and tricycles	26.07	25.51	29.15	25.24	24.73
Other entertainment	42.89	44.58	44.58	34.88	52.36
Fees for recreational lessons	6.02	4.30	3.49	7.14	8.33
Community antenna or cable TV	3.53	3.69	3.24	4.40	2.29
VCRs and video disc players	2.52	2.56	3.11	2.86	1.30
Pet purchase, supplies, and medicine	2.33	2.92	0.87	0.88	5.68
Athletic gear, game tables, exercise equipment	5.00	9.77	7.35	1.03	9.20
Photographic equipment	2.10	1.81	2.17	1.98	2.49
PERSONAL CARE PRODUCTS AND SERVICES	**15.77**	**18.78**	**14.99**	**12.54**	**19.11**
Cosmetics, perfume, bath preparation	9.98	11.39	9.70	8.03	12.17
EDUCATION	**199.83**	**332.46**	**185.63**	**172.82**	**142.70**
College tuition	155.43	297.25	154.50	109.13	107.92
Elementary and high school tuition	10.44	9.79	8.15	14.70	6.45
Other school expenses including rentals	15.75	6.40	5.65	29.96	11.32
College books and supplies	9.97	12.05	7.95	9.69	10.72
Miscellaneous school supplies	6.20	5.43	7.89	6.69	4.28
ALL OTHER GIFTS	**74.21**	**63.60**	**86.89**	**65.93**	**83.72**
Gifts of trip expenses	40.70	39.95	46.41	31.74	49.98
Legal fees	4.50	2.32	1.52	7.19	5.14
Funeral expenses	21.80	12.73	33.92	20.88	18.61
Cemetery lots, vaults, and maintenance fees	2.24	3.35	1.20	2.90	1.27
Miscellaneous personal services	2.49	0.14	0.99	2.45	6.21

Note: (–) means sample is too small to make a reliable estimate. Expenditures for items in a given category may not add to category total because categories with annual spending of less than $2.00 for the average household are omitted. Spending on gifts is also included in the product and service categories in other chapters.
Source: Bureau of Labor Statistics, unpublished tables from the 2003 Consumer Expenditure Survey

Table 6.22 Gifts for Nonhousehold Members: Indexed spending by region, 2003

(indexed average annual spending of consumer units (CU) on selected gifts of products and services for nonhousehold members by region in which consumer unit lives, 2003; index definition: an index of 100 is the average for all consumer units; an index of 132 means that spending by consumer units in that group is 32 percent above the average for all consumer units; an index of 68 indicates spending that is 32 percent below the average for all consumer units)

	total consumer units	Northeast	Midwest	South	West
Average spending of CU, total	$40,817	$42,162	$40,280	$37,625	$45,381
Average spending of CU, index	100	103	99	92	111
Gifts, spending index	**100**	**116**	**104**	**86**	**105**
FOOD	**100**	**157**	**85**	**75**	**106**
Fresh fruit other than apples, bananas, and citrus	100	182	59	103	66
Candy and chewing gum	100	133	112	54	132
Board (including at school)	100	133	66	106	96
Catered affairs	100	216	69	45	120
ALCOHOLIC BEVERAGES	**100**	**109**	**100**	**90**	**108**
Beer and ale	100	104	128	75	106
Wine	100	127	88	84	114
HOUSING	**100**	**98**	**97**	**91**	**119**
Housekeeping supplies	**100**	**131**	**106**	**62**	**127**
Laundry and cleaning supplies	100	145	124	70	83
Other household products	100	204	93	53	91
Miscellaneous household products	100	140	94	56	141
Lawn and garden supplies	100	277	90	48	38
Postage and stationery	100	96	110	65	148
Stationery, stationery supplies, giftwrap	100	94	121	59	147
Postage	100	107	87	76	145
Household textiles	**100**	**80**	**144**	**76**	**110**
Bathroom linens	100	108	154	76	72
Bedroom linens	100	77	127	95	101
Appliances and miscellaneous housewares	**100**	**61**	**99**	**106**	**126**
Major appliances	100	66	100	75	169
Small appliances and miscellaneous housewares	100	59	99	117	110
China and other dinnerware	100	22	180	42	175
Glassware	100	52	62	169	73
Nonelectric cookware	100	58	93	115	119
Tableware, nonelectric kitchenware	100	59	75	144	92
Small electric kitchen appliances	100	76	142	91	91
Miscellaneous household equipment	**100**	**98**	**104**	**79**	**131**
Infants' equipment	100	65	11	79	259
Household decorative items	100	114	135	62	110
Indoor plants, fresh flowers	100	110	108	91	98
Computers and computer hardware, nonbusiness use	100	133	65	109	92
Miscellaneous household equipment and parts	100	25	84	59	249
Other housing	**100**	**95**	**81**	**111**	**107**
Repair or maintenance services	100	119	94	109	76
Materials for additions, finishing basements, remodeling rooms	100	–	4	70	336
Housing while attending school	100	126	91	87	109
Lodging on trips	100	134	139	67	82
Utility: natural gas (renter)	100	183	114	71	60
Electricity (renter)	100	60	80	163	53
Day care centers, nurseries, and preschools	100	89	56	158	61
Bedroom furniture other than mattresses and springs	100	80	113	63	163
APPAREL AND SERVICES	**100**	**117**	**107**	**84**	**103**
Men and boys, aged 2 or older	**100**	**125**	**86**	**80**	**125**
Men's suits	100	170	65	103	72
Men's coats and jackets	100	199	149	53	36
Men's accessories	100	107	75	84	147
Men's sweaters and vests	100	141	115	79	84
Men's active sportswear	100	119	68	55	189
Men's shirts	100	120	62	80	155
Men's pants	100	152	79	67	130
Boys' shirts	100	111	96	65	150
Boys' pants	100	75	100	105	114
Women and girls, aged 2 or older	**100**	**110**	**120**	**82**	**99**
Women's coats and jackets	100	59	92	93	156
Women's dresses	100	64	174	74	95
Women's vests and sweaters	100	139	145	56	88

	total consumer units	Northeast	Midwest	South	West
Women's shirts, tops, blouses	100	100	128	86	91
Women's pants	100	93	115	109	76
Women's active sportswear	100	117	190	62	48
Women's sleepwear	100	108	117	102	71
Women's undergarments	100	47	170	107	59
Women's accessories	100	160	100	44	136
Girls' dresses and suits	100	137	23	113	128
Girls' shirts, blouses, sweaters	100	182	123	49	85
Girls' skirts and pants	100	101	106	102	90
Girls' active sportswear	100	126	80	100	99
Girls' accessories	100	170	48	34	200
Children under age 2	**100**	**115**	**97**	**94**	**100**
Infant dresses, outerwear	100	106	108	93	98
Infant underwear	100	119	83	94	110
Infant nightwear, loungewear	100	150	93	97	69
Infant accessories	100	83	130	102	80
Other apparel products and services	**100**	**122**	**118**	**83**	**88**
Jewelry and watches	100	112	109	97	86
Jewelry	100	114	110	97	83
All other apparel products and services	100	133	128	69	90
Men's footwear	100	77	148	69	118
Boys' footwear	100	196	87	73	72
Women's footwear	100	143	134	71	72
Girls' footwear	100	141	144	68	68
TRANSPORTATION	**100**	**54**	**96**	**78**	**181**
New cars	100	76	–	79	260
New trucks	100	–	–	63	351
Used cars	100	–	214	97	74
Used trucks	100	63	336	20	16
Airline fares	100	116	90	92	110
Ship fares	100	150	63	89	114
HEALTH CARE	**100**	**63**	**179**	**89**	**67**
Physician's services	100	120	87	83	122
Dental services	100	76	110	56	182
Hospital services other than room	100	–	123	133	110
Care in convalescent or nursing home	100	47	253	87	9
Nonprescription drugs	100	89	156	30	161
Prescription drugs	100	39	184	121	32
ENTERTAINMENT	**100**	**102**	**107**	**87**	**112**
Toys, games, hobbies, and tricycles	100	98	112	97	95
Other entertainment	100	104	104	81	122
Fees for recreational lessons	100	71	58	119	138
Community antenna or cable TV	100	105	92	125	65
VCRs and video disc players	100	102	123	113	52
Pet purchase, supplies, and medicine	100	125	37	38	244
Athletic gear, game tables, exercise equipment	100	163	123	17	153
Photographic equipment	100	86	103	94	119
PERSONAL CARE PRODUCTS AND SERVICES	**100**	**119**	**95**	**80**	**121**
Cosmetics, perfume, bath preparation	100	114	97	80	122
EDUCATION	**100**	**166**	**93**	**86**	**71**
College tuition	100	191	99	70	69
Elementary and high school tuition	100	94	78	141	62
Other school expenses including rentals	100	41	36	190	72
College books and supplies	100	121	80	97	108
Miscellaneous school supplies	100	88	127	108	69
ALL OTHER GIFTS	**100**	**86**	**117**	**89**	**113**
Gifts of trip expenses	100	98	114	78	123
Legal fees	100	52	34	160	114
Funeral expenses	100	58	156	96	85
Cemetery lots, vaults, and maintenance fees	100	150	54	129	57
Miscellaneous personal services	100	6	40	98	249

Note: (–) means sample is too small to make a reliable estimate. Categories with annual spending of less than $2.00 for the average household are omitted. Spending on gifts is also included in the product and service categories in other chapters.
Source: Calculations by New Strategist based on the 2003 Consumer Expenditure Survey

Table 6.23 Gifts for Nonhousehold Members: Total spending by region, 2003

(total annual spending on selected gifts of products and services for nonhousehold members by region in which consumer units live, 2003; numbers in thousands)

	total consumer units	Northeast	Midwest	South	West
Number of consumer units	115,356	22,182	26,438	41,325	25,412
Total spending of all consumer units	$4,708,523,919	$935,243,917	$1,064,932,951	$1,554,834,529	$1,153,213,586
Gifts, total spending	**116,164,646**	**25,926,322**	**27,591,226**	**35,637,440**	**26,917,153**
FOOD	**8,950,472**	**2,707,979**	**1,748,081**	**2,405,528**	**2,081,243**
Fresh fruit other than apples, bananas, and citrus	272,240	95,383	37,013	100,833	39,643
Candy and chewing gum	1,085,500	276,831	278,392	210,344	315,871
Board (including at school)	1,927,599	493,771	292,140	734,345	406,846
Catered affairs	2,932,350	1,216,017	463,194	475,651	777,353
ALCOHOLIC BEVERAGES	**1,858,385**	**390,847**	**428,031**	**597,560**	**440,136**
Beer and ale	453,349	90,946	132,983	122,322	105,714
Wine	1,105,110	270,177	222,608	333,906	278,261
HOUSING	**25,427,923**	**4,801,294**	**5,663,020**	**8,257,975**	**6,678,782**
Housekeeping supplies	**4,794,195**	**1,210,915**	**1,163,272**	**1,062,466**	**1,343,278**
Laundry and cleaning supplies	259,551	72,535	73,762	65,294	47,266
Other household products	1,431,568	562,757	304,830	273,572	286,647
Miscellaneous household products	642,533	173,241	138,271	128,934	200,247
Lawn and garden supplies	625,230	333,617	129,546	107,032	52,603
Postage and stationery	3,101,923	575,401	784,680	723,601	1,009,365
Stationery, stationery supplies, giftwrap	2,206,760	399,941	612,833	469,452	714,840
Postage	827,103	169,692	165,502	226,048	265,047
Household textiles	**1,467,328**	**224,704**	**483,287**	**399,200**	**354,243**
Bathroom linens	380,675	78,968	134,569	104,139	60,735
Bedroom linens	686,368	101,150	199,343	232,660	151,964
Appliances and miscellaneous housewares	**2,827,376**	**330,955**	**642,972**	**1,072,384**	**783,452**
Major appliances	767,117	98,044	175,020	205,799	285,885
Small appliances and miscellaneous housewares	2,061,412	232,911	467,953	866,585	497,567
China and other dinnerware	235,326	9,760	97,292	35,540	90,721
Glassware	248,015	24,844	35,427	150,010	39,897
Nonelectric cookware	417,589	46,582	89,360	172,739	109,526
Tableware, nonelectric kitchenware	587,162	66,990	100,993	302,086	119,436
Small electric kitchen appliances	263,012	38,375	85,659	85,956	52,603
Miscellaneous household equipment	**6,544,146**	**1,237,756**	**1,562,486**	**1,841,442**	**1,891,669**
Infants' equipment	541,020	68,099	13,748	152,903	309,264
Household decorative items	2,181,382	477,800	677,077	486,809	529,078
Indoor plants, fresh flowers	1,252,766	265,519	310,382	406,225	271,146
Computers and computer hardware, nonbusiness use	927,462	237,347	138,800	363,247	187,286
Miscellaneous household equipment and parts	499,491	23,957	95,706	105,792	273,687
Other housing	**9,794,878**	**1,797,407**	**1,811,003**	**3,882,071**	**2,306,139**
Repair or maintenance services	482,188	110,245	104,430	187,616	80,302
Materials for additions, finishing basements, remodeling rooms	257,244	–	2,644	64,467	190,336
Housing while attending school	3,233,429	781,028	671,790	1,006,264	773,795
Lodging on trips	287,236	74,088	91,211	69,426	52,095
Utility: natural gas (renter)	325,304	114,681	85,130	82,650	42,692
Electricity (renter)	1,101,650	126,881	201,458	643,430	129,347
Day care centers, nurseries, and preschools	1,094,728	187,216	141,443	617,809	148,152
Bedroom furniture other than mattresses and springs	296,465	45,695	76,935	67,360	106,476
APPAREL AND SERVICES	**25,971,250**	**5,856,492**	**6,388,214**	**7,787,283**	**5,900,666**
Men and boys, aged 2 or older	**6,409,179**	**1,542,758**	**1,267,702**	**1,834,417**	**1,760,035**
Men's suits	337,993	110,688	49,968	124,388	53,365
Men's coats and jackets	455,656	174,129	155,455	86,369	36,085
Men's accessories	318,383	65,437	54,462	95,874	103,173
Men's sweaters and vests	264,165	71,648	69,532	74,385	49,045
Men's active sportswear	471,806	108,026	73,762	92,981	196,435
Men's shirts	965,530	223,151	136,949	276,464	329,594
Men's pants	695,597	203,187	126,109	166,540	199,230
Boys' shirts	424,510	90,724	93,591	98,767	140,274
Boys' pants	487,956	70,539	111,304	183,483	122,486
Women and girls, aged 2 or older	**9,260,780**	**1,955,565**	**2,543,864**	**2,711,333**	**2,026,353**
Women's coats and jackets	817,874	92,277	172,640	272,745	280,803
Women's dresses	549,095	67,433	218,642	145,051	114,608
Women's vests and sweaters	814,413	217,605	271,254	163,234	157,554

	total consumer units	Northeast	Midwest	South	West
Women's shirts, tops, blouses	$980,526	$189,434	$288,174	$302,912	$197,197
Women's pants	740,586	132,427	195,377	288,449	123,756
Women's active sportswear	377,214	84,957	164,444	84,303	40,151
Women's sleepwear	648,301	134,645	173,962	238,032	100,886
Women's undergarments	362,218	33,051	141,443	138,852	46,758
Women's accessories	524,870	151,929	119,764	83,477	157,809
Girls' dresses and suits	244,555	54,550	12,955	99,180	68,867
Girls' shirts, blouses, sweaters	625,230	219,158	175,548	110,751	116,895
Girls' skirts and pants	528,330	102,481	128,224	192,988	104,443
Girls' active sportswear	238,787	37,673	43,623	85,130	52,095
Girls' accessories	258,397	84,513	28,553	31,407	113,592
Children under age 2	**4,476,966**	**988,430**	**995,391**	**1,505,470**	**988,527**
Infant dresses, outerwear	1,371,583	278,606	339,200	457,468	296,304
Infant underwear	2,242,521	512,404	428,560	757,901	545,850
Infant nightwear, loungewear	287,236	82,739	61,072	100,007	43,963
Infant accessories	456,810	72,979	135,891	166,127	80,810
Other apparel products and services	**5,824,324**	**1,369,739**	**1,580,992**	**1,736,063**	**1,125,752**
Jewelry and watches	2,981,953	643,943	745,023	1,031,472	561,859
Jewelry	2,800,844	612,001	705,366	973,204	511,035
All other apparel products and services	2,841,218	725,573	335,970	704,178	563,892
Men's footwear	582,548	86,066	198,021	143,811	150,947
Boys' footwear	472,960	177,900	94,384	124,388	75,474
Women's footwear	920,541	253,762	282,622	233,900	146,373
Girls' footwear	678,293	184,111	224,194	164,887	101,394
TRANSPORTATION	**6,890,214**	**712,929**	**1,511,989**	**1,915,414**	**2,748,816**
New cars	1,332,362	194,314	–	375,231	762,614
New trucks	1,511,164	–	–	342,998	1,168,444
Used cars	1,542,310	–	755,598	534,332	252,849
Used trucks	436,046	53,237	335,763	31,820	15,501
Airline fares	839,792	186,551	172,640	278,117	203,042
Ship fares	431,431	124,441	61,865	137,199	108,255
HEALTH CARE	**5,524,399**	**666,569**	**2,264,943**	**1,768,710**	**818,775**
Physician's services	384,135	88,728	76,670	114,884	103,427
Dental services	422,203	51,666	106,810	84,716	169,244
Hospital services other than room	253,783	–	71,647	121,082	61,243
Care in convalescent or nursing home	2,349,802	214,500	1,350,235	728,973	45,996
Nonprescription drugs	356,450	61,222	127,167	38,846	126,552
Prescription drugs	333,379	25,066	140,915	144,638	23,379
ENTERTAINMENT	**7,956,103**	**1,554,736**	**1,949,274**	**2,484,459**	**1,958,757**
Toys, games, hobbies, and tricycles	3,007,331	565,863	770,668	1,043,043	628,439
Other entertainment	4,947,619	988,874	1,178,606	1,441,416	1,330,572
Fees for recreational lessons	694,443	95,383	92,269	295,061	211,682
Community antenna or cable TV	407,207	81,852	85,659	181,830	58,193
VCRs and video disc players	290,697	55,786	82,222	118,190	33,036
Pet purchase, supplies, and medicine	268,779	64,771	23,001	36,366	144,340
Athletic gear, game tables, exercise equipment	692,136	216,718	194,319	42,565	233,790
Photographic equipment	242,248	40,149	57,370	81,824	63,276
PERSONAL CARE PRODUCTS AND SERVICES	**1,819,164**	**416,578**	**396,306**	**518,216**	**485,623**
Cosmetics, perfume, bath preparation	1,151,253	252,553	256,449	331,840	309,264
EDUCATION	**23,051,589**	**7,374,528**	**4,907,686**	**7,141,787**	**3,626,292**
College tuition	17,929,783	6,593,500	4,084,671	4,509,797	2,742,463
Elementary and high school tuition	1,204,317	217,162	215,470	607,478	163,907
Other school expenses including rentals	1,816,857	141,965	149,375	1,238,097	287,664
College books and supplies	1,150,099	267,293	210,182	400,439	272,417
Miscellaneous school supplies	715,207	120,448	203,596	276,464	108,763
ALL OTHER GIFTS	**8,560,569**	**1,410,775**	**2,297,198**	**2,724,557**	**2,127,493**
Gifts of trip expenses	4,694,989	886,171	1,226,988	1,311,656	1,270,092
Legal fees	519,102	51,462	40,186	297,127	130,618
Funeral expenses	2,514,761	282,277	896,777	862,866	472,917
Cemetery lots, vaults, and maintenance fees	258,397	74,310	31,726	119,843	32,273
Miscellaneous personal services	287,236	3,105	26,174	101,246	157,809

Note: Numbers may not add to total because of rounding. (–) means sample is too small to make a reliable estimate. Expenditures for items in a given category may not add to category total because categories with annual spending of less than $2.00 for the average household are omitted. Spending on gifts is also included in the product and service categories in other chapters.

Source: Calculations by New Strategist based on the 2003 Consumer Expenditure Survey

Table 6.24 Gifts for Nonhousehold Members: Market shares by region, 2003

(percentage of total annual spending on selected gifts of products and services for nonhousehold members accounted for by consumer units by region, 2003)

	total consumer units	Northeast	Midwest	South	West
Share of total consumer units	100.0%	19.2%	22.9%	35.8%	22.0%
Share of total before-tax income	100.0	21.5	23.4	32.8	22.5
Share of total spending	100.0	19.9	22.6	33.0	24.5
Share of gifts spending	100.0	22.3	23.8	30.7	23.2
FOOD	100.0	30.3	19.5	26.9	23.3
Fresh fruit other than apples, bananas, and citrus	100.0	35.0	13.6	37.0	14.6
Candy and chewing gum	100.0	25.5	25.6	19.4	29.1
Board (including at school)	100.0	25.6	15.2	38.1	21.1
Catered affairs	100.0	41.5	15.8	16.2	26.5
ALCOHOLIC BEVERAGES	100.0	21.0	23.0	32.2	23.7
Beer and ale	100.0	20.1	29.3	27.0	23.3
Wine	100.0	24.4	20.1	30.2	25.2
HOUSING	100.0	18.9	22.3	32.5	26.3
Housekeeping supplies	100.0	25.3	24.3	22.2	28.0
Laundry and cleaning supplies	100.0	27.9	28.4	25.2	18.2
Other household products	100.0	39.3	21.3	19.1	20.0
Miscellaneous household products	100.0	27.0	21.5	20.1	31.2
Lawn and garden supplies	100.0	53.4	20.7	17.1	8.4
Postage and stationery	100.0	18.5	25.3	23.3	32.5
Stationery, stationery supplies, giftwrap	100.0	18.1	27.8	21.3	32.4
Postage	100.0	20.5	20.0	27.3	32.0
Household textiles	100.0	15.3	32.9	27.2	24.1
Bathroom linens	100.0	20.7	35.4	27.4	16.0
Bedroom linens	100.0	14.7	29.0	33.9	22.1
Appliances and miscellaneous housewares	100.0	11.7	22.7	37.9	27.7
Major appliances	100.0	12.8	22.8	26.8	37.3
Small appliances and miscellaneous housewares	100.0	11.3	22.7	42.0	24.1
China and other dinnerware	100.0	4.1	41.3	15.1	38.6
Glassware	100.0	10.0	14.3	60.5	16.1
Nonelectric cookware	100.0	11.2	21.4	41.4	26.2
Tableware, nonelectric kitchenware	100.0	11.4	17.2	51.4	20.3
Small electric kitchen appliances	100.0	14.6	32.6	32.7	20.0
Miscellaneous household equipment	100.0	18.9	23.9	28.1	28.9
Infants' equipment	100.0	12.6	2.5	28.3	57.2
Household decorative items	100.0	21.9	31.0	22.3	24.3
Indoor plants, fresh flowers	100.0	21.2	24.8	32.4	21.6
Computers and computer hardware, nonbusiness use	100.0	25.6	15.0	39.2	20.2
Miscellaneous household equipment and parts	100.0	4.8	19.2	21.2	54.8
Other housing	100.0	18.4	18.5	39.6	23.5
Repair or maintenance services	100.0	22.9	21.7	38.9	16.7
Materials for additions, finishing basements, remodeling rooms	100.0	–	1.0	25.1	74.0
Housing while attending school	100.0	24.2	20.8	31.1	23.9
Lodging on trips	100.0	25.8	31.8	24.2	18.1
Utility: natural gas (renter)	100.0	35.3	26.2	25.4	13.1
Electricity (renter)	100.0	11.5	18.3	58.4	11.7
Day care centers, nurseries, and preschools	100.0	17.1	12.9	56.4	13.5
Bedroom furniture other than mattresses and springs	100.0	15.4	26.0	22.7	35.9
APPAREL AND SERVICES	100.0	22.5	24.6	30.0	22.7
Men and boys, aged 2 or older	100.0	24.1	19.8	28.6	27.5
Men's suits	100.0	32.7	14.8	36.8	15.8
Men's coats and jackets	100.0	38.2	34.1	19.0	7.9
Men's accessories	100.0	20.6	17.1	30.1	32.4
Men's sweaters and vests	100.0	27.1	26.3	28.2	18.6
Men's active sportswear	100.0	22.9	15.6	19.7	41.6
Men's shirts	100.0	23.1	14.2	28.6	34.1
Men's pants	100.0	29.2	18.1	23.9	28.6
Boys' shirts	100.0	21.4	22.0	23.3	33.0
Boys' pants	100.0	14.5	22.8	37.6	25.1
Women and girls, aged 2 or older	100.0	21.1	27.5	29.3	21.9
Women's coats and jackets	100.0	11.3	21.1	33.3	34.3
Women's dresses	100.0	12.3	39.8	26.4	20.9
Women's vests and sweaters	100.0	26.7	33.3	20.0	19.3

	total consumer units	Northeast	Midwest	South	West
Women's shirts, tops, blouses	100.0%	19.3%	29.4%	30.9%	20.1%
Women's pants	100.0	17.9	26.4	38.9	16.7
Women's active sportswear	100.0	22.5	43.6	22.3	10.6
Women's sleepwear	100.0	20.8	26.8	36.7	15.6
Women's undergarments	100.0	9.1	39.0	38.3	12.9
Women's accessories	100.0	30.9	22.8	15.9	30.1
Girls' dresses and suits	100.0	26.4	5.3	40.6	28.2
Girls' shirts, blouses, sweaters	100.0	35.1	28.1	17.7	18.7
Girls' skirts and pants	100.0	19.4	24.3	36.5	19.8
Girls' active sportswear	100.0	24.2	18.3	35.7	21.8
Girls' accessories	100.0	32.7	11.1	12.2	44.0
Children under age 2	**100.0**	**22.1**	**22.2**	**33.6**	**22.1**
Infant dresses, outerwear	100.0	20.3	24.7	33.4	21.6
Infant underwear	100.0	22.8	19.1	33.8	24.3
Infant nightwear, loungewear	100.0	28.8	21.3	34.8	15.3
Infant accessories	100.0	16.0	29.7	36.4	17.7
Other apparel products and services	**100.0**	**23.5**	**27.1**	**29.8**	**19.3**
Jewelry and watches	100.0	21.6	25.0	34.6	18.8
Jewelry	100.0	21.9	25.2	34.7	18.2
All other apparel products and services	100.0	25.5	29.4	24.8	19.8
Men's footwear	100.0	14.8	34.0	24.7	25.9
Boys' footwear	100.0	37.6	20.0	26.3	16.0
Women's footwear	100.0	27.6	30.7	25.4	15.9
Girls' footwear	100.0	27.1	33.1	24.3	14.9
TRANSPORTATION	**100.0**	**10.3**	**21.9**	**27.8**	**39.9**
New cars	100.0	4.6	–	28.2	57.2
New trucks	100.0	–	–	22.7	77.3
Used cars	100.0	–	49.0	34.6	16.4
Used trucks	100.0	12.2	77.0	7.3	3.6
Airline fares	100.0	22.2	20.6	33.1	24.2
Ship fares	100.0	28.8	14.3	31.8	25.1
HEALTH CARE	**100.0**	**12.1**	**41.0**	**32.0**	**14.8**
Physician's services	100.0	23.1	20.0	29.9	26.9
Dental services	100.0	14.6	25.3	20.1	40.1
Hospital services other than room	100.0	–	28.2	47.7	24.1
Care in convalescent or nursing home	100.0	9.1	57.9	31.0	2.0
Nonprescription drugs	100.0	17.2	35.7	10.9	35.5
Prescription drugs	100.0	7.5	42.3	43.4	7.0
ENTERTAINMENT	**100.0**	**19.5**	**24.5**	**31.2**	**24.6**
Toys, games, hobbies, and tricycles	100.0	18.8	25.6	34.7	20.9
Other entertainment	100.0	20.0	23.8	29.1	26.9
Fees for recreational lessons	100.0	13.7	13.3	42.5	30.5
Community antenna or cable TV	100.0	20.1	21.0	44.7	14.3
VCRs and video disc players	100.0	19.5	28.3	40.7	11.4
Pet purchase, supplies, and medicine	100.0	24.1	8.6	13.5	53.7
Athletic gear, game tables, exercise equipment	100.0	31.3	28.1	6.1	33.8
Photographic equipment	100.0	16.6	23.7	33.8	26.1
PERSONAL CARE PRODUCTS AND SERVICES	**100.0**	**22.9**	**21.8**	**28.5**	**26.7**
Cosmetics, perfume, bath preparation	100.0	21.9	22.3	28.8	26.9
EDUCATION	**100.0**	**32.0**	**21.3**	**31.0**	**15.7**
College tuition	100.0	36.8	22.8	25.2	15.3
Elementary and high school tuition	100.0	38.0	17.9	50.4	13.6
Other school expenses including rentals	100.0	7.8	8.2	68.1	15.8
College books and supplies	100.0	33.2	8.3	34.8	23.7
Miscellaneous school supplies	100.0	16.8	29.2	38.7	15.2
ALL OTHER GIFTS	**100.0**	**16.5**	**26.8**	**31.8**	**24.9**
Gifts of trip expenses	100.0	18.9	26.1	27.9	27.1
Legal fees	100.0	9.9	7.7	57.2	25.2
Funeral expenses	100.0	11.2	35.7	34.3	18.8
Cemetery lots, vaults, and maintenance fees	100.0	28.8	12.3	46.4	12.5
Miscellaneous personal services	100.0	1.1	9.1	35.2	54.9

Note: Numbers may not add to total because of rounding. (–) means sample is too small to make a reliable estimate. Expenditures for items in a given category may not add to category total because categories with annual spending of less than $2.00 for the average household are omitted. Spending on gifts is also included in the product and service categories in other chapters.

Source: Calculations by New Strategist based on the 2003 Consumer Expenditure Survey

Table 6.25 Gifts for Nonhousehold Members: Average spending by education, 2003

(average annual spending of consumer units (CU) on selected gifts of products and services for nonhousehold members by education of consumer unit reference person, 2003)

	total consumer units	less than high school graduate	high school graduate	some college	associate's degree	college graduate total	bachelor's degree	master's, professional, doctorate
Number of consumer units (000)	115,356	17,721	31,552	24,514	10,981	30,589	19,557	11,032
Average number of persons per CU	2.5	2.6	2.5	2.3	2.6	2.5	2.5	2.4
Average before-tax income of CU	$51,128.00	$25,028.00	$40,113.00	$45,113.00	$54,087.00	$81,842.00	$74,921.00	$93,948.00
Average spending of CU, total	40,817.33	23,901.14	33,955.56	37,912.41	44,547.12	58,480.00	54,725.85	65,202.73
Gifts, average spending	**1,007.01**	**380.29**	**645.14**	**870.72**	**993.28**	**1,840.17**	**1,540.54**	**2,381.28**
FOOD	**77.59**	**17.05**	**53.96**	**61.97**	**77.74**	**147.26**	**130.63**	**177.97**
Fresh fruit other than apples, bananas, and citrus	2.36	1.65	1.62	3.10	1.15	3.31	1.63	6.52
Candy and chewing gum	9.41	4.41	6.88	7.55	5.56	16.98	17.44	16.10
Board (including at school)	16.71	2.21	3.51	9.62	6.34	48.12	32.57	75.69
Catered affairs	25.42	1.41	26.41	16.43	39.79	40.35	48.39	26.10
ALCOHOLIC BEVERAGES	**16.11**	**6.73**	**6.57**	**21.53**	**20.72**	**25.11**	**17.64**	**39.39**
Beer and ale	3.93	3.37	2.22	5.25	6.29	4.28	3.96	4.88
Wine	9.58	1.56	3.19	14.59	11.66	15.77	10.39	26.07
HOUSING	**220.43**	**92.90**	**145.65**	**186.04**	**225.35**	**390.66**	**336.20**	**490.77**
Housekeeping supplies	**41.56**	**9.77**	**31.73**	**33.40**	**58.38**	**67.85**	**49.35**	**103.22**
Laundry and cleaning supplies	2.25	0.86	2.45	1.30	3.43	3.06	3.22	2.76
Other household products	12.41	3.12	10.61	7.89	10.65	22.60	12.72	41.51
Miscellaneous household products	5.57	1.68	5.97	4.48	7.81	7.15	5.57	10.18
Lawn and garden supplies	5.42	0.50	3.22	2.82	1.34	13.21	5.20	28.52
Postage and stationery	26.89	5.79	18.67	24.21	44.30	42.18	33.41	58.96
Stationery, stationery supplies, giftwrap	19.13	4.83	15.31	16.13	41.35	25.31	21.43	32.72
Postage	7.17	0.96	3.36	7.14	2.11	15.68	11.35	23.95
Household textiles	**12.72**	**2.29**	**6.82**	**11.60**	**18.73**	**22.89**	**17.07**	**33.99**
Bathroom linens	3.30	0.92	1.61	2.50	6.63	5.73	5.73	5.75
Bedroom linens	5.95	0.81	2.94	5.44	9.09	10.94	6.73	19.00
Appliances and miscellaneous housewares	**24.51**	**9.02**	**13.06**	**23.71**	**31.64**	**42.43**	**40.37**	**46.11**
Major appliances	6.65	4.40	3.21	12.66	2.98	8.20	7.90	8.56
Small appliances and miscellaneous housewares	17.87	4.62	9.85	11.05	28.66	34.23	32.46	37.55
China and other dinnerware	2.04	0.53	1.99	0.30	2.16	4.06	3.42	5.26
Glassware	2.15	0.38	0.93	1.09	2.26	5.01	4.71	5.60
Nonelectric cookware	3.62	2.06	1.23	2.12	7.66	6.67	3.87	12.02
Tableware, nonelectric kitchenware	5.09	0.24	2.78	3.52	8.21	9.98	12.33	5.48
Small electric kitchen appliances	2.28	1.00	1.77	1.93	5.25	2.76	3.01	2.33
Miscellaneous household equipment	**56.73**	**22.82**	**40.50**	**47.93**	**51.94**	**99.60**	**98.61**	**101.54**
Infants' equipment	4.69	3.23	5.36	1.71	0.30	8.23	6.31	11.89
Household decorative items	18.91	6.59	10.57	20.51	26.73	29.90	30.10	29.50
Indoor plants, fresh flowers	10.86	5.23	8.44	10.10	11.44	17.03	15.07	20.51
Computers and computer hardware, nonbusiness use	8.04	2.36	6.66	4.52	3.44	17.21	19.77	12.67
Miscellaneous household equipment and parts	4.33	0.23	1.89	2.08	3.41	10.75	11.34	9.60
Other housing	**84.91**	**48.99**	**53.54**	**69.40**	**64.66**	**157.89**	**130.81**	**205.91**
Repair or maintenance services	4.18	6.67	0.97	5.59	9.65	2.97	3.87	1.37
Materials for additions, finishing basements, remodeling rooms	2.23	0.58	1.64	1.48	–	5.20	8.13	–
Housing while attending school	28.03	1.77	8.80	13.57	11.77	80.48	54.61	126.36
Lodging on trips	2.49	0.05	2.06	2.10	2.01	4.82	3.11	7.85
Utility: natural gas (renter)	2.82	5.75	2.77	1.47	1.15	2.86	4.04	0.76
Electricity (renter)	9.55	15.34	10.53	9.78	5.21	6.54	7.83	4.25
Day care centers, nurseries, and preschools	9.49	5.66	9.15	11.37	6.01	11.79	11.65	12.03
Bedroom furniture other than mattresses and springs	2.57	0.53	2.53	2.50	0.75	4.51	2.70	7.71
APPAREL AND SERVICES	**225.14**	**122.38**	**173.98**	**221.73**	**236.42**	**331.29**	**325.19**	**343.79**
Men and boys, aged 2 or older	**55.56**	**32.54**	**35.87**	**58.35**	**67.02**	**82.31**	**69.54**	**106.59**
Men's suits	2.93	0.38	1.55	2.19	3.44	6.24	6.44	5.88
Men's coats and jackets	3.95	1.03	–	6.40	0.45	8.72	4.31	17.14
Men's accessories	2.76	0.80	1.83	3.62	3.04	3.97	3.38	5.10
Men's sweaters and vests	2.29	0.63	1.88	2.50	1.71	3.73	4.20	2.90
Men's active sportswear	4.09	0.84	1.84	2.96	10.13	6.92	5.19	10.23
Men's shirts	8.37	4.34	6.00	9.85	12.83	10.30	8.73	13.31
Men's pants	6.03	7.07	3.71	4.84	12.31	6.82	5.27	9.79
Boys' shirts	3.68	3.82	3.03	3.93	2.33	4.51	3.32	6.80
Boys' pants	4.23	2.71	4.16	4.23	3.11	5.59	4.75	7.07
Women and girls, aged 2 or older	**80.28**	**41.68**	**63.13**	**78.72**	**81.89**	**117.71**	**118.79**	**115.51**
Women's coats and jackets	7.09	0.26	4.45	3.12	9.29	15.34	14.41	17.12
Women's dresses	4.76	5.78	1.66	5.04	4.55	7.32	10.87	0.52
Women's vests and sweaters	7.06	3.72	3.03	11.12	6.22	10.15	11.07	8.38

	total consumer units	less than high school graduate	high school graduate	some college	associate's degree	college graduate total	bachelor's degree	master's, professional, doctorate
Women's shirts, tops, blouses	$8.50	$5.43	$6.58	$7.41	$8.23	$12.73	$12.63	$12.91
Women's pants	6.42	2.35	5.67	6.75	1.99	10.30	13.44	4.30
Women's active sportswear	3.27	1.46	3.23	4.57	2.53	3.49	2.93	4.56
Women's sleepwear	5.62	1.11	5.76	6.41	4.90	3.22	4.47	0.82
Women's undergarments	3.14	1.93	3.11	3.63	1.05	4.04	5.44	1.36
Women's accessories	4.55	2.36	2.34	4.51	7.09	7.13	8.37	4.77
Girls' dresses and suits	2.12	1.48	1.75	0.85	2.20	3.70	3.32	4.42
Girls' shirts, blouses, sweaters	5.42	2.40	5.25	4.07	8.83	7.00	4.64	11.53
Girls' skirts and pants	4.58	4.04	4.13	3.96	5.86	5.38	4.98	6.10
Girls' active sportswear	2.07	1.39	1.17	3.05	2.07	2.59	1.33	5.00
Girls' accessories	2.24	0.79	2.16	0.73	–	4.81	2.93	8.40
Children under age 2	**38.81**	**25.14**	**37.18**	**35.39**	**32.44**	**51.97**	**50.82**	**54.13**
Infant dresses, outerwear	11.89	8.60	9.78	12.58	11.92	15.41	14.85	16.39
Infant underwear	19.44	12.58	19.54	15.19	13.72	27.54	28.13	26.40
Infant nightwear, loungewear	2.49	1.30	1.96	2.45	3.00	3.59	3.75	3.31
Infant accessories	3.96	1.99	5.13	4.17	2.82	3.92	2.56	6.53
Other apparel products and services	**50.49**	**23.02**	**37.79**	**49.26**	**55.08**	**79.29**	**86.04**	**67.57**
Jewelry and watches	25.85	4.93	19.25	15.16	22.87	54.42	62.88	39.41
Jewelry	24.28	3.90	17.77	13.86	20.61	52.49	60.63	38.05
All other apparel products and services	24.63	18.08	18.54	34.11	32.20	24.87	23.16	28.16
Men's footwear	5.05	2.73	4.14	7.38	7.56	4.28	1.54	9.51
Boys' footwear	4.10	5.98	1.72	6.39	6.09	2.98	2.22	4.44
Women's footwear	7.98	5.35	5.31	9.62	5.43	11.10	14.19	5.18
Girls' footwear	5.88	2.75	6.22	7.88	7.50	5.10	3.94	7.31
TRANSPORTATION	**59.73**	**4.77**	**28.20**	**88.83**	**97.24**	**87.15**	**71.63**	**114.55**
New cars	11.55	–	–	23.36	–	24.83	28.89	17.62
New trucks	13.10	–	–	44.27	38.80	–	–	–
Used cars	13.37	–	16.67	8.23	29.78	15.96	4.90	35.55
Used trucks	3.78	0.24	0.12	0.63	9.69	10.02	9.11	11.64
Airline fares	7.28	2.01	3.74	4.56	8.41	15.79	11.13	24.04
Ship fares	3.74	0.94	1.56	0.97	2.56	10.27	7.90	14.48
HEALTH CARE	**47.89**	**49.13**	**35.25**	**55.75**	**17.60**	**63.98**	**57.58**	**75.75**
Physician's services	3.33	1.61	4.13	1.56	2.24	5.29	3.08	9.21
Dental services	3.66	0.72	3.65	3.60	2.07	5.99	5.33	7.17
Hospital services other than room	2.20	0.29	6.31	0.44	0.23	1.20	0.32	2.75
Care in convalescent or nursing home	20.37	40.39	3.00	37.17	0.70	20.26	22.83	15.68
Nonprescription drugs	3.09	0.55	3.65	1.35	2.19	5.28	1.85	11.83
Prescription drugs	2.89	2.17	2.71	2.57	4.12	3.32	2.90	4.06
ENTERTAINMENT	**68.97**	**32.96**	**59.29**	**66.81**	**87.60**	**94.92**	**90.30**	**103.64**
Toys, games, hobbies, and tricycles	26.07	13.42	26.73	29.64	33.06	27.32	26.75	28.31
Other entertainment	42.89	19.54	32.51	37.16	54.54	67.60	63.55	75.33
Fees for recreational lessons	6.02	0.13	2.67	4.37	6.32	14.11	16.05	10.68
Community antenna or cable TV	3.53	5.71	3.49	3.07	2.96	2.88	3.38	2.00
VCRs and video disc players	2.52	0.16	2.80	2.71	1.47	3.82	3.95	3.58
Pet purchase, supplies, and medicine	2.33	–	0.44	0.73	2.03	6.64	1.65	16.18
Athletic gear, game tables, exercise equipment	6.00	8.79	1.34	7.87	17.34	4.58	6.12	1.62
Photographic equipment	2.10	–	1.10	1.69	1.96	4.73	4.72	4.76
PERSONAL CARE PRODUCTS AND SERVICES	**15.77**	**6.19**	**14.73**	**12.85**	**14.97**	**23.86**	**25.90**	**19.94**
Cosmetics, perfume, bath preparation	9.98	3.72	9.08	8.48	8.84	15.39	16.75	12.80
EDUCATION	**199.83**	**10.68**	**70.45**	**90.56**	**152.83**	**546.48**	**356.49**	**884.31**
College tuition	155.43	5.91	53.07	63.10	123.37	433.15	279.86	704.92
Elementary and high school tuition	10.44	0.28	5.39	2.55	3.05	30.50	21.00	47.34
Other school expenses including rentals	15.75	0.41	2.29	11.84	9.20	43.80	27.12	73.37
College books and supplies	9.97	1.19	4.36	9.15	9.57	21.65	17.85	28.39
Miscellaneous school supplies	6.20	0.45	4.12	2.88	6.23	13.53	6.35	27.25
ALL OTHER GIFTS	**74.21**	**37.35**	**55.87**	**63.34**	**61.68**	**127.01**	**126.70**	**128.45**
Gifts of trip expenses	40.70	11.06	21.04	38.84	32.42	82.61	78.65	89.63
Legal fees	4.50	–	4.05	5.76	6.25	5.94	8.36	1.65
Funeral expenses	21.80	21.87	24.38	15.76	21.17	24.18	31.37	11.44
Cemetery lots, vaults, and maintenance fees	2.24	2.64	3.55	0.98	0.19	2.40	3.17	1.05
Miscellaneous personal services	2.49	0.01	0.03	1.32	0.01	7.82	1.52	19.86

Note: (–) means sample is too small to make a reliable estimate. Expenditures for items in a given category may not add to category total because categories with annual spending of less than $2.00 for the average household are omitted. Spending on gifts is also included in the product and service categories in other chapters.
Source: Bureau of Labor Statistics, unpublished tables from the 2003 Consumer Expenditure Survey

(indexed average annual spending of consumer units (CU) on selected gifts of products and services for nonhousehold members by education of consumer unit reference person, 2003; index definition: an index of 100 is the average for all consumer units; an index of 132 means that spending by consumer units in that group is 32 percent above the average for all consumer units; an index of 68 indicates spending that is 32 percent below the average for all consumer units)

	total consumer units	less than high school graduate	high school graduate	some college	associate's degree	college graduate total	bachelor's degree	master's, professional, doctorate
Average spending of CU, total	$40,817	$23,901	$33,956	$37,912	$44,547	$58,480	$54,726	$65,203
Average spending of CU, index	100	59	83	93	109	143	134	160
Gifts, spending index	**100**	**38**	**64**	**86**	**99**	**183**	**153**	**236**
FOOD	**100**	**22**	**70**	**80**	**100**	**190**	**168**	**229**
Fresh fruit other than apples, bananas, and citrus	100	70	69	131	49	140	69	276
Candy and chewing gum	100	47	73	80	59	180	185	171
Board (including at school)	100	13	21	58	38	288	195	453
Catered affairs	100	6	104	65	157	159	190	103
ALCOHOLIC BEVERAGES	**100**	**42**	**41**	**134**	**129**	**156**	**109**	**245**
Beer and ale	100	86	56	134	160	109	101	124
Wine	100	16	33	152	122	165	108	272
HOUSING	**100**	**42**	**66**	**84**	**102**	**177**	**153**	**223**
Housekeeping supplies	**100**	**24**	**76**	**80**	**140**	**163**	**119**	**248**
Laundry and cleaning supplies	100	38	109	58	152	136	143	123
Other household products	100	25	85	64	86	182	102	334
Miscellaneous household products	100	30	107	80	140	128	100	183
Lawn and garden supplies	100	9	59	52	25	244	96	526
Postage and stationery	100	22	69	90	165	157	124	219
Stationery, stationery supplies, giftwrap	100	25	80	84	216	132	112	171
Postage	100	13	47	100	29	219	158	334
Household textiles	**100**	**18**	**54**	**91**	**147**	**180**	**134**	**267**
Bathroom linens	100	28	49	76	201	174	174	174
Bedroom linens	100	14	49	91	153	184	113	319
Appliances and miscellaneous housewares	**100**	**37**	**53**	**97**	**129**	**173**	**165**	**188**
Major appliances	100	66	48	190	45	123	119	129
Small appliances and miscellaneous housewares	100	26	55	62	160	192	182	210
China and other dinnerware	100	26	98	15	106	199	168	258
Glassware	100	18	43	51	105	233	219	260
Nonelectric cookware	100	57	34	59	212	184	107	332
Tableware, nonelectric kitchenware	100	5	55	69	161	196	242	108
Small electric kitchen appliances	100	44	78	85	230	121	132	102
Miscellaneous household equipment	**100**	**40**	**71**	**84**	**92**	**176**	**174**	**179**
Infants' equipment	100	69	114	36	6	175	135	254
Household decorative items	100	35	56	108	141	158	159	156
Indoor plants, fresh flowers	100	48	78	93	105	157	139	189
Computers and computer hardware, nonbusiness use	100	29	83	56	43	214	246	158
Miscellaneous household equipment and parts	100	5	44	48	79	248	262	222
Other housing	**100**	**58**	**63**	**82**	**76**	**186**	**154**	**243**
Repair or maintenance services	100	160	23	134	231	71	93	33
Materials for additions, finishing basements, remodeling rooms	100	26	74	66	–	233	365	–
Housing while attending school	100	6	31	48	42	287	195	451
Lodging on trips	100	2	83	84	81	194	125	315
Utility: natural gas (renter)	100	204	98	52	41	101	143	27
Electricity (renter)	100	161	110	102	55	68	82	45
Day care centers, nurseries, and preschools	100	60	96	120	63	124	123	127
Bedroom furniture other than mattresses and springs	100	21	98	97	29	175	105	300
APPAREL AND SERVICES	**100**	**54**	**77**	**98**	**105**	**147**	**144**	**153**
Men and boys, aged 2 or older	**100**	**59**	**65**	**105**	**121**	**148**	**125**	**192**
Men's suits	100	13	53	75	117	213	220	201
Men's coats and jackets	100	26	–	162	11	221	109	434
Men's accessories	100	29	66	131	110	144	122	185
Men's sweaters and vests	100	28	82	109	75	163	183	127
Men's active sportswear	100	21	45	72	248	169	127	250
Men's shirts	100	52	72	118	153	123	104	159
Men's pants	100	117	62	80	204	113	87	162
Boys' shirts	100	104	82	107	63	123	90	185
Boys' pants	100	64	98	100	74	132	112	167
Women and girls, aged 2 or older	**100**	**52**	**79**	**98**	**102**	**147**	**148**	**144**
Women's coats and jackets	100	4	63	44	131	216	203	241
Women's dresses	100	121	35	106	96	154	228	11
Women's vests and sweaters	100	53	43	158	88	144	157	119

	total consumer units	less than high school graduate	high school graduate	some college	associate's degree	college graduate total	bachelor's degree	master's, professional, doctorate
Women's shirts, tops, blouses	100	64	79	87	97	150	149	152
Women's pants	100	37	38	105	31	160	209	67
Women's active sportswear	100	45	99	140	77	107	90	139
Women's sleepwear	100	20	174	114	87	57	80	15
Women's undergarments	100	61	99	116	33	129	173	43
Women's accessories	100	52	51	99	156	157	184	105
Girls' dresses and suits	100	70	83	40	104	175	157	208
Girls' shirts, blouses, sweaters	100	44	97	75	163	129	86	213
Girls' skirts and pants	100	88	90	86	128	117	109	133
Girls' active sportswear	100	67	57	147	100	125	64	242
Girls' accessories	100	35	56	33	–	215	131	375
Children under age 2	**100**	**65**	**56**	**91**	**84**	**134**	**131**	**139**
Infant dresses, outerwear	100	72	82	106	100	130	125	138
Infant underwear	100	65	101	78	71	142	145	136
Infant nightwear, loungewear	100	52	79	98	120	144	151	133
Infant accessories	100	50	130	105	71	99	65	165
Other apparel products and services	**100**	**46**	**75**	**98**	**109**	**157**	**170**	**134**
Jewelry and watches	100	19	74	59	88	211	243	152
Jewelry	100	16	73	57	85	216	250	157
All other apparel products and services	100	73	75	138	131	101	94	114
Men's footwear	100	54	82	156	150	85	30	188
Boys' footwear	100	146	42	168	149	73	54	108
Women's footwear	100	67	73	121	68	139	178	65
Girls' footwear	100	47	106	134	128	87	67	124
TRANSPORTATION	**100**	**8**	**47**	**149**	**163**	**146**	**120**	**192**
New cars	100	–	–	202	–	215	250	153
New trucks	100	–	–	338	296	–	–	–
Used cars	100	–	125	62	223	119	37	266
Used trucks	100	6	3	17	256	265	241	308
Airline fares	100	28	51	63	116	217	153	330
Ship fares	100	25	42	26	68	275	211	387
HEALTH CARE	**100**	**103**	**74**	**116**	**37**	**134**	**120**	**158**
Physician's services	100	48	124	47	67	159	92	277
Dental services	100	20	100	98	57	164	146	196
Hospital services other than room	100	13	287	20	10	55	15	125
Care in convalescent or nursing home	100	198	15	182	3	99	112	77
Nonprescription drugs	100	18	118	44	71	171	60	383
Prescription drugs	100	75	94	89	143	115	100	140
ENTERTAINMENT	**100**	**48**	**86**	**97**	**127**	**138**	**131**	**150**
Toys, games, hobbies, and tricycles	100	51	103	114	127	105	103	109
Other entertainment	100	46	76	87	127	158	148	176
Fees for recreational lessons	100	2	44	73	105	234	267	177
Community antenna or cable TV	100	162	99	87	84	82	96	57
VCRs and video disc players	100	6	111	108	58	152	157	142
Pet purchase, supplies, and medicine	100	–	19	31	87	285	71	694
Athletic gear, game tables, exercise equipment	100	147	22	131	289	76	102	27
Photographic equipment	100	–	52	80	93	225	225	227
PERSONAL CARE PRODUCTS AND SERVICES	**100**	**39**	**93**	**81**	**95**	**151**	**164**	**126**
Cosmetics, perfume, bath preparation	100	37	91	85	89	154	168	128
EDUCATION	**100**	**5**	**35**	**45**	**76**	**273**	**178**	**443**
College tuition	100	4	34	41	79	279	180	454
Elementary and high school tuition	100	3	52	24	29	292	201	453
Other school expenses including rentals	100	3	16	75	58	278	172	466
College books and supplies	100	12	44	92	96	217	179	285
Miscellaneous school supplies	100	7	66	46	100	218	102	440
ALL OTHER GIFTS	**100**	**50**	**75**	**85**	**83**	**171**	**171**	**173**
Gifts of trip expenses	100	27	52	95	80	203	193	220
Legal fees	100	–	90	128	139	132	186	37
Funeral expenses	100	100	112	72	97	111	144	52
Cemetery lots, vaults, and maintenance fees	100	118	158	44	8	107	142	47
Miscellaneous personal services	100	0	1	53	0	314	61	798

Note: (–) means sample is too small to make a reliable estimate. Categories with annual spending of less than $2.00 for the average household are omitted. Spending on gifts is also included in the product and service categories in other chapters.
Source: Calculations by New Strategist based on the 2003 Consumer Expenditure Survey

Table 6.27 Gifts for Nonhousehold Members: Total spending by education, 2003

(total annual spending on selected gifts of products and services for nonhousehold members by consumer unit (CU) educational attainment group, 2003; numbers in thousands)

	total consumer units	less than high school graduate	high school graduate	some college	associate's degree	college graduate total	college graduate bachelor's degree	college graduate master's, professional, doctorate
Number of consumer units	115,356	17,721	31,552	24,514	10,981	30,589	19,557	11,032
Total spending of all CUs	$4,708,523,919	$423,552,102	$1,071,365,829	$929,384,819	$489,171,925	$1,788,844,720	$1,070,273,448	$719,316,517
Gifts, total spending	**116,164,646**	**6,739,119**	**20,355,457**	**21,344,830**	**10,907,208**	**56,288,960**	**30,128,341**	**26,270,281**
FOOD	**8,950,472**	**302,143**	**1,702,546**	**1,519,133**	**853,663**	**4,504,536**	**2,554,731**	**1,963,365**
Fresh fruit other than apples, bananas, and citrus	272,240	29,240	51,114	75,993	12,628	101,250	31,878	71,929
Candy and chewing gum	1,085,500	78,150	217,078	185,081	61,054	519,401	341,074	177,615
Board (including at school)	1,927,599	39,163	110,748	235,825	69,620	1,471,943	636,971	835,012
Catered affairs	2,932,350	24,987	833,288	402,765	436,934	1,234,266	946,363	287,935
ALCOHOLIC BEVERAGES	**1,858,385**	**119,262**	**207,297**	**527,786**	**227,526**	**768,090**	**344,985**	**434,550**
Beer and ale	453,349	59,720	70,045	128,699	69,070	130,921	77,446	53,836
Wine	1,105,110	27,645	100,651	357,659	128,038	482,389	203,197	287,604
HOUSING	**25,427,923**	**1,646,281**	**4,595,549**	**4,560,585**	**2,474,568**	**11,949,899**	**6,575,063**	**5,414,175**
Housekeeping supplies	**4,794,195**	**173,134**	**1,001,145**	**818,768**	**641,071**	**2,075,464**	**965,138**	**1,138,723**
Laundry and cleaning supplies	259,551	15,240	77,302	51,868	37,665	93,602	62,974	30,448
Other household products	1,431,568	55,290	334,767	193,415	116,948	691,311	248,765	457,938
Miscellaneous household products	642,533	29,771	188,365	109,823	85,762	218,711	108,932	112,306
Lawn and garden supplies	625,230	8,861	101,597	69,129	14,715	404,081	101,696	314,633
Postage and stationery	3,101,923	102,605	589,076	593,484	486,458	1,290,244	653,399	650,447
Stationery, stationery supplies, giftwrap	2,206,760	85,592	483,061	395,411	454,064	774,208	419,107	360,967
Postage	827,103	17,012	106,015	175,030	23,170	479,636	221,972	264,216
Household textiles	**1,467,328**	**40,581**	**215,185**	**284,362**	**205,674**	**700,182**	**333,838**	**374,978**
Bathroom linens	380,675	16,303	50,799	61,285	72,804	175,275	112,062	63,434
Bedroom linens	686,368	14,354	92,763	133,356	99,817	334,644	131,619	209,608
Appliances and miscellaneous housewares	**2,827,376**	**159,843**	**412,069**	**581,227**	**347,439**	**1,297,891**	**789,516**	**508,686**
Major appliances	767,117	77,972	101,282	310,347	32,723	250,830	154,500	94,434
Small appliances and miscellaneous housewares	2,061,412	81,871	310,787	270,880	314,715	1,047,061	634,820	414,252
China and other dinnerware	235,326	9,392	62,788	7,354	23,719	124,191	66,885	58,028
Glassware	248,015	6,734	29,343	26,720	24,817	153,251	92,113	61,779
Nonelectric cookware	417,589	36,505	38,809	51,970	84,114	204,029	75,686	132,605
Tableware, nonelectric kitchenware	587,162	4,253	87,715	86,289	90,154	305,278	241,138	60,455
Small electric kitchen appliances	263,012	17,721	55,847	47,312	57,650	84,426	58,867	25,705
Miscellaneous household equipment	**6,544,146**	**404,393**	**1,277,856**	**1,174,956**	**570,353**	**3,046,664**	**1,928,516**	**1,120,189**
Infants' equipment	541,020	57,239	169,119	41,919	3,294	251,747	123,405	131,170
Household decorative items	2,181,382	116,781	333,505	502,782	293,522	914,611	588,666	325,444
Indoor plants, fresh flowers	1,252,766	92,681	266,299	247,591	125,623	520,931	294,724	226,266
Computers and computer hardware, nonbusiness use	927,462	41,822	210,136	110,803	37,775	526,437	386,642	139,775
Miscellaneous household equipment and parts	499,491	4,076	59,633	50,989	37,445	328,832	221,776	105,907
Other housing	**9,794,878**	**868,152**	**1,689,294**	**1,701,272**	**710,031**	**4,829,697**	**2,558,251**	**2,271,599**
Repair or maintenance services	482,188	118,199	30,605	137,033	105,967	90,849	75,686	15,114
Materials for additions, finishing basements, remodeling rooms	257,244	10,278	51,745	36,281	–	159,063	158,998	–
Housing while attending school	3,233,429	31,366	277,658	332,655	129,246	2,461,803	1,068,008	1,394,004
Lodging on trips	287,236	886	64,997	51,479	22,072	147,439	60,822	86,601
Utility: natural gas (renter)	325,304	101,896	87,399	36,036	12,628	87,485	79,010	8,384
Electricity (renter)	1,101,650	271,840	332,243	239,747	57,211	200,052	153,131	46,886
Day care centers, nurseries, and preschools	1,094,728	100,301	288,701	278,724	65,996	360,644	227,839	132,715
Bedroom furniture other than mattresses and springs	296,465	9,392	79,827	61,285	8,236	137,956	52,804	85,057
APPAREL AND SERVICES	**25,971,250**	**2,168,696**	**5,489,417**	**5,435,489**	**2,596,128**	**10,133,830**	**6,359,741**	**3,792,691**
Men and boys, aged 2 or older	**6,409,179**	**576,641**	**1,131,770**	**1,430,392**	**735,947**	**2,517,781**	**1,359,994**	**1,175,901**
Men's suits	337,993	6,734	48,906	53,686	37,775	190,875	125,947	64,868
Men's coats and jackets	455,656	18,253	–	156,890	4,941	266,736	84,291	189,088
Men's accessories	318,383	14,177	57,740	88,741	33,382	121,438	66,103	56,263
Men's sweaters and vests	264,165	11,164	59,318	61,285	18,778	114,097	82,139	31,993
Men's active sportswear	471,806	14,886	58,056	72,561	111,238	211,676	101,501	112,857
Men's shirts	965,530	76,909	189,312	241,463	140,886	315,067	170,733	146,836
Men's pants	695,597	125,287	117,058	118,648	135,176	208,617	103,065	108,003
Boys' shirts	424,510	67,694	95,603	96,340	25,586	137,956	64,929	75,018
Boys' pants	487,956	48,024	131,256	103,694	34,151	170,993	92,896	77,996
Women and girls, aged 2 or older	**9,260,780**	**738,611**	**1,991,878**	**1,929,742**	**899,234**	**3,600,631**	**2,323,176**	**1,274,306**
Women's coats and jackets	817,874	4,607	140,406	76,484	102,013	469,235	281,816	188,868
Women's dresses	549,095	102,427	52,376	123,551	49,964	223,911	212,585	5,737
Women's vests and sweaters	814,413	65,922	95,603	272,596	68,302	310,478	216,496	92,448

	total consumer units	less than high school graduate	high school graduate	some college	associate's degree	college graduate total	bachelor's degree	master's, professional, doctorate
Women's shirts, tops, blouses	$980,526	$96,225	$210,767	$181,649	$90,374	$389,398	$247,005	$142,423
Women's pants	740,586	41,644	78,900	165,470	21,852	315,067	262,846	47,438
Women's active sportswear	377,214	25,873	01,913	112,029	27,782	106,756	57,302	50,306
Women's sleepwear	648,301	19,670	207,948	157,135	53,807	98,497	87,420	9,046
Women's undergarments	362,218	34,202	98,127	88,986	11,530	123,580	106,390	15,004
Women's accessories	524,870	41,822	73,832	110,558	77,855	218,100	163,692	52,623
Girls' dresses and suits	244,555	26,227	55,216	20,837	24,158	113,179	64,929	48,761
Girls' shirts, blouses, sweaters	625,230	42,530	165,648	99,772	96,962	214,123	90,744	127,199
Girls' skirts and pants	528,330	71,593	130,310	97,075	64,349	164,569	97,394	67,295
Girls' active sportswear	238,787	24,632	36,916	74,768	22,731	79,226	26,011	55,160
Girls' accessories	258,397	14,000	68,152	17,895	–	147,133	57,302	92,669
Children under age 2	**4,476,966**	**445,506**	**1,173,103**	**867,550**	**356,224**	**1,589,710**	**993,887**	**597,162**
Infant dresses, outerwear	1,371,583	152,401	308,579	308,386	130,894	471,376	290,421	180,814
Infant underwear	2,242,521	222,930	516,526	372,368	150,659	842,421	550,138	291,245
Infant nightwear, loungewear	287,236	23,037	51,842	60,059	32,943	109,815	73,339	36,516
Infant accessories	456,810	35,265	151,862	102,223	30,966	119,909	50,066	72,039
Other apparel products and services	**5,824,324**	**407,937**	**1,132,350**	**1,207,560**	**604,833**	**2,425,402**	**1,682,684**	**745,432**
Jewelry and watches	2,981,953	87,365	607,376	371,632	251,135	1,664,653	1,229,744	434,771
Jewelry	2,800,844	69,112	550,679	339,764	226,318	1,605,617	1,185,741	419,768
All other apparel products and services	2,841,218	320,396	524,974	836,173	353,588	760,748	452,940	310,661
Men's footwear	582,548	48,378	140,625	193,170	83,016	130,921	30,118	104,914
Boys' footwear	472,960	105,972	74,269	158,901	66,874	91,155	43,417	48,982
Women's footwear	920,541	94,807	153,317	235,825	59,627	339,538	277,514	57,146
Girls' footwear	678,293	48,733	196,253	193,170	82,358	156,004	77,055	80,644
TRANSPORTATION	**6,890,214**	**84,529**	**889,766**	**2,177,579**	**1,067,792**	**2,665,831**	**1,400,868**	**1,263,716**
New cars	1,332,362	–	–	572,647	–	759,525	565,002	194,384
New trucks	1,511,164	–	–	1,085,235	426,063	–	–	–
Used cars	1,542,310	–	525,972	201,750	327,014	488,200	95,829	392,188
Used trucks	436,046	4,253	3,786	15,444	106,406	306,502	178,164	128,412
Airline fares	839,792	35,619	118,004	111,784	92,350	483,000	217,669	265,209
Ship fares	431,431	16,658	49,221	23,779	28,111	314,149	154,500	159,743
HEALTH CARE	**5,524,399**	**870,633**	**1,115,363**	**1,366,656**	**193,266**	**1,957,084**	**1,126,092**	**835,674**
Physician's services	384,135	28,531	130,310	38,242	24,597	161,816	60,236	101,605
Dental services	422,203	12,759	115,165	88,250	22,731	183,228	104,239	79,099
Hospital services other than room	253,783	5,139	199,093	10,786	2,526	36,707	6,258	30,338
Care in convalescent or nursing home	2,349,802	715,751	94,972	911,185	7,687	619,733	446,486	172,982
Nonprescription drugs	356,450	9,747	115,480	33,339	24,048	161,510	36,180	130,509
Prescription drugs	333,379	38,455	83,506	63,001	45,242	101,555	56,715	44,790
ENTERTAINMENT	**7,956,103**	**584,084**	**1,870,718**	**1,637,780**	**961,936**	**2,903,508**	**1,765,997**	**1,143,356**
Toys, games, hobbies, and tricycles	3,007,331	237,816	844,963	726,595	363,032	835,691	523,150	312,316
Other entertainment	4,947,619	346,268	1,025,756	910,940	598,904	2,067,816	1,242,847	831,041
Fees for recreational lessons	694,443	2,304	84,244	107,126	69,400	431,611	313,890	117,822
Community antenna or cable TV	407,207	101,187	110,116	75,258	32,504	88,096	66,103	22,064
VCRs and video disc players	290,697	2,835	88,346	56,433	16,142	116,850	77,250	39,495
Pet purchase, supplies, and medicine	268,779	–	15,883	17,895	22,291	203,111	32,269	178,498
Athletic gear, game tables, exercise equipment	692,136	155,768	42,280	132,925	190,411	140,098	119,689	17,872
Photographic equipment	242,248	–	34,707	41,429	21,523	144,686	92,309	52,512
PERSONAL CARE PRODUCTS AND SERVICES	**1,819,164**	**109,693**	**464,761**	**315,005**	**164,386**	**729,854**	**506,526**	**219,978**
Cosmetics, perfume, bath preparation	1,151,253	65,922	286,492	207,879	97,072	470,765	327,580	141,210
EDUCATION	**23,051,589**	**189,260**	**2,222,838**	**2,229,988**	**1,678,226**	**16,716,277**	**6,971,875**	**9,755,708**
College tuition	17,929,783	104,731	1,674,465	1,546,833	1,354,726	13,249,625	5,473,222	7,776,677
Elementary and high school tuition	1,204,317	4,962	170,065	62,511	33,492	932,965	410,697	522,255
Other school expenses including rentals	1,816,857	7,266	78,564	290,246	101,025	1,339,798	530,386	809,418
College books and supplies	1,150,099	21,088	137,567	224,303	105,088	662,252	349,092	313,198
Miscellaneous school supplies	715,207	7,974	129,394	70,600	68,412	413,869	124,187	300,622
ALL OTHER GIFTS	**8,560,569**	**661,879**	**1,762,310**	**1,552,717**	**677,308**	**3,885,109**	**2,477,872**	**1,417,060**
Gifts of trip expenses	4,694,989	195,994	663,354	952,124	356,004	2,526,957	1,538,158	988,798
Legal fees	519,102	–	127,786	141,201	58,631	181,699	163,497	18,203
Funeral expenses	2,514,761	387,558	769,238	385,341	232,468	739,642	613,503	126,206
Cemetery lots, vaults, and maintenance fees	258,397	46,783	112,310	24,024	2,086	73,414	61,996	11,584
Miscellaneous personal services	287,236	177	947	32,358	110	239,206	29,727	219,096

Note: Numbers may not add to total because of rounding. (–) means sample is too small to make a reliable estimate. Expenditures for items in a given category may not add to category total because categories with annual spending of less than $2.00 for the average household are omitted. Spending on gifts is also included in the product and service categories in other chapters.

Source: Calculations by New Strategist based on the 2003 Consumer Expenditure Survey

Table 6.28 Gifts for Nonhousehold Members: Market shares by education, 2003

(percentage of total annual spending on selected gifts of products and services for nonhousehold members accounted for by consumer unit educational attainment groups, 2003)

	total consumer units	less than high school graduate	high school graduate	some college	associate's degree	college graduate total	bachelor's degree	master's, professional, doctorate
Share of total consumer units	100.0%	15.4%	27.4%	21.3%	9.5%	26.5%	17.0%	9.6%
Share of total before-tax income	100.0	7.5	21.5	18.8	10.1	42.4	24.8	17.6
Share of total spending	100.0	9.0	22.8	19.7	10.4	38.0	22.7	15.3
Share of gifts spending	100.0	5.8	17.5	18.4	9.4	48.5	25.9	22.6
FOOD	100.0	3.4	19.0	17.0	9.5	50.3	28.5	21.9
Fresh fruit other than apples, bananas, and citrus	100.0	10.7	18.8	27.9	4.6	37.2	11.7	26.4
Candy and chewing gum	100.0	7.2	20.0	17.1	5.6	47.8	31.4	16.4
Board (including at school)	100.0	2.0	5.7	12.2	3.6	76.4	33.0	43.3
Catered affairs	100.0	0.9	28.4	13.7	14.9	42.1	32.3	9.8
ALCOHOLIC BEVERAGES	100.0	6.4	11.2	28.4	12.2	41.3	18.6	23.4
Beer and ale	100.0	13.2	15.5	28.4	15.2	28.9	17.1	11.9
Wine	100.0	2.5	9.1	32.4	11.6	43.7	18.4	26.0
HOUSING	100.0	6.5	18.1	17.9	9.7	47.0	25.9	21.3
Housekeeping supplies	100.0	3.6	20.9	17.1	13.4	43.3	20.1	23.8
Laundry and cleaning supplies	100.0	5.9	29.8	12.3	14.5	36.1	24.3	11.7
Other household products	100.0	3.9	23.4	13.5	8.2	48.3	17.4	32.0
Miscellaneous household products	100.0	4.6	29.3	17.1	13.3	34.0	17.0	17.5
Lawn and garden supplies	100.0	1.4	16.2	11.1	2.4	64.6	16.3	50.3
Postage and stationery	100.0	3.3	19.0	19.1	15.7	41.6	21.1	21.0
Stationery, stationery supplies, giftwrap	100.0	3.9	21.9	17.9	20.6	35.1	19.0	16.4
Postage	100.0	2.1	12.8	21.2	2.8	58.0	26.8	31.9
Household textiles	100.0	2.8	14.7	19.4	14.0	47.7	22.8	25.6
Bathroom linens	100.0	4.3	13.3	16.1	19.1	46.0	29.4	16.7
Bedroom linens	100.0	2.1	13.5	19.4	14.5	48.8	19.2	30.5
Appliances and miscellaneous housewares	100.0	5.7	14.6	20.6	12.3	45.9	27.9	18.0
Major appliances	100.0	10.2	13.2	40.5	4.3	32.7	20.1	12.3
Small appliances and miscellaneous housewares	100.0	4.0	15.1	13.1	15.3	50.8	30.8	20.1
China and other dinnerware	100.0	4.0	26.7	3.1	10.1	52.8	28.4	24.7
Glassware	100.0	2.7	11.8	10.8	10.0	61.8	37.1	24.9
Nonelectric cookware	100.0	8.7	9.3	12.4	20.1	48.9	18.1	31.8
Tableware, nonelectric kitchenware	100.0	0.7	14.9	14.7	15.4	52.0	41.1	10.3
Small electric kitchen appliances	100.0	6.7	21.2	18.0	21.9	32.1	22.4	9.8
Miscellaneous household equipment	100.0	6.2	19.5	18.0	8.7	46.6	29.5	17.1
Infants' equipment	100.0	10.6	31.3	7.7	0.6	46.5	22.8	24.2
Household decorative items	100.0	5.4	15.3	23.0	13.5	41.9	27.0	14.9
Indoor plants, fresh flowers	100.0	7.4	21.3	19.8	10.0	41.6	23.5	18.1
Computers and computer hardware, nonbusiness use	100.0	4.5	22.7	11.9	4.1	56.8	41.7	15.1
Miscellaneous household equipment and parts	100.0	0.8	11.9	10.2	7.5	65.8	44.4	21.2
Other housing	100.0	8.9	17.2	17.4	7.2	49.3	26.1	23.2
Repair or maintenance services	100.0	24.5	6.3	28.4	22.0	18.8	15.7	3.1
Materials for additions, finishing basements, remodeling rooms	100.0	4.0	20.1	14.1	–	61.8	61.8	–
Housing while attending school	100.0	1.0	8.6	10.3	4.0	76.1	33.0	43.1
Lodging on trips	100.0	0.3	22.6	17.9	7.7	51.3	21.2	30.1
Utility: natural gas (renter)	100.0	31.3	26.9	11.1	3.9	26.9	24.3	2.6
Electricity (renter)	100.0	24.7	30.2	21.8	5.2	18.2	13.9	4.3
Day care centers, nurseries, and preschools	100.0	9.2	26.4	25.5	6.0	32.9	20.8	12.1
Bedroom furniture other than mattresses and springs	100.0	3.2	26.9	20.7	2.8	46.5	17.8	28.7
APPAREL AND SERVICES	100.0	8.4	21.1	20.9	10.0	39.0	24.5	14.6
Men and boys, aged 2 or older	100.0	9.0	17.7	22.3	11.5	39.3	21.2	18.3
Men's suits	100.0	2.0	14.5	15.9	11.2	56.5	37.3	19.2
Men's coats and jackets	100.0	4.0	–	34.4	1.1	58.5	18.5	41.5
Men's accessories	100.0	4.5	18.1	27.9	10.5	38.1	20.8	17.7
Men's sweaters and vests	100.0	4.2	22.5	23.2	7.1	43.2	31.1	12.1
Men's active sportswear	100.0	3.2	12.3	15.4	23.6	44.9	21.5	23.9
Men's shirts	100.0	8.0	19.6	25.0	14.6	32.6	17.7	15.2
Men's pants	100.0	18.0	16.8	17.1	19.4	30.0	14.8	15.5
Boys' shirts	100.0	15.9	22.5	22.7	6.0	32.5	15.3	17.7
Boys' pants	100.0	9.8	26.9	21.3	7.0	35.0	19.0	16.0
Women and girls, aged 2 or older	100.0	8.0	21.5	20.8	9.7	38.9	25.1	13.8
Women's coats and jackets	100.0	0.6	17.2	9.4	12.5	57.4	34.5	23.1
Women's dresses	100.0	18.7	9.5	22.5	9.1	40.8	38.7	1.0
Women's vests and sweaters	100.0	8.1	11.7	33.5	8.4	38.1	26.6	11.4

	total consumer units	less than high school graduate	high school graduate	some college	associate's degree	college graduate total	college graduate bachelor's degree	college graduate master's, professional, doctorate
Women's shirts, tops, blouses	100.0%	9.8%	21.5%	18.5%	9.2%	39.7%	25.2%	14.5%
Women's pants	100.0	5.6	24.2	22.3	3.0	42.5	35.5	6.4
Women's active sportswear	100.0	6.9	27.0	29.7	7.4	28.3	15.2	13.3
Women's sleepwear	100.0	3.0	47.5	24.2	8.3	15.2	13.5	1.4
Women's undergarments	100.0	9.4	27.1	24.6	3.2	34.1	29.4	4.1
Women's accessories	100.0	8.0	14.1	21.1	14.8	41.6	31.2	10.0
Girls' dresses and suits	100.0	10.7	22.5	8.5	9.9	46.3	26.5	19.9
Girls' shirts, blouses, sweaters	100.0	6.8	25.5	16.0	15.5	34.2	14.5	20.3
Girls' skirts and pants	100.0	13.6	24.7	18.4	12.2	31.1	18.4	12.7
Girls' active sportswear	100.0	10.3	15.5	31.3	9.5	33.2	10.9	23.1
Girls' accessories	100.0	5.4	26.4	6.9	–	56.9	22.2	35.9
Children under age 2	**100.0**	**10.0**	**26.2**	**19.4**	**8.0**	**35.5**	**22.2**	**13.3**
Infant dresses, outerwear	100.0	11.1	22.5	22.5	9.5	34.4	21.2	13.2
Infant underwear	100.0	9.9	27.5	16.6	6.7	37.6	24.5	13.0
Infant nightwear, loungewear	100.0	8.0	21.5	20.9	11.5	38.2	25.5	12.7
Infant accessories	100.0	7.7	35.4	22.4	6.8	26.2	11.0	15.8
Other apparel products and services	**100.0**	**7.0**	**20.5**	**20.7**	**10.4**	**41.6**	**28.9**	**12.8**
Jewelry and watches	100.0	2.9	20.4	12.5	8.4	55.8	41.2	14.6
Jewelry	100.0	2.5	20.0	12.1	8.1	57.3	42.3	15.0
All other apparel products and services	100.0	11.3	20.6	29.4	12.4	26.8	15.9	10.9
Men's footwear	100.0	8.3	22.4	33.2	14.3	22.5	5.2	18.0
Boys' footwear	100.0	22.4	11.5	35.7	14.1	19.3	9.2	10.4
Women's footwear	100.0	10.3	19.9	25.6	6.5	36.9	30.1	6.2
Girls' footwear	100.0	7.2	28.9	28.5	12.1	23.0	11.4	11.9
TRANSPORTATION	**100.0**	**1.2**	**12.9**	**31.6**	**15.5**	**38.7**	**20.3**	**18.3**
New cars	100.0	–	–	43.0	–	57.0	42.4	14.6
New trucks	100.0	–	–	71.8	28.2	–	–	–
Used cars	100.0	–	34.1	13.1	21.2	31.7	6.2	25.4
Used trucks	100.0	1.0	0.9	3.5	24.4	70.3	40.9	29.4
Airline fares	100.0	4.2	14.1	13.3	11.0	57.5	25.9	31.6
Ship fares	100.0	3.9	11.4	5.5	6.5	72.8	35.8	37.0
HEALTH CARE	**100.0**	**15.8**	**20.2**	**24.7**	**3.5**	**35.4**	**20.4**	**15.1**
Physician's services	100.0	7.4	33.9	10.0	6.4	42.1	15.7	26.5
Dental services	100.0	3.0	27.3	20.9	5.4	43.4	24.7	18.7
Hospital services other than room	100.0	2.0	78.5	4.3	1.0	14.5	2.5	12.0
Care in convalescent or nursing home	100.0	30.5	4.0	38.8	0.3	26.4	19.0	7.4
Nonprescription drugs	100.0	2.7	32.4	9.4	6.7	45.3	10.2	36.6
Prescription drugs	100.0	11.5	25.6	18.9	13.6	30.5	17.0	13.4
ENTERTAINMENT	**100.0**	**7.3**	**23.5**	**20.6**	**12.1**	**36.5**	**22.2**	**14.4**
Toys, games, hobbies, and tricycles	100.0	7.9	28.1	24.2	12.1	27.8	17.4	10.4
Other entertainment	100.0	7.0	20.7	18.4	12.1	41.8	25.1	16.8
Fees for recreational lessons	100.0	0.3	12.1	15.4	10.0	62.2	45.2	17.0
Community antenna or cable TV	100.0	24.8	27.0	18.5	8.0	21.6	16.2	5.4
VCRs and video disc players	100.0	1.0	33.4	22.9	5.6	40.2	26.6	13.6
Pet purchase, supplies, and medicine	100.0	–	5.2	6.7	8.3	75.6	12.0	66.4
Athletic gear, game tables, exercise equipment	100.0	22.5	6.1	27.9	27.5	20.2	17.3	2.6
Photographic equipment	100.0	–	14.3	17.1	8.9	59.7	38.1	21.7
PERSONAL CARE PRODUCTS AND SERVICES	**100.0**	**6.0**	**25.5**	**17.3**	**9.0**	**40.1**	**27.8**	**12.1**
Cosmetics, perfume, bath preparation	100.0	5.7	24.9	18.1	8.4	40.9	28.5	12.3
EDUCATION	**100.0**	**0.8**	**9.6**	**9.6**	**7.3**	**72.5**	**30.2**	**42.3**
College tuition	100.0	0.6	9.3	8.6	7.6	73.9	30.5	43.4
Elementary and high school tuition	100.0	0.4	14.1	5.2	2.8	77.5	34.1	43.4
Other school expenses including rentals	100.0	0.4	4.3	16.0	5.6	73.7	29.2	44.6
College books and supplies	100.0	1.8	12.0	19.5	9.1	57.6	30.4	27.2
Miscellaneous school supplies	100.0	1.1	18.2	9.9	9.6	57.9	17.4	42.0
ALL OTHER GIFTS	**100.0**	**7.7**	**20.6**	**18.1**	**7.9**	**45.4**	**28.9**	**16.6**
Gifts of trip expenses	100.0	4.2	14.1	20.3	7.6	53.8	32.8	21.1
Legal fees	100.0	–	24.6	27.2	13.2	35.0	31.5	3.5
Funeral expenses	100.0	15.4	30.6	15.4	9.2	29.4	24.4	5.0
Cemetery lots, vaults, and maintenance fees	100.0	18.1	43.3	9.3	0.8	28.4	24.0	4.5
Miscellaneous personal services	100.0	0.1	0.3	11.3	0.0	83.3	10.3	76.3

Note: Numbers may not add to total because of rounding. (–) means sample is too small to make a reliable estimate. Expenditures for items in a given category may not add to category total because categories with annual spending of less than $2.00 for the average household are omitted. Spending on gifts is also included in the product and service categories in other chapters.
Source: Calculations by New Strategist based on the 2003 Consumer Expenditure Survey

Spending on Health Care, 2003

American households spent 9 percent more on out-of-pocket health care costs in 2003 than in 2000, after adjusting for inflation. Out-of-pocket spending on health insurance rose a substantial 19 percent during those years, while prescription drug spending was up 7 percent. Out-of-pocket spending on medical services fell 3 percent, however, as managed care limited services. Out-of-pocket health care costs absorbed 5.9 percent of the household budget in 2003, up from 5.4 percent in 2000.

Not surprisingly, out-of-pocket health care spending rises with age, peaking among house-holders aged 75 or older at more than $3,800 in 2003. Householders aged 75 or older spend more than any other age group on out-of-pocket health insurance costs ($2,031). The oldest age group also spends the most out-of-pocket on prescription drugs ($823). Householders aged 55 to 64 spend the most on medical services ($742).

Out-of-pocket spending on health care rises with income, largely because household size also grows with income. In 2003, households with incomes of $100,000 or more spent $3,809 out-of-pocket on health care, 53 percent more than the average household. Spending on health care is below average only for households with incomes below $40,000.

Married couples without children at home, most of them older empty-nesters, spend the most out-of-pocket on health care, $3,713 in 2003—54 percent more than the average household. Married couples with children at home spend just 14 percent more than the average household on health care overall, but they spend 44 percent more than average on physician services.

Asians, blacks and Hispanics spend far less than the average household out-of-pocket on almost every health care category, while whites and others and non-Hispanics spend more. One factor behind these differences is the older age of the white and other and non-Hispanic popula-tions. There are some exceptions, however. Asian households spend more than twice the average on vitamins, for example.

Households in the Northeast spend 12 percent less than average out-of-pocket on health care, while households in the Midwest spend 7 percent more. Households in the South spend 16 percent more than average out-of-pocket on prescription drugs, while those in the West spend 16 percent less than average on this item. Average household out-of-pocket spending on dental services is 37 percent above average in the West and 16 percent below average in the South.

College graduates spend the most on out-of-pocket health care costs, an average of $3,031 in 2003—25 percent more than the average household. They spend 47 percent more than average out-of-pocket on medical services and 58 percent more on eyeglasses and contact lenses. But college graduates spend only an average amount out-of-pocket on prescription drugs.

Table 7.1 Health Care: Average spending by age, 2003

(average annual out-of-pocket spending of consumer units (CU) on health care, by age of consumer unit reference person, 2003)

	total consumer units	under 25	25 to 34	35 to 44	45 to 54	55 to 64	65 to 74	75+
Number of consumer units (000)	115,356	8,584	19,737	24,413	23,131	16,580	11,495	11,417
Average number of persons per CU	2.5	1.8	2.9	3.2	2.6	2.1	1.9	1.5
Average before-tax income of CU	$51,128.00	$20,680.00	$50,389.00	$61,091.00	$68,028.00	$58,672.00	$35,314.00	$25,492.00
Average spending of CU, total	40,817.33	22,395.53	40,525.22	47,175.06	50,100.86	44,190.65	33,629.17	25,016.38
Health care, average spending	2,416.39	546.26	1,467.74	2,104.68	2,479.46	3,059.00	3,625.67	3,856.38
HEALTH INSURANCE	1,251.62	280.62	809.56	1,109.48	1,165.96	1,571.83	1,973.71	2,031.33
Commercial health insurance	249.19	77.76	195.08	307.16	294.30	382.86	179.51	132.35
Traditional fee-for-service health plan (not BCBS)	81.75	25.36	39.14	83.20	79.71	156.56	76.71	95.31
Preferred-provider health plan (not BCBS)	167.44	52.40	155.93	223.96	214.59	226.30	102.80	37.05
Blue Cross, Blue Shield	350.88	81.14	254.96	342.95	380.66	527.14	350.24	420.85
Traditional fee-for-service health plan	63.91	10.53	30.54	68.02	68.88	121.14	50.94	72.80
Preferred-provider health plan	124.05	32.11	114.32	129.94	151.13	218.59	68.88	60.84
Health maintenance organization	109.20	32.92	96.55	129.64	139.97	143.48	68.10	73.97
Commercial Medicare supplement	46.84	5.46	10.84	9.58	15.12	29.53	154.47	200.89
Other BCBS health insurance	6.88	0.11	2.71	5.77	5.56	14.40	7.85	12.35
Health maintenance plans (HMOs)	278.97	80.46	287.53	335.75	349.81	367.08	175.41	124.87
Medicare payments	215.02	9.89	20.14	35.91	53.80	137.09	859.04	880.52
Commercial Medicare supplements/ other health insurance	157.55	31.38	51.86	87.72	87.40	157.66	409.52	472.75
Commercial Medicare supplement (not BCBS)	102.12	14.30	25.90	36.07	34.64	68.25	325.70	401.96
Other health insurance (not BCBS)	55.43	17.07	25.96	51.65	52.76	89.41	83.81	70.79
MEDICAL SERVICES	590.82	128.54	394.32	597.84	717.80	742.05	681.34	695.11
Physician's services	143.63	41.43	126.67	148.97	182.64	193.74	132.01	98.28
Dental services	227.24	34.16	121.41	247.22	286.90	274.88	306.51	242.82
Eye care services	34.60	11.26	30.30	31.44	47.25	41.29	38.52	27.07
Service by professionals other than physician	38.54	9.55	20.01	42.93	52.34	49.97	34.59	42.45
Lab tests, X-rays	28.93	4.18	21.40	35.56	42.04	38.70	21.13	13.52
Hospital room	26.06	5.45	20.74	24.16	26.00	43.92	36.05	18.97
Hospital services other than room	43.34	17.66	35.71	46.43	43.18	69.71	43.88	30.74
Care in convalescent or nursing home	32.80	1.63	2.69	8.32	21.43	13.24	40.81	204.00
Other medical services	14.40	3.20	15.40	12.82	16.03	16.59	17.11	15.27
DRUGS	466.85	99.77	202.04	300.64	459.01	626.66	837.93	970.51
Nonprescription drugs	70.30	33.82	55.03	65.73	67.11	78.46	108.47	92.91
Nonprescription vitamins	48.02	11.57	26.83	36.58	64.22	62.61	76.92	54.94
Prescription drugs	348.53	54.38	120.18	198.33	327.69	485.59	652.54	822.66
MEDICAL SUPPLIES	107.10	37.33	61.82	96.72	136.69	118.46	132.68	159.42
Eyeglasses and contact lenses	50.97	20.77	32.23	46.75	73.24	62.70	59.94	43.90
Hearing aids	14.40	2.70	3.21	8.99	15.57	11.86	16.06	53.79
Topicals and dressings	30.10	12.40	22.00	33.82	31.63	29.41	32.59	46.47
Medical equipment for general use	3.10	0.62	0.72	1.90	2.98	5.28	7.36	4.43
Supportive, convalescent medical equipment	5.25	0.55	2.27	3.00	7.23	5.31	13.64	6.18
Rental of medical equipment	2.13	0.15	0.80	1.11	4.67	2.58	2.44	1.98
Rental of supportive, convalescent medical equipment	1.15	0.14	0.59	1.15	1.37	1.32	0.64	2.68

Note: Subcategories may not add to total because some are not shown.
Source: Bureau of Labor Statistics, unpublished tables from the 2003 Consumer Expenditure Survey

Table 7.2 Health Care: Indexed spending by age, 2003

(indexed average annual out-of-pocket spending of consumer units (CU) on health care, by age of consumer unit reference person, 2003; index definition: an index of 100 is the average for all consumer units; an index of 132 means that spending by consumer units in that group is 32 percent above the average for all consumer units; an index of 68 indicates spending that is 32 percent below the average for all consumer units)

	total consumer units	under 25	25 to 34	35 to 44	45 to 54	55 to 64	65 to 74	75+
Average spending of CU, total	$40,817	$22,396	$40,525	$47,175	$50,101	$44,191	$33,629	$25,016
Average spending of CU, index	100	55	99	116	123	108	82	61
Health care, spending index	100	23	61	87	103	127	150	160
HEALTH INSURANCE	100	22	65	89	93	126	158	162
Commercial health insurance	100	31	78	123	118	154	72	53
Traditional fee-for-service health plan (not BCBS)	100	31	48	102	98	192	94	117
Preferred-provider health plan (not BCBS)	100	31	93	134	128	135	61	22
Blue Cross, Blue Shield	100	23	73	98	108	150	100	120
Traditional fee-for-service health plan	100	16	48	106	108	190	80	114
Preferred-provider health plan	100	26	92	105	122	176	56	49
Health maintenance organization	100	30	88	119	128	131	62	68
Commercial Medicare supplement	100	12	23	20	32	63	330	429
Other BCBS health insurance	100	2	39	84	81	209	114	180
Health maintenance plans (HMOs)	100	29	113	120	125	132	63	45
Medicare payments	100	5	9	17	25	64	400	410
Commercial Medicare supplements/ other health insurance	100	20	33	56	55	100	260	300
Commercial Medicare supplement (not BCBS)	100	14	25	35	34	67	319	394
Other health insurance (not BCBS)	100	31	47	93	95	161	151	128
MEDICAL SERVICES	100	22	67	101	121	126	115	118
Physician's services	100	29	88	104	127	135	92	68
Dental services	100	15	53	109	126	121	135	107
Eye care services	100	33	88	91	137	119	111	78
Service by professionals other than physician	100	25	52	111	136	130	90	110
Lab tests, X-rays	100	14	74	123	145	134	73	47
Hospital room	100	21	80	93	100	169	138	73
Hospital services other than room	100	41	82	107	100	161	101	71
Care in convalescent or nursing home	100	5	8	25	65	40	124	622
Other medical services	100	22	107	89	111	115	119	106
DRUGS	100	21	43	64	98	134	179	208
Nonprescription drugs	100	48	78	93	95	112	154	132
Nonprescription vitamins	100	24	56	76	134	130	160	114
Prescription drugs	100	16	34	57	94	139	187	236
MEDICAL SUPPLIES	100	35	53	90	128	111	124	149
Eyeglasses and contact lenses	100	41	63	92	144	123	118	86
Hearing aids	100	19	22	62	108	82	112	374
Topicals and dressings	100	41	73	112	105	98	108	154
Medical equipment for general use	100	20	23	61	96	170	237	143
Supportive, convalescent medical equipment	100	10	43	57	138	101	260	118
Rental of medical equipment	100	7	35	52	219	121	115	93
Rental of supportive, convalescent medical equipment	100	12	51	100	119	115	56	233

Source: Calculations by New Strategist based on the 2003 Consumer Expenditure Survey

Table 7.3 Health Care: Total spending by age, 2003

(total annual out-of-pocket spending on health care, by consumer unit (CU) age groups, 2003; numbers in thousands)

	total consumer units	under 25	25 to 34	35 to 44	45 to 54	55 to 64	65 to 74	75+
Number of consumer units	115,356	8,584	19,737	24,413	23,131	16,580	11,495	11,417
Total spending of all CUs	$4,708,523,919	$192,243,230	$799,846,267	$1,151,684,740	$1,158,882,993	$732,680,977	$386,567,309	$285,612,010
Health care, total spending	278,745,085	4,689,096	28,968,784	51,381,553	57,352,389	50,718,220	41,677,077	44,028,290
HEALTH INSURANCE	**144,381,877**	**2,408,842**	**15,978,286**	**27,085,735**	**26,969,821**	**26,060,941**	**22,687,796**	**23,191,695**
Commercial health insurance	**28,745,562**	**667,492**	**3,850,294**	**7,498,697**	**6,807,453**	**6,347,819**	**2,063,467**	**1,511,040**
Traditional fee-for-service health plan (not BCBS)	9,430,353	217,690	772,506	2,031,162	1,843,772	2,595,765	881,781	1,088,154
Preferred-provider health plan (not BCBS)	19,315,209	449,802	3,077,590	5,467,535	4,963,681	3,752,054	1,181,686	423,000
Blue Cross, Blue Shield	**40,476,113**	**696,506**	**5,032,146**	**8,372,438**	**8,805,046**	**8,739,981**	**4,026,009**	**4,804,844**
Traditional fee-for-service health plan	7,372,402	90,390	602,768	1,660,572	1,593,263	2,008,501	585,555	831,158
Preferred-provider health plan	14,309,912	275,632	2,256,334	3,172,225	3,495,788	3,624,222	791,776	694,610
Health maintenance organization	12,596,875	282,585	1,905,607	3,164,901	3,237,646	2,378,898	782,810	844,515
Commercial Medicare supplement	5,403,275	46,869	213,949	233,877	349,741	489,607	1,775,633	2,293,561
Other BCBS health insurance	793,649	944	53,487	140,863	128,608	238,752	90,236	141,000
Health maintenance plans (HMOs)	**32,180,863**	**690,669**	**5,674,980**	**8,196,665**	**8,091,455**	**6,086,186**	**2,016,338**	**1,425,641**
Medicare payments	**24,803,847**	**84,896**	**397,503**	**876,671**	**1,244,448**	**2,272,952**	**9,874,665**	**10,052,897**
Commercial Medicare supplements/ other health insurance	**18,174,338**	**269,366**	**1,023,561**	**2,141,508**	**2,021,649**	**2,614,003**	**4,707,432**	**5,397,387**
Commercial Medicare supplement (not BCBS)	11,780,155	122,751	511,188	880,577	801,258	1,131,585	3,743,922	4,589,177
Other health insurance (not BCBS)	6,394,183	146,529	512,373	1,260,931	1,220,392	1,482,418	963,396	808,209
MEDICAL SERVICES	**68,154,632**	**1,103,387**	**7,782,694**	**14,595,068**	**16,603,432**	**12,303,189**	**7,832,003**	**7,936,071**
Physician's services	16,568,582	355,635	2,500,086	3,636,805	4,224,646	3,212,209	1,517,455	1,122,063
Dental services	26,213,497	293,229	2,396,269	6,035,382	6,636,284	4,557,510	3,523,332	2,772,276
Eye care services	3,991,318	96,656	598,031	767,545	1,092,940	684,588	442,787	309,058
Service by professionals other than physician	4,445,820	81,977	394,937	1,048,050	1,210,677	828,503	397,612	484,652
Lab tests, X-rays	3,337,249	35,881	422,372	868,126	972,427	641,646	242,889	154,358
Hospital room	3,006,177	46,783	409,345	539,818	601,406	728,194	414,395	216,580
Hospital services other than room	4,999,529	151,593	704,808	1,133,496	998,797	1,155,792	504,401	350,959
Care in convalescent or nursing home	3,783,677	13,992	53,093	203,116	495,697	219,519	469,111	2,329,068
Other medical services	1,661,126	27,469	303,950	312,975	370,790	275,062	196,679	174,338
DRUGS	**53,853,949**	**856,426**	**3,987,663**	**7,339,524**	**10,617,360**	**10,390,023**	**9,632,005**	**11,080,313**
Nonprescription drugs	8,109,527	290,311	1,086,127	1,604,666	1,552,321	1,300,867	1,246,863	1,060,753
Nonprescription vitamins	5,539,395	99,317	529,544	893,028	1,485,473	1,038,074	884,195	627,250
Prescription drugs	40,205,027	466,798	2,371,993	4,841,830	7,579,797	8,051,082	7,500,947	9,392,309
MEDICAL SUPPLIES	**12,354,628**	**320,441**	**1,220,141**	**2,361,225**	**3,161,776**	**1,964,067**	**1,525,157**	**1,820,098**
Eyeglasses and contact lenses	5,879,695	178,290	636,124	1,141,308	1,694,114	1,039,566	689,010	501,206
Hearing aids	1,661,126	23,177	63,356	219,473	360,150	196,639	184,610	614,120
Topicals and dressings	3,472,216	106,442	434,214	825,648	731,634	487,618	374,622	530,548
Medical equipment for general use	357,604	5,322	14,211	46,385	68,930	87,542	84,603	50,577
Supportive, convalescent medical equipment	605,619	4,721	44,803	73,239	167,237	88,040	156,792	70,557
Rental of medical equipment	245,708	1,288	15,790	27,098	108,022	42,776	28,048	22,606
Rental of supportive, convalescent medical equipment	132,659	1,202	11,645	28,075	31,689	21,886	7,357	30,598

Note: Numbers may not add to total because of rounding and missing subcategories.
Source: Calculations by New Strategist based on the 2003 Consumer Expenditure Survey

Table 7.4 Health Care: Market shares by age, 2003

(percentage of total annual out-of-pocket spending on health care accounted for by consumer unit age groups, 2003)

	total consumer units	under 25	25 to 34	35 to 44	45 to 54	55 to 64	65 to 74	75+
Share of total consumer units	100.0%	7.4%	17.1%	21.2%	20.1%	14.4%	10.0%	9.9%
Share of total before-tax income	100.0	3.0	16.9	25.3	26.7	16.5	6.9	4.9
Share of total spending	100.0	4.1	17.0	24.5	24.6	15.6	8.2	6.1
Share of health care spending	100.0	1.7	10.4	18.4	20.6	18.2	15.0	15.8
HEALTH INSURANCE	**100.0**	**1.7**	**11.1**	**18.8**	**18.7**	**18.1**	**15.7**	**16.1**
Commercial health insurance	**100.0**	**2.3**	**13.4**	**26.1**	**23.7**	**22.1**	**7.2**	**5.3**
Traditional fee-for-service health plan (not BCBS)	100.0	2.3	8.2	21.5	19.6	27.5	9.4	11.5
Preferred-provider health plan (not BCBS)	100.0	2.3	5.9	28.3	25.7	19.4	6.1	2.2
Blue Cross, Blue Shield	**100.0**	**1.7**	**12.4**	**20.7**	**21.8**	**21.6**	**9.9**	**11.9**
Traditional fee-for-service health plan	100.0	1.2	8.2	22.5	21.6	27.2	7.9	11.3
Preferred-provider health plan	100.0	1.9	15.8	22.2	24.4	25.3	5.5	4.9
Health maintenance organization	100.0	2.2	15.1	25.1	25.7	18.9	6.2	6.7
Commercial Medicare supplement	100.0	0.9	4.0	4.3	6.5	9.1	32.9	42.4
Other BCBS health insurance	100.0	0.1	6.7	17.7	16.2	30.1	11.4	17.8
Health maintenance plans (HMOs)	**100.0**	**2.1**	**17.6**	**25.5**	**25.1**	**18.9**	**6.3**	**4.4**
Medicare payments	**100.0**	**0.3**	**1.6**	**3.5**	**5.0**	**9.2**	**39.8**	**40.5**
Commercial Medicare supplements/ other health insurance	**100.0**	**1.5**	**5.6**	**11.8**	**11.1**	**14.4**	**25.9**	**29.7**
Commercial Medicare supplement (not BCBS)	100.0	1.0	4.3	7.5	6.8	9.6	31.8	39.0
Other health insurance (not BCBS)	100.0	2.3	8.0	19.7	19.1	23.2	15.1	12.6
MEDICAL SERVICES	**100.0**	**1.6**	**11.4**	**21.4**	**24.4**	**18.1**	**11.5**	**11.6**
Physician's services	100.0	2.1	15.1	22.0	25.5	19.4	9.2	6.8
Dental services	100.0	1.1	9.1	23.0	25.3	17.4	13.4	10.6
Eye care services	100.0	2.4	15.0	19.2	27.4	17.2	11.1	7.7
Service by professionals other than physician	100.0	1.8	3.9	23.6	27.2	18.6	8.9	10.9
Lab tests, X-rays	100.0	1.1	12.7	25.0	29.1	19.2	7.3	4.6
Hospital room	100.0	1.6	13.6	19.6	20.0	24.2	13.8	7.2
Hospital services other than room	100.0	3.0	14.1	22.7	20.0	23.1	10.1	7.0
Care in convalescent or nursing home	100.0	0.4	.4	5.4	13.1	5.8	12.4	61.6
Other medical services	100.0	1.7	13.3	18.8	22.3	16.6	11.8	10.5
DRUGS	**100.0**	**1.6**	**7.4**	**13.6**	**19.7**	**19.3**	**17.9**	**20.6**
Nonprescription drugs	100.0	3.6	13.4	19.8	19.1	16.0	15.4	13.1
Nonprescription vitamins	100.0	1.8	9.5	16.1	26.8	18.7	16.0	11.3
Prescription drugs	100.0	1.2	5.9	12.0	18.9	20.0	18.7	23.4
MEDICAL SUPPLIES	**100.0**	**2.6**	**9.9**	**19.1**	**25.6**	**15.9**	**12.3**	**14.7**
Eyeglasses and contact lenses	100.0	3.0	10.3	19.4	28.8	17.7	11.7	8.5
Hearing aids	100.0	1.4	3.3	13.2	21.7	11.8	11.1	37.0
Topicals and dressings	100.0	3.1	12.5	23.8	21.1	14.0	10.8	15.3
Medical equipment for general use	100.0	1.5	4.0	13.0	19.3	24.5	23.7	14.1
Supportive, convalescent medical equipment	100.0	0.8	7.4	12.1	27.6	14.5	25.9	11.7
Rental of medical equipment	100.0	0.5	6.4	11.0	44.0	17.4	11.4	9.2
Rental of supportive, convalescent medical equipment	100.0	0.9	8.8	21.2	23.9	16.5	5.5	23.1

Note: Numbers may not add to total because of rounding.
Source: Calculations by New Strategist based on the 2003 Consumer Expenditure Survey

Table 7.5 Health Care: Average spending by income, 2003

(average annual out-of-pocket spending on health care, by before-tax income of consumer units (CU), 2003; complete income reporters only)

	total complete reporters	under $20,000	$20,000–$39,999	$40,000–$49,999	$50,000–$69,999	$70,000–$79,999	$80,000–$99,999	$100,000 or more
Number of consumer units (000)	97,391	27,100	23,941	8,891	13,890	5,121	6,909	11,537
Average number of persons per CU	2.5	1.8	2.4	2.6	2.8	3.0	3.0	3.1
Average before-tax income of CU	$51,128.00	$10,752.55	$29,072.57	$44,294.00	$58,900.00	$74,560.00	$88,832.00	$154,665.00
Average spending of CU, total	42,741.66	19,862.52	31,684.32	39,756.91	49,788.99	57,128.14	65,957.39	93,514.86
Health care, average spending	**2,495.46**	**1,595.26**	**2,364.65**	**2,629.34**	**2,811.06**	**2,700.11**	**3,335.48**	**3,809.23**
HEALTH INSURANCE	**1,267.17**	**828.88**	**1,225.70**	**1,354.82**	**1,461.18**	**1,399.53**	**1,577.48**	**1,837.07**
Commercial health insurance	**252.96**	**80.37**	**193.31**	**268.01**	**356.67**	**361.53**	**405.77**	**505.97**
Traditional fee-for-service health plan (not BCBS)	83.00	43.21	75.71	102.06	103.24	137.27	103.68	116.09
Preferred-provider health plan (not BCBS)	169.96	37.16	117.59	165.95	253.43	224.26	302.09	389.89
Blue Cross, Blue Shield	**355.50**	**163.22**	**333.80**	**414.97**	**470.59**	**433.70**	**442.76**	**580.80**
Traditional fee-for-service health plan	63.73	29.19	57.36	69.35	92.67	57.60	87.20	107.54
Preferred-provider health plan	127.06	33.94	89.95	145.96	179.18	192.15	211.95	265.79
Health maintenance organization	110.74	37.65	112.13	162.94	151.42	164.22	118.14	162.12
Commercial Medicare supplement	47.23	58.19	70.50	32.95	38.73	11.10	19.48	27.10
Other BCBS health insurance	6.74	4.24	3.87	3.77	8.58	8.63	6.00	18.25
Health maintenance plans (HMOs)	**282.42**	**95.25**	**233.66**	**321.48**	**380.24**	**383.32**	**498.72**	**501.05**
Medicare payments	**219.23**	**341.05**	**277.02**	**180.67**	**130.93**	**96.41**	**89.58**	**81.33**
Commercial Medicare supplements/ other health insurance	**157.07**	**149.00**	**187.91**	**169.68**	**122.75**	**124.58**	**140.65**	**167.92**
Commercial Medicare supplement (not BCBS)	99.22	120.82	132.03	89.78	72.57	59.91	60.57	60.36
Other health insurance (not BCBS)	57.85	28.17	55.88	79.90	50.18	64.67	80.08	107.56
MEDICAL SERVICES	**611.55**	**283.36**	**513.75**	**659.63**	**716.87**	**716.40**	**1,031.91**	**1,122.18**
Physician's services	148.16	56.42	125.31	171.12	181.50	173.74	261.39	274.08
Dental services	236.28	88.29	203.86	220.82	282.68	302.65	420.87	467.22
Eye care services	36.88	13.12	26.85	36.96	52.36	46.96	47.63	83.86
Service by professionals other than physician	39.90	20.96	24.92	45.40	43.27	43.78	60.55	93.09
Lab tests, X-rays	30.10	14.03	21.39	30.22	31.01	29.29	106.18	39.52
Hospital room	26.26	13.61	23.10	46.07	30.78	41.99	26.40	34.75
Hospital services other than room	43.19	26.57	33.11	50.80	69.62	64.15	60.10	38.35
Care in convalescent or nursing home	34.97	41.52	34.96	15.19	9.58	0.74	30.77	83.16
Other medical services	14.07	8.43	20.16	19.87	16.08	13.11	18.02	5.88
DRUGS	**501.29**	**419.96**	**514.35**	**515.51**	**508.40**	**445.83**	**554.68**	**642.04**
Nonprescription drugs	81.04	59.02	83.77	78.04	86.92	95.45	89.36	111.22
Nonprescription vitamins	56.11	45.98	43.04	47.25	52.28	53.71	82.58	107.00
Prescription drugs	364.15	314.96	387.54	390.23	369.20	296.67	382.74	423.82
MEDICAL SUPPLIES	**115.45**	**63.05**	**110.86**	**99.39**	**124.61**	**138.34**	**171.41**	**207.94**
Eyeglasses and contact lenses	54.05	22.36	42.88	53.73	64.34	68.97	83.40	115.36
Hearing aids	14.24	5.12	21.27	6.69	12.85	19.19	24.54	20.23
Topicals and dressings	35.47	24.72	35.81	23.67	36.34	36.88	54.66	58.17
Medical equipment for general use	3.00	2.48	3.29	2.71	3.93	4.60	0.10	3.77
Supportive, convalescent medical equipment	5.19	3.82	4.05	10.64	4.97	4.83	5.36	6.89
Rental of medical equipment	2.29	4.07	1.98	0.71	0.68	2.79	1.79	2.01
Rental of supportive, convalescent medical equipment	1.20	0.48	1.58	1.23	1.51	1.09	1.57	1.51

Note: Subcategories may not add to total because some are not shown.
Source: Bureau of Labor Statistics, unpublished tables from the 2003 Consumer Expenditure Survey; calculations by New Strategist

Table 7.6 Health Care: Indexed spending by income, 2003

(indexed average annual out-of-pocket spending of consumer units (CU) on health care, by before-tax income of consumer unit, 2003; complete income reporters only; index definition: an index of 100 is the average for all consumer units; an index of 132 means that spending by consumer units in that group is 32 percent above the average for all consumer units; an index of 68 indicates spending that is 32 percent below the average for all consumer units)

	total complete reporters	under $20,000	$20,000– $39,999	$40,000– $49,999	$50,000– $69,999	$70,000– $79,999	$80,000– $99,999	$100,000 or more
Average spending of CU, total	$42,742	$19,863	$31,684	$39,757	$49,789	$57,128	$65,957	$93,515
Average spending of CU, index	100	46	74	93	116	134	154	219
Health care, spending index	**100**	**64**	**95**	**105**	**113**	**108**	**134**	**153**
HEALTH INSURANCE	**100**	**65**	**97**	**107**	**115**	**110**	**124**	**145**
Commercial health insurance	**100**	**32**	**76**	**105**	**141**	**143**	**160**	**200**
Traditional fee-for-service health plan (not BCBS)	100	52	91	123	124	165	125	140
Preferred-provider health plan (not BCBS)	100	22	69	98	149	132	178	229
Blue Cross, Blue Shield	**100**	**46**	**94**	**117**	**132**	**122**	**125**	**163**
Traditional fee-for-service health plan	100	46	90	109	145	90	137	169
Preferred-provider health plan	100	27	71	115	141	151	167	209
Health maintenance organization	100	34	101	147	137	148	107	146
Commercial Medicare supplement	100	123	149	70	82	24	41	57
Other BCBS health insurance	100	63	57	56	127	128	89	271
Health maintenance plans (HMOs)	**100**	**34**	**83**	**114**	**135**	**136**	**177**	**177**
Medicare payments	**100**	**156**	**126**	**82**	**60**	**44**	**41**	**37**
Commercial Medicare supplements/ other health insurance	**100**	**95**	**120**	**108**	**78**	**79**	**90**	**107**
Commercial Medicare supplement (not BCBS)	100	122	133	90	73	60	61	61
Other health insurance (not BCBS)	100	49	97	138	87	112	138	186
MEDICAL SERVICES	**100**	**46**	**84**	**108**	**117**	**117**	**169**	**183**
Physician's services	100	38	85	115	123	117	176	185
Dental services	100	37	86	93	120	128	178	198
Eye care services	100	36	73	100	142	127	129	227
Service by professionals other than physician	100	53	62	114	108	110	152	233
Lab tests, X-rays	100	47	71	100	103	97	353	131
Hospital room	100	52	88	175	117	160	101	132
Hospital services other than room	100	62	77	141	161	149	139	89
Care in convalescent or nursing home	100	119	100	43	27	2	88	238
Other medical services	100	60	143	141	114	93	128	42
DRUGS	**100**	**84**	**103**	**103**	**101**	**89**	**111**	**128**
Nonprescription drugs	100	73	103	96	107	118	110	137
Nonprescription vitamins	100	82	77	84	93	96	147	191
Prescription drugs	100	86	106	107	101	81	105	116
MEDICAL SUPPLIES	**100**	**55**	**96**	**86**	**108**	**120**	**148**	**180**
Eyeglasses and contact lenses	100	41	79	99	119	128	154	213
Hearing aids	100	36	149	47	90	135	172	142
Topicals and dressings	100	70	101	67	102	104	154	164
Medical equipment for general use	100	83	110	90	131	153	3	126
Supportive, convalescent medical equipment	100	74	78	205	96	93	103	133
Rental of medical equipment	100	178	86	31	30	122	78	88
Rental of supportive, convalescent medical equipment	100	40	132	103	126	91	131	126

Source: Calculations by New Strategist based on the 2003 Consumer Expenditure Survey

Table 7.7 Health Care: Total spending by income, 2003

(total annual out-of-pocket spending on health care, by before-tax income group of consumer units (CU), 2003; complete income reporters only; numbers in thousands)

	total complete reporters	under $20,000	$20,000– $39,999	$40,000– $49,999	$50,000– $69,999	$70,000– $79,999	$80,000– $99,999	$100,000 or more
Number of consumer units	97,391	27,100	23,941	8,891	13,890	5,121	6,909	11,537
Total spending of all CUs	$4,162,653,009	$538,274,380	$758,554,310	$353,478,687	$691,569,071	$292,553,205	$455,699,608	$1,078,880,940
Health care, total spending	**243,035,345**	**43,231,512**	**56,612,146**	**23,377,462**	**39,045,623**	**13,827,263**	**23,044,831**	**43,947,087**
HEALTH INSURANCE	**123,410,953**	**22,462,672**	**29,344,428**	**12,045,705**	**20,295,790**	**7,166,993**	**10,898,809**	**21,194,277**
Commercial health insurance	**24,636,027**	**2,177,985**	**4,628,036**	**2,382,877**	**4,954,146**	**1,851,395**	**2,803,465**	**5,837,376**
Traditional fee-for-service health plan (not BCBS)	8,083,453	1,171,077	1,812,604	907,415	1,434,004	702,960	716,325	1,339,330
Preferred-provider health plan (not BCBS)	16,552,574	1,007,026	2,815,324	1,475,461	3,520,143	1,148,435	2,087,140	4,498,161
Blue Cross, Blue Shield	**34,622,501**	**4,423,248**	**7,991,536**	**3,689,498**	**6,536,495**	**2,220,978**	**3,059,029**	**6,700,690**
Traditional fee-for-service health plan	6,206,728	791,086	1,373,157	616,591	1,287,186	294,970	602,465	1,240,689
Preferred-provider health plan	12,374,500	919,864	2,153,451	1,297,730	2,488,810	984,000	1,464,363	3,066,419
Health maintenance organization	10,785,079	1,020,396	2,684,418	1,448,700	2,103,224	840,971	816,229	1,870,378
Commercial Medicare supplement	4,599,777	1,577,049	1,687,895	292,958	537,960	56,843	134,587	312,653
Other BCBS health insurance	656,415	114,843	92,615	33,519	119,176	44,194	41,454	210,550
Health maintenance plans (HMOs)	**27,505,166**	**2,581,241**	**5,594,040**	**2,858,279**	**5,281,534**	**1,962,982**	**3,445,656**	**5,780,614**
Medicare payments	**21,351,029**	**9,242,339**	**6,632,159**	**1,606,337**	**1,818,618**	**493,716**	**618,908**	**938,304**
Commercial Medicare supplements/ other health insurance	**15,297,204**	**4,037,788**	**4,498,657**	**1,508,625**	**1,704,998**	**637,974**	**971,751**	**1,937,293**
Commercial Medicare supplement (not BCBS)	9,663,135	3,274,343	3,161,017	798,234	1,007,997	306,799	418,478	696,373
Other health insurance (not BCBS)	5,634,069	763,371	1,337,772	710,391	697,000	331,175	553,273	1,240,920
MEDICAL SERVICES	**59,559,466**	**7,679,067**	**12,299,705**	**5,864,770**	**9,957,324**	**3,668,684**	**7,129,466**	**12,946,591**
Physician's services	14,429,451	1,528,864	3,000,033	1,521,428	2,521,035	889,723	1,805,944	3,162,061
Dental services	23,011,545	2,392,755	4,880,516	1,963,311	3,926,425	1,549,871	2,907,791	5,390,317
Eye care services	3,591,780	355,669	642,874	328,611	727,280	240,482	329,076	967,493
Service by professionals other than physician	3,885,901	567,887	596,499	403,651	601,020	224,197	418,340	1,073,979
Lab tests, X-rays	2,931,469	380,080	512,155	268,686	430,729	149,994	733,598	455,942
Hospital room	2,557,488	368,809	552,954	409,608	427,534	215,031	182,398	400,911
Hospital services other than room	4,206,317	720,030	792,805	540,573	967,022	328,512	415,231	442,444
Care in convalescent or nursing home	3,405,763	1,125,155	836,858	135,054	133,066	3,790	212,590	959,417
Other medical services	1,370,291	228,497	482,751	176,664	223,351	67,136	124,500	67,838
DRUGS	**48,821,134**	**11,381,010**	**12,314,152**	**4,583,399**	**7,061,676**	**2,283,095**	**3,832,284**	**7,407,215**
Nonprescription drugs	7,892,567	1,599,519	2,005,620	693,854	1,207,319	488,799	617,388	1,283,145
Nonprescription vitamins	5,464,609	1,246,152	1,030,356	420,100	726,169	275,049	570,545	1,234,459
Prescription drugs	35,464,933	8,535,342	9,278,044	3,469,535	5,128,188	1,519,247	2,644,351	4,889,611
MEDICAL SUPPLIES	**11,243,791**	**1,708,709**	**2,653,993**	**883,676**	**1,730,833**	**708,439**	**1,184,272**	**2,399,004**
Eyeglasses and contact lenses	5,263,984	606,010	1,026,591	477,713	893,683	353,195	576,211	1,330,908
Hearing aids	1,386,848	138,868	509,110	59,481	178,487	98,272	169,547	233,394
Topicals and dressings	3,454,459	669,933	857,215	210,450	504,763	188,862	377,646	671,107
Medical equipment for general use	292,173	67,249	78,779	24,095	54,588	23,557	691	43,494
Supportive, convalescent medical equipment	505,459	103,430	96,994	94,600	69,033	24,734	37,032	79,490
Rental of medical equipment	223,025	110,389	47,332	6,313	9,445	14,288	12,367	23,189
Rental of supportive, convalescent medical equipment	116,869	13,028	37,865	10,936	20,974	5,582	10,847	17,421

Note: Numbers may not add to total because of rounding and missing subcategories.
Source: Calculations by New Strategist based on the 2003 Consumer Expenditure Survey

Table 7.8 Health Care: Market shares by income, 2003

(percentage of total annual out-of-pocket spending on health care accounted for by before-tax income group of consumer units, 2003; complete income reporters only)

	total complete reporters	under $20,000	$20,000–$39,999	$40,000–$49,999	$50,000–$69,999	$70,000–$79,999	$80,000–$99,999	$100,000 or more
Share of total consumer units	100.0%	27.8%	24.6%	9.1%	14.3%	5.3%	7.1%	11.8%
Share of total before-tax income	100.0	5.9	14.0	7.9	16.4	7.7	12.3	35.8
Share of total spending	100.0	12.9	18.2	8.5	16.6	7.0	10.9	25.9
Share of health care spending	100.0	17.8	23.3	9.6	16.1	5.7	9.5	18.1
HEALTH INSURANCE	**100.0**	**18.2**	**23.8**	**9.8**	**16.4**	**5.8**	**8.8**	**17.2**
Commercial health insurance	**100.0**	**8.8**	**18.8**	**9.7**	**20.1**	**7.5**	**11.4**	**23.7**
Traditional fee-for-service health plan (not BCBS)	100.0	14.5	22.4	11.2	17.7	8.7	8.9	16.6
Preferred-provider health plan (not BCBS)	100.0	6.1	17.0	8.9	21.3	6.9	12.6	27.2
Blue Cross, Blue Shield	**100.0**	**12.8**	**23.1**	**10.7**	**18.9**	**6.4**	**8.8**	**19.4**
Traditional fee-for-service health plan	100.0	12.7	22.1	9.9	20.7	4.8	9.7	20.0
Preferred-provider health plan	100.0	7.4	17.4	10.5	20.1	8.0	11.8	24.8
Health maintenance organization	100.0	9.5	24.9	13.4	19.5	7.8	7.6	17.3
Commercial Medicare supplement	100.0	34.3	36.7	6.4	11.7	1.2	2.9	6.8
Other BCBS health insurance	100.0	17.5	14.1	5.1	18.2	6.7	6.3	32.1
Health maintenance plans (HMOs)	**100.0**	**9.4**	**20.3**	**10.4**	**19.2**	**7.1**	**12.5**	**21.0**
Medicare payments	**100.0**	**43.3**	**31.1**	**7.5**	**8.5**	**2.3**	**2.9**	**4.4**
Commercial Medicare supplements/ other health insurance	**100.0**	**26.4**	**29.4**	**9.9**	**11.1**	**4.2**	**6.4**	**12.7**
Commercial Medicare supplement (not BCBS)	100.0	33.9	32.7	8.3	10.4	3.2	4.3	7.2
Other health insurance (not BCBS)	100.0	13.5	23.7	12.6	12.4	5.9	9.8	22.0
MEDICAL SERVICES	**100.0**	**12.9**	**20.7**	**9.8**	**16.7**	**6.2**	**12.0**	**21.7**
Physician's services	100.0	10.6	20.8	10.5	17.5	6.2	12.5	21.9
Dental services	100.0	10.4	21.2	8.5	17.1	6.7	12.6	23.4
Eye care services	100.0	9.9	17.9	9.1	20.2	6.7	9.2	26.9
Service by professionals other than physician	100.0	14.6	15.4	10.4	15.5	5.8	10.8	27.6
Lab tests, X-rays	100.0	13.0	17.5	9.2	14.7	5.1	25.0	15.6
Hospital room	100.0	14.4	21.5	16.0	16.7	8.4	7.1	15.7
Hospital services other than room	100.0	17.1	18.3	12.9	23.0	7.8	9.9	10.5
Care in convalescent or nursing home	100.0	33.0	24.6	4.0	3.9	0.1	6.2	28.2
Other medical services	100.0	16.7	35.2	12.9	16.3	4.9	9.1	5.0
DRUGS	**100.0**	**23.3**	**25.2**	**9.4**	**14.5**	**4.7**	**7.8**	**15.2**
Nonprescription drugs	100.0	20.3	25.4	8.8	15.3	6.2	7.8	16.3
Nonprescription vitamins	100.0	22.8	18.9	7.7	13.3	5.0	10.4	22.6
Prescription drugs	100.0	24.1	26.2	9.8	14.5	4.3	7.5	13.8
MEDICAL SUPPLIES	**100.0**	**15.2**	**23.6**	**7.9**	**15.4**	**6.3**	**10.5**	**21.3**
Eyeglasses and contact lenses	100.0	11.5	19.5	9.1	17.0	6.7	10.9	25.3
Hearing aids	100.0	10.0	35.7	4.3	12.9	7.1	12.2	16.8
Topicals and dressings	100.0	19.4	24.3	6.1	14.6	5.5	10.9	19.4
Medical equipment for general use	100.0	23.0	27.0	8.2	18.7	8.1	0.2	14.9
Supportive, convalescent medical equipment	100.0	20.5	19.2	18.7	13.7	4.9	7.3	15.7
Rental of medical equipment	100.0	49.5	21.2	2.8	4.2	6.4	5.5	10.4
Rental of supportive, convalescent medical equipment	100.0	11.1	32.4	9.4	17.9	4.8	9.3	14.9

Note: Numbers may not add to total because of rounding.
Source: Calculations by New Strategist based on the 2003 Consumer Expenditure Survey

Table 7.9 Health Care: Average spending by high-income consumer units, 2003

(average annual out-of-pocket spending on health care, by before-tax income of high-income consumer units (CU), 2003; complete income reporters only)

	total complete reporters	$100,000 or more	$100,000–$119,999	$120,000–$149,999	$150,000 or more
Number of consumer units (000)	97,391	11,537	4,384	3,151	4,002
Average number of persons per CU	2.5	3.1	3.1	3.1	3.1
Average before-tax income of CU	$51,128.00	$154,665.00	$108,087.00	$131,885.00	$223,634.00
Average spending of CU, total	42,741.66	93,514.86	75,601.50	86,451.46	118,674.11
Health care, average spending	**2,495.46**	**3,809.23**	**3,464.95**	**3,478.15**	**4,447.00**
HEALTH INSURANCE	**1,267.17**	**1,837.07**	**1,668.97**	**1,717.97**	**2,115.02**
Commercial health insurance	**252.96**	**505.97**	**432.72**	**529.76**	**567.50**
Traditional fee-for-service health plan (not BCBS)	83.00	116.09	102.34	135.32	115.99
Preferred-provider health plan (not BCBS)	169.96	389.89	330.37	394.44	451.51
Blue Cross, Blue Shield	**355.50**	**580.80**	**480.65**	**566.86**	**701.50**
Traditional fee-for-service health plan	63.73	107.54	53.56	93.27	177.91
Preferred-provider health plan	127.06	265.79	202.88	309.04	300.66
Health maintenance organization	110.74	162.12	190.84	133.30	153.35
Commercial Medicare supplement	47.23	27.10	14.76	19.76	46.40
Other BCBS health insurance	6.74	18.25	18.61	11.48	23.18
Health maintenance plans (HMOs)	**282.42**	**501.05**	**527.84**	**405.13**	**547.23**
Medicare payments	**219.23**	**81.33**	**84.15**	**85.13**	**75.24**
Commercial Medicare supplements/ other health insurance	**157.07**	**167.92**	**143.61**	**131.09**	**223.54**
Commercial Medicare supplement (not BCBS)	99.22	60.36	57.40	45.20	75.53
Other health insurance (not BCBS)	57.85	107.56	86.21	85.89	148.01
MEDICAL SERVICES	**611.55**	**1,122.18**	**971.56**	**890.42**	**1,469.71**
Physician's services	148.16	274.08	210.30	231.19	377.72
Dental services	236.28	467.22	524.50	420.27	441.43
Eye care services	36.88	83.86	52.92	46.33	147.32
Service by professionals other than physician	39.90	93.09	58.02	93.46	131.23
Lab tests, X-rays	30.10	39.52	39.90	29.81	46.76
Hospital room	26.26	34.75	33.83	42.60	29.59
Hospital services other than room	43.19	38.35	29.84	31.12	53.37
Care in convalescent or nursing home	34.97	83.16	8.92	9.80	222.26
Other medical services	14.07	5.88	–	–	–
DRUGS	**501.29**	**642.04**	**621.59**	**678.18**	**635.98**
Nonprescription drugs	81.04	111.22	88.25	121.38	128.30
Nonprescription vitamins	56.11	107.00	132.48	93.90	89.47
Prescription drugs	364.15	423.82	400.86	462.90	418.21
MEDICAL SUPPLIES	**115.45**	**207.94**	**202.84**	**191.58**	**226.30**
Eyeglasses and contact lenses	54.05	115.36	100.40	123.51	125.33
Hearing aids	14.24	20.23	26.12	12.89	19.56
Topicals and dressings	35.47	58.17	63.55	42.51	64.49
Medical equipment for general use	3.00	3.77	2.02	2.81	6.43
Supportive, convalescent medical equipment	5.19	6.89	8.17	5.42	6.66
Rental of medical equipment	2.29	2.01	1.17	3.04	2.11
Rental of supportive, convalescent medical equipment	1.20	1.51	1.39	1.40	1.72

Note: Subcategories may not add to total because some are not shown. (–) means sample is too small to make a reliable estimate.
Source: Bureau of Labor Statistics, unpublished tables from the 2003 Consumer Expenditure Survey; calculations by New Strategist

Table 7.10 Health Care: Indexed spending by high-income consumer units, 2003

(indexed average annual out-of-pocket spending of consumer units (CU) on health care, by before-tax income of high-income consumer unit, 2003; complete income reporters only; index definition: an index of 100 is the average for all consumer units, an index of 132 means that spending by consumer units in that group is 32 percent above the average for all consumer units; an index of 68 indicates spending that is 32 percent below the average for all consumer units)

	total complete reporters	$100,000 or more	$100,000–$119,999	$120,000–$149,999	$150,000 or more
Average spending of CU, total	$42,742	$93,515	$75,602	$86,451	$118,674
Average spending of CU, index	100	219	177	202	278
Health care, spending index	100	153	139	139	178
HEALTH INSURANCE	100	145	132	136	167
Commercial health insurance	100	200	171	209	224
Traditional fee-for-service health plan (not BCBS)	100	140	123	163	140
Preferred-provider health plan (not BCBS)	100	229	194	232	266
Blue Cross, Blue Shield	100	163	135	159	197
Traditional fee-for-service health plan	100	169	84	146	279
Preferred-provider health plan	100	209	160	243	237
Health maintenance organization	100	146	172	120	138
Commercial Medicare supplement	100	57	31	42	98
Other BCBS health insurance	100	271	276	170	344
Health maintenance plans (HMOs)	100	177	187	143	194
Medicare payments	100	37	38	39	34
Commercial Medicare supplements/ other health insurance	100	107	91	83	142
Commercial Medicare supplement (not BCBS)	100	61	58	46	76
Other health insurance (not BCBS)	100	186	149	148	256
MEDICAL SERVICES	100	183	159	146	240
Physician's services	100	185	142	156	255
Dental services	100	198	222	178	187
Eye care services	100	227	143	126	399
Service by professionals other than physician	100	233	145	234	329
Lab tests, X-rays	100	131	133	99	155
Hospital room	100	132	129	162	113
Hospital services other than room	100	89	69	72	124
Care in convalescent or nursing home	100	238	26	28	636
Other medical services	100	42	–	–	–
DRUGS	100	128	124	135	127
Nonprescription drugs	100	137	109	150	158
Nonprescription vitamins	100	191	236	167	159
Prescription drugs	100	116	110	127	115
MEDICAL SUPPLIES	100	180	176	166	196
Eyeglasses and contact lenses	100	213	186	229	232
Hearing aids	100	142	183	91	137
Topicals and dressings	100	164	179	120	182
Medical equipment for general use	100	126	67	94	214
Supportive, convalescent medical equipment	100	133	157	104	128
Rental of medical equipment	100	88	51	133	92
Rental of supportive, convalescent medical equipment	100	126	116	117	143

Note: (–) means sample is too small to make a reliable estimate.
Source: Calculations by New Strategist based on the 2003 Consumer Expenditure Survey

Table 7.11 Health Care: Total spending by high-income consumer units, 2003

(total annual out-of-pocket spending on health care, by before-tax income group of high-income consumer units (CU), 2003; complete income reporters only; numbers in thousands)

	total complete reporters	$100,000 or more	$100,000–$119,999	$120,000–$149,999	$150,000 or more
Number of consumer units	97,391	11,537	4,384	3,151	4,002
Total spending of all CUs	$4,162,653,009	$1,078,880,940	$331,436,976	$272,408,550	$474,933,788
Health care, total spending	243,035,345	43,947,087	15,190,341	10,959,651	17,796,894
HEALTH INSURANCE	123,410,953	21,194,277	7,316,764	5,413,323	8,464,310
Commercial health insurance	24,636,027	5,837,376	1,897,044	1,669,274	2,271,135
Traditional fee-for-service health plan (not BCBS)	8,083,453	1,339,330	448,659	426,393	464,192
Preferred-provider health plan (not BCBS)	16,552,574	4,498,161	1,448,342	1,242,880	1,806,943
Blue Cross, Blue Shield	34,622,501	6,700,690	2,107,170	1,786,176	2,807,403
Traditional fee-for-service health plan	6,206,728	1,240,689	234,807	293,894	711,996
Preferred-provider health plan	12,374,500	3,066,419	889,426	973,785	1,203,241
Health maintenance organization	10,785,079	1,870,378	836,643	420,028	613,707
Commercial Medicare supplement	4,599,777	312,653	64,708	62,264	185,693
Other BCBS health insurance	656,415	210,550	81,586	36,173	92,766
Health maintenance plans (HMOs)	27,505,166	5,780,614	2,314,051	1,276,565	2,190,014
Medicare payments	21,351,029	938,304	368,914	268,245	301,110
Commercial Medicare supplements/ other health insurance	15,297,204	1,937,293	629,586	413,065	894,607
Commercial Medicare supplement (not BCBS)	9,663,135	696,373	251,642	142,425	302,271
Other health insurance (not BCBS)	5,634,069	1,240,920	377,945	270,639	592,336
MEDICAL SERVICES	59,559,466	12,946,591	4,259,319	2,805,713	5,881,779
Physician's services	14,429,451	3,162,061	921,955	728,480	1,511,635
Dental services	23,011,545	5,390,317	2,299,408	1,324,271	1,766,603
Eye care services	3,591,780	967,493	232,001	145,986	589,575
Service by professionals other than physician	3,885,901	1,073,979	254,360	294,492	525,182
Lab tests, X-rays	2,931,469	455,942	174,922	93,931	187,134
Hospital room	2,557,488	400,911	148,311	134,233	118,419
Hospital services other than room	4,206,317	442,444	130,819	98,059	213,587
Care in convalescent or nursing home	3,405,763	959,417	39,105	30,880	889,485
Other medical services	1,370,291	67,838	–	–	–
DRUGS	48,821,134	7,407,215	2,725,051	2,136,945	2,545,192
Nonprescription drugs	7,892,567	1,283,145	386,888	382,468	513,457
Nonprescription vitamins	5,464,609	1,234,459	580,792	295,879	358,059
Prescription drugs	35,464,933	4,889,611	1,757,370	1,458,598	1,673,676
MEDICAL SUPPLIES	11,243,791	2,399,004	889,251	603,669	905,653
Eyeglasses and contact lenses	5,263,984	1,330,908	440,154	389,180	501,571
Hearing aids	1,386,848	233,394	114,510	40,616	78,279
Topicals and dressings	3,454,459	671,107	278,603	133,949	258,089
Medical equipment for general use	292,173	43,494	8,856	8,854	25,733
Supportive, convalescent medical equipment	505,459	79,490	35,817	17,078	26,653
Rental of medical equipment	223,025	23,189	5,129	9,579	8,444
Rental of supportive, convalescent medical equipment	116,869	17,421	6,094	4,411	6,883

Note: Numbers may not add to total because of rounding and missing subcategories. (–) means sample is too small to make a reliable estimate.
Source: Calculations by New Strategist based on the 2003 Consumer Expenditure Survey

Table 7.12 Health Care: Market shares by high-income consumer units, 2003

(percentage of total annual out-of-pocket spending on health care accounted for by before-tax income group of high-income consumer units, 2003; complete income reporters only)

	total complete reporters	$100,000 or more	$100,000–$119,999	$120,000–$149,999	$150,000 or more
Share of total consumer units	100.0%	11.8%	4.5%	3.2%	4.1%
Share of total before-tax income	100.0	35.8	9.5	8.3	18.0
Share of total spending	100.0	25.9	8.0	6.5	11.4
Share of health care spending	100.0	18.1	6.3	4.5	7.3
HEALTH INSURANCE	100.0	17.2	5.9	4.4	6.9
Commercial health insurance	100.0	23.7	7.7	6.8	9.2
Traditional fee-for-service health plan (not BCBS)	100.0	16.6	5.6	5.3	5.7
Preferred-provider health plan (not BCBS)	100.0	27.2	8.7	7.5	10.9
Blue Cross, Blue Shield	100.0	19.4	6.1	5.2	8.1
Traditional fee-for-service health plan	100.0	20.0	3.8	4.7	11.5
Preferred-provider health plan	100.0	24.8	7.2	7.9	9.7
Health maintenance organization	100.0	17.3	7.8	3.9	5.7
Commercial Medicare supplement	100.0	6.8	1.4	1.4	4.0
Other BCBS health insurance	100.0	32.1	12.4	5.5	14.1
Health maintenance plans (HMOs)	100.0	21.0	8.4	4.6	8.0
Medicare payments	100.0	4.4	1.7	1.3	1.4
Commercial Medicare supplements/ other health insurance	100.0	12.7	4.1	2.7	5.8
Commercial Medicare supplement (not BCBS)	100.0	7.2	2.6	1.5	3.1
Other health insurance (not BCBS)	100.0	22.0	6.7	4.8	10.5
MEDICAL SERVICES	100.0	21.7	7.2	4.7	9.9
Physician's services	100.0	21.9	6.4	5.0	10.5
Dental services	100.0	23.4	10.0	5.8	7.7
Eye care services	100.0	26.9	6.5	4.1	16.4
Service by professionals other than physician	100.0	27.6	6.5	7.6	13.5
Lab tests, X-rays	100.0	15.6	6.0	3.2	6.4
Hospital room	100.0	15.7	5.8	5.2	4.6
Hospital services other than room	100.0	10.5	3.1	2.3	5.1
Care in convalescent or nursing home	100.0	28.2	1.1	0.9	26.1
Other medical services	100.0	5.0	–	–	–
DRUGS	100.0	15.2	5.6	4.4	5.2
Nonprescription drugs	100.0	16.3	4.9	4.8	6.5
Nonprescription vitamins	100.0	22.6	10.6	5.4	6.6
Prescription drugs	100.0	13.8	5.0	4.1	4.7
MEDICAL SUPPLIES	100.0	21.3	7.9	5.4	8.1
Eyeglasses and contact lenses	100.0	25.3	8.4	7.4	9.5
Hearing aids	100.0	16.8	8.3	2.9	5.6
Topicals and dressings	100.0	19.4	8.1	3.9	7.5
Medical equipment for general use	100.0	14.9	3.0	3.0	8.8
Supportive, convalescent medical equipment	100.0	15.7	7.1	3.4	5.3
Rental of medical equipment	100.0	10.4	2.3	4.3	3.8
Rental of supportive, convalescent medical equipment	100.0	14.9	5.2	3.8	5.9

Note: Numbers may not add to total because of rounding. (–) means sample is too small to make a reliable estimate
Source: Calculations by New Strategist based on the 2003 Consumer Expenditure Survey

Table 7.13 Health Care: Average spending by household type, 2003

(average annual out-of-pocket spending of consumer units (CU) on health care, by type of consumer unit, 2003)

	total married couples	married couples, no children	married couples with children				single parent, at least one child <18	single person
			total	oldest child under 6	oldest child 6 to 17	oldest child 18 or older		
Number of consumer units (000)	58,448	25,132	28,584	5,496	15,047	8,041	6,999	33,929
Average number of persons per CU	3.2	2.0	3.9	3.5	4.1	4.0	2.9	1.0
Average before-tax income of CU	$69,472.00	$62,930.00	$75,557.00	$66,317.00	$77,508.00	$78,307.00	$29,154.00	$27,131.00
Average spending of CU, total	53,030.03	47,895.65	57,702.32	51,503.24	59,183.18	59,180.36	30,534.75	23,657.35
Health care, average spending	**3,201.74**	**3,712.69**	**2,759.95**	**2,177.48**	**2,764.42**	**3,150.92**	**1,200.65**	**1,557.54**
HEALTH INSURANCE	**1,662.76**	**1,906.49**	**1,455.04**	**1,253.43**	**1,428.92**	**1,641.71**	**644.16**	**778.54**
Commercial health insurance	**367.41**	**359.84**	**381.99**	**353.74**	**383.32**	**398.81**	**161.35**	**102.38**
Traditional fee-for-service health plan (not BCBS)	112.79	129.35	97.37	75.27	91.26	123.90	49.43	43.24
Preferred-provider health plan (not BCBS)	254.61	230.48	284.62	278.47	292.07	274.91	111.92	59.13
Blue Cross, Blue Shield	**479.53**	**517.03**	**458.26**	**407.69**	**476.99**	**457.76**	**209.02**	**193.94**
Traditional fee-for-service health plan	87.69	101.72	74.93	78.40	82.07	59.22	36.46	32.51
Preferred-provider health plan	182.85	175.17	195.38	206.42	188.99	199.80	83.97	48.44
Health maintenance organization	146.90	129.61	162.92	110.62	182.83	161.42	69.18	55.91
Commercial Medicare supplement	55.07	103.14	17.69	6.42	13.29	33.62	15.04	49.03
Other BCBS health insurance	7.03	7.38	7.32	5.83	9.81	3.70	4.37	8.05
Health maintenance plans (HMOs)	**400.25**	**319.63**	**464.49**	**410.18**	**461.63**	**506.95**	**189.21**	**114.10**
Medicare payments	**230.32**	**428.27**	**52.43**	**13.93**	**20.32**	**138.84**	**37.47**	**226.95**
Commercial Medicare supplements/ other health insurance	**185.25**	**281.72**	**97.88**	**67.90**	**86.67**	**139.34**	**47.10**	**141.19**
Commercial Medicare supplement (not BCBS)	112.29	196.48	40.10	22.74	24.35	81.43	19.27	100.76
Other health insurance (not BCBS)	72.96	85.23	57.78	45.16	62.32	57.91	27.83	40.42
MEDICAL SERVICES	**809.34**	**846.94**	**783.30**	**536.41**	**844.13**	**838.20**	**329.51**	**359.72**
Physician's services	200.24	197.83	206.97	169.71	211.65	223.70	87.50	74.20
Dental services	327.93	357.17	314.84	149.68	354.45	353.58	165.66	103.48
Eye care services	46.95	44.70	50.85	31.16	52.12	61.95	15.48	18.82
Service by professionals other than physician	49.62	48.22	53.43	37.89	54.33	62.36	15.53	31.22
Lab tests, X-rays	43.31	43.96	29.33	26.68	28.97	31.82	8.16	14.49
Hospital room	39.51	41.80	36.08	45.47	35.18	31.34	7.44	13.42
Hospital services other than room	62.96	61.54	64.28	60.29	70.61	55.18	21.77	20.98
Care in convalescent or nursing home	21.00	30.85	11.04	11.22	14.54	4.37	–	70.47
Other medical services	15.52	15.56	16.47	4.31	22.29	13.89	7.98	12.32
DRUGS	**584.06**	**792.20**	**391.05**	**295.69**	**361.17**	**513.55**	**164.37**	**356.49**
Nonprescription drugs	86.67	90.45	83.03	35.40	77.89	91.79	47.67	46.80
Nonprescription vitamins	58.57	77.64	45.37	33.57	44.87	55.06	11.21	40.95
Prescription drugs	438.83	624.11	262.65	176.72	238.42	366.71	105.49	268.74
MEDICAL SUPPLIES	**145.58**	**167.06**	**130.56**	**91.95**	**130.20**	**157.45**	**62.61**	**62.80**
Eyeglasses and contact lenses	68.94	68.16	71.22	36.37	70.95	95.54	33.67	28.32
Hearing aids	22.52	35.82	13.06	6.33	13.33	17.16	4.37	6.60
Topicals and dressings	39.85	44.65	35.79	41.76	35.00	33.00	20.08	19.11
Medical equipment for general use	3.87	4.75	3.13	1.78	2.90	4.48	2.43	1.99
Supportive, convalescent medical equipment	7.15	9.97	4.67	4.21	5.03	4.31	1.31	2.55
Rental of medical equipment	1.78	1.99	1.65	0.78	1.83	1.89	0.60	3.64
Rental of supportive, convalescent medical equipment	1.47	1.73	1.05	0.71	1.15	1.09	0.16	0.60

Note: Average spending figures for total consumer units can be found on Average Spending by Age and Average Spending by Region tables. Subcategories may not add to total because some are not shown. (–) means sample is too small to make a reliable estimate.
Source: Bureau of Labor Statistics, unpublished tables from the 2003 Consumer Expenditure Survey

Table 7.14 Health Care: Indexed spending by household type, 2003

(indexed average annual out-of-pocket spending of consumer units (CU) on health care, by type of consumer unit, 2003; index definition: an index of 100 is the average for all consumer units; an index of 132 means that spending by consumer units in that group is 32 percent above the average for all consumer units; an index of 68 indicates spending that is 32 percent below the average for all consumer units)

	total married couples	married couples, no children	married couples with children				single parent, at least one child <18	single person
			total	oldest child under 6	oldest child 6 to 17	oldest child 18 or older		
Average spending of CU, total	$53,030	$47,896	$57,702	$51,503	$59,183	$59,180	$30,535	$23,657
Average spending of CU, index	130	117	141	126	145	145	75	58
Health care, spending index	**133**	**154**	**114**	**90**	**114**	**130**	**50**	**64**
HEALTH INSURANCE	**133**	**152**	**116**	**100**	**114**	**131**	**51**	**62**
Commercial health insurance	**147**	**144**	**153**	**142**	**154**	**160**	**65**	**41**
Traditional fee-for-service health plan (not BCBS)	138	158	119	92	112	152	60	53
Preferred-provider health plan (not BCBS)	152	138	170	166	174	164	67	35
Blue Cross, Blue Shield	**137**	**147**	**131**	**116**	**136**	**130**	**60**	**55**
Traditional fee-for-service health plan	137	159	117	123	128	93	57	51
Preferred-provider health plan	147	141	158	166	152	161	68	39
Health maintenance organization	135	119	149	101	167	148	63	51
Commercial Medicare supplement	118	220	38	14	28	72	32	105
Other BCBS health insurance	102	107	106	85	143	54	64	117
Health maintenance plans (HMOs)	**143**	**115**	**167**	**147**	**165**	**182**	**68**	**41**
Medicare payments	**107**	**199**	**24**	**6**	**9**	**65**	**17**	**106**
Commercial Medicare supplements/ other health insurance	**118**	**179**	**62**	**43**	**55**	**88**	**30**	**90**
Commercial Medicare supplement (not BCBS)	110	192	39	22	24	80	19	99
Other health insurance (not BCBS)	132	154	104	81	112	104	50	73
MEDICAL SERVICES	**137**	**143**	**133**	**91**	**143**	**142**	**56**	**61**
Physician's services	139	138	144	118	147	156	61	52
Dental services	144	157	139	66	156	156	73	46
Eye care services	136	129	147	90	151	179	45	54
Service by professionals other than physician	129	125	139	98	141	162	40	81
Lab tests, X-rays	150	152	101	92	100	110	28	50
Hospital room	152	160	138	174	135	120	29	51
Hospital services other than room	145	142	148	139	163	127	50	48
Care in convalescent or nursing home	64	94	34	34	44	13	–	215
Other medical services	108	108	114	30	155	96	55	86
DRUGS	**125**	**170**	**84**	**63**	**77**	**110**	**35**	**76**
Nonprescription drugs	123	129	118	121	111	131	68	67
Nonprescription vitamins	122	162	94	70	93	115	23	85
Prescription drugs	126	179	75	51	68	105	30	77
MEDICAL SUPPLIES	**136**	**156**	**122**	**86**	**122**	**147**	**58**	**59**
Eyeglasses and contact lenses	135	134	140	71	139	187	66	56
Hearing aids	156	249	91	44	93	119	30	46
Topicals and dressings	132	148	119	139	116	110	67	63
Medical equipment for general use	125	153	111	57	94	145	78	64
Supportive, convalescent medical equipment	136	190	89	80	96	82	25	49
Rental of medical equipment	84	93	77	37	86	89	28	171
Rental of supportive, convalescent medical equipment	128	150	91	62	100	95	14	52

Note: Spending index for total consumer units is 100. (–) means sample is too small to make a reliable estimate.
Source: Calculations by New Strategist based on the 2003 Consumer Expenditure Survey

Table 7.15 Health Care: Total spending by household type, 2003

(total annual out-of-pocket spending on health care, by consumer unit (CU) type, 2003; numbers in thousands)

	total married couples	married couples, no children	married couples with children total	oldest child under 6	oldest child 6 to 17	oldest child 18 or older	single parent, at least one child <18	single person
Number of consumer units	58,448	25,132	28,584	5,496	15,047	8,041	6,999	33,929
Total spending of all CUs	$3,099,499,193	$1,203,713,476	$1,649,363,115	$283,061,807	$890,529,309	$475,869,275	$213,712,715	$802,670,228
Health care, total spending	**187,135,300**	**93,307,325**	**78,890,411**	**11,967,430**	**41,596,228**	**25,336,548**	**8,403,349**	**52,845,775**
HEALTH INSURANCE	**97,184,996**	**47,913,907**	**41,590,863**	**6,888,851**	**21,500,959**	**13,200,990**	**4,508,476**	**26,415,084**
Commercial health insurance	**21,474,380**	**9,043,499**	**10,918,802**	**1,944,155**	**5,767,816**	**3,206,831**	**1,129,289**	**3,473,651**
Traditional fee-for-service health plan (not BCBS)	6,592,350	3,250,824	2,783,224	413,684	1,373,189	996,280	345,961	1,467,090
Preferred-provider health plan (not BCBS)	14,881,445	5,792,423	8,135,578	1,530,471	4,394,777	2,210,551	783,328	2,006,222
Blue Cross, Blue Shield	**28,027,569**	**12,993,998**	**13,098,904**	**2,240,664**	**7,177,269**	**3,680,848**	**1,462,931**	**6,580,190**
Traditional fee-for-service health plan	5,125,305	2,556,427	2,141,799	430,886	1,234,907	476,188	255,184	1,103,032
Preferred-provider health plan	10,687,217	4,402,372	5,584,742	1,134,484	2,843,733	1,606,592	587,706	1,643,521
Health maintenance organization	8,586,011	3,257,359	4,656,905	607,968	2,751,043	1,297,978	484,191	1,896,970
Commercial Medicare supplement	3,218,731	2,592,114	505,651	35,284	199,975	270,338	105,265	1,663,539
Other BCBS health insurance	410,889	185,474	209,235	32,042	147,611	29,752	30,586	273,128
Health maintenance plans (HMOs)	**23,393,812**	**8,032,941**	**13,276,982**	**2,254,349**	**6,946,147**	**4,076,385**	**1,324,281**	**3,871,299**
Medicare payments	**13,461,743**	**10,763,282**	**1,498,659**	**76,559**	**305,755**	**1,116,412**	**262,253**	**7,700,187**
Commercial Medicare supplements/ other health insurance	**10,827,492**	**7,080,187**	**2,797,802**	**373,178**	**1,304,123**	**1,120,433**	**329,653**	**4,790,436**
Commercial Medicare supplement (not BCBS)	6,563,126	4,937,935	1,146,218	124,979	366,394	654,779	134,871	3,418,686
Other health insurance (not BCBS)	4,264,366	2,142,000	1,651,584	248,199	937,729	465,654	194,782	1,371,410
MEDICAL SERVICES	**47,304,304**	**21,285,296**	**22,389,847**	**2,948,109**	**12,701,624**	**6,739,966**	**2,306,240**	**12,204,940**
Physician's services	11,703,628	4,971,864	5,916,030	932,726	3,184,698	1,798,772	612,413	2,517,532
Dental services	19,166,853	8,976,396	8,999,387	822,641	5,333,409	2,843,137	1,159,454	3,510,973
Eye care services	2,744,134	1,123,400	1,453,496	171,255	784,250	498,140	108,345	638,544
Service by professionals other than physician	2,900,190	1,211,865	1,527,243	208,243	817,504	501,437	108,694	1,059,263
Lab tests, X-rays	2,531,383	1,104,803	838,369	146,633	435,912	255,865	57,112	491,631
Hospital room	2,309,280	1,050,518	1,031,311	249,903	529,353	252,005	52,073	455,327
Hospital services other than room	3,679,886	1,546,623	1,837,380	331,354	1,062,469	443,702	152,368	711,830
Care in convalescent or nursing home	1,227,408	775,322	315,567	61,665	218,783	35,139	–	2,390,977
Other medical services	907,113	391,054	470,778	23,688	335,398	111,689	55,852	418,005
DRUGS	**34,137,139**	**19,909,570**	**11,177,773**	**1,625,112**	**5,434,525**	**4,129,456**	**1,150,426**	**12,095,349**
Nonprescription drugs	5,065,688	2,273,189	2,373,330	469,358	1,172,011	738,083	333,642	1,587,877
Nonprescription vitamins	3,423,299	1,951,248	1,296,856	184,501	675,159	442,737	78,459	1,389,393
Prescription drugs	25,648,736	15,685,133	7,507,588	971,253	3,587,506	2,948,715	738,325	9,118,079
MEDICAL SUPPLIES	**8,508,860**	**4,198,552**	**3,731,927**	**505,357**	**1,959,119**	**1,266,055**	**438,207**	**2,130,741**
Eyeglasses and contact lenses	4,029,405	1,712,997	2,035,752	199,890	1,067,585	768,237	235,656	960,869
Hearing aids	1,316,249	900,228	373,307	34,790	200,577	137,984	30,586	223,931
Topicals and dressings	2,329,153	1,122,144	1,023,021	229,513	526,645	265,353	140,540	648,383
Medical equipment for general use	226,194	119,377	89,468	9,783	43,636	36,024	17,008	67,519
Supportive, convalescent medical equipment	417,903	250,566	133,487	23,138	75,686	34,657	9,169	86,519
Rental of medical equipment	104,037	50,013	47,164	4,287	27,536	15,197	4,199	123,502
Rental of supportive, convalescent medical equipment	85,919	43,478	30,013	3,902	17,304	8,765	1,120	20,357

Note: Total spending figures for total consumer units can be found on Total Spending by Age and Total Spending by Region tables. Spending by type of consumer unit will not add to total because not all types of consumer units are shown. Numbers may not add to category total because of rounding and missing subcategories. (–) means sample is too small to make a reliable estimate.

Source: Calculations by New Strategist based on the 2003 Consumer Expenditure Survey

Table 7.16 Health Care: Market shares by household type, 2003

(percentage of total annual out-of-pocket spending on health care accounted for by types of consumer units, 2003)

	total married couples	married couples, no children	married couples with children				single parent, at least one child <18	single person
			total	oldest child under 6	oldest child 6 to 17	oldest child 18 or older		
Share of total consumer units	50.7%	21.8%	24.8%	4.8%	13.0%	7.0%	6.1%	29.4%
Share of total before-tax income	68.8	26.8	36.6	6.2	19.8	10.7	3.5	15.6
Share of total spending	65.8	25.6	35.0	6.0	18.9	10.1	4.5	17.0
Share of health care spending	**67.1**	**33.5**	**28.3**	**4.3**	**14.9**	**9.1**	**3.0**	**19.0**
HEALTH INSURANCE	**67.3**	**33.2**	**28.8**	**4.8**	**14.9**	**9.1**	**3.1**	**18.3**
Commercial health insurance	**74.7**	**31.5**	**38.0**	**6.8**	**20.1**	**11.2**	**3.9**	**12.1**
Traditional fee-for-service health plan (not BCBS)	69.9	34.5	29.5	4.4	14.6	10.6	3.7	15.6
Preferred-provider health plan (not BCBS)	77.0	30.0	42.1	7.9	22.8	11.4	4.1	10.4
Blue Cross, Blue Shield	**69.2**	**32.1**	**32.4**	**5.5**	**17.7**	**9.1**	**3.6**	**16.3**
Traditional fee-for-service health plan	69.5	34.7	29.1	5.8	16.8	6.5	3.5	15.0
Preferred-provider health plan	74.7	30.8	39.0	7.9	19.9	11.2	4.1	11.5
Health maintenance organization	68.2	25.9	37.0	4.8	21.8	10.3	3.8	15.1
Commercial Medicare supplement	59.6	48.0	9.4	0.7	3.7	5.0	1.9	30.8
Other BCBS health insurance	51.8	23.4	26.4	4.0	18.6	3.7	3.9	34.4
Health maintenance plans (HMOs)	**72.7**	**25.0**	**41.3**	**7.0**	**21.6**	**12.7**	**4.1**	**12.0**
Medicare payments	**54.3**	**43.4**	**6.0**	**0.3**	**1.2**	**4.5**	**1.1**	**31.0**
Commercial Medicare supplements/ other health insurance	**59.6**	**39.0**	**15.4**	**2.1**	**7.2**	**6.2**	**1.8**	**26.4**
Commercial Medicare supplement (not BCBS)	55.7	41.9	9.7	1.1	3.1	5.6	1.1	29.0
Other health insurance (not BCBS)	66.7	33.5	25.8	3.9	14.7	7.3	3.0	21.4
MEDICAL SERVICES	**69.4**	**31.2**	**32.9**	**4.3**	**18.6**	**9.9**	**3.4**	**17.9**
Physician's services	70.6	30.0	35.7	5.6	19.2	10.9	3.7	15.2
Dental services	73.1	34.2	34.3	3.1	20.3	10.8	4.4	13.4
Eye care services	68.8	28.1	36.4	4.3	19.6	12.5	2.7	16.0
Service by professionals other than physician	65.2	27.3	34.4	4.7	18.4	11.3	2.4	23.8
Lab tests, X-rays	75.9	33.1	25.1	4.4	13.1	7.7	1.7	14.7
Hospital room	76.8	34.9	34.3	8.3	17.6	8.4	1.7	15.1
Hospital services other than room	73.6	30.9	36.8	6.6	21.3	8.9	3.0	14.2
Care in convalescent or nursing home	32.4	20.5	8.3	1.6	5.8	0.9	–	63.2
Other medical services	54.6	23.5	28.3	1.4	20.2	6.7	3.4	25.2
DRUGS	**63.4**	**37.0**	**20.8**	**3.0**	**10.1**	**7.7**	**2.1**	**22.5**
Nonprescription drugs	62.5	28.0	29.3	5.8	14.5	9.1	4.1	19.6
Nonprescription vitamins	61.8	35.2	23.4	3.3	12.2	8.0	1.4	25.1
Prescription drugs	63.8	39.0	18.7	2.4	8.9	7.3	1.8	22.7
MEDICAL SUPPLIES	**68.9**	**34.0**	**30.2**	**4.1**	**15.9**	**10.2**	**3.5**	**17.2**
Eyeglasses and contact lenses	68.5	29.1	34.6	3.4	18.2	13.1	4.0	16.3
Hearing aids	79.2	54.2	22.5	2.1	12.1	8.3	1.8	13.5
Topicals and dressings	67.1	32.3	29.5	5.6	15.2	7.6	4.0	18.7
Medical equipment for general use	63.3	33.4	25.0	2.7	12.2	10.1	4.8	18.9
Supportive, convalescent medical equipment	69.0	41.4	22.0	3.8	12.5	5.7	1.5	14.3
Rental of medical equipment	42.3	20.4	19.2	1.7	11.2	6.2	1.7	50.3
Rental of supportive, convalescent medical equipment	64.8	32.8	22.6	2.9	13.0	6.6	0.8	15.3

Note: Market share for total consumer units is 100.0%. Market shares by type of consumer unit will not add to total because not all types of consumer units are shown. (–) means sample is too small to make a reliable estimate.
Source: Calculations by New Strategist based on the 2003 Consumer Expenditure Survey

Table 7.17 Health Care: Average spending by race and Hispanic origin, 2003

(average annual out-of-pocket spending of consumer units (CU) on health care, by race and Hispanic origin of consumer unit reference person, 2003)

	total consumer units	race Asian	race black	race white and other	Hispanic origin Hispanic	Hispanic origin non-Hispanic
Number of consumer units (000)	115,356	3,573	13,743	98,041	11,727	103,629
Average number of persons per CU	2.5	2.8	2.6	2.5	3.3	2.4
Average before-tax income of CU	$51,128.00	$60,393.00	$34,485.00	$53,039.00	$37,150.00	$52,797.00
Average spending of CU, total	40,817.33	44,922.85	28,707.56	42,360.25	34,574.75	41,520.78
Health care, average spending	**2,416.39**	**1,955.29**	**1,309.18**	**2,588.04**	**1,439.35**	**2,527.40**
HEALTH INSURANCE	**1,251.62**	**1,070.63**	**774.01**	**1,325.17**	**746.94**	**1,308.74**
Commercial health insurance	**249.19**	**235.12**	**105.26**	**269.88**	**113.39**	**264.56**
Traditional fee-for-service health plan (not BCBS)	81.75	74.63	35.52	88.49	26.14	88.05
Preferred-provider health plan (not BCBS)	167.44	160.49	69.75	181.39	87.25	176.51
Blue Cross, Blue Shield	**350.88**	**302.57**	**213.94**	**371.84**	**179.72**	**370.25**
Traditional fee-for-service health plan	63.91	54.18	22.99	70.00	13.13	69.66
Preferred-provider health plan	124.05	121.75	59.05	133.25	87.12	128.23
Health maintenance organization	109.20	106.47	104.31	109.99	69.61	113.68
Commercial Medicare supplement	46.84	19.90	23.61	51.08	7.98	51.24
Other BCBS health insurance	6.88	0.27	3.98	7.53	1.88	7.45
Health maintenance plans (HMOs)	**278.97**	**300.72**	**234.00**	**284.49**	**267.61**	**280.26**
Medicare payments	**215.02**	**124.42**	**159.73**	**226.07**	**131.30**	**224.49**
Commercial Medicare supplements/ other health insurance	**157.55**	**107.80**	**61.06**	**172.89**	**54.92**	**169.17**
Commercial Medicare supplement (not BCBS)	102.12	71.05	41.77	111.72	34.50	109.78
Other health insurance (not BCBS)	55.43	36.75	19.30	61.18	20.42	59.39
MEDICAL SERVICES	**590.82**	**475.87**	**228.68**	**645.78**	**364.56**	**616.45**
Physician's services	143.63	99.18	71.03	155.43	98.71	148.72
Dental services	227.24	283.82	68.19	247.48	118.07	239.60
Eye care services	34.60	18.95	12.75	38.24	23.49	35.86
Service by professionals other than physician	38.54	15.73	10.33	43.33	17.94	40.88
Lab tests, X-rays	28.93	8.42	13.35	31.87	21.01	29.83
Hospital room	26.06	16.86	20.50	27.18	14.89	27.33
Hospital services other than room	43.34	21.66	24.21	46.81	46.34	43.00
Care in convalescent or nursing home	32.80	2.05	0.94	38.39	2.98	36.17
Other medical services	14.40	9.21	7.38	15.57	21.13	13.64
DRUGS	**466.85**	**340.00**	**263.08**	**499.68**	**262.52**	**490.36**
Nonprescription drugs	70.30	96.09	41.64	73.26	58.78	71.75
Nonprescription vitamins	48.02	117.00	17.83	49.50	27.99	50.53
Prescription drugs	348.53	126.91	203.61	376.92	175.75	368.08
MEDICAL SUPPLIES	**107.10**	**68.79**	**43.41**	**117.41**	**65.33**	**111.86**
Eyeglasses and contact lenses	50.97	39.71	23.14	55.28	30.55	53.28
Hearing aids	14.40	0.81	0.99	16.78	2.77	15.72
Topicals and dressings	30.10	24.20	15.92	32.30	27.40	30.44
Medical equipment for general use	3.10	1.23	0.80	3.49	1.32	3.30
Supportive, convalescent medical equipment	5.25	2.06	1.66	5.87	1.90	5.63
Rental of medical equipment	2.13	0.45	0.44	2.43	0.85	2.27
Rental of supportive, convalescent medical equipment	1.15	0.34	0.46	1.27	0.55	1.22

Note: Other races include Native Americans and Pacific Islanders. Subcategories may not add to total because some are not shown.
Source: Bureau of Labor Statistics, unpublished tables from the 2003 Consumer Expenditure Survey

Table 7.18 Health Care: Indexed spending by race and Hispanic origin, 2003

(indexed average annual out-of-pocket spending of consumer units (CU) on health care, by race and Hispanic origin of consumer unit reference person, 2003; index definition: an index of 100 is the average for all consumer units; an index of 132 means that spending by consumer units in that group is 32 percent above the average for all consumer units; an index of 68 indicates spending that is 32 percent below the average for all consumer units)

	total consumer units	race			Hispanic origin	
		Asian	black	white and other	Hispanic	non-Hispanic
Average spending of CU, total	$40,817	$44,923	$28,708	$42,360	$34,575	$41,521
Average spending of CU, index	100	110	70	104	85	102
Health care, spending index	**100**	81	54	107	60	105
HEALTH INSURANCE	**100**	86	62	106	60	105
Commercial health insurance	**100**	94	42	108	46	106
Traditional fee-for-service health plan (not BCBS)	100	91	43	108	32	108
Preferred-provider health plan (not BCBS)	100	96	42	108	52	105
Blue Cross, Blue Shield	**100**	86	61	106	51	106
Traditional fee-for-service health plan	100	85	36	110	21	109
Preferred-provider health plan	100	98	48	107	70	103
Health maintenance organization	100	98	96	101	64	104
Commercial Medicare supplement	100	42	50	109	17	109
Other BCBS health insurance	100	4	58	109	27	108
Health maintenance plans (HMOs)	**100**	108	84	102	96	100
Medicare payments	**100**	58	74	105	61	104
Commercial Medicare supplements/ other health insurance	**100**	68	39	110	35	107
Commercial Medicare supplement (not BCBS)	100	70	41	109	34	108
Other health insurance (not BCBS)	100	66	35	110	37	107
MEDICAL SERVICES	**100**	81	39	109	62	104
Physician's services	100	69	49	108	69	104
Dental services	100	125	30	109	52	105
Eye care services	100	55	37	111	68	104
Service by professionals other than physician	100	41	27	112	47	106
Lab tests, X-rays	100	29	46	110	73	103
Hospital room	100	65	79	104	57	105
Hospital services other than room	100	50	56	108	107	99
Care in convalescent or nursing home	100	6	3	117	9	110
Other medical services	100	54	51	108	147	95
DRUGS	**100**	73	56	107	56	105
Nonprescription drugs	100	137	59	104	84	102
Nonprescription vitamins	100	244	37	103	58	105
Prescription drugs	100	36	58	108	50	106
MEDICAL SUPPLIES	**100**	64	41	110	61	104
Eyeglasses and contact lenses	100	78	45	108	60	105
Hearing aids	100	5	7	117	19	109
Topicals and dressings	100	80	53	107	91	101
Medical equipment for general use	100	40	26	113	43	106
Supportive, convalescent medical equipment	100	39	32	112	36	107
Rental of medical equipment	100	21	21	114	40	107
Rental of supportive, convalescent medical equipment	100	30	40	110	48	106

Note: Other races include Native Americans and Pacific Islanders.
Source: Calculations by New Strategist based on the 2003 Consumer Expenditure Survey

Table 7.19 Health Care: Total spending by race and Hispanic origin, 2003

(total annual out-of-pocket spending on health care, by consumer unit race and Hispanic origin groups, 2003; numbers in thousands)

	total consumer units	race Asian	race black	race white and other	Hispanic origin Hispanic	Hispanic origin non-Hispanic
Number of consumer units	115,356	3,573	13,743	98,041	11,727	103,629
Total spending of all consumer units	$4,708,523,919	$160,509,343	$394,527,997	$4,153,041,270	$405,458,093	$4,302,756,911
Health care, total spending	**278,745,085**	**6,986,251**	**17,992,061**	**253,734,030**	**16,879,257**	**261,911,935**
HEALTH INSURANCE	**144,381,877**	**3,825,361**	**10,637,219**	**129,920,992**	**8,759,365**	**135,623,417**
Commercial health insurance	**28,745,562**	**840,084**	**1,446,588**	**26,459,305**	**1,329,725**	**27,416,088**
Traditional fee-for-service health plan (not BCBS)	9,430,353	266,653	488,151	8,675,648	306,544	9,124,533
Preferred-provider health plan (not BCBS)	19,315,209	573,431	958,574	17,783,657	1,023,181	18,291,555
Blue Cross, Blue Shield	**40,476,113**	**1,081,083**	**2,940,177**	**36,455,565**	**2,107,576**	**38,368,637**
Traditional fee-for-service health plan	7,372,402	193,585	315,952	6,862,870	153,976	7,218,796
Preferred-provider health plan	14,309,912	435,013	811,524	13,063,963	1,021,656	13,288,347
Health maintenance organization	12,596,875	380,417	1,433,532	10,783,530	816,316	11,780,545
Commercial Medicare supplement	5,403,275	71,103	324,472	5,007,934	93,581	5,309,950
Other BCBS health insurance	793,649	965	54,697	738,249	22,047	772,036
Health maintenance plans (HMOs)	**32,180,863**	**1,074,473**	**3,215,862**	**27,891,684**	**3,138,262**	**29,043,064**
Medicare payments	**24,803,847**	**444,553**	**2,195,169**	**22,164,129**	**1,539,755**	**23,263,674**
Commercial Medicare supplements/ other health insurance	**18,174,338**	**385,169**	**839,148**	**16,950,308**	**644,047**	**17,530,918**
Commercial Medicare supplement (not BCBS)	11,780,155	253,862	574,045	10,953,141	404,582	11,376,392
Other health insurance (not BCBS)	6,394,183	131,308	265,240	5,998,148	239,465	6,154,526
MEDICAL SERVICES	**68,154,632**	**1,700,284**	**3,142,749**	**63,312,917**	**4,275,195**	**63,882,097**
Physician's services	16,568,582	354,370	976,165	15,238,513	1,157,572	15,411,705
Dental services	26,213,497	1,014,089	937,135	24,263,187	1,384,607	24,829,508
Eye care services	3,991,318	67,708	175,223	3,749,088	275,467	3,716,136
Service by professionals other than physician	4,445,820	56,203	141,965	4,248,117	210,382	4,236,354
Lab tests, X-rays	3,337,249	30,085	183,469	3,124,567	246,384	3,091,253
Hospital room	3,006,177	60,241	281,732	2,664,754	174,615	2,832,181
Hospital services other than room	4,999,529	77,391	332,718	4,589,299	543,429	4,456,047
Care in convalescent or nursing home	3,783,677	7,325	12,918	3,763,794	34,946	3,748,261
Other medical services	1,661,126	32,907	101,423	1,526,498	247,792	1,413,500
DRUGS	**53,853,949**	**1,214,820**	**3,615,508**	**48,989,127**	**3,078,572**	**50,815,516**
Nonprescription drugs	8,109,527	343,330	572,259	7,182,484	689,313	7,435,381
Nonprescription vitamins	5,539,395	418,041	245,038	4,853,030	328,239	5,236,373
Prescription drugs	40,205,027	453,449	2,798,212	36,953,614	2,061,020	38,143,762
MEDICAL SUPPLIES	**12,354,628**	**245,787**	**596,584**	**11,510,994**	**766,125**	**11,591,940**
Eyeglasses and contact lenses	5,879,695	141,884	318,013	5,419,706	358,260	5,521,353
Hearing aids	1,661,126	2,894	13,606	1,645,128	32,484	1,629,048
Topicals and dressings	3,472,216	86,467	218,789	3,166,724	321,320	3,154,467
Medical equipment for general use	357,604	4,395	10,994	342,163	15,480	341,976
Supportive, convalescent medical equipment	605,619	7,360	22,813	575,501	22,281	583,431
Rental of medical equipment	245,708	1,608	6,047	238,240	9,968	235,238
Rental of supportive, convalescent medical equipment	132,659	1,215	6,322	124,512	6,450	126,427

Note: Other races include Native Americans and Pacific Islanders. Numbers may not add to total because of rounding and missing subcategories.
Source: Calculations by New Strategist based on the 2003 Consumer Expenditure Survey

Table 7.20 Health Care: Market shares by race and Hispanic origin, 2003

(percentage of total annual out-of-pocket spending on health care accounted for by consumer unit race and Hispanic origin groups, 2003)

	total consumer units	race			Hispanic origin	
		Asian	black	white and other	Hispanic	non-Hispanic
Share of total consumer units	100.0%	3.1%	11.9%	85.0%	10.2%	89.8%
Share of total before-tax income	100.0	3.7	8.0	88.2	7.4	92.8
Share of total spending	100.0	3.4	8.4	88.2	8.6	91.4
Share of health care spending	100.0	2.5	6.5	91.0	6.1	94.0
HEALTH INSURANCE	**100.0**	**2.6**	**7.4**	**90.0**	**6.1**	**93.9**
Commercial health insurance	**100.0**	**2.9**	**5.0**	**92.0**	**4.6**	**95.4**
Traditional fee-for-service health plan (not BCBS)	100.0	2.8	5.2	92.0	3.3	96.8
Preferred-provider health plan (not BCBS)	100.0	3.0	5.0	92.1	5.3	94.7
Blue Cross, Blue Shield	**100.0**	**2.7**	**7.3**	**90.1**	**5.2**	**94.8**
Traditional fee-for-service health plan	100.0	2.6	4.3	93.1	2.1	97.9
Preferred-provider health plan	100.0	3.0	5.7	91.3	7.1	92.9
Health maintenance organization	100.0	3.0	11.4	85.6	6.5	93.5
Commercial Medicare supplement	100.0	1.3	6.0	92.7	1.7	98.3
Other BCBS health insurance	100.0	0.1	6.9	93.0	2.8	97.3
Health maintenance plans (HMOs)	**100.0**	**3.3**	**10.0**	**86.7**	**9.8**	**90.2**
Medicare payments	**100.0**	**1.8**	**8.9**	**89.4**	**6.2**	**93.8**
Commercial Medicare supplements/ other health insurance	**100.0**	**2.1**	**4.6**	**93.3**	**3.5**	**96.5**
Commercial Medicare supplement (not BCBS)	100.0	2.2	4.9	93.0	3.4	96.6
Other health insurance (not BCBS)	100.0	2.1	4.1	93.8	3.7	96.3
MEDICAL SERVICES	**100.0**	**2.5**	**4.6**	**92.9**	**6.3**	**93.7**
Physician's services	100.0	2.1	5.9	92.0	7.0	93.0
Dental services	100.0	3.9	3.6	92.6	5.3	94.7
Eye care services	100.0	1.7	4.4	93.9	6.9	93.1
Service by professionals other than physician	100.0	1.3	3.2	95.6	4.7	95.3
Lab tests, X-rays	100.0	0.9	5.5	93.6	7.4	92.6
Hospital room	100.0	2.0	9.4	88.6	5.8	94.2
Hospital services other than room	100.0	1.5	6.7	91.8	10.9	89.1
Care in convalescent or nursing home	100.0	0.2	0.3	99.5	0.9	99.1
Other medical services	100.0	2.0	6.1	91.9	14.9	85.1
DRUGS	**100.0**	**2.3**	**6.7**	**91.0**	**5.7**	**94.4**
Nonprescription drugs	100.0	4.2	7.1	88.6	8.5	91.7
Nonprescription vitamins	100.0	7.5	4.4	87.6	5.9	94.5
Prescription drugs	100.0	1.1	7.0	91.9	5.1	94.9
MEDICAL SUPPLIES	**100.0**	**2.0**	**4.8**	**93.2**	**6.2**	**93.8**
Eyeglasses and contact lenses	100.0	2.4	5.4	92.2	6.1	93.9
Hearing aids	100.0	0.2	0.8	99.0	2.0	98.1
Topicals and dressings	100.0	2.5	6.3	91.2	9.3	90.8
Medical equipment for general use	100.0	1.2	3.1	95.7	4.3	95.6
Supportive, convalescent medical equipment	100.0	1.2	3.8	95.0	3.7	96.3
Rental of medical equipment	100.0	0.7	2.5	97.0	4.1	95.7
Rental of supportive, convalescent medical equipment	100.0	0.9	4.8	93.9	4.9	95.3

Note: Other races include Native Americans and Pacific Islanders. Numbers may not add to total because of rounding.
Source: Calculations by New Strategist based on the 2003 Consumer Expenditure Survey

Table 7.21 Health Care: Average spending by region, 2003

(average annual out-of-pocket spending of consumer units (CU) on health care, by region in which consumer unit lives, 2003)

	total consumer units	Northeast	Midwest	South	West
Number of consumer units (000)	115,356	22,182	26,438	41,325	25,412
Average number of persons per CU	2.5	2.4	2.5	2.5	2.6
Average before-tax income of CU	$48,596.00	$54,219.00	$49,591.00	$44,461.00	$49,667.00
Average spending of CU, total	40,817.33	42,162.29	40,280.39	37,624.55	45,380.67
Health care, average spending	**2,416.39**	**2,126.67**	**2,586.41**	**2,396.39**	**2,524.59**
HEALTH INSURANCE	**1,251.62**	**1,236.69**	**1,332.45**	**1,223.35**	**1,226.54**
Commercial health insurance	**249.19**	**189.47**	**289.40**	**277.91**	**212.78**
Traditional fee-for-service health plan (not BCBS)	81.75	101.37	82.10	84.43	59.91
Preferred-provider health plan (not BCBS)	167.44	88.10	207.30	193.48	152.86
Blue Cross, Blue Shield	**350.88**	**372.26**	**373.96**	**352.79**	**305.11**
Traditional fee-for-service health plan	63.91	91.46	75.91	56.95	38.70
Preferred-provider health plan	124.05	62.14	143.33	144.53	124.75
Health maintenance organization	109.20	173.45	87.76	94.74	98.93
Commercial Medicare supplement	46.84	38.08	58.32	51.46	35.02
Other BCBS health insurance	6.88	7.14	8.64	5.11	7.71
Health maintenance plans (HMOs)	**278.97**	**310.01**	**260.23**	**225.31**	**358.64**
Medicare payments	**215.02**	**219.12**	**221.42**	**216.59**	**202.22**
Commercial Medicare supplements/ other health insurance	**157.55**	**145.82**	**187.43**	**150.74**	**147.79**
Commercial Medicare supplement (not BCBS)	102.12	74.68	134.49	102.58	91.66
Other health insurance (not BCBS)	55.43	71.15	52.95	48.16	56.13
MEDICAL SERVICES	**590.82**	**448.14**	**621.37**	**562.93**	**728.96**
Physician's services	143.63	114.41	150.92	152.18	147.66
Dental services	227.24	207.75	220.02	190.67	311.24
Eye care services	34.60	25.36	36.86	30.40	47.15
Service by professionals other than physician	38.54	25.89	44.27	32.66	53.19
Lab tests, X-rays	28.93	12.12	26.26	25.94	51.26
Hospital room	26.06	20.94	20.87	30.71	28.39
Hospital services other than room	43.34	18.37	42.55	51.70	52.37
Care in convalescent or nursing home	32.80	11.30	65.89	29.05	23.24
Other medical services	14.40	5.98	13.65	19.36	14.46
DRUGS	**466.85**	**357.96**	**513.09**	**520.43**	**426.49**
Nonprescription drugs	70.30	58.42	72.58	72.48	74.76
Nonprescription vitamins	48.02	45.89	47.88	42.04	59.58
Prescription drugs	348.53	253.65	392.63	405.91	292.15
MEDICAL SUPPLIES	**107.10**	**83.88**	**119.50**	**89.68**	**142.60**
Eyeglasses and contact lenses	50.97	50.18	59.77	41.40	58.06
Hearing aids	14.40	5.12	16.83	11.32	25.00
Topicals and dressings	30.10	25.47	32.40	25.92	38.37
Medical equipment for general use	3.10	–	3.54	2.77	6.17
Supportive, convalescent medical equipment	5.25	2.10	4.96	4.18	10.04
Rental of medical equipment	2.13	0.93	0.80	3.16	2.88
Rental of supportive, convalescent medical equipment	1.15	0.42	1.20	0.93	2.08

Note: Subcategories may not add to total because some are not shown. (–) means sample is too small to make a reliable estimate.
Source: Bureau of Labor Statistics, unpublished tables from the 2003 Consumer Expenditure Survey

Table 7.22 Health Care: Indexed spending by region, 2003

(indexed average annual out-of-pocket spending of consumer units (CU) on health care, by region in which consumer unit lives, 2003; index definition: an index of 100 is the average for all consumer units; an index of 132 means that spending by consumer units in that group is 32 percent above the average for all consumer units; an index of 68 indicates spending that is 32 percent below the average for all consumer units)

	total consumer units	Northeast	Midwest	South	West
Average spending of CU, total	$40,817	$42,162	$40,280	$37,625	$45,381
Average spending of CU, index	100	103	99	92	111
Health care, spending index	100	88	107	99	104
HEALTH INSURANCE	100	99	106	98	98
Commercial health insurance	100	76	116	112	85
Traditional fee-for-service health plan (not BCBS)	100	124	100	103	73
Preferred-provider health plan (not BCBS)	100	53	124	116	91
Blue Cross, Blue Shield	100	106	107	101	87
Traditional fee-for-service health plan	100	143	119	89	61
Preferred-provider health plan	100	50	116	117	101
Health maintenance organization	100	159	80	87	91
Commercial Medicare supplement	100	81	125	110	75
Other BCBS health insurance	100	104	126	74	112
Health maintenance plans (HMOs)	100	111	93	81	129
Medicare payments	100	102	103	101	94
Commercial Medicare supplements/ other health insurance	100	93	119	96	94
Commercial Medicare supplement (not BCBS)	100	73	132	100	90
Other health insurance (not BCBS)	100	128	96	87	101
MEDICAL SERVICES	100	76	105	95	123
Physician's services	100	80	105	106	103
Dental services	100	91	97	84	137
Eye care services	100	73	107	88	136
Service by professionals other than physician	100	67	115	85	138
Lab tests, X-rays	100	42	91	90	177
Hospital room	100	80	80	118	109
Hospital services other than room	100	42	98	119	121
Care in convalescent or nursing home	100	54	201	89	71
Other medical services	100	42	95	134	100
DRUGS	100	77	110	111	91
Nonprescription drugs	100	83	103	103	106
Nonprescription vitamins	100	96	100	88	124
Prescription drugs	100	73	113	116	84
MEDICAL SUPPLIES	100	78	112	84	133
Eyeglasses and contact lenses	100	93	117	81	114
Hearing aids	100	35	117	79	174
Topicals and dressings	100	85	108	86	127
Medical equipment for general use	100	–	114	89	199
Supportive, convalescent medical equipment	100	40	94	80	191
Rental of medical equipment	100	44	38	148	135
Rental of supportive, convalescent medical equipment	100	37	104	81	181

(–) means sample is too small to make a reliable estimate.
Source: Calculations by New Strategist based on the 2003 Consumer Expenditure Survey

Table 7.23 Health Care: Total spending by region, 2003

(total annual out-of-pocket spending on health care, by region in which consumer units live, 2003; numbers in thousands)

	total consumer units	Northeast	Midwest	South	West
Number of consumer units	115,356	22,182	26,438	41,325	25,412
Total spending of all consumer units	$4,708,523,919	$935,243,917	$1,064,932,951	$1,554,834,529	$1,153,213,586
Health care, total spending	**278,745,085**	**47,173,794**	**68,379,508**	**99,030,817**	**64,154,881**
HEALTH INSURANCE	**144,381,877**	**27,432,258**	**35,227,313**	**50,554,939**	**31,168,834**
Commercial health insurance	**28,745,562**	**4,202,824**	**7,651,157**	**11,484,631**	**5,407,165**
Traditional fee-for-service health plan (not BCBS)	9,430,353	2,248,589	2,170,560	3,489,070	1,522,433
Preferred-provider health plan (not BCBS)	19,315,209	1,954,234	5,480,597	7,995,561	3,884,478
Blue Cross, Blue Shield	**40,476,113**	**8,257,471**	**9,886,754**	**14,579,047**	**7,753,455**
Traditional fee-for-service health plan	7,372,402	2,028,766	2,006,909	2,353,459	983,444
Preferred-provider health plan	14,309,912	1,378,389	3,789,359	5,972,702	3,170,147
Health maintenance organization	12,596,875	3,847,468	2,320,199	3,915,131	2,514,009
Commercial Medicare supplement	5,403,275	844,691	1,541,864	2,126,585	889,928
Other BCBS health insurance	793,649	158,379	228,424	211,171	195,927
Health maintenance plans (HMOs)	**32,180,863**	**6,876,642**	**6,879,961**	**9,310,936**	**9,113,760**
Medicare payments	**24,803,847**	**4,860,520**	**5,853,902**	**8,950,582**	**5,138,815**
Commercial Medicare supplements/ other health insurance	**18,174,338**	**3,234,579**	**4,955,274**	**6,229,331**	**3,755,639**
Commercial Medicare supplement (not BCBS)	11,780,155	1,656,552	3,555,647	4,239,119	2,329,264
Other health insurance (not BCBS)	6,394,183	1,578,249	1,399,892	1,990,212	1,426,376
MEDICAL SERVICES	**68,154,632**	**9,940,641**	**16,427,780**	**23,263,082**	**18,524,332**
Physician's services	16,568,582	2,537,843	3,990,023	6,288,839	3,752,336
Dental services	26,213,497	4,608,311	5,816,889	7,879,438	7,909,231
Eye care services	3,991,318	562,536	974,505	1,256,280	1,198,176
Service by professionals other than physician	4,445,820	574,292	1,170,410	1,349,675	1,351,664
Lab tests, X-rays	3,337,249	268,846	694,262	1,071,971	1,302,619
Hospital room	3,006,177	464,491	551,761	1,269,091	721,447
Hospital services other than room	4,999,529	407,483	1,124,937	2,136,503	1,330,826
Care in convalescent or nursing home	3,783,677	250,657	1,742,000	1,200,491	590,575
Other medical services	1,661,126	132,648	360,879	800,052	367,458
DRUGS	**53,853,949**	**7,940,269**	**13,565,073**	**21,506,770**	**10,837,964**
Nonprescription drugs	8,109,527	1,295,872	1,918,870	2,995,236	1,899,801
Nonprescription vitamins	5,539,395	1,017,932	1,265,851	1,737,303	1,514,047
Prescription drugs	40,205,027	5,626,464	10,380,352	16,774,231	7,424,116
MEDICAL SUPPLIES	**12,354,628**	**1,860,626**	**3,159,341**	**3,706,026**	**3,623,751**
Eyeglasses and contact lenses	5,879,695	1,113,093	1,580,199	1,710,855	1,475,421
Hearing aids	1,661,126	113,572	444,952	467,799	635,300
Topicals and dressings	3,472,216	564,976	856,591	1,071,144	975,058
Medical equipment for general use	357,604	–	93,591	114,470	156,792
Supportive, convalescent medical equipment	605,619	46,582	131,132	172,739	255,136
Rental of medical equipment	245,708	20,629	21,150	130,587	73,187
Rental of supportive, convalescent medical equipment	132,659	9,316	31,726	38,432	52,857

Note: Numbers may not add to total because of rounding and missing subcategories. (–) means sample is too small to make a reliable estimate.
Source: Calculations by New Strategist based on the 2003 Consumer Expenditure Survey

Table 7.24 Health Care: Market shares by region, 2003

(percentage of total annual out-of-pocket spending on health care accounted for by consumer units by region, 2003)

	total consumer units	Northeast	Midwest	South	West
Share of total consumer units	100.0%	19.2%	22.9%	35.8%	22.0%
Share of total before-tax income	100.0	21.5	23.4	32.8	22.5
Share of total spending	100.0	19.9	22.6	33.0	24.5
Share of health care spending	100.0	16.9	24.5	35.5	23.0
HEALTH INSURANCE	100.0	19.0	24.4	35.0	21.6
Commercial health insurance	100.0	14.6	26.6	40.0	18.8
Traditional fee-for-service health plan (not BCBS)	100.0	23.8	23.0	37.0	16.1
Preferred-provider health plan (not BCBS)	100.0	10.1	28.4	41.4	20.1
Blue Cross, Blue Shield	100.0	20.4	24.4	36.0	19.2
Traditional fee-for-service health plan	100.0	27.5	27.2	31.9	13.3
Preferred-provider health plan	100.0	9.6	26.5	41.7	22.2
Health maintenance organization	100.0	30.5	18.4	31.1	20.0
Commercial Medicare supplement	100.0	15.6	28.5	39.4	16.5
Other BCBS health insurance	100.0	20.0	28.8	26.6	24.7
Health maintenance plans (HMOs)	100.0	21.4	21.4	28.9	28.3
Medicare payments	100.0	19.6	23.6	36.1	20.7
Commercial Medicare supplements/ other health insurance	100.0	17.8	27.3	34.3	20.7
Commercial Medicare supplement (not BCBS)	100.0	14.1	30.2	36.0	19.8
Other health insurance (not BCBS)	100.0	24.7	21.9	31.1	22.3
MEDICAL SERVICES	100.0	14.6	24.1	34.1	27.2
Physician's services	100.0	15.3	24.1	38.0	22.6
Dental services	100.0	17.6	22.2	30.1	30.2
Eye care services	100.0	14.1	24.4	31.5	30.0
Service by professionals other than physician	100.0	12.9	26.3	30.4	30.4
Lab tests, X-rays	100.0	8.1	20.8	32.1	39.0
Hospital room	100.0	15.5	18.4	42.2	24.0
Hospital services other than room	100.0	8.2	22.5	42.7	26.6
Care in convalescent or nursing home	100.0	6.6	46.0	31.7	15.6
Other medical services	100.0	8.0	21.7	48.2	22.1
DRUGS	100.0	14.7	25.2	39.9	20.1
Nonprescription drugs	100.0	16.0	23.7	36.9	23.4
Nonprescription vitamins	100.0	18.4	22.9	31.4	27.3
Prescription drugs	100.0	14.0	25.8	41.7	18.5
MEDICAL SUPPLIES	100.0	15.1	25.6	30.0	29.3
Eyeglasses and contact lenses	100.0	18.9	26.9	29.1	25.1
Hearing aids	100.0	6.8	26.8	28.2	38.2
Topicals and dressings	100.0	16.3	24.7	30.8	28.1
Medical equipment for general use	100.0	–	26.2	32.0	43.8
Supportive, convalescent medical equipment	100.0	7.7	21.7	28.5	42.1
Rental of medical equipment	100.0	8.4	8.6	53.1	29.8
Rental of supportive, convalescent medical equipment	100.0	7.0	23.9	29.0	39.8

Note: Numbers may not add to total because of rounding. (–) means sample is too small to make a reliable estimate
Source: Calculations by New Strategist based on the 2003 Consumer Expenditure Survey

Table 7.25 Health Care: Average spending by education, 2003

(average annual out-of-pocket spending of consumer units (CU) on health care, by education of consumer unit reference person, 2003)

	total consumer units	less than high school graduate	high school graduate	some college	associate's degree	college graduate total	college graduate bachelor's degree	college graduate master's, professional, doctorate
Number of consumer units (000)	115,356	17,721	31,552	24,514	10,981	30,589	19,557	11,032
Average number of persons per CU	2.5	2.6	2.5	2.3	2.6	2.5	2.5	2.4
Average before-tax income of CU	$51,128.00	$25,028.00	$40,113.00	$45,113.00	$54,087.00	$81,842.00	$74,921.00	$93,948.00
Average spending of CU, total	40,817.33	23,901.14	33,955.56	37,912.41	44,547.12	58,480.00	54,725.85	65,202.73
Health care, average spending	**2,416.39**	**1,796.77**	**2,286.62**	**2,249.11**	**2,439.49**	**3,031.19**	**2,812.25**	**3,420.44**
HEALTH INSURANCE	**1,251.62**	**975.76**	**1,245.58**	**1,128.66**	**1,279.86**	**1,506.08**	**1,424.64**	**1,650.45**
Commercial health insurance	**249.19**	**105.85**	**231.23**	**219.32**	**274.13**	**365.74**	**379.30**	**341.72**
Traditional fee-for-service health plan (not BCBS)	81.75	49.08	94.85	69.84	72.05	100.20	106.10	89.74
Preferred-provider health plan (not BCBS)	167.44	56.77	136.38	149.48	202.09	265.54	273.19	251.98
Blue Cross, Blue Shield	**350.88**	**195.34**	**344.56**	**320.75**	**363.19**	**467.24**	**443.30**	**509.69**
Traditional fee-for-service health plan	63.91	25.42	65.72	52.18	58.74	95.60	72.55	136.46
Preferred-provider health plan	124.05	46.70	98.42	116.76	155.86	189.73	188.26	192.32
Health maintenance organization	109.20	66.20	114.85	102.45	103.56	135.73	136.06	135.14
Commercial Medicare supplement	46.84	52.21	57.15	45.37	36.37	38.04	37.64	38.75
Other BCBS health insurance	6.88	4.81	8.43	3.99	8.66	8.16	8.79	7.03
Health maintenance plans (HMOs)	**278.97**	**140.97**	**253.48**	**269.38**	**377.50**	**357.53**	**344.01**	**381.51**
Medicare payments	**215.02**	**372.04**	**255.38**	**171.04**	**130.79**	**147.92**	**127.67**	**183.81**
Commercial Medicare supplements/ other health insurance	**157.55**	**161.57**	**160.93**	**148.17**	**134.24**	**167.64**	**130.36**	**233.72**
Commercial Medicare supplement (not BCBS)	102.12	139.16	113.27	101.22	71.31	80.96	61.67	115.15
Other health insurance (not BCBS)	55.43	22.41	47.66	46.95	62.93	86.68	68.69	118.58
MEDICAL SERVICES	**590.82**	**317.09**	**498.53**	**568.42**	**571.76**	**869.21**	**781.83**	**1,024.20**
Physician's services	143.63	83.58	127.71	130.96	147.53	203.61	184.81	236.93
Dental services	227.24	71.88	189.49	234.98	214.43	354.60	312.75	428.79
Eye care services	34.60	13.24	29.80	30.67	40.17	53.08	51.15	56.51
Service by professionals other than physician	38.54	17.97	26.00	28.30	36.89	72.20	73.68	69.58
Lab tests, X-rays	28.93	17.71	19.97	24.22	25.08	49.84	30.47	84.19
Hospital room	26.06	31.59	27.79	11.79	26.29	32.43	27.56	41.05
Hospital services other than room	43.34	28.00	45.49	43.30	57.47	44.97	49.74	36.52
Care in convalescent or nursing home	32.80	41.53	17.17	44.87	10.18	42.31	38.53	49.01
Other medical services	14.40	10.93	11.75	19.26	13.72	15.50	13.14	19.68
DRUGS	**466.85**	**444.73**	**447.01**	**444.21**	**482.50**	**510.49**	**474.42**	**575.22**
Nonprescription drugs	70.30	51.38	58.61	65.48	95.78	87.14	88.24	85.04
Nonprescription vitamins	48.02	23.57	29.40	54.95	59.53	70.46	63.79	83.21
Prescription drugs	348.53	369.78	359.01	323.79	327.19	352.89	322.38	406.98
MEDICAL SUPPLIES	**107.10**	**59.19**	**95.50**	**107.81**	**105.37**	**145.42**	**131.37**	**170.57**
Eyeglasses and contact lenses	50.97	20.10	41.65	48.38	50.83	80.60	73.79	92.68
Hearing aids	14.40	14.69	11.88	17.87	14.96	13.86	10.29	20.20
Topicals and dressings	30.10	15.72	29.79	26.32	33.58	39.09	37.37	42.38
Medical equipment for general use	3.10	2.31	2.94	4.38	0.97	3.46	3.43	3.51
Supportive, convalescent medical equipment	5.25	4.10	4.75	7.89	1.96	5.49	4.13	7.91
Rental of medical equipment	2.13	1.44	3.32	1.86	2.15	1.50	1.19	2.05
Rental of supportive, convalescent medical equipment	1.15	0.83	1.16	1.13	0.92	1.42	1.18	1.85

Note: Subcategories may not add to total because some are not shown.
Source: Bureau of Labor Statistics, unpublished tables from the 2003 Consumer Expenditure Survey

Table 7.26 Health Care: Indexed spending by education, 2003

(indexed average annual out-of-pocket spending of consumer units (CU) on health care, by education of consumer unit reference person, 2003; index definition: an index of 100 is the average for all consumer units; an index of 132 means that spending by consumer units in that group is 32 percent above the average for all consumer units; an index of 68 indicates spending that is 32 percent below the average for all consumer units)

	total consumer units	less than high school graduate	high school graduate	some college	associate's degree	college graduate total	bachelor's degree	master's, professional, doctorate
Average spending of CU, total	$40,817	$23,901	$33,956	$37,912	$44,547	$58,480	$54,726	$65,203
Average spending of CU, index	100	59	83	93	109	143	134	160
Health care, spending index	100	74	95	93	101	125	116	142
HEALTH INSURANCE	100	78	100	90	102	120	114	132
Commercial health insurance	100	42	93	88	110	147	152	137
Traditional fee-for-service health plan (not BCBS)	100	60	116	85	88	123	130	110
Preferred-provider health plan (not BCBS)	100	34	81	89	121	159	163	150
Blue Cross, Blue Shield	100	56	98	91	104	133	126	145
Traditional fee-for-service health plan	100	40	103	82	92	150	114	214
Preferred-provider health plan	100	38	79	94	126	153	152	155
Health maintenance organization	100	61	105	94	95	124	125	124
Commercial Medicare supplement	100	111	122	97	78	81	80	83
Other BCBS health insurance	100	70	123	58	126	119	128	102
Health maintenance plans (HMOs)	100	51	91	97	135	128	123	137
Medicare payments	100	173	119	80	61	69	59	85
Commercial Medicare supplements/ other health insurance	100	103	102	94	85	106	83	148
Commercial Medicare supplement (not BCBS)	100	136	111	99	70	79	60	113
Other health insurance (not BCBS)	100	40	86	85	114	156	124	214
MEDICAL SERVICES	100	54	84	96	97	147	132	173
Physician's services	100	58	89	91	103	142	129	165
Dental services	100	32	83	103	94	156	138	189
Eye care services	100	38	86	89	116	153	148	163
Service by professionals other than physician	100	47	67	73	96	187	191	181
Lab tests, X-rays	100	61	59	84	87	172	105	291
Hospital room	100	121	137	45	101	124	106	158
Hospital services other than room	100	65	105	100	133	104	115	84
Care in convalescent or nursing home	100	127	52	137	31	129	117	149
Other medical services	100	76	82	134	95	108	91	137
DRUGS	100	95	96	95	103	109	102	123
Nonprescription drugs	100	73	85	93	136	124	126	121
Nonprescription vitamins	100	49	61	114	124	147	133	173
Prescription drugs	100	106	103	93	94	101	92	117
MEDICAL SUPPLIES	100	55	89	101	98	136	123	159
Eyeglasses and contact lenses	100	39	82	95	100	158	145	182
Hearing aids	100	102	83	124	104	96	71	140
Topicals and dressings	100	52	99	87	112	130	124	141
Medical equipment for general use	100	75	95	141	31	112	111	113
Supportive, convalescent medical equipment	100	78	90	150	37	105	79	151
Rental of medical equipment	100	68	155	87	101	70	56	96
Rental of supportive, convalescent medical equipment	100	72	101	98	80	123	103	161

Source: Calculations by New Strategist based on the 2003 Consumer Expenditure Survey

Table 7.27 Health Care: Total spending by education, 2003

(total annual out-of-pocket spending on health care, by consumer unit (CU) educational attainment groups, 2003; numbers in thousands)

	total consumer units	less than high school graduate	high school graduate	some college	associate's degree	college graduate total	bachelor's degree	master's, professional, doctorate
Number of consumer units	115,356	17,721	31,552	24,514	10,981	30,589	19,557	11,032
Total spending of all CUs	$4,708,523,919	$423,552,102	$1,071,365,829	$929,384,819	$489,171,925	$1,788,844,720	$1,070,273,448	$719,316,517
Health care, total spending	278,745,085	31,840,561	72,147,434	55,134,683	26,788,040	92,721,071	54,999,173	37,734,294
HEALTH INSURANCE	**144,381,877**	**17,291,443**	**39,300,540**	**27,667,971**	**14,054,143**	**46,069,481**	**27,861,684**	**18,207,764**
Commercial health insurance	**28,745,562**	**1,875,768**	**7,295,769**	**5,376,410**	**3,010,222**	**11,187,621**	**7,417,970**	**3,769,855**
Traditional fee-for-service health plan (not BCBS)	9,430,353	869,747	2,992,707	1,712,058	791,181	3,065,018	2,074,998	990,012
Preferred-provider health plan (not BCBS)	19,315,209	1,006,021	4,303,062	3,664,353	2,219,150	8,122,603	5,342,777	2,779,843
Blue Cross, Blue Shield	**40,476,113**	**3,461,620**	**10,871,557**	**7,862,866**	**3,988,189**	**14,292,404**	**8,669,618**	**5,622,900**
Traditional fee-for-service health plan	7,372,402	450,468	2,073,597	1,279,141	645,024	2,924,308	1,418,860	1,505,427
Preferred-provider health plan	14,309,912	827,571	3,105,348	2,862,255	1,711,499	5,803,651	3,681,801	2,121,674
Health maintenance organization	12,596,875	1,173,130	3,623,747	2,511,459	1,137,192	4,151,845	2,660,925	1,490,864
Commercial Medicare supplement	5,403,275	925,213	1,803,197	1,112,200	399,379	1,163,606	736,125	427,490
Other BCBS health insurance	793,649	85,238	265,983	97,811	95,095	249,606	171,906	77,555
Health maintenance plans (HMOs)	**32,180,863**	**2,498,129**	**7,997,801**	**6,603,581**	**4,145,328**	**10,936,485**	**6,727,804**	**4,208,818**
Medicare payments	**24,803,847**	**6,592,921**	**8,057,750**	**4,192,875**	**1,436,205**	**4,524,725**	**2,496,842**	**2,027,792**
Commercial Medicare supplements/ other health insurance	**18,174,338**	**2,863,182**	**5,077,663**	**3,632,239**	**1,474,089**	**5,127,940**	**2,549,451**	**2,578,399**
Commercial Medicare supplement (not BCBS)	11,780,155	2,466,054	3,573,895	2,431,307	783,055	2,476,485	1,206,080	1,270,335
Other health insurance (not BCBS)	6,394,183	397,128	1,503,768	1,150,932	691,034	2,651,455	1,343,370	1,308,175
MEDICAL SERVICES	**68,154,632**	**5,619,152**	**15,729,619**	**13,934,248**	**6,278,497**	**26,588,265**	**15,290,249**	**11,298,974**
Physician's services	16,568,582	1,481,121	4,029,506	3,210,353	1,620,027	6,228,226	3,614,329	2,613,812
Dental services	26,213,497	1,273,785	5,978,788	5,760,300	2,354,656	10,846,859	6,116,452	4,730,411
Eye care services	3,991,318	234,626	940,250	751,844	441,107	1,623,664	1,000,341	623,418
Service by professionals other than physician	4,445,820	318,446	820,352	693,746	405,089	2,208,526	1,440,960	767,607
Lab tests, X-rays	3,337,249	313,839	630,093	593,729	275,403	1,524,556	595,902	928,784
Hospital room	3,006,177	559,806	876,830	289,020	288,690	992,001	538,991	452,864
Hospital services other than room	4,999,529	496,188	1,435,300	1,061,456	631,078	1,375,587	972,765	402,889
Care in convalescent or nursing home	3,783,677	735,953	541,748	1,099,943	111,787	1,294,221	753,531	540,678
Other medical services	1,661,126	193,691	370,736	472,140	150,659	474,130	256,979	217,110
DRUGS	**53,853,949**	**7,881,060**	**14,104,060**	**10,889,364**	**5,298,333**	**15,615,379**	**9,278,232**	**6,345,827**
Nonprescription drugs	8,109,527	910,505	1,849,263	1,605,177	1,051,760	2,665,525	1,725,710	938,161
Nonprescription vitamins	5,539,395	417,684	927,629	1,347,044	653,699	2,155,301	1,247,541	917,973
Prescription drugs	40,205,027	6,552,871	11,327,484	7,937,388	3,592,873	10,794,552	6,304,786	4,489,803
MEDICAL SUPPLIES	**12,354,628**	**1,048,906**	**3,013,216**	**2,642,854**	**1,157,068**	**4,448,252**	**2,569,203**	**1,881,728**
Eyeglasses and contact lenses	5,879,695	356,192	1,314,141	1,185,987	558,164	2,465,473	1,443,111	1,022,446
Hearing aids	1,661,126	260,321	374,838	438,065	164,276	423,964	201,242	222,846
Topicals and dressings	3,472,216	278,574	939,934	645,208	368,742	1,195,724	730,845	467,536
Medical equipment for general use	357,604	40,936	92,763	107,371	10,652	105,838	67,081	38,722
Supportive, convalescent medical equipment	605,619	72,656	149,872	193,415	21,523	167,934	80,770	87,263
Rental of medical equipment	245,708	25,518	104,753	45,596	23,609	45,884	23,273	22,616
Rental of supportive, convalescent medical equipment	132,659	14,708	36,600	27,701	10,103	43,436	23,077	20,409

Note: Numbers may not add to total because of rounding and missing subcategories.
Source: Calculations by New Strategist based on the 2003 Consumer Expenditure Survey

Table 7.28 Health Care: Market shares by education, 2003

(percentage of total annual out-of-pocket spending on health care accounted for by consumer unit educational attainment groups, 2003)

	total consumer units	less than high school graduate	high school graduate	some college	associate's degree	college graduate total	bachelor's degree	master's, professional, doctorate
Share of total consumer units	100.0%	15.4%	27.4%	21.3%	9.5%	26.5%	17.0%	9.6%
Share of total before-tax income	100.0	7.5	21.5	18.8	10.1	42.4	24.8	17.6
Share of total spending	100.0	9.0	22.8	19.7	10.4	38.0	22.7	15.3
Share of health care spending	100.0	11.4	25.9	19.8	9.6	33.3	19.7	13.5
HEALTH INSURANCE	100.0	12.0	27.2	19.2	9.7	31.9	19.3	12.6
Commercial health insurance	100.0	6.5	25.4	18.7	10.5	38.9	25.8	13.1
Traditional fee-for-service health plan (not BCBS)	100.0	9.2	31.7	18.2	8.4	32.5	22.0	10.5
Preferred-provider health plan (not BCBS)	100.0	5.2	22.3	19.0	11.5	42.1	27.7	14.4
Blue Cross, Blue Shield	100.0	8.6	26.9	19.4	9.9	35.3	21.4	13.9
Traditional fee-for-service health plan	100.0	6.1	28.1	17.4	8.7	39.7	19.2	20.4
Preferred-provider health plan	100.0	5.8	21.7	20.0	12.0	40.6	25.7	14.8
Health maintenance organization	100.0	9.3	28.8	19.9	9.0	33.0	21.1	11.8
Commercial Medicare supplement	100.0	17.1	33.4	20.6	7.4	21.5	13.6	7.9
Other BCBS health insurance	100.0	10.7	33.5	12.3	12.0	31.5	21.7	9.8
Health maintenance plans (HMOs)	100.0	7.8	24.9	20.5	12.9	34.0	20.9	13.1
Medicare payments	100.0	26.6	32.5	16.9	5.8	18.2	10.1	8.2
Commercial Medicare supplements/ other health insurance	100.0	15.8	27.9	20.0	8.1	28.2	14.0	14.2
Commercial Medicare supplement (not BCBS)	100.0	20.9	39.3	21.1	6.6	21.0	10.2	10.8
Other health insurance (not BCBS)	100.0	6.2	23.5	18.0	10.8	41.5	21.0	20.5
MEDICAL SERVICES	100.0	8.2	23.1	20.4	9.2	39.0	22.4	16.6
Physician's services	100.0	8.9	24.3	19.4	9.8	37.6	21.8	15.8
Dental services	100.0	4.9	22.8	22.0	9.0	41.4	23.3	18.0
Eye care services	100.0	5.9	23.6	18.8	11.1	40.7	25.1	15.6
Service by professionals other than physician	100.0	7.2	18.5	15.6	9.1	49.7	32.4	17.3
Lab tests, X-rays	100.0	9.4	18.9	17.8	8.3	45.7	17.9	27.8
Hospital room	100.0	18.6	29.2	9.6	9.6	33.0	17.9	15.1
Hospital services other than room	100.0	9.9	28.7	21.2	12.6	27.5	19.5	8.1
Care in convalescent or nursing home	100.0	19.5	14.3	29.1	3.0	34.2	19.9	14.3
Other medical services	100.0	11.7	22.3	28.4	9.1	28.5	15.5	13.1
DRUGS	100.0	14.6	26.2	20.2	9.8	29.0	17.2	11.8
Nonprescription drugs	100.0	11.2	22.8	19.8	13.0	32.9	21.3	11.6
Nonprescription vitamins	100.0	7.5	16.7	24.3	11.8	38.9	22.5	16.6
Prescription drugs	100.0	16.3	28.2	19.7	8.9	26.8	15.7	11.2
MEDICAL SUPPLIES	100.0	8.5	24.4	21.4	9.4	36.0	20.8	15.2
Eyeglasses and contact lenses	100.0	6.1	22.4	20.2	9.5	41.9	24.5	17.4
Hearing aids	100.0	15.7	22.6	26.4	9.9	25.5	12.1	13.4
Topicals and dressings	100.0	8.0	27.1	18.6	10.6	34.4	21.0	13.5
Medical equipment for general use	100.0	11.4	25.9	30.0	3.0	29.6	18.8	10.8
Supportive, convalescent medical equipment	100.0	12.0	24.7	31.9	3.6	27.7	13.3	14.4
Rental of medical equipment	100.0	10.4	42.6	18.6	9.6	18.7	9.5	9.2
Rental of supportive, convalescent medical equipment	100.0	11.1	27.6	20.9	7.6	32.7	17.4	15.4

Note: Numbers may not add to total because of rounding.
Source: Calculations by New Strategist based on the 2003 Consumer Expenditure Survey

Spending on Household Operations, 2003

Americans are spending more on housing than ever before as homeownership rates reach record highs. In 2003, housing costs—including shelter, utilities, and all household operations (household services, housekeeping supplies, furniture, and equipment)—absorbed 32.5 percent of average household expenditures. That figure was higher than the 32.4 percent in 2000. Not all housing categories are experiencing spending gains, however. Spending on household furnishings and equipment fell 3 percent between 2000 and 2003, after adjusting for inflation—despite the rise in homeownership. Spending on household services also fell 3 percent during those years, while spending on housekeeping supplies rose 3 percent.

Overall housing costs are highest for householders aged 35 to 44, at $16,098 in 2003. The 35-to-44 age group spends the most on household services, $949 in 2003, because of the high cost of day care. Householders aged 45 to 64 spend the most on furnishings and equipment—more than $1,800 in 2003. These older householders also spend the most on housekeeping supplies.

Households with incomes of $100,000 or more spent $28,941 on housing in 2003, more than twice the $13,653 spent by the average income-reporting household. The most affluent households spend far more than average on just about every category of household operations. They account for 58 percent of spending on housekeeping services and 52 percent of spending on office furniture for home use.

Among household types, married couples with children under age 18 spend the most on housing, more than $19,000 in 2003. Behind this figure is the high cost of housing for recent homebuyers—many married couples with children under age 18 are new homeowners. In addition, these householders spend the most on day care. Married couples with preschoolers spent an average of $1,481 on day care centers in 2003.

Asian households spend 22 percent more than the average household on housing, while the spending of black and Hispanic households is below average. Asian households spend fully 65 percent more than average on day care centers, and they spend 45 percent more on major appliances. Hispanics spend 25 percent more than average on laundry and cleaning supplies. Blacks spend 59 percent more than average on home security system service fees.

Households in the West spend the most on housing, $15,371 in 2003, because of the high cost of housing in California. Spending on housing is lowest in the South, at $12,006. Southern households spend the most on termite and pest control services, however. Households in the West spend the most on computer hardware and software. Midwesterners are the biggest spenders on water softening services.

Not surprisingly, college graduates (who dominate the nation's affluent households) spend the most on housing, an average of $19,631 in 2003. They spend far more than the average household on almost every category of household operations. They spend more than twice the average on housekeeping services. They spend less than average on window air conditioners.

Table 8.1 Housing: Household Operations: Average spending by age, 2003

(average annual spending of consumer units (CU) on household services, supplies, furnishings, and equipment, by age of consumer unit reference person, 2003)

	total consumer units	under 25	25 to 34	35 to 44	45 to 54	55 to 64	65 to 74	75+
Number of consumer units (000)	115,356	8,584	19,737	24,413	23,131	16,580	11,495	11,417
Average number of persons per CU	2.5	1.8	2.9	3.2	2.6	2.1	1.9	1.5
Average before-tax income of CU	$51,128.00	$20,680.00	$50,389.00	$61,091.00	$68,028.00	$58,672.00	$35,314.00	$25,492.00
Average spending of CU, total	40,817.33	22,395.53	40,525.22	47,175.06	50,100.86	44,190.65	33,629.17	25,016.38
Housing, average spending	13,431.87	7,094.92	14,392.28	16,097.66	15,623.93	13,713.92	10,760.59	8,677.59
HOUSEHOLD SERVICES	707.15	229.91	871.68	949.34	633.00	604.31	503.80	768.06
Personal services	293.53	134.86	570.65	521.09	121.48	71.39	36.96	376.69
Babysitting and child care in your own home	36.05	16.71	65.12	87.91	24.65	0.58	0.26	0.14
Babysitting and child care in someone else's home	23.99	29.04	67.75	36.38	9.64	2.20	2.90	–
Day care centers, nurseries, and preschools	188.82	89.11	437.77	392.41	78.94	45.12	6.74	12.74
Other household services	413.61	95.04	301.03	428.25	511.53	532.92	466.83	391.37
Housekeeping services	93.13	2.79	44.02	84.47	124.35	141.08	113.31	111.26
Gardening, lawn care service	83.70	3.46	28.89	70.14	97.91	113.22	137.20	142.24
Water softening service	3.23	0.41	3.62	3.23	3.59	2.76	5.03	2.86
Nonclothing laundry and dry cleaning, sent out	1.00	0.44	1.08	0.90	1.22	1.55	0.80	0.51
Nonclothing laundry and dry cleaning, coin-operated	3.62	5.02	6.06	3.72	2.74	2.81	2.36	2.33
Termite/pest control services	11.30	0.64	9.45	10.50	11.34	13.79	13.10	18.75
Home security system service fee	15.54	2.53	14.41	20.08	15.34	16.08	20.06	12.69
Other home services	14.83	2.23	5.07	14.48	15.55	25.50	23.73	16.05
Termite/pest control products	1.52	0.11	0.98	1.50	1.72	1.84	1.64	2.58
Moving, storage, and freight express	30.46	8.93	39.41	34.88	34.20	37.97	25.07	8.70
Appliance repair, including service center	11.75	0.42	6.93	10.96	15.61	13.17	18.80	13.30
Reupholstering and furniture repair	5.20	0.86	1.78	4.12	4.95	11.61	5.43	7.63
Repairs/rentals of lawn/garden equipment, hand/power tools, etc.	6.08	0.20	3.18	5.66	6.64	7.61	10.00	9.12
Appliance rental	1.63	2.73	2.96	1.78	1.97	0.63	0.45	0.16
Repair of computer systems for nonbusiness use	4.20	0.85	2.71	5.52	5.86	5.21	4.90	0.98
Computer information services	123.92	63.03	128.82	151.71	165.06	134.86	84.55	42.21
HOUSEKEEPING SUPPLIES	528.84	224.97	454.83	597.11	617.55	618.30	590.20	373.15
Laundry and cleaning supplies	132.28	73.04	140.17	149.08	154.25	139.05	123.39	81.01
Soaps and detergents	74.15	48.63	81.48	83.07	86.50	72.87	64.99	46.71
Other laundry cleaning products	58.13	24.41	58.69	66.01	67.75	66.18	58.40	34.29
Other household products	263.37	100.57	203.77	310.90	312.12	308.38	312.72	176.39
Cleansing and toilet tissue, paper towels, and napkins	75.23	39.52	68.15	88.41	79.29	84.29	79.46	61.71
Miscellaneous household products	106.32	43.24	87.10	125.82	134.47	116.86	118.93	60.17
Lawn and garden supplies	81.82	17.81	48.52	96.68	98.37	107.24	114.32	54.51
Postage and stationery	133.19	51.36	110.88	137.12	151.18	170.86	154.09	115.75
Stationery, stationery supplies, giftwrap	59.55	27.71	57.49	68.94	69.82	60.05	67.13	37.61
Postage	68.94	22.76	52.22	58.90	78.58	102.90	83.33	73.47
Delivery services	4.70	0.89	1.17	9.27	2.78	7.92	3.63	4.68
HOUSEHOLD FURNISHINGS AND EQUIPMENT	1,497.05	736.51	1,570.65	1,730.64	1,801.37	1,830.94	1,179.77	657.44
Household textiles	113.48	41.73	108.73	107.63	154.78	139.94	124.28	54.16
Bathroom linens	20.30	6.93	20.54	21.90	26.07	27.37	13.46	11.57
Bedroom linens	53.45	24.07	53.87	48.28	77.15	56.19	59.12	26.78
Kitchen and dining room linens	7.37	2.51	6.27	7.14	10.17	9.71	8.80	2.85
Curtains and draperies	15.24	4.37	16.31	15.42	19.60	17.88	20.31	3.37
Slipcovers and decorative pillows	4.35	0.51	2.25	4.11	4.99	8.13	5.88	3.21
Sewing materials for household items	11.27	2.55	7.94	9.27	14.61	18.74	15.37	6.12
Other linens	1.51	0.80	1.54	1.52	2.19	1.91	1.33	0.24
Furniture	400.82	202.80	498.58	517.56	449.67	446.98	225.45	141.64
Mattresses and springs	44.89	30.07	48.45	45.03	54.16	58.48	28.93	27.12
Other bedroom furniture	79.44	42.02	117.92	95.82	82.04	89.70	29.59	36.01
Sofas	92.17	50.73	111.88	148.68	89.63	99.40	41.00	14.56
Living room chairs	38.76	17.00	38.61	38.00	49.68	45.22	44.83	19.41
Living room tables	17.51	11.41	23.51	21.53	18.76	19.23	8.30	7.32
Kitchen and dining room furniture	49.42	15.15	57.28	71.52	75.27	31.85	24.41	12.63

	total consumer units	under 25	25 to 34	35 to 44	45 to 54	55 to 64	65 to 74	75+
Infants' furniture	$8.17	$10.34	$22.78	$6.99	$4.20	$4.75	$2.96	$2.03
Outdoor furniture	15.35	2.75	9.61	17.04	15.65	33.61	11.32	8.04
Wall units, cabinets, and other furniture	55.13	23.32	68.53	72.95	60.30	64.74	34.10	14.52
Floor coverings	**51.76**	**7.71**	**31.55**	**61.39**	**61.96**	**75.65**	**55.50**	**40.12**
Wall-to-wall carpeting	29.50	3.92	12.80	31.88	29.04	51.58	40.18	30.62
Floor coverings, nonpermanent	22.26	3.79	18.75	29.52	32.91	24.07	15.32	9.50
Major appliances	**195.70**	**67.38**	**215.59**	**208.68**	**216.55**	**231.21**	**219.16**	**110.36**
Dishwashers (built-in), garbage disposals, range hoods	13.50	2.78	11.44	15.89	16.51	14.82	12.28	13.25
Refrigerators and freezers	47.56	16.32	50.55	54.72	45.84	55.89	53.93	35.52
Washing machines	28.68	14.83	23.88	39.54	32.09	27.65	26.86	11.95
Clothes dryers	19.43	10.99	21.16	28.11	20.36	18.05	15.47	8.33
Cooking stoves, ovens	30.49	5.67	21.94	27.87	36.83	56.09	30.14	19.95
Microwave ovens	7.56	4.55	6.29	8.52	9.50	7.95	7.76	5.27
Window air conditioners	5.40	1.39	6.01	6.20	5.62	5.90	7.53	2.44
Electric floor-cleaning equipment	30.24	7.68	63.15	19.21	32.83	24.86	36.08	8.88
Sewing machines	8.95	1.75	5.24	5.50	13.58	13.15	18.67	2.65
Miscellaneous household appliances	2.24	1.13	0.04	1.07	1.38	5.25	9.02	–
Small appliances and misc. housewares	**87.76**	**47.59**	**68.71**	**92.45**	**111.20**	**127.00**	**78.53**	**46.59**
Housewares	65.25	33.50	47.01	69.09	85.98	98.80	52.38	35.60
Plastic dinnerware	1.56	1.38	2.06	1.86	2.21	1.31	0.53	0.30
China and other dinnerware	7.04	1.53	3.76	5.53	7.94	13.99	10.29	5.19
Flatware	3.99	2.92	3.50	4.00	5.46	5.00	3.39	1.81
Glassware	8.89	9.55	4.49	7.78	10.13	19.23	5.02	5.00
Silver serving pieces	6.51	2.85	5.66	7.82	7.23	8.38	7.34	2.94
Other serving pieces	1.44	0.92	1.44	1.27	2.54	1.76	0.67	0.25
Nonelectric cookware	15.26	6.06	13.53	18.41	12.14	25.97	13.96	11.31
Tableware, nonelectric kitchenware	20.56	8.28	12.57	22.41	38.33	23.17	11.18	8.79
Small appliances	22.51	14.09	21.70	23.35	25.21	28.20	26.14	10.99
Small electric kitchen appliances	15.66	10.39	16.37	14.76	20.07	18.70	15.03	7.58
Portable heating and cooling equipment	6.85	3.70	5.34	8.59	5.14	9.50	11.11	3.41
Miscellaneous household equipment	**647.53**	**369.30**	**547.09**	**742.93**	**807.22**	**810.15**	**476.86**	**264.57**
Window coverings	24.34	2.29	41.02	27.78	18.31	29.47	15.26	18.64
Infants' equipment	13.08	5.68	23.52	15.55	11.64	11.87	12.50	–
Laundry and cleaning equipment	14.03	6.90	12.73	14.77	17.36	18.00	14.80	6.75
Outdoor equipment	23.74	0.86	17.28	35.33	33.47	19.68	28.85	8.17
Clocks	4.02	2.76	2.29	8.72	2.26	5.41	1.73	1.99
Lamps and lighting fixtures	13.66	5.77	12.81	20.59	16.54	12.61	9.70	5.97
Other household decorative items	126.78	49.01	93.62	149.94	130.27	231.64	119.64	44.60
Telephones and accessories	26.78	11.95	19.94	38.63	41.05	24.33	16.62	8.69
Lawn and garden equipment	55.39	6.40	62.52	37.77	86.79	75.42	42.12	38.22
Power tools	24.38	0.99	28.79	39.80	25.76	23.98	20.43	3.02
Office furniture for home use	12.61	4.56	13.28	13.25	18.16	19.60	5.63	1.76
Hand tools	7.22	4.08	9.40	8.90	9.19	6.12	4.33	2.71
Indoor plants and fresh flowers	40.31	17.15	30.04	37.14	53.81	55.73	42.57	30.22
Closet and storage items	9.57	3.72	10.78	12.54	10.14	13.42	4.38	4.08
Rental of furniture	2.70	10.11	4.03	4.12	0.67	0.06	2.37	0.09
Luggage	6.18	1.66	4.98	8.29	8.75	7.61	4.30	1.74
Computers and computer hardware, nonbusiness use	136.77	116.14	151.31	153.24	181.26	166.11	71.71	24.67
Computer software and accessories, nonbusiness use	17.98	18.07	18.25	20.73	22.12	22.90	12.22	1.83
Telephone answering devices	0.93	0.35	1.23	0.83	1.43	0.96	0.59	0.22
Calculators	1.27	2.93	0.59	1.93	2.00	0.74	0.31	0.09
Business equipment for home use	1.08	0.36	0.87	1.90	0.88	1.17	0.83	0.79
Other hardware	38.35	85.94	47.05	39.99	51.47	16.00	13.50	10.52
Smoke alarms	1.13	0.34	2.16	0.97	1.23	1.16	0.81	0.30
Other household appliances	6.67	1.91	3.90	6.30	8.58	10.25	5.13	8.31
Miscellaneous household equipment and parts	38.57	9.39	34.64	43.91	54.09	35.91	26.52	41.18

Note: Subcategories may not add to total because some are not shown. (–) means sample is too small to make a reliable estimate.
Source: Bureau of Labor Statistics, unpublished tables from the 2003 Consumer Expenditure Survey

Table 8.2 Housing: Household Operations: Indexed spending by age, 2003

(indexed average annual spending of consumer units (CU) on household services, supplies, furnishings, and equipment, by age of consumer unit reference person, 2003; index definition: an index of 100 is the average for all consumer units; an index of 132 means that spending by consumer units in that group is 32 percent above the average for all consumer units; an index of 68 indicates spending that is 32 percent below the average for all consumer units)

	total consumer units	under 25	25 to 34	35 to 44	45 to 54	55 to 64	65 to 74	75+
Average spending of CU, total	$40,817	$22,396	$40,525	$47,175	$50,101	$44,191	$33,629	$25,016
Average spending of CU, index	100	55	99	116	123	108	82	61
Housing, spending index	100	53	107	120	116	102	80	65
HOUSEHOLD SERVICES	100	33	123	134	90	85	71	109
Personal services	100	46	194	178	41	24	13	128
Babysitting and child care in your own home	100	46	181	244	68	2	1	0
Babysitting and child care in someone else's home	100	121	282	152	40	9	12	–
Day care centers, nurseries, and preschools	100	47	232	208	42	24	4	7
Other household services	100	23	73	104	124	129	113	95
Housekeeping services	100	3	47	91	134	151	122	119
Gardening, lawn care service	100	4	35	84	117	135	164	170
Water softening service	100	13	112	100	111	85	156	89
Nonclothing laundry and dry cleaning, sent out	100	44	108	90	122	155	80	51
Nonclothing laundry and dry cleaning, coin-operated	100	139	167	103	76	78	65	64
Termite/pest control services	100	6	84	93	100	122	116	166
Home security system service fee	100	16	93	129	99	103	129	82
Other home services	100	15	34	98	105	172	160	108
Termite/pest control products	100	7	64	99	113	121	108	170
Moving, storage, and freight express	100	29	129	115	112	125	82	29
Appliance repair, including service center	100	4	59	93	133	112	160	113
Reupholstering and furniture repair	100	17	34	79	95	223	104	147
Repairs/rentals of lawn/garden equipment, hand/power tools, etc.	100	3	52	93	109	125	164	150
Appliance rental	100	167	182	109	121	39	28	10
Repair of computer systems for nonbusiness use	100	20	65	131	140	124	117	23
Computer information services	100	51	104	122	133	109	68	34
HOUSEKEEPING SUPPLIES	100	43	86	113	117	117	112	71
Laundry and cleaning supplies	100	55	106	113	117	105	93	61
Soaps and detergents	100	66	110	112	117	98	88	63
Other laundry cleaning products	100	42	101	114	117	114	100	59
Other household products	100	38	77	118	119	117	119	67
Cleansing and toilet tissue, paper towels, and napkins	100	53	91	118	105	112	106	82
Miscellaneous household products	100	41	82	118	126	110	112	57
Lawn and garden supplies	100	22	59	118	120	131	140	67
Postage and stationery	100	39	83	103	114	128	116	87
Stationery, stationery supplies, giftwrap	100	47	97	116	117	101	113	63
Postage	100	33	76	85	114	149	121	107
Delivery services	100	19	25	197	59	169	77	100
HOUSEHOLD FURNISHINGS AND EQUIPMENT	100	49	105	116	120	122	79	44
Household textiles	100	37	96	95	136	123	110	48
Bathroom linens	100	34	101	108	128	135	66	57
Bedroom linens	100	45	101	90	144	105	111	50
Kitchen and dining room linens	100	34	85	97	138	132	119	39
Curtains and draperies	100	29	107	101	129	117	133	22
Slipcovers and decorative pillows	100	12	52	94	115	187	135	74
Sewing materials for household items	100	23	70	82	130	166	136	54
Other linens	100	53	102	101	145	126	88	16
Furniture	100	51	124	129	112	112	56	35
Mattresses and springs	100	67	108	100	121	130	64	60
Other bedroom furniture	100	53	148	121	103	113	37	45
Sofas	100	55	121	161	97	108	44	16
Living room chairs	100	44	100	98	128	117	116	50
Living room tables	100	65	134	123	107	110	47	42
Kitchen and dining room furniture	100	31	116	145	152	64	49	26

	total consumer units	under 25	25 to 34	35 to 44	45 to 54	55 to 64	65 to 74	75+
Infants' furniture	100	127	279	86	51	58	36	25
Outdoor furniture	100	18	63	111	102	219	74	52
Wall units, cabinets, and other furniture	100	42	124	132	109	117	62	26
Floor coverings	**100**	**15**	**61**	**119**	**120**	**146**	**107**	**78**
Wall-to-wall carpeting	100	13	43	108	98	175	136	104
Floor coverings, nonpermanent	100	17	84	133	148	108	69	43
Major appliances	**100**	**34**	**110**	**107**	**111**	**118**	**112**	**56**
Dishwashers (built-in), garbage disposals, range hoods	100	21	85	118	122	110	91	98
Refrigerators and freezers	100	34	106	115	96	118	113	75
Washing machines	100	52	101	138	112	96	94	42
Clothes dryers	100	57	109	145	105	93	80	43
Cooking stoves, ovens	100	19	72	91	121	184	99	65
Microwave ovens	100	60	83	113	126	105	103	70
Window air conditioners	100	26	111	115	104	109	139	45
Electric floor-cleaning equipment	100	25	209	64	109	82	119	29
Sewing machines	100	20	59	63	152	147	209	30
Miscellaneous household appliances	100	50	2	48	62	234	403	–
Small appliances and misc. housewares	**100**	**54**	**73**	**105**	**127**	**145**	**89**	**53**
Housewares	100	51	72	106	132	151	80	55
Plastic dinnerware	100	88	132	119	142	84	34	19
China and other dinnerware	100	22	53	79	113	199	146	74
Flatware	100	73	88	100	137	125	85	45
Glassware	100	107	51	88	114	216	56	56
Silver serving pieces	100	44	87	120	111	129	113	45
Other serving pieces	100	64	100	88	176	122	47	17
Nonelectric cookware	100	40	89	121	80	170	91	74
Tableware, nonelectric kitchenware	100	40	61	109	186	113	54	43
Small appliances	100	63	96	104	112	125	116	49
Small electric kitchen appliances	100	66	105	94	128	119	96	48
Portable heating and cooling equipment	100	54	78	125	75	139	162	50
Miscellaneous household equipment	**100**	**57**	**100**	**115**	**125**	**125**	**74**	**41**
Window coverings	100	9	169	114	75	121	63	77
Infants' equipment	100	43	180	119	89	91	96	–
Laundry and cleaning equipment	100	49	91	105	124	128	105	48
Outdoor equipment	100	4	73	149	141	83	122	34
Clocks	100	69	57	217	56	135	43	50
Lamps and lighting fixtures	100	42	94	151	121	92	71	44
Other household decorative items	100	39	74	118	103	183	94	35
Telephones and accessories	100	45	74	144	153	91	62	32
Lawn and garden equipment	100	12	113	68	157	136	76	69
Power tools	100	4	118	163	106	98	84	12
Office furniture for home use	100	36	105	105	144	155	45	14
Hand tools	100	57	130	123	127	85	60	38
Indoor plants and fresh flowers	100	43	75	92	133	138	106	75
Closet and storage items	100	39	113	131	106	140	46	43
Rental of furniture	100	374	149	153	25	2	88	3
Luggage	100	27	81	134	142	123	70	28
Computers and computer hardware, nonbusiness use	100	85	111	112	133	121	52	18
Computer software and accessories, nonbusiness use	100	101	102	115	123	127	68	10
Telephone answering devices	100	38	133	89	154	103	63	24
Calculators	100	231	46	152	157	58	24	7
Business equipment for home use	100	33	81	176	81	108	77	73
Other hardware	100	224	123	104	134	42	35	27
Smoke alarms	100	30	191	86	109	103	72	27
Other household appliances	100	29	58	94	129	154	77	125
Miscellaneous household equipment and parts	100	24	93	114	140	93	69	107

Note: (–) means sample is too small to make a reliable estimate.
Source: Calculations by New Strategist based on the 2003 Consumer Expenditure Survey

Table 8.3 Housing: Household Operations: Total spending by age, 2003

(total annual spending on household services, supplies, furnishings, and equipment, by consumer unit (CU) age groups, 2003; numbers in thousands)

	total consumer units	under 25	25 to 34	35 to 44	45 to 54	55 to 64	65 to 74	75+
Number of consumer units	115,356	8,584	19,737	24,413	23,131	16,580	11,495	11,417
Total spending of all CUs	$4,708,523,919	$192,243,230	$799,846,267	$1,151,684,740	$1,158,882,993	$732,680,977	$386,567,309	$285,612,010
Housing, total spending	1,549,446,796	60,902,793	284,060,430	392,992,174	361,397,125	227,376,794	123,692,982	99,072,045
HOUSEHOLD SERVICES	81,573,995	1,973,547	17,204,348	23,176,237	14,641,923	10,019,460	5,791,181	8,768,941
Personal services	33,860,447	1,157,638	11,262,919	12,721,370	2,809,954	1,183,646	424,855	4,300,670
Babysitting and child care in your own home	4,158,584	143,439	1,285,273	2,145,147	570,179	9,616	2,989	1,598
Babysitting and child care in someone else's home	2,767,390	249,279	1,337,182	888,145	222,983	36,476	33,336	–
Day care centers, nurseries, and preschools	21,781,520	764,920	8,640,266	9,579,905	1,825,961	748,090	77,476	145,453
Other household services	47,712,395	815,823	5,941,429	10,454,867	11,832,200	8,835,814	5,366,211	4,468,271
Housekeeping services	10,743,104	23,949	868,823	2,062,166	2,876,340	2,339,106	1,302,498	1,270,255
Gardening, lawn care service	9,655,297	29,701	570,202	1,712,328	2,264,756	1,877,188	1,577,114	1,623,954
Water softening service	372,600	3,519	71,448	78,854	83,040	45,761	57,820	32,653
Nonclothing laundry and dry cleaning, sent out	115,356	3,777	21,316	21,972	28,220	25,699	9,196	5,823
Nonclothing laundry and dry cleaning, coin-operated	417,589	43,092	119,606	90,816	63,379	46,590	27,128	26,602
Termite/pest control services	1,303,523	5,494	186,515	256,337	262,306	228,638	150,585	214,069
Home security system service fee	1,792,632	21,718	284,410	490,213	354,830	266,606	230,590	144,882
Other home services	1,710,729	19,142	100,067	353,500	359,687	422,790	272,776	183,243
Termite/pest control products	175,341	944	19,342	36,620	39,785	30,507	18,852	29,456
Moving, storage, and freight express	3,513,744	76,655	777,835	851,525	791,080	629,543	288,180	99,328
Appliance repair, including service center	1,355,433	3,605	136,777	267,566	361,075	218,359	216,106	151,846
Reupholstering and furniture repair	599,851	7,382	35,132	190,582	114,498	192,494	62,418	87,112
Repairs/rentals of lawn/garden equipment, hand/power tools, etc.	701,364	1,717	62,764	138,178	153,590	126,174	114,950	104,123
Appliance rental	188,030	23,434	58,422	43,455	45,568	10,445	5,173	1,827
Repair of computer systems for nonbusiness use	484,495	7,296	53,487	134,760	135,548	86,382	56,326	11,189
Computer information services	14,294,916	541,050	2,542,520	3,703,696	3,818,003	2,235,979	971,902	481,912
HOUSEKEEPING SUPPLIES	61,004,867	1,931,142	8,976,980	14,577,246	14,284,549	10,251,414	6,784,349	4,260,254
Laundry and cleaning supplies	15,259,292	626,975	2,766,535	3,639,490	3,567,957	2,305,449	1,418,368	924,891
Soaps and detergents	8,553,647	417,440	1,608,171	2,027,988	2,000,832	1,208,185	747,060	533,288
Other laundry cleaning products	6,705,644	209,535	1,158,365	1,611,502	1,567,125	1,097,264	671,308	391,489
Other household products	30,381,310	863,293	4,021,808	7,590,002	7,219,648	5,112,940	3,594,716	2,013,845
Cleansing and toilet tissue, paper towels, and napkins	8,678,232	339,240	1,345,077	2,158,353	1,834,057	1,397,528	913,393	704,543
Miscellaneous household products	12,264,650	371,172	1,719,093	3,071,644	3,110,426	1,937,539	1,367,100	686,961
Lawn and garden supplies	9,438,428	152,881	957,639	2,360,249	2,275,396	1,778,039	1,314,108	622,341
Postage and stationery	15,364,266	440,874	2,188,439	3,347,511	3,496,945	2,832,859	1,771,265	1,321,518
Stationery, stationery supplies, giftwrap	6,869,450	237,863	1,134,680	1,683,032	1,615,006	995,629	771,659	429,393
Postage	7,952,643	195,372	1,030,666	1,437,926	1,817,634	1,706,082	957,878	838,807
Delivery services	542,173	7,640	23,092	226,309	64,304	131,314	41,727	53,432
HOUSEHOLD FURNISHINGS, EQUIPMENT	172,693,700	6,322,202	30,999,919	42,250,114	41,667,489	30,356,985	13,561,456	7,505,992
Household textiles	13,090,599	358,210	2,146,004	2,627,571	3,580,216	2,320,205	1,428,599	618,345
Bathroom linens	2,341,727	59,487	405,398	534,645	603,025	453,795	154,723	132,095
Bedroom linens	6,165,778	206,617	1,063,232	1,178,660	1,784,557	931,630	679,584	305,747
Kitchen and dining room linens	850,174	21,546	123,751	174,309	235,242	160,992	101,156	32,538
Curtains and draperies	1,758,025	37,512	321,910	376,448	453,368	296,450	233,463	38,475
Slipcovers and decorative pillows	501,799	4,378	44,408	100,337	115,424	134,795	67,591	36,649
Sewing materials for household items	1,300,062	21,889	156,712	226,309	337,944	310,709	176,678	69,872
Other linens	174,188	6,867	30,395	37,108	50,657	31,668	15,288	2,740
Furniture	46,236,992	1,740,835	9,840,473	12,635,192	10,401,317	7,410,928	2,591,548	1,617,104
Mattresses and springs	5,178,331	258,121	956,258	1,099,317	1,252,775	969,598	332,550	309,629
Other bedroom furniture	9,163,881	360,700	2,327,387	2,339,254	1,897,667	1,487,226	340,137	411,126
Sofas	10,632,363	435,466	2,208,176	3,629,725	2,073,232	1,648,052	471,295	166,232
Living room chairs	4,471,199	145,928	762,046	927,694	1,149,148	749,748	515,321	221,604
Living room tables	2,019,884	97,943	464,017	525,612	433,938	318,833	95,409	83,572
Kitchen and dining room furniture	5,700,894	130,048	1,130,535	1,746,018	1,741,070	528,073	280,593	144,197

	total consumer units	under 25	25 to 34	35 to 44	45 to 54	55 to 64	65 to 74	75+
Infants' furniture	$942,459	$88,759	$449,609	$170,647	$97,150	$78,755	$34,025	$23,177
Outdoor furniture	1,770,715	23,606	189,673	415,998	362,000	557,254	130,123	91,793
Wall units, cabinets, and other furniture	6,359,576	200,179	,352,577	1,780,928	1,394,799	1,073,389	391,980	165,775
Floor coverings	**5,970,827**	**66,183**	**622,702**	**1,498,714**	**1,433,197**	**1,254,277**	**637,973**	**458,050**
Wall-to-wall carpeting	3,403,002	33,649	252,634	778,286	671,724	855,196	461,869	349,589
Floor coverings, nonpermanent	2,567,825	32,533	370,069	720,672	761,241	399,081	176,103	108,462
Major appliances	**22,575,169**	**578,390**	**4,262,995**	**5,094,505**	**5,009,018**	**3,833,462**	**2,519,244**	**1,259,980**
Dishwashers (built-in), garbage disposals, range hoods	1,557,306	23,864	225,791	387,923	381,893	245,716	141,159	151,275
Refrigerators and freezers	5,486,331	140,091	997,705	1,335,879	1,060,325	926,656	619,925	405,532
Washing machines	3,308,410	127,301	570,005	965,290	742,274	458,437	308,756	136,433
Clothes dryers	2,241,367	94,338	417,635	686,249	470,947	299,269	177,828	95,104
Cooking stoves, ovens	3,517,204	48,671	433,030	680,390	851,915	929,972	346,459	227,769
Microwave ovens	872,091	39,057	124,146	207,999	219,745	131,811	89,201	60,168
Window air conditioners	622,922	11,932	118,619	151,361	129,996	97,822	86,557	27,857
Electric floor-cleaning equipment	3,488,365	65,925	1,246,392	468,974	759,391	412,179	414,740	101,383
Sewing machines	1,032,436	15,022	103,422	136,713	314,119	218,027	214,612	30,255
Miscellaneous household appliances	258,397	9,700	789	26,122	31,921	87,045	103,685	–
Small appliances and misc. housewares	**10,123,643**	**408,513**	**1,356,129**	**2,256,982**	**2,572,167**	**2,105,660**	**902,702**	**531,918**
Housewares	7,526,979	287,564	927,836	1,686,694	1,988,803	1,638,104	602,108	406,445
Plastic dinnerware	179,955	11,846	40,658	45,408	51,120	21,720	6,092	3,425
China and other dinnerware	812,106	13,134	74,211	135,004	183,660	231,954	118,284	59,254
Flatware	460,270	25,065	69,080	97,652	126,295	82,900	38,968	20,665
Glassware	1,025,515	81,977	88,619	189,933	234,317	318,833	57,705	57,085
Silver serving pieces	750,968	24,464	111,711	190,910	167,237	138,940	84,373	33,566
Other serving pieces	166,113	7,897	28,421	31,005	58,753	29,181	7,702	2,854
Nonelectric cookware	1,760,333	52,019	267,042	449,443	280,810	430,583	160,470	129,126
Tableware, nonelectric kitchenware	2,371,719	71,076	248,094	547,095	886,611	384,159	128,514	100,355
Small appliances	2,596,664	120,949	428,293	570,044	583,133	467,556	300,479	125,473
Small electric kitchen appliances	1,806,475	89,188	323,095	360,336	464,239	310,046	172,770	86,541
Portable heating and cooling equipment	790,189	31,761	105,396	209,708	118,893	157,510	127,709	38,932
Miscellaneous household equipment	**74,696,471**	**3,170,071**	**12,771,615**	**18,137,150**	**18,671,806**	**13,432,287**	**5,481,506**	**3,020,596**
Window coverings	2,807,765	19,657	409,612	578,193	423,529	488,613	175,414	212,813
Infants' equipment	1,508,856	48,757	464,214	379,856	269,245	196,805	143,688	–
Laundry and cleaning equipment	1,618,445	59,230	251,252	360,530	401,554	298,440	170,126	77,065
Outdoor equipment	2,738,551	7,382	141,055	362,511	774,195	326,294	331,631	93,277
Clocks	463,731	23,692	45,198	212,831	52,276	89,698	19,886	22,720
Lamps and lighting fixtures	1,575,763	49,530	252,831	502,664	382,587	209,074	111,502	68,159
Other household decorative items	14,624,834	420,702	1,847,778	3,660,485	3,013,275	3,840,591	1,375,262	509,198
Telephones and accessories	3,089,234	102,579	393,556	943,074	949,528	403,391	191,047	99,214
Lawn and garden equipment	6,389,569	54,938	1,233,957	922,079	2,007,539	1,250,464	484,169	436,358
Power tools	2,812,379	8,498	568,228	971,637	595,855	397,588	234,843	34,479
Office furniture for home use	1,454,639	39,143	252,107	323,472	420,059	324,968	64,717	20,094
Hand tools	832,870	35,023	135,528	217,276	212,574	101,470	49,773	30,940
Indoor plants and fresh flowers	4,650,000	147,216	592,899	906,699	1,244,679	924,003	489,342	345,022
Closet and storage items	1,103,957	31,932	212,765	306,139	234,548	222,504	50,348	46,581
Rental of furniture	311,461	86,784	79,540	100,582	15,498	995	27,243	1,028
Luggage	712,900	14,249	98,290	202,384	202,396	126,174	49,429	19,866
Computers and computer hardware, nonbusiness use	15,777,240	996,946	2,936,405	3,741,048	4,192,725	2,754,104	824,306	281,657
Computer software and accessories, nonbusiness use	2,074,101	155,113	350,200	506,081	511,658	379,682	140,469	20,893
Telephone answering devices	107,281	3,004	25,263	20,263	33,077	15,917	6,782	2,512
Calculators	146,502	25,151	1,645	47,117	46,262	12,269	3,563	1,028
Business equipment for home use	124,584	3,090	7,171	46,385	20,355	19,399	9,541	9,019
Other hardware	4,423,903	737,709	928,626	976,275	1,190,553	265,280	155,183	120,107
Smoke alarms	130,352	2,919	42,632	23,681	28,451	19,233	9,311	3,425
Other household appliances	769,425	16,395	76,974	153,802	198,464	169,945	58,969	94,875
Miscellaneous household equipment and parts	4,449,281	80,604	683,690	1,071,975	1,251,156	595,388	304,847	470,152

Note: Numbers may not add to total because of rounding and missing subcategories. (–) means sample is too small to make a reliable estimate.
Source: Calculations by New Strategist based on the 2003 Consumer Expenditure Survey

Table 8.4 Housing: Household Operations: Market shares by age, 2003

(percentage of total annual spending on household services, supplies, furnishings, and equipment accounted for by consumer unit age groups, 2003)

	total consumer units	under 25	25 to 34	35 to 44	45 to 54	55 to 64	65 to 74	75+
Share of total consumer units	100.0%	7.4%	17.1%	21.2%	20.1%	14.4%	10.0%	9.9%
Share of total before-tax income	100.0	3.0	16.9	25.3	26.7	16.5	6.9	4.9
Share of total spending	100.0	4.1	17.0	24.5	24.6	15.6	8.2	6.1
Share of housing spending	100.0	3.9	18.3	25.4	23.3	14.7	8.0	6.4
HOUSEHOLD SERVICES	100.0	2.4	21.1	28.4	17.9	12.3	7.1	10.7
Personal services	100.0	3.4	33.3	37.6	8.3	3.5	1.3	12.7
Babysitting and child care in your own home	100.0	3.4	30.9	51.6	13.7	0.2	0.1	0.0
Babysitting and child care in someone else's home	100.0	9.0	48.3	32.1	8.1	1.3	1.2	–
Day care centers, nurseries, and preschools	100.0	3.5	39.7	44.0	8.4	3.4	0.4	0.7
Other household services	100.0	1.7	12.5	21.9	24.8	18.5	11.2	9.4
Housekeeping services	100.0	0.2	8.1	19.2	26.8	21.8	12.1	11.8
Gardening, lawn care service	100.0	0.3	5.9	17.7	23.5	19.4	16.3	16.8
Water softening service	100.0	0.9	19.2	21.2	22.3	12.3	15.5	8.8
Nonclothing laundry and dry cleaning, sent out	100.0	3.3	18.5	19.0	24.5	22.3	8.0	5.0
Nonclothing laundry and dry cleaning, coin-operated	100.0	10.3	28.6	21.7	15.2	11.2	6.5	6.4
Termite/pest control services	100.0	0.4	14.3	19.7	20.1	17.5	11.6	16.4
Home security system service fee	100.0	1.2	15.9	27.3	19.8	14.9	12.9	8.1
Other home services	100.0	1.1	5.8	20.7	21.0	24.7	15.9	10.7
Termite/pest control products	100.0	0.5	11.0	20.9	22.7	17.4	10.8	16.8
Moving, storage, and freight express	100.0	2.2	22.1	24.2	22.5	17.9	8.2	2.8
Appliance repair, including service center	100.0	0.3	10.1	19.7	26.6	16.1	15.9	11.2
Reupholstering and furniture repair	100.0	1.2	5.9	16.8	19.1	32.1	10.4	14.5
Repairs/rentals of lawn/garden equipment, hand/power tools, etc.	100.0	0.2	8.9	19.7	21.9	18.0	16.4	14.8
Appliance rental	100.0	12.5	31.1	23.1	24.2	5.6	2.8	1.0
Repair of computer systems for nonbusiness use	100.0	1.5	11.0	27.8	28.0	17.8	11.6	2.3
Computer information services	100.0	3.8	17.8	25.9	26.7	15.6	6.8	3.4
HOUSEKEEPING SUPPLIES	100.0	3.2	14.7	23.9	23.4	16.8	11.1	7.0
Laundry and cleaning supplies	100.0	4.1	18.1	23.9	23.4	15.1	9.3	6.1
Soaps and detergents	100.0	4.9	18.8	23.7	23.4	14.1	8.7	6.2
Other laundry cleaning products	100.0	3.1	17.3	24.0	23.4	16.4	10.0	5.8
Other household products	100.0	2.8	13.2	25.0	23.8	16.8	11.8	6.6
Cleansing and toilet tissue, paper towels, and napkins	100.0	3.9	15.5	24.9	21.1	16.1	10.5	8.1
Miscellaneous household products	100.0	3.0	14.0	25.0	25.4	15.8	11.1	5.6
Lawn and garden supplies	100.0	1.6	10.1	25.0	24.1	18.8	13.9	6.6
Postage and stationery	100.0	2.9	14.2	21.8	22.8	18.4	11.5	8.6
Stationery, stationery supplies, giftwrap	100.0	3.5	16.5	24.5	23.5	14.5	11.2	6.3
Postage	100.0	2.5	13.0	18.1	22.9	21.5	12.0	10.5
Delivery services	100.0	1.4	4.3	41.7	11.9	24.2	7.7	9.9
HOUSEHOLD FURNISHINGS AND EQUIPMENT	100.0	3.7	18.0	24.5	24.1	17.6	7.9	4.3
Household textiles	100.0	2.7	16.4	20.1	27.3	17.7	10.9	4.7
Bathroom linens	100.0	2.5	17.3	22.8	25.8	19.4	6.6	5.6
Bedroom linens	100.0	3.4	17.2	19.1	28.9	15.1	11.0	5.0
Kitchen and dining room linens	100.0	2.5	14.6	20.5	27.7	18.9	11.9	3.8
Curtains and draperies	100.0	2.1	18.3	21.4	25.8	16.9	13.3	2.2
Slipcovers and decorative pillows	100.0	0.9	8.8	20.0	23.0	26.9	13.5	7.3
Sewing materials for household items	100.0	1.7	12.1	17.4	26.0	23.9	13.6	5.4
Other linens	100.0	3.9	17.4	21.3	29.1	18.2	8.8	1.6
Furniture	100.0	3.8	21.3	27.3	22.5	16.0	5.6	3.5
Mattresses and springs	100.0	5.0	18.5	21.2	24.2	18.7	6.4	6.0
Other bedroom furniture	100.0	3.9	25.4	25.5	20.7	16.2	3.7	4.5
Sofas	100.0	4.1	20.8	34.1	19.5	15.5	4.4	1.6
Living room chairs	100.0	3.3	17.0	20.7	25.7	16.8	11.5	5.0
Living room tables	100.0	4.8	23.0	26.0	21.5	15.8	4.7	4.1
Kitchen and dining room furniture	100.0	2.3	19.8	30.6	30.5	9.3	4.9	2.5

	total consumer units	under 25	25 to 34	35 to 44	45 to 54	55 to 64	65 to 74	75+
Infants' furniture	100.0%	9.4%	47.7%	18.1%	10.3%	8.4%	3.6%	2.5%
Outdoor furniture	100.0	1.3	10.7	23.5	20.4	31.5	7.3	5.2
Wall units, cabinets, and other furniture	100.0	3.1	21.3	28.0	21.9	16.9	6.2	2.6
Floor coverings	**100.0**	**1.1**	**10.4**	**25.1**	**24.0**	**21.0**	**10.7**	**7.7**
Wall-to-wall carpeting	100.0	1.0	7.4	22.9	19.7	25.1	13.6	10.3
Floor coverings, nonpermanent	100.0	1.3	14.4	28.1	29.6	15.5	6.9	4.2
Major appliances	**100.0**	**2.6**	**18.9**	**22.6**	**22.2**	**17.0**	**11.2**	**5.6**
Dishwashers (built-in), garbage disposals, range hoods	100.0	1.5	14.5	24.9	24.5	15.8	9.1	9.7
Refrigerators and freezers	100.0	2.6	18.2	24.3	19.3	16.9	11.3	7.4
Washing machines	100.0	3.8	17.2	29.2	22.4	13.9	9.3	4.1
Clothes dryers	100.0	4.2	18.6	30.6	21.0	13.4	7.9	4.2
Cooking stoves, ovens	100.0	1.4	12.3	19.3	24.2	26.4	9.9	6.5
Microwave ovens	100.0	4.5	14.2	23.9	25.2	15.1	10.2	6.9
Window air conditioners	100.0	1.9	19.0	24.3	20.9	15.7	13.9	4.5
Electric floor-cleaning equipment	100.0	1.9	25.7	13.4	21.8	11.8	11.9	2.9
Sewing machines	100.0	1.5	10.0	13.2	30.4	21.1	20.8	2.9
Miscellaneous household appliances	100.0	3.8	0.3	10.1	12.4	33.7	40.1	–
Small appliances and misc. housewares	**100.0**	**4.0**	**13.4**	**22.3**	**25.4**	**20.8**	**8.9**	**5.3**
Housewares	100.0	3.8	12.3	22.4	26.4	21.8	8.0	5.4
Plastic dinnerware	100.0	6.6	22.6	25.2	28.4	12.1	3.4	1.9
China and other dinnerware	100.0	1.6	9.1	16.6	22.6	28.6	14.6	7.3
Flatware	100.0	5.4	15.0	21.2	27.4	18.0	8.5	4.5
Glassware	100.0	8.0	8.6	18.5	22.8	31.1	5.6	5.6
Silver serving pieces	100.0	3.3	14.9	25.4	22.3	18.5	11.2	4.5
Other serving pieces	100.0	4.8	17.1	18.7	35.4	17.6	4.6	1.7
Nonelectric cookware	100.0	3.0	15.2	25.5	16.0	24.5	9.1	7.3
Tableware, nonelectric kitchenware	100.0	3.0	11.5	23.1	37.4	16.2	5.4	4.2
Small appliances	100.0	4.7	15.5	22.0	22.5	18.0	11.6	4.8
Small electric kitchen appliances	100.0	4.9	17.9	19.9	25.7	17.2	9.6	4.8
Portable heating and cooling equipment	100.0	4.0	13.3	26.5	15.0	19.9	16.2	4.9
Miscellaneous household equipment	**100.0**	**4.2**	**17.1**	**24.3**	**25.0**	**18.0**	**7.3**	**4.0**
Window coverings	100.0	0.7	28.8	24.2	15.1	17.4	6.2	7.6
Infants' equipment	100.0	3.2	30.8	25.2	17.8	13.0	9.5	–
Laundry and cleaning equipment	100.0	3.7	15.5	22.3	24.8	18.4	10.5	4.8
Outdoor equipment	100.0	0.3	12.5	31.5	28.3	11.9	12.1	3.4
Clocks	100.0	5.1	9.7	45.9	11.3	19.3	4.3	4.9
Lamps and lighting fixtures	100.0	3.1	16.0	31.9	24.3	13.3	7.1	4.3
Other household decorative items	100.0	2.9	12.6	25.0	20.6	26.3	9.4	3.5
Telephones and accessories	100.0	3.3	12.7	30.5	30.7	13.1	6.2	3.2
Lawn and garden equipment	100.0	0.9	19.3	14.4	31.4	19.6	7.6	6.8
Power tools	100.0	0.3	20.2	34.5	21.2	14.1	8.4	1.2
Office furniture for home use	100.0	2.7	18.0	22.2	28.9	22.3	4.4	1.4
Hand tools	100.0	4.2	22.3	26.1	25.5	12.2	6.0	3.7
Indoor plants and fresh flowers	100.0	3.2	12.8	19.5	26.8	19.9	10.5	7.4
Closet and storage items	100.0	2.9	19.3	27.7	21.2	20.2	4.6	4.2
Rental of furniture	100.0	27.9	25.5	32.3	5.0	0.3	8.7	0.3
Luggage	100.0	2.0	13.8	28.4	28.4	17.7	6.9	2.8
Computers and computer hardware, nonbusiness use	100.0	6.3	18.9	23.7	26.6	17.5	5.2	1.8
Computer software and accessories, nonbusiness use	100.0	7.5	17.4	24.4	24.7	18.3	6.8	1.0
Telephone answering devices	100.0	2.8	23.5	18.9	30.8	14.8	6.3	2.3
Calculators	100.0	17.2	7.9	32.2	31.6	8.4	2.4	0.7
Business equipment for home use	100.0	2.5	13.8	37.2	16.3	15.6	7.7	7.2
Other hardware	100.0	16.7	21.0	22.1	26.9	6.0	3.5	2.7
Smoke alarms	100.0	2.2	32.7	13.2	21.8	14.8	7.1	2.6
Other household appliances	100.0	2.1	10.0	20.0	25.8	22.1	7.7	12.3
Miscellaneous household equipment and parts	100.0	1.8	15.4	24.1	28.1	13.4	6.9	10.6

Note: Numbers may not add to total because of rounding. (–) means sample is too small to make a reliable estimate.
Source: Calculations by New Strategist based on the 2003 Consumer Expenditure Survey

Table 8.5 Housing: Household Operations: Average spending by income, 2003

(average annual spending on household services, supplies, furnishings, and equipment, by before-tax income of consumer units (CU), 2003; complete income reporters only)

	total complete reporters	under $20,000	$20,000– $39,999	$40,000– $49,999	$50,000– $69,999	$70,000– $79,999	$80,000– $99,999	$100,000 or more
Number of consumer units (000)	97,391	27,100	23,941	8,891	13,890	5,121	6,909	11,537
Average number of persons per CU	2.5	1.8	2.4	2.6	2.8	3.0	3.0	3.1
Average before-tax income of CU	$51,128.00	$10,752.55	$29,072.57	$44,294.00	$58,900.00	$74,560.00	$88,832.00	$154,665.00
Average spending of CU, total	42,741.66	19,862.52	31,684.32	39,756.91	49,788.99	57,128.14	65,957.39	93,514.86
Housing, average spending	13,652.50	7,329.14	10,471.06	12,727.58	15,106.04	17,080.57	19,840.62	28,941.39
HOUSEHOLD SERVICES	**729.81**	**286.84**	**429.83**	**560.02**	**749.02**	**911.51**	**1,167.75**	**2,157.97**
Personal services	**303.13**	**123.01**	**155.39**	**229.05**	**316.12**	**429.17**	**569.13**	**858.99**
Babysitting and child care in your own home	37.42	7.28	13.15	21.16	22.92	19.83	28.05	201.96
Babysitting and child care in someone else's home	24.17	7.00	19.41	30.73	41.13	16.75	46.32	39.00
Day care centers, nurseries, and preschools	198.17	31.55	95.31	168.94	242.22	371.55	486.69	522.77
Other household services	**426.69**	**163.83**	**274.44**	**330.97**	**432.91**	**482.34**	**598.62**	**1,298.98**
Housekeeping services	94.64	22.09	41.96	44.69	55.14	53.98	117.78	464.62
Gardening, lawn care service	87.05	40.91	56.21	57.02	69.62	88.88	102.80	293.34
Water softening service	3.40	1.47	2.60	3.32	3.53	5.52	6.90	6.48
Nonclothing laundry and dry cleaning, sent out	1.08	0.37	0.90	0.44	0.88	1.01	1.43	3.61
Nonclothing laundry and dry cleaning, coin-operated	3.78	4.90	4.89	3.48	3.39	1.45	1.78	1.76
Termite/pest control services	11.78	5.85	7.24	9.89	16.72	15.52	16.90	25.92
Home security system service fee	16.27	5.06	9.73	13.81	19.44	14.67	28.64	47.53
Other home services	14.29	5.66	12.06	8.08	9.03	22.11	25.66	40.03
Termite/pest control products	1.56	1.04	0.92	0.96	1.67	1.67	2.12	4.02
Moving, storage, and freight express	33.64	12.68	19.98	27.80	44.90	53.08	40.42	89.49
Appliance repair, including service center	12.53	5.04	8.29	11.89	16.27	14.63	25.38	26.31
Reupholstering and furniture repair	5.42	3.43	2.03	3.94	3.94	6.25	8.11	18.03
Repairs/rentals of lawn/garden equipment, hand/power tools, etc.	5.70	3.59	4.61	7.18	5.08	5.66	7.22	11.62
Appliance rental	1.83	2.80	1.95	1.06	0.97	1.00	0.03	2.37
Repair of computer systems for nonbusiness use	4.13	1.27	4.63	2.56	7.57	5.62	2.39	7.29
Computer information services	127.46	46.45	94.60	134.85	171.21	191.30	211.05	249.14
HOUSEKEEPING SUPPLIES	**581.95**	**326.54**	**456.76**	**541.53**	**627.62**	**769.14**	**897.09**	**1,185.81**
Laundry and cleaning supplies	**145.41**	**106.54**	**132.32**	**124.64**	**158.84**	**226.16**	**212.61**	**192.40**
Soaps and detergents	79.98	59.03	76.17	56.53	85.28	123.79	112.67	104.08
Other laundry cleaning products	65.43	47.50	56.16	58.11	73.56	102.38	99.94	88.32
Other household products	**287.28**	**142.47**	**207.42**	**287.72**	**282.71**	**349.99**	**468.67**	**686.76**
Cleansing and toilet tissue, paper towels, and napkins	80.52	56.79	72.86	79.95	88.03	119.83	109.02	111.97
Miscellaneous household products	117.27	50.71	78.05	158.33	116.21	170.56	193.19	261.13
Lawn and garden supplies	89.49	34.97	56.51	49.44	78.46	59.60	166.46	313.66
Postage and stationery	**149.26**	**77.53**	**117.01**	**129.17**	**186.07**	**192.99**	**215.80**	**306.65**
Stationery, stationery supplies, giftwrap	68.54	30.69	47.50	65.92	93.88	97.42	102.33	144.92
Postage	74.87	45.91	65.19	58.54	83.73	92.95	89.70	152.01
Delivery services	5.85	1.29	4.33	4.71	8.47	2.62	23.78	9.72
HOUSEHOLD FURNISHINGS, EQUIPMENT	**1,599.87**	**554.98**	**1,040.41**	**1,450.04**	**1,833.84**	**2,054.83**	**3,097.57**	**4,008.38**
Household textiles	**126.29**	**50.87**	**86.33**	**140.36**	**138.48**	**183.35**	**211.38**	**289.96**
Bathroom linens	23.05	9.81	13.75	28.47	23.79	44.33	52.19	43.37
Bedroom linens	59.59	23.87	42.81	66.87	61.65	93.36	102.39	132.33
Kitchen and dining room linens	8.83	4.20	7.10	9.91	14.01	9.66	12.90	13.82
Curtains and draperies	16.14	3.91	11.68	15.19	15.82	16.96	19.58	52.82
Slipcovers and decorative pillows	5.30	–	3.75	5.13	4.94	2.03	4.10	17.20
Sewing materials for household items	11.89	5.55	6.72	13.74	16.34	14.41	17.48	26.32
Other linens	1.48	0.59	0.53	1.05	1.93	2.59	2.76	4.10
Furniture	**418.92**	**122.02**	**248.07**	**333.69**	**493.29**	**578.84**	**868.11**	**1,107.04**
Mattresses and springs	46.78	19.09	38.91	34.07	53.65	53.55	93.57	98.62
Other bedroom furniture	83.35	26.99	45.75	57.30	121.95	140.91	147.61	203.33
Sofas	96.30	20.86	59.83	90.77	116.80	132.58	226.65	234.63
Living room chairs	39.38	15.69	23.80	57.89	46.54	39.56	71.42	85.24
Living room tables	18.40	5.06	13.21	16.90	19.75	19.28	36.81	48.60
Kitchen and dining room furniture	51.02	9.69	24.74	24.22	48.26	84.31	93.10	186.63

	total complete reporters	under $20,000	$20,000–$39,999	$40,000–$49,999	$50,000–$69,999	$70,000–$79,999	$80,000–$99,999	$100,000 or more
Infants' furniture	$8.35	$3.30	$4.52	$4.47	$9.76	$14.26	$20.13	$19.76
Outdoor furniture	16.41	4.16	6.25	9.43	11.31	11.49	40.66	65.43
Wall units, cabinets, and other furniture	58.94	17.18	31.06	38.64	65.27	82.91	138.17	164.81
Floor coverings	**54.30**	**19.73**	**22.19**	**32.28**	**40.95**	**58.19**	**97.98**	**207.30**
Wall-to-wall carpeting	30.08	12.69	11.41	23.65	24.01	34.26	60.78	101.70
Floor coverings, nonpermanent	24.22	7.04	10.78	8.63	16.93	23.94	37.20	105.59
Major appliances	**205.16**	**78.58**	**179.76**	**220.27**	**221.29**	**232.46**	**346.38**	**423.86**
Dishwashers (built-in), garbage disposals, range hoods	13.82	4.68	10.68	10.97	17.76	18.51	26.42	29.61
Refrigerators and freezers	50.71	22.78	40.17	43.09	52.34	65.70	110.46	99.71
Washing machines	29.87	12.47	22.62	29.27	37.34	31.42	56.21	60.80
Clothes dryers	19.50	6.04	15.21	23.94	23.81	21.02	39.76	38.57
Cooking stoves, ovens	32.24	7.31	23.80	26.63	40.62	41.33	54.27	88.06
Microwave ovens	7.83	4.33	6.25	6.38	10.51	7.91	12.22	14.51
Window air conditioners	5.87	4.06	5.97	4.83	6.20	6.63	7.52	8.97
Electric floor-cleaning equipment	33.13	7.51	49.06	59.24	15.19	28.69	24.41	57.32
Sewing machines	8.65	5.08	4.53	2.87	15.36	6.50	12.98	20.31
Miscellaneous household appliances	1.90	–	–	0.95	0.65	4.63	1.38	2.61
Small appliances and misc. housewares	**94.65**	**46.78**	**72.94**	**67.55**	**107.50**	**134.22**	**170.16**	**203.46**
Housewares	71.10	35.88	54.22	44.68	82.67	86.66	136.76	157.68
Plastic dinnerware	1.61	0.78	1.28	1.18	1.91	1.65	2.63	3.57
China and other dinnerware	7.85	3.51	7.85	2.18	10.54	6.20	17.79	16.29
Flatware	4.19	1.76	2.56	2.61	4.44	5.87	7.38	11.57
Glassware	9.65	2.78	6.05	8.04	11.89	9.91	23.90	24.66
Silver serving pieces	7.09	4.30	4.84	3.82	9.15	12.34	15.43	11.90
Other serving pieces	1.51	0.48	0.77	0.66	1.39	2.72	3.06	4.78
Nonelectric cookware	15.88	15.05	13.57	5.70	17.79	21.62	14.73	29.27
Tableware, nonelectric kitchenware	23.32	7.81	17.30	20.50	25.57	26.34	51.83	55.64
Small appliances	23.56	10.90	18.72	22.87	24.83	47.56	33.41	45.77
Small electric kitchen appliances	16.28	7.81	13.56	14.18	18.04	23.35	22.27	34.62
Portable heating and cooling equipment	7.27	3.08	5.16	8.69	6.79	24.20	11.14	11.15
Miscellaneous household equipment	**700.53**	**237.00**	**431.14**	**655.88**	**832.34**	**867.76**	**1,403.56**	**1,776.76**
Window coverings	26.51	5.36	7.68	33.33	17.06	46.43	69.44	82.96
Infants' equipment	14.90	7.13	16.62	11.27	8.33	25.15	44.30	18.72
Laundry and cleaning equipment	15.53	8.96	13.95	13.73	13.75	22.12	20.31	33.19
Outdoor equipment	25.58	9.47	16.59	12.60	24.79	7.89	50.81	91.26
Clocks	3.96	2.21	1.19	4.74	4.84	3.89	13.09	7.09
Lamps and lighting fixtures	14.81	4.44	8.57	10.80	12.25	20.93	41.53	39.56
Other household decorative items	142.75	50.37	82.52	146.16	140.40	131.18	329.13	398.94
Telephones and accessories	27.78	13.95	19.61	38.76	26.39	40.17	27.21	67.10
Lawn and garden equipment	52.55	18.99	50.54	81.16	88.12	66.64	79.47	89.77
Power tools	30.91	3.52	18.29	30.09	46.67	5.76	83.92	88.97
Office furniture for home use	12.05	1.98	4.20	6.95	10.37	22.19	13.19	52.81
Hand tools	7.67	3.07	9.13	7.14	7.68	10.04	15.92	9.84
Indoor plants and fresh flowers	42.47	14.93	30.99	33.45	44.71	63.77	71.21	108.54
Closet and storage items	10.91	4.77	8.61	8.06	13.65	12.64	20.83	23.31
Rental of furniture	3.08	3.34	5.12	4.78	1.15	2.46	1.29	0.56
Luggage	6.68	1.32	2.93	3.41	7.70	8.44	14.32	22.99
Computers and computer hardware, nonbusiness use	141.82	52.67	79.88	126.48	172.64	248.50	207.20	367.93
Computer software and accessories, nonbusiness use	19.26	7.68	13.82	15.01	18.62	31.98	31.32	48.92
Telephone answering devices	0.99	0.50	0.53	1.38	1.08	1.56	1.38	2.20
Calculators	1.31	1.01	0.66	0.72	1.11	1.72	2.48	3.21
Business equipment for home use	1.23	0.45	1.09	1.30	2.60	0.80	1.27	1.84
Other hardware	45.69	5.97	23.89	10.45	105.99	16.45	140.65	103.63
Smoke alarms	1.23	0.46	0.61	2.42	1.51	0.80	1.83	2.90
Other household appliances	7.14	3.47	3.36	2.91	7.25	18.30	10.68	19.59
Miscellaneous household equipment and parts	43.73	11.89	30.78	43.81	53.66	57.95	110.80	90.91

Note: Subcategories may not add to total because some are not shown. (–) means sample is too small to make a reliable estimate.
Source: Bureau of Labor Statistics, unpublished tables from the 2003 Consumer Expenditure Survey; calculations by New Strategist

Table 8.6 Housing: Household Operations: Indexed spending by income, 2003

(indexed average annual spending of consumer units (CU) on household services, supplies, furnishings, and equipment, by before-tax income of consumer unit, 2003; complete income reporters only; index definition: an index of 100 is the average for all consumer units; an index of 132 means that spending by consumer units in that group is 32 percent above the average for all consumer units; an index of 68 indicates spending that is 32 percent below the average for all consumer units)

	total complete reporters	under $20,000	$20,000–$39,999	$40,000–$49,999	$50,000–$69,999	$70,000–$79,999	$80,000–$99,999	$100,000 or more
Average spending of CU, total	$42,742	$19,863	$31,684	$39,757	$49,789	$57,128	$65,957	$93,515
Average spending of CU, index	100	46	74	93	116	134	154	219
Housing, spending index	100	54	77	93	111	125	145	212
HOUSEHOLD SERVICES	100	39	59	77	103	125	160	296
Personal services	100	41	51	76	104	142	188	283
Babysitting and child care in your own home	100	19	35	57	61	53	75	540
Babysitting and child care in someone else's home	100	29	80	127	170	69	192	161
Day care centers, nurseries, and preschools	100	16	48	85	122	187	246	264
Other household services	100	38	64	78	101	113	140	304
Housekeeping services	100	23	44	47	58	57	124	491
Gardening, lawn care service	100	47	65	66	80	102	118	337
Water softening service	100	43	76	98	104	162	203	191
Nonclothing laundry and dry cleaning, sent out	100	35	84	41	81	94	132	334
Nonclothing laundry and dry cleaning, coin-operated	100	130	129	92	90	38	47	47
Termite/pest control services	100	50	61	84	142	132	143	220
Home security system service fee	100	31	60	85	119	90	176	292
Other home services	100	40	84	57	63	155	180	280
Termite/pest control products	100	66	59	62	107	107	136	258
Moving, storage, and freight express	100	38	59	83	133	158	120	266
Appliance repair, including service center	100	40	66	95	130	117	203	210
Reupholstering and furniture repair	100	63	37	73	73	115	150	333
Repairs/rentals of lawn/garden equipment, hand/power tools, etc.	100	63	81	126	89	99	127	204
Appliance rental	100	153	107	58	53	55	2	130
Repair of computer systems for nonbusiness use	100	31	112	62	183	136	58	177
Computer information services	100	36	74	106	134	150	166	195
HOUSEKEEPING SUPPLIES	100	56	78	93	108	132	154	204
Laundry and cleaning supplies	100	73	91	86	109	156	146	132
Soaps and detergents	100	74	95	83	107	155	141	130
Other laundry cleaning products	100	73	86	89	112	156	153	135
Other household products	100	50	72	100	98	122	163	239
Cleansing and toilet tissue, paper towels, and napkins	100	71	90	99	109	149	135	139
Miscellaneous household products	100	43	67	135	99	145	165	223
Lawn and garden supplies	100	39	63	55	88	67	186	350
Postage and stationery	100	52	78	87	125	129	145	205
Stationery, stationery supplies, giftwrap	100	45	69	96	137	142	149	211
Postage	100	61	87	78	112	124	120	203
Delivery services	100	22	74	81	145	45	406	166
HOUSEHOLD FURNISHINGS AND EQUIPMENT	100	35	65	91	115	128	194	251
Household textiles	100	40	68	111	110	145	167	230
Bathroom linens	100	43	60	124	103	192	226	188
Bedroom linens	100	40	72	112	103	157	172	222
Kitchen and dining room linens	100	48	80	112	159	109	146	157
Curtains and draperies	100	24	72	94	98	105	121	327
Slipcovers and decorative pillows	100	–	71	97	93	38	77	325
Sewing materials for household items	100	47	57	116	137	121	147	221
Other linens	100	40	36	71	130	175	186	277
Furniture	100	29	59	80	118	138	207	264
Mattresses and springs	100	41	83	73	115	114	200	211
Other bedroom furniture	100	32	55	69	146	169	177	244
Sofas	100	22	62	94	121	138	235	244
Living room chairs	100	40	60	147	118	100	181	216
Living room tables	100	27	72	92	107	105	200	264
Kitchen and dining room furniture	100	19	48	47	95	165	182	366

	total complete reporters	under $20,000	$20,000– $39,999	$40,000– $49,999	$50,000– $69,999	$70,000– $79,999	$80,000– $99,999	$100,000 or more
Infants' furniture	100	40	54	54	117	171	241	237
Outdoor furniture	100	25	38	57	69	70	248	399
Wall units, cabinets, and other furniture	100	29	53	66	111	141	234	280
Floor coverings	**100**	**36**	**41**	**59**	**75**	**107**	**180**	**382**
Wall-to-wall carpeting	100	42	38	79	80	114	202	338
Floor coverings, nonpermanent	100	29	44	36	70	99	154	436
Major appliances	**100**	**38**	**88**	**107**	**108**	**113**	**169**	**207**
Dishwashers (built-in), garbage disposals, range hoods	100	34	77	79	129	134	191	214
Refrigerators and freezers	100	45	79	85	103	130	218	197
Washing machines	100	42	76	98	125	105	188	204
Clothes dryers	100	31	78	123	122	108	204	198
Cooking stoves, ovens	100	23	74	83	126	128	168	273
Microwave ovens	100	55	80	81	134	101	156	185
Window air conditioners	100	69	102	82	106	113	128	153
Electric floor-cleaning equipment	100	23	148	209	46	87	74	173
Sewing machines	100	59	52	33	178	75	150	235
Miscellaneous household appliances	100	–	–	50	34	244	73	137
Small appliances and misc. housewares	**100**	**49**	**77**	**71**	**114**	**142**	**180**	**215**
Housewares	100	50	76	63	116	122	192	222
Plastic dinnerware	100	48	80	73	119	102	163	222
China and other dinnerware	100	45	00	28	134	79	227	208
Flatware	100	42	61	62	106	140	176	276
Glassware	100	29	63	83	123	103	248	256
Silver serving pieces	100	61	68	54	129	174	218	168
Other serving pieces	100	32	51	44	92	180	203	317
Nonelectric cookware	100	95	85	36	112	136	93	184
Tableware, nonelectric kitchenware	100	33	74	88	110	113	222	239
Small appliances	100	46	79	97	105	202	142	194
Small electric kitchen appliances	100	48	83	87	111	143	137	213
Portable heating and cooling equipment	100	42	71	120	93	333	153	153
Miscellaneous household equipment	**100**	**34**	**52**	**94**	**119**	**124**	**200**	**254**
Window coverings	100	20	29	145	64	175	262	313
Infants' equipment	100	48	112	76	56	169	297	126
Laundry and cleaning equipment	100	58	90	88	89	142	131	214
Outdoor equipment	100	37	65	49	97	31	199	357
Clocks	100	56	30	120	122	98	331	179
Lamps and lighting fixtures	100	30	58	73	83	141	280	267
Other household decorative items	100	35	58	102	98	92	231	279
Telephones and accessories	100	50	71	140	95	145	98	242
Lawn and garden equipment	100	36	58	154	168	127	151	171
Power tools	100	11	59	97	151	19	271	288
Office furniture for home use	100	16	35	58	86	184	109	438
Hand tools	100	40	119	93	100	131	208	128
Indoor plants and fresh flowers	100	35	73	79	105	150	168	256
Closet and storage items	100	44	79	74	125	116	191	214
Rental of furniture	100	109	165	155	37	80	42	18
Luggage	100	20	44	51	115	126	214	344
Computers and computer hardware, nonbusiness use	100	37	55	39	122	175	146	259
Computer software and accessories, nonbusiness use	100	40	72	73	97	166	163	254
Telephone answering devices	100	51	54	139	109	158	139	222
Calculators	100	77	50	55	85	131	189	245
Business equipment for home use	100	37	89	106	211	65	103	150
Other hardware	100	13	52	23	232	36	308	227
Smoke alarms	100	37	50	197	123	65	149	236
Other household appliances	100	49	47	41	102	256	150	274
Miscellaneous household equipment and parts	100	27	70	100	123	133	253	208

Note: (–) means sample is too small to make a reliable estimate.
Source: Calculations by New Strategist based on the 2003 Consumer Expenditure Survey

Table 8.7 Housing: Household Operations: Total spending by income, 2003

(total annual spending on household services, supplies, furnishings, and equipment, by before-tax income group of consumer units (CU), 2003; complete income reporters only; numbers in thousands)

	total complete reporters	under $20,000	$20,000–$39,999	$40,000–$49,999	$50,000–$69,999	$70,000–$79,999	$80,000–$99,999	$100,000 or more
Number of consumer units	97,391	27,100	23,941	8,891	13,890	5,121	6,909	11,537
Total spending of all CUs	$4,162,653,009	$538,274,380	$758,554,310	$353,478,687	$691,569,071	$292,553,205	$455,699,608	$1,078,880,940
Housing, total spending	1,329,630,628	198,619,804	250,687,762	113,160,914	209,822,896	87,469,599	137,078,844	333,896,816
HOUSEHOLD SERVICES	**71,076,926**	**7,773,414**	**10,290,496**	**4,979,138**	**10,403,888**	**4,667,843**	**8,067,985**	**24,896,500**
Personal services	**29,522,134**	**3,333,573**	**3,720,090**	**2,036,484**	**4,390,907**	**2,197,780**	**3,932,119**	**9,910,168**
Babysitting and child care in your own home	3,644,371	197,254	314,787	188,134	318,359	101,549	193,797	2,330,013
Babysitting and child care in someone else's home	2,353,940	189,590	464,583	273,220	571,296	85,777	320,025	449,943
Day care centers, nurseries, and preschools	19,299,974	855,020	2,281,740	1,502,046	3,364,436	1,902,708	3,362,541	6,031,197
Other household services	**41,555,766**	**4,439,886**	**6,570,406**	**2,942,654**	**6,013,120**	**2,470,063**	**4,135,866**	**14,986,332**
Housekeeping services	9,217,084	598,708	1,004,634	397,339	765,895	276,432	813,742	5,360,321
Gardening, lawn care service	8,477,887	1,108,683	1,345,655	506,965	967,022	455,154	710,245	3,384,264
Water softening service	331,129	39,941	62,217	29,518	49,032	28,268	47,672	74,760
Nonclothing laundry and dry cleaning, sent out	105,182	10,147	21,654	3,912	12,223	5,172	9,880	41,649
Nonclothing laundry and dry cleaning, coin-operated	368,138	132,660	117,141	30,941	47,087	7,425	12,298	20,305
Termite/pest control services	1,147,266	158,583	173,333	87,932	232,241	79,478	116,762	299,039
Home security system service fee	1,584,552	137,219	232,939	122,785	270,022	75,125	197,874	548,354
Other home services	1,391,717	153,265	288,768	71,839	125,427	113,225	177,285	461,826
Termite/pest control products	151,930	28,079	22,104	8,535	23,196	8,552	14,647	46,379
Moving, storage, and freight express	3,276,233	343,638	478,402	247,170	623,661	271,823	279,262	1,032,446
Appliance repair, including service center	1,220,309	136,457	198,557	105,714	225,990	74,920	175,350	303,538
Reupholstering and furniture repair	527,859	92,941	48,631	35,031	54,727	32,006	56,032	208,012
Repairs/rentals of lawn/garden equipment, hand/power tools, etc.	555,129	97,247	110,326	63,837	70,561	28,985	49,883	134,060
Appliance rental	178,226	75,827	46,784	9,424	13,473	5,121	207	27,343
Repair of computer systems for nonbusiness use	402,225	34,476	110,822	22,761	105,147	28,780	16,513	84,105
Computer information services	12,413,457	1,258,763	2,264,819	1,198,951	2,378,107	979,647	1,458,144	2,874,328
HOUSEKEEPING SUPPLIES	**56,676,692**	**8,849,324**	**10,935,299**	**4,814,743**	**8,717,642**	**3,938,766**	**6,197,995**	**13,680,690**
Laundry and cleaning supplies	**14,161,625**	**2,887,163**	**3,167,960**	**1,108,174**	**2,206,288**	**1,158,165**	**1,468,922**	**2,219,719**
Soaps and detergents	7,789,332	1,599,838	1,823,571	591,518	1,184,539	633,929	778,437	1,200,771
Other laundry cleaning products	6,372,293	1,287,326	1,344,520	516,656	1,021,748	524,288	690,485	1,018,948
Other household products	**27,978,486**	**3,861,006**	**4,965,798**	**2,558,119**	**3,926,842**	**1,792,299**	**3,238,041**	**7,923,150**
Cleansing and toilet tissue, paper towels, and napkins	7,841,923	1,538,961	1,744,295	710,835	1,222,737	613,649	753,219	1,291,798
Miscellaneous household products	11,421,043	1,374,304	1,868,698	1,407,712	1,614,157	873,438	1,334,750	3,012,657
Lawn and garden supplies	8,715,521	947,659	1,352,805	439,571	1,089,809	305,212	1,150,072	3,618,695
Postage and stationery	**14,536,581**	**2,101,198**	**2,801,410**	**1,148,450**	**2,584,512**	**988,302**	**1,490,962**	**3,537,821**
Stationery, stationery supplies, giftwrap	6,675,179	831,627	1,137,187	586,095	1,303,993	498,888	706,998	1,671,942
Postage	7,291,664	1,244,066	1,560,604	520,479	1,163,010	475,997	619,737	1,753,739
Delivery services	569,737	35,090	103,750	41,877	117,648	13,417	164,296	112,140
HOUSEHOLD FURNISHINGS, EQUIPMENT	**155,812,939**	**15,039,848**	**24,908,549**	**12,892,306**	**25,472,038**	**10,522,784**	**21,401,111**	**46,244,680**
Household textiles	**12,299,509**	**1,378,460**	**2,066,712**	**1,247,941**	**1,923,487**	**938,935**	**1,460,424**	**3,345,269**
Bathroom linens	2,244,863	265,862	329,085	253,127	330,443	227,014	360,581	500,360
Bedroom linens	5,803,530	646,929	1,024,827	594,541	856,319	478,097	707,413	1,526,691
Kitchen and dining room linens	859,963	113,703	170,037	88,110	194,599	49,469	89,126	159,441
Curtains and draperies	1,571,891	106,045	279,564	135,054	219,740	86,852	135,278	609,384
Slipcovers and decorative pillows	516,172	–	89,689	45,611	68,617	10,396	28,327	198,436
Sewing materials for household items	1,157,979	150,375	160,867	122,162	226,963	73,794	120,769	303,654
Other linens	144,139	15,962	12,751	9,336	26,808	13,263	19,069	47,302
Furniture	**40,799,038**	**3,306,703**	**5,938,956**	**2,966,838**	**6,851,798**	**2,964,240**	**5,997,772**	**12,771,920**
Mattresses and springs	4,555,951	517,260	931,518	302,916	745,199	274,230	646,475	1,137,779
Other bedroom furniture	8,117,540	731,348	1,095,410	509,454	1,693,886	721,600	1,019,837	2,345,818
Sofas	9,378,753	565,393	1,432,304	807,036	1,622,352	678,942	1,565,925	2,706,926
Living room chairs	3,835,258	425,110	569,758	514,700	646,441	202,587	493,441	983,414
Living room tables	1,791,994	137,021	316,152	150,258	274,328	98,733	254,320	560,698
Kitchen and dining room furniture	4,968,889	262,542	592,281	215,340	670,331	431,752	643,228	2,153,150

	total complete reporters	under $20,000	$20,000– $39,999	$40,000– $49,999	$50,000– $69,999	$70,000– $79,999	$80,000– $99,999	$100,000 or more
Infants' furniture	$813,215	$89,548	$108,259	$39,743	$135,566	$73,025	$139,078	$227,971
Outdoor furniture	1,598,186	112,724	149,656	83,842	157,096	58,840	280,920	754,866
Wall units, cabinets, and other furniture	5,740,226	465,646	743,509	343,548	906,600	424,582	954,617	1,901,413
Floor coverings	**5,288,331**	**534,615**	**531,162**	**287,001**	**568,796**	**297,991**	**676,944**	**2,391,620**
Wall-to-wall carpeting	2,929,521	343,823	273,173	210,272	333,499	175,445	419,929	1,173,313
Floor coverings, nonpermanent	2,358,810	190,836	257,989	76,729	235,158	122,597	257,015	1,218,192
Major appliances	**19,980,738**	**2,129,552**	**4,303,610**	**1,958,421**	**3,073,718**	**1,190,428**	**2,393,139**	**4,890,073**
Dishwashers (built-in), garbage disposals, range hoods	1,345,944	126,881	255,627	97,534	246,686	94,790	182,536	341,611
Refrigerators and freezers	4,938,698	617,341	961,591	383,113	727,003	336,450	763,168	1,150,354
Washing machines	2,909,069	337,993	541,503	260,240	518,653	160,902	388,355	701,450
Clothes dryers	1,899,125	163,759	364,156	212,851	330,721	107,643	274,702	444,982
Cooking stoves, ovens	3,139,886	198,103	569,812	236,767	564,212	211,651	374,951	1,015,948
Microwave ovens	762,572	117,409	149,657	56,725	145,984	40,507	84,428	167,402
Window air conditioners	571,685	110,007	142,950	42,944	86,113	33,952	51,956	103,487
Electric floor-cleaning equipment	3,226,564	203,562	1,174,567	615,613	210,989	146,921	168,649	661,301
Sewing machines	842,432	137,596	108,504	25,517	213,350	33,287	89,679	234,316
Miscellaneous household appliances	185,043	–	–	8,446	9,029	23,710	9,534	30,112
Small appliances and misc. housewares	**9,218,058**	**1,267,851**	**1,746,299**	**600,587**	**1,493,175**	**687,341**	**1,175,635**	**2,347,318**
Housewares	6,924,500	972,467	1,298,017	397,250	1,148,286	443,786	944,875	1,819,154
Plastic dinnerware	156,800	21,124	30,714	10,491	26,530	8,450	18,171	41,187
China and other dinnerware	764,519	95,026	187,915	19,382	146,401	31,750	122,911	187,938
Flatware	408,068	47,677	61,310	23,205	61,672	30,060	50,988	133,483
Glassware	939,823	75,265	144,819	71,484	165,152	50,749	165,125	284,502
Silver serving pieces	690,502	116,453	115,972	33,964	127,094	63,193	106,606	137,290
Other serving pieces	147,060	13,031	18,356	5,868	19,307	13,929	21,142	55,147
Nonelectric cookware	1,546,569	407,755	324,840	50,679	247,103	110,716	101,770	337,688
Tableware, nonelectric kitchenware	2,271,158	211,654	414,090	182,266	355,167	134,887	358,093	641,919
Small appliances	2,294,532	295,312	448,282	203,337	344,889	243,555	230,830	528,048
Small electric kitchen appliances	1,585,525	211,687	324,672	125,074	250,576	119,575	153,863	399,411
Portable heating and cooling equipment	708,033	83,500	123,478	77,263	94,313	123,928	76,966	128,638
Miscellaneous household equipment	**68,225,317**	**6,422,821**	**10,321,810**	**5,831,429**	**11,561,203**	**4,443,799**	**9,697,196**	**20,498,480**
Window coverings	2,581,835	145,365	183,907	340,792	236,963	237,768	479,761	957,110
Infants' equipment	1,451,126	193,315	397,858	100,202	115,704	128,793	306,069	215,973
Laundry and cleaning equipment	1,512,482	242,790	333,889	122,073	190,988	113,277	140,322	382,913
Outdoor equipment	2,491,262	256,723	397,215	112,027	344,333	40,405	351,046	1,052,867
Clocks	385,668	59,872	28,475	42,143	67,228	19,921	90,439	81,797
Lamps and lighting fixtures	1,442,361	120,371	205,363	96,023	170,153	107,183	286,931	456,404
Other household decorative items	13,902,565	1,365,089	1,975,518	1,299,509	1,950,156	671,773	2,273,959	4,602,571
Telephones and accessories	2,705,522	378,157	469,429	344,615	366,557	205,711	187,994	774,133
Lawn and garden equipment	5,117,897	514,731	731,175	721,594	1,223,987	341,263	549,058	1,035,676
Power tools	3,010,356	95,453	437,812	267,530	648,246	29,497	579,803	1,026,447
Office furniture for home use	1,173,562	53,532	100,450	61,792	144,039	113,635	91,130	609,269
Hand tools	746,989	83,194	218,572	63,482	106,675	51,415	109,991	113,524
Indoor plants and fresh flowers	4,136,196	404,662	741,825	297,404	621,022	326,566	491,990	1,252,226
Closet and storage items	1,062,536	129,266	206,123	71,661	189,599	64,729	143,914	268,927
Rental of furniture	299,964	90,618	122,686	42,499	15,974	12,598	8,913	6,461
Luggage	650,572	35,692	70,217	30,318	106,953	43,221	98,937	265,236
Computers and computer hardware, nonbusiness use	13,811,992	1,427,441	1,912,451	1,124,534	2,397,970	1,272,569	1,431,545	4,244,808
Computer software and accessories, nonbusiness use	1,875,751	208,139	330,865	133,454	258,632	163,770	216,390	564,390
Telephone answering devices	96,417	13,602	12,745	12,270	15,001	7,989	9,534	25,381
Calculators	127,582	27,239	15,712	6,402	15,418	8,808	17,134	37,034
Business equipment for home use	119,791	12,294	26,173	11,558	36,114	4,097	8,774	21,228
Other hardware	4,449,795	161,714	572,039	92,911	1,472,201	84,240	971,751	1,195,579
Smoke alarms	119,791	12,433	14,650	21,516	20,974	4,097	12,643	33,457
Other household appliances	695,372	94,015	80,505	25,873	100,703	93,714	73,788	226,010
Miscellaneous household equipment and parts	4,258,908	322,159	736,836	389,515	745,337	296,762	765,517	1,048,829

Note: Numbers may not add to total because of rounding and missing subcategories. (–) means sample is too small to make a reliable estimate.
Source: Calculations by New Strategist based on the 2003 Consumer Expenditure Survey

Table 8.8 Housing: Household Operations: Market shares by income, 2003

(percentage of total annual spending on household services, supplies, furnishings, and equipment accounted for by before-tax income group of consumer units, 2003; complete income reporters only)

	total complete reporters	under $20,000	$20,000– $39,999	$40,000– $49,999	$50,000– $69,999	$70,000– $79,999	$80,000– $99,999	$100,000 or more
Share of total consumer units	100.0%	27.8%	24.6%	9.1%	14.3%	5.3%	7.1%	11.8%
Share of total before-tax income	100.0	5.9	14.0	7.9	16.4	7.7	12.3	35.8
Share of total spending	100.0	12.9	18.2	8.5	16.6	7.0	10.9	25.9
Share of housing spending	100.0	14.9	18.9	8.5	15.8	6.6	10.3	25.1
HOUSEHOLD SERVICES	100.0	10.9	14.5	7.0	14.6	6.6	11.4	35.0
Personal services	100.0	11.3	12.6	6.9	14.9	7.4	13.3	33.6
Babysitting and child care in your own home	100.0	5.4	8.6	5.2	8.7	2.8	5.3	63.9
Babysitting and child care in someone else's home	100.0	8.1	19.7	11.6	24.3	3.6	13.6	19.1
Day care centers, nurseries, and preschools	100.0	4.4	11.8	7.8	17.4	9.9	17.4	31.2
Other household services	100.0	10.7	15.8	7.1	14.5	5.9	10.0	36.1
Housekeeping services	100.0	6.5	10.9	4.3	8.3	3.0	8.8	58.2
Gardening, lawn care service	100.0	13.1	15.9	6.0	11.4	5.4	8.4	39.9
Water softening service	100.0	12.1	18.8	8.9	14.8	8.5	14.4	22.6
Nonclothing laundry and dry cleaning, sent out	100.0	9.6	20.6	3.7	11.6	4.9	9.4	39.6
Nonclothing laundry and dry cleaning, coin-operated	100.0	36.0	31.8	8.4	12.8	2.0	3.3	5.5
Termite/pest control services	100.0	13.8	15.1	7.7	20.2	6.9	10.2	26.1
Home security system service fee	100.0	8.7	14.7	7.7	17.0	4.7	12.5	34.6
Other home services	100.0	11.0	20.7	5.2	9.0	8.1	12.7	33.2
Termite/pest control products	100.0	18.5	14.5	5.6	15.3	5.6	9.6	30.5
Moving, storage, and freight express	100.0	10.5	14.6	7.5	19.0	8.3	8.5	31.5
Appliance repair, including service center	100.0	11.2	16.3	8.7	18.5	6.1	14.4	24.9
Reupholstering and furniture repair	100.0	17.6	9.2	6.6	10.4	6.1	10.6	39.4
Repairs/rentals of lawn/garden equipment, hand/power tools, etc.	100.0	17.5	19.9	11.5	12.7	5.2	9.0	24.1
Appliance rental	100.0	42.5	26.2	5.3	7.6	2.9	0.1	15.3
Repair of computer systems for nonbusiness use	100.0	8.6	27.6	5.7	26.1	7.2	4.1	20.9
Computer information services	100.0	10.1	18.2	9.7	19.2	7.9	11.7	23.2
HOUSEKEEPING SUPPLIES	100.0	15.6	19.3	8.5	15.4	6.9	10.9	24.1
Laundry and cleaning supplies	100.0	20.4	22.4	7.8	15.6	8.2	10.4	15.7
Soaps and detergents	100.0	20.5	23.4	7.6	15.2	8.1	10.0	15.4
Other laundry cleaning products	100.0	20.2	21.1	8.1	16.0	8.2	10.8	16.0
Other household products	100.0	13.8	17.7	9.1	14.0	6.4	11.6	28.3
Cleansing and toilet tissue, paper towels, and napkins	100.0	19.6	22.2	9.1	15.6	7.8	9.6	16.5
Miscellaneous household products	100.0	12.0	16.4	12.3	14.1	7.6	11.7	26.4
Lawn and garden supplies	100.0	10.9	15.5	5.0	12.5	3.5	13.2	41.5
Postage and stationery	100.0	14.5	19.3	7.9	17.8	6.8	10.3	24.3
Stationery, stationery supplies, giftwrap	100.0	12.5	17.0	8.8	19.5	7.5	10.6	25.0
Postage	100.0	17.1	21.4	7.1	15.9	6.5	8.5	24.1
Delivery services	100.0	6.2	18.2	7.4	20.6	2.4	28.8	19.7
HOUSEHOLD FURNISHINGS AND EQUIPMENT	100.0	9.7	16.0	8.3	16.3	6.8	13.7	29.7
Household textiles	100.0	11.2	16.8	10.1	15.6	7.6	11.9	27.2
Bathroom linens	100.0	11.8	14.7	11.3	14.7	10.1	16.1	22.3
Bedroom linens	100.0	11.1	17.7	10.2	14.8	8.2	12.2	26.3
Kitchen and dining room linens	100.0	13.2	19.8	10.2	22.6	5.8	10.4	18.5
Curtains and draperies	100.0	6.7	17.8	8.6	14.0	5.5	8.6	38.8
Slipcovers and decorative pillows	100.0	–	17.4	8.8	13.3	2.0	5.5	38.4
Sewing materials for household items	100.0	13.0	13.9	10.5	19.6	6.4	10.4	26.2
Other linens	100.0	11.1	8.8	6.5	18.6	9.2	13.2	32.8
Furniture	100.0	8.1	14.6	7.3	16.8	7.3	14.7	31.3
Mattresses and springs	100.0	11.4	20.4	6.6	16.4	6.0	14.2	25.0
Other bedroom furniture	100.0	9.0	13.5	6.3	20.9	8.9	12.6	28.9
Sofas	100.0	6.0	15.3	8.6	17.3	7.2	16.7	28.9
Living room chairs	100.0	11.1	14.9	13.4	16.9	5.3	12.9	25.6
Living room tables	100.0	7.6	17.6	8.4	15.3	5.5	14.2	31.3
Kitchen and dining room furniture	100.0	5.3	11.9	4.3	13.5	8.7	12.9	43.3

	total complete reporters	under $20,000	$20,000–$39,999	$40,000–$49,999	$50,000–$69,999	$70,000–$79,999	$80,000–$99,999	$100,000 or more
Infants' furniture	100.0%	11.0%	13.3%	4.9%	16.7%	9.0%	17.1%	28.0%
Outdoor furniture	100.0	7.1	9.4	5.2	9.8	3.7	17.6	47.2
Wall units, cabinets, and other furniture	100.0	8.1	13.0	6.0	15.8	7.4	16.6	33.1
Floor coverings	**100.0**	**10.1**	**10.0**	**5.4**	**10.8**	**5.6**	**12.8**	**45.2**
Wall-to-wall carpeting	100.0	11.7	9.3	7.2	11.4	6.0	14.3	40.1
Floor coverings, nonpermanent	100.0	8.1	10.9	3.3	10.0	5.2	10.9	51.6
Major appliances	**100.0**	**10.7**	**21.5**	**9.8**	**15.4**	**6.0**	**12.0**	**24.5**
Dishwashers (built-in), garbage disposals, range hoods	100.0	9.4	19.0	7.2	18.3	7.0	13.6	25.4
Refrigerators and freezers	100.0	12.5	19.5	7.3	14.7	6.8	15.5	23.3
Washing machines	100.0	11.6	18.6	8.9	17.8	5.5	13.3	24.1
Clothes dryers	100.0	8.6	19.2	11.2	17.4	5.7	14.5	23.4
Cooking stoves, ovens	100.0	6.3	18.1	7.5	18.0	6.7	11.9	32.4
Microwave ovens	100.0	15.4	19.6	7.4	19.1	5.3	11.1	22.0
Window air conditioners	100.0	19.2	25.0	7.5	15.1	5.9	9.1	18.1
Electric floor-cleaning equipment	100.0	6.3	36.4	19.1	6.5	4.6	5.2	20.5
Sewing machines	100.0	16.3	12.9	3.0	25.3	4.0	10.6	27.8
Miscellaneous household appliances	100.0	–	–	4.6	4.9	12.8	5.2	16.3
Small appliances and misc. housewares	**100.0**	**13.8**	**18.9**	**6.5**	**16.2**	**7.5**	**12.8**	**25.5**
Housewares	100.0	14.0	18.7	5.7	16.6	6.4	13.6	26.3
Plastic dinnerware	100.0	13.5	19.6	6.7	16.9	5.4	11.6	26.3
China and other dinnerware	100.0	12.4	24.6	2.5	19.1	4.2	16.1	24.6
Flatware	100.0	11.7	15.0	5.7	15.1	7.4	12.5	32.7
Glassware	100.0	8.0	15.4	7.6	17.6	5.4	17.6	30.3
Silver serving pieces	100.0	16.9	16.8	4.9	18.4	9.2	15.4	19.9
Other serving pieces	100.0	8.9	12.5	4.0	13.1	9.5	14.4	37.5
Nonelectric cookware	100.0	26.4	21.0	3.3	16.0	7.2	6.6	21.8
Tableware, nonelectric kitchenware	100.0	9.3	18.2	8.0	15.6	5.9	15.8	28.3
Small appliances	100.0	12.9	19.5	8.9	15.0	10.6	10.1	23.0
Small electric kitchen appliances	100.0	13.4	20.5	8.0	15.8	7.5	9.7	25.2
Portable heating and cooling equipment	100.0	11.8	17.4	10.9	13.3	17.5	10.9	18.2
Miscellaneous household equipment	**100.0**	**9.4**	**15.1**	**8.5**	**16.9**	**6.5**	**14.2**	**30.0**
Window coverings	100.0	5.6	7.1	13.2	9.2	9.2	18.6	37.1
Infants' equipment	100.0	13.3	27.4	6.9	8.0	8.9	21.1	14.9
Laundry and cleaning equipment	100.0	16.1	22.1	8.1	12.6	7.5	9.3	25.3
Outdoor equipment	100.0	10.3	15.9	4.5	13.8	1.6	14.1	42.3
Clocks	100.0	15.5	7.4	10.9	17.4	5.2	23.4	21.2
Lamps and lighting fixtures	100.0	8.3	14.2	6.7	11.8	7.4	19.9	31.6
Other household decorative items	100.0	9.8	14.2	9.3	14.0	4.8	16.4	33.1
Telephones and accessories	100.0	14.0	17.4	12.7	13.5	7.6	6.9	28.6
Lawn and garden equipment	100.0	10.1	14.3	14.1	23.9	6.7	10.7	20.2
Power tools	100.0	3.2	14.5	8.9	21.5	1.0	19.3	34.1
Office furniture for home use	100.0	4.6	8.6	5.3	12.3	9.7	7.8	51.9
Hand tools	100.0	11.1	29.3	8.5	14.3	6.9	14.7	15.2
Indoor plants and fresh flowers	100.0	9.8	17.9	7.2	15.0	7.9	11.9	30.3
Closet and storage items	100.0	12.2	19.4	6.7	17.8	6.1	13.5	25.3
Rental of furniture	100.0	30.2	40.9	14.2	5.3	4.2	3.0	2.2
Luggage	100.0	5.5	10.8	4.7	16.4	6.6	15.2	40.8
Computers and computer hardware, nonbusiness use	100.0	10.3	13.8	8.1	17.4	9.2	10.4	30.7
Computer software and accessories, nonbusiness use	100.0	11.1	17.6	7.1	13.8	8.7	11.5	30.1
Telephone answering devices	100.0	14.1	13.2	12.7	15.6	8.3	9.9	26.3
Calculators	100.0	21.3	12.3	5.0	12.1	6.9	13.4	29.0
Business equipment for home use	100.0	10.3	21.8	9.5	30.1	3.4	7.3	17.7
Other hardware	100.0	3.6	12.9	2.1	33.1	1.9	21.8	26.9
Smoke alarms	100.0	10.4	12.2	18.0	17.5	3.4	10.6	27.9
Other household appliances	100.0	13.5	11.6	3.7	14.5	13.5	10.6	32.5
Miscellaneous household equipment and parts	100.0	7.6	17.3	9.1	17.5	7.0	18.0	24.6

Note: Numbers may not add to total because of rounding. (–) means sample is too small to make a reliable estimate.
Source: Calculations by New Strategist based on the 2003 Consumer Expenditure Survey

Table 8.9 Housing: Household Operations: Average spending by high-income consumer units, 2003

(average annual spending on household services, supplies, furnishings, and equipment, by before-tax income of high-income consumer units (CU), 2003; complete income reporters only)

	total complete reporters	$100,000 or more	$100,000–$119,999	$120,000–$149,999	$150,000 or more
Number of consumer units (000)	97,391	11,537	4,384	3,151	4,002
Average number of persons per CU	2.5	3.1	3.1	3.1	3.1
Average before-tax income of CU	$51,128.00	$154,665.00	$108,087.00	$131,885.00	$223,634.00
Average spending of CU, total	42,741.66	93,514.86	75,601.50	86,451.46	118,674.11
Housing, average spending	13,652.50	28,941.39	23,204.37	26,719.05	36,970.78
HOUSEHOLD SERVICES	**729.81**	**2,157.97**	**1,438.03**	**1,847.93**	**3,190.81**
Personal services	**303.13**	**858.99**	**677.41**	**824.81**	**1,084.83**
Babysitting and child care in your own home	37.42	201.96	105.02	87.18	398.54
Babysitting and child care in someone else's home	24.17	39.00	32.82	48.72	38.10
Day care centers, nurseries, and preschools	198.17	522.77	481.72	448.47	626.27
Other household services	**426.69**	**1,298.98**	**760.62**	**1,023.12**	**2,105.98**
Housekeeping services	94.64	464.62	127.29	309.60	956.27
Gardening, lawn care service	87.05	293.34	171.11	195.81	504.05
Water softening service	3.40	6.48	7.52	5.84	5.84
Nonclothing laundry and dry cleaning, sent out	1.08	3.61	2.01	2.89	5.93
Nonclothing laundry and dry cleaning, coin-operated	3.78	1.76	2.75	1.97	0.53
Termite/pest control services	11.78	25.92	15.89	21.41	40.45
Home security system service fee	16.27	47.53	33.85	47.76	62.33
Other home services	14.29	40.03	26.46	41.60	53.66
Termite/pest control products	1.56	4.02	2.55	2.86	6.56
Moving, storage, and freight express	33.64	89.49	89.55	90.61	88.56
Appliance repair, including service center	12.53	26.31	21.43	28.18	30.19
Reupholstering and furniture repair	5.42	18.03	11.45	12.03	29.96
Repairs/rentals of lawn/garden equipment, hand/power tools, etc.	5.70	11.62	5.61	19.78	11.78
Appliance rental	1.83	2.37	1.72	4.78	1.18
Repair of computer systems for nonbusiness use	4.13	7.29	5.96	8.21	8.02
Computer information services	127.46	249.14	234.43	225.86	283.58
HOUSEKEEPING SUPPLIES	**581.95**	**1,185.81**	**1,071.69**	**1,083.08**	**1,389.64**
Laundry and cleaning supplies	**145.41**	**192.40**	**169.63**	**164.72**	**238.65**
Soaps and detergents	79.98	104.08	97.85	80.65	129.05
Other laundry cleaning products	65.43	88.32	71.78	84.07	109.60
Other household products	**287.28**	**686.76**	**646.71**	**593.67**	**802.59**
Cleansing and toilet tissue, paper towels, and napkins	80.52	111.97	115.32	80.04	133.13
Miscellaneous household products	117.27	261.13	248.75	177.79	339.30
Lawn and garden supplies	89.49	313.66	282.63	335.84	330.16
Postage and stationery	**149.26**	**306.65**	**255.35**	**324.70**	**348.39**
Stationery, stationery supplies, giftwrap	68.54	144.92	142.26	154.97	140.01
Postage	74.87	152.01	108.34	154.39	197.62
Delivery services	5.85	9.72	4.75	15.33	10.76
HOUSEHOLD FURNISHINGS AND EQUIPMENT	**1,599.87**	**4,008.38**	**3,177.25**	**3,514.16**	**5,304.22**
Household textiles	**126.29**	**289.96**	**268.58**	**279.92**	**321.29**
Bathroom linens	23.05	43.37	48.56	58.68	25.83
Bedroom linens	59.59	132.33	148.17	119.73	124.89
Kitchen and dining room linens	8.83	13.82	11.46	13.49	16.64
Curtains and draperies	16.14	52.82	22.85	60.00	80.00
Slipcovers and decorative pillows	5.30	17.20	12.59	2.80	33.41
Sewing materials for household items	11.89	26.32	22.45	21.16	34.62
Other linens	1.48	4.10	2.50	4.06	5.89
Furniture	**418.92**	**1,107.04**	**796.85**	**974.37**	**1,551.36**
Mattresses and springs	46.78	98.62	85.84	87.09	121.70
Other bedroom furniture	83.35	203.33	130.98	183.43	298.26
Sofas	96.30	234.63	164.26	207.20	333.34
Living room chairs	39.38	85.24	86.97	57.60	105.11
Living room tables	18.40	48.60	30.42	84.94	39.91
Kitchen and dining room furniture	51.02	186.63	103.16	139.50	315.19

	total complete reporters	$100,000 or more	$100,000– $119,999	$120,000– $149,999	$150,000 or more
Infants' furniture	$8.35	$19.76	$6.18	$45.56	$14.32
Outdoor furniture	16.41	65.43	23.29	43.45	128.91
Wall units, cabinets, and other furniture	58.94	164.81	165.75	125.62	194.64
Floor coverings	**54.30**	**207.30**	**140.12**	**192.85**	**292.28**
Wall-to-wall carpeting	30.08	101.70	87.55	135.28	90.77
Floor coverings, nonpermanent	24.22	105.59	52.56	57.57	201.52
Major appliances	**205.16**	**423.86**	**283.89**	**352.86**	**632.40**
Dishwashers (built-in), garbage disposals, range hoods	13.82	29.61	29.11	25.16	33.64
Refrigerators and freezers	50.71	99.71	69.10	90.01	140.90
Washing machines	29.87	60.30	49.43	75.06	62.01
Clothes dryers	19.50	38.57	32.53	40.12	43.94
Cooking stoves, ovens	32.24	88.06	42.26	75.74	147.96
Microwave ovens	7.83	14.51	8.54	23.20	14.22
Window air conditioners	5.87	8.97	5.10	9.19	13.03
Electric floor-cleaning equipment	33.13	57.32	35.89	5.30	121.01
Sewing machines	8.65	20.31	7.98	3.81	46.82
Miscellaneous household appliances	1.90	2.61	3.96	4.08	–
Small appliances and misc. housewares	**94.65**	**203.46**	**152.16**	**149.33**	**301.52**
Housewares	71.10	157.68	113.23	116.91	237.73
Plastic dinnerware	1.61	3.57	3.13	4.02	3.70
China and other dinnerware	7.85	16.29	25.02	11.34	10.64
Flatware	4.19	11.57	5.59	11.93	17.83
Glassware	9.65	24.66	9.22	6.02	55.93
Silver serving pieces	7.09	11.90	8.30	13.88	14.28
Other serving pieces	1.51	4.78	3.68	3.77	6.79
Nonelectric cookware	15.88	29.27	38.49	29.68	18.94
Tableware, nonelectric kitchenware	23.32	55.64	19.80	36.27	109.62
Small appliances	23.56	45.77	38.93	32.42	63.79
Small electric kitchen appliances	16.28	34.62	27.77	27.07	48.08
Portable heating and cooling equipment	7.27	11.15	11.17	5.35	15.71
Miscellaneous household equipment	**700.53**	**1,776.76**	**1,535.66**	**1,564.84**	**2,205.36**
Window coverings	26.51	82.96	37.59	102.98	116.89
Infants' equipment	14.90	18.72	6.97	24.05	27.35
Laundry and cleaning equipment	15.53	33.19	29.55	24.66	43.76
Outdoor equipment	25.58	91.26	43.99	74.15	155.93
Clocks	3.96	7.09	4.78	0.85	14.45
Lamps and lighting fixtures	14.81	39.56	25.16	38.37	56.26
Other household decorative items	142.75	398.94	419.13	331.63	429.25
Telephones and accessories	27.78	67.10	26.04	87.22	96.12
Lawn and garden equipment	52.55	89.77	80.70	97.68	93.48
Power tools	30.91	88.97	92.26	36.28	126.29
Office furniture for home use	12.05	52.81	28.80	26.41	99.92
Hand tools	7.67	9.84	9.52	7.59	11.97
Indoor plants and fresh flowers	42.47	108.54	92.37	97.07	135.29
Closet and storage items	10.91	23.31	24.31	25.43	20.58
Rental of furniture	3.08	0.56	0.64	1.15	–
Luggage	6.68	22.99	15.70	19.70	33.56
Computers and computer hardware, nonbusiness use	141.82	367.93	259.63	374.97	481.03
Computer software and accessories, nonbusiness use	19.26	48.92	39.55	58.13	51.94
Telephone answering devices	0.99	2.20	2.96	1.27	2.10
Calculators	1.31	3.21	3.49	3.48	2.69
Business equipment for home use	1.23	1.84	2.23	2.47	0.92
Other hardware	45.69	103.63	231.81	33.50	18.73
Smoke alarms	1.23	2.90	2.75	1.47	4.21
Other household appliances	7.14	19.59	7.95	30.56	23.71
Miscellaneous household equipment and parts	43.73	90.91	47.74	63.77	158.92

Note: Subcategories may not add to total because some are not shown. (–) means sample is too small to make a reliable estimate.
Source: Bureau of Labor Statistics, unpublished tables from the 2003 Consumer Expenditure Survey; calculations by New Strategist

Table 8.10 Housing: Household Operations: Indexed spending by high-income consumer units, 2003

(indexed average annual spending of high-income consumer units (CU) on household services, supplies, furnishings, and equipment, by before-tax income of consumer unit, 2003; complete income reporters only; index definition: an index of 100 is the average for all consumer units; an index of 132 means that spending by consumer units in that group is 32 percent above the average for all consumer units; an index of 68 indicates spending that is 32 percent below the average for all consumer units)

	total complete reporters	$100,000 or more	$100,000–$119,999	$120,000–$149,999	$150,000 or more
Average spending of CU, total	$42,742	$93,515	$75,602	$86,451	$118,674
Average spending of CU, index	100	219	177	202	278
Housing, spending index	100	212	170	196	271
HOUSEHOLD SERVICES	100	296	197	253	437
Personal services	100	283	223	272	358
Babysitting and child care in your own home	100	540	281	233	1065
Babysitting and child care in someone else's home	100	161	136	202	158
Day care centers, nurseries, and preschools	100	264	243	226	316
Other household services	100	304	178	240	494
Housekeeping services	100	491	134	327	1010
Gardening, lawn care service	100	337	197	225	579
Water softening service	100	191	221	172	172
Nonclothing laundry and dry cleaning, sent out	100	334	186	268	549
Nonclothing laundry and dry cleaning, coin-operated	100	47	73	52	14
Termite/pest control services	100	220	135	182	343
Home security system service fee	100	292	208	294	383
Other home services	100	280	185	291	376
Termite/pest control products	100	258	163	183	421
Moving, storage, and freight express	100	266	266	269	263
Appliance repair, including service center	100	210	171	225	241
Reupholstering and furniture repair	100	333	211	222	553
Repairs/rentals of lawn/garden equipment, hand/power tools, etc.	100	204	98	347	207
Appliance rental	100	130	94	261	64
Repair of computer systems for nonbusiness use	100	177	144	199	194
Computer information services	100	195	184	177	222
HOUSEKEEPING SUPPLIES	100	204	184	186	239
Laundry and cleaning supplies	100	132	117	113	164
Soaps and detergents	100	130	122	101	161
Other laundry cleaning products	100	135	110	128	168
Other household products	100	239	225	207	279
Cleansing and toilet tissue, paper towels, and napkins	100	139	143	99	165
Miscellaneous household products	100	223	212	152	289
Lawn and garden supplies	100	350	316	375	369
Postage and stationery	100	205	171	218	233
Stationery, stationery supplies, giftwrap	100	211	208	226	204
Postage	100	203	145	206	264
Delivery services	100	166	81	262	184
HOUSEHOLD FURNISHINGS AND EQUIPMENT	100	251	199	220	332
Household textiles	100	230	213	222	254
Bathroom linens	100	188	211	255	112
Bedroom linens	100	222	249	201	210
Kitchen and dining room linens	100	157	130	153	188
Curtains and draperies	100	327	142	372	496
Slipcovers and decorative pillows	100	325	238	53	630
Sewing materials for household items	100	221	189	178	291
Other linens	100	277	169	274	398
Furniture	100	264	190	233	370
Mattresses and springs	100	211	183	186	260
Other bedroom furniture	100	244	157	220	358
Sofas	100	244	171	215	346
Living room chairs	100	216	221	146	267
Living room tables	100	264	165	462	217
Kitchen and dining room furniture	100	366	202	273	618

	total complete reporters	$100,000 or more	$100,000– $119,999	$120,000– $149,999	$150,000 or more
Infants' furniture	100	237	74	546	171
Outdoor furniture	100	399	142	265	786
Wall units, cabinets, and other furniture	100	280	281	213	330
Floor coverings	**100**	**382**	**258**	**355**	**538**
Wall-to-wall carpeting	100	338	291	450	302
Floor coverings, nonpermanent	100	436	217	238	832
Major appliances	**100**	**207**	**138**	**172**	**308**
Dishwashers (built-in), garbage disposals, range hoods	100	214	211	182	243
Refrigerators and freezers	100	197	136	177	278
Washing machines	100	204	165	251	208
Clothes dryers	100	198	167	206	225
Cooking stoves, ovens	100	273	131	235	459
Microwave ovens	100	185	109	296	182
Window air conditioners	100	153	87	157	222
Electric floor-cleaning equipment	100	173	108	16	365
Sewing machines	100	235	92	44	541
Miscellaneous household appliances	100	137	208	215	–
Small appliances and misc. housewares	**100**	**215**	**161**	**158**	**319**
Housewares	100	222	159	164	334
Plastic dinnerware	100	222	194	250	230
China and other dinnerware	100	208	319	144	136
Flatware	100	276	133	285	426
Glassware	100	256	96	62	580
Silver serving pieces	100	168	117	196	201
Other serving pieces	100	317	244	250	450
Nonelectric cookware	100	184	242	187	119
Tableware, nonelectric kitchenware	100	239	85	156	470
Small appliances	100	194	165	138	271
Small electric kitchen appliances	100	213	171	166	295
Portable heating and cooling equipment	100	153	154	74	216
Miscellaneous household equipment	**100**	**254**	**219**	**223**	**315**
Window coverings	100	313	142	388	441
Infants' equipment	100	126	47	161	184
Laundry and cleaning equipment	100	214	190	159	282
Outdoor equipment	100	357	172	290	610
Clocks	100	179	121	21	365
Lamps and lighting fixtures	100	267	170	259	380
Other household decorative items	100	279	294	232	301
Telephones and accessories	100	242	94	314	346
Lawn and garden equipment	100	171	154	186	178
Power tools	100	288	298	117	409
Office furniture for home use	100	438	239	219	829
Hand tools	100	128	124	99	156
Indoor plants and fresh flowers	100	256	217	229	319
Closet and storage items	100	214	223	233	189
Rental of furniture	100	18	21	37	–
Luggage	100	344	235	295	502
Computers and computer hardware, nonbusiness use	100	259	183	264	339
Computer software and accessories, nonbusiness use	100	254	205	302	270
Telephone answering devices	100	222	299	128	212
Calculators	100	245	266	266	205
Business equipment for home use	100	150	181	201	75
Other hardware	100	227	507	73	41
Smoke alarms	100	236	224	120	342
Other household appliances	100	274	111	428	332
Miscellaneous household equipment and parts	100	208	109	146	363

Note: (–) means sample is too small to make a reliable estimate.
Source: Calculations by New Strategist based on the 2003 Consumer Expenditure Survey

Table 8.11 Housing: Household Operations: Total spending by high-income consumer units, 2003

(total annual spending on household services, supplies, furnishings, and equipment, by before-tax income group of high-income consumer units (CU), 2003; complete income reporters only; numbers in thousands)

	total complete reporters	$100,000 or more	$100,000–$119,999	$120,000–$149,999	$150,000 or more
Number of consumer units	97,391	11,537	4,384	3,151	4,002
Total spending of all CUs	$4,162,653,009	$1,078,880,940	$331,436,976	$272,408,550	$474,933,788
Housing, total spending	1,329,630,628	333,896,816	101,727,958	84,191,727	147,957,062
HOUSEHOLD SERVICES	**71,076,926**	**24,896,500**	**6,304,324**	**5,822,827**	**12,769,622**
Personal services	**29,522,134**	**9,910,168**	**2,969,765**	**2,598,976**	**4,341,490**
Babysitting and child care in your own home	3,644,371	2,330,013	460,408	274,704	1,594,957
Babysitting and child care in someone else's home	2,353,940	449,943	143,883	153,517	152,476
Day care centers, nurseries, and preschools	19,299,974	6,031,197	2,111,860	1,413,129	2,506,333
Other household services	**41,555,766**	**14,986,332**	**3,334,558**	**3,223,851**	**8,428,132**
Housekeeping services	9,217,084	5,360,321	558,039	975,550	3,826,993
Gardening, lawn care service	8,477,887	3,384,264	750,146	616,997	2,017,208
Water softening service	331,129	74,760	32,968	18,402	23,372
Nonclothing laundry and dry cleaning, sent out	105,182	41,649	8,812	9,106	23,732
Nonclothing laundry and dry cleaning, coin-operated	368,138	20,305	12,056	6,207	2,121
Termite/pest control services	1,147,266	299,039	69,662	67,463	161,881
Home security system service fee	1,584,552	548,354	148,398	150,492	249,445
Other home services	1,391,717	461,826	116,001	131,082	214,747
Termite/pest control products	151,930	46,379	11,179	9,012	26,253
Moving, storage, and freight express	3,276,233	1,032,446	392,587	285,512	354,417
Appliance repair, including service center	1,220,309	303,538	93,949	88,795	120,820
Reupholstering and furniture repair	527,859	208,012	50,197	37,907	119,900
Repairs/rentals of lawn/garden equipment, hand/power tools, etc.	555,129	134,060	24,594	62,327	47,144
Appliance rental	178,226	27,343	7,540	15,062	4,722
Repair of computer systems for nonbusiness use	402,225	84,105	26,129	25,870	32,096
Computer information services	12,413,457	2,874,328	1,027,741	711,685	1,134,887
HOUSEKEEPING SUPPLIES	**56,676,692**	**13,680,690**	**4,698,289**	**3,412,785**	**5,561,339**
Laundry and cleaning supplies	**14,161,625**	**2,219,719**	**743,658**	**519,033**	**955,077**
Soaps and detergents	7,789,332	1,200,771	428,974	254,128	516,458
Other laundry cleaning products	6,372,293	1,018,948	314,684	264,905	438,619
Other household products	**27,978,486**	**7,923,150**	**2,835,177**	**1,870,654**	**3,211,965**
Cleansing and toilet tissue, paper towels, and napkins	7,841,923	1,291,798	505,563	252,206	532,786
Miscellaneous household products	11,421,043	3,012,657	1,090,520	560,216	1,357,879
Lawn and garden supplies	8,715,521	3,618,695	1,239,050	1,058,232	1,321,300
Postage and stationery	**14,536,581**	**3,537,821**	**1,119,454**	**1,023,130**	**1,394,257**
Stationery, stationery supplies, giftwrap	6,675,179	1,671,942	623,668	488,310	560,320
Postage	7,291,664	1,753,739	474,963	486,483	790,875
Delivery services	569,737	112,140	20,824	48,305	43,062
HOUSEHOLD FURNISHINGS AND EQUIPMENT	**155,812,939**	**46,244,680**	**13,929,064**	**11,073,118**	**21,227,488**
Household textiles	**12,299,509**	**3,345,269**	**1,177,455**	**882,028**	**1,285,803**
Bathroom linens	2,244,863	500,360	212,887	184,901	103,372
Bedroom linens	5,803,530	1,526,691	649,577	377,269	499,810
Kitchen and dining room linens	859,963	159,441	50,241	42,507	66,593
Curtains and draperies	1,571,891	609,384	100,174	189,060	320,160
Slipcovers and decorative pillows	516,172	198,436	55,195	8,823	133,707
Sewing materials for household items	1,157,979	303,654	98,421	66,675	138,549
Other linens	144,139	47,302	10,960	12,793	23,572
Furniture	**40,799,038**	**12,771,920**	**3,493,390**	**3,070,240**	**6,208,543**
Mattresses and springs	4,555,951	1,137,779	376,323	274,421	487,043
Other bedroom furniture	8,117,540	2,345,818	574,216	577,988	1,193,637
Sofas	9,378,753	2,706,926	720,116	652,887	1,334,027
Living room chairs	3,835,258	983,414	381,276	181,498	420,650
Living room tables	1,791,994	560,698	133,361	267,646	159,720
Kitchen and dining room furniture	4,968,889	2,153,150	452,253	439,565	1,261,390

	total complete reporters	$100,000 or more	$100,000–$119,999	$120,000–$149,999	$150,000 or more
Infants' furniture	$813,215	$227,971	$27,093	$143,560	$57,309
Outdoor furniture	1,598,186	754,866	102,103	136,911	515,898
Wall units, cabinets, and other furniture	5,740,226	1,901,413	726,648	395,829	778,949
Floor coverings	**5,288,331**	**2,391,620**	**614,286**	**607,670**	**1,169,705**
Wall-to-wall carpeting	2,929,521	1,173,313	383,819	426,267	363,262
Floor coverings, nonpermanent	2,358,810	1,218,192	230,423	181,403	806,483
Major appliances	**19,980,738**	**4,890,073**	**1,244,574**	**1,111,862**	**2,530,865**
Dishwashers (built-in), garbage disposals, range hoods	1,345,944	341,611	127,618	79,279	134,627
Refrigerators and freezers	4,938,698	1,150,354	302,934	283,622	563,882
Washing machines	2,909,069	731,450	216,701	236,514	248,164
Clothes dryers	1,899,125	444,982	142,612	126,418	175,848
Cooking stoves, ovens	3,139,886	1,015,943	185,268	238,657	592,136
Microwave ovens	762,572	157,402	37,439	73,103	56,908
Window air conditioners	571,685	103,487	22,358	28,958	52,146
Electric floor-cleaning equipment	3,226,564	661,301	157,342	16,700	484,282
Sewing machines	842,432	234,316	34,984	12,005	187,374
Miscellaneous household appliances	185,043	30,112	17,361	12,856	–
Small appliances and misc. housewares	**9,218,058**	**2,347,318**	**657,069**	**470,539**	**1,206,683**
Housewares	6,924,500	1,819,154	496,400	368,383	951,395
Plastic dinnerware	156,800	41,187	13,722	12,667	14,807
China and other dinnerware	764,519	187,938	109,688	35,732	42,581
Flatware	408,068	133,483	24,507	37,591	71,356
Glassware	939,823	284,502	40,420	18,969	223,832
Silver serving pieces	690,502	137,290	36,387	43,736	57,149
Other serving pieces	147,060	55,147	16,133	11,879	27,174
Nonelectric cookware	1,546,569	337,688	168,740	93,522	75,798
Tableware, nonelectric kitchenware	2,271,158	641,919	86,803	114,287	438,699
Small appliances	2,294,532	523,048	170,669	102,155	255,288
Small electric kitchen appliances	1,585,525	399,411	121,744	85,298	192,416
Portable heating and cooling equipment	708,033	123,638	48,969	16,858	62,871
Miscellaneous household equipment	**68,225,317**	**20,498,480**	**6,732,333**	**4,930,811**	**8,825,851**
Window coverings	2,581,835	957,110	164,795	324,490	467,794
Infants' equipment	1,451,126	215,973	30,556	75,782	109,455
Laundry and cleaning equipment	1,512,482	382,913	129,547	77,704	175,128
Outdoor equipment	2,491,262	1,052,867	192,852	233,647	624,032
Clocks	385,668	81,797	20,956	2,678	57,829
Lamps and lighting fixtures	1,442,361	456,404	110,301	120,904	225,153
Other household decorative items	13,902,565	4,602,571	1,837,466	1,044,966	1,717,859
Telephones and accessories	2,705,522	774,133	114,159	274,830	384,672
Lawn and garden equipment	5,117,897	1,035,676	353,789	307,790	374,107
Power tools	3,010,356	1,026,447	404,468	114,318	505,413
Office furniture for home use	1,173,562	609,269	126,259	83,218	399,880
Hand tools	746,989	113,524	41,736	23,916	47,904
Indoor plants and fresh flowers	4,136,196	1,252,226	404,950	305,868	541,431
Closet and storage items	1,062,536	268,927	106,575	80,130	82,361
Rental of furniture	299,964	6,461	2,806	3,624	–
Luggage	650,572	265,236	68,829	62,075	134,307
Computers and computer hardware, nonbusiness use	13,811,992	4,244,808	1,138,218	1,181,530	1,925,082
Computer software and accessories, nonbusiness use	1,875,751	564,390	173,387	183,168	207,864
Telephone answering devices	96,417	25,381	12,977	4,002	8,404
Calculators	127,582	37,034	15,300	10,965	10,765
Business equipment for home use	119,791	21,228	9,776	7,783	3,682
Other hardware	4,449,795	1,195,579	1,016,255	105,559	74,957
Smoke alarms	119,791	33,457	12,056	4,632	16,848
Other household appliances	695,372	226,010	34,853	96,295	94,887
Miscellaneous household equipment and parts	4,258,908	1,048,829	209,292	200,939	635,998

Note: Numbers may not add to total because of rounding and missing subcategories. (–) means sample is too small to make a reliable estimate.
Source: Calculations by New Strategist based on the 2003 Consumer Expenditure Survey

Table 8.12 Housing: Household Operations: Market shares by high-income consumer units, 2003

(percentage of total annual spending on household services, supplies, furnishings, and equipment accounted for by before-tax income group of high-income consumer units, 2003; complete income reporters only)

	total complete reporters	$100,000 or more	$100,000– $119,999	$120,000– $149,999	$150,000 or more
Share of total consumer units	100.0%	11.8%	4.5%	3.2%	4.1%
Share of total before-tax income	100.0	35.8	9.5	8.3	18.0
Share of total spending	100.0	25.9	8.0	6.5	11.4
Share of housing spending	100.0	25.1	7.7	6.3	11.1
HOUSEHOLD SERVICES	100.0	35.0	8.9	8.2	18.0
Personal services	100.0	33.6	10.1	8.8	14.7
Babysitting and child care in your own home	100.0	63.9	12.6	7.5	43.8
Babysitting and child care in someone else's home	100.0	19.1	6.1	6.5	6.5
Day care centers, nurseries, and preschools	100.0	31.2	10.9	7.3	13.0
Other household services	100.0	36.1	8.0	7.8	20.3
Housekeeping services	100.0	58.2	6.1	10.6	41.5
Gardening, lawn care service	100.0	39.9	8.8	7.3	23.8
Water softening service	100.0	22.6	10.0	5.6	7.1
Nonclothing laundry and dry cleaning, sent out	100.0	39.6	8.4	8.7	22.6
Nonclothing laundry and dry cleaning, coin-operated	100.0	5.5	3.3	1.7	0.6
Termite/pest control services	100.0	26.1	6.1	5.9	14.1
Home security system service fee	100.0	34.6	9.4	9.5	15.7
Other home services	100.0	33.2	8.3	9.4	15.4
Termite/pest control products	100.0	30.5	7.4	5.9	17.3
Moving, storage, and freight express	100.0	31.5	12.0	8.7	10.8
Appliance repair, including service center	100.0	24.9	7.7	7.3	9.9
Reupholstering and furniture repair	100.0	39.4	9.5	7.2	22.7
Repairs/rentals of lawn/garden equipment, hand/power tools, etc.	100.0	24.1	4.4	11.2	8.5
Appliance rental	100.0	15.3	4.2	8.5	2.6
Repair of computer systems for nonbusiness use	100.0	20.9	6.5	6.4	8.0
Computer information services	100.0	23.2	8.3	5.7	9.1
HOUSEKEEPING SUPPLIES	100.0	24.1	8.3	6.0	9.8
Laundry and cleaning supplies	100.0	15.7	5.3	3.7	6.7
Soaps and detergents	100.0	15.4	5.5	3.3	6.6
Other laundry cleaning products	100.0	16.0	4.9	4.2	6.9
Other household products	100.0	28.3	10.1	6.7	11.5
Cleansing and toilet tissue, paper towels, and napkins	100.0	16.5	6.4	3.2	6.8
Miscellaneous household products	100.0	26.4	9.5	4.9	11.9
Lawn and garden supplies	100.0	41.5	14.2	12.1	15.2
Postage and stationery	100.0	24.3	7.7	7.0	9.6
Stationery, stationery supplies, giftwrap	100.0	25.0	9.3	7.3	8.4
Postage	100.0	24.1	6.5	6.7	10.8
Delivery services	100.0	19.7	3.7	8.5	7.6
HOUSEHOLD FURNISHINGS AND EQUIPMENT	100.0	29.7	8.9	7.1	13.6
Household textiles	100.0	27.2	9.6	7.2	10.5
Bathroom linens	100.0	22.3	9.5	8.2	4.6
Bedroom linens	100.0	26.3	11.2	6.5	8.6
Kitchen and dining room linens	100.0	18.5	5.8	4.9	7.7
Curtains and draperies	100.0	38.8	6.4	12.0	20.4
Slipcovers and decorative pillows	100.0	38.4	10.7	1.7	25.9
Sewing materials for household items	100.0	26.2	8.5	5.8	12.0
Other linens	100.0	32.8	7.6	8.9	16.4
Furniture	100.0	31.3	8.6	7.5	15.2
Mattresses and springs	100.0	25.0	8.3	6.0	10.7
Other bedroom furniture	100.0	28.9	7.1	7.1	14.7
Sofas	100.0	28.9	7.7	7.0	14.2
Living room chairs	100.0	25.6	9.9	4.7	11.0
Living room tables	100.0	31.3	7.4	14.9	8.9
Kitchen and dining room furniture	100.0	43.3	9.1	8.8	25.4

	total complete reporters	$100,000 or more	$100,000– $119,999	$120,000– $149,999	$150,000 or more
Infants' furniture	100.0%	28.0%	3.3%	17.7%	7.0%
Outdoor furniture	100.0	47.2	6.4	8.6	32.3
Wall units, cabinets, and other furniture	100.0	33.1	12.7	6.9	13.6
Floor coverings	**100.0**	**45.2**	**11.6**	**11.5**	**22.1**
Wall-to-wall carpeting	100.0	40.1	13.1	14.6	12.4
Floor coverings, nonpermanent	100.0	51.6	9.8	7.7	34.2
Major appliances	**100.0**	**24.5**	**6.2**	**5.6**	**12.7**
Dishwashers (built-in), garbage disposals, range hoods	100.0	25.4	9.5	5.9	10.0
Refrigerators and freezers	100.0	23.3	6.1	5.7	11.4
Washing machines	100.0	24.1	7.4	8.1	8.5
Clothes dryers	100.0	23.4	7.5	6.7	9.3
Cooking stoves, ovens	100.0	32.4	5.9	7.6	18.9
Microwave ovens	100.0	22.0	4.9	9.6	7.5
Window air conditioners	100.0	18.1	3.9	5.1	9.1
Electric floor-cleaning equipment	100.0	20.5	4.9	0.5	15.0
Sewing machines	100.0	27.8	4.2	1.4	22.2
Miscellaneous household appliances	100.0	16.3	9.4	6.9	–
Small appliances and misc. housewares	**100.0**	**25.5**	**7.2**	**5.1**	**13.1**
Housewares	100.0	26.3	7.2	5.3	13.7
Plastic dinnerware	100.0	26.3	8.8	8.1	9.4
China and other dinnerware	100.0	24.6	14.3	4.7	5.6
Flatware	100.0	32.7	6.0	9.2	17.5
Glassware	100.0	30.3	4.3	2.0	23.8
Silver serving pieces	100.0	19.9	5.3	6.3	8.3
Other serving pieces	100.0	37.5	11.0	8.1	18.5
Nonelectric cookware	100.0	21.8	10.9	6.0	4.9
Tableware, nonelectric kitchenware	100.0	28.3	3.8	5.0	19.3
Small appliances	100.0	23.0	7.4	4.5	11.1
Small electric kitchen appliances	100.0	25.2	7.7	5.4	12.1
Portable heating and cooling equipment	100.0	18.2	6.9	2.4	8.9
Miscellaneous household equipment	**100.0**	**30.0**	**9.9**	**7.2**	**12.9**
Window coverings	100.0	37.1	6.4	12.6	18.1
Infants' equipment	100.0	14.9	2.1	5.2	7.5
Laundry and cleaning equipment	100.0	25.3	8.6	5.1	11.6
Outdoor equipment	100.0	42.3	7.7	9.4	25.0
Clocks	100.0	21.2	5.4	0.7	15.0
Lamps and lighting fixtures	100.0	31.6	7.6	8.4	15.6
Other household decorative items	100.0	33.1	13.2	7.5	12.4
Telephones and accessories	100.0	28.6	4.2	10.2	14.2
Lawn and garden equipment	100.0	20.2	6.9	6.0	7.3
Power tools	100.0	34.1	13.4	3.8	16.8
Office furniture for home use	100.0	51.9	10.8	7.1	34.1
Hand tools	100.0	15.2	5.6	3.2	6.4
Indoor plants and fresh flowers	100.0	30.3	9.8	7.4	13.1
Closet and storage items	100.0	25.3	10.0	7.5	7.8
Rental of furniture	100.0	2.2	0.9	1.2	–
Luggage	100.0	40.8	10.6	9.5	20.6
Computers and computer hardware, nonbusiness use	100.0	30.7	8.2	8.6	13.9
Computer software and accessories, nonbusiness use	100.0	30.1	9.2	9.8	11.1
Telephone answering devices	100.0	26.3	13.5	4.2	8.7
Calculators	100.0	29.0	12.0	8.6	8.4
Business equipment for home use	100.0	17.7	8.2	6.5	3.1
Other hardware	100.0	26.9	22.8	2.4	1.7
Smoke alarms	100.0	27.9	10.1	3.9	14.1
Other household appliances	100.0	32.5	5.0	13.8	13.6
Miscellaneous household equipment and parts	100.0	24.6	4.9	4.7	14.9

Note: Numbers may not add to total because of rounding. (–) means sample is too small to make a reliable estimate.
Source: Calculations by New Strategist based on the 2003 Consumer Expenditure Survey

Table 8.13 Housing: Household Operations: Average spending by household type, 2003

(average annual spending of consumer units (CU) on household services, supplies, furnishings, and equipment, by type of consumer unit, 2003)

	total married couples	married couples, no children	married couples with children				single parent, at least one child <18	single person
			total	oldest child under 6	oldest child 6 to 17	oldest child 18 or older		
Number of consumer units (000)	58,448	25,132	28,584	5,496	15,047	8,041	6,999	33,929
Average number of persons per CU	3.2	2.0	3.9	3.5	4.1	4.0	2.9	1.0
Average before-tax income of CU	$69,472.00	$62,930.00	$75,557.00	$66,317.00	$77,508.00	$78,307.00	$29,154.00	$27,131.00
Average spending of CU, total	53,030.03	47,895.65	57,702.32	51,503.24	59,183.18	59,180.36	30,534.75	23,657.35
Housing, average spending	**16,647.97**	**14,352.35**	**18,679.27**	**19,303.20**	**19,234.53**	**17,214.61**	**11,772.50**	**8,767.66**
HOUSEHOLD SERVICES	**970.13**	**596.47**	**1,316.07**	**2,364.65**	**1,286.30**	**655.53**	**725.08**	**343.36**
Personal services	**416.35**	**68.17**	**725.01**	**1,850.46**	**652.48**	**91.56**	**478.44**	**92.74**
Babysitting and child care in your own home	61.59	1.60	116.57	211.21	140.06	7.95	52.75	0.25
Babysitting and child care in someone else's home	32.01	0.95	57.67	157.85	46.03	10.99	55.10	0.70
Day care centers, nurseries, and preschools	293.05	8.47	549.33	1,481.41	464.42	71.21	369.72	9.72
Other household services	**553.78**	**528.30**	**591.07**	**514.18**	**633.82**	**563.98**	**246.63**	**250.62**
Housekeeping services	135.76	109.40	163.95	114.34	190.66	147.87	49.60	51.27
Gardening, lawn care service	105.66	124.45	92.20	97.42	95.93	81.65	34.67	70.13
Water softening service	4.31	3.74	4.98	5.66	5.07	4.36	1.18	1.69
Nonclothing laundry and dry cleaning, sent out	1.19	1.59	0.98	0.90	1.01	0.99	0.32	0.86
Nonclothing laundry and dry cleaning, coin-operated	2.82	1.84	3.13	4.35	3.26	2.06	6.12	3.49
Termite/pest control services	15.64	17.39	14.45	28.16	13.32	7.19	5.75	6.86
Home security system service fee	20.56	21.95	20.69	17.32	24.51	15.83	9.35	9.33
Other home services	18.95	18.60	17.92	17.07	14.34	25.20	7.32	10.93
Termite/pest control products	2.06	2.24	1.95	3.80	1.82	0.94	0.56	1.10
Moving, storage, and freight express	42.14	38.36	46.37	58.71	54.23	23.23	13.59	11.19
Appliance repair, including service center	16.74	15.87	17.11	10.48	15.61	24.45	4.47	5.03
Reupholstering and furniture repair	7.09	11.30	4.46	2.81	4.40	5.70	0.44	3.03
Repairs/rentals of lawn/garden equipment, hand/power tools, etc.	7.95	7.72	9.09	8.51	10.71	6.46	2.82	3.34
Appliance rental	1.50	1.34	1.64	0.83	2.12	1.29	6.73	0.49
Repair of computer systems for nonbusiness use	5.67	3.95	7.87	2.82	5.95	14.92	2.33	2.88
Computer information services	161.70	142.93	181.40	139.89	189.20	195.16	100.15	68.60
HOUSEKEEPING SUPPLIES	**698.92**	**659.25**	**734.26**	**645.33**	**727.65**	**813.15**	**348.85**	**283.83**
Laundry and cleaning supplies	**171.41**	**149.18**	**185.17**	**151.55**	**183.11**	**214.10**	**122.27**	**67.91**
Soaps and detergents	96.00	81.59	105.17	84.80	105.97	118.53	72.16	34.51
Other laundry cleaning products	75.41	67.59	80.00	66.75	77.14	95.57	50.11	33.40
Other household products	**360.38**	**335.72**	**384.95**	**351.98**	**388.87**	**401.21**	**161.28**	**122.60**
Cleansing and toilet tissue, paper towels, and napkins	95.37	84.54	103.56	79.38	106.55	115.24	68.60	38.97
Miscellaneous household products	144.53	117.20	167.71	167.49	168.40	166.46	62.04	47.17
Lawn and garden supplies	120.48	133.98	113.69	105.12	113.92	119.51	30.64	36.46
Postage and stationery	**167.12**	**174.35**	**164.14**	**141.79**	**155.67**	**197.84**	**65.30**	**93.33**
Stationery, stationery supplies, giftwrap	74.23	66.66	81.77	77.47	82.87	82.68	32.09	38.38
Postage	89.10	102.56	79.31	62.89	69.58	111.21	30.16	48.78
Delivery services	3.79	5.13	3.07	1.43	3.22	3.96	3.05	6.18
HOUSEHOLD FURNISHINGS AND EQUIPMENT	**2,055.20**	**2,020.65**	**2,121.62**	**2,300.02**	**2,182.96**	**1,879.59**	**950.71**	**768.56**
Household textiles	**156.69**	**168.41**	**148.67**	**125.33**	**142.22**	**178.20**	**66.66**	**52.06**
Bathroom linens	26.87	30.03	26.45	16.92	27.55	31.21	11.87	7.39
Bedroom linens	74.00	77.82	68.40	61.66	64.14	82.03	38.22	26.42
Kitchen and dining room linens	10.43	12.45	8.75	4.59	9.21	10.88	3.56	2.93
Curtains and draperies	22.52	22.78	24.75	21.88	22.08	31.73	7.10	5.80
Slipcovers and decorative pillows	4.43	5.28	3.63	6.95	2.61	3.28	0.56	3.08
Sewing materials for household items	16.51	17.81	14.94	11.12	15.02	17.41	3.92	5.65
Other linens	1.92	2.24	1.75	2.22	1.62	1.68	1.44	0.80
Furniture	**564.28**	**541.57**	**595.40**	**743.75**	**623.86**	**440.74**	**278.01**	**193.76**
Mattresses and springs	62.87	65.88	62.16	69.83	56.46	67.58	30.29	24.39
Other bedroom furniture	107.73	97.62	109.48	144.87	103.54	96.42	57.15	38.25
Sofas	128.59	116.63	143.68	161.99	163.89	93.37	81.34	41.14
Living room chairs	50.59	60.47	44.46	52.71	46.33	35.32	19.75	26.02
Living room tables	23.56	27.54	20.98	25.42	22.28	15.53	10.35	10.92
Kitchen and dining room furniture	75.35	55.83	96.03	90.58	122.32	50.57	19.67	22.06

	total married couples	married couples, no children	married couples with children				single parent, at least one child <18	single person
			total	oldest child under 6	oldest child 6 to 17	oldest child 18 or older		
Infants' furniture	$12.61	$9.65	$15.94	$59.40	$6.35	$4.19	$7.17	$1.54
Outdoor furniture	24.73	29.28	20.04	15.57	24.77	14.25	5.93	4.60
Wall units, cabinets, and other furniture	78.25	78.66	82.61	123.38	77.93	63.51	46.36	24.84
Floor coverings	**71.32**	**73.49**	**72.23**	**49.58**	**79.09**	**74.86**	**38.35**	**26.15**
Wall-to-wall carpeting	39.49	46.17	35.85	18.09	35.79	48.09	31.62	15.62
Floor coverings, nonpermanent	31.83	27.32	36.38	31.48	43.30	26.77	6.74	10.52
Major appliances	**270.50**	**250.73**	**282.04**	**345.14**	**290.59**	**221.41**	**162.82**	**91.21**
Dishwashers (built-in), garbage disposals, range hoods	18.88	19.69	18.54	19.65	18.63	17.63	13.38	7.12
Refrigerators and freezers	64.72	59.53	69.13	70.73	75.01	57.04	32.27	20.42
Washing machines	38.38	32.46	40.37	44.14	46.32	28.46	31.37	13.10
Clothes dryers	25.47	22.14	28.54	35.11	32.01	17.92	24.62	7.98
Cooking stoves, ovens	48.05	54.49	43.79	31.49	46.80	46.54	12.85	9.63
Microwave ovens	9.43	10.83	8.55	9.34	9.30	6.61	4.21	5.54
Window air conditioners	6.41	6.31	5.47	6.74	6.27	3.13	7.85	3.68
Electric floor-cleaning equipment	39.15	25.30	51.79	121.30	41.21	22.23	34.17	17.28
Sewing machines	14.24	11.61	11.14	4.70	11.54	14.79	0.06	4.38
Miscellaneous household appliances	3.88	6.91	1.80	–	0.25	6.29	0.50	0.66
Small appliances and misc. housewares	**116.69**	**126.71**	**108.40**	**97.86**	**91.86**	**149.36**	**48.96**	**47.75**
Housewares	87.37	96.14	80.50	71.79	65.81	116.74	36.85	35.45
Plastic dinnerware	1.84	1.24	2.37	2.72	2.50	1.87	1.50	1.00
China and other dinnerware	10.53	11.91	10.05	4.94	8.82	16.32	4.75	2.81
Flatware	5.04	4.95	4.52	5.27	3.63	5.65	2.41	2.70
Glassware	10.13	12.42	8.94	6.94	9.29	9.70	4.20	8.58
Silver serving pieces	8.25	10.20	6.85	5.26	5.55	10.67	3.58	4.20
Other serving pieces	2.03	2.15	1.96	2.28	1.66	2.30	0.87	0.53
Nonelectric cookware	19.99	20.47	18.24	14.59	15.03	27.47	4.33	9.04
Tableware, nonelectric kitchenware	29.56	32.80	27.57	29.78	19.33	42.75	15.20	6.59
Small appliances	29.32	30.56	27.90	26.08	26.05	32.63	12.11	12.30
Small electric kitchen appliances	20.03	19.60	19.60	20.41	18.50	21.10	8.33	9.45
Portable heating and cooling equipment	9.29	10.97	8.30	5.67	7.55	11.53	3.78	2.85
Miscellaneous household equipment	**875.72**	**859.73**	**914.90**	**938.36**	**955.33**	**815.01**	**355.91**	**357.64**
Window coverings	39.65	46.94	37.35	79.71	34.20	14.29	7.77	9.01
Infants' equipment	22.85	16.62	29.10	65.91	18.44	23.74	9.44	1.39
Laundry and cleaning equipment	18.37	16.79	19.35	20.96	18.53	19.86	11.10	6.92
Outdoor equipment	29.65	28.40	30.85	9.50	45.89	15.89	11.08	13.79
Clocks	4.76	3.36	5.35	4.07	7.24	2.50	1.37	1.39
Lamps and lighting fixtures	18.41	16.96	20.73	20.13	19.75	22.97	7.03	9.09
Other household decorative items	170.70	183.70	164.42	164.31	169.75	153.65	93.75	56.26
Telephones and accessories	33.50	25.51	35.81	27.53	41.31	30.69	37.28	8.51
Lawn and garden equipment	80.53	95.46	73.83	88.36	74.15	63.29	10.03	30.56
Power tools	40.28	27.72	50.40	46.89	65.37	22.47	6.88	6.79
Office furniture for home use	20.51	25.28	17.43	15.59	22.22	9.75	7.05	3.57
Hand tools	10.34	8.55	12.16	21.39	10.52	8.93	3.73	3.98
Indoor plants and fresh flowers	53.71	63.38	47.34	38.04	45.52	57.12	18.40	24.64
Closet and storage items	12.00	10.29	13.49	14.47	15.06	9.57	2.72	6.70
Rental of furniture	1.80	0.65	2.66	3.43	3.23	1.09	9.25	1.87
Luggage	8.87	8.38	8.98	5.12	9.26	11.09	3.87	3.28
Computers and computer hardware, nonbusiness use	183.56	171.79	198.50	166.39	193.22	230.34	69.09	87.87
Computer software and accessories, nonbusiness use	23.11	20.61	26.55	22.86	26.17	29.80	10.06	13.44
Telephone answering devices	1.03	1.10	1.04	1.48	0.67	1.44	1.11	0.81
Calculators	1.56	0.50	2.66	0.72	3.15	3.06	1.07	1.10
Business equipment for home use	1.15	1.03	1.07	0.74	1.38	0.72	1.89	0.89
Other hardware	35.16	18.83	52.04	74.68	55.36	28.63	4.05	40.46
Smoke alarms	1.28	1.20	1.38	1.44	1.32	1.48	0.61	1.05
Other household appliances	10.13	11.81	8.41	5.94	10.77	5.67	1.88	2.78
Miscellaneous household equipment and parts	52.81	54.88	53.96	38.70	62.89	46.98	25.41	21.49

Note: Average spending figures for total consumer units can be found on Average Spending by Age and Average Spending by Region tables. Subcategories may not add to total because some are not shown. (–) means sample is too small to make a reliable estimate.
Source: Bureau of Labor Statistics, unpublished tables from the 2003 Consumer Expenditure Survey

Table 8.14 Housing: Household Operations: Indexed spending by household type, 2003

(indexed average annual spending of consumer units (CU) on household services, supplies, furnishings, and equipment, by type of consumer unit, 2003; index definition: an index of 100 is the average for all consumer units; an index of 132 means that spending by consumer units in that group is 32 percent above the average for all consumer units; an index of 68 indicates spending that is 32 percent below the average for all consumer units)

	total married couples	married couples, no children	married couples with children				single parent, at least one child <18	single person
			total	oldest child under 6	oldest child 6 to 17	oldest child 18 or older		
Average spending of CU, total	$53,030	$47,896	$57,702	$51,503	$59,183	$59,180	$30,535	$23,657
Average spending of CU, index	130	117	141	126	145	145	75	58
Housing, spending index	**124**	**107**	**139**	**144**	**143**	**128**	**88**	**65**
HOUSEHOLD SERVICES	**137**	**84**	**186**	**334**	**182**	**93**	**103**	**49**
Personal services	**142**	**23**	**247**	**630**	**222**	**31**	**163**	**32**
Babysitting and child care in your own home	171	4	323	586	389	22	146	1
Babysitting and child care in someone else's home	133	4	240	658	192	46	230	3
Day care centers, nurseries, and preschools	155	4	291	785	246	38	196	5
Other household services	**134**	**128**	**143**	**124**	**153**	**136**	**60**	**61**
Housekeeping services	146	117	176	123	205	159	53	55
Gardening, lawn care service	126	149	110	116	115	98	41	84
Water softening service	133	116	154	175	157	135	37	52
Nonclothing laundry and dry cleaning, sent out	119	159	98	90	101	99	32	86
Nonclothing laundry and dry cleaning, coin-operated	78	51	86	120	90	57	169	96
Termite/pest control services	138	154	128	249	118	64	51	61
Home security system service fee	132	141	133	111	158	102	60	60
Other home services	128	125	121	115	97	170	49	74
Termite/pest control products	136	147	128	250	120	62	37	72
Moving, storage, and freight express	138	126	152	193	178	76	45	37
Appliance repair, including service center	142	135	146	89	133	208	38	43
Reupholstering and furniture repair	136	217	86	54	85	110	8	58
Repairs/rentals of lawn/garden equipment, hand/power tools, etc.	131	127	150	140	176	106	46	55
Appliance rental	92	82	101	51	130	79	413	30
Repair of computer systems for nonbusiness use	135	94	187	67	142	355	55	69
Computer information services	130	115	146	113	153	157	81	55
HOUSEKEEPING SUPPLIES	**132**	**125**	**139**	**122**	**138**	**154**	**66**	**54**
Laundry and cleaning supplies	**130**	**113**	**140**	**115**	**138**	**162**	**92**	**51**
Soaps and detergents	129	110	142	114	143	160	97	47
Other laundry cleaning products	130	116	138	115	133	164	86	57
Other household products	**137**	**127**	**146**	**134**	**148**	**152**	**61**	**47**
Cleansing and toilet tissue, paper towels, and napkins	127	112	138	106	142	153	91	52
Miscellaneous household products	136	110	158	158	158	157	58	44
Lawn and garden supplies	147	164	139	128	139	146	37	45
Postage and stationery	**125**	**131**	**123**	**106**	**117**	**149**	**49**	**70**
Stationery, stationery supplies, giftwrap	125	112	137	130	139	139	54	64
Postage	129	149	115	91	101	161	44	71
Delivery services	81	109	65	30	69	84	65	131
HOUSEHOLD FURNISHINGS AND EQUIPMENT	**137**	**135**	**142**	**154**	**146**	**126**	**64**	**51**
Household textiles	**138**	**148**	**131**	**110**	**125**	**157**	**59**	**46**
Bathroom linens	132	148	130	83	136	154	58	36
Bedroom linens	138	146	128	115	120	153	72	49
Kitchen and dining room linens	142	169	119	62	125	148	48	40
Curtains and draperies	148	149	162	144	145	208	47	38
Slipcovers and decorative pillows	102	121	83	160	60	75	13	71
Sewing materials for household items	146	158	133	99	133	154	35	50
Other linens	127	148	116	147	107	111	95	53
Furniture	**141**	**135**	**149**	**186**	**156**	**110**	**69**	**48**
Mattresses and springs	140	147	138	156	126	151	67	54
Other bedroom furniture	136	123	138	182	130	121	72	48
Sofas	140	127	156	176	178	101	88	45
Living room chairs	131	156	115	136	120	91	51	67
Living room tables	135	157	120	145	127	89	59	62
Kitchen and dining room furniture	152	113	194	183	248	102	40	45

	total married couples	married couples, no children	married couples with children				single parent, at least one child <18	single person
			total	oldest child under 6	oldest child 6 to 17	oldest child 18 or older		
Infants' furniture	154	118	195	727	78	51	88	19
Outdoor furniture	161	191	131	101	161	93	39	30
Wall units, cabinets, and other furniture	142	143	150	224	141	115	84	45
Floor coverings	**138**	**142**	**140**	**96**	**153**	**145**	**74**	**51**
Wall-to-wall carpeting	134	157	122	61	121	163	107	53
Floor coverings, nonpermanent	143	123	163	41	195	120	30	47
Major appliances	**138**	**128**	**144**	**176**	**148**	**113**	**83**	**47**
Dishwashers (built-in), garbage disposals, range hoods	140	146	137	146	138	131	99	53
Refrigerators and freezers	136	125	145	149	158	120	68	43
Washing machines	134	113	143	154	162	99	109	46
Clothes dryers	131	114	147	181	165	92	127	41
Cooking stoves, ovens	158	179	144	103	153	153	42	32
Microwave ovens	125	143	113	124	123	87	56	73
Window air conditioners	119	117	101	125	116	58	145	68
Electric floor-cleaning equipment	129	84	171	401	136	74	113	57
Sewing machines	159	130	124	53	129	165	1	49
Miscellaneous household appliances	173	308	80	–	11	281	22	29
Small appliances and misc. housewares	**133**	**144**	**124**	**112**	**105**	**170**	**56**	**54**
Housewares	134	147	123	110	101	179	56	54
Plastic dinnerware	118	79	152	174	160	120	96	64
China and other dinnerware	150	169	143	70	125	232	67	40
Flatware	126	124	113	132	91	142	60	68
Glassware	114	140	101	78	104	109	47	97
Silver serving pieces	127	157	105	81	85	164	55	65
Other serving pieces	141	149	136	158	115	160	60	37
Nonelectric cookware	131	134	120	96	98	180	28	59
Tableware, nonelectric kitchenware	144	160	134	145	94	208	74	32
Small appliances	130	136	124	116	116	145	54	55
Small electric kitchen appliances	128	125	125	130	118	135	53	60
Portable heating and cooling equipment	136	160	121	83	110	168	55	42
Miscellaneous household equipment	**135**	**133**	**141**	**145**	**148**	**126**	**55**	**55**
Window coverings	163	193	153	327	141	59	32	37
Infants' equipment	175	127	222	504	141	181	72	11
Laundry and cleaning equipment	131	120	138	149	132	142	79	49
Outdoor equipment	125	120	130	40	193	67	47	58
Clocks	118	84	133	101	180	62	34	35
Lamps and lighting fixtures	135	124	152	147	145	168	51	67
Other household decorative items	135	145	130	130	134	121	74	44
Telephones and accessories	125	95	134	103	154	115	139	32
Lawn and garden equipment	145	172	133	160	134	114	18	55
Power tools	165	114	207	192	268	92	28	28
Office furniture for home use	163	200	138	124	176	77	56	28
Hand tools	143	118	168	296	146	124	52	55
Indoor plants and fresh flowers	133	157	117	94	113	142	46	61
Closet and storage items	125	108	141	151	157	100	28	70
Rental of furniture	67	24	99	127	120	40	343	69
Luggage	144	136	145	83	150	179	63	53
Computers and computer hardware, nonbusiness use	134	126	145	122	141	168	51	64
Computer software and accessories, nonbusiness use	129	115	148	127	146	166	56	75
Telephone answering devices	111	118	112	159	72	155	119	87
Calculators	123	39	209	57	248	241	84	87
Business equipment for home use	106	95	99	65	128	67	175	82
Other hardware	92	49	136	195	144	75	11	106
Smoke alarms	113	106	122	127	117	131	54	93
Other household appliances	152	177	126	89	161	85	28	42
Miscellaneous household equipment and parts	137	142	140	100	163	122	66	56

Note: Spending index for total consumer units is 100. (–) means sample is too small to make a reliable estimate.
Source: Calculations by New Strategist based on the 2003 Consumer Expenditure Survey

Table 8.15 Housing: Household Operations: Total spending by household type, 2003

(total annual spending on household services, supplies, furnishings, and equipment, by consumer unit (CU) type, 2003; numbers in thousands)

	total married couples	married couples, no children	married couples with children				single parent, at least one child <18	single person
			total	oldest child under 6	oldest child 6 to 17	oldest child 18 or older		
Number of consumer units	58,448	25,132	28,584	5,496	15,047	8,041	6,999	33,929
Total spending of all CUs	$3,099,499,193	$1,203,713,476	$1,649,363,115	$283,061,807	$890,529,309	$475,869,275	$213,712,715	$802,670,228
Housing, total spending	973,040,551	360,703,260	533,928,254	106,090,387	289,421,973	138,422,679	82,395,728	297,477,936
HOUSEHOLD SERVICES	**56,702,158**	**14,990,484**	**37,618,545**	**12,996,116**	**19,354,956**	**5,271,117**	**5,074,835**	**11,649,861**
Personal services	**24,334,825**	**1,713,248**	**20,723,686**	**10,170,128**	**9,817,867**	**736,234**	**3,348,602**	**3,146,575**
Babysitting and child care in your own home	3,599,812	40,211	3,332,037	1,160,810	2,107,483	63,926	369,197	8,482
Babysitting and child care in someone else's home	1,870,920	23,875	1,648,439	867,544	692,613	88,371	385,645	23,750
Day care centers, nurseries, and preschools	17,128,186	212,868	15,702,049	8,141,829	6,988,128	572,600	2,587,670	329,790
Other household services	**32,367,333**	**13,277,236**	**16,895,145**	**2,825,933**	**9,537,090**	**4,534,963**	**1,726,163**	**8,503,286**
Housekeeping services	7,934,900	2,749,441	4,686,347	628,413	2,868,861	1,189,023	347,150	1,739,540
Gardening, lawn care service	6,175,616	3,127,677	2,635,445	535,420	1,443,459	656,548	242,655	2,379,441
Water softening service	251,911	93,994	142,348	31,107	76,288	35,059	8,259	57,340
Nonclothing laundry and dry cleaning, sent out	69,553	39,960	28,012	4,946	15,197	7,961	2,240	29,179
Nonclothing laundry and dry cleaning, coin-operated	164,823	46,243	89,468	23,908	49,053	16,564	42,834	118,412
Termite/pest control services	914,127	437,045	413,039	154,767	200,426	57,815	40,244	232,753
Home security system service fee	1,201,691	551,647	591,403	95,191	368,802	127,289	65,441	316,558
Other home services	1,107,590	467,455	512,225	93,817	215,774	202,633	51,233	370,844
Termite/pest control products	120,403	56,296	55,739	20,885	27,386	7,559	3,919	37,322
Moving, storage, and freight express	2,462,999	964,064	1,325,440	322,670	815,999	186,792	95,116	379,666
Appliance repair, including service center	978,420	398,845	489,072	57,598	234,884	196,602	31,286	170,663
Reupholstering and furniture repair	414,396	283,992	127,485	15,444	66,207	45,834	3,080	102,805
Repairs/rentals of lawn/garden equipment, hand/power tools, etc.	464,662	194,019	259,829	46,771	161,153	51,945	19,737	113,323
Appliance rental	87,672	33,677	46,878	4,562	31,900	10,373	47,103	16,625
Repair of computer systems for nonbusiness use	331,400	99,271	224,956	15,499	89,530	119,972	16,308	97,716
Computer information services	9,451,042	3,592,117	5,185,138	768,835	2,846,892	1,569,282	700,950	2,327,529
HOUSEKEEPING SUPPLIES	**40,850,476**	**16,568,271**	**20,988,088**	**3,546,734**	**10,948,950**	**6,538,539**	**2,441,601**	**9,630,068**
Laundry and cleaning supplies	**10,018,572**	**3,749,192**	**5,292,899**	**832,919**	**2,755,256**	**1,721,578**	**855,768**	**2,304,118**
Soaps and detergents	5,611,008	2,050,520	3,006,179	456,061	1,594,531	953,100	505,048	1,170,890
Other laundry cleaning products	4,407,564	1,698,672	2,286,720	366,858	1,160,726	768,478	350,720	1,133,229
Other household products	**21,063,490**	**8,437,315**	**11,003,411**	**1,934,482**	**5,851,327**	**3,226,130**	**1,128,799**	**4,159,695**
Cleansing and toilet tissue, paper towels, napkins	5,574,186	2,124,659	2,960,159	436,272	1,603,258	926,645	480,131	1,322,213
Miscellaneous household products	8,447,489	2,945,470	4,793,823	920,525	2,533,915	1,338,505	434,218	1,600,431
Lawn and garden supplies	7,041,815	3,367,185	3,249,715	577,740	1,714,154	960,980	214,449	1,237,051
Postage and stationery	**9,767,830**	**4,381,764**	**4,691,778**	**779,278**	**2,342,366**	**1,590,831**	**457,035**	**3,166,594**
Stationery, stationery supplies, giftwrap	4,338,595	1,675,299	2,337,314	425,775	1,246,945	664,830	224,598	1,302,195
Postage	5,207,717	2,577,538	2,266,997	345,643	1,046,970	894,240	211,090	1,655,057
Delivery services	221,518	128,927	87,753	7,859	48,451	31,842	21,347	209,681
HOUSEHOLD FURNISHINGS, EQUIPMENT	**120,122,330**	**50,782,976**	**60,644,386**	**12,640,910**	**32,846,999**	**15,113,783**	**6,654,019**	**26,076,472**
Household textiles	**9,158,217**	**4,232,480**	**4,249,583**	**688,814**	**2,139,984**	**1,432,906**	**466,553**	**1,766,344**
Bathroom linens	1,570,498	754,714	756,047	92,992	414,545	250,960	83,078	250,735
Bedroom linens	4,325,152	1,955,772	1,955,146	338,883	965,115	659,603	267,502	896,404
Kitchen and dining room linens	609,613	312,893	250,110	25,237	138,583	87,486	24,916	99,412
Curtains and draperies	1,316,249	572,507	707,454	120,252	332,238	255,141	49,693	196,788
Slipcovers and decorative pillows	258,925	132,697	103,760	38,197	39,273	26,374	3,919	104,501
Sewing materials for household items	964,976	447,601	427,045	61,116	226,006	139,994	27,436	191,699
Other linens	112,220	56,296	50,022	12,201	24,376	13,509	10,079	27,143
Furniture	**32,981,037**	**13,610,737**	**17,018,914**	**4,087,650**	**9,387,221**	**3,543,990**	**1,945,792**	**6,574,083**
Mattresses and springs	3,674,626	1,655,696	1,776,781	383,786	849,554	543,411	212,000	827,528
Other bedroom furniture	6,296,603	2,453,386	3,129,376	796,206	1,557,966	775,313	399,993	1,297,784
Sofas	7,515,828	2,931,145	4,106,949	890,297	2,466,053	750,788	569,299	1,395,839
Living room chairs	2,956,884	1,519,732	1,270,845	289,694	697,128	284,008	138,230	882,833
Living room tables	1,377,035	692,135	599,692	139,708	335,247	124,877	72,440	370,505
Kitchen and dining room furniture	4,404,057	1,403,120	2,744,922	497,828	1,840,549	406,633	137,670	748,474

	total married couples	married couples, no children	married couples with children				single parent, at least one child <18	single person
			total	oldest child under 6	oldest child 6 to 17	oldest child 18 or older		
Infants' furniture	$737,029	$242,524	$455,629	$326,462	$95,548	$33,692	$50,183	$52,251
Outdoor furniture	1,445,419	735,865	572,823	85,573	372,714	114,584	41,504	156,073
Wall units, cabinets, and other furniture	4,573,556	1,976,883	2,361,324	678,096	1,172,613	510,684	324,474	842,796
Floor coverings	**4,168,511**	**1,846,951**	**2,064,622**	**272,492**	**1,190,067**	**601,949**	**268,412**	**887,243**
Wall-to-wall carpeting	2,308,112	1,160,344	1,024,736	99,423	538,532	386,692	221,308	529,971
Floor coverings, nonpermanent	1,860,400	686,606	1,039,886	173,014	651,535	215,258	47,173	356,933
Major appliances	**15,810,184**	**6,301,346**	**8,061,831**	**1,896,889**	**4,372,508**	**1,780,358**	**1,139,577**	**3,094,664**
Dishwashers (built-in), garbage disposals, range hoods	1,103,498	494,849	529,947	107,996	280,326	141,763	93,647	241,574
Refrigerators and freezers	3,782,755	1,496,108	1,976,012	388,732	1,128,675	458,659	225,858	692,830
Washing machines	2,243,234	815,785	1,168,228	242,593	696,977	228,847	219,559	444,470
Clothes dryers	1,488,671	556,422	818,646	192,965	481,654	144,095	172,315	270,753
Cooking stoves, ovens	2,808,426	1,369,443	1,251,693	173,069	704,200	374,228	89,937	326,736
Microwave ovens	551,165	272,180	244,393	51,333	139,937	53,151	29,466	187,967
Window air conditioners	374,652	158,583	155,354	37,043	94,345	25,168	54,942	124,859
Electric floor-cleaning equipment	2,288,239	635,840	1,480,365	666,665	620,087	178,751	239,156	586,293
Sewing machines	832,300	291,783	318,426	25,831	173,642	118,926	420	148,609
Miscellaneous household appliances	226,778	173,662	51,451	–	3,762	50,578	3,500	22,393
Small appliances and misc. housewares	**6,820,297**	**3,184,476**	**3,098,506**	**537,839**	**1,382,217**	**1,201,004**	**342,671**	**1,620,110**
Housewares	5,106,602	2,416,190	2,301,012	394,558	990,243	938,706	257,913	1,202,783
Plastic dinnerware	107,544	31,164	67,744	14,949	37,618	15,037	10,499	33,929
China and other dinnerware	615,457	299,322	287,269	27,150	132,715	131,229	33,245	95,340
Flatware	294,578	124,403	129,200	28,964	54,621	45,432	16,868	91,608
Glassware	592,078	312,139	255,541	38,142	139,787	77,998	29,396	291,111
Silver serving pieces	482,196	256,346	195,800	28,909	83,511	85,797	25,056	142,502
Other serving pieces	118,649	54,034	56,025	12,531	24,978	18,494	6,089	17,982
Nonelectric cookware	1,168,376	514,452	521,372	80,187	226,156	220,886	30,306	306,718
Tableware, nonelectric kitchenware	1,727,723	824,330	788,061	163,671	290,859	343,753	106,385	223,592
Small appliances	1,713,695	768,034	797,494	143,336	391,974	262,378	84,758	417,327
Small electric kitchen appliances	1,170,713	492,587	560,246	112,173	278,370	169,665	58,302	320,629
Portable heating and cooling equipment	542,982	275,698	237,247	31,162	113,605	92,713	26,456	96,698
Miscellaneous household equipment	**51,184,083**	**21,606,734**	**26,151,502**	**5,157,227**	**14,374,851**	**6,553,495**	**2,491,014**	**12,134,368**
Window coverings	2,317,463	1,179,696	1,067,612	438,086	514,607	114,906	54,382	305,700
Infants' equipment	1,335,537	417,694	831,794	362,241	277,467	190,893	66,071	47,161
Laundry and cleaning equipment	1,073,690	421,966	553,386	115,196	278,821	159,694	77,689	234,789
Outdoor equipment	1,732,983	713,749	881,816	52,212	690,507	127,771	77,549	467,881
Clocks	278,212	84,444	153,210	22,369	108,940	20,103	9,589	47,161
Lamps and lighting fixtures	1,076,028	426,239	592,546	110,634	297,178	184,702	49,203	308,415
Other household decorative items	9,977,074	4,616,748	4,699,781	903,048	2,554,228	1,235,500	656,156	1,908,846
Telephones and accessories	1,958,008	641,117	1,023,593	151,305	621,592	246,778	260,923	288,736
Lawn and garden equipment	4,706,817	2,399,101	2,210,357	485,627	1,115,735	508,915	70,200	1,036,870
Power tools	2,354,285	696,659	1,440,634	257,707	983,622	180,681	48,153	230,378
Office furniture for home use	1,198,768	635,337	498,219	85,683	334,344	78,400	49,343	121,127
Hand tools	604,352	214,879	347,581	117,559	158,294	71,806	26,106	135,037
Indoor plants and fresh flowers	3,139,242	1,592,866	1,353,167	209,058	684,939	459,302	128,782	836,011
Closet and storage items	701,376	258,608	385,598	79,527	226,608	76,952	19,037	227,324
Rental of furniture	105,206	16,336	76,033	18,851	48,602	8,765	64,741	63,447
Luggage	518,434	210,606	256,684	28,140	139,335	89,175	27,086	111,287
Computers and computer hardware, nonbusiness use	10,728,715	4,317,426	5,673,924	914,479	2,907,381	1,852,164	483,561	2,981,341
Computer software and accessories, nonbusiness use	1,350,733	517,971	758,905	125,639	393,780	239,622	70,410	456,006
Telephone answering devices	60,201	27,645	29,727	8,134	10,081	11,579	7,769	27,482
Calculators	91,179	12,566	76,033	3,957	47,398	24,605	7,489	37,322
Business equipment for home use	67,215	25,886	30,585	4,067	20,765	5,790	13,228	30,197
Other hardware	2,055,032	473,236	1,487,511	410,441	833,002	230,214	28,346	1,372,767
Smoke alarms	74,813	30,158	39,446	7,914	19,862	11,901	4,269	35,625
Other household appliances	592,078	296,809	240,391	32,646	162,056	45,592	13,158	94,323
Miscellaneous household equipment and parts	3,086,639	1,379,244	1,542,393	212,695	946,306	377,766	177,845	729,134

Note: Total spending figures for total consumer units can be found on Total Spending by Age and Total Spending by Region tables. Spending by type of consumer unit will not add to total because not all types of consumer units are shown. Numbers may not add to category total because of rounding and missing subcategories. (–) means sample is too small to make a reliable estimate.
Source: Calculations by New Strategist based on the 2003 Consumer Expenditure Survey

Table 8.16 Housing: Household Operations: Market shares by household type, 2003

(percentage of total annual spending on household services, supplies, furnishings, and equipment accounted for by types of consumer units, 2003)

	total married couples	married couples, no children	married couples with children				single parent, at least one child <18	single person
			total	oldest child under 6	oldest child 6 to 17	oldest child 18 or older		
Share of total consumer units	50.7%	21.8%	24.8%	4.8%	13.0%	7.0%	6.1%	29.4%
Share of total before-tax income	68.8	26.8	36.6	6.2	19.8	10.7	3.5	15.6
Share of total spending	65.8	25.6	35.0	6.0	18.9	10.1	4.5	17.0
Share of housing spending	62.8	23.3	34.5	6.8	18.7	8.9	5.3	19.2
HOUSEHOLD SERVICES	**69.5**	**18.4**	**46.1**	**15.9**	**23.7**	**6.5**	**6.2**	**14.3**
Personal services	**71.9**	**5.1**	**61.2**	**30.0**	**29.0**	**2.2**	**9.9**	**9.3**
Babysitting and child care in your own home	86.6	1.0	80.1	27.9	50.7	1.5	8.9	0.2
Babysitting and child care in someone else's home	67.6	0.9	59.6	31.3	25.0	3.2	13.9	0.9
Day care centers, nurseries, and preschools	78.6	1.0	72.1	37.4	32.1	2.6	11.9	1.5
Other household services	**67.8**	**27.8**	**35.4**	**5.9**	**20.0**	**9.5**	**3.6**	**17.8**
Housekeeping services	73.9	25.6	43.6	5.8	26.7	11.1	3.2	16.2
Gardening, lawn care service	64.0	32.4	27.3	5.5	14.9	6.8	2.5	24.6
Water softening service	67.6	25.2	38.2	8.3	20.5	9.4	2.2	15.4
Nonclothing laundry and dry cleaning, sent out	60.3	34.6	24.3	4.3	13.2	6.9	1.9	25.3
Nonclothing laundry and dry cleaning, coin-operated	39.5	11.1	21.4	5.7	11.7	4.0	10.3	28.4
Termite/pest control services	70.1	33.5	31.7	11.9	15.4	4.4	3.1	17.9
Home security system service fee	67.0	30.8	33.0	5.3	20.6	7.1	3.7	17.7
Other home services	64.7	27.3	29.9	5.5	12.6	11.8	3.0	21.7
Termite/pest control products	68.7	32.1	31.8	11.9	15.6	4.3	2.2	21.3
Moving, storage, and freight express	70.1	27.4	37.7	9.2	23.2	5.3	2.7	10.8
Appliance repair, including service center	72.2	29.4	36.1	4.2	17.3	14.5	2.3	12.6
Reupholstering and furniture repair	69.1	47.3	21.3	2.6	11.0	7.6	0.5	17.1
Repairs/rentals of lawn/garden equipment, hand/power tools, etc.	66.3	27.7	37.0	6.7	23.0	7.4	2.8	16.2
Appliance rental	46.6	17.9	24.9	2.4	17.0	5.5	25.1	8.8
Repair of computer systems for nonbusiness use	68.4	20.5	46.4	3.2	18.5	24.8	3.4	20.2
Computer information services	66.1	25.1	36.3	5.4	19.9	11.0	4.9	16.3
HOUSEKEEPING SUPPLIES	**67.0**	**27.2**	**34.4**	**5.8**	**17.9**	**10.7**	**4.0**	**15.8**
Laundry and cleaning supplies	**65.7**	**24.6**	**34.7**	**5.5**	**18.1**	**11.3**	**5.6**	**15.1**
Soaps and detergents	65.6	24.0	35.1	5.4	18.6	11.1	5.9	13.7
Other laundry cleaning products	65.7	25.3	34.1	5.5	17.3	11.5	5.2	16.9
Other household products	**69.3**	**27.8**	**36.2**	**6.4**	**19.3**	**10.6**	**3.7**	**13.7**
Cleansing and toilet tissue, paper towels, and napkins	64.2	24.5	34.1	5.0	18.5	10.7	5.5	15.2
Miscellaneous household products	68.9	24.0	39.1	7.5	20.7	10.9	3.5	13.0
Lawn and garden supplies	74.6	35.7	34.4	6.1	18.2	10.2	2.3	13.1
Postage and stationery	**63.6**	**28.5**	**30.5**	**5.1**	**15.2**	**10.4**	**3.0**	**20.6**
Stationery, stationery supplies, giftwrap	63.2	24.4	34.0	6.2	18.2	9.7	3.3	19.0
Postage	65.5	32.4	28.5	4.3	13.2	11.2	2.7	20.8
Delivery services	40.9	23.8	16.2	1.4	8.9	5.9	3.9	38.7
HOUSEHOLD FURNISHINGS AND EQUIPMENT	**69.6**	**29.4**	**35.1**	**7.3**	**19.0**	**8.8**	**3.9**	**15.1**
Household textiles	**70.0**	**32.3**	**32.5**	**5.3**	**16.3**	**10.9**	**3.6**	**13.5**
Bathroom linens	67.1	32.2	32.3	4.0	17.7	10.7	3.5	10.7
Bedroom linens	70.1	31.7	31.7	5.5	15.7	10.7	4.3	14.5
Kitchen and dining room linens	71.7	36.8	29.4	3.0	16.3	10.3	2.9	11.7
Curtains and draperies	74.9	32.6	40.2	6.8	18.9	14.5	2.8	11.2
Slipcovers and decorative pillows	51.6	26.4	20.7	7.6	7.8	5.3	0.8	20.8
Sewing materials for household items	74.2	34.4	32.8	4.7	17.4	10.8	2.1	14.7
Other linens	64.4	32.3	28.7	7.0	14.0	7.8	5.8	15.6
Furniture	**71.3**	**29.4**	**36.8**	**8.8**	**20.3**	**7.7**	**4.2**	**14.2**
Mattresses and springs	71.0	32.0	34.3	7.4	16.4	10.5	4.1	16.0
Other bedroom furniture	68.7	26.8	34.1	8.7	17.0	8.5	4.4	14.2
Sofas	70.7	27.6	38.6	8.4	23.2	7.1	5.4	13.1
Living room chairs	66.1	34.0	28.4	6.5	15.6	6.4	3.1	19.7
Living room tables	68.2	34.3	29.7	6.9	16.6	6.2	3.6	18.3
Kitchen and dining room furniture	77.3	24.6	48.1	8.7	32.3	7.1	2.4	13.1

	total married couples	married couples, no children	married couples with children				single parent, at least one child <18	single person
			total	oldest child under 6	oldest child 6 to 17	oldest child 18 or older		
Infants' furniture	78.2%	25.7%	48.3%	34.6%	10.1%	3.6%	5.3%	5.5%
Outdoor furniture	81.6	41.6	32.3	4.8	21.0	6.5	2.3	8.8
Wall units, cabinets, and other furniture	71.9	31.1	37.1	10.7	18.4	8.0	5.1	13.3
Floor coverings	**69.8**	**30.9**	**34.6**	**4.6**	**19.9**	**10.1**	**4.5**	**14.9**
Wall-to-wall carpeting	67.8	34.1	30.1	2.9	15.8	11.4	6.5	15.6
Floor coverings, nonpermanent	72.5	26.7	40.5	6.7	25.4	8.4	1.8	13.9
Major appliances	**70.0**	**27.9**	**35.7**	**8.4**	**19.4**	**7.9**	**5.0**	**13.7**
Dishwashers (built-in), garbage disposals, range hoods	70.9	31.8	34.0	6.9	18.0	9.1	6.0	15.5
Refrigerators and freezers	68.9	27.3	36.0	7.1	20.6	8.4	4.1	12.6
Washing machines	67.8	24.7	35.3	7.3	21.1	6.9	6.6	13.4
Clothes dryers	66.4	24.8	36.5	8.6	21.5	6.4	7.7	12.1
Cooking stoves, ovens	79.8	38.9	35.6	4.9	20.0	10.6	2.6	9.3
Microwave ovens	63.2	31.2	28.0	5.9	16.0	6.1	3.4	21.6
Window air conditioners	60.1	25.5	25.1	5.9	15.1	4.0	8.8	20.0
Electric floor-cleaning equipment	65.6	18.2	42.4	19.1	17.8	5.1	6.9	16.8
Sewing machines	80.6	28.3	30.8	2.5	16.8	11.5	0.0	14.4
Miscellaneous household appliances	87.8	67.2	19.9	–	1.5	19.6	1.4	8.7
Small appliances and misc. housewares	**67.4**	**31.5**	**30.6**	**5.3**	**13.7**	**11.9**	**3.4**	**16.0**
Housewares	67.3	32.1	30.6	5.2	13.2	12.5	3.4	16.0
Plastic dinnerware	59.8	17.3	37.6	8.3	20.9	8.4	5.8	18.9
China and other dinnerware	75.8	36.9	35.4	3.3	16.3	16.2	4.1	11.7
Flatware	64.0	27.0	28.1	6.3	11.9	9.9	3.7	19.9
Glassware	57.7	30.4	24.9	3.7	13.6	7.6	2.9	28.4
Silver serving pieces	64.2	34.1	26.1	3.8	11.1	11.4	3.3	19.0
Other serving pieces	71.4	32.5	33.7	7.5	15.0	11.1	3.7	10.8
Nonelectric cookware	66.4	29.2	29.5	4.6	12.8	12.5	1.7	17.4
Tableware, nonelectric kitchenware	72.8	34.8	33.2	6.9	12.3	14.5	4.5	9.4
Small appliances	66.0	29.6	30.7	5.5	15.1	10.1	3.3	16.1
Small electric kitchen appliances	64.8	27.3	31.0	6.2	15.4	9.4	3.2	17.7
Portable heating and cooling equipment	68.7	34.9	30.0	3.9	14.4	11.7	3.3	12.2
Miscellaneous household equipment	**68.5**	**28.9**	**35.0**	**6.9**	**19.2**	**8.8**	**3.3**	**16.2**
Window coverings	82.5	42.0	38.0	15.6	18.3	4.1	1.9	10.9
Infants' equipment	88.5	27.7	55.1	24.0	18.4	12.7	4.4	3.1
Laundry and cleaning equipment	66.3	26.1	34.2	7.1	17.2	9.9	4.8	14.5
Outdoor equipment	63.3	26.1	32.2	1.9	25.2	4.7	2.8	17.1
Clocks	60.0	18.2	33.0	4.8	23.5	4.3	2.1	10.2
Lamps and lighting fixtures	68.3	27.0	37.6	7.0	18.9	11.7	3.1	19.6
Other household decorative items	68.2	31.6	32.1	6.2	17.5	8.4	4.5	13.1
Telephones and accessories	63.4	20.8	33.1	4.9	20.1	8.0	8.4	9.3
Lawn and garden equipment	73.7	37.5	33.0	7.5	17.5	8.0	1.1	16.2
Power tools	83.7	24.8	51.2	9.2	35.0	6.4	1.7	8.2
Office furniture for home use	82.4	43.7	34.3	5.9	23.0	5.4	3.4	8.3
Hand tools	72.6	25.8	41.7	14.1	19.0	8.6	3.1	16.2
Indoor plants and fresh flowers	67.5	34.3	29.1	4.5	14.7	9.9	2.8	18.0
Closet and storage items	63.5	23.4	34.9	7.2	20.5	7.0	1.7	20.6
Rental of furniture	33.8	5.2	24.4	6.1	15.6	2.8	20.8	20.4
Luggage	72.7	29.5	36.0	3.9	19.5	12.5	3.8	15.6
Computers and computer hardware, nonbusiness use	68.0	27.4	36.0	5.8	18.4	11.7	3.1	18.9
Computer software and accessories, nonbusiness use	65.1	25.0	36.6	6.1	19.0	11.6	3.4	22.0
Telephone answering devices	56.1	25.8	27.7	7.6	9.4	10.8	7.2	25.6
Calculators	62.2	8.6	51.9	2.7	32.4	16.8	5.1	25.5
Business equipment for home use	54.0	20.8	24.5	3.3	16.7	4.6	10.6	24.2
Other hardware	46.5	10.7	33.6	9.3	18.8	5.2	0.6	31.0
Smoke alarms	57.4	23.1	30.3	6.1	15.2	9.1	3.3	27.3
Other household appliances	77.0	38.6	31.2	4.2	21.1	5.9	1.7	12.3
Miscellaneous household equipment and parts	69.4	31.0	34.7	4.8	21.3	8.5	4.0	16.4

Note: Market share for total consumer units is 100.0%. Market shares by type of consumer unit will not add to total because not all types of consumer units are shown. (–) means sample is too small to make a reliable estimate.
Source: Calculations by New Strategist based on the 2003 Consumer Expenditure Survey

Table 8.17 Housing: Household Operations: Average spending by race and Hispanic origin, 2003

(average annual spending of consumer units (CU) on household services, supplies, furnishings, and equipment, by race and Hispanic origin of consumer unit reference person, 2003)

	total consumer units	race			Hispanic origin	
		Asian	black	white and other	Hispanic	non-Hispanic
Number of consumer units (000)	115,356	3,573	13,743	98,041	11,727	103,629
Average number of persons per CU	2.5	2.8	2.6	2.5	3.3	2.4
Average before-tax income of CU	$51,128.00	$60,393.00	$34,485.00	$53,039.00	$37,150.00	$52,797.00
Average spending of CU, total	40,817.33	44,922.85	28,707.56	42,360.25	34,574.75	41,520.78
Housing, average spending	13,431.87	16,326.15	10,622.26	13,719.46	12,300.40	13,561.68
HOUSEHOLD SERVICES	707.15	783.28	452.58	740.06	454.37	735.77
Personal services	293.53	380.77	247.07	296.86	238.00	299.82
Babysitting and child care in your own home	36.05	41.33	7.89	39.81	38.64	35.76
Babysitting and child care in someone else's home	23.99	26.77	38.43	21.86	40.35	22.14
Day care centers, nurseries, and preschools	188.82	311.10	197.92	183.09	151.36	193.06
Other household services	413.61	402.51	205.50	443.19	216.36	435.95
Housekeeping services	93.13	51.75	18.13	105.15	35.31	99.67
Gardening, lawn care service	83.70	109.95	35.04	89.56	39.02	88.76
Water softening service	3.23	1.33	1.34	3.57	2.92	3.27
Nonclothing laundry and dry cleaning, sent out	1.00	0.14	0.68	1.08	0.19	1.10
Nonclothing laundry and dry cleaning, coin-operated	3.62	4.16	5.20	3.37	11.57	2.72
Termite/pest control services	11.30	12.49	3.89	12.30	3.55	12.18
Home security system service fee	15.54	15.94	24.70	14.25	9.04	16.28
Other home services	14.83	11.34	8.56	15.84	5.06	15.94
Termite/pest control products	1.52	1.99	0.41	1.66	0.37	1.65
Moving, storage, and freight express	30.46	32.63	12.46	32.91	10.94	32.67
Appliance repair, including service center	11.75	8.72	8.16	12.36	9.12	12.04
Reupholstering and furniture repair	5.20	0.27	0.79	6.00	3.71	5.37
Repairs/rentals of lawn/garden equipment, hand/power tools, etc.	6.08	1.37	1.62	6.88	2.07	6.54
Appliance rental	1.63	–	3.08	1.49	1.07	1.70
Repair of computer systems for nonbusiness use	4.20	9.24	3.54	4.11	1.03	4.56
Computer information services	123.92	141.18	76.90	129.88	80.20	128.87
HOUSEKEEPING SUPPLIES	528.84	470.73	357.06	554.93	475.67	535.52
Laundry and cleaning supplies	132.28	96.31	136.71	133.08	165.46	128.12
Soaps and detergents	74.15	66.10	83.33	73.20	102.32	70.62
Other laundry cleaning products	58.13	30.21	53.39	59.88	63.14	57.50
Other household products	263.37	227.96	167.65	278.03	199.46	271.40
Cleansing and toilet tissue, paper towels, and napkins	75.23	70.20	65.79	76.74	90.51	73.32
Miscellaneous household products	106.32	78.85	55.30	114.47	76.61	110.05
Lawn and garden supplies	81.82	78.91	46.56	86.82	32.35	88.03
Postage and stationery	133.19	146.45	52.69	143.82	110.75	136.00
Stationery, stationery supplies, giftwrap	59.55	60.84	22.06	64.70	52.22	60.47
Postage	68.94	81.61	29.80	73.87	57.20	70.41
Delivery services	4.70	4.00	0.83	5.26	1.33	5.12
HOUSEHOLD FURNISHINGS AND EQUIPMENT	1,497.05	1,634.46	784.98	1,591.21	1,208.42	1,530.81
Household textiles	113.48	67.39	61.45	122.49	88.88	116.51
Bathroom linens	20.30	13.72	14.02	21.43	13.97	21.09
Bedroom linens	53.45	31.08	30.18	57.55	47.90	54.14
Kitchen and dining room linens	7.37	3.62	4.81	7.87	3.88	7.81
Curtains and draperies	15.24	11.43	6.80	16.56	16.16	15.13
Slipcovers and decorative pillows	4.35	2.90	2.02	4.72	–	4.86
Sewing materials for household items	11.27	4.29	2.39	12.77	4.24	12.07
Other linens	1.51	0.36	1.24	1.60	2.47	1.41
Furniture	400.82	334.30	233.58	426.68	402.56	400.62
Mattresses and springs	44.89	51.24	20.01	48.14	49.81	44.33
Other bedroom furniture	79.44	68.88	52.49	83.60	100.63	77.04
Sofas	92.17	93.08	52.51	97.69	97.31	91.58
Living room chairs	38.76	21.35	16.12	42.57	21.61	40.70
Living room tables	17.51	10.07	14.15	18.25	13.41	17.97
Kitchen and dining room furniture	49.42	31.93	36.10	51.92	47.90	49.59

		race			Hispanic origin	
	total consumer units	Asian	black	white and other	Hispanic	non-Hispanic
Infants' furniture	$8.17	$7.16	$6.38	$8.45	$12.93	$7.63
Outdoor furniture	15.35	7.07	6.00	16.96	9.55	16.01
Wall units, cabinets, and other furniture	55.13	43.54	29.81	59.10	49.42	55.77
Floor coverings	**51.76**	**20.67**	**11.23**	**58.58**	**19.27**	**55.44**
Wall-to-wall carpeting	29.50	5.15	4.63	33.87	9.36	31.79
Floor coverings, nonpermanent	22.26	15.51	6.60	24.70	9.91	23.66
Major appliances	**195.70**	**282.90**	**118.25**	**203.32**	**200.86**	**194.65**
Dishwashers (built-in), garbage disposals, range hoods	13.50	18.83	4.33	14.59	9.27	13.99
Refrigerators and freezers	47.56	64.75	32.08	49.10	43.37	48.03
Washing machines	28.58	33.93	20.50	29.64	26.56	28.92
Clothes dryers	19.43	24.66	11.82	20.30	15.65	19.86
Cooking stoves, ovens	30.49	51.44	16.72	31.67	16.96	32.03
Microwave ovens	7.56	11.18	5.35	7.73	7.89	7.52
Window air conditioners	5.40	4.77	4.20	5.60	7.65	5.15
Electric floor-cleaning equipment	30.24	50.55	20.34	30.81	69.88	25.26
Sewing machines	8.95	13.50	0.86	9.92	1.95	9.74
Miscellaneous household appliances	2.24	–	1.66	2.41	0.61	2.45
Small appliances and misc. housewares	**87.76**	**127.61**	**42.66**	**92.49**	**82.14**	**88.45**
Housewares	65.25	101.07	31.91	68.48	61.57	65.72
Plastic dinnerware	1.56	2.04	0.85	1.64	2.25	1.48
China and other dinnerware	7.04	1.66	4.88	7.55	4.84	7.31
Flatware	3.99	5.33	2.13	4.28	3.71	4.03
Glassware	8.89	6.87	3.44	9.73	6.24	9.22
Silver serving pieces	6.51	7.45	2.68	7.00	6.44	6.52
Other serving pieces	1.44	1.89	0.49	1.56	1.36	1.45
Nonelectric cookware	15.26	46.59	8.30	15.00	20.02	14.67
Tableware, nonelectric kitchenware	20.56	31.24	9.14	21.72	16.70	21.04
Small appliances	22.51	26.54	10.75	24.01	20.57	22.73
Small electric kitchen appliances	15.66	20.35	8.27	16.52	13.64	15.89
Portable heating and cooling equipment	6.85	6.19	2.48	7.48	6.93	6.84
Miscellaneous household equipment	**647.53**	**801.59**	**317.82**	**687.65**	**414.73**	**675.15**
Window coverings	24.34	65.12	8.71	25.05	26.77	24.07
Infants' equipment	13.03	4.01	8.56	14.06	15.39	12.79
Laundry and cleaning equipment	14.03	11.11	8.68	14.89	17.41	13.61
Outdoor equipment	23.74	29.53	2.54	26.45	11.05	25.33
Clocks	4.02	2.89	0.49	4.55	2.89	4.16
Lamps and lighting fixtures	13.66	17.64	4.16	14.85	8.10	14.29
Other household decorative items	126.78	220.84	46.63	134.20	95.04	130.76
Telephones and accessories	26.78	64.29	11.70	27.40	17.49	27.94
Lawn and garden equipment	55.39	20.53	21.53	61.40	18.71	59.54
Power tools	24.38	11.57	28.86	24.26	10.31	26.14
Office furniture for home use	12.61	26.82	2.59	13.50	14.19	12.43
Hand tools	7.22	2.74	0.99	8.25	6.32	7.32
Indoor plants and fresh flowers	40.31	32.35	13.04	44.42	23.20	42.24
Closet and storage items	9.57	9.27	2.22	10.60	8.21	9.74
Rental of furniture	2.70	6.62	6.16	2.08	2.87	2.68
Luggage	6.18	13.61	3.77	6.25	5.51	6.25
Computers and computer hardware, nonbusiness use	136.77	159.95	59.40	146.77	74.34	143.83
Computer software and accessories, nonbusiness use	17.98	31.39	7.39	18.98	10.39	18.84
Telephone answering devices	0.93	1.04	0.59	0.97	0.88	0.93
Calculators	1.27	2.33	0.34	1.28	0.52	1.36
Business equipment for home use	1.08	0.41	0.54	1.17	0.94	1.10
Other hardware	38.35	17.43	58.62	36.36	5.99	42.42
Smoke alarms	1.13	1.20	1.68	1.04	0.67	1.17
Other household appliances	6.67	2.83	1.55	7.52	5.06	6.85
Miscellaneous household equipment and parts	38.57	46.07	16.40	41.35	32.46	39.34

Note: Other races include Native Americans and Pacific Islanders. Subcategories may not add to total because some are not shown. (–) means sample is too small to make a reliable estimate.
Source: Bureau of Labor Statistics, unpublished tables from the 2003 Consumer Expenditure Survey

Table 8.18 Housing: Household Operations: Indexed spending by race and Hispanic origin, 2003

(indexed average annual spending of consumer units (CU) on household services, supplies, furnishings, and equipment, by race and Hispanic origin of consumer unit reference person, 2003; index definition: an index of 100 is the average for all consumer units; an index of 132 means that spending by consumer units in that group is 32 percent above the average for all consumer units; an index of 68 indicates spending that is 32 percent below the average for all consumer units)

		race			Hispanic origin	
	total consumer units	Asian	black	white and other	Hispanic	non-Hispanic
Average spending of CU, total	$40,817	$44,923	$28,708	$42,360	$34,575	$41,521
Average spending of CU, index	100	110	70	104	85	102
Housing, spending index	100	122	79	102	92	101
HOUSEHOLD SERVICES	100	111	64	105	64	104
Personal services	100	130	84	101	81	102
Babysitting and child care in your own home	100	115	22	110	107	99
Babysitting and child care in someone else's home	100	112	160	91	168	92
Day care centers, nurseries, and preschools	100	165	105	97	80	102
Other household services	100	97	50	107	52	105
Housekeeping services	100	56	19	113	38	107
Gardening, lawn care service	100	131	42	107	47	106
Water softening service	100	41	41	111	90	101
Nonclothing laundry and dry cleaning, sent out	100	14	68	108	19	110
Nonclothing laundry and dry cleaning, coin-operated	100	115	144	93	320	75
Termite/pest control services	100	111	34	109	31	108
Home security system service fee	100	103	159	92	58	105
Other home services	100	76	58	107	34	107
Termite/pest control products	100	131	27	109	24	109
Moving, storage, and freight express	100	107	41	108	36	107
Appliance repair, including service center	100	74	69	105	78	102
Reupholstering and furniture repair	100	5	15	115	71	103
Repairs/rentals of lawn/garden equipment, hand/power tools, etc.	100	23	27	113	34	108
Appliance rental	100	–	189	91	66	104
Repair of computer systems for nonbusiness use	100	220	84	98	25	109
Computer information services	100	114	62	105	65	104
HOUSEKEEPING SUPPLIES	100	89	68	105	90	101
Laundry and cleaning supplies	100	73	103	101	125	97
Soaps and detergents	100	89	112	99	138	95
Other laundry cleaning products	100	52	92	103	109	99
Other household products	100	87	64	106	76	103
Cleansing and toilet tissue, paper towels, and napkins	100	93	87	102	120	97
Miscellaneous household products	100	74	52	108	72	104
Lawn and garden supplies	100	96	57	106	40	108
Postage and stationery	100	110	40	108	83	102
Stationery, stationery supplies, giftwrap	100	102	37	109	88	102
Postage	100	118	43	107	83	102
Delivery services	100	85	18	112	28	109
HOUSEHOLD FURNISHINGS AND EQUIPMENT	100	109	52	106	81	102
Household textiles	100	59	54	108	78	103
Bathroom linens	100	68	69	106	69	104
Bedroom linens	100	58	56	108	90	101
Kitchen and dining room linens	100	49	65	107	53	106
Curtains and draperies	100	75	45	109	106	99
Slipcovers and decorative pillows	100	67	46	109	–	112
Sewing materials for household items	100	38	21	113	38	107
Other linens	100	24	82	106	164	93
Furniture	100	83	58	106	100	100
Mattresses and springs	100	114	45	107	111	99
Other bedroom furniture	100	87	66	105	127	97
Sofas	100	101	57	106	106	99
Living room chairs	100	55	42	110	56	105
Living room tables	100	58	81	104	77	103
Kitchen and dining room furniture	100	65	73	105	97	100

	total consumer units	race			Hispanic origin	
		Asian	black	white and other	Hispanic	non-Hispanic
Infants' furniture	100	88	78	103	158	93
Outdoor furniture	100	46	39	110	62	104
Wall units, cabinets, and other furniture	100	79	54	107	90	101
Floor coverings	**100**	**40**	**22**	**113**	**37**	**107**
Wall-to-wall carpeting	100	17	16	115	32	108
Floor coverings, nonpermanent	100	70	30	111	45	106
Major appliances	**100**	**145**	**66**	**104**	**103**	**99**
Dishwashers (built-in), garbage disposals, range hoods	100	139	32	108	69	104
Refrigerators and freezers	100	136	67	103	91	101
Washing machines	100	118	71	103	93	101
Clothes dryers	100	127	61	104	81	102
Cooking stoves, ovens	100	169	55	104	56	105
Microwave ovens	100	148	71	102	104	99
Window air conditioners	100	88	78	104	142	95
Electric floor-cleaning equipment	100	167	67	102	231	84
Sewing machines	100	151	10	111	22	109
Miscellaneous household appliances	100	–	74	108	27	109
Small appliances and misc. housewares	**100**	**145**	**49**	**105**	**94**	**101**
Housewares	100	155	49	105	94	101
Plastic dinnerware	100	131	54	105	144	95
China and other dinnerware	100	24	69	107	69	104
Flatware	100	83	53	107	93	101
Glassware	100	77	39	109	70	104
Silver serving pieces	100	114	41	108	99	100
Other serving pieces	100	131	34	108	94	101
Nonelectric cookware	100	305	54	98	131	96
Tableware, nonelectric kitchenware	100	152	44	106	81	102
Small appliances	100	118	48	107	91	101
Small electric kitchen appliances	100	130	53	105	87	101
Portable heating and cooling equipment	100	90	36	109	101	100
Miscellaneous household equipment	**100**	**124**	**49**	**106**	**64**	**104**
Window coverings	100	268	36	103	110	99
Infants' equipment	100	31	65	107	118	98
Laundry and cleaning equipment	100	79	62	106	124	97
Outdoor equipment	100	124	11	111	47	107
Clocks	100	72	12	113	72	103
Lamps and lighting fixtures	100	129	30	109	59	105
Other household decorative items	100	174	37	106	75	103
Telephones and accessories	100	240	44	102	65	104
Lawn and garden equipment	100	37	39	111	34	107
Power tools	100	47	118	100	42	107
Office furniture for home use	100	213	21	107	113	99
Hand tools	100	38	14	114	88	101
Indoor plants and fresh flowers	100	80	32	110	58	105
Closet and storage items	100	97	23	111	86	102
Rental of furniture	100	245	228	77	106	99
Luggage	100	220	61	101	89	101
Computers and computer hardware, nonbusiness use	100	117	43	107	54	105
Computer software and accessories, nonbusiness use	100	175	41	106	58	105
Telephone answering devices	100	112	53	104	95	100
Calculators	100	183	74	101	41	107
Business equipment for home use	100	38	59	108	87	102
Other hardware	100	45	153	95	16	111
Smoke alarms	100	106	149	92	59	104
Other household appliances	100	42	23	113	76	103
Miscellaneous household equipment and parts	100	119	43	107	84	102

Note: Other races include Native Americans and Pacific Islanders. (–) means sample is too small to make a reliable estimate.
Source: Calculations by New Strategist based on the 2003 Consumer Expenditure Survey

Table 8.19 Housing: Household Operations: Total spending by race and Hispanic origin, 2003

(total annual spending on household services, supplies, furnishings, and equipment, by consumer unit race and Hispanic origin groups, 2003; numbers in thousands)

	total consumer units	race			Hispanic origin	
		Asian	black	white and other	Hispanic	non-Hispanic
Number of consumer units	115,356	3,573	13,743	98,041	11,727	103,629
Total spending of all consumer units	$4,708,523,919	$160,509,343	$394,527,997	$4,153,041,270	$405,458,093	$4,302,756,911
Housing, total spending	1,549,446,796	58,333,334	145,981,719	1,345,069,578	144,246,791	1,405,383,337
HOUSEHOLD SERVICES	**81,573,995**	**2,798,659**	**6,219,807**	**72,556,222**	**5,328,397**	**76,247,109**
Personal services	**33,860,447**	**1,360,491**	**3,395,483**	**29,104,451**	**2,791,026**	**31,070,047**
Babysitting and child care in your own home	4,158,584	147,672	108,432	3,903,012	453,131	3,705,773
Babysitting and child care in someone's home	2,767,390	95,649	528,143	2,143,176	473,184	2,294,346
Day care centers, nurseries, and preschools	21,781,520	1,111,560	2,720,015	17,950,327	1,774,999	20,006,615
Other household services	**47,712,395**	**1,438,168**	**2,824,187**	**43,450,791**	**2,537,254**	**45,177,063**
Housekeeping services	10,743,104	184,903	249,161	10,309,011	414,080	10,328,702
Gardening, lawn care service	9,655,297	392,851	481,555	8,780,552	457,588	9,198,110
Water softening service	372,600	4,752	18,416	350,006	34,243	338,867
Nonclothing laundry and dry cleaning, sent out	115,356	500	9,345	105,884	2,228	113,992
Nonclothing laundry and dry cleaning, coin-operated	417,589	14,864	71,464	330,398	135,681	281,871
Termite/pest control services	1,303,523	44,627	53,460	1,205,904	41,631	1,262,201
Home security system service fee	1,792,632	56,954	339,452	1,397,084	106,012	1,687,080
Other home services	1,710,729	40,518	117,640	1,552,969	59,339	1,651,846
Termite/pest control products	175,341	7,110	5,635	162,748	4,339	170,988
Moving, storage, and freight express	3,513,744	116,587	171,238	3,226,529	128,293	3,385,559
Appliance repair, including service center	1,355,433	31,157	112,143	1,211,787	106,950	1,247,693
Reupholstering and furniture repair	599,851	965	10,857	588,246	43,507	556,488
Repairs/rentals of lawn/garden equipment, hand/power tools, etc.	701,364	4,895	22,264	674,522	24,275	677,734
Appliance rental	188,030	–	42,328	145,702	12,548	176,169
Repair of computer systems for nonbusiness use	484,495	33,015	48,650	402,949	12,079	472,548
Computer information services	14,294,916	504,436	1,056,837	12,733,565	940,505	13,354,669
HOUSEKEEPING SUPPLIES	**61,004,867**	**1,681,918**	**4,907,076**	**54,405,892**	**5,578,182**	**55,495,402**
Laundry and cleaning supplies	**15,259,292**	**344,116**	**1,878,806**	**13,047,296**	**1,940,349**	**13,276,947**
Soaps and detergents	8,553,647	236,175	1,145,204	7,176,601	1,199,907	7,318,280
Other laundry cleaning products	6,705,644	107,940	733,739	5,870,695	740,443	5,958,668
Other household products	**30,381,310**	**814,501**	**2,304,014**	**27,258,339**	**2,339,067**	**28,124,911**
Cleansing and toilet tissue, paper towels, and napkins	8,678,232	250,825	904,152	7,523,666	1,061,411	7,598,078
Miscellaneous household products	12,264,650	281,731	759,988	11,222,753	898,405	11,404,371
Lawn and garden supplies	9,438,428	281,945	639,874	8,511,920	379,368	9,122,461
Postage and stationery	**15,364,266**	**523,266**	**724,119**	**14,100,257**	**1,298,765**	**14,093,544**
Stationery, stationery supplies, giftwrap	6,869,450	217,381	303,171	6,343,253	612,384	6,266,446
Postage	7,952,643	291,593	409,541	7,242,289	670,784	7,296,518
Delivery services	542,173	14,292	11,407	515,696	15,597	530,580
HOUSEHOLD FURNISHINGS AND EQUIPMENT	**172,693,700**	**5,839,926**	**10,787,980**	**156,003,820**	**14,171,141**	**158,636,309**
Household textiles	**13,090,599**	**240,784**	**844,507**	**12,009,042**	**1,042,296**	**12,073,815**
Bathroom linens	2,341,727	49,022	192,677	2,101,019	163,826	2,185,536
Bedroom linens	6,165,778	111,049	414,764	5,642,260	561,723	5,610,474
Kitchen and dining room linens	850,174	12,934	66,104	771,583	45,501	809,342
Curtains and draperies	1,758,025	40,839	93,452	1,623,559	189,508	1,567,907
Slipcovers and decorative pillows	501,799	10,362	27,761	462,754	–	503,637
Sewing materials for household items	1,300,062	15,328	32,846	1,251,984	49,722	1,250,802
Other linens	174,188	1,286	17,041	156,866	28,966	146,117
Furniture	**46,236,992**	**1,194,454**	**3,210,090**	**41,832,134**	**4,720,821**	**41,515,850**
Mattresses and springs	5,178,331	183,081	274,997	4,719,694	584,122	4,593,874
Other bedroom furniture	9,163,881	246,108	721,370	8,196,228	1,180,088	7,983,578
Sofas	10,632,363	332,575	721,645	9,577,625	1,141,154	9,490,344
Living room chairs	4,471,199	76,284	221,537	4,173,605	253,420	4,217,700
Living room tables	2,019,884	35,980	194,463	1,789,248	157,259	1,862,213
Kitchen and dining room furniture	5,700,894	114,086	496,122	5,090,289	561,723	5,138,962

		race			Hispanic origin	
	total consumer units	Asian	black	white and other	Hispanic	non-Hispanic
Infants' furniture	$942,459	$25,583	$87,680	$828,446	$151,630	$790,689
Outdoor furniture	1,770,715	25,261	82,458	1,662,775	111,993	1,659,100
Wall units, cabinets, and other furniture	6,359,576	155,568	409,679	5,794,223	579,548	5,779,389
Floor coverings	**5,970,827**	**73,854**	**154,334**	**5,743,242**	**225,979**	**5,745,192**
Wall-to-wall carpeting	3,403,002	18,401	63,630	3,320,649	109,765	3,294,366
Floor coverings, nonpermanent	2,567,825	55,417	90,704	2,421,613	116,215	2,451,862
Major appliances	**22,575,169**	**1,010,802**	**1,625,110**	**19,933,696**	**2,355,485**	**20,171,385**
Dishwashers (built-in), garbage disposals, range hoods	1,557,306	67,280	59,507	1,430,418	108,709	1,449,770
Refrigerators and freezers	5,486,331	231,352	440,875	4,813,813	508,600	4,977,301
Washing machines	3,308,410	121,232	281,732	2,905,935	311,469	2,996,951
Clothes dryers	2,241,367	88,110	162,442	1,990,232	183,528	2,058,072
Cooking stoves, ovens	3,517,204	183,795	229,783	3,104,958	198,890	3,319,237
Microwave ovens	872,091	39,046	73,525	757,857	92,526	779,290
Window air conditioners	622,922	17,043	57,721	549,030	89,712	533,689
Electric floor-cleaning equipment	3,488,365	180,515	279,533	3,020,643	819,483	2,617,669
Sewing machines	1,032,436	48,236	11,819	972,567	22,868	1,009,346
Miscellaneous household appliances	258,397	–	22,313	235,584	7,153	253,891
Small appliances and misc. housewares	**10,123,643**	**455,951**	**586,276**	**9,067,812**	**963,256**	**9,165,985**
Housewares	7,526,979	361,023	438,539	6,713,848	722,031	6,810,498
Plastic dinnerware	179,955	7,289	11,682	160,787	26,386	153,371
China and other dinnerware	812,106	5,831	67,066	740,210	56,759	757,528
Flatware	460,270	11,598	29,273	419,615	43,507	417,625
Glassware	1,025,515	24,247	47,276	953,939	73,176	955,459
Silver serving pieces	750,968	26,619	36,831	686,287	75,522	675,661
Other serving pieces	166,113	6,553	6,734	152,944	15,949	150,262
Nonelectric cookware	1,760,333	166,466	114,067	1,470,615	234,775	1,520,237
Tableware, nonelectric kitchenware	2,371,719	111,021	125,611	2,129,451	195,841	2,180,354
Small appliances	2,596,664	94,827	147,737	2,353,964	241,224	2,355,487
Small electric kitchen appliances	1,806,475	72,711	113,655	1,619,637	159,956	1,646,665
Portable heating and cooling equipment	790,189	22,117	34,083	733,347	81,268	708,822
Miscellaneous household equipment	**74,696,471**	**2,864,031**	**4,367,800**	**67,417,894**	**4,863,539**	**69,965,119**
Window coverings	2,807,765	232,674	119,702	2,455,927	313,932	2,494,350
Infants' equipment	1,508,856	14,328	117,640	1,378,456	180,479	1,325,415
Laundry and cleaning equipment	1,618,445	39,696	119,289	1,459,830	204,167	1,410,391
Outdoor equipment	2,738,551	105,511	34,907	2,593,184	129,583	2,624,923
Clocks	463,731	10,326	6,734	446,087	33,891	431,097
Lamps and lighting fixtures	1,575,763	63,028	57,171	1,455,909	94,989	1,480,858
Other household decorative items	14,624,834	789,051	640,836	13,157,102	1,114,534	13,550,528
Telephones and accessories	3,089,234	229,708	160,793	2,686,323	205,105	2,895,394
Lawn and garden equipment	6,389,569	73,354	295,837	6,019,717	219,412	6,170,071
Power tools	2,812,379	41,340	396,623	2,378,475	120,905	2,708,862
Office furniture for home use	1,454,639	95,828	35,594	1,323,554	166,406	1,288,108
Hand tools	832,870	9,740	13,606	808,838	74,115	758,564
Indoor plants and fresh flowers	4,650,000	115,557	179,209	4,354,981	272,066	4,377,289
Closet and storage items	1,103,957	33,122	30,509	1,039,235	96,279	1,009,346
Rental of furniture	311,461	23,653	84,657	203,925	33,656	277,726
Luggage	712,900	48,629	51,811	612,756	64,616	647,681
Computers and computer hardware, nonbusiness use	15,777,240	571,501	816,334	14,389,478	871,785	14,904,959
Computer software and accessories, nonbusiness use	2,074,101	112,156	101,561	1,860,818	121,844	1,952,370
Telephone answering devices	107,281	3,716	8,108	95,100	10,320	96,375
Calculators	146,502	8,325	12,918	125,492	6,098	140,935
Business equipment for home use	124,584	1,465	8,796	114,708	11,023	113,992
Other hardware	4,423,903	62,277	805,615	3,564,771	70,245	4,395,942
Smoke alarms	130,352	4,288	23,088	101,963	7,857	121,246
Other household appliances	769,425	10,112	21,302	737,268	59,339	709,859
Miscellaneous household equipment and parts	4,449,281	164,608	225,385	4,053,995	380,658	4,076,765

Note: Other races include Native Americans and Pacific Islanders. Numbers may not add to total because of rounding and missing subcategories. (–) means sample is too small to make a reliable estimate.
Source: Calculations by New Strategist based on the 2003 Consumer Expenditure Survey

Table 8.20 Housing: Household Operations: Market shares by race and Hispanic origin, 2003

(percentage of total annual spending on household services, supplies, furnishings, and equipment accounted for by consumer unit race and Hispanic origin groups, 2003)

	total consumer units	race			Hispanic origin	
		Asian	black	white and other	Hispanic	non-Hispanic
Share of total consumer units	100.0%	3.1%	11.9%	85.0%	10.2%	89.8%
Share of total before-tax income	100.0	3.7	8.0	88.2	7.4	92.8
Share of total spending	100.0	3.4	8.4	88.2	8.6	91.4
Share of housing spending	100.0	3.8	9.4	86.8	9.3	90.7
HOUSEHOLD SERVICES	100.0	3.4	7.6	88.9	6.5	93.5
Personal services	100.0	4.0	10.0	86.0	8.2	91.8
Babysitting and child care in your own home	100.0	3.6	2.6	93.9	10.9	89.1
Babysitting and child care in someone else's home	100.0	3.5	19.1	77.4	17.1	82.9
Day care centers, nurseries, and preschools	100.0	5.1	12.5	82.4	8.1	91.9
Other household services	100.0	3.0	5.9	91.1	5.3	94.7
Housekeeping services	100.0	1.7	2.3	96.0	3.9	96.1
Gardening, lawn care service	100.0	4.1	5.0	90.9	4.7	95.3
Water softening service	100.0	1.3	4.9	93.9	9.2	90.9
Nonclothing laundry and dry cleaning, sent out	100.0	0.4	8.1	91.8	1.9	98.8
Nonclothing laundry and dry cleaning, coin-operated	100.0	3.6	17.1	79.1	32.5	67.5
Termite/pest control services	100.0	3.4	4.1	92.5	3.2	96.8
Home security system service fee	100.0	3.2	18.9	77.9	5.9	94.1
Other home services	100.0	2.4	6.9	90.8	3.5	96.6
Termite/pest control products	100.0	4.1	3.2	92.8	2.5	97.5
Moving, storage, and freight express	100.0	3.3	4.9	91.8	3.7	96.4
Appliance repair, including service center	100.0	2.3	8.3	89.4	7.9	92.1
Reupholstering and furniture repair	100.0	0.2	1.8	98.1	7.3	92.8
Repairs/rentals of lawn/garden equipment, hand/power tools, etc.	100.0	0.7	3.2	96.2	3.5	96.6
Appliance rental	100.0	–	22.5	77.5	6.7	93.7
Repair of computer systems for nonbusiness use	100.0	6.8	10.0	83.2	2.5	97.5
Computer information services	100.0	3.5	7.4	89.1	6.6	93.4
HOUSEKEEPING SUPPLIES	100.0	2.8	8.0	89.2	9.1	91.0
Laundry and cleaning supplies	100.0	2.3	12.3	85.5	12.7	87.0
Soaps and detergents	100.0	2.8	13.4	83.9	14.0	85.6
Other laundry cleaning products	100.0	1.6	10.9	87.5	11.0	88.9
Other household products	100.0	2.7	7.6	89.7	7.7	92.6
Cleansing and toilet tissue, paper towels, and napkins	100.0	2.9	10.4	86.7	12.2	87.6
Miscellaneous household products	100.0	2.3	6.2	91.5	7.3	93.0
Lawn and garden supplies	100.0	3.0	6.8	90.2	4.0	96.7
Postage and stationery	100.0	3.4	4.7	91.8	8.5	91.7
Stationery, stationery supplies, giftwrap	100.0	3.2	4.4	92.3	8.9	91.2
Postage	100.0	3.7	5.1	91.1	8.4	91.7
Delivery services	100.0	2.6	2.1	95.1	2.9	97.9
HOUSEHOLD FURNISHINGS AND EQUIPMENT	100.0	3.4	6.2	90.3	8.2	91.9
Household textiles	100.0	1.8	6.5	91.7	8.0	92.2
Bathroom linens	100.0	2.1	8.2	89.7	7.0	93.3
Bedroom linens	100.0	1.8	6.7	91.5	9.1	91.0
Kitchen and dining room linens	100.0	1.5	7.8	90.8	5.4	95.2
Curtains and draperies	100.0	2.3	5.3	92.4	10.8	89.2
Slipcovers and decorative pillows	100.0	2.1	5.5	92.2	–	100.0
Sewing materials for household items	100.0	1.2	2.5	96.3	3.8	96.2
Other linens	100.0	0.7	9.8	90.1	16.6	83.9
Furniture	100.0	2.6	6.9	90.5	10.2	89.8
Mattresses and springs	100.0	3.5	5.3	91.1	11.3	88.7
Other bedroom furniture	100.0	2.7	7.9	89.4	12.9	87.1
Sofas	100.0	3.1	6.8	90.1	10.7	89.3
Living room chairs	100.0	1.7	5.0	93.3	5.7	94.3
Living room tables	100.0	1.8	9.6	88.6	7.8	92.2
Kitchen and dining room furniture	100.0	2.0	8.7	89.3	9.9	90.1

	total consumer units	race			Hispanic origin	
		Asian	black	white and other	Hispanic	non-Hispanic
Infants' furniture	100.0%	2.7%	9.3%	87.9%	16.1%	83.9%
Outdoor furniture	100.0	1.4	4.7	93.9	6.3	93.7
Wall units, cabinets, and other furniture	100.0	2.4	6.4	91.1	9.1	90.9
Floor coverings	**100.0**	**1.2**	**2.6**	**96.2**	**3.8**	**96.2**
Wall-to-wall carpeting	100.0	0.5	1.9	97.6	3.2	96.8
Floor coverings, nonpermanent	100.0	2.2	3.5	94.3	4.5	95.5
Major appliances	**100.0**	**4.5**	**7.2**	**88.3**	**10.4**	**89.4**
Dishwashers (built-in), garbage disposals, range hoods	100.0	4.3	3.8	91.9	7.0	93.1
Refrigerators and freezers	100.0	4.2	8.0	87.7	9.3	90.7
Washing machines	100.0	3.7	8.5	87.8	9.4	90.6
Clothes dryers	100.0	3.9	7.2	88.8	8.2	91.8
Cooking stoves, ovens	100.0	5.2	6.5	88.3	5.7	94.4
Microwave ovens	100.0	4.6	8.4	86.9	10.6	89.4
Window air conditioners	100.0	2.7	9.3	88.1	14.4	85.7
Electric floor-cleaning equipment	100.0	5.2	8.0	86.6	23.5	75.0
Sewing machines	100.0	4.7	1.1	94.2	2.2	97.8
Miscellaneous household appliances	100.0	–	8.8	91.2	2.8	98.3
Small appliances and misc. housewares	**100.0**	**4.5**	**5.8**	**89.6**	**9.5**	**90.5**
Housewares	100.0	4.8	5.8	89.2	9.6	90.5
Plastic dinnerware	100.0	4.1	6.5	89.3	14.7	85.2
China and other dinnerware	100.0	0.7	8.3	91.1	7.0	93.3
Flatware	100.0	2.6	6.4	91.2	9.5	90.7
Glassware	100.0	2.4	4.6	93.0	7.1	93.2
Silver serving pieces	100.0	3.5	4.9	91.4	10.1	90.0
Other serving pieces	100.0	4.1	4.1	92.1	9.6	90.5
Nonelectric cookware	100.0	9.5	5.5	83.5	13.3	86.4
Tableware, nonelectric kitchenware	100.0	4.7	5.3	89.8	8.3	91.9
Small appliances	100.0	3.7	5.7	90.7	9.3	90.7
Small electric kitchen appliances	100.0	4.0	6.3	89.7	8.9	91.2
Portable heating and cooling equipment	100.0	2.8	4.3	92.8	10.3	89.7
Miscellaneous household equipment	**100.0**	**3.8**	**5.8**	**90.3**	**6.5**	**93.7**
Window coverings	100.0	8.3	4.3	87.5	11.2	88.8
Infants' equipment	100.0	0.9	7.8	91.4	12.0	87.8
Laundry and cleaning equipment	100.0	2.5	7.4	90.2	12.6	87.1
Outdoor equipment	100.0	3.9	1.3	94.7	4.7	95.9
Clocks	100.0	2.2	1.5	96.2	7.3	93.0
Lamps and lighting fixtures	100.0	4.0	3.6	92.4	6.0	94.0
Other household decorative items	100.0	5.4	4.4	90.0	7.6	92.7
Telephones and accessories	100.0	7.4	5.2	87.0	6.6	93.7
Lawn and garden equipment	100.0	1.1	4.6	94.2	3.4	96.6
Power tools	100.0	1.5	14.1	84.6	4.3	96.3
Office furniture for home use	100.0	6.5	2.4	91.0	11.4	88.6
Hand tools	100.0	1.2	1.6	97.1	8.9	91.1
Indoor plants and fresh flowers	100.0	2.5	3.9	93.7	5.9	94.1
Closet and storage items	100.0	3.0	2.3	94.1	8.7	91.4
Rental of furniture	100.0	7.6	27.2	65.5	10.8	89.2
Luggage	100.0	6.8	7.3	86.0	9.1	90.9
Computers and computer hardware, nonbusiness use	100.0	3.6	5.2	91.2	5.5	94.5
Computer software and accessories, nonbusiness use	100.0	5.4	4.9	89.7	5.9	94.1
Telephone answering devices	100.0	3.5	7.6	88.6	9.6	89.8
Calculators	100.0	5.7	8.8	85.7	4.2	96.2
Business equipment for home use	100.0	1.2	7.1	92.1	8.8	91.5
Other hardware	100.0	1.4	18.2	80.6	1.6	99.4
Smoke alarms	100.0	3.3	17.7	78.2	6.0	93.0
Other household appliances	100.0	1.3	2.8	95.8	7.7	92.3
Miscellaneous household equipment and parts	100.0	3.7	5.1	91.1	8.6	91.6

Note: Other races include Native Americans and Pacific Islanders. Numbers may not add to total because of rounding. (–) means sample is too small to make a reliable estimate.
Source: Calculations by New Strategist based on the 2003 Consumer Expenditure Survey

Table 8.21 Housing: Household Operations: Average spending by region, 2003

(average annual spending of consumer units (CU) on household services, supplies, furnishings, and equipment, by region in which consumer unit lives, 2003)

	total consumer units	Northeast	Midwest	South	West
Number of consumer units (000)	115,356	22,182	26,438	41,325	25,412
Average number of persons per CU	2.5	2.4	2.5	2.5	2.6
Average before-tax income of CU	$48,596.00	$54,219.00	$49,591.00	$44,461.00	$49,667.00
Average spending of CU, total	40,817.33	42,162.29	40,280.39	37,624.55	45,380.67
Housing, average spending	13,431.87	14,811.03	12,634.36	12,006.35	15,371.39
HOUSEHOLD SERVICES	**707.15**	**813.23**	**614.24**	**666.13**	**777.92**
Personal services	**293.53**	**373.49**	**274.16**	**264.53**	**291.05**
Babysitting and child care in your own home	36.05	66.30	38.05	21.88	30.62
Babysitting and child care in someone else's home	23.99	25.54	34.60	12.89	29.65
Day care centers, nurseries, and preschools	188.82	205.50	193.87	177.73	187.03
Other household services	**413.61**	**439.74**	**340.08**	**401.60**	**486.87**
Housekeeping services	93.13	111.77	71.88	84.86	112.41
Gardening, lawn care service	83.70	90.75	58.99	85.70	100.00
Water softening service	3.23	2.75	6.19	1.82	2.89
Nonclothing laundry and dry cleaning, sent out	1.00	1.89	0.80	0.62	1.07
Nonclothing laundry and dry cleaning, coin-operated	3.62	5.78	2.70	2.60	4.32
Termite/pest control services	11.30	2.84	4.07	17.77	15.69
Home security system service fee	15.54	14.39	12.64	19.91	12.47
Other home services	14.83	16.10	12.62	10.55	22.99
Termite/pest control products	1.52	0.44	0.77	2.10	2.30
Moving, storage, and freight express	30.46	25.77	21.24	30.47	44.14
Appliance repair, including service center	11.75	12.74	12.44	10.33	12.46
Reupholstering and furniture repair	5.20	5.46	5.90	4.61	5.20
Repairs/rentals of lawn/garden equipment, hand/power tools, etc.	6.08	7.35	5.05	7.85	3.16
Appliance rental	1.63	1.54	2.44	1.16	1.67
Repair of computer systems for nonbusiness use	4.20	5.00	2.93	4.79	3.87
Computer information services	123.92	131.33	117.28	113.52	141.27
HOUSEKEEPING SUPPLIES	**528.84**	**523.13**	**575.23**	**495.68**	**537.04**
Laundry and cleaning supplies	**132.28**	**125.07**	**144.81**	**131.72**	**126.06**
Soaps and detergents	74.15	71.86	77.95	74.40	71.70
Other laundry cleaning products	58.13	53.21	66.86	57.32	54.36
Other household products	**263.37**	**257.06**	**283.66**	**258.01**	**255.69**
Cleansing and toilet tissue, paper towels, and napkins	75.23	75.54	74.44	73.62	78.39
Miscellaneous household products	106.32	102.29	122.80	100.02	102.23
Lawn and garden supplies	81.82	79.23	86.42	84.37	75.07
Postage and stationery	**133.19**	**141.00**	**146.76**	**105.95**	**155.30**
Stationery, stationery supplies, giftwrap	59.55	57.12	68.04	48.85	69.67
Postage	68.94	79.67	77.22	53.68	75.03
Delivery services	4.70	4.21	1.50	3.42	10.59
HOUSEHOLD FURNISHINGS AND EQUIPMENT	**1,497.05**	**1,451.63**	**1,504.35**	**1,293.56**	**1,857.98**
Household textiles	**113.48**	**126.32**	**105.45**	**90.96**	**147.12**
Bathroom linens	20.30	22.83	21.30	15.81	24.18
Bedroom linens	53.45	67.18	40.47	42.84	72.29
Kitchen and dining room linens	7.37	8.26	7.33	5.40	9.78
Curtains and draperies	15.24	17.34	16.32	13.61	14.91
Slipcovers and decorative pillows	4.35	2.49	3.58	3.46	8.20
Sewing materials for household items	11.27	7.24	14.44	8.51	15.98
Other linens	1.51	0.98	2.00	1.33	1.78
Furniture	**400.82**	**390.69**	**410.54**	**357.19**	**470.50**
Mattresses and springs	44.89	35.57	45.89	42.73	55.49
Other bedroom furniture	79.44	90.42	75.67	63.56	99.58
Sofas	92.17	78.69	102.64	78.86	114.66
Living room chairs	38.76	29.25	37.56	39.11	47.75
Living room tables	17.51	14.15	17.40	17.01	21.35
Kitchen and dining room furniture	49.42	74.33	39.06	45.66	44.55

	total consumer units	Northeast	Midwest	South	West
Infants' furniture	$8.17	$5.28	$10.61	$7.28	$9.59
Outdoor furniture	15.35	14.26	19.65	14.16	13.76
Wall units, cabinets, and other furniture	55.13	48.74	62.05	48.82	63.76
Floor coverings	**51.76**	**65.88**	**43.74**	**37.75**	**70.58**
Wall-to-wall carpeting	29.50	32.34	28.76	18.33	45.97
Floor coverings, nonpermanent	22.26	33.54	14.98	19.42	24.62
Major appliances	**195.70**	**176.47**	**195.23**	**178.93**	**240.48**
Dishwashers (built-in), garbage disposals, range hoods	13.50	19.82	12.78	7.24	18.91
Refrigerators and freezers	47.56	43.40	50.00	46.80	49.86
Washing machines	28.68	28.07	24.12	25.84	38.59
Clothes dryers	19.43	15.28	18.57	17.49	27.10
Cooking stoves, ovens	30.49	27.59	33.47	23.45	41.39
Microwave ovens	7.56	6.74	7.90	6.30	9.95
Window air conditioners	5.40	9.56	4.07	2.70	7.59
Electric floor-cleaning equipment	30.24	17.01	30.35	37.82	29.57
Sewing machines	8.95	1.85	10.17	9.01	13.77
Miscellaneous household appliances	2.24	4.35	2.07	1.35	2.02
Small appliances and misc. housewares	**87.76**	**75.46**	**86.79**	**86.92**	**101.12**
Housewares	65.25	50.07	62.41	68.36	76.67
Plastic dinnerware	1.56	1.51	1.19	1.28	2.45
China and other dinnerware	7.04	3.41	8.79	4.98	11.61
Flatware	3.99	4.59	4.01	1.96	6.77
Glassware	8.89	7.24	7.11	12.42	6.62
Silver serving pieces	6.51	5.78	5.08	7.72	6.76
Other serving pieces	1.44	1.16	0.98	1.38	2.24
Nonelectric cookware	15.26	10.31	12.70	17.79	18.30
Tableware, nonelectric kitchenware	20.56	16.06	22.55	20.83	21.92
Small appliances	22.51	25.39	24.38	18.56	24.45
Small electric kitchen appliances	15.66	15.86	16.58	12.37	19.87
Portable heating and cooling equipment	6.85	9.53	7.80	6.19	4.58
Miscellaneous household equipment	**647.53**	**616.82**	**662.61**	**541.81**	**828.18**
Window coverings	24.34	13.55	19.60	17.68	49.53
Infants' equipment	13.08	12.36	6.58	13.45	20.10
Laundry and cleaning equipment	14.03	14.01	14.36	12.18	16.67
Outdoor equipment	23.74	16.15	28.37	20.85	30.02
Clocks	4.02	5.13	3.20	3.42	4.87
Lamps and lighting fixtures	13.66	5.39	14.02	11.16	15.86
Other household decorative items	126.78	118.14	150.96	100.86	149.79
Telephones and accessories	26.78	22.51	19.40	23.28	44.01
Lawn and garden equipment	55.39	90.92	49.62	56.91	27.90
Power tools	24.38	18.59	28.90	19.65	32.13
Office furniture for home use	12.61	10.50	8.82	15.69	13.38
Hand tools	7.22	5.10	10.67	5.87	7.66
Indoor plants and fresh flowers	40.31	47.24	42.73	32.12	45.04
Closet and storage items	9.57	5.09	15.29	6.85	10.81
Rental of furniture	2.70	3.29	2.11	3.11	2.14
Luggage	6.18	7.02	7.02	4.58	7.16
Computers and computer hardware, nonbusiness use	136.77	114.42	127.43	104.52	194.87
Computer software and accessories, nonbusiness use	17.98	15.96	13.76	14.51	23.54
Telephone answering devices	0.93	0.80	1.01	0.77	1.21
Calculators	1.27	1.61	1.48	1.05	1.12
Business equipment for home use	1.08	0.46	1.51	0.79	1.66
Other hardware	38.35	15.62	53.57	29.82	55.53
Smoke alarms	1.13	1.96	1.34	0.54	1.12
Other household appliances	6.67	7.63	6.37	6.61	6.24
Miscellaneous household equipment and parts	38.57	25.34	28.49	35.53	65.83

Note: Subcategories may not add to total because some are not shown.
Source: Bureau of Labor Statistics, unpublished tables from the 2003 Consumer Expenditure Survey

Table 8.22 Housing: Household Operations: Indexed spending by region, 2003

(indexed average annual spending of consumer units (CU) on household services, supplies, furnishings, and equipment, by region in which consumer unit lives, 2003; index definition: an index of 100 is the average for all consumer units; an index of 132 means that spending by consumer units in that group is 32 percent above the average for all consumer units; an index of 68 indicates spending that is 32 percent below the average for all consumer units)

	total consumer units	Northeast	Midwest	South	West
Average spending of CU, total	$40,817	$42,162	$40,280	$37,625	$45,381
Average spending of CU, index	100	103	99	92	111
Housing, spending index	**100**	**110**	**94**	**89**	**114**
HOUSEHOLD SERVICES	**100**	**115**	**87**	**94**	**110**
Personal services	**100**	**127**	**93**	**90**	**99**
Babysitting and child care in your own home	100	184	106	61	85
Babysitting and child care in someone else's home	100	106	144	54	124
Day care centers, nurseries, and preschools	100	109	103	94	99
Other household services	**100**	**106**	**82**	**97**	**118**
Housekeeping services	100	120	77	91	121
Gardening, lawn care service	100	108	70	102	119
Water softening service	100	85	192	56	89
Nonclothing laundry and dry cleaning, sent out	100	189	80	62	107
Nonclothing laundry and dry cleaning, coin-operated	100	160	75	72	119
Termite/pest control services	100	25	36	157	139
Home security system service fee	100	93	81	128	80
Other home services	100	109	85	71	155
Termite/pest control products	100	29	51	138	151
Moving, storage, and freight express	100	85	70	100	145
Appliance repair, including service center	100	108	106	88	106
Reupholstering and furniture repair	100	105	113	89	100
Repairs/rentals of lawn/garden equipment, hand/power tools, etc.	100	121	83	129	52
Appliance rental	100	94	150	71	102
Repair of computer systems for nonbusiness use	100	119	70	114	92
Computer information services	100	106	95	92	114
HOUSEKEEPING SUPPLIES	**100**	**99**	**109**	**94**	**102**
Laundry and cleaning supplies	**100**	**95**	**109**	**100**	**95**
Soaps and detergents	100	97	105	100	97
Other laundry cleaning products	100	92	115	99	94
Other household products	**100**	**98**	**108**	**98**	**97**
Cleansing and toilet tissue, paper towels, and napkins	100	100	99	98	104
Miscellaneous household products	100	96	116	94	96
Lawn and garden supplies	100	97	106	103	92
Postage and stationery	**100**	**106**	**110**	**80**	**117**
Stationery, stationery supplies, giftwrap	100	96	114	82	117
Postage	100	116	112	78	109
Delivery services	100	90	32	73	225
HOUSEHOLD FURNISHINGS AND EQUIPMENT	**100**	**97**	**100**	**86**	**124**
Household textiles	**100**	**111**	**93**	**80**	**130**
Bathroom linens	100	112	105	78	119
Bedroom linens	100	126	76	80	135
Kitchen and dining room linens	100	112	99	73	133
Curtains and draperies	100	114	107	89	98
Slipcovers and decorative pillows	100	57	82	80	189
Sewing materials for household items	100	64	128	76	142
Other linens	100	65	132	88	118
Furniture	**100**	**97**	**102**	**89**	**117**
Mattresses and springs	100	79	102	95	124
Other bedroom furniture	100	114	95	80	125
Sofas	100	85	111	86	124
Living room chairs	100	75	97	101	123
Living room tables	100	81	99	97	122
Kitchen and dining room furniture	100	150	79	92	90

	total consumer units	Northeast	Midwest	South	West
Infants' furniture	100	65	130	89	117
Outdoor furniture	100	93	128	92	90
Wall units, cabinets, and other furniture	100	88	113	89	116
Floor coverings	**100**	**127**	**85**	**73**	**136**
Wall-to-wall carpeting	100	110	97	62	156
Floor coverings, nonpermanent	100	151	67	87	111
Major appliances	**100**	**90**	**100**	**91**	**123**
Dishwashers (built-in), garbage disposals, range hoods	100	147	95	54	140
Refrigerators and freezers	100	91	105	98	105
Washing machines	100	98	84	90	135
Clothes dryers	100	79	96	90	139
Cooking stoves, ovens	100	90	110	77	136
Microwave ovens	100	89	104	83	132
Window air conditioners	100	177	75	50	141
Electric floor-cleaning equipment	100	56	100	125	98
Sewing machines	100	21	114	101	154
Miscellaneous household appliances	100	194	92	60	90
Small appliances and misc. housewares	**100**	**86**	**99**	**99**	**115**
Housewares	100	77	96	105	118
Plastic dinnerware	100	97	76	82	157
China and other dinnerware	100	48	125	71	165
Flatware	100	115	101	49	170
Glassware	100	81	80	140	74
Silver serving pieces	100	89	78	119	104
Other serving pieces	100	81	68	96	156
Nonelectric cookware	100	68	83	117	120
Tableware, nonelectric kitchenware	100	78	110	101	107
Small appliances	100	113	108	82	109
Small electric kitchen appliances	100	101	106	79	127
Portable heating and cooling equipment	100	139	114	90	67
Miscellaneous household equipment	**100**	**95**	**102**	**84**	**128**
Window coverings	100	56	81	73	203
Infants' equipment	100	94	50	103	154
Laundry and cleaning equipment	100	100	102	87	119
Outdoor equipment	100	68	120	88	126
Clocks	100	128	80	85	121
Lamps and lighting fixtures	100	113	103	82	116
Other household decorative items	100	93	119	80	118
Telephones and accessories	100	84	72	87	164
Lawn and garden equipment	100	164	90	103	50
Power tools	100	76	119	81	132
Office furniture for home use	100	83	70	124	106
Hand tools	100	71	148	81	106
Indoor plants and fresh flowers	100	117	106	80	112
Closet and storage items	100	64	160	72	113
Rental of furniture	100	122	78	115	79
Luggage	100	114	114	74	116
Computers and computer hardware, nonbusiness use	100	103	93	76	142
Computer software and accessories, nonbusiness use	100	89	110	81	131
Telephone answering devices	100	86	109	83	130
Calculators	100	127	117	83	88
Business equipment for home use	100	43	140	73	154
Other hardware	100	41	140	78	145
Smoke alarms	100	173	119	48	99
Other household appliances	100	114	96	99	94
Miscellaneous household equipment and parts	100	56	74	92	171

Source: Calculations by New Strategist based on the 2003 Consumer Expenditure Survey

Table 8.23 Housing: Household Operations: Total spending by region, 2003

(total annual spending on household services, supplies, furnishings, and equipment, by region in which consumer units live, 2003; numbers in thousands)

	total consumer units	Northeast	Midwest	South	West
Number of consumer units	115,356	22,182	26,438	41,325	25,412
Total spending of all consumer units	$4,708,523,919	$935,243,917	$1,064,932,951	$1,554,834,529	$1,153,213,586
Housing, total spending	**1,549,446,796**	**328,538,267**	**334,027,210**	**496,162,414**	**390,617,763**
HOUSEHOLD SERVICES	**81,573,995**	**18,039,068**	**16,239,277**	**27,527,822**	**19,768,503**
Personal services	**33,860,447**	**8,284,755**	**7,248,242**	**10,931,702**	**7,396,163**
Babysitting and child care in your own home	4,158,584	1,470,667	1,005,966	904,191	778,115
Babysitting and child care in someone else's home	2,767,390	566,528	914,755	532,679	753,466
Day care centers, nurseries, and preschools	21,781,520	4,558,401	5,125,535	7,344,692	4,752,806
Other household services	**47,712,395**	**9,754,313**	**8,991,035**	**16,596,120**	**12,372,340**
Housekeeping services	10,743,104	2,479,282	1,900,363	3,506,840	2,856,563
Gardening, lawn care service	9,655,297	2,013,017	1,559,578	3,541,553	2,541,200
Water softening service	372,600	61,001	163,651	75,212	73,441
Nonclothing laundry and dry cleaning, sent out	115,356	41,924	21,150	25,622	27,191
Nonclothing laundry and dry cleaning, coin-operated	417,589	128,212	71,383	107,445	109,780
Termite/pest control services	1,303,523	62,997	107,603	734,345	398,714
Home security system service fee	1,792,632	319,199	334,176	822,781	316,888
Other home services	1,710,729	357,130	333,648	435,979	584,222
Termite/pest control products	175,341	9,760	20,357	86,783	58,448
Moving, storage, and freight express	3,513,744	571,630	561,543	1,259,173	1,121,686
Appliance repair, including service center	1,355,433	282,599	328,889	426,887	316,634
Reupholstering and furniture repair	599,851	121,114	155,984	190,508	132,142
Repairs/rentals of lawn/garden equipment, hand/power tools, etc.	701,364	163,038	133,512	324,401	80,302
Appliance rental	188,030	34,160	64,509	47,937	42,438
Repair of computer systems for nonbusiness use	484,495	110,910	77,463	197,947	98,344
Computer information services	14,294,916	2,913,162	3,100,649	4,691,214	3,589,953
HOUSEKEEPING SUPPLIES	**61,004,867**	**11,604,070**	**15,207,931**	**20,483,976**	**13,647,260**
Laundry and cleaning supplies	**15,259,292**	**2,774,303**	**3,828,487**	**5,443,329**	**3,203,437**
Soaps and detergents	8,553,647	1,593,999	2,060,842	3,074,580	1,822,040
Other laundry cleaning products	6,705,644	1,180,304	1,767,645	2,368,749	1,381,396
Other household products	**30,381,310**	**5,702,105**	**7,499,403**	**10,662,263**	**6,497,594**
Cleansing and toilet tissue, paper towels, and napkins	8,678,232	1,675,628	1,968,045	3,042,347	1,992,047
Miscellaneous household products	12,264,650	2,268,997	3,246,586	4,133,327	2,597,869
Lawn and garden supplies	9,438,428	1,757,480	2,284,772	3,486,590	1,907,679
Postage and stationery	**15,364,266**	**3,127,662**	**3,880,041**	**4,378,384**	**3,946,484**
Stationery, stationery supplies, giftwrap	6,869,450	1,267,036	1,798,842	2,018,726	1,770,454
Postage	7,952,643	1,767,240	2,041,542	2,218,326	1,906,662
Delivery services	542,173	93,386	39,657	141,332	269,113
HOUSEHOLD FURNISHINGS AND EQUIPMENT	**172,693,700**	**32,200,057**	**39,772,005**	**53,456,367**	**47,214,988**
Household textiles	**13,090,599**	**2,802,030**	**2,787,887**	**3,758,922**	**3,738,613**
Bathroom linens	2,341,727	506,415	563,129	653,348	614,462
Bedroom linens	6,165,778	1,490,187	1,069,946	1,770,363	1,837,033
Kitchen and dining room linens	850,174	183,223	193,791	223,155	248,529
Curtains and draperies	1,758,025	384,636	431,468	562,433	378,893
Slipcovers and decorative pillows	501,799	55,233	94,648	142,985	208,378
Sewing materials for household items	1,300,062	160,598	381,765	351,676	406,084
Other linens	174,188	21,738	52,876	54,962	45,233
Furniture	**46,236,992**	**8,666,286**	**10,853,857**	**14,760,877**	**11,956,346**
Mattresses and springs	5,178,331	789,014	1,213,240	1,765,817	1,410,112
Other bedroom furniture	9,163,881	2,005,696	2,000,563	2,626,617	2,530,527
Sofas	10,632,363	1,745,502	2,713,596	3,258,890	2,913,740
Living room chairs	4,471,199	648,824	993,011	1,616,221	1,213,423
Living room tables	2,019,884	313,875	460,021	702,938	542,546
Kitchen and dining room furniture	5,700,894	1,648,788	1,032,668	1,886,900	1,132,105

	total consumer units	Northeast	Midwest	South	West
Infants' furniture	$942,459	$117,121	$280,507	$300,846	$243,70
Outdoor furniture	1,770,715	316,315	519,507	585,162	349,669
Wall units, cabinets, and other furniture	6,359,576	1,081,151	1,640,478	2,017,487	1,620,269
Floor coverings	**5,970,827**	**1,461,350**	**1,156,398**	**1,560,019**	**1,793,579**
Wall-to-wall carpeting	3,403,002	717,366	760,357	757,487	1,168,190
Floor coverings, nonpermanent	2,567,825	743,984	396,041	802,532	625,643
Major appliances	**22,575,169**	**3,914,458**	**5,161,491**	**7,394,282**	**6,111,078**
Dishwashers (built-in), garbage disposals, range hoods	1,557,306	439,647	337,878	299,193	480,541
Refrigerators and freezers	5,486,331	962,699	1,321,900	1,934,010	1,267,042
Washing machines	3,308,410	622,649	637,685	1,067,838	980,649
Clothes dryers	2,241,367	338,941	490,954	722,774	688,665
Cooking stoves, ovens	3,517,204	612,001	884,880	969,071	1,051,803
Microwave ovens	872,091	149,507	208,860	260,348	252,849
Window air conditioners	622,922	212,060	107,603	111,578	192,877
Electric floor-cleaning equipment	3,488,365	377,316	802,393	1,562,912	751,433
Sewing machines	1,032,436	41,037	268,874	372,338	349,923
Miscellaneous household appliances	258,397	96,492	54,727	55,789	51,332
Small appliances and misc. housewares	**10,123,643**	**1,673,854**	**2,294,554**	**3,591,969**	**2,569,661**
Housewares	7,526,979	1,110,653	1,649,996	2,824,977	1,948,338
Plastic dinnerware	179,955	33,495	31,461	52,896	62,259
China and other dinnerware	812,106	75,641	232,390	205,799	295,033
Flatware	460,270	101,815	106,016	80,997	172,039
Glassware	1,025,515	160,598	187,974	513,257	168,227
Silver serving pieces	750,968	128,212	134,305	319,029	171,785
Other serving pieces	166,113	25,731	25,909	57,029	56,923
Nonelectric cookware	1,760,333	228,696	335,763	735,172	465,040
Tableware, nonelectric kitchenware	2,371,719	356,243	596,177	860,800	557,031
Small appliances	2,596,664	563,201	644,558	766,992	621,323
Small electric kitchen appliances	1,806,475	351,807	438,342	511,190	504,936
Portable heating and cooling equipment	790,189	211,394	206,216	255,802	116,387
Miscellaneous household equipment	**74,696,471**	**13,682,301**	**17,518,083**	**22,390,298**	**21,045,710**
Window coverings	2,807,765	300,566	518,185	730,626	1,258,656
Infants' equipment	1,508,856	274,170	173,962	555,821	510,781
Laundry and cleaning equipment	1,618,445	310,770	379,650	503,339	423,618
Outdoor equipment	2,738,551	358,461	750,046	861,626	762,868
Clocks	463,731	113,794	84,602	141,332	123,756
Lamps and lighting fixtures	1,575,763	341,381	370,661	461,187	403,034
Other household decorative items	14,624,834	2,620,581	3,991,080	4,168,040	3,806,463
Telephones and accessories	3,089,234	499,317	512,897	962,046	1,118,382
Lawn and garden equipment	6,389,569	2,016,787	1,311,854	2,351,806	708,995
Power tools	2,812,379	412,363	764,058	812,036	816,488
Office furniture for home use	1,454,639	232,911	233,183	648,389	340,013
Hand tools	832,870	113,128	282,093	242,578	194,656
Indoor plants and fresh flowers	4,650,000	1,047,878	129,696	1,327,359	1,144,556
Closet and storage items	1,103,957	135,088	404,237	283,076	274,704
Rental of furniture	311,461	72,979	55,784	128,521	54,382
Luggage	712,900	155,718	185,595	189,269	181,950
Computers and computer hardware, nonbusiness use	15,777,240	1,136,978	3,368,994	4,319,289	4,952,036
Computer software and accessories, nonbusiness use	2,074,101	354,025	522,415	599,626	598,198
Telephone answering devices	107,281	17,746	26,702	31,820	30,749
Calculators	146,502	35,713	39,128	43,391	28,461
Business equipment for home use	124,584	10,204	39,921	32,647	42,184
Other hardware	4,423,903	346,483	1,416,284	1,232,312	1,411,128
Smoke alarms	130,352	43,477	35,427	22,316	28,461
Other household appliances	769,425	169,249	168,410	273,158	158,571
Miscellaneous household equipment and parts	4,449,281	562,092	753,219	1,468,277	1,672,872

Note: Numbers may not add to total because of rounding and missing subcategories.
Source: Calculations by New Strategist based on the 2003 Consumer Expenditure Survey

Table 8.24 Housing: Household Operations: Market shares by region, 2003

(percentage of total annual spending on household services, supplies, furnishings, and equipment accounted for by consumer units by region, 2003)

	total consumer units	Northeast	Midwest	South	West
Share of total consumer units	100.0%	19.2%	22.9%	35.8%	22.0%
Share of total before-tax income	100.0	21.5	23.4	32.8	22.5
Share of total spending	100.0	19.9	22.6	33.0	24.5
Share of housing spending	100.0	21.2	21.6	32.0	25.2
HOUSEHOLD SERVICES	**100.0**	**22.1**	**19.9**	**33.7**	**24.2**
Personal services	**100.0**	**24.5**	**21.4**	**32.3**	**21.8**
Babysitting and child care in your own home	100.0	35.4	24.2	21.7	18.7
Babysitting and child care in someone else's home	100.0	20.5	33.1	19.2	27.2
Day care centers, nurseries, and preschools	100.0	20.9	23.5	33.7	21.8
Other household services	**100.0**	**20.4**	**18.8**	**34.8**	**25.9**
Housekeeping services	100.0	23.1	17.7	32.6	26.6
Gardening, lawn care service	100.0	20.8	16.2	36.7	26.3
Water softening service	100.0	16.4	43.9	20.2	19.7
Nonclothing laundry and dry cleaning, sent out	100.0	36.3	18.3	22.2	23.6
Nonclothing laundry and dry cleaning, coin-operated	100.0	30.7	17.1	25.7	26.3
Termite/pest control services	100.0	4.8	8.3	56.3	30.6
Home security system service fee	100.0	17.8	18.6	45.9	17.7
Other home services	100.0	20.9	19.5	25.5	34.2
Termite/pest control products	100.0	5.6	11.6	49.5	33.3
Moving, storage, and freight express	100.0	16.3	16.0	35.8	31.9
Appliance repair, including service center	100.0	20.8	24.3	31.5	23.4
Reupholstering and furniture repair	100.0	20.2	26.0	31.8	22.0
Repairs/rentals of lawn/garden equipment, hand/power tools, etc.	100.0	23.2	19.0	46.3	11.4
Appliance rental	100.0	18.2	34.3	25.5	22.6
Repair of computer systems for nonbusiness use	100.0	22.9	16.0	40.9	20.3
Computer information services	100.0	20.4	21.7	32.8	25.1
HOUSEKEEPING SUPPLIES	**100.0**	**19.0**	**24.9**	**33.6**	**22.4**
Laundry and cleaning supplies	**100.0**	**18.2**	**25.1**	**35.7**	**21.0**
Soaps and detergents	100.0	18.6	24.1	35.9	21.3
Other laundry cleaning products	100.0	17.6	26.4	35.3	20.6
Other household products	**100.0**	**18.8**	**24.7**	**35.1**	**21.4**
Cleansing and toilet tissue, paper towels, and napkins	100.0	19.3	22.7	35.1	23.0
Miscellaneous household products	100.0	18.5	26.5	33.7	21.2
Lawn and garden supplies	100.0	18.6	24.2	36.9	20.2
Postage and stationery	**100.0**	**20.4**	**25.3**	**28.5**	**25.7**
Stationery, stationery supplies, giftwrap	100.0	18.4	26.2	29.4	25.8
Postage	100.0	22.2	25.7	27.9	24.0
Delivery services	100.0	17.2	7.3	26.1	49.6
HOUSEHOLD FURNISHINGS AND EQUIPMENT	**100.0**	**18.6**	**23.0**	**31.0**	**27.3**
Household textiles	**100.0**	**21.4**	**21.3**	**28.7**	**28.6**
Bathroom linens	100.0	21.6	24.0	27.9	26.2
Bedroom linens	100.0	24.2	17.4	28.7	29.8
Kitchen and dining room linens	100.0	21.6	22.8	26.2	29.2
Curtains and draperies	100.0	21.9	24.5	32.0	21.6
Slipcovers and decorative pillows	100.0	11.0	18.9	28.5	41.5
Sewing materials for household items	100.0	12.4	29.4	27.1	31.2
Other linens	100.0	12.5	30.4	31.6	26.0
Furniture	**100.0**	**18.7**	**23.5**	**31.9**	**25.9**
Mattresses and springs	100.0	15.2	23.4	34.1	27.2
Other bedroom furniture	100.0	21.9	21.8	28.7	27.6
Sofas	100.0	16.4	25.5	30.7	27.4
Living room chairs	100.0	14.5	22.2	36.1	27.1
Living room tables	100.0	15.5	22.8	34.8	26.9
Kitchen and dining room furniture	100.0	28.9	18.1	33.1	19.9

	total consumer units	Northeast	Midwest	South	West
Infants' furniture	100.0%	12.4%	29.8%	31.9%	25.9%
Outdoor furniture	100.0	17.9	29.3	33.0	19.7
Wall units, cabinets, and other furniture	100.0	17.0	25.8	31.7	25.5
Floor coverings	**100.0**	**24.5**	**19.4**	**26.1**	**30.0**
Wall-to-wall carpeting	100.0	21.1	22.3	22.3	34.3
Floor coverings, nonpermanent	100.0	29.0	15.4	31.3	24.4
Major appliances	**100.0**	**17.3**	**22.9**	**32.8**	**27.1**
Dishwashers (built-in), garbage disposals, range hoods	100.0	28.2	21.7	19.2	30.9
Refrigerators and freezers	100.0	17.5	24.1	35.3	23.1
Washing machines	100.0	18.8	19.3	32.3	29.6
Clothes dryers	100.0	15.1	21.9	32.2	30.7
Cooking stoves, ovens	100.0	17.4	25.2	27.6	29.9
Microwave ovens	100.0	17.1	23.9	29.9	29.0
Window air conditioners	100.0	34.0	17.3	17.9	31.0
Electric floor-cleaning equipment	100.0	10.8	23.0	44.8	21.5
Sewing machines	100.0	4.0	26.0	36.1	33.9
Miscellaneous household appliances	100.0	37.3	21.2	21.6	19.9
Small appliances and misc. housewares	**100.0**	**16.5**	**22.7**	**35.5**	**25.4**
Housewares	100.0	14.8	21.9	37.5	25.9
Plastic dinnerware	100.0	18.6	17.5	29.4	34.6
China and other dinnerware	100.0	9.3	28.6	25.3	36.3
Flatware	100.0	22.1	23.0	17.6	37.4
Glassware	100.0	15.7	18.3	50.0	16.4
Silver serving pieces	100.0	17.1	17.9	42.5	22.9
Other serving pieces	100.0	15.5	15.6	34.3	34.3
Nonelectric cookware	100.0	13.0	19.1	41.8	26.4
Tableware, nonelectric kitchenware	100.0	15.0	25.1	36.3	23.5
Small appliances	100.0	21.7	24.8	29.5	23.9
Small electric kitchen appliances	100.0	19.5	24.3	28.3	28.0
Portable heating and cooling equipment	100.0	26.8	26.1	32.4	14.7
Miscellaneous household equipment	**100.0**	**18.3**	**23.5**	**30.0**	**28.2**
Window coverings	100.0	10.7	18.5	26.0	44.8
Infants' equipment	100.0	18.2	11.5	36.8	33.9
Laundry and cleaning equipment	100.0	19.2	23.5	31.1	26.2
Outdoor equipment	100.0	13.1	27.4	31.5	27.9
Clocks	100.0	24.5	18.2	30.5	26.7
Lamps and lighting fixtures	100.0	21.7	23.5	29.3	25.6
Other household decorative items	100.0	17.9	27.3	28.5	26.0
Telephones and accessories	100.0	16.2	16.6	31.1	36.2
Lawn and garden equipment	100.0	31.6	20.5	36.8	11.1
Power tools	100.0	14.7	27.2	28.9	29.0
Office furniture for home use	100.0	16.0	16.0	44.6	23.4
Hand tools	100.0	13.6	33.9	29.1	23.4
Indoor plants and fresh flowers	100.0	22.5	24.3	28.5	24.6
Closet and storage items	100.0	12.2	36.6	25.6	24.9
Rental of furniture	100.0	23.4	17.9	41.3	17.5
Luggage	100.0	21.8	26.0	26.5	25.5
Computers and computer hardware, nonbusiness use	100.0	19.9	21.4	27.4	31.4
Computer software and accessories, nonbusiness use	100.0	17.1	25.2	28.9	28.8
Telephone answering devices	100.0	16.5	24.9	29.7	28.7
Calculators	100.0	24.4	26.7	29.6	19.4
Business equipment for home use	100.0	8.2	32.0	26.2	33.9
Other hardware	100.0	7.8	32.0	27.9	31.9
Smoke alarms	100.0	33.4	27.2	17.1	21.8
Other household appliances	100.0	22.0	21.9	35.5	20.6
Miscellaneous household equipment and parts	100.0	12.6	16.9	33.0	37.6

Note: Numbers may not add to total because of rounding.
Source: Calculations by New Strategist based on the 2003 Consumer Expenditure Survey

Table 8.25 Housing: Household Operations: Average spending by education, 2003

(average annual spending of consumer units (CU) on household services, supplies, furnishings, and equipment, by education of consumer unit reference person, 2003)

	total consumer units	less than high school graduate	high school graduate	some college	associate's degree	college graduate total	bachelor's degree	master's, professional, doctorate
Number of consumer units (000)	115,356	17,721	31,552	24,514	10,981	30,589	19,557	11,032
Average number of persons per CU	2.5	2.6	2.5	2.3	2.6	2.5	2.5	2.4
Average before-tax income of CU	$51,128.00	$25,028.00	$40,113.00	$45,113.00	$54,087.00	$81,842.00	$74,921.00	$93,948.00
Average spending of CU, total	40,817.33	23,901.14	33,955.56	37,912.41	44,547.12	58,480.00	54,725.85	65,202.73
Housing, average spending	**13,431.87**	**8,350.94**	**10,923.45**	**12,259.77**	**14,059.62**	**19,631.09**	**18,357.09**	**21,907.58**
HOUSEHOLD SERVICES	**707.15**	**237.07**	**447.25**	**651.93**	**718.41**	**1,287.85**	**1,177.37**	**1,483.63**
Personal services	**293.53**	**81.84**	**199.47**	**238.45**	**333.05**	**543.15**	**515.95**	**591.36**
Babysitting and child care in your own home	36.05	13.38	8.78	22.97	18.64	94.06	76.70	124.83
Babysitting and child care in someone else's home	23.99	15.52	24.20	22.29	28.29	28.49	36.95	13.49
Day care centers, nurseries, and preschools	188.82	32.20	120.54	156.95	260.47	349.81	361.03	329.90
Other household services	**413.61**	**155.23**	**247.78**	**413.48**	**385.35**	**744.71**	**661.42**	**892.27**
Housekeeping services	93.13	20.31	31.48	95.06	59.85	209.31	175.71	268.88
Gardening, lawn care service	83.70	29.62	49.02	79.07	68.20	160.07	141.41	193.15
Water softening service	3.23	1.44	3.26	2.14	5.26	4.40	3.42	6.14
Nonclothing laundry and dry cleaning, sent out	1.00	0.12	0.42	1.22	0.56	2.10	1.83	2.58
Nonclothing laundry and dry cleaning, coin-operated	3.62	6.50	3.48	3.61	2.52	2.49	2.74	2.03
Termite/pest control services	11.30	4.01	7.23	9.56	18.23	18.64	15.93	23.44
Home security system service fee	15.54	6.47	11.93	13.59	13.68	26.76	23.36	32.80
Other home services	14.83	5.85	10.51	12.82	12.01	27.12	23.60	33.36
Termite/pest control products	1.52	0.45	1.04	1.29	1.91	2.68	1.98	3.91
Moving, storage, and freight express	30.46	21.89	11.58	26.19	16.85	63.21	53.21	80.94
Appliance repair, including service center	11.75	6.84	10.47	10.62	11.26	16.99	15.68	19.33
Reupholstering and furniture repair	5.20	3.70	1.30	5.92	6.89	8.90	5.19	15.46
Repairs/rentals of lawn/garden equipment, hand/power tools, etc.	6.08	5.29	5.08	5.56	9.17	6.87	7.30	6.12
Appliance rental	1.63	2.07	2.11	2.25	1.20	0.56	0.35	0.92
Repair of computer systems for nonbusiness use	4.20	0.50	4.64	5.13	5.23	4.79	4.78	4.80
Computer information services	123.92	40.16	93.46	131.94	151.35	187.58	181.72	197.98
HOUSEKEEPING SUPPLIES	**528.84**	**322.51**	**477.39**	**480.53**	**639.22**	**683.03**	**638.83**	**767.56**
Laundry and cleaning supplies	**132.28**	**114.21**	**130.93**	**136.97**	**149.02**	**133.91**	**135.32**	**131.22**
Soaps and detergents	74.15	70.97	74.53	79.17	77.65	70.61	72.66	66.68
Other laundry cleaning products	58.13	43.24	56.41	57.80	71.38	63.31	62.66	64.54
Other household products	**263.37**	**153.17**	**238.48**	**224.98**	**329.89**	**349.84**	**336.21**	**375.91**
Cleansing and toilet tissue, paper towels, and napkins	75.23	67.02	72.91	73.77	86.36	79.25	78.09	81.46
Miscellaneous household products	106.32	50.47	100.77	94.73	133.25	139.30	140.71	136.60
Lawn and garden supplies	81.82	35.68	64.81	56.48	110.27	131.30	117.42	157.85
Postage and stationery	**133.19**	**55.13**	**107.97**	**118.58**	**160.32**	**199.27**	**167.29**	**260.43**
Stationery, stationery supplies, giftwrap	59.55	20.15	45.99	54.95	85.78	87.88	76.72	109.24
Postage	68.94	34.42	57.40	60.35	67.98	104.10	88.67	133.62
Delivery services	4.70	0.57	4.58	3.28	6.56	7.28	1.91	17.57
HOUSEHOLD FURNISHINGS AND EQUIPMENT	**1,497.05**	**614.74**	**1,080.02**	**1,396.09**	**1,669.64**	**2,429.12**	**2,149.32**	**2,936.95**
Household textiles	**113.48**	**53.74**	**67.54**	**123.86**	**127.37**	**179.62**	**181.41**	**175.88**
Bathroom linens	20.30	9.37	13.47	20.32	21.46	32.26	35.82	25.45
Bedroom linens	53.45	26.86	28.23	65.95	59.76	81.25	83.94	76.11
Kitchen and dining room linens	7.37	3.60	3.81	6.92	14.34	11.03	9.31	14.32
Curtains and draperies	15.24	7.00	10.37	12.65	12.30	28.15	24.33	34.93
Slipcovers and decorative pillows	4.35	1.94	2.15	5.31	3.44	7.35	6.93	8.16
Sewing materials for household items	11.27	4.56	8.56	11.08	14.80	16.84	17.66	15.39
Other linens	1.51	0.42	0.95	1.63	1.27	2.73	3.42	1.51
Furniture	**400.82**	**190.64**	**278.12**	**353.11**	**407.23**	**685.08**	**589.89**	**853.85**
Mattresses and springs	44.89	29.54	26.92	49.09	55.58	65.10	55.30	82.48
Other bedroom furniture	79.44	39.12	59.76	68.82	63.49	137.32	127.14	155.37
Sofas	92.17	49.15	63.80	77.93	106.79	152.50	128.49	195.08
Living room chairs	38.76	20.41	30.49	35.53	35.37	61.75	56.68	70.74
Living room tables	17.51	8.27	10.26	15.14	15.88	32.80	28.60	40.25
Kitchen and dining room furniture	49.42	15.45	26.33	37.52	49.12	102.54	74.78	151.76

	total consumer units	less than high school graduate	high school graduate	some college	associate's degree	college graduate total	bachelor's degree	master's professional, doctorate
Infants' furniture	$8.17	$4.27	$6.45	$5.34	$10.77	$13.53	$11.34	$17.42
Outdoor furniture	15.35	4.68	6.23	12.23	12.09	34.57	29.85	42.92
Wall units, cabinets, and other furniture	55.13	19.75	47.38	51.46	58.14	84.96	77.71	97.83
Floor coverings	**51.76**	**10.10**	**41.58**	**39.39**	**50.50**	**96.77**	**75.05**	**135.27**
Wall-to-wall carpeting	29.50	5.90	30.35	26.78	34.98	42.52	38.32	49.98
Floor coverings, nonpermanent	22.26	4.20	11.24	12.61	15.52	54.25	36.74	85.29
Major appliances	**195.70**	**107.57**	**168.36**	**134.67**	**203.36**	**277.09**	**250.18**	**326.57**
Dishwashers (built-in), garbage disposals, range hoods	13.50	5.98	10.91	10.00	15.14	22.75	21.44	25.07
Refrigerators and freezers	47.56	35.78	41.22	50.39	53.01	56.57	52.32	64.10
Washing machines	28.68	18.29	22.53	27.91	34.14	39.71	39.44	40.20
Clothes dryers	19.43	13.09	14.11	20.22	20.19	27.68	30.54	22.63
Cooking stoves, ovens	30.49	13.26	21.73	28.50	33.59	50.02	40.02	67.74
Microwave ovens	7.56	4.39	6.41	7.40	7.59	10.69	9.53	12.73
Window air conditioners	5.40	7.54	4.13	3.71	12.35	4.35	3.42	6.00
Electric floor-cleaning equipment	30.24	6.88	38.93	22.75	11.10	44.01	35.22	60.82
Sewing machines	8.95	1.70	6.03	9.93	12.98	13.92	16.24	9.81
Miscellaneous household appliances	2.24	–	0.84	1.81	1.04	5.46	1.66	12.73
Small appliances and misc. housewares	**87.76**	**42.32**	**66.97**	**68.10**	**118.44**	**137.24**	**118.91**	**171.74**
Housewares	65.25	29.95	47.44	47.20	92.16	105.86	89.75	136.42
Plastic dinnerware	1.56	0.85	1.02	1.75	1.67	2.35	2.32	2.38
China and other dinnerware	7.04	4.84	5.22	4.36	14.83	9.50	7.31	13.70
Flatware	3.99	1.65	2.42	3.56	4.22	7.24	6.17	9.14
Glassware	8.89	1.76	5.12	4.88	9.44	18.96	14.57	27.37
Silver serving pieces	6.51	2.74	4.84	6.17	7.36	10.04	10.66	8.86
Other serving pieces	1.44	0.40	0.44	0.44	1.51	2.74	2.15	3.80
Nonelectric cookware	15.26	11.03	13.55	9.16	23.97	20.82	17.68	26.81
Tableware, nonelectric kitchenware	20.56	6.67	14.32	15.52	29.16	34.20	28.88	44.37
Small appliances	22.51	12.38	19.52	20.90	26.28	31.38	29.16	35.32
Small electric kitchen appliances	15.66	9.17	12.59	15.05	19.61	21.65	20.20	24.23
Portable heating and cooling equipment	6.85	3.21	6.93	5.85	6.67	9.73	8.97	11.08
Miscellaneous household equipment	**647.53**	**210.37**	**457.45**	**626.97**	**762.74**	**1,053.31**	**933.88**	**1,273.64**
Window coverings	24.34	3.86	10.10	22.20	26.34	51.90	45.10	63.95
Infants' equipment	13.08	8.29	11.05	12.58	4.41	20.54	18.16	25.09
Laundry and cleaning equipment	14.03	10.05	12.61	15.49	16.90	15.49	12.50	21.22
Outdoor equipment	23.74	7.02	14.96	30.83	27.76	34.51	41.21	21.69
Clocks	4.02	1.16	3.62	1.83	6.16	6.74	4.65	10.74
Lamps and lighting fixtures	13.66	4.43	8.75	11.40	10.24	27.13	20.91	38.15
Other household decorative items	126.78	39.46	75.04	123.49	170.66	211.21	203.50	225.95
Telephones and accessories	26.78	15.39	19.84	18.48	24.43	46.17	40.74	56.56
Lawn and garden equipment	55.39	17.37	59.57	50.54	120.38	53.57	57.05	47.39
Power tools	24.38	8.25	13.49	46.35	9.31	32.13	24.87	46.02
Office furniture for home use	12.61	0.90	4.42	14.61	6.63	28.38	19.54	44.06
Hand tools	7.22	5.66	8.18	5.37	10.37	7.47	8.12	6.32
Indoor plants and fresh flowers	40.31	16.86	27.42	34.10	48.55	69.20	66.41	74.13
Closet and storage items	9.57	3.88	5.99	10.63	10.81	14.85	14.92	14.71
Rental of furniture	2.70	4.38	4.10	1.59	1.60	1.58	1.39	1.90
Luggage	6.18	2.14	3.59	4.72	4.89	12.82	11.46	15.23
Computers and computer hardware, nonbusiness use	136.77	35.43	77.12	147.01	130.93	250.88	219.82	305.95
Computer software and accessories, nonbusiness use	17.98	5.31	8.81	19.85	17.09	33.61	29.75	40.45
Telephone answering devices	0.93	0.28	0.82	1.36	0.88	1.08	0.92	1.36
Calculators	1.27	0.30	0.68	1.95	1.31	1.88	1.90	1.86
Business equipment for home use	1.08	0.81	0.38	1.31	0.75	1.90	1.75	2.16
Other hardware	38.35	1.63	50.20	16.83	34.68	60.76	18.99	140.65
Smoke alarms	1.13	0.43	0.90	1.35	1.04	1.61	1.82	1.21
Other household appliances	6.67	3.12	4.28	4.98	15.43	9.41	8.48	11.06
Miscellaneous household equipment and parts	38.57	13.95	31.51	27.95	61.20	58.52	59.92	55.83

Note: Subcategories may not add to total because some are not shown. (–) means sample is too small to make a reliable estimate.
Source: Bureau of Labor Statistics, unpublished tables from the 2003 Consumer Expenditure Survey

Table 8.26 Housing: Household Operations: Indexed spending by education, 2003

(indexed average annual spending of consumer units (CU) on household services, supplies, furnishings, and equipment, by education of consumer unit reference person, 2003; index definition: an index of 100 is the average for all consumer units; an index of 132 means that spending by consumer units in that group is 32 percent above the average for all consumer units; an index of 68 indicates spending that is 32 percent below the average for all consumer units)

	total consumer units	less than high school graduate	high school graduate	some college	associate's degree	college graduate total	bachelor's degree	master's, professional, doctorate
Average spending of CU, total	$40,817	$23,901	$33,956	$37,912	$44,547	$58,480	$54,726	$65,203
Average spending of CU, index	100	59	83	93	109	143	134	160
Housing, spending index	100	62	81	91	105	146	137	163
HOUSEHOLD SERVICES	100	34	63	92	102	182	166	210
Personal services	100	28	68	81	113	185	176	201
Babysitting and child care in your own home	100	37	24	64	52	261	213	346
Babysitting and child care in someone else's home	100	65	101	93	118	119	154	56
Day care centers, nurseries, and preschools	100	17	64	83	138	185	191	175
Other household services	100	38	60	100	93	180	160	216
Housekeeping services	100	22	34	102	64	225	189	289
Gardening, lawn care service	100	35	59	94	81	191	169	231
Water softening service	100	45	101	66	163	136	106	190
Nonclothing laundry and dry cleaning, sent out	100	12	42	122	56	210	183	258
Nonclothing laundry and dry cleaning, coin-operated	100	180	96	100	70	69	76	56
Termite/pest control services	100	35	64	85	161	165	141	207
Home security system service fee	100	42	77	87	88	172	150	211
Other home services	100	39	71	86	81	183	159	225
Termite/pest control products	100	30	68	85	126	176	130	257
Moving, storage, and freight express	100	72	38	86	55	208	175	266
Appliance repair, including service center	100	58	89	90	96	145	133	165
Reupholstering and furniture repair	100	71	25	114	133	171	100	297
Repairs/rentals of lawn/garden equipment, hand/power tools, etc.	100	87	84	91	151	113	120	101
Appliance rental	100	127	129	138	74	34	21	56
Repair of computer systems for nonbusiness use	100	12	110	122	125	114	114	114
Computer information services	100	32	75	106	122	151	147	160
HOUSEKEEPING SUPPLIES ·	100	61	90	91	121	129	121	145
Laundry and cleaning supplies	100	86	99	104	113	101	102	99
Soaps and detergents	100	96	101	107	105	95	98	90
Other laundry cleaning products	100	74	97	99	123	109	108	111
Other household products	100	58	91	85	125	133	128	143
Cleansing and toilet tissue, paper towels, and napkins	100	89	97	98	115	105	104	108
Miscellaneous household products	100	47	95	89	125	131	132	128
Lawn and garden supplies	100	44	79	69	135	160	144	193
Postage and stationery	100	41	81	89	120	150	126	196
Stationery, stationery supplies, giftwrap	100	34	77	92	144	148	129	183
Postage	100	50	83	88	99	151	129	194
Delivery services	100	12	97	70	140	155	41	374
HOUSEHOLD FURNISHINGS AND EQUIPMENT	100	41	72	93	112	162	144	196
Household textiles	100	47	60	109	112	158	160	155
Bathroom linens	100	46	66	100	106	159	176	125
Bedroom linens	100	50	53	123	112	152	157	142
Kitchen and dining room linens	100	49	52	94	195	150	126	194
Curtains and draperies	100	46	68	85	81	185	160	229
Slipcovers and decorative pillows	100	45	49	122	79	169	159	188
Sewing materials for household items	100	40	76	98	131	149	157	137
Other linens	100	28	63	108	84	181	226	100
Furniture	100	48	69	88	102	171	147	213
Mattresses and springs	100	66	60	109	124	145	123	184
Other bedroom furniture	100	49	75	87	80	173	160	196
Sofas	100	53	69	85	116	165	139	212
Living room chairs	100	53	79	92	91	159	146	183
Living room tables	100	47	59	86	91	187	163	230
Kitchen and dining room furniture	100	31	53	76	99	207	151	307

	total consumer units	less than high school graduate	high school graduate	some college	associate's degree	college graduate total	bachelor's degree	master's, professional, doctorate
Infants' furniture	100	52	79	65	132	166	139	213
Outdoor furniture	100	30	41	80	79	225	194	280
Wall units, cabinets, and other furniture	100	36	87	93	105	154	141	177
Floor coverings	**100**	**20**	**80**	**76**	**98**	**187**	**145**	**261**
Wall-to-wall carpeting	100	20	103	91	119	144	130	169
Floor coverings, nonpermanent	100	19	50	57	70	244	165	383
Major appliances	**100**	**55**	**86**	**94**	**104**	**142**	**128**	**167**
Dishwashers (built-in), garbage disposals, range hoods	100	44	81	74	112	169	159	186
Refrigerators and freezers	100	75	87	106	111	119	110	135
Washing machines	100	64	79	97	119	138	138	140
Clothes dryers	100	67	73	104	104	142	157	116
Cooking stoves, ovens	100	43	71	93	110	164	131	222
Microwave ovens	100	58	85	98	100	141	126	168
Window air conditioners	100	140	76	69	229	81	63	111
Electric floor-cleaning equipment	100	23	129	75	37	146	116	201
Sewing machines	100	19	67	111	145	156	181	110
Miscellaneous household appliances	100	–	38	81	46	244	74	568
Small appliances and misc. housewares	**100**	**48**	**76**	**78**	**135**	**156**	**135**	**196**
Housewares	100	46	73	72	141	162	138	209
Plastic dinnerware	100	54	65	112	107	151	149	153
China and other dinnerware	100	69	74	62	211	135	104	195
Flatware	100	41	61	89	106	181	155	229
Glassware	100	20	58	55	106	213	164	308
Silver serving pieces	100	42	74	95	113	154	164	136
Other serving pieces	100	28	31	126	105	190	149	264
Nonelectric cookware	100	72	89	60	157	136	116	176
Tableware, nonelectric kitchenware	100	32	72	75	142	166	140	216
Small appliances	100	55	87	93	117	139	130	157
Small electric kitchen appliances	100	59	80	96	125	138	129	155
Portable heating and cooling equipment	100	47	101	85	97	142	131	162
Miscellaneous household equipment	**100**	**32**	**71**	**97**	**118**	**163**	**144**	**197**
Window coverings	100	16	41	91	108	213	185	263
Infants' equipment	100	63	84	96	34	157	139	192
Laundry and cleaning equipment	100	72	90	110	120	110	89	151
Outdoor equipment	100	30	63	130	117	145	174	91
Clocks	100	29	90	46	153	168	116	267
Lamps and lighting fixtures	100	32	64	83	75	199	153	279
Other household decorative items	100	31	59	97	135	167	161	178
Telephones and accessories	100	57	74	69	91	172	152	211
Lawn and garden equipment	100	31	108	91	217	97	103	86
Power tools	100	34	55	190	38	132	102	189
Office furniture for home use	100	7	35	116	53	225	155	349
Hand tools	100	78	113	74	144	103	112	88
Indoor plants and fresh flowers	100	42	68	85	120	172	165	184
Closet and storage items	100	41	63	111	113	155	156	154
Rental of furniture	100	162	152	59	59	59	51	70
Luggage	100	35	58	76	79	207	185	246
Computers and computer hardware, nonbusiness use	100	26	56	107	96	183	161	224
Computer software and accessories, nonbusiness use	100	30	49	110	95	187	165	225
Telephone answering devices	100	30	88	146	95	116	99	146
Calculators	100	24	54	154	103	148	150	146
Business equipment for home use	100	75	35	121	69	176	162	200
Other hardware	100	4	131	44	90	158	50	367
Smoke alarms	100	38	30	119	92	142	161	107
Other household appliances	100	47	64	75	231	141	127	166
Miscellaneous household equipment and parts	100	36	82	72	159	152	155	145

Note: (–) means sample is too small to make a reliable estimate.
Source: Calculations by New Strategist based on the 2003 Consumer Expenditure Survey

Table 8.27 Housing: Household Operations: Total spending by education, 2003

(total annual spending on household services, supplies, furnishings, and equipment, by consumer unit (CU) educational attainment group, 2003; numbers in thousands)

	total consumer units	less than high school graduate	high school graduate	some college	associate's degree	college graduate total	bachelor's degree	master's, professional, doctorate
Number of consumer units	115,356	17,721	31,552	24,514	10,981	30,589	19,557	11,032
Total spending of all CUs	$4,708,523,919	$423,552,102	$1,071,365,829	$929,384,819	$489,171,925	$1,788,844,720	$1,070,273,448	$719,316,517
Housing, total spending	1,549,446,796	147,987,008	344,656,694	300,536,002	154,388,687	600,495,412	359,009,609	241,684,423
HOUSEHOLD SERVICES	81,573,995	4,201,117	14,111,632	15,981,412	7,888,860	39,394,044	23,025,825	16,367,406
Personal services	33,860,447	1,450,287	6,293,677	5,845,363	3,657,222	16,614,415	10,090,434	6,523,884
Babysitting and child care in your own home	4,158,584	237,107	277,027	563,987	204,686	2,877,201	1,500,022	1,377,125
Babysitting and child care in someone else's home	2,767,390	275,030	763,558	546,417	310,652	871,481	722,631	148,822
Day care centers, nurseries, and preschools	21,781,520	570,616	3,803,278	3,847,472	2,860,221	10,700,338	7,060,664	3,639,457
Other household services	47,712,395	2,750,831	7,817,955	10,136,049	4,231,528	22,779,934	12,935,391	9,843,523
Housekeeping services	10,743,104	359,914	993,257	2,330,301	657,213	6,402,584	3,436,360	2,966,284
Gardening, lawn care service	9,655,297	524,896	1,546,679	1,938,322	748,904	4,896,381	2,765,555	2,130,831
Water softening service	372,600	25,518	102,860	52,460	57,760	134,592	66,885	67,736
Nonclothing laundry and dry cleaning, sent out	115,356	2,127	13,252	29,907	6,149	64,237	35,789	28,463
Nonclothing laundry and dry cleaning, coin-operated	417,589	115,187	109,801	88,496	27,672	76,167	53,586	22,395
Termite/pest control services	1,303,523	71,061	228,121	234,354	200,184	570,179	311,543	258,590
Home security system service fee	1,792,632	114,655	376,415	333,145	150,220	818,562	456,852	361,850
Other home services	1,710,729	103,668	331,612	314,269	131,882	829,574	461,545	368,028
Termite/pest control products	175,341	7,974	32,814	31,623	20,974	81,979	38,723	43,135
Moving, storage, and freight express	3,513,744	387,913	365,372	642,022	185,030	1,933,531	1,040,628	892,930
Appliance repair, including service center	1,355,433	121,212	330,349	260,339	123,646	519,707	306,654	213,249
Reupholstering and furniture repair	599,851	65,568	41,018	145,123	75,659	272,242	101,501	170,555
Repairs/rentals of lawn/garden equipment, hand/power tools, etc.	701,364	93,744	160,284	136,298	100,696	210,146	142,766	67,516
Appliance rental	188,030	36,682	66,575	55,157	13,177	17,130	6,845	10,149
Repair of computer systems for nonbusiness use	484,495	8,861	146,401	125,757	57,431	146,521	93,482	52,954
Computer information services	14,294,916	711,675	2,948,850	3,234,377	1,661,974	5,737,885	3,553,898	2,184,115
HOUSEKEEPING SUPPLIES	61,004,867	5,715,200	15,062,609	11,779,712	7,019,275	20,893,205	12,493,598	8,467,722
Laundry and cleaning supplies	15,259,292	2,023,915	4,131,103	3,357,683	1,636,389	4,096,173	2,646,453	1,447,619
Soaps and detergents	8,553,647	1,257,659	2,351,571	1,940,773	852,675	2,159,889	1,421,012	735,614
Other laundry cleaning products	6,705,644	766,256	1,779,848	1,416,909	783,824	1,936,590	1,225,442	712,005
Other household products	30,381,310	2,714,326	7,524,521	5,515,160	3,622,522	10,701,256	6,575,259	4,147,039
Cleansing and toilet tissue, paper towels, napkins	8,678,232	1,187,661	2,300,456	1,808,398	948,319	2,424,178	1,527,206	898,667
Miscellaneous household products	12,264,650	894,379	3,179,495	2,322,211	1,463,218	4,261,048	2,751,865	1,506,971
Lawn and garden supplies	9,438,428	632,285	2,044,885	1,384,551	1,210,875	4,016,336	2,296,383	1,741,401
Postage and stationery	15,364,266	976,959	3,406,669	2,906,870	1,760,474	6,095,470	3,271,691	2,873,064
Stationery, stationery supplies, giftwrap	6,869,450	357,078	1,451,076	1,347,044	941,950	2,688,161	1,500,413	1,205,136
Postage	7,952,643	609,957	1,811,085	1,479,420	746,488	3,184,315	1,734,119	1,474,096
Delivery services	542,173	10,101	144,508	80,406	72,035	222,688	37,354	193,832
HOUSEHOLD FURNISHINGS, EQUIPMENT	172,693,700	10,893,808	34,076,791	34,223,750	18,334,317	74,304,352	42,034,251	32,400,432
Household textiles	13,090,599	952,327	2,131,022	3,036,304	1,398,650	5,494,396	3,547,835	1,940,308
Bathroom linens	2,341,727	166,046	425,005	498,124	235,652	986,801	700,532	280,764
Bedroom linens	6,165,778	475,986	890,713	1,616,698	656,225	2,485,356	1,641,615	839,646
Kitchen and dining room linens	850,174	63,796	120,213	169,637	157,468	337,397	182,076	157,978
Curtains and draperies	1,758,025	124,047	327,194	310,102	135,066	861,080	475,822	385,348
Slipcovers and decorative pillows	501,799	34,379	67,837	130,169	37,775	224,829	135,530	90,021
Sewing materials for household items	1,300,062	80,808	270,085	271,615	162,519	515,119	345,377	169,782
Other linens	174,188	7,443	29,974	39,958	13,946	83,508	66,885	16,658
Furniture	46,236,992	3,378,331	8,775,242	8,656,139	4,471,793	20,955,912	11,536,479	9,419,673
Mattresses and springs	5,178,331	523,478	849,380	1,203,392	610,324	1,991,344	1,081,502	909,919
Other bedroom furniture	9,163,881	693,246	1,885,548	1,637,053	697,184	4,200,481	2,486,477	1,714,042
Sofas	10,632,363	870,987	2,013,018	1,910,376	1,172,661	4,664,823	2,512,879	2,152,123
Living room chairs	4,471,199	361,686	962,020	870,982	388,398	1,888,871	1,108,491	780,404
Living room tables	2,019,884	146,553	323,724	371,142	174,378	1,003,319	559,330	444,038
Kitchen and dining room furniture	5,700,894	273,789	830,764	919,765	539,387	3,136,596	1,462,472	1,674,216

	total consumer units	less than high school graduate	high school graduate	some college	associate's degree	college graduate total	bachelor's degree	master's professional doctorate
Infants' furniture	$942,459	$75,669	$203,510	$130,905	$118,265	$413,869	$221,776	$192,177
Outdoor furniture	1,770,715	82,934	196,569	301,032	132,760	1,057,462	583,776	473,493
Wall units, cabinets, and other furniture	6,359,576	349,990	1,510,710	1,261,490	638,435	2,598,841	1,519,774	1,079,261
Floor coverings	**5,970,827**	**178,982**	**1,311,932**	**965,606**	**554,541**	**2,960,098**	**1,467,753**	**1,492,299**
Wall-to-wall carpeting	3,403,002	104,554	957,603	656,485	384,115	1,300,644	749,424	551,379
Floor coverings, nonpermanent	2,567,825	74,428	354,644	309,122	170,425	1,659,453	718,524	940,919
Major appliances	**22,575,169**	**1,906,248**	**5,312,095**	**4,527,000**	**2,233,096**	**8,475,906**	**4,892,770**	**3,602,720**
Dishwashers (built-in), garbage disposals, range hoods	1,557,306	105,972	344,232	245,140	166,252	695,900	419,302	276,572
Refrigerators and freezers	5,486,331	634,057	1,303,729	1,235,260	582,103	1,730,420	1,023,222	707,151
Washing machines	3,308,410	324,117	710,867	684,186	374,891	1,214,689	771,328	443,486
Clothes dryers	2,241,367	231,968	445,199	495,673	221,706	846,704	597,271	249,654
Cooking stoves, ovens	3,517,204	234,980	635,625	693,649	368,852	1,530,062	782,671	747,308
Microwave ovens	872,091	77,795	202,248	181,404	83,346	326,996	186,378	140,437
Window air conditioners	622,922	133,616	130,310	90,947	135,615	133,062	66,885	66,192
Electric floor-cleaning equipment	3,488,365	121,920	1,228,319	557,694	121,889	1,346,222	688,798	670,966
Sewing machines	1,032,436	30,126	190,259	243,424	142,533	425,799	317,606	108,224
Miscellaneous household appliances	258,397	–	26,504	44,370	11,420	167,016	32,465	140,437
Small appliances and misc. housewares	**10,123,643**	**749,953**	**2,113,037**	**1,669,403**	**1,300,590**	**4,198,034**	**2,325,523**	**1,894,636**
Housewares	7,526,979	530,744	1,496,827	1,157,061	1,012,009	3,238,152	1,755,241	1,504,985
Plastic dinnerware	179,955	15,063	32,183	42,900	18,338	71,884	45,372	26,256
China and other dinnerware	812,106	85,770	164,701	106,881	162,848	290,596	142,962	151,138
Flatware	460,270	29,240	76,356	87,270	46,340	221,464	120,667	100,832
Glassware	1,025,515	31,189	161,546	119,628	103,661	579,967	284,945	301,946
Silver serving pieces	750,968	48,556	152,712	151,251	80,820	307,114	208,478	97,744
Other serving pieces	166,113	7,088	13,883	44,370	16,581	83,814	42,048	41,922
Nonelectric cookware	1,760,333	195,463	427,530	224,548	263,215	636,863	345,768	295,768
Tableware, nonelectric kitchenware	2,371,719	118,199	467,601	380,457	320,206	1,046,144	564,806	489,490
Small appliances	2,596,664	219,386	615,895	512,343	288,581	959,883	570,282	389,650
Small electric kitchen appliances	1,806,475	162,502	397,240	368,936	215,337	662,252	395,051	267,305
Portable heating and cooling equipment	790,189	56,884	218,655	143,407	73,243	297,631	175,426	122,235
Miscellaneous household equipment	**74,696,471**	**3,727,967**	**14,433,462**	**15,369,543**	**8,375,648**	**32,219,700**	**18,263,891**	**14,050,796**
Window coverings	2,807,765	68,403	318,675	544,211	289,240	1,587,569	882,021	705,496
Infants' equipment	1,508,856	146,907	348,650	308,386	48,426	628,298	355,155	276,793
Laundry and cleaning equipment	1,618,445	178,096	397,871	379,722	185,579	473,824	244,463	234,099
Outdoor equipment	2,738,551	124,401	472,018	755,767	304,833	1,055,626	805,944	239,284
Clocks	463,731	20,556	114,218	44,861	67,643	206,170	90,940	118,484
Lamps and lighting fixtures	1,575,763	78,504	276,080	279,460	112,445	829,880	408,937	420,871
Other household decorative items	14,624,834	699,271	2,367,662	3,027,234	1,874,017	6,460,703	3,979,850	2,492,680
Telephones and accessories	3,089,234	272,726	625,992	453,019	268,266	1,412,294	796,752	623,970
Lawn and garden equipment	6,389,569	307,814	1,879,553	1,241,389	1,321,893	1,638,653	1,115,727	522,806
Power tools	2,812,379	146,198	425,636	1,136,224	102,233	982,825	486,383	507,693
Office furniture for home use	1,454,639	15,949	139,460	358,150	72,804	868,116	382,144	486,070
Hand tools	832,870	100,301	258,095	131,640	113,873	228,500	158,803	69,722
Indoor plants and fresh flowers	4,650,000	298,776	865,156	835,927	533,128	2,116,759	1,298,780	817,802
Closet and storage items	1,103,957	68,757	188,996	260,584	118,705	454,247	291,790	162,281
Rental of furniture	311,461	77,618	129,363	38,977	17,570	48,331	27,184	20,961
Luggage	712,900	37,923	113,272	115,796	53,697	392,151	224,123	168,017
Computers and computer hardware, nonbusiness use	15,777,240	627,855	2,433,290	3,603,803	1,437,742	7,674,168	4,299,020	3,375,240
Computer software and accessories, nonbusiness use	2,074,101	94,099	277,973	486,603	187,665	1,028,096	581,821	446,244
Telephone answering devices	107,281	4,962	25,873	33,339	9,663	33,036	17,992	15,004
Calculators	146,502	5,316	21,455	48,047	14,385	57,507	37,158	20,520
Business equipment for home use	124,584	14,354	11,990	32,113	8,236	58,119	34,225	23,829
Other hardware	4,423,903	28,885	1,583,910	413,796	380,821	1,858,588	371,387	1,551,651
Smoke alarms	130,352	7,620	28,597	33,094	11,420	49,248	35,594	13,349
Other household appliances	769,425	55,290	135,043	122,080	169,437	287,842	165,843	122,014
Miscellaneous household equipment and parts	4,449,281	247,208	994,204	685,166	672,037	1,790,068	1,171,855	615,917

Note: Numbers may not add to total because of rounding and missing subcategories. (–) means sample is too small to make a reliable estimate.
Source: Calculations by New Strategist based on the 2003 Consumer Expenditure Survey

Table 8.28 Housing: Household Operations: Market shares by education, 2003

(percentage of total annual spending on household services, supplies, furnishings, and equipment accounted for by consumer unit educational attainment groups, 2003)

	total consumer units	less than high school graduate	high school graduate	some college	associate's degree	college graduate total	bachelor's degree	master's, professional, doctorate
Share of total consumer units	100.0%	15.4%	27.4%	21.3%	9.5%	26.5%	17.0%	9.6%
Share of total before-tax income	100.0	7.5	21.5	18.8	10.1	42.4	24.8	17.6
Share of total spending	100.0	9.0	22.8	19.7	10.4	38.0	22.7	15.3
Share of housing spending	100.0	9.6	22.2	19.4	10.0	38.8	23.2	15.6
HOUSEHOLD SERVICES	100.0	5.2	17.3	19.6	9.7	48.3	28.2	20.1
Personal services	100.0	4.3	18.6	17.3	10.8	49.1	29.8	19.3
Babysitting and child care in your own home	100.0	5.7	6.7	13.5	4.9	69.2	36.1	33.1
Babysitting and child care in someone else's home	100.0	9.9	27.6	19.7	11.2	31.5	26.1	5.4
Day care centers, nurseries, and preschools	100.0	2.6	17.5	17.7	13.1	49.1	32.4	16.7
Other household services	100.0	5.8	16.4	21.2	8.9	47.7	27.1	20.6
Housekeeping services	100.0	3.4	9.2	21.7	6.1	59.6	32.0	27.6
Gardening, lawn care service	100.0	5.4	16.0	20.1	7.8	50.7	28.6	22.1
Water softening service	100.0	6.8	27.6	14.1	15.5	36.1	18.0	18.2
Nonclothing laundry and dry cleaning, sent out	100.0	1.8	11.5	25.9	5.3	55.7	31.0	24.7
Nonclothing laundry and dry cleaning, coin-operated	100.0	27.6	26.3	21.2	6.6	18.2	12.8	5.4
Termite/pest control services	100.0	5.5	17.5	18.0	15.4	43.7	23.9	19.8
Home security system service fee	100.0	6.4	21.0	18.6	8.4	45.7	25.5	20.2
Other home services	100.0	6.1	19.4	18.4	7.7	48.5	27.0	21.5
Termite/pest control products	100.0	4.5	18.7	18.0	12.0	46.8	22.1	24.6
Moving, storage, and freight express	100.0	11.0	10.4	18.3	5.3	55.0	29.6	25.4
Appliance repair, including service center	100.0	8.9	24.4	19.2	9.1	38.3	22.6	15.7
Reupholstering and furniture repair	100.0	10.9	6.8	24.2	12.6	45.4	16.9	28.4
Repairs/rentals of lawn/garden equipment, hand/power tools, etc.	100.0	13.4	22.9	19.4	14.4	30.0	20.4	9.6
Appliance rental	100.0	19.5	35.4	29.3	7.0	9.1	3.6	5.4
Repair of computer systems for nonbusiness use	100.0	1.8	30.2	26.0	11.9	30.2	19.3	10.9
Computer information services	100.0	5.0	20.6	22.6	11.6	40.1	24.9	15.3
HOUSEKEEPING SUPPLIES	100.0	9.4	24.7	19.3	11.5	34.2	20.5	13.9
Laundry and cleaning supplies	100.0	13.3	27.1	22.0	10.7	26.8	17.3	9.5
Soaps and detergents	100.0	14.7	27.5	22.7	10.0	25.3	16.6	8.6
Other laundry cleaning products	100.0	11.4	26.5	21.1	11.7	28.9	18.3	10.6
Other household products	100.0	8.9	24.8	18.2	11.9	35.2	21.6	13.6
Cleansing and toilet tissue, paper towels, and napkins	100.0	13.7	26.5	20.8	10.9	27.9	17.6	10.4
Miscellaneous household products	100.0	7.3	25.9	18.9	11.9	34.7	22.4	12.3
Lawn and garden supplies	100.0	6.7	21.7	14.7	12.8	42.6	24.3	18.5
Postage and stationery	100.0	6.4	22.2	18.9	11.5	39.7	21.3	18.7
Stationery, stationery supplies, giftwrap	100.0	5.2	21.1	19.6	13.7	39.1	21.8	17.5
Postage	100.0	7.7	22.8	18.6	9.4	40.0	21.8	18.5
Delivery services	100.0	1.9	26.7	14.8	13.3	41.1	6.9	35.8
HOUSEHOLD FURNISHINGS AND EQUIPMENT	100.0	6.3	19.7	19.8	10.6	43.0	24.3	18.8
Household textiles	100.0	7.3	16.3	23.2	10.7	42.0	27.1	14.8
Bathroom linens	100.0	7.1	18.1	21.3	10.1	42.1	29.9	12.0
Bedroom linens	100.0	7.7	14.4	26.2	10.6	40.3	26.6	13.6
Kitchen and dining room linens	100.0	7.5	14.1	20.0	18.5	39.7	21.4	18.6
Curtains and draperies	100.0	7.1	18.6	17.6	7.7	49.0	27.1	21.9
Slipcovers and decorative pillows	100.0	6.9	13.5	25.9	7.5	44.8	27.0	17.9
Sewing materials for household items	100.0	6.2	20.8	20.9	12.5	39.6	26.6	13.1
Other linens	100.0	4.3	17.2	22.9	8.0	47.9	38.4	9.6
Furniture	100.0	7.3	19.0	18.7	9.7	45.3	25.0	20.4
Mattresses and springs	100.0	10.1	16.4	23.2	11.8	38.5	20.9	17.6
Other bedroom furniture	100.0	7.6	20.6	18.4	7.6	45.8	27.1	18.7
Sofas	100.0	8.2	18.9	18.0	11.0	43.9	23.6	20.2
Living room chairs	100.0	8.1	21.5	19.5	8.7	42.2	24.8	17.5
Living room tables	100.0	7.3	16.0	18.4	8.6	49.7	27.7	22.0
Kitchen and dining room furniture	100.0	4.8	14.6	16.1	9.5	55.0	25.7	29.4

	total consumer units	less than high school graduate	high school graduate	some college	associate's degree	college graduate total	bachelor's degree	master's, professional, doctorate
Infants' furniture	100.0%	8.0%	21.6%	13.5%	12.5%	43.9%	23.5%	20.4%
Outdoor furniture	100.0	4.7	11.1	17.0	7.5	59.7	33.0	26.7
Wall units, cabinets, and other furniture	100.0	5.5	25.8	19.8	10.0	40.9	23.9	17.0
Floor coverings	**100.0**	**3.0**	**22.0**	**16.2**	**9.3**	**49.6**	**24.6**	**25.0**
Wall-to-wall carpeting	100.0	3.1	28.1	19.3	11.3	38.2	22.0	16.2
Floor coverings, nonpermanent	100.0	2.9	13.8	12.0	6.6	64.6	28.0	36.6
Major appliances	**100.0**	**8.4**	**23.5**	**20.1**	**9.9**	**37.5**	**21.7**	**16.0**
Dishwashers (built-in), garbage disposals, range hoods	100.0	6.8	22.1	15.7	10.7	44.7	26.9	17.8
Refrigerators and freezers	100.0	11.6	23.8	22.5	10.6	31.5	18.7	12.9
Washing machines	100.0	9.8	21.5	20.7	11.3	36.7	23.3	13.4
Clothes dryers	100.0	10.3	19.9	22.1	9.9	37.8	26.6	11.1
Cooking stoves, ovens	100.0	6.7	19.5	19.9	10.5	43.5	22.3	21.2
Microwave ovens	100.0	8.9	23.2	20.8	9.6	37.5	21.4	16.1
Window air conditioners	100.0	21.4	20.9	14.6	21.8	21.4	10.7	10.6
Electric floor-cleaning equipment	100.0	3.5	35.2	16.0	3.5	38.6	19.7	19.2
Sewing machines	100.0	2.9	18.4	23.6	13.8	41.2	30.8	10.5
Miscellaneous household appliances	100.0	–	10.3	17.2	4.4	64.6	12.6	54.3
Small appliances and misc. housewares	**100.0**	**7.4**	**20.9**	**16.5**	**12.8**	**41.5**	**23.0**	**18.7**
Housewares	100.0	7.1	19.9	15.4	13.4	43.0	23.3	20.0
Plastic dinnerware	100.0	8.4	17.9	23.8	10.2	39.9	25.2	14.6
China and other dinnerware	100.0	10.6	20.3	13.2	20.1	35.8	17.6	18.6
Flatware	100.0	6.4	16.6	13.0	10.1	48.1	26.2	21.9
Glassware	100.0	3.0	15.8	11.7	10.1	56.6	27.8	29.4
Silver serving pieces	100.0	6.5	20.3	20.1	10.8	40.9	27.8	13.0
Other serving pieces	100.0	4.3	8.4	26.7	10.0	50.5	25.3	25.2
Nonelectric cookware	100.0	11.1	24.3	12.8	15.0	36.2	19.6	16.8
Tableware, nonelectric kitchenware	100.0	5.0	19.7	16.0	13.5	44.1	23.8	20.6
Small appliances	100.0	8.4	23.7	19.7	11.1	37.0	22.0	15.0
Small electric kitchen appliances	100.0	9.0	22.0	20.4	11.9	36.7	21.9	14.8
Portable heating and cooling equipment	100.0	7.2	27.7	18.1	9.3	37.7	22.2	15.5
Miscellaneous household equipment	**100.0**	**5.0**	**19.3**	**20.6**	**11.2**	**43.1**	**24.5**	**18.8**
Window coverings	100.0	2.4	11.3	19.4	10.3	56.5	31.4	25.1
Infants' equipment	100.0	9.7	23.1	20.4	3.2	41.6	23.5	18.3
Laundry and cleaning equipment	100.0	11.0	24.6	23.5	11.5	29.3	15.1	14.5
Outdoor equipment	100.0	4.5	17.2	27.6	11.1	38.5	29.4	8.7
Clocks	100.0	4.4	24.6	9.7	14.6	44.5	19.6	25.6
Lamps and lighting fixtures	100.0	5.0	17.5	17.7	7.1	52.7	26.0	26.7
Other household decorative items	100.0	4.8	15.2	20.7	12.8	44.2	27.2	17.0
Telephones and accessories	100.0	8.8	20.3	14.7	8.7	45.7	25.8	20.2
Lawn and garden equipment	100.0	4.8	29.4	19.4	20.7	25.6	17.5	8.2
Power tools	100.0	5.2	15.1	40.4	3.6	34.9	17.3	18.1
Office furniture for home use	100.0	1.1	9.6	24.6	5.0	59.7	26.3	33.4
Hand tools	100.0	12.0	31.0	15.8	13.7	27.4	19.1	8.4
Indoor plants and fresh flowers	100.0	6.4	18.6	18.0	11.5	45.5	27.9	17.6
Closet and storage items	100.0	6.2	17.1	23.6	10.8	41.1	26.4	14.7
Rental of furniture	100.0	24.9	41.5	12.5	5.6	15.5	8.7	6.7
Luggage	100.0	5.3	15.9	16.2	7.5	55.0	31.4	23.6
Computers and computer hardware, nonbusiness use	100.0	4.0	15.4	22.8	9.1	48.6	27.2	21.4
Computer software and accessories, nonbusiness use	100.0	4.5	13.4	23.5	9.0	49.6	28.1	21.5
Telephone answering devices	100.0	4.6	24.1	31.1	9.0	30.8	16.8	14.0
Calculators	100.0	3.6	14.6	32.8	9.8	39.3	25.4	14.0
Business equipment for home use	100.0	11.5	9.6	25.8	6.6	46.7	27.5	19.1
Other hardware	100.0	0.7	35.8	9.4	8.6	42.0	8.4	35.1
Smoke alarms	100.0	5.8	21.8	25.4	8.8	37.8	27.3	10.2
Other household appliances	100.0	7.2	17.5	15.9	22.0	37.4	21.6	15.9
Miscellaneous household equipment and parts	100.0	5.6	22.3	15.4	15.1	40.2	26.3	13.8

Note: Numbers may not add to total because of rounding. (–) means sample is too small to make a reliable estimate.
Source: Calculations by New Strategist based on the 2003 Consumer Expenditure Survey

Spending on Shelter and Utilities, 2003

Housing is by far Americans' biggest expense. In 2003, housing costs—including shelter, utilities, and household operations—absorbed 32.9 percent of average household expenditures. That figure was up from 32.4 percent in 2000. Spending on shelter rose 4 percent between 2000 and 2003, after adjusting for inflation. Spending on owned homes rose 7 percent while spending on rented homes barely increased—up just 0.3 percent. Spending on "other lodging," such as hotels and motels, fell 13 percent because of the struggling economy. Spending on utilities and fuels increased 13 percent because of rising energy prices.

Overall housing costs are highest for householders aged 35 to 44, at $16,098 in 2003. This age group spends much more than any other on mortgage interest—$4,410 in 2003. Second in spending on mortgage interest are householders aged 45 to 54, devoting $3,885 to this item in 2003. Spending on maintenance and repair services for owned homes is greatest among householders aged 65 to 74. Householders aged 25 to 34 spend the most on rent.

Households with incomes of $100,000 or more spent $28,941 on housing in 2003, more than twice the $13,653 spent by the average income-reporting household. They devote more than $8,000 to mortgage interest alone. The most affluent households account for a large share of the market in a number of shelter categories: 41 percent of the market for lodging while on trips, 49 percent of the market for owned vacation homes, and 51 percent of the market for housing while attending school.

Among household types, married couples with children under age 18 spend the most on housing, more than $19,000 in 2003. Behind this figure is the high cost of housing for recent home-buyers—many married couples with young children are new homeowners. This household type spends more than twice as much as the average household on mortgage interest. Married couples without children at home (most of them empty-nesters) spend nearly twice the average on owned vacation homes and 67 percent more than average on lodging while on trips.

Asian households spend 22 percent more than the average household on housing, while the spending of black and Hispanic households is below average. Asians spend 50 percent more than average on mortgage interest, in part because many Asians live in California, where housing costs are high. Blacks spend 35 percent more than the average household on rent, while Hispanics spend 64 percent more. Blacks spend 19 percent more than average on residential telephone service, while Hispanics spend more than three times the average on phone cards.

Households in the West spend the most on housing, $15,371 in 2003, because of the high cost of housing in California. Housing costs are lowest in the South, at $12,006. Western households spend 38 percent more than the average household on mortgage interest. Households in the Northeast spend 20 percent more than average on lodging while on trips, while households in the South spend 22 percent more than average on electricity.

Not surprisingly, college graduates (who dominate the nation's affluent households) spend the most on housing, an average of $19,631 in 2003. They spend far more than the average household on almost every shelter category. They spend 70 percent more than average on mortgage interest, and more than twice the average on lodging while on trips and owned vacation homes.

Table 9.1 Housing: Shelter and Utilities: Average spending by age, 2003

(average annual spending of consumer units (CU) on shelter and utilities, by age of consumer unit reference person, 2003)

	total consumer units	under 25	25 to 34	35 to 44	45 to 54	55 to 64	65 to 74	75+
Number of consumer units (000)	115,356	8,584	19,737	24,413	23,131	16,580	11,495	11,417
Average number of persons per CU	2.5	1.8	2.9	3.2	2.6	2.1	1.9	1.5
Average before-tax income of CU	$51,128.00	$20,680.00	$50,389.00	$61,091.00	$68,028.00	$58,672.00	$35,314.00	$25,492.00
Average spending of CU, total	40,817.33	22,395.53	40,525.22	47,175.06	50,100.86	44,190.65	33,629.17	25,016.38
Housing, average spending	**13,431.87**	**7,094.92**	**14,392.28**	**16,097.66**	**15,623.93**	**13,713.92**	**10,760.59**	**8,677.59**
SHELTER	**7,887.40**	**4,574.38**	**8,915.03**	**9,678.28**	**9,237.25**	**7,571.49**	**5,763.89**	**4,634.61**
Owned dwellings*	**5,262.95**	**765.42**	**4,837.04**	**6,940.46**	**6,893.19**	**5,769.28**	**4,300.24**	**2,725.11**
Mortgage interest and charges	2,954.01	449.01	3,373.38	4,540.62	4,088.31	2,739.41	1,348.78	349.82
Mortgage interest	2,830.50	446.48	3,311.40	4,409.65	3,885.01	2,535.15	1,234.01	315.03
Interest paid, home equity loan	64.00	1.37	33.98	79.21	98.56	99.43	57.01	16.02
Interest paid, home equity line of credit	58.47	1.16	28.00	51.76	100.81	104.83	57.76	16.24
Property taxes	1,343.82	229.65	910.01	1,479.00	1,625.29	1,769.63	1,471.75	1,325.05
Maintenance, repairs, insurance, other expenses	965.11	86.76	553.65	920.84	1,179.59	1,260.24	1,479.70	1,050.24
Homeowner's insurance	287.43	34.18	196.19	300.03	354.08	366.14	366.29	279.92
Ground rent	40.58	13.46	38.80	40.54	40.22	42.50	55.13	47.41
Maintenance and repair services	516.31	26.91	230.22	443.54	631.81	698.12	962.52	587.12
Painting and papering	60.58	1.42	24.24	65.11	69.89	103.24	93.23	44.52
Plumbing and water heating	48.43	1.30	25.73	44.70	56.97	59.95	78.95	66.39
Heat, air conditioning, electrical work	85.39	7.69	51.88	74.28	93.34	118.21	138.61	108.09
Roofing and gutters	97.98	1.56	28.67	79.27	89.60	156.04	184.11	176.27
Other repair and maintenance services	172.07	10.93	85.11	120.41	260.96	182.10	373.51	156.56
Repair, replacement of hard-surface flooring	45.89	4.02	11.08	53.53	54.34	68.61	88.84	27.81
Repair of built-in appliances	5.97	–	3.51	6.24	6.72	9.96	5.28	7.48
Maintenance and repair materials	78.80	7.64	65.34	108.52	110.28	95.42	51.64	31.43
Paints, wallpaper, and supplies	12.22	2.85	10.48	13.90	19.18	14.25	9.34	4.54
Tools, equipment for painting, wallpapering	1.31	0.31	1.13	1.49	2.06	1.53	1.00	0.49
Plumbing supplies and equipment	5.37	0.26	2.95	5.63	5.12	10.55	5.16	6.08
Electrical supplies, heating and cooling equipment	3.38	0.15	2.91	4.90	2.61	6.52	3.01	0.78
Hard-surface flooring, repair and replacement	15.40	1.05	17.85	21.30	19.39	18.35	7.37	5.05
Roofing and gutters	6.91	0.05	7.24	9.12	12.55	3.07	4.68	3.14
Plaster, paneling, siding, windows, doors, screens, awnings	16.81	0.02	8.93	20.70	33.34	19.93	8.29	5.25
Patio, walk, fence, driveway, masonry, brick, and stucco materials	1.42	–	1.17	2.08	1.69	2.52	0.55	0.28
Miscellaneous supplies and equipment	15.84	2.90	12.52	29.35	13.94	18.62	12.24	5.84
Property management and security	36.52	4.04	20.37	24.25	38.49	52.98	36.16	87.59
Property management	33.03	3.86	18.90	22.10	36.16	49.20	31.30	74.66
Management and upkeep services for security	3.49	0.18	1.47	2.15	2.33	3.78	4.86	12.93
Parking	5.47	0.53	2.72	3.96	4.71	5.08	7.96	16.77
Rented dwellings	**2,179.49**	**3,592.77**	**3,835.41**	**2,315.06**	**1,656.44**	**1,179.47**	**1,044.95**	**1,618.64**
Rent	2,109.74	3,526.93	3,743.37	2,236.85	1,590.87	1,140.30	1,000.91	1,523.74
Rent as pay	32.98	45.20	29.36	41.84	32.04	16.66	32.90	36.82
Maintenance, insurance, and other expenses	36.77	20.64	62.68	36.38	33.53	22.51	11.14	58.08
Tenant's insurance	9.67	7.97	12.55	8.67	9.54	8.52	7.17	12.60
Maintenance and repair services	16.88	5.35	33.30	7.89	17.41	7.86	2.39	42.97
Maintenance and repair materials	10.23	7.32	16.83	19.82	6.58	6.13	1.58	2.51
Other lodging	**444.96**	**216.19**	**242.58**	**422.76**	**687.62**	**622.75**	**418.71**	**290.86**
Owned vacation homes	150.29	9.55	54.49	128.61	245.51	223.72	183.26	135.34
Mortgage interest and charges	61.55	0.32	32.74	67.51	123.38	74.61	45.07	17.07
Property taxes	58.90	7.57	14.41	43.11	78.16	99.16	81.97	87.41
Maintenance, insurance, and other expenses	29.84	1.66	7.34	17.99	43.97	49.95	56.22	30.86
Housing while attending school	52.90	140.38	10.15	30.33	123.89	49.71	20.79	2.41
Lodging on trips	241.77	66.27	177.95	263.82	318.22	349.33	214.66	153.11

	total consumer units	under 25	25 to 34	35 to 44	45 to 54	55 to 64	65 to 74	75+
UTILITIES, FUELS, PUBLIC SERVICES	**$2,811.43**	**$1,329.14**	**$2,580.10**	**$3,142.29**	**$3,334.75**	**$3,088.88**	**$2,722.93**	**$2,244.32**
Natural gas	**392.01**	**117.93**	**341.19**	**427.09**	**467.74**	**431.90**	**411.02**	**380.44**
Electricity	**1,027.91**	**470.15**	**915.40**	**1,144.88**	**1,198.93**	**1,153.15**	**1,046.09**	**845.07**
Fuel oil and other fuels	**109.52**	**23.45**	**61.52**	**108.67**	**129.31**	**146.15**	**140.00**	**135.04**
Fuel oil	57.54	10.38	28.31	62.01	64.73	71.25	73.84	83.15
Bottled and tank gas	42.42	11.22	28.56	37.66	51.94	61.39	56.68	38.66
Wood and other fuels	9.10	1.84	4.22	8.97	11.40	13.38	8.53	12.98
Telephone services	**955.70**	**615.62**	**1,001.39**	**1,096.67**	**1,155.95**	**981.46**	**773.48**	**571.84**
Residential telephone and pay phones	619.60	277.66	591.70	695.68	724.34	680.45	585.89	495.63
Cellular phone service	316.10	313.38	376.56	379.35	413.09	284.93	172.93	71.16
Pager service	1.12	0.34	1.14	1.43	1.49	1.39	0.87	0.12
Phone cards	18.88	24.25	31.58	20.22	17.02	14.70	13.79	4.94
Water and other public services	**326.29**	**102.00**	**260.91**	**364.97**	**382.81**	**376.23**	**352.34**	**311.92**
Water and sewerage maintenance	236.30	78.12	192.10	270.11	277.34	269.48	251.23	213.01
Trash and garbage collection	87.63	23.88	66.65	92.30	102.53	104.09	98.44	96.89
Septic tank cleaning	2.35	–	2.16	2.56	2.95	2.67	2.67	2.02

* See appendix for information about mortgage principal reduction.
Note: Subcategories may not add to total because some are not shown. (–) means sample is too small to make a reliable estimate.
Source: Bureau of Labor Statistics, unpublished tables from the 2003 Consumer Expenditure Survey

Table 9.2 Housing: Shelter and Utilities: Indexed spending by age, 2003

(indexed average annual spending of consumer units (CU) on shelter and utilities, by age of consumer unit reference person, 2003; index definition: an index of 100 is the average for all consumer units; an index of 132 means that spending by consumer units in that group is 32 percent above the average for all consumer units; an index of 68 indicates spending that is 32 percent below the average for all consumer units)

	total consumer units	under 25	25 to 34	35 to 44	45 to 54	55 to 64	65 to 74	75+
Average spending of CU, total	$40,817	$22,396	$40,525	$47,175	$50,101	$44,191	$33,629	$25,016
Average spending of CU, index	100	55	99	116	123	108	82	61
Housing, spending index	100	53	107	120	116	102	80	65
SHELTER	100	58	113	123	117	96	73	59
Owned dwellings*	100	15	92	132	131	110	82	52
Mortgage interest and charges	100	15	114	154	138	93	46	12
Mortgage interest	100	16	117	156	137	90	44	11
Interest paid, home equity loan	100	2	53	124	154	155	89	25
Interest paid, home equity line of credit	100	2	48	89	172	179	99	28
Property taxes	100	17	68	110	121	132	110	99
Maintenance, repairs, insurance, other expenses	100	9	57	95	122	131	153	109
Homeowner's insurance	100	12	68	104	123	127	127	97
Ground rent	100	33	96	100	99	105	136	117
Maintenance and repair services	100	5	45	86	122	135	186	114
Painting and papering	100	2	40	108	115	170	154	74
Plumbing and water heating	100	3	53	92	118	124	163	137
Heat, air conditioning, electrical work	100	9	61	87	109	138	162	127
Other repair and maintenance services	100	6	50	70	152	106	217	91
Repair, replacement of hard-surface flooring	100	9	24	117	118	150	194	61
Repair of built-in appliances	100	–	59	105	113	167	88	125
Maintenance and repair materials	100	10	83	138	140	121	66	40
Paints, wallpaper, and supplies	100	23	86	114	157	117	76	37
Tools, equipment for painting, wallpapering	100	24	86	114	157	117	76	37
Plumbing supplies and equipment	100	5	55	105	95	197	96	113
Electrical supplies, heating and cooling equipment	100	4	86	145	77	193	89	23
Hard-surface flooring, repair and replacement	100	7	116	138	126	119	48	33
Roofing and gutters	100	1	105	132	182	44	68	45
Plaster, paneling, siding, windows, doors, screens, awnings	100	0	53	123	198	119	49	31
Patio, walk, fence, driveway, masonry, brick, and stucco materials	100	–	82	147	119	178	39	20
Miscellaneous supplies and equipment	100	18	79	185	88	118	77	37
Property management and security	100	11	56	66	105	145	99	240
Property management	100	12	57	67	110	149	95	226
Management and upkeep services for security	100	5	42	62	67	108	139	371
Parking	100	10	50	72	86	93	146	307
Rented dwellings	100	165	176	106	76	54	48	74
Rent	100	167	177	106	75	54	47	72
Rent as pay	100	137	89	127	97	51	100	112
Maintenance, insurance, and other expenses	100	56	171	99	91	61	30	158
Tenant's insurance	100	82	130	90	99	88	74	130
Maintenance and repair services	100	32	197	47	103	47	14	255
Maintenance and repair materials	100	72	165	194	64	60	15	25
Other lodging	100	49	55	95	155	140	94	65
Owned vacation homes	100	6	36	86	163	149	122	90
Mortgage interest and charges	100	1	53	110	201	121	73	28
Property taxes	100	13	25	73	133	168	139	148
Maintenance, insurance, and other expenses	100	6	25	60	147	167	188	103
Housing while attending school	100	265	19	57	234	94	39	5
Lodging on trips	100	27	74	109	132	145	89	63

	total consumer units	under 25	25 to 34	35 to 44	45 to 54	55 to 64	65 to 74	75+
UTILITIES, FUELS, AND PUBLIC SERVICES	100	47	92	112	119	110	97	80
Natural gas	100	30	87	109	119	110	105	97
Electricity	100	46	89	111	117	112	102	82
Fuel oil and other fuels	100	21	55	99	118	133	128	123
Fuel oil	100	18	49	108	113	124	128	145
Bottled and tank gas	100	26	68	89	122	145	134	91
Wood and other fuels	100	20	46	99	125	147	94	143
Telephone services	100	64	105	115	121	103	81	60
Residential telephone and pay phones	100	45	96	112	117	110	95	80
Cellular phone service	100	99	119	120	131	90	55	23
Pager service	100	30	102	128	133	124	78	11
Phone cards	100	128	157	107	90	78	73	26
Water and other public services	100	31	80	112	117	115	108	96
Water and sewerage maintenance	100	33	81	114	117	114	106	90
Trash and garbage collection	100	27	76	105	117	119	112	111
Septic tank cleaning	100	–	92	109	126	114	114	86

* See appendix for information about mortgage principal reduction.
Note: (–) means sample is too small to make a reliable estimate.
Source: Calculations by New Strategist based on the 2003 Consumer Expenditure Survey

Table 9.3 Housing: Shelter and Utilities: Total spending by age, 2003

(total annual spending on shelter and utilities, by consumer unit (CU) age groups, 2003; numbers in thousands)

	total consumer units	under 25	25 to 34	35 to 44	45 to 54	55 to 64	65 to 74	75+
Number of consumer units	115,356	8,584	19,737	24,413	23,131	16,580	11,495	11,417
Total spending of all CUs	$4,708,523,920	$192,243,230	$799,846,267	$1,151,684,740	$1,158,882,993	$732,680,977	$386,567,309	$285,612,011
Housing, total spending	1,549,446,796	60,902,793	284,060,430	392,992,174	361,397,125	227,376,794	123,692,982	99,072,045
SHELTER	909,858,914	39,266,478	175,955,947	236,275,850	213,666,830	125,535,304	66,255,916	52,913,342
Owned dwellings*	607,112,860	6,570,365	95,468,659	169,437,450	159,446,378	95,654,662	49,431,259	31,112,581
Mortgage interest and charges	340,762,778	3,854,302	66,580,401	110,850,156	94,566,699	45,419,418	15,504,226	3,993,895
Mortgage interest	326,515,158	3,832,584	65,357,102	107,652,785	89,864,166	42,032,787	14,184,945	3,596,698
Interest paid, home equity loan	7,382,784	11,760	670,663	1,933,754	2,279,791	1,648,549	655,330	182,900
Interest paid, home equity line of credit	6,744,865	9,957	552,636	1,263,617	2,331,836	1,738,081	663,951	185,412
Property taxes	155,017,700	1,971,316	17,960,867	36,106,827	37,594,583	29,340,465	16,917,766	15,128,096
Maintenance, repairs, insurance, other expenses	111,331,229	744,748	10,927,390	22,480,467	27,285,096	20,894,779	17,009,152	11,990,590
Homeowner's insurance	33,156,775	293,401	3,872,202	7,324,632	8,190,225	6,070,601	4,210,504	3,195,847
Ground rent	4,681,147	115,541	765,796	989,703	930,329	704,650	633,719	541,280
Maintenance and repair services	59,559,456	230,995	4,543,852	10,828,142	14,614,397	11,574,830	11,064,167	6,703,149
Painting and papering	6,988,267	12,189	478,425	1,589,530	1,616,626	1,711,719	1,071,679	508,285
Plumbing and water heating	5,586,691	11,159	507,833	1,091,261	1,317,773	993,971	907,530	757,975
Heat, air conditioning, electrical work	9,850,249	66,011	1,023,956	1,815,398	2,159,048	1,959,922	1,593,322	1,234,064
Roofing and gutters	11,302,581	13,391	565,860	1,935,219	2,072,538	2,587,143	2,116,345	2,012,475
Other repair and maintenance services	19,849,307	93,823	1,679,816	2,939,569	6,036,266	3,019,218	4,293,498	1,787,446
Repair, replacement of hard-surface flooring	5,293,687	34,508	218,686	1,306,828	1,256,939	1,137,554	1,021,216	317,507
Repair of built-in appliances	688,675	–	69,277	152,337	155,440	165,137	60,694	85,399
Maintenance and repair materials	9,090,053	65,582	1,289,616	2,649,299	2,550,887	1,582,064	593,602	358,836
Paints, wallpaper, and supplies	1,409,650	24,464	206,844	339,341	443,653	236,265	107,363	51,833
Tools, equipment for painting, wallpapering	151,116	2,661	22,303	35,375	47,650	25,367	11,495	5,594
Plumbing supplies and equipment	619,462	2,232	58,224	137,445	118,431	174,919	59,314	69,415
Electrical supplies, heating and cooling equipment	389,903	1,288	57,435	119,624	60,372	108,102	34,600	8,905
Hard-surface flooring, repair and replacement	1,776,482	9,013	352,306	519,997	448,510	304,243	84,718	57,656
Roofing and gutters	797,110	429	142,896	222,647	290,294	50,901	53,797	35,849
Plaster, paneling, siding, windows, doors, screens, awnings	1,939,134	172	176,251	505,349	771,188	330,439	95,294	59,939
Patio, walk, fence, driveway, masonry, brick, and stucco materials	163,806	–	23,092	50,779	39,091	41,782	6,322	3,197
Miscellaneous supplies and equipment	1,827,239	24,894	247,107	716,522	322,446	308,720	140,699	66,675
Property management and security	4,212,801	34,679	402,043	592,015	890,312	878,408	415,659	1,000,015
Property management	3,810,209	33,134	373,029	539,527	836,417	815,736	359,794	852,393
Management and upkeep services for security	402,592	1,545	29,013	52,488	53,895	62,672	55,866	147,622
Parking	630,997	4,550	53,685	96,676	108,947	84,226	91,500	191,463
Rented dwellings	251,417,248	30,840,338	75,699,487	56,517,560	38,315,114	19,555,613	12,011,700	18,480,013
Rent	243,371,167	30,275,167	73,882,894	54,608,219	36,798,414	18,906,174	11,505,460	17,396,540
Rent as pay	3,804,441	387,997	579,478	1,021,440	741,117	276,223	378,186	420,374
Maintenance, insurance, and other expenses	4,241,640	177,174	1,237,115	888,145	775,582	373,216	128,054	663,099
Tenant's insurance	1,115,493	68,415	247,699	211,661	220,670	141,262	82,419	143,854
Maintenance and repair services	1,947,209	45,924	657,242	192,619	402,711	130,319	27,473	490,589
Maintenance and repair materials	1,180,092	62,835	332,174	483,866	152,202	101,635	18,162	28,657
Other lodging	51,328,806	1,855,775	4,787,802	10,320,840	15,905,338	10,325,195	4,813,072	3,320,749
Owned vacation homes	17,336,853	81,977	1,075,469	3,139,756	5,678,892	3,709,278	2,106,574	1,545,177
Mortgage interest and charges	7,100,162	2,747	646,189	1,648,122	2,853,903	1,237,034	518,080	194,888
Property taxes	6,794,468	64,981	284,410	1,052,444	1,807,919	1,644,073	942,245	997,960
Maintenance, insurance, and other expenses	3,442,223	14,249	144,870	439,190	1,017,070	828,171	646,249	352,329
Housing while attending school	6,102,332	1,205,022	200,331	740,446	2,865,700	824,192	238,981	27,515
Lodging on trips	27,889,620	568,862	3,512,199	6,440,638	7,360,747	5,791,891	2,467,517	1,748,057

	total consumer units	under 25	25 to 34	35 to 44	45 to 54	55 to 64	65 to 74	75+
UTILITIES, FUELS, PUBLIC SERVICES	$324,315,319	$11,409,338	$53,923,434	$76,712,726	$77,136,102	$51,213,630	$31,300,080	$25,623,401
Natural gas	45,220,706	1,012,311	5,734,067	10,426,548	10,819,294	7,160,902	4,724,675	4,343,484
Electricity	118,575,586	4,035,768	13,067,250	27,949,955	27,732,450	19,119,227	12,024,805	9,648,164
Fuel oil and other fuels	12,633,789	201,295	,214,220	2,652,961	2,991,070	2,423,167	1,609,300	1,541,752
Fuel oil	6,637,584	89,102	553,755	1,513,850	1,497,270	1,181,325	848,791	949,324
Bottled and tank gas	4,893,402	96,313	565,662	919,394	1,201,424	1,017,846	651,537	441,381
Wood and other fuels	1,049,740	15,795	83,290	218,985	263,693	221,840	98,052	148,193
Telephone services	110,245,729	5,284,482	15,758,513	26,773,005	26,738,279	16,272,607	8,891,153	6,528,697
Residential telephone and pay phones	71,474,578	2,383,433	11,678,383	16,983,536	16,754,709	11,281,861	6,734,806	5,658,608
Cellular phone service	36,464,032	2,690,054	7,434,138	9,261,072	9,555,185	4,724,139	1,987,830	812,434
Pager service	129,199	2,919	22,500	34,911	34,465	23,046	10,001	1,370
Phone cards	2,177,921	208,162	623,295	493,631	393,690	243,726	158,516	56,400
Water and other public services	37,639,509	875,568	5,149,581	8,910,013	8,854,778	6,237,893	4,050,148	3,561,191
Water and sewerage maintenance	27,258,623	670,582	3,791,478	6,594,195	6,415,152	4,467,978	2,887,889	2,431,935
Trash and garbage collection	10,108,646	204,986	1,315,471	2,253,320	2,371,621	1,725,812	1,131,568	1,106,193
Septic tank cleaning	271,087	–	42,632	62,497	68,236	44,269	30,692	23,062

* See appendix for information about mortgage principal reduction.
Note: Numbers may not add to total because of rounding and missing subcategories. (–) means sample is too small to make a reliable estimate.
Source: Calculations by New Strategist based on the 2003 Consumer Expenditure Survey

Table 9.4 Housing: Shelter and Utilities: Market shares by age, 2003

(percentage of total annual spending on shelter and utilities accounted for by consumer unit age groups, 2003)

	total consumer units	under 25	25 to 34	35 to 44	45 to 54	55 to 64	65 to 74	75+
Share of total consumer units	100.0%	7.4%	17.1%	21.2%	20.1%	14.4%	10.0%	9.9%
Share of total before-tax income	100.0	3.0	16.9	25.3	26.7	16.5	6.9	4.9
Share of total spending	100.0	4.1	17.0	24.5	24.6	15.6	8.2	6.1
Share of housing spending	**100.0**	**3.9**	**18.3**	**25.4**	**23.3**	**14.7**	**8.0**	**6.4**
SHELTER	**100.0**	**4.3**	**19.3**	**26.0**	**23.5**	**13.8**	**7.3**	**5.8**
Owned dwellings*	**100.0**	**1.1**	**15.7**	**27.9**	**26.3**	**15.8**	**8.1**	**5.1**
Mortgage interest and charges	100.0	1.1	19.5	32.5	27.8	13.3	4.6	1.2
Mortgage interest	100.0	1.2	20.0	33.0	27.5	12.9	4.3	1.1
Interest paid, home equity loan	100.0	0.2	9.1	26.2	30.9	22.3	8.9	2.5
Interest paid, home equity line of credit	100.0	0.1	8.2	18.7	34.6	25.8	9.8	2.7
Property taxes	100.0	1.3	11.6	23.3	24.3	18.9	10.9	9.8
Maintenance, repairs, insurance, other expenses	100.0	0.7	9.8	20.2	24.5	18.8	15.3	10.8
Homeowner's insurance	100.0	0.9	11.7	22.1	24.7	18.3	12.7	9.6
Ground rent	100.0	2.5	16.4	21.1	19.9	15.1	13.5	11.6
Maintenance and repair services	100.0	0.4	7.6	18.2	24.5	19.4	18.6	11.3
Painting and papering	100.0	0.2	6.8	22.7	23.1	24.5	15.3	7.3
Plumbing and water heating	100.0	0.2	9.1	19.5	23.6	17.8	16.2	13.6
Heat, air conditioning, electrical work	100.0	0.7	10.4	18.4	21.9	19.9	16.2	12.5
Roofing and gutters	100.0	0.1	5.0	17.1	18.3	22.9	18.7	17.8
Other repair and maintenance services	100.0	0.5	8.5	14.8	30.4	15.2	21.6	9.0
Repair, replacement of hard-surface flooring	100.0	0.7	4.1	24.7	23.7	21.5	19.3	6.0
Repair of built-in appliances	100.0	–	10.1	22.1	22.6	24.0	8.8	12.4
Maintenance and repair materials	100.0	0.7	14.2	29.1	28.1	17.4	6.5	3.9
Paints, wallpaper, and supplies	100.0	1.7	14.7	24.1	31.5	16.8	7.6	3.7
Tools, equipment for painting, wallpapering	100.0	1.8	14.8	24.1	31.5	16.8	7.6	3.7
Plumbing supplies and equipment	100.0	0.4	9.4	22.2	19.1	28.2	9.6	11.2
Electrical supplies, heating and cooling equipment	100.0	0.3	14.7	30.7	15.5	27.7	8.9	2.3
Hard-surface flooring, repair and replacement	100.0	0.5	19.8	29.3	25.2	17.1	4.8	3.2
Roofing and gutters	100.0	0.1	17.9	27.9	36.4	6.4	6.7	4.5
Plaster, paneling, siding, windows, doors, screens, awnings	100.0	0.0	9.1	26.1	39.8	17.0	4.9	3.1
Patio, walk, fence, driveway, masonry, brick, and stucco materials	100.0	–	14.1	31.0	23.9	25.5	3.9	2.0
Miscellaneous supplies and equipment	100.0	1.4	13.5	39.2	17.6	16.9	7.7	3.6
Property management and security	100.0	0.8	9.5	14.1	21.1	20.9	9.9	23.7
Property management	100.0	0.9	9.8	14.2	22.0	21.4	9.4	22.4
Management and upkeep services for security	100.0	0.4	7.2	13.0	13.4	15.6	13.9	36.7
Parking	100.0	0.7	8.5	15.3	17.3	13.3	14.5	30.3
Rented dwellings	**100.0**	**12.3**	**30.1**	**22.5**	**15.2**	**7.8**	**4.8**	**7.4**
Rent	100.0	12.4	30.4	22.4	15.1	7.8	4.7	7.1
Rent as pay	100.0	10.2	15.2	26.8	19.5	7.3	9.9	11.1
Maintenance, insurance, and other expenses	100.0	4.2	29.2	20.9	18.3	8.8	3.0	15.6
Tenant's insurance	100.0	6.1	22.2	19.0	19.8	12.7	7.4	12.9
Maintenance and repair services	100.0	2.4	33.8	9.9	20.7	6.7	1.4	25.2
Maintenance and repair materials	100.0	5.3	28.1	41.0	12.9	8.6	1.5	2.4
Other lodging	**100.0**	**3.6**	**9.3**	**20.1**	**31.0**	**20.1**	**9.4**	**6.5**
Owned vacation homes	100.0	0.5	6.2	18.1	32.8	21.4	12.2	8.9
Mortgage interest and charges	100.0	0.0	9.1	23.2	40.2	17.4	7.3	2.7
Property taxes	100.0	1.0	4.2	15.5	26.6	24.2	13.9	14.7
Maintenance, insurance, and other expenses	100.0	0.4	4.2	12.8	29.5	24.1	18.8	10.2
Housing while attending school	100.0	19.7	3.3	12.1	47.0	13.5	3.9	0.5
Lodging on trips	100.0	2.0	12.6	23.1	26.4	20.8	8.8	6.3

	total consumer units	under 25	25 to 34	35 to 44	45 to 54	55 to 64	65 to 74	75+
UTILITIES, FUELS, PUBLIC SERVICES	100.0%	3.5%	15.7%	23.7%	23.8%	15.8%	9.7%	7.9%
Natural gas	100.0	2.2	14.9	23.1	23.9	15.8	10.4	9.6
Electricity	100.0	3.4	15.2	23.6	23.4	16.1	10.1	8.1
Fuel oil and other fuels	100.0	1.6	9.6	21.0	23.7	19.2	12.7	12.2
Fuel oil	100.0	1.3	3.4	22.8	22.6	17.8	12.8	14.3
Bottled and tank gas	100.0	2.0	11.6	18.8	24.6	20.8	13.3	9.0
Wood and other fuels	100.0	1.5	7.9	20.9	25.1	21.1	9.3	14.1
Telephone services	100.0	4.8	17.9	24.3	24.3	14.8	8.1	5.9
Residential telephone and pay phones	100.0	3.3	16.3	23.8	23.4	15.8	9.4	7.9
Cellular phone service	100.0	7.4	20.4	25.4	26.2	13.0	5.5	2.2
Pager service	100.0	2.3	17.4	27.0	26.7	17.8	7.7	1.1
Phone cards	100.0	9.6	28.6	22.7	18.1	11.2	7.3	2.6
Water and other public services	100.0	2.3	13.7	23.7	23.5	16.6	10.8	9.5
Water and sewerage maintenance	100.0	2.5	13.9	24.2	23.5	16.4	10.6	8.9
Trash and garbage collection	100.0	2.0	13.0	22.3	23.5	17.1	11.2	10.9
Septic tank cleaning	100.0	–	15.7	23.1	25.2	16.3	11.3	8.5

See appendix for information about mortgage principal reduction.
Note: Numbers may not add to total because of rounding. (–) means sample is too small to make a reliable estimate.
Source: Calculations by New Strategist based on the 2003 Consumer Expenditure Survey

Table 9.5 Housing: Shelter and Utilities: Average spending by income, 2003

(average annual spending on shelter and utilities, by before-tax income of consumer units (CU), 2003; complete income reporters only)

	total complete reporters	under $20,000	$20,000– $39,999	$40,000– $49,999	$50,000– $69,999	$70,000– $79,999	$80,000– $99,999	$100,000 or more
Number of consumer units (000)	97,391	27,100	23,941	8,891	13,890	5,121	6,909	11,537
Average number of persons per CU	2.5	1.8	2.4	2.6	2.8	3.0	3.0	3.1
Average before-tax income of CU	$51,128.00	$10,752.56	$29,072.57	$44,294.00	$58,900.00	$74,560.00	$88,832.00	$154,665.00
Average spending of CU, total	42,741.66	19,862.52	31,684.32	39,756.91	49,788.99	57,128.14	65,957.39	93,514.86
Housing, average spending	**13,652.50**	**7,329.14**	**10,471.06**	**12,727.58**	**15,106.04**	**17,080.57**	**19,840.62**	**28,941.39**
SHELTER	**7,921.27**	**4,310.83**	**6,028.26**	**7,269.49**	**8,678.84**	**9,912.48**	**10,899.35**	**17,253.15**
Owned dwellings*	**5,246.50**	**1,673.73**	**3,065.41**	**4,577.88**	**6,253.16**	**7,642.51**	**8,858.27**	**14,241.65**
Mortgage interest and charges	2,946.67	579.62	1,550.78	2,635.44	3,820.61	4,763.57	5,358.91	8,340.06
Mortgage interest	2,818.69	546.54	1,478.20	2,513.30	3,640.96	4,575.68	5,125.00	8,021.92
Interest paid, home equity loan	66.37	18.65	45.44	78.17	90.44	109.71	130.71	126.06
Interest paid, home equity line of credit	60.38	14.43	27.13	43.97	82.66	78.19	103.20	189.58
Property taxes	1,310.38	620.04	823.96	1,055.64	1,408.74	1,697.13	2,038.63	3,411.45
Maintenance, repairs, insurance, other expenses	989.45	474.08	690.68	886.80	1,023.80	1,181.81	1,460.73	2,490.15
Homeowner's insurance	290.66	137.73	237.52	300.79	333.08	407.60	429.70	566.13
Ground rent	43.97	50.16	70.87	49.63	37.01	14.04	13.42	9.20
Maintenance and repair services	529.88	239.41	297.19	410.24	506.20	555.01	785.49	1,651.51
Painting and papering	63.49	25.35	28.00	37.94	31.56	74.01	116.06	248.67
Plumbing and water heating	51.86	29.22	41.37	42.18	53.77	62.48	52.85	126.61
Heat, air conditioning, electrical work	86.93	37.19	53.26	54.50	89.53	89.22	162.03	249.51
Roofing and gutters	99.55	69.89	65.55	102.97	97.68	92.99	104.65	239.25
Other repair and maintenance services	176.19	60.67	88.49	121.84	185.78	169.48	281.83	599.52
Repair, replacement of hard-surface flooring	45.59	15.77	17.01	43.26	41.14	62.94	55.94	168.03
Repair of built-in appliances	6.28	1.31	3.42	7.54	6.74	3.89	12.14	19.92
Maintenance and repair materials	84.58	27.82	52.96	87.17	111.50	142.04	175.24	169.31
Paints, wallpaper, and supplies	12.23	4.18	7.08	15.98	16.88	20.42	22.26	23.72
Tools, equipment for painting, wallpapering	1.31	0.45	0.76	1.72	1.81	2.19	2.39	2.55
Plumbing supplies and equipment	5.90	4.47	4.46	8.47	8.34	5.56	7.38	6.60
Electrical supplies, heating and cooling equipment	3.70	1.34	1.95	1.64	1.66	4.00	12.33	11.59
Hard-surface flooring, repair and replacement	17.42	4.04	8.71	19.77	21.40	27.16	45.39	39.24
Roofing and gutters	6.98	3.92	11.00	5.19	11.22	13.39	2.71	1.78
Plaster, paneling, siding, windows, doors, screens, awnings	18.46	5.67	8.84	15.12	31.35	26.49	46.40	35.24
Patio, walk, fence, driveway, masonry, brick, and stucco materials	1.62	0.83	1.81	0.87	1.72	4.89	2.91	1.35
Miscellaneous supplies and equipment	16.80	2.90	8.35	18.34	16.83	37.82	33.30	46.55
Property management and security	35.40	16.39	26.35	35.53	32.43	53.37	50.52	85.28
Property management	32.63	15.33	23.99	33.50	30.53	46.98	45.82	78.77
Management and upkeep services for security	2.77	1.06	2.36	2.02	1.91	6.38	4.71	6.50
Parking	4.96	2.56	5.79	3.44	3.58	9.75	6.36	8.72
Rented dwellings	**2,219.83**	**2,496.13**	**2,786.34**	**2,388.94**	**1,986.39**	**1,712.61**	**1,356.65**	**1,288.00**
Rent	2,143.93	2,388.52	2,708.73	2,305.43	1,915.32	1,672.43	1,334.70	1,242.06
Rent as pay	35.87	85.49	28.23	10.65	14.73	23.00	0.07	7.21
Maintenance, insurance, and other expenses	40.03	22.13	49.39	72.86	56.35	17.18	21.88	38.73
Tenant's insurance	10.62	7.33	10.71	14.89	14.06	11.17	12.93	9.16
Maintenance and repair services	17.90	10.18	22.13	32.94	35.40	2.11	6.44	8.46
Maintenance and repair materials	11.51	4.62	16.55	25.03	6.89	3.91	2.52	21.12
Other lodging	**454.93**	**140.96**	**176.51**	**302.67**	**439.29**	**557.36**	**684.43**	**1,723.49**
Owned vacation homes	156.58	43.70	61.89	105.08	144.89	159.23	203.77	642.54
Mortgage interest and charges	65.34	14.51	17.41	44.44	54.35	67.01	85.04	301.01
Property taxes	59.71	23.28	33.60	46.22	60.37	60.62	80.66	196.15
Maintenance, insurance, and other expenses	31.52	5.90	10.89	14.42	30.17	31.61	38.07	145.38
Housing while attending school	53.24	39.81	5.36	22.21	18.27	58.69	83.92	229.39
Lodging on trips	245.11	57.45	109.25	175.38	276.13	339.44	396.74	851.55

	total complete reporters	under $20,000	$20,000– $39,999	$40,000– $49,999	$50,000– $69,999	$70,000– $79,999	$80,000– $99,999	$100,000 or more
UTILITIES, FUELS, PUBLIC SERVICES	**$2,819.61**	**$1,849.96**	**$2,515.81**	**$2,906.50**	**$3,216.72**	**$3,432.63**	**$3,778.86**	**$4,336.08**
Natural gas	**387.07**	**261.61**	**336.16**	**381.92**	**423.32**	**468.13**	**472.31**	**660.73**
Electricity	**1,021.26**	**715.74**	**945.64**	**1,067.73**	**1,152.74**	**1,186.35**	**1,335.26**	**1,440.40**
Fuel oil and other fuels	**111.84**	**73.73**	**98.66**	**105.66**	**118.70**	**152.53**	**158.29**	**179.28**
Fuel oil	57.92	31.23	50.70	40.53	58.36	85.14	93.71	114.90
Bottled and tank gas	43.69	31.18	39.25	51.10	48.05	61.73	53.62	57.37
Wood and other fuels	9.78	11.00	8.03	12.91	12.19	5.66	9.93	7.00
Telephone services	**969.60**	**603.61**	**851.60**	**1,002.08**	**1,145.68**	**1,189.64**	**1,349.94**	**1,511.73**
Residential telephone and pay phones	620.68	448.15	582.40	653.51	694.10	724.41	786.51	846.35
Cellular phone service	327.73	135.76	243.49	326.91	431.23	446.36	546.35	645.92
Pager service	1.16	0.11	1.35	1.24	1.87	1.17	1.10	2.38
Phone cards	20.03	19.59	24.36	20.42	18.48	17.71	15.98	17.08
Water and other public services	**329.83**	**195.27**	**283.74**	**349.11**	**376.27**	**435.97**	**463.05**	**543.93**
Water and sewerage maintenance	238.54	143.26	205.32	259.41	271.78	309.36	326.71	390.98
Trash and garbage collection	88.62	51.22	76.19	87.65	102.12	123.19	130.48	146.33
Septic tank cleaning	2.67	0.78	2.23	2.06	2.37	3.42	5.87	6.62

See appendix for information about mortgage principal reduction.
Note: Subcategories may not add to total because some are not shown.
Source: Bureau of Labor Statistics, unpublished tables from the 2003 Consumer Expenditure Survey; calculations by New Strategist

Table 9.6 Housing: Shelter and Utilities: Indexed spending by income, 2003

(indexed average annual spending of consumer units (CU) on shelter and utilities, by before-tax income of consumer unit, 2003; complete income reporters only; index definition: an index of 100 is the average for all consumer units; an index of 132 means that spending by consumer units in that group is 32 percent above the average for all consumer units; an index of 68 indicates spending that is 32 percent below the average for all consumer units)

	total complete reporters	under $20,000	$20,000–$39,999	$40,000–$49,999	$50,000–$69,999	$70,000–$79,999	$80,000–$99,999	$100,000 or more
Average spending of CU, total	$42,742	$19,863	$31,684	$39,757	$49,789	$57,128	$65,957	$93,515
Average spending of CU, index	100	47	74	93	117	134	154	219
Housing, spending index	**100**	**54**	**77**	**93**	**111**	**125**	**145**	**212**
SHELTER	**100**	**54**	**76**	**92**	**110**	**125**	**138**	**218**
Owned dwellings*	**100**	**32**	**58**	**87**	**119**	**146**	**169**	**272**
Mortgage interest and charges	100	20	53	89	130	162	182	283
Mortgage interest	100	19	52	89	129	162	182	285
Interest paid, home equity loan	100	28	69	118	136	165	197	190
Interest paid, home equity line of credit	100	24	45	73	137	130	171	314
Property taxes	100	47	63	81	108	130	156	260
Maintenance, repairs, insurance, other expenses	100	48	70	90	104	119	148	252
Homeowner's insurance	100	47	82	104	115	140	148	195
Ground rent	100	114	161	113	84	32	31	21
Maintenance and repair services	100	45	56	77	96	105	148	312
Painting and papering	100	40	44	60	50	117	183	392
Plumbing and water heating	100	56	80	81	104	121	102	244
Heat, air conditioning, electrical work	100	43	61	63	103	103	186	287
Roofing and gutters	100	70	66	103	98	93	105	240
Other repair and maintenance services	100	34	50	69	105	96	160	340
Repair, replacement of hard-surface flooring	100	35	38	95	90	138	123	369
Repair of built-in appliances	100	21	55	120	107	62	193	317
Maintenance and repair materials	100	33	63	103	132	168	207	200
Paints, wallpaper, and supplies	100	34	58	131	138	167	182	194
Tools, equipment for painting, wallpapering	100	34	58	131	138	167	182	195
Plumbing supplies and equipment	100	76	76	144	141	94	125	112
Electrical supplies, heating and cooling equipment	100	36	53	44	45	108	333	313
Hard-surface flooring, repair and replacement	100	23	50	114	123	156	261	225
Roofing and gutters	100	56	158	74	161	192	39	26
Plaster, paneling, siding, windows, doors, screens, awnings	100	31	48	82	170	144	251	191
Patio, walk, fence, driveway, masonry, brick, and stucco materials	100	51	112	54	106	302	180	83
Miscellaneous supplies and equipment	100	17	50	109	100	225	198	277
Property management and security	100	46	74	100	92	151	143	241
Property management	100	47	74	103	94	144	140	241
Management and upkeep services for security	100	38	85	73	69	230	170	235
Parking	100	52	117	69	72	197	128	176
Rented dwellings	**100**	**112**	**126**	**108**	**90**	**77**	**61**	**58**
Rent	100	111	126	108	89	78	62	58
Rent as pay	100	238	79	30	41	64	0	20
Maintenance, insurance, and other expenses	100	55	123	182	141	43	55	97
Tenant's insurance	100	69	101	140	132	105	122	86
Maintenance and repair services	100	57	124	184	198	12	36	47
Maintenance and repair materials	100	40	144	218	60	34	22	184
Other lodging	**100**	**31**	**39**	**67**	**97**	**123**	**150**	**379**
Owned vacation homes	100	28	40	67	93	102	130	410
Mortgage interest and charges	100	22	27	68	83	103	130	461
Property taxes	100	39	56	77	101	102	135	329
Maintenance, insurance, and other expenses	100	19	35	46	96	100	121	461
Housing while attending school	100	75	10	42	34	110	158	431
Lodging on trips	100	23	45	72	113	139	162	347

	total complete reporters	under $20,000	$20,000— $39,999	$40,000— $49,999	$50,000— $69,999	$70,000— $79,999	$80,000— $99,999	$100,000 or more
UTILITIES, FUELS, AND PUBLIC SERVICES	**100**	**66**	**89**	**103**	**114**	**122**	**134**	**154**
Natural gas	**100**	**68**	**87**	**99**	**109**	**121**	**122**	**171**
Electricity	**100**	**70**	**93**	**105**	**113**	**116**	**131**	**141**
Fuel oil and other fuels	**100**	**66**	**88**	**95**	**106**	**136**	**142**	**160**
Fuel oil	100	54	88	70	101	147	162	198
Bottled and tank gas	100	71	90	117	110	141	123	131
Wood and other fuels	100	113	82	132	125	58	102	72
Telephone services	**100**	**62**	**88**	**103**	**118**	**123**	**139**	**156**
Residential telephone and pay phones	100	72	94	105	112	117	127	136
Cellular phone service	100	41	74	100	132	136	167	197
Pager service	100	10	116	107	161	101	95	205
Phone cards	100	98	122	102	92	88	80	85
Water and other public services	**100**	**59**	**86**	**106**	**114**	**132**	**140**	**165**
Water and sewerage maintenance	100	60	86	109	114	130	137	164
Trash and garbage collection	100	58	86	99	115	139	147	165
Septic tank cleaning	100	29	84	77	89	128	220	248

See appendix for information about mortgage principal reduction.
Source: Calculations by New Strategist based on the 2003 Consumer Expenditure Survey

Table 9.7 Housing: Shelter and Utilities: Total spending by income, 2003

(total annual spending on shelter and utilities, by before-tax income group of consumer units (CU), 2003; complete income reporters only; numbers in thousands)

	total complete reporters	under $20,000	$20,000–$39,999	$40,000–$49,999	$50,000–$69,999	$70,000–$79,999	$80,000–$99,999	$100,000 or more
Number of consumer units	97,391	27,100	23,941	8,891	13,890	5,121	6,909	11,537
Total spending of all CUs	$4,162,653,009	$538,274,380	$758,554,310	$353,478,687	$691,569,071	$292,553,205	$455,699,608	$1,078,880,940
Housing, total spending	1,329,630,628	198,619,804	250,687,762	113,160,914	209,822,896	87,469,599	137,078,844	333,896,816
SHELTER	771,460,407	116,823,380	144,322,487	64,633,036	120,549,088	50,761,810	75,303,609	199,049,592
Owned dwellings*	510,961,882	45,358,182	73,388,989	40,701,931	86,856,392	39,137,294	61,201,787	164,305,916
Mortgage interest and charges	286,979,138	15,707,729	37,127,122	23,431,697	53,068,273	24,394,242	37,024,709	96,219,272
Mortgage interest	274,515,038	14,811,129	35,389,685	22,345,750	50,572,934	23,432,057	35,408,625	92,548,891
Interest paid, home equity loan	6,463,841	505,432	1,087,960	695,010	1,256,212	561,825	903,075	1,454,354
Interest paid, home equity line of credit	5,880,469	391,012	649,478	390,937	1,148,147	400,411	713,009	2,187,185
Property taxes	127,619,219	16,802,990	19,726,457	9,385,695	19,567,399	8,691,003	14,084,895	39,357,899
Maintenance, repairs, insurance, other expenses	96,363,525	12,847,581	16,535,517	7,884,539	14,220,582	6,052,049	10,092,184	28,728,861
Homeowner's insurance	28,307,668	3,732,586	5,686,527	2,674,324	4,626,481	2,087,320	2,968,797	6,531,442
Ground rent	4,282,282	1,359,296	1,696,611	441,260	514,069	71,899	92,719	106,140
Maintenance and repair services	51,605,543	6,488,055	7,115,065	3,647,444	7,031,118	2,842,206	5,426,950	19,053,471
Painting and papering	6,183,355	687,107	670,228	337,325	438,368	379,005	801,859	2,868,906
Plumbing and water heating	5,050,697	791,909	990,527	375,022	746,865	319,960	365,141	1,460,700
Heat, air conditioning, electrical work	8,466,200	1,007,717	1,275,054	484,560	1,243,572	456,896	1,119,465	2,878,597
Roofing and gutters	9,695,274	1,894,116	1,569,334	915,506	1,356,775	476,202	723,027	2,760,227
Other repair and maintenance services	17,159,320	1,644,271	2,118,568	1,085,279	2,580,484	867,907	1,947,164	6,916,662
Repair, replacement of hard-surface flooring	4,440,056	427,247	409,321	384,625	571,435	322,316	386,490	1,938,562
Repair of built-in appliances	611,616	35,535	81,925	67,038	93,619	19,921	83,875	229,817
Maintenance and repair materials	8,237,331	753,953	1,267,861	775,029	1,548,735	727,387	1,210,733	1,953,330
Paints, wallpaper, and supplies	1,191,092	113,281	169,480	142,078	234,463	104,571	153,794	273,658
Tools, equipment for painting, wallpapering	127,582	12,176	18,262	15,293	25,141	11,215	16,513	29,419
Plumbing supplies and equipment	574,607	121,208	106,673	75,307	115,843	28,473	50,988	76,144
Electrical supplies, heating and cooling equipment	360,347	36,383	46,596	14,581	23,057	20,484	85,188	133,714
Hard-surface flooring, repair and replacement	1,696,551	109,535	208,423	175,775	297,246	139,086	313,600	452,712
Roofing and gutters	679,789	106,290	263,340	45,144	155,846	68,570	18,723	20,536
Plaster, paneling, siding, windows, doors, screens, awnings	1,797,838	153,629	211,689	134,432	435,452	135,655	320,578	406,564
Patio, walk, fence, driveway, masonry, brick, and stucco materials	157,773	22,464	43,411	7,735	23,891	25,042	20,105	15,575
Miscellaneous supplies and equipment	1,636,169	78,681	199,987	163,061	233,769	193,676	230,070	537,047
Property management and security	3,447,641	444,129	630,876	315,897	450,453	273,308	349,043	983,875
Property management	3,177,868	415,387	574,313	297,849	424,062	240,585	316,570	908,770
Management and upkeep services for security	269,773	28,814	56,563	17,960	26,530	32,672	32,541	74,991
Parking	483,059	69,417	138,709	30,585	49,726	49,930	43,941	100,603
Rented dwellings	216,191,464	67,645,166	66,707,665	21,240,066	27,590,957	8,770,276	9,373,095	14,859,656
Rent	208,799,487	64,728,818	64,849,583	20,497,578	26,603,795	8,564,514	9,221,442	14,329,646
Rent as pay	3,493,415	2,316,642	675,805	94,689	204,600	117,783	484	83,182
Maintenance, insurance, and other expenses	3,898,562	599,787	1,182,385	647,798	782,702	87,979	151,169	446,828
Tenant's insurance	1,034,292	198,601	256,404	132,387	195,293	57,202	89,333	105,679
Maintenance and repair services	1,743,299	275,922	529,829	292,870	491,706	10,805	44,494	97,603
Maintenance and repair materials	1,120,970	125,139	396,152	222,542	95,702	20,023	17,411	243,661
Other lodging	44,306,088	3,819,960	4,225,832	2,691,039	6,101,738	2,854,241	4,728,727	19,883,904
Owned vacation homes	15,249,483	1,184,242	1,481,755	934,266	2,012,522	815,417	1,407,847	7,412,984
Mortgage interest and charges	6,363,528	393,346	416,758	395,116	754,922	343,158	587,541	3,472,752
Property taxes	5,815,217	630,904	804,301	410,942	838,539	310,435	557,280	2,262,983
Maintenance, insurance, and other expenses	3,069,764	159,999	260,804	128,208	419,061	161,875	263,026	1,677,249
Housing while attending school	5,185,097	1,078,774	128,328	197,469	253,770	300,552	579,803	2,646,472
Lodging on trips	23,871,508	1,556,989	2,615,643	1,559,304	3,835,446	1,738,272	2,741,077	9,824,332

	total complete reporters	under $20,000	$20,000–$39,999	$40,000–$49,999	$50,000–$69,999	$70,000–$79,999	$80,000–$99,999	$100,000 or more
UTILITIES, FUELS, PUBLIC SERVICES	$274,604,638	$50,133,804	$60,231,063	$25,841,692	$44,680,241	$17,578,498	$26,108,144	$50,025,355
Natural gas	37,697,134	7,089,714	8,048,038	3,395,651	5,879,915	2,397,294	3,263,190	7,622,842
Electricity	99,461,533	19,396,474	22,639,516	9,493,187	16,011,559	6,075,298	9,225,311	16,617,895
Fuel oil and other fuels	10,892,209	1,998,196	2,362,115	939,423	1,648,743	781,106	1,093,626	2,068,353
Fuel oil	5,640,887	846,429	1,213,835	360,352	810,620	436,002	647,442	1,325,601
Bottled and tank gas	4,255,013	844,853	939,570	454,330	667,415	316,119	370,461	661,878
Wood and other fuels	952,484	298,040	192,247	114,783	169,319	28,985	68,606	80,759
Telephone services	94,430,314	16,357,737	20,388,175	8,909,493	15,913,495	6,092,146	9,326,736	17,440,829
Residential telephone and pay phones	60,448,646	12,144,775	13,943,290	5,810,357	9,641,049	3,709,704	5,433,998	9,764,340
Cellular phone service	31,917,952	3,679,089	5,829,412	2,906,557	5,989,785	2,285,810	3,774,732	7,451,979
Pager service	112,974	2,997	32,270	11,025	25,974	5,992	7,600	27,458
Phone cards	1,950,742	530,760	583,203	181,554	256,687	90,693	110,406	197,052
Water and other public services	32,122,474	5,291,680	6,793,088	3,103,937	5,226,390	2,232,602	3,199,213	6,275,320
Water and sewerage maintenance	23,231,649	3,882,474	4,915,595	2,306,414	3,775,024	1,584,233	2,257,239	4,510,736
Trash and garbage collection	8,630,790	1,388,165	1,824,167	779,296	1,418,447	630,856	901,486	1,688,209
Septic tank cleaning	260,034	21,041	53,434	18,316	32,919	17,514	40,556	76,375

* See appendix for information about mortgage principal reduction.
Note: Numbers may not add to total because of rounding and missing subcategories.
Source: Calculations by New Strategist based on the 2003 Consumer Expenditure Survey

Table 9.8 Housing: Shelter and Utilities: Market shares by income, 2003

(percentage of total annual spending on shelter and utilities accounted for by before-tax income group of consumer units, 2003; complete income reporters only)

	total complete reporters	under $20,000	$20,000–$39,999	$40,000–$49,999	$50,000–$69,999	$70,000–$79,999	$80,000–$99,999	$100,000 or more
Share of total consumer units	100.0%	27.8%	24.6%	9.1%	14.3%	5.3%	7.1%	11.8%
Share of total before-tax income	100.0	5.9	14.0	7.9	16.4	7.7	12.3	35.8
Share of total spending	100.0	12.9	18.2	8.5	16.6	7.0	10.9	25.9
Share of housing spending	100.0	14.9	18.9	8.5	15.8	6.6	10.3	25.1
SHELTER	100.0	15.1	18.7	8.4	15.6	6.6	9.8	25.8
Owned dwellings*	100.0	8.9	14.4	8.0	17.0	7.7	12.0	32.2
Mortgage interest and charges	100.0	5.5	12.9	8.2	18.5	8.5	12.9	33.5
Mortgage interest	100.0	5.4	12.9	8.1	18.4	8.5	12.9	33.7
Interest paid, home equity loan	100.0	7.8	16.8	10.8	19.4	8.7	14.0	22.5
Interest paid, home equity line of credit	100.0	6.7	11.1	6.6	19.5	6.8	12.1	37.2
Property taxes	100.0	13.2	15.5	7.4	15.3	6.8	11.0	30.8
Maintenance, repairs, insurance, other expenses	100.0	13.3	17.2	8.2	14.8	6.3	10.5	29.8
Homeowner's insurance	100.0	13.2	20.1	9.4	16.3	7.4	10.5	23.1
Ground rent	100.0	31.7	39.6	10.3	12.0	1.7	2.2	2.5
Maintenance and repair services	100.0	12.6	13.8	7.1	13.6	5.5	10.5	36.9
Painting and papering	100.0	11.1	10.8	5.5	7.1	6.1	13.0	46.4
Plumbing and water heating	100.0	15.7	19.6	7.4	14.8	6.3	7.2	28.9
Heat, air conditioning, electrical work	100.0	11.9	15.1	5.7	14.7	5.4	13.2	34.0
Roofing and gutters	100.0	19.5	16.2	9.4	14.0	4.9	7.5	28.5
Other repair and maintenance services	100.0	9.6	12.3	6.3	15.0	5.1	11.3	40.3
Repair, replacement of hard-surface flooring	100.0	9.6	9.2	8.7	12.9	7.3	8.7	43.7
Repair of built-in appliances	100.0	5.8	13.4	11.0	15.3	3.3	13.7	37.6
Maintenance and repair materials	100.0	9.2	15.4	9.4	18.8	8.8	14.7	23.7
Paints, wallpaper, and supplies	100.0	9.5	14.2	11.9	19.7	8.8	12.9	23.0
Tools, equipment for painting, wallpapering	100.0	9.5	14.3	12.0	19.7	8.8	12.9	23.1
Plumbing supplies and equipment	100.0	21.1	18.6	13.1	20.2	5.0	8.9	13.3
Electrical supplies, heating and cooling equipment	100.0	10.1	12.9	4.1	6.4	5.7	23.6	37.1
Hard-surface flooring, repair and replacement	100.0	6.5	12.3	10.4	17.5	8.2	18.5	26.7
Roofing and gutters	100.0	15.6	38.7	6.8	22.9	10.1	2.8	3.0
Plaster, paneling, siding, windows, doors, screens, awnings	100.0	8.5	11.8	7.5	24.2	7.5	17.8	22.6
Patio, walk, fence, driveway, masonry, brick, and stucco materials	100.0	14.2	27.5	4.9	15.1	15.9	12.7	9.9
Miscellaneous supplies and equipment	100.0	4.8	12.2	10.0	14.3	11.8	14.1	32.8
Property management and security	100.0	12.9	18.3	9.2	13.1	7.9	10.1	28.5
Property management	100.0	13.1	18.1	9.4	13.3	7.6	10.0	28.6
Management and upkeep services for security	100.0	10.7	21.0	6.7	9.8	12.1	12.1	27.8
Parking	100.0	14.4	28.7	6.3	10.3	10.3	9.1	20.8
Rented dwellings	100.0	31.3	30.9	9.8	12.8	4.1	4.3	6.9
Rent	100.0	31.0	31.1	9.8	12.7	4.1	4.4	6.9
Rent as pay	100.0	66.3	19.3	2.7	5.9	3.4	0.0	2.4
Maintenance, insurance, and other expenses	100.0	15.4	30.3	16.6	20.1	2.3	3.9	11.5
Tenant's insurance	100.0	19.2	24.8	12.8	18.9	5.5	8.6	10.2
Maintenance and repair services	100.0	15.8	30.4	16.8	28.2	0.6	2.6	5.6
Maintenance and repair materials	100.0	11.2	35.3	19.9	8.5	1.8	1.6	21.7
Other lodging	100.0	8.6	9.5	6.1	13.8	6.4	10.7	44.9
Owned vacation homes	100.0	7.8	9.7	6.1	13.2	5.3	9.2	48.6
Mortgage interest and charges	100.0	6.2	6.6	6.2	11.9	5.4	9.2	54.6
Property taxes	100.0	10.9	13.8	7.1	14.4	5.3	9.6	38.9
Maintenance, insurance, and other expenses	100.0	5.2	8.5	4.2	13.7	5.3	8.6	54.6
Housing while attending school	100.0	20.8	2.5	3.8	4.9	5.8	11.2	51.0
Lodging on trips	100.0	6.5	11.0	6.5	16.1	7.3	11.5	41.2

	total complete reporters	under $20,000	$20,000–$39,999	$40,000–$49,999	$50,000–$69,999	$70,000–$79,999	$80,000–$99,999	$100,000 or more
UTILITIES, FUELS, PUBLIC SERVICES	**100.0%**	**18.3%**	**21.9%**	**9.4%**	**16.3%**	**6.4%**	**9.5%**	**18.2%**
Natural gas	**100.0**	**18.8**	**21.4**	**9.0**	**15.6**	**6.4**	**8.7**	**20.2**
Electricity	**100.0**	**19.5**	**22.8**	**9.5**	**16.1**	**6.1**	**9.3**	**16.7**
Fuel oil and other fuels	**100.0**	**18.3**	**21.7**	**8.6**	**15.1**	**7.2**	**10.0**	**19.0**
Fuel oil	100.0	15.0	21.5	6.4	14.4	7.7	11.5	23.5
Bottled and tank gas	100.0	19.9	22.1	10.7	15.7	7.4	8.7	15.6
Wood and other fuels	100.0	31.3	20.2	12.1	17.8	3.0	7.2	8.5
Telephone services	**100.0**	**17.3**	**21.6**	**9.4**	**16.9**	**6.5**	**9.9**	**18.5**
Residential telephone and pay phones	100.0	20.1	23.1	9.5	16.0	6.1	9.0	16.2
Cellular phone service	100.0	11.5	18.3	9.1	18.8	7.2	11.8	23.3
Pager service	100.0	2.7	28.6	9.3	23.0	5.3	6.7	24.3
Phone cards	100.0	27.2	29.9	9.3	13.2	4.7	5.7	10.1
Water and other public services	**100.0**	**16.5**	**21.1**	**9.7**	**16.3**	**7.0**	**10.0**	**19.5**
Water and sewerage maintenance	100.0	16.7	21.2	9.9	16.3	6.8	9.7	19.4
Trash and garbage collection	100.0	16.1	21.1	9.0	16.4	7.3	10.4	19.6
Septic tank cleaning	100.0	8.1	20.5	7.0	12.7	6.7	15.6	29.4

* See appendix for information about mortgage principal reduction.
Note: Numbers may not add to total because of rounding.
Source: Calculations by New Strategist based on the 2003 Consumer Expenditure Survey

Table 9.9 Housing: Shelter and Utilities: Average spending by high-income consumer units, 2003

(average annual spending on shelter and utilities, by before-tax income of high-income consumer units (CU), 2003; complete income reporters only)

	total complete reporters	$100,000 or more	$100,000–$119,999	$120,000–$149,999	$150,000 or more
Number of consumer units (000)	97,391	11,537	4,384	3,151	4,002
Average number of persons per CU	2.5	3.1	3.1	3.1	3.1
Average before-tax income of CU	$51,128.00	$154,665.00	$108,087.00	$131,885.00	$223,634.00
Average spending of CU, total	42,741.66	93,514.86	75,601.50	86,451.46	118,674.11
Housing, average spending	**13,652.50**	**28,941.39**	**23,204.37**	**26,719.05**	**36,970.78**
SHELTER	**7,921.27**	**17,253.15**	**13,622.89**	**16,127.66**	**22,116.74**
Owned dwellings*	**5,246.50**	**14,241.65**	**11,269.44**	**13,210.95**	**18,309.66**
Mortgage interest and charges	2,946.67	8,340.06	6,815.10	7,766.05	10,462.82
Mortgage interest	2,818.69	8,021.92	6,519.10	7,474.41	10,099.56
Interest paid, home equity loan	66.37	126.06	139.58	131.05	107.32
Interest paid, home equity line of credit	60.38	189.58	156.42	160.59	248.73
Property taxes	1,310.38	3,411.45	2,515.50	2,831.04	4,850.10
Maintenance, repairs, insurance, other expenses	989.45	2,490.15	1,938.84	2,613.86	2,996.73
Homeowner's insurance	290.66	566.13	464.79	531.80	704.20
Ground rent	43.97	9.20	12.29	–	13.06
Maintenance and repair services	529.88	1,651.51	1,270.18	1,791.25	1,959.27
Painting and papering	63.49	248.67	134.05	169.90	436.26
Plumbing and water heating	51.86	126.61	96.48	112.49	170.72
Heat, air conditioning, electrical work	86.93	249.51	218.19	236.07	294.42
Roofing and gutters	99.55	239.25	209.02	356.26	180.22
Other repair and maintenance services	176.19	599.52	449.22	757.49	639.79
Repair, replacement of hard-surface flooring	45.59	168.03	140.81	139.66	220.21
Repair of built-in appliances	6.28	19.92	22.40	19.37	17.64
Maintenance and repair materials	84.58	169.31	151.91	216.66	151.08
Paints, wallpaper, and supplies	12.23	23.72	24.07	24.65	22.60
Tools, equipment for painting, wallpapering	1.31	2.55	2.59	2.65	2.43
Plumbing supplies and equipment	5.90	6.60	11.56	3.91	3.29
Electrical supplies, heating and cooling equipment	3.70	11.59	14.67	11.11	8.58
Hard-surface flooring, repair and replacement	17.42	39.24	28.74	98.77	3.87
Roofing and gutters	6.98	1.78	2.22	2.07	1.06
Plaster, paneling, siding, windows, doors, screens, awnings	18.46	35.24	34.03	29.87	40.79
Patio, walk, fence, driveway, masonry, brick, and stucco materials	1.62	1.35	1.13	0.17	2.51
Miscellaneous supplies and equipment	16.80	46.55	32.90	43.47	63.92
Property management and security	35.40	85.28	37.16	63.56	155.10
Property management	32.63	78.77	33.94	60.67	142.15
Management and upkeep services for security	2.77	6.50	3.22	2.89	12.95
Parking	4.96	8.72	2.51	10.59	14.03
Rented dwellings	**2,219.83**	**1,288.00**	**1,272.25**	**1,561.52**	**1,089.87**
Rent	2,143.93	1,242.06	1,203.28	1,516.06	1,068.78
Rent as pay	35.87	7.21	9.68	12.94	–
Maintenance, insurance, and other expenses	40.03	38.73	59.30	32.52	21.09
Tenant's insurance	10.62	9.16	9.60	8.20	9.42
Maintenance and repair services	17.90	8.46	5.51	9.67	10.74
Maintenance and repair materials	11.51	21.12	44.19	14.65	0.93
Other lodging	**454.93**	**1,723.49**	**1,081.19**	**1,355.20**	**2,717.21**
Owned vacation homes	156.58	642.54	407.15	477.06	1,030.76
Mortgage interest and charges	65.34	301.01	152.59	207.99	536.87
Property taxes	59.71	196.15	124.60	125.13	330.48
Maintenance, insurance, and other expenses	31.52	145.38	129.96	143.94	163.41
Housing while attending school	53.24	229.39	187.33	178.13	315.84
Lodging on trips	245.11	851.55	486.72	700.01	1,370.61

	total complete reporters	$100,000 or more	$100,000–$119,999	$120,000–$149,999	$150,000 or more
UTILITIES, FUELS, AND PUBLIC SERVICES	**$2,819.61**	**$4,336.08**	**$3,894.50**	**$4,146.21**	**$4,969.38**
Natural gas	**387.07**	**660.73**	**570.29**	**607.66**	**801.60**
Electricity	**1,021.26**	**1,440.40**	**1,300.02**	**1,348.51**	**1,666.56**
Fuel oil and other fuels	**111.84**	**179.28**	**159.48**	**188.99**	**193.34**
Fuel oil	57.92	114.90	97.74	108.31	138.91
Bottled and tank gas	43.69	57.37	49.69	75.50	51.51
Wood and other fuels	9.78	7.00	12.05	5.14	2.92
Telephone services	**969.60**	**1,511.73**	**1,387.56**	**1,493.70**	**1,661.97**
Residential telephone and pay phones	620.68	846.35	756.89	836.46	952.16
Cellular phone service	327.73	645.92	607.87	635.15	696.09
Pager service	1.16	2.38	3.46	1.54	1.84
Phone cards	20.03	17.08	19.34	20.55	11.88
Water and other public services	**329.83**	**543.93**	**477.15**	**507.34**	**645.90**
Water and sewerage maintenance	238.54	390.98	344.06	369.45	459.33
Trash and garbage collection	88.62	146.33	125.00	132.17	180.84
Septic tank cleaning	2.67	6.62	8.08	5.72	5.73

See appendix for information about mortgage principal reduction.

Note: Subcategories may not add to total because some are not shown. (–) means sample is too small to make a reliable estimate.

Source: Bureau of Labor Statistics, unpublished tables from the 2003 Consumer Expenditure Survey, calculations by New Strategist

Table 9.10 Housing: Shelter and Utilities: Indexed spending by high-income consumer units, 2003

(indexed average annual spending of consumer units (CU) on shelter and utilities, by before-tax income of high-income consumer unit, 2003; complete income reporters only; index definition: an index of 100 is the average for all consumer units; an index of 132 means that spending by consumer units in that group is 32 percent above the average for all consumer units, an index of 68 indicates spending that is 32 percent below the average for all consumer units)

	total complete reporters	$100,000 or more	$100,000–$119,999	$120,000–$149,999	$150,000 or more
Average spending of CU, total	$42,742	$93,515	$75,602	$86,452	$118,674
Average spending of CU, index	100	219	177	202	278
Housing, spending index	**100**	**212**	**170**	**196**	**271**
SHELTER	**100**	**218**	**172**	**204**	**279**
Owned dwellings*	**100**	**272**	**215**	**252**	**349**
Mortgage interest and charges	100	283	231	264	355
Mortgage interest	100	285	231	265	358
Interest paid, home equity loan	100	190	210	198	162
Interest paid, home equity line of credit	100	314	259	266	412
Property taxes	100	260	192	216	370
Maintenance, repairs, insurance, other expenses	100	252	196	264	303
Homeowner's insurance	100	195	160	183	242
Ground rent	100	21	28	–	30
Maintenance and repair services	100	312	240	338	370
Painting and papering	100	392	211	268	687
Plumbing and water heating	100	244	186	217	329
Heat, air conditioning, electrical work	100	287	251	272	339
Roofing and gutters	100	240	210	358	181
Other repair and maintenance services	100	340	255	430	363
Repair, replacement of hard-surface flooring	100	369	309	306	483
Repair of built-in appliances	100	317	357	308	281
Maintenance and repair materials	100	200	180	256	179
Paints, wallpaper, and supplies	100	194	197	202	185
Tools, equipment for painting, wallpapering	100	195	198	202	186
Plumbing supplies and equipment	100	112	196	66	56
Electrical supplies, heating and cooling equipment	100	313	397	300	232
Hard-surface flooring, repair and replacement	100	225	165	567	22
Roofing and gutters	100	26	32	30	15
Plaster, paneling, siding, windows, doors, screens, awnings	100	191	184	162	221
Patio, walk, fence, driveway, masonry, brick, and stucco materials	100	83	70	11	155
Miscellaneous supplies and equipment	100	277	196	259	381
Property management and security	100	241	105	180	438
Property management	100	241	104	186	436
Management and upkeep services for security	100	235	116	104	468
Parking	100	176	51	214	283
Rented dwellings	**100**	**58**	**57**	**70**	**49**
Rent	100	58	56	71	50
Rent as pay	100	20	27	36	–
Maintenance, insurance, and other expenses	100	97	148	81	53
Tenant's insurance	100	86	90	77	89
Maintenance and repair services	100	47	31	54	60
Maintenance and repair materials	100	184	384	127	8
Other lodging	**100**	**379**	**238**	**298**	**597**
Owned vacation homes	100	410	260	305	658
Mortgage interest and charges	100	461	234	318	822
Property taxes	100	329	209	210	554
Maintenance, insurance, and other expenses	100	461	412	457	518
Housing while attending school	100	431	352	335	593
Lodging on trips	100	347	199	286	559

	total complete reporters	$100,000 or more	$100,000– $119,999	$120,000– $149,999	$150,000 or more
UTILITIES, FUELS, AND PUBLIC SERVICES	100	154	138	147	176
Natural gas	100	171	147	157	207
Electricity	100	141	127	132	163
Fuel oil and other fuels	100	160	143	169	173
Fuel oil	100	198	169	187	240
Bottled and tank gas	100	131	114	173	118
Wood and other fuels	100	72	123	53	30
Telephone services	100	156	143	154	171
Residential telephone and pay phones	100	136	122	135	153
Cellular phone service	100	197	186	194	212
Pager service	100	205	298	133	159
Phone cards	100	85	97	103	59
Water and other public services	100	155	145	154	196
Water and sewerage maintenance	100	164	144	155	193
Trash and garbage collection	100	165	141	149	204
Septic tank cleaning	100	248	303	214	215

* See appendix for information about mortgage principal reduction.
Note: (–) means sample is too small to make a reliable estimate.
Source: Calculations by New Strategist based on the 2003 Consumer Expenditure Survey

Table 9.11 Housing: Shelter and Utilities: Total spending by high-income consumer units, 2003

(total annual spending on shelter and utilities, by before-tax income group of high-income consumer units (CU), 2003; complete income reporters only; numbers in thousands)

	total complete reporters	$100,000 or more	$100,000–$119,999	$120,000–$149,999	$150,000 or more
Number of consumer units	97,391	11,537	4,384	3,151	4,002
Total spending of all CUs	$4,162,653,009	$1,078,880,940	$331,436,976	$272,408,551	$474,933,788
Housing, total spending	1,329,630,628	333,896,816	101,727,958	84,191,727	147,957,062
SHELTER	771,460,407	199,049,592	59,722,750	50,818,257	88,511,194
Owned dwellings*	510,961,882	164,305,916	49,405,225	41,627,704	73,275,259
Mortgage interest and charges	286,979,138	96,219,272	29,877,398	24,470,824	41,872,206
Mortgage interest	274,515,038	92,548,891	28,579,734	23,551,866	40,418,439
Interest paid, home equity loan	6,463,841	1,454,354	611,919	412,939	429,495
Interest paid, home equity line of credit	5,880,469	2,187,185	685,745	506,019	995,418
Property taxes	127,619,219	39,357,899	11,027,952	8,920,607	19,410,100
Maintenance, repairs, insurance, other expenses	96,363,525	28,728,861	8,499,875	8,236,273	11,992,914
Homeowner's insurance	28,307,668	6,531,442	2,037,639	1,675,702	2,818,208
Ground rent	4,282,282	106,140	53,879	–	52,266
Maintenance and repair services	51,605,543	19,053,471	5,568,469	5,644,229	7,840,999
Painting and papering	6,183,355	2,868,906	587,675	535,355	1,745,913
Plumbing and water heating	5,050,697	1,460,700	422,968	354,456	683,221
Heat, air conditioning, electrical work	8,466,200	2,878,597	956,545	743,857	1,178,269
Roofing and gutters	9,695,274	2,760,227	916,344	1,122,575	721,240
Other repair and maintenance services	17,159,320	6,916,662	1,969,381	2,386,851	2,560,440
Repair, replacement of hard-surface flooring	4,440,056	1,938,562	617,311	440,069	881,280
Repair of built-in appliances	611,616	229,817	98,202	61,035	70,595
Maintenance and repair materials	8,237,331	1,953,330	665,973	682,696	604,622
Paints, wallpaper, and supplies	1,191,092	273,658	105,523	77,672	90,445
Tools, equipment for painting, wallpapering	127,582	29,419	11,355	8,350	9,725
Plumbing supplies and equipment	574,607	76,144	50,679	12,320	13,167
Electrical supplies, heating and cooling equipment	360,347	133,714	64,313	35,008	34,337
Hard-surface flooring, repair and replacement	1,696,551	452,712	125,996	311,224	15,488
Roofing and gutters	679,789	20,536	9,733	6,523	4,242
Plaster, paneling, siding, windows, doors, screens, awnings	1,797,838	406,564	149,188	94,120	163,242
Patio, walk, fence, driveway, masonry, brick, and stucco materials	157,773	15,575	4,954	536	10,045
Miscellaneous supplies and equipment	1,636,169	537,047	144,234	136,974	255,808
Property management and security	3,447,641	983,875	162,909	200,278	620,710
Property management	3,177,868	908,770	148,793	191,171	568,884
Management and upkeep services for security	269,773	74,991	14,117	9,106	51,826
Parking	483,059	100,603	11,004	33,369	56,148
Rented dwellings	216,191,464	14,859,656	5,577,544	4,920,350	4,361,660
Rent	208,799,487	14,329,646	5,275,180	4,777,105	4,277,258
Rent as pay	3,493,415	83,182	42,437	40,774	–
Maintenance, insurance, and other expenses	3,898,562	446,828	259,971	102,471	84,402
Tenant's insurance	1,034,292	105,679	42,086	25,838	37,699
Maintenance and repair services	1,743,299	97,603	24,156	30,470	42,982
Maintenance and repair materials	1,120,970	243,661	193,729	46,162	3,722
Other lodging	44,306,088	19,883,904	4,739,937	4,270,235	10,874,274
Owned vacation homes	15,249,483	7,412,984	1,784,946	1,503,216	4,125,102
Mortgage interest and charges	6,363,528	3,472,752	668,955	655,377	2,148,554
Property taxes	5,815,217	2,262,983	546,246	394,285	1,322,581
Maintenance, insurance, and other expenses	3,069,764	1,677,249	569,745	453,555	653,967
Housing while attending school	5,185,097	2,646,472	821,255	561,288	1,263,992
Lodging on trips	23,871,508	9,824,332	2,133,781	2,205,732	5,485,181

	total complete reporters	$100,000 or more	$100,000– $119,999	$120,000– $149,999	$150,000 or more
UTILITIES, FUELS, AND PUBLIC SERVICES	$274,604,638	$50,025,355	$17,073,488	$13,064,708	$19,887,459
Natural gas	37,697,134	7,622,842	2,500,151	1,914,737	3,208,003
Electricity	99,461,533	16,617,895	5,699,288	4,249,155	6,669,573
Fuel oil and other fuels	10,892,209	2,068,353	699,160	595,508	773,747
Fuel oil	5,640,887	1,325,601	428,492	341,285	555,918
Bottled and tank gas	4,255,013	661,878	217,841	237,901	206,143
Wood and other fuels	952,484	80,759	52,827	16,196	11,686
Telephone services	94,430,314	17,440,829	6,083,063	4,706,649	6,651,204
Residential telephone and pay phones	60,448,646	9,764,340	3,318,206	2,635,686	3,810,544
Cellular phone service	31,917,952	7,451,979	2,664,902	2,001,358	2,785,752
Pager service	112,974	27,458	15,169	4,853	7,364
Phone cards	1,950,742	197,052	84,787	64,753	47,544
Water and other public services	32,122,474	6,275,320	2,091,826	1,598,628	2,584,892
Water and sewerage maintenance	23,231,649	4,510,736	1,508,359	1,164,137	1,838,239
Trash and garbage collection	8,630,790	1,688,209	548,000	416,468	723,722
Septic tank cleaning	260,034	76,375	35,423	18,024	22,932

* See appendix for information about mortgage principal reduction.
Note: Numbers may not add to total because of rounding and missing subcategories. (–) means sample is too small to make a reliable estimate.
Source: Calculations by New Strategist based on the 2003 Consumer Expenditure Survey

Table 9.12 Housing: Shelter and Utilities: Market shares by high-income consumer units, 2003

(percentage of total annual spending on shelter and utilities accounted for by before-tax income group of high-income consumer units, 2003; complete income reporters only)

	total complete reporters	$100,000 or more	$100,000–$119,999	$120,000–$149,999	$150,000 or more
Share of total consumer units	100.0%	11.8%	4.5%	3.2%	4.1%
Share of total before-tax income	100.0	35.8	9.5	8.3	18.0
Share of total spending	100.0	25.9	8.0	6.5	11.4
Share of housing spending	100.0	25.1	7.7	6.3	11.1
SHELTER	100.0	25.8	7.7	6.6	11.5
Owned dwellings*	100.0	32.2	9.7	8.1	14.3
Mortgage interest and charges	100.0	33.5	10.4	8.5	14.6
Mortgage interest	100.0	33.7	10.4	8.6	14.7
Interest paid, home equity loan	100.0	22.5	9.5	6.4	6.6
Interest paid, home equity line of credit	100.0	37.2	11.7	8.6	16.9
Property taxes	100.0	30.8	8.6	7.0	15.2
Maintenance, repairs, insurance, other expenses	100.0	29.8	8.8	8.5	12.4
Homeowner's insurance	100.0	23.1	7.2	5.9	10.0
Ground rent	100.0	2.5	1.3	–	1.2
Maintenance and repair services	100.0	36.9	10.8	10.9	15.2
Painting and papering	100.0	46.4	9.5	8.7	28.2
Plumbing and water heating	100.0	28.9	8.4	7.0	13.5
Heat, air conditioning, electrical work	100.0	34.0	11.3	8.8	13.9
Roofing and gutters	100.0	28.5	9.5	11.6	7.4
Other repair and maintenance services	100.0	40.3	11.5	13.9	14.9
Repair, replacement of hard-surface flooring	100.0	43.7	13.9	9.9	19.8
Repair of built-in appliances	100.0	37.6	16.1	10.0	11.5
Maintenance and repair materials	100.0	23.7	8.1	8.3	7.3
Paints, wallpaper, and supplies	100.0	23.0	8.9	6.5	7.6
Tools, equipment for painting, wallpapering	100.0	23.1	8.9	6.5	7.6
Plumbing supplies and equipment	100.0	13.3	8.8	2.1	2.3
Electrical supplies, heating and cooling equipment	100.0	37.1	17.8	9.7	9.5
Hard-surface flooring, repair and replacement	100.0	26.7	7.4	18.3	0.9
Roofing and gutters	100.0	3.0	1.4	1.0	0.6
Plaster, paneling, siding, windows, doors, screens, awnings	100.0	22.6	8.3	5.2	9.1
Patio, walk, fence, driveway, masonry, brick, and stucco materials	100.0	9.9	3.1	0.3	6.4
Miscellaneous supplies and equipment	100.0	32.8	8.8	8.4	15.6
Property management and security	100.0	28.5	4.7	5.8	18.0
Property management	100.0	28.6	4.7	6.0	17.9
Management and upkeep services for security	100.0	27.8	5.2	3.4	19.2
Parking	100.0	20.8	2.3	6.9	11.6
Rented dwellings	100.0	6.9	2.6	2.3	2.0
Rent	100.0	6.9	2.5	2.3	2.1
Rent as pay	100.0	2.4	1.2	1.2	–
Maintenance, insurance, and other expenses	100.0	11.5	6.7	2.6	2.2
Tenant's insurance	100.0	10.2	4.1	2.5	3.6
Maintenance and repair services	100.0	5.6	1.4	1.7	2.5
Maintenance and repair materials	100.0	21.7	17.3	4.1	0.3
Other lodging	100.0	44.9	10.7	9.6	24.5
Owned vacation homes	100.0	48.6	11.7	9.9	27.1
Mortgage interest and charges	100.0	54.6	10.5	10.3	33.8
Property taxes	100.0	38.9	9.4	6.8	22.7
Maintenance, insurance, and other expenses	100.0	54.6	18.6	14.8	21.3
Housing while attending school	100.0	51.0	15.8	10.8	24.4
Lodging on trips	100.0	41.2	8.9	9.2	23.0

	total complete reporters	$100,000 or more	$100,000–$119,999	$120,000–$149,999	$150,000 or more
UTILITIES, FUELS, AND PUBLIC SERVICES	100.0%	18.2%	6.2%	4.8%	7.2%
Natural gas	100.0	20.2	6.6	5.1	8.5
Electricity	100.0	16.7	5.7	4.3	6.7
Fuel oil and other fuels	100.0	19.0	6.4	5.5	7.1
Fuel oil	100.0	23.5	7.6	6.1	9.9
Bottled and tank gas	100.0	15.6	5.1	5.6	4.8
Wood and other fuels	100.0	8.5	5.5	1.7	1.2
Telephone services	100.0	18.5	6.4	5.0	7.0
Residential telephone and pay phones	100.0	16.2	5.5	4.4	6.3
Cellular phone service	100.0	23.3	8.4	6.3	8.7
Pager service	100.0	24.3	13.4	4.3	6.5
Phone cards	100.0	10.1	4.3	3.3	2.4
Water and other public services	100.0	19.5	6.5	5.0	8.1
Water and sewerage maintenance	100.0	19.4	6.5	5.0	7.9
Trash and garbage collection	100.0	19.6	6.4	4.8	8.4
Septic tank cleaning	100.0	29.4	13.6	6.9	8.8

See appendix for information about mortgage principal reduction.
Note: Numbers may not add to total because of rounding. (–) means sample is too small to make a reliable estimate.
Source: Calculations by New Strategist based on the 2003 Consumer Expenditure Survey

Table 9.13 Housing: Shelter and Utilities: Average spending by household type, 2003

(average annual spending of consumer units (CU) on shelter and utilities, by type of consumer unit, 2003)

	total married couples	married couples, no children	married couples with children total	oldest child under 6	oldest child 6 to 17	oldest child 18 or older	single parent, at least one child <18	single person
Number of consumer units (000)	58,448	25,132	28,584	5,496	15,047	8,041	6,999	33,929
Average number of persons per CU	3.2	2.0	3.9	3.5	4.1	4.0	2.9	1.0
Average before-tax income of CU	$69,472.00	$62,930.00	$75,557.00	$66,317.00	$77,508.00	$78,307.00	$29,154.00	$27,131.00
Average spending of CU, total	53,030.03	47,895.65	57,702.32	51,503.24	59,183.18	59,180.36	30,534.75	23,657.35
Housing, average spending	**16,647.97**	**14,352.35**	**18,679.27**	**19,303.20**	**19,234.53**	**17,214.61**	**11,772.50**	**8,767.66**
SHELTER	**9,480.09**	**8,000.65**	**10,812.49**	**10,963.13**	**11,292.33**	**9,811.68**	**7,152.44**	**5,613.57**
Owned dwellings*	**7,433.18**	**5,972.56**	**8,772.56**	**8,440.34**	**9,213.38**	**8,174.75**	**3,233.54**	**2,692.09**
Mortgage interest and charges	4,348.66	2,924.22	5,609.91	5,852.56	5,952.52	4,803.00	1,937.52	1,230.19
Mortgage interest	4,155.16	2,743.87	5,398.73	5,732.37	5,745.68	4,521.50	1,889.45	1,187.54
Interest paid, home equity loan	95.92	84.04	112.46	59.44	122.93	129.08	33.25	23.61
Interest paid, home equity line of credit	95.53	95.16	98.73	60.75	83.91	152.42	14.82	19.04
Property taxes	1,840.64	1,742.46	1,955.75	1,617.92	2,022.80	2,061.16	675.15	802.47
Maintenance, repairs, insurance, other expenses	1,243.87	1,305.89	1,206.90	969.86	1,238.06	1,310.59	620.87	659.43
Homeowner's insurance	391.03	402.20	391.33	353.86	400.52	399.73	149.26	178.49
Ground rent	36.73	40.08	29.60	33.89	32.21	21.80	52.60	43.34
Maintenance and repair services	662.08	710.21	626.83	422.97	640.40	740.74	372.39	334.38
Painting and papering	76.65	61.87	83.81	91.27	87.30	72.19	38.02	40.23
Plumbing and water heating	56.98	61.84	56.90	30.04	55.93	77.05	49.08	30.52
Heat, air conditioning, electrical work	115.41	129.26	110.37	107.60	114.99	103.60	32.13	52.24
Roofing and gutters	133.96	163.34	117.46	31.44	92.66	222.65	58.58	56.31
Other repair and maintenance services	206.49	208.82	192.39	132.65	223.36	175.28	180.48	124.03
Repair, replacement of hard-surface flooring	64.75	76.41	58.47	27.71	56.65	82.91	12.17	27.05
Repair of built-in appliances	7.84	8.67	7.43	2.26	9.52	7.05	1.93	4.00
Maintenance and repair materials	116.00	99.48	131.04	112.15	141.90	123.61	31.42	39.71
Paints, wallpaper, and supplies	16.81	9.98	21.78	14.42	22.54	25.40	7.10	6.61
Tools, equipment for painting, wallpapering	1.81	1.07	2.34	1.55	2.42	2.73	0.76	0.71
Plumbing supplies and equipment	7.51	7.75	5.65	4.61	5.29	7.04	2.58	1.98
Electrical supplies, heating and cooling equipment	4.17	4.47	3.80	2.78	4.26	3.65	0.83	1.86
Hard-surface flooring, repair and replacement	22.43	21.40	24.66	17.81	25.95	26.93	7.64	8.13
Roofing and gutters	10.67	8.11	12.32	1.89	17.87	9.07	2.40	4.27
Plaster, paneling, siding, windows, doors, screens, awnings	25.08	19.83	29.89	33.95	26.85	32.80	5.50	9.26
Patio, walk, fence, driveway, masonry, brick, and stucco materials	2.05	1.61	2.68	1.95	3.69	1.29	0.03	0.64
Miscellaneous supplies and equipment	25.23	24.88	27.74	33.21	32.72	14.69	4.58	6.25
Property management and security	34.04	47.32	26.09	45.48	20.56	23.20	11.93	53.96
Property management	30.61	41.59	24.31	42.09	18.97	22.14	10.56	48.73
Management and upkeep services for security	3.43	5.73	1.78	3.39	1.59	1.06	1.37	5.23
Parking	3.99	6.60	2.01	1.50	2.47	1.50	3.28	9.55
Rented dwellings	**1,405.03**	**1,280.11**	**1,455.46**	**2,203.62**	**1,487.90**	**883.46**	**3,724.16**	**2,679.14**
Rent	1,358.85	1,232.94	1,411.13	2,163.52	1,437.32	847.92	3,505.32	2,600.59
Rent as pay	10.97	10.95	10.58	15.37	10.53	7.40	135.60	45.82
Maintenance, insurance, and other expenses	35.21	36.23	33.75	24.73	40.05	28.14	83.23	32.73
Tenant's insurance	8.68	11.37	6.63	9.79	7.05	3.71	11.45	11.69
Maintenance and repair services	14.49	16.19	11.31	5.94	9.29	18.76	65.87	15.24
Maintenance and repair materials	12.04	8.67	15.81	9.00	23.71	5.67	5.91	5.80
Other lodging	**641.88**	**747.98**	**584.47**	**319.17**	**591.05**	**753.46**	**194.75**	**242.34**
Owned vacation homes	210.17	285.51	146.24	82.83	134.44	211.65	72.30	87.38
Mortgage interest and charges	85.74	108.04	66.51	44.10	55.23	102.93	41.76	31.06
Property taxes	76.80	105.37	56.87	25.67	59.11	74.01	26.83	44.34
Maintenance, insurance, and other expenses	47.63	72.10	22.86	13.06	20.10	34.70	3.71	11.98
Housing while attending school	72.62	58.77	93.49	1.05	61.81	215.94	17.84	43.52
Lodging on trips	359.08	403.70	344.74	235.30	394.80	325.88	104.60	111.43

	total married couples	married couples, no children	married couples with children				single parent, at least one child <18	single person
			total	oldest child under 5	oldest child 6 to 17	oldest child 18 or older		
UTILITIES, FUELS, PUBLIC SERVICES	$3,443.64	$3,075.34	$3,694.82	$3,030.08	$3,745.30	$4,054.66	$2,595.42	$1,758.33
Natural gas	473.36	412.97	517.25	429.29	517.00	577.85	335.40	253.70
Electricity	1,258.86	1,152.68	1,331.31	1,055.46	1,378.49	1,431.55	1,022.07	621.31
Fuel oil and other fuels	142.59	136.99	145.85	92.47	151.72	171.35	62.05	70.45
Fuel oil	74.51	70.64	78.59	40.55	86.23	90.29	31.04	38.18
Bottled and tank gas	57.13	56.27	55.78	40.80	54.57	68.29	27.57	25.14
Wood and other fuels	10.41	9.72	10.72	9.27	10.52	12.07	3.38	6.93
Telephone services	1,145.40	990.84	1,252.30	1,093.71	1,237.88	1,387.68	932.29	622.65
Residential telephone and pay phones	724.37	662.22	757.95	650.67	761.68	824.29	636.17	429.11
Cellular phone service	399.09	311.85	471.48	419.56	451.74	543.90	281.77	179.45
Pager service	1.60	1.41	1.83	1.74	2.19	1.23	0.74	0.49
Phone cards	20.33	15.36	21.04	21.74	22.27	18.27	13.62	13.61
Water and other public services	423.42	381.86	448.10	359.16	460.21	486.22	243.61	190.23
Water and sewerage maintenance	309.91	270.04	333.70	268.57	340.83	364.85	184.12	129.06
Trash and garbage collection	110.32	108.47	111.07	89.32	115.75	117.18	58.17	60.44
Septic tank cleaning	3.20	3.35	3.33	1.27	3.63	4.19	1.33	0.73

* See appendix for information about mortgage principal reduction.

Note: Average spending figures for total consumer units can be found on Average Spending by Age and Average Spending by Region tables. Subcategories may not add to total because some are not shown.

Source: Bureau of Labor Statistics, unpublished tables from the 2003 Consumer Expenditure Survey

Table 9.14 Housing: Shelter and Utilities: Indexed spending by household type, 2003

(indexed average annual spending of consumer units (CU) on shelter and utilities, by type of consumer unit, 2003; index definition: an index of 100 is the average for all consumer units; an index of 132 means that spending by consumer units in that group is 32 percent above the average for all consumer units; an index of 68 indicates spending that is 32 percent below the average for all consumer units)

	total married couples	married couples, no children	married couples with children				single parent, at least one child <18	single person
			total	oldest child under 6	oldest child 6 to 17	oldest child 18 or older		
Average spending of CU, total	$53,030	$47,896	$57,702	$51,503	$59,183	$59,180	$30,535	$23,657
Average spending of CU, index	130	117	141	126	145	145	75	58
Housing, spending index	**124**	**107**	**139**	**144**	**143**	**128**	**88**	**65**
SHELTER	**120**	**101**	**137**	**139**	**143**	**124**	**91**	**71**
Owned dwellings*	**141**	**114**	**167**	**160**	**175**	**155**	**61**	**51**
Mortgage interest and charges	147	99	190	198	202	163	66	42
Mortgage interest	147	97	191	203	203	160	67	42
Interest paid, home equity loan	150	131	176	93	192	202	52	37
Interest paid, home equity line of credit	163	163	169	104	144	261	25	33
Property taxes	137	130	146	120	151	153	50	60
Maintenance, repairs, insurance, other expenses	129	135	125	101	128	136	64	68
Homeowner's insurance	136	140	136	123	139	139	52	62
Ground rent	91	99	73	84	79	54	130	107
Maintenance and repair services	128	138	121	82	124	144	72	65
Painting and papering	127	102	138	151	144	119	63	66
Plumbing and water heating	118	128	118	62	116	159	101	63
Heat, air conditioning, electrical work	135	151	129	126	135	121	38	61
Roofing and gutters	137	167	120	32	95	227	60	58
Other repair and maintenance services	120	121	112	77	130	102	105	72
Repair, replacement of hard-surface flooring	141	167	127	60	123	181	27	59
Repair of built-in appliances	131	145	125	38	160	118	32	67
Maintenance and repair materials	147	126	166	142	180	157	40	50
Paints, wallpaper, and supplies	138	82	178	118	185	208	58	54
Tools, equipment for painting, wallpapering	138	82	179	118	185	208	58	54
Plumbing supplies and equipment	140	144	105	86	99	131	48	37
Electrical supplies, heating and cooling equipment	123	132	112	82	126	108	25	55
Hard-surface flooring, repair and replacement	146	139	160	116	169	175	50	53
Roofing and gutters	154	117	178	27	259	131	35	62
Plaster, paneling, siding, windows, doors, screens, awnings	149	118	178	202	160	195	33	55
Patio, walk, fence, driveway, masonry, brick, and stucco materials	144	113	189	137	260	91	2	45
Miscellaneous supplies and equipment	159	157	175	210	207	93	29	40
Property management and security	93	130	71	125	56	64	33	148
Property management	93	126	74	127	57	67	32	148
Management and upkeep services for security	98	164	51	97	46	30	39	150
Parking	73	121	37	27	45	27	60	175
Rented dwellings	**65**	**59**	**67**	**101**	**68**	**41**	**171**	**123**
Rent	64	58	67	103	68	40	166	123
Rent as pay	33	33	32	47	32	22	411	139
Maintenance, insurance, and other expenses	96	99	92	67	109	77	226	89
Tenant's insurance	90	118	69	101	73	38	118	121
Maintenance and repair services	86	96	67	35	55	111	390	90
Maintenance and repair materials	118	85	155	88	232	55	58	57
Other lodging	**144**	**168**	**131**	**72**	**133**	**169**	**44**	**55**
Owned vacation homes	140	190	97	55	90	141	48	58
Mortgage interest and charges	139	176	108	72	90	167	68	51
Property taxes	130	179	97	44	100	126	46	75
Maintenance, insurance, and other expenses	160	242	77	44	67	116	12	40
Housing while attending school	137	111	177	2	117	408	34	82
Lodging on trips	149	167	143	97	163	135	43	46

	total married couples	married couples, no children	married couples with children				single parent, at least one child <18	single person
			total	oldest child under 6	oldest child 6 to 17	oldest child 18 or older		
UTILITIES, FUELS, AND PUBLIC SERVICES	**123**	**109**	**131**	**108**	**133**	**144**	**92**	**63**
Natural gas	**121**	**105**	**132**	**110**	**132**	**147**	**86**	**65**
Electricity	**123**	**112**	**130**	**103**	**134**	**139**	**99**	**60**
Fuel oil and other fuels	**130**	**125**	**133**	**84**	**139**	**157**	**57**	**64**
Fuel oil	130	123	137	71	150	157	54	66
Bottled and tank gas	135	133	132	95	129	161	65	59
Wood and other fuels	114	107	118	102	116	133	37	76
Telephone services	**120**	**104**	**131**	**114**	**130**	**145**	**98**	**65**
Residential telephone and pay phones	117	107	122	105	123	133	103	69
Cellular phone service	126	99	149	133	143	172	89	57
Pager service	143	126	163	155	196	110	66	44
Phone cards	108	81	111	115	118	97	72	72
Water and other public services	**130**	**117**	**137**	**110**	**141**	**149**	**75**	**58**
Water and sewerage maintenance	131	114	141	114	144	154	78	55
Trash and garbage collection	126	124	127	102	132	134	66	69
Septic tank cleaning	136	143	142	54	155	178	57	31

* See appendix for information about mortgage principal reduction.
Note: Spending index for total consumer units is 100.
Source: Calculations by New Strategist based on the 2003 Consumer Expenditure Survey

Table 9.15 Housing: Shelter and Utilities: Total spending by household type, 2003

(total annual spending on shelter and utilities, by consumer unit (CU) type, 2003; numbers in thousands)

	total married couples	married couples, no children	married couples with children total	oldest child under 6	oldest child 6 to 17	oldest child 18 or older	single parent, at least one child <18	single person
Number of consumer units	58,448	25,132	28,584	5,496	15,047	8,041	6,999	33,929
Total spending of all CUs	$3,099,499,193	$1,203,713,476	$1,649,363,115	$283,061,807	$890,529,310	$475,869,275	$213,712,715	$802,670,228
Housing, total spending	973,040,551	360,703,260	533,928,254	106,090,387	289,421,973	138,422,679	82,395,728	297,477,936
SHELTER	**554,092,300**	**201,072,336**	**309,064,214**	**60,253,363**	**169,915,690**	**78,895,719**	**50,059,928**	**190,462,817**
Owned dwellings*	434,454,505	150,102,378	250,754,855	46,388,109	138,633,729	65,733,165	22,631,547	91,339,922
Mortgage interest and charges	254,170,480	73,491,497	160,353,667	32,165,670	89,567,568	38,620,923	13,560,703	41,739,117
Mortgage interest	242,860,792	68,958,941	154,317,298	31,505,106	86,455,247	36,357,382	13,224,261	40,292,045
Interest paid, home equity loan	5,606,332	2,112,093	3,214,557	326,682	1,849,728	1,037,932	232,717	801,064
Interest paid, home equity line of credit	5,583,537	2,391,561	2,822,098	333,882	1,262,594	1,225,609	103,725	646,008
Property taxes	107,581,727	43,791,505	55,903,158	8,892,088	30,437,072	16,573,788	4,725,375	27,227,005
Maintenance, repairs, insurance, other expenses	72,701,714	32,819,628	34,498,030	5,330,351	18,629,089	10,538,454	4,345,469	22,373,801
Homeowner's insurance	22,854,921	10,108,090	11,185,777	1,944,815	6,026,624	3,214,229	1,044,671	6,055,987
Ground rent	2,146,795	1,007,291	846,086	186,259	484,664	175,294	368,147	1,470,483
Maintenance and repair services	38,697,252	17,848,998	17,917,309	2,324,643	9,636,099	5,956,290	2,606,358	11,345,179
Painting and papering	4,480,039	1,554,917	2,395,625	501,620	1,313,603	580,480	266,102	1,364,964
Plumbing and water heating	3,330,367	1,554,163	1,626,430	165,100	841,579	619,559	343,511	1,035,513
Heat, air conditioning, electrical work	6,745,484	3,248,562	3,154,816	591,370	1,730,255	833,048	224,878	1,772,451
Roofing and gutters	7,829,694	4,105,061	3,357,477	172,794	1,394,255	1,790,329	410,001	1,910,542
Other repair and maintenance services	12,068,928	5,248,064	5,499,276	729,044	3,360,898	1,409,427	1,263,180	4,208,214
Repair, replacement of hard-surface flooring	3,784,508	1,920,336	1,671,307	152,294	852,413	666,679	85,178	917,779
Repair of built-in appliances	458,232	217,894	212,379	12,421	143,247	56,689	13,508	135,716
Maintenance and repair materials	6,779,968	2,500,131	3,745,647	616,376	2,135,169	993,948	219,909	1,347,321
Paints, wallpaper, and supplies	982,511	250,817	622,560	79,252	339,159	204,241	49,693	224,271
Tools, equipment for painting, wallpapering	105,791	26,891	66,887	8,519	36,414	21,952	5,319	24,090
Plumbing supplies and equipment	438,945	194,773	161,500	25,337	79,599	56,609	18,057	67,179
Electrical supplies, heating and cooling equipment	243,728	112,340	108,619	15,279	64,100	29,350	5,809	63,108
Hard-surface flooring, repair and replacement	1,310,989	537,825	704,881	97,884	390,470	216,544	53,472	275,843
Roofing and gutters	623,640	203,821	352,155	10,387	268,890	72,932	16,798	144,877
Plaster, paneling, siding, windows, doors, screens, awnings	1,465,876	498,368	854,376	186,589	404,012	263,745	38,495	314,183
Patio, walk, fence, driveway, masonry, brick, and stucco materials	119,818	40,463	76,605	10,717	55,523	10,373	210	21,715
Miscellaneous supplies and equipment	1,474,643	625,284	792,920	182,522	492,338	118,122	32,055	212,056
Property management and security	1,989,570	1,189,246	745,757	249,958	309,366	186,551	83,498	1,830,809
Property management	1,789,093	1,045,240	694,877	231,327	285,442	178,028	73,909	1,653,360
Management and upkeep services for security	200,477	144,006	50,880	18,631	23,925	8,524	9,589	177,449
Parking	233,208	165,871	57,454	8,244	37,166	12,062	22,957	324,022
Rented dwellings	**82,121,193**	**32,171,725**	**41,602,869**	**12,111,096**	**22,388,431**	**7,103,902**	**26,065,396**	**90,900,541**
Rent	79,422,065	30,986,248	40,335,740	11,890,706	21,627,354	6,818,125	24,533,735	88,235,418
Rent as pay	641,175	275,195	302,419	84,474	158,445	59,503	949,064	1,554,627
Maintenance, insurance, and other expenses	2,057,954	910,532	964,710	135,916	602,632	226,274	582,527	1,110,496
Tenant's insurance	507,329	285,751	189,512	53,806	106,081	29,832	80,139	396,630
Maintenance and repair services	846,912	406,887	323,285	32,646	139,787	150,849	461,024	517,078
Maintenance and repair materials	703,714	217,894	451,913	49,464	356,764	45,593	41,364	196,788
Other lodging	**37,516,602**	**18,798,233**	**16,706,491**	**1,754,158**	**8,893,529**	**6,058,572**	**1,363,055**	**8,222,354**
Owned vacation homes	12,284,016	7,175,437	4,180,124	455,234	2,022,919	1,701,878	506,028	2,964,716
Mortgage interest and charges	5,011,332	2,715,261	1,901,122	242,374	831,046	827,660	292,278	1,053,835
Property taxes	4,488,806	2,648,159	1,625,572	141,082	889,428	595,114	187,783	1,504,412
Maintenance, insurance, and other expenses	2,783,878	1,812,017	653,430	71,778	302,445	279,023	25,966	406,469
Housing while attending school	4,244,494	1,477,008	2,672,318	5,771	930,055	1,736,374	124,862	1,476,590
Lodging on trips	20,987,508	10,145,788	9,854,048	1,293,209	5,940,556	2,620,401	732,095	3,780,709

	total married couples	married couples, no children	married couples with children				single parent, at least one child <18	single person
			total	oldest child under 6	oldest child 6 to 17	oldest child 18 or older		
UTILITIES, FUELS, PUBLIC SERVICES	**$201,273,871**	**$77,289,445**	**$105,612,735**	**$16,653,320**	**$56,355,529**	**$32,603,521**	**$18,165,345**	**$59,658,379**
Natural gas	27,666,945	10,378,762	14,785,074	2,359,378	7,779,299	4,646,492	2,347,465	8,607,787
Electricity	73,577,849	28,969,154	38,054,165	5,800,808	20,742,139	11,511,094	7,153,468	21,080,427
Fuel oil and other fuels	8,334,100	3,442,833	4,168,976	508,215	2,282,931	1,377,825	434,288	2,390,298
Fuel oil	4,354,961	1,775,325	2,246,417	222,863	1,297,503	726,022	217,249	1,295,409
Bottled and tank gas	3,339,134	1,414,178	1,594,416	224,237	821,115	549,120	192,962	852,975
Wood and other fuels	608,444	244,283	306,421	50,948	158,294	97,055	23,657	235,128
Telephone services	**66,946,339**	**24,901,791**	**35,795,743**	**6,011,030**	**18,626,380**	**11,158,335**	**6,525,098**	**21,125,892**
Residential telephone and pay phones	42,337,978	16,642,913	21,655,243	3,576,082	11,460,999	6,628,116	4,452,554	14,559,273
Cellular phone service	23,326,012	7,837,414	13,476,784	2,305,902	6,797,332	4,373,500	1,972,108	6,088,559
Pager service	93,517	35,436	52,309	9,563	32,953	9,890	5,179	16,625
Phone cards	1,188,248	386,028	601,407	119,483	335,097	146,909	95,326	461,774
Water and other public services	**24,748,052**	**9,596,906**	**12,808,490**	**1,973,943**	**6,924,780**	**3,909,695**	**1,705,026**	**6,454,314**
Water and sewerage maintenance	18,113,620	6,786,645	9,538,481	1,476,061	5,128,469	2,933,759	1,288,656	4,378,877
Trash and garbage collection	6,447,983	2,726,068	3,174,825	490,903	1,741,690	942,244	407,132	2,050,669
Septic tank cleaning	187,034	84,192	95,185	6,980	54,621	33,692	9,309	24,768

* See appendix for information about mortgage principal reduction.
Note: Total spending figures for total consumer units can be found on Total Spending by Age and Total Spending by Region tables. Spending by type of consumer unit will not add to total because not all types of consumer units are shown. Numbers may not add to category total because of rounding and missing subcategories.
Source: Calculations by New Strategist based on the 2003 Consumer Expenditure Survey

Table 9.16 Housing: Shelter and Utilities: Market shares by household type, 2003

(percentage of total annual spending on shelter and utilities accounted for by types of consumer units, 2003)

	total married couples	married couples, no children	married couples with children				single parent, at least one child <18	single person
			total	oldest child under 6	oldest child 6 to 17	oldest child 18 or older		
Share of total consumer units	50.7%	21.8%	24.8%	4.8%	13.0%	7.0%	6.1%	29.4%
Share of total before-tax income	68.8	26.8	36.6	6.2	19.8	10.7	3.5	15.6
Share of total spending	65.8	25.6	35.0	6.0	18.9	10.1	4.5	17.1
Share of housing spending	**62.8**	**23.3**	**34.5**	**6.8**	**18.7**	**8.9**	**5.3**	**19.2**
SHELTER	**60.9**	**22.1**	**34.0**	**6.6**	**18.7**	**8.7**	**5.5**	**20.9**
Owned dwellings*	**71.6**	**24.7**	**41.3**	**7.6**	**22.8**	**10.8**	**3.7**	**15.1**
Mortgage interest and charges	74.6	21.6	47.1	9.4	26.3	11.3	4.0	12.2
Mortgage interest	74.4	21.1	47.3	9.6	26.5	11.1	4.1	12.3
Interest paid, home equity loan	75.9	28.6	43.5	4.4	25.1	14.1	3.2	10.9
Interest paid, home equity line of credit	82.8	35.5	41.8	5.0	18.7	18.2	1.5	9.6
Property taxes	69.4	28.3	36.1	5.7	19.6	10.7	3.1	17.6
Maintenance, repairs, insurance, other expenses	65.3	29.5	31.0	4.8	16.7	9.5	3.9	20.1
Homeowner's insurance	68.9	30.5	33.7	5.9	18.2	9.7	3.2	18.3
Ground rent	45.9	21.5	18.1	4.0	10.4	3.7	7.9	31.4
Maintenance and repair services	65.0	30.0	30.1	3.9	16.2	10.0	4.4	19.1
Painting and papering	64.1	22.3	34.3	7.2	18.8	8.3	3.8	19.5
Plumbing and water heating	59.6	27.8	29.1	3.0	15.1	11.1	6.1	18.5
Heat, air conditioning, electrical work	68.5	33.0	32.0	6.0	17.6	8.5	2.3	18.0
Roofing and gutters	69.3	36.3	29.7	1.5	12.3	15.8	3.6	16.9
Other repair and maintenance services	60.8	26.4	27.7	3.7	16.9	7.1	6.4	21.2
Repair, replacement of hard-surface flooring	71.5	36.3	31.6	2.9	16.1	12.6	1.6	17.3
Repair of built-in appliances	66.5	31.6	30.8	1.8	20.8	8.2	2.0	19.7
Maintenance and repair materials	74.6	27.5	41.2	6.8	23.5	10.9	2.4	14.8
Paints, wallpaper, and supplies	69.7	17.8	44.2	5.6	24.1	14.5	3.5	15.9
Tools, equipment for painting, wallpapering	70.0	17.8	44.3	5.6	24.1	14.5	3.5	15.9
Plumbing supplies and equipment	70.9	31.4	26.1	4.1	12.9	9.1	2.9	10.8
Electrical supplies, heating and cooling equipment	62.5	28.8	27.9	3.9	16.4	7.5	1.5	16.2
Hard-surface flooring, repair and replacement	73.8	30.3	39.7	5.5	22.0	12.2	3.0	15.5
Roofing and gutters	78.2	25.6	44.2	1.3	33.7	9.2	2.1	18.2
Plaster, paneling, siding, windows, doors, screens, awnings	75.6	25.7	44.1	9.6	20.8	13.6	2.0	16.2
Patio, walk, fence, driveway, masonry, brick, and stucco materials	73.1	24.7	46.8	6.5	33.9	6.3	0.1	13.3
Miscellaneous supplies and equipment	80.7	34.2	43.4	10.0	26.9	6.5	1.8	11.6
Property management and security	47.2	28.2	17.7	5.9	7.3	4.4	2.0	43.5
Property management	47.0	27.4	18.2	6.1	7.5	4.7	1.9	43.4
Management and upkeep services for security	49.8	35.8	12.6	4.6	5.9	2.1	2.4	44.1
Parking	37.0	26.3	9.1	1.3	5.9	1.9	3.6	51.4
Rented dwellings	**32.7**	**12.8**	**16.5**	**4.8**	**8.9**	**2.8**	**10.4**	**36.2**
Rent	32.6	12.7	16.6	4.9	8.9	2.8	10.1	36.3
Rent as pay	16.9	7.2	8.0	2.2	4.2	1.6	24.9	40.9
Maintenance, insurance, and other expenses	48.5	21.5	22.7	3.2	14.2	5.3	13.7	26.2
Tenant's insurance	45.5	25.6	17.0	4.8	9.5	2.7	7.2	35.6
Maintenance and repair services	43.5	20.9	16.6	1.7	7.2	7.7	23.7	26.6
Maintenance and repair materials	59.6	18.5	38.3	4.2	30.2	3.9	3.5	16.7
Other lodging	**73.1**	**36.6**	**32.5**	**3.4**	**17.3**	**11.8**	**2.7**	**16.0**
Owned vacation homes	70.9	41.4	24.1	2.5	11.7	9.8	2.9	17.1
Mortgage interest and charges	70.6	38.2	26.8	3.4	11.7	11.7	4.1	14.8
Property taxes	66.1	39.0	23.9	2.1	13.1	8.8	2.8	22.1
Maintenance, insurance, and other expenses	80.9	52.6	19.0	2.1	8.8	8.1	0.8	11.8
Housing while attending school	69.6	24.2	43.8	0.1	15.2	28.5	2.1	24.2
Lodging on trips	75.3	36.4	35.3	4.6	21.3	9.4	2.6	13.6

	total married couples	married couples, no children	married couples with children				single parent, at least one child <18	single person
			total	oldest child under 6	oldest child 6 to 17	oldest child 18 or older		
UTILITIES, FUELS, PUBLIC SERVICES	**62.1%**	**23.8%**	**32.6%**	**5.1%**	**17.4%**	**10.1%**	**5.6%**	**18.4%**
Natural gas	**61.2**	**23.0**	**32.7**	**5.2**	**17.2**	**10.3**	**5.2**	**19.0**
Electricity	**62.1**	**24.4**	**32.1**	**4.9**	**17.5**	**9.7**	**6.0**	**17.8**
Fuel oil and other fuels	**66.0**	**27.3**	**33.0**	**4.0**	**18.1**	**10.9**	**3.4**	**18.9**
Fuel oil	65.6	26.7	33.8	3.4	19.5	10.9	3.3	19.5
Bottled and tank gas	68.2	28.9	32.6	4.6	16.8	11.2	3.9	17.4
Wood and other fuels	58.0	23.3	29.2	4.9	15.1	9.2	2.3	22.4
Telephone services	**60.7**	**22.6**	**32.5**	**5.5**	**16.9**	**10.1**	**5.9**	**19.2**
Residential telephone and pay phones	59.2	23.3	30.3	5.0	16.0	9.3	6.2	20.4
Cellular phone service	64.0	21.5	37.0	6.3	18.6	12.0	5.4	16.7
Pager service	72.4	27.4	40.5	7.4	25.5	7.7	4.0	12.9
Phone cards	54.6	17.7	27.6	5.5	15.4	6.7	4.4	21.2
Water and other public services	**65.8**	**25.5**	**34.0**	**5.2**	**18.4**	**10.4**	**4.5**	**17.1**
Water and sewerage maintenance	66.5	24.9	35.0	5.4	18.8	10.8	4.7	16.1
Trash and garbage collection	63.8	27.0	31.4	4.9	17.2	9.3	4.0	20.3
Septic tank cleaning	69.0	31.1	35.1	2.6	20.1	12.4	3.4	9.1

* See appendix for information about mortgage principal reduction.
Note: Market share for total consumer units is 100.0%. Market shares by type of consumer unit will not add to total because not all types of consumer units are shown.
Source: Calculations by New Strategist based on the 2003 Consumer Expenditure Survey

Table 9.17 Housing: Shelter and Utilities: Average spending by race and Hispanic origin, 2003

(average annual spending of consumer units (CU) on shelter and utilities, by race and Hispanic origin of consumer unit reference person, 2003)

		race			Hispanic origin	
	total consumer units	Asian	black	white and other	Hispanic	non-Hispanic
Number of consumer units (000)	115,356	3,573	13,743	98,041	11,727	103,629
Average number of persons per CU	2.5	2.8	2.6	2.5	3.3	2.4
Average before-tax income of CU	$51,128.00	$60,393.00	$34,485.00	$53,039.00	$37,150.00	$52,797.00
Average spending of CU, total	40,817.33	44,922.85	28,707.56	42,360.25	34,574.75	41,520.78
Housing, average spending	13,431.87	16,326.15	10,622.26	13,719.46	12,300.40	13,561.68
SHELTER	**7,887.40**	**10,901.62**	**6,117.31**	**8,025.66**	**7,671.90**	**7,911.78**
Owned dwellings*	5,262.95	6,834.76	3,041.69	5,517.02	3,888.52	5,418.49
Mortgage interest and charges	2,954.01	4,347.69	1,847.96	3,058.26	2,470.93	3,008.68
Mortgage interest	2,830.50	4,244.39	1,791.31	2,924.64	2,412.91	2,877.76
Interest paid, home equity loan	64.00	21.31	42.01	68.64	42.89	66.39
Interest paid, home equity line of credit	58.47	81.99	14.64	63.76	15.13	63.38
Property taxes	1,343.82	1,713.06	747.72	1,413.92	779.38	1,407.70
Maintenance, repairs, insurance, other expenses	965.11	774.02	446.01	1,044.84	638.22	1,002.10
Homeowner's insurance	287.43	290.08	180.85	302.28	170.76	300.64
Ground rent	40.58	50.13	14.31	43.91	59.47	38.44
Maintenance and repair services	516.31	338.46	211.36	565.53	287.58	542.19
Painting and papering	60.58	52.17	26.67	65.64	40.74	62.83
Plumbing and water heating	48.43	24.77	32.81	51.49	27.52	50.80
Heat, air conditioning, electrical work	85.39	31.31	29.54	95.18	30.94	91.55
Roofing and gutters	97.98	63.29	46.55	106.46	49.26	103.50
Other repair and maintenance services	172.07	138.76	57.46	189.35	81.17	182.36
Repair, replacement of hard-surface flooring	45.89	23.15	16.53	50.83	56.94	44.64
Repair of built-in appliances	5.97	5.02	1.80	6.59	1.03	6.53
Maintenance and repair materials	78.80	46.04	22.87	87.83	98.91	76.52
Paints, wallpaper, and supplies	12.22	4.77	4.73	13.54	11.70	12.28
Tools, equipment for painting, wallpapering	1.31	0.51	0.51	1.45	1.26	1.32
Plumbing supplies and equipment	5.37	1.96	3.38	5.78	9.18	4.94
Electrical supplies, heating and cooling equipment	3.38	0.91	1.94	3.68	3.76	3.34
Hard-surface flooring, repair and replacement	15.40	12.88	2.81	17.25	32.34	13.48
Roofing and gutters	6.91	2.66	0.27	7.99	14.39	6.06
Plaster, paneling, siding, windows, doors, screens, awnings	16.81	12.91	4.22	18.71	13.42	17.19
Patio, walk, fence, driveway, masonry, brick, and stucco materials	1.42	–	0.39	1.62	0.21	1.56
Miscellaneous supplies and equipment	15.84	9.28	4.62	17.65	12.60	16.21
Property management and security	36.52	44.55	14.45	39.32	18.70	38.54
Property management	33.03	42.59	13.24	35.45	17.20	34.82
Management and upkeep services for security	3.49	1.96	1.22	3.87	1.50	3.72
Parking	5.47	4.75	2.17	5.96	2.80	5.77
Rented dwellings	**2,179.49**	**3,660.82**	**2,946.36**	**2,018.01**	**3,559.71**	**2,023.30**
Rent	2,109.74	3,584.04	2,843.26	1,953.18	3,451.86	1,957.85
Rent as pay	32.98	26.89	88.32	25.45	66.55	29.18
Maintenance, insurance, and other expenses	36.77	49.88	14.79	39.38	41.30	36.26
Tenant's insurance	9.67	7.51	8.20	9.96	4.53	10.25
Maintenance and repair services	16.88	42.09	4.50	17.69	10.38	17.61
Maintenance and repair materials	10.23	0.29	2.09	11.73	26.38	8.40
Other lodging	**444.96**	**406.05**	**129.25**	**490.63**	**223.66**	**470.00**
Owned vacation homes	150.29	59.36	48.04	167.94	114.47	154.34
Mortgage interest and charges	61.55	29.47	22.74	68.17	49.69	62.90
Property taxes	58.90	21.09	18.06	66.00	26.71	62.54
Maintenance, insurance, and other expenses	29.84	8.80	7.24	33.77	38.07	28.91
Housing while attending school	52.90	80.69	17.69	56.82	14.26	57.27
Lodging on trips	241.77	265.99	63.52	265.87	94.93	258.38

	total consumer units	race			Hispanic origin	
		Asian	black	white and other	Hispanic	non-Hispanic
UTILITIES, FUELS, AND PUBLIC SERVICES	$2,811.43	$2,536.06	$2,910.33	$2,807.60	$2,490.05	$2,847.80
Natural gas	392.01	384.95	465.16	382.01	300.85	402.33
Electricity	1,027.91	779.94	1,094.20	1,027.66	860.44	1,046.87
Fuel oil and other fuels	109.52	26.73	46.25	121.41	56.51	115.52
Fuel oil	57.54	21.20	20.13	64.11	22.83	61.47
Bottled and tank gas	42.42	2.93	19.17	47.12	25.42	44.34
Wood and other fuels	9.10	2.60	6.94	9.64	8.05	9.22
Telephone services	955.70	1,026.33	1,026.75	943.16	967.60	954.35
Residential telephone and pay phones	619.60	606.32	735.73	603.81	603.22	621.45
Cellular phone service	316.10	368.45	272.11	320.36	303.30	317.55
Pager service	1.12	2.25	0.75	1.13	0.99	1.13
Phone cards	18.88	49.30	18.15	17.87	60.09	14.21
Water and other public services	326.29	318.11	277.96	333.36	304.65	328.73
Water and sewerage maintenance	236.30	234.83	221.91	238.37	231.10	236.89
Trash and garbage collection	87.63	82.18	55.23	92.37	72.48	89.35
Septic tank cleaning	2.35	1.11	0.82	2.61	1.08	2.50

* See appendix for information about mortgage principal reduction.
Note: Other races include Native Americans and Pacific Islanders. Subcategories may not add to total because some are not shown. (–) means sample is too small to make a reliable estimate.
Source: Bureau of Labor Statistics, unpublished tables from the 2003 Consumer Expenditure Survey

Table 9.18 Housing: Shelter and Utilities: Indexed spending by race and Hispanic origin, 2003

(indexed average annual spending of consumer units (CU) on shelter and utilities, by race and Hispanic origin of consumer unit reference person, 2003; index definition: an index of 100 is the average for all consumer units; an index of 132 means that spending by consumer units in that group is 32 percent above the average for all consumer units; an index of 68 indicates spending that is 32 percent below the average for all consumer units)

		race			Hispanic origin	
	total consumer units	Asian	black	white and other	Hispanic	non-Hispanic
Average spending of CU, total	$40,817	$44,923	$28,708	$42,360	$34,575	$41,521
Average spending of CU, index	100	110	70	104	85	102
Housing, spending index	**100**	**122**	**79**	**102**	**92**	**101**
SHELTER	**100**	**138**	**78**	**102**	**97**	**100**
Owned dwellings*	**100**	**130**	**58**	**105**	**74**	**103**
Mortgage interest and charges	100	147	63	104	84	102
Mortgage interest	100	150	63	103	85	102
Interest paid, home equity loan	100	33	66	107	67	104
Interest paid, home equity line of credit	100	140	25	109	26	108
Property taxes	100	128	56	105	58	105
Maintenance, repairs, insurance, other expenses	100	80	46	108	66	104
Homeowner's insurance	100	101	63	105	59	105
Ground rent	100	124	35	108	147	95
Maintenance and repair services	100	66	41	110	56	105
Painting and papering	100	86	44	108	67	104
Plumbing and water heating	100	51	68	106	57	105
Heat, air conditioning, electrical work	100	37	35	112	36	107
Roofing and gutters	100	65	48	109	50	106
Other repair and maintenance services	100	81	33	110	47	106
Repair, replacement of hard-surface flooring	100	50	36	111	124	97
Repair of built-in appliances	100	84	30	110	17	109
Maintenance and repair materials	100	58	29	112	126	97
Paints, wallpaper, and supplies	100	39	39	111	96	101
Tools, equipment for painting, wallpapering	100	39	39	111	96	101
Plumbing supplies and equipment	100	37	63	108	171	92
Electrical supplies, heating and cooling equipment	100	27	57	109	111	99
Hard-surface flooring, repair and replacement	100	84	18	112	210	88
Roofing and gutters	100	39	4	116	208	88
Plaster, paneling, siding, windows, doors, screens, awnings	100	77	25	111	80	102
Patio, walk, fence, driveway, masonry, brick, and stucco materials	100	–	28	114	15	110
Miscellaneous supplies and equipment	100	59	29	111	80	102
Property management and security	100	122	40	108	51	106
Property management	100	129	40	107	52	105
Management and upkeep services for security	100	56	35	111	43	107
Parking	100	87	40	109	51	106
Rented dwellings	**100**	**168**	**135**	**93**	**163**	**93**
Rent	100	170	135	93	164	93
Rent as pay	100	82	268	77	202	89
Maintenance, insurance, and other expenses	100	136	40	107	112	99
Tenant's insurance	100	78	85	103	47	106
Maintenance and repair services	100	249	27	105	62	104
Maintenance and repair materials	100	3	20	115	258	82
Other lodging	**100**	**91**	**29**	**110**	**50**	**106**
Owned vacation homes	100	40	32	112	76	103
Mortgage interest and charges	100	48	37	111	81	102
Property taxes	100	36	31	112	45	106
Maintenance, insurance, and other expenses	100	30	24	113	128	97
Housing while attending school	100	153	33	107	27	108
Lodging on trips	100	110	26	110	39	107

	total consumer units	race			Hispanic origin	
		Asian	black	white and other	Hispanic	non-Hispanic
UTILITIES, FUELS, AND PUBLIC SERVICES	100	90	104	100	89	101
Natural gas	100	98	119	97	77	103
Electricity	100	76	106	100	84	102
Fuel oil and other fuels	100	24	42	111	52	106
Fuel oil	100	37	35	111	40	107
Bottled and tank gas	100	7	45	111	60	105
Wood and other fuels	100	29	76	106	89	101
Telephone services	100	107	107	99	101	100
Residential telephone and pay phones	100	98	119	98	97	100
Cellular phone service	100	117	86	101	96	101
Pager service	100	201	67	101	88	101
Phone cards	100	261	96	95	318	75
Water and other public services	100	98	85	102	93	101
Water and sewerage maintenance	100	99	94	101	98	100
Trash and garbage collection	100	94	63	105	83	102
Septic tank cleaning	100	47	35	111	46	106

See appendix for information about mortgage principal reduction.
Note: Other races include Native Americans and Pacific Islanders. (–) means sample is too small to make a reliable estimate.
Source: Calculations by New Strategist based on the 2003 Consumer Expenditure Survey

Table 9.19 Housing: Shelter and Utilities: Total spending by race and Hispanic origin, 2003

(total annual spending on shelter and utilities, by consumer unit race and Hispanic origin groups, 2003; numbers in thousands)

		race			Hispanic origin	
	total consumer units	Asian	black	white and other	Hispanic	non-Hispanic
Number of consumer units	115,356	3,573	13,743	98,041	11,727	103,629
Total spending of all consumer units	$4,708,523,920	$160,509,343	$394,527,997	$4,153,041,270	$405,458,093	$4,302,756,911
Housing, total spending	1,549,446,796	58,333,334	145,981,719	1,345,069,578	144,246,791	1,405,383,337
SHELTER	909,858,914	38,951,488	84,070,191	786,843,732	89,968,371	819,889,850
Owned dwellings*	607,112,860	24,420,598	41,801,946	540,894,158	45,600,674	561,512,700
Mortgage interest and charges	340,762,778	15,534,296	25,396,514	299,834,869	28,976,596	311,786,500
Mortgage interest	326,515,158	15,165,206	24,617,973	286,734,630	28,296,196	298,219,391
Interest paid, home equity loan	7,382,784	76,141	577,343	6,729,534	502,971	6,879,929
Interest paid, home equity line of credit	6,744,865	292,950	201,198	6,251,094	177,430	6,568,006
Property taxes	155,017,700	6,120,763	10,275,916	138,622,131	9,139,789	145,878,543
Maintenance, repairs, insurance, other expenses	111,331,229	2,765,574	6,129,515	102,437,158	7,484,406	103,846,621
Homeowner's insurance	33,156,775	1,036,456	2,485,422	29,635,834	2,002,503	31,155,023
Ground rent	4,681,147	179,115	196,662	4,304,980	697,405	3,983,499
Maintenance and repair services	59,559,456	1,209,318	2,904,721	55,445,127	3,372,451	56,186,608
Painting and papering	6,988,267	186,403	366,526	6,435,411	477,758	6,511,010
Plumbing and water heating	5,586,691	88,503	450,908	5,048,131	322,727	5,264,353
Heat, air conditioning, electrical work	9,850,249	111,871	405,968	9,331,542	362,833	9,487,235
Roofing and gutters	11,302,581	226,135	639,737	10,437,445	577,672	10,725,602
Other repair and maintenance services	19,849,307	495,790	789,673	18,564,063	951,881	18,897,784
Repair, replacement of hard-surface flooring	5,293,687	82,715	227,172	4,983,424	667,735	4,625,999
Repair of built-in appliances	688,675	17,937	24,737	646,090	12,079	676,697
Maintenance and repair materials	9,090,053	164,501	314,302	8,610,941	1,159,918	7,929,691
Paints, wallpaper, and supplies	1,409,650	17,043	65,004	1,327,475	137,206	1,272,564
Tools, equipment for painting, wallpapering	151,116	1,822	7,009	142,160	14,776	136,790
Plumbing supplies and equipment	619,462	7,003	46,451	566,677	107,654	511,927
Electrical supplies, heating and cooling equipment	389,903	3,251	26,661	360,791	44,094	346,121
Hard-surface flooring, repair and replacement	1,776,482	46,020	38,618	1,691,207	379,251	1,396,919
Roofing and gutters	797,110	9,504	3,711	783,348	168,752	627,992
Plaster, paneling, siding, windows, doors, screens, awnings	1,939,134	46,127	57,996	1,834,347	157,376	1,781,383
Patio, walk, fence, driveway, masonry, brick, and stucco materials	163,806	–	5,360	158,446	2,463	161,661
Miscellaneous supplies and equipment	1,827,239	33,157	63,493	1,730,424	147,760	1,679,826
Property management and security	4,212,801	159,177	198,586	3,854,972	219,295	3,993,862
Property management	3,810,209	152,174	181,957	3,475,554	201,704	3,608,362
Management and upkeep services for security	402,592	7,003	16,767	379,419	17,591	385,500
Parking	630,997	16,972	29,822	584,324	32,836	597,939
Rented dwellings	251,417,248	13,080,110	40,491,826	197,847,718	41,744,719	209,672,556
Rent	243,371,167	12,805,775	39,074,922	191,491,720	40,479,962	202,890,038
Rent as pay	3,804,441	96,078	1,213,782	2,495,144	780,432	3,023,894
Maintenance, insurance, and other expenses	4,241,640	178,221	203,259	3,860,855	484,325	3,757,588
Tenant's insurance	1,115,493	26,833	112,693	976,488	53,123	1,062,197
Maintenance and repair services	1,947,209	150,388	61,844	1,734,345	121,726	1,824,907
Maintenance and repair materials	1,180,092	1,036	28,723	1,150,021	309,358	870,484
Other lodging	51,328,806	1,450,817	1,776,283	48,101,856	2,622,861	48,705,630
Owned vacation homes	17,336,853	212,093	660,214	16,465,006	1,342,390	15,994,100
Mortgage interest and charges	7,100,162	105,296	312,516	6,683,455	582,715	6,518,264
Property taxes	6,794,468	75,355	248,199	6,470,706	313,228	6,480,958
Maintenance, insurance, and other expenses	3,442,223	31,442	99,499	3,310,845	446,447	2,995,914
Housing while attending school	6,102,332	288,305	243,114	5,570,690	167,227	5,934,833
Lodging on trips	27,889,620	950,382	872,955	26,066,161	1,113,244	26,775,661

	total consumer units	race			Hispanic origin	
		Asian	black	white and other	Hispanic	non-Hispanic
UTILITIES, FUELS, AND PUBLIC SERVICES	$324,315,319	$9,061,342	$39,996,665	$275,259,912	$29,200,816	$295,114,666
Natural gas	45,220,706	1,375,426	6,392,694	37,452,642	3,528,068	41,693,056
Electricity	118,575,586	2,786,726	15,037,591	100,752,814	10,090,380	108,486,091
Fuel oil and other fuels	12,633,789	95,506	635,614	11,903,158	662,693	11,971,222
Fuel oil	6,637,584	75,748	276,647	6,285,409	267,727	6,370,075
Bottled and tank gas	4,893,402	10,469	263,453	4,619,692	298,100	4,594,910
Wood and other fuels	1,049,740	9,290	95,376	945,115	94,402	955,459
Telephone services	110,245,729	3,667,077	14,110,625	92,468,350	11,347,045	98,898,336
Residential telephone and pay phones	71,474,578	2,166,381	10,111,137	59,198,136	7,073,961	64,400,242
Cellular phone service	36,464,032	1,316,508	3,739,608	31,408,415	3,556,799	32,907,389
Pager service	129,199	8,039	10,307	110,786	11,610	117,101
Phone cards	2,177,921	176,149	249,436	1,751,993	704,675	1,472,568
Water and other public services	37,639,509	1,136,607	3,820,004	32,682,948	3,572,631	34,065,961
Water and sewerage maintenance	27,258,623	839,048	3,049,709	23,370,033	2,710,110	24,548,674
Trash and garbage collection	10,108,646	293,629	759,026	9,056,047	849,973	9,259,251
Septic tank cleaning	271,087	3,966	11,269	255,887	12,665	259,073

* See appendix for information about mortgage principal reduction.
Note: Other races include Native Americans and Pacific Islanders. Numbers may not add to total because of rounding and missing subcategories. (–) means sample is too small to make a reliable estimate.
Source: Calculations by New Strategist based on the 2003 Consumer Expenditure Survey

Table 9.20 Housing: Shelter and Utilities: Market shares by race and Hispanic origin, 2003

(percentage of total annual spending on shelter and utilities accounted for by consumer unit race and Hispanic origin groups, 2003)

	total consumer units	race			Hispanic origin	
		Asian	black	white and other	Hispanic	non-Hispanic
Share of total consumer units	100.0%	3.1%	11.9%	85.0%	10.2%	89.8%
Share of total before-tax income	100.0	3.7	8.0	88.2	7.4	92.8
Share of total spending	100.0	3.4	8.4	88.2	8.6	91.4
Share of housing spending	100.0	3.8	9.4	86.8	9.3	90.7
SHELTER	**100.0**	**4.3**	**9.2**	**86.5**	**9.9**	**90.1**
Owned dwellings*	**100.0**	**4.0**	**6.9**	**89.1**	**7.5**	**92.5**
Mortgage interest and charges	100.0	4.6	7.5	88.0	8.5	91.5
Mortgage interest	100.0	4.6	7.5	87.8	8.7	91.3
Interest paid, home equity loan	100.0	1.0	7.8	91.2	6.8	93.2
Interest paid, home equity line of credit	100.0	4.3	3.0	92.7	2.6	97.4
Property taxes	100.0	3.9	6.6	89.4	5.9	94.1
Maintenance, repairs, insurance, other expenses	100.0	2.5	5.5	92.0	6.7	93.3
Homeowner's insurance	100.0	3.1	7.5	89.4	6.0	94.0
Ground rent	100.0	3.8	4.2	92.0	14.9	85.1
Maintenance and repair services	100.0	2.0	4.9	93.1	5.7	94.3
Painting and papering	100.0	2.7	5.2	92.1	6.8	93.2
Plumbing and water heating	100.0	1.6	8.1	90.4	5.8	94.2
Heat, air conditioning, electrical work	100.0	1.1	4.1	94.7	3.7	96.3
Roofing and gutters	100.0	2.0	5.7	92.3	5.1	94.9
Other repair and maintenance services	100.0	2.5	4.0	93.5	4.8	95.2
Repair, replacement of hard-surface flooring	100.0	1.6	4.3	94.1	12.6	87.4
Repair of built-in appliances	100.0	2.6	3.6	93.8	1.8	98.3
Maintenance and repair materials	100.0	1.8	3.5	94.7	12.8	87.2
Paints, wallpaper, and supplies	100.0	1.2	4.6	94.2	9.7	90.3
Tools, equipment for painting, wallpapering	100.0	1.2	4.6	94.1	9.8	90.5
Plumbing supplies and equipment	100.0	1.1	7.5	91.5	17.4	82.6
Electrical supplies, heating and cooling equipment	100.0	0.8	6.8	92.5	11.3	88.8
Hard-surface flooring, repair and replacement	100.0	2.6	2.2	95.2	21.3	78.6
Roofing and gutters	100.0	1.2	0.5	98.3	21.2	78.8
Plaster, paneling, siding, windows, doors, screens, awnings	100.0	2.4	3.0	94.6	8.1	91.9
Patio, walk, fence, driveway, masonry, brick, and stucco materials	100.0	–	3.3	96.7	1.5	98.7
Miscellaneous supplies and equipment	100.0	1.8	3.5	94.7	8.1	91.9
Property management and security	100.0	3.8	4.7	91.5	5.2	94.8
Property management	100.0	4.0	4.8	91.2	5.3	94.7
Management and upkeep services for security	100.0	1.7	4.2	94.2	4.4	95.8
Parking	100.0	2.7	4.7	92.6	5.2	94.8
Rented dwellings	**100.0**	**5.2**	**16.1**	**78.7**	**16.6**	**83.4**
Rent	100.0	5.3	16.1	78.7	16.6	83.4
Rent as pay	100.0	2.5	31.9	65.6	20.5	79.5
Maintenance, insurance, and other expenses	100.0	4.2	4.8	91.0	11.4	88.6
Tenant's insurance	100.0	2.4	10.1	87.5	4.8	95.2
Maintenance and repair services	100.0	7.7	3.2	89.1	6.3	93.7
Maintenance and repair materials	100.0	0.1	2.4	97.5	26.2	73.8
Other lodging	**100.0**	**2.8**	**3.5**	**93.7**	**5.1**	**94.9**
Owned vacation homes	100.0	1.2	3.8	95.0	7.7	92.3
Mortgage interest and charges	100.0	1.5	4.4	94.1	8.2	91.8
Property taxes	100.0	1.1	3.7	95.2	4.6	95.4
Maintenance, insurance, and other expenses	100.0	0.9	2.9	96.2	13.0	87.0
Housing while attending school	100.0	4.7	4.0	91.3	2.7	97.3
Lodging on trips	100.0	3.4	3.1	93.5	4.0	96.0

	total consumer units	race			Hispanic origin	
		Asian	black	white and other	Hispanic	non-Hispanic
UTILITIES, FUELS, AND PUBLIC SERVICES	100.0%	2.8%	12.3%	84.9%	9.0%	91.0%
Natural gas	100.0	3.0	14.1	82.8	7.8	92.2
Electricity	100.0	2.4	12.7	85.0	8.5	91.5
Fuel oil and other fuels	100.0	0.8	5.0	94.2	5.2	94.8
Fuel oil	100.0	1.1	4.2	94.7	4.0	96.0
Bottled and tank gas	100.0	0.2	5.4	94.4	6.1	93.9
Wood and other fuels	100.0	0.9	9.1	90.0	9.0	91.0
Telephone services	100.0	3.3	12.8	83.9	10.3	89.7
Residential telephone and pay phones	100.0	3.0	14.1	82.8	9.9	90.1
Cellular phone service	100.0	3.6	10.3	86.1	9.8	90.2
Pager service	100.0	6.2	8.0	85.7	9.0	90.6
Phone cards	100.0	8.1	11.5	80.4	32.4	67.6
Water and other public services	100.0	3.0	10.1	86.8	9.5	90.5
Water and sewerage maintenance	100.0	3.2	11.2	85.7	9.9	90.1
Trash and garbage collection	100.0	2.9	7.5	89.6	8.4	91.6
Septic tank cleaning	100.0	1.5	4.2	94.4	4.7	95.6

* See appendix for information about mortgage principal reduction.
Note: Other races include Native Americans and Pacific Islanders. Numbers may not add to total because of rounding. (–) means sample is too small to make a reliable estimate.
Source: Calculations by New Strategist based on the 2003 Consumer Expenditure Survey

Table 9.21 Housing: Shelter and Utilities: Average spending by region, 2003

(average annual spending of consumer units (CU) on shelter and utilities, by region in which consumer unit lives, 2003)

	total consumer units	Northeast	Midwest	South	West
Number of consumer units (000)	115,356	22,182	26,438	41,325	25,412
Average number of persons per CU	2.5	2.4	2.5	2.5	2.6
Average before-tax income of CU	$48,596.00	$54,219.00	$49,591.00	$44,461.00	$49,667.00
Average spending of CU, total	40,817.33	42,162.29	40,280.39	37,624.55	45,380.67
Housing, average spending	13,431.87	14,811.03	12,634.36	12,006.35	15,371.39
SHELTER	**7,887.40**	**9,133.80**	**7,085.69**	**6,659.80**	**9,629.83**
Owned dwellings*	**5,262.95**	**5,932.06**	**4,907.97**	**4,527.53**	**6,244.13**
Mortgage interest and charges	2,954.01	2,901.30	2,577.90	2,567.45	4,019.96
Mortgage interest	2,830.50	2,718.57	2,442.27	2,474.75	3,910.66
Interest paid, home equity loan	64.00	106.97	58.36	51.73	52.31
Interest paid, home equity line of credit	58.47	75.76	77.27	40.98	52.27
Property taxes	1,343.82	2,004.26	1,426.99	1,017.65	1,211.23
Maintenance, repairs, insurance, other expenses	965.11	1,026.50	903.09	942.43	1,012.93
Homeowner's insurance	287.43	239.71	303.74	316.01	265.65
Ground rent	40.58	17.73	30.82	33.61	82.01
Maintenance and repair services	516.31	618.08	452.26	502.45	516.63
Painting and papering	60.58	49.31	47.10	65.37	76.65
Plumbing and water heating	48.43	61.35	39.79	42.72	55.45
Heat, air conditioning, electrical work	85.39	102.51	71.09	100.04	61.48
Roofing and gutters	97.98	135.95	95.94	84.08	89.58
Other repair and maintenance services	172.07	213.03	157.38	159.41	172.19
Repair, replacement of hard-surface flooring	45.89	44.58	37.62	44.89	57.24
Repair of built-in appliances	5.97	11.35	3.34	5.94	4.05
Maintenance and repair materials	78.80	82.49	85.04	58.90	101.45
Paints, wallpaper, and supplies	12.22	14.79	11.32	10.21	14.19
Tools, equipment for painting, wallpapering	1.31	1.59	1.22	1.10	1.52
Plumbing supplies and equipment	5.37	5.97	3.85	4.96	7.11
Electrical supplies, heating and cooling equipment	3.38	3.60	2.58	3.81	3.33
Hard-surface flooring, repair and replacement	15.40	7.30	17.56	15.16	20.61
Roofing and gutters	6.91	6.91	8.36	5.69	7.36
Plaster, paneling, siding, windows, doors, screens, awnings	16.81	13.90	23.28	9.88	23.86
Patio, walk, fence, driveway, masonry, brick, and stucco materials	1.42	3.03	1.13	0.54	1.76
Miscellaneous supplies and equipment	15.84	25.40	15.74	7.39	21.33
Property management and security	36.52	62.52	26.95	26.02	40.88
Property management	33.03	59.36	25.06	22.02	36.24
Management and upkeep services for security	3.49	3.15	1.88	4.00	4.64
Parking	5.47	5.98	4.29	5.44	6.32
Rented dwellings	**2,179.49**	**2,664.43**	**1,719.81**	**1,802.20**	**2,847.99**
Rent	2,109.74	2,589.77	1,658.98	1,742.05	2,757.62
Rent as pay	32.98	40.96	35.99	30.40	27.08
Maintenance, insurance, and other expenses	36.77	33.70	24.84	29.75	63.30
Tenant's insurance	9.67	8.82	11.24	9.17	9.59
Maintenance and repair services	16.88	17.01	7.38	13.03	32.90
Maintenance and repair materials	10.23	7.86	6.22	7.55	20.81
Other lodging	**444.96**	**537.31**	**457.90**	**330.06**	**537.71**
Owned vacation homes	150.29	193.32	151.56	101.67	190.48
Mortgage interest and charges	61.55	67.24	62.15	44.58	83.57
Property taxes	58.90	92.00	57.84	37.17	66.42
Maintenance, insurance, and other expenses	29.84	34.08	31.57	19.91	40.48
Housing while attending school	52.90	53.33	52.39	42.68	69.66
Lodging on trips	241.77	290.67	253.95	185.71	277.57

	total consumer units	Northeast	Midwest	South	West
UTILITIES, FUELS, AND PUBLIC SERVICES	$2,811.43	$2,889.24	$2,854.86	$2,891.19	$2,568.62
Natural gas	392.01	511.52	593.21	243.36	320.10
Electricity	1,027.91	926.48	930.81	1,251.39	854.07
Fuel oil and other fuels	109.52	287.44	99.29	60.90	43.92
Fuel oil	57.54	242.74	13.45	16.24	8.94
Bottled and tank gas	42.42	24.75	80.65	37.17	26.61
Wood and other fuels	9.10	17.92	5.01	7.49	8.28
Telephone services	955.70	931.99	916.81	1,002.17	941.28
Residential telephone and pay phones	619.60	636.64	594.03	654.68	574.28
Cellular phone service	316.10	276.69	305.53	328.51	341.33
Pager service	1.12	0.88	0.92	1.33	1.19
Phone cards	18.88	17.78	16.33	17.64	24.48
Water and other public services	326.29	231.82	314.73	333.37	409.24
Water and sewerage maintenance	236.30	174.60	226.12	246.26	284.56
Trash and garbage collection	87.63	54.36	86.34	84.68	122.81
Septic tank cleaning	2.35	2.86	2.28	2.43	1.86

See appendix for information about mortgage principal reduction.
Note: Subcategories may not add to total because some are not shown.
Source: Bureau of Labor Statistics, unpublished tables from the 2003 Consumer Expenditure Survey

Table 9.22 Housing: Shelter and Utilities: Indexed spending by region, 2003

(indexed average annual spending of consumer units (CU) on shelter and utilities, by region in which consumer unit lives, 2003; index definition: an index of 100 is the average for all consumer units; an index of 132 means that spending by consumer units in that group is 32 percent above the average for all consumer units; an index of 68 indicates spending that is 32 percent below the average for all consumer units)

	total consumer units	Northeast	Midwest	South	West
Average spending of CU, total	$40,817	$42,162	$40,280	$37,625	$45,381
Average spending of CU, index	100	103	99	92	111
Housing, spending index	100	110	94	89	114
SHELTER	100	116	90	84	122
Owned dwellings*	100	113	93	86	119
Mortgage interest and charges	100	98	87	87	136
Mortgage interest	100	96	86	87	138
Interest paid, home equity loan	100	167	91	81	82
Interest paid, home equity line of credit	100	130	132	70	89
Property taxes	100	149	106	76	90
Maintenance, repairs, insurance, other expenses	100	106	94	98	105
Homeowner's insurance	100	83	106	110	92
Ground rent	100	44	76	83	202
Maintenance and repair services	100	120	88	97	100
Painting and papering	100	81	78	108	127
Plumbing and water heating	100	127	82	88	115
Heat, air conditioning, electrical work	100	120	83	117	72
Roofing and gutters	100	139	98	86	91
Other repair and maintenance services	100	124	92	93	100
Repair, replacement of hard-surface flooring	100	97	82	98	125
Repair of built-in appliances	100	190	56	100	68
Maintenance and repair materials	100	105	108	75	129
Paints, wallpaper, and supplies	100	121	93	84	116
Tools, equipment for painting, wallpapering	100	121	93	84	116
Plumbing supplies and equipment	100	111	72	92	132
Electrical supplies, heating and cooling equipment	100	107	76	113	99
Hard-surface flooring, repair and replacement	100	47	114	98	134
Roofing and gutters	100	100	121	82	107
Plaster, paneling, siding, windows, doors, screens, awnings	100	83	139	59	142
Patio, walk, fence, driveway, masonry, brick, and stucco materials	100	213	80	38	124
Miscellaneous supplies and equipment	100	160	99	47	135
Property management and security	100	171	74	71	112
Property management	100	180	76	67	110
Management and upkeep services for security	100	90	54	115	133
Parking	100	109	78	100	116
Rented dwellings	100	122	79	83	131
Rent	100	123	79	83	131
Rent as pay	100	124	109	92	82
Maintenance, insurance, and other expenses	100	92	68	81	172
Tenant's insurance	100	91	116	95	99
Maintenance and repair services	100	101	44	77	195
Maintenance and repair materials	100	77	61	74	203
Other lodging	100	121	103	74	121
Owned vacation homes	100	129	101	68	127
Mortgage interest and charges	100	109	101	72	136
Property taxes	100	156	98	63	113
Maintenance, insurance, and other expenses	100	114	106	67	136
Housing while attending school	100	101	99	81	132
Lodging on trips	100	120	105	77	115

	total consumer units	Northeast	Midwest	South	West
UTILITIES, FUELS, AND PUBLIC SERVICES	**100**	**103**	**102**	**103**	**91**
Natural gas	**100**	**131**	**151**	**62**	**82**
Electricity	**100**	**90**	**91**	**122**	**83**
Fuel oil and other fuels	**100**	**263**	**91**	**56**	**40**
Fuel oil	100	422	23	28	16
Bottled and tank gas	100	58	190	88	63
Wood and other fuels	100	197	55	82	91
Telephone services	100	98	96	105	99
Residential telephone and pay phones	**100**	**103**	**96**	**106**	**93**
Cellular phone service	100	88	97	104	108
Pager service	100	79	82	119	106
Phone cards	100	94	87	93	130
Water and other public services	**100**	**71**	**97**	**102**	**125**
Water and sewerage maintenance	100	74	96	104	120
Trash and garbage collection	100	62	99	97	140
Septic tank cleaning	100	122	97	103	79

* See appendix for information about mortgage principal reduction.
Source: Calculations by New Strategist based on the 2003 Consumer Expenditure Survey

Table 9.23 Housing: Shelter and Utilities: Total spending by region, 2003

(total annual spending on shelter and utilities, by region in which consumer units live, 2003; numbers in thousands)

	total consumer units	Northeast	Midwest	South	West
Number of consumer units	115,356	22,182	26,438	41,325	25,412
Total spending of all consumer units	$4,708,523,920	$935,243,917	$1,064,932,951	$1,554,834,529	$1,153,213,586
Housing, total spending	**1,549,446,796**	**328,538,268**	**334,027,210**	**496,162,414**	**390,617,763**
SHELTER	**909,858,914**	**202,605,952**	**187,331,472**	**275,216,235**	**244,713,240**
Owned dwellings*	**607,112,860**	**131,584,955**	**129,756,911**	**187,100,177**	**158,675,832**
Mortgage interest and charges	340,762,778	64,356,637	68,154,520	106,099,871	102,155,224
Mortgage interest	326,515,158	60,303,320	64,568,734	102,269,044	99,377,692
Interest paid, home equity loan	7,382,784	2,372,809	1,542,922	2,137,742	1,329,302
Interest paid, home equity line of credit	6,744,865	1,680,508	2,042,864	1,693,499	1,328,285
Property taxes	155,017,700	44,458,495	37,726,762	42,054,386	30,779,777
Maintenance, repairs, insurance, other expenses	111,331,229	22,769,823	23,875,893	38,945,920	25,740,577
Homeowner's insurance	33,156,775	5,317,247	8,030,278	13,059,113	6,750,698
Ground rent	4,681,147	393,287	814,819	1,388,933	2,084,038
Maintenance and repair services	59,559,456	13,710,251	11,956,850	20,763,746	13,128,602
Painting and papering	6,988,267	1,093,794	1,245,230	2,701,415	1,947,830
Plumbing and water heating	5,586,691	1,360,866	1,051,968	1,765,404	1,409,095
Heat, air conditioning, electrical work	9,850,249	2,273,877	1,879,477	4,134,153	1,562,330
Roofing and gutters	11,302,581	3,015,643	2,536,462	3,474,606	2,276,407
Other repair and maintenance services	19,849,307	4,725,432	4,160,812	6,587,618	4,375,692
Repair, replacement of hard-surface flooring	5,293,687	988,874	994,598	1,855,079	1,454,583
Repair of built-in appliances	688,675	251,766	88,303	245,471	102,919
Maintenance and repair materials	9,090,053	1,829,793	2,248,288	2,434,043	2,578,047
Paints, wallpaper, and supplies	1,409,650	328,072	299,278	421,928	360,596
Tools, equipment for painting, wallpapering	151,116	35,269	32,254	45,458	38,626
Plumbing supplies and equipment	619,462	132,427	101,786	204,972	180,679
Electrical supplies, heating and cooling equipment	389,903	79,855	68,210	157,448	84,622
Hard-surface flooring, repair and replacement	1,776,482	161,929	464,251	626,487	523,741
Roofing and gutters	797,110	153,278	221,022	235,139	187,032
Plaster, paneling, siding, windows, doors, screens, awnings	1,939,134	308,330	615,477	408,291	606,330
Patio, walk, fence, driveway, masonry, brick, and stucco materials	163,806	67,212	29,875	22,316	44,725
Miscellaneous supplies and equipment	1,827,239	563,423	416,134	305,392	542,038
Property management and security	4,212,801	1,386,819	712,504	1,075,277	1,038,843
Property management	3,810,209	1,316,724	662,536	909,977	920,931
Management and upkeep services for security	402,592	69,873	49,703	165,300	117,912
Parking	630,997	132,648	113,419	224,808	160,604
Rented dwellings	**251,417,248**	**59,102,386**	**45,468,337**	**74,475,915**	**72,373,122**
Rent	243,371,167	57,446,278	43,860,113	71,990,216	70,076,639
Rent as pay	3,804,441	908,575	951,504	1,256,280	688,157
Maintenance, insurance, and other expenses	4,241,640	747,533	656,720	1,229,419	1,608,580
Tenant's insurance	1,115,493	195,645	297,163	378,950	243,701
Maintenance and repair services	1,947,209	377,316	195,112	538,465	836,055
Maintenance and repair materials	1,180,092	174,351	164,444	312,004	528,824
Other lodging	**51,328,806**	**11,918,610**	**12,105,960**	**13,639,730**	**13,664,287**
Owned vacation homes	17,336,853	4,288,224	4,006,943	4,201,513	4,840,478
Mortgage interest and charges	7,100,162	1,491,518	1,643,122	1,842,269	2,123,681
Property taxes	6,794,468	2,040,744	1,529,174	1,536,050	1,687,865
Maintenance, insurance, and other expenses	3,442,223	755,963	834,648	822,781	1,028,678
Housing while attending school	6,102,332	1,182,966	1,385,087	1,763,751	1,770,200
Lodging on trips	27,889,620	6,447,642	6,713,930	7,674,466	7,053,609

	total consumer units	Northeast	Midwest	South	West
UTILITIES, FUELS, AND PUBLIC SERVICES	**$324,315,319**	**$64,089,122**	**$75,476,789**	**$119,478,427**	**$65,273,771**
Natural gas	**45,220,706**	**11,346,537**	**15,683,286**	**10,056,852**	**8,134,381**
Electricity	**118,575,586**	**20,551,179**	**24,608,755**	**51,713,692**	**21,703,627**
Fuel oil and other fuels	**12,633,789**	**6,375,994**	**2,625,029**	**2,516,693**	**1,116,095**
Fuel oil	6,637,584	5,384,459	355,591	671,118	227,183
Bottled and tank gas	4,893,402	549,005	2,132,225	1,536,050	676,213
Wood and other fuels	1,049,740	397,501	132,454	309,524	210,411
Telephone services	**110,245,729**	**20,673,402**	**24,238,623**	**41,414,675**	**23,919,807**
Residential telephone and pay phones	71,474,578	14,121,949	15,704,965	27,054,651	14,593,603
Cellular phone service	36,464,032	6,137,538	8,077,602	13,575,676	8,673,878
Pager service	129,199	19,520	24,323	54,962	30,240
Phone cards	2,177,921	394,396	431,733	728,973	622,086
Water and other public services	**37,639,509**	**5,142,231**	**8,320,832**	**13,776,515**	**10,399,607**
Water and sewerage maintenance	27,258,623	3,872,977	5,978,161	10,176,695	7,231,239
Trash and garbage collection	10,108,646	1,205,814	2,282,657	3,499,401	3,120,848
Septic tank cleaning	271,087	63,441	60,279	100,420	47,266

* See appendix for information about mortgage principal reduction.
Note: Numbers may not add to total because of rounding and missing subcategories.
Source: Calculations by New Strategist based on the 2003 Consumer Expenditure Survey

Table 9.24 Housing: Shelter and Utilities: Market shares by region, 2003

(percentage of total annual spending on shelter and utilities accounted for by consumer units by region, 2003)

	total consumer units	Northeast	Midwest	South	West
Share of total consumer units	100.0%	19.2%	22.9%	35.8%	22.0%
Share of total before-tax income	100.0	21.5	23.4	32.8	22.5
Share of total spending	100.0	19.9	22.6	33.0	24.5
Share of housing spending	100.0	21.2	21.6	32.0	25.2
SHELTER	100.0	22.3	20.6	30.2	26.9
Owned dwellings*	100.0	21.7	21.4	30.8	26.1
Mortgage interest and charges	100.0	18.9	20.0	31.1	30.0
Mortgage interest	100.0	18.5	19.8	31.3	30.4
Interest paid, home equity loan	100.0	32.1	20.9	29.0	18.0
Interest paid, home equity line of credit	100.0	24.9	30.3	25.1	19.7
Property taxes	100.0	28.7	24.3	27.1	19.9
Maintenance, repairs, insurance, other expenses	100.0	20.5	21.4	35.0	23.1
Homeowner's insurance	100.0	16.0	24.2	39.4	20.4
Ground rent	100.0	8.4	17.4	29.7	44.5
Maintenance and repair services	100.0	23.0	20.1	34.9	22.0
Painting and papering	100.0	15.7	17.8	38.7	27.9
Plumbing and water heating	100.0	24.4	18.8	31.6	25.2
Heat, air conditioning, electrical work	100.0	23.1	19.1	42.0	15.9
Roofing and gutters	100.0	26.7	22.4	30.7	20.1
Other repair and maintenance services	100.0	23.8	21.0	33.2	22.1
Repair, replacement of hard-surface flooring	100.0	18.7	18.8	35.0	27.5
Repair of built-in appliances	100.0	36.6	12.8	35.6	14.9
Maintenance and repair materials	100.0	20.1	24.7	26.8	28.4
Paints, wallpaper, and supplies	100.0	23.3	21.2	29.9	25.6
Tools, equipment for painting, wallpapering	100.0	23.3	21.3	30.1	25.6
Plumbing supplies and equipment	100.0	21.4	16.4	33.1	29.2
Electrical supplies, heating and cooling equipment	100.0	20.5	17.5	40.4	21.7
Hard-surface flooring, repair and replacement	100.0	9.1	26.1	35.3	29.5
Roofing and gutters	100.0	19.2	27.7	29.5	23.5
Plaster, paneling, siding, windows, doors, screens, awnings	100.0	15.9	31.7	21.1	31.3
Patio, walk, fence, driveway, masonry, brick, and stucco materials	100.0	41.0	18.2	13.6	27.3
Miscellaneous supplies and equipment	100.0	30.8	22.8	16.7	29.7
Property management and security	100.0	32.9	16.9	25.5	24.7
Property management	100.0	34.6	17.4	23.9	24.2
Management and upkeep services for security	100.0	17.4	12.3	41.1	29.3
Parking	100.0	21.0	18.0	35.6	25.5
Rented dwellings	100.0	23.5	18.1	29.6	28.8
Rent	100.0	23.6	18.0	29.6	28.8
Rent as pay	100.0	23.9	25.0	33.0	18.1
Maintenance, insurance, and other expenses	100.0	17.6	15.5	29.0	37.9
Tenant's insurance	100.0	17.5	26.6	34.0	21.8
Maintenance and repair services	100.0	19.4	10.0	27.7	42.9
Maintenance and repair materials	100.0	14.8	13.9	26.4	44.8
Other lodging	100.0	23.2	23.6	26.6	26.6
Owned vacation homes	100.0	24.7	23.1	24.2	27.9
Mortgage interest and charges	100.0	21.0	23.1	25.9	29.9
Property taxes	100.0	30.0	22.5	22.6	24.8
Maintenance, insurance, and other expenses	100.0	22.0	24.2	23.9	29.9
Housing while attending school	100.0	19.4	22.7	28.9	29.0
Lodging on trips	100.0	23.1	24.1	27.5	25.3

	total consumer units	Northeast	Midwest	South	West
UTILITIES, FUELS, AND PUBLIC SERVICES	100.0%	19.8%	23.3%	36.8%	20.1%
Natural gas	100.0	25.1	34.7	22.2	18.0
Electricity	100.0	17.3	20.8	43.6	18.3
Fuel oil and other fuels	100.0	50.5	20.8	19.9	8.8
Fuel oil	100.0	81.1	5.4	10.1	3.4
Bottled and tank gas	100.0	11.2	43.6	31.4	13.3
Wood and other fuels	100.0	37.9	12.6	29.5	20.1
Telephone services	100.0	18.8	22.0	37.6	21.7
Residential telephone and pay phones	100.0	19.8	22.0	37.9	20.4
Cellular phone service	100.0	15.8	22.2	37.2	23.8
Pager service	100.0	15.1	18.8	42.5	23.4
Phone cards	100.0	18.1	19.8	33.5	28.6
Water and other public services	100.0	13.7	22.1	36.6	27.6
Water and sewerage maintenance	100.0	14.2	21.9	37.3	26.5
Trash and garbage collection	100.0	11.9	22.6	34.6	30.9
Septic tank cleaning	100.0	23.4	22.2	37.0	17.4

* See appendix for information about mortgage principal reduction.
Note: Numbers may not add to total because of rounding.
Source: Calculations by New Strategist based on the 2003 Consumer Expenditure Survey

Table 9.25 Housing: Shelter and Utilities: Average spending by education, 2003

(average annual spending of consumer units (CU) on shelter and utilities, by education of consumer unit reference person, 2003)

	total consumer units	less than high school graduate	high school graduate	some college	associate's degree	college graduate total	bachelor's degree	master's, professional, doctorate
Number of consumer units (000)	115,356	17,721	31,552	24,514	10,981	30,589	19,557	11,032
Average number of persons per CU	2.5	2.6	2.5	2.3	2.6	2.5	2.5	2.4
Average before-tax income of CU	$51,128.00	$25,028.00	$40,113.00	$45,113.00	$54,087.00	$81,842.00	$74,921.00	$93,948.00
Average spending of CU, total	40,817.33	23,901.14	33,955.56	37,912.41	44,547.12	58,480.00	54,725.85	65,202.73
Housing, average spending	**13,431.87**	**8,350.94**	**10,923.45**	**12,259.77**	**14,059.62**	**19,631.09**	**18,357.09**	**21,907.58**
SHELTER	**7,887.40**	**4,865.39**	**6,178.38**	**7,120.82**	**8,031.92**	**11,963.38**	**11,232.93**	**13,258.37**
Owned dwellings*	**5,262.95**	**2,427.33**	**4,039.63**	**4,364.99**	**5,617.52**	**8,759.85**	**7,994.58**	**10,116.58**
Mortgage interest and charges	2,954.01	1,144.35	2,209.69	2,496.91	3,378.83	4,983.97	4,667.91	5,544.31
Mortgage interest	2,830.50	1,091.46	2,096.43	2,399.08	3,229.82	4,797.54	4,494.24	5,335.25
Interest paid, home equity loan	64.00	38.21	67.68	44.81	99.91	77.62	76.94	78.84
Interest paid, home equity line of credit	58.47	14.67	45.57	48.12	49.10	108.81	96.73	130.23
Property taxes	1,343.82	766.41	1,057.39	1,085.69	1,300.40	2,196.24	1,966.85	2,602.92
Maintenance, repairs, insurance, other expenses	965.11	516.58	772.55	782.39	938.29	1,579.63	1,359.82	1,969.34
Homeowner's insurance	287.43	179.95	261.67	259.01	292.41	397.27	352.16	477.25
Ground rent	40.58	56.98	59.64	41.09	36.16	12.59	8.78	19.34
Maintenance and repair services	516.31	225.94	356.99	373.50	485.66	974.30	817.82	1,251.71
Painting and papering	60.58	19.17	31.24	39.78	37.90	139.64	121.63	171.58
Plumbing and water heating	48.43	18.63	37.31	48.17	50.98	76.48	61.35	103.29
Heat, air conditioning, electrical work	85.39	48.50	59.45	58.72	108.93	146.42	119.35	194.41
Roofing and gutters	97.98	61.09	97.64	58.78	93.45	152.76	132.93	187.92
Other repair and maintenance services	172.07	60.13	108.39	109.66	147.24	361.54	311.13	450.90
Repair, replacement of hard-surface flooring	45.89	15.42	18.41	54.49	40.35	86.96	63.18	129.12
Repair of built-in appliances	5.97	3.00	4.56	3.89	6.80	10.50	8.25	14.48
Maintenance and repair materials	78.80	42.00	73.73	73.33	98.17	102.77	115.99	79.33
Paints, wallpaper, and supplies	12.22	7.24	9.88	15.95	11.03	14.96	15.80	13.46
Tools, equipment for painting, wallpapering	1.31	0.78	1.06	1.71	1.18	1.61	1.70	1.45
Plumbing supplies and equipment	5.37	5.21	5.08	4.96	5.60	6.02	7.07	4.16
Electrical supplies, heating and cooling equipment	3.38	6.74	2.41	3.14	1.25	3.40	2.04	5.82
Hard-surface flooring, repair and replacement	15.40	4.49	18.33	14.47	30.86	13.89	13.05	15.37
Roofing and gutters	6.91	2.39	9.51	3.18	3.47	11.06	13.53	6.68
Plaster, paneling, siding, windows, doors, screens, awnings	16.81	8.22	12.67	16.25	23.40	24.13	29.61	14.42
Patio, walk, fence, driveway, masonry, brick, and stucco materials	1.42	2.50	1.05	0.45	2.58	1.56	1.96	0.84
Miscellaneous supplies and equipment	15.84	4.43	13.75	13.06	18.70	25.80	30.71	17.10
Property management and security	36.52	10.20	17.57	30.06	22.79	81.43	56.12	126.30
Property management	33.03	9.13	16.17	26.64	20.74	73.79	48.08	119.37
Management and upkeep services for security	3.49	1.07	1.40	3.42	2.05	7.64	8.04	6.93
Parking	5.47	1.51	2.95	5.39	3.10	11.28	8.95	15.41
Rented dwellings	**2,179.49**	**2,345.88**	**1,917.20**	**2,372.88**	**2,070.66**	**2,237.74**	**2,406.40**	**1,938.72**
Rent	2,109.74	2,244.20	1,850.53	2,290.57	2,006.75	2,191.25	2,352.06	1,906.17
Rent as pay	32.98	76.63	36.52	27.70	16.75	14.11	17.04	8.91
Maintenance, insurance, and other expenses	36.77	25.05	30.15	54.61	47.15	32.38	37.30	23.65
Tenant's insurance	9.67	2.92	7.43	11.74	11.16	13.71	15.35	10.79
Maintenance and repair services	16.88	16.91	8.26	33.84	25.22	9.15	10.65	6.49
Maintenance and repair materials	10.23	5.23	14.46	9.03	10.76	9.52	11.30	6.37
Other lodging	**444.96**	**92.18**	**221.55**	**382.95**	**343.74**	**965.79**	**831.95**	**1,203.06**
Owned vacation homes	150.29	45.41	73.36	115.98	110.63	332.14	296.61	395.13
Mortgage interest and charges	61.55	9.51	19.75	51.82	31.62	153.38	130.32	194.27
Property taxes	58.90	26.45	35.70	42.82	54.48	116.08	97.63	148.79
Maintenance, insurance, and other expenses	29.84	9.46	17.91	21.33	24.53	62.68	68.66	52.07
Housing while attending school	52.90	4.49	17.52	64.62	25.19	117.99	87.18	172.60
Lodging on trips	241.77	42.28	130.67	202.36	207.91	515.66	448.16	635.34

	total consumer units	less than high school graduate	high school graduate	some college	associate's degree	college graduate		
						total	bachelor's degree	master's, professional, doctorate
UTILITIES, FUELS, AND PUBLIC SERVICES	$2,811.43	$2,311.23	$2,740.41	$2,610.40	$3,000.43	$3,267.71	$3,158.65	$3,461.07
Natural gas	392.01	312.72	380.67	351.25	384.28	485.08	470.21	511.45
Electricity	1,027.91	903.13	1,045.81	943.14	1,091.84	1,126.74	1,089.50	1,192.78
Fuel oil and other fuels	109.52	100.89	116.24	87.95	131.66	116.93	105.14	137.84
Fuel oil	57.54	43.60	54.88	39.90	73.41	76.82	66.71	94.73
Bottled and tank gas	42.42	45.02	50.27	39.61	49.14	32.66	32.27	33.35
Wood and other fuels	9.10	11.81	9.97	8.17	9.11	7.38	6.04	9.75
Telephone services	955.70	734.78	897.14	926.25	1,055.16	1,131.97	1,107.35	1,175.61
Residential telephone and pay phones	619.60	551.99	609.31	572.05	661.32	692.52	679.11	716.23
Cellular phone service	316.10	146.64	272.22	338.03	373.21	421.47	410.72	440.52
Pager service	1.12	0.91	1.26	0.88	2.18	0.90	1.02	0.69
Phone cards	18.88	35.24	14.35	15.29	18.45	17.08	16.50	18.12
Water and other public services	326.29	259.71	300.55	301.81	337.49	406.99	386.45	443.40
Water and sewerage maintenance	236.30	195.19	219.66	217.33	245.39	289.23	275.92	312.84
Trash and garbage collection	87.63	63.26	78.71	82.61	89.68	114.25	107.26	126.64
Septic tank cleaning	2.35	1.26	2.19	1.88	2.42	3.51	3.28	3.92

* See appendix for information about mortgage principal reduction.
Note: Subcategories may not add to total because some are not shown.
Source: Bureau of Labor Statistics, unpublished tables from the 2003 Consumer Expenditure Survey

Table 9.26 Housing: Shelter and Utilities: Indexed spending by education, 2003

(indexed average annual spending of consumer units (CU) on shelter and utilities, by education of consumer unit reference person, 2003; index definition: an index of 100 is the average for all consumer units; an index of 132 means that spending by consumer units in that group is 32 percent above the average for all consumer units; an index of 68 indicates spending that is 32 percent below the average for all consumer units)

	total consumer units	less than high school graduate	high school graduate	some college	associate's degree	college graduate total	bachelor's degree	master's, professional, doctorate
Average spending of CU, total	$40,817	$23,901	$33,956	$37,912	$44,547	$58,480	$54,726	$65,203
Average spending of CU, index	100	59	83	93	109	143	134	160
Housing, spending index	**100**	**62**	**81**	**91**	**105**	**146**	**137**	**163**
SHELTER	**100**	**62**	**78**	**90**	**102**	**152**	**142**	**168**
Owned dwellings*	**100**	**46**	**77**	**83**	**107**	**166**	**152**	**192**
Mortgage interest and charges	100	39	75	85	114	169	158	188
Mortgage interest	100	39	74	85	114	170	159	189
Interest paid, home equity loan	100	60	106	70	156	121	120	123
Interest paid, home equity line of credit	100	25	78	82	84	186	165	223
Property taxes	100	57	79	81	97	163	146	194
Maintenance, repairs, insurance, other expenses	100	54	80	81	97	164	141	204
Homeowner's insurance	100	63	91	90	102	138	123	166
Ground rent	100	140	147	101	89	31	22	48
Maintenance and repair services	100	44	69	72	94	189	158	242
Painting and papering	100	32	52	66	63	231	201	283
Plumbing and water heating	100	39	77	100	105	158	127	213
Heat, air conditioning, electrical work	100	57	70	69	128	172	140	228
Roofing and gutters	100	62	100	60	95	156	136	192
Other repair and maintenance services	100	35	63	64	86	210	181	262
Repair, replacement of hard-surface flooring	100	34	40	119	88	190	138	281
Repair of built-in appliances	100	50	76	65	114	176	138	243
Maintenance and repair materials	100	53	94	93	125	130	147	101
Paints, wallpaper, and supplies	100	59	81	131	90	122	129	110
Tools, equipment for painting, wallpapering	100	60	81	131	90	123	130	111
Plumbing supplies and equipment	100	97	95	92	104	112	132	78
Electrical supplies, heating and cooling equipment	100	199	71	93	37	101	60	172
Hard-surface flooring, repair and replacement	100	29	119	94	200	90	85	100
Roofing and gutters	100	35	138	46	50	160	196	97
Plaster, paneling, siding, windows, doors, screens, awnings	100	49	75	97	139	144	176	86
Patio, walk, fence, driveway, masonry, brick, and stucco materials	100	176	74	32	182	110	138	59
Miscellaneous supplies and equipment	100	28	87	82	118	163	194	108
Property management and security	100	28	48	82	62	223	154	346
Property management	100	28	49	81	63	223	146	361
Management and upkeep services for security	100	31	40	98	59	219	230	199
Parking	100	28	54	99	57	206	164	282
Rented dwellings	**100**	**108**	**88**	**109**	**95**	**103**	**110**	**89**
Rent	100	106	88	109	95	104	112	90
Rent as pay	100	232	111	84	51	43	52	27
Maintenance, insurance, and other expenses	100	68	82	149	128	88	101	64
Tenant's insurance	100	30	77	121	115	142	159	112
Maintenance and repair services	100	100	49	201	149	54	63	38
Maintenance and repair materials	100	51	141	88	105	93	111	62
Other lodging	**100**	**21**	**50**	**86**	**77**	**217**	**187**	**270**
Owned vacation homes	100	30	49	77	74	221	197	263
Mortgage interest and charges	100	16	32	84	51	249	212	316
Property taxes	100	45	61	73	93	197	166	253
Maintenance, insurance, and other expenses	100	32	60	72	82	210	230	175
Housing while attending school	100	9	33	122	48	223	165	326
Lodging on trips	100	18	54	84	86	213	185	263

	total consumer units	less than high school graduate	high school graduate	some college	associate's degree	college graduate total	bachelor's degree	master's, professional, doctorate
UTILITIES, FUELS, AND PUBLIC SERVICES	100	82	98	93	107	116	112	123
Natural gas	100	80	97	90	98	124	120	131
Electricity	100	88	102	92	106	110	106	116
Fuel oil and other fuels	100	92	106	80	120	107	96	126
Fuel oil	100	76	95	69	128	134	116	165
Bottled and tank gas	100	106	119	93	116	77	76	79
Wood and other fuels	100	130	110	90	100	81	66	107
Telephone services	100	77	94	97	110	118	116	123
Residential telephone and pay phones	100	89	98	92	107	112	110	116
Cellular phone service	100	46	86	107	118	133	130	139
Pager service	100	81	113	79	195	80	91	62
Phone cards	100	187	76	31	98	91	87	96
Water and other public services	100	80	92	93	103	125	118	136
Water and sewerage maintenance	100	83	93	92	104	122	117	132
Trash and garbage collection	100	72	90	94	102	130	122	145
Septic tank cleaning	100	54	93	80	103	149	140	167

See appendix for information about mortgage principal reduction.
Source: Calculations by New Strategist based on the 2003 Consumer Expenditure Survey

Table 9.27 Housing: Shelter and Utilities: Total spending by education, 2003

(total annual spending on shelter and utilities, by consumer unit (CU) educational attainment group, 2003; numbers in thousands)

	total consumer units	less than high school graduate	high school graduate	some college	associate's degree	college graduate total	bachelor's degree	master's, professional, doctorate
Number of consumer units	115,356	17,721	31,552	24,514	10,981	30,589	19,557	11,032
Total spending of all CUs	$4,708,523,920	$423,552,102	$1,071,365,829	$929,384,819	$489,171,925	$1,788,844,720	$1,070,273,448	$719,316,517
Housing, total spending	**1,549,446,796**	**147,987,008**	**344,656,694**	**300,536,002**	**154,388,687**	**600,495,412**	**359,009,609**	**241,684,423**
SHELTER	**909,858,914**	**86,219,576**	**194,940,246**	**174,559,782**	**88,198,514**	**365,947,831**	**219,682,412**	**146,266,338**
Owned dwellings*	607,112,860	43,014,715	127,458,406	107,003,365	61,685,987	267,955,052	156,350,001	111,606,111
Mortgage interest and charges	340,762,778	20,279,026	69,720,139	61,209,252	37,102,932	152,454,658	91,290,316	61,164,828
Mortgage interest	326,515,158	19,341,763	66,146,559	58,811,047	35,466,653	146,751,951	87,893,852	58,858,478
Interest paid, home equity loan	7,382,784	677,119	2,135,439	1,098,472	1,097,112	2,374,318	1,504,716	869,763
Interest paid, home equity line of credit	6,744,865	259,967	1,437,825	1,179,614	539,167	3,328,389	1,891,749	1,436,697
Property taxes	155,017,700	13,581,552	33,362,769	26,614,605	14,279,692	67,180,785	38,465,685	28,715,413
Maintenance, repairs, insurance, other expenses	111,331,229	9,154,314	24,375,498	19,179,509	10,303,363	48,319,302	26,594,000	21,725,759
Homeowner's insurance	33,156,775	3,188,894	8,256,212	6,349,371	3,210,954	12,152,092	6,887,193	5,265,022
Ground rent	4,681,147	1,009,743	1,881,761	1,007,280	397,073	385,116	171,711	213,359
Maintenance and repair services	59,559,456	4,003,883	11,263,749	9,155,979	5,333,033	29,802,863	15,994,106	13,808,865
Painting and papering	6,988,267	339,712	985,685	975,167	416,180	4,271,448	2,378,718	1,892,871
Plumbing and water heating	5,586,691	330,142	1,177,205	1,180,839	559,811	2,339,447	1,199,822	1,139,495
Heat, air conditioning, electrical work	9,850,249	859,469	1,875,766	1,439,462	1,196,160	4,478,841	2,334,128	2,144,731
Roofing and gutters	11,302,581	1,082,576	3,080,737	1,440,933	1,026,174	4,672,776	2,599,712	2,073,133
Other repair and maintenance services	19,849,307	1,065,564	3,419,921	2,688,205	1,616,842	11,059,147	6,084,769	4,974,329
Repair, replacement of hard-surface flooring	5,293,687	273,258	580,872	1,335,768	443,083	2,660,019	1,235,611	1,424,452
Repair of built-in appliances	688,675	53,163	143,877	95,360	74,671	321,185	161,345	159,743
Maintenance and repair materials	9,090,053	744,282	2,326,329	1,797,612	1,078,005	3,143,632	2,268,416	875,169
Paints, wallpaper, and supplies	1,409,650	128,300	311,734	390,998	121,120	457,611	309,001	148,491
Tools, equipment for painting, wallpapering	151,116	13,822	33,445	41,919	12,958	49,248	33,247	15,996
Plumbing supplies and equipment	619,462	92,326	160,284	121,589	61,494	184,146	138,268	45,893
Electrical supplies, heating and cooling equipment	389,903	119,440	76,040	76,974	13,726	104,003	39,896	64,206
Hard-surface flooring, repair and replacement	1,776,482	79,567	578,348	354,718	338,874	424,881	255,219	169,562
Roofing and gutters	797,110	42,353	300,060	77,955	38,104	338,314	264,606	73,694
Plaster, paneling, siding, windows, doors, screens, awnings	1,939,134	145,667	399,764	398,353	256,955	738,113	579,083	159,081
Patio, walk, fence, driveway, masonry, brick, and stucco materials	163,806	44,303	33,130	11,031	28,331	47,719	38,332	9,267
Miscellaneous supplies and equipment	1,827,239	78,504	433,840	320,153	205,345	789,196	600,596	188,647
Property management and security	4,212,801	180,754	554,369	736,391	250,257	2,490,862	1,097,539	1,393,342
Property management	3,810,209	161,793	510,196	653,053	227,746	2,257,162	940,301	1,316,890
Management and upkeep services for security	402,592	18,962	44,173	83,838	22,511	233,700	157,238	76,452
Parking	630,997	26,759	93,078	132,131	34,041	345,044	175,035	170,003
Rented dwellings	**251,417,248**	**41,571,340**	**60,491,494**	**58,168,780**	**22,737,918**	**68,450,229**	**47,061,965**	**21,387,959**
Rent	243,371,167	39,769,468	58,387,923	56,151,033	22,036,122	67,028,146	45,999,237	21,028,867
Rent as pay	3,804,441	1,357,960	1,152,279	679,038	183,932	431,611	333,251	98,295
Maintenance, insurance, and other expenses	4,241,640	443,911	951,293	1,338,710	517,754	990,472	729,476	260,907
Tenant's insurance	1,115,493	51,745	234,431	287,794	122,548	419,375	300,200	119,035
Maintenance and repair services	1,947,209	299,662	260,620	829,554	276,941	279,889	208,282	71,598
Maintenance and repair materials	1,180,092	92,681	456,242	221,361	118,156	291,207	220,994	70,274
Other lodging	**51,328,806**	**1,633,522**	**6,990,346**	**9,387,636**	**3,774,609**	**29,542,550**	**16,270,446**	**13,272,158**
Owned vacation homes	17,336,853	804,711	2,314,655	2,843,134	1,214,828	10,159,831	5,800,802	4,359,074
Mortgage interest and charges	7,100,162	168,527	623,152	1,270,316	347,219	4,691,741	2,548,668	2,143,187
Property taxes	6,794,468	468,721	1,126,406	1,049,690	598,245	3,550,771	1,909,350	1,641,451
Maintenance, insurance, and other expenses	3,442,223	167,641	565,096	522,884	269,364	1,917,319	1,342,784	574,436
Housing while attending school	6,102,332	79,567	552,791	1,584,095	276,611	3,609,196	1,704,979	1,904,123
Lodging on trips	27,889,620	749,244	4,122,900	4,960,653	2,283,060	15,773,524	8,764,665	7,009,071

	total consumer units	less than high school graduate	high school graduate	some college	associate's degree	college graduate		
						total	bachelor's degree	master's, professional, doctorate
UTILITIES, FUELS, PUBLIC SERVICES	$324,315,319	$40,957,307	$86,465,416	$63,991,346	$32,947,722	$99,955,981	$61,773,718	$38,182,524
Natural gas	45,220,706	5,541,711	12,010,900	8,610,543	4,219,779	14,838,112	9,195,897	5,642,316
Electricity	118,575,586	16,004,367	32,997,397	23,120,134	11,989,495	34,465,850	21,307,352	13,158,749
Fuel oil and other fuels	12,633,789	1,787,872	3,667,605	2,156,006	1,445,759	3,576,772	2,056,223	1,520,651
Fuel oil	6,637,584	772,636	1,731,574	978,109	806,115	2,349,847	1,304,648	1,045,061
Bottled and tank gas	4,893,402	797,799	1,585,119	971,000	539,606	999,037	631,104	367,917
Wood and other fuels	1,049,740	209,285	314,573	200,279	100,037	225,747	118,124	107,562
Telephone services	110,245,729	13,021,036	28,306,561	22,706,093	11,586,712	34,625,830	21,656,444	12,969,330
Residential telephone and pay phones	71,474,578	9,781,815	19,224,949	14,023,234	7,261,955	21,183,494	13,281,354	7,902,001
Cellular phone service	36,464,032	2,598,607	8,589,085	8,286,467	4,098,219	12,892,346	8,032,451	4,859,817
Pager service	129,199	16,126	39,756	21,572	23,939	27,530	19,948	7,612
Phone cards	2,177,921	624,488	452,771	374,819	202,600	522,460	322,691	199,900
Water and other public services	37,639,509	4,602,321	9,482,954	7,398,570	3,705,978	12,449,417	7,557,803	4,891,589
Water and sewerage maintenance	27,258,623	3,458,962	6,930,712	5,327,628	2,694,628	8,847,257	5,396,167	3,451,251
Trash and garbage collection	10,108,646	1,121,031	2,483,458	2,025,102	984,776	3,494,793	2,097,684	1,397,093
Septic tank cleaning	271,087	22,329	69,099	46,086	26,574	107,367	64,147	43,245

See appendix for information about mortgage principal reduction.
Note: Numbers may not add to total because of rounding and missing subcategories.
Source: Calculations by New Strategist based on the 2003 Consumer Expenditure Survey

Table 9.28 Housing: Shelter and Utilities: Market shares by education, 2003

(percentage of total annual spending on shelter and utilities accounted for by consumer unit educational attainment groups, 2003)

	total consumer units	less than high school graduate	high school graduate	some college	associate's degree	college graduate total	college graduate bachelor's degree	college graduate master's, professional, doctorate
Share of total consumer units	100.0%	15.4%	27.4%	21.3%	9.5%	26.5%	17.0%	9.6%
Share of total before-tax income	100.0	7.5	21.5	18.8	10.1	42.4	24.8	17.6
Share of total spending	100.0	9.0	22.8	19.7	10.4	38.0	22.7	15.3
Share of housing spending	100.0	9.6	22.2	19.4	10.0	38.8	23.2	15.6
SHELTER	100.0	9.5	21.4	19.2	9.7	40.2	24.1	16.1
Owned dwellings*	100.0	7.1	21.0	17.6	10.2	44.1	25.8	18.4
Mortgage interest and charges	100.0	6.0	20.5	18.0	10.9	44.7	26.8	18.0
Mortgage interest	100.0	5.9	20.3	18.0	10.9	44.9	26.9	18.0
Interest paid, home equity loan	100.0	9.2	28.9	14.9	14.9	32.2	20.4	11.8
Interest paid, home equity line of credit	100.0	3.9	21.3	17.5	8.0	49.3	28.1	21.3
Property taxes	100.0	8.8	21.5	17.2	9.2	43.3	24.8	18.5
Maintenance, repairs, insurance, other expenses	100.0	8.2	21.9	17.2	9.3	43.4	23.9	19.5
Homeowner's insurance	100.0	9.6	24.9	19.2	9.7	36.7	20.8	15.9
Ground rent	100.0	21.6	40.2	21.5	8.5	8.2	3.7	4.6
Maintenance and repair services	100.0	6.7	18.9	15.4	9.0	50.0	26.9	23.2
Painting and papering	100.0	4.9	14.1	14.0	6.0	61.1	34.0	27.1
Plumbing and water heating	100.0	5.9	21.1	21.1	10.0	41.9	21.5	20.4
Heat, air conditioning, electrical work	100.0	8.7	19.0	14.6	12.1	45.5	23.7	21.8
Roofing and gutters	100.0	9.6	27.3	12.7	9.1	41.3	23.0	18.3
Other repair and maintenance services	100.0	5.4	17.2	13.5	8.1	55.7	30.7	25.1
Repair, replacement of hard-surface flooring	100.0	5.2	11.0	25.2	8.4	50.2	23.3	26.9
Repair of built-in appliances	100.0	7.7	20.9	13.8	10.8	46.6	23.4	23.2
Maintenance and repair materials	100.0	8.2	25.6	19.8	11.9	34.6	25.0	9.6
Paints, wallpaper, and supplies	100.0	9.1	22.1	27.7	8.6	32.5	21.9	10.5
Tools, equipment for painting, wallpapering	100.0	9.1	22.1	27.7	8.6	32.6	22.0	10.6
Plumbing supplies and equipment	100.0	14.9	25.9	19.6	9.9	29.7	22.3	7.4
Electrical supplies, heating and cooling equipment	100.0	30.6	19.5	19.7	3.5	26.7	10.2	16.5
Hard-surface flooring, repair and replacement	100.0	4.5	32.6	20.0	19.1	23.9	14.4	9.5
Roofing and gutters	100.0	5.3	37.6	9.8	4.8	42.4	33.2	9.2
Plaster, paneling, siding, windows, doors, screens, awnings	100.0	7.5	20.6	20.5	13.3	38.1	29.9	8.2
Patio, walk, fence, driveway, masonry, brick, and stucco materials	100.0	27.1	20.2	6.7	17.3	29.1	23.4	5.7
Miscellaneous supplies and equipment	100.0	4.3	23.7	17.5	11.2	43.2	32.9	10.3
Property management and security	100.0	4.3	13.2	17.5	5.9	59.1	26.1	33.1
Property management	100.0	4.2	13.4	17.1	6.0	59.2	24.7	34.6
Management and upkeep services for security	100.0	4.7	11.0	20.8	5.6	58.1	39.1	19.0
Parking	100.0	4.2	14.8	20.9	5.4	54.7	27.7	26.9
Rented dwellings	100.0	16.5	24.1	23.1	9.0	27.2	18.7	8.5
Rent	100.0	16.3	24.0	23.1	9.1	27.5	18.9	8.6
Rent as pay	100.0	35.7	30.3	17.8	4.8	11.3	8.8	2.6
Maintenance, insurance, and other expenses	100.0	10.5	22.4	31.6	12.2	23.4	17.2	6.2
Tenant's insurance	100.0	4.6	21.0	25.8	11.0	37.6	26.9	10.7
Maintenance and repair services	100.0	15.4	13.4	42.6	14.2	14.4	10.7	3.7
Maintenance and repair materials	100.0	7.9	38.7	18.8	10.0	24.7	18.7	6.0
Other lodging	100.0	3.2	13.6	18.3	7.4	57.6	31.7	25.9
Owned vacation homes	100.0	4.6	13.4	16.4	7.0	58.6	33.5	25.1
Mortgage interest and charges	100.0	2.4	8.8	17.9	4.9	66.1	35.9	30.2
Property taxes	100.0	6.9	16.6	15.5	8.8	52.3	28.1	24.2
Maintenance, insurance, and other expenses	100.0	4.9	16.4	15.2	7.8	55.7	39.0	16.7
Housing while attending school	100.0	1.3	9.1	26.0	4.5	59.1	27.9	31.2
Lodging on trips	100.0	2.7	14.8	17.8	8.2	56.6	31.4	25.1

	total consumer units	less than high school graduate	high school graduate	some college	associate's degree	college graduate		
						total	bachelor's degree	master's, professional, doctorate
UTILITIES, FUELS, PUBLIC SERVICES	100.0%	12.6%	26.7%	19.7%	10.2%	30.8%	19.1%	11.8%
Natural gas	100.0	12.3	26.6	19.0	9.3	32.8	20.3	12.5
Electricity	100.0	13.5	27.8	19.5	10.1	29.1	18.0	11.1
Fuel oil and other fuels	100.0	14.2	29.0	17.1	11.4	28.3	16.3	12.0
Fuel oil	100.0	11.6	26.1	14.7	12.1	35.4	19.7	15.7
Bottled and tank gas	100.0	16.3	32.4	19.8	11.0	20.4	12.9	7.5
Wood and other fuels	100.0	19.9	30.0	19.1	9.5	21.5	11.3	10.2
Telephone services	100.0	11.8	25.7	20.6	10.5	31.4	19.6	11.8
Residential telephone and pay phones	100.0	13.7	26.9	19.6	10.2	29.6	18.6	11.1
Cellular phone service	100.0	7.1	23.6	22.7	11.2	35.4	22.0	13.3
Pager service	100.0	12.5	30.8	16.7	18.5	21.3	15.4	5.9
Phone cards	100.0	28.7	20.8	17.2	9.3	24.0	14.8	9.2
Water and other public services	100.0	12.2	25.2	19.7	9.8	33.1	20.1	13.0
Water and sewerage maintenance	100.0	12.7	25.4	19.5	9.9	32.5	19.8	12.7
Trash and garbage collection	100.0	11.1	24.6	20.0	9.7	34.6	20.8	13.8
Septic tank cleaning	100.0	8.2	25.5	17.0	9.8	39.6	23.7	16.0

* See appendix for information about mortgage principal reduction.
Note: Numbers may not add to total because of rounding.
Source: Calculations by New Strategist based on the 2003 Consumer Expenditure Survey

Spending on Personal Care, Reading, Education, and Tobacco, 2003

The average household spent 13 percent less on personal care products and services in 2003 than in 2000, after adjusting for inflation. Spending on reading material also fell during those years—down a substantial 19 percent as Internet use cut household spending on books and newspapers. Not surprisingly, spending on education rose 16 percent as college tuition soared. The average household spent 9 percent less on tobacco in 2003 than in 2000 as smoking declined in popularity.

Spending on personal care products and services is highest among householders aged 35 to 44, at $616 in 2003. This is the age when household size peaks. The biggest spenders on reading material are householders aged 55 to 64. This age group spends 42 percent more than the average household on magazine subscriptions. Householders aged 65 or older are the biggest spenders on newspaper subscriptions, however. Education spending is greatest for the youngest householders, who are most likely to be paying their way through college. Householders aged 45 to 54 (the parents of college students) are the second-biggest spenders on education.

Households with incomes of $100,000 or more spend twice as much as the average household on personal care products and services. This high-income group also spends more than twice the average on reading material and more than three times the average on education. Households with incomes of $100,000 or more spend 24 percent less than average on tobacco, however. Households with incomes below $50,000 account for the 61 percent majority of spending on tobacco.

Not surprisingly, spending on education is highest among married couples with children aged 18 or older at home, many of whom have children in college. Couples with school-aged or older children at home spend the most on personal care products and services because they have the largest households. Married couples without children at home spend the most on reading material—particularly newspaper and magazine subscriptions. Tobacco spending is highest for couples with adult children at home.

Asian, black, and Hispanic householders spend about an average amount on personal care products and services, but on a number of individual personal care items their spending is well above average. Blacks spend more than three times the average on wigs and hairpieces, for example. Asian households spend more than three times the average on college tuition.

Households in the Northeast spend 25 percent more than average on newspaper subscriptions, while households in the South spend 26 percent less than average on this item. Households in the West spend the most on books—38 percent more than average. Spending on tobacco is greatest in the Midwest—25 percent above average. Household spending on education is 33 percent above average in the Northeast and 26 percent below average in the South.

College graduates spend more than other householders on personal care products and services, reading material, and education. They spend twice the average on college tuition and more than twice the average on books not purchased through book clubs. Householders with no more than a high school diploma spend the most on tobacco, 31 percent more than the average household.

Table 10.1 Personal Care, Reading, Education, Tobacco: Average spending by age, 2003

(average annual spending of consumer units (CU) on personal care, reading, education, and tobacco products, by age of consumer unit reference person, 2003)

	total consumer units	under 25	25 to 34	35 to 44	45 to 54	55 to 64	65 to 74	75+
Number of consumer units (000)	115,356	8,584	19,737	24,413	23,131	16,580	11,495	11,417
Average number of persons per CU	2.5	1.8	2.9	3.2	2.6	2.1	1.9	1.5
Average before-tax income of CU	$51,128.00	$20,680.00	$50,389.00	$61,091.00	$68,028.00	$58,672.00	$35,314.00	$25,492.00
Average spending of CU, total	40,817.33	22,395.53	40,525.22	47,175.06	50,100.86	44,190.65	33,629.17	25,016.38
PERSONAL CARE PRODUCTS AND SERVICES	**526.92**	**325.76**	**498.15**	**602.10**	**615.81**	**549.50**	**490.50**	**386.97**
Personal care products	**270.49**	**199.09**	**268.11**	**333.12**	**318.35**	**268.54**	**222.87**	**144.18**
Hair care products	55.65	47.85	59.64	71.77	61.62	49.56	45.83	25.43
Hair accessories	6.75	5.83	7.68	11.20	7.13	5.12	3.20	1.25
Wigs and hairpieces	1.84	1.46	1.64	1.19	3.18	1.21	3.11	0.78
Oral hygiene products	28.22	35.34	22.96	30.87	26.45	30.85	29.77	24.46
Shaving products	14.80	9.50	13.59	18.81	19.55	14.98	8.15	9.01
Cosmetics, perfume, and bath products	123.43	73.29	122.64	153.55	152.23	128.54	96.86	57.36
Deodorants, feminine hygiene, misc. products	30.11	24.97	27.90	39.15	36.11	25.47	22.49	20.30
Electric personal care appliances	9.68	0.85	12.06	6.59	12.09	12.80	13.47	5.60
Personal care services	**256.43**	**126.68**	**230.04**	**268.97**	**297.46**	**280.95**	**267.64**	**242.79**
READING	**127.27**	**52.94**	**98.77**	**113.54**	**150.48**	**167.97**	**148.96**	**133.82**
Newspaper subscriptions	41.54	4.80	16.05	29.31	47.24	56.31	67.77	80.03
Newspaper, nonsubscription	9.71	4.63	8.27	10.44	11.66	12.24	9.96	6.60
Magazine subscriptions	14.45	5.95	9.95	11.04	16.19	20.51	21.07	16.96
Magazines, nonsubscription	7.73	7.95	8.61	8.95	9.50	7.02	5.22	3.45
Books purchased through book clubs	5.69	0.87	5.21	4.44	7.05	6.28	8.52	6.34
Books not purchased through book clubs	47.81	28.73	50.62	48.71	58.42	65.09	36.31	20.39
EDUCATION	**783.33**	**1,489.67**	**683.75**	**694.37**	**1,376.83**	**742.94**	**176.35**	**80.54**
College tuition	467.71	1,152.49	461.22	232.95	869.15	452.47	107.08	37.93
Elementary and high school tuition	124.91	2.83	54.01	208.28	256.79	112.16	23.27	14.63
Other school tuition	21.36	28.73	19.55	39.95	25.83	11.38	4.34	1.75
Other school expenses including rentals	44.75	27.81	37.49	59.55	51.68	84.97	3.74	7.23
Books, supplies for college	54.65	242.65	54.62	27.73	72.57	39.28	8.70	3.18
Books, supplies for elementary, high school	14.09	2.95	12.06	30.12	20.50	5.53	4.15	1.19
Books, supplies for day care, nursery school	3.02	2.10	5.35	4.49	2.53	0.97	3.18	0.32
Miscellaneous school expenses and supplies	52.85	30.11	39.46	91.30	77.78	36.19	21.89	14.31
TOBACCO PRODUCTS AND SMOKING SUPPLIES	**289.70**	**229.77**	**284.57**	**312.31**	**384.78**	**336.94**	**219.42**	**104.73**
Cigarettes	266.78	215.33	258.51	287.97	359.36	314.09	197.64	87.77
Other tobacco products	21.42	13.98	24.93	22.98	23.36	21.46	18.23	16.80
Smoking accessories	1.42	0.46	1.14	1.36	1.65	1.39	3.55	0.16

Note: Subcategories may not add to total because some are not shown.
Source: Bureau of Labor Statistics, unpublished tables from the 2003 Consumer Expenditure Survey

Table 10.2 Personal Care, Reading, Education, Tobacco: Indexed spending by age, 2003

(indexed average annual spending of consumer units (CU) on personal care, reading, education, and tobacco products, by age of consumer unit reference person, 2003; index definition: an index of 100 is the average for all consumer units; an index of 132 means that spending by consumer units in that group is 32 percent above the average for all consumer units; an index of 68 indicates spending that is 32 percent below the average for all consumer units)

	total consumer units	under 25	25 to 34	35 to 44	45 to 54	55 to 64	65 to 74	75+
Average spending of CU, total	$40,817	$22,396	$40,525	$47,175	$50,101	$44,191	$33,629	$25,016
Average spending of CU, index	100	55	99	116	123	108	82	61
PERSONAL CARE PRODUCTS AND SERVICES	100	62	95	114	117	104	93	73
Personal care products	100	74	99	123	118	99	82	53
Hair care products	100	86	107	129	111	89	82	46
Hair accessories	100	86	114	166	106	76	47	19
Wigs and hairpieces	100	79	89	65	173	66	169	42
Oral hygiene products	100	125	81	109	94	109	105	87
Shaving products	100	64	92	127	132	101	55	61
Cosmetics, perfume, and bath products	100	59	99	124	123	104	78	46
Deodorants, feminine hygiene, misc. products	100	83	93	130	120	85	75	67
Electric personal care appliances	100	9	125	68	125	132	139	58
Personal care services	100	49	90	105	116	110	104	95
READING	100	42	78	89	118	132	117	105
Newspaper subscriptions	100	12	39	71	114	136	163	193
Newspaper, nonsubscription	100	48	85	103	120	126	103	68
Magazine subscriptions	100	41	69	76	112	142	146	117
Magazines, nonsubscription	100	103	111	116	123	91	68	45
Books purchased through book clubs	100	15	92	78	124	110	150	111
Books not purchased through book clubs	100	60	106	102	122	136	76	43
EDUCATION	100	190	87	89	176	95	23	10
College tuition	100	246	99	50	186	97	23	8
Elementary and high school tuition	100	2	43	167	206	90	19	12
Other school tuition	100	135	92	187	121	53	20	8
Other school expenses including rentals	100	62	84	133	115	190	8	16
Books, supplies for college	100	444	100	51	133	72	16	6
Books, supplies for elementary, high school	100	21	86	214	145	39	29	8
Books, supplies for day care, nursery school	100	70	177	149	84	32	105	11
Miscellaneous school expenses and supplies	100	57	75	173	147	68	41	27
TOBACCO PRODUCTS AND SMOKING SUPPLIES	100	79	98	108	133	116	76	36
Cigarettes	100	81	97	108	135	118	74	33
Other tobacco products	100	65	116	107	109	100	85	78
Smoking accessories	100	32	80	96	116	98	250	11

Source: Calculations by New Strategist based on the 2003 Consumer Expenditure Survey

Table 10.3 Personal Care, Reading, Education, Tobacco: Total spending by age, 2003

(total annual spending on personal care, reading, education, and tobacco products, by consumer unit (CU) age groups, 2003; numbers in thousands)

	total consumer units	under 25	25 to 34	35 to 44	45 to 54	55 to 64	65 to 74	75+
Number of consumer units	115,356	8,584	19,737	24,413	23,131	16,580	11,495	11,417
Total spending of all CUs	$4,708,523,919	$192,243,230	$799,846,267	$1,151,684,740	$1,158,882,993	$732,680,977	$386,567,309	$285,612,010
PERSONAL CARE PRODUCTS AND SERVICES	60,783,384	2,796,324	9,831,987	14,699,067	14,244,301	9,110,710	5,638,298	4,418,036
Personal care products	31,202,644	1,708,989	5,291,687	8,132,459	7,363,754	4,452,393	2,561,891	1,646,103
Hair care products	6,419,561	410,744	1,177,115	1,752,121	1,425,332	821,705	526,816	290,334
Hair accessories	778,653	50,045	151,580	273,426	164,924	84,890	36,784	14,271
Wigs and hairpieces	212,255	12,533	32,369	29,051	73,557	20,062	35,749	8,905
Oral hygiene products	3,255,346	303,359	453,162	753,629	611,815	511,493	342,206	279,260
Shaving products	1,707,269	81,548	268,226	459,209	452,211	248,368	93,684	102,867
Cosmetics, perfume, and bath products	14,238,391	629,121	2,420,546	3,748,616	3,521,232	2,131,193	1,113,406	654,879
Deodorants, feminine hygiene, misc. products	3,473,369	214,342	550,662	955,769	835,260	422,293	258,523	231,765
Electric personal care appliances	1,116,646	7,296	238,028	160,882	279,654	212,224	154,838	63,935
Personal care services	29,580,739	1,087,421	4,540,299	6,566,365	6,880,547	4,658,151	3,076,522	2,771,933
READING	14,681,358	454,437	1,949,423	2,771,852	3,480,753	2,784,943	1,712,295	1,527,823
Newspaper subscriptions	4,791,888	41,203	316,779	715,545	1,092,708	933,620	779,016	913,703
Newspaper, nonsubscription	1,120,107	39,744	163,225	254,872	269,707	202,939	114,490	75,352
Magazine subscriptions	1,666,894	51,075	196,383	269,520	374,491	340,056	242,200	193,632
Magazines, nonsubscription	891,702	68,243	169,936	218,496	219,745	116,392	60,004	39,389
Books purchased through book clubs	656,376	7,468	102,830	108,394	163,074	104,122	97,937	72,384
Books not purchased through book clubs	5,515,170	246,618	999,087	1,189,157	1,351,313	1,079,192	417,383	232,793
EDUCATION	90,361,815	12,787,327	13,495,174	16,951,655	31,847,455	12,317,945	2,027,143	919,525
College tuition	53,953,155	9,892,974	9,103,099	5,687,008	20,104,309	7,501,953	1,230,885	433,047
Elementary and high school tuition	14,409,118	24,293	1,065,995	5,084,740	5,939,809	1,859,613	267,489	167,031
Other school tuition	2,464,004	246,618	385,858	975,299	597,474	188,680	49,888	19,980
Other school expenses including rentals	5,162,181	238,721	739,940	1,453,794	1,195,410	1,408,803	42,991	82,545
Books, supplies for college	6,304,205	2,082,908	1,078,035	676,972	1,678,617	651,262	100,007	36,306
Books, supplies for elementary, high school	1,625,366	25,323	238,028	735,320	474,186	91,687	47,704	13,586
Books, supplies for day care, nursery school	348,375	18,026	105,593	109,614	58,521	16,083	36,554	3,653
Miscellaneous school expenses and supplies	6,096,565	258,464	778,822	2,228,907	1,799,129	600,030	251,626	163,377
TOBACCO PRODUCTS AND SMOKING SUPPLIES	33,418,633	1,972,346	5,616,558	7,624,424	8,900,346	5,586,465	2,522,233	1,195,702
Cigarettes	30,774,674	1,848,393	5,102,212	7,030,212	8,312,356	5,207,612	2,271,872	1,002,070
Other tobacco products	2,470,926	120,004	492,043	561,011	540,340	355,807	209,554	191,806
Smoking accessories	163,806	3,949	22,500	33,202	38,166	23,046	40,807	1,827

Note: Numbers may not add to total because of rounding and missing subcategories.
Source: Calculations by New Strategist based on the 2003 Consumer Expenditure Survey

Table 10.4 Personal Care, Reading, Education, Tobacco: Market shares by age, 2003

(percentage of total annual spending on personal care, reading, education, and tobacco products accounted for by consumer unit age groups, 2003)

	total consumer units	under 25	25 to 34	35 to 44	45 to 54	55 to 64	65 to 74	75+
Share of total consumer units	100.0%	7.4%	17.1%	21.2%	20.1%	14.4%	10.0%	9.9%
Share of total before-tax income	100.0	3.0	16.9	25.3	26.7	16.5	6.9	4.9
Share of total spending	100.0	4.1	17.0	24.5	24.6	15.6	8.2	6.1
PERSONAL CARE PRODUCTS AND SERVICES	100.0	4.6	16.2	24.2	23.4	15.0	9.3	7.3
Personal care products	100.0	5.5	17.0	26.1	23.6	14.3	8.2	5.3
Hair care products	100.0	6.4	18.3	27.3	22.2	12.8	8.2	4.5
Hair accessories	100.0	6.4	19.5	35.1	21.2	10.9	4.7	1.8
Wigs and hairpieces	100.0	5.9	15.2	13.7	34.7	9.5	16.8	4.2
Oral hygiene products	100.0	9.3	13.9	23.2	18.8	15.7	10.5	8.6
Shaving products	100.0	4.8	15.7	26.9	26.5	14.5	5.5	6.0
Cosmetics, perfume, and bath products	100.0	4.4	17.0	26.3	24.7	15.0	7.8	4.6
Deodorants, feminine hygiene, misc. products	100.0	6.2	15.9	27.5	24.0	12.2	7.4	6.7
Electric personal care appliances	100.0	0.7	21.3	14.4	25.0	19.0	13.9	5.7
Personal care services	100.0	3.7	15.3	22.2	23.3	15.7	10.4	9.4
READING	100.0	3.1	13.3	18.9	23.7	19.0	11.7	10.4
Newspaper subscriptions	100.0	0.9	6.6	14.9	22.8	19.5	16.3	19.1
Newspaper, nonsubscription	100.0	3.5	14.6	22.8	24.1	18.1	10.2	6.7
Magazine subscriptions	100.0	3.1	11.8	16.2	22.5	20.4	14.5	11.6
Magazines, nonsubscription	100.0	7.7	19.1	24.5	24.6	13.1	6.7	4.4
Books purchased through book clubs	100.0	1.1	15.7	16.5	24.8	15.9	14.9	11.0
Books not purchased through book clubs	100.0	4.5	18.1	21.6	24.5	19.6	7.6	4.2
EDUCATION	100.0	14.2	14.9	18.8	35.2	13.6	2.2	1.0
College tuition	100.0	18.3	16.9	10.5	37.3	13.9	2.3	0.8
Elementary and high school tuition	100.0	0.2	7.4	35.3	41.2	12.9	1.9	1.2
Other school tuition	100.0	10.0	15.7	39.6	24.2	7.7	2.0	0.8
Other school expenses including rentals	100.0	4.6	14.3	28.2	23.2	27.3	0.8	1.6
Books, supplies for college	100.0	33.0	17.1	10.7	26.6	10.3	1.6	0.6
Books, supplies for elementary, high school	100.0	1.6	14.6	45.2	29.2	5.6	2.9	0.8
Books, supplies for day care, nursery school	100.0	5.2	30.3	31.5	16.8	4.6	10.5	1.0
Miscellaneous school expenses and supplies	100.0	4.2	12.8	36.6	29.5	9.8	4.1	2.7
TOBACCO PRODUCTS AND SMOKING SUPPLIES	100.0	5.9	16.8	22.8	26.6	16.7	7.5	3.6
Cigarettes	100.0	6.0	16.6	22.8	27.0	16.9	7.4	3.3
Other tobacco products	100.0	4.9	19.9	22.7	21.9	14.4	8.5	7.8
Smoking accessories	100.0	2.4	13.7	20.3	23.3	14.1	24.9	1.1

Note: Numbers may not add to total because of rounding.
Source: Calculations by New Strategist based on the 2003 Consumer Expenditure Survey

Table 10.5 Personal Care, Reading, Education, Tobacco: Average spending by income, 2003

(average annual spending on personal care, reading, education, and tobacco products, by before-tax income of consumer units (CU), 2003; complete income reporters only)

	total complete reporters	under $20,000	$20,000– $39,999	$40,000– $49,999	$50,000– $69,999	$70,000– $79,999	$80,000– $99,999	$100,000 or more
Number of consumer units (000)	97,391	27,100	23,941	8,891	13,890	5,121	6,909	11,537
Average number of persons per CU	2.5	1.8	2.4	2.6	2.8	3.0	3.0	3.1
Average before-tax income of CU	$51,128.00	$10,752.55	$29,072.57	$44,294.00	$58,900.00	$74,560.00	$88,832.00	$154,665.00
Average spending of CU, total	42,741.66	19,862.52	31,684.32	39,756.91	49,788.99	57,128.14	65,957.39	93,514.86
PERSONAL CARE PRODUCTS AND SERVICES	**559.25**	**310.86**	**414.58**	**532.84**	**636.73**	**722.16**	**871.26**	**1,131.22**
Personal care products	**301.31**	**183.08**	**218.09**	**292.37**	**353.76**	**394.22**	**477.58**	**569.03**
Hair care products	61.78	38.40	52.35	64.77	69.58	87.08	91.80	98.68
Hair accessories	7.58	4.57	6.49	6.51	10.45	10.08	10.95	11.61
Wigs and hairpieces	1.97	1.26	1.69	0.80	2.02	0.50	2.68	5.30
Oral hygiene products	31.64	25.07	26.92	27.71	35.69	33.11	44.30	48.07
Shaving products	16.88	8.82	12.37	23.08	23.42	22.26	16.66	30.98
Cosmetics, perfume, and bath products	136.81	79.12	84.42	129.31	155.87	191.47	226.34	297.59
Deodorants, feminine hygiene, misc. products	33.81	24.45	25.00	34.73	45.20	43.84	52.37	45.13
Electric personal care appliances	10.84	1.91	8.86	5.46	11.54	5.87	32.48	31.66
Personal care services	**257.94**	**127.78**	**196.49**	**240.47**	**282.97**	**327.94**	**393.67**	**562.19**
READING	**133.31**	**63.96**	**99.06**	**128.78**	**143.87**	**180.44**	**202.39**	**295.78**
Newspaper subscriptions	42.55	24.94	35.59	33.29	42.80	55.04	59.30	85.74
Newspaper, nonsubscription	10.53	6.39	10.40	11.93	13.31	12.47	10.31	15.33
Magazine subscriptions	15.43	6.62	10.76	16.38	18.50	25.09	21.67	33.35
Magazines, nonsubscription	8.47	3.78	6.86	7.33	9.46	12.11	13.89	17.65
Books purchased through book clubs	6.19	2.74	4.96	8.74	9.24	4.79	11.38	8.74
Books not purchased through book clubs	49.82	19.46	30.38	46.04	50.51	68.57	85.72	133.70
EDUCATION	**791.90**	**507.74**	**281.63**	**399.93**	**599.75**	**855.21**	**1,081.72**	**2,858.41**
College tuition	461.10	359.83	145.80	234.03	331.24	454.21	582.71	1,614.86
Elementary and high school tuition	126.44	12.85	26.52	37.38	92.32	99.41	227.66	661.67
Other school tuition	22.81	12.61	9.15	15.58	12.95	49.18	40.02	70.55
Other school expenses including rentals	47.43	10.61	18.43	27.92	33.52	54.27	54.70	218.52
Books, supplies for college	57.42	74.42	29.43	32.23	44.04	61.77	65.35	104.35
Books, supplies for elementary, high school	14.93	4.68	11.82	12.68	20.78	25.12	20.35	32.38
Books, supplies for day care, nursery school	3.32	1.32	2.37	5.66	3.11	13.09	1.95	4.91
Miscellaneous school expenses and supplies	58.45	31.41	38.11	34.44	61.78	98.17	88.98	151.17
TOBACCO PRODUCTS AND SMOKING SUPPLIES	**307.18**	**252.62**	**323.77**	**414.98**	**345.18**	**325.25**	**357.69**	**233.76**
Cigarettes	282.56	235.43	304.95	385.07	310.97	285.23	330.95	203.45
Other tobacco products	22.97	15.73	17.13	28.26	32.49	37.50	25.50	28.56
Smoking accessories	1.65	1.46	1.68	1.65	1.71	2.52	1.24	1.75

Note: Subcategories may not add to total because some are not shown.
Source: Bureau of Labor Statistics, unpublished tables from the 2003 Consumer Expenditure Survey; calculations by New Strategist

Table 10.6 Personal Care, Reading, Education, Tobacco: Indexed spending by income, 2003

(indexed average annual spending of consumer units (CU) on personal care, reading, education, and tobacco products, by before-tax income of consumer unit, 2003; complete income reporters only; index definition: an index of 100 is the average for all consumer units; an index of 132 means that spending by consumer units in that group is 32 percent above the average for all consumer units; an index of 68 indicates spending that is 32 percent below the average for all consumer units)

	total complete reporters	under $20,000	$20,000–$39,999	$40,000–$49,999	$50,000–$69,999	$70,000–$79,999	$80,000–$99,999	$100,000 or more
Average spending of CU, total	$42,742	$19,863	$31,684	$39,757	$49,789	$57,128	$65,957	$93,515
Average spending of CU, index	100	46	74	93	116	134	154	219
PERSONAL CARE PRODUCTS AND SERVICES	**100**	**56**	**74**	**95**	**114**	**129**	**156**	**202**
Personal care products	**100**	**61**	**72**	**97**	**117**	**131**	**159**	**189**
Hair care products	100	62	85	105	113	141	149	160
Hair accessories	100	60	86	86	138	133	144	153
Wigs and hairpieces	100	64	86	41	103	25	136	269
Oral hygiene products	100	79	85	88	113	105	140	152
Shaving products	100	52	73	137	139	132	99	184
Cosmetics, perfume, and bath products	100	58	62	95	114	140	165	218
Deodorants, feminine hygiene, misc. products	100	72	74	103	134	130	155	133
Electric personal care appliances	100	18	82	50	106	54	300	292
Personal care services	**100**	**50**	**76**	**93**	**110**	**127**	**153**	**218**
READING	**100**	**48**	**74**	**97**	**108**	**135**	**152**	**222**
Newspaper subscriptions	100	59	84	90	101	129	139	202
Newspaper, nonsubscription	100	61	99	113	126	118	98	146
Magazine subscriptions	100	43	70	106	120	163	140	216
Magazines, nonsubscription	100	45	81	87	112	143	164	208
Books purchased through book clubs	100	44	80	141	149	77	184	141
Books not purchased through book clubs	100	39	61	92	101	138	172	268
EDUCATION	**100**	**64**	**36**	**51**	**76**	**108**	**137**	**361**
College tuition	100	78	32	51	72	99	126	350
Elementary and high school tuition	100	10	21	30	73	79	180	523
Other school tuition	100	55	40	68	57	216	175	309
Other school expenses including rentals	100	22	39	59	71	114	115	461
Books, supplies for college	100	130	51	56	77	108	114	182
Books, supplies for elementary, high school	100	31	79	85	139	168	136	217
Books, supplies for day care, nursery school	100	40	71	170	94	394	59	148
Miscellaneous school expenses and supplies	100	54	65	59	106	168	152	259
TOBACCO PRODUCTS AND SMOKING SUPPLIES	**100**	**82**	**105**	**135**	**112**	**106**	**116**	**76**
Cigarettes	100	83	108	136	110	101	117	72
Other tobacco products	100	68	75	123	141	163	111	124
Smoking accessories	100	89	102	100	104	153	75	106

Source: Calculations by New Strategist based on the 2003 Consumer Expenditure Survey

Table 10.7 Personal Care, Reading, Education, Tobacco: Total spending by income, 2003

(total annual spending on personal care, reading, education, and tobacco products, by before-tax income group of consumer units (CU), 2003; complete income reporters only; numbers in thousands)

	total complete reporters	under $20,000	$20,000– $39,999	$40,000– $49,999	$50,000– $69,999	$70,000– $79,999	$80,000– $99,999	$100,000 or more
Number of consumer units	97,391	27,100	23,941	8,891	13,890	5,121	6,909	11,537
Total spending of all CUs	$4,162,653,009	$538,274,380	$758,554,310	$353,478,687	$691,569,071	$292,553,205	$455,699,608	$1,078,880,940
PERSONAL CARE PRODUCTS AND SERVICES	**54,465,917**	**8,424,430**	**9,925,398**	**4,737,430**	**8,844,180**	**3,698,181**	**6,019,535**	**13,050,885**
Personal care products	**29,344,882**	**4,961,536**	**5,221,388**	**2,599,452**	**4,913,726**	**2,018,801**	**3,299,600**	**6,564,899**
Hair care products	6,016,816	1,040,637	1,253,230	575,870	966,466	445,937	634,246	1,138,471
Hair accessories	738,224	123,859	155,311	57,830	145,151	51,620	75,654	133,945
Wigs and hairpieces	191,860	34,251	40,555	7,113	28,058	2,561	18,516	61,146
Oral hygiene products	3,081,451	679,524	644,410	246,370	495,734	169,556	306,069	554,584
Shaving products	1,643,960	239,125	296,142	205,204	325,304	113,993	115,104	357,416
Cosmetics, perfume, and bath products	13,324,063	2,144,017	2,021,183	1,149,695	2,165,034	980,518	1,563,783	3,433,296
Deodorants, feminine hygiene, misc. products	3,292,790	662,554	598,621	308,784	627,828	224,505	361,824	520,665
Electric personal care appliances	1,055,718	51,728	212,068	48,545	160,291	30,060	224,404	365,261
Personal care services	**25,121,035**	**3,462,965**	**4,704,118**	**2,138,019**	**3,930,453**	**1,679,381**	**2,719,866**	**6,485,986**
READING	**12,983,194**	**1,733,252**	**2,371,572**	**1,144,983**	**1,998,354**	**924,033**	**1,398,313**	**3,412,414**
Newspaper subscriptions	4,143,987	675,869	852,112	340,436	594,492	281,860	409,704	989,182
Newspaper, nonsubscription	1,025,527	173,290	248,980	106,070	184,876	63,859	71,232	176,862
Magazine subscriptions	1,502,743	179,495	257,639	145,635	256,965	128,486	149,718	384,759
Magazines, nonsubscription	824,902	102,515	164,201	65,171	131,399	62,015	95,966	203,628
Books purchased through book clubs	602,850	74,261	118,656	77,707	128,344	24,530	78,624	100,833
Books not purchased through book clubs	4,852,020	527,380	727,281	409,342	701,584	351,147	592,239	1,542,497
EDUCATION	**77,123,933**	**13,759,709**	**6,742,572**	**3,555,778**	**8,330,528**	**4,379,530**	**7,473,603**	**32,977,476**
College tuition	44,906,990	9,751,488	3,490,514	2,080,761	4,600,924	2,326,009	4,025,943	18,630,640
Elementary and high school tuition	12,314,118	348,302	634,886	332,346	1,282,325	509,079	1,572,903	7,633,687
Other school tuition	2,221,489	341,863	219,145	138,522	179,876	251,851	276,498	813,935
Other school expenses including rentals	4,619,255	287,575	441,138	248,237	465,593	277,917	377,922	2,521,065
Books, supplies for college	5,592,191	2,016,848	704,633	286,557	611,716	316,324	451,503	1,203,886
Books, supplies for elementary, high school	1,454,048	126,941	283,018	112,738	288,634	128,640	140,598	373,568
Books, supplies for day care, nursery school	323,338	35,733	56,775	50,323	43,198	67,034	13,473	56,647
Miscellaneous school expenses and supplies	5,692,504	851,078	912,463	306,206	858,124	502,729	614,763	1,744,048
TOBACCO PRODUCTS AND SMOKING SUPPLIES	**29,916,567**	**6,845,911**	**7,751,344**	**3,685,587**	**4,794,550**	**1,665,605**	**2,471,280**	**2,696,889**
Cigarettes	27,518,801	6,380,090	7,300,840	3,423,657	4,319,373	1,460,663	2,286,534	2,347,203
Other tobacco products	2,237,071	426,284	410,183	251,260	451,286	192,038	176,180	329,497
Smoking accessories	160,695	39,581	40,321	14,670	23,752	12,905	8,567	20,190

Note: Numbers may not add to total because of rounding and missing subcategories.
Source: Calculations by New Strategist based on the 2003 Consumer Expenditure Survey

Table 10.8 Personal Care, Reading, Education, Tobacco: Market shares by income, 2003

(percentage of total annual spending on personal care, reading, education, and tobacco products accounted for by before-tax income group of consumer units, 2003; complete income reporters only)

	total complete reporters	under $20,000	$20,000–$39,999	$40,000–$49,999	$50,000–$69,999	$70,000–$79,999	$80,000–$99,999	$100,000 or more
Share of total consumer units	100.0%	27.8%	24.6%	9.1%	14.3%	5.3%	7.1%	11.8%
Share of total before-tax income	100.0	5.9	14.0	7.9	16.4	7.7	12.3	35.8
Share of total spending	100.0	12.9	18.2	8.5	16.6	7.0	10.9	25.9
PERSONAL CARE PRODUCTS AND SERVICES	100.0	15.5	18.2	8.7	16.2	6.8	11.1	24.0
Personal care products	100.0	16.9	17.8	8.9	16.7	6.9	11.2	22.4
Hair care products	100.0	17.3	20.8	9.6	16.1	7.4	10.5	18.9
Hair accessories	100.0	16.8	21.0	7.8	19.7	7.0	10.2	18.1
Wigs and hairpieces	100.0	17.9	21.1	3.7	14.6	1.3	9.7	31.9
Oral hygiene products	100.0	22.1	20.9	8.0	16.1	5.5	9.9	18.0
Shaving products	100.0	14.5	18.0	12.5	19.8	6.9	7.0	21.7
Cosmetics, perfume, and bath products	100.0	16.1	15.2	8.6	16.2	7.4	11.7	25.8
Deodorants, feminine hygiene, misc. products	100.0	20.1	18.2	9.4	19.1	6.8	11.0	15.8
Electric personal care appliances	100.0	4.9	20.1	4.6	15.2	2.8	21.3	34.6
Personal care services	100.0	13.8	18.7	8.5	15.6	6.7	10.8	25.8
READING	100.0	13.3	18.3	8.8	15.4	7.1	10.8	26.3
Newspaper subscriptions	100.0	16.3	20.6	8.2	14.3	6.8	9.9	23.9
Newspaper, nonsubscription	100.0	16.9	24.3	10.3	18.0	6.2	6.9	17.2
Magazine subscriptions	100.0	11.9	17.1	9.7	17.1	8.6	10.0	25.6
Magazines, nonsubscription	100.0	12.4	19.9	7.9	15.9	7.5	11.6	24.7
Books purchased through book clubs	100.0	12.3	19.7	12.9	21.3	4.1	13.0	16.7
Books not purchased through book clubs	100.0	10.9	15.0	8.4	14.5	7.2	12.2	31.8
EDUCATION	100.0	17.8	8.7	4.6	10.8	5.7	9.7	42.8
College tuition	100.0	21.7	7.8	4.6	10.2	5.2	9.0	41.5
Elementary and high school tuition	100.0	2.8	5.2	2.7	10.4	4.1	12.8	62.0
Other school tuition	100.0	15.4	9.9	6.2	8.1	11.3	12.4	36.6
Other school expenses including rentals	100.0	6.2	9.5	5.4	10.1	6.0	8.2	54.6
Books, supplies for college	100.0	36.1	12.6	5.1	10.9	5.7	8.1	21.5
Books, supplies for elementary, high school	100.0	8.7	19.5	7.8	19.9	8.8	9.7	25.7
Books, supplies for day care, nursery school	100.0	11.1	17.6	15.6	13.4	20.7	4.2	17.5
Miscellaneous school expenses and supplies	100.0	15.0	16.0	5.4	15.1	8.8	10.8	30.6
TOBACCO PRODUCTS AND SMOKING SUPPLIES	100.0	22.9	25.9	12.3	16.0	5.6	8.3	9.0
Cigarettes	100.0	23.2	26.5	12.4	15.7	5.3	8.3	8.5
Other tobacco products	100.0	19.1	18.3	11.2	20.2	8.6	7.9	14.7
Smoking accessories	100.0	24.6	25.1	9.1	14.8	8.0	5.3	12.6

Note: Numbers may not add to total because of rounding.
Source: Calculations by New Strategist based on the 2003 Consumer Expenditure Survey

Table 10.9 Personal Care, Reading, Education, Tobacco: Average spending by high-income consumer units, 2003

(average annual spending on personal care, reading, education, and tobacco products, by before-tax income of high-income consumer units (CU), 2003; complete income reporters only)

	total complete reporters	$100,000 or more	$100,000– $119,999	$120,000– $149,999	$150,000 or more
Number of consumer units (000)	97,391	11,537	4,384	3,151	4,002
Average number of persons per CU	2.5	3.1	3.1	3.1	3.1
Average before-tax income of CU	$51,128.00	$154,665.00	$108,087.00	$131,885.00	$223,634.00
Average spending of CU, total	42,741.66	93,514.86	75,601.50	86,451.46	118,674.11
PERSONAL CARE PRODUCTS AND SERVICES	**559.25**	**1,131.22**	**874.37**	**1,139.39**	**1,405.43**
Personal care products	**301.31**	**569.03**	**430.33**	**613.70**	**685.04**
Hair care products	61.78	98.68	73.66	125.06	105.39
Hair accessories	7.58	11.61	7.88	12.20	15.21
Wigs and hairpieces	1.97	5.30	0.25	17.10	1.54
Oral hygiene products	31.64	48.07	42.69	54.31	49.07
Shaving products	16.88	30.98	25.54	33.88	34.65
Cosmetics, perfume, and bath products	136.81	297.59	224.76	302.18	373.22
Deodorants, feminine hygiene, misc. products	33.81	45.13	37.09	43.00	55.53
Electric personal care appliances	10.84	31.66	18.46	25.97	50.44
Personal care services	**257.94**	**562.19**	**444.04**	**525.69**	**720.39**
READING	**133.31**	**295.78**	**227.78**	**293.31**	**372.22**
Newspaper subscriptions	42.55	85.74	71.17	84.54	102.66
Newspaper, nonsubscription	10.53	15.33	14.66	18.35	13.69
Magazine subscriptions	15.43	33.35	27.11	37.09	37.25
Magazines, nonsubscription	8.47	17.65	13.11	15.44	24.36
Books purchased through book clubs	6.19	8.74	7.08	11.38	8.47
Books not purchased through book clubs	49.82	133.70	94.53	125.61	182.99
EDUCATION	**791.90**	**2,858.41**	**2,092.61**	**2,165.22**	**4,242.77**
College tuition	461.10	1,614.86	1,272.05	1,354.79	2,195.25
Elementary and high school tuition	126.44	661.67	387.46	342.79	1,213.21
Other school tuition	22.81	70.55	39.90	34.41	132.58
Other school expenses including rentals	47.43	218.52	107.38	201.46	353.73
Books, supplies for college	57.42	104.35	113.95	82.28	111.23
Books, supplies for elementary, high school	14.93	32.38	28.61	30.88	37.68
Books, supplies for day care, nursery school	3.32	4.91	1.76	6.43	7.15
Miscellaneous school expenses and supplies	58.45	151.17	141.51	112.17	191.94
TOBACCO PRODUCTS AND SMOKING SUPPLIES	**307.18**	**233.76**	**243.07**	**258.74**	**203.90**
Cigarettes	282.56	203.45	222.47	233.04	159.32
Other tobacco products	22.97	28.56	20.17	22.58	42.45
Smoking accessories	1.65	1.75	0.43	3.12	2.13

Note: Subcategories may not add to total because some are not shown.
Source: Bureau of Labor Statistics, unpublished tables from the 2003 Consumer Expenditure Survey; calculations by New Strategist

Table 10.10 Personal Care, Reading, Education, Tobacco: Indexed spending by high-income consumer units, 2003

(indexed average annual spending of consumer units (CU) on personal care, reading, education, and tobacco products, by before-tax income of high-income consumer unit, 2003; complete income reporters only; index definition: an index of 100 is the average for all consumer units; an index of 132 means that spending by consumer units in that group is 32 percent above the average for all consumer units; an index of 68 indicates spending that is 32 percent below the average for all consumer units)

	total complete reporters	$100,000 or more	$100,000–$119,999	$120,000–$149,999	$150,000 or more
Average spending of CU, total	$42,742	$93,515	$75,602	$86,451	$118,674
Average spending of CU, index	100	219	177	202	278
PERSONAL CARE PRODUCTS AND SERVICES	100	202	156	204	251
Personal care products	100	189	143	204	227
Hair care products	100	160	119	202	171
Hair accessories	100	153	104	161	201
Wigs and hairpieces	100	269	13	868	78
Oral hygiene products	100	152	135	172	155
Shaving products	100	184	151	201	205
Cosmetics, perfume, and bath products	100	218	164	221	273
Deodorants, feminine hygiene, misc. products	100	133	110	127	164
Electric personal care appliances	100	292	170	240	465
Personal care services	100	218	172	204	279
READING	100	222	171	220	279
Newspaper subscriptions	100	202	167	199	241
Newspaper, nonsubscription	100	146	139	174	130
Magazine subscriptions	100	216	176	240	241
Magazines, nonsubscription	100	208	155	182	288
Books purchased through book clubs	100	141	114	184	137
Books not purchased through book clubs	100	268	190	252	367
EDUCATION	100	361	264	273	536
College tuition	100	350	276	294	476
Elementary and high school tuition	100	523	306	271	960
Other school tuition	100	309	175	151	581
Other school expenses including rentals	100	461	226	425	746
Books, supplies for college	100	182	198	143	194
Books, supplies for elementary, high school	100	217	192	207	252
Books, supplies for day care, nursery school	100	148	53	194	215
Miscellaneous school expenses and supplies	100	259	242	192	328
TOBACCO PRODUCTS AND SMOKING SUPPLIES	100	76	79	84	66
Cigarettes	100	72	79	82	56
Other tobacco products	100	124	88	98	185
Smoking accessories	100	06	26	189	129

Source: Calculations by New Strategist based on the 2003 Consumer Expenditure Survey

Table 10.11 Personal Care, Reading, Education, Tobacco: Total spending by high-income consumer units, 2003

(total annual spending on personal care, reading, education, and tobacco products, by before-tax income group of high-income consumer units (CU), 2003; complete income reporters only; numbers in thousands)

	total complete reporters	$100,000 or more	$100,000–$119,999	$120,000–$149,999	$150,000 or more
Number of consumer units	97,391	11,537	4,384	3,151	4,002
Total spending of all CUs	$4,162,653,009	$1,078,880,940	$331,436,976	$272,408,550	$474,933,788
PERSONAL CARE PRODUCTS AND SERVICES	**54,465,917**	**13,050,885**	**3,833,238**	**3,590,218**	**5,624,531**
Personal care products	**29,344,882**	**6,564,899**	**1,886,567**	**1,933,769**	**2,741,530**
Hair care products	6,016,816	1,138,471	322,925	394,064	421,771
Hair accessories	738,224	133,945	34,546	38,442	60,870
Wigs and hairpieces	191,860	61,146	1,096	53,882	6,163
Oral hygiene products	3,081,451	554,584	187,153	171,131	196,378
Shaving products	1,643,960	357,416	111,967	106,756	138,669
Cosmetics, perfume, and bath products	13,324,063	3,433,296	985,348	952,169	1,493,626
Deodorants, feminine hygiene, misc. products	3,292,790	520,665	162,603	135,493	222,231
Electric personal care appliances	1,055,718	365,261	80,929	81,831	201,861
Personal care services	**25,121,035**	**6,485,986**	**1,946,671**	**1,656,449**	**2,883,001**
READING	**12,983,194**	**3,412,414**	**998,588**	**924,220**	**1,489,624**
Newspaper subscriptions	4,143,987	989,182	312,009	266,386	410,845
Newspaper, nonsubscription	1,025,527	176,862	64,269	57,821	54,787
Magazine subscriptions	1,502,743	384,759	118,850	116,871	149,075
Magazines, nonsubscription	824,902	203,628	57,474	48,651	97,489
Books purchased through book clubs	602,850	100,833	31,039	35,858	33,897
Books not purchased through book clubs	4,852,020	1,542,497	414,420	395,797	732,326
EDUCATION	**77,123,933**	**32,977,476**	**9,174,002**	**6,822,608**	**16,979,566**
College tuition	44,906,990	18,630,640	5,576,667	4,268,943	8,785,391
Elementary and high school tuition	12,314,118	7,633,687	1,698,625	1,080,131	4,855,266
Other school tuition	2,221,489	813,935	174,922	108,426	530,585
Other school expenses including rentals	4,619,255	2,521,065	470,754	634,800	1,415,627
Books, supplies for college	5,592,191	1,203,886	499,557	259,264	445,142
Books, supplies for elementary, high school	1,454,048	373,568	125,426	97,303	150,795
Books, supplies for day care, nursery school	323,338	56,647	7,716	20,261	28,614
Miscellaneous school expenses and supplies	5,692,504	1,744,048	620,380	353,448	768,144
TOBACCO PRODUCTS AND SMOKING SUPPLIES	**29,916,567**	**2,696,889**	**1,065,619**	**815,290**	**816,008**
Cigarettes	27,518,801	2,347,203	975,308	734,309	637,599
Other tobacco products	2,237,071	329,497	88,425	71,150	169,885
Smoking accessories	160,695	20,190	1,885	9,831	8,524

Note: Numbers may not add to total because of rounding and missing subcategories.
Source: Calculations by New Strategist based on the 2003 Consumer Expenditure Survey

Table 10.12 Personal Care, Reading, Education, Tobacco: Market shares by high-income consumer units, 2003

(percentage of total annual spending on personal care, reading, education, and tobacco products accounted for by before-tax income group of high-income consumer units, 2003; complete income reporters only)

	total complete reporters	$100,000 or more	$100,000–$119,999	$120,000–$149,999	$150,000 or more
Share of total consumer units	100.0%	11.8%	4.5%	3.2%	4.1%
Share of total before-tax income	100.0	35.8	9.5	8.3	18.0
Share of total spending	100.0	25.9	8.0	6.5	11.4
PERSONAL CARE PRODUCTS AND SERVICES	100.0	24.0	7.0	6.6	10.3
Personal care products	100.0	22.4	6.4	6.6	9.3
Hair care products	100.0	18.9	5.4	6.5	7.0
Hair accessories	100.0	18.1	4.7	5.2	8.2
Wigs and hairpieces	100.0	31.9	0.6	28.1	3.2
Oral hygiene products	100.0	18.0	6.1	5.6	6.4
Shaving products	100.0	21.7	6.8	6.5	8.4
Cosmetics, perfume, and bath products	100.0	25.8	7.4	7.1	11.2
Deodorants, feminine hygiene, misc. products	100.0	15.8	4.9	4.1	6.7
Electric personal care appliances	100.0	34.6	7.7	7.8	19.1
Personal care services	100.0	25.8	7.7	6.6	11.5
READING	100.0	26.3	7.7	7.1	11.5
Newspaper subscriptions	100.0	23.9	7.5	6.4	9.9
Newspaper, nonsubscription	100.0	17.2	6.3	5.6	5.3
Magazine subscriptions	100.0	25.6	7.9	7.8	9.9
Magazines, nonsubscription	100.0	24.7	7.0	5.9	11.8
Books purchased through book clubs	100.0	16.7	5.1	5.9	5.6
Books not purchased through book clubs	100.0	31.8	8.5	8.2	15.1
EDUCATION	100.0	42.8	11.9	8.8	22.0
College tuition	100.0	41.5	12.4	9.5	19.6
Elementary and high school tuition	100.0	62.0	13.8	8.8	39.4
Other school tuition	100.0	36.6	7.9	4.9	23.9
Other school expenses including rentals	100.0	54.6	10.2	13.7	30.6
Books, supplies for college	100.0	21.5	8.9	4.6	8.0
Books, supplies for elementary, high school	100.0	25.7	8.6	6.7	10.4
Books, supplies for day care, nursery school	100.0	17.5	2.4	6.3	8.8
Miscellaneous school expenses and supplies	100.0	30.6	10.9	6.2	13.5
TOBACCO PRODUCTS AND SMOKING SUPPLIES	100.0	9.0	3.6	2.7	2.7
Cigarettes	100.0	8.5	3.5	2.7	2.3
Other tobacco products	100.0	14.7	4.0	3.2	7.6
Smoking accessories	100.0	12.6	1.2	6.1	5.3

Note: Numbers may not add to total because of rounding.
Source: Calculations by New Strategist based on the 2003 Consumer Expenditure Survey

Table 10.13 Personal Care, Reading, Education, Tobacco: Average spending by household type, 2003

(average annual spending of consumer units (CU) on personal care, reading, education, and tobacco products, by type of consumer unit, 2003)

	total married couples	married couples, no children	married couples with children				single parent, at least one child <18	single person
			total	oldest child under 6	oldest child 6 to 17	oldest child 18 or older		
Number of consumer units (000)	58,448	25,132	28,584	5,496	15,047	8,041	6,999	33,929
Average number of persons per CU	3.2	2.0	3.9	3.5	4.1	4.0	2.9	1.0
Average before-tax income of CU	$69,472.00	$62,930.00	$75,557.00	$66,317.00	$77,508.00	$78,307.00	$29,154.00	$27,131.00
Average spending of CU, total	53,030.03	47,895.65	57,702.32	51,503.24	59,183.18	59,180.36	30,534.75	23,657.35
PERSONAL CARE PRODUCTS AND SERVICES	**667.88**	**616.64**	**712.74**	**558.67**	**713.28**	**821.39**	**459.02**	**315.81**
Personal care products	**337.65**	**282.88**	**378.31**	**307.06**	**371.88**	**443.43**	**262.77**	**163.32**
Hair care products	68.87	53.24	80.38	62.48	85.57	82.97	56.93	32.56
Hair accessories	8.88	4.98	11.76	9.61	13.98	8.83	7.74	3.45
Wigs and hairpieces	2.20	1.49	2.95	0.94	1.19	7.61	3.65	0.43
Oral hygiene products	33.80	32.64	33.85	23.90	35.19	38.43	20.71	21.77
Shaving products	19.53	16.20	21.83	26.59	19.15	23.80	9.00	8.54
Cosmetics, perfume, and bath products	154.19	130.76	170.90	154.57	157.18	210.88	129.18	75.24
Deodorants, feminine hygiene, misc. products	35.42	26.72	42.09	24.92	45.41	47.95	32.34	17.39
Electric personal care appliances	14.76	16.85	14.55	4.06	14.21	22.95	3.22	3.95
Personal care services	**330.23**	**333.77**	**334.43**	**251.61**	**341.40**	**377.96**	**196.25**	**152.49**
READING	**162.81**	**186.42**	**149.49**	**121.09**	**150.52**	**166.98**	**63.96**	**93.09**
Newspaper subscriptions	56.14	70.78	45.65	33.50	42.94	59.03	11.33	29.65
Newspaper, nonsubscription	10.65	10.64	10.50	7.94	10.14	12.93	8.33	8.50
Magazine subscriptions	19.08	24.03	16.01	11.68	15.81	19.34	5.91	10.26
Magazines, nonsubscription	9.06	8.38	9.95	8.84	10.18	10.28	5.86	5.62
Books purchased through book clubs	6.75	7.44	5.91	8.08	6.03	4.22	2.49	5.02
Books not purchased through book clubs	60.55	65.01	60.69	50.88	64.05	61.10	30.03	34.02
EDUCATION	**1,052.98**	**609.68**	**1,509.72**	**412.95**	**1,437.86**	**2,393.20**	**492.67**	**498.45**
College tuition	589.24	440.72	759.38	224.63	487.34	1,633.88	185.68	382.43
Elementary and high school tuition	218.23	21.68	408.91	48.17	583.91	327.98	103.02	9.55
Other school tuition	29.44	15.77	43.21	17.57	52.58	43.19	27.11	7.81
Other school expenses including rentals	67.39	60.29	80.92	54.68	81.72	97.37	31.26	11.75
Books, supplies for college	52.33	33.06	70.35	26.56	39.62	157.80	26.25	65.28
Books, supplies for elementary, high school	20.30	1.50	36.86	2.54	56.78	23.06	35.87	0.66
Books, supplies for day care, nursery school	4.30	3.67	4.88	2.84	6.10	4.00	2.77	1.39
Miscellaneous school expenses and supplies	71.76	32.98	105.20	35.97	129.81	105.92	80.71	19.57
TOBACCO PRODUCTS AND SMOKING SUPPLIES	**300.12**	**274.61**	**298.25**	**219.66**	**291.10**	**365.37**	**230.42**	**193.40**
Cigarettes	271.53	247.02	267.06	173.92	264.73	335.09	221.57	176.02
Other tobacco products	26.84	26.12	29.34	43.58	24.88	27.95	7.94	16.41
Smoking accessories	1.59	1.46	1.52	2.16	1.50	1.10	0.92	0.97

Note: Average spending figures for total consumer units can be found on Average Spending by Age and Average Spending by Region tables. Subcategories may not add to total because some are not shown.
Source: Bureau of Labor Statistics, unpublished tables from the 2003 Consumer Expenditure Survey

Table 10.14 Personal Care, Reading, Education, Tobacco: Indexed spending by household type, 2003

(indexed average annual spending of consumer units (CU) on personal care, reading, education, and tobacco products, by type of consumer unit, 2003; index definition: an index of 100 is the average for all consumer units; an index of 132 means that spending by consumer units in that group is 32 percent above the average for all consumer units; an index of 68 indicates spending that is 32 percent below the average for all consumer units)

| | total married couples | married couples, no children | married couples with children | | | | single parent, at least one child <18 | single person |
			total	oldest child under 6	oldest child 6 to 17	oldest child 18 or older		
Average spending of CU, total	$53,030	$47,896	$57,702	$51,503	$59,183	$59,180	$30,535	$23,657
Average spending of CU, index	130	117	141	126	145	145	75	58
PERSONAL CARE PRODUCTS AND SERVICES	127	117	135	106	135	156	87	60
Personal care products	125	105	140	114	137	164	97	60
Hair care products	124	96	144	112	154	149	102	59
Hair accessories	132	74	174	142	207	131	115	51
Wigs and hairpieces	120	81	160	51	65	414	198	23
Oral hygiene products	120	116	120	85	125	136	73	77
Shaving products	132	109	148	180	129	161	61	58
Cosmetics, perfume, and bath products	125	106	138	125	127	171	105	61
Deodorants, feminine hygiene, misc. products	118	89	140	83	151	159	107	58
Electric personal care appliances	152	174	150	42	147	237	33	41
Personal care services	129	130	130	98	133	147	77	59
READING	128	146	117	95	118	131	50	73
Newspaper subscriptions	135	170	110	81	103	142	27	71
Newspaper, nonsubscription	110	110	108	82	104	133	86	88
Magazine subscriptions	132	166	111	81	109	134	41	71
Magazines, nonsubscription	117	108	129	114	132	133	76	73
Books purchased through book clubs	119	131	104	142	106	74	44	88
Books not purchased through book clubs	127	136	127	106	134	128	63	71
EDUCATION	134	78	193	53	184	306	63	64
College tuition	126	94	152	48	104	349	40	82
Elementary and high school tuition	175	17	327	39	467	263	82	8
Other school tuition	138	74	202	82	246	202	127	37
Other school expenses including rentals	151	135	181	122	183	218	70	26
Books, supplies for college	96	60	129	49	72	289	48	119
Books, supplies for elementary, high school	144	11	262	18	403	164	255	5
Books, supplies for day care, nursery school	142	122	162	94	202	132	92	46
Miscellaneous school expenses and supplies	136	62	199	68	246	200	153	37
TOBACCO PRODUCTS AND SMOKING SUPPLIES	104	95	103	76	100	126	80	67
Cigarettes	102	93	100	65	99	126	83	66
Other tobacco products	125	122	137	203	116	130	37	77
Smoking accessories	112	103	107	152	106	77	65	68

Note: Spending index for total consumer units is 100.
Source: Calculations by New Strategist based on the 2003 Consumer Expenditure Survey

Table 10.15 Personal Care, Reading, Education, Tobacco: Total spending by household type, 2003

(total annual spending on personal care, reading, education, and tobacco products, by consumer unit (CU) type, 2003; numbers in thousands)

	total married couples	married couples, no children	married couples with children				single parent, at least one child <18	single person
			total	oldest child under 6	oldest child 6 to 17	oldest child 18 or older		
Number of consumer units	58,448	25,132	28,584	5,496	15,047	8,041	6,999	33,929
Total spending of all CUs	$3,099,499,193	$1,203,713,476	$1,649,363,115	$283,061,807	$890,529,309	$475,869,275	$213,712,715	$802,670,228
PERSONAL CARE PRODUCTS AND SERVICES	**39,036,250**	**15,497,396**	**20,372,960**	**3,070,450**	**10,732,724**	**6,604,797**	**3,212,681**	**10,715,117**
Personal care products	**19,734,967**	**7,109,340**	**10,813,613**	**1,687,602**	**5,595,678**	**3,565,621**	**1,839,127**	**5,541,284**
Hair care products	4,025,314	1,338,028	2,297,582	343,390	1,287,572	667,162	398,453	1,104,728
Hair accessories	519,018	125,157	336,148	52,817	210,357	71,002	54,172	117,055
Wigs and hairpieces	128,586	37,447	84,323	5,166	17,906	61,192	25,546	14,589
Oral hygiene products	1,975,542	820,308	967,568	131,354	529,504	309,016	144,949	738,634
Shaving products	1,141,489	407,138	623,989	146,139	288,150	191,376	62,991	289,754
Cosmetics, perfume, and bath products	9,012,097	3,286,260	4,885,006	849,517	2,365,087	1,695,686	904,131	2,552,818
Deodorants, feminine hygiene, misc. products	2,070,228	671,527	1,203,101	136,960	683,284	385,566	226,348	590,025
Electric personal care appliances	862,692	423,474	415,897	22,314	213,818	184,541	22,537	134,020
Personal care services	**19,301,283**	**8,388,308**	**9,559,347**	**1,382,849**	**5,137,046**	**3,039,176**	**1,373,554**	**5,173,833**
READING	**9,515,919**	**4,685,107**	**4,273,022**	**665,511**	**2,264,874**	**1,342,686**	**447,656**	**3,158,451**
Newspaper subscriptions	3,281,271	1,778,843	1,304,860	184,116	646,118	474,660	79,299	1,005,995
Newspaper, nonsubscription	622,471	267,404	300,132	43,638	152,577	103,970	58,302	288,397
Magazine subscriptions	1,115,188	603,922	457,630	64,193	237,893	155,513	41,364	348,112
Magazines, nonsubscription	529,539	210,606	284,411	48,585	153,178	82,661	41,014	190,681
Books purchased through book clubs	394,524	186,982	168,931	44,408	90,733	33,933	17,428	170,324
Books not purchased through book clubs	3,539,026	1,633,831	1,734,763	279,636	963,760	491,305	210,180	1,154,265
EDUCATION	**61,544,575**	**15,322,478**	**43,153,836**	**2,269,573**	**21,635,479**	**19,243,721**	**3,448,197**	**16,911,910**
College tuition	34,439,900	11,076,175	21,706,118	1,234,566	7,333,005	13,138,029	1,299,574	12,975,467
Elementary and high school tuition	12,755,107	544,862	11,688,283	264,742	8,786,094	2,637,287	721,037	324,022
Other school tuition	1,720,709	396,332	1,235,115	96,565	791,171	347,291	189,743	264,985
Other school expenses including rentals	3,938,811	1,515,208	2,313,017	300,521	1,229,641	782,952	218,789	398,666
Books, supplies for college	3,058,584	830,864	2,010,884	145,974	596,162	1,268,870	183,724	2,214,885
Books, supplies for elementary, high school	1,186,494	37,698	1,053,606	13,960	854,369	185,425	251,054	22,393
Books, supplies for day care, nursery school	251,326	92,234	139,490	15,609	91,787	32,164	19,387	47,161
Miscellaneous school expenses and supplies	4,194,228	828,853	3,007,037	197,691	1,953,251	851,703	564,889	663,991
TOBACCO PRODUCTS AND SMOKING SUPPLIES	**17,541,414**	**6,901,499**	**8,525,178**	**1,207,251**	**4,380,182**	**2,937,940**	**1,612,710**	**6,561,869**
Cigarettes	15,870,385	6,208,107	7,633,643	955,864	3,983,392	2,694,459	1,550,768	5,972,183
Other tobacco products	1,568,744	656,448	838,655	239,516	374,369	224,746	55,572	556,775
Smoking accessories	92,932	36,693	43,448	11,871	22,571	8,845	6,439	32,911

Note: Total spending figures for total consumer units can be found on Total Spending by Age and Total Spending by Region tables. Spending by type of consumer unit will not add to total because not all types of consumer units are shown. Numbers may not add to category total because of rounding and missing subcategories.
Source: Calculations by New Strategist based on the 2003 Consumer Expenditure Survey

Table 10.16 Personal Care, Reading, Education, Tobacco: Market shares by household type, 2003

(percentage of total annual spending on personal care, reading, education, and tobacco products accounted for by types of consumer units, 2003)

	total married couples	married couples, no children	married couples with children				single parent, at least one child <18	single person
			total	oldest child under 6	oldest child 6 to 17	oldest child 18 or older		
Share of total consumer units	50.7%	21.8%	24.8%	4.8%	13.0%	7.0%	6.1%	29.4%
Share of total before-tax income	68.8	26.8	36.6	6.2	19.8	10.7	3.5	15.6
Share of total spending	65.8	25.6	35.0	6.0	18.9	10.1	4.5	17.0
PERSONAL CARE PRODUCTS AND SERVICES	**64.2**	**25.5**	**33.5**	**5.1**	**17.7**	**10.9**	**5.3**	**17.6**
Personal care products	**63.2**	**22.8**	**34.7**	**5.4**	**17.9**	**11.4**	**5.9**	**17.8**
Hair care products	62.7	20.8	35.8	5.3	20.1	10.4	6.2	17.2
Hair accessories	66.7	16.1	43.2	6.8	27.0	9.1	7.0	15.0
Wigs and hairpieces	60.6	17.6	39.7	2.4	8.4	28.8	12.0	6.9
Oral hygiene products	60.7	25.2	29.7	4.0	16.3	9.5	4.5	22.7
Shaving products	66.9	23.8	36.5	8.6	16.9	11.2	3.7	17.0
Cosmetics, perfume, and bath products	63.3	23.1	34.3	6.0	15.6	11.9	6.3	17.9
Deodorants, feminine hygiene, misc. products	59.6	19.3	34.6	3.9	19.7	11.1	6.5	17.0
Electric personal care appliances	77.3	37.9	37.2	2.0	19.1	16.5	2.0	12.0
Personal care services	**65.2**	**28.4**	**32.3**	**4.7**	**17.4**	**10.3**	**4.6**	**17.5**
READING	**64.8**	**31.9**	**29.1**	**4.5**	**15.4**	**9.1**	**3.0**	**21.5**
Newspaper subscriptions	68.5	37.1	27.2	3.8	13.5	9.9	1.7	21.0
Newspaper, nonsubscription	55.6	23.9	26.8	3.9	13.6	9.3	5.2	25.7
Magazine subscriptions	66.9	36.2	27.5	3.9	14.3	9.3	2.5	20.9
Magazines, nonsubscription	59.4	23.6	31.9	5.4	17.2	9.3	4.6	21.4
Books purchased through book clubs	60.1	28.5	25.7	6.8	13.8	5.2	2.7	25.9
Books not purchased through book clubs	64.2	29.6	31.5	5.1	17.5	8.9	3.8	20.9
EDUCATION	**68.1**	**17.0**	**47.8**	**2.5**	**23.9**	**21.3**	**3.8**	**18.7**
College tuition	63.8	20.5	40.2	2.3	13.6	24.4	2.4	24.0
Elementary and high school tuition	88.5	3.8	81.1	1.8	61.0	18.3	5.0	2.2
Other school tuition	69.8	16.1	50.1	3.9	32.1	14.1	7.7	10.8
Other school expenses including rentals	76.3	29.4	44.8	5.8	23.8	15.2	4.2	7.7
Books, supplies for college	48.5	13.2	31.9	2.3	9.5	20.1	2.9	35.1
Books, supplies for elementary, high school	73.0	2.3	64.8	0.9	52.6	11.4	15.4	1.4
Books, supplies for day care, nursery school	72.1	26.5	40.0	4.5	26.3	9.2	5.6	13.5
Miscellaneous school expenses and supplies	68.8	13.6	49.3	3.2	32.0	14.0	9.3	10.9
TOBACCO PRODUCTS AND SMOKING SUPPLIES	**52.5**	**20.7**	**25.5**	**3.6**	**13.1**	**8.8**	**4.8**	**19.6**
Cigarettes	51.6	20.2	24.8	3.1	12.9	8.8	5.0	19.4
Other tobacco products	63.5	26.6	33.9	9.7	15.2	9.1	2.2	22.5
Smoking accessories	56.7	22.4	26.5	7.2	13.8	5.4	3.9	20.1

Note: Market share for total consumer units is 100.0%. Market shares by type of consumer unit will not add to total because not all types of consumer units are shown.
Source: Calculations by New Strategist based on the 2003 Consumer Expenditure Survey

Table 10.17 Personal Care, Reading, Education, Tobacco: Average spending by race and Hispanic origin, 2003

(average annual spending of consumer units (CU) on personal care, reading, education, and tobacco products, by race and Hispanic origin of consumer unit reference person, 2003)

	total consumer units	race			Hispanic origin	
		Asian	black	white and other	Hispanic	non-Hispanic
Number of consumer units (000)	115,356	3,573	13,743	98,041	11,727	103,629
Average number of persons per CU	2.5	2.8	2.6	2.5	3.3	2.4
Average before-tax income of CU	$51,128.00	$60,393.00	$34,485.00	$53,039.00	$37,150.00	$52,797.00
Average spending of CU, total	40,817.33	44,922.85	28,707.56	42,360.25	34,574.75	41,520.78
PERSONAL CARE PRODUCTS AND SERVICES	526.92	519.84	460.57	536.27	489.94	530.73
Personal care products	270.49	300.58	194.73	279.80	298.83	266.91
Hair care products	55.65	57.93	42.97	57.32	63.61	54.65
Hair accessories	6.75	5.10	7.10	6.76	8.68	6.51
Wigs and hairpieces	1.84	0.09	5.97	1.33	0.39	2.00
Oral hygiene products	28.22	25.19	20.29	29.44	29.53	28.06
Shaving products	14.80	15.79	8.62	15.62	15.54	14.71
Cosmetics, perfume, and bath products	123.43	172.37	80.34	127.48	135.84	121.87
Deodorants, feminine hygiene, misc. products	30.11	23.31	25.98	30.95	33.84	29.64
Electric personal care appliances	9.68	0.80	3.47	10.89	11.39	9.47
Personal care services	256.43	219.26	265.83	256.47	191.11	263.82
READING	127.27	111.02	52.47	138.34	48.11	136.23
Newspaper subscriptions	41.54	22.96	15.70	45.85	10.23	45.09
Newspaper, nonsubscription	9.71	12.14	8.71	9.76	6.31	10.10
Magazine subscriptions	14.45	12.87	4.91	15.85	4.77	15.55
Magazines, nonsubscription	7.73	7.13	4.36	8.23	4.30	8.12
Books purchased through book clubs	5.69	1.80	3.09	6.19	2.06	6.10
Books not purchased through book clubs	47.81	54.12	15.62	52.09	20.35	50.92
EDUCATION	783.33	1,890.11	442.40	790.75	476.53	818.12
College tuition	467.71	1,419.85	254.34	462.91	204.27	497.52
Elementary and high school tuition	124.91	165.41	65.50	131.76	65.74	131.60
Other school tuition	21.36	26.01	23.01	20.96	25.22	20.92
Other school expenses including rentals	44.75	102.49	15.77	46.71	70.16	41.87
Books, supplies for college	54.65	112.97	36.09	55.13	46.22	55.60
Books, supplies for elementary, high school	14.09	11.57	15.33	14.01	16.23	13.85
Books, supplies for day care, nursery school	3.02	2.72	2.43	3.11	1.49	3.19
Miscellaneous school expenses and supplies	52.85	49.09	29.93	56.17	47.20	53.56
TOBACCO PRODUCTS AND SMOKING SUPPLIES	289.70	118.99	179.85	311.32	171.45	303.08
Cigarettes	266.78	112.65	169.69	286.00	163.12	278.51
Other tobacco products	21.42	4.71	8.44	23.84	6.68	23.08
Smoking accessories	1.42	1.63	0.99	1.48	1.65	1.40

Note: Other races include Native Americans and Pacific Islanders. Subcategories may not add to total because some are not shown.
Source: Bureau of Labor Statistics, unpublished tables from the 2003 Consumer Expenditure Survey

Table 10.18 Personal Care, Reading, Education, Tobacco: Indexed spending by race and Hispanic origin, 2003

(indexed average annual spending of consumer units (CU) on personal care, reading, education, and tobacco products, by race and Hispanic origin of consumer unit reference person, 2003; index definition: an index of 100 is the average for all consumer units; an index of 132 means that spending by consumer units in that group is 32 percent above the average for all consumer units; an index of 68 indicates spending that is 32 percent below the average for all consumer units)

	total consumer units	race			Hispanic origin	
		Asian	black	white and other	Hispanic	non-Hispanic
Average spending of CU, total	$40,817	$44,923	$28,708	$42,360	$34,575	$41,521
Average spending of CU, index	100	110	70	104	85	102
PERSONAL CARE PRODUCTS AND SERVICES	**100**	**99**	**87**	**102**	**93**	**101**
Personal care products	**100**	**111**	**72**	**103**	**110**	**99**
Hair care products	100	104	77	103	114	98
Hair accessories	100	76	105	100	129	96
Wigs and hairpieces	100	5	324	72	21	109
Oral hygiene products	100	39	72	104	105	99
Shaving products	100	107	58	106	105	99
Cosmetics, perfume, and bath products	100	140	65	103	110	99
Deodorants, feminine hygiene, misc. products	100	77	85	103	112	98
Electric personal care appliances	100	8	36	113	118	98
Personal care services	**100**	**86**	**104**	**100**	**75**	**103**
READING	**100**	**87**	**41**	**109**	**38**	**107**
Newspaper subscriptions	100	55	38	110	25	109
Newspaper, nonsubscription	100	125	90	101	65	104
Magazine subscriptions	100	89	34	110	33	108
Magazines, nonsubscription	100	92	56	106	56	105
Books purchased through book clubs	100	32	54	109	36	107
Books not purchased through book clubs	100	113	33	109	43	107
EDUCATION	**100**	**241**	**56**	**101**	**61**	**104**
College tuition	100	304	54	99	44	106
Elementary and high school tuition	100	132	52	105	53	105
Other school tuition	100	122	108	98	118	98
Other school expenses including rentals	100	229	35	104	157	94
Books, supplies for college	100	207	66	101	85	102
Books, supplies for elementary, high school	100	82	109	99	115	98
Books, supplies for day care, nursery school	100	90	80	103	49	106
Miscellaneous school expenses and supplies	100	93	57	106	89	101
TOBACCO PRODUCTS AND SMOKING SUPPLIES	**100**	**41**	**62**	**107**	**59**	**105**
Cigarettes	100	42	64	107	61	104
Other tobacco products	100	22	39	111	31	108
Smoking accessories	100	115	70	104	116	99

Note: Other races include Native Americans and Pacific Islanders.
Source: Calculations by New Strategist based on the 2003 Consumer Expenditure Survey

Table 10.19 Personal Care, Reading, Education, Tobacco: Total spending by race and Hispanic origin, 2003

(total annual spending on personal care, reading, education, and tobacco products, by consumer unit race and Hispanic origin groups, 2003; numbers in thousands)

	total consumer units	race			Hispanic origin	
		Asian	black	white and other	Hispanic	non-Hispanic
Number of consumer units	115,356	3,573	13,743	98,041	11,727	103,629
Total spending of all consumer units	$4,708,523,919	$160,509,343	$394,527,997	$4,153,041,270	$405,458,093	$4,302,756,911
PERSONAL CARE PRODUCTS AND SERVICES	**60,783,384**	**1,857,388**	**6,329,614**	**52,576,447**	**5,745,526**	**54,999,019**
Personal care products	**31,202,644**	**1,073,972**	**2,676,174**	**27,431,872**	**3,504,379**	**27,659,616**
Hair care products	6,419,561	206,984	590,537	5,619,710	745,954	5,663,325
Hair accessories	778,653	18,222	97,575	662,757	101,790	674,625
Wigs and hairpieces	212,255	322	82,046	130,395	4,574	207,258
Oral hygiene products	3,255,346	90,004	278,845	2,886,327	346,298	2,907,830
Shaving products	1,707,269	56,418	118,465	1,531,400	182,238	1,524,383
Cosmetics, perfume, and bath products	14,238,391	615,878	1,104,113	12,498,267	1,592,996	12,629,266
Deodorants, feminine hygiene, misc. products	3,473,369	83,287	357,043	3,034,369	396,842	3,071,564
Electric personal care appliances	1,116,646	2,858	47,688	1,067,666	133,571	981,367
Personal care services	**29,580,739**	**783,416**	**3,653,302**	**25,144,575**	**2,241,147**	**27,339,403**
READING	**14,681,358**	**396,674**	**721,095**	**13,562,992**	**564,186**	**14,117,379**
Newspaper subscriptions	4,791,888	82,036	215,765	4,495,180	119,967	4,672,632
Newspaper, nonsubscription	1,120,107	43,376	119,702	956,880	73,997	1,046,653
Magazine subscriptions	1,666,894	45,985	67,478	1,553,950	55,938	1,611,431
Magazines, nonsubscription	891,702	25,475	59,919	806,877	50,426	841,467
Books purchased through book clubs	656,376	6,431	42,466	606,874	24,158	632,137
Books not purchased through book clubs	5,515,170	193,371	214,666	5,106,956	238,644	5,276,789
EDUCATION	**90,361,815**	**6,753,363**	**6,079,903**	**77,525,921**	**5,588,267**	**84,780,957**
College tuition	53,953,155	5,073,124	3,495,395	45,384,159	2,395,474	51,557,500
Elementary and high school tuition	14,409,118	591,010	900,167	12,917,882	770,933	13,637,576
Other school tuition	2,464,004	92,934	316,226	2,054,939	295,755	2,167,919
Other school expenses including rentals	5,162,181	366,197	216,727	4,579,495	822,766	4,338,946
Books, supplies for college	6,304,205	403,642	495,985	5,405,000	542,022	5,761,772
Books, supplies for elementary, high school	1,625,366	41,340	210,680	1,373,554	190,329	1,435,262
Books, supplies for day care, nursery school	348,375	9,719	33,395	304,908	17,473	330,577
Miscellaneous school expenses and supplies	6,096,565	175,399	411,328	5,506,963	553,514	5,550,369
TOBACCO PRODUCTS AND SMOKING SUPPLIES	**33,418,633**	**425,151**	**2,471,679**	**30,522,124**	**2,010,594**	**31,407,877**
Cigarettes	30,774,674	402,498	2,332,050	28,039,726	1,912,908	28,861,713
Other tobacco products	2,470,926	16,829	115,991	2,337,297	78,336	2,391,757
Smoking accessories	163,806	5,824	13,606	145,101	19,350	145,081

Note: Other races include Native Americans and Pacific Islanders. Numbers may not add to total because of rounding and missing subcategories.
Source: Calculations by New Strategist based on the 2003 Consumer Expenditure Survey

Table 10.20 Personal Care, Reading, Education, Tobacco: Market shares by race and Hispanic origin, 2003

(percentage of total annual spending on personal care, reading, education, and tobacco products accounted for by consumer unit race and Hispanic origin groups, 2003)

	total consumer units	race			Hispanic origin	
		Asian	black	white and other	Hispanic	non-Hispanic
Share of total consumer units	100.0%	3.1%	11.9%	85.0%	10.2%	89.8%
Share of total before-tax income	100.0	3.7	8.0	88.2	7.4	92.8
Share of total spending	100.0	3.4	8.4	88.2	8.6	91.4
PERSONAL CARE PRODUCTS AND SERVICES	100.0	3.2	10.4	86.5	9.5	90.5
Personal care products	100.0	3.4	8.6	87.9	11.2	88.6
Hair care products	100.0	3.2	9.2	87.5	11.6	88.2
Hair accessories	100.0	2.3	12.5	85.1	13.1	86.6
Wigs and hairpieces	100.0	0.2	38.7	61.4	2.2	97.6
Oral hygiene products	100.0	2.8	8.6	88.7	10.6	89.3
Shaving products	100.0	3.3	6.9	89.7	10.7	89.3
Cosmetics, perfume, and bath products	100.0	4.3	7.8	87.8	11.2	88.7
Deodorants, feminine hygiene, misc. products	100.0	2.4	10.3	87.4	11.4	88.4
Electric personal care appliances	100.0	0.3	4.3	95.6	12.0	87.9
Personal care services	100.0	2.6	12.4	85.0	7.6	92.4
READING	100.0	2.7	4.9	92.4	3.8	96.2
Newspaper subscriptions	100.0	1.7	4.5	93.8	2.5	97.5
Newspaper, nonsubscription	100.0	3.9	10.7	85.4	6.6	93.4
Magazine subscriptions	100.0	2.8	4.0	93.2	3.4	96.7
Magazines, nonsubscription	100.0	2.9	6.7	90.5	5.7	94.4
Books purchased through book clubs	100.0	1.0	6.5	92.5	3.7	96.3
Books not purchased through book clubs	100.0	3.5	3.9	92.6	4.3	95.7
EDUCATION	100.0	7.5	6.7	85.8	6.2	93.8
College tuition	100.0	9.4	6.5	84.1	4.4	95.6
Elementary and high school tuition	100.0	4.1	6.2	89.7	5.4	94.6
Other school tuition	100.0	3.8	12.8	83.4	12.0	88.0
Other school expenses including rentals	100.0	7.1	4.2	88.7	15.9	84.1
Books, supplies for college	100.0	6.4	7.9	85.7	8.6	91.4
Books, supplies for elementary, high school	100.0	2.5	13.0	84.5	11.7	88.3
Books, supplies for day care, nursery school	100.0	2.8	9.6	87.5	5.0	94.9
Miscellaneous school expenses and supplies	100.0	2.9	6.7	90.3	9.1	91.0
TOBACCO PRODUCTS AND SMOKING SUPPLIES	100.0	1.3	7.4	91.3	6.0	94.0
Cigarettes	100.0	1.3	7.6	91.1	6.2	93.8
Other tobacco products	100.0	0.7	4.7	94.6	3.2	96.8
Smoking accessories	100.0	3.6	8.3	88.6	11.8	88.6

Note: Other races include Native Americans and Pacific Islanders. Numbers may not add to total because of rounding.
Source: Calculations by New Strategist based on the 2003 Consumer Expenditure Survey

Table 10.21 Personal Care, Reading, Education, Tobacco: Average spending by region, 2003

(average annual spending of consumer units (CU) on personal care, reading, education, and tobacco products, by region in which consumer unit lives, 2003)

	total consumer units	Northeast	Midwest	South	West
Number of consumer units (000)	115,356	22,182	26,438	41,325	25,412
Average number of persons per CU	2.5	2.4	2.5	2.5	2.6
Average before-tax income of CU	$48,596.00	$54,219.00	$49,591.00	$44,461.00	$49,667.00
Average spending of CU, total	40,817.33	42,162.29	40,280.39	37,624.55	45,380.67
PERSONAL CARE PRODUCTS AND SERVICES	526.92	531.67	498.97	494.03	605.51
Personal care products	270.49	248.71	251.06	253.29	337.84
Hair care products	55.65	48.50	49.43	59.73	62.08
Hair accessories	6.75	6.13	6.07	7.96	6.08
Wigs and hairpieces	1.84	1.66	1.06	1.25	3.77
Oral hygiene products	28.22	25.29	26.83	25.71	36.31
Shaving products	14.80	13.20	15.53	12.76	18.69
Cosmetics, perfume, and bath products	123.43	113.88	111.15	108.74	168.41
Deodorants, feminine hygiene, misc. products	30.11	28.96	32.73	26.96	33.33
Electric personal care appliances	9.68	11.10	8.25	10.19	9.16
Personal care services	256.43	282.96	247.92	240.73	267.67
READING	127.27	153.02	141.14	93.29	145.61
Newspaper subscriptions	41.54	51.80	51.39	30.77	39.86
Newspaper, nonsubscription	9.71	17.21	10.95	6.89	6.46
Magazine subscriptions	14.45	16.95	15.71	10.51	17.39
Magazines, nonsubscription	7.73	7.69	8.50	6.73	8.59
Books purchased through book clubs	5.69	6.09	5.73	4.58	7.09
Books not purchased through book clubs	47.81	51.82	48.82	33.75	66.13
EDUCATION	783.33	1,039.57	796.05	580.94	875.02
College tuition	467.71	690.28	480.63	294.79	541.18
Elementary and high school tuition	124.91	175.67	138.05	102.94	102.64
Other school tuition	21.36	27.67	17.11	21.79	19.56
Other school expenses including rentals	44.75	35.91	30.92	54.51	50.97
Books, supplies for college	54.65	52.69	50.35	42.21	81.06
Books, supplies for elementary, high school	14.09	8.99	13.41	17.78	13.25
Books, supplies for day care, nursery school	3.02	1.37	3.80	2.59	4.34
Miscellaneous school expenses and supplies	52.85	47.01	61.77	44.31	62.02
TOBACCO PRODUCTS AND SMOKING SUPPLIES	289.70	305.78	363.42	274.57	223.54
Cigarettes	266.78	286.20	339.09	248.37	204.52
Other tobacco products	21.42	18.88	21.92	24.79	17.61
Smoking accessories	1.42	0.70	2.05	1.41	1.42

Note: Subcategories may not add to total because some are not shown.
Source: Bureau of Labor Statistics, unpublished tables from the 2003 Consumer Expenditure Survey

Table 10.22 Personal Care, Reading, Education, Tobacco: Indexed spending by region, 2003

(indexed average annual spending of consumer units (CU) on personal care, reading, education, and tobacco products, by region in which consumer unit lives, 2003; index definition: an index of 100 is the average for all consumer units; an index of 132 means that spending by consumer units in that group is 32 percent above the average for all consumer units; an index of 68 indicates spending that is 32 percent below the average for all consumer units)

	total consumer units	Northeast	Midwest	South	West
Average spending of CU, total	$40,817	$42,162	$40,280	$37,625	$45,381
Average spending of CU, index	100	103	99	92	111
PERSONAL CARE PRODUCTS AND SERVICES	**100**	**101**	**95**	**94**	**115**
Personal care products	**100**	**92**	**93**	**94**	**125**
Hair care products	100	87	89	107	112
Hair accessories	100	91	90	118	90
Wigs and hairpieces	100	90	58	68	205
Oral hygiene products	100	90	95	91	129
Shaving products	100	89	105	86	126
Cosmetics, perfume, and bath products	100	92	90	88	136
Deodorants, feminine hygiene, misc. products	100	96	109	90	111
Electric personal care appliances	100	115	85	105	95
Personal care services	**100**	**110**	**97**	**94**	**104**
READING	**100**	**120**	**111**	**73**	**114**
Newspaper subscriptions	100	125	124	74	96
Newspaper, nonsubscription	100	177	113	71	67
Magazine subscriptions	100	117	109	73	120
Magazines, nonsubscription	100	99	110	87	111
Books purchased through book clubs	100	107	101	80	125
Books not purchased through book clubs	100	108	102	71	138
EDUCATION	**100**	**133**	**102**	**74**	**112**
College tuition	100	148	103	63	116
Elementary and high school tuition	100	141	111	82	82
Other school tuition	100	130	80	102	92
Other school expenses including rentals	100	80	69	122	114
Books, supplies for college	100	96	92	77	148
Books, supplies for elementary, high school	100	64	95	126	94
Books, supplies for day care, nursery school	100	45	126	86	144
Miscellaneous school expenses and supplies	100	89	117	84	117
TOBACCO PRODUCTS AND SMOKING SUPPLIES	**100**	**106**	**125**	**95**	**77**
Cigarettes	100	107	127	93	77
Other tobacco products	100	88	102	116	82
Smoking accessories	100	49	144	99	100

Source: Calculations by New Strategist based on the 2003 Consumer Expenditure Survey

Table 10.23 Personal Care, Reading, Education, Tobacco: Total spending by region, 2003

(total annual spending on personal care, reading, education, and tobacco products, by region in which consumer units live, 2003; numbers in thousands)

	total consumer units	Northeast	Midwest	South	West
Number of consumer units	115,356	22,182	26,438	41,325	25,412
Total spending of all consumer units	$4,708,523,919	$935,243,917	$1,064,932,951	$1,554,834,529	$1,153,213,586
PERSONAL CARE PRODUCTS AND SERVICES	**60,783,384**	**11,793,504**	**13,191,769**	**20,415,790**	**15,387,220**
Personal care products	**31,202,644**	**5,516,885**	**6,637,524**	**10,467,209**	**8,585,190**
Hair care products	6,419,561	1,075,827	1,306,830	2,468,342	1,577,577
Hair accessories	778,653	135,976	160,479	328,947	154,505
Wigs and hairpieces	212,255	36,822	28,024	51,656	95,803
Oral hygiene products	3,255,346	560,983	709,332	1,062,466	922,710
Shaving products	1,707,269	292,802	410,582	527,307	474,950
Cosmetics, perfume, and bath products	14,238,391	2,526,086	2,938,584	4,493,681	4,279,635
Deodorants, feminine hygiene, misc. products	3,473,369	642,391	865,316	1,114,122	846,982
Electric personal care appliances	1,116,646	246,220	218,114	421,102	232,774
Personal care services	**29,580,739**	**6,276,619**	**6,554,509**	**9,948,167**	**6,802,030**
READING	**14,681,358**	**3,394,290**	**3,731,459**	**3,855,209**	**3,700,241**
Newspaper subscriptions	4,791,888	1,149,028	1,358,649	1,271,570	1,012,922
Newspaper, nonsubscription	1,120,107	381,752	289,496	284,729	164,162
Magazine subscriptions	1,666,894	375,985	415,341	434,326	441,915
Magazines, nonsubscription	891,702	170,580	224,723	278,117	218,289
Books purchased through book clubs	656,376	135,088	151,490	189,269	180,171
Books not purchased through book clubs	5,515,170	1,149,471	1,290,703	1,394,719	1,680,496
EDUCATION	**90,361,815**	**23,059,742**	**21,045,970**	**24,007,346**	**22,236,008**
College tuition	53,953,155	15,311,791	12,706,896	12,182,197	13,752,466
Elementary and high school tuition	14,409,118	3,896,712	3,649,766	4,253,996	2,608,288
Other school tuition	2,464,004	613,776	452,354	900,472	497,059
Other school expenses including rentals	5,162,181	796,556	817,463	2,252,626	1,295,250
Books, supplies for college	6,304,205	1,168,770	1,331,153	1,744,328	2,059,897
Books, supplies for elementary, high school	1,625,366	199,416	354,534	734,759	336,709
Books, supplies for day care, nursery school	348,375	30,389	100,464	107,032	110,288
Miscellaneous school expenses and supplies	6,096,565	1,042,776	1,633,075	1,831,111	1,576,052
TOBACCO PRODUCTS AND SMOKING SUPPLIES	**33,418,633**	**6,782,812**	**9,608,098**	**11,346,605**	**5,680,598**
Cigarettes	30,774,674	6,348,488	8,964,861	10,263,890	5,197,262
Other tobacco products	2,470,926	418,796	579,521	1,024,447	447,505
Smoking accessories	163,806	15,527	54,198	58,268	36,085

Note: Numbers may not add to total because of rounding and missing subcategories.
Source: Calculations by New Strategist based on the 2003 Consumer Expenditure Survey

Table 10.24 Personal Care, Reading, Education, Tobacco: Market shares by region, 2003

(percentage of total annual spending on personal care, reading, education, and tobacco products accounted for by consumer units by region, 2003)

	total consumer units	Northeast	Midwest	South	West
Share of total consumer units	100.0%	19.2%	22.9%	35.8%	22.0%
Share of total before-tax income	100.0	21.5	23.4	32.8	22.5
Share of total spending	100.0	19.9	22.6	33.0	24.5
PERSONAL CARE PRODUCTS AND SERVICES	100.0	19.4	21.7	33.6	25.3
Personal care products	100.0	17.7	21.3	33.5	27.5
Hair care products	100.0	16.8	20.4	38.5	24.6
Hair accessories	100.0	17.5	20.6	42.2	19.8
Wigs and hairpieces	100.0	17.3	13.2	24.3	45.1
Oral hygiene products	100.0	17.2	21.8	32.6	28.3
Shaving products	100.0	17.2	24.0	30.9	27.8
Cosmetics, perfume, and bath products	100.0	17.7	20.6	31.6	30.1
Deodorants, feminine hygiene, misc. products	100.0	18.5	24.9	32.1	24.4
Electric personal care appliances	100.0	22.0	19.5	37.7	20.8
Personal care services	100.0	21.2	22.2	33.6	23.0
READING	100.0	23.1	25.4	26.3	25.2
Newspaper subscriptions	100.0	24.0	28.4	26.5	21.1
Newspaper, nonsubscription	100.0	34.1	25.8	25.4	14.7
Magazine subscriptions	100.0	22.6	24.9	26.1	26.5
Magazines, nonsubscription	100.0	19.1	25.2	31.2	24.5
Books purchased through book clubs	100.0	20.6	23.1	28.8	27.4
Books not purchased through book clubs	100.0	20.8	23.4	25.3	30.5
EDUCATION	100.0	25.5	23.3	26.6	24.6
College tuition	100.0	28.4	23.6	22.6	25.5
Elementary and high school tuition	100.0	27.0	25.3	29.5	18.1
Other school tuition	100.0	24.9	18.4	36.5	20.2
Other school expenses including rentals	100.0	15.4	15.8	43.6	25.1
Books, supplies for college	100.0	18.5	21.1	27.7	32.7
Books, supplies for elementary, high school	100.0	12.3	21.8	45.2	20.7
Books, supplies for day care, nursery school	100.0	8.7	28.8	30.7	31.7
Miscellaneous school expenses and supplies	100.0	17.1	26.8	30.0	25.9
TOBACCO PRODUCTS AND SMOKING SUPPLIES	100.0	20.3	28.8	34.0	17.0
Cigarettes	100.0	20.6	29.1	33.4	16.9
Other tobacco products	100.0	16.9	23.5	41.5	18.1
Smoking accessories	100.0	9.5	33.1	35.6	22.0

Note: Numbers may not add to total because of rounding.
Source: Calculations by New Strategist based on the 2003 Consumer Expenditure Survey

Table 10.25 Personal Care, Reading, Education, Tobacco: Average spending by education, 2003

(average annual spending of consumer units (CU) on personal care, reading, education, and tobacco products, by education of consumer unit reference person, 2003)

	total consumer units	less than high school graduate	high school graduate	some college	associate's degree	college graduate		
						total	bachelor's degree	master's, professional, doctorate
Number of consumer units (000)	115,356	17,721	31,552	24,514	10,981	30,589	19,557	11,032
Average number of persons per CU	2.5	2.6	2.5	2.3	2.6	2.5	2.5	2.4
Average before-tax income of CU	$51,128.00	$25,028.00	$40,113.00	$45,113.00	$54,087.00	$81,842.00	$74,921.00	$93,948.00
Average spending of CU, total	40,817.33	23,901.14	33,955.56	37,912.41	44,547.12	58,480.00	54,725.85	65,202.73
PERSONAL CARE PRODUCTS AND SERVICES	**526.92**	**305.45**	**436.33**	**517.54**	**591.95**	**724.83**	**694.06**	**781.38**
Personal care products	**270.49**	**157.32**	**226.50**	**271.52**	**326.42**	**352.47**	**337.96**	**380.18**
Hair care products	55.65	32.00	49.19	58.67	76.56	65.17	63.62	68.13
Hair accessories	6.75	3.77	6.15	6.51	10.18	7.93	8.75	6.36
Wigs and hairpieces	1.84	2.06	0.99	1.65	6.73	0.98	0.75	1.41
Oral hygiene products	28.22	18.24	24.37	27.32	31.38	36.72	37.77	34.72
Shaving products	14.80	10.68	13.23	16.44	19.14	15.89	17.18	13.43
Cosmetics, perfume, and bath products	123.43	62.65	100.15	120.57	134.44	175.50	163.14	199.12
Deodorants, feminine hygiene, misc. products	30.11	21.21	26.49	29.45	32.82	37.80	36.57	40.16
Electric personal care appliances	9.68	6.70	5.93	10.81	15.16	12.48	10.19	16.86
Personal care services	**256.43**	**148.13**	**209.83**	**246.03**	**265.53**	**372.36**	**356.10**	**401.20**
READING	**127.27**	**41.66**	**83.34**	**117.99**	**125.34**	**230.32**	**194.13**	**294.46**
Newspaper subscriptions	41.54	21.43	35.70	37.42	39.76	63.18	54.62	78.35
Newspaper, nonsubscription	9.71	6.13	9.85	10.41	9.65	11.10	10.56	12.06
Magazine subscriptions	14.45	3.07	8.82	14.16	15.14	26.85	22.20	35.09
Magazines, nonsubscription	7.73	2.71	5.55	7.97	9.66	12.01	12.11	11.83
Books purchased through book clubs	5.69	1.67	4.94	3.91	7.74	9.49	7.28	13.40
Books not purchased through book clubs	47.81	6.62	18.42	43.71	42.86	107.06	86.66	143.22
EDUCATION	**783.33**	**102.24**	**327.88**	**859.36**	**775.50**	**1,586.96**	**1,338.96**	**2,028.85**
College tuition	467.71	37.68	172.17	527.93	495.99	963.26	825.16	1,208.09
Elementary and high school tuition	124.91	9.68	54.96	93.45	90.26	301.45	228.83	430.20
Other school tuition	21.36	2.90	8.99	31.06	13.33	39.92	34.86	48.88
Other school expenses including rentals	44.75	4.54	15.19	39.23	41.32	104.19	86.43	135.66
Books, supplies for college	54.65	9.40	23.14	101.33	61.63	73.45	75.83	69.22
Books, supplies for elementary, high school	14.09	10.94	11.65	12.86	13.37	19.68	17.61	23.35
Books, supplies for day care, nursery school	3.02	1.94	1.69	2.08	3.91	5.44	6.58	3.42
Miscellaneous school expenses and supplies	52.85	25.15	40.09	51.44	55.70	79.57	63.65	110.03
TOBACCO PRODUCTS AND SMOKING SUPPLIES	**289.70**	**341.70**	**380.34**	**305.04**	**318.10**	**143.68**	**157.51**	**119.14**
Cigarettes	266.78	318.17	355.06	282.65	288.63	125.38	137.85	103.27
Other tobacco products	21.42	21.96	23.82	20.50	27.14	17.30	18.44	15.27
Smoking accessories	1.42	1.57	1.46	1.47	2.33	1.01	1.22	0.60

Note: Subcategories may not add to total because some are not shown.
Source: Bureau of Labor Statistics, unpublished tables from the 2003 Consumer Expenditure Survey

Table 10.26 Personal Care, Reading, Education, Tobacco: Indexed spending by education, 2003

(indexed average annual spending of consumer units (CU) on personal care, reading, education, and tobacco products, by education of consumer unit reference person, 2003; index definition: an index of 100 is the average for all consumer units; an index of 132 means that spending by consumer units in that group is 32 percent above the average for all consumer units; an index of 68 indicates spending that is 32 percent below the average for all consumer units)

	total consumer units	less than high school graduate	high school graduate	some college	associate's degree	college graduate total	bachelor's degree	master's, professional, doctorate
Average spending of CU, total	$40,817	$23,901	$33,956	$37,912	$44,547	$58,480	$54,726	$65,203
Average spending of CU, index	100	59	83	93	109	143	134	160
PERSONAL CARE PRODUCTS AND SERVICES	**100**	**58**	**83**	**98**	**112**	**138**	**132**	**148**
Personal care products	**100**	**58**	**84**	**100**	**121**	**130**	**125**	**141**
Hair care products	100	58	88	105	138	117	114	122
Hair accessories	100	56	91	96	151	117	130	94
Wigs and hairpieces	100	112	54	90	366	53	41	77
Oral hygiene products	100	65	86	97	111	130	134	123
Shaving products	100	72	89	111	129	107	116	91
Cosmetics, perfume, and bath products	100	51	81	98	109	142	132	161
Deodorants, feminine hygiene, misc. products	100	70	83	98	109	126	121	133
Electric personal care appliances	100	69	61	112	157	129	105	174
Personal care services	**100**	**58**	**82**	**96**	**104**	**145**	**139**	**156**
READING	**100**	**33**	**65**	**93**	**98**	**181**	**153**	**231**
Newspaper subscriptions	100	52	86	90	96	152	131	189
Newspaper, nonsubscription	100	63	101	107	99	114	109	124
Magazine subscriptions	100	21	61	98	105	186	154	243
Magazines, nonsubscription	100	35	72	103	125	155	157	153
Books purchased through book clubs	100	29	87	59	136	167	128	236
Books not purchased through book clubs	100	14	39	91	90	224	181	300
EDUCATION	**100**	**13**	**42**	**110**	**99**	**203**	**171**	**259**
College tuition	100	8	37	113	106	206	176	258
Elementary and high school tuition	100	8	44	75	72	241	183	344
Other school tuition	100	14	42	145	62	187	163	229
Other school expenses including rentals	100	10	34	88	92	233	193	303
Books, supplies for college	100	17	42	185	113	134	139	127
Books, supplies for elementary, high school	100	78	83	91	95	140	125	166
Books, supplies for day care, nursery school	100	64	56	69	129	180	218	113
Miscellaneous school expenses and supplies	100	48	76	97	105	151	120	208
TOBACCO PRODUCTS AND SMOKING SUPPLIES	**100**	**118**	**131**	**105**	**110**	**50**	**54**	**41**
Cigarettes	100	119	133	106	108	47	52	39
Other tobacco products	100	103	111	96	127	81	86	71
Smoking accessories	100	111	103	104	164	71	86	42

Source: Calculations by New Strategist based on the 2003 Consumer Expenditure Survey

Table 10.27 Personal Care, Reading, Education, Tobacco: Total spending by education, 2003

(total annual spending on personal care, reading, education, and tobacco products, by consumer unit (CU) educational attainment group, 2003; numbers in thousands)

	total consumer units	less than high school graduate	high school graduate	some college	associate's degree	college graduate total	bachelor's degree	master's, professional, doctorate
Number of consumer units	115,356	17,721	31,552	24,514	10,981	30,589	19,557	11,032
Total spending of all CUs	$4,708,523,919	$423,552,102	$1,071,365,829	$929,384,819	$489,171,925	$1,788,844,720	$1,070,273,448	$719,316,517
PERSONAL CARE PRODUCTS AND SERVICES	**60,783,384**	**5,412,879**	**13,767,084**	**12,686,976**	**6,500,203**	**22,171,825**	**13,573,731**	**8,620,184**
Personal care products	**31,202,644**	**2,787,868**	**7,146,528**	**6,656,041**	**3,584,418**	**10,781,705**	**6,609,484**	**4,194,146**
Hair care products	6,419,561	567,072	1,552,043	1,438,236	840,705	1,993,485	1,244,216	751,610
Hair accessories	778,653	66,808	194,045	159,586	111,787	242,571	171,124	70,164
Wigs and hairpieces	212,255	36,505	31,236	40,448	73,902	29,977	14,668	15,555
Oral hygiene products	3,255,346	323,231	768,922	669,722	344,584	1,123,228	738,668	383,031
Shaving products	1,707,269	189,260	417,433	403,010	210,176	486,059	335,989	148,160
Cosmetics, perfume, and bath products	14,238,391	1,110,221	3,159,933	2,958,104	1,476,286	5,368,370	3,190,529	2,196,692
Deodorants, feminine hygiene, misc. products	3,473,369	375,862	835,812	721,937	360,396	1,156,264	715,199	443,045
Electric personal care appliances	1,116,646	118,731	187,103	264,996	166,472	381,751	199,286	186,000
Personal care services	**29,580,739**	**2,625,012**	**6,620,556**	**6,031,179**	**2,915,785**	**11,390,120**	**6,964,248**	**4,426,038**
READING	**14,681,358**	**738,257**	**2,629,544**	**2,892,407**	**1,376,359**	**7,045,258**	**3,796,600**	**3,248,483**
Newspaper subscriptions	4,791,888	379,761	1,126,406	917,314	436,605	1,932,613	1,068,203	864,357
Newspaper, nonsubscription	1,120,107	108,630	310,787	255,191	105,967	339,538	206,522	133,046
Magazine subscriptions	1,666,894	54,403	278,289	347,118	166,252	821,315	434,165	387,113
Magazines, nonsubscription	891,702	48,024	175,114	195,377	106,076	367,374	236,835	130,509
Books purchased through book clubs	656,376	29,594	155,867	95,850	84,993	290,290	142,375	147,829
Books not purchased through book clubs	5,515,170	117,313	581,188	1,071,507	470,646	3,274,858	1,694,810	1,580,003
EDUCATION	**90,361,815**	**1,811,795**	**10,345,270**	**21,066,351**	**8,515,766**	**48,543,519**	**26,186,041**	**22,382,273**
College tuition	53,953,155	667,727	5,432,308	12,941,676	5,446,466	29,465,160	16,137,654	13,327,649
Elementary and high school tuition	14,409,118	171,539	1,734,098	2,290,833	991,145	9,221,054	4,475,228	4,745,966
Other school tuition	2,464,004	51,391	283,652	761,405	146,377	1,221,113	681,757	539,244
Other school expenses including rentals	5,162,181	80,453	479,275	961,684	453,735	3,187,068	1,690,312	1,496,601
Books, supplies for college	6,304,205	166,577	730,113	2,484,004	676,759	2,246,762	1,483,007	763,635
Books, supplies for elementary, high school	1,625,366	193,868	367,581	315,250	146,816	601,992	344,399	257,597
Books, supplies for day care, nursery school	348,375	34,379	53,323	50,989	42,936	166,404	128,685	37,729
Miscellaneous school expenses and supplies	6,096,565	445,683	1,264,920	1,261,000	611,642	2,433,967	1,244,803	1,213,851
TOBACCO PRODUCTS AND SMOKING SUPPLIES	**33,418,633**	**6,055,266**	**12,000,488**	**7,477,751**	**3,493,056**	**4,395,028**	**3,080,423**	**1,314,352**
Cigarettes	30,774,674	5,638,291	11,202,853	6,928,882	3,169,446	3,835,249	2,695,932	1,139,275
Other tobacco products	2,470,926	389,153	751,569	502,537	298,024	529,190	360,631	168,459
Smoking accessories	163,806	27,822	46,066	36,036	25,586	30,895	23,860	6,619

Note: Numbers may not add to total because of rounding and missing subcategories.
Source: Calculations by New Strategist based on the 2003 Consumer Expenditure Survey

Table 10.28 Personal Care, Reading, Education, Tobacco: Market shares by education, 2003

(percentage of total annual spending on personal care, reading, education, and tobacco products accounted for by consumer unit educational attainment groups, 2003)

	total consumer units	less than high school graduate	high school graduate	some college	associate's degree	college graduate total	bachelor's degree	master's, professional, doctorate
Share of total consumer units	100.0%	15.4%	27.4%	21.3%	9.5%	26.5%	17.0%	9.6%
Share of total before-tax income	100.0	7.5	21.5	18.8	10.1	42.4	24.8	17.6
Share of total spending	100.0	9.0	22.8	19.7	10.4	38.0	22.7	15.3
PERSONAL CARE PRODUCTS AND SERVICES	**100.0**	**8.9**	**22.6**	**20.9**	**10.7**	**36.5**	**22.3**	**14.2**
Personal care products	**100.0**	**8.9**	**22.9**	**21.3**	**11.5**	**34.6**	**21.2**	**13.4**
Hair care products	100.0	8.8	24.2	22.4	13.1	31.1	19.4	11.7
Hair accessories	100.0	8.6	24.9	20.5	14.4	31.2	22.0	9.0
Wigs and hairpieces	100.0	17.2	14.7	19.1	34.8	14.1	6.9	7.3
Oral hygiene products	100.0	9.9	23.6	20.6	10.6	34.5	22.7	11.8
Shaving products	100.0	11.1	24.5	23.6	12.3	28.5	19.7	8.7
Cosmetics, perfume, and bath products	100.0	7.8	22.2	20.8	10.4	37.7	22.4	15.4
Deodorants, feminine hygiene, misc. products	100.0	10.8	24.1	20.8	10.4	33.3	20.6	12.8
Electric personal care appliances	100.0	10.6	16.8	23.7	14.9	34.2	17.8	16.7
Personal care services	**100.0**	**8.9**	**22.4**	**20.4**	**9.9**	**38.5**	**23.5**	**15.0**
READING	**100.0**	**5.0**	**17.9**	**19.7**	**9.4**	**48.0**	**25.9**	**22.1**
Newspaper subscriptions	100.0	7.9	23.5	19.1	9.1	40.3	22.3	18.0
Newspaper, nonsubscription	100.0	9.7	27.7	22.8	9.5	30.3	18.4	11.9
Magazine subscriptions	100.0	3.3	16.7	20.8	10.0	49.3	26.0	23.2
Magazines, nonsubscription	100.0	5.4	19.6	21.9	11.9	41.2	26.6	14.6
Books purchased through book clubs	100.0	4.5	23.7	14.6	12.9	44.2	21.7	22.5
Books not purchased through book clubs	100.0	2.1	10.5	19.4	8.5	59.4	30.7	28.6
EDUCATION	**100.0**	**2.0**	**11.4**	**23.3**	**9.4**	**53.7**	**29.0**	**24.8**
College tuition	100.0	1.2	10.1	24.0	10.1	54.6	29.9	24.7
Elementary and high school tuition	100.0	1.2	12.0	15.9	6.9	64.0	31.1	32.9
Other school tuition	100.0	2.1	11.5	30.9	5.9	49.6	27.7	21.9
Other school expenses including rentals	100.0	1.6	9.3	18.6	8.8	61.7	32.7	29.0
Books, supplies for college	100.0	2.6	11.6	39.4	10.7	35.6	23.5	12.1
Books, supplies for elementary, high school	100.0	11.9	22.6	19.4	9.0	37.0	21.2	15.8
Books, supplies for day care, nursery school	100.0	9.9	15.3	14.6	12.3	47.8	36.9	10.8
Miscellaneous school expenses and supplies	100.0	7.3	20.7	20.7	10.0	39.9	20.4	19.9
TOBACCO PRODUCTS AND SMOKING SUPPLIES	**100.0**	**18.1**	**35.9**	**22.4**	**10.5**	**13.2**	**9.2**	**3.9**
Cigarettes	100.0	18.3	36.4	22.5	10.3	12.5	8.8	3.7
Other tobacco products	100.0	15.7	30.4	20.3	12.1	21.4	14.6	6.8
Smoking accessories	100.0	17.0	23.1	22.0	15.6	18.9	14.6	4.0

Note: Numbers may not add to total because of rounding.
Source: Calculations by New Strategist based on the 2003 Consumer Expenditure Survey

Spending on Transportation, 2003

Transportation is the second-largest household expenditure category. The $7,781 devoted to transportation in 2003 consumed 19.1 percent of the average household budget. Spending trends have been mixed in the transportation category during the past three years. Households devoted much more to new cars and trucks, spending on this item climbing by a substantial 20 percent between 2000 and 2003. Partly as a result, spending on used cars and trucks fell 15 percent and spending on leased vehicles fell 36 percent. Spending on vehicle maintenance and repairs declined 7 percent as warranties on new cars and trucks reduced repair bills. Gasoline and motor oil spending by the average household fell 3 percent between 2000 and 2003—a trend that has now most certainly reversed. Spending on public transportation fell 16 percent between 2000 and 2003.

Householders aged 45 to 54 spend the most on transportation—$9,766 in 2003, or 26 percent more than the average household. These are also the most affluent households, which accounts for their above-average spending. Householders aged 55 to 64 spend the most on new cars, however. Spending on public transportation also peaks in the 55-to-64 age group. Householders aged 55 to 64 spend 42 percent more than the average household on airline fares and 69 percent more on intercity train fares. Householders aged 65 to 74 spend 83 percent more than average on ship fares.

Households with incomes of $100,000 or more spend 93 percent more than the average household on transportation. They spend more than twice the average on new cars and trucks, more than three times the average on airline fares, and nearly four times the average on ship fares. Households with incomes below $70,000 control 70 percent of spending on used cars and trucks.

Married couples with children aged 18 or older at home spend the most on transportation because they are more likely to have two or more vehicles. In 2003 this household type spent twice the average on used cars. Married couples without children at home (most of them empty-nesters) spend 54 percent more than the average household on airline fares and 67 percent more than average on ship fares.

Asians, blacks, and Hispanics spend less than the average household on transportation, but on some categories their spending is well above average. Asians spend more than twice the average on airline fares. They also spend more than twice the average on intracity mass transit fares. Blacks spend 80 percent more than average on this item, while Hispanics spend 66 percent more.

Households in the West spend the most on transportation, $8,645 in 2003. Households in the South spend the most on new trucks, however—12 percent more than the average household. Households in the Northeast spend 40 percent more than the average household on public transportation.

Because they dominate affluent households, college graduates spend 29 percent more than average on transportation. They spend 50 percent more than average on new cars and more than twice the average on public transportation. Households headed by college graduates control 58 percent of the market for airline fares and 53 percent of the market for ship fares.

Table 11.1 Transportation: Average spending by age, 2003

(average annual spending of consumer units (CU) on transportation, by age of consumer unit reference person, 2003)

	total consumer units	under 25	25 to 34	35 to 44	45 to 54	55 to 64	65 to 74	75+
Number of consumer units (000)	115,356	8,584	19,737	24,413	23,131	16,580	11,495	11,417
Average number of persons per CU	2.5	1.8	2.9	3.2	2.6	2.1	1.9	1.5
Average before-tax income of CU	$51,128.00	$20,680.00	$50,389.00	$61,091.00	$68,028.00	$58,672.00	$35,314.00	$25,492.00
Average spending of CU, total	40,817.33	22,395.53	40,525.22	47,175.06	50,100.86	44,190.65	33,629.17	25,016.38
Transportation, average spending	**7,780.55**	**4,674.19**	**8,106.28**	**8,892.09**	**9,766.12**	**8,680.23**	**6,015.36**	**3,622.22**
VEHICLE PURCHASES	**3,731.76**	**2,240.74**	**3,932.04**	**4,255.49**	**4,632.43**	**4,289.18**	**2,769.81**	**1,721.10**
Cars and trucks, new	**2,052.46**	**991.01**	**1,756.69**	**2,220.54**	**2,568.79**	**2,624.31**	**1,899.77**	**1,279.70**
New cars	944.91	564.46	636.16	903.58	1,190.24	1,290.63	901.52	897.66
New trucks	1,107.55	426.54	1,120.53	1,316.96	1,378.55	1,333.69	998.25	382.03
Cars and trucks, used	**1,611.45**	**1,230.54**	**2,079.57**	**1,937.13**	**1,950.76**	**1,645.19**	**831.87**	**440.74**
Used cars	816.42	794.76	901.49	847.23	1,118.76	812.97	454.05	377.11
Used trucks	795.03	435.78	1,178.08	1,089.90	832.00	832.22	377.81	63.64
Other vehicles	**67.85**	**19.19**	**95.78**	**97.82**	**112.88**	**19.68**	**38.17**	**0.66**
GASOLINE AND MOTOR OIL	**1,332.76**	**947.11**	**1,388.49**	**1,582.36**	**1,644.38**	**1,411.45**	**1,019.34**	**562.62**
Gasoline	1,220.61	872.46	1,279.37	1,463.26	1,518.63	1,257.30	907.54	520.14
Diesel fuel	14.73	2.18	14.88	16.36	18.64	23.78	11.00	2.00
Gasoline on trips	86.95	65.02	82.98	88.76	95.18	120.14	90.24	38.27
Motor oil	8.96	6.79	10.41	11.40	10.96	9.02	5.92	1.83
Motor oil on trips	0.88	0.66	0.84	0.90	0.96	1.21	0.91	0.39
OTHER VEHICLE EXPENSES	**2,330.98**	**1,299.01**	**2,446.06**	**2,643.03**	**3,013.23**	**2,484.32**	**1,856.51**	**1,112.39**
Vehicle finance charges	**370.59**	**224.25**	**483.34**	**476.44**	**485.24**	**336.35**	**191.39**	**57.32**
Automobile finance charges	174.48	118.76	218.71	200.14	238.36	172.21	97.02	36.92
Truck finance charges	177.99	99.39	246.41	252.21	224.18	145.73	73.14	18.95
Motorcycle and plane finance charges	2.77	2.20	3.88	4.16	4.62	0.91	0.04	0.06
Other vehicle finance charges	15.35	3.90	14.34	19.93	18.07	17.50	21.19	1.38
Maintenance and repairs	**618.92**	**352.25**	**557.78**	**677.09**	**781.79**	**727.91**	**600.67**	**330.20**
Coolant, additives, brake and transmission fluids	2.95	2.91	3.27	3.16	4.37	2.40	2.16	0.65
Tires—purchased, replaced, installed	87.97	56.48	88.22	99.15	108.72	100.93	66.24	48.31
Parts, equipment, and accessories	47.58	45.81	48.09	64.04	56.15	49.49	28.19	12.26
Vehicle products	4.20	5.01	3.65	3.00	6.25	6.41	2.21	1.54
Miscellaneous auto repair, servicing	40.05	11.26	26.50	34.59	49.52	44.67	88.69	21.60
Body work and painting	31.51	9.64	30.74	29.74	44.24	38.21	27.71	21.35
Clutch and transmission repair	37.77	24.77	36.86	43.04	54.31	36.82	29.67	13.89
Drive shaft and rear-end repair	7.70	5.53	6.03	8.90	11.99	9.48	5.87	0.24
Brake work	44.30	28.10	35.83	50.24	57.13	53.45	42.47	21.02
Repair to steering or front-end	13.03	6.94	13.45	6.43	14.93	13.15	10.06	8.61
Repair to engine cooling system	15.87	8.30	17.77	15.55	18.28	16.37	15.26	13.92
Motor tune-up	38.08	23.67	30.85	42.67	45.88	42.26	45.01	22.81
Lube, oil change, and oil filters	55.94	35.10	55.01	59.74	67.94	65.76	51.94	30.57
Front-end alignment, wheel balance, rotation	7.94	3.83	6.95	9.33	10.20	10.55	5.82	3.49
Shock absorber replacement	3.06	2.18	0.79	4.22	4.19	2.95	5.40	0.68
Gas tank repair, replacement	8.16	10.69	4.20	8.43	3.17	19.44	13.22	1.43
Tire repair and other repair work	44.14	21.14	33.65	51.17	58.02	52.80	37.90	30.07
Vehicle air conditioning repair	12.18	4.05	8.54	10.51	15.20	14.41	21.50	9.41
Exhaust system repair	10.90	4.31	10.70	14.21	11.83	11.48	10.31	6.99
Electrical system repair	25.11	8.87	22.23	26.19	29.61	35.10	23.65	17.80
Motor repair, replacement	70.37	30.74	62.29	75.40	95.31	87.46	61.28	37.17
Auto repair service policy	8.11	2.91	10.16	7.38	6.46	14.34	6.12	6.40
Vehicle insurance	**905.26**	**504.29**	**909.56**	**996.83**	**1,197.13**	**932.47**	**724.36**	**554.88**
Vehicle rental, leases, licenses, other charges	**436.21**	**218.22**	**495.38**	**492.68**	**549.08**	**487.59**	**340.09**	**169.99**
Leased and rented vehicles	270.13	107.11	339.65	319.04	332.93	300.79	187.44	79.48
Rented vehicles	32.95	9.47	26.06	38.99	47.78	42.61	24.35	14.16
Auto rental	5.60	1.21	8.71	5.50	6.94	4.76	5.14	2.71
Auto rental on trips	21.95	5.40	13.30	25.67	32.99	31.67	15.67	11.18
Truck rental	2.22	1.42	1.70	3.34	3.80	1.85	0.94	–
Truck rental on trips	2.29	1.43	2.33	3.00	3.19	2.14	1.99	0.06

	total consumer units	under 25	25 to 34	35 to 44	45 to 54	55 to 64	65 to 74	75+
Leased vehicles	$237.19	$97.64	$313.58	$280.04	$285.15	$258.18	$163.09	$65.33
Car lease payments	132.32	67.57	129.24	147.88	176.15	145.81	125.99	51.07
Truck lease payments	86.11	23.69	123.96	122.90	91.26	97.90	33.72	14.08
Vehicle registration, state	81.20	45.70	75.71	82.57	105.32	94.84	77.93	48.87
Vehicle registration, local	6.97	4.70	6.86	6.30	9.04	7.96	5.87	5.75
Driver's license	7.17	5.31	6.45	8.52	8.45	7.20	6.43	5.11
Vehicle inspection	8.36	3.61	6.53	9.58	10.83	8.74	8.28	7.02
Parking fees	28.12	31.86	31.08	35.27	33.78	25.67	18.94	6.28
Parking fees in home city, excluding residence	23.61	28.78	27.31	29.57	27.96	19.79	16.02	4.95
Parking fees on trips	4.51	3.08	3.77	5.70	5.82	5.88	2.93	1.33
Tolls	13.00	7.18	12.39	11.82	22.57	16.14	7.06	2.41
Tolls on trips	3.75	2.09	3.96	4.06	4.39	4.57	3.77	1.42
Towing charges	4.67	9.11	5.85	5.58	4.86	3.51	2.26	1.06
Automobile service clubs	12.83	1.53	6.90	9.85	16.92	18.17	22.11	12.58
PUBLIC TRANSPORTATION	**385.05**	**187.33**	**339.69**	**411.20**	**476.08**	**495.28**	**369.71**	**226.11**
Airline fares	252.56	115.70	209.41	271.86	308.65	359.34	231.21	141.59
Intercity bus fares	8.96	6.19	7.22	6.83	9.97	10.16	14.42	9.26
Intracity mass transit fares	48.94	33.80	53.69	68.12	62.59	35.33	29.15	14.50
Local transportation on trips	8.33	3.80	7.12	7.33	10.03	10.34	9.96	7.96
Taxi fares and limousine service on trips	4.89	2.23	4.18	4.30	5.89	6.07	5.85	4.68
Taxi fares and limousine service	16.69	13.48	25.03	13.09	25.02	11.94	9.09	9.08
Intercity train fares	16.07	5.09	13.24	12.39	18.99	27.10	18.85	12.35
Ship fares	27.90	6.24	14.44	25.84	33.59	34.99	51.18	26.58
School bus	0.70	0.80	0.36	1.44	1.34	–	–	0.11

Note: Subcategories may not add to total because some are not shown. (–) means sample is too small to make a reliable estimate.
Source: Bureau of Labor Statistics, unpublished tables from the 2003 Consumer Expenditure Survey

Table 11.2 Transportation: Indexed spending by age, 2003

(indexed average annual spending of consumer units (CU) on transportation, by age of consumer unit reference person, 2003; index definition: an index of 100 is the average for all consumer units; an index of 132 means that spending by consumer units in that group is 32 percent above the average for all consumer units; an index of 68 indicates spending that is 32 percent below the average for all consumer units)

	total consumer units	under 25	25 to 34	35 to 44	45 to 54	55 to 64	65 to 74	75+
Average spending of CU, total	$40,817	$22,396	$40,525	$47,175	$50,101	$44,191	$33,629	$25,016
Average spending of CU, index	100	55	99	116	123	108	82	61
Transportation, spending index	100	60	104	114	126	112	77	47
VEHICLE PURCHASES	100	60	105	114	124	115	74	46
Cars and trucks, new	100	48	86	108	125	128	93	62
New cars	100	60	67	96	126	137	95	95
New trucks	100	39	101	119	124	120	90	34
Cars and trucks, used	100	76	129	120	121	102	52	27
Used cars	100	97	110	104	137	100	56	46
Used trucks	100	55	148	137	105	105	48	8
Other vehicles	100	28	141	144	166	29	56	1
GASOLINE AND MOTOR OIL	100	71	104	119	123	106	76	42
Gasoline	100	71	105	120	124	103	74	43
Diesel fuel	100	15	101	114	127	161	75	14
Gasoline on trips	100	75	95	102	109	138	104	44
Motor oil	100	76	116	127	122	101	66	20
Motor oil on trips	100	75	95	102	109	138	103	44
OTHER VEHICLE EXPENSES	100	56	105	113	129	107	80	48
Vehicle finance charges	100	61	130	129	131	91	52	15
Automobile finance charges	100	68	125	115	137	99	56	21
Truck finance charges	100	56	138	142	126	82	41	11
Motorcycle and plane finance charges	100	79	140	150	167	33	1	2
Other vehicle finance charges	100	25	93	130	118	114	138	9
Maintenance and repairs	100	57	90	109	126	118	97	53
Coolant, additives, brake and transmission fluids	100	99	111	107	148	81	73	22
Tires—purchased, replaced, installed	100	64	100	113	124	115	75	55
Parts, equipment, and accessories	100	96	101	135	118	104	59	26
Vehicle products	100	119	87	71	149	153	53	37
Miscellaneous auto repair, servicing	100	28	66	86	124	112	221	54
Body work and painting	100	31	98	94	140	121	88	68
Clutch and transmission repair	100	66	98	114	144	97	79	37
Drive shaft and rear-end repair	100	72	78	116	156	123	76	3
Brake work	100	63	81	113	129	121	96	47
Repair to steering or front-end	100	53	103	126	115	101	77	66
Repair to engine cooling system	100	52	112	98	115	103	96	88
Motor tune-up	100	62	81	112	120	111	118	60
Lube, oil change, and oil filters	100	63	98	107	121	118	93	55
Front-end alignment, wheel balance, rotation	100	48	88	118	128	133	73	44
Shock absorber replacement	100	71	26	138	137	96	176	22
Gas tank repair, replacement	100	131	51	103	39	238	162	18
Tire repair and other repair work	100	48	76	116	131	120	86	68
Vehicle air conditioning repair	100	33	70	86	125	118	177	77
Exhaust system repair	100	40	98	130	109	105	95	64
Electrical system repair	100	35	89	104	118	140	94	71
Motor repair, replacement	100	44	89	107	135	124	87	53
Auto repair service policy	100	36	125	91	80	177	75	79
Vehicle insurance	100	56	100	110	132	103	80	61
Vehicle rental, leases, licenses, other charges	100	50	114	113	126	112	78	39
Leased and rented vehicles	100	40	126	118	123	111	69	29
Rented vehicles	100	29	79	118	145	129	74	43
Auto rental	100	22	156	98	124	85	92	48
Auto rental on trips	100	25	61	117	150	144	71	51
Truck rental	100	64	77	150	171	83	42	–
Truck rental on trips	100	62	102	131	139	93	87	3

	total consumer units	under 25	25 to 34	35 to 44	45 to 54	55 to 64	65 to 74	75+
Leased vehicles	100	41	132	118	120	109	69	28
Car lease payments	100	51	98	112	133	110	95	39
Truck lease payments	100	28	144	143	106	114	39	16
Vehicle registration, state	100	56	93	102	130	117	96	60
Vehicle registration, local	100	67	98	90	130	114	84	82
Driver's license	100	74	90	119	118	100	90	71
Vehicle inspection	100	43	78	115	130	105	99	84
Parking fees	100	113	111	125	120	91	67	22
Parking fees in home city, excluding residence	100	122	116	125	118	84	68	21
Parking fees on trips	100	68	84	126	129	130	65	29
Tolls	100	55	95	91	174	124	54	19
Tolls on trips	100	56	106	108	117	122	101	38
Towing charges	100	195	125	119	104	75	48	23
Automobile service clubs	100	12	54	77	132	142	172	98
PUBLIC TRANSPORTATION	**100**	**49**	**88**	**107**	**124**	**129**	**96**	**59**
Airline fares	100	46	83	103	122	142	92	56
Intercity bus fares	100	69	81	76	111	113	161	103
Intracity mass transit fares	100	69	120	139	128	72	60	30
Local transportation on trips	100	46	85	88	120	124	120	96
Taxi fares and limousine service on trips	100	46	85	88	120	124	120	96
Taxi fares and limousine service	100	81	150	78	150	72	54	54
Intercity train fares	100	32	82	77	118	169	117	77
Ship fares	100	22	52	93	120	125	183	95
School bus	100	114	51	206	191	–	–	16

Note: (–) means sample is too small to make a reliable estimate.
Source: Calculations by New Strategist based on the 2003 Consumer Expenditure Survey

Table 11.3 Transportation: Total spending by age, 2003

(total annual spending on transportation, by consumer unit (CU) age groups, 2003; numbers in thousands)

	total consumer units	under 25	25 to 34	35 to 44	45 to 54	55 to 64	65 to 74	75+
Number of consumer units	115,356	8,584	19,737	24,413	23,131	16,580	11,495	11,417
Total spending of all CUs	$4,708,523,919	$192,243,230	$799,846,267	$1,151,684,740	$1,158,882,993	$732,680,977	$386,567,309	$285,612,010
Transportation, total spending	897,533,126	40,123,247	159,993,648	217,082,593	225,900,122	143,918,213	69,146,563	41,354,886
VEHICLE PURCHASES	430,480,907	19,234,512	77,606,673	103,889,277	107,152,738	71,114,604	31,838,966	19,649,799
Cars and trucks, new	236,763,576	8,506,830	34,671,791	54,210,043	59,418,681	43,511,060	21,837,856	14,610,335
New cars	109,001,038	4,845,325	12,555,890	22,059,099	27,531,441	21,398,645	10,362,972	10,248,584
New trucks	127,762,538	3,661,419	22,115,901	32,150,944	31,887,240	22,112,580	11,474,884	4,361,637
Cars and trucks, used	185,890,426	10,562,955	41,044,473	47,291,155	45,123,030	27,277,250	9,562,346	5,031,929
Used cars	94,178,946	6,822,220	17,792,708	20,683,426	25,878,038	13,479,043	5,219,305	4,305,465
Used trucks	91,711,481	3,740,736	23,251,765	26,607,729	19,244,992	13,798,208	4,342,926	726,578
Other vehicles	7,826,905	164,727	1,890,410	2,388,080	2,611,027	326,294	438,764	7,535
GASOLINE AND MOTOR OIL	153,741,863	8,129,992	27,404,627	38,630,155	38,036,154	23,401,841	11,717,313	6,423,433
Gasoline	140,804,687	7,489,197	25,250,926	35,722,566	35,127,431	20,846,034	10,432,172	5,938,438
Diesel fuel	1,699,194	18,713	293,687	411,603	431,162	394,272	126,445	22,834
Gasoline on trips	10,030,204	558,132	1,637,776	2,166,898	2,201,609	1,991,921	1,037,309	436,929
Motor oil	1,033,590	58,285	205,462	278,308	253,516	149,552	68,050	20,893
Motor oil on trips	101,513	5,665	16,579	21,972	22,206	20,062	10,460	4,453
OTHER VEHICLE EXPENSES	268,892,529	11,150,702	48,277,886	64,524,291	69,699,023	41,190,026	21,340,582	12,700,157
Vehicle finance charges	42,749,780	1,924,962	9,539,682	11,631,330	11,224,086	5,576,683	2,200,028	654,422
Automobile finance charges	20,127,315	1,019,436	4,316,679	4,886,018	5,513,505	2,855,242	1,115,245	421,516
Truck finance charges	20,532,214	853,164	4,863,394	6,157,203	5,185,508	2,416,203	840,744	216,352
Motorcycle and plane finance charges	319,536	18,885	76,580	101,558	106,865	15,088	460	685
Other vehicle finance charges	1,770,715	33,478	283,029	486,551	417,977	290,150	243,579	15,755
Maintenance and repairs	71,396,136	3,023,714	11,008,904	16,529,798	18,083,584	12,068,748	6,904,702	3,769,893
Coolant, additives, brake and transmission fluids	340,300	24,979	64,540	77,145	101,082	39,792	24,829	7,421
Tires—purchased, replaced, installed	10,147,867	484,824	1,741,198	2,420,549	2,514,802	1,673,419	761,429	551,555
Parts, equipment, and accessories	5,488,638	393,233	949,152	1,563,409	1,298,806	820,544	324,044	139,972
Vehicle products	484,495	43,006	72,040	73,239	144,569	106,278	25,404	17,582
Miscellaneous auto repair, servicing	4,620,008	96,656	523,031	844,446	1,145,447	740,629	1,019,492	246,607
Body work and painting	3,634,868	82,750	606,715	726,043	1,023,315	633,522	318,526	243,753
Clutch and transmission repair	4,356,996	212,626	727,506	1,050,736	1,256,245	610,476	341,057	158,582
Drive shaft and rear-end repair	888,241	47,470	119,014	217,276	277,341	157,178	67,476	2,740
Brake work	5,110,271	241,210	707,177	1,226,509	1,321,474	886,201	488,193	239,985
Repair to steering or front-end	1,503,089	59,573	265,463	401,106	345,346	218,027	115,640	98,300
Repair to engine cooling system	1,830,700	71,247	350,726	379,622	422,835	271,415	175,414	158,925
Motor tune-up	4,392,756	203,183	608,886	1,041,703	1,061,250	700,671	517,390	260,422
Lube, oil change, and oil filters	6,453,015	301,298	1,085,732	1,458,433	1,571,520	1,090,301	597,050	349,018
Front-end alignment, wheel balance, rotation	915,927	32,877	137,172	227,773	235,936	174,919	66,901	39,845
Shock absorber replacement	352,989	18,713	15,592	103,023	96,919	48,911	62,073	7,764
Gas tank repair, replacement	941,305	91,763	82,895	205,802	73,325	322,315	151,964	16,326
Tire repair and other repair work	5,091,814	181,466	664,150	1,249,213	1,342,061	875,424	435,661	343,309
Vehicle air conditioning repair	1,405,036	34,765	168,554	256,581	351,591	238,918	247,143	107,434
Exhaust system repair	1,257,380	36,997	211,186	346,909	273,640	190,338	118,513	79,805
Electrical system repair	2,896,589	76,140	438,754	639,376	684,909	581,958	271,857	203,223
Motor repair, replacement	8,117,602	263,872	1,229,418	1,840,740	2,204,616	1,450,087	704,414	424,370
Auto repair service policy	935,537	24,979	200,528	180,168	149,426	237,757	70,349	73,069
Vehicle insurance	104,427,173	4,328,825	17,951,986	24,335,611	27,690,814	15,460,353	8,326,518	6,335,065
Vehicle rental, leases, licenses, other charges	50,319,441	1,873,200	9,777,315	12,027,797	12,700,769	8,084,242	3,909,335	1,940,776
Leased and rented vehicles	31,161,116	919,432	6,703,672	7,788,724	7,701,004	4,987,098	2,154,623	907,423
Rented vehicles	3,800,980	81,290	514,346	951,863	1,105,199	706,474	279,903	161,665
Auto rental	645,994	10,387	171,909	134,272	160,529	78,921	59,084	30,940
Auto rental on trips	2,532,064	46,354	262,502	626,682	763,092	525,089	180,127	127,642
Truck rental	256,090	12,189	33,553	81,539	87,898	30,673	10,805	–
Truck rental on trips	264,165	12,275	45,987	73,239	73,788	35,481	22,875	685

	total consumer units	under 25	25 to 34	35 to 44	45 to 54	55 to 64	65 to 74	75+
Leased vehicles	$27,361,290	$838,142	$6,189,128	$6,836,617	$6,595,805	$4,280,624	$1,874,720	$745,873
Car lease payments	15,263,906	580,021	2,550,810	3,610,194	4,074,526	2,417,530	1,448,255	583,066
Truck lease payments	9,933,305	203,355	2,445,599	3,000,358	2,110,935	1,623,182	387,611	160,751
Vehicle registration, state	9,366,907	392,289	1,494,288	2,013,223	2,436,157	1,572,447	895,805	557,949
Vehicle registration, local	804,031	40,345	135,396	153,802	209,104	131,977	67,476	65,648
Driver's license	827,103	45,581	127,304	207,999	195,457	119,376	73,913	58,341
Vehicle inspection	964,376	30,988	128,883	233,877	250,509	144,909	95,179	80,147
Parking fees	3,243,811	273,486	513,426	861,047	781,365	425,609	217,715	71,699
Parking fees in home city, excluding residence	2,723,555	247,048	539,017	721,892	646,743	328,118	184,150	56,514
Parking fees on trips	520,256	26,439	74,408	139,154	134,622	97,490	33,680	15,185
Tolls	1,499,628	61,633	244,541	288,562	522,067	267,601	81,155	27,515
Tolls on trips	432,585	17,941	78,159	99,117	101,545	75,771	43,336	16,212
Towing charges	538,713	78,200	115,461	136,225	112,417	58,196	25,979	12,102
Automobile service clubs	1,480,017	13,134	136,185	240,468	391,377	301,259	254,154	143,626
PUBLIC TRANSPORTATION	**44,417,828**	**1,608,041**	**6,704,462**	**10,038,626**	**11,012,206**	**8,211,742**	**4,249,816**	**2,581,498**
Airline fares	29,134,311	993,169	4,133,125	6,635,918	7,139,383	5,957,857	2,657,759	1,616,533
Intercity bus fares	1,033,590	53,135	142,501	165,741	230,616	168,453	165,758	105,721
Intracity mass transit fares	5,645,523	290,139	1,158,365	1,663,014	1,447,769	585,771	335,079	165,547
Local transportation on trips	960,915	32,619	140,527	178,947	232,004	171,437	114,490	90,879
Taxi fares and limousine service on trips	564,091	19,142	82,501	104,976	136,242	100,641	67,246	53,432
Taxi fares and limousine service	1,925,292	115,712	494,017	319,566	578,738	197,965	104,490	103,666
Intercity train fares	1,853,771	43,693	261,318	302,477	439,258	449,318	216,681	141,000
Ship fares	3,218,432	53,564	285,002	630,832	776,970	580,134	588,314	303,464
School bus	80,749	6,867	7,105	35,155	30,996	–	–	1,256

Note: Numbers may not add to total because of rounding and missing subcategories. (–) means sample is too small to make a reliable estimate.
Source: Calculations by New Strategist based on the 2003 Consumer Expenditure Survey

Table 11.4 Transportation: Market shares by age, 2003

(percentage of total annual spending on transportation accounted for by consumer unit age groups, 2003)

	total consumer units	under 25	25 to 34	35 to 44	45 to 54	55 to 64	65 to 74	75+
Share of total consumer units	100.0%	7.4%	17.1%	21.2%	20.1%	14.4%	10.0%	9.9%
Share of total before-tax income	100.0	3.0	16.9	25.3	26.7	16.5	6.9	4.9
Share of total spending	100.0	4.1	17.0	24.5	24.6	15.6	8.2	6.1
Share of transportation spending	**100.0**	**4.5**	**17.8**	**24.2**	**25.2**	**16.0**	**7.7**	**4.6**
VEHICLE PURCHASES	**100.0**	**4.5**	**18.0**	**24.1**	**24.9**	**16.5**	**7.4**	**4.6**
Cars and trucks, new	**100.0**	**3.6**	**14.6**	**22.9**	**25.1**	**18.4**	**9.2**	**6.2**
New cars	100.0	4.4	11.5	20.2	25.3	19.6	9.5	9.4
New trucks	100.0	2.9	17.3	25.2	25.0	17.3	9.0	3.4
Cars and trucks, used	**100.0**	**5.7**	**22.1**	**25.4**	**24.3**	**14.7**	**5.1**	**2.7**
Used cars	100.0	7.2	18.9	22.0	27.5	14.3	5.5	4.6
Used trucks	100.0	4.1	25.4	29.0	21.0	15.0	4.7	0.8
Other vehicles	**100.0**	**2.1**	**24.2**	**30.5**	**33.4**	**4.2**	**5.6**	**0.1**
GASOLINE AND MOTOR OIL	**100.0**	**5.3**	**17.8**	**25.1**	**24.7**	**15.2**	**7.6**	**4.2**
Gasoline	100.0	5.3	17.9	25.4	24.9	14.8	7.4	4.2
Diesel fuel	100.0	1.1	17.3	24.2	25.4	23.2	7.4	1.3
Gasoline on trips	100.0	5.6	16.3	21.6	21.9	19.9	10.3	4.4
Motor oil	100.0	5.6	19.9	26.9	24.5	14.5	6.6	2.0
Motor oil on trips	100.0	5.6	16.3	21.6	21.9	19.8	10.3	4.4
OTHER VEHICLE EXPENSES	**100.0**	**4.1**	**18.0**	**24.0**	**25.9**	**15.3**	**7.9**	**4.7**
Vehicle finance charges	**100.0**	**4.5**	**22.3**	**27.2**	**26.3**	**13.0**	**5.1**	**1.5**
Automobile finance charges	100.0	5.1	21.4	24.3	27.4	14.2	5.5	2.1
Truck finance charges	100.0	4.2	23.7	30.0	25.3	11.8	4.1	1.1
Motorcycle and plane finance charges	100.0	5.9	24.0	31.8	33.4	4.7	0.1	0.2
Other vehicle finance charges	100.0	1.9	16.0	27.5	23.6	16.4	13.8	0.9
Maintenance and repairs	**100.0**	**4.2**	**15.4**	**23.2**	**25.3**	**16.9**	**9.7**	**5.3**
Coolant, additives, brake and transmission fluids	100.0	7.3	19.0	22.7	29.7	11.7	7.3	2.2
Tires—purchased, replaced, installed	100.0	4.8	17.2	23.9	24.8	16.5	7.5	5.4
Parts, equipment, and accessories	100.0	7.2	17.3	28.5	23.7	14.9	5.9	2.6
Vehicle products	100.0	8.9	14.9	15.1	29.8	21.9	5.2	3.6
Miscellaneous auto repair, servicing	100.0	2.1	11.3	18.3	24.8	16.0	22.1	5.3
Body work and painting	100.0	2.3	16.7	20.0	28.2	17.4	8.8	6.7
Clutch and transmission repair	100.0	4.9	16.7	24.1	28.8	14.0	7.8	3.6
Drive shaft and rear-end repair	100.0	5.3	13.4	24.5	31.2	17.7	7.6	0.3
Brake work	100.0	4.7	13.8	24.0	25.9	17.3	9.6	4.7
Repair to steering or front-end	100.0	4.0	17.7	26.7	23.0	14.5	7.7	6.5
Repair to engine cooling system	100.0	3.9	19.2	20.7	23.1	14.8	9.6	8.7
Motor tune-up	100.0	4.6	13.9	23.7	24.2	16.0	11.8	5.9
Lube, oil change, and oil filters	100.0	4.7	16.8	22.6	24.4	16.9	9.3	5.4
Front-end alignment, wheel balance, rotation	100.0	3.6	15.0	24.9	25.8	19.1	7.3	4.4
Shock absorber replacement	100.0	5.3	4.4	29.2	27.5	13.9	17.6	2.2
Gas tank repair, replacement	100.0	9.7	8.8	21.9	7.8	34.2	16.1	1.7
Tire repair and other repair work	100.0	3.6	13.0	24.5	26.4	17.2	8.6	6.7
Vehicle air conditioning repair	100.0	2.5	12.0	18.3	25.0	17.0	17.6	7.6
Exhaust system repair	100.0	2.9	16.8	27.6	21.8	15.1	9.4	6.3
Electrical system repair	100.0	2.6	15.1	22.1	23.6	20.1	9.4	7.0
Motor repair, replacement	100.0	3.3	15.1	22.7	27.2	17.9	8.7	5.2
Auto repair service policy	100.0	2.7	21.4	19.3	16.0	25.4	7.5	7.8
Vehicle insurance	**100.0**	**4.1**	**17.2**	**23.3**	**26.5**	**14.8**	**8.0**	**6.1**
Vehicle rental, leases, licenses, other charges	**100.0**	**3.7**	**19.4**	**23.9**	**25.2**	**16.1**	**7.8**	**3.9**
Leased and rented vehicles	100.0	3.0	21.5	25.0	24.7	16.0	6.9	2.9
Rented vehicles	100.0	2.1	13.5	25.0	29.1	18.6	7.4	4.3
Auto rental	100.0	1.6	26.6	20.8	24.8	12.2	9.1	4.8
Auto rental on trips	100.0	1.8	10.4	24.7	30.1	20.7	7.1	5.0
Truck rental	100.0	4.8	13.1	31.8	34.3	12.0	4.2	–
Truck rental on trips	100.0	4.6	17.4	27.7	27.9	13.4	8.7	0.3

	total consumer units	under 25	25 to 34	35 to 44	45 to 54	55 to 64	65 to 74	75+
Leased vehicles	100.0%	3.1%	22.6%	25.0%	24.1%	15.6%	6.9%	2.7%
Car lease payments	100.0	3.8	16.7	23.7	26.7	15.8	9.5	3.8
Truck lease payments	100.0	2.0	24.6	30.2	21.3	16.3	3.9	1.6
Vehicle registration, state	100.0	4.2	16.0	21.5	26.0	16.8	9.6	6.0
Vehicle registration, local	100.0	5.0	16.8	19.1	26.0	16.4	8.4	8.2
Driver's license	100.0	5.5	15.4	25.1	23.6	14.4	8.9	7.1
Vehicle inspection	100.0	3.2	13.4	24.3	26.0	15.0	9.9	8.3
Parking fees	100.0	8.4	18.9	26.5	24.1	13.1	6.7	2.2
Parking fees in home city, excluding residence	100.0	9.1	19.8	26.5	23.7	12.0	6.8	2.1
Parking fees on trips	100.0	5.1	14.3	26.7	25.9	18.7	6.5	2.9
Tolls	100.0	4.1	16.3	19.2	34.8	17.8	5.4	1.8
Tolls on trips	100.0	4.1	18.1	22.9	23.5	17.5	10.0	3.7
Towing charges	100.0	14.5	21.4	25.3	20.9	10.8	4.8	2.2
Automobile service clubs	100.0	0.9	9.2	16.2	26.4	20.4	17.2	9.7
PUBLIC TRANSPORTATION	**100.0**	**3.6**	**15.1**	**22.6**	**24.8**	**18.5**	**9.6**	**5.8**
Airline fares	100.0	3.4	14.2	22.8	24.5	20.4	9.1	5.5
Intercity bus fares	100.0	5.1	13.8	16.1	22.3	16.3	16.0	10.2
Intracity mass transit fares	100.0	5.1	20.5	29.5	25.6	10.4	5.9	2.9
Local transportation on trips	100.0	3.4	14.6	18.6	24.1	17.8	11.9	9.5
Taxi fares and limousine service on trips	100.0	3.4	14.6	18.6	24.2	17.8	11.9	9.5
Taxi fares and limousine service	100.0	6.0	25.7	16.6	30.1	10.3	5.4	5.4
Intercity train fares	100.0	2.4	14.1	16.3	23.7	24.2	11.7	7.6
Ship fares	100.0	1.7	8.9	19.6	24.1	18.0	18.3	9.4
School bus	100.0	8.5	8.8	43.5	38.4	–	–	1.6

Note: Numbers may not add to total because of rounding. (–) means sample is too small to make a reliable estimate.
Source: Calculations by New Strategist based on the 2003 Consumer Expenditure Survey

Table 11.5 Transportation: Average spending by income, 2003

(average annual spending on transportation, by before-tax income of consumer unit (CU), 2003; complete income reporters only)

	total complete reporters	under $20,000	$20,000–$39,999	$40,000–$49,999	$50,000–$69,999	$70,000–$79,999	$80,000–$99,999	$100,000 or more
Number of consumer units (000)	97,391	27,100	23,941	8,891	13,890	5,121	6,909	11,537
Average number of persons per CU	2.5	1.8	2.4	2.6	2.8	3.0	3.0	3.1
Average before-tax income of CU	$51,128.00	$10,752.55	$29,072.57	$44,294.00	$58,900.00	$74,560.00	$88,832.00	$154,665.00
Average spending of CU, total	42,741.66	19,862.52	31,684.32	39,756.91	49,788.99	57,128.14	65,957.39	93,514.86
Transportation, average spending	**8,041.00**	**3,150.87**	**6,225.52**	**7,949.42**	**10,656.37**	**11,539.51**	**13,295.31**	**15,525.91**
VEHICLE PURCHASES	**3,871.43**	**1,312.12**	**2,902.39**	**3,685.79**	**5,406.88**	**5,698.10**	**6,833.83**	**7,603.62**
Cars and trucks, new	**2,154.02**	**525.96**	**1,341.13**	**1,425.02**	**2,654.37**	**3,538.21**	**4,473.69**	**5,620.95**
New cars	988.81	296.80	665.43	905.01	1,037.01	1,716.54	1,532.09	2,643.58
New trucks	1,165.20	229.16	675.69	520.01	1,617.35	1,821.67	2,941.59	2,977.37
Cars and trucks, used	**1,649.48**	**773.97**	**1,544.01**	**2,178.97**	**2,607.57**	**2,104.52**	**2,143.88**	**1,865.29**
Used cars	823.82	526.66	826.78	908.67	1,002.97	875.70	1,317.39	915.97
Used trucks	825.66	247.30	717.23	1,270.30	1,604.61	1,228.82	826.49	949.31
Other vehicles	**67.94**	**16.78**	**38.40**	**81.80**	**144.94**	**55.38**	**216.26**	**117.38**
GASOLINE AND MOTOR OIL	**1,353.47**	**689.01**	**1,168.01**	**1,493.57**	**1,712.47**	**1,860.93**	**2,038.23**	**2,123.48**
Gasoline	1,233.75	633.74	1,076.17	1,387.36	1,556.28	1,682.44	1,825.79	1,909.77
Diesel fuel	16.32	4.53	12.66	7.97	18.46	24.93	42.28	36.11
Gasoline on trips	92.07	41.32	68.99	86.35	124.30	137.84	156.10	166.10
Motor oil	9.54	5.99	9.48	11.02	12.17	14.33	12.49	9.82
Motor oil on trips	0.93	0.42	0.70	0.87	1.26	1.39	1.58	1.68
OTHER VEHICLE EXPENSES	**2,415.84**	**988.58**	**1,891.85**	**2,486.27**	**3,103.87**	**3,531.14**	**3,841.66**	**4,631.67**
Vehicle finance charges	**382.96**	**105.50**	**288.68**	**405.91**	**560.03**	**625.75**	**755.85**	**668.41**
Automobile finance charges	177.68	58.80	155.52	197.05	248.04	257.12	300.52	294.48
Truck finance charges	185.83	43.08	118.66	191.72	291.00	344.83	397.36	332.08
Motorcycle and plane finance charges	2.82	1.55	1.23	3.69	3.91	3.76	5.81	5.85
Other vehicle finance charges	16.63	2.47	13.26	13.45	17.09	20.04	52.16	36.00
Maintenance and repairs	**656.70**	**314.37**	**523.10**	**685.48**	**800.24**	**919.46**	**1,058.84**	**1,190.85**
Coolant, additives, brake and transmission fluids	3.21	2.51	3.47	4.02	3.52	3.62	3.90	2.72
Tires—purchased, replaced, installed	92.25	39.40	76.57	91.64	122.55	137.23	145.21	161.19
Parts, equipment, and accessories	52.36	20.84	45.10	81.94	67.66	73.15	107.20	58.18
Vehicle products	4.53	2.41	3.75	3.19	11.08	2.10	8.69	3.32
Miscellaneous auto repair, servicing	46.50	29.74	28.59	40.60	37.85	50.93	110.39	101.28
Body work and painting	33.97	13.00	19.72	33.25	32.02	50.40	72.14	85.57
Clutch and transmission repair	40.65	18.90	32.94	39.19	50.98	82.78	46.43	74.26
Drive shaft and rear-end repair	7.54	2.57	4.24	5.46	10.08	4.35	8.01	25.76
Brake work	45.72	24.08	33.27	46.01	47.54	64.73	72.85	95.33
Repair to steering or front-end	13.70	7.30	9.82	9.49	21.33	18.38	22.82	23.28
Repair to engine cooling system	16.48	11.50	15.71	18.50	15.63	22.79	20.99	23.72
Motor tune-up	39.93	20.55	31.42	30.17	44.32	51.55	53.89	91.80
Lube, oil change, and oil filters	59.01	26.49	46.33	64.16	76.84	83.84	92.77	105.05
Front-end alignment, wheel balance, rotation	8.24	4.12	7.68	10.38	10.40	9.33	8.89	13.97
Shock absorber replacement	3.19	2.17	2.80	2.72	3.21	1.60	4.70	6.50
Gas tank repair, replacement	7.90	1.65	7.10	5.09	4.26	54.99	4.28	12.91
Tire repair and other repair work	44.07	18.69	42.10	46.61	54.33	52.75	63.34	78.07
Vehicle air conditioning repair	12.46	7.74	12.13	11.37	12.93	15.59	14.75	21.76
Exhaust system repair	11.51	7.86	11.48	9.16	8.00	23.01	22.38	14.54
Electrical system repair	25.92	13.40	25.19	28.34	33.32	32.73	34.20	38.07
Motor repair, replacement	75.94	38.03	56.57	89.54	110.21	79.50	126.85	121.42
Auto repair service policy	8.88	1.71	7.14	9.99	18.72	4.12	14.15	16.28
Vehicle insurance	**929.49**	**420.59**	**806.77**	**982.54**	**1,158.38**	**1,284.17**	**1,420.97**	**1,611.28**
Vehicle rental, leases, licenses, other charges	**446.69**	**148.12**	**273.32**	**412.34**	**585.22**	**701.76**	**605.99**	**1,161.13**
Leased and rented vehicles	269.22	72.94	131.86	237.92	367.15	463.01	316.85	807.04
Rented vehicles	33.88	7.74	24.61	25.50	33.48	39.71	59.17	103.70
Auto rental	6.24	1.74	7.84	5.78	10.88	4.31	4.33	10.25
Auto rental on trips	21.87	4.22	12.33	16.57	17.94	30.71	32.63	81.58
Truck rental	2.57	1.21	1.96	1.07	2.39	1.38	9.96	4.49
Truck rental on trips	2.16	0.50	2.38	2.08	2.25	2.37	6.84	2.65

	total complete reporters	under $20,000	$20,000–$39,999	$40,000–$49,999	$50,000–$69,999	$70,000–$79,999	$80,000–$99,999	$100,000 or more
Leased vehicles	$235.35	$65.19	$107.25	$212.42	$333.67	$423.29	$257.68	$703.34
Car lease payments	130.57	36.46	54.98	118.07	157.91	206.76	166.38	429.94
Truck lease payments	88.35	18.07	51.37	72.25	164.60	184.47	85.92	209.54
Vehicle registration, state	86.06	35.47	75.14	96.00	106.37	127.45	140.46	144.43
Vehicle registration, local	7.45	2.91	8.36	8.42	11.88	7.91	11.25	7.65
Driver's license	7.69	4.39	6.14	9.57	9.99	9.48	10.61	11.89
Vehicle inspection	9.11	4.69	8.14	8.49	11.25	12.15	14.66	14.72
Parking fees	29.05	13.28	12.49	22.18	32.49	34.82	46.11	88.82
Parking fees in home city, excluding residence	24.50	11.85	10.66	18.09	27.23	28.88	37.08	75.08
Parking fees on trips	4.55	1.42	1.83	4.09	5.26	5.94	9.03	13.74
Tolls	15.26	3.02	2.50	7.73	21.64	17.53	30.01	40.24
Tolls on trips	4.00	1.54	2.52	3.21	4.42	4.72	6.96	10.83
Towing charges	5.19	4.76	5.06	5.31	5.15	5.10	3.89	7.19
Automobile service clubs	13.68	5.11	11.10	13.52	14.88	19.60	25.20	28.28
PUBLIC TRANSPORTATION	**400.26**	**161.15**	**263.27**	**283.78**	**433.15**	**449.33**	**581.60**	**1,167.14**
Airline fares	255.77	82.14	144.85	194.23	307.47	297.42	375.85	788.56
Intercity bus fares	9.43	6.93	10.24	9.77	9.61	7.51	8.95	14.30
Intracity mass transit fares	52.72	43.25	42.76	37.70	35.72	55.87	71.60	114.99
Local transportation on trips	8.81	2.97	4.08	6.92	12.23	9.10	13.79	26.54
Taxi fares and limousine service on trips	5.17	1.74	2.40	4.05	7.18	5.34	8.10	15.59
Taxi fares and limousine service	19.94	17.15	19.34	11.56	17.00	24.37	23.30	34.88
Intercity train fares	15.98	4.07	5.11	13.35	22.21	19.61	37.54	46.49
Ship fares	31.69	2.70	33.77	6.14	20.68	30.04	42.32	122.74
School bus	0.76	0.24	0.72	0.04	1.03	0.06	0.15	3.05

Note: Subcategories may not add to total because some are not shown.
Source: Bureau of Labor Statistics, unpublished tables from the 2003 Consumer Expenditure Survey; calculations by New Strategist

Table 11.6 Transportation: Indexed spending by income, 2003

(indexed average annual spending of consumer units (CU) on transportation, by before-tax income of consumer unit, 2003; complete income reporters only; index definition: an index of 100 is the average for all consumer units; an index of 132 means that spending by consumer units in that group is 32 percent above the average for all consumer units; an index of 68 indicates spending that is 32 percent below the average for all consumer units)

	total complete reporters	under $20,000	$20,000–$39,999	$40,000–$49,999	$50,000–$69,999	$70,000–$79,999	$80,000–$99,999	$100,000 or more
Average spending of CU, total	$42,742	$19,863	$31,684	$39,757	$49,789	$57,128	$65,957	$93,515
Average spending of CU, index	100	46	74	93	116	134	154	219
Transportation, spending index	**100**	**39**	**77**	**99**	**133**	**144**	**165**	**193**
VEHICLE PURCHASES	**100**	**34**	**75**	**95**	**140**	**147**	**177**	**196**
Cars and trucks, new	**100**	**24**	**62**	**66**	**123**	**164**	**208**	**261**
New cars	100	30	67	92	105	174	155	267
New trucks	100	20	58	45	139	156	252	256
Cars and trucks, used	**100**	**47**	**94**	**132**	**158**	**128**	**130**	**113**
Used cars	100	64	100	110	122	106	160	111
Used trucks	100	30	87	154	194	149	100	115
Other vehicles	**100**	**25**	**57**	**120**	**213**	**82**	**318**	**173**
GASOLINE AND MOTOR OIL	**100**	**51**	**86**	**110**	**127**	**137**	**151**	**157**
Gasoline	100	51	87	112	126	136	148	155
Diesel fuel	100	28	78	29	113	153	259	221
Gasoline on trips	100	45	75	94	135	150	170	180
Motor oil	100	63	99	116	128	150	131	103
Motor oil on trips	100	45	75	94	135	149	170	181
OTHER VEHICLE EXPENSES	**100**	**41**	**78**	**103**	**128**	**146**	**159**	**192**
Vehicle finance charges	**100**	**28**	**75**	**106**	**146**	**163**	**197**	**175**
Automobile finance charges	100	33	88	111	140	145	169	166
Truck finance charges	100	23	64	103	157	186	214	179
Motorcycle and plane finance charges	100	55	44	131	139	133	206	207
Other vehicle finance charges	100	15	80	81	103	121	314	216
Maintenance and repairs	**100**	**48**	**80**	**104**	**122**	**140**	**161**	**181**
Coolant, additives, brake and transmission fluids	100	78	108	125	110	113	121	85
Tires—purchased, replaced, installed	100	43	83	99	133	149	157	175
Parts, equipment, and accessories	100	40	86	156	129	140	205	111
Vehicle products	100	53	83	70	245	46	192	73
Miscellaneous auto repair, servicing	100	64	61	87	81	110	237	218
Body work and painting	100	38	58	98	94	148	212	252
Clutch and transmission repair	100	47	81	96	125	204	114	183
Drive shaft and rear-end repair	100	34	56	72	134	58	106	342
Brake work	100	53	73	101	104	142	159	209
Repair to steering or front-end	100	53	72	69	156	134	167	170
Repair to engine cooling system	100	70	95	112	95	138	127	144
Motor tune-up	100	51	79	76	111	129	135	230
Lube, oil change, and oil filters	100	45	79	109	130	142	157	178
Front-end alignment, wheel balance, rotation	100	50	93	126	126	113	108	170
Shock absorber replacement	100	68	88	85	101	50	147	204
Gas tank repair, replacement	100	21	90	64	54	696	54	163
Tire repair and other repair work	100	42	96	106	123	120	144	177
Vehicle air conditioning repair	100	62	97	91	104	125	118	175
Exhaust system repair	100	68	100	80	70	200	194	126
Electrical system repair	100	52	97	109	129	126	132	147
Motor repair, replacement	100	50	74	118	145	105	167	160
Auto repair service policy	100	19	80	113	211	46	159	183
Vehicle insurance	100	45	87	106	125	138	153	173
Vehicle rental, leases, licenses, other charges	**100**	**33**	**61**	**92**	**131**	**157**	**136**	**260**
Leased and rented vehicles	**100**	**27**	**49**	**88**	**136**	**172**	**118**	**300**
Rented vehicles	100	23	73	75	99	117	175	306
Auto rental	100	28	126	93	174	69	69	164
Auto rental on trips	100	19	56	76	82	140	149	373
Truck rental	100	47	76	42	93	54	388	175
Truck rental on trips	100	23	110	96	104	110	317	123

	total complete reporters	under $20,000	$20,000–$39,999	$40,000–$49,999	$50,000–$69,999	$70,000–$79,999	$80,000–$99,999	$100,000 or more
Leased vehicles	100	28	46	90	142	180	109	299
Car lease payments	100	28	42	90	121	158	127	329
Truck lease payments	100	20	58	32	186	209	97	237
Vehicle registration, state	100	41	87	112	124	148	163	168
Vehicle registration, local	100	39	112	113	159	106	151	103
Driver's license	100	57	80	124	130	123	138	155
Vehicle inspection	100	51	89	93	123	133	161	162
Parking fees	100	46	43	76	112	120	159	306
Parking fees in home city, excluding residence	100	48	44	74	111	118	151	306
Parking fees on trips	100	31	40	50	116	131	198	302
Tolls	100	20	82	51	142	115	197	264
Tolls on trips	100	38	63	80	111	118	174	271
Towing charges	100	92	98	102	99	98	75	139
Automobile service clubs	100	37	81	93	109	143	184	207
PUBLIC TRANSPORTATION	**100**	**40**	**66**	**71**	**108**	**112**	**145**	**292**
Airline fares	100	32	57	76	120	116	147	308
Intercity bus fares	100	74	109	104	102	80	95	152
Intracity mass transit fares	100	82	81	72	68	106	136	218
Local transportation on trips	100	34	45	79	139	103	157	301
Taxi fares and limousine service on trips	100	34	46	79	139	103	157	302
Taxi fares and limousine service	100	86	97	58	85	122	117	175
Intercity train fares	100	25	32	84	139	123	235	291
Ship fares	100	9	107	19	65	95	134	387
School bus	100	32	94	5	136	8	20	401

Source: Calculations by New Strategist based on the 2003 Consumer Expenditure Survey

Table 11.7 Transportation: Total spending by income, 2003

(total annual spending on transportation, by before-tax income group of consumer units (CU), 2003; complete income reporters only; numbers in thousands)

	total complete reporters	under $20,000	$20,000– $39,999	$40,000– $49,999	$50,000– $69,999	$70,000– $79,999	$80,000– $99,999	$100,000 or more
Number of consumer units	97,391	27,100	23,941	8,891	13,890	5,121	6,909	11,537
Total spending of all CUs	$4,162,653,009	$538,274,380	$758,554,310	$353,478,687	$691,569,071	$292,553,205	$455,699,608	$1,078,880,940
Transportation, total spending	783,121,031	85,388,464	149,045,167	70,678,293	148,016,979	59,093,831	91,857,297	179,122,424
VEHICLE PURCHASES	377,042,439	35,558,577	69,486,200	32,770,359	75,101,563	29,179,970	47,214,931	87,722,964
Cars and trucks, new	209,782,162	14,253,639	32,107,961	12,669,853	36,869,199	18,119,173	30,908,724	64,848,900
New cars	96,301,195	8,043,315	15,931,116	8,046,444	14,404,069	8,790,401	10,585,210	30,498,982
New trucks	113,479,993	6,210,206	16,176,737	4,623,409	22,464,992	9,328,772	20,323,445	34,349,918
Cars and trucks, used	160,644,507	20,974,493	36,965,093	19,373,222	36,219,147	10,777,247	14,812,067	21,519,851
Used cars	80,232,654	14,272,620	19,793,844	8,078,985	13,931,253	4,484,460	9,101,848	10,567,546
Used trucks	80,411,853	6,701,717	17,171,117	11,294,237	22,288,033	6,292,787	5,710,219	10,952,189
Other vehicles	6,616,745	454,795	919,334	727,284	2,013,217	283,601	1,494,140	1,354,213
GASOLINE AND MOTOR OIL	131,815,797	18,672,211	27,963,233	13,279,331	23,786,208	9,529,823	14,082,131	24,498,589
Gasoline	120,156,146	17,174,252	25,764,632	12,335,018	21,616,729	8,615,775	12,614,383	22,033,016
Diesel fuel	1,589,421	122,809	303,132	70,861	256,409	127,667	292,113	416,601
Gasoline on trips	8,966,789	1,119,842	1,651,740	767,738	1,726,527	705,879	1,078,495	1,916,296
Motor oil	929,110	162,430	227,056	97,979	169,041	73,384	86,293	113,293
Motor oil on trips	90,574	11,333	16,672	7,735	17,501	7,118	10,916	19,382
OTHER VEHICLE EXPENSES	235,281,073	26,790,442	45,292,890	22,105,427	43,112,754	18,082,968	26,542,029	53,435,577
Vehicle finance charges	37,296,857	2,858,926	6,911,220	3,608,946	7,778,817	3,204,466	5,222,168	7,711,446
Automobile finance charges	17,304,433	1,593,615	3,723,243	1,751,972	3,445,276	1,316,712	2,076,293	3,397,416
Truck finance charges	18,098,170	1,167,551	2,840,925	1,704,583	4,041,990	1,765,874	2,745,360	3,831,207
Motorcycle and plane finance charges	274,643	41,889	29,540	32,808	54,310	19,255	40,141	67,491
Other vehicle finance charges	1,619,612	66,930	317,380	119,584	237,380	102,625	360,373	415,332
Maintenance and repairs	63,956,670	8,519,431	12,523,444	6,094,603	11,115,334	4,708,555	7,315,526	13,738,836
Coolant, additives, brake and transmission fluids	312,625	68,040	83,097	35,742	48,893	18,538	26,945	31,381
Tires—purchased, replaced, installed	8,984,320	1,067,858	1,833,123	814,771	1,702,220	702,755	1,003,256	1,859,649
Parts, equipment, and accessories	5,099,393	564,687	1,079,714	728,529	939,797	374,601	740,645	671,223
Vehicle products	441,181	65,228	89,668	28,362	153,901	10,754	60,039	38,303
Miscellaneous auto repair, servicing	4,528,682	805,929	684,515	360,975	525,737	260,813	762,685	1,168,467
Body work and painting	3,308,372	352,219	472,141	295,626	444,758	258,098	498,415	987,221
Clutch and transmission repair	3,958,944	512,311	788,511	348,438	708,112	423,916	320,785	856,738
Drive shaft and rear-end repair	734,328	69,686	101,394	48,545	140,011	22,276	55,341	297,193
Brake work	4,452,717	652,438	796,533	409,075	660,331	331,482	503,321	1,099,822
Repair to steering or front-end	1,334,257	197,814	234,986	84,376	296,274	94,124	157,663	268,581
Repair to engine cooling system	1,605,004	311,525	376,000	164,484	217,101	116,708	145,020	273,658
Motor tune-up	3,888,823	556,960	752,183	268,241	615,605	263,988	372,326	1,059,097
Lube, oil change, and oil filters	5,747,043	717,827	1,109,251	570,447	1,067,308	429,345	640,948	1,211,962
Front-end alignment, wheel balance, rotation	802,502	111,740	183,825	92,289	144,456	47,779	61,421	161,172
Shock absorber replacement	310,677	58,871	67,120	24,184	44,587	8,194	32,472	74,991
Gas tank repair, replacement	769,389	44,651	170,091	45,255	59,171	281,604	29,571	148,943
Tire repair and other repair work	4,292,021	506,407	1,007,977	414,410	754,644	270,133	437,616	900,694
Vehicle air conditioning repair	1,213,492	209,780	290,427	101,091	179,598	79,836	101,908	251,045
Exhaust system repair	1,120,970	213,034	274,731	81,442	111,120	117,834	154,623	167,748
Electrical system repair	2,524,375	363,048	603,168	251,971	462,815	167,610	236,288	439,214
Motor repair, replacement	7,395,873	1,030,521	1,354,347	796,100	1,530,817	407,120	876,407	1,400,823
Auto repair service policy	864,832	46,253	170,858	88,821	260,021	21,099	97,762	187,822
Vehicle insurance	90,523,961	11,398,072	19,314,814	8,735,763	16,089,898	6,576,235	9,817,482	18,589,337
Vehicle rental, leases, licenses, other charges	43,503,586	4,013,939	6,543,544	3,666,115	8,128,706	3,593,713	4,186,785	13,395,957
Leased and rented vehicles	26,219,605	1,976,580	3,156,743	2,115,347	5,099,714	2,371,074	2,189,117	9,310,820
Rented vehicles	3,299,607	209,839	589,186	226,721	465,037	203,355	408,806	1,196,387
Auto rental	607,720	47,102	187,656	51,390	151,123	22,072	29,916	118,254
Auto rental on trips	2,129,941	114,454	295,131	147,324	249,187	157,266	225,441	941,188
Truck rental	250,295	32,695	46,996	9,513	33,197	7,067	68,814	51,801
Truck rental on trips	210,365	13,440	57,036	18,493	31,253	12,137	47,258	30,573

	total complete reporters	under $20,000	$20,000–$39,999	$40,000–$49,999	$50,000–$69,999	$70,000–$79,999	$80,000–$99,999	$100,000 or more
Leased vehicles	$22,920,972	$1,766,697	$2,567,665	$1,888,626	$4,634,676	$2,167,668	$1,780,311	$8,114,434
Car lease payments	12,716,343	988,159	1,316,175	1,049,760	2,193,370	1,058,818	1,149,519	4,960,218
Truck lease payments	8,604,495	489,665	1,229,895	642,375	2,286,294	944,671	593,621	2,417,463
Vehicle registration, state	8,381,469	961,232	1,798,974	853,536	1,477,479	652,671	970,438	1,666,866
Vehicle registration, local	725,563	78,869	200,142	74,862	165,013	40,507	77,726	88,258
Driver's license	748,937	119,054	147,041	85,087	138,761	48,547	73,304	137,175
Vehicle inspection	887,232	126,994	194,902	75,485	156,263	62,220	101,286	169,825
Parking fees	2,829,209	359,844	299,018	197,202	451,286	178,313	318,574	1,024,716
Parking fees in home city, excluding residence	2,386,080	321,270	255,285	160,838	378,225	147,894	256,186	866,198
Parking fees on trips	443,129	38,530	43,734	36,364	73,061	30,419	62,388	158,518
Tolls	1,486,187	81,946	299,371	68,727	300,580	89,771	207,339	464,249
Tolls on trips	389,564	41,651	60,367	28,540	61,394	24,171	48,087	124,946
Towing charges	505,459	129,131	121,247	47,211	71,534	26,117	26,876	82,951
Automobile service clubs	1,332,309	138,527	265,738	120,206	206,683	100,372	174,107	326,266
PUBLIC TRANSPORTATION	**38,981,722**	**4,367,108**	**6,302,845**	**2,523,088**	**6,016,454**	**2,301,019**	**4,018,274**	**13,465,294**
Airline fares	24,909,696	2,226,078	3,467,861	1,726,899	4,270,758	1,523,088	2,596,748	9,097,617
Intercity bus fares	918,397	187,849	245,110	86,865	133,483	38,459	61,836	164,979
Intracity mass transit fares	5,134,454	1,172,157	1,023,607	335,191	496,151	286,110	494,684	1,326,640
Local transportation on trips	858,015	80,361	97,773	61,526	169,875	46,601	95,275	306,192
Taxi fares and limousine service on trips	503,511	47,179	57,493	36,097	99,730	27,346	55,963	179,862
Taxi fares and limousine service	1,941,977	464,828	463,125	102,780	236,130	124,799	160,980	402,411
Intercity train fares	1,556,308	110,166	122,323	118,695	308,497	100,423	259,364	536,355
Ship fares	3,086,321	73,101	808,470	54,591	287,245	153,835	292,389	1,416,051
School bus	74,017	6,583	17,190	355	14,307	307	1,036	35,188

Note: Numbers may not add to total because of rounding and missing subcategories.
Source: Calculations by New Strategist based on the 2003 Consumer Expenditure Survey

Table 11.8 Transportation: Market shares by income, 2003

(percentage of total annual spending on transportation accounted for by before-tax income group of consumer units, 2003; complete income reporters only)

	total complete reporters	under $20,000	$20,000– $39,999	$40,000– $49,999	$50,000– $69,999	$70,000– $79,999	$80,000– $99,999	$100,000 or more
Share of total consumer units	100.0%	27.8%	24.6%	9.1%	14.3%	5.3%	7.1%	11.8%
Share of total before-tax income	100.0	5.9	14.0	7.9	16.4	7.7	12.3	35.8
Share of total spending	100.0	12.9	18.2	8.5	16.6	7.0	10.9	25.9
Share of transportation spending	100.0	10.9	19.0	9.0	18.9	7.5	11.7	22.9
VEHICLE PURCHASES	100.0	9.4	18.4	8.7	19.9	7.7	12.5	23.3
Cars and trucks, new	100.0	6.8	15.3	6.0	17.6	8.6	14.7	30.9
New cars	100.0	8.4	16.5	8.4	15.0	9.1	11.0	31.7
New trucks	100.0	5.5	14.3	4.1	19.8	8.2	17.9	30.3
Cars and trucks, used	100.0	13.1	23.0	12.1	22.5	6.7	9.2	13.4
Used cars	100.0	17.8	24.7	10.1	17.4	5.6	11.3	13.2
Used trucks	100.0	8.3	21.4	14.0	27.7	7.8	7.1	13.6
Other vehicles	100.0	6.9	13.9	11.0	30.4	4.3	22.6	20.5
GASOLINE AND MOTOR OIL	100.0	14.2	21.2	10.1	18.0	7.2	10.7	18.6
Gasoline	100.0	14.3	21.4	10.3	18.0	7.2	10.5	18.3
Diesel fuel	100.0	7.7	19.1	4.5	16.1	8.0	18.4	26.2
Gasoline on trips	100.0	12.5	18.4	8.6	19.3	7.9	12.0	21.4
Motor oil	100.0	17.5	24.4	10.5	18.2	7.9	9.3	12.2
Motor oil on trips	100.0	12.5	18.4	8.5	19.3	7.9	12.1	21.4
OTHER VEHICLE EXPENSES	100.0	11.4	19.3	9.4	18.3	7.7	11.3	22.7
Vehicle finance charges	100.0	7.7	18.5	9.7	20.9	8.6	14.0	20.7
Automobile finance charges	100.0	9.2	21.5	10.1	19.9	7.6	12.0	19.6
Truck finance charges	100.0	6.5	15.7	9.4	22.3	9.8	15.2	21.2
Motorcycle and plane finance charges	100.0	15.3	10.8	11.9	19.8	7.0	14.6	24.6
Other vehicle finance charges	100.0	4.1	19.6	7.4	14.7	6.3	22.3	25.6
Maintenance and repairs	100.0	13.3	19.6	9.5	17.4	7.4	11.4	21.5
Coolant, additives, brake and transmission fluids	100.0	21.8	26.6	11.4	15.6	5.9	8.6	10.0
Tires—purchased, replaced, installed	100.0	11.9	20.4	9.1	18.9	7.8	11.2	20.7
Parts, equipment, and accessories	100.0	11.1	21.2	14.3	18.4	7.3	14.5	13.2
Vehicle products	100.0	14.8	20.3	6.4	34.9	2.4	13.6	8.7
Miscellaneous auto repair, servicing	100.0	17.8	15.1	8.0	11.6	5.8	16.8	25.8
Body work and painting	100.0	10.6	14.3	8.9	13.4	7.8	15.1	29.8
Clutch and transmission repair	100.0	12.9	19.9	8.8	17.9	10.7	8.1	21.6
Drive shaft and rear-end repair	100.0	9.5	13.8	6.6	19.1	3.0	7.5	40.5
Brake work	100.0	14.7	17.9	9.2	14.8	7.4	11.3	24.7
Repair to steering or front-end	100.0	14.8	17.6	6.3	22.2	7.1	11.8	20.1
Repair to engine cooling system	100.0	19.4	23.4	10.2	13.5	7.3	9.0	17.1
Motor tune-up	100.0	14.3	19.3	6.9	15.8	6.8	9.6	27.2
Lube, oil change, and oil filters	100.0	12.5	19.3	9.9	18.6	7.5	11.2	21.1
Front-end alignment, wheel balance, rotation	100.0	13.9	22.9	11.5	18.0	6.0	7.7	20.1
Shock absorber replacement	100.0	18.9	21.6	7.8	14.4	2.6	10.5	24.1
Gas tank repair, replacement	100.0	5.8	22.1	5.9	7.7	36.6	3.8	19.4
Tire repair and other repair work	100.0	11.8	23.5	9.7	17.6	6.3	10.2	21.0
Vehicle air conditioning repair	100.0	17.3	23.9	8.3	14.8	6.6	8.4	20.7
Exhaust system repair	100.0	19.0	24.5	7.3	9.9	10.5	13.8	15.0
Electrical system repair	100.0	14.4	23.9	10.0	18.3	6.6	9.4	17.4
Motor repair, replacement	100.0	13.9	18.3	10.8	20.7	5.5	11.8	18.9
Auto repair service policy	100.0	5.3	19.8	10.3	30.1	2.4	11.3	21.7
Vehicle insurance	100.0	12.6	21.3	9.7	17.8	7.3	10.8	20.5
Vehicle rental, leases, licenses, other charges	100.0	9.2	15.0	8.4	18.7	8.3	9.6	30.8
Leased and rented vehicles	100.0	7.5	12.0	8.1	19.5	9.0	8.3	35.5
Rented vehicles	100.0	6.4	17.9	6.9	14.1	6.2	12.4	36.3
Auto rental	100.0	7.8	30.9	8.5	24.9	3.6	4.9	19.5
Auto rental on trips	100.0	5.4	13.9	6.9	11.7	7.4	10.6	44.2
Truck rental	100.0	13.1	18.8	3.8	13.3	2.8	27.5	20.7
Truck rental on trips	100.0	6.4	27.1	8.8	14.9	5.8	22.5	14.5

	total complete reporters	under $20,000	$20,000–$39,999	$40,000–$49,999	$50,000–$69,999	$70,000–$79,999	$80,000–$99,999	$100,000 or more
Leased vehicles	100.0%	7.7%	11.2%	8.2%	20.2%	9.5%	7.8%	35.4%
Car lease payments	100.0	7.8	10.4	8.3	17.2	8.3	9.0	39.0
Truck lease payments	100.0	5.7	14.3	7.5	26.6	11.0	6.9	28.1
Vehicle registration, state	100.0	11.5	21.5	10.2	17.6	7.8	11.6	19.9
Vehicle registration, local	100.0	10.9	27.6	10.3	22.7	5.6	10.7	12.2
Driver's license	100.0	15.9	19.6	11.4	18.5	6.5	9.8	18.3
Vehicle inspection	100.0	14.3	22.0	8.5	17.6	7.0	11.4	19.1
Parking fees	100.0	12.7	10.6	7.0	16.0	6.3	11.3	36.2
Parking fees in home city, excluding residence	100.0	13.5	10.7	6.7	15.9	6.2	10.7	36.3
Parking fees on trips	100.0	8.7	9.9	8.2	16.5	6.9	14.1	35.8
Tolls	100.0	5.5	20.1	4.6	20.2	6.0	14.0	31.2
Tolls on trips	100.0	10.7	15.5	7.3	15.8	6.2	12.3	32.1
Towing charges	100.0	25.5	24.0	9.3	14.2	5.2	5.3	16.4
Automobile service clubs	100.0	10.4	19.9	9.0	15.5	7.5	13.1	24.5
PUBLIC TRANSPORTATION	**100.0**	**11.2**	**16.2**	**6.5**	**15.4**	**5.9**	**10.3**	**34.5**
Airline fares	100.0	8.9	13.9	6.9	17.1	6.1	10.4	36.5
Intercity bus fares	100.0	20.5	26.7	9.5	14.5	4.2	6.7	18.0
Intracity mass transit fares	100.0	22.8	19.9	6.5	9.7	5.6	9.6	25.8
Local transportation on trips	100.0	9.4	11.4	7.2	19.8	5.4	11.1	35.7
Taxi fares and limousine service on trips	100.0	9.4	11.4	7.2	19.8	5.4	11.1	35.7
Taxi fares and limousine service	100.0	23.9	23.8	5.3	12.2	6.4	8.3	20.7
Intercity train fares	100.0	7.1	7.9	7.6	19.8	6.5	16.7	34.5
Ship fares	100.0	2.4	26.2	1.8	9.3	5.0	9.5	45.9
School bus	100.0	8.9	23.2	0.5	19.3	0.4	1.4	47.5

Note: Numbers may not add to total because of rounding.
Source: Calculations by New Strategist based on the 2003 Consumer Expenditure Survey

Table 11.9 Transportation: Average spending by high-income consumer units, 2003

(average annual spending on transportation, by before-tax income of high-income consumer unit (CU), 2003; complete income reporters only)

	total complete reporters	$100,000 or more	$100,000– $119,999	$120,000– $149,999	$150,000 or more
Number of consumer units (000)	97,391	11,537	4,384	3,151	4,002
Average number of persons per CU	2.5	3.1	3.1	3.1	3.1
Average before-tax income of CU	$51,128.00	$154,665.00	$108,087.00	$131,885.00	$223,634.00
Average spending of CU, total	42,741.66	93,514.86	75,601.50	86,451.46	118,674.11
Transportation, average spending	**8,041.00**	**15,525.91**	**14,177.75**	**15,784.97**	**16,799.23**
VEHICLE PURCHASES	**3,871.43**	**7,603.62**	**7,295.40**	**7,932.09**	**7,682.63**
Cars and trucks, new	**2,154.02**	**5,620.95**	**5,663.88**	**5,076.10**	**6,002.97**
New cars	988.81	2,643.58	2,457.53	2,199.11	3,197.42
New trucks	1,165.20	2,977.37	3,206.35	2,876.99	2,805.55
Cars and trucks, used	**1,649.48**	**1,865.29**	**1,508.40**	**2,652.94**	**1,636.03**
Used cars	823.82	915.97	742.35	1,239.34	851.55
Used trucks	825.66	949.31	766.05	1,413.60	784.48
Other vehicles	**67.94**	**117.38**	**123.12**	**203.05**	**43.63**
GASOLINE AND MOTOR OIL	**1,353.47**	**2,123.48**	**2,062.67**	**2,195.46**	**2,133.43**
Gasoline	1,233.75	1,909.77	1,865.18	1,971.48	1,910.03
Diesel fuel	16.32	36.11	25.79	40.40	44.04
Gasoline on trips	92.07	166.10	157.41	172.33	170.72
Motor oil	9.54	9.82	12.71	9.50	6.91
Motor oil on trips	0.93	1.68	1.59	1.74	1.72
OTHER VEHICLE EXPENSES	**2,415.84**	**4,631.67**	**4,190.95**	**4,611.54**	**5,130.38**
Vehicle finance charges	**382.96**	**668.41**	**721.06**	**675.73**	**604.94**
Automobile finance charges	177.68	294.48	313.68	275.89	288.08
Truck finance charges	185.83	332.08	354.47	353.85	290.40
Motorcycle and plane finance charges	2.82	5.85	5.69	9.83	2.88
Other vehicle finance charges	16.63	36.00	47.23	36.16	23.58
Maintenance and repairs	**656.70**	**1,190.85**	**1,052.04**	**1,220.58**	**1,319.65**
Coolant, additives, brake and transmission fluids	3.21	2.72	3.68	2.42	1.90
Tires—purchased, replaced, installed	92.25	161.19	150.19	182.83	156.20
Parts, equipment, and accessories	52.36	58.18	59.12	65.96	51.02
Vehicle products	4.53	3.32	1.31	4.32	4.72
Miscellaneous auto repair, servicing	46.50	101.28	83.55	102.12	119.90
Body work and painting	33.97	85.57	66.68	49.69	134.52
Clutch and transmission repair	40.65	74.26	57.04	74.56	92.89
Drive shaft and rear-end repair	7.54	25.76	15.66	14.22	45.91
Brake work	45.72	95.33	105.25	99.13	81.48
Repair to steering or front-end	13.70	23.28	23.36	25.09	21.75
Repair to engine cooling system	16.48	23.72	15.79	15.50	38.89
Motor tune-up	39.93	91.80	65.65	109.23	106.72
Lube, oil change, and oil filters	59.01	105.05	98.77	111.78	106.63
Front-end alignment, wheel balance, rotation	8.24	13.97	16.09	9.67	15.02
Shock absorber replacement	3.19	6.50	6.56	5.13	7.53
Gas tank repair, replacement	7.90	12.91	4.73	14.52	20.56
Tire repair and other repair work	44.07	78.07	74.06	66.24	91.77
Vehicle air conditioning repair	12.46	21.76	20.70	18.70	25.33
Exhaust system repair	11.51	14.54	14.73	15.61	13.50
Electrical system repair	25.92	38.07	35.52	40.08	39.28
Motor repair, replacement	75.94	121.42	121.30	112.72	128.40
Auto repair service policy	8.88	16.28	12.30	22.53	15.73
Vehicle insurance	**929.49**	**1,611.28**	**1,583.39**	**1,600.02**	**1,650.70**
Vehicle rental, leases, licenses, other charges	**446.69**	**1,161.13**	**834.45**	**1,115.20**	**1,555.09**
Leased and rented vehicles	269.22	807.04	540.58	752.67	1,141.77
Rented vehicles	33.88	103.70	57.58	68.67	181.81
Auto rental	6.24	10.25	10.22	3.14	15.89
Auto rental on trips	21.87	81.58	43.60	58.74	141.16
Truck rental	2.57	4.49	0.91	6.68	6.69
Truck rental on trips	2.16	2.65	2.61	0.10	4.71

	total complete reporters	$100,000 or more	$100,000– $119,999	$120,000– $149,999	$150,000 or more
Leased vehicles	$235.35	$703.34	$483.01	$684.00	$959.96
Car lease payments	130.57	429.94	267.56	406.45	626.35
Truck lease payments	88.35	209.54	151.93	236.27	251.61
Vehicle registration, state	86.06	144.48	127.17	154.53	155.52
Vehicle registration, local	7.45	7.65	3.45	14.68	6.73
Driver's license	7.69	11.89	12.19	11.27	12.07
Vehicle inspection	9.11	14.72	15.30	15.02	13.84
Parking fees	29.05	88.82	64.31	86.49	117.49
Parking fees in home city, excluding residence	24.50	75.08	53.27	75.63	98.54
Parking fees on trips	4.55	13.74	11.04	10.86	18.95
Tolls	15.26	40.24	35.46	33.37	50.78
Tolls on trips	4.00	10.83	9.02	11.22	12.52
Towing charges	5.19	7.19	6.74	5.10	9.33
Automobile service clubs	13.68	28.28	20.24	30.85	35.06
PUBLIC TRANSPORTATION	**400.26**	**1,167.14**	**628.72**	**1,045.88**	**1,852.79**
Airline fares	255.77	788.56	397.45	659.37	1,318.79
Intercity bus fares	9.43	14.30	9.53	11.48	21.74
Intracity mass transit fares	52.72	114.99	76.24	114.23	158.04
Local transportation on trips	8.81	26.54	17.47	18.92	42.49
Taxi fares and limousine service on trips	5.17	15.59	10.26	11.11	24.95
Taxi fares and limousine service	19.94	34.88	17.17	72.14	25.20
Intercity train fares	15.98	45.49	24.94	37.67	77.05
Ship fares	31.69	122.74	73.80	116.90	180.96
School bus	0.76	3.05	1.86	4.07	3.57

Note: Subcategories may not add to total because some are not shown.
Source: Bureau of Labor Statistics, unpublished tables from the 2003 Consumer Expenditure Survey; calculations by New Strategist

Table 11.10 Transportation: Indexed spending by high-income consumer units, 2003

(indexed average annual spending of consumer units (CU) on transportation, by before-tax income of high-income consumer unit, 2003; complete income reporters only; index definition: an index of 100 is the average for all consumer units; an index of 132 means that spending by consumer units in that group is 32 percent above the average for all consumer units; an index of 68 indicates spending that is 32 percent below the average for all consumer units)

	total complete reporters	$100,000 or more	$100,000–$119,999	$120,000–$149,999	$150,000 or more
Average spending of CU, total	$42,742	$93,515	$75,602	$86,451	$118,674
Average spending of CU, index	100	219	177	202	278
Transportation, spending index	100	193	176	196	209
VEHICLE PURCHASES	100	196	188	205	198
Cars and trucks, new	100	261	263	236	279
New cars	100	267	249	222	323
New trucks	100	256	275	247	241
Cars and trucks, used	100	113	91	161	99
Used cars	100	111	90	150	103
Used trucks	100	115	93	171	95
Other vehicles	100	173	181	299	64
GASOLINE AND MOTOR OIL	100	157	152	162	158
Gasoline	100	155	151	160	155
Diesel fuel	100	221	158	248	270
Gasoline on trips	100	180	171	187	185
Motor oil	100	103	133	100	72
Motor oil on trips	100	181	171	187	185
OTHER VEHICLE EXPENSES	100	192	173	191	212
Vehicle finance charges	100	175	188	176	158
Automobile finance charges	100	166	177	155	162
Truck finance charges	100	179	191	190	156
Motorcycle and plane finance charges	100	207	202	349	102
Other vehicle finance charges	100	216	284	217	142
Maintenance and repairs	100	181	160	186	201
Coolant, additives, brake and transmission fluids	100	85	115	75	59
Tires—purchased, replaced, installed	100	175	163	198	169
Parts, equipment, and accessories	100	111	113	126	97
Vehicle products	100	73	29	95	104
Miscellaneous auto repair, servicing	100	218	180	220	258
Body work and painting	100	252	196	146	396
Clutch and transmission repair	100	183	140	183	229
Drive shaft and rear-end repair	100	342	208	189	609
Brake work	100	209	230	217	178
Repair to steering or front-end	100	170	171	183	159
Repair to engine cooling system	100	144	96	94	236
Motor tune-up	100	230	164	274	267
Lube, oil change, and oil filters	100	178	167	189	181
Front-end alignment, wheel balance, rotation	100	170	195	117	182
Shock absorber replacement	100	204	206	161	236
Gas tank repair, replacement	100	163	60	184	260
Tire repair and other repair work	100	177	168	150	208
Vehicle air conditioning repair	100	175	166	150	203
Exhaust system repair	100	126	128	136	117
Electrical system repair	100	147	137	155	152
Motor repair, replacement	100	160	160	148	169
Auto repair service policy	100	183	139	254	177
Vehicle insurance	100	173	170	172	178
Vehicle rental, leases, licenses, other charges	100	260	187	250	348
Leased and rented vehicles	100	300	201	280	424
Rented vehicles	100	306	170	203	537
Auto rental	100	164	164	50	255
Auto rental on trips	100	373	199	269	645
Truck rental	100	175	35	260	260
Truck rental on trips	100	123	121	5	218

	total complete reporters	$100,000 or more	$100,000– $119,999	$120,000– $149,999	$150,000 or more
Leased vehicles	100	299	205	291	408
Car lease payments	100	329	205	311	480
Truck lease payments	100	237	172	267	285
Vehicle registration, state	100	168	148	180	181
Vehicle registration, local	100	103	46	197	90
Driver's license	100	155	159	147	157
Vehicle inspection	100	162	168	165	152
Parking fees	100	306	221	298	404
Parking fees in home city, excluding residence	100	306	217	309	402
Parking fees on trips	100	302	243	239	416
Tolls	100	264	232	219	333
Tolls on trips	100	271	226	281	313
Towing charges	100	139	130	98	180
Automobile service clubs	100	207	148	226	256
PUBLIC TRANSPORTATION	**100**	**292**	**157**	**261**	**463**
Airline fares	100	308	155	258	516
Intercity bus fares	100	152	101	122	231
Intracity mass transit fares	100	218	145	217	300
Local transportation on trips	100	301	198	215	482
Taxi fares and limousine service on trips	100	302	198	215	483
Taxi fares and limousine service	100	175	86	362	126
Intercity train fares	100	291	156	236	482
Ship fares	100	387	233	369	571
School bus	100	401	245	536	470

Source: Calculations by New Strategist based on the 2003 Consumer Expenditure Survey

Table 11.11 Transportation: Total spending by high-income consumer units, 2003

(total annual spending on transportation, by before-tax income group of high-income consumer units (CU), 2003; complete income reporters only; numbers in thousands)

	total complete reporters	$100,000 or more	$100,000–$119,999	$120,000–$149,999	$150,000 or more
Number of consumer units	97,391	11,537	4,384	3,151	4,002
Total spending of all CUs	$4,162,653,009	$1,078,880,940	$331,436,976	$272,408,550	$474,933,788
Transportation, total spending	783,121,031	179,122,424	62,155,256	49,738,440	67,230,518
VEHICLE PURCHASES	377,042,439	87,722,964	31,983,034	24,994,016	30,745,885
Cars and trucks, new	209,782,162	64,848,900	24,830,450	15,994,791	24,023,886
New cars	96,301,195	30,498,982	10,773,812	6,929,396	12,796,075
New trucks	113,479,993	34,349,918	14,056,638	9,065,395	11,227,811
Cars and trucks, used	160,644,507	21,519,851	6,612,826	8,359,414	6,547,392
Used cars	80,232,654	10,567,546	3,254,462	3,905,160	3,407,903
Used trucks	80,411,853	10,952,189	3,358,363	4,454,254	3,139,489
Other vehicles	6,616,745	1,354,213	539,758	639,811	174,607
GASOLINE AND MOTOR OIL	131,815,797	24,498,589	9,042,745	6,917,894	8,537,987
Gasoline	120,156,146	22,033,016	8,176,949	6,212,133	7,643,940
Diesel fuel	1,589,421	416,601	113,063	127,300	176,248
Gasoline on trips	8,966,789	1,916,296	690,085	543,012	683,221
Motor oil	929,110	113,293	55,721	29,935	27,654
Motor oil on trips	90,574	19,382	6,971	5,483	6,883
OTHER VEHICLE EXPENSES	235,281,073	53,435,577	18,373,125	14,530,963	20,531,781
Vehicle finance charges	37,296,857	7,711,446	3,161,127	2,129,225	2,420,970
Automobile finance charges	17,304,433	3,397,416	1,375,173	869,329	1,152,896
Truck finance charges	18,098,170	3,831,207	1,553,996	1,114,981	1,162,181
Motorcycle and plane finance charges	274,643	67,491	24,945	30,974	11,526
Other vehicle finance charges	1,619,612	415,332	207,056	113,940	94,367
Maintenance and repairs	63,956,670	13,738,836	4,612,143	3,846,048	5,281,239
Coolant, additives, brake and transmission fluids	312,625	31,381	16,133	7,625	7,604
Tires—purchased, replaced, installed	8,984,320	1,859,649	658,433	576,097	625,112
Parts, equipment, and accessories	5,099,393	671,223	259,182	207,840	204,182
Vehicle products	441,181	38,303	5,743	13,612	18,889
Miscellaneous auto repair, servicing	4,528,682	1,168,467	366,283	321,780	479,840
Body work and painting	3,308,372	987,221	292,325	156,573	538,349
Clutch and transmission repair	3,958,944	856,738	250,063	234,939	371,746
Drive shaft and rear-end repair	734,328	297,193	68,653	44,807	183,732
Brake work	4,452,717	1,099,822	461,416	312,359	326,083
Repair to steering or front-end	1,334,257	268,581	102,410	79,059	87,044
Repair to engine cooling system	1,605,004	273,658	69,223	48,841	155,638
Motor tune-up	3,888,823	1,059,097	287,810	344,184	427,093
Lube, oil change, and oil filters	5,747,043	1,211,962	433,008	352,219	426,733
Front-end alignment, wheel balance, rotation	802,502	161,172	70,539	30,470	60,110
Shock absorber replacement	310,677	74,991	28,759	16,165	30,135
Gas tank repair, replacement	769,389	148,943	20,736	45,753	82,281
Tire repair and other repair work	4,292,021	900,694	324,679	208,722	367,264
Vehicle air conditioning repair	1,213,492	251,045	90,749	58,924	101,371
Exhaust system repair	1,120,970	167,748	64,576	49,187	54,027
Electrical system repair	2,524,375	439,214	155,720	126,292	157,199
Motor repair, replacement	7,395,873	1,400,823	531,779	355,181	513,857
Auto repair service policy	864,832	187,822	53,923	70,992	62,951
Vehicle insurance	90,523,961	18,589,337	6,941,582	5,041,663	6,606,101
Vehicle rental, leases, licenses, other charges	43,503,586	13,395,957	3,658,229	3,513,995	6,223,470
Leased and rented vehicles	26,219,605	9,310,820	2,369,903	2,371,663	4,569,364
Rented vehicles	3,299,607	1,196,387	252,431	216,379	727,604
Auto rental	607,720	118,254	44,804	9,894	63,592
Auto rental on trips	2,129,941	941,188	191,142	185,090	564,922
Truck rental	250,295	51,801	3,989	21,049	26,773
Truck rental on trips	210,365	30,573	11,442	315	18,849

	total complete reporters	$100,000 or more	$100,000– $119,999	$120,000– $149,999	$150,000 or more
Leased vehicles	$22,920,972	$8,114,434	$2,117,516	$2,155,284	$3,841,760
Car lease payments	12,716,343	4,960,218	1,172,983	1,280,724	2,506,653
Truck lease payments	8,604,495	2,417,463	666,061	744,487	1,006,943
Vehicle registration, state	8,381,469	1,666,866	557,513	486,924	622,391
Vehicle registration, local	725,563	88,258	15,125	46,257	26,933
Driver's license	748,937	137,175	53,441	35,512	48,304
Vehicle inspection	887,232	169,825	67,075	47,328	55,388
Parking fees	2,829,209	1,024,716	281,935	272,530	470,195
Parking fees in home city, excluding residence	2,386,080	866,198	233,536	238,310	394,357
Parking fees on trips	443,129	158,518	48,399	34,220	75,838
Tolls	1,486,187	464,249	155,457	105,149	203,222
Tolls on trips	389,564	124,946	39,544	35,354	50,105
Towing charges	505,459	82,951	29,548	16,070	37,339
Automobile service clubs	1,332,309	326,266	88,732	97,208	140,310
PUBLIC TRANSPORTATION	**38,981,722**	**13,465,294**	**2,756,308**	**3,295,568**	**7,414,866**
Airline fares	24,909,696	9,097,617	1,742,421	2,077,675	5,277,798
Intercity bus fares	918,397	164,979	41,780	36,173	87,003
Intracity mass transit fares	5,134,454	1,326,640	334,236	359,939	632,476
Local transportation on trips	858,015	306,192	76,588	59,617	170,045
Taxi fares and limousine service on trips	503,511	179,862	44,980	35,008	99,850
Taxi fares and limousine service	1,941,977	402,411	75,273	227,313	100,850
Intercity train fares	1,556,308	536,355	109,337	118,698	308,354
Ship fares	3,086,321	1,416,051	323,539	368,352	724,202
School bus	74,017	35,188	8,154	12,825	14,287

Note: Numbers may not add to total because of rounding and missing subcategories.
Source: Calculations by New Strategist based on the 2003 Consumer Expenditure Survey

Table 11.12 Transportation: Market shares by high-income consumer units, 2003

(percentage of total annual spending on transportation accounted for by before-tax income group of high-income consumer units, 2003; complete income reporters only)

	total complete reporters	$100,000 or more	$100,000–$119,999	$120,000–$149,999	$150,000 or more
Share of total consumer units	100.0%	11.8%	4.5%	3.2%	4.1%
Share of total before-tax income	100.0	35.8	9.5	8.3	18.0
Share of total spending	100.0	25.9	8.0	6.5	11.4
Share of transportation spending	100.0	22.9	7.9	6.4	8.6
VEHICLE PURCHASES	100.0	23.3	8.5	6.6	8.2
Cars and trucks, new	100.0	30.9	11.8	7.6	11.5
New cars	100.0	31.7	11.2	7.2	13.3
New trucks	100.0	30.3	12.4	8.0	9.9
Cars and trucks, used	100.0	13.4	4.1	5.2	4.1
Used cars	100.0	13.2	4.1	4.9	4.2
Used trucks	100.0	13.6	4.2	5.5	3.9
Other vehicles	100.0	20.5	8.2	9.7	2.6
GASOLINE AND MOTOR OIL	100.0	18.6	6.9	5.2	6.5
Gasoline	100.0	18.3	6.8	5.2	6.4
Diesel fuel	100.0	26.2	7.1	8.0	11.1
Gasoline on trips	100.0	21.4	7.7	6.1	7.6
Motor oil	100.0	12.2	6.0	3.2	3.0
Motor oil on trips	100.0	21.4	7.7	6.1	7.6
OTHER VEHICLE EXPENSES	100.0	22.7	7.8	6.2	8.7
Vehicle finance charges	100.0	20.7	8.5	5.7	6.5
Automobile finance charges	100.0	19.6	7.9	5.0	6.7
Truck finance charges	100.0	21.2	8.6	6.2	6.4
Motorcycle and plane finance charges	100.0	24.6	9.1	11.3	4.2
Other vehicle finance charges	100.0	25.6	12.8	7.0	5.8
Maintenance and repairs	100.0	21.5	7.2	6.0	8.3
Coolant, additives, brake and transmission fluids	100.0	10.0	5.2	2.4	2.4
Tires—purchased, replaced, installed	100.0	20.7	7.3	6.4	7.0
Parts, equipment, and accessories	100.0	13.2	5.1	4.1	4.0
Vehicle products	100.0	8.7	1.3	3.1	4.3
Miscellaneous auto repair, servicing	100.0	25.8	8.1	7.1	10.6
Body work and painting	100.0	29.8	8.8	4.7	16.3
Clutch and transmission repair	100.0	21.6	6.3	5.9	9.4
Drive shaft and rear-end repair	100.0	40.5	9.3	6.1	25.0
Brake work	100.0	24.7	10.4	7.0	7.3
Repair to steering or front-end	100.0	20.1	7.7	5.9	6.5
Repair to engine cooling system	100.0	17.1	4.3	3.0	9.7
Motor tune-up	100.0	27.2	7.4	8.9	11.0
Lube, oil change, and oil filters	100.0	21.1	7.5	6.1	7.4
Front-end alignment, wheel balance, rotation	100.0	20.1	8.8	3.8	7.5
Shock absorber replacement	100.0	24.1	9.3	5.2	9.7
Gas tank repair, replacement	100.0	19.4	2.7	5.9	10.7
Tire repair and other repair work	100.0	21.0	7.6	4.9	8.6
Vehicle air conditioning repair	100.0	20.7	7.5	4.9	8.4
Exhaust system repair	100.0	15.0	5.8	4.4	4.8
Electrical system repair	100.0	17.4	6.2	5.0	6.2
Motor repair, replacement	100.0	18.9	7.2	4.8	6.9
Auto repair service policy	100.0	21.7	6.2	8.2	7.3
Vehicle insurance	100.0	20.5	7.7	5.6	7.3
Vehicle rental, leases, licenses, other charges	100.0	30.8	8.4	8.1	14.3
Leased and rented vehicles	100.0	35.5	9.0	9.0	17.4
Rented vehicles	100.0	36.3	7.7	6.6	22.1
Auto rental	100.0	19.5	7.4	1.6	10.5
Auto rental on trips	100.0	44.2	9.0	8.7	26.5
Truck rental	100.0	20.7	1.6	8.4	10.7
Truck rental on trips	100.0	14.5	5.4	0.1	9.0

	total complete reporters	$100,000 or more	$100,000– $119,999	$120,000– $149,999	$150,000 or more
Leased vehicles	100.0%	35.4%	9.2%	9.4%	16.8%
Car lease payments	100.0	39.0	9.2	10.1	19.7
Truck lease payments	100.0	28.1	7.7	8.7	11.7
Vehicle registration, state	100.0	19.9	6.7	5.8	7.4
Vehicle registration, local	100.0	12.2	2.1	6.4	3.7
Driver's license	100.0	18.3	7.1	4.7	6.4
Vehicle inspection	100.0	19.1	7.6	5.3	6.2
Parking fees	100.0	36.2	10.0	9.6	16.6
Parking fees in home city, excluding residence	100.0	36.3	9.8	10.0	16.5
Parking fees on trips	100.0	35.8	10.9	7.7	17.1
Tolls	100.0	31.2	10.5	7.1	13.7
Tolls on trips	100.0	32.1	10.2	9.1	12.9
Towing charges	100.0	16.4	5.8	3.2	7.4
Automobile service clubs	100.0	24.5	6.7	7.3	10.5
PUBLIC TRANSPORTATION	**100.0**	**34.5**	**7.1**	**8.5**	**19.0**
Airline fares	100.0	36.5	7.0	8.3	21.2
Intercity bus fares	100.0	18.0	4.5	3.9	9.5
Intracity mass transit fares	100.0	25.8	6.5	7.0	12.3
Local transportation on trips	100.0	35.7	8.9	6.9	19.8
Taxi fares and limousine service on trips	100.0	35.7	8.9	7.0	19.8
Taxi fares and limousine service	100.0	20.7	3.9	11.7	5.2
Intercity train fares	100.0	34.5	7.0	7.6	19.8
Ship fares	100.0	45.9	10.5	11.9	23.5
School bus	100.0	47.5	11.0	17.3	19.3

Note: Numbers may not add to total because of rounding.
Source: Calculations by New Strategist based on the 2003 Consumer Expenditure Survey

Table 11.13 Transportation: Average spending by household type, 2003

(average annual spending of consumer units (CU) on transportation, by type of consumer unit, 2003)

	total married couples	married couples, no children	married couples with children total	oldest child under 6	oldest child 6 to 17	oldest child 18 or older	single parent, at least one child <18	single person
Number of consumer units (000)	58,448	25,132	28,584	5,496	15,047	8,041	6,999	33,929
Average number of persons per CU	3.2	2.0	3.9	3.5	4.1	4.0	2.9	1.0
Average before-tax income of CU	$69,472.00	$62,930.00	$75,557.00	$66,317.00	$77,508.00	$78,307.00	$29,154.00	$27,131.00
Average spending of CU, total	53,030.03	47,895.65	57,702.32	51,503.24	59,183.18	59,180.36	30,534.75	23,657.35
Transportation, average spending	**10,627.27**	**9,579.85**	**11,546.19**	**9,832.30**	**11,525.92**	**12,754.96**	**4,592.43**	**3,839.22**
VEHICLE PURCHASES	**5,308.15**	**4,932.61**	**5,712.93**	**4,953.03**	**5,849.39**	**5,976.93**	**1,734.41**	**1,691.66**
Cars and trucks, new	**3,019.94**	**3,248.96**	**2,996.73**	**2,499.07**	**3,188.14**	**2,978.67**	**449.52**	**1,027.27**
New cars	1,320.20	1,589.97	1,164.27	705.02	1,102.80	1,593.14	247.02	542.90
New trucks	1,699.74	1,658.99	1,832.47	1,794.05	2,085.35	1,385.53	202.50	484.37
Cars and trucks, used	**2,193.50**	**1,604.36**	**2,607.10**	**2,352.97**	**2,552.74**	**2,882.51**	**1,267.59**	**619.79**
Used cars	990.27	808.90	1,049.09	651.95	881.38	1,634.35	891.86	376.98
Used trucks	1,203.23	795.46	1,558.01	1,701.02	1,671.37	1,248.16	375.73	242.81
Other vehicles	**94.71**	**79.28**	**109.09**	**100.99**	**108.50**	**115.75**	**17.30**	**44.60**
GASOLINE AND MOTOR OIL	**1,740.49**	**1,462.55**	**1,949.06**	**1,612.96**	**1,926.89**	**2,220.48**	**992.68**	**673.86**
Gasoline	1,588.19	1,301.81	1,803.21	1,495.57	1,772.86	2,070.24	936.94	613.67
Diesel fuel	22.20	21.02	22.01	14.79	24.54	22.21	3.22	7.35
Gasoline on trips	115.78	129.26	106.90	90.99	114.40	103.76	45.98	48.22
Motor oil	11.94	9.15	13.49	10.70	12.18	17.84	6.07	4.13
Motor oil on trips	1.17	1.31	1.08	0.92	1.16	1.05	0.46	0.49
OTHER VEHICLE EXPENSES	**3,077.95**	**2,638.09**	**3,417.95**	**2,924.54**	**3,261.06**	**4,048.80**	**1,631.71**	**1,217.37**
Vehicle finance charges	**519.66**	**399.29**	**612.96**	**603.23**	**596.67**	**650.07**	**227.05**	**143.93**
Automobile finance charges	221.21	181.44	247.07	231.45	207.00	332.72	134.37	86.24
Truck finance charges	269.38	189.74	334.12	350.71	357.18	279.65	87.14	52.81
Motorcycle and plane finance charges	3.28	1.54	4.34	5.25	3.56	5.19	2.94	1.48
Other vehicle finance charges	25.78	26.57	27.42	15.82	28.94	32.52	2.60	3.40
Maintenance and repairs	**793.50**	**734.09**	**833.39**	**652.27**	**809.19**	**1,003.39**	**475.85**	**362.36**
Coolant, additives, brake and transmission fluids	3.64	2.44	4.18	3.11	4.25	4.79	2.71	1.73
Tires—purchased, replaced, installed	113.85	98.20	125.05	106.52	125.32	137.22	70.05	50.55
Parts, equipment, and accessories	61.93	44.41	78.10	51.40	76.46	99.43	38.12	25.01
Vehicle products	5.47	3.33	6.44	0.37	9.92	3.82	1.86	1.85
Miscellaneous auto repair, servicing	58.67	68.96	40.34	37.31	38.44	46.45	13.74	15.31
Body work and painting	40.34	34.02	45.85	23.08	41.44	69.66	24.83	19.32
Clutch and transmission repair	48.63	47.36	48.82	29.06	49.70	60.69	43.17	15.80
Drive shaft and rear-end repair	9.72	7.16	11.61	2.22	9.29	22.37	17.27	4.26
Brake work	55.65	46.12	62.33	56.02	58.15	74.47	36.28	25.19
Repair to steering or front-end	16.17	11.05	20.24	14.19	21.85	21.34	12.83	7.25
Repair to engine cooling system	19.89	19.84	20.33	22.39	19.25	20.94	12.07	10.38
Motor tune-up	47.41	45.10	51.86	48.39	50.68	56.45	25.96	26.11
Lube, oil change, and oil filters	71.57	70.38	74.71	64.18	72.24	86.52	38.97	34.02
Front-end alignment, wheel balance, rotation	10.59	8.28	12.44	9.04	12.56	14.54	6.04	4.28
Shock absorber replacement	3.89	3.79	3.91	1.87	3.47	6.14	2.98	2.04
Gas tank repair, replacement	8.39	13.59	3.98	6.49	4.71	0.65	1.10	8.69
Tire repair and other repair work	56.97	51.07	60.84	48.42	63.72	63.95	28.53	28.44
Vehicle air conditioning repair	15.06	17.15	13.39	14.06	12.13	15.28	7.94	8.78
Exhaust system repair	12.63	13.87	11.52	12.02	8.20	17.39	15.30	6.59
Electrical system repair	31.67	34.11	32.10	29.91	31.13	35.44	27.97	14.93
Motor repair, replacement	85.51	80.47	87.42	45.16	88.30	114.67	45.94	48.73
Auto repair service policy	12.63	13.39	11.58	27.07	5.49	12.38	2.20	3.11
Vehicle insurance	**1,172.96**	**979.81**	**1,308.92**	**1,006.45**	**1,174.89**	**1,766.42**	**612.00**	**492.90**
Vehicle rental, leases, licenses, other charges	**591.83**	**524.90**	**662.68**	**662.58**	**680.30**	**628.91**	**316.80**	**218.17**
Leased and rented vehicles	371.43	313.11	426.98	461.88	447.45	364.84	230.85	118.05
Rented vehicles	43.42	51.69	37.07	36.52	39.80	32.36	26.30	20.10
Auto rental	5.18	4.50	5.77	7.44	7.36	1.67	7.53	5.98
Auto rental on trips	30.44	37.76	24.93	20.94	25.83	25.99	12.75	11.81
Truck rental	3.59	4.85	2.69	2.26	3.58	1.30	0.85	0.82
Truck rental on trips	3.17	2.39	3.50	5.88	2.71	3.34	5.17	0.35

	total married couples	married couples, no children	married couples with children				single parent, at least one child <18	single person
			total	oldest child under 6	oldest child 6 to 17	oldest child 18 or older		
Leased vehicles	$328.02	$261.42	$389.91	$425.36	$407.65	$332.48	$204.54	$97.95
Car lease payments	178.07	159.44	198.93	201.76	189.91	213.88	119.14	64.33
Truck lease payments	122.83	78.06	167.33	166.60	197.81	110.80	68.53	30.53
Vehicle registration, state	110.82	105.50	118.43	107.35	112.74	136.65	44.70	43.48
Vehicle registration, local	9.78	8.68	11.06	8.23	11.26	12.62	5.01	2.88
Driver's license	9.09	8.05	10.10	8.56	9.03	13.14	4.57	4.49
Vehicle inspection	10.87	9.64	12.15	7.51	12.24	15.16	4.24	5.16
Parking fees	33.20	33.24	34.69	33.43	34.07	36.71	13.30	24.58
Parking fees in home city, excluding residence	26.89	25.16	29.52	27.92	28.92	31.74	11.26	21.74
Parking fees on trips	6.31	8.08	5.17	5.51	5.15	4.97	2.04	2.84
Tolls	19.29	17.88	22.12	12.15	30.40	12.55	3.73	3.81
Tolls on trips	5.24	5.40	5.35	5.32	5.27	5.52	1.31	2.14
Towing charges	4.84	3.27	6.31	5.83	5.06	8.98	4.78	4.24
Automobile service clubs	17.27	20.12	15.49	12.52	12.76	22.75	4.33	9.34
PUBLIC TRANSPORTATION	**500.69**	**546.60**	**466.25**	**341.78**	**488.59**	**508.75**	**233.62**	**256.33**
Airline fares	347.08	389.30	318.29	254.60	341.45	318.47	108.55	160.72
Intercity bus fares	9.72	11.79	7.55	3.51	7.07	11.19	6.56	8.02
Intracity mass transit fares	46.45	30.59	54.96	53.50	46.83	71.18	59.63	40.17
Local transportation on trips	11.25	14.18	9.63	5.71	9.30	12.93	3.95	5.84
Taxi fares and limousine service on trips	6.61	8.33	5.66	3.35	5.46	7.60	2.32	3.43
Taxi fares and limousine service	13.33	16.55	11.50	2.55	18.98	3.23	20.62	18.81
Intercity train fares	22.73	29.11	18.33	9.09	16.95	27.23	5.22	8.72
Ship fares	42.46	46.73	33.17	9.46	39.96	54.44	24.79	10.62
School bus	1.05	0.04	2.05	–	2.58	2.47	1.99	–

Note: Average spending figures for total consumer units can be found on Average Spending by Age and Average Spending by Region tables. Subcategories may not add to total because some are not shown. (–) means sample is too small to make a reliable estimate.
Source: Bureau of Labor Statistics, unpublished tables from the 2003 Consumer Expenditure Survey

Table 11.14 Transportation: Indexed spending by household type, 2003

(indexed average annual spending of consumer units (CU) on transportation, by type of consumer unit, 2003; index definition: an index of 100 is the average for all consumer units; an index of 132 means that spending by consumer units in that group is 32 percent above the average for all consumer units; an index of 68 indicates spending that is 32 percent below the average for all consumer units)

	total married couples	married couples, no children	married couples with children	oldest child under 6	oldest child 6 to 17	oldest child 18 or older	single parent, at least one child <18	single person
			total					
Average spending of CU, total	$53,030	$47,896	$57,702	$51,503	$59,183	$59,180	$30,535	$23,657
Average spending of CU, index	130	117	141	126	145	145	75	58
Transportation, spending index	**137**	**123**	**148**	**126**	**148**	**164**	**59**	**49**
VEHICLE PURCHASES	**142**	**132**	**153**	**133**	**157**	**160**	**46**	**45**
Cars and trucks, new	**147**	**158**	**146**	**122**	**155**	**145**	**22**	**50**
New cars	140	168	123	75	117	169	26	57
New trucks	153	150	165	162	188	125	18	44
Cars and trucks, used	**136**	**100**	**162**	**146**	**158**	**179**	**79**	**38**
Used cars	121	99	128	80	108	200	109	46
Used trucks	151	100	196	214	210	157	47	31
Other vehicles	**140**	**117**	**161**	**149**	**160**	**171**	**25**	**66**
GASOLINE AND MOTOR OIL	**131**	**110**	**146**	**121**	**145**	**167**	**74**	**51**
Gasoline	130	107	148	123	145	170	77	50
Diesel fuel	151	143	149	100	167	151	22	50
Gasoline on trips	133	149	123	105	132	119	53	55
Motor oil	133	102	151	119	136	199	68	46
Motor oil on trips	133	149	123	105	132	119	52	56
OTHER VEHICLE EXPENSES	**132**	**113**	**147**	**125**	**140**	**174**	**70**	**52**
Vehicle finance charges	**140**	**108**	**165**	**153**	**161**	**175**	**61**	**39**
Automobile finance charges	127	104	142	133	119	191	77	49
Truck finance charges	151	107	188	197	201	157	49	30
Motorcycle and plane finance charges	118	56	157	190	129	187	106	53
Other vehicle finance charges	168	173	179	103	189	212	17	22
Maintenance and repairs	**128**	**119**	**135**	**105**	**131**	**162**	**77**	**59**
Coolant, additives, brake and transmission fluids	123	83	142	105	144	162	92	59
Tires—purchased, replaced, installed	129	112	142	121	142	156	80	57
Parts, equipment, and accessories	130	93	164	108	161	209	80	53
Vehicle products	130	79	153	9	236	91	44	44
Miscellaneous auto repair, servicing	146	172	101	93	96	116	34	38
Body work and painting	128	108	146	73	132	221	79	61
Clutch and transmission repair	129	125	129	77	132	161	114	42
Drive shaft and rear-end repair	126	93	151	29	121	291	224	55
Brake work	126	104	141	126	131	168	82	57
Repair to steering or front-end	124	85	155	109	168	164	98	56
Repair to engine cooling system	125	125	128	141	121	132	76	65
Motor tune-up	125	118	136	127	133	148	68	69
Lube, oil change, and oil filters	128	126	134	115	129	155	70	61
Front-end alignment, wheel balance, rotation	133	104	157	114	158	183	76	54
Shock absorber replacement	127	124	128	61	113	201	97	67
Gas tank repair, replacement	103	167	49	80	58	8	13	106
Tire repair and other repair work	129	116	138	110	144	145	65	64
Vehicle air conditioning repair	124	141	110	115	100	125	65	72
Exhaust system repair	116	127	106	110	75	160	140	60
Electrical system repair	126	136	128	119	124	141	111	59
Motor repair, replacement	122	114	124	64	125	163	65	69
Auto repair service policy	156	165	143	334	68	153	27	38
Vehicle insurance	**130**	**108**	**145**	**111**	**130**	**195**	**68**	**54**
Vehicle rental, leases, licenses, other charges	**136**	**120**	**152**	**152**	**156**	**144**	**73**	**50**
Leased and rented vehicles	138	116	158	171	166	135	85	44
Rented vehicles	132	157	113	111	121	98	80	61
Auto rental	93	80	103	133	131	30	134	107
Auto rental on trips	139	172	114	95	118	118	58	54
Truck rental	162	218	121	102	161	59	38	37
Truck rental on trips	138	104	153	257	118	146	226	15

	total married couples	married couples, no children	married couples with children				single parent, at least one child <18	single person
			total	oldest child under 6	oldest child 6 to 17	oldest child 18 or older		
Leased vehicles	138	110	164	179	172	140	86	41
Car lease payments	135	120	150	152	144	162	90	49
Truck lease payments	143	91	194	193	230	129	80	35
Vehicle registration, state	136	130	146	132	139	168	55	54
Vehicle registration, local	140	125	159	118	162	181	72	41
Driver's license	127	112	141	119	126	183	64	63
Vehicle inspection	130	115	145	90	146	181	51	62
Parking fees	118	118	123	119	121	131	47	87
Parking fees in home city, excluding residence	114	107	125	118	122	134	48	92
Parking fees on trips	140	179	115	122	114	110	45	63
Tolls	148	138	170	93	234	97	29	29
Tolls on trips	140	144	143	142	141	147	35	57
Towing charges	104	70	135	125	108	192	102	91
Automobile service clubs	135	157	121	96	99	177	34	73
PUBLIC TRANSPORTATION	**130**	**142**	**121**	**89**	**127**	**132**	**61**	**67**
Airline fares	137	154	126	101	135	126	43	64
Intercity bus fares	108	132	84	39	79	125	73	90
Intracity mass transit fares	95	63	112	109	96	145	122	82
Local transportation on trips	135	170	116	69	112	155	47	70
Taxi fares and limousine service on trips	135	170	116	69	112	155	47	70
Taxi fares and limousine service	80	99	70	15	114	19	124	113
Intercity train fares	141	181	114	57	105	169	32	54
Ship fares	152	167	137	34	143	195	89	38
School bus	150	6	293	–	369	353	284	–

Note: Spending index for total consumer units is 100. (–) means sample is too small to make a reliable estimate.
Source: Calculations by New Strategist based on the 2003 Consumer Expenditure Survey

Table 11.15 Transportation: Total spending by household type, 2003

(total annual spending on transportation, by consumer unit (CU) type, 2003; numbers in thousands)

	total married couples	married couples, no children	married couples with children total	oldest child under 6	oldest child 6 to 17	oldest child 18 or older	single parent, at least one child <18	single person
Number of consumer units	58,448	25,132	28,584	5,496	15,047	8,041	6,999	33,929
Total spending of all CUs	$3,099,499,193	$1,203,713,476	$1,649,363,115	$283,061,807	$890,529,309	$475,869,275	$213,712,715	$802,670,228
Transportation, total spending	621,142,677	240,760,790	330,036,295	54,038,321	173,430,518	102,562,633	32,142,418	130,260,895
VEHICLE PURCHASES	310,250,751	123,966,355	163,298,391	27,221,853	88,015,771	48,060,494	12,139,136	57,396,332
Cars and trucks, new	176,509,453	81,652,863	85,658,530	13,734,889	47,971,943	23,951,485	3,146,190	34,854,244
New cars	77,163,050	39,959,126	33,279,494	3,874,790	16,593,832	12,810,439	1,728,893	18,420,054
New trucks	99,346,404	41,693,737	52,379,322	9,860,099	31,378,261	11,141,047	1,417,298	16,434,190
Cars and trucks, used	128,205,688	40,320,776	74,521,346	12,931,923	38,411,079	23,178,263	8,871,862	21,028,855
Used cars	57,879,301	20,329,275	29,987,189	3,583,117	13,262,125	13,141,808	6,242,128	12,790,554
Used trucks	70,326,387	19,991,501	44,534,158	9,348,806	25,149,104	10,036,455	2,629,734	8,238,300
Other vehicles	5,535,610	1,992,465	3,118,229	555,041	1,632,600	930,746	121,083	1,513,233
GASOLINE AND MOTOR OIL	101,728,160	36,756,807	55,711,931	8,864,828	28,993,914	17,854,880	6,947,767	22,863,396
Gasoline	92,826,529	32,717,089	51,542,955	8,219,653	26,676,224	16,646,800	6,557,643	20,821,209
Diesel fuel	1,297,546	528,275	629,134	81,286	369,253	178,591	22,537	249,378
Gasoline on trips	6,767,109	3,248,562	3,055,630	500,081	1,721,377	834,334	321,814	1,636,056
Motor oil	697,869	229,958	385,598	58,807	183,272	143,451	42,484	140,127
Motor oil on trips	68,384	32,923	30,871	5,056	17,455	8,443	3,220	16,625
OTHER VEHICLE EXPENSES	179,900,022	66,300,478	97,698,683	16,073,272	49,069,170	32,556,401	11,420,338	41,304,147
Vehicle finance charges	30,373,088	10,034,956	17,520,849	3,315,352	8,978,093	5,227,213	1,589,123	4,883,401
Automobile finance charges	12,929,282	4,559,950	7,062,249	1,272,049	3,114,729	2,675,402	940,456	2,926,037
Truck finance charges	15,744,722	4,768,546	9,550,486	1,927,502	5,374,487	2,248,666	609,893	1,791,790
Motorcycle and plane finance charges	191,709	38,703	124,055	28,854	53,567	41,733	20,577	50,215
Other vehicle finance charges	1,506,789	667,757	783,773	86,947	435,460	261,493	18,197	115,359
Maintenance and repairs	46,378,488	18,449,150	23,821,620	3,584,876	12,175,882	8,068,259	3,330,474	12,294,512
Coolant, additives, brake and transmission fluids	212,751	61,322	119,481	17,093	63,950	38,516	18,967	58,697
Tires—purchased, replaced, installed	6,654,305	2,467,962	3,574,429	585,434	1,885,690	1,103,386	490,280	1,715,111
Parts, equipment, and accessories	3,619,685	1,116,112	2,232,410	282,494	1,150,494	799,517	266,802	848,564
Vehicle products	319,711	83,690	184,081	2,034	149,266	30,717	13,018	62,769
Miscellaneous auto repair, servicing	3,429,144	1,733,103	1,153,079	205,056	578,407	373,504	96,166	519,453
Body work and painting	2,357,792	854,991	1,310,576	126,848	623,548	560,136	173,785	655,508
Clutch and transmission repair	2,842,326	1,190,252	1,395,471	159,714	747,836	488,008	302,147	536,078
Drive shaft and rear-end repair	568,115	179,945	331,860	12,201	139,787	179,877	120,873	144,538
Brake work	3,252,631	1,159,088	1,781,641	307,886	874,983	598,813	253,924	854,672
Repair to steering or front-end	945,104	277,709	578,540	77,988	328,777	171,595	89,797	245,985
Repair to engine cooling system	1,162,531	498,619	581,113	123,055	289,655	168,379	84,478	352,183
Motor tune-up	2,771,020	1,133,453	1,482,366	265,951	762,582	453,914	181,694	885,886
Lube, oil change, and oil filters	4,183,123	1,768,790	2,135,511	352,733	1,086,995	695,707	272,751	1,154,265
Front-end alignment, wheel balance, rotation	618,964	208,093	355,585	49,684	188,990	116,916	42,274	145,216
Shock absorber replacement	227,363	95,250	111,763	10,278	52,213	49,372	20,857	69,215
Gas tank repair, replacement	490,379	341,544	113,764	35,669	70,871	5,227	7,699	294,843
Tire repair and other repair work	3,329,783	1,283,491	1,739,051	266,116	958,795	514,222	199,681	964,941
Vehicle air conditioning repair	880,227	431,014	382,740	77,274	182,520	122,866	55,572	297,897
Exhaust system repair	738,198	348,581	329,288	66,062	123,385	139,833	107,085	223,592
Electrical system repair	1,851,048	857,253	917,546	164,385	468,413	284,973	195,762	506,560
Motor repair, replacement	4,997,888	2,022,372	2,498,813	248,199	1,328,650	922,061	321,534	1,653,360
Auto repair service policy	738,198	336,517	331,003	148,777	82,608	99,548	15,398	105,519
Vehicle insurance	68,557,166	24,624,585	37,414,169	5,531,449	17,678,570	14,203,783	4,283,388	16,723,604
Vehicle rental, leases, licenses, other charges	34,591,280	13,191,787	18,942,045	3,641,540	10,236,474	5,057,065	2,217,283	7,402,290
Leased and rented vehicles	21,709,341	7,869,081	12,204,796	2,538,492	6,732,780	2,933,678	1,615,719	4,005,318
Rented vehicles	2,537,812	1,299,073	1,059,609	200,714	598,871	260,207	184,074	681,973
Auto rental	302,761	113,094	164,930	40,890	110,746	13,428	52,702	202,895
Auto rental on trips	1,779,157	948,984	712,599	115,086	388,664	208,986	89,237	400,701
Truck rental	209,828	121,890	76,891	12,421	53,868	10,453	5,949	27,822
Truck rental on trips	185,280	60,065	100,044	32,316	40,777	26,857	36,185	11,875

	total married couples	married couples, no children	married couples with children				single parent, at least one child <18	single person
			total	oldest child under 6	oldest child 6 to 17	oldest child 18 or older		
Leased vehicles	$19,172,113	$6,570,007	$11,145,187	$2,337,779	$6,133,910	$2,673,472	$1,431,575	$3,323,346
Car lease payments	10,407,835	4,007,046	5,686,215	1,108,873	2,857,576	1,719,809	833,861	2,182,653
Truck lease payments	7,179,168	1,961,804	4,782,961	915,634	2,976,447	890,943	479,641	1,035,852
Vehicle registration, state	6,477,207	2,651,426	3,385,203	589,996	1,696,399	1,098,803	312,855	1,475,233
Vehicle registration, local	571,621	218,146	316,139	45,232	169,429	101,477	35,065	97,716
Driver's license	531,292	202,313	288,698	47,046	135,874	105,659	31,985	152,341
Vehicle inspection	635,330	242,272	347,296	41,275	184,175	121,902	29,676	175,074
Parking fees	1,940,474	835,388	991,579	183,731	512,651	295,185	93,087	833,975
Parking fees in home city, excluding residence	1,571,667	632,321	843,800	153,448	435,159	255,221	78,809	737,616
Parking fees on trips	368,807	203,067	147,779	30,283	77,492	39,964	14,278	96,358
Tolls	1,127,462	449,360	632,278	66,776	457,429	100,915	26,106	129,269
Tolls on trips	306,268	135,713	152,924	29,239	79,298	44,386	9,169	72,608
Towing charges	282,888	82,182	180,365	32,042	76,138	72,208	33,455	143,859
Automobile service clubs	1,009,397	505,656	442,766	67,711	192,000	182,933	30,306	316,897
PUBLIC TRANSPORTATION	**29,264,329**	**13,737,151**	**13,327,290**	**1,878,423**	**7,351,814**	**4,090,859**	**1,635,106**	**8,697,021**
Airline fares	20,286,132	9,783,888	9,098,001	1,399,282	5,137,798	2,560,817	759,741	5,453,069
Intercity bus fares	568,115	296,306	215,809	19,291	106,382	89,979	45,913	272,111
Intracity mass transit fares	2,714,910	768,788	1,570,977	294,036	704,651	572,358	417,350	1,362,928
Local transportation on trips	657,540	356,372	275,264	31,382	139,937	103,970	27,646	198,145
Taxi fares and limousine service on trips	386,341	209,350	161,785	18,412	82,157	61,112	16,238	116,376
Taxi fares and limousine service	779,112	415,935	331,574	14,015	285,592	25,972	144,319	638,204
Intercity train fares	1,328,523	731,593	523,945	49,959	255,047	218,956	36,535	295,861
Ship fares	2,481,702	1,174,418	1,091,051	51,992	601,278	437,752	173,505	360,326
School bus	61,370	1,005	58,597	–	38,821	19,861	13,928	–

Note: Total spending figures for total consumer units can be found on Total Spending by Age and Total Spending by Region tables. Spending by type of consumer unit will not add to total because not all types of consumer units are shown. Numbers may not add to category total because of rounding and missing subcategories. (–) means sample is too small to make a reliable estimate.
Source: Calculations by New Strategist based on the 2003 Consumer Expenditure Survey

Table 11.16 Transportation: Market shares by household type, 2003

(percentage of total annual spending on transportation accounted for by types of consumer units, 2003)

	total married couples	married couples, no children	married couples with children total	oldest child under 6	oldest child 6 to 17	oldest child 18 or older	single parent, at least one child <18	single person
Share of total consumer units	50.7%	21.8%	24.8%	4.8%	13.0%	7.0%	6.1%	29.4%
Share of total before-tax income	68.8	26.8	36.6	6.2	19.8	10.7	3.5	15.6
Share of total spending	65.8	25.6	35.0	6.0	18.9	10.1	4.5	17.0
Share of transportation spending	69.2	26.8	36.8	6.0	19.3	11.4	3.6	14.5
VEHICLE PURCHASES	**72.1**	**28.8**	**37.9**	**6.3**	**20.4**	**11.2**	**2.8**	**13.3**
Cars and trucks, new	**74.6**	**34.5**	**36.2**	**5.8**	**20.3**	**10.1**	**1.3**	**14.7**
New cars	70.8	36.7	30.5	3.6	15.2	11.8	1.6	16.9
New trucks	77.8	32.6	41.0	7.7	24.6	8.7	1.1	12.9
Cars and trucks, used	**69.0**	**21.7**	**40.1**	**7.0**	**20.7**	**12.5**	**4.8**	**11.3**
Used cars	61.5	21.6	31.8	3.8	14.1	14.0	6.6	13.6
Used trucks	76.7	21.8	48.6	10.2	27.4	10.9	2.9	9.0
Other vehicles	**70.7**	**25.5**	**39.8**	**7.1**	**20.9**	**11.9**	**1.5**	**19.3**
GASOLINE AND MOTOR OIL	**66.2**	**23.9**	**36.2**	**5.8**	**18.9**	**11.6**	**4.5**	**14.9**
Gasoline	65.9	23.2	36.6	5.8	18.9	11.8	4.7	14.8
Diesel fuel	76.4	31.1	37.0	4.8	21.7	10.5	1.3	14.7
Gasoline on trips	67.5	32.4	30.5	5.0	17.2	8.3	3.2	16.3
Motor oil	67.5	22.2	37.3	5.7	17.7	13.9	4.1	13.6
Motor oil on trips	67.4	32.4	30.4	5.0	17.2	8.3	3.2	16.4
OTHER VEHICLE EXPENSES	**66.9**	**24.7**	**36.3**	**6.0**	**18.2**	**12.1**	**4.2**	**15.4**
Vehicle finance charges	**71.0**	**23.5**	**41.0**	**7.8**	**21.0**	**12.2**	**3.7**	**11.4**
Automobile finance charges	64.2	22.7	35.1	6.3	15.5	13.3	4.7	14.5
Truck finance charges	76.7	23.2	46.5	9.4	26.2	11.0	3.0	8.7
Motorcycle and plane finance charges	60.0	12.1	38.8	9.0	16.8	13.1	6.4	15.7
Other vehicle finance charges	85.1	37.7	44.3	4.9	24.6	14.8	1.0	6.5
Maintenance and repairs	**65.0**	**25.8**	**33.4**	**5.0**	**17.1**	**11.3**	**4.7**	**17.2**
Coolant, additives, brake and transmission fluids	62.5	18.0	35.1	5.0	18.8	11.3	5.6	17.2
Tires—purchased, replaced, installed	65.6	24.3	35.2	5.8	18.6	10.9	4.8	16.9
Parts, equipment, and accessories	65.9	20.3	40.7	5.1	21.0	14.6	4.9	15.5
Vehicle products	66.0	17.3	38.0	0.4	30.8	6.3	2.7	13.0
Miscellaneous auto repair, servicing	74.2	37.5	25.0	4.4	12.5	8.1	2.1	11.2
Body work and painting	64.9	23.5	36.1	3.5	17.2	15.4	4.8	18.0
Clutch and transmission repair	65.2	27.3	32.0	3.7	17.2	11.2	6.9	12.3
Drive shaft and rear-end repair	64.0	20.3	37.4	1.4	15.7	20.3	13.6	16.3
Brake work	63.6	22.7	34.9	6.0	17.1	11.7	5.0	16.7
Repair to steering or front-end	62.9	18.5	38.5	5.2	21.9	11.4	6.0	16.4
Repair to engine cooling system	63.5	27.2	31.7	6.7	15.8	9.2	4.6	19.2
Motor tune-up	63.1	25.8	33.7	6.1	17.4	10.3	4.1	20.2
Lube, oil change, and oil filters	64.8	27.4	33.1	5.5	16.8	10.8	4.2	17.9
Front-end alignment, wheel balance, rotation	67.6	22.7	38.8	5.4	20.6	12.8	4.6	15.9
Shock absorber replacement	64.4	27.0	31.7	2.9	14.8	14.0	5.9	19.6
Gas tank repair, replacement	52.1	36.3	12.1	3.8	7.5	0.6	0.8	31.3
Tire repair and other repair work	65.4	25.2	34.2	5.2	18.8	10.1	3.9	19.0
Vehicle air conditioning repair	62.6	30.7	27.2	5.5	13.0	8.7	4.0	21.2
Exhaust system repair	58.7	27.7	26.2	5.3	9.8	11.1	8.5	17.8
Electrical system repair	63.9	29.6	31.7	5.7	16.2	9.8	6.8	17.5
Motor repair, replacement	61.6	24.9	30.8	3.1	16.4	11.4	4.0	20.4
Auto repair service policy	78.9	36.0	35.4	15.9	8.8	10.6	1.6	11.3
Vehicle insurance	**65.7**	**23.6**	**35.8**	**5.3**	**16.9**	**13.6**	**4.1**	**16.0**
Vehicle rental, leases, licenses, other charges	**68.7**	**26.2**	**37.6**	**7.2**	**20.3**	**10.0**	**4.4**	**14.7**
Leased and rented vehicles	69.7	25.3	39.2	8.1	21.6	9.4	5.2	12.9
Rented vehicles	66.8	34.2	27.9	5.3	15.8	6.8	4.8	17.9
Auto rental	46.9	17.5	25.5	6.3	17.1	2.1	8.2	31.4
Auto rental on trips	70.3	37.5	28.1	4.5	15.3	8.3	3.5	15.8
Truck rental	81.9	47.6	30.0	4.9	21.0	4.1	2.3	10.9
Truck rental on trips	70.1	22.7	37.9	12.2	15.4	10.2	13.7	4.5

	total married couples	married couples, no children	married couples with children				single parent, at least one child <18	single person
			total	oldest child under 6	oldest child 6 to 17	oldest child 18 or older		
Leased vehicles	70.1%	24.0%	40.7%	8.5%	22.4%	9.8%	5.2%	12.1%
Car lease payments	68.2	26.3	37.3	7.3	18.7	11.3	5.5	14.3
Truck lease payments	72.3	19.7	48.2	9.2	30.0	9.0	4.8	10.4
Vehicle registration, state	69.1	28.3	36.1	6.3	18.1	11.7	3.3	15.7
Vehicle registration, local	71.1	27.1	39.3	5.6	21.1	12.6	4.4	12.2
Driver's license	64.2	24.5	34.9	5.7	16.4	12.8	3.9	18.4
Vehicle inspection	65.9	25.1	36.0	4.3	19.1	12.6	3.1	18.2
Parking fees	59.8	25.8	30.6	5.7	15.8	9.1	2.9	25.7
Parking fees in home city, excluding residence	57.7	23.2	31.0	5.6	16.0	9.4	2.9	27.1
Parking fees on trips	70.9	39.0	28.4	5.8	14.9	7.7	2.7	18.5
Tolls	75.2	30.0	42.2	4.5	30.5	6.7	1.7	8.6
Tolls on trips	70.8	31.4	35.4	6.8	18.3	10.3	2.1	16.8
Towing charges	52.5	15.3	33.5	5.9	14.1	13.4	6.2	26.7
Automobile service clubs	68.2	34.2	29.9	4.6	13.0	12.4	2.0	21.4
PUBLIC TRANSPORTATION	**65.9**	**30.9**	**30.0**	**4.2**	**16.6**	**9.2**	**3.7**	**19.6**
Airline fares	69.6	33.6	31.2	4.8	17.6	8.8	2.6	18.7
Intercity bus fares	55.0	28.7	20.9	1.9	10.3	8.7	4.4	26.3
Intracity mass transit fares	48.1	13.6	27.8	5.2	12.5	10.1	7.4	24.1
Local transportation on trips	68.4	37.1	28.6	3.3	14.6	10.8	2.9	20.6
Taxi fares and limousine service on trips	68.5	37.1	28.7	3.3	14.6	10.8	2.9	20.6
Taxi fares and limousine service	40.5	21.6	17.2	0.7	14.8	1.3	7.5	33.1
Intercity train fares	71.7	39.5	28.3	2.7	13.8	11.8	2.0	16.0
Ship fares	77.1	36.5	33.9	1.6	18.7	13.6	5.4	11.2
School bus	76.0	1.2	72.6	–	48.1	24.6	17.2	–

Note: Market share for total consumer units is 100.0%. Market shares by type of consumer unit will not add to total because not all types of consumer units are shown. (–) means sample is too small to make a reliable estimate.
Source: Calculations by New Strategist based on the 2003 Consumer Expenditure Survey

Table 11.17 Transportation: Average spending by race and Hispanic origin, 2003

(average annual spending by consumer units (CU) on transportation, by race and Hispanic origin of consumer unit reference person, 2003)

	total consumer units	race Asian	race black	race white and other	Hispanic origin Hispanic	Hispanic origin non-Hispanic
Number of consumer units (000)	115,356	3,573	13,743	98,041	11,727	103,629
Average number of persons per CU	2.5	2.8	2.6	2.5	3.3	2.4
Average before-tax income of CU	$51,128.00	$60,393.00	$34,485.00	$53,039.00	$37,150.00	$52,797.00
Average spending of CU, total	40,817.33	44,922.85	28,707.56	42,360.25	34,574.75	41,520.78
Transportation, average spending	**7,780.55**	**7,453.96**	**5,073.60**	**8,171.94**	**6,779.59**	**7,893.97**
VEHICLE PURCHASES	**3,731.76**	**2,992.15**	**2,096.74**	**3,987.90**	**3,062.61**	**3,807.49**
Cars and trucks, new	**2,052.46**	**2,156.04**	**929.22**	**2,206.13**	**1,440.72**	**2,121.69**
New cars	944.91	1,547.66	480.14	988.09	662.29	976.89
New trucks	1,107.55	608.38	449.09	1,218.05	778.42	1,144.80
Cars and trucks, used	**1,611.45**	**836.11**	**1,163.74**	**1,702.47**	**1,561.96**	**1,617.05**
Used cars	816.42	509.30	563.84	863.02	793.50	819.02
Used trucks	795.03	326.81	599.90	839.45	768.46	798.04
Other vehicles	**67.85**	–	**3.77**	**79.30**	**59.94**	**68.74**
GASOLINE AND MOTOR OIL	**1,332.76**	**1,312.71**	**1,015.59**	**1,377.95**	**1,328.34**	**1,333.26**
Gasoline	1,220.61	1,237.06	975.04	1,254.44	1,255.63	1,216.65
Diesel fuel	14.73	7.54	2.17	16.75	3.71	15.98
Gasoline on trips	86.95	61.78	33.31	95.39	57.23	90.31
Motor oil	8.96	5.71	4.74	9.68	11.20	8.71
Motor oil on trips	0.88	0.62	0.54	0.96	0.58	0.91
OTHER VEHICLE EXPENSES	**2,330.98**	**2,383.01**	**1,728.39**	**2,413.58**	**2,057.30**	**2,362.03**
Vehicle finance charges	**370.59**	**282.29**	**307.76**	**382.62**	**331.39**	**375.03**
Automobile finance charges	174.48	196.10	191.33	171.33	169.09	175.09
Truck finance charges	177.99	83.46	115.43	190.21	156.77	180.39
Motorcycle and plane finance charges	2.77	2.03	0.44	3.13	2.77	2.77
Other vehicle finance charges	15.35	0.71	0.57	17.95	2.76	16.77
Maintenance and repairs	**618.92**	**545.75**	**412.70**	**650.55**	**520.36**	**630.24**
Coolant, additives, brake and transmission fluids	2.95	2.49	2.63	3.01	3.80	2.85
Tires—purchased, replaced, installed	87.97	85.57	55.75	92.57	83.22	88.50
Parts, equipment, and accessories	47.58	31.49	18.37	52.27	54.33	46.82
Vehicle products	4.20	2.16	1.79	4.61	9.02	3.59
Miscellaneous auto repair, servicing	40.05	9.06	11.84	45.18	26.55	41.75
Body work and painting	31.51	33.64	15.82	33.63	20.79	32.72
Clutch and transmission repair	37.77	14.84	31.71	39.46	34.21	38.17
Drive shaft and rear-end repair	7.70	0.08	5.40	8.30	2.48	8.29
Brake work	44.30	54.03	42.77	44.16	34.01	45.47
Repair to steering or front-end	13.03	15.14	9.37	13.47	5.99	13.83
Repair to engine cooling system	15.87	10.92	14.66	16.21	11.93	16.31
Motor tune-up	38.08	31.49	25.01	40.15	36.96	38.21
Lube, oil change, and oil filters	55.94	58.97	35.33	58.58	44.88	57.19
Front-end alignment, wheel balance, rotation	7.94	9.33	5.35	8.25	8.54	7.87
Shock absorber replacement	3.06	3.40	2.00	3.20	3.93	2.96
Gas tank repair, replacement	8.16	0.68	3.09	9.16	5.12	8.54
Tire repair and other repair work	44.14	65.43	30.78	45.23	30.53	45.68
Vehicle air conditioning repair	12.18	10.42	6.71	13.01	11.24	12.29
Exhaust system repair	10.90	2.87	8.86	11.48	7.30	11.31
Electrical system repair	25.11	27.60	16.46	26.23	14.38	26.32
Motor repair, replacement	70.37	70.27	63.51	71.33	68.82	70.54
Auto repair service policy	8.11	5.88	4.48	8.71	2.36	8.77
Vehicle insurance	**905.26**	**989.47**	**729.90**	**926.78**	**812.17**	**915.80**
Vehicle rental, leases, licenses, other charges	**436.21**	**565.49**	**278.04**	**453.64**	**393.37**	**440.96**
Leased and rented vehicles	270.13	363.83	194.34	277.34	245.62	272.91
Rented vehicles	32.95	47.43	26.78	33.29	19.06	34.52
Auto rental	5.60	11.95	7.89	5.05	2.27	5.98
Auto rental on trips	21.95	25.02	12.00	23.23	15.25	22.70
Truck rental	2.22	7.56	3.65	1.83	0.78	2.39
Truck rental on trips	2.29	2.82	3.23	2.14	0.76	2.47

		race			Hispanic origin	
	total consumer units	Asian	black	white and other	Hispanic	non-Hispanic
Leased vehicles	$237.19	$316.40	$167.56	$244.06	$226.56	$238.39
Car lease payments	132.32	214.33	81.17	136.50	84.73	137.71
Truck lease payments	86.11	90.62	64.16	89.02	100.40	84.49
Vehicle registration, state	81.20	88.42	37.88	87.01	67.82	82.72
Vehicle registration, local	6.97	11.04	4.34	7.19	7.67	6.89
Driver's license	7.17	8.46	3.51	7.64	5.24	7.39
Vehicle inspection	8.36	10.16	5.16	8.74	9.27	8.26
Parking fees	28.12	38.49	15.31	29.54	21.54	28.87
Parking fees in home city, excluding residence	23.61	32.76	13.69	24.67	19.36	24.09
Parking fees on trips	4.51	5.73	1.62	4.88	2.18	4.78
Tolls	13.00	19.52	6.81	13.60	20.39	12.07
Tolls on trips	3.75	4.48	1.76	4.00	3.05	3.82
Towing charges	4.67	2.91	3.86	4.85	7.52	4.35
Automobile service clubs	12.83	18.19	5.06	13.73	5.26	13.59
PUBLIC TRANSPORTATION	**385.05**	**766.09**	**232.88**	**392.52**	**331.35**	**391.18**
Airline fares	252.56	528.87	88.21	265.53	197.38	258.81
Intercity bus fares	8.96	16.23	8.64	8.74	12.50	8.55
Intracity mass transit fares	48.94	113.25	88.16	41.10	81.10	45.30
Local transportation on trips	8.33	13.72	3.09	8.87	5.85	8.61
Taxi fares and limousine service on trips	4.89	8.05	1.81	5.21	3.43	5.06
Taxi fares and limousine service	16.69	14.77	31.55	14.71	11.74	17.31
Intercity train fares	16.07	25.25	4.84	17.31	9.54	16.81
Ship fares	27.90	44.85	5.71	30.39	7.37	30.22
School bus	0.70	1.09	0.88	0.67	2.44	0.51

Note: Other races include Native Americans and Pacific Islanders. Subcategories may not add to total because some are not shown. (–) means sample is too small to make a reliable estimate.
Source: Bureau of Labor Statistics, unpublished tables from the 2003 Consumer Expenditure Survey

(indexed average annual spending of consumer units (CU) on transportation, by race and Hispanic origin of consumer unit reference person, 2003; index definition: an index of 100 is the average for all consumer units; an index of 132 means that spending by consumer units in that group is 32 percent above the average for all consumer units; an index of 68 indicates spending that is 32 percent below the average for all consumer units)

	total consumer units	race			Hispanic origin	
		Asian	black	white and other	Hispanic	non-Hispanic
Average spending of CU, total	$40,817	$44,923	$28,708	$42,360	$34,575	$41,521
Average spending of CU, index	100	110	70	104	85	102
Transportation, spending index	**100**	**96**	**65**	**105**	**87**	**101**
VEHICLE PURCHASES	**100**	**80**	**56**	**107**	**82**	**102**
Cars and trucks, new	**100**	**105**	**45**	**107**	**70**	**103**
New cars	100	164	51	105	70	103
New trucks	100	55	41	110	70	103
Cars and trucks, used	**100**	**52**	**72**	**106**	**97**	**100**
Used cars	100	62	69	106	97	100
Used trucks	100	41	75	106	97	100
Other vehicles	**100**	–	**6**	**117**	**88**	**101**
GASOLINE AND MOTOR OIL	**100**	**98**	**76**	**103**	**100**	**100**
Gasoline	100	101	80	103	103	100
Diesel fuel	100	51	15	114	25	108
Gasoline on trips	100	71	38	110	66	104
Motor oil	100	64	53	108	125	97
Motor oil on trips	100	70	39	109	66	103
OTHER VEHICLE EXPENSES	**100**	**102**	**74**	**104**	**88**	**101**
Vehicle finance charges	**100**	**76**	**83**	**103**	**89**	**101**
Automobile finance charges	100	112	110	98	97	100
Truck finance charges	100	47	65	107	88	101
Motorcycle and plane finance charges	100	73	16	113	100	100
Other vehicle finance charges	100	5	4	117	18	109
Maintenance and repairs	**100**	**88**	**67**	**105**	**84**	**102**
Coolant, additives, brake and transmission fluids	100	84	89	102	129	97
Tires—purchased, replaced, installed	100	97	63	105	95	101
Parts, equipment, and accessories	100	66	39	110	114	98
Vehicle products	100	51	43	110	215	85
Miscellaneous auto repair, servicing	100	23	30	113	66	104
Body work and painting	100	107	50	107	66	104
Clutch and transmission repair	100	39	84	104	91	101
Drive shaft and rear-end repair	100	1	70	108	32	108
Brake work	100	122	97	100	77	103
Repair to steering or front-end	100	116	72	103	46	106
Repair to engine cooling system	100	69	92	102	75	103
Motor tune-up	100	83	66	105	97	100
Lube, oil change, and oil filters	100	105	65	105	80	102
Front-end alignment, wheel balance, rotation	100	118	67	104	108	99
Shock absorber replacement	100	111	65	105	128	97
Gas tank repair, replacement	100	8	38	112	63	105
Tire repair and other repair work	100	148	70	102	69	103
Vehicle air conditioning repair	100	86	55	107	92	101
Exhaust system repair	100	26	81	105	67	104
Electrical system repair	100	110	66	104	57	105
Motor repair, replacement	100	100	90	101	98	100
Auto repair service policy	100	73	55	107	29	108
Vehicle insurance	**100**	**109**	**81**	**102**	**90**	**101**
Vehicle rental, leases, licenses, other charges	**100**	**130**	**64**	**104**	**90**	**101**
Leased and rented vehicles	100	135	72	103	91	101
Rented vehicles	100	144	81	101	58	105
Auto rental	100	213	141	90	41	107
Auto rental on trips	100	114	55	106	69	103
Truck rental	100	341	164	82	35	108
Truck rental on trips	100	123	141	93	33	108

	total consumer units	race			Hispanic origin	
		Asian	black	white and other	Hispanic	non-Hispanic
Leased vehicles	100	133	71	103	96	101
Car lease payments	100	162	61	103	64	104
Truck lease payments	100	105	75	103	117	98
Vehicle registration, state	100	109	47	107	84	102
Vehicle registration, local	100	158	62	103	110	99
Driver's license	100	118	49	107	73	103
Vehicle inspection	100	122	62	105	111	99
Parking fees	100	137	54	105	77	103
Parking fees in home city, excluding residence	100	139	58	104	82	102
Parking fees on trips	100	127	36	108	48	106
Tolls	100	150	52	105	157	93
Tolls on trips	100	119	47	107	81	102
Towing charges	100	62	33	104	161	93
Automobile service clubs	100	142	39	107	41	107
PUBLIC TRANSPORTATION	**100**	**199**	**60**	**102**	**86**	**102**
Airline fares	100	209	35	105	78	102
Intercity bus fares	100	181	96	98	140	95
Intracity mass transit fares	100	231	180	84	166	93
Local transportation on trips	100	165	37	106	70	103
Taxi fares and limousine service on trips	100	165	37	107	70	103
Taxi fares and limousine service	100	88	89	88	70	104
Intercity train fares	100	157	30	108	59	105
Ship fares	100	161	20	109	26	108
School bus	100	156	126	96	349	73

Note: Other races include Native Americans and Pacific Islanders. (–) means sample is too small to make a reliable estimate.
Source: Calculations by New Strategist based on the 2003 Consumer Expenditure Survey

Table 11.19 Transportation: Total spending by race and Hispanic origin, 2003

(total annual spending on transportation, by consumer unit race and Hispanic origin groups, 2003; numbers in thousands)

	total consumer units	race			Hispanic origin	
		Asian	black	white and other	Hispanic	non-Hispanic
Number of consumer units	115,356	3,573	13,743	98,041	11,727	103,629
Total spending of all consumer units	$4,708,523,919	$160,509,343	$394,527,997	$4,153,041,270	$405,458,093	$4,302,756,911
Transportation, total spending	897,533,126	26,632,999	69,726,485	801,185,170	79,504,252	818,044,217
VEHICLE PURCHASES	430,480,907	10,690,952	28,815,498	390,977,704	35,915,227	394,566,381
Cars and trucks, new	236,763,576	7,703,531	12,770,270	216,291,191	16,895,323	219,868,613
New cars	109,001,038	5,529,789	6,598,564	96,873,332	7,766,675	101,234,134
New trucks	127,762,538	2,173,742	6,171,844	119,418,840	9,128,531	118,634,479
Cars and trucks, used	185,890,426	2,987,421	15,993,279	166,911,861	18,317,105	167,573,274
Used cars	94,178,946	1,819,729	7,748,853	84,611,344	9,305,375	84,874,224
Used trucks	91,711,481	1,167,692	8,244,426	82,300,517	9,011,730	82,700,087
Other vehicles	7,826,905	–	51,811	7,774,651	702,916	7,123,457
GASOLINE AND MOTOR OIL	153,741,863	4,690,313	13,957,253	135,095,596	15,577,443	138,164,401
Gasoline	140,804,687	4,420,015	13,399,975	122,986,552	14,724,773	126,080,223
Diesel fuel	1,699,194	26,940	29,822	1,642,187	43,507	1,655,991
Gasoline on trips	10,030,204	220,740	457,779	9,352,131	671,136	9,358,735
Motor oil	1,033,590	20,402	65,142	949,037	131,342	902,609
Motor oil on trips	101,513	2,215	4,673	94,119	6,802	94,302
OTHER VEHICLE EXPENSES	268,892,529	8,514,495	23,753,264	236,629,797	24,125,957	244,774,807
Vehicle finance charges	42,749,780	1,008,622	4,229,546	37,512,447	3,886,211	38,863,984
Automobile finance charges	20,127,315	700,665	2,629,448	16,797,365	1,982,918	18,144,402
Truck finance charges	20,532,214	298,203	1,586,354	18,648,379	1,838,442	18,693,635
Motorcycle and plane finance charges	319,536	7,253	6,047	306,868	32,484	287,052
Other vehicle finance charges	1,770,715	2,537	7,834	1,759,836	32,367	1,737,858
Maintenance and repairs	71,396,136	1,949,965	5,671,736	63,780,573	6,102,262	65,311,141
Coolant, additives, brake and transmission fluids	340,300	8,897	36,144	295,103	44,563	295,343
Tires—purchased, replaced, installed	10,147,867	305,742	766,172	9,075,655	975,921	9,171,167
Parts, equipment, and accessories	5,488,638	112,514	252,459	5,124,603	637,128	4,851,910
Vehicle products	484,495	7,718	24,600	451,969	105,778	372,028
Miscellaneous auto repair, servicing	4,620,008	32,371	162,717	4,429,492	311,352	4,326,511
Body work and painting	3,634,868	120,196	217,414	3,297,119	243,804	3,390,741
Clutch and transmission repair	4,356,996	53,023	435,791	3,868,698	401,181	3,955,519
Drive shaft and rear-end repair	888,241	286	74,212	813,740	29,083	859,084
Brake work	5,110,271	193,049	587,788	4,329,491	398,835	4,712,011
Repair to steering or front-end	1,503,089	54,095	128,772	1,320,612	70,245	1,433,189
Repair to engine cooling system	1,830,700	39,017	201,472	1,589,245	139,903	1,690,189
Motor tune-up	4,392,756	112,514	343,712	3,936,346	433,430	3,959,664
Lube, oil change, and oil filters	6,453,015	210,700	499,283	5,743,242	526,308	5,926,543
Front-end alignment, wheel balance, rotation	915,927	33,336	73,525	808,838	100,149	815,560
Shock absorber replacement	352,989	12,148	27,486	313,731	46,087	306,742
Gas tank repair, replacement	941,305	2,430	42,466	898,056	60,042	884,992
Tire repair and other repair work	5,091,814	233,781	423,010	4,434,394	358,025	4,733,773
Vehicle air conditioning repair	1,405,036	37,231	92,216	1,275,513	131,811	1,273,600
Exhaust system repair	1,257,380	10,255	121,763	1,125,511	85,607	1,172,044
Electrical system repair	2,896,589	98,615	226,210	2,571,615	168,634	2,727,515
Motor repair, replacement	8,117,602	251,075	872,818	6,993,265	807,052	7,309,990
Auto repair service policy	935,537	21,009	61,569	853,937	27,676	908,826
Vehicle insurance	104,427,173	3,535,376	10,031,016	90,862,438	9,524,318	94,903,438
Vehicle rental, leases, licenses, other charges	50,319,441	2,020,496	3,821,104	44,475,319	4,613,050	45,696,244
Leased and rented vehicles	31,161,116	1,299,965	2,670,815	27,190,691	2,880,386	28,281,390
Rented vehicles	3,800,980	169,467	368,038	3,263,785	223,517	3,577,273
Auto rental	645,994	42,697	108,432	495,107	26,620	619,701
Auto rental on trips	2,532,064	89,396	164,916	2,277,492	178,837	2,352,378
Truck rental	256,090	27,012	50,162	179,415	9,147	247,673
Truck rental on trips	264,165	10,076	44,390	209,808	8,913	255,964

	total consumer units	race			Hispanic origin	
		Asian	black	white and other	Hispanic	non-Hispanic
Leased vehicles	$27,361,290	$1,130,497	$2,302,777	$23,927,886	$2,656,869	$24,704,117
Car lease payments	15,263,906	765,801	1,115,519	13,382,597	993,629	14,270,750
Truck lease payments	9,933,305	323,785	881,751	8,727,610	1,177,391	8,755,614
Vehicle registration, state	9,366,907	315,925	520,585	8,530,547	795,325	8,572,191
Vehicle registration, local	804,031	39,446	59,645	704,915	89,946	714,004
Driver's license	827,103	30,228	48,238	749,033	61,449	765,818
Vehicle inspection	964,376	36,302	70,914	856,878	108,709	855,976
Parking fees	3,243,811	137,525	210,405	2,896,131	252,600	2,991,769
Parking fees in home city, excluding residence	2,723,555	117,051	188,142	2,418,671	227,035	2,496,423
Parking fees on trips	520,256	20,473	22,264	478,440	25,565	495,347
Tolls	1,499,628	69,745	93,590	1,333,358	239,114	1,250,802
Tolls on trips	432,585	15,007	24,138	392,164	35,767	395,863
Towing charges	538,713	10,397	53,048	475,499	88,187	450,786
Automobile service clubs	1,480,017	64,993	69,540	1,346,103	61,684	1,418,681
PUBLIC TRANSPORTATION	**44,417,828**	**2,737,240**	**3,200,470**	**38,483,053**	**3,885,741**	**40,537,592**
Airline fares	29,134,311	1,889,653	1,212,270	26,032,827	2,314,675	26,820,221
Intercity bus fares	1,033,590	57,990	118,740	856,878	146,588	886,028
Intracity mass transit fares	5,645,523	404,642	1,211,583	4,029,485	951,060	4,694,394
Local transportation on trips	960,915	49,022	42,466	869,624	68,603	892,246
Taxi fares and limousine service on trips	564,091	28,798	24,875	510,794	40,224	524,363
Taxi fares and limousine service	1,925,292	52,773	433,592	1,442,183	137,675	1,793,818
Intercity train fares	1,853,771	90,218	66,515	1,697,090	111,876	1,742,003
Ship fares	3,218,432	60,249	78,473	2,979,466	86,428	3,131,668
School bus	80,749	3,895	12,094	65,687	28,614	52,851

Note: Other races include Native Americans and Pacific Islanders. Numbers may not add to total because of rounding and missing subcategories. (–) means sample is too small to make a reliable estimate.
Source: Calculations by New Strategist based on the 2003 Consumer Expenditure Survey

Table 11.20 Transportation: Market shares by race and Hispanic origin, 2003

(percentage of total annual spending on transportation accounted for by consumer unit race and Hispanic origin groups, 2003)

	total consumer units	race			Hispanic origin	
		Asian	black	white and other	Hispanic	non-Hispanic
Share of total consumer units	100.0%	3.1%	11.9%	85.0%	10.2%	89.8%
Share of total before-tax income	100.0	3.7	8.0	88.2	7.4	92.8
Share of total spending	100.0	3.4	8.4	88.2	8.6	91.4
Share of transportation spending	100.0	3.0	7.8	89.3	8.9	91.1
VEHICLE PURCHASES	100.0	2.5	6.7	90.8	8.3	91.7
Cars and trucks, new	100.0	3.3	5.4	91.4	7.1	92.9
New cars	100.0	5.1	6.1	88.9	7.1	92.9
New trucks	100.0	1.7	4.8	93.5	7.1	92.9
Cars and trucks, used	100.0	1.6	8.6	89.8	9.9	90.1
Used cars	100.0	1.9	8.2	89.8	9.9	90.1
Used trucks	100.0	1.3	9.0	89.7	9.8	90.2
Other vehicles	100.0	–	0.7	99.3	9.0	91.0
GASOLINE AND MOTOR OIL	100.0	3.1	9.1	87.9	10.1	89.9
Gasoline	100.0	3.1	9.5	87.3	10.5	89.5
Diesel fuel	100.0	1.6	1.8	96.6	2.6	97.5
Gasoline on trips	100.0	2.2	4.6	93.2	6.7	93.3
Motor oil	100.0	2.0	6.3	91.8	12.7	87.3
Motor oil on trips	100.0	2.2	4.6	92.7	6.7	92.9
OTHER VEHICLE EXPENSES	100.0	3.2	8.8	88.0	9.0	91.0
Vehicle finance charges	100.0	2.4	9.9	87.7	9.1	90.9
Automobile finance charges	100.0	3.5	13.1	83.5	9.9	90.1
Truck finance charges	100.0	1.5	7.7	90.8	9.0	91.0
Motorcycle and plane finance charges	100.0	2.3	1.9	96.0	10.2	89.8
Other vehicle finance charges	100.0	0.1	0.4	99.4	1.8	98.1
Maintenance and repairs	100.0	2.7	7.9	89.3	8.5	91.5
Coolant, additives, brake and transmission fluids	100.0	2.6	10.6	86.7	13.1	86.8
Tires—purchased, replaced, installed	100.0	3.0	7.6	89.4	9.6	90.4
Parts, equipment, and accessories	100.0	2.0	4.6	93.4	11.6	88.4
Vehicle products	100.0	1.6	5.1	93.3	21.8	76.8
Miscellaneous auto repair, servicing	100.0	0.7	3.5	95.9	6.7	93.6
Body work and painting	100.0	3.3	6.0	90.7	6.7	93.3
Clutch and transmission repair	100.0	1.2	10.0	88.8	9.2	90.8
Drive shaft and rear-end repair	100.0	0.0	8.4	91.6	3.3	96.7
Brake work	100.0	3.8	11.5	84.7	7.8	92.2
Repair to steering or front-end	100.0	3.6	8.6	87.9	4.7	95.3
Repair to engine cooling system	100.0	2.1	11.0	86.8	7.6	92.3
Motor tune-up	100.0	2.6	7.8	89.6	9.9	90.1
Lube, oil change, and oil filters	100.0	3.3	7.7	89.0	8.2	91.8
Front-end alignment, wheel balance, rotation	100.0	3.6	8.0	88.3	10.9	89.0
Shock absorber replacement	100.0	3.4	7.8	88.9	13.1	86.9
Gas tank repair, replacement	100.0	0.3	4.5	95.4	6.4	94.0
Tire repair and other repair work	100.0	4.6	8.3	87.1	7.0	93.0
Vehicle air conditioning repair	100.0	2.6	6.6	90.8	9.4	90.6
Exhaust system repair	100.0	0.8	9.7	89.5	6.8	93.2
Electrical system repair	100.0	3.4	7.8	88.8	5.8	94.2
Motor repair, replacement	100.0	3.1	10.8	86.1	9.9	90.1
Auto repair service policy	100.0	2.2	6.6	91.3	3.0	97.1
Vehicle insurance	100.0	3.4	9.6	87.0	9.1	90.9
Vehicle rental, leases, licenses, other charges	100.0	4.0	7.6	88.4	9.2	90.8
Leased and rented vehicles	100.0	4.2	8.6	87.3	9.2	90.8
Rented vehicles	100.0	4.5	9.7	85.9	5.9	94.1
Auto rental	100.0	6.6	16.8	76.6	4.1	95.9
Auto rental on trips	100.0	3.5	6.5	89.9	7.1	92.9
Truck rental	100.0	10.5	19.6	70.1	3.6	96.7
Truck rental on trips	100.0	3.8	16.8	79.4	3.4	96.9

	total consumer units	race			Hispanic origin	
		Asian	black	white and other	Hispanic	non-Hispanic
Leased vehicles	100.0%	4.1%	8.4%	87.5%	9.7%	90.3%
Car lease payments	100.0	5.0	7.3	87.7	6.5	93.5
Truck lease payments	100.0	3.3	8.9	87.9	11.9	88.1
Vehicle registration, state	100.0	3.4	5.6	91.1	8.5	91.5
Vehicle registration, local	100.0	4.9	7.4	87.7	11.2	88.8
Driver's license	100.0	3.7	5.8	90.6	7.4	92.6
Vehicle inspection	100.0	3.8	7.4	88.9	11.3	88.8
Parking fees	100.0	4.2	6.5	89.3	7.8	92.2
Parking fees in home city, excluding residence	100.0	4.3	6.9	88.8	8.3	91.7
Parking fees on trips	100.0	3.9	4.3	92.0	4.9	95.2
Tolls	100.0	4.7	6.2	88.9	15.9	83.4
Tolls on trips	100.0	3.7	5.6	90.7	8.3	91.5
Towing charges	100.0	1.9	9.8	88.3	16.4	83.7
Automobile service clubs	100.0	4.4	4.7	91.0	4.2	95.9
PUBLIC TRANSPORTATION	**100.0**	**6.2**	**7.2**	**86.6**	**8.7**	**91.3**
Airline fares	100.0	6.5	4.2	89.4	7.9	92.1
Intercity bus fares	100.0	5.6	11.5	82.9	14.2	85.7
Intracity mass transit fares	100.0	7.2	21.5	71.4	16.8	83.2
Local transportation on trips	100.0	5.1	4.4	90.5	7.1	92.9
Taxi fares and limousine service on trips	100.0	5.1	4.4	90.6	7.1	93.0
Taxi fares and limousine service	100.0	2.7	22.5	74.9	7.2	93.2
Intercity train fares	100.0	4.9	3.6	91.5	6.0	94.0
Ship fares	100.0	5.0	2.4	92.6	2.7	97.3
School bus	100.0	4.8	15.0	81.3	35.4	65.5

Note: Other races include Native Americans and Pacific Islanders. Numbers may not add to total because of rounding. (–) means sample is too small to make a reliable estimate.
Source: Calculations by New Strategist based on the 2003 Consumer Expenditure Survey

Table 11.21 Transportation: Average spending by region, 2003

(average annual spending of consumer units (CU) on transportation, by region in which consumer unit lives, 2003)

	total consumer units	Northeast	Midwest	South	West
Number of consumer units (000)	115,356	22,182	26,438	41,325	25,412
Average number of persons per CU	2.5	2.4	2.5	2.5	2.6
Average before-tax income of CU	$48,596.00	$54,219.00	$49,591.00	$44,461.00	$49,667.00
Average spending of CU, total	40,817.33	42,162.29	40,280.39	37,624.55	45,380.67
Transportation, average spending	7,780.55	7,043.27	7,817.00	7,621.19	8,645.19
VEHICLE PURCHASES	3,731.76	3,040.28	3,775.45	3,892.69	4,028.20
Cars and trucks, new	2,052.46	1,687.88	2,039.44	2,208.33	2,130.78
New cars	944.91	982.10	813.48	970.38	1,007.77
New trucks	1,107.55	705.78	1,225.97	1,237.95	1,123.02
Cars and trucks, used	1,611.45	1,294.28	1,653.92	1,626.53	1,819.62
Used cars	816.42	763.26	856.41	774.81	888.90
Used trucks	795.03	531.02	797.50	851.73	930.72
Other vehicles	67.85	58.12	82.09	57.83	77.81
GASOLINE AND MOTOR OIL	1,332.76	1,157.16	1,357.22	1,321.31	1,479.12
Gasoline	1,220.61	1,088.75	1,232.82	1,222.42	1,320.08
Diesel fuel	14.73	6.06	10.55	14.16	27.57
Gasoline on trips	86.95	55.96	99.69	74.91	120.32
Motor oil	8.96	5.83	10.52	9.06	9.93
Motor oil on trips	0.88	0.57	1.01	0.76	1.22
OTHER VEHICLE EXPENSES	2,330.98	2,306.82	2,313.53	2,153.72	2,658.60
Vehicle finance charges	370.59	267.83	390.61	407.64	379.24
Automobile finance charges	174.48	157.25	176.64	180.38	177.69
Truck finance charges	177.99	101.00	192.34	211.61	175.61
Motorcycle and plane finance charges	2.77	2.17	3.09	2.51	3.39
Other vehicle finance charges	15.35	7.41	18.54	13.14	22.55
Maintenance and repairs	618.92	564.52	579.78	554.71	811.48
Coolant, additives, brake and transmission fluids	2.95	1.84	3.99	2.83	3.01
Tires—purchased, replaced, installed	87.97	78.26	77.27	84.44	113.30
Parts, equipment, and accessories	47.58	31.43	51.93	41.37	67.26
Vehicle products	4.20	3.74	2.38	4.86	5.48
Miscellaneous auto repair, servicing	40.05	28.07	37.76	28.30	71.76
Body work and painting	31.51	36.23	28.42	26.46	38.81
Clutch and transmission repair	37.77	27.00	27.20	36.54	60.16
Drive shaft and rear-end repair	7.70	8.12	3.17	7.29	12.72
Brake work	44.30	56.72	40.67	34.42	53.32
Repair to steering or front-end	13.03	13.85	15.59	9.51	15.39
Repair to engine cooling system	15.87	14.37	15.58	13.90	20.67
Motor tune-up	38.08	37.50	33.07	30.93	55.44
Lube, oil change, and oil filters	55.94	47.86	63.54	50.18	64.46
Front-end alignment, wheel balance, rotation	7.94	7.99	9.08	6.91	8.36
Shock absorber replacement	3.06	3.24	3.56	2.07	3.99
Gas tank repair, replacement	8.16	14.59	6.08	8.10	4.86
Tire repair and other repair work	44.14	54.38	36.17	36.97	55.13
Vehicle air conditioning repair	12.18	7.00	8.76	14.62	16.31
Exhaust system repair	10.90	11.79	13.03	8.94	11.11
Electrical system repair	25.11	19.90	29.16	23.49	28.07
Motor repair, replacement	70.37	53.60	63.41	71.62	90.22
Auto repair service policy	8.11	7.05	8.46	7.25	10.09
Vehicle insurance	905.26	923.87	859.56	905.44	936.28
Vehicle rental, leases, licenses, other charges	436.21	550.60	483.59	285.93	531.60
Leased and rented vehicles	270.13	378.10	304.46	167.85	306.51
Rented vehicles	32.95	33.67	33.99	25.13	43.95
Auto rental	5.60	4.37	3.81	7.23	5.89
Auto rental on trips	21.95	25.25	25.51	12.96	29.97
Truck rental	2.22	0.84	1.33	2.08	4.59
Truck rental on trips	2.29	1.57	3.21	1.83	2.71

	total consumer units	Northeast	Midwest	South	West
Leased vehicles	$237.19	$344.43	$270.47	$142.72	$262.56
Car lease payments	132.32	190.58	149.07	77.44	153.30
Truck lease payments	86.11	100.27	111.64	60.18	89.33
Vehicle registration, state	81.20	38.49	107.38	57.35	130.04
Vehicle registration, local	6.97	3.68	8.48	8.60	5.61
Driver's license	7.17	11.62	6.00	6.09	6.28
Vehicle inspection	8.36	15.21	2.33	6.35	11.92
Parking fees	28.12	44.44	28.91	16.52	31.94
Parking fees in home city, excluding residence	23.61	39.47	23.80	13.46	26.07
Parking fees on trips	4.51	4.97	5.10	3.06	5.87
Tolls	13.00	31.24	4.20	9.65	11.84
Tolls on trips	3.75	7.85	3.60	2.62	2.14
Towing charges	4.67	3.14	4.76	3.92	7.13
Automobile service clubs	12.83	16.84	13.47	6.98	18.18
PUBLIC TRANSPORTATION	**385.05**	**539.01**	**370.80**	**253.47**	**479.27**
Airline fares	252.56	277.82	257.37	180.63	342.49
Intercity bus fares	8.96	10.86	9.16	6.83	10.54
Intracity mass transit fares	48.94	150.78	24.73	16.04	38.74
Local transportation on trips	8.33	10.00	9.07	5.69	10.39
Taxi fares and limousine service on trips	4.89	5.87	5.33	3.34	6.10
Taxi fares and limousine service	16.69	36.27	14.61	9.56	13.20
Intercity train fares	16.07	19.44	17.87	12.95	16.32
Ship fares	27.90	27.43	32.28	17.99	39.87
School bus	0.70	0.54	0.39	0.43	1.62

Note: Subcategories may not add to total because some are not shown.
Source: Bureau of Labor Statistics, unpublished tables from the 2003 Consumer Expenditure Survey

Table 11.22 Transportation: Indexed spending by region, 2003

(indexed average annual spending of consumer units (CU) on transportation, by region in which consumer unit lives, 2003; index definition: an index of 100 is the average for all consumer units; an index of 132 means that spending by consumer units in that group is 32 percent above the average for all consumer units; an index of 68 indicates spending that is 32 percent below the average for all consumer units)

	total consumer units	Northeast	Midwest	South	West
Average spending of CU, total	$40,817	$42,162	$40,280	$37,625	$45,381
Average spending of CU, index	100	103	99	92	111
Transportation, spending index	100	91	100	98	111
VEHICLE PURCHASES	100	81	101	104	108
Cars and trucks, new	100	82	99	108	104
New cars	100	104	86	103	107
New trucks	100	64	111	112	101
Cars and trucks, used	100	80	103	101	113
Used cars	100	93	105	95	109
Used trucks	100	67	100	107	117
Other vehicles	100	86	121	85	115
GASOLINE AND MOTOR OIL	100	87	102	99	111
Gasoline	100	89	101	100	108
Diesel fuel	100	41	72	96	187
Gasoline on trips	100	64	115	86	138
Motor oil	100	65	117	101	111
Motor oil on trips	100	65	115	86	139
OTHER VEHICLE EXPENSES	100	99	99	92	114
Vehicle finance charges	100	72	105	110	102
Automobile finance charges	100	90	101	103	102
Truck finance charges	100	57	108	119	99
Motorcycle and plane finance charges	100	78	112	91	122
Other vehicle finance charges	100	48	121	86	147
Maintenance and repairs	100	91	94	90	131
Coolant, additives, brake and transmission fluids	100	62	135	96	102
Tires—purchased, replaced, installed	100	89	88	96	129
Parts, equipment, and accessories	100	66	109	87	141
Vehicle products	100	89	57	116	130
Miscellaneous auto repair, servicing	100	70	94	71	179
Body work and painting	100	115	90	84	123
Clutch and transmission repair	100	71	72	97	159
Drive shaft and rear-end repair	100	105	41	95	165
Brake work	100	128	92	78	120
Repair to steering or front-end	100	106	120	73	118
Repair to engine cooling system	100	91	98	88	130
Motor tune-up	100	98	87	81	146
Lube, oil change, and oil filters	100	86	114	90	115
Front-end alignment, wheel balance, rotation	100	101	114	87	105
Shock absorber replacement	100	106	116	68	130
Gas tank repair, replacement	100	179	75	99	60
Tire repair and other repair work	100	123	82	84	125
Vehicle air conditioning repair	100	57	72	120	134
Exhaust system repair	100	108	120	82	102
Electrical system repair	100	79	116	94	112
Motor repair, replacement	100	76	90	102	128
Auto repair service policy	100	87	104	89	124
Vehicle insurance	100	102	95	100	103
Vehicle rental, leases, licenses, other charges	100	126	111	66	122
Leased and rented vehicles	100	140	113	62	113
Rented vehicles	100	102	103	76	133
Auto rental	100	78	68	129	105
Auto rental on trips	100	115	116	59	137
Truck rental	100	38	60	94	207
Truck rental on trips	100	69	140	80	118

	total consumer units	Northeast	Midwest	South	West
Leased vehicles	100	145	114	60	111
Car lease payments	100	144	113	59	116
Truck lease payments	100	116	130	70	104
Vehicle registration, state	100	47	132	71	160
Vehicle registration, local	100	53	122	123	80
Driver's license	100	162	84	85	88
Vehicle inspection	100	182	28	76	143
Parking fees	100	158	103	59	114
Parking fees in home city, excluding residence	100	167	101	57	110
Parking fees on trips	100	110	113	68	130
Tolls	100	240	32	74	91
Tolls on trips	100	209	96	70	57
Towing charges	100	67	102	84	153
Automobile service clubs	100	131	105	54	142
PUBLIC TRANSPORTATION	**100**	**140**	**96**	**66**	**124**
Airline fares	100	110	102	72	136
Intercity bus fares	100	121	102	76	118
Intracity mass transit fares	100	308	51	33	79
Local transportation on trips	100	120	109	68	125
Taxi fares and limousine service on trips	100	120	109	68	125
Taxi fares and limousine service	100	217	88	57	79
Intercity train fares	100	121	111	81	102
Ship fares	100	98	116	64	143
School bus	100	77	56	61	231

Source: Calculations by New Strategist based on the 2003 Consumer Expenditure Survey

Table 11.23 Transportation: Total spending by region, 2003

(total annual spending on transportation, by region in which consumer units live, 2003; numbers in thousands)

	total consumer units	Northeast	Midwest	South	West
Number of consumer units	115,356	22,182	26,438	41,325	25,412
Total spending of all consumer units	$4,708,523,919	$935,243,917	$1,064,932,951	$1,554,834,529	$1,153,213,586
Transportation, total spending	897,533,126	156,233,815	206,665,846	314,945,677	219,691,568
VEHICLE PURCHASES	**430,480,907**	**67,439,491**	**99,815,347**	**160,865,414**	**102,364,618**
Cars and trucks, new	**236,763,576**	**37,440,554**	**53,918,715**	**91,259,237**	**54,147,381**
New cars	109,001,038	21,784,942	21,506,784	40,100,954	25,609,451
New trucks	127,762,538	15,655,612	32,412,195	51,158,284	28,538,184
Cars and trucks, used	**185,890,426**	**28,709,719**	**43,726,337**	**67,216,352**	**46,240,183**
Used cars	94,178,946	16,930,633	22,641,768	32,019,023	22,588,727
Used trucks	91,711,481	11,779,086	21,084,305	35,197,742	23,651,457
Other vehicles	**7,826,905**	**1,289,218**	**2,170,295**	**2,389,825**	**1,977,308**
GASOLINE AND MOTOR OIL	**153,741,863**	**25,668,123**	**35,882,182**	**54,603,136**	**37,587,397**
Gasoline	140,804,687	24,150,653	32,593,295	50,516,507	33,545,873
Diesel fuel	1,699,194	134,423	278,921	585,162	700,609
Gasoline on trips	10,030,204	1,241,305	2,635,604	3,095,656	3,057,572
Motor oil	1,033,590	129,321	278,128	374,405	252,341
Motor oil on trips	101,513	12,644	26,702	31,407	31,003
OTHER VEHICLE EXPENSES	**268,892,529**	**51,169,881**	**61,165,106**	**89,002,479**	**67,560,343**
Vehicle finance charges	**42,749,780**	**5,941,005**	**10,326,947**	**16,845,723**	**9,637,247**
Automobile finance charges	20,127,315	3,488,120	4,670,008	7,454,204	4,515,458
Truck finance charges	20,532,214	2,240,382	5,085,085	8,744,783	4,462,601
Motorcycle and plane finance charges	319,536	48,135	81,693	103,726	86,147
Other vehicle finance charges	1,770,715	164,369	490,161	543,011	573,041
Maintenance and repairs	**71,396,136**	**12,522,183**	**15,328,224**	**22,923,391**	**20,621,330**
Coolant, additives, brake and transmission fluids	340,300	40,815	105,488	116,950	76,490
Tires—purchased, replaced, installed	10,147,867	1,735,963	2,042,864	3,489,483	2,879,180
Parts, equipment, and accessories	5,488,638	697,180	1,372,925	1,709,615	1,709,211
Vehicle products	484,495	82,961	62,922	200,840	139,258
Miscellaneous auto repair, servicing	4,620,008	622,649	998,299	1,169,498	1,823,565
Body work and painting	3,634,868	803,654	751,368	1,093,460	986,240
Clutch and transmission repair	4,356,996	598,914	719,114	1,510,016	1,528,786
Drive shaft and rear-end repair	888,241	180,118	83,808	301,259	323,241
Brake work	5,110,271	1,258,163	1,075,233	1,422,407	1,354,968
Repair to steering or front-end	1,503,089	307,221	412,168	393,001	391,091
Repair to engine cooling system	1,830,700	318,755	411,904	574,418	525,266
Motor tune-up	4,392,756	831,825	874,305	1,278,182	1,408,841
Lube, oil change, and oil filters	6,453,015	1,061,631	1,679,871	2,073,689	1,638,058
Front-end alignment, wheel balance, rotation	915,927	177,234	240,057	285,556	212,444
Shock absorber replacement	352,989	71,870	94,119	85,543	101,394
Gas tank repair, replacement	941,305	323,635	160,743	334,733	123,502
Tire repair and other repair work	5,091,814	1,206,257	956,262	1,527,785	1,400,964
Vehicle air conditioning repair	1,405,036	155,274	231,597	604,172	414,470
Exhaust system repair	1,257,380	261,526	344,487	369,446	282,327
Electrical system repair	2,896,589	441,422	770,932	970,724	713,315
Motor repair, replacement	8,117,602	1,188,955	1,676,434	2,959,697	2,292,671
Auto repair service policy	935,537	156,383	223,665	299,606	256,407
Vehicle insurance	**104,427,173**	**20,493,284**	**22,725,047**	**37,417,308**	**23,792,747**
Vehicle rental, leases, licenses, other charges	**50,319,441**	**12,213,409**	**12,785,152**	**11,816,057**	**13,509,019**
Leased and rented vehicles	31,161,116	8,387,014	8,049,313	6,936,401	7,789,032
Rented vehicles	3,800,980	746,868	898,628	1,038,497	1,116,857
Auto rental	645,994	96,935	100,729	298,780	149,677
Auto rental on trips	2,532,064	560,096	674,433	535,572	761,598
Truck rental	256,090	18,633	35,163	85,956	116,641
Truck rental on trips	264,165	34,826	84,866	75,625	68,867

	total consumer units	Northeast	Midwest	South	West
Leased vehicles	$27,361,290	$7,640,146	$7,150,686	$5,897,904	$6,672,175
Car lease payments	15,263,906	4,227,446	3,941,113	3,200,208	3,895,660
Truck lease payments	9,933,305	2,224,189	2,951,538	2,486,939	2,270,054
Vehicle registration, state	9,366,907	853,785	2,838,912	2,369,989	3,304,576
Vehicle registration, local	804,031	81,630	224,194	355,395	142,561
Driver's license	827,103	257,755	158,628	251,669	159,587
Vehicle inspection	964,376	337,388	61,601	262,414	302,911
Parking fees	3,243,811	985,768	764,323	682,689	811,659
Parking fees in home city, excluding residence	2,723,555	875,524	629,224	556,235	662,491
Parking fees on trips	520,256	110,245	134,834	126,455	149,168
Tolls	1,499,628	692,966	111,040	398,786	300,878
Tolls on trips	432,585	174,129	95,177	108,272	54,382
Towing charges	538,713	69,651	125,845	161,994	181,188
Automobile service clubs	1,480,017	373,545	356,120	288,449	461,990
PUBLIC TRANSPORTATION	**44,417,828**	**11,956,320**	**9,803,210**	**10,474,648**	**12,179,209**
Airline fares	29,134,311	6,162,603	6,804,348	7,464,535	8,703,356
Intercity bus fares	1,033,590	240,897	242,172	282,250	267,842
Intracity mass transit fares	5,645,523	3,344,602	653,812	662,853	984,461
Local transportation on trips	960,915	221,820	239,793	235,139	264,031
Taxi fares and limousine service on trips	564,091	130,208	140,915	138,026	155,013
Taxi fares and limousine service	1,925,292	804,541	386,259	395,067	335,438
Intercity train fares	1,853,771	431,218	472,447	535,159	414,724
Ship fares	3,218,432	608,452	853,419	743,437	1,013,176
School bus	80,749	11,978	10,311	17,770	41,167

Note: Numbers may not add to total because of rounding and missing subcategories.
Source: Calculations by New Strategist based on the 2003 Consumer Expenditure Survey

Table 11.24 Transportation: Market shares by region, 2003

(percentage of total annual spending on transportation accounted for by consumer units by region, 2003)

	total consumer units	Northeast	Midwest	South	West
Share of total consumer units	100.0%	19.2%	22.9%	35.8%	22.0%
Share of total before-tax income	100.0	21.5	23.4	32.8	22.5
Share of total spending	100.0	19.9	22.6	33.0	24.5
Share of transportation spending	100.0	17.4	23.0	35.1	24.5
VEHICLE PURCHASES	100.0	**15.7**	**23.2**	**37.4**	**23.8**
Cars and trucks, new	100.0	**15.8**	**22.8**	**38.5**	**22.9**
New cars	100.0	20.0	19.7	36.8	23.5
New trucks	100.0	12.3	25.4	40.0	22.3
Cars and trucks, used	100.0	**15.4**	**23.5**	**36.2**	**24.9**
Used cars	100.0	18.0	24.0	34.0	24.0
Used trucks	100.0	12.8	23.0	38.4	25.8
Other vehicles	100.0	**16.5**	**27.7**	**30.5**	**25.3**
GASOLINE AND MOTOR OIL	100.0	**16.7**	**23.3**	**35.5**	**24.4**
Gasoline	100.0	17.2	23.1	35.9	23.8
Diesel fuel	100.0	7.9	16.4	34.4	41.2
Gasoline on trips	100.0	12.4	26.3	30.9	30.5
Motor oil	100.0	12.5	26.9	36.2	24.4
Motor oil on trips	100.0	12.5	26.3	30.9	30.5
OTHER VEHICLE EXPENSES	100.0	**19.0**	**22.7**	**33.1**	**25.1**
Vehicle finance charges	100.0	**13.9**	**24.2**	**39.4**	**22.5**
Automobile finance charges	100.0	17.3	23.2	37.0	22.4
Truck finance charges	100.0	10.9	24.8	42.6	21.7
Motorcycle and plane finance charges	100.0	15.1	25.6	32.5	27.0
Other vehicle finance charges	100.0	9.3	27.7	30.7	32.4
Maintenance and repairs	100.0	**17.5**	**21.5**	**32.1**	**28.9**
Coolant, additives, brake and transmission fluids	100.0	12.0	31.0	34.4	22.5
Tires—purchased, replaced, installed	100.0	17.1	20.1	34.4	28.4
Parts, equipment, and accessories	100.0	12.7	25.0	31.1	31.1
Vehicle products	100.0	17.1	13.0	41.5	28.7
Miscellaneous auto repair, servicing	100.0	13.5	21.6	25.3	39.5
Body work and painting	100.0	22.1	20.7	30.1	27.1
Clutch and transmission repair	100.0	13.7	16.5	34.7	35.1
Drive shaft and rear-end repair	100.0	20.3	9.4	33.9	36.4
Brake work	100.0	24.6	21.0	27.8	26.5
Repair to steering or front-end	100.0	20.4	27.4	26.1	26.0
Repair to engine cooling system	100.0	17.4	22.5	31.4	28.7
Motor tune-up	100.0	18.9	19.9	29.1	32.1
Lube, oil change, and oil filters	100.0	16.5	26.0	32.1	25.4
Front-end alignment, wheel balance, rotation	100.0	19.4	26.2	31.2	23.2
Shock absorber replacement	100.0	20.4	26.7	24.2	28.7
Gas tank repair, replacement	100.0	34.4	17.1	35.6	13.1
Tire repair and other repair work	100.0	23.7	18.8	30.0	27.5
Vehicle air conditioning repair	100.0	11.1	16.5	43.0	29.5
Exhaust system repair	100.0	20.8	27.4	29.4	22.5
Electrical system repair	100.0	15.2	26.6	33.5	24.6
Motor repair, replacement	100.0	14.6	20.7	36.5	28.2
Auto repair service policy	100.0	16.7	23.9	32.0	27.4
Vehicle insurance	100.0	**19.6**	**21.8**	**35.8**	**22.8**
Vehicle rental, leases, licenses, other charges	100.0	**24.3**	**25.4**	**23.5**	**26.8**
Leased and rented vehicles	100.0	26.9	25.8	22.3	25.0
Rented vehicles	100.0	19.6	23.6	27.3	29.4
Auto rental	100.0	15.0	15.6	46.3	23.2
Auto rental on trips	100.0	22.1	26.6	21.2	30.1
Truck rental	100.0	7.3	13.7	33.6	45.5
Truck rental on trips	100.0	13.2	32.1	28.6	26.1

	total consumer units	Northeast	Midwest	South	West
Leased vehicles	100.0%	27.9%	26.1%	21.6%	24.4%
Car lease payments	100.0	27.7	25.8	21.0	25.5
Truck lease payments	100.0	22.4	29.7	25.0	22.9
Vehicle registration, state	100.0	9.1	30.3	25.3	35.3
Vehicle registration, local	100.0	10.2	27.9	44.2	17.7
Driver's license	100.0	31.2	19.2	30.4	19.3
Vehicle inspection	100.0	35.0	6.4	27.2	31.4
Parking fees	100.0	30.4	23.6	21.0	25.0
Parking fees in home city, excluding residence	100.0	32.1	23.1	20.4	24.3
Parking fees on trips	100.0	21.2	25.9	24.3	28.7
Tolls	100.0	46.2	7.4	26.6	20.1
Tolls on trips	100.0	40.3	22.0	25.0	12.6
Towing charges	100.0	12.9	23.4	30.1	33.6
Automobile service clubs	100.0	25.2	24.1	19.5	31.2
PUBLIC TRANSPORTATION	**100.0**	**26.9**	**22.1**	**23.6**	**27.4**
Airline fares	100.0	21.2	23.4	25.6	29.9
Intercity bus fares	100.0	23.3	23.4	27.3	25.9
Intracity mass transit fares	100.0	59.2	11.6	11.7	17.4
Local transportation on trips	100.0	23.1	25.0	24.5	27.5
Taxi fares and limousine service on trips	100.0	23.1	25.0	24.5	27.5
Taxi fares and limousine service	100.0	41.8	20.1	20.5	17.4
Intercity train fares	100.0	23.3	25.5	28.9	22.4
Ship fares	100.0	18.9	26.5	23.1	31.5
School bus	100.0	14.8	12.8	22.0	51.0

Note: Numbers may not add to total because of rounding.
Source: Calculations by New Strategist based on the 2003 Consumer Expenditure Survey

Table 11.25 Transportation: Average spending by education, 2003

(average annual spending of consumer units (CU) on transportation, by education of consumer unit reference person, 2003)

	total consumer units	less than high school graduate	high school graduate	some college	associate's degree	college graduate total	bachelor's degree	master's, professional, doctorate
Number of consumer units (000)	115,356	17,721	31,552	24,514	10,981	30,589	19,557	11,032
Average number of persons per CU	2.5	2.6	2.5	2.3	2.6	2.5	2.5	2.4
Average before-tax income of CU	$51,128.00	$25,028.00	$40,113.00	$45,113.00	$54,087.00	$81,842.00	$74,921.00	$93,948.00
Average spending of CU, total	40,817.33	23,901.14	33,955.56	37,912.41	44,547.12	58,480.00	54,725.85	65,202.73
Transportation, average spending	**7,780.55**	**4,411.76**	**7,295.96**	**7,264.63**	**9,379.95**	**10,068.13**	**9,717.16**	**10,694.46**
VEHICLE PURCHASES	**3,731.76**	**2,058.87**	**3,658.84**	**3,382.10**	**4,833.41**	**4,660.87**	**4,576.88**	**4,809.77**
Cars and trucks, new	**2,052.46**	**719.02**	**1,968.71**	**1,757.44**	**2,809.69**	**2,875.95**	**2,733.92**	**3,127.75**
New cars	944.91	418.81	756.50	905.18	1,115.99	1,414.46	1,356.31	1,517.55
New trucks	1,107.55	300.21	1,212.21	852.26	1,693.70	1,461.50	1,377.61	1,610.21
Cars and trucks, used	**1,611.45**	**1,309.96**	**1,652.59**	**1,561.86**	**1,875.23**	**1,688.73**	**1,742.43**	**1,593.54**
Used cars	816.42	612.48	836.92	737.14	962.31	924.60	918.32	935.73
Used trucks	795.03	697.49	815.67	824.72	912.92	764.13	824.11	657.81
Other vehicles	**67.85**	**29.89**	**37.54**	**62.81**	**148.49**	**96.19**	**100.54**	**88.48**
GASOLINE AND MOTOR OIL	**1,332.76**	**941.93**	**1,305.87**	**1,330.90**	**1,530.35**	**1,517.42**	**1,501.89**	**1,544.96**
Gasoline	1,220.61	893.81	1,210.31	1,204.51	1,410.76	1,365.22	1,367.54	1,361.11
Diesel fuel	14.73	4.45	17.47	19.50	16.96	13.22	12.40	14.68
Gasoline on trips	86.95	33.42	66.06	95.65	90.70	131.19	113.99	161.69
Motor oil	8.96	9.92	10.07	9.05	11.01	6.46	6.81	5.84
Motor oil on trips	0.88	0.34	0.67	0.97	0.92	1.33	1.15	1.63
OTHER VEHICLE EXPENSES	**2,330.98**	**1,263.40**	**2,130.90**	**2,243.28**	**2,682.67**	**3,096.67**	**2,967.19**	**3,330.23**
Vehicle finance charges	**370.59**	**192.32**	**383.57**	**399.64**	**479.05**	**398.28**	**398.32**	**398.20**
Automobile finance charges	174.48	97.61	166.99	177.48	210.01	211.58	203.76	225.46
Truck finance charges	177.99	88.03	192.27	197.48	249.96	173.93	179.32	164.38
Motorcycle and plane finance charges	2.77	0.94	2.80	3.56	5.53	2.20	2.67	1.37
Other vehicle finance charges	15.35	5.75	21.51	21.12	13.56	10.56	12.57	6.99
Maintenance and repairs	**618.92**	**347.91**	**544.05**	**572.31**	**688.59**	**862.88**	**789.47**	**996.32**
Coolant, additives, brake and transmission fluids	2.95	3.11	3.36	3.08	3.51	2.11	2.35	1.69
Tires—purchased, replaced, installed	87.97	46.00	79.67	88.19	88.33	120.52	115.56	129.32
Parts, equipment, and accessories	47.58	32.61	52.04	58.06	68.68	35.70	39.85	28.33
Vehicle products	4.20	4.02	4.49	2.26	11.10	3.24	3.30	3.13
Miscellaneous auto repair, servicing	40.05	43.41	25.21	22.98	34.27	67.79	45.07	111.26
Body work and painting	31.51	16.91	20.37	26.99	39.53	52.20	45.12	64.74
Clutch and transmission repair	37.77	23.99	36.86	28.87	46.96	50.53	49.65	52.08
Drive shaft and rear-end repair	7.70	1.13	5.44	5.10	13.81	13.72	13.55	14.04
Brake work	44.30	20.90	36.47	45.59	50.54	62.67	57.84	71.23
Repair to steering or front-end	13.03	9.35	9.60	13.19	13.39	18.46	19.02	17.45
Repair to engine cooling system	15.87	9.19	12.13	15.79	18.65	22.64	20.86	25.81
Motor tune-up	38.08	18.39	24.13	34.89	41.87	65.08	55.12	82.75
Lube, oil change, and oil filters	55.94	27.60	46.42	58.04	61.45	78.52	74.71	85.28
Front-end alignment, wheel balance, rotation	7.94	6.09	6.89	6.17	8.31	11.37	11.73	10.74
Shock absorber replacement	3.06	2.14	3.92	2.78	2.31	3.21	2.82	3.89
Gas tank repair, replacement	8.16	1.97	15.35	3.93	6.31	7.44	3.50	14.99
Tire repair and other repair work	44.14	21.74	35.84	39.00	48.19	68.33	61.69	80.11
Vehicle air conditioning repair	12.18	4.63	9.54	13.29	15.29	17.28	12.25	26.21
Exhaust system repair	10.90	6.35	10.74	9.23	15.35	13.45	11.78	16.41
Electrical system repair	25.11	11.60	24.27	24.41	23.47	34.94	28.67	46.06
Motor repair, replacement	70.37	36.55	73.43	61.95	70.78	93.39	95.87	89.01
Auto repair service policy	8.11	0.23	6.71	8.50	6.49	14.40	10.22	21.81
Vehicle insurance	**905.26**	**587.89**	**891.79**	**860.56**	**1,011.87**	**1,100.58**	**1,097.41**	**1,106.21**
Vehicle rental, leases, licenses, other charges	**436.21**	**135.27**	**311.48**	**410.78**	**503.15**	**734.93**	**681.99**	**829.51**
Leased and rented vehicles	270.13	54.62	185.92	241.76	322.76	485.69	452.75	544.08
Rented vehicles	32.95	5.53	13.03	29.85	30.15	72.87	59.38	96.79
Auto rental	5.60	1.64	2.84	8.10	4.44	9.16	9.20	9.11
Auto rental on trips	21.95	2.32	7.73	17.65	21.16	51.69	42.32	68.31
Truck rental	2.22	0.96	1.27	2.19	1.68	4.16	2.53	7.05
Truck rental on trips	2.29	0.61	1.03	1.82	2.61	4.84	4.71	5.08

	total consumer units	less than high school graduate	high school graduate	some college	associate's degree	college graduate		
						total	bachelor's degree	master's, professional, doctorate
Leased vehicles	$237.19	$49.1■	$172.89	$211.92	$292.61	$412.82	$393.37	$447.29
Car lease payments	132.32	26.1□	80.50	117.35	186.79	239.74	234.44	249.13
Truck lease payments	86.11	22.2■	81.69	79.29	89.73	131.85	127.09	140.29
Vehicle registration, state	81.20	39.7■	70.42	88.84	91.68	106.44	107.10	105.27
Vehicle registration, local	6.97	4.4■	5.70	7.73	11.96	7.32	7.09	7.75
Driver's license	7.17	4.5□	6.73	6.94	8.67	8.82	7.72	10.78
Vehicle inspection	8.36	5.5	7.09	8.36	10.26	10.64	10.21	11.41
Parking fees	28.12	6.5□	13.15	25.73	27.68	58.16	48.53	75.24
Parking fees in home city, excluding residence	23.61	5.8□	10.51	21.07	24.38	49.19	41.41	62.98
Parking fees on trips	4.51	0.7□	2.65	4.66	3.30	8.97	7.12	12.26
Tolls	13.00	11.1■	7.57	10.87	8.09	22.53	17.37	32.40
Tolls on trips	3.75	1.28	2.10	3.36	3.90	7.12	5.93	9.24
Towing charges	4.67	3.5□	3.12	6.52	4.92	5.35	5.13	5.74
Automobile service clubs	12.83	3.90	9.67	10.67	13.23	22.85	20.16	27.62
PUBLIC TRANSPORTATION	**385.05**	**147.55**	**200.36**	**308.34**	**333.52**	**793.17**	**671.20**	**1,009.50**
Airline fares	252.56	73.5□	122.30	195.26	205.31	553.53	456.42	725.69
Intercity bus fares	8.96	6.2□	5.92	7.24	7.55	15.52	14.08	18.08
Intracity mass transit fares	48.94	48.1□	33.62	40.15	38.20	76.10	68.02	90.43
Local transportation on trips	8.33	1.1□	4.55	7.50	4.98	18.25	16.16	21.97
Taxi fares and limousine service on trips	4.89	0.6□	2.67	4.40	2.92	10.72	9.49	12.90
Taxi fares and limousine service	16.69	8.74	7.23	20.50	27.75	24.09	23.40	25.43
Intercity train fares	16.07	2.7□	7.56	10.21	13.26	38.29	36.79	40.95
Ship fares	27.90	5.64	16.17	21.91	33.31	55.75	46.40	72.33
School bus	0.70	0.6□	0.33	1.16	0.24	0.92	0.46	1.73

Note: Subcategories may not add to total because some are not shown.
Source: Bureau of Labor Statistics, unpublished tables from the 2003 Consumer Expenditure Survey

Table 11.26 Transportation: Indexed spending by education, 2003

(indexed average annual spending of consumer units (CU) on transportation, by education of consumer unit reference person, 2003; index definition: an index of 100 is the average for all consumer units; an index of 132 means that spending by consumer units in that group is 32 percent above the average for all consumer units; an index of 68 indicates spending that is 32 percent below the average for all consumer units)

	total consumer units	less than high school graduate	high school graduate	some college	associate's degree	college graduate total	bachelor's degree	master's, professional, doctorate
Average spending of CU, total	$40,817	$23,901	$33,956	$37,912	$44,547	$58,480	$54,726	$65,203
Average spending of CU, index	100	59	83	93	109	143	134	160
Transportation, spending index	**100**	**57**	**94**	**93**	**121**	**129**	**125**	**137**
VEHICLE PURCHASES	**100**	**55**	**98**	**91**	**130**	**125**	**123**	**129**
Cars and trucks, new	**100**	**35**	**96**	**86**	**137**	**140**	**133**	**152**
New cars	100	44	80	96	118	150	144	161
New trucks	100	27	109	77	153	132	124	145
Cars and trucks, used	**100**	**81**	**103**	**97**	**116**	**105**	**108**	**99**
Used cars	100	75	103	90	118	113	112	115
Used trucks	100	88	103	104	115	96	104	83
Other vehicles	**100**	**44**	**55**	**93**	**219**	**142**	**148**	**130**
GASOLINE AND MOTOR OIL	**100**	**71**	**98**	**100**	**115**	**114**	**113**	**116**
Gasoline	100	73	99	99	116	112	112	112
Diesel fuel	100	30	119	132	115	90	84	100
Gasoline on trips	100	38	76	110	104	151	131	186
Motor oil	100	111	112	101	123	72	76	65
Motor oil on trips	100	39	76	110	105	151	131	185
OTHER VEHICLE EXPENSES	**100**	**54**	**91**	**96**	**115**	**133**	**127**	**143**
Vehicle finance charges	**100**	**52**	**104**	**108**	**129**	**107**	**107**	**107**
Automobile finance charges	100	56	96	102	120	121	117	129
Truck finance charges	100	49	108	111	140	98	101	92
Motorcycle and plane finance charges	100	34	101	129	200	79	96	49
Other vehicle finance charges	100	37	140	138	88	69	82	46
Maintenance and repairs	**100**	**56**	**88**	**92**	**111**	**139**	**128**	**161**
Coolant, additives, brake and transmission fluids	100	105	114	104	119	72	80	57
Tires—purchased, replaced, installed	100	52	91	100	100	137	131	147
Parts, equipment, and accessories	100	69	109	122	144	75	84	60
Vehicle products	100	96	107	54	264	77	79	75
Miscellaneous auto repair, servicing	100	108	63	57	86	169	113	278
Body work and painting	100	54	65	86	125	166	143	205
Clutch and transmission repair	100	64	98	76	124	134	131	138
Drive shaft and rear-end repair	100	15	71	66	179	178	176	182
Brake work	100	47	82	103	114	141	131	161
Repair to steering or front-end	100	72	74	101	103	142	146	134
Repair to engine cooling system	100	58	76	99	118	143	131	163
Motor tune-up	100	48	63	92	110	171	145	217
Lube, oil change, and oil filters	100	49	83	104	110	140	134	152
Front-end alignment, wheel balance, rotation	100	77	87	78	105	143	148	135
Shock absorber replacement	100	70	128	91	75	105	92	127
Gas tank repair, replacement	100	24	188	48	77	91	43	184
Tire repair and other repair work	100	49	81	88	109	155	140	181
Vehicle air conditioning repair	100	38	78	109	126	142	101	215
Exhaust system repair	100	58	99	85	141	123	108	151
Electrical system repair	100	46	97	97	93	139	114	183
Motor repair, replacement	100	52	104	88	101	133	136	126
Auto repair service policy	100	3	83	105	80	178	126	269
Vehicle insurance	**100**	**65**	**99**	**95**	**112**	**122**	**121**	**122**
Vehicle rental, leases, licenses, other charges	**100**	**31**	**71**	**94**	**115**	**168**	**156**	**190**
Leased and rented vehicles	100	20	69	89	119	180	168	201
Rented vehicles	100	17	40	91	92	221	180	294
Auto rental	100	29	51	145	79	164	164	163
Auto rental on trips	100	11	35	80	96	235	193	311
Truck rental	100	43	57	99	76	187	114	318
Truck rental on trips	100	27	45	79	114	211	206	222

	total consumer units	less than high school graduate	high school graduate	some college	associate's degree	college graduate total	college graduate bachelor's degree	college graduate master's, professional, doctorate
Leased vehicles	100	21	73	89	123	174	166	189
Car lease payments	100	20	61	89	141	181	177	188
Truck lease payments	100	26	95	92	104	153	148	163
Vehicle registration, state	100	49	87	109	113	131	132	130
Vehicle registration, local	100	64	82	111	172	105	102	111
Driver's license	100	63	94	97	121	123	108	150
Vehicle inspection	100	66	85	100	123	127	122	136
Parking fees	100	23	47	92	98	207	173	268
Parking fees in home city, excluding residence	100	25	45	89	103	208	175	267
Parking fees on trips	100	16	59	103	73	199	158	272
Tolls	100	86	58	84	62	173	134	249
Tolls on trips	100	34	56	90	104	190	158	246
Towing charges	100	76	67	140	105	115	110	123
Automobile service clubs	100	30	75	83	103	178	157	215
PUBLIC TRANSPORTATION	**100**	**38**	**52**	**80**	**87**	**206**	**174**	**262**
Airline fares	100	29	48	77	81	219	181	287
Intercity bus fares	100	70	66	81	84	173	157	202
Intracity mass transit fares	100	98	69	82	78	155	139	185
Local transportation on trips	100	14	55	90	60	219	194	264
Taxi fares and limousine service on trips	100	14	55	90	60	219	194	264
Taxi fares and limousine service	100	52	43	123	166	144	140	152
Intercity train fares	100	17	47	64	83	238	229	255
Ship fares	100	20	58	79	119	200	166	259
School bus	100	94	47	166	34	131	66	247

Source: Calculations by New Strategist based on the 2003 Consumer Expenditure Survey

Table 11.27 Transportation: Total spending by education, 2003

(total annual spending on transportation, by consumer unit (CU) educational attainment group, 2003; numbers in thousands)

	total consumer units	less than high school graduate	high school graduate	some college	associate's degree	college graduate total	bachelor's degree	master's, professional, doctorate
Number of consumer units	115,356	17,721	31,552	24,514	10,981	30,589	19,557	11,032
Total spending of all CUs	$4,708,523,919	$423,552,102	$1,071,365,829	$929,384,819	$489,171,925	$1,788,844,720	$1,070,273,448	$719,316,517
Transportation, total spending	897,533,126	78,180,799	230,202,130	178,085,140	103,001,231	307,974,029	190,038,498	117,981,283
VEHICLE PURCHASES	430,480,907	36,485,235	115,443,720	82,908,799	53,075,675	142,571,352	89,510,042	53,061,383
Cars and trucks, new	236,763,576	12,741,753	62,116,738	43,081,884	30,853,206	87,972,435	53,467,273	34,505,338
New cars	109,001,038	7,421,732	23,869,088	22,189,583	12,254,686	43,266,917	26,525,355	16,741,612
New trucks	127,762,538	5,320,021	38,247,650	20,892,302	18,598,520	44,705,824	26,941,919	17,763,837
Cars and trucks, used	185,890,426	23,213,801	52,142,520	38,287,436	20,591,901	51,656,562	34,076,704	17,579,933
Used cars	94,178,946	10,853,758	26,406,500	18,070,250	10,567,126	28,282,589	17,959,584	10,322,973
Used trucks	91,711,481	12,360,220	25,736,020	20,217,186	10,024,775	23,373,973	16,117,119	7,256,960
Other vehicles	7,826,905	529,681	1,184,462	1,539,724	1,630,569	2,942,356	1,966,261	976,111
GASOLINE AND MOTOR OIL	153,741,863	16,691,942	41,202,810	32,625,683	16,804,773	46,416,360	29,372,463	17,043,999
Gasoline	140,804,687	15,839,207	38,187,701	29,527,358	15,491,556	41,760,715	26,744,980	15,015,766
Diesel fuel	1,699,194	78,858	551,213	478,023	186,238	404,387	242,507	161,950
Gasoline on trips	10,030,204	592,236	2,084,325	2,344,764	995,977	4,012,971	2,229,302	1,783,764
Motor oil	1,033,590	175,792	317,729	221,852	120,901	197,605	133,183	64,427
Motor oil on trips	101,513	6,025	21,140	23,779	10,103	40,683	22,491	17,982
OTHER VEHICLE EXPENSES	268,892,529	22,388,711	67,234,157	54,991,766	29,458,399	94,724,039	58,029,335	36,739,097
Vehicle finance charges	42,749,780	3,408,103	12,102,401	9,796,775	5,260,448	12,182,987	7,789,944	4,392,942
Automobile finance charges	20,127,315	1,729,747	5,268,868	4,350,745	2,306,120	6,472,021	3,984,934	2,487,275
Truck finance charges	20,532,214	1,559,980	6,066,503	4,841,025	2,744,811	5,320,345	3,506,961	1,813,440
Motorcycle and plane finance charges	319,536	16,658	88,346	87,270	60,725	67,296	52,217	15,114
Other vehicle finance charges	1,770,715	101,896	678,684	517,736	148,902	323,020	245,831	77,114
Maintenance and repairs	71,396,136	6,165,313	17,165,866	14,029,607	7,561,407	26,394,636	15,439,665	10,991,402
Coolant, additives, brake and transmission fluids	340,300	55,112	106,015	75,503	38,543	64,543	45,959	18,644
Tires—purchased, replaced, installed	10,147,867	815,166	2,513,748	2,161,890	969,952	3,686,586	2,260,007	1,426,658
Parts, equipment, and accessories	5,488,638	577,882	1,641,966	1,423,283	754,175	1,092,027	779,346	312,537
Vehicle products	484,495	71,238	141,668	55,402	121,889	99,108	64,538	34,530
Miscellaneous auto repair, servicing	4,620,008	769,269	795,426	563,332	376,319	2,073,628	881,434	1,227,420
Body work and painting	3,634,868	299,662	642,714	661,633	434,079	1,596,746	882,412	714,212
Clutch and transmission repair	4,356,996	425,127	1,163,007	707,719	515,668	1,545,662	971,005	574,547
Drive shaft and rear-end repair	888,241	20,025	171,643	125,021	151,648	419,681	264,997	154,889
Brake work	5,110,271	370,369	1,150,701	1,117,593	554,980	1,917,013	1,131,177	785,809
Repair to steering or front-end	1,503,089	165,691	302,899	323,340	147,036	564,673	371,974	192,508
Repair to engine cooling system	1,830,700	162,856	382,726	387,076	204,796	692,535	407,959	284,736
Motor tune-up	4,392,756	325,889	761,350	855,293	459,774	1,990,732	1,077,982	912,898
Lube, oil change, and oil filters	6,453,015	489,100	1,464,644	1,422,793	674,782	2,401,848	1,461,103	940,809
Front-end alignment, wheel balance, rotation	915,927	107,921	217,393	151,251	91,252	347,797	229,404	118,484
Shock absorber replacement	352,989	37,923	123,684	68,149	25,366	98,191	55,151	42,914
Gas tank repair, replacement	941,305	34,910	484,323	96,340	69,290	227,582	68,450	165,370
Tire repair and other repair work	5,091,814	385,255	1,130,824	956,046	529,174	2,090,146	1,206,471	883,774
Vehicle air conditioning repair	1,405,036	82,048	301,006	325,791	167,899	528,578	239,573	289,149
Exhaust system repair	1,257,380	112,528	338,868	226,264	168,558	411,422	230,381	181,035
Electrical system repair	2,896,589	205,564	765,767	598,387	257,724	1,068,780	560,699	508,134
Motor repair, replacement	8,117,602	647,703	2,316,863	1,518,642	777,235	2,856,707	1,874,930	981,958
Auto repair service policy	935,537	4,076	211,714	208,369	71,267	440,482	199,873	240,608
Vehicle insurance	104,427,173	10,417,999	28,137,758	21,095,768	11,111,344	33,665,642	21,462,047	12,203,709
Vehicle rental, leases, licenses, other charges	50,319,441	2,397,120	9,827,817	10,069,861	5,525,090	22,480,774	13,337,678	9,151,154
Leased and rented vehicles	31,161,116	967,921	5,866,148	5,926,505	3,544,228	14,856,771	8,854,432	6,002,291
Rented vehicles	3,800,980	97,997	411,123	731,743	331,077	2,229,020	1,161,295	1,067,787
Auto rental	645,994	29,062	89,608	198,563	48,756	280,195	179,924	100,502
Auto rental on trips	2,532,064	41,113	243,897	432,672	232,358	1,581,145	827,652	753,596
Truck rental	256,090	17,012	40,071	53,686	18,448	127,250	49,479	77,776
Truck rental on trips	264,165	10,810	32,499	44,615	28,660	148,051	92,113	56,043

	total consumer units	less than high school graduate	high school graduate	some college	associate's degree	college graduate total	bachelor's degree	master's, professional, doctorate
Leased vehicles	$27,361,290	$870,101	$5,455,025	$5,195,007	$3,213,150	$12,627,751	$7,693,137	$4,934,503
Car lease payments	15,263,906	463,050	2,539,936	2,876,963	2,051,141	7,333,407	4,584,943	2,748,402
Truck lease payments	9,933,305	393,406	2,577,483	1,943,715	985,325	4,033,160	2,485,499	1,547,679
Vehicle registration, state	9,366,907	704,587	2,221,892	2,177,824	1,006,738	3,255,893	2,094,555	1,161,339
Vehicle registration, local	804,031	79,036	179,846	189,493	131,333	223,911	138,659	85,498
Driver's license	827,103	80,276	212,345	170,127	95,205	269,795	150,980	118,925
Vehicle inspection	964,376	97,643	223,704	204,937	112,665	325,467	199,677	125,875
Parking fees	3,243,811	115,718	414,909	630,745	303,954	1,779,056	949,101	830,048
Parking fees in home city, excluding residence	2,723,555	103,136	331,612	516,510	267,717	1,504,673	809,855	694,795
Parking fees on trips	520,256	12,582	83,613	114,235	36,237	274,383	139,246	135,252
Tolls	1,499,628	197,412	238,849	266,467	88,836	689,170	339,705	357,437
Tolls on trips	432,585	22,683	66,259	82,367	42,826	217,794	115,973	101,936
Towing charges	538,713	62,555	98,442	159,831	54,027	163,651	100,327	63,324
Automobile service clubs	1,480,017	69,112	305,108	261,564	145,279	698,959	394,269	304,704
PUBLIC TRANSPORTATION	**44,417,828**	**2,614,734**	**6,321,759**	**7,558,647**	**3,662,383**	**24,262,277**	**13,126,658**	**11,136,804**
Airline fares	29,134,311	1,303,025	3,858,810	4,786,604	2,254,509	16,931,929	8,926,206	8,005,812
Intercity bus fares	1,033,590	111,111	186,788	177,481	82,907	474,741	275,363	199,459
Intracity mass transit fares	5,645,523	853,266	1,060,778	984,237	419,474	2,327,823	1,330,267	997,624
Local transportation on trips	960,915	20,734	143,562	183,855	54,685	558,249	316,041	242,373
Taxi fares and limousine service on trips	564,091	12,227	84,244	107,862	32,065	327,914	185,596	142,313
Taxi fares and limousine service	1,925,292	154,882	228,121	502,537	304,723	736,889	457,634	280,544
Intercity train fares	1,853,771	47,847	238,533	250,288	145,608	1,171,253	719,502	451,760
Ship fares	3,218,432	99,946	510,196	537,102	365,777	1,705,337	907,445	797,945
School bus	80,749	11,696	10,412	28,436	2,635	28,142	8,996	19,085

Note: Numbers may not add to total because of rounding and missing subcategories.
Source: Calculations by New Strategist based on the 2003 Consumer Expenditure Survey

Table 11.28 Transportation: Market shares by education, 2003

(percentage of total annual spending on transportation accounted for by consumer unit educational attainment groups, 2003)

	total consumer units	less than high school graduate	high school graduate	some college	associate's degree	college graduate total	bachelor's degree	master's, professional, doctorate
Share of total consumer units	100.0%	15.4%	27.4%	21.3%	9.5%	26.5%	17.0%	9.6%
Share of total before-tax income	100.0	7.5	21.5	18.8	10.1	42.4	24.8	17.6
Share of total spending	100.0	9.0	22.8	19.7	10.4	38.0	22.7	15.3
Share of transportation spending	100.0	8.7	25.6	19.8	11.5	34.3	21.2	13.1
VEHICLE PURCHASES	100.0	8.5	26.8	19.3	12.3	33.1	20.8	12.3
Cars and trucks, new	100.0	5.4	26.2	18.2	13.0	37.2	22.6	14.6
New cars	100.0	6.8	21.9	20.4	11.2	39.7	24.3	15.4
New trucks	100.0	4.2	29.9	16.4	14.6	35.0	21.1	13.9
Cars and trucks, used	100.0	12.5	28.1	20.6	11.1	27.8	18.3	9.5
Used cars	100.0	11.5	28.0	19.2	11.2	30.0	19.1	11.0
Used trucks	100.0	13.5	28.1	22.0	10.9	25.5	17.6	7.9
Other vehicles	100.0	6.8	15.1	19.7	20.8	37.6	25.1	12.5
GASOLINE AND MOTOR OIL	100.0	10.9	26.8	21.2	10.9	30.2	19.1	11.1
Gasoline	100.0	11.2	27.1	21.0	11.0	29.7	19.0	10.7
Diesel fuel	100.0	4.6	32.4	28.1	11.0	23.8	14.3	9.5
Gasoline on trips	100.0	5.9	20.8	23.4	9.9	40.0	22.2	17.8
Motor oil	100.0	17.0	30.7	21.5	11.7	19.1	12.9	6.2
Motor oil on trips	100.0	5.9	20.8	23.4	10.0	40.1	22.2	17.7
OTHER VEHICLE EXPENSES	100.0	8.3	25.0	20.5	11.0	35.2	21.6	13.7
Vehicle finance charges	100.0	8.0	28.3	22.9	12.3	28.5	18.2	10.3
Automobile finance charges	100.0	8.6	26.2	21.6	11.5	32.2	19.8	12.4
Truck finance charges	100.0	7.6	29.5	23.6	13.4	25.9	17.1	8.8
Motorcycle and plane finance charges	100.0	5.2	27.6	27.3	19.0	21.1	16.3	4.7
Other vehicle finance charges	100.0	5.8	38.3	29.2	8.4	18.2	13.9	4.4
Maintenance and repairs	100.0	8.6	24.0	19.7	10.6	37.0	21.6	15.4
Coolant, additives, brake and transmission fluids	100.0	16.2	31.2	22.2	11.3	19.0	13.5	5.5
Tires—purchased, replaced, installed	100.0	8.0	24.8	21.3	9.6	36.3	22.3	14.1
Parts, equipment, and accessories	100.0	10.5	29.9	25.9	13.7	19.9	14.2	5.7
Vehicle products	100.0	14.7	29.2	11.4	25.2	20.5	13.3	7.1
Miscellaneous auto repair, servicing	100.0	16.7	17.2	12.2	8.1	44.9	19.1	26.6
Body work and painting	100.0	8.2	17.7	18.2	11.9	43.9	24.3	19.6
Clutch and transmission repair	100.0	9.8	26.7	16.2	11.8	35.5	22.3	13.2
Drive shaft and rear-end repair	100.0	2.3	19.3	14.1	17.1	47.2	29.8	17.4
Brake work	100.0	7.2	22.5	21.9	10.9	37.5	22.1	15.4
Repair to steering or front-end	100.0	11.0	20.2	21.5	9.8	37.6	24.7	12.8
Repair to engine cooling system	100.0	8.9	20.9	21.1	11.2	37.8	22.3	15.6
Motor tune-up	100.0	7.4	17.3	19.5	10.5	45.3	24.5	20.8
Lube, oil change, and oil filters	100.0	7.6	22.7	22.0	10.5	37.2	22.6	14.6
Front-end alignment, wheel balance, rotation	100.0	11.8	23.7	16.5	10.0	38.0	25.0	12.9
Shock absorber replacement	100.0	10.7	35.0	19.3	7.2	27.8	15.6	12.2
Gas tank repair, replacement	100.0	3.7	51.5	10.2	7.4	24.2	7.3	17.6
Tire repair and other repair work	100.0	7.6	22.2	18.8	10.4	41.0	23.7	17.4
Vehicle air conditioning repair	100.0	5.8	21.4	23.2	11.9	37.6	17.1	20.6
Exhaust system repair	100.0	8.9	27.0	18.0	13.4	32.7	18.3	14.4
Electrical system repair	100.0	7.1	26.4	20.7	8.9	36.9	19.4	17.5
Motor repair, replacement	100.0	8.0	28.5	18.7	9.6	35.2	23.1	12.1
Auto repair service policy	100.0	0.4	22.6	22.3	7.6	47.1	21.4	25.7
Vehicle insurance	100.0	10.0	26.9	20.2	10.6	32.2	20.6	11.7
Vehicle rental, leases, licenses, other charges	100.0	4.8	19.5	20.0	11.0	44.7	26.5	18.2
Leased and rented vehicles	100.0	3.1	18.8	19.0	11.4	47.7	28.4	19.3
Rented vehicles	100.0	2.6	10.8	19.3	8.7	58.6	30.6	28.1
Auto rental	100.0	4.5	13.9	30.7	7.5	43.4	27.9	15.6
Auto rental on trips	100.0	1.6	9.6	17.1	9.2	62.4	32.7	29.8
Truck rental	100.0	6.6	15.6	21.0	7.2	49.7	19.3	30.4
Truck rental on trips	100.0	4.1	12.3	16.9	10.8	56.0	34.9	21.2

	total consumer units	less than high school graduate	high school graduate	some college	associate's degree	college graduate		
						total	bachelor's degree	master's, professional, doctorate
Leased vehicles	100.0%	3.2%	19.9%	19.0%	11.7%	46.2%	28.1%	18.0%
Car lease payments	100.0	3.0	16.6	18.8	13.4	48.0	30.0	18.0
Truck lease payments	100.0	4.0	25.9	19.6	9.9	40.6	25.0	15.6
Vehicle registration, state	100.0	7.5	23.7	23.3	10.7	34.8	22.4	12.4
Vehicle registration, local	100.0	9.8	22.4	23.6	16.3	27.8	17.2	10.6
Driver's license	100.0	9.7	25.7	20.6	11.5	32.6	18.3	14.4
Vehicle inspection	100.0	10.1	23.2	21.3	11.7	33.7	20.7	13.1
Parking fees	100.0	3.6	12.8	19.4	9.4	54.8	29.3	25.6
Parking fees in home city, excluding residence	100.0	3.8	12.2	19.0	9.8	55.2	29.7	25.5
Parking fees on trips	100.0	2.4	16.1	22.0	7.0	52.7	26.8	26.0
Tolls	100.0	13.2	15.9	17.8	5.9	46.0	22.7	23.8
Tolls on trips	100.0	5.2	15.3	19.0	9.9	50.3	26.8	23.6
Towing charges	100.0	11.6	18.3	29.7	10.0	30.4	18.6	11.8
Automobile service clubs	100.0	4.7	20.6	17.7	9.8	47.2	26.6	20.6
PUBLIC TRANSPORTATION	**100.0**	**5.9**	**14.2**	**17.0**	**8.2**	**54.6**	**29.6**	**25.1**
Airline fares	100.0	4.5	13.2	16.4	7.7	58.1	30.6	27.5
Intercity bus fares	100.0	10.7	18.1	17.2	8.0	45.9	26.6	19.3
Intracity mass transit fares	100.0	15.1	18.8	17.4	7.4	41.2	23.6	17.7
Local transportation on trips	100.0	2.2	14.9	19.1	5.7	58.1	32.9	25.2
Taxi fares and limousine service on trips	100.0	2.2	14.9	19.1	5.7	58.1	32.9	25.2
Taxi fares and limousine service	100.0	8.0	11.8	26.1	15.8	38.3	23.8	14.6
Intercity train fares	100.0	2.6	12.9	13.5	7.9	63.2	38.8	24.4
Ship fares	100.0	3.1	15.9	16.7	11.4	53.0	28.2	24.8
School bus	100.0	14.5	12.9	35.2	3.3	34.9	11.1	23.6

Note: Numbers may not add to total because of rounding.
Source: Calculations by New Strategist based on the 2003 Consumer Expenditure Survey

Appendix A

About the Consumer Expenditure Survey

History

The Consumer Expenditure Survey (CEX) is an ongoing study of the day-to-day spending of American households. In taking the survey, government interviewers collect spending data on products and services as well as the amount and sources of household income, changes in saving and debt, and demographic and economic characteristics of household members. Data collection for the CEX is done by the Bureau of the Census, under contract with the Bureau of Labor Statistics (BLS). The BLS is responsible for analysis and release of the survey data.

Since the late 19th century, the federal government has conducted expenditure surveys about every ten years. Although the results have been used for a variety of purposes, their primary application is to track consumer prices. Beginning in 1980, the CEX became a continuous survey with annual release of data (with a lag time of about two years between data collection and release). The survey is used to update prices for the market basket of products and services used in calculating the Consumer Price Index.

Description of the Consumer Expenditure Survey

The CEX is two surveys: an interview survey and a diary survey. In the interview portion of the survey, respondents are asked each quarter for five consecutive quarters to report their expenditures for the previous three months. The purchase of big-ticket items such as houses, cars, and major appliances, or recurring expenses such as insurance premiums, utility payments, and rent are recorded by the interview survey. About 95 percent of all expenditures are covered by the interview component.

Expenditures on small, frequently purchased items are recorded during a two-week period by the diary survey. These detailed records include expenses for food and beverages purchased in grocery stores and at restaurants, as well as other items such as tobacco, housekeeping supplies, nonprescription drugs, and personal care products and services. The diary survey is intended to capture expenditures respondents are likely to forget or recall incorrectly over longer periods of time.

The average spending figures shown in this book are the integrated data from both the diary and interview components of the survey. Integrated data provide a more complete accounting of consumer expenditures than either component of the survey is designed to do alone.

Data collection and processing

Two separate, nationally representative samples are used for the interview and diary surveys. For the interview survey, about 7,500 consumer units are interviewed on a rotating panel basis each quarter for five consecutive quarters. Another 7,500 consumer units keep weekly diaries of spending for two consecutive weeks. Data collection is carried out in 105 areas of the country.

The data are reviewed, audited, and cleaned by the BLS, and then weighted to reflect the number and characteristics of all U.S. consumer units. As with any sample survey, the CEX is subject to two major types of error. Nonsampling error occurs when respondents misinterpret questions or interviewers are inconsistent in the way they ask questions or record answers. Respondents may forget items, recall expenses incorrectly, or deliberately give wrong answers. A respondent may remember how much he or she spent at the grocery store but forget the items picked up at a local convenience store. Most surveys of alcohol consumption or spending on alcohol suffer from this type of underreporting, for example. Nonsampling error can also be caused by mistakes during the various stages of data processing and refinement.

Sampling error occurs when a sample does not accurately represent the population it is supposed to represent. This kind of error is present in every sample-based survey and is minimized by using a proper sampling procedure. Standard error tables documenting the extent of sampling error in the CEX are available from the BLS at http://www.bls.gov/cex/csxstnderror.htm.

Although the CEX is the best source of information about the spending behavior of American households, it should be treated with caution because of the above problems. Comparisons with consumption data from other sources show that CEX data tend to underestimate expenditures except for rent, fuel, telephone service, furniture, transportation, and personal care services. Despite these problems, the data reveal important spending patterns by demographic segment that can be used to better understand consumer behavior.

The definition of consumer units

The CEX uses consumer units as its sampling unit instead of households, which are the sampling units used by the Census Bureau. The term "household" is used interchangeably with the term "consumer unit" in this book for convenience, although they are not exactly the same. Some households contain more than one consumer unit.

Consumer units are defined by the BLS as either: 1) members of a household who are related by blood, marriage, adoption, or other legal arrangements; 2) a person living alone or sharing a household with others or living as a roomer in a private home or lodging house or in permanent living quarters in a hotel or motel, but who is financially independent; or 3) two persons or more living together who pool their income to make joint expenditure decisions. The BLS defines financial independence in terms of "the three major expenses categories: housing, food, and other living expenses. To be considered financially independent, at least two of the three major expense categories have to be provided by the respondent."

The Census Bureau uses households as its sampling unit in the decennial census and in the monthly Current Population Survey. The Census Bureau's household "consists of all persons who occupy a housing unit. A house, an apartment or other groups of rooms, or a single room is regarded as a housing unit when it is occupied or intended for occupancy as separate living quarters; that is, when the occupants do not live and eat with any other persons in the structure and there is direct access from the outside or through a common hall."

The definition goes on to specify that "a household includes the related family members and all the unrelated persons, if any, such as lodgers, foster children, wards, or employees who share the housing unit. A person living alone in a housing unit or a group of unrelated persons sharing a housing unit as partners is also counted as a household. The count of households excludes group quarters."

Because there can be more than one consumer unit in a household, consumer units outnumber households by several million. Most of the excess consumer units are headed by young adults, under age 25.

For more information

If you want to know more about the Consumer Expenditure Survey, contact the CEX specialists at the Bureau of Labor Statistics at (202) 691-6900, or visit the Consumer Expenditure Survey home page at http://www.bls.gov/cex/. The CEX web site includes news releases, technical documentation, and current and historical CEX data. The detailed average spending data shown in Chapters 2 through 11 of *Household Spending* are available only by special request from the BLS.

Appendix B

Mortgage Principal and Capital Improvements

The spending statistics reported by the Consumer Expenditure Survey do not include spending on mortgage principal reduction or capital improvements. Because the survey treats home equity as an asset, principal reduction and capital improvements are regarded as asset accumulation rather than expenditures. The following table shows the average amounts spent by households in 2003 for mortgage principal reduction and capital improvements. Adding these figures to expenditures for the category "owned dwellings" gives a more complete picture of the average amount households devote to housing.

(average annual reduction in mortgage principal and change in capital improvement for owned homes, by age of consumer unit (CU) reference person, average before-tax income of consumer unit, type of consumer unit, race and Hispanic origin of consumer unit reference person, region in which consumer unit lives, and educational attainment of consumer unit reference person, 2003)

AGE OF REFERENCE PERSON	total consumer units	under 25	25 to 34	35 to 44	45 to 54	55 to 64	65 or older total	65 to 74	75 or older
Reduction of mortgage principal	−$1,131.11	−$134.23	−$957.14	−$1,601.97	−$1,765.60	−$1,278.50	−$405.57	−$646.46	−$163.04
Change in capital improvements	1,005.04	64.77	725.08	1,321.44	1,366.67	1,378.73	630.91	918.60	341.26

BEFORE-TAX INCOME OF CONSUMER UNIT	complete income reporters	under $20,000	$20,000–$39,999	$40,000–$49,999	$50,000–$69,999	$70,000–$79,999	$80,000–$99,999	$100,000 or more
Reduction of mortgage principal	−$1,122.56	−$252.02	−$559.29	$929.98	$1,358.18	−$1,682.49	−$1,975.83	−$3,483.01
Change in capital improvements	1,060.27	130.30	354.21	374.15	986.58	1,603.75	1,765.88	4,642.77

TYPE OF CONSUMER UNIT	total consumer units	total married couples	married couples, no children	married couples with children total	oldest child under 6	oldest child 6 to 17	oldest child 18 or older	single parent with child under 18	single person
Reduction of mortgage principal	−$1,131.11	−$1,717.58	−$1,248.14	−$2,150.09	−$1,904.75	−$2,289.25	−$2,057.35	−$550.62	−$440.37
Change in capital improvements	1,006.04	1,664.00	1,130.21	2,119.49	1,673.16	2,632.23	1,465.06	216.57	343.50

RACE/HISPANIC ORIGIN OF REFERENCE PERSON	total consumer units	race Asian	black	white and other	Hispanic origin Hispanic	non-Hispanic
Reduction of mortgage principal	−$1,131.11	−$2,012.36	−$582.47	−$1,175.90	−$788.71	−$1,169.86
Change in capital improvements	1,006.04	1,321.96	161.92	1,112.85	427.28	1,071.54

REGION	total consumer units	Northeast	Midwest	South	West
Reduction of mortgage principal	−1,131.11	−1,222.18	−1,049.33	−973.87	−1,392.41
Change in capital improvements	1,006.04	1,363.16	1,251.93	673.52	979.23

EDUCATIONAL ATTAINMENT OF REFERENCE PERSON	total consumer units	less than high school graduate	high school graduate	some college	associate's degree	college graduate total	bachelor's degree	master's, professional, doctorate
Reduction of mortgage principal	−$1,131.11	−$440.37	−$788.32	−$853.49	−$1,371.78	−$2,020.94	−$1,885.53	−$2,261.01
Change in capital improvements	1,006.04	306.34	567.33	868.99	946.54	1,995.11	1,454.54	2,953.47

Source: Bureau of Labor Statistics, 2003 Consumer Expenditue Survey

Appendix C

Percent Reporting Expenditure and Amount Spent, Average Quarter 2003

(percent of consumer units reporting expenditure and amount spent by purchasers during an average quarter, 2003)

	percent reporting expenditure during quarter	average amount spent by purchasers per quarter
FOOD	**99.48%**	**$1,318.91**
Food at home	**98.77**	**971.80**
Grocery stores	98.26	910.92
Convenience stores	23.69	235.18
Food prepared by CU on trips	10.69	84.85
Food away from home	**80.37**	**438.22**
Meals at restaurants, carryouts, and other	76.68	335.82
Board (including at school)	1.19	698.53
Catered affairs	0.89	1,359.27
Food on trips	25.10	213.12
School lunches	9.25	153.70
Meals as pay	1.87	351.34
ALCOHOLIC BEVERAGES	**37.95**	**196.22**
At home	**30.12**	**131.23**
Beer and wine	29.29	114.88
Other alcoholic beverages	7.79	75.48
Away from home	**25.18**	**138.76**
Alcoholic beverages at restaurants, taverns	19.44	136.96
Alcoholic beverages purchased on trips	11.90	69.87
HOUSING	**99.52**	**3,167.12**
Shelter	**97.58**	**2,020.75**
Owned Dwellings	67.02	**1,963.20**
Mortgage interest and charges	41.74	1,769.29
Mortgage interest	39.27	1,801.95
Interest paid, home equity loan	3.26	490.80
Interest paid, home equity line of credit	3.51	416.45
Property taxes	65.79	510.65
Maintenance, repairs, insurance, other expenses	35.87	672.64
Homeowners insurance	24.78	289.98
Ground rent	1.31	774.43
Maintenance and repair services	11.72	1,101.34
Painting and papering	1.12	1,352.23
Plumbing and water heating	3.56	340.01
Heat, air conditioning, electrical work	3.68	580.01
Roofing and gutters	1.38	1,775.00
Other repair and maintenance services	3.85	1,117.34
Repair/replacement of hard surface flooring	0.63	1,821.03
Repair of built-in appliances	0.94	158.78
Maintenance and repair materials	6.01	327.79
Paints, wallpaper and supplies	2.61	117.05
Tools/equipment for painting, wallpapering	2.61	12.55
Plumbing supplies and equipment	0.86	156.10
Electrical supplies, heating/cooling equipment	0.47	179.79
Hard surface flooring, repair and replacement	0.47	819.15
Roofing and gutters	0.34	508.09
Plaster, paneling, siding, windows, doors, screens, awnings	0.89	472.19
Patio, walk, fence, driveway, masonry, brick, and stucco work	0.35	101.43
Landscape maintenance	0.02	162.50
Miscellaneous supplies and equipment	1.60	247.50
Insulation, other maintenance/repair	1.58	229.59
Finish basement, remodel rooms, build patios, walks, etc.	0.03	1,108.33
Property management and security	4.17	218.94
Property management	3.91	211.19
Management and upkeep services for security	0.95	91.84
Parking	1.01	135.40

	percent reporting expenditure during quarter	average amount spent by purchasers per quarter
RENTED DWELLINGS	**31.53%**	**$1,728.11**
Rent	31.02	1,700.31
Rent as pay	0.67	1,230.60
Maintenance, insurance, and other expenses	3.47	264.91
Tenant's insurance	2.40	100.73
Maintenance and repair services	0.52	811.54
Maintenance and repair materials	0.75	336.51
OTHER LODING	**18.61**	**597.74**
Owned vacation homes	4.50	834.94
Mortgage interest and charges	1.23	1,251.02
Mortgage interest	1.20	1,268.54
Interest paid, home equity loan	0.01	475.00
Interest paid, home equity line of credit	0.03	400.00
Property taxes	4.09	360.02
Maintenance, insurance and other expenses	1.35	552.59
Homeowners and related insurance	0.62	293.55
Ground rent	0.11	913.64
Maintenance and repair services	0.63	528.97
Maintenance and repair materials	0.05	170.00
Property management and security	0.52	209.62
Property management	0.50	194.50
Management and upkeep services for security	0.15	78.33
Parking	0.12	108.33
Housing while attending school	1.04	1,271.63
Lodging on out-of-town trips	14.72	410.61
Utilities, fuels, public services	**97.25**	**722.73**
Natural gas	50.40	194.45
Electricity	90.55	283.80
Fuel oil and other fuels	10.68	256.37
Fuel oil	3.79	379.55
Coal	0.08	140.63
Bottled gas	6.03	175.87
Wood and other fuels	1.62	140.43
Telephone services	94.66	252.40
Telephone services in home city, excl. mobile car phones	89.49	173.09
Cellular phone service	42.14	187.53
Pager service	0.44	63.64
Phone cards	9.88	47.77
Water and other public services	60.32	135.23
Water and sewerage maintenance	53.55	110.32
Trash and garbage collection	37.49	58.44
Septic tank cleaning	0.47	125.00
Household services	**58.13**	**303.32**
Personal services	8.01	916.14
Babysitting and child care in your own home	1.79	503.49
Babysitting and child care in someone else's home	1.09	550.23
Care for elderly, invalids, handicapped, etc.	0.35	2,754.29
Adult day care centers	0.10	1,525.00
Day care centers, nursery and preschools	5.45	866.15
Other household services	55.31	186.11
Housekeeping services	5.72	407.04
Gardening, lawn care service	12.58	166.34
Water softening service	1.37	58.94
Nonclothing laundry and dry cleaning, sent out	0.59	42.37
Nonclothing laundry and dry cleaning, coin-operated	4.63	19.55
Termite/pest control services	2.52	112.10
Home security system service fee	4.10	94.76
Other home services	2.00	185.38
Termite/pest control products	1.50	25.33
Moving, storage, and freight express	1.70	447.94
Appliance repair, including service center	2.39	122.91
Reupholstering and furniture repair	0.62	209.68
Repairs/rentals of lawn/garden equip., hand/power tools, etc.	1.14	133.33
Appliance rental	0.26	156.73
Rental of office equipment for nonbusiness use	0.04	381.25

	percent reporting expenditure during quarter	average amount spent by purchasers per quarter
Repair of computer systems for nonbusiness use	0.51%	$205.88
Computer information services	41.28	75.05
Household furnishings and equipment	**50.54**	**595.36**
Household textiles	19.26	108.76
Bathroom linens	6.73	43.43
Bedroom linens	9.92	95.72
Kitchen and dining room linens	2.40	27.08
Curtains and draperies	2.45	155.51
Slipcovers and decorative pillows	1.33	65.98
Sewing materials for household items	3.88	72.62
Other linens	0.76	49.67
Furniture	10.97	913.45
Mattress and springs	1.66	676.05
Other bedroom furniture	2.44	813.93
Sofas	2.21	1,042.65
Living room chairs	2.02	479.70
Living room tables	1.60	273.59
Kitchen and dining room furniture	1.61	767.39
Infants' furniture	0.81	252.16
Outdoor furniture	1.40	274.11
Wall units, cabinets, and other furniture	3.38	407.77
Floor coverings	3.42	378.36
Wall-to-wall carpeting (renter)	0.03	1,591.67
Wall-to-wall carpeting, replacement (owner)	0.44	1,567.61
Floor coverings, nonpermanent	3.03	183.66
Major appliances	7.98	556.20
Dishwashers (built-in), garbage disposals, range hoods (renter)	0.04	293.75
Dishwashers (built-in), garbage disposals, range hoods (owner)	0.77	423.05
Refrigerators and freezers (renter)	0.29	406.03
Refrigerators and freezers (owner)	1.38	776.27
Washing machines (renter)	0.31	387.01
Washing machines (owner)	1.04	574.04
Clothes dryers (renter)	0.28	307.14
Clothes dryers (owner)	0.87	459.48
Cooking stoves, ovens (renter)	0.14	271.43
Cooking stoves, ovens (owner)	0.92	787.23
Microwave ovens (renter)	0.52	76.44
Microwave ovens (owner)	0.94	158.78
Window air conditioners (renter)	0.17	188.24
Window air conditioners (owner)	0.38	271.05
Electric floor cleaning equipment	2.14	167.29
Sewing machines	0.38	588.82
Small appliances and miscellaneous housewares	15.41	84.30
Housewares	9.53	77.28
Plastic dinnerware	1.62	24.07
China and other dinnerware	2.73	79.49
Flatware	1.69	59.02
Glassware	2.31	35.50
Silver serving pieces	0.19	53.95
Other serving pieces	0.93	38.71
Nonelectric cookware	3.72	67.88
Small appliances	7.76	72.52
Small electric kitchen appliances	6.59	59.41
Portable heating and cooling equipment	1.48	115.71
Miscellaneous household equipment	34.73	315.07
Window coverings	1.90	320.26
Infants' equipment	0.63	113.49
Outdoor equipment	0.93	204.03
Clocks	1.91	57.07
Lamps and lighting fixtures	3.73	91.56
Other household decorative items	8.65	169.83
Telephones and accessories	4.55	77.03
Lawn and garden equipment	2.74	505.38
Power tools	2.21	189.25
Small miscellaneous furnishings	1.12	281.47
Hand tools	2.01	89.80
Indoor plants and fresh flowers	13.12	76.81

	percent reporting expenditure during quarter	average amount spent by purchasers per quarter
Closet and storage items	1.89%	$68.12
Rental of furniture	0.23	293.48
Luggage	1.65	93.64
Computers and computer hardware, nonbusiness use	4.56	749.84
Computer software and accessories, nonbusiness use	4.08	110.17
Telephone answering devices	0.44	52.84
Calculators	0.39	35.67
Business equipment for home use	0.32	84.38
Smoke alarms (owner)	0.57	43.86
Smoke alarms (renter)	0.08	40.63
Other household appliances (owner)	0.86	161.05
Other household appliances (renter)	0.32	88.28
APPAREL AND SERVICES	**74.93**	**394.42**
Men and boys'	**37.01**	**203.72**
MEN'S APPAREL	**30.46**	**186.00**
Suits	1.63	363.19
Sportcoats and tailored jackets	1.56	160.69
Coats and jackets	4.66	117.92
Underwear	6.95	28.42
Hosiery	6.58	16.60
Nightwear	1.45	34.83
Accessories	4.84	38.43
Sweaters and vests	3.40	85.22
Active sportswear	3.69	67.07
Shirts	16.41	75.29
Pants	16.99	89.71
Shorts and shorts sets	4.81	51.87
Uniforms	0.58	113.36
Costumes	0.85	120.29
BOYS' (AGED 2 TO 15) APPAREL	**11.72**	**159.90**
Coats and jackets	2.43	65.95
Sweaters	1.30	50.96
Shirts	6.27	59.61
Underwear	3.38	27.15
Nightwear	1.31	30.92
Hosiery	3.09	15.13
Accessories	1.54	22.08
Suits, sportcoats, and vests	0.63	94.85
Pants	6.87	77.98
Shorts and shorts sets	3.49	55.73
Uniforms	0.73	115.41
Active sportswear	1.90	60.92
Costumes	1.22	54.30
Women and girls'	**45.86**	**242.22**
WOMEN'S APPAREL	**40.68**	**217.20**
Coats and jackets	6.63	113.42
Dresses	8.83	110.73
Sportcoats and tailored jackets	1.61	84.78
Sweaters and vests	9.32	74.89
Shirts, blouses, and tops	21.10	69.79
Skirts	5.13	49.56
Pants	20.32	83.55
Shorts and shorts sets	5.97	52.97
Active sportswear	5.33	65.76
Nightwear	5.90	43.94
Undergarments	11.31	43.66
Hosiery	10.38	19.05
Suits	3.45	160.72
Accessories	7.69	48.60
Uniforms	1.54	91.88
Costumes	1.25	128.00
GIRLS' (AGED 2 TO 15) APPAREL	**12.33**	**184.29**
Coats and jackets	2.64	64.30
Dresses and suits	3.50	64.39
Shirts, blouses, and sweaters	7.05	80.43
Skirts and pants	6.94	84.55

	percent reporting expenditure during quarter	average amount spent by purchasers per quarter
Shorts and shorts sets	3.46%	$55.49
Active sportswear	2.15	61.28
Underwear and nightwear	4.30	37.03
Hosiery	2.76	14.31
Accessories	2.03	25.12
Uniforms	0.65	100.38
Costumes	1.45	67.24
Children under age two	13.35	118.13
Coats, jackets, and snowsuits	1.27	41.14
Outerwear including dresses	7.44	68.92
Underwear	7.60	101.02
Nightwear and loungewear	2.79	36.47
Accessories	3.92	36.35
Footwear	**31.08**	**96.61**
Men's	11.29	88.15
Boys'	5.67	61.99
Women's	17.64	75.61
Girls'	5.70	56.54
Other apparel products and services	**40.86**	**154.84**
Material for making clothes	1.47	56.12
Sewing patterns and notions	1.86	21.37
Watches	4.02	106.47
Jewelry	7.69	390.64
Shoe repair and other shoe services	0.93	30.91
Coin-operated apparel laundry and dry cleaning	14.49	62.82
Apparel alteration, repair, and tailoring services	2.80	50.18
Clothing rental	0.51	120.59
Watch and jewelry repair	2.12	42.34
Professional laundry, dry cleaning	18.81	81.31
Clothing storage	0.11	109.09
TRANSPORTATION	**93.79**	**2,058.48**
Vehicle purchases	**6.70**	**13,924.48**
Cars and trucks, new	2.02	25,401.73
New cars	1.02	23,159.56
New trucks	1.01	27,414.60
Cars and trucks, used	4.55	8,854.12
Used cars	2.81	7,263.52
Used trucks	1.84	10,802.04
Other vehicles	0.23	7,375.00
New motorcycles	0.12	7,527.08
Used motorcycles	0.10	6,317.50
Gasoline and motor oil	**89.41**	**372.48**
Gasoline	88.63	344.30
Diesel fuel	1.24	296.98
Gasoline on out-of-town trips	22.09	98.40
Motor oil	10.86	20.63
Motor oil on out-of-town trips	22.09	1.00
Other vehicle expenses	**79.03**	**721.06**
Vehicle finance charges	34.06	272.01
Automobile finance charges	20.38	214.03
Truck finance charges	16.95	262.52
Motorcycle and plane finance charges	0.70	98.93
Other vehicle finance charges	1.27	302.17
Maintenance and repairs	49.84	291.11
Coolant, additives, brake, transmission fluids	6.11	12.07
Tires	8.09	271.85
Parts, equipment, and accessories	10.54	112.86
Vehicle audio equipment	0.18	213.89
Body work and painting	1.42	554.75
Clutch, transmission repair	1.55	609.19
Drive shaft and rear-end repair	0.29	663.79
Brake work	4.50	246.11
Repair to steering or front-end	1.11	293.47
Repair to engine cooling system	1.56	254.33
Motor tune-up	4.70	202.55
Lube, oil change, and oil filters	31.63	44.21

	percent reporting expenditure during quarter	average amount spent by purchasers per quarter
Front-end alignment, wheel balance, rotation	2.18%	S91.06
Shock absorber replacement	0.36	212.50
Repair tires and other repair work	7.27	151.79
Exhaust system repair	1.22	223.36
Electrical system repair	2.68	234.24
Motor repair, replacement	2.88	610.85
Auto repair service policy	0.34	596.32
Vehicle accessories, including labor	0.79	307.91
Vehicle audio equipment, including labor	0.39	293.59
Vehicle air conditioning repair	1.18	258.05
Vehicle insurance	50.95	444.19
Vehicle rental, leases, licenses, other charges	38.43	275.31
Leased and rented vehicles	6.85	985.88
Rented vehicles	3.00	274.58
Auto rental	0.61	229.51
Auto rental, out-of-town trips	1.96	279.97
Truck rental	0.28	198.21
Truck rental, out-of-town trips	0.21	272.62
Leased vehicles	4.08	1,453.37
Car lease payments	2.57	1,287.16
Cash downpayment (car lease)	0.08	3,478.13
Termination fee (car lease)	0.04	381.25
Truck lease payments	1.71	1,258.92
Cash downpayment (truck lease)	0.04	2,887.50
Termination fee (truck lease)	0.03	2,000.00
Vehicle registration, state	15.22	125.15
Vehicle registration, local	1.98	88.01
Driver's license	5.90	30.38
Vehicle inspection	5.57	37.52
Parking fees	11.44	61.45
Parking fees in home city, excluding residence	9.13	64.65
Parking fees, out-of-town trips	3.15	35.79
Tolls on out-of-town trips	7.07	13.26
Towing charges	1.23	94.92
Automobile service clubs	4.18	76.73
Public transportation	**18.12**	**523.30**
Airline fares	9.92	636.49
Intercity bus fares	4.15	53.98
Intracity mass transit fares	7.04	173.79
Local transportation on out-of-town trips	5.07	41.08
Taxi fares and limousine service on trips	5.07	24.11
Taxi fares and limousine service	2.86	95.63
Intercity train fares	3.61	111.29
Ship fares	2.18	319.95
School bus	0.10	175.00
HEALTH CARE	**78.60**	**720.96**
Health insurance	**64.68**	**483.77**
Commercial health insurance	13.89	448.51
Traditional fee for service health plan (not BCBS)	4.43	461.34
Preferred provider health plan (not BCBS)	9.65	433.33
Blue Cross, Blue Shield	19.12	458.79
Traditional fee for service health plan	3.23	499.30
Preferred provider health plan	7.07	438.65
Health maintenance organization	6.33	431.28
Commercial Medicare supplement	2.46	476.02
Other BCBS health insurance	0.71	242.25
Health maintenance plans (HMOs)	17.04	409.29
Medicare payments	23.09	232.81
Commercial Medicare supplements/other health insurance	13.03	302.28
Commercial Medicare supplement (not BCBS)	5.72	446.33
Other health insurance (not BCBS)	7.77	178.35
Medical Services	**40.69**	**362.23**
Physician's services	26.80	133.98
Dental services	14.25	398.67
Eye care services	7.32	118.17
Service by professionals other than physician	5.83	165.27

	percent reporting expenditure during quarter	average amount spent by purchasers per quarter
Lab tests, x-rays	4.60%	$157.23
Hospital room	1.61	404.66
Hospital services other than room	2.54	426.57
Care in convalescent or nursing home	0.33	2,484.85
Other medical services	2.23	161.44
Prescription drugs	**44.54**	**195.63**
Medical supplies	**8.60**	**223.84**
Eyeglasses and contact lenses	7.04	181.00
Hearing aids	0.81	444.44
Medical equipment for general use	1.20	64.58
Supportive/convalescent medical equipment	0.84	156.25
Rental of medical equipment	0.67	79.48
Rental of supportive, convalescent medical equipment	0.64	44.92
ENTERTAINMENT	**88.15**	**547.06**
Fees and admissions	**47.22**	**261.79**
Recreation expenses, out of town trips	8.86	64.53
Social, recreation, civic club membership	10.46	227.20
Fees for participant sports	11.07	148.44
Participant sports, out-of-town trips	4.44	134.18
Movie, theater, opera, ballet	30.44	74.48
Movie, other admissions, out-of-town trips	9.83	115.23
Admission to sports events	6.50	129.42
Admission to sports events, out-of-town trips	9.83	38.40
Fees for recreational lessons	6.74	294.36
Other entertainment services, out-of-town trips	8.86	64.53
Television, radios, sound equipment	**80.91**	**224.28**
Televisions	74.58	200.24
Community antenna or cable TV	68.92	153.73
Black and white TV	0.09	94.44
Color TV, console	0.97	1,456.19
Color TV, portable, table model	2.50	346.50
VCRs and video disc players	3.38	179.44
Video cassettes, tapes, and discs	16.06	55.92
Video game hardware and software	4.12	113.47
Repair of TV, radio, and sound equipment	0.53	122.64
Rental of televisions	0.07	207.14
Radios and sound equipment	36.57	87.85
Radios	1.16	82.11
Tape recorders and players	0.36	73.61
Sound components and component systems	1.54	276.79
Compact disc, tape, record, video mail order clubs	1.84	59.51
Records, CDs, audio tapes, needles	16.46	50.59
Rental of VCR, radio, sound equipment	0.06	120.83
Musical instruments and accessories	1.39	419.42
Rental and repair of musical instruments	0.35	163.57
Rental of video cassettes, tapes, discs, films	25.72	34.76
Sound equipment accessories	1.04	151.44
Satellite dishes	0.15	151.67
Pets, toys, and playground equipment	**36.55**	**198.78**
Pets	27.72	168.34
Pet purchase, supplies, and medicines	22.78	96.51
Pet services	4.88	125.61
Veterinary services	8.37	221.57
Toys, games, hobbies, and tricycles	14.24	175.65
Playground equipment	0.34	287.50
Other entertainment supplies, equipment, services	**30.21**	**345.91**
Unmotored recreational vehicles	0.22	6,850.00
Boat without motor and boat trailers	0.11	1,579.55
Trailer and other attachable campers	0.11	12,118.18
Motorized recreational vehicles	0.29	14,425.00
Motorized camper	0.05	41,945.00
Other vehicle	0.10	4,385.00
Motor boats	0.15	10,981.67
Rental of recreational vehicles	0.40	263.13
Rental of noncamper trailer	0.02	100.00
Boat and trailer rental, out-of-town trips	0.07	214.29

	percent reporting expenditure during quarter	average amount spent by purchasers per quarter
Rental of camper on out-of-town trips	0.02%	$462.50
Rental of other vehicles, out-of-town trips	0.24	257.29
Rental of boat	0.04	275.00
Rental of other RVs	0.03	208.33
Outboard motors	0.05	560.00
Docking and landing fees	0.43	207.56
Sports, recreation, exercise equipment	10.50	246.60
Athletic gear, game tables, exercise equipment	5.61	204.63
Bicycles	1.43	193.36
Camping equipment	1.01	109.16
Hunting and fishing equipment	1.96	201.28
Winter sports equipment	0.46	265.76
Water sports equipment	0.48	233.33
Other sports equipment	1.15	326.30
Rental and repair of miscellaneous sports equipment	0.41	122.56
Photographic equipment and supplies	24.27	80.27
Film	16.81	21.76
Film processing	17.01	32.73
Repair and rental of photographic equipment	0.09	161.11
Photographic equipment	2.16	302.20
Photographer fees	2.31	155.19
PERSONAL CARE PRODUCTS AND SERVICES	**73.39**	**89.61**
Wigs and hairpieces	0.65	70.77
Electric personal care appliances	3.15	40.16
Personal care services	72.70	88.09
READING	**48.82**	**65.14**
Newspaper subscriptions	22.27	46.63
Newspaper, nonsubscriptions	14.09	17.23
Magazine subscriptions	8.17	44.22
Magazines, nonsubscriptions	10.26	18.84
Books purchased through book clubs	2.45	58.06
Books not purchased through book clubs	19.39	61.64
Encyclopedia and other reference book sets	0.06	104.17
EDUCATION	**14.81**	**1,233.09**
College tuition	5.05	2,315.40
Elementary/high school tuition	1.73	1,805.06
Other schools tuition	0.79	675.95
Other school expenses including rentals	3.66	305.67
Books, supplies for college	4.57	298.96
Books, supplies for elementary, high school	3.90	90.32
Books, supplies for day care, nursery school	0.63	119.84
TOBACCO PRODUCTS AND SMOKING SUPPLIES	**23.16**	**311.09**
Cigarettes	20.82	320.34
Other tobacco products	3.18	168.40
FINANCIAL PRODUCTS AND SERVICES		
Miscellaneous financial products and services	**41.57**	**351.17**
Lotteries and gambling losses	13.15	91.86
Legal fees	2.25	1,201.00
Funeral expenses	1.39	1,034.35
Safe deposit box rental	2.39	36.40
Checking accounts, other bank service charges	14.96	33.44
Cemetery lots, vaults, and maintenance fees	0.69	480.80
Accounting fees	5.02	231.28
Finance charges, except mortgage and vehicles	6.94	687.61
Occupational expenses	5.48	158.26
Expenses for other properties	4.56	293.04
Interest paid, home equity line of credit (other property)	0.02	662.50
Credit card memberships	0.89	65.73
Shopping club membership fees	2.78	44.24
Cash contributions	**48.59**	**704.82**
Support for college students	2.05	781.43
Alimony expenditures	0.34	3,101.47
Child support expenditures	3.24	1,281.79
Gifts to non-household members of stocks, bonds, mutual funds	0.31	1,990.32
Cash contributions to charities	15.92	218.99

	percent reporting expenditure during quarter	average amount spent by purchasers per quarter
Cash contributions to religious organizations	31.69%	$445.26
Cash contributions to educational organizations	2.18	692.32
Cash contributions to political organizations	1.35	122.59
Other cash gifts	12.54	601.42
Personal insurance and pensions	**76.94**	**1,317.66**
Life and other personal insurance	35.28	281.53
Life, endowment, annuity, other personal insurance	34.37	276.56
Other nonhealth insurance	2.32	184.05
Pensions and Social Security	**68.36**	**1,337.75**
Deductions for government retirement	2.72	640.07
Deductions for railroad retirement	0.07	1,221.43
Deductions for private pensions	10.82	1,111.88
Nonpayroll deposit to retirement plans	7.86	1,234.57
Deductions for Social Security	68.06	997.47
PERSONAL TAXES	**60.79**	**1,041.18**
Federal income taxes	55.74	826.64
State and local income taxes	39.88	314.40
Other taxes	16.32	286.67
GIFTS	**30.95**	**584.98**
Food	**1.07**	**1,008.88**
Housing	**12.13**	**280.63**
Household textiles	2.68	71.83
Appliances and miscellaneous housewares	2.28	139.91
Major appliances	0.42	283.93
Small appliances and miscellaneous housewares	1.94	102.84
Miscellaneous household equipment	6.17	128.36
Other housing	3.68	570.79
Apparel and services	**17.85**	**213.04**
Males aged two or older	5.05	189.26
Females aged two or older	6.57	194.56
Children under age two	8.45	81.42
Other apparel products and services	5.16	170.69
Jewelry and watches	2.38	271.53
All other apparel products and services	3.04	77.14
Transportation	**1.20**	**1,199.79**
Health care	**1.45**	**726.55**
Entertainment	**7.98**	**183.90**
Toys, games, hobbies, and tricycles	4.59	141.99
Other entertainment	4.14	197.04
Education	**2.02**	**2,396.41**
All other gifts	**4.54**	**224.12**

Source: Calculations by New Strategist based on the 2003 Consumer Expenditure Survey

Appendix D

Spending by Product and Service
Ranked by Amount Spent, 2003

*(average annual spending of consumer units on products and services,
ranked by amount spent, 2003)*

Mortgage interest	$2,830.50
Social Security	2,715.50
Rent	2,109.74
Federal income taxes	1,843.07
Property taxes	1,343.82
Gasoline and motor oil	1,332.76
Health insurance	1,251.62
New trucks	1,107.55
Electricity	1,027.91
New cars	944.91
Vehicle insurance	905.26
Used cars	816.42
Used trucks	795.03
Residential telephone and pay phones	619.60
Vehicle maintenance and repairs	618.92
Cash contributions to churches, religious organizations	564.41
Apparel, women's	528.63
Dinner at full-service restaurants	517.42
Maintenance and repair services, owned homes	516.31
State and local income taxes	501.53
Pensions, deductions for private	481.22
College tuition	467.71
Cable service and community antenna	423.79
Life, endowment, annuity, other personal insurance	397.30
Natural gas	392.01
Retirement accounts, nonpayroll deposits	388.15
Vehicle finance charges	370.59
Lunch at fast food restaurants and take-outs	369.02
Drugs, prescription	348.53
Cellular phone service	316.10
Cash gifts to non-household members	301.67
Homeowner's insurance	287.43
Apparel, men's	282.18
Apparel, children's	276.76
Cigarettes	266.78
Personal care services	256.43
Airline fares	252.56
Beef	245.55
Lodging on trips	241.77
Vehicle leasing	237.19
Water and sewerage maintenance	236.30
Dental services	227.24
Dinner at fast food restaurants and take-outs	215.93
Medicare payments	215.02
Restaurant meals on trips	213.97
Lunch at full-service restaurants	210.10
Recreation expenses on trips	195.71
Finance charges, except mortgage and vehicle	190.88
Day care centers, nurseries, and preschools	188.82
Taxes, except federal, state, and local	187.14
Snacks at fast food restaurants and take-outs	180.26
Fresh vegetables	171.96
Fresh fruits	170.88
Pork	170.61
Child support expenditures	166.12
Vacation homes, owned	150.29
Poultry	144.61
Physician's services	143.63

Cash contributions to charities and other organizations	$139.45
Shoes, women's	138.40
Computers and computer hardware, nonbusiness use	136.77
Carbonated drinks	133.91
Laundry and cleaning supplies	132.28
Decorative items for the home	126.78
Elementary and high school tuition	124.91
Fish and seafood	124.46
Computer information services	123.92
Cosmetics, perfume, and bath products	123.43
Home equity loan, line of credit interest	122.47
Jewelry	120.16
Milk, fresh	112.58
Beer and ale at home	111.17
Legal fees	108.09
Household products, except cleaning supplies and paper products	106.32
Toys, games, hobbies, and tricycles	100.05
Pet food	99.82
Cheese	97.04
Prepared food, excluding frozen	95.13
Social, recreation, civic club membership	95.06
Housekeeping services	93.13
Breakfast at fast food restaurants and take-outs	92.82
Sofas	92.17
Television sets	91.49
Movie, theater, opera, ballet tickets	90.69
Wine at home	89.93
Breakfast at full-service restaurants	89.42
State and local vehicle registration	88.17
Trash and garbage collection	87.63
Cereals, ready-to-eat and cooked	86.21
Camper, motorized	83.89
Gardening, lawn care service	83.70
Shoes, men's	83.38
Lawn and garden supplies	81.82
Bedroom furniture, except mattresses and springs	79.44
Fees for recreational lessons	79.36
Potato chips and other snacks	79.27
Maintenance and repair materials, owned homes	78.30
Pet purchase, supplies, and medicines	75.73
Candy and chewing gum	75.31
Cleansing and toilet tissue, paper towels, and napkins	75.23
Veterinarian services	74.18
Lunch at employer and school cafeterias	73.48
Shoes, children's	72.14
Drugs, nonprescription	70.30
Frozen prepared foods, except meals	69.94
Deductions for government retirement	69.64
Lunch meats (cold cuts)	69.31
Postage	68.94
Motorboats	65.89
Fees for participant sports	65.73
Cash support for college students	64.39
Laundry and dry cleaning of apparel, professional	61.18
Cash contributions to educational institutions	60.37
Beer and ale at restaurants, bars	60.33
Babysitting and child care	60.04
Stationery, stationery supplies, giftwrap	59.55
Nonalcoholic beverages and ice, except fruit drinks	58.72
Ice cream and related products	58.09
Fuel oil	57.54
Funeral expenses	57.51
Vegetables, canned and dried	57.40
School lunches	56.87
Hair care products	55.65
Lawn and garden equipment	55.39

Wall units and cabinets	$55.13
Books, supplies for college	54.65
Athletic gear, game tables, exercise equipment	54.52
Fruit juice, canned and bottled	53.82
Bedroom linens	53.45
Trailers and other attachable campers	53.32
Housing while attending school	52.90
Eyeglasses and contact lenses	50.97
Kitchen and dining room furniture	49.42
Bread, other than white	49.06
Mass transit fares, intracity	48.94
Catered affairs	48.39
Vitamins, nonprescription	48.02
Books, except book clubs	47.81
Refrigerators and freezers	47.56
Accounting fees	46.44
Cookies	45.06
Mattresses and springs	44.89
Hospital services other than room	43.34
Bottled/tank gas	42.42
Alimony expenditures	42.18
Newspaper subscriptions	41.54
Ground rent	40.58
Plants and fresh flowers, indoor	40.31
Living room chairs	38.76
Whiskey and other alcoholic beverages at restaurants, bars	38.75
Medical services by professionals other than physician	38.54
Sauces and gravies	38.46
Coffee	38.08
Eggs	37.34
Biscuits and rolls	37.24
Cakes and cupcakes	36.71
Laundry and dry cleaning of apparel, coin-operated	36.41
Groceries purchased on trips	36.28
Video cassettes, tapes, and discs	35.92
Rental of video cassettes, tapes, discs, films	35.76
Lottery and gambling losses	35.37
Soups, canned and packaged	35.19
Frozen meals	34.85
Occupational expenses	34.69
Eye care services	34.60
Admission to sports events	33.65
Bread, white	33.50
Records, CDs, audio tapes, needles	33.31
Alcoholic beverages on trips	33.26
Board (including at school)	33.25
Property management, owned home	33.03
Vehicle rental	32.95
Convalescent or nursing home care	32.80
Snacks at vending machines, mobile vendors	31.33
Hunting and fishing equipment	30.49
Cooking stoves, ovens	30.49
Moving, storage, and freight express	30.46
Electric floor-cleaning equipment	30.24
Deodorants, feminine hygiene and misc. personal products	30.11
Topicals and dressings	30.10
Floor coverings, wall-to-wall	29.50
Lab tests, X-rays	28.93
Washing machines	28.68
Dairy, except milk, cream, and ice cream (I.e. yogurt)	28.26
Oral hygiene products	28.22
Parking fees	28.12
Ship fares	27.90
Pasta, cornmeal, and other cereal products	27.75
Sweetrolls, coffee cakes, doughnuts	27.65
Vegetables, frozen	26.79
Telephones and accessories	26.78

Baby food	$26.76
Snacks at full-service restaurants	26.66
Nuts	26.41
Fats and oils	26.29
Meals as pay	26.28
Salad dressings	26.17
Photographic equipment	26.11
Hospital room	26.06
Alcoholic beverage at home, except beer, whiskey, and wine	24.70
Gifts to non–CU members of stocks, bonds, and mutual funds	24.68
Bakery products, frozen and refrigerated	24.56
Pet services	24.52
Crackers	24.52
Power tools	24.38
Window coverings	24.34
VCRs and video disc players	24.26
Outdoor equipment	23.74
Musical instruments and accessories	23.32
Frankfurters	22.74
Film processing	22.27
Floor coverings, nonpermanent	22.26
Taxi fares and limousine service	21.58
Tobacco products, except cigarettes	21.42
School tuition except elementary, high school, college	21.36
Jams, preserves, other sweets	21.20
Fruit juice, fresh	20.77
Salt, spices, and other seasonings	20.77
Tableware, nonelectric kitchenware	20.56
Prepared salads	20.51
Bathroom linens	20.30
Checking accounts, other bank service charges	20.01
Baking needs	19.58
Clothes dryers	19.43
Fruit-flavored drinks, noncarbonated	19.29
Phone cards	18.88
Wine at restaurants, bars	18.78
Videogame hardware and software	18.70
Butter	18.08
Computer software and accessories, nonbusiness use	17.98
Tea	17.71
Living room tables	17.51
Sound components and component systems	17.47
Watches	17.12
Sugar	16.89
Maintenance and repair services, rented homes	16.88
Tolls	16.75
Train fares, intercity	16.07
Rice	16.05
Fruit, canned	15.96
Small electric kitchen appliances	15.66
Home security system service fee	15.54
Outdoor furniture	15.35
Nonelectric cookware	15.26
Curtains and draperies	15.24
Shaving products	14.80
Film	14.63
Magazine subscriptions	14.45
Hearing aids	14.40
Photographer fees	14.34
Whiskey at home	14.29
Books, supplies for elementary, high school	14.09
Laundry and cleaning equipment	14.03
Cream	13.95
Lamps and lighting fixtures	13.66
Dishwashers (built-in), garbage disposals, range hoods	13.50
Cemetery lots, vaults, and maintenance fees	13.27
Infants' equipment	13.08

Automobile service clubs	$12.83
Flour mixes, prepared	12.79
Peanut butter	12.64
Office furniture for home use	12.61
Appliance repair, including service center	11.75
Olives, pickles, relishes	11.41
Termite/pest control services	11.30
Sewing materials for household items	11.27
Prepared desserts	11.10
Bicycles	11.06
Nondairy cream and imitation milk	11.02
Maintenance and repair materials, rented homes	10.23
Snacks at employer and school cafeterias	10.16
Lamb and organ meats	9.96
Pies, tarts, turnovers	9.72
Newspaper, nonsubscription	9.71
Electric personal care appliances	9.68
Tenant's insurance	9.67
Margarine	9.61
Closet and storage items	9.57
Camping equipment	9.31
Wood and other fuels	9.10
Bus fares, intercity	8.96
Sewing machines	8.95
Glassware	8.89
Vegetable juices	8.67
Vehicle inspection	8.36
Medical equipment	8.35
Local transportation on trips	8.33
Infants' furniture	8.17
Fruit juice, frozen	7.88
Magazines, nonsubscription	7.73
Microwave ovens	7.56
Kitchen and dining room linens	7.37
Flour	7.32
Hand tools	7.22
Driver's license	7.17
China and other dinnerware	7.04
Boat without motor and boat trailers	6.95
Portable heating and cooling equipment	6.85
Hair accessories	6.75
Cash contributions to political organizations	6.62
Silver serving pieces	6.51
Fruit, dried	6.30
Luggage	6.18
Repairs/rentals of lawn equipment, tools, etc.	6.08
Books purchased through book clubs	5.69
Artificial sweeteners	5.67
Apparel repair and tailoring	5.62
Lunch at vending machines, mobile vendors	5.56
Sound equipment accessories	5.54
Parking, owned home	5.47
Radios	5.46
Air conditioners, window	5.40
Material for making clothes	5.33
Reupholstering and furniture repair	5.20
Sewing patterns and notions	4.99
Pinball, electronic video games	4.97
Shopping club membership fees	4.92
Winter sports equipment	4.89
Delivery services	4.70
Towing charges	4.67
Water sports equipment	4.48
Compact disc, tape, record, video mail order clubs	4.38
Slipcovers and decorative pillows	4.35
Breakfast at employer and school cafeterias	4.27
Rental of recreational vehicles	4.21

Repair of computer systems for nonbusiness use	$4.20
Clocks	4.02
Flatware	3.99
Tape recorders and players	3.93
Playground equipment	3.91
Fruit, frozen	3.66
Laundry and dry cleaning, nonapparel, coin-operated	3.62
Watch and jewelry repair	3.59
Docking and landing fees	3.57
Bread and cracker products	3.57
Management and upkeep services for security, owned home	3.49
Safe deposit box rental	3.48
Deductions for railroad retirement	3.42
Rental of medical equipment	3.28
Water softening service	3.23
Books, supplies for day care, nursery school	3.02
Dinner at employer and school cafeterias	2.83
Rental of furniture	2.70
Repair of TV, radio, and sound equipment	2.60
Clothing rental	2.46
Septic tank cleaning	2.35
Credit card memberships	2.34
Fireworks	2.33
Rental and repair of musical instruments	2.29
Rental and repair of miscellaneous sports equipment	2.01
Wigs and hairpieces	1.84
Appliance rental	1.63
Plastic dinnerware	1.56
Termite/pest control products	1.52
Smoking accessories	1.42
Breakfast at vending machines, mobile vendors	1.37
Dinner at vending machines, mobile vendors	1.32
Calculators	1.27
Shoe repair and other shoe services	1.15
Smoke alarms	1.13
Pager service	1.12
Business equipment for home use	1.03
Laundry and dry cleaning, nonapparel, sent out	1.00
Telephone answering devices	0.93
Satellite dishes	0.91
School bus	0.70
Rental of television sets	0.58
Repair and rental of photographic equipment	0.58
Clothing storage	0.48
Rental of VCR, radio, sound equipment	0.29

Source: Calculations by New Strategist based on the 2003 Consumer Expenditure Survey

Glossary

age The age of the reference person, also called the householder or head of household.

alcoholic beverages Includes beer and ale, wine, whiskey, gin, vodka, rum, and other alcoholic beverages.

apparel, accessories, and related services Includes the following:

• *men's and boys' apparel* Includes coats, jackets, sweaters, vests, sport coats, tailored jackets, slacks, shorts and short sets, sportswear, shirts, underwear, nightwear, hosiery, uniforms, and other accessories.

• *women's and girls' apparel* Includes coats, jackets, furs, sport coats, tailored jackets, sweaters, vests, blouses, shirts, dresses, dungarees, culottes, slacks, shorts, sportswear, underwear, nightwear, uniforms, hosiery, and other accessories.

• *infants' apparel* Includes coats, jackets, snowsuits, underwear, diapers, dresses, crawlers, sleeping garments, hosiery, footwear, and other accessories for children.

• *footwear* Includes articles such as shoes, slippers, boots, and other similar items. It excludes footwear for babies and footwear used for sports such as bowling or golf shoes.

• *other apparel products and services* Includes material for making clothes, shoe repair, alterations and sewing patterns and notions, clothing rental, clothing storage, dry cleaning, sent-out laundry, watches, jewelry, and repairs to watches and jewelry.

average spending The average amount spent per household. The Bureau of Labor Statistics calculates the average for all households in a segment, not just for those who purchased an item. For items purchased by most households—such as bread—average spending figures are an accurate account of actual spending. For products and services purchased by few households during a year's time—such as cars—the average amount spent is much less than what purchasers spend. See the Percent Reporting Appendix for the percentage of consumer units reporting an expenditure and the average amount spent by purchasers.

baby boom People born from 1946 through 1964, aged 38 to 56 in 2002.

baby bust People born from 1965 through 1976, aged 26 to 37 in 2001. Also known as Generation X.

cash contributions Includes cash contributed to persons or organizations outside the consumer unit including alimony and child support payments, care of students away from home, and contributions to religious, educational, charitable, or political organizations.

complete income reporters Respondents who provided values for major sources of income, such as wages and salaries, self-employment income, and Social Security income. Even complete income reporters may not have given a full accounting of all income from all sources.

consumer unit Defined as follows:

• All members of a household who are related by blood, marriage, adoption, or other legal arrangements.

• A person living alone or sharing a household with others or living as a roomer in a private home or lodging house or in permanent living quarters in a hotel or motel, but who is financially independent.

• Two persons or more living together who pool their income to make joint expenditure decisions. Financial independence is determined by the three major expense categories: housing, food, and other living expenses. To be considered financially independent, at least two of the three major expense categories have to be provided by the respondent. For convenience, called households in the text of this book.

consumer unit, composition of The classification of interview households by type according to: (1) relationship of other household members to the reference person; (2) age of the children to the reference person; and (3) combination of relationship to the reference person and age of the children. Stepchildren and adopted children are included with the reference person's own children.

earner A consumer unit member aged 14 or older who worked at least one week during the 12 months prior to the interview date.

education Includes tuition, fees, books, supplies, and equipment for public and private nursery schools, elementary and high schools, colleges and universities, and other schools.

education of reference person The number of years of formal education of the reference person based on the highest grade completed. If the respondent was enrolled at the time of interview, the grade being attended is the one recorded. Those not reporting their education are classified under no school or not reported.

entertainment Includes the following:

• *fees and admissions* Includes fees for participant sports; admissions to sporting events, movies, concerts, plays; health, swimming, tennis, and country club memberships, and other social recreational and fraternal organizations; recreational lessons or instructions; and recreational expenses on trips.

• *television, radio, and sound equipment* Includes television sets, video recorders, video cassettes, tapes, discs, disc players, video game hardware, video game cartridges, cable TV, radios, phonographs, tape recorders and players, sound components, records and tapes, and records and tapes through record clubs, musical instruments, and rental and repair of TV and sound equipment.

• *pets, toys, hobbies, and playground equipment* Includes pet food, pet services, veterinary expenses, toys, games, hobbies, and playground equipment.

• *other entertainment equipment and services* Includes indoor exercise equipment, athletic shoes, bicycles, trailers, campers, camping equipment, rental of cameras and trailers, hunting and fishing equipment, sports equipment, winter sports equipment, water sports equipment, boats, boat motors and boat trailers, rental of boat, landing and docking fees, rental and repair of sports equipment, photographic equipment, film and film processing, photographer fees, repair and rental of photo equipment, fireworks, pinball and electronic video games.

expenditure The transaction cost including excise and sales taxes of goods and services acquired during the survey period. The full cost of each purchase is recorded even though full payment may not have been made at the date of purchase. Expenditure estimates include gifts. Excluded from expenditures are purchases or portions of purchases directly assignable to business purposes and periodic credit or installment payments on goods and services already acquired.

federal income tax Includes federal income tax withheld in the survey year to pay for income earned in survey year plus additional tax paid in survey year to cover any underpayment or under withholding of tax in the year prior to the survey.

financial products and services Includes union dues, professional dues and fees, other occupational expenses, funerals, cemetery lots, and unclassified fees and personal services.

food Includes the following:

• *food at home* Refers to the total expenditures for food at grocery stores or other food stores during the interview period. It is calculated by multiplying the number of visits to a grocery or other food store by the average amount spent per visit. It excludes the purchase of nonfood items.

• *food away from home* Includes all meals (breakfast, lunch, brunch, and dinner) at restaurants, carryouts, and vending machines, including tips, plus meals as pay, special catered affairs such as weddings, bar mitzvahs, and confirmations, and meals away from home on trips.

generation X People born from 1965 through 1976, aged 26 to 37 in 2002. Also known as the baby bust.

gifts for nonhousehold members Includes gift expenditures for people outside of the consumer unit. The amount spent on gifts is also included in individual product and service categories.

health care Includes the following:

• *health insurance* Includes health maintenance plans (HMOs), Blue Cross/Blue Shield, commercial health insurance, Medicare, Medicare supplemental insurance, and other health insurance.

• *medical services* Includes hospital room and services, physicians' services, services of a practitioner other than a physician, eye and dental care, lab tests, X-rays, nursing, therapy services, care in convalescent or nursing home, and other medical care.

• *drugs* Includes prescription and non-prescription drugs, internal and respiratory over-the-counter drugs.

• *medical supplies* Includes eyeglasses and contact lenses, topicals and dressings, antiseptics, bandages, cotton, first aid kits, contraceptives; medical equipment for general use such as syringes, ice bags, thermometers, vaporizers, heating pads; supportive or convalescent medical equipment such as hearing aids, braces, canes, crutches, and walkers.

Hispanic origin The self-identified Hispanic origin of the consumer unit reference person. All consumer units are included in one of two Hispanic origin groups based on the reference person's Hispanic origin: Hispanic or non-Hispanic. Hispanics may be of any race.

household According to the Census Bureau, all the people who occupy a household. A group of unrelated people who share a housing unit as roommates or unmarried partners is also counted as a household. Households do not include group quarters such as college dormitories, prisons, or nursing homes. A household may contain more than one consumer unit. The terms "household" and "consumer unit" are used interchangeably in this book.

household furnishings and equipment Includes the following:

• *household textiles* Includes bathroom, kitchen, dining room, and other linens, curtains and drapes, slipcovers and decorative pillows, and sewing materials.

• *furniture* Includes living room, dining room, kitchen, bedroom, nursery, porch, lawn, and other outdoor furniture.

• *carpet, rugs, and other floor coverings* Includes installation and replacement of wall-to-wall carpets, room-size rugs, and other soft floor coverings.

• *major appliances* Includes refrigerators, freezers, dishwashers, stoves, ovens, garbage disposals, vacuum cleaners, microwaves, air-conditioners, sewing machines, washing machines and dryers, and floor cleaning equipment.

• *small appliances and miscellaneous housewares* Includes small electrical kitchen appliances, portable heating and cooling equipment, china and other dinnerware, flatware, glassware, silver and other serving pieces, nonelectric cookware, and plastic dinnerware. Excludes personal care appliances.

• *miscellaneous household equipment* Includes typewriters, luggage, lamps and other light fixtures, window coverings, clocks, lawn mowers and gardening equipment, other hand and power tools, telephone answering devices, telephone accessories, computers and computer hardware for home use, calculators, office equipment for home use, floral arrangements and house plants, rental of furniture, closet and storage items, household decorative items, infants' equipment, outdoor equipment, smoke alarms, other household appliances and small miscellaneous furnishing.

household services Includes the following:

• *personal services* Includes baby sitting, day care, and care of elderly and handicapped persons.

• *other household services* Includes housekeeping services, gardening and lawn care services, coin-operated laundry and dry-cleaning of household textiles, termite and pest control products, moving, storage, and freight expenses, repair of household appliances and other household equipment, reupholstering and furniture repair, rental and repair of lawn and gardening tools, and rental of other household equipment.

housekeeping supplies Includes soaps, detergents, other laundry cleaning products, cleansing and toilet tissue, paper towels, napkins, and miscellaneous household products; lawn and garden supplies, postage, stationery, stationery supplies, and gift wrap.

housing tenure "Owner" includes households living in their own homes, cooperatives, condominiums, or townhouses. "Renter" includes households paying rent as well as families living rent free in lieu of wages.

income before taxes The total money earnings and selected money receipts accruing to a consumer unit during the 12 months prior to the interview date. Income includes the following components:

• *wages and salaries* Includes total money earnings for all members of the consumer unit aged 14 or older from all jobs, including civilian wages and salaries, Armed Forces pay and allowances, piece-rate payments, commissions, tips, National Guard or Reserve pay (received for training periods), and cash bonuses before deductions for taxes, pensions, union dues, etc.

• *self-employment income* Includes net business and farm income, which consists of net income (gross receipts minus operating expenses) from a profession or unincorporated business or from the operation of a farm by an owner, tenant, or sharecropper. If the business or farm is a partnership, only an appropriate share of net income is recorded. Losses are also recorded.

• *Social Security, private and government retirement* Includes the following: payments by the federal government made under retirement, survivor, and disability insurance programs to retired persons, dependents of deceased insured workers, or to disabled workers; and private pensions or retirement benefits received by retired persons or their survivors, either directly or through an insurance company.

• *interest, dividends, rental income, and other property income* Includes interest income on savings or bonds; payments made by a corporation to its stockholders, periodic receipts from estates or trust funds; net income or loss from the rental of property, real estate, or farms, and net income or loss from roomers or boarders.

• *unemployment and workers' compensation and veterans' benefits* Includes income from unemployment compensation and workers' compensation, and veterans' payments including educational benefits, but excluding military retirement.

• *public assistance, supplemental security income, and food stamps* Includes public assistance or welfare, including money received from job training grants; supplemental security income paid by federal, state, and local welfare agencies to low-income persons who are aged 65 or older, blind, or disabled; and the value of food stamps obtained.

• *regular contributions for support* Includes alimony and child support as well as any regular contributions from persons outside the consumer unit.

• *other income* Includes money income from care of foster children, cash scholarships, fellowships, or stipends not based on working; and meals and rent as pay.

indexed spending The indexed spending figures compare the spending of each demographic segment with that of the average household. To compute an index, the amount spent on an item by a demographic segment is divided by the amount spent on the item by the average household. That figure is then multiplied by 100. An index of 100 is the average for all households. An index of 132 means average spending by households in a segment is 32 percent above average (100 plus 32). An index of 75 means average spending by households in a segment is 25 percent below average (100 minus 25). Indexed spending figures identify the consumer units that spend the most on a product or service.

life and other personal insurance Includes premiums from whole life and term insurance; endowments; income and other life insurance; mortgage guarantee insurance; mortgage life insurance; premiums for personal life liability, accident and disability; and other non-health insurance other than homes and vehicles.

market share The market share is the percentage of total household spending on an item that is accounted for by a demographic segment. Market shares are calculated by dividing a demographic segment's total spending on an item by the total spending of all

households on the item. Total spending on an item for all households is calculated by multiplying average spending by the total number of households (112,108,000 in 2002). Total spending on an item for each demographic segment is calculated by multiplying the segment's average spending by the number of households in the segment. Market shares reveal the demographic segments that account for the largest share of spending on a product or service.

metropolitan statistical area (MSA) As defined by the Office of Management and Budget, a large population nucleus, together with adjacent communities which have a high degree of economic and social integration with the nucleus.

millennial generation People born from 1977 through 1994, and aged 8 through 25 in 2002.

occupation The occupation in which the reference person received the most earnings during the survey period. The occupational categories follow those of the Census of Population. Categories shown in the tables include the following:

• *self-employed* Includes all occupational categories; the reference person is self-employed in own business, professional practice, or farm.

• *wage and salary earners, managers, and professionals* Includes executives, administrators, managers, and professional specialties such as architects, engineers, natural and social scientists, lawyers, teachers, writers, health diagnosis and treatment workers, entertainers, and athletes.

• *wage and salary earners, technical, sales, and clerical workers* Includes technicians and related support workers; sales representatives, sales workers, cashiers, and sales-related occupations; and administrative support, including clerical.

• *retired* People who did not work either full- or part-time during the survey period.

personal care Includes products for the hair, oral hygiene products, shaving needs, cosmetics and bath products, suntan lotions and hand creams, electric personal care appliances, incontinence products, other personal care products, personal care services such as hair care services (haircuts, bleaching, tinting, coloring, conditioning treatments, permanents, press, and curls), styling and other services for wigs and hairpieces, body massages or slenderizing treatments, facials, manicures, pedicures, shaves, electrolysis.

race The self-identified race of the consumer unit reference person. All consumer units are included in one of two racial groups based on the reference person's race: black or "white and other." The "other" group includes American Indians, Alaskan natives, Asians, and Pacific Islanders. Hispanics may be of any race.

reading Includes subscriptions for newspapers, magazines, and books through book clubs; purchase of single-copy newspapers and magazines, books, and encyclopedias and other reference books.

reference person The first member mentioned by the respondent when asked to "Start with the name of the person or one of the persons who owns or rents the home." It is with respect to this person that the relationship of other consumer unit members is determined. Also called the householder or head of household.

region Consumer units are classified according to their address at the time of their participation in the survey. The four major census regions of the United States are the following state groupings:

• *Northeast* Connecticut, Maine, Massachusetts, New Hampshire, New Jersey, New York, Pennsylvania, Rhode Island, and Vermont.

• *Midwest* Illinois, Indiana, Iowa, Kansas, Michigan, Minnesota, Missouri, Nebraska, North Dakota, Ohio, South Dakota, and Wisconsin.

• *South* Alabama, Arkansas, Delaware, District of Columbia, Florida, Georgia, Kentucky, Louisiana, Maryland, Mississippi, North Carolina, Oklahoma, South Carolina, Tennessee, Texas, Virginia, and West Virginia.

• *West* Alaska, Arizona, California, Colorado, Hawaii, Idaho, Montana, Nevada, New Mexico, Oregon, Utah, Washington, and Wyoming.

retirement, pensions, and Social Security Includes all Social Security contributions paid by employees; employees' contributions to railroad retirement, government retirement and private pensions programs; retirement programs for self-employed.

shelter Includes the following:

• *owned dwellings* Includes interest on mortgages, property taxes and insurance, refinancing and prepayment charges, ground rent, expenses for property management/security, homeowners' insurance, fire insurance and extended coverage, landscaping expenses for repairs and maintenance contracted out (including periodic maintenance and service contracts), and expenses of materials for owner-performed repairs and maintenance for dwellings used or maintained by the consumer unit, but not dwellings maintained for business or rent.

• *rented dwellings* Includes rent paid for dwellings, rent received as pay, parking fees, maintenance, and other expenses.

• *other lodging* Includes all expenses for vacation homes, school, college, hotels, motels, cottages, trailer camps, and other lodging while out of town.

• *utilities, fuels, and public services* Includes natural gas, electricity, fuel oil, coal, bottled gas, wood, and other fuels; telephone services; water, garbage and trash collection, sewerage maintenance, septic tank cleaning, and other public services.

size of consumer unit The number of people whose usual place of residence at the time of the interview is in the consumer unit.

state and local income taxes Includes state and local income taxes withheld in the survey year to pay for income earned in survey year plus additional taxes paid in the survey year to cover any underpayment or under withholding of taxes in the year prior to the survey.

tobacco and smoking supplies Includes cigarettes, cigars, snuff, loose smoking tobacco, chewing tobacco, and smoking accessories such as cigarette or cigar holders, pipes, flints, lighters, pipe cleaners, and other smoking products and accessories.

transportation Includes the following:

• *vehicle purchases (net outlay)* Includes the net outlay (purchase price minus trade-in value) on new and used domestic and imported cars and trucks and other vehicles, including motorcycles and private planes.

• *gasoline and motor oil* Includes gasoline, diesel fuel, and motor oil.

• *other vehicle expenses* Includes vehicle finance charges, maintenance and repairs, vehicle insurance, and vehicle rental licenses and other charges.

• *vehicle finance charges* Includes the dollar amount of interest paid for a loan contracted for the purchase of vehicles described above.

• *maintenance and repairs* Includes tires, batteries, tubes, lubrication, filters, coolant, additives, brake and transmission fluids, oil change, brake adjustment and repair, front-end alignment, wheel balancing, steering repair, shock absorber replacement, clutch and transmission repair, electrical system repair, repair to cooling system, drive train repair, drive shaft and rear-end repair, tire repair, other maintenance and services, and auto repair policies.

• *vehicle insurance* Includes the premium paid for insuring cars, trucks, and other vehicles.

• *vehicle rental, licenses, and other charges* Includes leased and rented cars, trucks, motorcycles, and aircraft, inspection fees, state and local registration, drivers' license fees, parking fees, towing charges, and tolls on trips.

• *public transportation* Includes fares for mass transit, buses, trains, airlines, taxis, private school buses, and fares paid on trips for trains, boats, taxis, buses, and trains.

Index

accounting fees, 177–206
admissions
    to entertainment events, 1–60, 119–176
    to movies, theater, opera, ballet, 119–176
    to sporting events, 119–176
air conditioners, window units, 525–554
    maintenance and repair of, 467–524
airline fares, 555–612
    gifts of, 321–378
alarms, smoke, 525–554
alcoholic beverages, 1–60, 207–320. *See also* Beer; Wine; *and*
    Whiskey.
    at catered affairs, 207–320
    at home, 207–320
    from fast-food restaurants, 207–320
    from full-service restaurants, 207–320
    gifts of, 1–60, 321–378
    purchased on trips, 207–320
alimony, 177–206
apparel
    boys', 1–60, 61–118
    gifts of, 1–60, 321–378
    girls', 1–60, 61–118
    infants', 1–60, 61–118
    men's, 1–60, 61–118
    repair, 61–118
    shoes, 1–60, 61–118
    shoes, gifts of, 321–378
    women's, 1–60, 61–118
apples, 207–320
appliances
    gifts of, 1–60, 321–378
    kitchen, 525–554
    major, 1–60, 525–554
    personal care, 525–554
    repair, 525–554
    small, 1–60, 525–554
artificial sweeteners, 207–320
athletic gear, 119–176
    gifts of, 321–378
audio tapes, 119–176
auto rental, 555–612
    on trips, 555–612
automobile service clubs, 555–612
automobiles. *See* Cars *and* Trucks.

baby food, 207–320
babysitting. *See also* Day care centers, nursery schools,
    and preschools.
    other home, 525–554
    own home, 525–554
bacon, 207–320
bakery products, 1–60, 207–320
    frozen and refrigerated, 207–320
baking needs, 207–320
ballet tickets, 119–176
bananas, 207–320
bank service charges, 177–206
bath products, 525–554
    gifts of, 321–378
bathroom linens, 525–554
    gifts of, 321–378
bedroom furniture, 525–554
    gifts of, 321–378

bedroom linens, 525–554
    gifts of, 321–378
beds. *See* Mattresses and springs.
beef, 1–60, 207–320
beer and ale, 207–320
    gifts of, 321–378
bicycles, 119–176
biscuits and rolls, 207–320
blouses and tops, 61–118
Blue Cross, Blue Shield. *See* Health insurance.
board, including at school, 207–320
    gifts of, 321–378
boats, 119–176
bologna, 207–320
books, 525–554
    and supplies for college, 525–554
    and supplies for college, gifts of, 321–378
    and supplies for daycare and nursery school, 525–554
    and supplies for elementary and high school, 525–554
    purchased through book clubs, 525–554
boys' apparel, 1–60, 61–118
    gifts of, 1–60, 321–378
bread, 207–320
bread and cracker products, 207–320
breakfast and brunch, at restaurants, 207–320
bus fares, intercity, 555–612
business equipment and office furniture for home use, 525–554
butter, 207–320

cabinets, 525–554
cable TV and community antenna, 119–176
    gifts of, 321–378
cafeterias, meals from, 207–320
cakes, 207–320
    gifts of, 321–378
calculators, 525–554
campers, motorized, 119–176
camping equipment, 119–176
candy, 207–320
    gifts of, 321–378
carbonated drinks, 207–320
carpeting, wall-to-wall, 525–554
cars
    gifts of, 321–378
    lease payments, 555–612
    new, 1–60, 555–612
    rental, 555–612
    used, 1–60, 555–612
catered affairs, 207–320
    gifts of, 321–378
CD, tape, record, video mail order clubs, 119–176
CDs, 119–176
cellular phone service, 467–524
cemetery lots, vaults, maintenance fees, 177–206
cereal, 1–60, 207–320
chairs, living room, 525–554
charitable contributions, 177–206
checking accounts, 177–206
cheese, 207–320
chewing gum, 207–320
    gifts of, 321–378
chicken. *See* Poultry.
child care. *See* Babysitting; *and* Day care centers, nursery
    schools, and preschools.